W9-APR-277

Dana Facaros & Michael Pauls

TUSCANY, UMBRIA & THE MARCHES

'...the enduring charm of Tuscany, Umbria
and the Marches is in that dreamy glass
of wine, in those hills that look exactly
as they did when Piero painted them,
in the bartender who's a dead ringer for
Lorenzo de'Medici, in those bewitching
Etruscan smiles that might have
been smiled yesterday.'

CADOGANguides

1 Basilica of San Francesco, Assisi

2 Onion Grain Vines, The Marches
3 Canaiolo grapes, Chianti, Tuscany
4 Chianti barrels, Tuscany

5 Ploughed fields, Tuscany

8

9 Salami-curing room
10 Pecorino cheese with herbs
11 Panforte
12 The Palio, Siena
13 The Leaning Tower (left) and the Cathedral
  (right), Pisa
14 Ponte Vecchio, Florence

15

18

19 A view over the rooftops of Lucca, Tuscany

20 Village square, The Marches

About the authors

Dana Facaros and Michael Pauls are professional travel writers. They spent three years in a tiny Italian village, where they suffered massive overdoses of food, art and wine, and enjoyed every minute of it. They reckon they could whip 98 per cent of the world's non-Italian population at Trivial Pursuit (except for the sport questions). They now live in southwest France. They have written over 40 guides for Cadogan.

About the updaters

Nicky Swallow, a professional musician, has lived in Italy for 18 years. Her enthusiasm for Italian life has led to an intimate knowledge of the country, where she has travelled extensively. She is a regular contributor to travel guides and magazines.

Helen Holubov moved to Florence in 1988 for one year. She has lived there ever since and has spent the subsequent time teaching English, working freelance for travel guides and trying to think of a good reason to leave.

Contents

Reference

Maps and Plans

Cadogan Guides
Network House, 1, Ariel Way,
London, W12 7SL
info@cadoganguides.co.uk
www.cadoganguides.com

The Globe Pequot Press
246 Goose Lane, PO Box 480, Guilford,
Connecticut 06437–0480

Copyright © Dana Facaros and Michael Pauls
1989, 1990, 1992, 1994, 1996, 1998, 2001, 2003,
2005

Cover and photo essay design by Kicca Tommasi
Book design by Andrew Barker
Cover photographs: © Alamy images
Photo essay: © John Ferro Sims
Maps © Cadogan Guides,
    drawn by Map Creation Ltd
Managing Editor: Natalie Pomier
Editor: Antonia Cunningham
Editorial Assistant: Nicola Jessop
Art Director: Sarah Rianhard-Gardner
Proofreading: Anna Amari-Parker and
    James Alexander
Indexing: Isobel McLean
Production: Navigator Guides Ltd

Printed in Italy by Legoprint
A catalogue record for this book is available
    from the British Library
ISBN 1-86011-186-6

The author and publishers have made every effort
to ensure the accuracy of the information in this
book at the time of going to press. However, they
cannot accept any responsibility for any loss, injury
or inconvenience resulting from the use of
information contained in this guide.

Please help us to keep this guide up to date. We
have done our best to ensure that the information
in this guide is correct at the time of going to press.
But places and facilities are constantly changing,
and standards and prices in hotels and restaurants
fluctuate. We would be delighted to receive any
comments concerning existing entries or
omissions. Authors of the best letters will receive a
copy of the Cadogan Guide of their choice.

All rights reserved. No part of this publication may
be reproduced, stored in a retrieval system, or
transmitted, in any form or by any means,
electronic or mechanical, including photocopying
and recording, or by any information storage and
retrieval system except as may be expressly
permitted by the UK 1988 Copyright Design &
Patents Act and the USA 1976 Copyright Act or in
writing from the publisher. Requests for permission
should be addressed to Cadogan Guides, Network
House, 1, Ariel Way, London, W12 7SL in the UK, or The
Globe Pequot Press, 246 Goose Lane, PO Box 480,
Guilford, Connecticut 06437–0480, in the USA.

Introduction

A glass of wine before dinner on the terrace, olives glinting in the last flash of the setting sun as geometric vineyards lose their rigid order in the melting darkness, and only the black daggers of cypresses stand out against the first stars of the evening – where could you be but Tuscany? It needs no introduction, this famous twilit land, where Titans of art five hundred years ago mimicked and then outdid nature, while nature utters a gentle retort by rivalling art. Neighbouring Umbria is most familiar as the land of St Francis of Assisi, converting many with its mystical eloquence; a land that, as the nun on the bus put it, 'speaks in silences'. Umbria has much in common with Tuscany – wine, art and lavish natural beauty, and a remarkable sense of continuity, of a land and people in perfect agreement. Long over-shadowed, the Marches nevertheless share many of the region's best features: transcendent Renaissance art, ageless hill towns, sandy beaches, as well as a few surprises, all traditionally free of mass tourism. Though no longer a best-kept secret, the Marches still offer a seductive slice of central Italian gentility.

Travellers have been flocking to central Italy ever since the Middle Ages, to learn, see and understand. Most have come with their Baedekers in hand, and even today it is hard to escape the generations of worthy opinions or avoid treading on those same old grapes of purple prose. After all, most of what we call Western civilization was either rediscovered or invented here, leaving works that have lost none of the power; at times it seems the artists of the early 1400s descended from space with their secret messages for the imagination. To the mass of accumulated opinion we now add ours, for better or worse, but mostly in the hope of provoking some of your own.

But at the end of the day – or rather, at the beginning of the new millennium, when times seem to be changing faster than we can or care to – the enduring charm of Tuscany, Umbria and the Marches is in that dreamy glass of wine, in those hills that look exactly as they did when Piero painted them, in the bartender who's a dead ringer for Lorenzo de' Medici, in those bewitching Etruscan smiles that might have been smiled only yesterday. Things have stayed the same, not by accident, or economic reason, or by decree of some Tuscan National Trust, but because that's the way people like them. They make as few concessions to the 21st century as possible, and their Brigadoon may not be for everyone. They're not catching up with the world; the world's catching up with them.

A Guide to the Guide

This **Introduction** contains an overview of **Tuscany, Umbria and the Marches** and suggestions for themed itineraries. A chapter on **History and Art** provides a detailed background to the development and culture of the region, one of the most artistically rich in the world. Following this is **Topics**, a series of short essays, which gives more insights into the people and customs of central Italy. Then comes **Food and Drink**, introducing the gastronomic specialities of the region and its wines, along with a list of vocabulary to help you make sense of the menu. There is a comprehensive **Travel** section which includes details of special-interest holidays, followed by the

Chapter Divisions

N

40 km
20 miles

EMILIA ROMAGNA

Pontremoli

Viareggio

10 LUCCA, THE GARFAGNANA & LUNIGIANA

Lucca

Pisa

Livorno

Isola di Gorgona

Isola di Capraia

11 THE TUSCAN COAST

Piombino

Isola d'Elba

Isola Pianosa

Isola di Montecristo

Isola del Giglio

Isola di Giannutri

Orbetello

Viareggio

Pistoia

Prato

07 FLORENCE

08 CHIANTI & THE MUGELLO

09 THE VALDARNO, PRATO & PISTOIA

Castellina in Chianti

12 SIENA

Siena

13 HILL TOWNS WEST OF SIENA

Massa Marittima

T U S C A N Y

14 SOUTHERN TUSCANY

Pienza

15 AREZZO & ITS PROVINCE

Arezzo

17 NORTHERN UMBRIA

Gubbio

16 PERUGIA, LAKE TRASIMENO & ASSISI

Perugia

Assisi

Deruta

Foligno

18 THE VALLE UMBRA: SPELLO TO SPOLETO

U M B R I A

Todi

19 THE TIBER VALLEY: TODI, ORVIETO, AMELIA

Orvieto

Amelia

Narni

Terni

Spoleto

20 THE VALNERINA: NARNI TO NORCIA

Norcia

Ascoli Piceno

21 THE MARCHES

T H E   M A R C H E S

Ancona

Pesaro

L A Z I O

A B R U Z Z I

Practical A–Z, which covers everything you are likely to need, on subjects ranging from climate, insurance and health to tourist offices.

The largest section of the book is devoted to **Tuscany**, starting in the treasure-house of **Florence** and then moving out to the delights of the surrounding countryside with its villages and hill towns, and other major art centres including Pisa, Siena and Arezzo.

Umbria, 'the green heart of Italy', follows, and the chapter tours its peaceful land-scape and lovely towns such as Perugia, Assisi and Orvieto. The guide ends with a section on **The Marches** – less well known, but one of the most civilized corners of Italy, containing Renaissance Urbino and Ascoli Piceno and scores of other fine old towns in the valleys leading up to the Sibilline Mountains.

The chapters are divided into sections which focus on a key city or town and the area around it, or on a journey between two featured places. Each section begins with a practical listings guide to the best places to stay and eat out, as well as information on how best to get around, local tourist offices and, where appropriate, details of any sports and activities, festivals, entertainment and nightlife relevant to the area.

The book concludes with a **Glossary** of architectural, artistic and historical terms, followed by two **Charts**, one of which shows the genealogy of the prominent Medici family, the other charting the progress of artistic influence from the 13th century through to the 16th. A chapter on **Language** supplies essential vocabulary for travel-ling around, booking hotels and a guide to Italian pronunciation. To enrich your appreciation of the area, there are also some suggestions for **Further Reading**.

Itineraries

10 Days of Roman and Etruscan Sites

1 **Florence** (Archaeology Museum and Etruscan tombs at Sesto Fiorentino) and **Fiesole** (Etruscan Walls, Roman theatre and museum).
2 **Volterra** (museum, Etruscan arch and Roman theatre).
3–4 The Etruscan cities of the coast: **Populonia**, **Vetulonia**, **Roselle** and **Ansedonia**, with stops at the Archaeology Museum in **Grosseto** and 'Frontone' (temple pediment) in **Orbetello**.
5 **Chiusi** (fine museum and only painted Etruscan tombs in Tuscany).
6 **Arezzo** (Roman amphitheatre and museum).
7 **Cortona** (Etruscan walls, gate, tombs and museum).
8 **Perugia** (gates, tombs and museum).
9 **Assisi** (Temple of Minerva – only complete Roman temple façade) and **Spello** (Roman Gates).
10 Roman ruins at *Carsulae* near San Gemini, and **Orvieto** (Etruscan tombs).

Early Medieval Art and Architecture, in Two Weeks

The best in Tuscany and Umbria, before 1200:
1 **Florence** (Baptistry, San Miniato).
2 **Pistoia** (Sant'Andrea, San Giovanni Fuorcivitas).
3 The bizarre **Pieve di Castelvecchio**, near Pescia, and Barga cathedral.
4 **Lucca** (Cathedral and San Michele).
5 **Pisa** (Piazza of Miracles, Museums and San Piero a Grado).
6 **Rosia**, **Sovicille** and the other churches just west of Siena.
7 **Sant'Antimo**, outside Montalcino and **Abbadia San Salvatore** (town and abbey).
8 The well-preserved medieval town of **Sovana**, near Pitigliano.
9 **Lugnano in Teverina** (Santa Maria Assunta), **Terni** (San Salvatore) and **Ferentillo** (San Pietro in Valle).
10–11 **Spoleto** (San Pietro, Cathedral, San Salvatore); **Bevagna** (San Salvatore and San Michele); **Foligno** (Cathedral façade and Santa Maria Infraportas), **Tempietto di Clitunno**; **Spello** (Santa Claudio).
12 **Perugia** (Sant'Angelo) and **Arezzo** (Santa Maria della Pieve).
13 **Grópina**, near Loro Ciuffenna in the Valdarno, and **Poppi** (Castle).
14 **Stia** (San Pietro and Castello di Romena).

13-Day Tour of High Medieval Art and Architecture

1–2 **Florence**: Orsanmichele, Bargello, Cathedral, Palazzo Vecchio, Palazzo Davanzati.
2 **Empoli** (Collegiata and museum) and **Certaldo** (Boccaccio's well-preserved home town).
3 **San Gimignano**: Collegiata frescoes and the city itself – a genuine, extraordinary medieval monument.
4 **Volterra**: civic buildings and art in Cathedral, San Francesco.

5 Massa Marittima and **San Galgano**.

6–8 Siena: Palazzo Pubblico, Cathedral – and nearly everything else!

9 Down the highway to **Orvieto**: Cathedral and more.

10 Todi: Civic buildings and San Fortunato.

11 Perugia: Palazzo dei Priori, Fontana Maggiore, many churches.

12 Assisi: Great hoard of trecento frescoes in San Francesco, many good churches.

13 The thoroughly medieval city of **Gubbio**.

13 Days Shooting a Renaissance Loop Outside Florence

Renaissance art somehow seems especially rarefied out in the provinces. Once you've paid your respects to Great Aunt Florence, visit:

1 Impruneta (Collegiata), **Certosa di Galluzzo**, **Lastra a Signa** (Alberti's church) and **Poggio a Caiano**, the archetypal Renaissance villa.

2 Prato (Santa Maria delle Carceri, Filippo Lippi's fresco cycle in the Cathedral, Donatello and Michelozzo's pulpit).

3 Lucca, for the sculpture of Matteo Civitali and Jacopo della Quercia.

4 San Gimignano, which has much of the best painting outside Florence, by Gozzoli, Ghirlandaio, Sodoma and more.

5 Siena, for the Sienese side of the Renaissance (Cathedral, especially pavements, tombs, Piccolomini Library and the Pinacoteca).

6–7 The exquisite monastic complex and frescoes at **Monte Oliveto Maggiore**, on the way to Pius II's planned city of **Pienza**; nearby **Montepulciano** for the best of classic Renaissance temples, Sangallo's San Biagio, as well as other churches and palaces.

8 Orvieto (Cathedral frescoes by Angelico and Signorelli) and **Città della Pieve** (Perugino).

9 Perugia (Pinacoteca, San Bernardino and others).

10 Cortona (two Renaissance temples, Signorelli and Fra Angelico) and **Monte San Savino**.

11 Arezzo (Piero della Francesca's frescoes and S. Maria delle Grazie).

12 More Pieros in **Monterchi** and **Sansepolcro**.

13 La Verna (Andrea della Robbia) and over the Passo di Consuma to Florence.

Villas and Gardens, in a Week or So

A 'Two-Centre Holiday' as all are located near Florence and Lucca. Do check the opening hours and do the necessary telephoning before setting out. In **Florence** itself there are beautiful walks around the Boboli Gardens, the villas and gardens of **Arcetri**, the **Villa Stibbert and Garden**, and the villas and gardens in and around **Fiesole**. Then:

1 Medici villas and gardens of **La Petraia**, **Castello** and **Careggi**.

2 Into the Mugello: Gardens of **Pratolino**, and Medici Villas at **Cafaggiolo** and **Trebbio**.

3 More Medici villas and gardens: **Poggio a Caiano**, **Villa Artimino** and **Cerreto Guidi**.

4–5 Villas in Chianti, although only the **Castello di Brolio** and **Badia a Coltibuono** are open to the public; other striking estates include: Villa Tattali, Palazzo al Bosco, Villa Le Corti, Poggio Torselli, Vignamaggio and several around Castellina.

6–7 From **Lucca**, **Castello Garzoni**, with fabulous gardens, near Collodi, and the three villas northeast of Lucca itself: **Villa Mansi**, **Villa Torrigiani** and **Villa Pecci-Blunt**. Other possibilities: the Medici **Villa della Magia** in Quarrata, southeast of Pistoia, and **Fosdinovo** castle up in the Lunigiana.

Nature and Scenery

For Tuscany and Umbria at their least civilized: start with the grandest of all, south Umbria's **Piano Grande** around **Norcia**, in the shadow of snow-capped **Monti Sibillini**; also the **Cascata delle Marmore** and the **Valnerina** north of Arrone and any of the side roads through the mountains. Southern Tuscany's **Monte Amiata** is an isolated patch of lovely mountain forests. **Mediterranean Coastal Scenery**: maquis and pine forests, on **Monte Argentario**, with side trips to **Giglio** and the surrounding marshlands with wildlife reserves and exotic birds, like the **Monti dell'Uccellina**. Further north, there are ancient coastal forests around **Pietrasanta** and **San Rossore**. **Coastal Mountains**: the **Apuan Alps**, lush, streaked with marble, are located along the coast from Carrara down, while a bit further inland are the dense oak and chestnut forests of the **Garfagnana**. **Serious Apennines**: the entire ridge between Tuscany and Emilia-Romagna, around **Abetone**, **Firenzuola**, **Camaldoli** (with ancient forests), **Pratomagno** (Monte Secchieta, and its panoramic roads), and the enchanting **Casentino**.

Two Weeks of Wine

For the best of Tuscan and Umbrian DOC wines, and some of the most ravishing scenery:

1 **Florence** to **Carmignano**, **Cerreto Guidi** and **Vinci** (wines: Carmignano and Chianti).
2 **Montecatini Alta**, **Collodi** and **Montecarlo** (wines: Bianco della Valdinievole and Montecarlo).
3 South of the Arno to **San Miniato** and environs, and **Certaldo** (wines: Bianco Pisano di S. Torpè and Chianti).
4 **San Gimignano** and **Colle di Val d'Elsa** (wines: Vernaccia di San Gimignano and Chianti Colli Senesi).
5 **Barberino Val d'Elsa** and **San Casciano** to the Florence–Siena wine route, the Chiantigiana and **Greve in Chianti** (wines: Chianti, Chianti Colli Fiorentini and Chianti Classico).
6 **Panzano** and **Radda in Chianti** (wine: Chianti Classico).
7 **Gaiole in Chianti**, **Castello di Brolio** and **Siena**, with a stop at the Enoteca Nazionale (wines: Chianti Classico and Chianti Colli Senesi).
8 **Montalcino** (wine: Brunello).
9 **Montepulciano** (wine: Vino Nobile).
10 **Cortona** (wine: Bianco Vergine della Valdichiana).
11 **Tuoro** and **Passignano** on Lake Trasimeno, to **Perugia** (wines: Colli del Trasimeno and Colli Perugini).
12 **Torgiano** and its wine museum, **Bevagna** and **Montefalco** (wines: Torgiana, Montefalco and Sagrantino).

13 Orvieto (wine: Orvieto Classico).

14 Sovana, Pitigliano, Saturnia (wines: Morellino di Scansano and Bianco di Pitigliano).

15 Check in at the spa at **Chianciano Terme** for liver repairs!

Ten Days of Curiosities

The unexpected, unique side of Tuscany and Umbria doesn't jump out at you; you'll have to look for it. In **Florence** you spend:

1–3 seeing **Galileo's Forefinger** at the Museum of the History of Science; gruesomely realistic **wax anatomical models** at La Specola museum; a **151-kilo topaz** at the Museum of Mineralogy; a **16th-century Mexican Bishop's mitre** made out of feathers, in the Museo degli Argenti; **Islamic and Japanese armour** in the Villa Stibbert; or an ornate **Mozarabic Synagogue** or onion-domed **Russian Orthodox Church**. From there, head to Tuscany's northernmost town, **Pontrémoli**...

4 to see the mysterious **Neolithic statue-*steles***, and then down to **Carrara** for the eerie, almost black whiteness of the **marble quarries**.

5 Pisa – the **Leaning Tower** is only one of a score of oddities in the Piazza of Miracles; also take a look at the **Turkish war pennants** in Santo Stefano.

6 Volterra, to see the balze and the unusual **Etruscan sculpture** in the Guarnacci Museum, on your way to the geothermal carnival of the **Metal Hills** – **geysers and sulphur lakes** around Larderello and Monterotondo.

7 Detour to Elba for **Napoleon's Death Mask**, or even better, inland to **San Galgano**, with its ruined Gothic abbey and genuine **Sword in the stone**.

8 If it's Saturday or Sunday, try the **Giardino dei Tarocchi** (at Capalbio, east of Orbetello), a bizarre collection of colossal modern sculptures, covered in bright ceramics and mirrors, dedicated to the 22 major arcana of the Tarot deck.

9 Orvieto, for one of the world's most remarkable wells, **Pozzo di San Patrizio**, and a dip over the border into Lazio for the **Bomarzo Monster Park**, a Renaissance 'Sacred Wood' full of strange stone creatures.

10 If you're still game, **Terni** for the paintings of **Orneore Metelli**, a shoemaker who never learned the lessons of perspective, and **Ferentillo** up the Valnerina road for the **Chinese and Napoleonic mummies**.

Discover the Marches in 9 Days

1–2 One day in **Urbino** to see the **Palazzo Ducale** and the town, another for excursions to outlying villages: **Urbania, Fermignano** or **San Leo**.

3 To **Fossombrone** with a look at the nearby **Gola del Furlo**.

4 A drive south through the mountains for a look at **Fabriano, Genga**'s caves and Romanesque church, ending up in **Jesi**.

5 Ancona and a rest on the beaches around **Monte Conero**.

6 Art at **Loreto** and accordions in **Castelfidardo**.

7 Inland again for pretty towns and picture galleries: **Tolentino, Camerino** and **San Severino Marche**.

8 A scenic drive south along the flank of **Monti Sibillini**.

9 Ascoli Piceno.

History and Art

02

Historical Outline

At times, the history of Tuscany and Umbria has been a small part of a bigger story – that of Rome, or modern Italy. However, the crucial eras of the Middle Ages and the Renaissance provided a tremendous chronicle of contending city states, each with a complex history of its own. For that reason, we have included detailed histories of the most important towns – Florence, Siena, Pisa and Perugia, and covered the rest to a lesser extent. Here is a brief historical outline for the region as a whole.

The Etruscans

Neolithic cultures seem to have occupied this region of Italy since about 4500 BC without distinguishing themselves artistically or politically. The dawn of history in these parts comes with the arrival of the **Etruscans**, though where they came from and precisely when they arrived remains one of the major mysteries of early Mediterranean history. According to their traditions, the Etruscans migrated from western Anatolia, c. 900 BC. Classical authors were divided on this point; some believed the migration theory, while others saw the Etruscans as the indigenous inhabitants of west-central Italy. Their language remains murky to modern scholars, but the discovery of Etruscan inscriptions on the Greek island of Lemnos, along with other clues, tends to support the Etruscan story.

Whatever it was, they were a talented people, and the great wealth they derived from intensive agriculture, manufacturing, and above all mining (Elba and the Metal Hills) allowed these talents to blossom into opulence by the 7th century BC. Though they gave their name to modern Tuscany, the real centre of Etruscan civilization lay to the south; roughly the coast from Orbetello to Cervéteri (Caere) in Lazio and around Lakes Bolsena and Trasimeno. Never a unified nation, the Etruscans preferred the general Mediterranean model of the independent city state; the 12 greatest dominated central Italy in a federation called the **Dodecapolis**. Which cities were members is uncertain, but the 14 possibilities include *Veii, Cervéteri, Tarquinia* and *Vulci* (in Lazio), *Roselle, Vetulonia* and *Populonia* (on or near the Tuscan coast), *Volterra, Fiesole, Arezzo, Chiusi, Orvieto, Cortona* and *Perugia*.

The Etruscans always maintained extremely close trade and cultural ties with classical Greece. They sold Elban iron and bought Greek culture wholesale; the artistic thieving magpies of antiquity, they adapted every style of Greek art, from the Minoan-style frescoes at Tarquinia to the classical bronzes now in the Florence Museum, and created something of their very own. In expressive portrait sculpture, however, they surpassed even the Greeks.

A considerable mythology has grown up around the Etruscans. Some historians and poets celebrate them as a nation of free peoples, devoted to art, good food and easy living. A less sentimental view depicts a slave society run for the benefit of a military, aristocratic élite. Whichever, the art they left behind gives them a place as the most enigmatic, vivid and fascinating people of early Italy. Echoes of their culture are clearly visible in everything that has happened in this part of Italy for the last 2,000 years.

The Romans

Etruscan kings once ruled in Rome, but after the establishment of the Republic, this precocious city was to prove the end of the Etruscan world. All of southern Etruria was swallowed up by 358 BC, and internal divisions between the Etruscan cities allowed the Romans to push their conquest inevitably northwards. After the conquest of an Etruscan city, Roman policy was often diabolically clever; by establishing veterans' colonies in new towns nearby to draw off trade, Rome was able to ensure the withering of Etruscan culture and the slow extinction of many of Etruria's greatest cities.

Four other cultures from this time deserve a mention; first the **Umbrii**, a peaceful, pastoral people indigenous to eastern Umbria and parts of the Marches. They adopted the Etruscan alphabet, but never had much to say in it – the only surviving inscription in Umbrian is in the museum of Gubbio. These earliest Umbrians had the good sense to avoid antagonizing Rome, and often allied themselves with the city in wars against other Italian tribes. The more war-like **Piceni**, most important of the tribes that occupied what is today the Marches, proved more antagonistic; in fact they played a leading role in the Social Wars of 92–89 BC, the last doomed attempt of the Italians to fight free of Roman imperialism. The wandering **Celts**, who occupied all northern Italy, often made themselves at home in the Apennines and northern Etruria; their influence on the region's culture is slight. And finally there was the unnamed culture of the rugged **Lunigiana**, around Pontrémoli, a people who carried their Neolithic customs and religion (*see* the statue-*steles* in the Pontrémoli museum, **Lucca, the Garfagnana and Lunigiana**, p.258) well into the modern era.

Under the empire, Etruria and Umbria were separate provinces, with the Tiber for a border. Both were relatively quiet, though the region experienced a north/south economic split to mirror the bigger one beginning across Italy. Southern Etruria, the old Etruscan heartland, shrivelled and died under Roman misrule, never to recover. The north became more prosperous, and important new cities appeared: Lucca, Pisa, Florence and, to a lesser extent, Assisi, Gubbio and Siena.

The Dark Ages

Later Italians' willingness to create fanciful stories about the 'barbarian invasions' makes it hard to define what did happen in this troubled time. The first (5th-century) campaigns of the **Goths** in Italy did not seem to cause too much damage, but the curtain finally came down on Roman civilization with the Greek-Gothic wars of 536–563, when Eastern Emperor Justinian and his generals Belisarius and Narsus attempted to recapture Italy for Byzantium. The chronicles of many cities record the devastation of the Gothic King, Totila (the sack of Florence, and a seven-year siege of Perugia), though the Imperial aggressors were undoubtedly just as bad. In any case, the damage to an already weakened society was fatal, and the wars opened the way for the conquest of much of Italy by the terrible **Lombards** (568), who established the Duchy of Spoleto, with loose control over much of central Italy. Lucca, the late Roman and Gothic capital of Etruria, alone managed to keep the Lombards out. By this time, low-lying cities like Florence had practically disappeared, while the remnants of the other towns survived under the control of local barons, or occasionally under their bishops. Feudal warfare and marauding became endemic. In the 800s even a band of Arabs came looting and pillaging up the Valnerina, almost in the centre of the peninsula.

By the 10th century, things were looking up. Florence had re-established itself, and built its famous baptistry. The old counts of Lucca extended their power to become counts of Tuscany, under the Attoni family, the lords of Canossa. As the leading power in the region, they made themselves a force to be reckoned with in European affairs. In 1077, the great Countess Matilda, allied with the Pope, humbled Emperor Henry IV at Canossa – the famous 'penance in the snow' – during the struggles over investiture. Perhaps most important of all was the growth of the maritime city of **Pisa**, which provided Tuscany with a new window on the world, building substantial wealth through trade and inviting new cultural influences from France, Byzantium and the Muslim world.

Medieval Tuscany

By 1000, with the new millennium, all of northern Italy was poised to rebuild the civilization that had been lost centuries before. In Tuscany and Umbria, as elsewhere, increasing trade had initiated a rebirth of towns, each doing its best to establish its independence from local nobles or bishops, and to increase its influence at the expense of its neighbours. Thus a thousand minor squabbles were played out against the background of the major issues of the day; first the conflict over investiture in the 11th century, evolving into the endless factional struggles of **Guelphs** and **Ghibellines** after 1215 (*see* **Topics**, p.33). Throughout, the cities were forced to choose sides between the partisans of the popes and those of the emperors. The Ghibellines' brightest hours came with the reigns of strong Hohenstaufen emperors **Frederick I Barbarossa** (1152–90) and his grandson **Frederick II** (1212–46), both of whom spent much time in Tuscany. An early Guelph wave came with the papacy of **Innocent III** (1198–1216), most powerful of the medieval pontiffs, and the Guelphs would come back to dominate Tuscany after the invasion of Charles of Anjou in 1261. Florence, Perugia, Arezzo and Lucca were the mainstays of the Guelphs, while Pisa, Pistoia and Siena usually supported the Ghibellines.

In truth, it was every city for itself. By 1200, most towns had become free *comuni*; their imposing public buildings can be seen in almost every corner of Tuscany and Umbria. All the trouble they caused fighting each other (at first with citizen militias, later increasingly with the use of hired *condottieri*) never troubled the booming economy. Florence and Siena became bankers to all Europe; great building programmes went up, beginning with the Pisa cathedral complex in the 1100s, and the now tamed and urbanized nobles built fantastical skyscraper skylines of tower-fortresses in the towns. Above all, it was a great age for culture, the age of Dante (b. 1265) and Giotto (b. 1266). Another feature of the time was the 13th-century religious revival, dominated by the figure of **St Francis of Assisi**.

Background of the Renaissance

Florence, biggest and richest of the Tuscan cities, increased its influence all through the 1300s, gaining Prato and Pistoia, and finally winning a seaport with the capture of declining Pisa in 1406. This set the stage for the relative political equilibrium of Tuscany during the early Renaissance, the height of the region's wealth and artistic achievement. Many Umbrian cities, notably Perugia, participated in both, though Umbria as a whole could not keep up. The popes, newly established in Rome, sent Cardinal Albornoz across the territory in the 1360s with the aim of binding the region more closely to the Papal State; he built a score of fortresses across Umbria.

The **Wars of Italy**, beginning in 1494, put an end to Renaissance tranquillity. Florence was once more lost in its internal convolutions, twice expelling the **Medici**, while French and Imperial armies marched over the two regions. When the dust had cleared, the last of the free cities (with the exception of Lucca) had been extinguished, and most of Tuscany came under the rule of the Grand Duke **Cosimo I** (1537–74), the Medici propped on a newly made throne by Emperor Charles V. Tuscany's economic and artistic decline was gentle compared with that of Umbria and the Marches; the majority of these latter two regions were incorporated into the Papal State during the 16th century.

The Modern Era

Though maintaining a relative independence, Tuscany had little to say in Italian affairs. After the Treaty of Câteau-Cambrésis in 1559, the Spaniards established a military enclave, called the Presidio, around Orbetello, precisely to keep an eye on central Italy. Cosimo I proved a vigorous ruler, though his successors gradually declined in ability. By 1600 it didn't matter. The total exhaustion of the Florentine economy kept pace with that of the Florentine imagination. By 1737, when the Medici dynasty became extinct, Tuscany was one of the torpid backwaters of Europe. It had no chance to decide its own destiny; the European powers agreed to bestow Tuscany on the House of Lorraine, cousins to the Austrian Habsburgs. Surprisingly enough, the Lorraines proved able and popular rulers, especially under the rule of the enlightened, progressive Peter Leopold (1765–90).

The languor of Lorraine and Papal rule was interrupted by Napoleon, who invaded central Italy twice and established a Kingdom of Etruria from 1801 to 1807. Austrian rule returned after 1815, continuing the series of well-meaning, intelligent Grand Dukes. By now, however, the Tuscans and the rest of the Italians wanted something better. In the tumult of the Risorgimento, one of the greatest and kindest of the Lorraines, Leopold II, saw the writing on the wall and allowed himself to be overthrown in 1859. Tuscany was almost immediately annexed to the new Italian kingdom, which liberated Umbria and the Marches in the same year.

Since then, the three regions have followed the history of modern Italy. The headstart Tuscany gained under the Lorraine dukes allowed it to keep up economically with northern Italy, while Umbria and the Marches had a hard job picking themselves up. Florence had a brief moment of glory (1865–70) as capital of Italy, awaiting the capture of Rome. Since then, the biggest affair has been the Second World War, with a long, tortuous campaign dragging across Tuscany and the Marches. The Germans based their Gothic Line on the Arno, blowing up all but one of Florence's bridges.

Art and Architecture

Etruscans

Although we have no way of knowing what life was like for the average man in Camars or Velathrii, their tomb sculptures and paintings convince us that they were a talented, likeable people. Almost all their art derives from the Greek; the Etruscans built classical temples (unfortunately of wood, with terracotta embellishments, so little survives), carved themselves sarcophagi decorated with scenes from Homer, and painted their pottery in red and black after the latest styles from Athens or Corinth. They excelled at portrait sculpture, and had a remarkable gift for capturing personality, sometimes seriously, though never heroically, often with an entirely intentional humour, and the serene smiles of people who truly enjoyed life.

Etruscan art in museums is often maddening; some of the works are among the finest productions of antiquity, while others – from the same time and city – are awkward and childish. Their talent for portraiture, among much else, was carried on by the Romans, and they bequeathed their love of fresco painting to the artists of the Middle Ages and Renaissance, who of course weren't even aware of the debt. After introducing yourself to the art of the Etruscans, it will be interesting to reconsider all that came later – in Tuscany, and indeed all Italy, you will find subtle reminders of this enigmatic people.

Romans and Dark Ages

After destroying the Etruscan nation, the Romans also began the extinction of its artistic tradition; by the time of the Empire, there was almost nothing left that could be called distinctively Etruscan. All of Tuscany, Umbria and the Marches contributed little under the Empire. In the chaos that followed, there was little room for art. What painting survived followed styles current in Byzantium.

Middle Ages

In both architecture and sculpture, the first main influence came from the north. Lombard masons filled Tuscany and Umbria with simple Romanesque churches; the first (Spoleto, Bevagna, Gropina, Abbadia S. Salvatore and in the Garfagnana, to name a few) follow the northern style, although it wasn't long before two distinctive Tuscan forms emerged: the Pisan style, characterized by blind rows of colonnades, black and white zebra stripes, and lozenge-shaped designs; and the 'Tuscan Romanesque' that developed around Florence, notable for its use of dark and light marble patterns and simple geometric patterns, often with intricate mosaic floors to match (the baptistry and San Miniato in Florence are the chief examples). In the cities in between – Lucca, Arezzo and Pistoia – there are interesting variations on the two different styles, often carrying an element such as stripes or arcades to remarkable extremes. The only real example of French Gothic in Tuscany is San Galgano built by Cistercians in the 1200s, although the style never caught on here or anywhere else in Italy.

From the large pool of talent working on Pisa's great cathedral complex in the 13th century emerged Italy's first great sculptor, **Nicola Pisano**, whose baptistry pulpit, with its realistic figures, was derived from ancient reliefs. His even more remarkable son, **Giovanni Pisano**, prefigures Donatello in the expressiveness of his statues and the vigour of his pulpits; his façade of Siena cathedral, though altered, is a unique work of art. **Arnolfo di Cambio**, a student of Nicola Pisano, became chief sculptor-architect of Florence during its building boom in the 1290s, designing its cathedral and Palazzo Vecchio with a hitherto unheard-of scale and grandeur, before moving on to embellish Orvieto with statues and tombs. Orvieto, however, hired the more imaginative **Lorenzo Maitani** in the early 1300s to create a remarkable cathedral façade as individualistic as Siena's, a unique combination of reliefs and mosaics.

Painting at first lagged behind the new realism and more complex composition of sculpture. The first to depart from Byzantine stylization, at least according to the account in Vasari's *Lives of the Artists* (*see* **Topics**, p.30), was **Cimabue**, in the late 1200s, who forsook Greek forms for a more 'Latin' or 'natural' way of painting. Cimabue found his greatest pupil, **Giotto**, as a young shepherd, chalk-sketching sheep on a piece of slate. Brought to Florence, Giotto soon eclipsed his master's fame (artistic celebrity being a recent Florentine invention) and achieved the greatest advances on the road to the new painting with a plain, rather severe approach that shunned Gothic prettiness while exploring new ideas in composition and expressing psychological depth in his subjects. Even more importantly, Giotto through his intuitive grasp of perspective was able to go further than any previous artist in representing his subjects as actual figures in space. In a sense Giotto actually invented space; it was this, despite his often awkward and graceless draughtsmanship, that so astounded his contemporaries. His followers, **Taddeo and Agnolo Gaddi** (father and son), **Giovanni da Milano** and **Maso di Banco**, filled Florence's churches with their own interpretations of the master's style. In the latter half of the 1300s, however, **Andrea Orcagna** appeared, regarded as the most important Florentine sculptor, painter and architect of his day. Inspired by the more elegant style of **Andrea Pisano**'s baptistry doors, Orcagna broke away from simple Giottesque forms to assume a more elaborate, detailed style in his sculpture, while the fragments of his frescoes that survive have a vivid dramatic power that must owe something to the time of the Black Death and the social upheavals ongoing as they were painted.

Siena never produced a Vasari to chronicle its accomplishments, though they were considerable; in the 13th and 14th centuries, Siena's Golden Age, the city's artists, like its soldiers, rivalled and often surpassed those of Florence. For whatever reason, it seemed purposefully to seek inspiration in different directions from Florence; at first from central Italian styles around Spoleto and then, with prosperity and the advent of **Guido da Siena** in the early 1200s, from the more elegant line and colour of Byzantium. Guido's work paved the way for the pivotal figure of **Duccio di Buoninsegna**, the catalyst who founded the essentials of Sienese art by uniting the beauty of Byzantine line and colour with the sweet finesse of western Gothic art. With Duccio's great followers **Pietro and Ambrogio Lorenzetti** and **Simone Martini**, the Sienese produced an increasingly elegant and rarefied art, almost oriental in its refined stylization. They were less innovative than the Florentines, though they brought the 'International Gothic' style – flowery and ornate, with all the bright tones of May – to its highest form in Italy. Simone Martini introduced the Sienese manner to Florence in the early 1400s, where it influenced most notably the work of **Lorenzo Monaco**, **Masolino** and the young goldsmith and sculptor **Ghiberti**. The Umbrian artists of the trecento, most of them anonymous, were also heavily influenced by the Sienese, using just as much colour, if less sophistication.

The Renaissance

Under the assaults of historians and critics over the last two centuries, the term 'Renaissance' has become a vague and controversial word. Nevertheless, however you choose to interpret this rebirth of the arts, and whatever dates you assign to it, Florence inescapably takes the credit for it. This is no small claim. Combining art, science and humanist scholarship to shape a visual revolution that often seemed pure sorcery to their contemporaries, a handful of Florentine geniuses taught the Western eye a new way of seeing. Perspective seems a simple enough trick to us now, but its discovery determined everything that followed, not only in art, but in science and philosophy as well.

Leading what scholars used self-assuredly to call the 'Early Renaissance' is a triumvirate of three geniuses: Brunelleschi, Donatello and Masaccio. **Brunelleschi**, neglecting his considerable talents in sculpture in favour of architecture and science, not only built the majestic dome of Florence cathedral, but threw the Pandora's box of perspective wide open by mathematically codifying the principles of foreshortening. His good friend **Donatello**, the greatest sculptor since the ancient Greeks, inspired a new generation of both sculptors and painters to explore new horizons in portraiture and three-dimensional representation. The first painter to incorporate Brunelleschi and Donatello's lessons of spatiality, perspective and expressiveness was the young prodigy **Masaccio** who, along with his master Masolino, painted the famous Brancacci Chapel in the Carmine, studied by nearly all Florentine artists right up to Michelangelo.

The new science of architecture, sculpture and painting introduced by this triumvirate ignited an explosion of talent unequalled before or since: a score of masters, most of them Tuscan, each following the dictates of his own genius to create a remarkable range of themes and styles. Among the most prominent are **Lorenzo Ghiberti**, who followed Donatello's advice on his second set of baptistry doors to cause a Renaissance revolution; **Leon Battista Alberti**, who took Brunelleschi's ideas to their most classical extreme in architecture, creating new forms in the process; **Paolo Uccello**, one of the most provocative of artists, who according to Vasari drove himself mad with the study of perspective and the possibilities of illusionism; **Piero della Francesca** of Sansepolcro, who explored the limits of perspective and geometrical forms to create the most compelling, haunting images of the quattrocento;

Fra (now Beato) **Angelico**, who combined Masaccio's innovations, International Gothic colours and his own deep faith to create the most purely spiritual art of his time; and **Andrea del Castagno**, who made use of perspective to create monumental, if often restless, figures.

Some of Donatello's gifted followers were **Agostino di Duccio**, **Benedetto da Maiano**, **Desiderio da Settignano**, **Antonio and Bernardo Rossellino**, **Mino da Fiesole** and, perhaps most famously, **Luca della Robbia**, who invented the coloured terra-cottas that were to be spread by his family throughout Tuscany. There are still more: **Benozzo Gozzoli**, whose enchanting springtime colours and delight in detail are a throwback to International Gothic; **Antonio and Piero Pollaiuolo**, sons of a poultry-man, whose new, dramatic use of line and form, often violent and writhing, would be echoed in Florentine Mannerism; **Fra Filippo Lippi**, a monk like Fra Angelico but far more earthly, the master of lovely Madonnas and teacher of his talented son **Filippino Lippi**; **Domenico Ghirlandaio**, whose gift of easy charm and flawless technique made him society's favoured fresco painter; **Andrea del Verrocchio**, who could cast in bronze, paint or carve with perfect detail; **Luca Signorelli**, who achieved apocalyptic grandeur in Orvieto cathedral; **Perugino** (Pietro Vannucci) of Umbria, who painted the stillness of his native region into his landscapes and taught the young **Raphael** of Urbino; and finally **Sandro Botticelli**, whose highly intellectual but lovely, melancholy and mytho-logical paintings are in a class of their own.

The 'Early Renaissance' came to a close near the end of the 1400s with the advent of **Leonardo da Vinci**, whose unique talent in painting, only one of his hundreds of interests, challenged the certainty of naturalism with a subtlety and chiaroscuro that approaches magic. One sole passion, however, obsessed the other great figure of the 'High Renaissance', **Michelangelo Buonarroti**: his consummate interest was the human body, at first graceful and serene as in most of his Florentine works and, later, contorted and anguished after he left for Rome.

Mannerism

Michelangelo left in Florence the seeds of the bold, neurotic avant-garde art that has come to be known as Mannerism. This first conscious 'movement' in Western art can be seen as a last fling amidst the growing intellectual and spiritual exhaustion of 1530s Florence, conquered once and for all by the Medici. The Mannerists' calculated exoticism and exaggerated, tortured poses, together with the brooding self-absorp-tion of Michelangelo, are a prelude to Florentine art's remarkably abrupt turn into decadence, and prophesy its final extinction. Foremost among the Mannerist painters are two surpassingly strange characters, **Jacopo Pontormo** and **Rosso Fiorentino**, who were not in such great demand as the coldly classical **Andrea del Sarto** and **Bronzino**, consummate perfectionists of the brush, both much less intense and demanding. There were also charming reactionaries working at the time, especially **Il Sodoma** and **Pinturicchio**, both of whom left their best works in Siena. In sculpture **Giambologna** and, to a lesser extent, **Bartolommeo Ammannati** specialized in virtuoso *contrapposto* figures, each one more impossible than the last. With their contemporary, **Giorgio Vasari**, Florentine art lost almost all imaginative and intellectual content, and became a virtuoso style of interior decoration perfectly adaptable to saccharine holy pictures, portraits of newly enthroned dukes, or absurd, mythological fountains and ballroom ceilings. In the cinquecento, with plenty of money to spend and a long Medici tradition of patronage to uphold, this tendency soon got out of hand. Under the reign of Cosimo I, indefatigable collector of *pietra dura* tables, silver and gold gimcracks, and exotic, stuffed animals, Florence gave birth to the artistic phenomenon modern critics call 'kitsch'.

The Rest Compressed

In the long, dark night of later Tuscan art a few artists stand out – the often whimsical architect and engineer, **Buontalenti**; **Pietro Tacca**, Giambologna's pupil with a taste for the grotesque; and the charming, Baroque fresco master **Pietro da Cortona**. Most of Tuscany, and particularly Florence, chose to sit out the Baroque – almost by choice, it seems, and we can race up to the 19th century until we reach the often delightful 'Tuscan Impressionists' or *Macchiaioli* ('Splatterers'; best collection in Modern Art section of Pitti Palace); and in the 20th century, **Modigliani** (from Livorno) of the oval faces; the Futurist **Gino Severini** (from Cortona); and **Alberto Burri**, one of the first to use junk as a medium (from Città di Castello, where there's a museum). There is an exceptionally good collection of contemporary Italian art at Macerata in the Marches; others include a museum dedicated to sculptor **Marino Marini** in Florence, and another to **Manzù**, in Orvieto, although newest and most entertaining of all is the late French artist Niki de Saint-Phalle's Giardino dei Tarocchi south of Orbetello.

Artists' Directory

This includes the principal architects, painters and sculptors of Tuscany, Umbria and the Marches. The works listed are far from exhaustive, bound to exasperate partisans of some artists and do scant justice to the rest, but we have tried to include only the best and most representative works that you'll find in these regions.

Agostino di Duccio (Florentine, 1418–81). A precocious and talented sculptor, his best work is in the Malatesta Temple at **Rimini** – he was exiled from Florence after being accused of theft (**Perugia**, S. Bernardino; **Florence**, Bargello; **Pontrémoli**, S. Francesco).

Alberti, **Leon Battista** (Florentine, b. Genoa 1404–72). Architect, theorist, and writer, also a sculptor and painter. His greatest contribution was recycling the classical orders and the principles of Vitruvius into Renaissance architecture; he was a consultant to the architecture-loving Duke of Urbino. (**Florence**, Palazzo Rucellai, façade of S. Maria Novella, SS. Annunziata; **Lastra a Signa**, S. Martino).

Allori, **Alessandro** (1535–1607). Florentine Mannerist painter, prolific follower of Michelangelo and Bronzino (**Florence**, SS. Annunziata, S. Spirito, Spedale degli Innocenti).

L'Alunno (Niccolò di Liberatore, *c.* 1430–1502). Painter of Foligno; genuine Renaissance polish without much to challenge the imagination (**Assisi**, cathedral museum; **Deruta**, Pinacoteca; **Foligno**, S. Niccoló; **Nocera Umbra**, Pinacoteca).

Ammannati, Bartolommeo (1511–92). Florentine architect and sculptor. Restrained, elegant architect (**Florence**, S. Trínita bridge, courtyard of Pitti Palace); neurotic, twisted Mannerist sculptor (**Florence**, Fountain of Neptune, Villa di Castello).

Andrea del Castagno (*c*. 1423–57). Precise, dry Florentine painter, one of the first and greatest slaves of perspective. Died of the plague (**Florence**, Uffizi, S. Apollonia, SS. Annunziata).

Angelico, Fra (or Beato) (Giovanni da Fiesole, *c*. 1387–1455). Monk first and painter second, but still one of the great visionary artists of the Renaissance (**Florence**, S. Marco – spectacular Annunciation and many more; **Cortona**, Cathedral Museum; **Fiesole**, S. Domenico; **Perugia**, National Museum).

Antonio da Fabriano (active *c*. 1450). One of the school of painters from the little Marches town of **Fabriano**; works there and in **Matelica**.

Arnolfo di Cambio (b. Colle di Val d'Elsa; *c*. 1245–1302). Architect and sculptor, pupil of Nicola Pisano and a key figure in his own right. Much of his best sculpture is in Rome, but he changed the face of Florence as main architect to the city's greatest building programme of the 1290s (**Florence**, cathedral and Palazzo Vecchio; **Orvieto**, Museo Civico, S. Domenico).

Baldovinetti, Alesso (Florentine, 1425–99). A delightful student of Fra Angelico who left few tracks; most famous for fresco work in **Florence** (SS. Annunziata, Uffizi, S. Niccolò sopr'Arno, S. Miniato).

Bandinelli, Baccio (1488–1559). Florence's comic relief of the late Renaissance; supremely serious, vain, and so awful it hurts; he was, of course, court sculptor to Cosimo I (**Florence**, Piazza della Signoria and SS. Annunziata).

Barna da Siena (active mid–late 1300s). One of the chief followers of Simone Martini, more dramatic and vigorous than the usual ethereal Sienese (**San Gimignano**, Collegiata).

Barocci, Federico (*c*. 1535–1612). Intense proto-Baroque painter of Urbino, inexplicably influential and popular in his time (**Urbino**, Palazzo Ducale and Duomo).

Bartolo di Fredi (Sienese, active *c*. 1353–1410). Student of Ambrogio Lorenzetti, a genuine pre-Raphaelite soul, entirely at home in the Sienese trecento; employs colours never before seen on this planet (**Montepulciano**, Duomo; **San Gimignano**, Collegiata).

Bartolommeo, Fra (*c*. 1472–1517). Florentine painter, master of the High Renaissance style (**Florence**, S. Marco, Pitti Palace).

Beccafumi, Domenico (*c*. 1486–1551). Sienese painter; odd mixture of Sienese conservatism and Florentine Mannerism (**Siena**, Pinacoteca, Palazzo Pubblico, cathedral pavement).

Benedetto da Maiano (Florentine, 1442–97). Sculptor, specialist in narrative reliefs (**Florence**, S. Croce, Strozzi Palace, Bargello; he also designed the loggia of S. Maria delle Grazie, **Arezzo**).

Berruguete, Pedro (*c*. 1450–1504). Spanish Renaissance painter who worked for the Duke of Urbino for many years and painted one of his most celebrated portraits (Ducal Palace, **Urbino**).

Bigarelli, Guido (13th century). Talented travelling sculptor from Como, who excelled in elaborate and sometimes bizarre pulpits (**Barga**, **Pistoia**, S. Bartolomeo, and **Pisa baptistry**).

Bonfigli, Benedetto (Perugia, *c.* 1420–96). Meticulous Umbrian painter, known for his painted banners in many **Perugia** churches; best works, especially the Cappella dei Priori frescoes, are in that city's National Gallery.

Botticelli, Sandro (Florentine, 1445–1510). Though technically excellent in every respect, and a master of both line and colour, there is more to Botticelli than this. Above every other quattrocento artist, his works reveal the imaginative soul of the Florentine Renaissance, particularly his great series of mythological paintings (**Florence**, Uffizi). Later, a little deranged and under the spell of Savonarola, he reverted to intense, though conventional, religious paintings. Almost forgotten in the philistine 1500s and not rediscovered until the 19th century, many of his best works are probably lost (**Florence**, Accademia; **Montelupo**, S. Giovanni Evangelista).

Bronzino, Agnolo (1503–72). Virtuoso Florentine Mannerist with a cool, glossy hyper-elegant style, at his best in portraiture; a close friend of Pontormo (**Florence**, Palazzo Vecchio, Uffizi, S. Lorenzo, SS. Annunziata).

Brunelleschi, Filippo (1377–1446). Florentine architect, credited in his own time with restoring the ancient Roman manner of building – but really deserves more credit for developing a brilliant, new approach of his own (**Florence**, Duomo cupola, Spedale degli Innocenti, S. Spirito, S. Croce's Pazzi Chapel, S. Lorenzo). Also a sculptor (he lost the competition for the baptistry doors to Ghiberti), and one of the first theorists on perspective.

Buontalenti, Bernardo (1536–1608). Late Florentine Mannerist architect and planner of the new city of **Livorno**, better known for his Medici villas (**Artimino**, also the fascinating grotto in **Florence**'s Boboli Gardens, and Belvedere Fort, Uffizi Tribuna).

Cellini, Benvenuto (1500–71). Goldsmith and sculptor. Though a native of Florence, Cellini spent much of his time in Rome. In 1545 he came to work for Cosimo I and to torment Bandinelli (*Perseus*, Loggia dei Lanzi; also works in the Bargello). As famed for his catty *Autobiography* as for his sculpture.

Cimabue (*c.* 1240–1302). Florentine painter credited by Vasari with initiating the 'rebirth of the arts'; one of the first painters to depart from the stylization of the Byzantine style (**Florence**, mosaics in baptistry, Crucifix in S. Croce; **Pisa**, cathedral mosaic; whatever is left in the upper church of S. Francesco in **Assisi**).

Civitali, Matteo (Lucchese, *c.* 1435–1501). Sweet yet imaginative sculptor, apparently self-taught. He would be much better known if all of his works weren't in Lucca (**Lucca**, cathedral, Guinigi Museum).

Cola dell'Amatrice (1489–1559). Architect and painter, a follower of Carlo Crivelli; worked mainly in **Ascoli Piceno** (cathedral façade and town hall).

Coppo di Marcovaldo (Florentine, active *c.* 1261–75). Another very early painter, as good as Cimabue if not as well known (**San Gimignano**; **Pistoia**, cathedral).

Crivelli, Carlo (1430–95). A refugee from Venice who painted all over the Marches; obsessively precise and something of an eccentric: fond of painting fruit and cucumbers above some of the most spiritual Madonnas and saints ever created (**Corridonia**, **Ancona**, **Ascoli Piceno**, **Macerata**). His brother **Vittore Crivelli** (d. 1501) copied him closely.

Daddi, Bernardo (active 1290–c. 1349). Florentine master of delicate altarpieces (**Florence**, Orsanmichele, S. Maria Novella's Spanish chapel).

De Magistris, Simone (active 1560–1600). Little-known painter of the Marches, one of the last to keep up something of the style and individuality of the Renaissance (**Sarnano**, **San Ginesio**, **Camerino**, **Osimo**, **Ascoli Piceno**).

Desiderio da Settignano (Florentine, 1428/31–61). Sculptor, follower of Donatello (**Florence**, S. Croce, Bargello, S. Lorenzo).

Dolci, Carlo (Florentine, 1616–86). Unsurpassed Baroque master of the 'whites of their eyes' school of religious art (**Florence**, Palazzo Corsini; **Prato**, Museo del Duomo).

Domenico di Bartolo (Sienese, c. 1400–46). An interesting painter, well out of the Sienese mainstream; the unique naturalism of his art is a Florentine influence. (Spedale di S. Maria della Scala, Pinacoteca in **Siena**).

Domenico Veneziano (Florentine 1404–61). Painter, teacher of Piero della Francesca; master of perspective with few surviving works (**Florence**, Uffizi).

Donatello (Florentine, 1386–1466). The greatest Renaissance sculptor, appearing as suddenly as a comet at the beginning of Florence's quattrocento. Never equalled in technical ability, expressiveness, nor imaginative content, his works influenced Renaissance painters as much as sculptors. A prolific worker, the favourite of Old Cosimo de' Medici, and a quiet fellow who lived with his mum, Donatello was the perfect model of the Early Renaissance artist: passionate about art, self-effacing, and a little eccentric (**Florence**, Bargello – the greatest works including the original *St George* from Orsanmichele, *David* and *Cupid-Atys*, also the great pulpits, the masterpiece of his old age in S. Lorenzo; other works in Palazzo Vecchio, and the Cathedral Museum; **Siena**, cathedral, baptistry).

Duccio di Buoninsegna (d. 1319). One of the first and greatest Sienese painters, Duccio was to Sienese art what Giotto was to Florence; ignored by Vasari, though his contributions to the new visual language of the Renaissance are comparable to Giotto's (**Siena**, parts of the great Maestà in the Cathedral Museum, also Pinacoteca; **Florence**, altarpiece in the Uffizi; **Massa Marittima**, cathedral; **Castelfiorentino**, Pinacoteca).

Francesco di Giorgio Martini (Sienese, 1439–1502). Architect – mostly of fortresses – sculptor and painter, his works are scattered all over Italy (**Siena**, cathedral, Pinacoteca; **Cortona**, S. Maria di Calcinaio; elegant castles at **San Leo** and **Mondavio** and in a score of other towns in the Marches).

Franciabigio (Florentine, 1482–1525). Most temperamental of Andrea del Sarto's pupils but only mildly Mannerist (**Florence**, Poggio a Caiano and SS. Annunziata).

Gaddi, Taddeo (c. 1300–c. 1366). Florentine; most important of the followers of Giotto. He and his son **Agnolo** (d. 1396) contributed some of the finest trecento fresco cycles (**Florence**, notably at S. Croce, and S. Ambrogio; **Prato**, cathedral).

Gentile da Fabriano (c. 1360–1427). Master nonpareil of the International Gothic style, from Fabriano in the Marches. Most of his work is lost (**Florence**, Uffizi).

Ghiberti, Lorenzo (1378–1455). Goldsmith and sculptor. The first artist to write an auto-biography was, naturally, a Florentine. He would probably be better known had he not spent most of his career working on the doors for the Florence baptistry after winning the famous competition of 1401 (also **Florence**, statues at Orsanmichele; **Siena**, baptistry).

Ghirlandaio, Domenico (Florentine, c. 1448–94). The painter of the quattrocento establishment, master of colourful, lively fresco cycles (with the help of a big workshop) in which he painted all the Medici and Florence's banking élite. A great portraitist with a distinctive, dry, restrained style (**Florence**, Ognissanti, S. Maria Novella, S. Trínita, Spedale degli Innocenti; **San Gimignano**, Collegiata; also **Narni**, museum).

Giambologna (1529–1608). A Fleming, born Jean Boulogne; court sculptor to the Medici after 1567 and one of the masters of Mannerist virtuosity; also a man with a taste for the outlandish (**Florence**, Loggia dei Lanzi, Bargello, Villa la Petraia; **Pratolino**, the *Appennino*).

Giotto (c. 1266–1337). Shepherd boy of the Mugello (discovered by Cimabue) who became the first great Florentine painter; he was even recognized as such in his own time. Invented an essential and direct approach to portraying narrative fresco cycles, but is even more important for his revolutionary treatment of space and of the human figure. (**Florence**, S. Croce, cathedral campanile, Horne Museum, S. Maria Novella; **Assisi**, lower church frescoes at S. Francesco; attribution of the great upper church to him or his followers is the longest-running battle in art history).

Giovanni da Milano (14th century). An innovative Lombard inspired by Giotto (**Florence**, S. Croce; **Prato**, Cathedral Museum).

Giovanni di Paolo (d. 1483). One of the best of the quattrocento Sienese painters; like most of them, a colourful, often eccentric, reactionary who continued the traditions of the Sienese trecento (**Siena**, Pinacoteca).

Giovanni di San Giovanni (1592–1633). One of Tuscany's more prolific, but likable Baroque fresco painters (**Florence**, Pitti Palace, Villa la Petraia).

Girolamo di Giovanni (c. 1420–73). Refined painter from **Camerino** (in the Marches), little known because his best works are still there.

Giuliano da Rimini (active 1350s). Recent studies attribute to this obscure figure the striking blue-green frescoes in the Basilica of S. Nicola at **Tolentino**.

Gozzoli, Benozzo (Florentine, d. 1497). Learned his trade from Fra Angelico, but few artists could have less in common. The most light-hearted and colourful of quattro-cento artists, Gozzoli created enchanting frescoes (**Florence**, Medici chapel; **San Gimignano**, S. Agostino; **Pisa**, Camposanto; **Montefalco**, S. Francesco; **Castelfiorentino**, Visitation Chapel; **Narni**, museum).

Guido da Siena (13th century). One of the founders of Sienese painting, still heavily Byzantine in style; little is known about his life (**Siena**, Palazzo Pubblico, Pinacoteca; **Grosseto**, museum).

Laurana, Luciano (c. 1420–79). Dalmatian architect who worked for the court of **Urbino**, designing much of the Palazzo Ducale, one of the masterpieces of the Renaissance.

Leonardo da Vinci (1452–1519). We could grieve that Florence's 'universal genius' spent so much time on his scientific interests and building fortifications, and that his meagre artistic output was largely unfinished or lost. All that is left in Tuscany is the *Annunciation* (**Florence**, Uffizi) and also models of all his gadgets at his birthplace, **Vinci**. As the pinnacle of the Renaissance marriage of science and art, Leonardo requires endless volumes of interpretation. As for his personal life, Vasari records him buying up caged birds in the market-place just to set them free.

Lippi, Filippino (Florentine, 1457–1504). Son and artistic heir of Fra Filippo. Often seems a neurotic Gozzoli, or at least one of the most thoughtful and serious artists of the quattrocento (**Florence**, S. Maria Novella, S. Maria del Carmine, Badia, Uffizi).

Lippi, Fra Filippo (Florentine, d. 1469). Never should have been a monk in the first place. A painter of exquisite, ethereal Madonnas, one of whom he ran off with (the model, at least, a brown-eyed nun named Lucrezia). The pope forgave them both. Lippi was a key figure in the increasingly complex, detailed painting of the middle 1400s (**Florence**, Uffizi; **Prato**, cathedral and Civic Museum; **Spoleto**, Duomo).

Lorenzetti, Ambrogio (Sienese, d. 1348). He could crank out golden Madonnas as well as any Sienese painter, but Lorenzetti was also a great innovator in subject matter and the treatment of landscapes. Created the first and greatest of secular frescoes, the *Allegories of Good and Bad Government* in **Siena**'s Palazzo Pubblico, while his last known work, the 1344 *Annunciation* in Siena's Pinacoteca is one of the 14th century's most revolutionary treatments of perspective (also **Massa Marittima**, museum).

Lorenzetti, Pietro (Sienese, d. 1348). Ambrogio's big brother, and also an innovator, standing square between Duccio di Buoninsegna and Giotto; one of the precursors of the Renaissance's new treatment of space (**Assisi**, S. Francesco; **Siena**, S. Spirito; **Arezzo**, Pieve di S. Maria; **Cortona**, Cathedral Museum). Both Lorenzettis seem to have died in Siena during the Black Death.

Lorenzo di Credi (1439–1537). One of the most important followers of Leonardo da Vinci, always technically perfect, if occasionally vacuous (**Florence**, Uffizi).

Lorenzo Monaco (b. Siena 1370–1425). A monk at S. Maria degli Angeli in Florence and a brilliant colourist, Lorenzo forms an uncommon connection between the Gothic style of Sienese painting and the new developments in early Renaissance Florence (**Florence**, Uffizi, S. Trínita).

Lotto, Lorenzo (*c.* 1480–1556). Venetian, pupil of Giovanni Bellini, best known there as one of the first great portraitists. Spent his declining years in the Marches, where he left a considerable amount of uninspired or magnificent religious work (**Jesi, Ancona, Recanati, Loreto**).

Maitani, Lorenzo (d. 1330). Sienese sculptor and architect, his reputation rests almost entirely on the great façade of **Orvieto** cathedral, where he spent most of his life as master of works.

Manetti, Rutilio (1571–1639). Quirky but somehow likeable Baroque painter, the last artist of any standing produced by Siena (**Massa Marittima**, cathedral).

Margarito d'Arezzo (Arezzo, 13th century). Also called Margaritone. A near contemporary of Giotto who stuck firmly to his Byzantine guns (**Arezzo**, museum).

Martini, Simone (Sienese, d. 1344). Possibly a pupil of Giotto, Martini took the Sienese version of International Gothic to an almost metaphysical perfection, creating luminous, lyrical, and exquisitely drawn altarpieces and frescoes perhaps unsurpassed in the trecento (**Assisi**, S. Francesco; **Siena**, Palazzo Pubblico; **Pisa**, Museo S. Matteo; **Florence**, Uffizi; **Orvieto**, Museo Civico).

Masaccio (Florentine, 1401–*c*. 1428). Though he died young and left little behind, this precocious 'shabby Tom' gets credit for inaugurating the Renaissance in painting by translating Donatello and Brunelleschi's perspective on to a flat surface. Also revolutionary in his use of light and shadow, and in expressing emotion in his subjects' faces (**Florence**, S. Maria del Carmine, S. Maria Novella; **Pisa**, Museo S. Matteo).

Maso di Banco (Florentine, active 1340s). One of the more colourful and original followers of Giotto (**Florence**, S. Croce).

Masolino (Florentine, d. 1447). Perhaps 'little Tom' also deserves much of the credit, along with Masaccio, for the new advances in art at the Carmine in **Florence**; art historians dispute endlessly how to attribute the frescoes. It's hard to tell, for this brilliant painter left little other work behind to prove his case (**Empoli**, civic museum; **Todi**, S. Fortunato; also attributed **Pistoia**, Tau chapel).

Matteo da Gualdo (*c*. 1430–1503). Umbrian painter, perhaps more representative of the lot than Perugino. Created conventional, colourful works; probably never heard of Florence (works in his home town, **Gualdo Tadino**).

Matteo di Giovanni (Sienese, 1435–95). One Sienese quattrocento painter who could keep up with the Florentines; a contemporary described him as 'Simone Martini come to life again' (**Siena**, Pinacoteca, cathedral pavement, S. Agostino, S. Maria delle Neve; **Grosseto**, Museum).

Melozzo da Forli (b. Forlí, in the Romagna, 1438–1494). Famous for his perspectives and illusionism, but unfortunately little of his work survives; the best preserved (outside Rome) is the S. Marco sacristy in **Loreto** (also **Urbino**, Ducal Palace).

Memmi, Lippo (Sienese, 1317–47). Brother-in-law and assistant of Simone Martini (**Siena**, S. Spirito; **San Gimignano**, museum).

Michelangelo Buonarroti (Florentine, 1475–1564). Born in Caprese (now Caprese Michelangelo) into a Florentine family of the minor nobility come down in the world, Michelangelo's early years and artistic training are obscure; he was apprenticed to Ghirlandaio but, showing a preference for sculpture, was sent to the court of Lorenzo de' Medici. Nicknamed Il Divino in his lifetime, he was a complex, difficult character, who seldom got along with mere mortals, popes, or patrons. What he couldn't express by means of the male nude in paint or marble, he did in his beautiful but difficult sonnets. In many ways he was the first modern artist, unsurpassed in technique but also the first genius to go over the top (**Florence**, Medici tombs and library in S. Lorenzo, three works in the Bargello, the *Pietà* in the Museo del Duomo, the *David* in the Accademia, Casa Buonarroti, and his only oil painting, in the Uffizi).

Michelozzo di Bartolomeo (Florentine, 1396–1472). Sculptor who worked with Donatello (**Prato**, pulpit of the Holy Girdle, and the tomb in **Florence's** baptistry), he is better known as the classicizing architect favoured by the elder Cosimo de' Medici

(**Florence**, Medici Palace, Chiostro of SS. Annunziata, library of S. Marco; Villas at **Trebbio** and **Cafaggiolo**; **Montepulciano**, S. Agostino; **Impruneta**, Tempietto).

Mino da Fiesole (Florentine, 1429–84). Sculptor of portrait busts and tombs; like the della Robbias a representative of the Florentine 'sweet style' (**Fiesole**, cathedral; **Empoli**, museum; **Volterra**, cathedral; **Florence**, Badia, Sant'Ambrogio; **Prato**, cathedral).

Nanni di Banco (Florentine, 1384–1421). Florentine sculptor at the dawn of the Renaissance (**Florence**, Orsanmichele, Porta della Mandorla).

Nelli, **Ottaviano** (*c*. 1375–*c*. 1440). A typical, often charming representative of the early Umbrian school; most of his work is in his home town, **Gubbio**.

Orcagna, **Andrea** (Florence, d. 1368). Sculptor, painter and architect who dominated the middle 1300s in Florence, though greatly disparaged by Vasari, who destroyed much of his work. Some believe he is the 'Master of the Triumph of Death' of Pisa's Camposanto (**Florence**, Orsanmichele, S. Croce, S. Maria Novella, *Crucifixion* in refectory of S. Spirito, also often given credit for the Loggia dei Lanzi).

Perugino (Pietro Vannucci, Perugia, *c*. 1450–1523). Perhaps the most distinctive of the Umbrian painters; created some works of genius, along with countless idyllic nativity scenes, each with its impeccably sweet Madonna and characteristic blue-green tinted background. Some of his later works are awful, although he may not always be responsible: in his cynical old age he let his workshop sign his name to anything (**Città della Pieve**, S. Maria dei Bianchi; **Perugia**, Pinacoteca, Collegio del Cambio; **Trevi**, Madonna delle Lacrime; **Florence**, Uffizi, S. Maddalena dei Pazzi, Cenacolo di Foligno; also in **Fano**).

Piero della Francesca (*c*. 1415–92). Painter, born in Sansepolcro, and one of the really unique quattrocento artists. Piero, a leading light in the famous court of Urbino, wrote two of the most important theoretical works on perspective, then illustrated them with a lifetime's work reducing painting to the bare essentials: geometry, light and colour. In his best work his reduction creates nothing dry or academic, but dreamlike, almost eerie scenes similar to those of Uccello. And, like Uccello or Botticelli, his subjects are often archetypes of immense psychological depth, not to be fully explained now or ever (**Arezzo**, S. Francesco and the cathedral; **Urbino**, Palazzo Ducale; **Sansepolcro**, civic museum; **Monterchi**; **Florence**, Uffizi; **Perugia**, National Gallery).

Piero di Cosimo (Florentine, 1462–1521). Painter better known for his personal eccentricities than his art, which in itself is pretty odd. Lived on hard-boiled eggs which he boiled with his glue (**Florence**, Uffizi; **Fiesole**, S. Francesco).

Pietro da Cortona (Cortona, 1596–1699). The most charming of Tuscan Baroque painters; his best is in Rome, but there are some florid ceilings in the Pitti Palace (**Florence**; works in **Cortona**; also **Perugia**, National Gallery).

Pinturicchio (Perugia, 1454–1513). This painter got his name for his use of gold and rich colours. Never an innovator, but, as an absolute virtuoso in colour, style and grace, no one could beat him. Another establishment artist, especially favoured by the popes and, like Perugino, slandered most vilely by Vasari (**Siena**, Piccolomini Library; **Spello**, S. Maria Maggiore; **Perugia**, National Gallery).

Pisano, Andrea (b. Pontedera, c. 1290–1348). Artistic heir of Giovanni and Nicola Pisano and teacher of Orcagna; probably a key figure in introducing new artistic ideas to **Florence** (baptistry, south doors). Not related to the other Pisani.

Pisano, Nicola (active c. 1258–78). The first great medieval Tuscan sculptor really came from down south in Puglia, which was then enjoying a flowering of classically orientated art under Emperor Frederick II. Nicola Pisano created a little Renaissance all his own, when he adapted the figures and composition of ancient reliefs to make his wonderful pulpit reliefs in **Siena** and **Pisa**'s baptistry. His son **Giovanni Pisano** (active c. 1265–1314) carried on the tradition, notably in the façade sculptures at **Siena** cathedral (also **Perugia**, S. Domenico, Fontana Maggiore; great relief pulpits in **Pisa** cathedral, Sant'Andrea, **Pistoia**).

Pollaiuolo, Antonio (Florentine, d. 1498). A sculptor, painter and goldsmith whose fame rests on his brilliant, unmistakable line; he occasionally worked with his less gifted brother **Piero** (**Florence**, Uffizi and Bargello).

Pontormo, Jacopo (Florentine, b. Pontormo, 1494–1556). You haven't seen pink and orange until you've seen the work of this determined Mannerist eccentric. After the initial shock, though, you'll meet an artist of real genius, one whose use of the human body as sole means for communicating ideas is equal to Michelangelo's (**Florence**, S. Felicità – his *Deposition* – and Uffizi; **Poggio a Caiano**; **Carmignano**).

Quercia, Jacopo della (Sienese, 1374–1438). Sculptor who learned his style from Pisano's cathedral pulpit; one of the unsuccessful contestants for the Florence baptistry doors. Maybe Siena's greatest sculptor, though his most celebrated work, that city's Fonte Gaia, is now ruined (**Lucca**, cathedral *tomb of Ilaria del Carretto*; **San Gimignano**, Collegiata; **Siena**, baptistry; **Volterra**, cathedral).

Raphael (Raffaello Sanzio, 1483–1520). Born in Urbino, Raphael spent time in Città di Castello, Perugia, and Florence before establishing himself in Rome. Only a few of the best works of this High Renaissance master remain in the region; those are in the Pitti Palace and Uffizi, **Florence**, and in **Perugia**'s San Severo; there's also a lovely portrait in the Ducal Palace, in **Urbino**.

Robbia, Luca della (Florentine, 1400–82). Greatest of the famous family of sculptors; he invented the coloured glaze for terracottas that we associate with the della Robbias, but was also a first-rate relief sculptor (the *cantorie* in **Florence's** cathedral museum; **Impruneta**, Collegiata). His nephew **Andrea della Robbia** (1435–1525; best works in convent of **La Verna** and the Tempietto at **Montevarchi**) and Andrea's son **Giovanni** (1469–1529; best work, **Pistoia**, Ospedale del Ceppo) carried on the sweet blue-and-white terracotta style in innumerable buildings across Tuscany.

Rosselli, Cosimo (Florentine, 1434–1507). Competent middle of the road Renaissance painter who occasionally excelled (**Florence**, S. Ambrogio).

Rossellino, Bernardo (1409–64). Florentine architect and sculptor best known as the planner and architect of the new town of **Pienza**. Also a sculptor (**Florence**, S. Croce, S. Miniato; **Empoli**, Pinacoteca). His brother **Antonio Rossellino** (1427–79) was also a talented sculptor (**Florence**, S. Croce).

Rossi, Vicenzo de' (1525–87). Florentine Mannerist sculptor of chunky male nudes (**Florence**, Palazzo Vecchio).

Rosso Fiorentino (Giovanni Battista di Jacopo, 1494–1540). Florentine Mannerist painter, he makes a fitting complement to Pontormo, both for his tortured soul and for the exaggerations of form and colour he used to create gripping, dramatic effects. Fled Italy after the Sack of Rome and worked for Francis I at Fontainebleau. (**Volterra** Pinacoteca has his masterpiece, the *Deposition*; **Florence**, Uffizi and S. Lorenzo; **Città di Castello**, Duomo).

Salimbeni, Iacopo (d. about 1427) and **Lorenzo** (d. 1420). Brothers from the Marches, charming masters of detail on the threshold of the Renaissance (**Urbino**, Oratorio di San Giovanni; **San Severino Marche**, Pinacoteca).

Salviati, Francesco (Florentine, 1510–63). Friend of Vasari and a similar sort of painter, though much more talented. Odd perspectives and decoration, often bizarre imagery (**Florence,** Palazzo Vecchio and Uffizi).

Sangallo, Antonio da (brother of Giuliano, 1455–1537). Architect at his best in palaces and churches in the monumental style: notably at the great temple of S. Biagio, **Montepulciano**; the son, **Antonio da Sangallo the Younger,** also an architect, and the family's best, practised mainly in Rome.

Sangallo, Giuliano da (Florentine, 1443–1516). Architect of humble origins who later became favourite of Lorenzo de' Medici. Often tripped up by an obsession, inherited from Alberti, with making architecture conform to philosophical principles (**Poggio a Caiano; Florence**, S. Maddalena dei Pazzi; **Prato**, S. Maria delle Carceri).

Il Sassetta (Stefano di Giovanni; active *c.* 1390–1450). One of the great Sienese quattrocento painters, though still working in a style the Florentines would have found hopelessly reactionary; an artist who studied Masaccio but preferred the Gothic elegance of Masolino. His masterpiece, the Borgo Sansepolcro polyptych, is dispersed through half the museums of Europe.

Signorelli, Luca (Cortona, d. 1523). A rarefied Umbrian painter and an important influence on Michelangelo. Imaginative, forceful compositions, combining geometrical rigour with a touch of unreality, much like his master Piero della Francesca (*The Last Judgement* in **Orvieto** cathedral; **Cortona**, civic and cathedral museums; **Monte Oliveto Maggiore**; **Sansepolcro**, museum; **Urbino**, Ducal Palace).

Il Sodoma (Giovanni Antonio Bazzi, 1477–1549). Born in Piedmont, but a Sienese by choice, he was probably not the libertine his nickname, and Vasari's biography, suggest. An endearing, serene artist, who usually eschewed Mannerist distortion, he got rich through his work, then blew it all feeding his exotic menagerie and died in the poorhouse (**Monte Oliveto Maggiore; Siena**, Pinacoteca and S. Domenico).

Spinello Aretino (Arezzo, late 14th century–1410). A link between Giotto and the International Gothic style; imaginative and colourful in his compositions (**Florence**, S. Miniato; **Siena**, Palazzo Pubblico; **Arezzo**, museum). His son **Parri di Spinello** did many fine works, all around **Arezzo** (S. Maria delle Grazie).

Tacca, Pietro (1580–1640). Born in Carrara, a pupil of Giambologna and one of the best early Baroque sculptors (**Livorno**, *Quattro Mori*; **Florence**, Piazza SS. Annunziata fountains; **Prato**, Piazza del Comune).

Taddeo di Bartolo (Volterra, 1363–1422). The greatest Sienese painter of the late 1300s; also the least conventional; never a consummate stylist, he often shows a remarkable imagination in composition and treatment of subject matter (**Siena**, Palazzo Pubblico, S. Spirito; **Perugia**, Pinacoteca; **Colle di Val d'Elsa**, museum and Collegiata; **Volterra**, Pinacoteca; **San Gimignano**, Museo Civico).

Talenti, Francesco (early 14th century). Chief architect of **Florence** cathedral and campanile after Arnolfo di Cambio and Giotto; his son **Simone** made the beautiful windows in **Orsanmichele** (and perhaps the Loggia dei Lanzi) in **Florence**.

Torrigiano, Pietro (1472–1528). Florentine portrait sculptor, famous for his work in Westminster Abbey and for breaking Michelangelo's nose (**Siena**, cathedral).

Uccello, Paolo (Florentine, 1397–1475). No artist has ever been more obsessed with the possibilities of artificial perspective. Like Piero della Francesca, he used the new technique to create a magic world of his own; contemplation of it made him increasingly eccentric in his later years. Uccello's provocative, visionary subjects (*Noah* fresco in S. Maria Novella, and *Battle of San Romano* in the Uffizi and cloister of San Miniato, **Florence**) put him up with Piero della Francesca and Botticelli as the most intellectually stimulating of quattrocento artists (also attributed frescoes, **Prato** cathedral, and a painting in the Ducal Palace, **Urbino**).

Vasari, Giorgio (Arezzo, 1511–74). Florentine sycophant, writer and artist. Also a pretty good architect (**Florence**, Uffizi, Corridoio, and Fish Loggia; also **Città di Castello**, palace).

Il Vecchietta (Lorenzo di Pietro, 1412–80). Sienese painter and sculptor, dry and linear, part Sienese Pollaiuolo and part Donatello. One wonders what he did to acquire his nickname, 'Little Old Woman' (**Siena**, Loggia della Mercanzia, baptistry; **Pienza** cathedral).

Verrocchio, Andrea del (1435–88). Florentine sculptor who worked in bronze; spent his life trying to outdo Donatello. Also a painter, a mystic alchemist in his spare time, and interestingly enough the master of both Botticelli and Leonardo (**Florence**, Uffizi, S. Lorenzo, Orsanmichele, Palazzo Vecchio, and Bargello).

Topics

The First Professional Philistine

Many who have seen Vasari's work in Florence will wonder how such a mediocre painter should rate so much attention. Ingratiating companion of the rich and famous, workmanlike over-achiever and tireless self-promoter, Vasari was the perfect man for his time. Born in Arezzo, in 1511, a fortunate introduction to Cardinal Silvio Passerini gave him the chance of an education in Florence with the young Medici heirs, Ippolito and Alessandro. In his early years, he became a fast and reliable frescoist gaining a reputation for customer satisfaction. In the 1530s, after various commissions around Italy, he returned to Florence just when Cosimo I was beginning his plans to remake the city. Vasari became Cosimo's court painter and architect, the most prolific fresco machine, painting over countless good frescoes of the 1300s.

But more than for his paintings, Vasari lives on through his book, the *Lives of the Painters, Sculptors and Architects*, a series of exhaustive, gossipy biographies of artists. Beginning with Cimabue, Vasari traces the rise of art out of Byzantine and Gothic barbarism, through Giotto and his followers, towards an ever-improving naturalism, finally culminating in the great age of Leonardo, Raphael, and Michelangelo, who not only mastered nature but outdid her. His book, being the first of its kind, and containing a mine of valuable information on dozens of Renaissance artists, naturally has had a tremendous influence on all subsequent criticism.

Much of Vasari's world seems quaint to us now: the idea of the artist striving for Virtue and Glory, the slavish worship of anything that survived from ancient Rome, artistic 'progress' and the conviction that art's purpose was to imitate nature. But many of Vasari's opinions have had a long career in the world of ideas. His blind disparagement of everything medieval lived on until the 1800s. His dismissal of Sienese, Umbrian and northern artists has not been entirely corrected even today. Vasari believed in a nice, tidy art that went by the book. With his interior decorator's concept of Beauty, he created a style of criticism in which virtuosity, not imagination, became the standard by which art was to be judged; history offers few more instructive examples of the stamina and resilience of dubious ideas.

Flora and Fauna

Tuscany has been cultivated so long and so intensively that wildlife is completely pushed to the fringes. Nevertheless, a great variety of birds and beasts complement the diversity of the landscape. Leaving aside Tuscany (*see* 'Landscapes', p.33–4), this region divides neatly into three: the coastal zone, the central hills and the mountains.

For nature-lovers, the coast will be by far the most interesting; the malaria mosquito kept much of the southern Maremma undeveloped for centuries, leaving it inhabited by vast stretches of pine forest, cork oak and holm oak, thriving wildlife (including wild horses) and marshlands. Its protected nesting grounds (*see* 'Monti dell'Uccellina' p.305, Orbetello's lagoons p.307 and Lago di Burano p.312) are Italy's greatest stopover for migrating waterfowl. Deforested land beyond the marshes is covered with the characteristic Mediterranean maquis (*macchia*, in Italian); *macchia alta* with shrub versions of pines, oaks, beech, cypress and laurel; or the *macchia bassa* in drier regions, thick patches of broom, heather, lentisk and fragrant plants.

As for the **animals**, the viper is the only really unpleasant thing you may meet; proliferating amid abandoned farmland, he's brownish-grey, about 18 inches long, and has a vaguely diamond-shaped head. Vipers object to being stepped on. If one bites you, you've got 30 minutes to get hold of the serum – buy it in any pharmacy and keep it in the fridge.

The region's other trademark animal, the boar, is shy but flourishes everywhere despite the Italians' best efforts to turn him into salami. There are also hares and rabbits, foxes and weasels, polecats, badgers and porcupines in the wilder areas. A few wolves, lynxes and deer survive in the higher reaches of the Apennines, and deer have also been reintroduced in the Maremma coastal parks. You can find all of these, and even wildcats, in the Val di Farma north of Roccastrada, in Tuscany. The only mountain goats are found on the island of Montecristo.

Many writers on this part of Italy comment on the absence of **birdsong**. They're exaggerating. Italian hunters shoot anything that flies, but there are still thrushes, starlings, wrens, and such, along with the white doves, ubiquitous in Umbria, that always make you think of Assisi and St Francis. Cuckoos announce the spring, pheasants lie low during the hunting season, and an occasional owl can be heard. Nightingales are rare, though there are supposedly some around Lago di Massacuccioli and the northern coasts – in the evening you're far more likely to see bats.

The **insect** world is well represented: lovely butterflies and moths; rather forbidding black bullet bees and wasps that resemble vintage fighter planes. The beetles reach disproportionate sizes – you may see a *diavolo*, a large black or red beetle with long, gracefully curving antlers that sing when you trap it; Leonardo drew one in his notebooks. There are enough mosquitoes, midges and little biting flies to be a nuisance in the summer, and, perhaps most alarming at first, the shiny black scorpion, who may crawl inside through the window or up drains (keep the plugs in) or come in with the firewood. Once inside they head for dark places like beds or shoes. One thwack with a shoe will do in even the largest scorpion. Getting stung is painful but not deadly; but visit the doctor, mainly to guard against infection or allergic reaction.

As for the **forests**, oaks, chestnuts and beeches predominate, along with tall, upright poplars ('Lombardy' type), pines, willows (not the weeping variety) and a few maples – with rounded leaves, not pointed as in northern Europe and America. Cypress trees are common; the tidier ones have been planted, while shaggier ones are the wild variety. Parasol or umbrella pines, that most characteristic Italian tree, make a grand sight isolated on a hill crest, or in groves along the Maremma. At higher altitudes, there are beeches, pines and firs – beautiful silver firs grow around Monte Amiata, while in the Casentino near Camaldoli is a vast stretch of old beech and pine forest. The Garfagnana's *Parco Naturale dell'Orecchiella* includes an ancient chestnut forest.

Many of the **wild flowers** are close cousins to those seen in northern Europe and America. There are a million varieties of buttercup, usually the tiny *ranuncolo* and *bottoncini d'oro*, and of bluebell, often called *campanella* or *campanellina*. Many of the common five-petalled pink blossoms in spring fields are wild geraniums (*geranio*), with pointed leaves like the anemone, and you'll see quite a few varieties of violet (*violette*) with round or spade-shaped leaves (a few are yellow). Daisies (*margherita*) come in all sizes. Tiniest of all are the wild pink and blue forget-me-nots (*non ti scordar di me*). Large swatches of lavender are among the charms of the Chianti hills.

The real star here is the bright red poppy. Dandelions and wild mustard are also plentiful, along with white, umbrella-like bunches of florets called *tragosellino* or *podragraria*, similar to Queen Anne's Lace. On a more exotic note, there are wild orchids, rhododendrons (in mountainous areas), five-petalled wild roses and water lilies in the coastal Maremma. The best wildflowers are in the Sibillini mountains; in early summer, the Piano Grande blooming is an unforgettable sight.

There are other **plants** to look for; a dozen kinds of greens that go into somewhat bitter salads, anise, fennel, mint, rosemary and sage are common. The Italians beat the bushes with fervour every spring looking for wild asparagus and repeat the performance in autumn searching for truffles and *porcini* (boletus) mushrooms.

A Florentine Puzzle

In a city as visually restrained as Florence, every detail of decoration stands out. In the Middle Ages and Renaissance, Florentine builders combined their passion for geometry with their love of making a little go a long way; they embellished buildings with simple geometrical designs. Though nothing special in themselves, they stand out like mystic hieroglyphs, symbols upon which to meditate while contemplating old Florence's remarkable journey through the western mind.

The city is full of them, incorporated into façades, mosaics, windows and friezes. Here are eight of them, a little exercise for the eye while tramping the hard pavements of Florence. Your job is to find them. Some are really obvious, others obscure. For No.6 you should be able to find at least three examples (two across the street from each other) and if you're clever you'll find not only No.5, a rather late addition to the cityscape, but also the medieval work that inspired it. Don't worry too much about the last one. But if you're an art historian or a Florentinophile, it's only fair that you seek out this hard one too. For the answers, *see* the last page of the Index, p.672.

Guelphs and Ghibellines

One medieval Italian writer claimed that the factional strife began with two brothers of Pistoia, named Guelf and Gibel. One murdered the other, starting the seemingly endless troubles that to many seemed a God-sent plague to punish the proud and wealthy Italians for their sins. However, most historians trace the roots of this party conflict to two great German houses, *Welf* and *Waiblingen*.

The chroniclers pinpoint the outbreak of the troubles to 1215, when a politically prominent Florentine noble named Buondelmonte dei Buondelmonti was assassinated by his enemies while crossing the Ponte Vecchio. It was the tinder that ignited a smouldering quarrel all over Italy, particularly in Tuscany. The atmosphere of city-states, each with its own internal struggles between nobles, the rich merchant class and the commoners, crystallized rapidly into parties. Initially the Guelphs, largely a creation of the newly-wealthy bourgeois, were all for free trade and the rights of the free cities; the Ghibellines were the party of the German emperors, nominal overlords of Italy. Naturally, the Guelphs found their protector in the emperors' bitter temporal rivals, the popes, which brought a religious angle into the story.

Before long, the labels Guelph and Ghibelline ceased to have any meaning at all. In the 13th and 14th centuries, the emperors and their Ghibelline allies helped the church root out heretical movements like the Patarenes, while the popes schemed to destroy the liberty of good Guelph cities, especially in Umbria, and incorporate them into the Papal State. In cities like Florence, where the Guelphs won a final victory, they themselves split into parties, battling with the same barbaric gusto. Black was the Ghibelline colour, white the Guelph, and cities arranged themselves like squares on a chessboard. When one suffered a revolution and changed from Guelph to Ghibelline, or vice versa, its nearest enemies would soon change the other way. Often the public buildings give us a clue as to the loyalties of a city in any given time. Simple, squared crenellations are Guelph (as in the Palazzo dei Priori in Perugia); ornate 'swallow-tail' crenellations (as in Frederick II's castle in Prato) are the mark of the Ghibelline.

The English looked on with bewilderment. Edmund Spenser, in his *Shepheards' Calendar* (1579), wrote this fanciful etymology: 'when all Italy was distraicte into the Factions of the Guelfes and the Gibelins, being two famous houses in Florence, the name began through their great mischiefes and many outrages, to be so odious or rather dreadfull in the peoples eares, that if theyr children at any time were frowarde and wanton, they would say to them the Guelfe or the Gibeline came. Which words nowe from them (as may thinge els) be come into our usage, and for Guelfes and Gibelines, we say *Elfes* and *Goblins*.'

Landscapes

There may be other regions in Italy that are lusher, others with taller mountains and more fertile valleys, and others that support more varied flora and enjoy a more temperate climate. Yet ultimately, it is the landscapes of Tuscany and Umbria that exert the most lasting charm. In the paintings of the Renaissance, the rolling hills, cypresses, poplars and parasol pines, vineyards and winding lanes of the background are often more beautiful than the nominally religious subject in the foreground. As early as Giotto, artists took care to relate the figures in their composition to the architecture and the landscape around them, epitomized in the paintings of Leonardo da Vinci, where each tree and rock takes on an almost mystic significance.

The tidy geometry and clipped hedges of an Italian garden are a perfect example of the Italian urge to order nature, and you'll find good examples in the Boboli Gardens and the Medici villas at Castello and Collodi. The Tuscans, in the vanguard of Italy in so many ways, were the first to order their entire territory. The vicious wars of the Middle Ages devastated the countryside (as is visible in the harsh, barren brown and grey hills of trecento painting); the Black Death in the 1300s depopulated the cultivated areas, giving the Tuscans the unique opportunity to arrange things just so. Not entirely by coincidence, the late 14th century was the time when the élite, weary of city strife, were discovering the joys of the country and building villas, playing the country squire and gentleman farmer whenever possible. And they planted everything in its place according to elegance and discipline, each tree with its own purpose; to act as a boundary marker, to offer shade, or to support a vine. Cypresses and parasol pines often stand strikingly along the crest of hills, not for aesthetics or as a study in perspective, but as a windbreak. Strongest is the sense that nothing has changed for centuries, that in the quattrocento Gozzoli and Fra Angelico painted the same scene you see today. Few landscapes anywhere are more ancient, or more civilized.

The countryside of Umbria is more dishevelled and rustic; its hills steeper, and its valleys narrower, planted with little evidence of elegant Tuscan precision. It is celebrated for its green, the 'mystical' colour to suit its mystical, saintly nature; in the autumn and winter, mists swirl romantically through the mountains. One feature, however, is just as artful as Tuscany – its tidy hill towns of pinkish grey stone. From some spots you can see several at a time, like an archipelago of islands crowned with villages, one behind the other, vanishing into the bluish haze of the horizon.

St Francis of Assisi

Francesco Bernardone was one of the most remarkable men who ever lived. Now the patron saint of all Italy, he remained closely attached to his native Umbria, in life as well as death; nearly every town in the region seems to have a legend about him, or at least a Franciscan church founded in the early days of his movement. His gentle spiritual revolution occurred amidst the sound and the fury that fills the chronicles of the 13th century. Francis taught that the natural world was a beautiful place, and that there was tremendous joy in living an ordinary humble life in it, in imitation of Christ.

Francis was born in 1182 to a merchant, Pietro Bernardone, and his Provençal wife, Madonna Pica. Some say Pietro was the richest man in Assisi; he travelled often through the south of France, trading fine cloth, and although he named his son Giovanni at the font he always called him Francesco after the country he loved. At one point Francis accompanied his father through Provence and up the Rhône to Bruges and Ghent, but most of all he used his father's wealth to finance a merry and dissipated youth; according to his first biographer, Tommaso da Celano, he was 'the first instigator of every evil, and behind none in foolishness'. He was also a poet in the troubadour tradition. His Francophile upbringing gave him an early taste for the cult of chivalry and mystic love, by 1200 all the rage among young Italians.

His conversion to saintliness did not happen overnight. In 1202, Francis joined the cavalry of Assisi in one of its many wars against Perugia, but was captured and spent a dismal year in a Perugian prison. He also suffered a long, severe illness. The two events that made him stop and think; he yearned for something more than the carefree life he had been living. Thinking it might be chivalry, he joined a band riding to the Fourth Crusade. He got as far as Spoleto when he fell ill again. He took this as a warning that he was on the wrong track, and changed his allegiance from a temporal lord to a spiritual one.

Francis began to spend his time alone in the countryside around Assisi, reflecting on the world's vanity. A revelation came to him while attending Mass one Sunday in 1205, as the priest read the words of the Gospel: '...and as ye go, preach, saying, the kingdom of Heaven is at hand. Heal the sick, cleanse the lepers, raise the dead, cast out devils: freely have ye received, freely give.' Francis took this message literally: he would live like Christ, in poverty and humility. The story goes that he took his final decision before the crucifix in the little church of San Damiano outside Assisi, which spoke to him, saying, 'Repair my house, which you see is in ruins.' Francis sold his father's pack horse and merchandise in Foligno to do just that; when his angry father hauled him before the bishop of Assisi and reproached him, Francis stripped off his rich clothes and declared that henceforth his only father was his father in heaven.

It has been commented that much of Franciscan legend comes in exemplary packages too tidy to be taken as a literal truth, but there is no doubt that this merchant's son who called himself 'God's Fool', kissing lepers and preaching to the world's outcasts, struck a chord in the hearts of many thirsting for something beyond the carrot and stick fare offered by the medieval Church. Although at first he was chased and stoned, Francis soon attracted a band of followers who lived with him in the Porziuncola, a chapel on the plain below Assisi, and wandered the area preaching, doing odd jobs to support themselves or begging their bread.

His visit in 1210 to Pope Innocent III is part of Franciscan legend. Innocent was perhaps chiefly responsible for the new worldly and militant direction of the Church, and he had little time for reformers or critics of its ambitions and corruption (in the previous year, he had declared the Albigensian Crusade against the other-worldly Cathars in southern France). His court scoffed at the shabby Umbrian holy man, but that night Innocent dreamt that his church of St John Lateran – then the seat of the popes – was collapsing, and that this same Francis came along to hold up its walls.

Dream or not, it did not occur to the pope that he might be able to harness such spiritual renewal within the institutions of the Church; unlike the Cathars and other heretics, Francis never attacked the papal hierarchy, explicitly at any rate, although his beliefs that a person could live by the Gospel in the 13th century and that the love of money was the root of all evil were harder to fit in the current scheme. Innocent nevertheless confirmed his First Rule for a simple lay order based on poverty, which Francis called the Frati Minori. As the movement quickly grew and the roads filled with begging friars, the Church tried to convince Francis to impose on it the discipline of a monastic rule. Francis resisted this, having no interest in organization; he never even took holy orders.

In the meantime, Francis spent his time travelling and preaching, mostly in Umbria, where many villages can show a humble stone in a cave where he rested his head, or tell a legend of his sway over the birds and beasts. In 1219, he went further afield, first in an unsuccessful attempt to reach Morocco, then to the Holy Land and Egypt, accompanying the Crusaders. At Damietta, on the Nile, he preached to Sultan Malik el Kamil. The story goes that Francis was on an apostolic mission to convert the infidels, but it's just as likely he went to learn from them, especially from the Sufi mystics. One of the more intriguing parallels was a Sufi brotherhood similar to the Friars Minor, founded some sixty years before Francis' birth by a holy man named Najmuddin Kubra, a wandering preacher with an uncanny influence over birds and animals.

Drawing on his troubadour days, Francis composed some of the first and finest vernacular verse in Italy, including the *Canticle of the Sun*, a poem in his native Umbrian dialect on the unity of all creation. His poetry became the foundation of a literary movement, based on Christian devotion: Tommaso da Celano, one of Francis's first followers and his autobiographer, composed the powerful *Dies Irae*, followed a later by Jacopone da Todi (*see* p.527), after Dante, the greatest poet of his century.

By 1221 Francis' extraordinary character and sanctity had inspired a movement of spiritual renewal that had spread across Italy and beyond. Unwilling to manage the growing organization, he turned the vicarship of the Friars Minor to Pieto Catani, who soon died, and then to Brother Elias. 'Henceforth I am dead to you,' he declared to the friars, and went to live in retreat with his early followers. But he wasn't quite dead; realizing the movement was slipping away from his intentions, he wrote a second Rule (1223) under Pope Honorius III that created the Franciscan order based on poverty as a supreme good, and confirmed it in his testament, urging his friars to remain 'wayfarers and pilgrims in this world'. At Christmas the same year, he reconstructed a manger scene in Greccio (a village just south of Umbria), to emphasize the humble, human, child side of Christ as opposed to the stern arbitrator of the Last Judgement. The Italians were charmed and have been making their Christmas *presepi* ever since.

During the last three years of his life, Francis spent most of his time at the sanctuary of La Verna in Tuscany, where in 1225 he received the stigmata seeming to confirm his life as a parallel of Christ's. Increasingly frail, he returned to Assisi a year later to meet his good Sister Death at age 44. Within two years he was canonized by Gregory IX, who as Cardinal Ugolino had been his friend and one of the Order's first protectors. Gregory also did much to diffuse Francis' dangerous legacy by declaring that his testament was not binding, and by directing the Franciscans down the path of the other new preaching order of the 13th century, the Dominicans. Huge churches, urban convents, university education, rich donations to be 'used' by the property-less friars soon came into being, explained away as being necessary for the times. The Order split into the 'Conventuals', who agreed, and the 'Spirituals', who wanted to hold on to their founder's prescription of poverty, the extremists going off on paths of esoteric mysticism that might have appalled Francis as much as his order's prosperity.

For the average Italian in the streets, though, these intermural disputes took nothing away from the humane Christianity of love and charity exemplified by Francis and preached by his friars. His native Assisi quickly became a place of pilgrimage, and his native land was well on its way to becoming *Umbria mistica*.

Trends in Taste

I took a quick walk through the city to see the Duomo and the Battistero. Once more, a completely new world opened up before me, but I did not wish to stay long. The location of the Boboli Gardens is marvellous. I hurried out of the city as quickly as I entered it.
Goethe, on Florence in *Italian Journey*

Goethe, the father of the Italian Grand Tour, en route from Venice to Rome, had little time for the city that likes to call itself 'The Capital of Culture'. Like most travellers in the 18th and early 19th centuries, he knew nothing of Giotto, Masaccio, Botticelli, or Piero della Francesca; it was Roman statues that wowed him, the very same ones the modern visitor to the Uffizi passes without a second glance. Shelley managed to fill pages on his visits to the museum without mentioning a single painting.

Some Tuscan attractions never change – the Leaning Tower, Michelangelo's *David*, the villas, gardens and the cheap wine. Others have gone through an amazing rise or fall in popularity, thanks in part to John Ruskin, whose *Mornings in Florence* brought to light the charms of the Romanesque architecture, Giotto, and the masters of the trecento; he considered Orcagna the master of them all (but in the 18th century, the Giottos in Santa Croce were whitewashed, while many works of Orcagna had been destroyed earlier, by Vasari). Botticelli went from total obscurity in the 18th century to become the darling of the Victorians. Livorno and Viareggio on the coast, and Bagni di Lucca near the Garfagnana, once hosted thriving English colonies – no more.

But Tuscany itself was very different then; where they played *pallone*, somewhere between lawn tennis and *jai alai*; where a herd of 150 camels, introduced by Grand Duke Ferdinand II in 1622, roamed the Pisan Park of San Rossore; where, as Robert and Elizabeth Browning found, the rent for a palazzo used to be laughably cheap.

But it's the story of the Venus de' Medici that is perhaps most instructive. The statue is a pleasant, if unremarkable Greek work of the 2nd century BC, but for two centuries it was Florence's chief attraction; the minute visitors arrived they would rush to gaze upon her; those prone to write gushed rapturously of her perfect beauty. Napoleon kidnapped her for France, asking the great neoclassical sculptor Canova to sculpt a replacement; later she was one of the things Florence managed to reclaim, though her reign was soon undermined – Ruskin called her an 'uninteresting little person'. Since then she has stood forlornly in the Uffizi's Tribunale, unnoticed and unloved.

Some things don't change. Over a hundred years after Goethe's tour of Florence, Aldous Huxley had no time for Florence, either: 'We came back through Florence and the spectacle of that second-rate provincial town with its repulsive Gothic architecture and its acres of Christmas card primitives made me almost sick. The only points about Florence are the country outside it, the Michelangelo tombs, Brunelleschi's dome, and a few rare pictures. The rest is simply dung when compared to Rome.'

Tuscany on Wheels

Tuscans have always loved a parade, and to the casual reader of Renaissance history, it seems they're forever proceeding somewhere or another, even to their own detriment – during outbreaks of plague, holy companies would parade through an afflicted area, invoking divine mercy, while in effect aiding the spread of the pestilence. They also had a great weakness for allegorical parade floats. During the centuries of endless war each Tuscan city rolled out its *Carroccio*, invented by a Milanese bishop in the 11th century. Drawn by six white oxen, this was a kind of holy ship of state in a hay cart; a mast held up a crucifix while a battle standard flew from the yard-arm, there was an altar for priests to say mass during the battle and a large bell with which to send signals over the din to the armies. The worst possible outcome of a battle was to lose one's *Carroccio* to the enemy, as Fiesole did to Florence. One, in Siena, is still in operation, rumbling out twice a year for the Palio.

Medieval clerical processions, by the time of Dante, became melded with the idea of the Roman 'triumph' (*trionfo*); in Purgatory, the poet finds Beatrice triumphing with a cast of characters from the Apocalypse. Savonarola wrote of a *Triumph of the Cross*; Petrarch and Bocaccio wrote allegorical triumphs of virtues, love and death. More interesting are the secular Roman-style Triumphs staged by the Medici, especially at Carnival (the name, according to Burckhardt, comes from a cart, the pagan *carrus navalis*, the ship of Isis, launched every 5 March to symbolize the reopening of navigation). You can get a hint of their splendour from the frescoes at Poggio a Caiano; the best artists of the day would be commissioned to design the decorations. The last relics of these parades are the huge satirical carnival floats at Viareggio. A lovely memory of Florence's processions remains in Gozzoli's fairy-tale frescoes in the chapel of the Medici palace, of the annual procession staged by the Compagnia de' Re Magi, the most splendid and aristocratic of pageants.

Umbria's Totem Tubers

Umbria's most valuable cash crop has neither seeds nor a planting season, and adamantly refuses to grow in straight rows. An aura of mystery surrounds its very nature; according to legend, it is spawned by lightning bolts flickering among the oaks. Truffles – *tartufi* – are the crop, and although they look a lot like granulated mud on your pasta, these earthy, aromatic and aphrodisiac tubers, actually a weird type of fungi, are the most prized gourmet delicacy in Italy. Even in their natural state they aren't much to look at, bulbous lumps from the size of a pea to a baby's fist, and they're very picky about where they grow. Umbria is one of their favourite spots – here are the proper calcareous soils, oak and beech forests and exposures, especially around Spoleto, Nórcia, and particularly in the Valnerina around Scheggino. This is the realm of the highest quality black truffle (*tuber melangosporum Vittadini*); within Europe, they grow here, around Perigord in France, and almost nowhere else. The rarer white truffle (*tuber magnatum Pico*), mostly from Piemonte, deigns to grow around Gubbio, and is avidly sought from October to December. The black truffle season is longer, extending into March. Out of season you can find them bottled in oil (never buy fresh except in season), but they are absolutely heavenly when fresh from the ground and offer a perfectly legitimate reason for visiting Umbria in the off season (serious fans might want to aim for the gastronomic February fair in Nórcia).

Except for saffron, truffles are the most expensive comestible in the world. Prices for a good white truffle can easily top a staggering €2,500 a kilo, while the black truffles are half as much, but still make a dent in the pocketbook. Not only do they stubbornly resist cultivation, they're fiendishly hard to track down. The vast majority are still brought to market by secretive truffle hunters and their specially trained hounds, who learn to love the scent as pups, because of the truffle juice rubbed around their mother's teats. They are gathered at night, when the truffles smell strongest, or perhaps because the best truffles are always on someone else's land. Truffle-hunting requires a dog and a special digging implement (*vanghetta*), and also a licence. And competition can be deadly – the 1997 season was marred in Umbria by a psycho truffle-dog poisoner. Fortunately, a little *tartufo* goes a long way, and Italians will travel far to look, dreamy-eyed, at glass jars of them at Umbria's truffle fairs.

Profits are such that imitations have made considerable headway. Beware of synthesized truffle aromas, which are nothing like the real thing, or cheap low-grade black truffles imported from China that lack the pungent, aromatic intensity of the Umbrian-grown. And you'd do well to steer clear of one local truffle product – the nubby black bottles of Tartufo liqueur, which tastes as vile as it looks.

After the Earthquakes: Art versus People

According to geologists, the earthquakes that jolted Umbria and the Marches twice on 26 September 1997, killing 11 and wounding many more, and the aftershocks that continued throughout 1998, were merely part of a million-year-old trend as the Apennines adjust to fit their crust. The 100,000 people in Umbria and the Marches whose homes were rendered uninhabitable obviously didn't find much comfort in the scientific long-range perspective. Luckily the government managed to respond quickly, so that by Christmas 1997 everyone was housed as close to their villages as possible, in rental accommodation, in prefab housing or, as a last resort, in shipping containers (fitted with doors, windows, room dividers, and soon with electricity and plumbing). People got on with their lives relatively quickly, and soon the skylines of the hill towns were dominated by cranes and scaffolding.

Although earthquakes are not uncommon in the region, this one grabbed the world's attention because it gravely damaged one of Italy's most precious and best loved treasures: the Basilica di San Francesco in Assisi. Billions of lire poured in from the state, charities and other sources to restore the art. Priority was given to a 'Jubilee list' of art and monuments on the official pilgrimage route, but nearly a third of the 1998 budget went to the big basilica; in Assisi everyone vowed it would reopen by Christmas 1999 and it did – an impressive feat.

Yet even by mid-2000, some people in Assisi were still living in a 'container village' on the outskirts of town. Less famous towns sometimes had two or three container villages; the worst-hit places were all but abandoned. Plenty of money was available for restoration, but a huge amount of it (in some cases, as much as half of a town's allotted sum) went to pay for the countless permits, licences, and opinions by various state experts required even before the real work could begin. Since the rebuilding of houses will in some cases take several years, in some places, such as Foligno, people have been moved out of containers and into wooden chalet-style buildings. Many feel these are a waste of time and money, when the resources could be poured into the final result. There has also been often bitter soul-searching about who Umbria really belongs to: the descendants of people who have lived there for generations, many just working their way out of real poverty, or the owners of second homes, who want the region to remain quaint and old and beautiful, and complain about the newish unattractive suburbs and small factories.

So was art given precedence over people in Umbria? In many cases the answer is yes, although the result isn't quite as cold and heartless as it may sound. Tourism is a major source of income in Umbria and 1998 was an economic disaster for the area, as tourists kept away, mainly because so many sights were closed. So repairing and reopening the major attractions benefited everybody. All kinds of restoration projects on buildings not directly damaged by the earthquakes have been undertaken, on buildings and art that otherwise would have been left to crumble slowly. Local authorities have benefited from the influx of expert restorers and of money, and from a heightened focus of attention on 'Art' in Umbria. Most of the work has now been completed and many things are in a much better state than they would have been had the earthquake never happened. Assisi is a particular example: the restoration has been so spectacular that those buildings will be in better condition than they have been for hundreds of years. Even the priceless frescoes inside the Basilica di San Francesco may shine again. On that note, at least in the long-range view of things, the disaster may have been a blessing in disguise.

Food and Drink

In Italy, the three Ms (the *Madonna*, *Mamma* and *Mangiare*) are still a force to be reckoned with, and in a country where millions of otherwise sane people spend much of their waking hours worrying about their digestion, standards both at home and in the restaurants are understandably high. Everybody is a gourmet, or at least thinks he or she is, and food is not only something to eat but a subject approaching the heights of philosophy – two Umbrian businessmen once overheard on a train heatedly discussed mushrooms for over *four* hours. Although ready-made pasta, tinned minestrone and frozen pizza in the *supermercato* tempt the virtue of the Italian cook, few give in (although many a working mother wishes she could at times).

For the visitor this national culinary obsession comes as an extra bonus to the senses – along with Italy's remarkable sights, music, and the warm sun on your back, you can enjoy some of the best tastes and smells the world can offer, prepared daily in Italy's kitchens and fermented in its countless wine cellars. Eating *all'Italiana* is not only delicious and wholesome, but now undeniably trendy. Foreigners flock here to learn the secrets of Italian cuisine and the even more elusive secret of how the Italians can live surrounded by such a plethora of delights, and still fit into their sleek Armani trousers.

Restaurant Generalities

Breakfast (*colazione*) in Italy is no lingering affair, but an early morning wake-up shot to the brain: a *cappuccino* (*espresso* with hot foamy milk, often sprinkled with chocolate – incidentally first thing in the morning is the only time of day at which any self-respecting Italian will touch the stuff), a *caffè latte* (white coffee) or a *caffè lungo* (a generous portion of *espresso*), accompanied by a croissant-type roll, called a *cornetto* or *briosca*, or a fancy pastry. This repast can be consumed in any bar and repeated during the morning as often as necessary. Breakfast in most Italian hotels seldom represents great value.

Lunch (*pranzo*), generally served around 1pm, is the most important meal of the day for the Italians, with a minimum of a first course (*primo piatto* – any kind of pasta dish, broth or soup, or rice dish or pizza), a second course (*secondo piatto* – a meat dish, accompanied by a *contorno* or side dish – a vegetable, salad, or potatoes usually), followed by fruit or dessert and coffee. You can, however, begin with a platter of *antipasti* – the appetizers Italians do so brilliantly, ranging from warm seafood delicacies, to raw ham (*prosciutto crudo*), salami in a hundred varieties, lovely vegetables, savoury toasts, olives, pâté and many many more. There are restaurants that specialise in *antipasti*, and they usually don't take it amiss if you decide to forget the pasta and meat and just nibble on these scrumptious hors-d'œuvres (though in the end it may well cost more than a full meal). Most Italians accompany their meal with wine and mineral water – *acqua minerale*, with or without bubbles (*con* or *senza gas*), which supposedly aids digestion – concluding their meals with a *digestivo* liqueur.

Cena, the **evening meal**, is usually eaten around 8pm – earlier in the north and later in the south. This is much the same as *pranzo* although lighter, without the pasta;

a pizza and beer, eggs or a fish dish. In restaurants, however, they offer all the courses whatever the time of day, so if you have only a sandwich for lunch you can have a full meal in the evening.

In Italy the various terms for types of **restaurants** – *ristorante, trattoria* or *osteria* – have been confused. A *trattoria* or *osteria* can be just as elaborate as a restaurant, though rarely is a *ristorante* as informal as a traditional *trattoria*. Unfortunately the old habit of posting menus and prices in the windows has fallen from fashion, so it's often difficult to judge variety or prices. Invariably the least expensive eating place is the *vino e cucina*, a simple establishment serving simple cuisine for simple everyday prices. It is essential to remember that the fancier the fittings, the fancier the **bill**, though neither of these points has anything at all to do with the quality of the food. If you're uncertain, do as you would at home – look for lots of locals.

People who haven't visited Italy for years and have fond memories of eating full meals for under a pound will be amazed at how much **prices** have risen; though in some respects eating out in Italy is still a bargain, especially when you figure out how much all that wine would have cost you at home. In many places you'll often find restaurants offering a *menu turistico* – full, set meals of usually meagre inspiration for a reasonable set price. More imaginative chefs often offer a *menu degustazione* – a set-price gourmet meal that allows you to taste their daily specialities and seasonal dishes. Both of these are cheaper than if you had ordered the same food *à la carte*.

As the pace of modern urban life militates against traditional lengthy home-cooked repasts with the family, followed by a siesta, alternatives to sit-down meals have mushroomed. Many office workers now behave much as their counterparts else-where in Europe and consume a rapid snack at lunchtime, returning home after a busy day to throw together some pasta and salad in the evenings.

The original Italian fast food alternative is known as the 'hot table' (*tavola calda*), a buffet serving hot and cold foods, where you can choose a simple prepared dish or a whole meal, depending on your appetite. The food in these can occasionally be truly impressive, though nowadays they are becoming harder to find among the growing number of international and made-in-Italy fast food franchises. However, bars often double as *paninotecas* (these make sandwiches to order), and if everywhere else is closed, you can always try the railway station bars – these will at least have sandwiches and drinks. Some of the station bars also prepare *cestini di viaggio*, full-course meals in a basket to help you survive long train trips.

Common snacks you'll encounter include *panini* of prosciutto, cheese and tomatoes, or other meats; *tramezzini*, little sandwiches on plain, square white bread that are always much better than they look; pizza, of course, or the traditional sandwich of Tuscany and Umbria, a hard roll filled with fat slices of warm *porchetta* (roast whole pig stuffed with fennel and garlic, complete with all the fat and gristle). Little shops that sell pizza by the slice (*al taglio*) are common in city centres; some, called *gastronomie*, offer other take-out delicacies as well. At any delicatessen (*pizzicheria*), or grocer's (*alimentari*) or market (*mercato*) you can buy the materials for countryside picnics; some places in smaller towns will make the sandwiches for you. The *rosticceria* is another very varied alternative to a restaurant meal – hot and cold food to take away, and usually of better quality than the *tavola calda*. Rarely do they have anywhere to sit down. Pastas, rice, roasted meats (always including spit-roasted chickens), veg, dessert and drinks are always good value.

Regional Specialities

Regional traditions are strong in Italy, not only in dialect but in the kitchen. Tuscany, Umbria and the Marches are no exception and firmly maintain their distinctive cuisine even when you wish they wouldn't – especially in the case of Umbrian bread, described by astonished visitors as 'tasty as chewy water' and 'scarcely distinguishable from a cricket bat'. Although neither Tuscany nor Umbria ranks among the great culinary regions of Italy, both offer good, honest, traditional dishes, often humble, rarely elaborate. The Medici may have put on some legendary feedbags, but the modern Tuscan is known by his fellow Italians as a *mangiafagioli*, or bean-eater. Some observers hold it as part of the austere Tuscan character, others as another sign of their famous alleged miserliness. Umbria and the Marches, historically poor areas, never had a choice one way or the other.

The truth is, although beans and tripe often appear on the menu, that most people when dining out want to try something different, from other regions, perhaps, or the recent concoctions of Italian nouvelle cuisine, or *cucina rivisitata*, or perhaps a recipe from the Middle Ages or Renaissance. Some of the country's finest restaurants are in Tuscany and Umbria, including two generally ranked among the top five in all Italy; in practice, the diversity of dishes in Tuscany, from traditional to bizarre, is almost endless. Umbria and the Marches are more conservative and not so sure about this newfangled *cucina rivisitata*.

Food

The Tuscans will tell you the basic simplicity of their kitchen is calculated to bring out the glories of their wine, which may well be true, as it tends to be the perfect complement to a glass of Chianti or Vino Nobile. Nearly all are born of thrift, like *bruschetta*, a Tuscan and Umbrian favourite that takes sliced stale bread, roasted over the fire, rubbed with garlic and covered with olive oil. *Acqua cotta*, popular in southern Tuscany, is *bruschetta* with an egg; another version adds mashed tomatoes. The other traditional Tusco-Umbrian *antipasto* is *crostini*, thin slices of toast with a piquant pâté spread of chicken livers, anchovies, capers and lemons, or other variations (in Umbria it's often spleen). Umbrians also like platters of prosciutto, salami, sliced stuffed rabbit and *capocollo* (cured neck of pork) which is better than it looks.

For *primo*, the traditional Tuscan relies mostly on **soups**. Perhaps most traditional is *ribollita* ('reboiled'), a thick, hearty soup made with chunks of yesterday's bread, beans, black cabbage and other vegetables. Similar is *pappa al pomodoro*, another bread-based soup flavoured with fresh tomatoes, basil and sludgy local olive oil. The prince of Tuscan soups is Livorno's *cacciucco*, a heavenly fish soup that you have to go to Livorno to try. Other first courses include the most Tuscan of pasta dishes, *pappardelle alla lepre* (wide egg noodles with a sauce of stewed hare); others are the simple but delicious *spaghetti con briciolata* (with olive oil, breadcrumbs and parsley); *pici* (in Siena and South Tuscany) – thick, hand-rolled spaghetti, often served '*all'aglione*' – with a garlic and tomato sauce; *crespelle* – pancakes stuffed with spinach and ricotta; *ravioli* stuffed with spinach and ricotta and served with melted butter and sage. *Panzanella* is another traditional dish in which stale bread is soaked and squeezed out and tomatoes, onions, basil, garlic and olive oil are added to make a 'bread salad'. Delicious *contorni* (side dishes) include *fagioli al fiasco* (beans with oil and black pepper simmered in an earthenware pot) or *fagioli all'uccelletto* (beans with garlic and tomatoes).

Umbrians are more fond of their pasta – *tagliatelle ai funghi* (with wild porcini mushrooms), or *ai tartufi* (with truffles); *tortellini con panna* (with cream sauce); *ciriole* or *pici* or *strangozzi* (various names for fat, home-made spaghetti) with various sauces, with wild asparagus holding pride of place in the spring and black truffles between November and March. In northern Umbria look for *baggiana*, a soup of fava beans, tomatoes and basil, and *strascinati*, home-made maccaroni served with sausage, eggs, and cheese. The real test of an Umbrian chef is eggs with truffles, a difficult dish to time correctly but superb when successful.

Florence's Most Ephemeral Art

Florence in its loftier moods likes to call itself the 'birthplace of international haute cuisine', a claim that has very much to do with Catherine de' Medici, a renowned trencherwoman, who brought a brigade of Florentine chefs with her to Paris and taught the Frenchies how to eat artichokes, but has little to do with the city's contribution to the Italian kitchen. Florentine food is on the whole extremely simple, with the emphasis on the individual flavours and fresh ingredients. A typical *primo* could be *pappardelle* (*see* above), usually served with a meat sauce, or game such as wild boar, rabbit and duck. Soups are also popular: try the *ribollita*, unique to the region, or *pappa al pomodoro* (*see* opposite).

The most famous main course in Florence is the *bistecca alla fiorentina*, a large steak on the bone, two inches thick, cut from loin of beef and cooked over coals. It is served charred on the outside and pink on the inside and simply seasoned with salt and black pepper. As for the vegetables, you could try *piselli alla fiorentina*, peas cooked with oil, parsley and diced bacon; or *tortino di carciofi*, a delicious omelette with fried artichokes; *fagioli all' uccelletto*, cannellini beans stewed with tomatoes, garlic and sage; and *spinaci saltati* – fresh spinach sauteed with garlic and olive oil. Florentine desserts tend to be sweet and fattening: *bomboloni alla crema* are vanilla-filled doughnuts and *le fritelle di San Giuseppe* are bits of deep-fried batter covered in sugar. If you prefer cheese, try the sturdy *pecorino toscano*. For better or worse, real Florentine soul food rarely turns up on many restaurant menus, and unless you make an effort you'll never learn what a Florentine cook can do with cockscombs, intestines, calves' feet and tripe.

Italian Menu Vocabulary

Antipasti

These before-meal treats can include almost anything. These are among the most common.

antipasto misto mixed antipasto
bruschetta garlic toast (sometimes with tomatoes)
carciofi (sott'olio) artichokes (in oil)
frutti di mare seafood
funghi (trifolati) mushrooms (with anchovies, garlic and lemon)
gamberi ai fagioli prawns (shrimps) with white beans
mozzarella (in carrozza) cow/buffalo cheese (fried with bread in batter)
olive olives
prosciutto (con melone) raw ham (with melon)
salami cured pork
salsicce sausages

Minestre (Soups) and Pasta

agnolotti ravioli with meat
cacciucco spiced fish soup
cannelloni meat/cheese rolled in pasta tubes
cappelletti small ravioli, often in broth
crespelle crêpes
fettuccine long strips of pasta
frittata omelette
gnocchi potato dumplings
lasagne sheets of pasta baked with meat and cheese sauce
minestra di verdura thick vegetable soup
minestrone soup with meat, vegetables and pasta
orecchiette ear-shaped pasta, served with turnip greens
panzerotti ravioli with mozzarella, anchovies and egg
pappardelle alla lepre pasta with hare sauce
pasta e fagioli soup with beans, bacon, and tomatoes
pastina in brodo tiny pasta in broth

penne all'arrabbiata quill-shaped pasta with tomatoes and hot peppers
polenta cake or pudding of corn semolina
risotto (alla Milanese) Italian rice (with stock, saffron and wine)
spaghetti all'Amatriciana with spicy pork, tomato, onion and chilli sauce
spaghetti alla Bolognese with ground meat, ham, mushrooms etc.
spaghetti alla carbonara with bacon, eggs and black pepper
spaghetti al pomodoro with tomato sauce
spaghetti al sugo/ragú with meat sauce
spaghetti alle vongole with clam sauce
stracciatella broth with eggs and cheese
tagliatelle flat egg noodles
tortellini pasta caps filled with
  al pomodoro meat and cheese, with tomato sauce
  con panna with cream
  in brodo in broth
vermicelli very thin spaghetti

Carne (Meat)

abbacchio milk-fed lamb
agnello lamb
animelle sweetbreads
anatra duck
arista pork loin
arrosto misto mixed roast meats
bistecca alla fiorentina Florentine beef steak
bocconcini veal mixed with ham and cheese and fried
bollito misto stew of boiled meats
braciola hop
brasato di manzo braised beef with veg
bresaola dried raw meat
capretto kid
capriolo roe-buck
carne di castrato/suino mutton/pork
carpaccio thinly sliced raw beef
cassoeula pork stew with cabbage
cervello (al burro nero) brains (in black butter sauce)

Neither Tuscany nor Umbria offer exceptional *secondi*: grilled meats, salad, and roast potatoes are typical *trattoria* standbys. Tuscany has its famous steak, *bistecca alla fiorentina (see p.45)*; otherwise, both Tuscans and Umbrians are content with grilled chops – lamb, pork or veal. *Fritto misto* is an interesting alternative, where lamb chops, liver, sweetbreads, artichokes and courgettes (*zucchini*) are dipped in batter and fried.

cervo venison
cinghiale boar
coniglio rabbit
cotoletta veal cutlet
  alla Milanese fried in breadcrumbs
  alla Bolognese with ham and cheese
fagiano pheasant
faraona guinea fowl
  alla creta in earthenware pot
fegato alla veneziana liver with filling
lepre (in salmi) hare (marinated in wine)
lombo di maiale pork loin
lumache snails
maiale (al latte) pork (cooked in milk)
manzo beef
osso buco braised veal knuckle
pancetta rolled pork
pernice partridge
petto di pollo boned chicken breast
  alla fiorentina fried in butter
  alla bolognese with ham and cheese
  alla sorpresa stuffed and deep fried
piccione pigeon
pizzaiola beef steak in tomato and oregano
pollo chicken
  alla cacciatora with tomatoes and
  mushrooms, cooked in wine
  alla diavola grilled
  alla Marengo fried with tomatoes, garlic
  and wine
polpette meatballs
quaglie quails
rane frogs
rognoni kidneys
saltimbocca veal scallop with prosciutto and
  sage, cooked in wine and butter
scaloppine thin slices of veal sautéed in butter
spezzatino pieces of beef/veal, usually stewed
spiedino meat on a skewer/stick
stufato beef and vegetables braised in wine
tacchino turkey
trippa tripe
uccelletti small birds on a skewer
vitello veal

Pesce (Fish)

acciughe or *alici* anchovies
anguilla eel
aragosta lobster
aringa herring
baccalà dried salt cod
bonito small tuna
branzino sea bass
calamari squid
cappe sante scallops
cefalo grey mullet
coda di rospo angler fish
cozze mussels
datteri di mare razor (or date) mussels
dentice dentex (perch-like fish)
dorato gilt head
fritto misto mixed fried delicacies, mainly fish
gamberetto shrimp
gamberi (di fiume) prawns (crayfish)
granchio crab
insalata di mare seafood salad
lampreda lamprey
merluzzo cod
nasello hake
orata bream
ostriche oysters
pesce spada swordfish
polipi/polpi octopus
pesce azzurro various small fish
pesce di San Pietro John Dory
rombo turbot
sarde sardines
seppie cuttlefish
sgombro mackerel
sogliola sole
squadro monkfish
stoccafisso wind-dried cod
tonno tuna
triglia red mullet (rouget)
trota trout
trota salmonata salmon trout
vongole small clams
zuppa di pesce mixed fish in sauce
  or stew

Otherwise, look for *arista di maiale* (pork loin with rosemary and garlic), *francesina* (meat, onion and tomato stew in Vernaccia di San Gimignano wine), *anatra* (duck, often served with truffles in Umbria), *piccione* (stuffed wild pigeon), *cinghiale* (boar), either roasted, in sausages or *stufato* (stewed). Both Tuscans and Umbrians are rather too fond of their *girarrosto*, a great spit of tiny birds and pork livers.

Contorni (Side Dishes, Vegetables)

asparagi asparagus
  alla fiorentina with fried eggs
broccoli broccoli
carciofi (alla giudia) artichokes (deep fried)
cardi cardoons/thistles
carote carrots
cavolfiore cauliflower
cavolo cabbage
ceci chickpeas
cetriolo cucumber
cipolla onion
fagioli white beans
fagiolini French (green) beans
fave broad beans
finocchio fennel
funghi (porcini) mushrooms (boletus)
insalata (mista/verde) salad (mixed/green)
lattuga lettuce
lenticchie lentils
melanzane aubergine/eggplant
patate (fritte) potatoes (fried)
peperoncini hot chilli peppers
peperoni sweet peppers
peperonata stewed peppers, onions, etc.
  (similar to ratatouille)
piselli (al prosciutto) peas (with ham)
pomodoro(i) tomato(es)
porri leeks
radicchio red chicory
radice radish
rapa turnip
rucola rocket
sedano celery
spinaci spinach
verdure greens
zucca pumpkin
zucchini courgettes

Formaggio (Cheese)

bel paese soft white cow's cheese
cacio/caciocavallo pale yellow, sharp cheese
caprino goat's cheese
fontina rich cow's milk cheese
groviera mild cheese (gruyère)
gorgonzola soft blue cheese
parmigiano parmesan cheese
pecorino sharp sheep's cheese
provolone sharp, tangy; *dolce* is less strong
stracchino soft white cheese

Frutta (Fruit, Nuts)

albicocche apricots
ananas pineapple
arance oranges
banane bananas
cachi persimmon
ciliege cherries
cocomero watermelon
datteri dates
fichi figs
fragole (con panna) strawberries (with cream)
lamponi raspberries
limone lemon
macedonia di frutta fruit salad
mandarino tangerine
mandorle almonds
melagrana pomegranate
mele apples
mirtilli bilberries
more blackberries
nespola medlar fruit
nocciole hazelnuts
noci walnuts
pera pear
pesca peach
pesca noce nectarine
pinoli pine nuts
pompelmo grapefruit
prugna/susina prune/plum
uva grapes

Dolci (Desserts)

amaretti macaroons
cannoli crisp pastry tubes filled with ricotta,
  cream, chocolate or fruit
coppa gelato assorted ice cream
crema caramella caramel-topped custard

In Tuscany it's fairly easy to find **seafood** as far inland as Florence – one traditional dish is *seppie in zimino*, or cuttlefish simmered with beets. In Umbria seafood is rare, though you can usually get trout. Hardy souls in Florence can try *cibreo* (cockscombs with chicken livers, beans and egg yolks).

crostata fruit flan
gelato (produzione propria) ice cream (home-made)
granita flavoured ice, often lemon or coffee
monte bianco chestnut pudding with cream
panettone sponge cake with candied fruit and raisins
panforte dense cake of chocolate, almonds and preserved fruit
saint honoré meringue cake
semifreddo refrigerated cake
sorbetto sorbet/sherbet
spumone a soft ice cream
tiramisù layers of sponge, mascarpone, coffee and chocolate
torrone nougat
torta cake, tart
torta millefoglie layered pastry and custard cream
zabaglione eggs and Marsala wine, served hot
zuppa inglese trifle

Bevande (Beverages)

acqua minerale mineral water
   con/senza gas with/without fizz
aranciata orange soda
birra (alla spina) beer (draught)
caffè (freddo) coffee (iced)
cioccolata chocolate
gassosa lemon-flavoured soda
latte (intero/scremato) milk (whole/skimmed)
limonata lemon soda
succo di frutta fruit juice
tè tea
vino wine
   rosso red
   bianco white
   rosato rosé

Cooking Terms (Miscellaneous)

aceto (balsamico) vinegar (balsamic)
affumicato smoked
aglio garlic

alla brace on embers
bicchiere glass
burro butter
cacciagione game
conto bill
costoletta/cotoletta chop
coltello knife
cucchiaio spoon
filetto fillet
forchetta fork
forno oven
fritto fried
ghiaccio ice
griglia grill
in bianco without tomato
magro lean meat/pasta without meat
marmellata jam
menta mint
miele honey
mostarda candied mustard sauce
olio oil
pane bread
pane tostato toasted bread
panini sandwiches (in roll)
panna cream
pepe pepper
piatto plate
prezzemolo parsley
ripieno stuffed
rosmarino rosemary
sale salt
salmi wine marinade
salsa sauce
salvia sage
senape mustard
tartufi truffles
tavola table
tazza cup
tovagliolo napkin
tramezzini finger sandwiches
umido cooked in sauce
uovo egg
zucchero sugar

Tuscany's tastiest **cheese** is *pecorino*, made from ewe's milk; the best is from around Pienza. When aged it becomes quite sharp and is grated over pasta dishes. Umbria's best cheeses come from Norcia; in fact, most cheese shops are named after the town.

Typical **desserts**, to be washed down with a glass of Vinsanto, include Siena's *panforte* (a rich, spicy dense cake full of nuts and candied fruit), *cenci*, a carnival sweet (deep-fried strips of dough), *castagnaccio* (chestnut cake, with pine nuts, raisins and rosemary), Florentine *zuccotto* (a cake of chocolate, nuts and candied fruits), *biscottini di Prato* (almond biscuits softened in wine), *crostate* (fruit tarts) or perhaps a *gelato ai Baci* (made with Perugia's famous hazelnut chocolates). In Assisi, the shops sell *rocciata*, a spicy strudel filled with a mixture of almonds, walnuts, prunes, figs, raisins and honey.

In the Marches, seafood is the obvious speciality, especially in *brodetto*, a stew concocted of a dozen different types of fish, and *stoccafisso*, made of cod from the North Sea, dried on the Norwegian coast and served mixed with potatoes. Around Macerata look for *vincigrassi*, a kind of lasagne made with chicken giblets, fresh tomatoes, mozzarella and Parmesan cheese.

Wine

Quaffing glass after glass of Chianti inspired Elizabeth Barrett Browning to write her best poetry, and there's no reason why the wines of Tuscany and Umbria shouldn't bring out the best in you as well. The first person to really celebrate Tuscan wines was a naturalist by the name of Francesco Redi in the 1600s, who, like many of us today, made a wine tour of the region, then composed a dithyrambic eulogy called 'Bacchus in Tuscany'. Modern Bacchuses in Tuscany will find quite a few treats, some of which are famous and some less so, along with plenty of cellars and *enoteche* (wine bars) where you can do your own survey – one particularly renowned place in Siena boasts a stock including not only every wine produced in Tuscany, Umbria, the Marches, but the rest of Italy as well.

Most Italian wines are named after the grape and the district they come from. If the label says DOC (*Denominazione di Origine Controllata*) it means that the wine comes from a specially defined area and was produced according to a certain traditional method; DOCG (the G stands for *Garantita*) means that a high quality is also guaranteed, a badge worn only by the noblest wines. *Classico* means that a wine comes from the oldest part of the zone of production; *Riserva*, or *Superiore*, means a wine has been aged longer. Most Tuscan farmers also make a cask of *Vinsanto*, a dessert wine that can be sweet or almost dry, and which according to tradition is holy only because priests are so fond of it.

Tuscan Wines

Tuscany produces 39 DOC and DOCG wines, including some of Italy's noblest reds: the dry, ruby **Brunello di Montalcino** and the garnet **Vino Nobile di Montepulciano**, a lovely deep red with the fragrance of violets. The famous Chianti may be drunk either young or as a *Riserva*, especially the higher octane **Chianti Classico**. There are seven other DOC Chianti wines (**Montalbano**, **Rufina**, **Colli Fiorentini**, **Colli Senesi**, **Colli Aretini**, **Colline Pisa** and simple **Chianti**). The chief grape in the Chianti region is Sangiovese, shared by all the classified red wines of Tuscany.

Lesser known DOC reds include a dry, bright red named **Rosso delle Colline Lucch** from the hills north of Lucca; the hearty **Pomino Rosso**, from a small area east of Rufina in the Mugello; **Carmignano**, a consistently fine ruby red that can take considerable ageing, produced just west of Florence; and **Morellino di Scansano**, from the hills south of Grosseto, a dry red to be drunk young or old. The three other DOC reds from the coast are **Parrina Rosso**, from Parrina near Orbetello, **Montescudaio Rosso**, and **Elba Rosso**, a happy island wine, little of which makes it to the mainland. All three have good white versions as well.

Of the Tuscan whites, the most notable is **Vernaccia di San Gimignano** (also a *Riserva*), dry and golden in colour, the perfect complement to seafood; delicious but more difficult to find are dry, straw-coloured **Montecarlo** from the hills east of Lucca and **Candia dei Colli Apuani**, a light wine that comes from mountains of marble near Carrara.

From the coast comes **Bolgheri**, white or rosé, both fairly dry. Cortona and its valley produce **Bianco Vergine Valdichiana**, a fresh and lively wine; from the hills around Montecatini comes the golden, dry **Bianco della Valdinievole**. **Bianco di Pitigliano**, of a yellow straw colour, is a celebrated accompaniment to lobster.

Umbrian Wines

Umbria has been a wine region ever since the Etruscans planted the first cuttings from the Greeks, but through much of its history the main concern was to produce wine rather than good wine. The one exception to the generally mediocre plonk was the still-reigning king of Umbrian vines, the celebrated **Orvieto** and **Orvieto Classico**, a delicate wine, dry with a slightly bitter aftertaste; Orvieto Classico comes from the old *zona* around the Paglia river.

The other DOC wines of Umbria are grown on the western hills of the region: the **Colli del Trasimeno** comes from the hills around Umbria's largest lake (Rosso, a garnet, slightly tannic wine; Bianco, dry and mellow with a deep straw colour); **Colli Perugini** from the hills of Perugia (a dry ruby red, a fruity light white, and a dry, intense rosé); **Colli Amerini**, from the Amelia region (the three primary colours, a Novella or new wine, and Malvasia); and **Colli Altotiberini** (a pleasant dry white and red, and a pale, fresh rosé). Those of **Torgiano**, from a small zone near the village of that name, include magnificent, dry, full-bodied reds that can take years of ageing, and a light and lively *bianco*. The area around Montefalco also produces three fine reds: a dry velvety *rosso*, the dry, garnet **Sagrantino**, with the aroma of blackberries, and the sweetish **Sagrantino Passito**, made from raisins.

One of the more unusual wines is the dessert wine **Vernaccia di Cannara**; only made in Cannara, it's unlike every other *vernaccia* in Italy, in that it's red. The most famous dessert wine here, however, is *vinsanto*, a rich, deep, unctious golden wine made from semi-dried grapes; it's sweet and strong, and holy only because priests are so fond of it. Although it is sometimes produced commercially, the best stuff is home-made; you'll know you're in with the locals when they serve you a glass from their precious cache, with the traditional biscuit or crunchy waffle (*cialde*).

Wines from the Marches

The rough and tumble slopes of the Marches conveniently produce a range of DOC white wines to go with the day's catch – wines still incognito outside Italy. The dry and delicate **Verdicchio** from the Jesi district and Matélica is the best known, and pale enough to mistake for water; as in Chianti, the oldest vineyards get to be called 'classic', for example, **Verdicchio dei Castelli di Jesi Classico**. Light golden **Falerio dei Colli Ascolani** is a dry wine consisting mainly of Trebbiano Toscano grapes, as is the pleasant **Bianco dei Colli Maceratesi**, from the province of Macerata and Loreto. Pinkish gold Biancame grapes form the base for **Bianchello del Metauro**, from the coast of Pesaro and hills along the Metauro river, a dry wine that is popular both as an aperitif and a table wine.

The red wines from the Marches are nearly all drunk young: there's the sprightly, fruity ruby **Lacrima di Morro D'Alba**, the pomegranate-coloured **Sangiovese dei Colli Pesaresi**, and **Rosso Conero** (made from Montepulciano grapes). The one wine that is aged for any time is **Rosso Piceno Superiore**, produced up in the hills east of Ascoli Piceno. If you can find it, try **Vernaccia di Serrapetrona**, a naturally sparkling red wine, either dry or dessert, grown in a tiny area near Serrapetrona. The quality of the Marches' other sparkling wines has improved enough to win them the prestigious Torgiano award.

Travel

Getting There

By Air from the UK and Ireland

From **London** there are several daily Alitalia and British Airways flights to the international airports at Pisa and Rome, as well as to Genoa (near the Lunigiana) and Bologna (just over the Apennines from the Mugello or Casentino). There are flights from **Gatwick** to Florence with Meridiana Italia and British Airways. British Airways also have direct flights from **Manchester** to Rome and Milan. Ryanair and easyJet fly from **London Stansted** to Rome Ciampino; easyJet also flies to Bologna and Ryanair to Pisa, and Ancona in the Marches.

From Ireland, there are direct flights most days from **Dublin** and **Cork** to Milan on either Alitalia or Aer Lingus, from where you can pick up a connecting flight to Florence, Perugia, Rome, Ancona or Rimini. Keep your eyes open for bargains and charters in the papers.

The carriers listed have a variety of **discounts** if booked in advance. Apex fares have fixed arrival and departure dates, and the stay in Italy must include at least one Saturday night. Children under the age of two usually travel free, and both British Airways and Alitalia offer cheaper tickets on some flights for students and those under 26. Alitalia often has promotional perks such as car hire (Jetdrive) or discounts on domestic flights, hotels, or tours within Italy. British Airways do a fly–drive package to Pisa and Florence. At the time of writing, Alitalia and BA fares start from £150 if booked well ahead. Ryanair and easyJet can be much cheaper if booked well in advance over the internet. See the airlines' own websites, or visit UK flight websites, including: *www.cheapflights.co.uk, www.ebookers.com, www.flightline.co.uk, www.airflights.co.uk, www.flights4less.co.uk, www.flightsdirect.com.*

By Air from the USA and Canada

From the **United States**, the major carriers fly only to Rome or Milan, though British Airways has a New York–London Gatwick–Pisa service that departs New York around 6pm and has you in Pisa around 1pm the next day. Your travel agent may be able to find a much cheaper fare from your home airport to your Italian airport by way of London, Brussels, Paris, Frankfurt or Amsterdam. From **Canada**, only Alitalia flies direct to Italy (from Toronto/Montréal to Rome/Milan).

To be eligible for Apex fares, you'll have to have fixed arrival and departure dates and spend at least a week in Italy, but no more than 90 days. Some Apex fares must be purchased at least 14 days (or sometimes 21 days) in advance and there are penalties to pay if you change your flight dates. At the time of writing the lowest midweek Apex between New York and Rome in the off-season is around $700, rising up into the $900 zone in summer; from Canada, low season fares start at around $900 and move up to $1,250. To sweeten the deal, some carriers, such as Alitalia, offer promotional packages that might include car rental (Jetdrive) or discounts on Italian hotels, domestic flights or excursions. Ask your travel agent for details. Children under the age of two usually travel for free and both British Airways and Alitalia offer cheaper tickets on some flights for students and under 26s.

It may be worth catching a cheap flight to London (New York–London fares are always very competitive) and then flying on from there using some of the British low-cost carriers such as easyJet and Ryanair (*see* box, opposite, for website details). Prices are rather more from Canada, so you may prefer to fly from the States.

For discounted flights, try looking through the small ads in newspaper travel pages (e.g. *New York Times, Chicago Tribune, Toronto Globe & Mail*). Numerous travel clubs and agencies also specialize in discount fares, but may require an annual membership fee. You could also do some initial research on your fare by visiting some of the US cheap flight websites including: *www.priceline.com* (bid for tickets), *www.expedia.com, www.hotwire.com, www.bestfares.com, www.travelocity.com, www.cheaptrips.com, www.courier.com* (courier flights), *www.ricksteves.com*. Other websites are listed in the box opposite.

Major Carriers

From the UK and Ireland

Only Alitalia, BA, Meridiana and Aer Lingus fly direct UK/Ireland–Italy.

Aer Lingus, Ireland **t** 0818 365 000;
UK **t** 0845 084 4444, *www.aerlingus.com*.
Alitalia, t 0870 544 8259; *www.alitalia.co.uk*.
British Airways, London **t** 0870 850 9850;
Dublin **t** 0845 890 626 747,
www.britishairways.com.
KLM Direct, t 0870 243 0541, *www.klm.com*.
Lufthansa, t 0845 773 7747,
www.lufthansa.com.
Meridiana, *www.meridiana.it*.
SN Brussels Airlines, t 0870 735 2345,
www.brussels-airlines.com.

From the USA and Canada

Air Canada, t 1 888 247 2262,
www.aircanada.ca.
Alitalia, (USA) **t** 800 223 5730, *www.alitaliausa.com*.
British Airways, t 800 AIRWAYS,
www.britishairways.com
Continental, t 800 231 0856, **t** 800 361 8071 (hearing impaired),
www.continental.com.
Delta, t 800 241 4141, *www.delta.com*.
Northwest Airlines, t 800 447 4747,
www.nwa.com.
United Airlines, t 800 864 8331, *www.ual.com*.

Low-cost Carriers

easyJet, t 0905 821 0905 (sales; calls charged at 65p per minute), *www.easyJet.com*. Operates flights from London Stansted to Bologna and Rome (7 times a week).
Ryanair, t 0871 246 0000 (UK only; Mon–Sat), *www.ryanair.com*. Offers flights from Stansted to Pisa, Rome and Ancona.

Discounts and Youth Fares

From the UK and Ireland

Budget Travel, 134 Lower Baggot Street, Dublin 2, **t** (01) 631 1111, *www.budgettravel.ie*.

Italflights, 125 High Holborn, London WC1V 6QA, **t** (020) 7405 6771.
Trailfinders, 215 Kensington High Street, London W8, **t** (020) 7937 1234; 4–5 Dawson St, Dublin 2, **t** (01) 677 7888, *www.trailfinders.co.uk*. Branches of this company can also be found in other major UK cities.
United Travel, 2 Old Dublin Road, Stillorgan, County Dublin, **t** (01) 283 2555, *www.unitedtravel.ie*

Besides saving 25% on regular flights, people under 26 have the choice of flying on special discount charters.
STA, 6 Wright's Lane, London W8 6TA, **t** 0870 160 0599, *www.statravel.co.uk*. Several branches in London, as well as in other major UK towns and cities.
USIT Now, 19–21 Aston Quay, Dublin 2, **t** (01) 602 1777, *www.usitnow.ie*. Ireland's no.1 specialist student travel agent also has other branches in Ireland.

From the USA and Canada

Airhitch, 2790 Broadway, Suite 100, New York, NY, 10025, **t** (212) 247 4482, or **t** 1 877 AIRHITCH, *www.air-hitch.org*.
Now Voyager, 74 Varick St, Suite 307, New York, NY 10013, **t** (212) 431 1616. For courier flights.
STA, toll free **t** 800 781 4040, *www.statravel.com*. Has branches at most universities and also at 10 Downing Street, New York, NY 10014, **t** (212) 627 3111, and ASUC Building, 2nd Floor, University of California, Berkeley, CA 94720, **t** (510) 642 3000.
TFI Tours, 34 West 32nd Street, NY, NY 10001, New York, **t** (212) 736 1140, outside New York, **t** (800) 745 8000, *www.lowestairprice.com*.
The Last Minute Club, 1300 Don Mills Rd, Toronto, Ontario M3B 2W6, **t** (416) 449 5400.
Travel Cuts, 187 College St, Toronto, Ontario M5T 1P7, **t** (866) 246 9762, *www.travelcuts.com*. Canada's largest specialist agent for student travel, with branches in most provinces.

Also see the following websites:
www.xfares.com (carry-on luggage only)
www.smarterliving.com

By Train

By Eurostar from London the journey time to Florence is about 17 hours. Services run daily and return fares cost around £225. The journey involves changing trains and stations in Paris, from where a sleeper or couchette is available on the evening train.

Eurostar, EPS House, Waterloo Station, London SE1, **t** 08705 186186, *www.eurostar.com.*

Travelling by train and ferry takes about 22 hours and costs around £176 for a second-class return (including the couchette). There are also Motorail links from Denderleeuw in Belgium to Bologna (contact Rail Choice, *see* below, for more details).

In an age of low-cost airlines, rail travel is not much of an economy unless you're able to take advantage of student, youth, family and young children or senior citizen discounts. **Interail** (UK) or **Eurail** (USA/Canada) passes offer unlimited travel for all ages throughout Europe for one or two months.

Rail Choice, 15 Colman House, Empire Square, High Street, London SE20 7EX, **t** 0870 165 7300, *sales@railchoice.co.uk.*

Rail Europe Travel Centre, (UK) 178 Piccadilly, London W1V 0BA, **t** 08708 371 371, *www.raileurope.co.uk.*

(USA/Canada) 226 Westchester Ave, White Plains, NY 10064, **t** 877 257 2887 or Canada **t** 800 361 RAIL, *www.raileurope.com.*

Citalia Holidays Ltd, The Atrium, London Rd, Crawley, W. Sussex, RH10 9SR, **t** 0870 901 4013, *www.citalia.com.*

Various youth fares and inclusive rail passes are also available within Italy, and if you're planning on doing a lot of train travel solely in Italy you can organize these before leaving home at Rail Choice (*see* above). They can even send rail passes and Motorail tickets from the UK to the USA by Fedex.

The **Trenitalia Pass** is available to travellers who are not resident in Italy; it allows first or second class travel on all Trenitalia trains for 4–10 days within a two month period (consecutive or non-consecutive). There are three versions of the pass available: **Trenitalia Pass** for adults over 26 (prices from £132 for 4-day, 2nd class pass up to £265 for 10-day, first class pass); **Trenitalia Pass Youth** for young people under 26 (from £109–178, depending on length of validity; 2nd class travel only); **Trenitalia Pass Saver** for groups of 2–5 people (from £113 for 4-day, second class pass up to £219 for 10-day, first class pass). Supplements are payable for Eurostar Italia upgrades, couchettes and travel on Artesia trains.

Rail Choice have further discounts for those students and under-26s using Eurostar (*see* 'Getting Around', p.59, for details on purchasing the rail passes in Italy).

By Coach

Usually more expensive than a cheap flight, the coach is the last refuge of aerophobic bargain-hunters. The journey time from London to Florence is around 30 hours; the return full fare is around £115. There are, again, discounts for students, senior citizens and children as well as off-peak travel.

Eurolines, 52 Grosvenor Gdns, London W1, **t** 0870 514 3219, *www.gobycoach.com. Open Mon–Fri 8am–8pm, Sun 10–12.*

By Car

Driving to Italy from the UK is a rather lengthy and expensive proposition, and if you're only staying for a short time compare your costs against Alitalia's or other airlines' fly-drive scheme. No matter how you cross the Channel, it is a good two-day drive – about 1,600km from Calais to Rome.

Eurotunnel trains, **t** 08705 353 535, *www.eurotunnel.com*, shuttle cars and their passengers through the Channel Tunnel from Folkestone to Calais on a simple drive-on-drive-off system (journey time 35mins). Eurotunnel runs 24 hours a day, year round, with a service at least once an hour through the night. Standard return fares range from £104 to £349, but special offers can bring them as low as £98. **Ferry information** is available from any travel agent or direct from the ferry companies.

You can cut many of the costly motorway tolls by going to Calais, travelling through France to Basle, Switzerland, and from there through the Gotthard Tunnel over the Alps. In the summer you can save the expensive tunnel tolls, and see some marvellous scenery, by taking one of the mountain passes instead.

To bring your car into Italy, you need your car registration (log book), valid driving licence and valid insurance (a Green Card is not necessary, but you'll need one if you go through Switzerland). If your driving licence is of the old-fashioned sort without a photograph the AA strongly recommends that you apply for an international driving permit as well (available from the AA or RAC).

Make sure everything is in excellent working order; it's not uncommon to be stopped, checked and fined by the police, and spare parts for some non-Italian cars are difficult to come by.

Foreign-plated cars are no longer entitled to free breakdown service from the **Italian Auto Club** (ACI), but their prices are fair. Phone ACI on **t** (06) 44 77 to find out the current rates (*see also* p.64).

Current motorway tunnel tolls are:
Fréjus Tunnel, *www.tunneldufrejus.com*, from Modane (France) to Bardonècchia. Prices from €29.30 one way.
Gran San Bernardo, *www.grandsaintbernard. ch*, from Bourg St Pierre (Switzerland) to Aosta. Prices from €18.20 one way.
Mont Blanc Tunnel, *www.tunnelmb.com*. €29.30 one way.

For more information on driving in Italy, contact a motoring organization:
AA, t 0870 600 0371, *www.theaa.com* (UK).
AAA, t 800 222 4357, *www.aaa.com* (USA).
RAC, t 0800 092 2222, *www.rac.co.uk*.

Passports and Customs Formalities

To get into Italy you need a valid passport. EU citizens do not need visas. Nationals from the USA, Canada, Australia and New Zealand do not need visas for stays of up to 90 days. If you plan to stay more than 90 days you must get a *permesso di soggiorno*. For this you will need to state your reason for staying, and be able to prove both a source of income and medical insurance. After a couple of exasperating days at some provincial Questura office filling out forms you should walk out with your permit.

According to Italian law, you must register with the police within eight days of your arrival. If you check into a hotel this is done automatically. Otherwise you should go to the local police station, but in practice few people do this. If you come to grief in the mesh of rules and forms you need to fill in, you can at least get someone to explain it to you in English by calling the Rome Police Office for visitors, **t** (06) 4686, ext. 2987.

EU nationals over the age of 17 can now import an unlimited quantity of goods for their personal use.

Arrivals from non-EU countries have to pass through Italian Customs, which are usually benign, although how the frontier police manage to recruit such ugly, mean-looking characters to hold the submachine guns and drug-sniffing dogs from such a famously good-looking population is a mystery. However, they'll leave you alone if you don't look suspicious (sadly, not being caucasian is often 'suspicious' enough) and aren't carrying more than 150 cigarettes or 75 cigars, or not more than a litre of hard liquor or three bottles of wine, a couple of cameras, a movie camera, 10 rolls of film for each, a tape-recorder, radio, record-player, one canoe less than 5.5m, sports equipment for personal use, and one television (though you'll have to pay for a licence for it at Customs). Pets must be accompanied by a bilingual Certificate of Health from your local Veterinary Inspector. US citizens may return with $400 worth of merchandise – keep your receipts.

There are no limits to the amount of money you may bring into Italy, and no-one is likely to check how much you leave with. If you want to ensure that your suitcase full of bank notes is legal, ask the Guardia di Finanza, **t** 117, 24-hour service.

Disabled Travellers

Recent access-for-all laws in Italy have improved the once dire situation: the number of ramps and stair lifts has increased probably a hundredfold in the past few years, and nearly every hotel has one or two rooms with facilities for the disabled – although the older ones may not have a lift, or not one large enough for a wheelchair. Although service

Specialist Organizations for Disabled Travellers

In Italy

CO.IN (Consorzio Cooperative Integrate), Via Ostiense 131L, 00154 ROMA, freephone **t** 800 810810, **t** 06 712 9011, **f** 06 2326 7505, *www.coinsociale.it/turismo*. Their tourist information centre (*open Mon–Fri 9–5*) offers advice and information on accessibility.

Centro Studi Consulenza Invalidi, Via Gozzadini 7, 20148 Milan. Publishes an annual guide, *Vacanze per Disabili*, with details of suitable accommodation in Italy.

In the UK and Ireland

RADAR (Royal Association for Disability & Rehabilitation), 25 Mortimer Street, London W1, **t** (020) 7723 4004, *www.radar.org.uk*. For information and books.

Holiday Care Service, Imperial Building, Victoria Rd, Horley, Surrey, RH6 7PZ, **t** (01293) 774535, *www.holidaycare.org.uk*. Information on accommodation, transportation, equipment hire, services, tour operators and contacts.

Royal National Institute for the Blind (RNIB), 224 Great Portland Street, London W15 5TB, **t** (020) 7388 1266. Its mobility unit offers a 'Plane Easy' audio cassette with advice for visually impaired people travelling by plane. Also advises on finding accommodation.

Tripscope, Alexandra House, Albany Road, Brentford, Middx TW8 0NE, **t** 08457 585641, **f** (020) 8580 7022, *www.justmobility.co.uk/tripscope*. Practical advice and information on every aspect of travel and transport for disabled travellers. Information can be provided by letter or tape.

Irish Wheelchair Association, Blackheath Drive, Clontarf, Dublin 3, **t** (01) 8833 8241, *www.iwa.ie*. Publishes guides with advice for disabled holiday-makers.

In the USA and Canada

American Foundation for the Blind, 15 West 16th Street, New York, NY 10011, **t** (212) 620 2000, toll free **t** 800 2323 5463. The best source of information in the USA for visually impaired travellers.

Federation for the Handicapped, 211 West 14th Street, New York, NY 10011, **t** (212) 747 4262. Organizes summer tours for members; there is a nominal annual fee.

SATH (Society for Accessible Travel and Hospitality), 347 5th Avenue, Suite 610, New York NY 10016, **t** (212) 447 7284, **f** (212) 725 8253, *www.sath.org*. Travel and access information. Website has good links and a list of relevant on-line publications.

Internet Sites

Emerging Horizons, *www.emerginghorizons.com*. International on-line travel newsletter for people with disabilities.

Access-Able Travel Source, *www.access-able.com*. Information for older and disabled travellers.

Access Ability, *www.access-ability.org/travel.html*. Information on travel agencies.

---

stations on the *autostrade* have equipped restrooms, you could get very stuck in the middle of a city – Florence, visited by zillions of tourists is notoriously lacking in accessible loos. Local tourist offices are helpful, and have been known to find someone to give you a hand on the spot, while the National Tourist Office can offer suggestions for hill towns that are particularly difficult to get around. Some of these, especially in Umbria, will tire out the fittest tourist. Italian churches are a problem in themselves. Long flights of steps in front were designed to impress on the would-be worshipper the feeling of going upwards to God – another raw deal for the disabled.

Getting Around

The republic has an excellent network of airports, railways, highways and byways, and you'll find getting around fairly easy – unless one union or another goes on strike (though to be fair, this rarely happens during the main holiday season). There's plenty of talk about passing a law to regulate strikes, but don't count on it happening soon. Instead, learn how to recognize the word in Italian: *sciopero* (SHO-PER-O) and be prepared to do as the Romans do when you hear it – quiver with resignation. There's always a day or two's notice, and usually strikes last only 12 or 24 hours – but this is long enough to throw a spanner in the works if you have to catch a plane, so keep your eyes and ears open for advance warnings.

By Train

FS information from anywhere in Italy, t 892 021 88088, open 7am–9pm, www.fs-on-line.com, www.trenitalia.com.

Italy's national railway, the FS (*Ferrovie dello Stato*) is well run and often a pleasure to ride. There are also several private rail lines around cities and in country districts. We have tried to list them all in the Getting Around sections of the Gazetteer chapters in this book. You may find that some of these private companies won't accept Interail or Eurail passes.

Train **fares** have increased greatly over the last couple of years and only those without extra supplements can still be called cheap. Possible FS unpleasantnesses you may encounter, besides a strike, are delays and crowding (especially on Friday nights, weekends and in the summer). Reserve a seat in advance (*fare una prenotazione*). The fee is small and can save you hours of standing. For the upper echelon trains (Eurostars and some intercities), reservations are mandatory. Do check when you purchase your ticket in advance that the date is correct; tickets are only valid the day they're purchased unless you specify otherwise.

Tickets may be purchased not only at stations, but at many travel agents (and some also on-line) and it's wise to buy them in advance as the queues can be long. Make sure that you ask which **platform** (*binario*) your train leaves from; the big permanent boards posted in the stations are not always correct.

Always remember to **stamp your ticket** (*convalidare*) in the not-very-obvious machine at the head of the platform before boarding the train. Failure to do so may result in a fine. If you get on a train without a ticket you can buy one from the conductor, with an added 20% penalty. You can also pay a conductor in order to move up to first class as long as there are places available.

There is a strict hierarchy of **trains**. A *Regionale* travels short-ish distances, and tends to stop at all the stations. There are only

a few *Espressi* trains left in service, but they are in poor condition, and mostly serve the long runs from the south of Italy. No supplement is required. *Intercity* trains link Italian cities, with minimum stops. Some carry an obligatory seat reservation requirement (free in this case), and all have a supplement. The true 'Kings of the Rails' are the super-swish and super-fast (Florence–Rome in 1½ hours) *Eurostars*. These make very few stops, offer both first and second class carriages, and carry a supplement that includes an obligatory seat reservation. So, the faster the train, the more you pay. Make sure you check all fares at the time of booking.

The Trenitalia pass has replaced the Flexicard (which no longer exists). First or second class passes are valid from 4–10 days, either consecutive or not, within a 2-month period. Second class passes cost from €174 for four days – €282 for ten days. These fares apply to individual travellers; for those travelling in groups of 2-5, the passes cost €149–€239 respectively.

Other **discounts**, available only once you're in Italy, are 15% off same-day return tickets and three-day returns (depending on the distance involved), and discounts for families of at least four travelling together. Senior citizens (60 and over) can also get a *Carta d'Argento* ('silver card') for €30, entitling them to a 20% reduction in fares. A *Carta Verde* bestows a 20% discount on people under 26 and costs €30. The *Carto Amicotreno*, €50 for one year, gets you discounts from 10 to 50 %.

Refreshments on routes of any great distance are provided by buffet cars or trolleys; you can usually get sandwiches and coffee from vendors along the tracks at intermediary stops. Station bars often have a good variety of take-away travellers' fare; at least consider investing in a plastic bottle of mineral water, since there's no drinking water on the trains.

Italy's stations also offer other facilities. All have a *deposito*, where you can leave your bags for hours or days for a fee. The larger ones have porters (who charge about €2.50 per piece) and luggage trolleys; major stations have an *albergo diurno* ('day hotel', where you can take a shower, get a shave and haircut, etc.), information offices, currency exchanges open at weekends (not at the most advantageous rates), hotel-finding and reservation services, kiosks with foreign papers, restaurants, etc. You can also arrange a rental car to await you at your destination, through hire firms Avis, Hertz or Maggiore.

By Coach and Bus

Intercity coach travel is often quicker than train travel, but also a bit more expensive. The Italians aren't dumb; you will find regular coach connections only where there is no train to offer competition. Coaches almost always depart from the vicinity of the train station, and tickets usually need to be purchased before you get on. In many regions they are the only means of public transport and are well used, with frequent departures. The base for all country bus lines will be the provincial capitals: we've done our best to explain the connections even for the most out-of-the-way routes, as well as listing coach companies in the relevant areas, in the listings for each chapter.

Courses for Foreigners and Specialist Holidays

The **Italian Institute**, 39 Belgrave Square, London SW1X 8NX, t (020) 7235 1461, *www.italculture.org.uk*, or 686 Park Avenue, New York, NY 10021, t (212) 879 4242, is the main source of information on courses for foreigners in Italy, including Italian government scholarships and language courses for business students. Graduate students should also contact their nearest Italian consulate to find out about scholarships – apparently many go unused each year because no one knows about them.

One obvious course to take, especially in this linguistically pure land of Dante, is **Italian language and culture**: there are special summer classes offered by the Scuola Lingua e Cultura per Stranieri of the University of Siena and the Università per Stranieri in Perugia (*see* opposite), and special classes in August for teachers of Italian. Similar courses are held in Cortona, Viareggio (run by the University of Pisa), Urbino (at the University of Urbino, Via Saffi 2, Urbino), and, not surprisingly, Florence – sometimes there seem to be more American students than Florentines in the city.

The following offer courses year-round:

British Institute, Piazza Strozzi 2, t 055 267781, f 055 2677 8223, *www.britishinstitute.it*. Runs courses on Florentine art and history, Dante, opera and language.

Centro Fiorenza, Via di Santo Spirito 14, t 055 239 8274, *www.centrofiorenza.com*. Offers history, literature and art at both basic and advanced levels. Also offers cooking courses.

Centro Linguistico Italiano Dante Alighieri, Piazza Repubblica 5, t 055 210808, f 055 287828, *www.clida.it*. Specializes in language courses.

Scuola Lorenzo de' Medici, Via Alloro 14r, t/f 055 289514, *www.lorenzodemedici.it*. Has classes in language and art.

Scuola Macchiavelli, Piazza Santo Spirito 4, t 055 239 6966, *www.centromachiavelli.it*. A smaller school than the others listed here, the Machiavelli is run by a co-operative of teachers and offers a more personal approach. You can learn Italian in classes with a maximum of 12 students or through individual lessons, enrol in courses in commercial Italian, art history, art and artisan practical courses in professional workshops, food and drink apprenticeships, cooking and opera singing.

Università per Stranieri, Ufficio Relazioni con lo studente, Palazzo Gallenga, Piazza Fortebraccio 4, 06122 Perugia, t 075 57461, *www.unistrapg.it*. Month-long courses in Italian year-round, for up to 4,000 students a year. Write in advance for details or contact the Italian Institute in your own country.

Music courses complement the regions' numerous music festivals: Certaldo's medieval music society, Ars Nova, sponsors a seminar in July. Siena's Accademia Musicale Chigiana, Via di Città, offers master classes for instrumentalists and conductors; in July and August Barga holds an International Opera workshop.

Art-lovers can take a course on medieval art at Florence's Università Internazionale dell'Arte, in the Villa Tornabuoni, Via Incontri 3;

City buses are the traveller's friend. Most cities label routes well; all charge flat fees for rides within the city limits and immediate suburbs, at the time of writing around €1. Bus tickets must always be purchased before you get on, either from a tobacconist's, a newspaper kiosk, many bars, or from ticket machines near the main stops. Once you are on, you must 'obliterate' your ticket in the machines at the front or back of the bus; controllers stage random checks to make sure you've punched your ticket. Fines for cheats are about €40, and the odds are about 12 to 1 against a check, so you may decide that you can take your chances. If you're good-hearted, you'll buy a ticket and help some overburdened municipal transit line meet its annual deficit.

By Taxi

Tariffs from town to town start at about €2.50 but as a rough guideline add €0.80 per km. There is a minimum charge of €4.50. Each piece of baggage will cost extra, and there are surcharges for trips outside the city limits, trips between 10pm and 6am, and trips on Sundays and holidays.

courses are offered from October to April in history of art, restoration and design, while the Istituto per l'Arte e il Restauro, in Palazzo Spinelli, Borgo Santa Croce 10, holds workshops in art restoration.

Paintings courses based in a villa near Greve, Chianti, run by Arte Vita, are open to students at all levels, *www.artevita.com*, under the guidance of two American artists.

In Spoleto, the Centro Italiano Studi di Alto Medioevo, in the Palazzo Ancaiani, offers classes on medieval art in April. Perugia's Accademia delle Belle Arti Pietro Vanucci, at Piazza San Francesco al Prato 5, has painting and sculpture courses.

A Taste of Florence, Via Taddea 31, t 055 292578, *www.divinacucina.com*. American cook Judy Witts has lived in Florence for many years, and her knowledge of the local food and culture is extensive. Courses are run from her home near the central market in Florence, and the day starts with a shopping session, progressing to the kitchen. Groups are limited to six, and day or week courses are offered.

Capezzana Wine and Culinary Centre, Via Capezana 100, 59011 Loc. Seano, Carmignano, t 055 870 6005, *www. cappezzana.it*. This wine- and olive oil-producing estate some 30km from Florence hosts courses for food professionals, skilled cooks and all those involved with food and wine. There is also accommodation available in a wing of the villa.

Worldwide Classroom, *www.worldwide.edu*. Database listing educational organizations around the world.

Specialist Tour Operators in the UK

Abercrombie & Kent, St George's House, Ambrose Street, Cheltenham, Gloucs GL0 3LG, t 0845 070 0610, *www.abercrombiekent. co.uk*. City breaks in all major cities.

Ace Study Tours, Babraham, Cambridge CB2 4AP, t (01223) 835055, f (01223) 837394, *ace@study-tours.org*, *www.study-tours.org*. Cultural tours through Tuscany and Umbria: Tuscan Villas and Gardens; Hill Towns of Umbria.

Alternative Travel, 69–71 Banbury Road, Oxford OX2 6PE, t (01865) 315678, f (01865) 315699, *info@atg-oxford.co.uk*, *www.atg-oxford.co.uk*. Offers walking, wild flower, garden and cycling tours: Piero della Francesca, the Palio in Siena, Renaissance Tuscany; also arranges truffle hunts and painting courses.

Arblaster & Clarke Wine Tours, Farnham Road, West Liss, Petersfield, Hants GU33 6JQ, t (01730) 893344, f (01730) 892888, *www. arblasterandclarke.com*. Tuscan wine tours, truffle hunts and gourmet cooking tours.

Bellini Travel, 15 Savile Row, London W1S 3PJ, t 0207 437 8918, *www.bellinitravel.com*. This small travel agency specialises in tailor-made tours to Tuscany and other parts of Italy for either individual travellers or small groups. Highly experienced staff have insider knowledge of accommodation (in hotels or villas) restaurants and some of the more unusual sights in the area plus access to villas and gardens that are not usually open to the public.

By Car

The advantages of driving in Tuscany, Umbria and the Marches generally outweigh the disadvantages. Before you bring your own car or hire one, consider the kind of holiday you're planning.

If it's a tour of the major art cities, you'd really be best off not driving at all: parking is impossible, traffic impossible, deciphering one-way streets, signals and signs impossible. In nearly every other case, however, a car gives you the freedom and possibility of making your way through Italy's delightful open countryside and stopping at the smaller towns and villages.

Be prepared to encounter some of the highest fuel costs in Europe, to spend a very long time looking for a place to park in any town bigger than a peanut, and face drivers who look at motoring as if it were a video game. The Italians, whether 21-year-old madcaps or elderly nuns, turn into aggressive starfighters once behind the wheel; their mission is to reach their destination in a certain allotted time (especially around lunch or dinner, if they think the pasta is already on the boil) regardless of minor nuisances such

---

British Airways Holidays, Astral Towers, Betts Way, Crawley, West Sussex, RH10 2XA, t 0870 243 3407, *www.britishairways.com/holidays*.

British Museum Traveller, 46 Bloomsbury Street, London WC1B 3QQ, t 0800 085 0864, f (020) 7436 7315, *www.britishmuseum traveller.co.uk*. Sometimes offers Tuscany art and architecture tours.

Citalia Holidays, the Atrium, London Road, Crawley, West Susses, RH10 9SR t 0870 901 4013, f 0870 901 4019, *italy@citalia.co.uk*, *www.citalia.co.uk*. Wide range of escorted or independent holidays throughout Italy.

Fine Art Travel, 15 Savile Row, London W1X 1AE, t (020) 7437 8553, f (020) 7437 1733, *www.bellini.com*. Cultural, art and historical tours, staying in private villas and palazzi.

Inscape Fine Art Study Tours, 1 Farley Lane, Stonesfield, Witney, Oxfordshire OX29 8HB, t (01993) 891726, f (01993) 891718, *www.inscapetours.co.uk*. Escorted art 'study' tours with guest lecturers in Florence, Siena and Southern Tuscany.

Italiatour, 9 Whyteleafe Business Village, Whyteleafe Hill, Whyteleafe, Surrey CR3 0AT, t (01883) 621900, f (01883) 625255, *www. italiatour.co.uk*. Offers resort holidays, city breaks, self-catering accommodation, watercolour and cookery courses, and horse-riding in Umbria.

JMB Travel Consultants, Suite Four, High Tree House, 4 Cromwell Road, Powick, Worcester WR2 5QJ, t (01905) 830099, f (01905) 830191, *www.jmb-travel.co.uk*. Opera in Macerata and Pesaro.

Kirker, 3 New Concordia Wharf, Mill Street, London SE1 2BB, t (020) 7231 3333, f (020)

7231 4771, *www.kirkerholidays.com*. For city breaks and tailor-made tours.

Magic of Italy, 227 Shepherds Bush Road, London W14 7AS, t 0870 027 0480, *www.magictravelgroup.co.uk*. Offers tailor-made city breaks and villa holidays.

Magnum, 7 Westleigh Park, Blaby, Leicester, t (0116) 277 7123. Organizes holidays in Florence especially suitable for elderly visitors.

Martin Randall Travel, Voysey House, Barley Mow Passage, Chiswick, London W4 4PH, t (020) 8742 3355, *www.martinrandall.com*. Imaginatively put together cultural tours with expert guides – art, archaeology, history, architecture, music; Medici Villas and Gardens; opera in Macerata and Pesaro.

Prospect Music and Art Tours, PO Box 4972, London W1 7FL, t (020) 7486 5704, f (020) 7486 5868, *www.prospecttours.com*. Art tours in Florence, Urbino and Umbria (*Art and Power in Urbino*); specialist holidays devoted to famous local cultural figures, such as Dante and Piero della Francesca.

Ramblers, Box 43, Welwyn Garden City, Hertfordshire AL8 6PQ, t (01707) 331133, f (01707) 333276, *www.ramblersholidays. co.uk*. Walking holidays.

Real Holidays Ltd, 66–68 Essex Road, London N1 8LR, t (020) 7359 3938. Designers of quirky holidays for demanding folk.

Sherpa Expeditions, 131a Heston Road, Hounslow, Middlesex, TW5 0RF, t (020) 8577 2717, f (020) 8572 9788 *www. sherpa-walking-holidays.co.uk*. Walking and cycling holidays in Tuscany and Umbria.

Simply Tuscany & Umbria, Kings Place, Wood Street, Kingston-upon-Thames, Surrey KT1

as other cars, road signs, traffic signals, solid no-passing lines, or blind curves on mountain roads. No matter how fast you trip along on the *autostrade* (Italy's toll motorways, official speed limit **130km/80miles** per hour), someone will pass you going twice as fast.

If you aren't intimidated, buy a good road map of Italy or a detailed one of the region you're travelling in (the Italian Touring Club produces excellent ones). Most petrol stations close for lunch in the afternoon, and few stay open late at night, though you may find a 'self-service' one where you feed a machine nice, smooth bank notes. *Autostrada* tolls are high – the website *www.autostrada.it* will help you calculate the cost for your journey. The rest stops and petrol stations along the motorways are open 24 hours. Other roads – from *superstrade* on down through the Italian grading system – are free of charge. The Italians are good about signposting, and roads are almost all excellently maintained. Some highways seem to be built of sheer bravura – suspended on cliffs, crossing valleys on enormous piers – feats of engineering that will remind you, more than almost anything else, that this is the land of the ancient Romans. Beware that you may be fined on the

---

1SG, **t** (020) 8541 2222, **f** (020) 8541 2280, *www.simply-travel.com*. Offers a wide range of places to stay, from opulent villas with pools to country house hotels, plus cookery and painting courses.

Specialtours, 81 Elizabeth St, London SW1W 9PG, **t** (020) 7730 2297. Cultural tours of Tuscany, Umbria and the Marches.

Tasting Places, Unit 40, Buspace Studios, Conlan Street, London W10 5AP, **t** (020) 7460 0077, **f** (020) 7460 0029, *www.tasting places.com*. Cookery courses near Orvieto and Arezzo.

Travelsphere, Compass House, Rockingham Road, Market Harborough, Leicestershire LE16 7QD, **t** 0870 240 2428, **f** (01858) 434 323, *www.travelsphere.co.uk*. Coach tours of the Tuscany coast.

Waymark, 44 Windsor Road, Slough, **t** (01753) 516477, **f** (01753) 517016, *www.waymark holidays.co.uk*. Walking tours of San Gimignano, Tuscany and the Marches.

In the USA/Canada

Abercrombie & Kent, Suite 212, 1520 Kensington Road, Oak Brook, IL 60523 2141, **t** 800 323 7308, **f** (630) 954 3324, *www. abercrombiekent.com*. Organizes city breaks and walking holidays.

Archaeological Tours Inc., Suite 904, 271 Madison Avenue, New York, NY 10016, **t** (212) 986 3054. Offers tours around the regions' Etruscan sites.

Bike Riders' Tours, PO Box 130254, Boston, MA 02113, **t** 800 473 7040, *www.bikeriderstours.com*; Cycling tours with stopovers at elegant hotels.

CIT Tours, 875 3rd Ave, mezz. level, New York, NY 10022, **t** 1-800 CIT-TOUR, *www.cittours. com*; and, in Canada, 80 Tiverton Court, Suite 401, Markham, Ontario L3R 0GA, **t** 800 387 0711. Custom tours.

Esplanade Tours, 160 Commonwealth Ave, Suite L3, Boston MA 02116, **t** 800 426 5492, *www.esplanadetours.com*. Art and architecture and FIT itineraries.

Europe Train Tours, 7578 N Broadway Suite 4, Red Hook, NY 12571, **t** 800 551 2085, *www.etttours.com*. Escorted tours by train and car.

Italiatour, 666 5th Avenue, New York, NY 10103, **t** 800 845 3365 (US) and **t** 888 515 5245 (Canada), *www.italiatourusa.com*. Fly–drive holidays and sightseeing tours organized by Alitalia.

Maupintour, 10650 W Charleston Blvd, Summerlin NV 89135, **t** 800 255 4266, *www.maupintour.com*. Escorted packages.

Trafalgar Tours, 11 East 26th Street, New York, NY 10010, **t** (212) 689 8977, *www.trafalgar tours.com*.

Travelguide International, 1145 Clark St, Stephen's Pt, Wisconsin 54481, **t** (715) 345 0505.

Travel Concepts, 307 Princeton, MA 01541, **t** (978) 464 0411, **f** (419) 821 7543. Gourmet wine and food holidays.

Specialist Tour Operators in Italy

Corymbus Viaggi, Via Massetana Romana 56, 53100 Siena, **t** 00 39 0577 271654, **f** 00 39 0577 271615, *corytrav@tin.it*. Etruscan tours, wine tours, art and cookery in Umbria and Tuscany, painting and stencil classes, mountain bike tours of Chianti.

spot for speeding, a burnt-out headlamp, etc; if you're especially unlucky you may be slapped with a *super multa*, or superfine, of €130–260 or more. You may even be fined for not having a portable triangle danger signal (these can be picked up at the border or from an ACI office). It is now law a) to keep head-lights dipped on the *autostrada* and in any rural area *at all times* and b) to carry a bright orange fluorescent jacket in the car at all times and to put it on if you break down.

The **Automobile Club of Italy** (ACI) (*Via Marsala 8, Rome, t 800 313535 or t 06 49981, f 06 499 82469, www.aci.it*) is a good friend to the foreign motorist. Besides having bushels of useful information and tips, they can be reached from anywhere by calling t 116 – also use this number if you have an accident, need an ambulance, or simply have to find the nearest service station. If you need major repairs, the ACI can make sure the prices charged are according to their guidelines.

Hiring a car is fairly simple if not particularly cheap (around €50 a day for a smallish car, €300 for a week). Italian car rental firms are called *autonoleggi*. There are both large inter-national firms through which you can reserve a car in advance, and local agencies, which often have lower prices. Air or rail travellers should check out possible discount packages.

Most companies will require a deposit amounting to the estimated cost of the hire, and there is 19% VAT added to the final cost. Petrol is as expensive as in the UK; diesel is significantly cheaper. Rates become more advantageous if you take the car for a week with unlimited mileage. If you need a car for more than three weeks, leasing is a more economic alternative. The National Tourist Office has a list of firms in Italy that hire caravans (trailers) and campers.

By Motorbike and Bicycle

The transport of choice for many Italians; motorbikes, mopeds and Vespas can be a delightful way to get between the cities and see the countryside. You should only consider it, however, if you've ridden them before – Italy's hills and aggravating traffic make it no place to learn. Helmets are compulsory. Hire costs for a *motorino* (moped) range from about €30 per day; scooters are somewhat more (from about €50).

Italians are keen cyclists as well, racing drivers up the steepest hills; if you're not training for the Tour de France, consider the hillyness of the region well before planning a bicycling tour – especially in the hot summer months. Bikes can be transported by train in Italy, either with you or within a couple of days; you need to apply at the luggage office (*ufficio bagagli*). Hire prices range from about €10 per day, and to buy one, upwards of €130, either in a bike shop or through the local clas-sified adverts. If you decide to bring your own bike, do check with the airlines first to see what their policies are on transporting them.

Practical A–Z

Children

Children are still the royalty of Italy: often spoiled, probably more fashionably dressed than you are, and never allowed to get dirty. If you're bringing your own *bambini* to Italy, they'll be warmly received. Many hotels offer them advantageous rates and have play areas, and most larger cities have permanent Luna Parks, or fun fairs. Other activities young children enjoy are the **Bomarzo Monster Park** in Lazio, close to the Umbrian border, **Pinocchio Park** in Collodi, near Pisa, **Città della Domenica** in Perugia, the **Pistoia Zoo** and the **Nature Park** in Cavriglia in the Valdarno. If a **circus** visits town, you're in for a treat; it will either be a showcase of daredevil skill or a family-run modern version of Fellini's *La Strada*.

Climate and When to Go

The climate in Tuscany, Umbria and the Marches is temperate along the coasts and in the valleys, and cooler up in the mountains; the higher Apennines and Monte Amiata have enough snow for skiing until April. Summers are hot and humid; in August the Italians head for the sea or mountains. Spring, especially May, when it rains less, is pleasantly warm. Autumn, too, is a classic time to visit, in October and November; before the rains, while the air is clear, the colours of the scenery are brilliant and rare. The hills of Tuscany and Umbria are never less than beautiful, but in October they're extraordinary – and it's the truffle season.

Winter can be agreeable for visiting the indoor city attractions and avoiding the crowds, particularly in Florence, where it seldom snows but may rain for days at a time. Umbria is not called the Green Heart of Italy for nothing: it can be hung over with mists for weeks on end, which depending on how one looks at it, can be terribly romantic or a big bore. The mountains, especially the Apuan Alps along the coast, also get a considerable amount of rain, with 80–120mm in a year.

Disabled Travellers

Recent access-for-all laws in Italy have improved the situation (*see* pp.57-8).

Eating Out

When you leave a restaurant you will be given a receipt (*ricevuto fiscale*) which, according to Italian law, you must take with you out of the door and carry for at least 300 metres. If you aren't given one, it means the restaurant is probably fudging its taxes and thus offering you lower prices. There is a slim chance the tax police may have their eye on both you and the restaurant; if you don't have a receipt they could slap you with a heavy fine.

Average Temperatures in °C (°F)

	January	April	July	October
Ancona	6 (42)	14 (56)	25 (77)	17 (62)
Florence	6 (42)	13 (55)	25 (77)	16 (60)
Livorno	9 (47)	15 (59)	24 (75)	15 (59)
Siena	5 (40)	12 (54)	25 (77)	15 (59)
Perugia	5 (40)	11 (52)	24 (75)	13 (55)
Terni	5 (40)	13 (55)	25 (77)	15 (59)

Average monthly rainfall in millimetres (inches)

	January	April	July	October
Ancona	68 (3)	57 (2)	28 (1)	101 (4)
Florence	61 (3)	74 (3)	23 (1)	96 (4)
Livorno	71 (3)	62 (3)	7 (¼)	110 (4)
Siena	70 (3)	61 (3)	21 (1)	112 (4)
Perugia	60 (3)	70 (3)	30 (1)	115 (4)
Terni	68 (3)	85 (3)	43 (2)	123 (5)

Restaurant Price Categories
very expensive over €60
expensive €40–60
moderate €25–40
cheap up to €25

When you eat out, mentally add to the bill (*conto*) the bread and cover charge (*pane e coperto*, between €1 and €3), and a 15% service charge. This is often included in the bill (*servizio compreso*); if not, it will say *servizio non compreso*. Additional tipping is at your own discretion, but never do it in family-owned and -run places.

In this book, prices quoted for meals are for an average complete meal, Italian-style with house wine, for one person. We have divided restaurants into price categories (*see* above). For further information about eating in Italy and a menu decoder, *see* **Food and Drink**, p.41.

Electricity

For electric appliances you need a 220AC adaptor with two round prongs on the plug. American appliances need transformers too.

Embassies and Consulates

If you have a choice, use the consulate in Florence if you're staying in Tuscany or the Marches; in Umbria, use the one in Rome.
UK: Via XX Settembre 80a, Rome,
   t 06 4220 0001.
   Lungarno Corsini 2, Florence, **t** 055 284133.
Ireland:Piazza Campitelli 3, Rome,
   t 06 697 9121.
USA: Via Vittorio Veneto 119a, Rome, **t** 06 46741.
   Lungarno Amerigo Vespucci 38, Florence,
   t 055 239 8276.
Canada: Via Zara 30, Rome, **t** 06 44598.
Australia: Via Alessandria 215, Rome, **t** 06 852721.
New Zealand: Via Zara 28, Rome, **t** 06 440 2928.

Insurance and Health

Emergencies, **t** 113
You can insure yourself against almost any mishap – cancelled flight, lost baggage, medical bills – for a price. While national health services in the UK and Australia have

reciprocal health care agreements v (pack an E-111 form, available at yo office), others should check their current pc cies to see if they cover you abroad, under what circumstances, and judge whether you need a special travel insurance policy. Travel agencies sell policies, as well as insurance companies, but they are not cheap.

Minor illnesses and problems that crop up in Italy can usually be handled free of charge in a public hospital clinic or *ambulatorio*. If you need minor aid, Italian pharmacists are highly trained and can probably diagnose your problem; look for a *farmacia* (they all have a list in the window with details of which ones are open during the night and on holidays). Extreme cases should head for the *Pronto Soccorso* (Accident and Emergency) of the nearest hospital. Italian doctors are not always great linguists; contact your embassy or consulate for a list of English-speaking doctors.

Lavatories

Italy's stakes in toilet cleanliness improve steadily; there are few holes in the ground, and paper is more common, though as ever they only exist in places like train and bus stations and bars. If you can't find one, try the nearest bar; they are legally obliged to let you use their *bagno*. In stations, motorway stops and smarter cafés, there are toilet attendants who expect a small tip. Don't get confused by Italian plurals: *signori* (gents), *signore* (ladies).

Maps and Publications

The maps in this guide are for orientation only and it is worth investing in a good, up-to-date regional map before you arrive from any of the following bookshops:
Stanford's, 12–14 Long Acre, London WC2 9LP,
   t (020) 7836 1321.
The Travel Bookshop, 13 Blenheim Crescent,
   London W11 2EE, **t** (020) 7229 5260.
The Complete Traveller, 199 Madison Ave, New
   York, NY 10016, **t** (212) 685 9007.
Excellent touring maps are produced by **Touring Club Italiano**, **Michelin** and the

Festivals

Although some festivals in Tuscany, Umbria and the Marches are clearly meant to pull the tourists in, or are just an excuse to hang out under the stars, this doesn't make them any less fun. There are several exceptions to this rule, and generally they add a note of pageantry or culture to your holiday. Some are great costume affairs, with roots dating back to the Middle Ages, and there are quite a few music festivals, antique fairs, and most of all, festivals devoted to food and drink. The following is a calendar of the major events. There are countles others, especially in the summer months. Look out for the banners and ask around when you arrive.

January

1 Feast of the Gift, the mayor's donation of gold, frankincense and myrrh, **Castiglione di Garfagnana**.

24 Feast of San Feliciano, procession with a traditional fair, **Foligno**.

27 Feast of Sant'Emiliano, with a procession of lights, **Trevi** (Perugia).

February

Carnival is celebrated in private parties nearly everywhere, and in **Viareggio** there's an enormous public one, with huge satirical floats, music and parades. **Fano**, on the Adriatic coast, has a contemporary carnival with music, dancing and costume parades, while more traditional Carnival celebrations take place in **Ascoli Piceno**. In **Bibbiena**, the last day of Carnival is celebrated with a grand dance called the Bello Ballo and a huge bonfire, the Bello Pomo.

5 Procession of Sant'Agata, **San Marino**: celebration of independence regained in 1740 after occupation;
Bruschetta festival, **Spello**, with olive-pickers parade and garlic toast feast, set to music.

14 St Valentine's Day, with a fair, music and fireworks, **Terni**. Romantic concerts all month.

Mid-Feb Dog show and 'dog love' products trade fair, **Ancona**.

March

19 Pancake festival, **Montefioralle**, near Greve-in-Chianti;
San Giuseppe, **Siena** (with rice fritters) and *Torrita di Siena*, donkey race and tournament.

March–April International Assembly of Church Choirs, **Loreto**.

April

2 *Palio* of the Golden Frog, **Fermignano** (Pesaro), with a race, flag-tossing and parade in costume.

Istituto Geografico de Agostini. These are available at major bookshops in Italy or sometimes on newsstands. Italian tourist offices can often supply good area maps and town plans.

Books are more expensive in Italy than in the UK, but some excellent shops stock English-language books. A few useful ones are:

Edison, Piazza della Repubblica 27, Florence, **t** 055 213110

Feltrinelli, Via Cavour 12–20r, Florence, **t** 055 219524.

The Paperback Exchange, Via Fiesolana 31r, Florence, **t** 055 247 8154.

Money and Banks

It's a good idea to bring some euros with you for when you arrive; you never know when unforeseen delays and/or public holidays might foul up your plans to find an open bank. **Traveller's cheques** are still the most secure way of financing an Italian holiday; it is easy to change them, and they'll insure you against any unpleasant surprises. You can now withdraw cash from most ATMs with any of the common debit or credit cards. Your bank may charge a small fee, but it won't work out any more expensive than normal commission rates. It's worth having a back-up (e.g. traveller's cheques) in case your card is rejected.

You can have money transferred to you through an Italian bank but this process may take over a week, even if it's sent urgent – *espressissimo*, so it's only worth doing if you are staying a while. You will need your passport as identification when you collect it. Sending cheques by post is inadvisable.

First 3 weeks Huge antiques fair, **Todi**.

Holy Week Religious rites, torchlight processions and so forth, **Assisi**, **Loreto** and many others.

Umbria Jazz, Gospel and Soul music festival, **Terni**.

Holy Thursday Trial of Jesus and re-enactment of Christ's Passion, Good Friday, **Sigillo** (Perugia).

Good Friday Way of the Cross candlelight procession, **Grassina**, near Florence; Evening procession of the Dead Christ, a 13th-century tradition against haunting ancient penitential chant, **Gubbio**; Procession of the Dead Christ, tradition dating from the 16th century, **Bevagna** (Perugia).

Easter Easter morning, *Scoppio del Carro*, 11am explosion of the cart in **Florence** (*see* p.85); Mary's girdle displayed from **Prato's** pulpit.

1st Sunday after Easter National Kite Festival, **San Miniato**.

2nd Sunday after Easter Donkey Palio, **Querceta**, near Lucca.

April–May *Cantamaggio*, parade of illumi-nated floats, **Terni**.

30 April–5 May Feast of San Pelligrino **Gualdo Tadino** (Perugia).

Early May *Calendimaggio*, in **Assisi**.

April–May *Corso dell'Anello*, medieval Tournament of the Ring, **Narni**.

May

All month Iris Festivals, **Florence**, **San Polo Robbiana** (Chianti).

First–third week Sword derring-do and *Palio*, **Camerino** (Macerata).

15 *Corsa dei Ceri*, race of tower shrines, **Gubbio**.

Fourth Sunday Historical parade and crossbow tournament, **Massa Marittima**.

Ascension Day Cricket Festival (insect, not sport) with floats and crickets sold in little cages, **Florence**.

Last Sunday Crossbow competition against Sansepolcro, in medieval costume, **Gubbio**; crossbow competition at **Montespertoli**, wine festival and cart processions.

Pentecost (Whitsuntide) Festival of the Piceni, celebrating the history of the Marches, **Monterubbiano** (Ascoli Piceno); *La Palombella*, **Orvieto**.

May and June *Maggio Musicale Fiorentino* music festival, **Florence**.

June

2 June new holiday, *Festa della Repubblica*.

Early June *Corpus Domini* processions, **Orvieto**; flower carpets in the streets, **Spello**; procession on sawdust designs in the streets, **Camaiore** (Lucca).

Second Sunday, garlic toast (*bruschetta*) festival, **Montecatini Terme**.

Most banks will also give you cash on a recognized credit card. **Credit and debit cards** are accepted in most hotels, resort-area restaurants, shops and most car-hire firms. From sad experience, Italians are wary of plastic, so you may be asked for some identifi-cation when paying by credit card.

Banking Hours

Banks are usually open 8.30am–1.20pm, and 3–4 or 4–5pm. They are closed on Saturdays, Sundays and national holidays.

American Express, Florence: Via Dante Alighieri 22R, t 50981, just off Piazza della Repubblica.

Official Holidays

Official holidays are treated the same as Sundays. Most museums, banks and shops, are closed on the following national holidays:

1 January New Year's Day *Capodanno*.

6 January Epiphany; better known to Italians as the day of *La Befana* – a kindly witch who brings the *bambini* the toys that Santa Claus or *Babbo Natale* somehow forgot.

Easter Monday Usually pretty dull.

25 April Liberation Day – even duller.

1 May Labour Day – lots of parades, speeches, picnics, music and drinking.

2 June is now a holiday.

15 August Assumption *Ferragosto*; the biggest of them all – woe to the innocent traveller on the road or train!

1 November All Saints *Ognissanti*; liveliest at the cemeteries.

8 December Immaculate Conception of the Virgin Mary – a dull one.

25 December Christmas Day.

26 December *Santo Stefano*.

Mid-June–August *Estate Fiesolana* – music, cinema, ballet and theatre, **Fiesole**.

Mid-June *Giostro della Quintana*, a medieval joust, **Foligno**.

16–17 *Festa di San Ranieri* – lights festival and historic regatta in **Pisa**.

18 *Festa del Barbarossa*, celebrating the meeting of the pope and emperor, with ballet, archery, snails, beans and *pici* at **San Quirico d'Orcia**.

Third Sunday *Palio di Rioni*, neighbourhood horse racing, in **Castiglion Fiorentina**.

24 St John the Baptist's Day, with fireworks, in **Florence** and a public holiday *Calcio in Costume*, Renaissance football game, in **Florence**. Also two other games in the month.

Last Sunday *Giocco del Ponte*, a traditional tug-of-war game, held on a bridge, with a cart in the middle, **Pisa**.

Last Sunday *La Bruscellata*, a week-long festival of dancing and singing old love songs around a flowering tree, **San Donato in Poggio** (Florence province).

Last week *Mercato delle Gaite*, **Bevagna**, medieval fair with archery.

June–July The Festival of Two Worlds, a renowned feast of contemporary culture with music, theatre and dance, **Spoleto**.

July

All month Umbria Jazz Festival, **Perugia**.

1 Versilian Historical Trophy, including a flag-throwing contest, **Querceta** (Lucca).

2 *Palio*, the worldfamous horse race around Il Campo, **Siena** (also on 16 August).

3 *Festa Medioevale*, the town of **Palazzuolo sul Senio** transforms every weekend in July.

2nd Sunday 16th-century archery contest in **Fivizzano** (Massa).

3rd Sunday Feast of San Paolino, **Lucca**, a torchlight parade and crossbow contest.

25 Joust of the Bear, a tournament dating back to the 1300s, **Pistoia**.

Last week Elban Wine Festival, **Le Ghiaie**.

Late July Medieval Festival, Monteriggione, near **Siena**.

July–August concert and theatre festival, **San Gimignano**; opera, ballet and concerts at the Sferisterio, **Macerata**; Puccini Opera Festival, **Torre del Lago**.

August

All month Folklore, religious festivals, **Assisi**.

August–September Festival of Chamber music, **Città di Castello**.

1–15 *Palio dei Colombi*, **Amelia**, crossbowmen in 14th-century dress free doves.

First weekend *Torneo della Quintana*, a 15th-century pageant/joust, **Ascoli Piceno**; Thanksgiving festival for San Sisto, **Pisa**.

Second weekend Battle for the Pail, **Sant'-Elpidio a Mare** (Ascoli Piceno): four teams in

Opening Hours and Museums

Although many shops in bigger towns are now open all day, this varies from region to region. Most of Italy closes down at 1pm until 3 or 4pm to eat and properly digest the main meal of the day. Afternoon hours are from 4 to 7, often from 5 to 8 in the hot summer months. Bars are often the only places open during the early afternoon. In any case, don't be surprised if you find anywhere in Italy unexpectedly closed (or open for that matter), whatever its official stated hours.

Museums and Galleries

Most major **museums** are now open all day from 9am to 7pm and tend to close on a Monday and often Sunday afternoons as well.

Where possible we have given opening hours for individual museums; but note that they can change at short notice, particularly in the summer. Many of Italy's museums are magnificent, many are run with shameful neglect, and many have been closed for years for 'restoration' with slim prospects of reopening in the foreseeable future. With two works of art per inhabitant, Italy has a hard time financing the preservation of its national heritage; it would be as well to enquire at the tourist office to find out exactly what is open and what is 'temporarily' closed before setting off on a wild-goose chase.

Entrance charges vary wildly; you should expect to pay between €2 and €5 for museum entrance; expensive ones run to €6.50 (Uffizi, Accademia) and €8.50 where there is a special exhibition. The good news is that state-run

medieval costume try to throw a ball into a
well and keep others from doing so.
Second Sunday Crossbow tournament,
Massa Marittima.
14 *Palio dei quartieri*, flag-tossing and
crossbow contest, **Gubbio**.
15 Beefsteak Festival, **Cortona**
Palio dell'Assunta, **Fermo** (Asoli Piceno),
re-enactment of 1182 event, with horse race.
16 *Palio*, dating from 1147, **Siena**.
17 *Palio Marinaro*, boat races, **Livorno**.
15–30 International choir contest, **Arezzo**.
Mid-Aug–Sept Rossini Opera Festival, big
name performers sing opera greats, **Pesaro**.

September

First Sunday Saracen's Joust, **Arezzo** (also June);
Palio dei Cerri between neighbourhoods and
Renaissance processions, **Cerreto Guidi**;
lantern festival, **Florence**.
Second Sunday *Giostra della Quintana*, jousting,
Foligno; crossbow contest with Gubbio,
Sansepolcro; eating, dancing, **Greve in Chianti**.
13 Holy Procession in honour of the *Volto
Santo* by torchlight in **Lucca**.
Mid-Sept *Sagra Musicale Umbra*, **Perugia**.
Third Sunday wine festival, **Impruneta**;
donkey race, **Carmignano**.
Last weekend Gioche delle Porti, donkey rides
and re-enactment of witch-burning in
costume, **Gualdo Tadino** (Perugia).

October

1 *Palio dei terzieri*, historical parade and cart
race, **Trevi** (Perugia).
3–4 Feast of San Francesco, religious and civic
rites in honour of Italy's patron saint, **Assisi**.
All month Wine festivals and *tartufo* festivals
in the Marches.

November

1–5 All Souls' Fair, **Perugia**.
11 San Martino, with wine and chestnuts,
Sigillo (Perugia).
22 Santa Cecilia, patroness of music, has
concerts held in her honour, **Siena**.
24 Offering of candles, with processions in
14th-century costume, **Amelia** (near Terni).

December

8 Fair of the Immaculate Conception,
Bagni di Lucca.
9–10 *Festa della Venuta*, **Loreto**, celebrating
the airborne arrival of the **Santa Casa**
(Holy House), with bonfires, religious
ceremonies, and a procession of aviators
bearing statue of the Madonna di Loreto, the
town's patron saint.
24 Christmas cribs and Franciscan rites, **Assisi**;
evergreen bonfire, **Camporgiano** (Lucca).
25–26 St Stephen's feast and display of the
holy girdle, **Prato**.
29–early Jan Umbria Jazz Winter, **Orvieto**.

museums and monuments are free if you're
under 18 or over 60 (bring ID). For one week of
the year – usually late spring – all state
museums are free of charge for the 'Settimana
dei Berri Culturali'.

Offices, Banks and Shops

Banks: *open Mon–Fri 8.30–1 and 3–4, closed
weekends and on local and national holidays*
(*see* Official Holidays, p.69).
Shops: *open Mon–Sat 8–1 and 3.30–7.30*. Some
supermarkets and department stores stay
open throughout the day.
  Government-run dispensers of red tape
(e.g. visa departments) often stay open for
quite limited periods, usually during the
mornings (*Mon–Fri*). It pays to get there as
soon as they open (or before) to spare your
nerves in an interminable queue. Anyway, take
something to read, or write your memoirs.

Food Shops

These are shut on Wednesday afternoons in
winter. They close on Saturday afternoons
from the end of June to the beginning of
September. Sunday opening is becoming more
usual, particularly for shops in the centre of
town. Bars are often the only places open
during the early afternoon and sometimes on
a Sunday.

Churches

Italy's churches have always been a prime
target for art thieves and as a consequence
are usually locked when there isn't a sacristan
or caretaker to keep an eye on things. All
churches, except for the really important
cathedrals and basilicas, close in the afternoon
at the same hours as the shops, and the little
ones tend to stay closed.

Always have a pocketful of coins for the light machines in churches, or whatever work of art you came to inspect will remain clouded in ecclesiastical gloom. Don't do your visiting during services, and don't come to see paintings and statues in churches the week preceding Easter – you will probably find them covered with mourning shrouds.

Photography

Film and developing are much more expensive than in the USA or UK. You are not allowed to take pictures in most of the museums, or in some of the churches. Most cities now offer one-hour processing if you need your pics in a hurry.

Police Business

Police/Emergency, t 113

The cities attract a fair amount of petty crime – pickpocketing, white-collar thievery (check your change) and car break-ins – but violent crime is rare. Nearly all mishaps can be avoided with adequate precautions.

Stay on the inside of the pavement and hold on to your property; pickpockets most often strike in crowds; don't carry too much cash and don't keep what you have in one place. Be extra careful in stations, don't leave valuables in hotel rooms, and park in garages, guarded car parks, or well-lit streets, with any temptations out of sight.

Purchasing small quantities of cannabis is legal, although 'small quantity' isn't specified, so if the police dislike you already, it may be enough to get you into big trouble.

Once the scourge of Italy, political terrorism has declined drastically, mainly thanks to the *Carabinieri,* the black-uniformed national police, technically part of the Italian army. Local matters are handled by the *Polizia Urbana;* the *Vigili Urbani* generally just direct traffic and hand out parking fines.

You probably won't encounter the *Guardia di Finanza,* the financial police, who are really after corrupt politicians (unless they catch you leaving a bar or restaurant without a receipt).

Post

City post offices are usually open Mon–Sat 8.10–6; elsewhere Mon–Sat 8.10–1.25.

The postal service in Italy used to have an extremely poor reputation, but has improved in the last couple of years. The new first-class mail, *posta prioritaria* (€0.62), is supposed to guarantee the arrival of a letter in Italy within 24 hours and to EU countries within 36. Or you can use registered delivery, *raccomandata,* for a €2.58 supplement. Stamps (*francobolli*) may also be purchased at tobacconists (*tabacchi,* identified by their blue signs with a white T). Airmail letters to and from North America can quite often take up to two weeks. This can be a nightmare if you're making hotel reservations and are sending a deposit – emailing, faxing or telephoning ahead is far more secure if time is short.

Ask for mail to be sent to you in Italy either care of your hotel or addressed *Fermo Posta* (poste restante: general delivery) to the central post office where you are staying, or if you're a card-holder, to an AmEx office. When you pick up your mail at the *Fermo Posta* window, bring your passport for identification. You will need to pay a nominal charge.

The Italian post has recently made the process of sending parcels a lot easier. You no longer have to wrap things in a certain way; the post offices have boxes if you want to use them. Whether they will be sent as a *lettera* or *pacco* depends on size, weight and contents. *Posta prioritaria* is good for parcels up to 2kg.

Sports and Activities

Bird-watching

The islands, and coastal parks near the Argentario are great places to go bird-watching; ecologically hyper-aware Giglio offers **nature appreciation** and classes for Italian speakers, based at the hotel Pardiui's Hermitage t 0564 809034. The bird park at Lago Burano near Capalbio is another place for bird-watching, t 0564 898829.

Boats and Sailing

The **sailing** is beautiful among the coves of the Tuscan archipelago and around the

Argentario; there's a good sailing school in Torre del Lago Puccini, **t** 0584 351211. You can bring your boat to Italy for six months without any paperwork if you bring it by car; if you arrive by sea you must report to the Port Authority of your first port to show passports and receive your '*Constituto*', which identifies you and allows you to purchase fuel tax-free. Boats with engines require a number plate, and if they're over 3 horsepower you need insurance. To leave your boat in Italy for an extended period, you must have a Navigation Licence; after a year you have to start paying taxes on it. All yachts must pay a daily berthing fee in Italian ports. The National Tourist office has a list of ports that charter yachts in Tuscan ports.

Clubs

Sports clubs are usually privately owned and open only to those paying an annual membership fee. Do not expect to be able to use a pool, gym or sailing club paying a daily rate. The best (cleanest) **swimming** is on the islands, especially on the beaches that look away from the mainland.

Fishing

Fishing in the sea is possible from the shore, boats, or underwater (but not with an aqualung) without a permit, though the Tyrhennian has been so thoroughly fished commercially that the government has begun to declare two- and three-month moratoria on all fishing to give the fish a break. Man-made lakes and streams are well stocked, however, and if you're more interested in the eating than the sport, there are trout farms where you can almost pick the fish out of the water with your hands. To fish in fresh water you need to purchase a year's membership card and you must be resident in Italy. The licence costs about €50 for a year and is available from the Federazione Italiana della Pesca Sportiva. Its offices in every province can inform you about local conditions and restrictions. Bait and equipment are readily available.

Gliding

Gliding and **hang-gliding** are big in Umbria, where the hills provide the necessary up-draughts; the centre for the sport is at Sigillo, near Gualdo Tadino, call 0759 220693 for info; the little airports at Foligno, **t** 0742 670201, and Perugia, S Egidio, **t** 075 592141, also offer gliding.

Golf

There are golf courses in Florence, Montecatini Terme, Punta Ala, Tirrenia, Orbetello, Portoferraio, on Elba, and in Umbria, one near Lake Trasimeno at Ellera.

Hunting

The most controversial sport in Italy is hunting, pitting avid enthusiasts against a burgeoning number of environmentalists who stage protests. The Apennines, especially in Umbria, are boar territory, and in autumn the woods are full of hunters. Pathetically tiny birds, as well as ducks and pigeons, are the other principal game.

Medieval Sports

Some **ancient sports** like the *palios* (two in Siena and one in Pesaro) are still popular, and not purely a tourist attraction; the rivalries between neighbourhoods and cities are intense. The Florentines play three games of Renaissance football a year (*calcio in costume*); Sansepolcro and Gubbio stage two annual crossbow matches, while in Lucca the archers compete from different city quarters. Arezzo, Narni, Foligno, Pistoia and Ascoli Piceno have annual jousts; in Pisa it's medieval tug-of-war.

Potholing

Spelunkers can find Tuscan caves to explore around Montecatini Alta, Monsummano and Sarteano. Monte Cucco near Gualdo Tadino has the most important caves in Umbria; the Centro Nazionale di Speleologia Monte Cucco is in Costacciaro, **t** 075 917 0400.

Riding

Horse riding is popular, and Agriturist (*see* 'Where to Stay', pp.76–7) has a number of villa and riding holidays on offer in Tuscany. The National Association of Equestrian Tourism (ANTE) isvery active here. Umbria's riding centre is at Corciano, near Lake Trasimeno, with day and longer excursions available. For more information, write directly to the local

Agriturist office. There are **race and trotting courses** in Florence and Montecatini Terme.

Rowing

Umbria's Lake Piediluco earns top billing for its international rowing championship; when there's enough water, you can try your skills in the Arno (*see* **Florence**, p.87). There is also the annual rowing race contested between the four old maritime republics of Venice, Amalfi, Genoa and Pisa, which alternates between the cities.

Skiing

Tuscany has major ski resorts at Abetone, north of Pistoia, and Monte Amiata. In Umbria there's skiing in the Monti Sibillini, along the border of the Marches; many people also head south into Lazio to Terminillo, east of Rieti.

Tennis

Tennis courts are nearly everywhere; each *comune* has at least one or two that you can hire by the hour.

Walking

Hiking and signed trails are best developed in Tuscany; April–October is the best and safest time to go. There are several scenic routes through the mountains: the four-day High Trail of the Apuan Alps, beginning from the Rifugio Carrara, above Carrara (for information call **t** 0585 841972, or the Italian Alpine Club (CAI) in Carrara, Via Giorgio, **t** 0585 776782. A second trail, the Grand Apennine Excursion from Lake Scaffaiolo, goes along the mountain ridge that separates Tuscany from Emilia-Romagna, departing from Pracchia, **t** 0187 625154 for information. There's a circular trail through the Garfagnana, starting from Castelnuovo di Garfagnana; contact the Comunità Montana Garfagnana, **t** 0583 644911. In southern Tuscany, trails cover Monte Amiata from Abbadia San Salvatore (Comunità Montana dell'Amiata, **t** 0564 969611). Other fine day trails are in the Casentino, from Badia Prataglia or Stia, or in the Nature Parks of Monti dell'Uccellina from Alberese or the Maremma. Maremmagica organizes trekking and walking tours with guides, **t** 0564 20298 for information. In Florence, you can get information from CAI,

Via Mezzetta 2, **t** 055 612 0467. In Umbria, the local CAI offices can suggest routes: in Perugia, at Via della Gabbia 9; in Spoleto, Vicolo Pianciani 4; in Terni, Via Fratelli Cervi 31; in the Marches, Macerata, Piazza Vittorio Veneto 14, and in most of the smaller mountain towns and villages.

Telephones

Public telephones for international calls may be found in the offices of **Telecom Italia**, Italy's telephone company. They are the only places where you can make reverse-charge calls (*a erre*, collect calls) but be prepared for a wait, as all these calls go through the operator in Rome. Rates for long-distance calls are among the highest in Europe. Calls within Italy are cheapest after 10pm; international calls after 11pm. Most phone booths now take only phone cards (*schede telefoniche*) available in €3, €5 and €10 amounts at tobacconists and newsstands – you will have to snap off the small perforated corner in order to use them. Try to avoid telephoning from hotels, which often add 25% to the bill.

As with most countries, Italy has a constant need for new telephone numbers and, as with other countries, this has forced the Italian telephone authorites to change numbers, usually by adding a digit to the area code, in order to cope with demand. Also, as elsewhere, it is usually realized after a couple of years that this renumbering has been based on a severe underestimation of the potential demand and that the numbers will have to change again. You now have to dial the full town prefix, including the zero, to call anywhere in Italy, even the town that you are in. In this book we have given all phone numbers with the full town prefix. NB: Mobile phone nos do NOT begin with an 'o'.

Direct calls may be made by dialling the international prefix (for the UK 0044, Ireland 00353, USA and Canada 001, Australia 0061, New Zealand 0064). Many places now have public fax machines, but the speed of transmission means that costs can be very high. **To call Italy** from abroad, dial **t** 0039 followed by the area prefix, including the initial zero, e.g. 0039 06 for Rome.

Tourist Offices

For more information before you travel, contact the Italian National Tourist Office in your own country:

UK, Italian State Tourist Board, 1 Princes Street, London W1R 8AY, **t** (020) 7408 1254, **f** (020) 7493 6695, *www.italiantourism.com*; Italian Embassy, 14 Three King's Yard, Davies Street, London W1Y 2EH, **t** (020) 7355 1557, **f** (020) 7312 2230, *www.embitaly.org.uk.*

USA, 630 Fifth Ave, Suite 1565, New York, NY 10111, **t** (212) 245 4822, **f** (212) 586 9249, *enitny@italiantourism.com*; 12400 Wilshire Blvd, Suite 550, Los Angeles, CA 90025, **t** (310) 820 1898, **f** (310) 820 6357, *enitla@earthlink.net*; 500 N. Michigan Ave, Suite 2240, Chicago 1 IL 60611, **t** (312) 644 0996, **f** (312) 644 3019, *enitch@italiantourism.com, www.italian tourism.com.*

Australia, Level 26, 44 Market Street, Sydney NSW 2000 , **t** (02) 92 621666, **f** (02) 92 625745, *lenitour@ihug.com.au.*

Canada, 175 Bloor Street East Suite 907 – South Tower Toronto M4W3R8 (ON), **t** (416) 925 4882, **f** (416) 9254799, *enit-canada@ on.aihn.com, www.italiantourism.com.*

New Zealand, c/o Italian Embassy, 34 Grant Road, Thorndon, Wellington, **t** (04) 736 065.

Tourist and travel information may also be available from **Alitalia** (Italy's national airline) or **CIT** (Italy's state-run travel agency) offices in some countries.

You can pick up more detailed information by writing directly to any of the city or provincial tourist offices (addresses are given in the text). These are usually helpful in sending out lists of flats, villas or farmhouses to hire, or at least lists of agents who handle the properties, and *agriturismo* (*see* p.76).

Where to Stay

Hotels

Tuscany, Umbria and the Marches are well endowed with hotels (*alberghi*) of every description. These are rated by the government's tourism bureaucracy, on a five-star scale: five at the top, one at the bottom. Ratings take into account such things as a restaurant on the premises, plumbing, air-conditioning, etc, but not character, style or charm. Use the stars, included here, as a quick reference only. Hotels may stay at a lower rating than they've earned, so a three-star hotel could turn out to be as comfortable as a four-star.

Breakfast is not always optional. You might well find that half- or full-board is obligatory, particularly during high season at hotels in seaside, lake or mountain resorts, spas or country villas. Otherwise, meal arrangements are optional. In the majority of cases hotel food is bland, just as it is anywhere else.

Prices

Prices listed here are for double rooms only in high season. For a single, count on paying two-thirds of a double; to add an extra bed in a double will add 35% to the bill. Taxes and service charges are included in the given rate. If rooms are listed without bath, it simply means the shower and lavatory are in the corridor. For rooms without bath, subtract 20–30%. Prices are by law listed on the door of each room and are printed in the hotel lists available from the local tourist office; any discrepancies should be reported to the tourist office. Room rates are seasonal: it could cost up to 50% less if you travel in the low season. In resorts, hotels may close down for several months of the year.

Hotel prices rise by 6–8% each year, and are often more expensive than in northern Europe. Each province or region sets its own price guidelines for accommodation. In

---

Hotel Price Categories

In Florence
luxury over €250
very expensive €180–250
expensive €130–180
moderate €75–130
inexpensive up to €75

Elsewhere in the Region
luxury over €230
very expensive €150–230
expensive €100–150
moderate €60–100
inexpensive up to €60

Florence, prices are slightly higher, and the price ranges reflect this. In general, the further south you go, the cheaper the rates.

The National Tourist office has a complete list and booking information for motels and five- and four-star hotels and chains. If you want to stay in a different kind of accommodation, you'll have to book ahead, several months in advance and preferably by fax rather than by post. A booking is valid once a deposit has been paid. If you have to cancel your reservation, the hotel will keep the deposit unless another agreement has been reached. If you come in the summer without reservations, start calling around for a place in the morning or put yourself at the mercy of one of the tourist office hotel finding services.

Besides classic hotels, there are an increasing number of alternatives, nearly always in historic buildings, in Umbria classified as *residenza d'epoca* or country houses.

Inexpensive Accommodation

Bargains are few and far between in Italy. Most cheaper places will always be around the railway station, though in large cities it may be worth looking for something in the historic centre. You could find anything in a one-star Italian hotel; they might be almost perfect, and memorably bad experiences will be few, and largely limited to major cities. In small towns the tourist office may have a list of *affitta camere* (rooms to rent). These vary from basic accommodation in someone's house to more upmarket places. Besides the youth hostels (*see* below), there are several city-run hostels, with dormitory-style rooms open to all. In some cities religious institutions may rent out extra rooms. Monasteries and convents in the country sometimes take guests as well; if you seek that kind of experience, bring a letter of introduction from your local priest or pastor, etc.

Youth and Student Hostels

You'll find hostels in Florence, Lucca, Perugia, Tavarnelle Val di Pesa, in Chianti, Abetone, Cortona, San Gimignano, Assisi, Foligno, Marina di Massa e Carrara, Ascoli Piceno and Pesaro. You can nearly always buy an IYHF card on the spot. There are no age limits, and senior citizens are often given added discounts.

Accommodation – a bunk bed in single-sex room and breakfast – costs around €10 per day. Curfews are common, and you usually can't check in before 5 or 6pm. Book in advance by sending your arrival and departure dates along with the number of guests (by sex) to the hostel, including international postal coupons for the reply. Avoid the spring, when noisy school groups descend on them for field trips.

The *Centro Turistico Studentesco e Giovanile* (CTS), with offices in most Italian cities (and one in London) can also book cheap accommodation for students.

Self-catering Holidays: Villas, Farmhouses and Flats

Renting a villa, farmhouse, cottage or flat has always been the choice way to visit Tuscany, and is becoming increasingly so in Umbria as well. The Internet has made finding a place easier than ever, with companies providing detailed listings and photos of their offerings online. Another place to look is the Sunday papers; or, if you're set on a particular area, write to its tourist office for a list of local rental agencies. These should provide photos to give you an idea of what to expect, and you should make sure all pertinent details are written down in your rental agreement so that you avoid any misunderstandings later.

In general minimum lets are for one week; rental prices (generally per week) usually include insurance, water and electricity, and sometimes linen and maid service. Don't be surprised if when you arrive the owner 'denounces' (*denunciare*) you to the police; according to Italian law, all visitors must be registered upon arrival. Common problems are water shortages, unruly insects (*see* **Topics**, p.29) and low kilowatts. Most companies offer all-inclusive packages, with flights and car-hire. Book as far in advance as possible for the summer season.

Rural Self-catering or *Agriturismo*

For a breath of rural seclusion, the gregarious Italians head for a spell on a **working farm**, in accommodation (sometimes self-catering) that often approximates to the French *gîte*. The real pull of the place may in

Self-catering Operators

In the UK

There is no shortage of choice of UK firms offering villas in Tuscany, Umbria and the Marches.

Accommodation Line, 46 Maddox St, London W1R 9PB, **t** (020) 7499 4433, **f** (020) 7409 2606.

Citalia, 3–5 Lansdowne Road, Croydon CR9 1LL, **t** (020) 8686 5533, **f** (020) 8681 0712, *ciao@citalia.co.uk, www.citalia.co.uk*.

CV Travel, 43 Cadogan Street, London SW3 2PR, **t** (020) 7591 2800, **f** (020) 7591 2802, *www.cvtravel.net*. Specialists in villa and hotel holidays for over 30 years, offering holidays that are distinctly unpackaged, for individuals who appreciate high levels of personal service, quality and product knowledge.

Inghams, 10–18 Putney Hill, London SW15 6AX, **t** (020) 8780 4400/4433, **f** (020) 8780 4405, *www.inghams.co.uk*.

Interhome, 383 Richmond Road, Twickenham, Middx TW1 2EF, **t** (020) 8891 1294, **f** (020) 8891 5331, *www.interhome.co.uk*.

Magic of Italy, **t** 0870 027 0840, **f** (020) 8748 3731, *www.magictravelgroup.co.uk*.

Simply Travel, Kings House, Wood St, Kingston-upon-Thames, London KT1 18G, **t** (020) 8541 2200, **f** (020) 8541 2280, *www.simply-travel.co.uk*. Luxury villas in Tuscany and Umbria.

Something Special Villa Holidays, Field House, Station Approach, Harlow, Essex CM20 2EW, **t** 0870 165 2608, *www.somethingspecial.co.uk*.

The Apartment Service, 5–6 Francis Grove, London SW19 4DT, **t** (020) 8947 3003, **f** (020) 8944 6744, *www.apartmentservice.com*. Apartments in Florence.

Topflight, D'Olier Chambers, D'Olier Street, Dublin 2, **t** (01) 240 1700, **f** (01) 679 9498, *www.topflight.ie*.

Travel à la Carte, First Floor, 30 High Street Thatcham, Berks RG19 3JD, **t** (01635) 863030,

fact be cooking by the hosts – a chance to sample home-grown produce. In Tuscany there are now hundreds of *agriturismo* farms offering rooms. They vary enormously in standard and price, from quite modest to very up-market. This branch of the Italian tourist industry is run by **Agriturist**. It has burgeoned in recent years, with several offices in each region. Prices, compared with the over-hyped 'Tuscan villa', are still reasonable. Local tourist offices will have information on this type of accommodation in their areas.

Associazione Regionale Agriturist, Via Degli Alfani 67, 50120 Firenze, **t** 055 287838, **f** 055 2302285.

Solemar, Via G Modena 19, Firenze, **t** 055 552131.

Turismo Verde, Via Jacopo Nardi 41, **t** 055 2338911, *www.turismoverde.it*.

Or write directly to the individual provincial **Agriturist** offices (UPA):

Tuscany

Via Fabio Fuzí 27, 52100 **Arezzo**, **t** 0575 905355, **f** 0575 902610.

Viale Amendola 46, 50121 **Firenze**, **t** 055 200 41225, **f** 055 239 6423.

Via Manin 20, 58100 **Grosseto**, **t** 0564 417418, **f** 0564 421828.

Via G Marradi 14, 57126 **Livorno**, **t** 0586 812744, **f** 0586 811792.

Viale Barsanti e Matteucci 208, 55100 **Lucca**, **t** 0583 342044, **f** 0583 341920.

Via Resistenza 52/M, **Aulla-Massa** 54011, **t/f** 0187 421028.

Via Lavagna 26, 56100 **Pisa**, **t** 050 26221, **f** 050 48533.

Via F Pacini 45, 51100 **Pistoia**, **t** 0573 21 231, **f** 0573 367439.

Via Marco Ronconi 214, 59100 **Prato**, **t** 0574 33939, **f** 0574 34437.

Via Massetana Romana 52, 53100 **Siena**, **t/f** 0577 47669.

Umbria

Via San Bartolomero 79, 06087 Ponte S. Giovanni, **Perugia**, **t** 075 5970729; **f** 075 5970740. *www.agrituristumbria.com*.

The Umbria tourist office publishes a complete guide, available from:

Azienda di Promozione Turistica, dell'Umbria, Via Mazzini 21, **Perugia**, **t** 075 575951, **f** 075 573 6828, *www.umbria2000.it*.

The Marches

Corso Mazzini 64, 60100 **Ancona**, **t** 071 201763.

Via Trieste 52, 63100 **Ascoli Piceno**, **t** 0736 257028.

f (01635) 867272, *www.anotheritaly.co.uk*.
The company's 'Another Italy' programme
offers villas and *agriturismi* of character
around the Marches and in Southern Tuscany.

Vacanze in Italia, Manor Courtyard, Bignor,
Pulborough, West Sussex RH20 1QD,
t (01798) 869421/014/0870 0772 772,
f (01798) 869014, *www.indiv-travellers.com*.

In the USA

At Home Abroad, 405 East 56th St 6H, New
York, NY 10022-2466, t (212) 421 9165, f (212)
752 1591, *www.athomeabroadinc.com*.

CIT North America Ltd, t (800) CIT-TOUR,
15 West 44th St, New York, NY 10173,
t 800 CIT-TOUR, *www.cit-tours.com*;
in Canada, 80 Tiverton Court, Suite 401,
Markham, Ontario L3R 0GA, t (905) 415 1060.

Hideaways International, 767 Islington St,
Portsmouth, NH 03801, t (603) 430 4433 or
toll free t 800 843 4433, f (603) 430 4444,
www.hideaways.com.

Homebase Abroad, 29 Mary's Lane, Scituate,
MA 02006, t (781) 545 5112, *www.homebase-
abroad. com*. Luxury villas.

Italianvillas.com website, *www.italianvillas.
com/search.htm*.

Rentals in Italy (and Elsewhere!), 700 E Main
St, Ventura, CA 93001, t (805) 641 1650,
f (805) 641 1630, *www.rentvillas.com*.

In Italy

Solo Affitti, Grosseto, t 0564 416743.

The Best in Italy, Via Ugo Foscolo 72, Firenze,
t 055 223064, *www.thebestinitaly.com*.

Toscana Vacanze, Piazza Silvio Pellico 1, 52047
Marciano della Chiana, t 0575 845348.

Toscanamare Villas, Via W della Gheradesca 5,
Castagneto Carducci (LI), t 0565 744012,
f 0565 744339, *www.toscanamare.it*. Villas
on the Etruscan coast.

Vela, Via Colombo 16, Castiglione della
Pescaia, t 0564 933495, *www.lavela
immobiliare.it*.

Corso Cavour 2, 62100 **Macerata**,
t 0733 231351.

Piazzale Matteotti 28, 61100 **Pesaro**,
t 0721 33168.

Alpine Refuges

The Club Alpino Italiano operates many of
the *Rifugi Alpini*, mountain huts in the
Apennines. Facilities range from basic to
grand; some are exclusively for hikers and
climbers, while others are reached by *funivie*,
used by skiers in winter and holiday-makers in
summer. Rates range from about €10–€28 a
night, depending on whether you are a CAI
member, but rise by 20% December–April.
Write to the club at Via E Petrella 19, Milan,
t 02 205 7231, *www.cai.it* for a list of huts, dates
available, and booking information.

Camping

Most official campsites are near the sea, the
mountains or the lakes; and there is usually
one within commuting distance of major
tourist centres. Details are published in the
Italian Touring Club's *Campeggi e Villaggi
Turistici*, available in Italian bookshops for €18;
ask for an abbreviated list free from:

**Centro Internazionale Prenotazioni
Federcampeggio**, Casella Postale 23, 50041,
Calenzano (Firenze), t 055 882391,
www.federcampeggio.it.

Camping prices vary enormously, so check
with the individual sites, and request a
booking form to reserve a space – in summer
the tents and caravans are packed cheek by
jowl. You may camp outside an official site if
you ask the landowner's permission. Hiring a
caravan is expensive: ask the tourist office for
a list of firms.

Florence

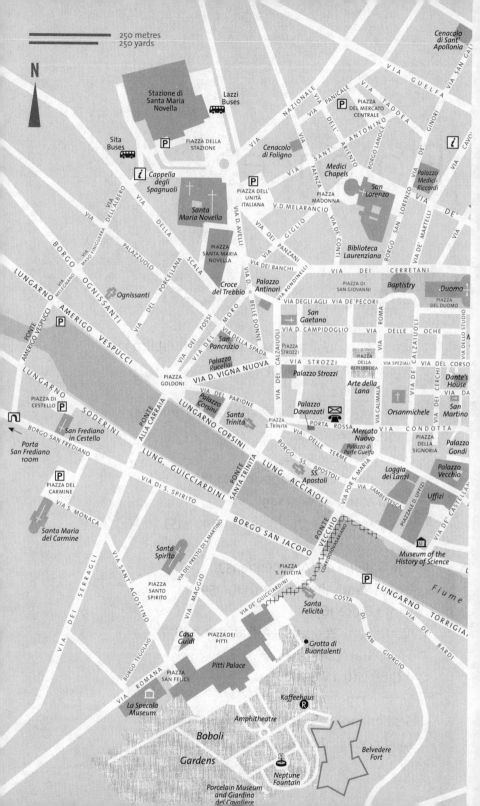

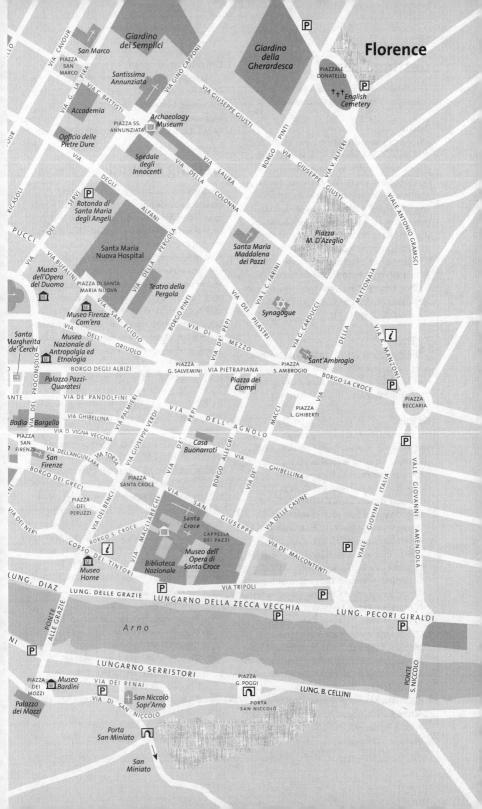

Getting There

Florence is the central transport node for Tuscany and harder to avoid than to reach.

By Air

Florence's **Vespucci airport** was lengthened in 1996, and now bustles with at least as much international traffic as Pisa. It is 6km out at Peretola, **t** 055 30615, flight information **t** 055 3061702 (recorded message in Italian and English). There is a regular bus to Florence, terminating at Santa Maria Novella Station (15mins). A taxi to the centre will cost €15–€20.

Alitalia: Lungarno Acciaioli 10/12r, **t** 055 27881 (reservations, **t** 848 865642), *www.alitalia.it*.

British Airways: t 199 712266 or contact Pisa office, **t** 050 40866, *www.britishairways.com*.

Meridiana (for London Gatwick): Peretola Airport 28r, **t** 199 111333.

By Train

The central station is **Santa Maria Novella**, call **t** 892021 for information, *www.frenitalic.com*. Many long-distance trains arriving at night use **Campo di Marte** station, bus nos.12 or 91.

By Bus

It's possible to reach nearly every city, town and village in Tuscany from Florence – once you know which of several bus companies to patronize. The tourist office has a complete list, but here are some of the most popular:

SITA (near station, Via S. Caterina da Siena 15, **t** 055 294955, **t** 800 373760, *www.sita-on-line.it*): towns in the Val d'Elsa, Chianti, Val di Pesa, Mugello and Casentino; Anghiari, Arezzo, Bibbiena, Castelfiorentino, Certaldo, Città di Castello, Consuma, Figline Valdarno, Firenzuola, Marina di Grosseto, Montevarchi, Poggibonsi (for San Gimignano and Volterra), Pontassieve, Poppi, Pratovecchio, Sansepolcro, Scarperia, Siena, Stia and Vallombrosa.

LAZZI (Piazza Stazione 47r, **t** 055 351061 Mon–Fri, **t** 166 845010 24-hour recorded message, *www.lazzi.it*): along the Arno to the coast, including Calenzano, Cerreto Guidi, Empoli, Forte dei Marmi, Livorno, Lucca, Marina di Carrara, Marina di Massa, Montecatini Terme, Montelupo, Montevarchi, Pescia, Pisa, Pistoia, Pontedera, Prato, Signa, Tirrenia, Torre del Lago, Viareggio.

CAP (Via Nazionale 13, **t** 055 214637): Borgo S. Lorenzo, Impruneta, Pistoia, Prato.

COPIT (Piazza S. Maria Novella, **t** 055 214637): Abetone, Cerreto Guidi, Pistoia, Poggio a Caiano, Vinci.

RAMA (Lazzi Station, **t** 055 239 8840): Grosseto.

Getting Around

Florence is a relatively easy city to get around, because nearly everything you'll want to see is within easy walking distance and large areas in the centre are pedestrian zones. In addition, there are no hills to climb, and it's hard to lose your way for very long.

Just to make life difficult, Florence has two sets of **address numbers** on every street – red ones for business, blue or black for residences; your hotel could be either. However, there has been some improvement in recent years: every major piazza, landmark or monument now has a plaque offering relevant background information, and helpful maps have been posted in strategic positions throughout the city.

By Bus

City buses (ATAF; *www.ataf.net*) can whizz or inch you across Florence, and are an excellent means of reaching sights on the periphery. Most useful lines begin at Santa Maria Novella station, and pass by Piazza del Duomo or Piazza San Marco. ATAF supply a comprehensive booklet, including a clear map, with details of all bus routes, available at the information/ticket booth at the station, tourist offices, some bars, and at ATAF's central office in Piazza della Stazione, **t** 800 424 500. Ticket prices: €1 for 60mins, €1.80 for 3hrs, €4.50 for 24hrs. The most useful buses for visitors are listed below.

6   Via Rondinella–Piazza San Marco–Duomo–Station–Soffiano

7   Station–Duomo–San Domenico–Fiesole

10 Station–Duomo–S. Marco–Ponte a Mensola–Settignano

11 Viale Calatafimi–S. Marco–Piazza Indipendenza–Station–Porta Romana–Poggio Imperiale

11a Viale Calatafimi–Duomo–Porta Romana–Poggio Imperiale

13 Station–Ponte Rosso–Parterre (car park)–Piazza Libertà–Viale Mazzini–Campo di

Marte–Piazzale Michelangelo–Porta Romana

14c Rovezzano–Duomo–Station–Careggi (hospital)

17 Cascine–station–Duomo–Via Lamarmora–Salviatino (for the youth hostel)

25 Station–S. Marco–Piazza Libertà–Via Bolognese–Pratolino

28 Station–Via R Giuliani–Castello–Sesto Fiorentino

37 Station–Ponte alla Carraia–Porta Romana–Certosa del Galluzzo

38 Porta Romana–Pian del Giullari (you need to book this one from the telephone near the bus stop at Porta Romana, **t** 0167 019794)

As part of the continuing campaign against city smog, a fleet of Lilliputian electric buses, routes A, B and D, have recently been introduced in the city. These mainly serve the centre, often taking circuitous routes 'round the houses', and are a good way of seeing some of the sights if you've had enough walking. Details of routes can be found on the ATAF maps.

By Taxi

Taxis in Florence don't cruise; you'll find them in ranks at the station and in the major *piazze*, or else ring for a radio taxi: **t** 055 4798 or 4390. Taxi meters start at €2.54 plus extras, adding €0.82 per km. There is a minimum charge of €4.55.

By Car

Until the late 1980s, Florence had of the most carcinogenic traffic problems in Italy. But in 1988, with great fanfares and accompanied by howls of protest, the city tried to do something about the cars that were choking it to death by enlarging the limited access zone, the *zona di traffico limitato* (ZTL).

Within the ZTL only buses, taxis, and cars belonging to residents are permitted; otherwise, you are permitted to pay to park in one of the city's **car parks** (there's the underground car park at the station, or the cheaper, big park at the Parterre, near Piazza Libertà) or take your chances on a side street or on metered parking areas as shown on the maps at the beginning of this chapter.

This new regulation was then followed by whole areas, especially around Piazza della Signoria and the Duomo, becoming totally traffic-free zones. The only danger is the odd ambulance or police car, the speeding mopeds (all of which you can easily hear) and the deadly silent bicycle.

Bicycle, Scooter, Golf Cart and Car Hire

Hiring a bike can save you tramping time and angst but it's not risk free. Watch out for cars and pedestrians. Electric golf cars holding up to four people have access to pedestrian zones.

Biancaneve, **t** 055 7139270.

You can hire a motorbike at:

Alinari, Via Guelfa 85r, **t** 055 280500.

Motorent, Via S. Zanobi 9r, **t** 055 490113.

Florence by Bike, Via S. Zanobi 120/122r, **t** 055 488992, *www.florencebybike.it*.

Between 8am and 7.30pm, visitors can now take advantage of one of the (almost) free bicycles supplied by the *comune* of Florence. There are various pick-up points around town, the most central being the Fortezza, the Parterre (for the car parks), Piazza Strozzi, Piazza Stazione, Piazza San Marco, the central market and Porta Romana. They cost about €1 for the day.

When you can't take any more art, hire a car and escape into the ravishing countryside. Most rental firms are within easy walking distance of the station.

Avis, Borgo Ognissanti 128r, **t** 055 213629.

Europcar, Borgo Ognissanti 53r, **t** 800 014410/199 100133.

Hertz, Via M Finiguerra 33, **t** 199 112211/055 239 8205.

Italy by Car, Borgo Ognissanti 134r, **t** 055 287161.

Maggiore-Budget, Via M Finiguerra 31r, **t** 055 210238.

Program, Borgo Ognissanti 135, **t** 055 282916.

Tourist Information

APT tourist service: *www.firenzeturismo.it*.

Florence becomes more tourist-friendly all the time and there is now a genuine effort on the part of the city administration to provide helpful tourist information. The *comune* publishes a leaflet listing bars and cafés that 'offer their clients a welcoming reception, politeness and, should they need it, bathroom facilities...'; believe it or not, finding a loo you could use in a bar or café used to be difficult.

In addition, there are two **guides for the disabled**, both available at the tourist office. The more comprehensive is in Italian, but it has a good map and covers access to sites and restaurants, etc. in great detail. (For further information on travel and specialist organizations, *see* pp.57–8.)

Florence

The main tourist office is a bit out of the way, near Piazza Beccaria on **Via Manzoni 16**, **t** 055 23320 (*open Mon–Fri 8–6, Sat 8–2*).

There is a branch at Via Camilla Cavour 1r, **t** 055 290832, *infoturismo@provincia.fi.it* (*open Mon–Sat 8.30–6.30, Sun 8.30–1.30*).

There is also an office at Borgo Santa Croce 29r, **t** 055 234 0444, **f** 055 226 4524 (*open Mon–Sat 9–7, Sun & hols 9–2*).

A new office has opened on the south side of the station in Piazza della Stazione, **t** 055 212245, **f** 055 238 1226, *www.comune.firenze.it* (*open Mon–Sat 8.30–7, Sun 8.30–2*).

In the summer, look out for the temporary mobile 'Tourist Help Points' run by the Vigili Urbani (the traffic police), in the centre of town.

Fiesole

Via Portigiani 3, **t** 055 598720/055 597 8373, **f** 055 598822, *www.comune.fiesole.fi.it* (*Mon–Sat 9–6, Sun 10–1 and 2–6, closes an hour earlier in winter*).

Practical A–Z

American Express: Via Dante Alighieri 22r, **t** 055 50981, just off Piazza della Repubblica.

Central Post Office: Via Pellicceria, near Piazza della Repubblica, **t** 055 27631 (*open Mon–Fri 8.15–7, Sat 8.15–12.30; telegram office open Mon–Sat 8.15–7; call **t** 160 for information*).

Consulates: **UK**, Lungarno Corsini 2, **t** 055 284133; **US**, Lung. Vespucci 38, **t** 055 239 8276.

E-mail services: you can send e-mail, use the Internet or fax from all over the city nowadays; one such service is **Internet Train**, Via Zannoni 1r, **t** 055 211103, *www.internettrain.it*, or Via Guelfa 24a, **t**/**f** 055 214794 (*opening hours differ from branch to branch*); they are also agents for the Swiss Post International if you want to avoid the bureaucratic slowpokes in the Posta Italiana. Mac users might try **Intotheweb**, Via de' Conti 23r, **t** 055 264 5628 (*open daily 10am–midnight*).

Libraries: British Institute Library, Lungarno Guicciardini 9, **t** 055 2677 8270 (*open 9.45–1 and 3.15–6.30, closed Sat and Sun*). American Library, Via S. Gallo 10 (*open 9–12.30, closed Sat and Sun*). There are so many other libraries in Florence that one, the Biblioteca del Servizio Beni Librari, Via G. Modena 13, **t** 055 438 2655, does nothing but dispense information on all the others.

Lost property in Italian is *Oggetti smarriti* or *Oggetti ritrovati*. The office is in Via Circondaria 17b, **t** 055 328 3942.

Medical: for an ambulance or first aid, Misericordia, Piazza del Duomo 20, **t** 055 212222. Doctor's night service, **t** 055 287788. For general medical **emergencies** call **t** 118. The general **hospital** Santa Maria Nuova, in Piazza S. M. Nuova, **t** 055 27581, is the most convenient. **Tourist Medical Service** (24hrs a day) is staffed by English- and French-speaking physicians at Via Lorenzo il Magnifico 59, ring first on **t** 055 475411. If you find yourself hospitalized while in Florence, the **AVO** (Association of Hospital Volunteers) provides volunteer interpreters to deal with language problems, **t** 055 425 0126/055 234 4567.

Pharmacies: open 24 hours every day in **S. Maria Novella** station, also **Molteni**, Via Calzaiuoli 7r and **Taverna**, Piazza S. Giovanni 20r, by the baptistry.

Police: emergency **t** 113. The *Ufficio Stranieri*, in the *questura*, Via Zara 2, **t** 055 49771 (*open Mon–Fri 8.30–12.30*), handles most foreigners' problems, and usually has someone around who speaks English. Go here for residents' permits, etc.

Tourist Aid Police: Via Pietrapiana 50, **t** 055 203911 (*open Mon–Fri 8.30–7.30, Sat 8.30–1.30*). Interpreters available to help you report thefts or resolve other problems.

Towed-away cars: there is one car pound if your car gets towed away: in the Ponte a Greve car park, near the Ponte al Indiano in the west of the city, **t** 055 783882 (*open 24hrs; bus 44*).

Festivals and Events

Traditional festivals in Florence date back for centuries. The following are listed roughly in the order they take place in the year:

Scoppio del Carro (Explosion of the Cart), *Easter Sunday*. Commemorates Florentine participation in the First Crusade, which took place in 1096. The Florentines were led by Pazzino de' Pazzi, who was the first over the walls of Jerusalem and upon returning home, received the special custody of the flame of Holy Saturday, with which the Florentines traditionally relit their family hearths. To make the event more colourful, the Pazzi constructed a decorated wooden ox cart to carry the flame. They lost the job after the Pazzi conspiracy in 1478, and since then the city has taken over the responsibility. In the morning, a firework-filled wooden float is pulled by white oxen from Il Prato to the cathedral, where, at 11am, during the singing of the Gloria, it is ignited by an iron 'dove' that descends on a wire from the high altar.

Maggio Musicale Fiorentino, Teatro del Maggio Musicale Fiorentino, Corso Italia 12 (off Lungarno Vespucci), t 055 211158, *www.maggiofiorentino.com* for ticket information, *late April–early July*. The city's big music festival, brings in big-name concert and opera stars. Some performances may also be held at Teatro della Pergola, or other venues.

Flower and Plant Show, Giardino di Orticoltura, Via Vittorio Emanuele 4, *late April*. A huge show, a must for horticulture fans. Centred around a 19th-century glasshouse.

International Iris festival, Piazzale Michelangelo, *May*.

Festa del Grillo (cricket festival), Cascine, Ascension Day, *May*. Michelangelo was thinking of the festival's little wooden cricket cages when he mocked Ammannati's gallery on the cathedral dome.

Calcio Storico in Costume, Piazza Santa Croce, *June*. Each June, four matches of historical football are played in 16th-century costume by 27-man teams from Florence's four quarters, in memory of a defiant football match played there in 1530, during the siege by Charles V. It's great fun with flag-throwing and a parade in historical costume as part of the pre-game ceremonies. The only fixed date is 24 June; the dates for the other matches are pulled out of a hat on Easter Sunday.

Festa di San Giovanni, *24 June*. The festival of Florence's patron saint, marked by a big firework display near Piazzale Michelangelo at 10pm.

Estate Fiesolana, *late June–Aug*. This is one of the annual cultural events generally adored by Florentines, when the old Roman theatre is made the venue for concerts, dance, theatre and films, for reasonable prices.

Summer concerts, Piazza Signoria, *summer months*. The piazza occasionally plays host to concerts and other events during the summer. Countless smaller-scale concerts are given, often outdoors or in cloisters, churches and villas. Look out for posters or ask at the tourist office.

Maggio Musicale **festival closing concert**, *late June–early July*. A free-for-all heralding the end of the annual music festival.

MaggioDanza **ballet company**, *late June–early July*. An evening of dance, held annually, also a free-for-all.

Florence Dance Festival, **t** 055 289276 for information, *July*. Presents an interesting combination of classical and contemporary dance performances. Usually held in Fiesole's Roman Theatre.

Festa delle Rificolona, *7 Sept*. A children's festival: Florentine kids gather in the evening in Piazza SS. Annunziata and along the river armed with paper lanterns, and then, after dark, they parade singing around the streets.

Shopping

Fashion

Although central Florence sometimes seems like one solid boutique, the city is no longer the queen of Italian fashion – the long lack of a central airport, more than anything else, sent most of the big designers to Milan. Even so, the big fashion names of the 1960s and 70s, and the international chain stores, are well represented in smart Via Tornabuoni, Via Calzaiuoli and around the Duomo, and the new overhaul of Gucci and the arrival of Prada has updated the city's slightly fusty image.

Leather

Via della Vigna Nuova. Leather is something Florence is still known for, and you'll see plenty of it in this central street.

The Leather School, entrance at Piazza Santa Croce 16 or Via S. Giuseppe 5r. An unusual institution, occupying part of Santa Croce's cloister, with less expensive goods.

Piazza Santa Croce and surrounding streets.

Jewellery

Ponte Vecchio. Florence is famous for jewellery. The shops on, and around, the bridge are forced, by the nature of their location, into wide-open competition. Good prices for Florentine brushed gold (although much of it is made in Arezzo these days) and antique jewellery are more common than you may think. Elsewhere, there are two other stores worth seeking out.

Il Gatto Bianco, Borgo SS. Apostoli 12r. Modern designs (earrings, rings, necklaces etc.) are crafted on the premises in silver, gold and other metals with pearls and precious stones.

Pepita Studio, Borgo degli Albizi 23r. Fun, chunky, young designs in plexiglass, wood and glass. Prices are very reasonable.

Marbled Paper

Florence is one of the few places in the world that makes marbled paper, an art brought from the Orient in the 12th century. Each sheet is hand-dipped to create a delicate, lightly coloured clouded design; no two sheets are alike. Stationery items or just sheets of marbled paper are available at:

Giulio Giannini e Figlio, Piazza Pitti 36r. The oldest manufacturer in Florence.

Il Papiro, with three shops at: Via Cavour 55r; Piazza del Duomo 24r; Lung. Acciaiuoli 42r.

La Bottega Artigiana del Libro, Lungarno Corsini 40r.

Il Torchio, Via dei Bardi 17, t 055 234 2862. Here the workbench is in the shop so you can see the artisans in action. These shops (and many others) also carry Florentine paper with its colourful Gothic patterns.

Books

Bookworms do better in Florence than most Italian cities, and prices of books in English seem to have come down in recent years, so there are a fair number of places to browse.

The Paperback Exchange, Via Fiesolana 31r. A wide selection in English, with many books about Florence.

Seeber, Via Tornabuoni 70r. An alternative to the Exchange, also has a good selection.

Feltrinelli, Via Cavour 12–20r. Books in English and an excellent range of art books.

BM Bookshop, Borgo Ognissanti 4r. Ditto here.

Franco Maria Ricci, Via delle Belle Donne 41r. A fabulous collection of art books.

Edition, Piazza della Republica 27r. Florence's biggest bookshop with plenty of titles in English, travel guides and maps (also in English), internet points, video services and a café.

Antiques and Art Galleries

Borgo Ognissanti and the various Lungarni are the place to look. Also check out: Piazza dei Ciompi's flea market and monthly flea market (2nd Sunday of month) held in Piazza Santo Spirito.

P. Bazzanti e Figli, Lungarno Corsini 44. Here you can pick up an exact replica of the bronze boar in the Mercato Nuovo.

Atelier Alice, Via Faenza 72r. Much easier to carry is an Italian carnival mask, available here, and for those who are keen to learn more about the art of the mask the shop runs five-lesson courses. Ring Prof A Dessi on t 055 215961 for details.

Via Maggio. This street is full of upmarket antique shops.

Serious collectors may want to check Florence's busy auction houses:

Casa d'Aste Pandolfini, Borgo degli Albizi 26, t 055 234 0888.

Casa d'Aste Pitti, Via Maggio 15, t 055 239 6382.

Sotheby's Italia, Via G Capponi 26, t 055 247 9021 (*call for appointment*).

Cloth

Casa dei Tessuti, Via de' Pecori 20–24r, t 055 215961. Keeps Florence's ancient cloth trade alive with lovely linens, silks and woollens. During the lunch break, you might catch a lecture on the history of Florence with special reference to the textile industry.

Silver, Crystal and Porcelain
A Poggi, Via Calzaiuoli 105r and 116r. One of the city's widest selections (including Florence's own Richard-Ginori).

Children's Toys and Clothes
Città del Sole, Via Cimatori 21r. The best toy shop in Florence.

Cirri, Via Por S. Maria 38–40r. If you happen to have or know the kinds of little girls who can wear white, this has a fairy-tale selection of dresses.

Anichini, Via di Parione 59r. Oldest kids' clothes shop in Florence; exquisitely produced dresses (made in store), silk party dresses, romper suits, Christening robes plus playwear.

Wine and Food
Millesimi, Borgo Tegolaio 33r. One of the best wine shops in town. Tastings by appointment.

Mercato Centrale. Good for a number of speciality food shops.

Allrientar Gastronomia, Borgo SS. Apostoli. Pick up items such as truffle cream here.

La Porta del Tartufo, Borgo Ognissanti 133r. Virtually confines itself to different types of truffles or 'truffled' foods ranging from *grappa* to salmon paste.

Il Procacci, Via Tornabuoni 64r. A high-quality *alimentari* (food shop) selling regional specialities as well as foreign foods. It's most famous as the venue for a lunch time *Prosecco* and *panino tartufato*, a glass of sparkling white wine and a truffle-filled sandwich. Also a bar.

Pitti Gola e Cantina, Piazza Pitti 16. Offers a good selection of wines, oils and vinegars, and cookery books (in both English and Italian) to go with them.

La Bottega del Brunello, Via Ricasoli 81r. Divided in two parts, one for display and one for tasting the wine and specialities on sale.

Casa del Vino, Via dell' Ariento 16r. With wine tastings plus snacks in the San Lorenzo street market.

Enoteca dei Giraldi, Via Giraldi. Exclusively in Tuscan wines from lesser-known producers, with over 140 labels (you can also eat there).

Le Volpi e L'Uva, Piazza de' Rossi 1. Situated behind the Ponte Vecchio on the square, this also stocks lesser-known labels.

Enoteca Murgia, Via dei Banchi 57, off Piazza S. Maria Novella. Good for wines and spirits in general.

Marchesi de' Frescobaldi, Via di S. Spirito 11. One of the largest wine suppliers in Italy; visit their ancient cellars.

Markets
Florence's lively street markets offer good bargains, fake designer glad rags and even some authentic labels.

San Lorenzo. Easily the largest and most boisterous: food (*open Mon–sat 8–2*) and clothes and party gifts (*open Tues–Sat*).

Sant'Ambrogio. A bustling food market.

Mercato Nuovo (Straw Market). The most touristic, but not flagrantly so.

Piazza Santo Spirito. Home to different markets on different days: Food, clothes and shoes (small). *Open daily exc Sun*. Craft and flea market (big). *Open every 2nd Sun of month*. Organic food market. *Open every 3rd Sun*.

Cascine, along the river. A weekly market where many Florentines buy their clothes. Here you may easily find designer clothes off the back of a lorry, shoes and lots more besides. *Open Tues am*.

Mercato delle Pulci (Flea Market), Piazza dei Ciompi. Perhaps the most fun market, offering all kinds of desirable junk. *Open Sun*.

Sports and Activities

On the Water
The one activity most summertime visitors begin to crave after tramping through the sights is a dip in a pool.

Piscina le Pavoniere, Cascine. The prettiest in Florence. *Open June–Sept 10–6.30*.

Bellariva, up the Arno at Lungarno Colombo 2. *Open June–Sept 11–5*.

Amici del Nuoto, Via del Romito 38, t 055 483951. *Open all year*.

Costoli, Via Paoli, near Campo di Marte, t 055 623 6027. *Open all year*.

If there's enough water in the Arno, you can try rowing or canoeing:

Società Canottieri Comunali, Lungarno Ferrucci 6, **t** 055 681 2151.

Società Canottieri Firenze, Lungarno dei Medici 8, **t** 055 238 1010 (membership only).

Horse-racing and Riding

Ippodromo Il Visarno, Cascine, **t** 055 422 6076. Florence's flat race course.

Ippodromo della Mulina, Cascine, **t** 055 4226076. Also at the Cascine, Florence's trotting course.

Maneggio Mirinelle, Via di Macia 21, **t/f** 055 887 8066. The nearest place to go riding in the Tuscan hills.

Centro Ippico Ugolino, Via Oliveta 12, **t** 055 230 1289. You can also ride here, near the golf course.

Golf

Golf Club Ugolino, on the Chiantigiana, **t** 055 230 1009, *www.golfugolino.it*. The nearest 18- hole golf course to Florence is in Gràssina, 7km southeast of the city; a lovely course.

Squash and Tennis

Centro Squash, Via Empoli 16, **t** 055 732 3055.

Circolo Tennis Firenze, Viale Visarno, **t** 055 354326.

Where to Stay

Florence ✉ 50100

Florence has some lovely hotels, and not all of them at Grand Ducal prices, although base rates are the highest in Tuscany. As in any city, the higher cost of living means you won't find much *inexpensive* accommodation. Florence, Venice and Rome are the most expensive places to stay in Italy, and you should count on having to pay around 25% more for a room here than you would anywhere else (*see* p.75).

Historic old palace-hotels are the rule rather than the exception; those listed below are some of the more atmospheric and charming, but to be honest, few are secrets, so reserve as far in advance as possible. Note that many hotels will try to lay down a heavy breakfast charge that is supposed to be optional.

There are almost 400 hotels in Florence but not enough for anyone who arrives in June and September without a reservation (Easter is even more busy). But don't despair; there are several hotel consortia that can help you find a room in nearly any price range for a small commission. If you're arriving by car or train, the most useful will be ITA.

ITA: in Santa Maria Novella station, **t** 055 282893, *open 8.30–7*. Bookings can be made by phone and a booking fee of between €3–€8 is charged, according to the category of hotel.

Florence Promhotels: Viale A. Volta 72, **t** 055 570481, **f** 055 587189. Free booking service.

For *agriturismo* or farmhouse accommodation in the surrounding countryside (self-catering or otherwise), contact: Agriturist Toscana, Piazza S. Firenze 3, **t/f** 055 287838, *www.agriturist.it*; or Turismo Verde Toscana, Via Jacopo Nardi 41, **t** 055 2338911.

Luxury

★★★★★**Excelsior**, Piazza Ognissanti 3, **t** 055 2715, **f** 055 210278, *www.westin.com/excelsiorflorence*. In the city the luxury leader is the former Florentine address of Napoleon's sister Caroline. Lots of marble, neoclassically plush, lush and green with plants, immaculately staffed, with decadently luxurious bedrooms, many of which have river views (for a price).

★★★★★**Helvetia & Bristol**, Via dei Pescioni 2, **t** 055 287814, **f** 055 288353, *www.charminghotels.it*. If you prefer luxury on a smaller scale, this has 52 exquisitely furnished bedrooms, each one different, all with rich fabrics adorning windows, walls and beds; Stravinsky, Bertrand Russell and Pirandello stayed here; added pluses are the restaurant and the winter garden.

★★★★★**The Savoy**, Piazza della Repubblica 7, **t** 055 283313, **f** 055 284840, *www.roccoforte hotels.com*. The old, crumbling Savoy reopened in spring 2000 under the Forte Group, now striking a minimalist tone with décor in shades of cream, beige and grey; it has a bar and restaurant where you can sit out on the piazza.

★★★★★**Villa La Vedetta**, Viale Michelangiolo 78, **t** 055 6580237, **f** 055 6582544, *www.villala vedettahotel.com*. This recently-opened luxury hotel occupies an elegant villa in a superb position near Piazzale Michelangelo with panoramic views over the city from its terraces and some of the rooms. Downstairs, cool grey and white marble prevail while the bedrooms are sumptuously-but not ostentatiously-done out in silks. The restaurant (which has just been awarded a Michelin star), serving creative gourmet fare, is superb; in summer you can eat on the terrace overlooking the city lights.

★★★★**Astoria**, Via del Giglio 9, **t** 055 239 8095, **f** 055 214632, *www.boscolohotels.com*. Recently refurbished, in a grand 16th-century palazzo near San Lorenzo market, this has more character than many of those located near the station. Public rooms are suitably impressive and some of the bedrooms likewise; avoid those on the lower floors by the street.

★★★★**Gallery Hotel Art**, Vicolo del'Oro 2, **t** 055 27263, **f** 055 268557, *galleryhotel@lungarnohotels.it*. Florence's most exciting hotel is a shrine to contemporary interior design. It is by no means stark, however, and the position (a mere two minutes from the Ponte Vecchio) is superb. It has a comfortable library, a smart bar and a restaurant serving trendy fusion food.

★★★★**J.K. Place**, Piazza Santa Maria Novella 7, **t** 055 2645181, **f** 055 2658387, *www.jkplace.com*. This tall, elegant townhouse stands on smartened up Piazza Santa Maria Novella with rooms that overlook Alberti's glorious church façade. The interior is luxuriously designer-chic (and attracts the fashion crowd), but manages to be warm and welcoming at the same time. Some of the bedrooms are on the small side, but are equipped with every mod con; there is a wonderful rooftop terrace and bar. Breakfast is served at a large communal table in a glassed-in courtyard and there is a selection of complimentary soft drinks and snacks available to guests.

★★★★**Kraft**, Via Solferino 2, **t** 055 284273, **f** 055 239 8267, *www.krafthotel.it*. Frequently used by upmarket tour groups, this is handy for the opera season (it is two minutes' walk from the Teatro del Maggio Musicale Fiorentino), and has the added advantage of a small rooftop pool. Bedrooms are light and sunny, and comfortably furnished with

cheerful fabrics. The suites on the top floor have great views. There is a restaurant.

★★★★**Lungarno**, Borgo San Jacopo 14, **t** 055 27261, **f** 055 268437, *www.lungarnohotels.com*. A discreet hotel enjoying a marvellous location on the river, only two minutes' walk from the Ponte Vecchio. The ground floor sitting/breakfast room and bar, and the new restaurant, which specializes in fish, look out on to the water. The building is modern, but incorporates a medieval tower, and has recently been refurbished; the smallish bedrooms are decorated in smart blue and cream. The best have balconies with 'The View'. Book ahead for these.

★★★★**Monna Lisa**, Borgo Pinti 27, **t** 055 247 9751, **f** 055 247 9755, *www.monnalisa.it*. This Renaissance palace, now owned by the descendants of sculptor Giovanni Dupre, may have a stern façade and, it is said, staff to match, but it is also one of the loveliest small hotels in Florence – well preserved and filled with family heirlooms and works of art. Rooms vary wildly; try to reserve one that overlooks the garden; breakfast is available, as is private parking.

Very Expensive

★★★★**Villa Carlotta**, Via Michele di Lando 3, **t** 055 233 6134, **f** 055 233 6147, *www.panoramichotelsitaly.it*. Located in a quiet residential district in the upper Oltrarno, close to the Porta Romana, this Tuscan-Edwardian building has 26 sophisticated rooms which have been tastefully refurnished and have every mod con. There's a garden and glassed-in veranda, where the large breakfasts are served; a private garage offers safe parking.

★★★**Aprile**, Via della Scala 6, **t** 055 216237, **f** 055 280947, *www.hotelaprile.it*. Convenient for the station and recently given a facelift, this was once a Medici palace and appropriately has a bust of Cosimo I above the door. Vaulted ceilings and frescoes remain intact, and the bedrooms all have period furniture although some are on the gloomy side; there's a shady courtyard.

★★★**Calzaiuoli**, Via Calzaiuoli 6, **t** 055 212456, **f** 055 268310, *www.calzaiuoli.it*. Just a few steps from Piazza Signoria and on a traffic-free street is a comfortable hotel with modern, nicely decorated rooms and wonderful views from the top floor.

***Beacci Tornabuoni**, Via Tornabuoni 3, **t** 055 212645, **f** 055 283594, *www.tornabuoni hotels.com*. Another excellent small hotel that puts you in the centre of fashionable Florence, on the top three floors of an elegant Renaissance palace. The rooms are comfortable, air-conditioned and equipped with minibars, though it's more fun to sit over your drink on the panoramic roof terrace.

***Hermitage**, Vicolo Marzio 1, **t** 055 287216, **f** 055 212208, *www.hermitagehotel.com*. Tucked away behind the Ponte Vecchio on the north side of the river, this little hotel is built upside down; the lift takes you to the fifth floor with its ravishing roof garden, reception and elegant blue and yellow sitting room. The bedrooms below are on the small side, but charmingly furnished with antiques and tasteful fabrics. Some have river views.

***Loggiato dei Serviti**, Piazza SS. Annunziata 3, **t** 055 289592, **f** 055 289595, *www.loggiato deiservitihotel.it*. Located on Florence's most beautiful square (now traffic-free), the front rooms of this delightful hotel overlook Brunelleschi's famous portico. The 16th-century building was originally a convent, and many of the architectural features remain. Rooms are furnished with antiques and tasteful fabrics; each is very different from the next. Recommended.

***Torre Guelfa**, Borgo SS. Apostoli 8, **t** 055 239 6338, **f** 055 239 8577, *www. torreguelfa.com*. Boasting the tallest privately owned tower in Florence, bang in the middle of the *centro storico*. There's a grand double salon, a sunny breakfast room, and stylish bedrooms in pastel shades with wrought iron and hand-painted furniture, as well as the chance to sip an *aperitivo* while contemplating a 360° view.

Casa Howard, Via della Scala 18, **t** 06 (yes...reservations are made through Rome) 6992 4555, *www.casahoward.com*. Following in the footsteps of the two very popular Casa Howards in Rome and only a stone's throw from the train station, this elegant guest house offers 11 individually-decorated rooms (there is one for kids, one with a library in it, one for dogs) at remarkably reasonable prices in a home-from-home

atmosphere. All rooms have tea and coffee-making facilities and some have a private terrace; there's even a Turkish hammam.

Expensive

****Villa Belvedere**, Via Benedetto Castelli 3, **t** 055 222501, **f** 055 223163, *www.villa-belvedere.com*. Not the more interesting building in this part of peripheral Florence (1km above Porta Romana), but a pleasant alternative to central accommodation, , nonetheless, with a beautiful garden, tennis court, a nice little pool and good views. Rooms are modern and comfortable with lots of wood and plenty of space. For trips into town, you can leave your car and catch a nearby bus. Light meals are served in the restaurant. Excellent value for a 4-star hotel.

***Hotel delle Arti**, Via dei Servi 38/A, **t** 055 2678553, **f** 055 290140, *www.hoteldellearti.it*. Under the same ownership as the Loggiato dei Serviti (*see* above), this nine-bedroom hotel has a simpler, more country look than its big sister up the road. The stylish bedrooms are decorated in restful shades of green and cream and have wood floors; a couple have pine four posters. The three corner rooms are particularly spacious and light and there is a pretty breakfast room on the top floor with a wrap around terrace.

***Morandi alla Crocetta**, Via Laura 50, **t** 055 234 4747, **f** 055 248 0954, *www.hotel morandi.it*. Small but popular, with 10 rooms in the university area northeast of Piazza San Marco. The building was a convent in the 16th century, and some of the comfortable and pleasant rooms still have the odd fresco. Two rooms have private terraces.

***Silla**, Via dei Renai 5, **t** 055 234 2888, **f** 055 234 1437, *www.hotelsilla.it*. Ten minutes' walk east of the Ponte Vecchio on the south bank of the river, this manages to be central, yet in a quiet and relatively green neighbourhood. The old-fashioned *pensione* is on the first floor of a 16th-century palazzo and the spacious breakfast terrace has great views over the Arno and beyond.

****Alessandra**, Borgo SS. Apostoli 17, **t** 055 283438, **f** 055 210619, *www.hotelalessandra. com*. A modest hotel in a palazzo designed by Michelangelo's pupil, Baccio d'Agnolo, on a central but quiet back street; there are 25 rooms of varying standards. Not all have private baths; the best have waxed parquet floors and antiques.

Casci, Via Cavour 13, t 055 211686, f 055 239 6461, *www.hotelcasci.com*. The Lombardis, owners of this 15th-century palazzo (once home to Rossini), run a relaxed and cheerful ship. The reception area is full of helpful information, the breakfast room has a frescoed ceiling while the recently refurbished bedrooms are bright and modern. The choice few look on to a garden at the back.

Relais Uffizi, Chiasso de' Baroncelli/Chiasso del Buco 16, t 055 267 6239, f 055 265 7909, *www.relaisuffizi.it*. The only hotel which overlooks Piazza della Signoria, the Relais Uffizi is hidden down a series of narrow lanes. The 13 rooms of varying shapes and sizes are decorated and furnished with style while the atmosphere is informal. You can relax in the sitting room and watch the ever-changing piazza below.

Moderate

***Locanda degli Artisti**, Via Faenza 56, t/f 055 213806, *www.hotelazzi.it*. This hotel, a stone's throw from the San Lorenzo market and the train station, offers pleasant rooms and has an arty, alternative feel to it. On the ground floor, bedrooms are a little more sophisticated (there are even a couple of suites) while upstairs, rooms are clean but quite Spartan and none have private baths. There's a sauna, a sunny terrace and a breakfast room where organic produce is served.

***Classic Hotel**, Viale Machiavelli 25, t 055 229351, f 055 229353, *www.classichotel.it*. A good alternative in a very pleasant location just above Porta Romana on the way to Piazzale Michelangelo, a five-minute walk to a bus stop for downtown. The pink-washed villa stands in a shady garden (a welcome respite from the heat of the city), and breakfast is served in the conservatory in summer.

Belletini, Via de' Conti 7, t 055 213561, f 055 28355, *www.firenze.net/hotelbelletini*. A friendly place near the Medici chapels, decorated in traditional Florentine style; a couple of rooms have stunning views of the nearby domes. There's a good, generous breakfast. An annexe around the corner houses an additional six stylishly furnished rooms, which are slightly more expensive. TV, air-conditioning, cots, and parking nearby.

Boboli, Via Romana 63, t 055 229 8645, f 055 233 7169, *www.hotelboboli.com*. As the name suggests, this modest hotel is located near the back entrance of the Boboli gardens. The brightest rooms are right at the top of the four-storey building. A lift has recently been installed. Or if you want quiet (Via Romana is quite noisy), go for a room on the inner courtyard. Breakfast is served on a little terrace in summer.

Residenza Johanna Cinque Giornate, Via Cinque Giornate 12, t/f 055 473377, *www.johanna.it*. Good value for money in a city where bargains are few and far between, located some way from the centre (near the Fortezza da Basso). The villa stands in its own garden and there are six comfortable rooms, each equipped with a breakfast tray and kettle, as well as a sitting room with plenty of reading material. Guests are left to themselves, but other facilities are of a three-star standard; parking available.

La Scaletta, Via Guicciardini 13, t 055 283028, f 055 289562, *www.lascaletta.com*. Between the Ponte Vecchio and the Pitti Palace is a friendly *pensione* with a roof garden and great views into Boboli. The 12 bedrooms (not all with bathrooms and some of which sleep up to four) are decently furnished, the nicest with some antique pieces. Very moderately priced dinner available.

Bavaria, Borgo degli Albizi 26, t/f 055 234 0313, *www.welcomehotels.com*. Housed in a grand, 16th-century palazzo whose façade is said to be frescoed by Vasari, this once-crummy hotel has had a facelift. While it is still on one floor and only a handful of rooms have private baths, the rooms are stylish, and some have splendid views of the city.

Maxim, Via dei Medici 4, t 055 217474, f 055 283729, *www.firenzealbergo.it/home/hotelmaxim*. This centrally located budget hotel has had a recent facelift. The reception area is bright and elegant, and the bedrooms (which sleep two or three) are well furnished and modern. All are ensuite and one even has a jacuzzi. Air-conditioning, and parking nearby.

*Sorelle Bandini, Piazza Santo Spirito 9, t 055 215308, f 055 282761. Remains popular, despite its state of disrepair and relatively high prices. This is partly due to the romantic loggia along one side of the fourth-storey hotel, but also to its location on Piazza Santo Spirito, bustling by day and lively (and noisy) at night. Expect uncomfortable beds, cavernous rooms, heavy Florentine furniture and a certain shabby charm.

Antica Dimora, Via San Gallo 72n, t 055 4627296, f 055 4634450, www. anticadimorafiernze.it. This delightful new guest house, situated ten minutes walk north of the Duomo, has six beautifully furnished rooms and the warm atmosphere of an elegant private apartment. Four posters are hung with fine linens and silks and all rooms have DVDs and modem connections. Prices are remarkably low for what is on offer.

Residenza Johlea, Via San Gallo 80, t 055 463 3292, f 055 463 4552, www.johanna.it. Really two small hotels a few doors from each other. A remarkable bargain in terms of what it offers for the price, the Johlea is under the same ownership as the Johannas (see below). Situated 10 mins' walk north of the central market, the rooms are comfortable and well furnished with taste and style and all have excellent bathrooms. Breakfast is supplied on trays in the rooms. On the top floor is a small sitting room and a roof terrace affording 360° views of the city. If all the rooms are full, there is a sister 'residenza' (the Johlea Due) a few doors down.

Inexpensive

*Dali, Via dell'Oriuolo 17, t/f 055 2340706, www.hoteldali.com. Just a few minutes walk from the Duomo, this little hotel is run by a genuinely friendly young couple who have decorated the rooms with care and attention to detail in spite of the low prices. Only three of the ten rooms have en suite bathrooms, but all are bright and homely. There's free parking in the internal courtyard. No breakfast.

*Orchidea, Borgo degli Albizi 11, t/f 055 248 0346, hotelorchidea@yahoo.it. Run by an Anglo-Italian family in a 12th-century building where Dante's in-laws once lived.

One of the seven cheerful rooms has a private shower; the best of the rest look on to a garden at the back.

*Scoti, Via de' Tornabuoni 7, t 055 292128, www.hotelscoti@hotmail.com. A simple and cheap pensione with a surprisingly upmarket address, which could be ideal if you would rather splurge on the wonderful clothes in the surrounding shops. A recent facelift means that all the simple rooms are now en suite; luckily the atmosphere has not been spoilt, and there are still wonderful faded floor-to-ceiling frescoes in the sitting room. The owners are friendly.

Istituto Gould, Via dei Serragli 49, t 055 212576, f 055 280274, gould.reception@ dada.it. An excellent budget choice near Santo Spirito, the Isitituto Gould is run by the Valdese church. Rooms vary in size from singles (a couple) to quads and not all have their own bathrooms; book early to secure singles or doubles. The best rooms have access to a terrace and the noisiest are on Via dei Serragli. No smoking is allowed in the building and you have to check in during office hours.

Residenza Johanna, Via Bonifacio Lupi 14, t 055 481896, f 055 482721, www.johanna.it. Only a tiny brass plaque over the bell identifies this building, just north of Piazza San Marco. There are no TVs or phones in the rooms, no doorman, and not all rooms have private baths, but the furnishings are comfortable, the bedrooms are prettily decorated and there's lots of reading material to hand. Breakfast is on a do-it-yourself tray in each room, and there are kettles out in the corridor.

Rooms to Let

Besides hotels, a number of institutions and private homes let rooms – there's a complete list in the back of the annual provincial hotel book. Many take women only, and fill up with students in the spring.

Youth Hostels

Archi Rossi, Via Faenza 94r, t 055 290804, www.hostelarchirossi.com. Purpose-built and fully wheelchair-accessible, this is the nearest hostel to the station, and is well equipped. You can book a place after 6am and occupy your room after 2.30pm. Phone bookings are accepted and there is a 12.30am curfew.

Ostello Europa Villa Camerata, Viale A Righe 2/4 (bus from the station), **t** 055 601451, *www.iyhf.org*. Has 500 beds for people with IYHF cards. Located in an old palazzo with gardens, it is a popular place, and you'd be wise to show up at 2pm to get a spot in the summer; maximum stay three days.

Ostello Santa Monaca, Via Santa Monaca 6, **t** 055 268338, *www.ostello.it*. Has 111 beds near the Carmine church; sign up for a place in the morning.

Camping

There are a few campsites within easy striking distance of Florence:

Camping Internazionale, Via S. Cristofano 2, **t** 055 237 4704, *www.florencecamping.com*. South of the city in Bottai Tavarnuzze, near the A1 exit Autostrada Firenze–Certosa. *Open end Mar–1st Nov.*

Camping Michelangelo, Viale Michelangelo 80, **t** 055 681 1977, **f** 055 689348, *www. ecvacanze.it*. Fine views over the city and free hot showers; arrive early to get a spot. On the other hand, there's no shade and the disco goes on until 1am. Bus 13 will take you there from the station. *Open all year.*

Camping Panoramico Fiesole, Via Peramonda 1, **t** 055 599069, *www.florencecamping.com*. A beautifully situated campsite, just above Fiesole on a hill with fabulous views over Florence, but packed and expensive in the summer. *Open all year.*

Mugello Verde International Camping, Via Masso Rondinaio 2, in San Piero a Sieve, **t** 055 848511, **f** 055 848 6910, *www. florencecamping.com*. 25km north of Florence on the road to Bologna, with a very pleasant setting among hills and forests, and frequent buses down to Florence. *Closed Nov–mid-Mar.*

Fiesole ✉ 50014

Many frequent visitors to Florence wouldn't stay anywhere else: it's cooler, quieter, and at night the city far below twinkles as if made of fairy lights.

*****Villa San Michele, Via Doccia 4, **t** 055 567 8200, **f** 055 567 8250, *www.orient/ expresshotels.com* (*luxury*). Built as a monastery in the 14th century, this hotel is the superb choice if money happens to be no object, set in a breathtaking location just below Fiesole with a façade and loggia reputedly designed by Michelangelo himself. After suffering bomb damage during the Second World War, it was carefully reconstructed to create one of the most beautiful hotels in Italy, set in a lovely Tuscan garden, complete with a pool. Each of its 29 rooms is richly and elegantly furnished and air-conditioned; the more plush suites have jacuzzis. The food is delicious, and the reasons to go down to Florence begin to seem insignificant; a stay here is complete in itself. Paradise, however, comes at a price.

****Villa Aurora, Piazza Mino 38, **t** 055 59363, **f** 055 59587, *www.aurorafiesole.com* (*very expensive*). An agreeable 19th-century villa, located right on Fiesole's famous piazza from where the no.7 bus will whisk you down to central Florence in 20mins. The 25 bedrooms have rustic antiques and splendid views over the city. Some of the bathrooms are poky. There is a restaurant – on a terrace overlooking Florence in the summer – and the bar next door (which can be noisy at times) is under the same ownership.

***Pensione Bencistà, Via Benedetto di Maiano 4, **t/f** 055 59163, *pensione bencista@iol.it* (*moderate – half board*). Another former monastery with views from its flower-decked terrace which are every bit as good as those at Villa San Michele (*see* p.119), and the welcome will be more friendly. Bedrooms, each one different from the next, are all comfortably furnished with solid antique pieces. The three little sitting rooms are particularly inviting in cooler weather when fires are lit. Half-board – breakfast and either lunch or dinner – is obligatory here, but prices are reasonable. NB: *No credit cards*.

***Villa Fiesole, Via Beato Angelico 35, **t** 055 597252, **f** 055 599133, *www.villafiesole.it* (*luxury*). This new hotel was once part of the San Michele convent, and shares part of its driveway with the hotel of the same name. The smart, neoclassical-style interiors are variations on a fresh blue and yellow colour scheme. Light meals are served in a sunny dining room or on the adjacent terrace, and there is a pool. The whole is wheelchair-accessible. The facilities (and prices) here are decidedly four-star.

*Villa Baccano, Via Bosconi 4, t/f 055 59341, www.villabaccano.it (inexpensive). In the hills 2km out of the centre of Fiesole, in a lovely garden setting.

*Villa Sorriso, Via Gramsci 21, t 055 59027, f 055 597 8075, www.paginegialle.it/albergosorriso.01 (inexpensive). An unpretentious, comfortable hotel in the centre of Fiesole, with a terrace overlooking Florence.

Le Cannelle, Via Gramsci 52–6, t 055 597 8336, f 055 597 8292, www.lecannelle.com (expensive–moderate). A new, friendly B&B run by two sisters on the main street. Rooms are comfortably rustic and there is a pretty breakfast room.

Villa Hotels in the Florentine Hills

If you're driving, you may consider lodging outside the city where parking is hassle-free and the summer heat is less intense.

Luxury

*****Villa La Massa, Via La Massa 6, t 055 62611, f 055 633102, www. villalamassa.com. A lovely choice, located up the Arno some 6km from Florence at Candeli. This is the former 15th-century villa of Count Giraldi, and retains the old dungeon (now one of two restaurants), the family chapel (now a bar), and other early-Renaissance amenities, combined with 20th-century features like tennis courts, a pool and air-conditioning. The recently refurbished interiors are fit for a Renaissance princeling, there's dining and dancing by the Arno in the summer, a shady garden, and a hotel bus to whizz you into the city. Excellent restaurant.

*****Grand Hotel Villa Cora, Viale Machiavelli 18–20, t 055 229 8451, f 055 229086, www.villacora.com. Near Piazzale Michelangelo is another luxury choice, an opulent 19th-century mansion set in a beautiful formal garden overlooking the Oltrarno. Built by the Baron Oppenheim, it later served as the residence of the wife of Napoleon III, Empress Eugénie. Its conversion to a hotel has dimmed little of its splendour; some of the bedrooms have frescoed ceilings and lavish 19th-century furnishings – all are air-conditioned and have frigo-bars, and there's a pretty pool. In the summer meals are served in the garden, and there's a fine view of Florence from the roof terrace.

****Torre di Bellosguardo, Via Roti Michelozzi 2, t 055 229 8145, f 055 229008, www.torrebellosguardo.com. In the 12th century a tower was built at Bellosguardo, enjoying one of the most breathtaking views over the city. It was later purchased by the Cavalcanti, friends of Dante, and a villa was added below the tower; after that, Cosimo I confiscated it, the Michelozzi purchased it from the Medici, Elizabeth Barrett Browning wrote about it, and finally, in 1988, it opened its doors as a small hotel. There are frescoes by Baroque master Poccetti in the entrance hall, and fine antiques adorn the rooms, each of which is unique and fitted out with modern bath. The large and beautiful terraced garden has a pool. For a splurge, reserve the two-level tower suite, with fabulous views in four directions. Superb formal gardens look down to the city below, and lunch is served around the pool.

Very Expensive

****Paggeria Medicea, Viale Papa Giovanni XXIII 3, Artimino, near Carmignano, t 055 871 8081, f 055 875 1470, www.artimino.com. You can play the Medici in the refurbished outbuildings of Grand Duke Ferdinand's villa, which has some unusual amenities – a hunting reserve and a lake stocked with fish, also a pool and tennis court, and pleasant modern rooms, many with balconies, all air-conditioned. A short walk across the gardens brings you to the restaurant Biagio Pignatta, which specializes in Medici dishes, in the former butcher's quarters.

***Villa le Rondini, Via Vecchia Bolognese 224, t 055 400081, f 055 268212, www.villalerondini.it. Occupying several buildings in a pleasant setting 7km north of Florence, surrounded by olive and cypress trees. The most interesting rooms are in the 16th-century villa. There is a very pleasant pool.

***Villa Villoresi**, Via Campi 2, Colonnata di Sesto Fiorentino, **t** 055 443212, **f** 055 443212, *www.ila-chateau.com/villores*. Contessa Cristina Villoresi's family home is a lovely oasis in the middle of one of Florence's more un-lovely suburbs, which hasn't been too pristinely restored, retaining much of its slightly faded appeal as well as its frescoed ceilings, antiques and chandeliers. The villa boasts the longest loggia in Tuscany, to which five of the best, and grandest, bedrooms have direct access. Other rooms are a good deal plainer and somewhat cheaper.

Villa Poggio San Felice, Via S. Matteo Arcetri 24, **t** 055 220016, **f** 055 233 5388, *www.villapoggiosanfelice.com*. A delightful alternative to city hotels, this is a 15th-century villa on a hill just south of Porta Romana, near the observatory. It was once owned by a Swiss hotel magnate, whose descendants have restored the house and gardens (designed by Porcinaie) and opened them up to guests. There are five double bedrooms, all furnished with family antiques, and all with stunning views. There is also a small pool. *Bed and breakfast only, closed Dec–Feb*.

Moderate

***Hermitage**, Via Gineparia 112, Bonistallo, **t** 055 877040, **f** 055 879 7057, *www.hotel hermitageprato.it*. Several miles from Florence, near Poggio a Caiano, this is a fine, affordable choice for families; there's a pool in the grounds and air-con rooms, not to mention gallons of fresh air and quiet.

Eating Out

Like any sophisticated city with many visitors, Florence has plenty of fine restaurants; even in the cheaper places standards are high, and if you don't care for anything fancier, there will be lots of good red Chianti to wash down your meal. By popular demand, the city centre is full of *tavole calde*, pizzerias and snack bars, where you can grab a sandwich or a salad instead of a full sit-down meal (one of the best pizza-by-the-slice places is just across from the Medici Chapels).

Please note that many of the best places are likely to close for all or part of August; you would also be wise to call ahead and reserve, even a day or two in advance.

Very Expensive

Alle Murate, Via Ghibellina 52r, **t** 055 240618, *www.caffeitaliano.it*. By the Bargello, this 'creative traditional' restaurant is elegant but relaxed, serving two set menus, one Tuscan and one different – spaghetti with sea bass, or pigeon stuffed with peppers and potatoes, or ducks' livers with ceps and rosemary. *Dinner only, closed Mon*.

Cibreo, Via dei Macci 118r, **t** 055 234 1100. One of the most Florentine of Florentine restaurants is close to the market of Sant' Ambrogio. The décor is simple – yet elegant – food is the main concern, and all of it is market-fresh. You can go native and order tripe, cockscombs and kidneys, or play it safe with prosciutto from the Casentino, a fragrant soup (no pasta here) of tomatoes, mussels and bell pepper, leg of lamb stuffed with artichokes, topped off with a delicious lemon *crostata*, cheesecake, or a chocolate cake to answer every chocaholic's dream. Booking is essential. *Open Tues–Sat 12.50–2.30 and 7.30–11.15, closed Aug*.

Don Chisciotte, Via C Ridolfi 4r, **t** 055 475430. A small place between the Fortezza Basso and Piazza dell'Indipendenza, serving inventive Italian food with a particular emphasis on fish and vegetables. Let yourself be tempted by tagliatelle with scampi and asparagus, fresh tuna steak with an onion cream, warm fish salad. *Closed Aug*.

Enoteca Pinchiorri, Via Ghibellina 87, near the Casa Buonarroti, **t** 055 242777. One of the finest gourmet restaurants in Italy, boasting two Michelin stars. The owners inherited the wine shop and converted it into a beautifully appointed restaurant, with meals served in a garden court in the summer; the cellars contain some 80,000 bottles of the best Italy and France have to offer. The cooking, a mixture of *nouvelle cuisine* and traditional Tuscan recipes, wins prizes every year. Italians tend to complain about the minute portions. Prices are reckoned to be over €200 excluding wine, but the sky's the limit if you go for a more interesting bottle.

Open Mon and Wed 7.30–10, Tues, Thurs–Sat 12.30–2 and 7.30–10, closed Aug.

Expensive

Beccofino, Piazza degli Scarlatti, **t** 055 290076, *www.beccofino.com*. On the river under the British Institute, you could almost be in London or New York once inside this trendy restaurant, but the food is decidedly Italian. Dishes are enhanced by a creative touch and are elegantly presented. Both fish and meat dishes are excellent and change with the seasons: octopus salad, pasta flavoured with courgettes and saffron, sea bass on a bed of truffle-flavoured mash, steak fillet with caramelized shallots, and a fabulous *bistecca alla Fiorentina*. You can also eat a light meal in the wine bar where prices are considerably lower. *Closed Mon.*

Buca Lapi, Via del Trebbio 1r, **t** 055 213768. Located since 1800 in the old wine cellar of the lovely Palazzo Antinori, serving traditional favourites, from *pappardelle al cinghiale* (wide pasta with boar) and a *bistecca fiorentina con fagioli* that is hard to beat, downed with many different Tuscan wines. *Closed Sun and Mon lunch.*

Coco Lezzone, Via del Parioncino 26r (off Lungarno Corsini), **t** 055 287178. In old Florentine dialect, this means big, smelly cook, but don't let this unpromising name put you off. The atmosphere is informal and the food is classic Tuscan using the highest quality fresh ingredients. *Open Mon–Sat 12.30–2 and 8–10.30.*

Oliviero, Via delle Terme 51r, **t** 055 212421. Five minutes from the Piazza della Signoria, this has somewhat passé décor and a slightly bizarre clientele, but it also has excellent food, serving curiosities such as *gnudi di fiori di zucchini e ricotta* (ravioli stripped of its pasta coating with ricotta cheese and courgette flowers) and boned pigeon stuffed with chestnuts. *Eves only, closed Sun.*

Pane e Vino, Via San Niccolò 70r (in the Oltrarno, just in from Ponte alla Grazie), **t** 055 247 6956. This pleasant and informal place has a superb wine list, and very knowledgeable staff to go with it. The *menu degustazione* changes daily, and offers seven small courses; with any luck, the superb porcini mushroom flan will be available. *Mon–Sat 7.30–midnight.*

Ristorante Ricchi, Piazza S. Spirito 8r, **t** 055 215864, *www.caffericchi.it*. This small fish restaurant has tables on magical Piazza Santo Spirito. Inside, the décor is contemporary and elegant, with tables lined up against the walls. The generous plate of *antipasto* is good and main courses include the catch of the day roasted on a bed of potatoes and tomatoes. There are a few meat dishes too. *Open Mon–Sat 8–10.30.*

Targa, Lungarno C Colombo 7, **t** 055 677377. From the rather dated ashes of Caffè Concerto has risen Targa with a re-vamped, more casual menu and a fresh approach to eating out. The space (a delightfully warm wood-and-glass room on the Arno) has not changed, but the food on offer is simpler (and a bit cheaper) while still providing a creative take on regional dishes such as crepes with talaggio cheese and artichokes, seared tuna fillet with braised leeks, rack of lamb with baby broad beans and asparagus. Save room for the sinful hot chocolate soufflé and choose a wine from a formidable list which includes labels from all of Italy and beyond. *Closed Sun and first 3 weeks in Aug.*

Taverna del Bronzino, Via delle Route 25–27r, **t** 055 495220. An elegant, traditional restaurant north of the Duomo, featuring plenty of Tuscan dishes – the *bistecca alla fiorentina* is succulent and tender – and delights like truffle-flavoured tortellini; there are several seafood choices for each course. *Open Mon–Sat 12.30–2.30 and 7.30–10.30, closed three weeks in Aug.*

Moderate

Angiolino, Via Santo Spirito 57r, **t** 055 239 8976. It has lost some of its genuinely 'characteristic' qualities after renovation, but it's still a reliable place to eat Tuscan standards. The vegetable *antipasti* are especially good, and the simple *pollastrina sulla griglia* (grilled spring chicken) is succulent and tasty. *Closed Mon.*

Antico Fattore, Via Lambertesca 1/3r, **t** 055 288975, *www.anticofattore.it*. This traditional Florentine *trattoria*, popular with locals and tourists alike, suffered serious damage in the 1993 Uffizi bomb, but it is back in business now and serving excellent and reasonably-priced local dishes. Try pasta with wild boar or deer sauce, *Il Fritto* (deep-fried rabbit, chicken and brains) and *involtini* with artichoke hearts. *Open Mon–Sat 12.15–2.45 and 7.15–10.30, closed 2 weeks in Aug.*

Antico Ristoro di Cambi, Via Sant' Onofrio 1r, **t** 055 217134. In the Oltrarno, some way to the west of the centre, is a place very popular with the Florentine *intellighenzia*. The food is genuinely Florentine, the classic soups – *ribollita* and *pappa al pomodoro* – are tasty and warming, and the *bistecca alla Fiorentina* impressive. *Open Mon–Sat noon–2.30 and 7.30–10.30.*

Baldovino, Via Giuseppe 22r (Piazza S. Croce), **t** 055 241773. An excellent *trattoria*/pizzeria where you can eat anything from a big salad, filled foccaccia or pizza (from a wood-burning oven) to a full menu of pasta, fish and steaks from the Val di Chiana. *Open Tues–Sun 11.30–2.30 and 7–11.30.*

Buca Mario, Piazza degli Ottaviani 16r, **t** 055 214179. Steep stairs take you down into one of Florence's traditional 'cellar restaurants'; a place full of Florentine atmosphere with a menu to match. The soups here are superb – *pappa al pomodoro* and *ribollita*, or you could try the tagliatelle with porcini. *Ossobuco* is also excellent (cooked in toma-to sauce, Florentine-style), or the *bistecca* is of the best quality. *Open Thurs–Tues 12.30–2.30 and 7.30–10.30.*

Cavolo Nero, Via dell' Ardiglione 22, **t** 055 294744. This little restaurant, tucked away in a side street near Piazza del Carmine, has quite a following among Florentine trendies. The interior is white on yellow with as many tables as possible crowded into the attrac-tive room and there is a pretty garden at the back. The food is mainly Mediterranean with a twist (curried monkfish, rabbit with wild fennel), but there are also plenty of local standards such as spaghetti with clams. *Open Mon–Sat noon–2.30 and 8–11, closed 2 weeks mid Aug.*

Coquinarius, Via della Oche 15r, **t** 055 230 2153. You can eat or drink just about anything at this café/wine bar/restaurant. It is a useful stop off for a light meal or snack in the centre of tourist land. Snacks include a series of hot *crostone* (toasted Tuscan bread with various toppings) and various salads, but you can also order a pasta dish or a *carpaccio*. Wines by the bottle or the glass. *Open Sept–April daily 9am–11pm; May–Aug Mon–Sat 9am–11pm.*

Finisterrae, Via de' Pepi 3–5r, **t** 055 2638675. A great place to go if you are tired of *ribollita* and the typical trattoria look, Finisterrae serves food from Mediterranean countries from southern Italy and France to Greece, Turkey, Tunisia and Spain. The standard of the food is not always up to scratch, but the atmosphere is wonderful with a series of rooms being decorated in the style of the various countries concerned. While you wait for a table, you can sip an aperitivo in the Moroccan-style bar and feast on excellent nibbles provided.

Il Latini, Via dei Palchetti 6r (by Palazzo Rucellai), **t** 055 210916, *www.illatini.com*. Something of an institution in Florence, crowded (prepare to queue; they don't accept bookings) and noisy but fun, where you eat huge portions of Florentine classics at long tables. Try one of the hearty soups followed by the *bistecca* or, more unusual, the *gran pezzo* – a vast rib-roast of beef. The house wine is good; try a *riserva*. *Closed Mon and all of Aug.*

La Vecchia Bettola, Viale Ariosto 32–34r, **t** 055 224158. A noisy *trattoria*, west of the Carmine, with great food; the menu changes daily, but you can nearly always find their classic *tagliolini con funghi porcini*. The grilled meats are tasty and succulent, and the ice cream comes from Vivoli. *Closed Sun and Mon.*

Osteria Santo Spirito, Piazza Santo Spirito 16r, **t** 055 238 2383. If there is no room at Borgo Antico, this is just a walk across the piazza. Sit outside and enjoy a choice of cold dish-es, pastas (try the gnocchi with melted cheese infused with truffle oil), vegetarian dishes and more. The decor inside is unusual for Florence – warm red paintwork with contemporary lighting. *Open daily 12.30–2.30 and 7.30–11.30.*

Sostanza, Via della Porcellana 25r, **t** 055 212691. Just west of Santa Maria Novella is one of the last authentic Florentine trattorias, a good place to eat *bistecca*. One of their most famous dishes is the simple, but delectable *petto di pollo al burro*, chicken breast sautéed in butter. *Open Mon–Fri 12.30–2 and 7.30–9.30.*

Zibibbo, Via di Terzollina 3r, **t** 055 433383. A wonderful restaurant serving traditional Tuscan fare but in a stylish, un-Tuscan setting (pink-varnished floorboards, contemporary furniture). Plenty of choice between meat and fish dishes; *pasta e fagioli*, delicious *spaghetti alle vongole*, *inzimino* (squid stew with Swiss chard), tripe *alla fiorentina*, *fricasée* of rabbit and pigeon wrapped in 'lardo' and cooked with prunes. Worth the trip up to the northernmost extremes of town. *Open Mon–Sat 1–3 and 8–11.*

Cheap

Aquacotta, Via dei Pilastri 51r, **t** 055 242907. This restaurant, north of Piazza S. Ambrogio, is named for the simple but delicious bread soup, one of the specialities; you could follow that by deep-fried rabbit accompanied by crisply fried courgette flowers. *Open Mon–Sat 7.30–10.*

Borgo Antico, Piazza Santo Spirito 6, **t** 055 210437. Popular with a young trendy crowd, so you may have to wait for a table, especially in summer. Inside, the music can be unbearably loud, but the pizza is decent, and there are plenty of other choices – interesting pastas, big salads and more substantial meat and fish dishes. *Open daily 12.30–2.30 and 7.30–11.30.*

La Casalinga, Via Michelozzi 9r, **t** 055 218624. A family-run *trattoria*, also near Piazza Santo Spirito, and always busy, which is not surprising given the quality of the simple home cooking and the low prices. The *ribollita* is excellent. *Open Mon–Sat noon–2.30 and 7–9.45.*

Trattoria Cibreo, Via de' Macci 114, **t** 055 234 1100. A little annexe to smart Cibreo (*see* p.95), this is one of the best deals in town; the food is the same (excluding the odd more extravagant dish), but served in a rustic setting on cheaper porcelain – and your bill will be a third of that of those dining next door. *Open Tues–Sat 12.50–2.30 and 7.30–11.15.*

Trattoria del Carmine, Piazza del Carmine 18r, **t** 055 218601. A traditional, bustling *trattoria* in the San Frediano district, often full. The long menu includes such staples as *ribollita*, *pasta e fagioli* and roast pork, but also features seasonal dishes such as risotto with asparagus or mushrooms, pasta with wild boar sauce and *ossobuco*. *Closed Sun and 3 weeks in Aug.*

Da Mario, Via della Rosina 2r, **t** 055 218550. Mario's *trattoria*, located at the back of the central market, is always buzzing, and there is usually a queue for the few rather cramped tables; don't expect a table to yourself. The food is pure Tuscan, excellent and cheap; *ribollita*, *spezzatino con patate* (beef stew with potatoes) and mixed boiled meats with a deliciously pungent *salsa verde*. *Open Mon–Sat noon–2pm, cash only.*

Il Pizzaiuolo, near the Sant'Ambrogio market at Via dei Macci 113r, **t** 055 241171. One of the best, boasting a real Neapolitan pizza maker, whose creations are puffy and light. There's lots more to choose from, but long queues. *Open Mon–Sat 12.30–3.30 and 7.30–1am, closed Aug.*

Da Ruggero, Via Senese 89r, **t** 055 220542. A tiny, family-run *trattoria* a little way from the centre of town; it's always full, so book. The traditional food is home cooked; try the excellent *pappardelle alla lepre* (with hare sauce) and good puddings. *Closed Tues and Wed, and 3 weeks July–Aug.*

Sabatino, Via Pisana 2r, **t** 055 225955. Just outside the old city gate of San Frediano, this simple, family-run *trattoria* feels as if it has always been this way. Cooking methods, too, are old-fashioned and suitably rustic, and prices are similarly retro. *Open Mon–Fri noon–2.30 and 7.30–10.30, closed Aug.*

Santa Lucia, Via Ponte alle Mosse 102r, **t** 055 353255. North of the Cascine there is a genuine Neapolitan pizzeria. It's a noisy, steamy and unromantic place but it makes up for its lack of glamour by serving what is possibly the best pizza in Florence, topped with the sweetest tomatoes and the creamiest *mozzarella di buffala*. *Open 7.30–1am, closed Wed and Aug; cash only.*

Al Tranvai, near the Carmine in Piazza Torquato Tasso 14r, **t** 055 225197. The two rows of tables in this cheerful little place are always full, and you may not get much elbow room. The menu changes daily, but the *crostini misti* are always on offer, and there's lots of offal: tripe, *lampredotto* (intestines), chicken gizzards etc. *Open Mon–Fri 7.30–10.30.*

There aren't many **vegetarian** restaurants as such in Florence, though non-meat eaters will find plenty of choice (pastas, risotto, etc.) to tempt them. Specifically **vegetarian** restaurants include:

Ruth's, Via Farini 2/A, **t** 055 248 0888. A new, bright and modern kosher vegetarian restaurant next to the synagogue, serving fish and Middle Eastern dishes. Try a *brick*, a savoury pastry, filled with fish, potatoes or cheese that tastes better than it sounds. *Open 12.30–2.30 and 8–10.30, closed Fri dinner and Sat lunch.*

Il Vegetariano, Via delle Ruote 30r, **t** 055 47030. Located to the west of San Marco; self-service with excellent fresh food including a wide choice of soups, salads and more substantial dishes. *Closed Sun lunch and Mon.*

Restaurants Around Florence

Biagio Pignatta, Artimino, **t** 055 875 1406 (*expensive*). Near the Medici villa in Artimino and named after a celebrated Medici chef, this serves Tuscan dishes with a Renaissance flavour – such as pork fillet with prunes and *vin santo* – on a terrace overlooking vines and olives. *Closed Wed, and Thurs lunch in winter.*

Bibé, Via delle Bagnese 1r, **t** 055 204 9085 (*moderate*). A couple of kilometres south of Porta Romana, occupying an old farm-house with a lovely garden (somewhat marred by its proximity to the road and mosquitoes). Try the *crespelle alla Fiorentina* – crêpes filled with ricotta and spinach – and the roast meats, fried chicken and rabbit. Desserts here are creative and divine. *Open 12.30–2 and 7.30–9.45, closed Wed and Thurs lunchtime.*

Centanni, Via di Centanni, Bagno a Ripoli, **t** 055 630122 (*expensive*). An elegant restaurant to the east of Florence, set in an olive grove with a lovely terrace for warm weather. Dishes are along traditional lines – home-made pasta with pigeon or wild boar sauce, *bistecca*, deep-fried chicken or brains

– and there is an excellent wine list. *Closed Sat lunch and Sun.*

Da Delfina, Via della Chiesa, Artimino, near Carmignano, **t** 055 871 8074 (*expensive*). In the same village, this is worth the drive out for its enchanting surroundings, lovely views, the charming atmosphere and sublime cooking – home-made tagliatelle with a sauce made from greens, risotto with garden vegetables, asparagus, succulent kid and lamb dishes. Outdoor seating too. *Open Tues–Sat 12.30–2.30 and 8–10.30, Sun 12.30–2.30.* NB: *No credit cards.*

Omero, Via Pian de' Giuliari 11r, **t** 055 220053. The main reason for a trip to Omero's rustic restaurant a ten-minute taxi ride from the centre of town is the wonderful view from the picture windows over hills dotted with elegant villas, olive groves and cypresses; make sure you get a table in the top room. The typically Tuscan food is reliable without being exceptional while the atmosphere is old-fashioned and charming. *Closed Tues.*

Cafés and *Gelaterie*

Caffè Italiano, Via Condotta 56r, **t** 055 291082. Right in the centre of town, a popular lunch time stop for locals who crowd in for the excellent hot and cold dishes. On two levels: downstairs for standing at the bar, upstairs for a longer sit. The atmosphere is old-fashioned, particularly in the tearoom upstairs. Newspapers are on offer for browsing.

Caffè Ricchi, Piazza Santo Spirito. A local institution. It continues to serve excellent light lunches and wonderful ice cream. The outside tables enjoy the benefit of one of the most beautiful piazzas in Florence, at a price. At *aperitivo* time (6pm–8pm) there's a great spread of 'free' nibbles to go with your Campari.

Capocaccia, Lungarno Corsini 12r, **t** 055 210751. Popular as a night spot as well as a day time bar and café, Capocaccia enjoys a great location on the river beside the British Consulate. It opens at lunchtimes (except at weekends when it does a brisk brunch trade) for light meals and is great for an aperitivo with free nibbles in the evening or as an evening venue for music and drinks. *Closed Mon.*

Dolci e Dolcezze, Piazza Cesare Beccaria 8r, **t** 055 234 5438. East of Sant' Ambrogio market, this has the most delicious cakes, pastries and marmalades in the city – the *crostate*, *torte* and *bavarese* are expensive but worth every euro. It now has another shop at Via del Corso 41r. *Closed Mon*.

Dolce Vita, t 055 284595. Piazza del Carmine. This is the place where fashionable young Florentines strut their latest togs – a favourite pastime since the 14th century. *Closed Mon and 2 weeks in Aug*.

Festa del Gelato, Via del Corso 75r. Boasts over 100 variations of ice cream.

Gelateria de' Ciompi, Via dell'Agnolo 121r. This traditional Florentine ice cream parlour, tucked around the corner from Santa Croce, prides itself on its authentic home-made recipes, some of which are over 50 years old.

Gilli, Piazza della Repubblica 36–39r. Many of Florence's grand old cafés were born in the last century, though this one, the oldest, dates back to 1733, when the Mercato Vecchio still occupied this area; its two panelled back rooms are especially pleasant in the winter. *Open Wed–Mon*.

Giubbe Rosse, Piazza della Repubblica 13–14r. Famous as the rendezvous of Florence's literati at the turn of the century; the chandelier-lit interior has changed little since.

Il Granduca, Via dei Calzaiuoli 57r. Yet another *gelato* option, with creamy concoctions that challenge those of nearby rival Perché No (Why Not). *Closed Wed*.

Hemingway, Piazza Piattellina 9r, **t** 055 284781 (*booking advised*). A beautifully appointed bar done out in pale blues with rattan furniture. You can enjoy teas and coffees, as well as cocktails, interesting light meals and an excellent brunch on Sundays. The owner is a chocaholic, so the hand-made chocolates and puddings are a dream. Try the *sette veli* chocolate cake. *Open weekdays 4.30–late, Sun 11–8*.

L'Oasi, Via dell'Oriuolo 5, near the Duomo. Sophisticated ice cream flavours, and a good choice of cakes.

Il Triangulo delle Bermude, Via Nazionale 61r. Has a superb choice of ice cream.

La Via del' Té, Piazza Ghiberti 22r. Looking on to the Sant' Ambrogio food market, this offers a huge range of teas to choose from plus sweet and savoury snacks.

Perché No, Via Tavolini 194. Arctic heaven near Via Calzaiuoli, with wonderful ice cream in 1940s surroundings.

Rivoire, Piazza della Signoria 5r. Florence's most elegant and classy watering hole, with a marble-detailed interior as lovely as the Piazza della Signoria itself. Terrace on the square.

Vivoli, Via Isola delle Stinche 7r, between the Bargello and S. Croce. Florence lays some claim to being the ice cream capital of the world, a reputation that owes much to the decadently delicious confections and rich *semifreddi* served here. *Closed Mon*.

Wine Bars

Florence is full of wine bars, from new-generation places to simple 'holes in the wall'.

Cantinetta dei Verazzano, Via dei Tavolini 18–20r. Part bakery (selling delicious bread and cakes), part wine bar, this centrally located place belongs to the Verazzano wine estate and serves its own very good wine exclusively; sip it with a plate of mixed *crostini* at hand.

Enoteca Baldovino, Via San Giuseppe 18r, **t** 055 234 7220. A bright and cheerful wine bar down the northern side of Santa Croce with snacks and pasta dishes. There is a comprehensive wine list and plenty of wines by the glass. *Open daily but closed Mon in winter*.

Enoteca dei Giraldi, Via dei Giraldi. Near the Bargello, this hosts art exhibitions and runs wine-tasting courses as well as supplying excellent food and drink.

Frescobaldi Wine Bar, Vicolo dei Gondi (off Via della Condotta), **t** 055 284724. One of Tuscany's best known wine growing families recently opened this pleasant little wine bar, annexe to a full-blown (and very elegant) restaurant. The wines on offer are, naturally, all Frescobaldi produced on their estates in Tuscany and the rest of Italy; some are the result of joint ventures in California and Chile. Delicious snacks include cheeses and cold meats, or you can pop next door for dinner. *Closed Sun*.

Fuori Porta, Via Monte alle Croci 10r, **t** 055 234 2483, *www.fuoriporta.it*. Possibly the most famous of all, where there are some 600 labels on the wine list and dozens of whiskeys and grappas. Among the snacks and hot dishes on offer, try one of the *crostoni*, a huge slab of local bread topped with something delicious and heated under the grill. *Closed Sun*.

Pitti Gola e Cantina, Piazza Pitti 16, **t** 055 212704. A delightful little place situated bang opposite the Pitti palace, with a good choice of wines from Tuscany and beyond, snacks and other more substantial dishes, as well as a few outside tables. *Closed Mon*.

Vini, Via dei Cimatori 38r. A hole in the wall and one of the last of its kind in Florence, where you can join the locals standing on the street, glass and *crostino* in hand. *Closed Sun*.

Le Volpi e L'Uva, Piazza dei Rossi, **t** 055 239 8132. The knowledgeable and helpful owners specialize in relatively unknown labels, and snacks include a marvellous selection of French and Italian cheeses.

Entertainment and Nightlife

Nightlife with Great Aunt Florence is still awaiting its Renaissance; according to the Florentines she's conservative, somewhat deaf and retires early – 1am is late in this city. However, there are plenty of people who wish it weren't so, and slowly, slowly, Florence by night is beginning to mean more than the old *passeggiata* over the Ponte Vecchio and an ice cream, and perhaps a late trip up to Fiesole to contemplate the lights.

Look for listings of concerts and events in Florence's daily, *La Nazione*. The tourist office's free *Florence Today* contains bilingual monthly information and a calendar, as does a booklet called *Florence Concierge Information*, available in hotels and tourist offices. The monthly *Firenze Spettacolo*, sold at newsstands, contains a brief section on events in English, but the comprehensive listings (including anything from ecology and trekking events, film societies, clubs, live music, opera and concerts) are easy to understand even in Italian. The annual *Guida locali di Firenze* also gives listings. For all current films being shown in Florence, look in the local paper.

Performance Arts

The opera and ballet season runs from September to Christmas and concerts from January to April at the **Teatro del Maggio Musicale Fiorentino**, and in the **Maggio Musicale** festival, which features all three, from mid-April until the end of June. There is usually more opera in July.

Classical Concerts

Concerts are held mainly in the following venues:

Teatro del Maggio Musicale Fiorentino, Via del Corso 16, **t** 055 211158, *www.maggio fiorentino.com*. Symphony concerts, recitals, opera and ballet are all held at Florence's municipal opera house.

Teatro della Pergola, Via della Pergola 12–32, **t** 055 226 4316, *www.amicimusica.fi.it*. The excellent chamber music series held here, in the stunning 18th-century Teatro della Pergola, is promoted by the Amici della Musica.

Teatro Verdi, Via Ghibellina 99, **t** 055 212320, *www.teatroverdifirenze.it*. The red and gold Teatro Verdi is home to Tuscany's regional orchestra who perform there regularly from late Nov–May.

Scuola di Musica di Fiesole, Villa la Torraccia, San Domenico, Fiesole, **t** 055 597851, *www. scuolamusica.fiesole.fi.it*. One of Italy's best known music schools promotes a series of chamber music concerts.

Many smaller events take place year-round in churches, cloisters and villas, with plenty of outdoor concerts in summer. Look out for posters: they are not always well publicized.

Rock and Jazz Concert Venues

Auditorium Flog, Via M Mercati 24b, **t** 055 487145, *www.flog.it*. One of the best places in Florence to hear live music year-round, often hosting ethnic music events. Look out for the Musica dei Popoli festival in November.

Teatro Verdi, Via Ghibellina 99, **t** 055 212320.

Tenax, Via Pratese 46, **t** 055 308160, *www.tenax.org*. A spacious venue on the outskirts of town, which is very popular and so usually crowded. Stages lots of live rock concerts, with bands ranging from inter-national names to local groups. DJs take over after the live music stops.

Palasport, Viale Paoli, **t** 055 678841, *www. boxoffice.it*. Big-name rock and jazz bands nearly always play at this venue in Campo di Marte, which seats 7,000.

Saschall, Lungarno Aldo Moro 3, **t** 055 650 4112, *www.saschall.it*. Risen from the ashes (not literally) of the old Teatro Tenda, this 3,000-seat venue plays host to all kinds of music (including musicals). See local press for details.

In the summer, there are lots of live music venues all over the city, many of them free, for when the Florentines move outdoors to cool off.

Musicus Concentus, Piazza del Carmine 14, **t** 055 287347, *www.musicusconcentus.com*. This venue brings big-name jazz performers in to Florence.

Box office, Via Alamanni 39, **t** 055 210804, *www.boxoffice.it*. A central ticket agency for all the major events in Tuscany and beyond, including classical, rock, jazz etc.

Cinemas

Summer is a great time to catch the latest **films**. English-language films are shown throughout the summer three evenings a week at the Odeon in Piazza Strozzi and open-air screens are erected in several venues in Florence with two different films in Italian each evening from mid-June until mid-Sept. Details appear in the local newspapers.

The following show original language (usually English) films:

Odeon Cinehall, Piazza Strozzi, **t** 055 214068, *www.cinehall.it*. Shows latest releases on Mon, Tues and Thurs.

Spazio Uno, Via del Sole 10, **t** 055 215634. Occasionally has original language films.

Clubs

Many clubs have themed evenings; keep an eye out for posters or handouts or buy the listings magazine *Firenze Spettacolo*. Places are somewhat seasonal as well.

Caffedecò, Piazza della Libertà 45–46r. There's often live jazz here, in elegant Art Deco surroundings, where Florence's swells put on the dog. *Closed Mon*.

Caffè La Torre, Lungarno Cellini 65r, **t** 055 680643. A small club which hosts regular jazz and Latin events.

Central Park, Parco delle Cascine. In summer, possibly the trendiest place in Florence, full of serious clubbers dancing to live music on three dance floors. *Open Tues–Sat 11pm–4am*.

"Ex-Mud", Corso dei Tintori 4. The old Mood club has been re-vamped and given an appropriate new name. Still a cool venue, it is located below ground in a cavernous basement with bar and decent dance space. *Open Wed–Sun 10pm–4am*.

Full-Up, Via della Vigna Vecchia 25r. Another possibility, with mirrored walls, disco lighting, and dated music. *Open Tues–Sat 11pm–4am*.

Girasol, Via del Romito 1, **t** 055 474948. If it's Latin sounds you are into, head north of the city to Girasol for live bands and DJs who supply a good mix of Cuban, Flamenco, Brazilian, Caribbean and salsa rhythms. The space is small, so be sure to arrive early. *Open Tues–Sun 8pm–2.30am*.

Jazz Club, Via Nuova de' Caccini 3, **t** 055 247 9700. A small club, with regular live jazz.

Lido, Lungarno Pecori Giraldi 1. A small place in a pretty setting on the Arno, playing a wide variety of music to a mixed crowd. *Closed Mon*.

Mago Merlino, Via dei Pilastri 31r. A relaxed tearoom/bar with live music, theatre, shows and games.

Maracanà, Via Faenza 4. Try this for live music with a Latin feel – samba, mambo and bossanova. *Closed June–Aug*.

Maramao, Via dei Macci 79r. Slick and cool; the music ranges from acid jazz to hip-hop and house. *Closed Mon*.

Rex Caffé, Via Fiesolana 25r, **t** 055 248 0331. The number one winter hotspot until Universale opened its doors, featuring an unusual décor, tapas, music and dancing. *Closed June–Aug*.

Rio Grande, Viale degli Olmi 1, **t** 055 331371. A huge and hugely popular venue with an outside dancefloor in summer where the music is mostly Latin. *Open Tue-Sat (winter also Mon)*.

Soulciety, Via San Zanobi 114b, **t** 055 830 3513. Popular with Florence's Senegalese community but otherwise a relatively little-known dance venue. It's a good alternative to the city's run-of-the-mill clubs and, with its Rococo décor, has an exotic feel to it. *Open Tues–Sun 11.30pm–4am, closed June–Sept.*

Universale, Via Pisana 77r, *www.universale firenze.it* A vast ex-cinema, with designer décor, a restaurant, several bars and a pizzeria, all accompanied by live music and a giant cinema screen. Fast becoming the hottest hang-out in town, these are chic, sleek surroundings for a sleek and chic crowd. *Open 7pm–3am, closed Mon and June–Sept.*

Yab, Via Sassetti 5r, **t** 055 215168, *www.yab.it*. Yab has been around for a long time, and so have some of the punters who hang out there – it is favoured by a decidedly older crowd. It has recently been completely redesigned and has a vast dance space and a great sound system. *Closed May–Sept.*

Pubs

Irish pubs are big in Florence, and you will also find the odd English and Scottish version.

The Fiddler's Elbow, Piazza Santa Maria Novella 7r, **t** 055 215056. One of the original pubs in Florence, with some live music and an ex-pat atmosphere. A handy place to wait for a train, but otherwise a bit grim. Terrace on the piazza.

James Joyce, Lungarno B. Cellini 1r, **t** 055 658 0856. An Irish pub with literary pretensions, the James Joyce enjoys a pleasant location with a big garden near the river. Books and magazines are on hand for browsing.

JJ Cathedral Pub, Piazza San Giovanni 44r, **t** 055 280260. An almost authentic atmosphere prevails in this pub sitting in the shadow of the Duomo; try and get the sole table on the tiny terrace overlooking the cathedral itself.

The Lion's Fountain, Borgo degli Albizi 34r, **t** 055 234 4412. A nice place which also serves food until late.

Il Rifrullo, Via S. Niccolò 55r, **t** 055 234 2621. Year-round, an older pub/wine bar; probably the most popular of all and one of the first to attract people to the Oltrarno. There's no word for 'cosy' in Italian, but the Rifrullo does the best it can.

Gay Clubs

There are a few gay clubs in Florence.

Crisco, Via Santí Egidio 43r, **t** 055 248 0580. *Closed Tues.*

Il Piccolo Café, Borgo Santa Croce 23, **t** 055 200 1057. A tiny, friendly, arty bar. *Open daily from 5pm.*

Silver Stud, Via della, Fornace 9, **t** 055 688466, *www.silverstud.it*. A new bar in the Oltrano. *Closed Sun.*

Tabasco, Piazza Santa Cecilia 3r, **t** 055 213000, *www.tabascogay.it*. Italy's first gay bar, opened in the 1970s.

Summer venues

In the summer, nightlife in Florence moves out of doors and a series of venues open up between late May and mid-September in some of the city's square and open spaces. A torrid Florentine summer evening is no time to sit indoors (unless there's air conditioning of course), and these venues usually incorporate food and drink and some kind of live entertainment. Admission is usually free.

Le Murate, Via dell'Agnolo, **t** 338 506 0253. Housed in the courtyard of a former prison, the Murate provides music and dancing, food, drink, film and live music.

Parterre, Piazza della Libertà. Club and live music venue.

Piazza Santissima Annunziata. Live music and dance, plus a bar and pizzeria, with the incomparable backdrop of Brunelleschi's loggia.

Le Rime Rampante. A great spot overlooking the river above Piazza Poggi with a bar, snacks and live music and dancing.

Discos

Auditorium Flog, Via M Mercanti 24b, **t** 055 490437. A favourite and usually packed student venue.

Jackie O, Via Erta Canina 24. An old favourite for the 30ish crowd which includes a piano bar. *Closed Mon, Tues, Wed.*

Space Electronic, Via Palazzuolo 37, **t** 055 293082. A high-tech noise box. *Open daily*.

Tenax, Via Pratese 46, **t** 055 308160, *www.tenax.org*. Lots of live music – the current place to go in Florence, out near the airport. *Closed Sun–Wed and mid-May–Sept.*

Fine balm let Arno be;
The walls of Florence all of silver rear'd,
And crystal pavements in the public way...
                14th-century madrigal by Lapo Gianni

Magari! – if only! – the modern Florentine would add to this vision, to this city of art and birthplace of the Renaissance, built by bankers and merchants whose sole preoccupation was making more florins. The precocious capital of Tuscany began to slip into legend back in the 14th century, during the lifetime of Dante; it was noted as *different* even before the Renaissance, before Boccaccio, Masaccio, Brunelleschi, Donatello, Leonardo da Vinci, Botticelli, Michelangelo, Machiavelli, the Medici...

This city of Florence is well populated, its good air a healthy tonic; its citizens are well
dressed, and its women lovely and fashionable, its buildings are very beautiful, and
every sort of useful craft is carried on in them, more so than any other Italian city. For
this many come from distant lands to see her, not out of necessity, but for the quality
of its manufactures and arts, and for the beauty and ornament of the city.
                Dino Compagni in his *Chronicle* of 1312

According to the tourist office, in 1997, 685 years after Dino, a grand total of over seven million tourists (Americans, Germans, French and Britons are still the top four groups) spent at least one night in a Florentine hotel. Some, perhaps, had orthodontist appointments. A large percentage of the others came to inhale the rarefied air of the cradle of Western civilization, to gaze at some of the loveliest things made by mortal hands and minds, to walk the streets of new Athens, the great humanist 'city built to the measure of man'. Calling Florence's visitors 'tourists', however, doesn't seem quite right; 'tourism' implies pleasure, a principle alien to this dour, intellectual, measured town. 'Pilgrims' is perhaps the better word, cultural pilgrims who throng the Uffizi, the Accademia, the Bargello to gaze upon the holy mysteries of our secular society, to buy postcards and replicas, the holy cards of our day.

Someone wrote a warning on a wall near Brunelleschi's Santo Spirito, in the Oltrarno: *'Turista con mappa/alla caccia del tesoro/per finire davanti ad un piatto/di spaghetti al pomodoro'* ('Tourist with a map, on a treasure hunt, only to end up in front of a plate of spaghetti with tomato sauce'). Unless you come with the right attitude, Florence can be as disenchanting as cold spaghetti. It only blossoms if you apply your mind as well as your vision, if you go slowly and do not let the art bedazzle until your eyes glaze over in dizzy excess (a common complaint, known in medical circles as the Stendhal syndrome). Realize that loving and hating Florence at the same time may be the only rational response. It is the capital of contradiction; you begin to like it because it goes out of its way to annoy.

History

The identity of Florence's first inhabitants is a matter of dispute. There seems to have been some kind of settlement along the Arno long before the Roman era, perhaps as early as 1000 BC; the original founders may have been either native Italics

Florentine Duality

Dante's *Vita Nuova*, the autobiography of his young soul, was only the beginning of Florentine analysis; Petrarch, the introspective 'first modern man', was a Florentine born in exile; Ghiberti was the first artist to write an autobiography, Cellini wrote one of the most readable; Alberti invented art criticism; Vasari invented art history; Michelangelo's personality, in his letters and sonnets, looms as large as his art. In many ways Florence broke away from the medieval idea of community and invented the modern concept of the individual, most famously expressed by Lorenzo de' Medici's friend, Pico della Mirandola, whose *Oration on the Dignity of Man* tells us what the God on the Sistine Chapel ceiling was saying when he created Adam: '...And I have created you neither celestial nor terrestrial, neither mortal nor immortal, so that, like a free and able sculptor and painter of yourself, you may mould yourself entirely in the form of your choice.'

To attempt to understand Florence, remember one historical constant: no matter what the issue, the city always takes both sides, vehemently and often violently, especially in the Punch and Judy days of Guelphs and Ghibellines. In the 1300s this was explained by the fact that the city was founded under the sign of Mars, the war god; but in medieval astronomy Mars is also connected with Aries, another Florentine symbol and the sign of the time of spring blossoms. (The Annunciation, at the beginning of spring, was Florence's most important festival.) One of the city's oldest symbols is the lily (or iris), flying on its oldest gonfalons. Perhaps even older is its *marzocco*, originally an equestrian statue of Mars on the Ponte Vecchio, later replaced by Donatello's grim lion.

Whatever dispute rocked the streets, Great Aunt Florence often expressed her schizophrenia in art, floral Florence versus stone Florence, epitomized by the irreconcilable differences between the two most famous works of art: Botticelli's graceful *Primavera* and Michelangelo's cold, perfect *David*. The 'city of flowers' seems a joke; it has nary a real flower, nor even a tree, in its stone streets; indeed, all effort has gone into keeping nature at bay, surpassing it with geometry and art. And yet the Florentines were perhaps the first since the Romans to discover the joys of the countryside. The rusticated stone palaces, like fortresses or prisons, hide charms as delightful as Gozzoli's frescoes in the Palazzo Medici-Riccordi. Luca della Robbia's dancing children and floral wreaths are contemporary with the naked, violent warriors of the Pollaiuolo brothers; the writhing, quarrelsome statuary in the Piazza della Signoria is sheltered by one of the most delicate *loggie* imaginable.

After 1500, all the good, bad and ugly symptoms of the Renaissance peaked in the mass fever of Mannerism. Then, drifting into a debilitating twilight, Florence gave birth to the artistic phenomenon known as kitsch – the Medici Princes' chapel is an early kitsch classic. Since then, worn out perhaps, or embarrassed, this city built by merchants has kept its own counsel, expressing its argumentative soul in overblown controversies about traffic, art restoration and the undesirability of fast-food counters and cheap *pensioni*. We who find her fascinating hope she some day comes to remember her proper role, bearing the torch of culture instead of merely collecting tickets for the culture torture.

or Etruscans. Throughout the period of Etruscan dominance, the village on the river lived in the shadow of *Faesulae* – Florence's present-day suburb of Fiesole was then an important city, the northernmost member of the Etruscan Dodecapolis. The Arno river cuts across central Italy like a wall. This narrow stretch of it, close to the mountain pass over to Emilia, was always the most logical place for a bridge.

Roman Florence can claim no less a figure than **Julius Caesar** for its founder. Like so many other Italian cities, it began as a planned urban enterprise in an under-developed province – a colony for army veterans in 59 BC. The origin of the name – so suggestive of springtime and flowers – is another mystery. First it was *Florentia*, then *Fiorenza* in the Middle Ages, and finally *Firenze*. One guess is that its foundation took place in April, when the Romans were celebrating the games of the Floralia.

The original street plan of *Florentia* can be seen today in the neat rectangle of blocks between Via Tornabuoni and Via del Proconsolo, between the Duomo and Piazza della Signoria. Its Forum occupied roughly the site of the modern Piazza della Repubblica, and the outline of its amphitheatre can be traced in the oval of streets just west of Piazza Santa Croce. Roman *Florentia* never really imposed itself on the historian. One writer mentions it as a major town and river crossing along the Via Cassia, connected to Rome and the thriving new cities of northern Italy, such as Bononia and Mediolanum (Bologna and Milan). At the height of the Empire, the municipal bound-aries had expanded out to Via de' Fossi, Via S. Egidio, and Via de' Benci. Nevertheless, Florentia did not play a significant role either in the Empire's heyday or in its decline.

After the fall of Rome, Florence weathered its troubles comparatively well. We hear of it withstanding sieges by the Goths around the year 400, when it was defended by the famous imperial general Stilicho, and again in 541, during the campaigns of Totila and Belisarius; all through the Greek–Gothic wars Florence seems to have taken the side of Constantinople. The Lombards arrived around 570; under their rule Florence was the seat of a duchy subject to the then Tuscan capital of Lucca. The next mention in the chronicles refers to Charlemagne spending Christmas with the Florentines in the year 786. Like the rest of Italy, Florence had undoubtedly declined; a new set of walls went up under Carolingian rule, about 800, enclosing an area scarcely larger than the original Roman settlement of 59 BC. Most likely throughout the Dark Ages the city was gradually increasing its relative importance and strength at the expense of its neighbours. The famous baptistry, erected some time between the 6th and 9th centuries, is the only important building from that troubled age in all Tuscany.

By the 1100s, Florence was the leading city of the County of Tuscany. **Countess Matilda**, ally of Pope Gregory VII against the emperors, oversaw the construction of a new set of walls in 1078, coinciding with the widest Roman-era boundaries. The city had recovered all the ground lost during the Dark Ages, and the momentum of growth did not abate. New walls again in the 1170s enclosed what was becoming one of the largest cities in Europe. In this period, Florence owed its growth and prosperity largely to the textile industry – weaving and 'finishing' cloth not only from Tuscany but wool shipped from as far afield as Spain and England. The capital gain from this trade, managed by the *Calimala* and the *Arte della Lana*, Florence's richest guilds, led naturally to an even more profitable business – banking and finance.

The Florentine Republic Battles with the Barons

In 1125, Florence once and for all conquered its ancient rival Fiesole. Wealth and influence brought with them increasing political responsibilities; the city often found itself at war with its neighbours. Since Countess Matilda's death in 1115, Florence had become a self-governing *comune*, largely independent of the emperor and local barons. The new city republic's hardest problems, however, were closer to home. The nobles of the county, encouraged in their anachronistic feudal behaviour by representatives of the imperial government, proved irreconcilable enemies to the new merchant republic, and Florence spent most of the 12th century trying to keep them in line. Often the city actually declared war on a noble clan, as with the Alberti, or the Counts of Guidi, and razed their castles whenever they captured one. To complicate the situation, nobles attracted by the stimulation of urban life – along with the opportunities for making money – often moved their families into Florence itself.

They brought their country habits with them: a boyish eagerness to brawl with their neighbours on the slightest pretext, and a complete disregard for the laws of the *comune*. Naturally, they couldn't feel secure without a little urban castle of their own, and before long Florence' skyline, like that of any prosperous Italian city of the Middle Ages, featured hundreds of tower-fortresses, built as much for status as for defence. Many were over 200ft in height. It wasn't uncommon for the honest citizen to come home from work hoping for a little peace and quiet, only to find siege engines in front of the house and a company of bowmen in the children's bedroom.

But just as Florence was able to break the power of the rural nobles, those in the town also eventually had to succumb. The last tower-fortresses were chopped down to size in the early 1300s. But even without the nobles raising all manner of hell, the Florentines managed to find brand new ways to keep the pot boiling. The rich merchants who dominated the government, familiarly known as the *popolari grossi*, resorted to every sort of murder and mayhem to beat down the demands of the lesser guilds, the *popolari minuti*, for a fair share of the wealth; the two only managed to settle their differences when confronted by murmurs of discontent from what was then one of Europe's largest urban proletariats. But even beyond simple class issues, the city born under the fiery sign of Mars always found a way to make trouble. Not only did Florentines pursue the Guelph–Ghibelline conflict with greater zest than almost any Tuscan city; according to the chronicles of the time, they actually started it. In 1215, men of the Amidei family murdered a prominent citizen named Buondelmonte dei Buondelmonti over a broken wedding engagement, the spark that ignited the factionalist struggles first in Florence, then quickly throughout Italy.

Guelphs and Ghibellines

In the 13th century, there was never a dull moment in Florence. Guelphs and Ghibellines, often more involved with some feud between powerful families than with real political issues, cast each other into exile and confiscated each other's property with every change of the wind. Religious strife occasionally pushed politics off the front page. In the 1240s, a curious foreshadowing of the Reformation saw Florence wrapped up in the **Patarene heresy**. This sect, closely related to the

Albigensians of southern France, was as obsessed with the presence of Evil in the world as John Calvin – or Florence's own future fire-and-brimstone preacher, Savonarola. Exploiting a streak of religious eccentricity that has always seemed to be present in the Florentine psyche, the Patarenes thrived in the city, even electing their own bishop. The established Church was up to the challenge; St Peter Martyr, a blood-thirsty Dominican, led his armies of axe-wielding monks to the assault in 1244, exterminating almost the entire Patarene community.

In 1248, with help from Emperor Frederick II, Florence's Ghibellines booted out the Guelphs – once and for all, they thought – but two years later the Guelphs were back, and it was the Ghibellines' turn to leave. The new Guelph regime, called the *primo popolo*, was for the first time completely in the control of the bankers and merchants. It passed the first measures to control the privileges of the turbulent, largely Ghibelline nobles, and forced them all to chop the tops off their tower-fortresses. The next decades witnessed a series of wars with the Ghibelline cities of Tuscany – Siena, Pisa and Pistoia, not just by coincidence Florence's habitual enemies. Usually the Florentines were the aggressors, and more often than not fortune favoured them. In 1260, however, the Sienese, reinforced by Ghibelline exiles from Florence and a few imperial cavalry, destroyed an invading Florentine army at the **Battle of Monteaperti**. Florence was at the Ghibellines' mercy. Only the refusal of Farinata degli Uberti, the leader of the exiles, to allow the city's destruction kept the Sienese from torching it – a famous episode recounted by Dante in the *Inferno*. (In a typical Florentine gesture of gratitude, Dante found a home for Uberti in one of the lower circles of hell.)

In Florence, a Ghibelline regime under Count Guido Novello made life rough for the wealthy Guelph bourgeoisie. As luck would have it, though, only a few years later the Guelphs were back in power, and Florence was winning on the battlefield again. The new Guelph government, the *secondo popolo*, earned a brief respite from factional strife. In 1289, Florence won a great victory over another old rival, Arezzo. This was the **Battle of Campaldino**, where the Florentine citizen army included young Dante Alighieri. In 1282, and again in 1293, Florence tried to clean up an increasingly corrupt government with a series of reforms. The 1293 Ordinamenti della Giustizia once and for all excluded the nobles from the important political offices. By now, however, the real threat to the Guelph merchants' rule did not come so much from the nobility, which had been steadily falling behind in wealth and power for two centuries, but from the lesser guilds, which had been excluded from a share of the power, and also from the growing working class employed in the textile mills and the foundries.

Despite all the troubles, the city's wealth and population grew tremendously throughout the 1200s. Its trade contacts spread across Europe, and crowned heads from London to Constantinople found Florentine bankers ready to float them a loan. About 1235 Florence minted modern Europe's first gold coin, the *florin*, which soon became a standard currency across the continent. By 1300 Florence counted over 100,000 souls – a little cramped, even inside the vast new circuit of walls built by the *comune* in the 1280s. It was not only one of the largest cities in Europe, but certainly one of the richest. Besides banking, the wool trade was also booming: by 1300 the wool guild, the Arte della Lana, had over 200 large workshops in the city alone.

Naturally, this new opulence created new possibilities for culture and art. Florence's golden age began perhaps in the 1290s, when the *comune* started its tremendous programme of public buildings – including the Palazzo della Signoria and the cathedral; important religious structures, such as Santa Croce, were under way at the same time. Cimabue was the artist of the day; Giotto was just beginning, and his friend Dante was hard at work on the *Commedia*.

As in so many other Italian cities, Florence developed its republican institutions slowly and painfully. At the beginning of the *comune* in 1115, the leaders were a class called the *boni homines*, which was made up mostly of nobles. Only a few decades later, these were calling themselves *consules*, evoking a memory of the ancient Roman republic. When the Ghibellines took over, the leading official was a *podestà* appointed by the Emperor. Later, under the Guelphs, the *podestà* and a new officer called the *capitano del popolo* were both elected by the citizens. With the reforms of the 1290s Florence's republican constitution was perfected – though it satisfied only a few citizens and guaranteed future trouble. Power was invested in the council of the richer guilds, the *Signoria*; the new Palazzo della Signoria was designed expressly as a symbol of their authority, replacing the old Bargello, which had been the seat of the *podestà*. The most novel feature of the government, designed to avoid the violent factionalism of the past, was the selection of officials by lot from among the guild members. In effect, politics was to be abolished.

Business as Usual: Riot, War, Plagues and Revolution

Despite the reforms of the Ordinamenti, Florence found little peace in the new century. As if following some strange and immutable law of city-state behaviour, no sooner had the Guelphs established total control than they themselves split into new factions. The radically anti-imperial **Blacks** and the more conciliatory **Whites** fought each other through the early 1300s with the same fervour that both had once exercised against the Ghibellines. The Whites, who included Dante among their partisans, came out losers when the Blacks conspired with the pope to bring Charles of Valois' French army into Florence; almost all the losing faction were forced into exile in 1302. Some of them must have sneaked back, for the chronicles of 1304 record the Blacks trying to burn them out of their houses with incendiary bombs, resulting in a fire that consumed a quarter of the city.

Beginning in 1313, Florence was involved in a constant series of inconclusive wars with Pisa, Lucca and Arezzo, among others. In 1325, the city was defeated and nearly destroyed by the great Lucchese general **Castruccio Castracani** (*see* p.227). Castruccio died of a common cold while the siege was already under way, another instance of Florence's famous good luck, but unfortunately one of the last. The factions may have been suppressed, but fate had found some more novel disasters for the city. One far-off monarch did more damage to Florence than its Italian enemies had ever managed – King Edward III of England, who in 1339 found it expedient to repudiate his foreign debts. Florence's two biggest banks, the Bardi and the Peruzzi, immediately went bust, and the city's standing as the centre of international finance was gravely damaged.

One constant throughout the history of the republic was the oppression of the poor. The ruling bankers and merchants exploited the labour of the masses and gave them only the bare minimum in return. In the 14th century, overcrowding, undernourishment and plenty of rats made Florence's poorer neighbourhoods a perfect breeding ground for epidemics. Famine, plagues and riots became common in the 1340s, causing a severe political crisis. At one point, in 1342, the Florentines gave over their government to a foreign dictator, Walter de Brienne, the French-Greek 'Duke of Athens'. He lasted only for a year before a popular revolt ended the experiment. The **Black Death** of 1348, which was the background for Boccaccio's *Decameron*, carried off perhaps one half of the population. Coming on the heels of a serious depression, it was a blow from which Florence would never really recover.

In the next two centuries, when the city was to stake its position as the great innovator in Western culture, it was already in relative decline, a politically decadent republic with a stagnant economy, barely holding its own among the changes in trade and diplomacy. For the time being, however, things didn't look too bad. Florence bought control of Prato, in 1350, and was successful in a defensive war against expansionist Milan in 1351. War was almost continuous for the last half of the century, a strain on the exchequer but not usually a threat to the city's survival; this was the heyday of the mercenary companies, led by *condottieri* like **Sir John Hawkwood** (Giovanni Acuto), immortalized in Florence's cathedral. Before the Florentines made him a better offer, Hawkwood was often in the employ of their enemies.

Throughout the century, the Guelph party had been steadily tightening its grip over the republic's affairs. Despite the selection of officials by lot, by the 1370s the party organization bore an uncanny resemblance to some of the big-city political machines common not so long ago in America. The merchants and the bankers who ran the party used it to turn the Florentine Republic into a profit-making business. With the increasingly limited opportunities for making money in trade and finance, the Guelph ruling class tried to make up the difference by soaking the poor. Wars and taxes stretched Florentine tolerance to breaking point, and finally, in 1378, came revolution. The **Ciompi Revolt** (*ciompi* – wage labourers in the textile industries) began in July, when a mob of workers seized the Bargello. Under the leadership of a wool-carder named Michele di Lando, they executed a few of the Guelph bosses and announced a new, reformed constitution. They were also foolish enough to believe the Guelph magnates when they promised to abide by the new arrangement if only the *ciompi* would go home. Before long di Lando was in exile, and the ruling class firmly back in the seat of power, more than ever determined to eliminate the last vestiges of democracy from the republic.

The Rise of the Medici

In 1393, Florentines celebrated the 100th anniversary of the great reform of the Ordinamenti, while watching their republic descend into oligarchy. In that year **Maso degli Albizzi** became *gonfaloniere* (the head of the Signoria) and served as virtual dictator for many years afterwards. The ruling class of merchants, more than a bit paranoid after the Ciompi Revolt, were relieved to see power concentrated in strong hands. In an atmosphere of repression and conspiracy, the Signoria's secret police hunted down malcontents while Florentine exiles plotted against the republic in foreign courts. Florence was almost constantly at war. In 1398 she defeated an attempt at conquest by Giangaleazzo Visconti of Milan. The imperialist policy of the Albizzi and their allies resulted in important territorial gains, including the conquest of Pisa in 1406, and the purchase of Livorno from the Genoese in 1421, but unsuccessful wars against Lucca finally disenchanted the Florentines with Albizzi rule. An emergency *parlamento* (the infrequent popular assembly usually called when a coming change of rulers was obvious) in 1434 decreed the recall from exile of the head of the popular opposition, **Cosimo de' Medici**.

Perhaps it was something that could only have happened in Florence – the darling of the plebeians, the great hope for reform, was also the head of Florence's biggest bank. The Medici family had their roots in the Mugello region north of Florence. Their name seems to suggest that they once were pharmacists (later enemies would jibe at the balls on the family arms as 'the pills'). For two centuries they had been active in Florentine politics; many had acquired reputations as troublemakers; their names turned up often in the lists of exiles and records of lawsuits. None of the Medici had ever been particularly rich until **Giovanni di Bicci de' Medici** (1360–1429) parlayed his wife's dowry into the founding of a bank. Good fortune – and a temporary monopoly on the handling of the pope's finances – made the Medici Bank Florence's biggest.

Giovanni had been content to stay on the fringe of politics; his son, **Cosimo** (known in Florentine history as '**il Vecchio**', the 'old man') took good care of the bank's affairs but aimed his sights much higher. His strategy was as old as Julius Caesar – the patrician reformer, cultivating the best men, winning the favour of the poor with largesse and gradually, carefully forming a party under a system specifically designed to prevent such things. In 1433 Rinaldo degli Albizzi had him exiled, but it was too late; continuing discontent forced his return only a year later, and for the next 35 years Cosimo would be the unchallenged ruler of Florence. Throughout this period, Cosimo occasionally held public office – this was done by lottery, with the electoral lists manipulated to ensure a majority of Medici supporters at all times. Nevertheless, he received ambassadors at the new family palace (built in 1444), entertained visiting popes and emperors, and made all the important decisions. A canny political godfather and usually a gentleman, Cosimo was also a useful patron to the great figures of the early Renaissance – including Donatello and Brunelleschi. His father had been one of the judges in the famous competition for the baptistry doors, and Cosimo was a member of the commission that picked Brunelleschi to design the cathedral dome.

Under Cosimo's leadership Florence began Europe's first progressive income tax, and invented the concept of the national debt – endlessly rolling over bonds to keep the republic afloat and the creditors happy. The poor, with fewer taxes to pay, were also happy, and the ruling classes were positively delighted; never in Florence's history had any government so successfully muted class conflict and the desire for a genuine democracy. Wars were few, and the internal friction negligible. Cosimo died in August 1464; his tomb in San Lorenzo bears the inscription *Pater patriae,* and no dissent was registered when his 40-year-old son **Piero** took up the boss's role.

Lorenzo il Magnifico

Piero didn't quite have the touch of his masterful father, but he survived a stiff political crisis in 1466, when he outmanoeuvred a new faction led by wealthy banker Luca Pitti. In 1469 he succumbed to the Medici family disease, the gout, and his 20-year-old son **Lorenzo** succeeded him in an equally smooth transition. He was to last for 23 years. Not necessarily more 'magnificent' than other contemporary princes, or other Medici, Lorenzo's honorific reveals something of the myth that was to grow up around him in later centuries. His long reign corresponded with the height of the Florentine Renaissance. It was a relatively peaceful time, and in the light of the disasters that were to follow, Florentines could not help looking back on it as a golden age.

As a ruler, Lorenzo showed many virtues. Still keeping up the pretence of being a private citizen, he lived relatively simply, always accessible to the concerns of his fellow citizens, who would often see him walking the city streets. In the field of foreign policy he was indispensable to Florence and indeed all Italy; he did more than anyone to keep the precarious peninsular balance of power from disintegrating. The most dramatic affair of his reign was the **Pazzi conspiracy**, an attempt to assassinate Lorenzo plotted by Pope Sixtus IV and the wealthy Pazzi family, the pope's bankers and ancient rivals of the Medici. In 1478, two of the Pazzi attacked Lorenzo and his brother Giuliano during mass at the cathedral. Giuliano was killed, but Lorenzo managed to escape into the sacristy. The botched murder aborted the planned revolt; Florentines showed little interest in the Pazzis' call to arms, and before nightfall most of the conspirators were dangling from the cornice of the Palazzo Vecchio.

Apparently, Lorenzo had angered the pope by starting a syndicate to mine for alum in Volterra, threatening the papal monopoly. Since Sixtus failed to murder Lorenzo, he had to settle for excommunicating him, and declaring war in alliance with King Ferrante of Naples. The war went badly for Florence and, in the most memorable act of his career, Lorenzo walked into the lion's cage, travelling to negotiate with the terrible Neapolitan, who had already murdered more than one important guest. As it turned out, Ferrante was only too happy to dump his papal entanglements; Florence found itself at peace once more, and Lorenzo returned home to a hero's welcome.

In other affairs, both foreign and domestic, Lorenzo was more a lucky ruler than a skilled one. Florence's economy was entering a long, slow decline, but for the moment the banks and mills were churning out just enough profit to keep up the accustomed level of opulence. The Medici Bank was on the ropes. Partly because of Lorenzo's neglect, it came close to collapsing on several occasions – and it seems that Lorenzo blithely made up the losses with public funds. Culturally, he was fortunate to be the nabob of Florence at its most artistically creative period; later historians and Medici propagandists gave him a reputation as an art patron that is entirely undeserved. His own tastes tended towards bric-a-brac, jewellery, antique statues and vases; there is little evidence that he appreciated the extraordinary talents of the great artists around him. Perhaps because he was too nearsighted to see anything clearly, he did not commission a single important canvas or fresco in Florence (except for Luca Signorelli's mysterious *Pan*, lost in Berlin during the last war). His favourite architect was the hack Giuliano da Sangallo.

Lorenzo was brought up with some of the leading humanist scholars of Tuscany for tutors and his real interests were literary. His well-formed lyrics and winsome pastorals have earned him a place among Italy's greatest 15th-century poets; they neatly reflect the private side of Lorenzo, the retiring, scholarly family man who enjoyed life better in one of the many rural Medici villas than in the busy city. In this, he was perfectly in tune with his class and his age. Plenty of Florentine bankers were learning the joys of country life, reading Horace or Catullus in their geometrical gardens and pestering their tenant farmers with well-meant advice.

Back in town, they had thick, new walls of rusticated sandstone between them and the bustle of the streets. The late 15th century was the great age of palace-building in Florence. Following the example of Cosimo de' Medici, the bankers and merchants erected dozens of palaces (some of the best can be seen around Via Tornabuoni), each with blank walls and iron-barred windows to the street. Historians always note a turning inward, a 'privatization' of Florentine life in this period. In a city that had become a republic only in name, civic interest and public life ceased to matter so much. The rich began to assume the airs of an aristocracy, and did everything they could to distance themselves from their fellow citizens. Ironically, just at the time when Florence's artists were creating their greatest achievements, the republican ethos, the civic soul that had made Florence great, began to disintegrate.

Savonarola

Lorenzo's death, in 1492, was followed by another apparently smooth transition of power to his son **Piero**. But after 58 years of Medicean quiet and stability, the city was ready for a change. The opportunity came soon enough, when the timid and inept Piero allowed the invading King of France, **Charles VIII**, to occupy Pisa and the Tuscan coast. A spontaneous revolt chased Piero and the rest of the Medici into exile, while a mob sacked the family's palace. A new regime, under **Piero Capponi**, dealt sternly with the French and tried to pump new life into the long-dormant republican constitution.

The Florence that threw out the Medici was a city in the mood for some radical reform. Already, the dominating figure on the political stage was an intense Dominican friar from Ferrara named **Girolamo Savonarola**. Perhaps not surprisingly, this oversophisticated and overstimulated city was also in the mood to be told how wicked and decadent it was, and Savonarola was happy to oblige. A spellbinding revival preacher with a touch of erudition, Savonarola packed as many as 10,000 into the Duomo to hear his weekly sermons, which were laced with political sarcasm and social criticism. Though an insufferable prig, he was also a sincere democrat. There is a story that the dying Lorenzo called Savonarola to his bedside for the last rites, and that the friar refused him absolution unless he 'restored the liberty of the Florentines', a proposal that only made the dying despot sneer with contempt.

Savonarola also talked Charles VIII into leaving Florence in peace. Pisa, however, took advantage of the confusion to revolt, and the restored republic's attempts to recapture it were in vain. Things were going badly. Piero Capponi's death in 1496 left Florence without an able leader, and Savonarolan extremists became ever more influential. The French invasion and the incessant wars that followed cost the city dearly in trade, while the Medici, now in Rome, intrigued to destroy the republic. Worst of all, Savonarola's attacks on clerical corruption made him another bitter enemy in Rome – **Pope Alexander VI**, the most corrupt cleric who ever lived – who scraped together a league of allies to make war on Florence in 1497.

This war proceeded without serious reverses for either side, but Savonarola was able to exploit it brilliantly, convincing the Florentines that they were on a moral crusade against the hated and dissolute Borgias, Medici, French, Venetians and Milanese. The year 1497 was undoubtedly the high point of Savonarola's career. The good friar's spies – mostly children – kept a close eye on any Florentines who were suspected of enjoying themselves, and collected books, fancy clothes and works of art for the famous **Bonfire of Vanities**. It was a climactic moment in the history of Florence's delicate psyche. Somehow the spell had been broken; like the deranged old Michelangelo, taking a hammer to his own work, the Florentines gathered the objects that had once been their greatest pride and put them to the torch. The bonfire was held in the centre of the Piazza della Signoria; a visiting Venetian offered to buy the whole lot, but the Florentines had someone sketch his portrait and threw that on the flames, too.

One vanity the Florentines could not quite bring themselves to part with was their violent factionalism. On one side were the Piagnoni ('weepers') of Savonarola's party, on the other the party of the Arrabbiati ('the angry'), including the gangs of young delinquents who would demonstrate their opposition to piety and holiness by sneaking into the cathedral and filling Savonarola's pulpit with cow dung. A Medicean party was also gathering strength, a sort of fifth column sowing discontent within the city and undermining the war effort. Three times, unsuccessfully, the exiled Medici attempted to seize the city with bands of mercenaries. The Pisan revolt continued, and Pope Alexander had excommunicated Savonarola and was threatening to place all Florence under an interdict. In the long hangover after the Bonfire of Vanities, the Florentines were growing weary of their preacher. When the Arrabbiati won the elections of 1498, his doom was sealed. A kangaroo court found the new scapegoat guilty of heresy and treason. After some gratuitous torture and public mockery, the very spot where the Bonfire of Vanities had been held now witnessed a bonfire of Savonarola.

Pope Alexander still wasn't happy. He sent an army under his son, Cesare Borgia, to menace the city. Florence weathered this threat, and the relatively democratic 'Savonarolan' constitution of 1494 seemed to be working out well. Under a new and innovative idea, borrowed from Venice and designed to circumvent party strife, a public-spirited gentleman named **Piero Soderini** was elected *gonfaloniere* for life in 1502. With the help of his friend and adviser, **Niccolò Machiavelli**, Soderini managed to keep the ship of state on an even keel. Pisa finally surrendered in 1509. Serious trouble returned in 1512, and once more the popes were behind it. As France's only ally in Italy, Florence ran foul of Julius II. Papal and Spanish armies invaded Florentine territory and, after their gruesome sack of Prato, designed specifically to overawe Florence, the frightened and politically apathetic city was ready to submit to the pope's conditions – the expulsion of Soderini, a change of alliance and the return of the Medici.

The End of the Republic

At first, the understanding was that the Medici would live in Florence as private citizens. But **Giuliano de' Medici**, son of Lorenzo and current leader, soon united the upper classes for a rolling back of Savonarolan democracy. With hired soldiers to intimidate the populace, a rigged *parlamento* in September 1512 restored Medici control. The democratic Grand Council was abolished; its new meeting hall in the Palazzo Vecchio (where Leonardo and Michelangelo were to have their 'Battle of the Frescoes') became apartments for soldiers. Soldiers were everywhere, and the Medicean restoration took on the aspect of a police state. Hundreds of political prisoners were tortured in the Palazzo Vecchio's dungeons, among them Machiavelli.

Giuliano died in 1516, succeeded by his nephew **Lorenzo, Duke of Urbino**, a snotty young sport with a tyrant's bad manners. Nobody mourned much when syphilis carried him off in 1519, but the family paid Michelangelo to give both Lorenzo and Giuliano fancy tombs. Ever since Giuliano's death, however, the real Medici boss had been not Lorenzo, but his uncle Giovanni, who in that year became **Pope Leo X**. The Medici, original masters of nepotism, had been planning this for years. Back in the 1470s, Lorenzo il Magnifico realized that the surest way of maintaining the family fortunes would be to get a Medici on the papal throne. He had little Giovanni ordained at the age of eight, purchased him a cardinal's hat at 13, and used bribery and diplomacy to help him accumulate dozens of benefices all over France and Italy. For his easy-going civility (as exemplified in his famous quote: 'God has given us the papacy so let us enjoy it'), and his patronage of scholars and artists, Leo became one of the best-remembered Renaissance popes. On the other side of the coin was his criminal mismanagement of the Church. Upper-class Florentines descended on Rome like a plague of locusts, occupying all the important sinecures and rapidly emptying the papal treasury. Their rapacity, plus the tremendous expenses involved in building the new St Peter's, caused Leo to step up the sale of indulgences all over Europe – disgusting reformers like Luther and greatly hastening the onset of the Reformation.

Back in Florence, Lorenzo Duke of Urbino's successor Giulio, bastard son of Lorenzo il Magnifico's murdered brother Giuliano, was little more than a puppet; Leo found enough time between banquets to manage the city's affairs. Giulio himself became pope in 1523, as **Clement VII**, thanks to the new financial interdependence between Florence and Rome, and now the Medici presence in Florence was reduced to two more unattractive young bastards, Ippolito and Alessandro, under the guardianship of Cardinal Silvio Passerini. Clement attempted to run the city from Rome as Leo had done, but high taxes and the lack of a strong hand made the new Medici regime increasingly precarious; its end followed after the sack of Rome in 1527. With Clement a prisoner in the Vatican and unable to intervene, a delegation of Florentine notables informed Cardinal Passerini and the Medicis that it was time to go. For the third time in less than a century, Florence had succeeded in getting rid of the Medici.

The new republic, though initiated by the disillusioned wealthy classes, soon found radical Savonarolan democrats gaining the upper hand. The Grand Council met and extended the franchise to include most of the citizens. Vanities were cursed again, books were banned and carnival parades forbidden; the Council officially pronounced

Jesus Christ 'King of the Florentines', just as it had done in the heyday of the Savonarolan camp meetings. In an intense atmosphere of republican virtue and pious crusade, Florence rushed headlong into the apocalyptic climax of its history. This time it did not take the Medici long to recover. In order to get Florence back, the witless Clement became allied to his former enemy, **Emperor Charles V**, a sordid deal that would eventually betray all Italy to Spanish control. Imperial troops were to help subdue Florence, and Clement's illegitimate son Alessandro was to wed Charles' illegitimate daughter. Charles' troops put Florence under siege in December 1529. The city had few resources for the struggle, and no friends, but a heroic resistance kept the imperialists at bay all through the winter and spring. Citizens gave up their gold and silver to be minted into the republic's last coins. The councillors debated seizing little Catherine de' Medici, future Queen of France, but then a prisoner of the republic, and dangling her from the walls to give the enemy a good target. Few artists were left in Florence, but Michelangelo stayed to help with his city's fortifications (by night he was working on the Medici tombs in San Lorenzo; both sides gave him safe passage when he wanted to leave Florence).

In August of 1530, the Florentines' skilful commander, Francesco Ferruccio, was killed in a skirmish near Pistoia; at about the same time the republic realized that its mercenary captain within the walls, Malatesta Baglioni, had sold them out to the pope and emperor. When they tried to arrest him, Baglioni only laughed, and directed his men to turn their artillery on the city. The inevitable capitulation came on 12 August; after almost 400 years, the Florentine republic had breathed its last.

At first, this third Medici return seemed to be just another dreary round of history repeating itself. Again, a packed *parlamento* gutted the constitution and legitimized the Medici takeover. Again the family and its minions combed the city, taking back every penny's worth of property that had been confiscated from them. This time, however, was to be different. Florence had gone from being a large fish in a small Italian pond to a minuscule but hindersome nuisance in the pan-European world of papal and imperial politics. Charles V didn't much like republics, or disorderly politicking, or indeed anyone who might conceivably say no to him. The orders came down from the emperor in Brussels; it was to be Medici for ever.

Cosimo I: the Medici as Grand Dukes

At first little was changed; the shell of the republican constitution was maintained, but with the 20-year-old illegitimate **Alessandro** as 'Duke of the Florentine Republic'; the harsh reality was under construction above the city's west end – the Fortezza da Basso, with its Spanish garrison, demanded by Charles V as insurance that Florence would never again be able to assert its independence. If any further symbolism was necessary, Alessandro ordered the great bell to be removed from the tower of the Palazzo Vecchio – the bell that had always summoned the citizens to political assemblies and the mustering of the army. In 1537, Alessandro was treacherously murdered by his jealous cousin Lorenzaccio de' Medici. With no legitimate heirs in the direct line Florence was in danger of falling under direct imperial rule, as had happened to Milan two years earlier, upon the extinction of the Sforza dukes. The assassination was kept secret while the Medici and the diplomats angled for a solution. The only reasonable choice turned out to be 18-year-old **Cosimo de' Medici**, heir of the family's cadet branch. This son of a famous mercenary commander, Giovanni of the Black Bands, had grown up on a farm; both the elder statesmen of the family and the imperial representatives thought they would easily be able to manipulate him.

It soon became clear that they had picked the wrong boy. Right from the start, young Cosimo had a surprisingly complete idea of how he meant to rule Florence, and also the will and strength of personality to see his commands carried out. No one ever admitted liking him; his puritanical court dismayed even the old partisans of Savonarola, and Florentines enjoyed grumbling over his high taxes, going to support 'colonels, spies, Spaniards, and women to serve Madame' (his Spanish consort Eleanor of Toledo). More surprising, when bowing and scraping Italians were everywhere else losing their liberty, Cosimo held his own against both pope and Spaniard. To back up his growing independence, Cosimo put his domains on an almost permanent war footing. New fortresses were built, a big fleet begun, and a paid standing army took the place of mercenaries and citizen levies. The skeleton of the old republic was revamped into a modern, bureaucratic state, governed scientifically and rationally as any in Europe. Early in his reign Cosimo defeated the last-ditch effort of the republican exiles, unreconstructed oligarchs led by the banker Filippo Strozzi, at the **Battle of Montemurlo**, the last threat ever to Medici rule. Cosimo's masterstroke came in 1557, when with the help of an Imperial army he took the entire Republic of Siena. Now the Medicis controlled roughly the boundaries of modern Tuscany; Cosimo was able to cap off his reign in 1569 by purchasing the title of Grand Duke of Tuscany.

Knick-knacks and Tedium: the Later Medici

For all Cosimo's efforts, Florence was entering a very evident decline. Banking and trade did well throughout the late 16th century, a prosperous time for almost all of Italy, but there were few opportunities for growth. More than ever, wealth was going into land, palaces and government bonds; the tradition of mercantile venture was becoming a thing of the past. For culture and art, Cosimo's reign turned out to be a disaster. It wasn't what he intended; indeed the Duke brought to the field his accustomed energy and compulsion to improve and organize. Academies were founded, and research underwritten. Cosimo's emphasis on art as political propaganda helped change the Florentine artist from a guild artisan to a flouncing courtier, ready to roll over at his master's command. The city had as great an influence in its age of decay as in its age of greatness. The cute, well-educated Florentine pranced across Europe, praised as the paragon of culture and refinement. Even in England – though that honest nation soon found him out:

A little Apish hatte, couched fast to the Pate, like an Oyster,
French Camarick Ruffes, deepe with a witnesse, starched to the purpose,
Delicate in speach, queynte in arraye: conceited in all poyntes:
In Courtyly guyles, a passing singular odde man...
                        Mirror of Tuscanism, Gabriel Harvey, 1580

Michelangelo, despite frequent entreaties, always refused to work for Cosimo. Most of the other talented Florentines eventually left for Rome or further afield, leaving lapdogs like **Giorgio Vasari** to carry on the grand traditions of Florentine art. Vasari, with help from such artists as Ammannati and Bandinelli, transformed much of the city – especially the interiors of its churches and public buildings. Florence began to fill up with equestrian statues of Medici, pageants and plaster triumphal arches displaying the triumphs of the Medici, sculptural allegories (like Cellini's *Perseus*) reminding us of the inevitability of the Medici and, best of all, portraits of semi-divine Medici floating in the clouds with little Cupids and Virtues. It was all the same to Cosimo and his successors, whose personal tastes tended more to engraved jewels, exotic taxidermy and sculptures made of seashells. But it helped to hasten the extinction of Florentine culture. Cosimo grew ill, abdicating most responsibility to his son **Francesco** from 1564 to his death 10 years later. Francesco, the genuine oddball among the Medici, was a moody, melancholic sort who cared little for government, preferring to lock himself up in the family palaces to pursue his passion for alchemy, as well as occasional researches into such subjects as perpetual motion and poisons – he received consignments of crates of scorpions every now and then. Despite his lack of interest, Francesco was a capable ruler, best known for his founding of Livorno.

Later Medici followed the general course established by other great families, such as the Habsburgs and Bourbons – each one was worse than the last. Francesco's death in 1587 gave the throne to his brother, **Ferdinando I**, founder of the Medici Chapels at San Lorenzo and another indefatigable collector of bric-a-brac. Next came **Cosimo II** (1609–21), a sickly nonentity who eventually succumbed to tuberculosis, and **Ferdinando II** (1621–70), whose long and uneventful reign oversaw the impoverishment of Florence and most of Tuscany. For this the Medici do not deserve much blame. A long string of bad harvests, beginning in the 1590s, plagues that recurred with terrible frequency as late as the 1630s, and general trade patterns that redistributed wealth and power from the Mediterranean to northern Europe, all set the stage for the collapse of the Florentine economy. The fatal blow came in the 1630s, when the long-deteriorating wool trade collapsed with sudden finality. Banking was going too, partly a victim of the age's continuing inflation, partly of high taxes and lack of worthwhile investments. Florence, by the mid-century, found itself with no prospects at all, a pensioner city drawing a barely respectable income from its glorious past.

With **Cosimo III** (1670–1723), the line of the Medici crossed over into the ridiculous. A religious crank and anti-Semite, this Cosimo temporarily wiped out free thought in the universities, allowed Tuscany to fill up with nuns and Jesuits, and decreed fantastical laws like the one that forbade any man to enter a house where an unmarried woman lived. To support his lavish court and pay the big tributes demanded by Spain and Austria (something earlier Medici would have scorned) Cosimo taxed what was left of the Florentine economy into an early grave. His heir **Gian Gastone** (1723–37), was an obese drunkard, senile and slobbering at the age of 50. He had to be carried up and down stairs on the rare occasions that he got out of bed (mainly to disprove rumours that he was dead); on the one occasion he appeared in public, the chronicles report him vomiting repeatedly out of the carriage window.

As a footnote on the Medici there is Gian Gastone's perfectly sensible sister, **Anna Maria Ludovica**. As the very last surviving Medici, it fell to her to dispose of the family's vast wealth and hoards of art. When she died, in 1743, her will revealed that the whole bundle was to become the property of the future rulers of Tuscany – whoever they should be – with the provision that not one bit of it should ever, ever, be moved outside Florence. Without her, the great collections of the Uffizi and the Bargello might long ago have been packed away to Vienna or to Paris.

Post-Medici Florence

When Gian Gastone died in 1737, Tuscany's fate had already been decided by the powers of Europe. The Grand Duchy would fall to **Francis Stephen**, Duke of Lorraine and husband-to-be of the Austrian Empress Maria Theresa; his troops had been installed in the Fortezza da Basso a year before. For most of the next century, Florence slumbered under benign Austrian rule. Already the first Grand Tourists were arriving on their way to Rome and Naples, sons of the Enlightenment like Goethe, who didn't stop because 'nothing in Florence could interest him', or relics like the Pretender Charles Edward Stuart, 'Bonnie Prince Charlie', who stayed two years. Napoleon's men occupied the city for most of two decades without making much impression.

After the Napoleonic Wars, the Habsburg restoration brought back the Lorraine dynasty. From 1824 to 1859, Florence and Tuscany were ruled by **Leopold II**, that most likeable of all Grand Dukes. This was when Florence first became popular among the northern Europeans and the time when the Brownings, Dostoevsky, Leigh Hunt and dozens of other artists and writers took up residence, rediscovering the glories of the city and of the early Renaissance. Grand Duke Leopold was decent enough to let himself be overthrown in 1859, during the tumults of the Risorgimento. In 1865, when only the Papal State remained to be incorporated into the Kingdom of Italy, Florence briefly became the new nation's capital. King Vittorio Emanuele moved into the Pitti Palace, and the Italian Parliament met in the great hall of the Palazzo Vecchio.

It was not meant to last. When the Italian troops entered Rome in 1870, Florence's brief hour as a major capital was at an end, but it had given the staid old city a jolt towards the modern world. In an unusual flurry of exertion, Florence finally threw up a façade for its cathedral, and levelled the picturesque though squalid market area and Jewish ghetto to build the dolorous Piazza della Repubblica. Fortunately, the city regained its senses before too much damage was done. Throughout the 20th century, Florence's role as a museum city was confirmed with each passing year. The Second World War allowed the city to resume briefly its ancient delight in black-and-white political epic. In 1944–5, Florence offered some of the most outrageous spectacles of Fascist fanaticism, and also some of the most courageous stories of the Resistance – including that of the German consul Gerhard Wolf, who used his position to protect Florentines from the Nazi terror, often at great personal risk.

In August 1944, the Allied armies were poised to advance through northern Tuscany. For the Germans, the Arno made a convenient defensive line, requiring that all the bridges of Florence be demolished. They all were, except for the Ponte Vecchio, saved in a last-minute deal, though the buildings on either side of it were destroyed to provide piles of rubble around the bridge approaches. After the war, all were repaired; the city had the Ponte della Trínita rebuilt stone by stone exactly as it was. No sooner was the war damage redeemed, however, than a greater disaster attacked Florence's heritage. The flood of 1966, when water reached 21ft, did more damage than Nazis or Napoleons; an international effort was raised to preserve and restore the city's art and monuments. Since then the Arno has been deepened under the Ponte Vecchio and 18ft earthen walls have been erected around Ponte Amerigo Vespucci; video screens and computers monitor every fluctuation in the water level. Should another flood occur, Florence will have time to protect herself. Far more insoluble is terrorism, which touched the city in May 1993, when a bomb destroyed the Gregoriophilus library opposite the Uffizi, damaged the Vasari Corridor and killed a family. Florence, shocked by this intrusion from the outside world into its holy of holies, repaired most of the damage in record time with funds raised by a national subscription.

Careful planning has saved the best of Florence's immediate countryside from post-war suburbanization – but much of the other territory around the city has been coated by a suburban sprawl that is not exactly attractive. A new airport extension is being built, which the Florentines hope will help make up some of the economic ground they've lost to Milan, and a whole new satellite city is planned – a new Florence ('Firenze Nuova'), nothing less than 'the greatest urban planning operation of the century,' they say, with some of the old audacity of Brunelleschi. The buildings on the marshland (northwest of the city) have been demolished, the land flattened and the project for a new city to include housing, shops, leisure facilities, a new law court and a new Fiat factory (Fiat along with the insurance group, La Fondiaria, are the sponsors) is already under way, with some apartment blocks nearing completion. The law court building was actually started in 1999. Work is progressing and the main structure is up, but it will be a while before it's finished.

Meanwhile Florence works hard to preserve what it already has. Although new measures to control the city's bugbear – the traffic problems of a city of 500,000 that receives seven million visitors a year – have been enacted to protect the historic centre, pollution from nearby industry continues to eat away at monuments; Donatello's statue of St Mark at Orsanmichele, perfectly intact 50 years ago, is now a mutilated leper. Private companies, banks and even individuals finance 90 per cent of the art restoration in Florence, with techniques invented by the city's innovative Institute of Restoration. Increasingly, copies are made to replace original works. Naturally, half the city is for them, and the other half against.

Piazza del Duomo

Tour groups circle around the three great spiritual monuments of medieval Florence like sharks around their prey. Postcard vendors prey, and sax players play to a human carnival from a hundred nations that mills about the cathedral good-naturedly while ambulances of a medieval brotherhood dedicated to first aid stand at the ready in case anyone swoons from ecstasy or art-glut.

The Baptistry

Open Mon–Sat 12–7, Sun 8.30–2; adm.

To begin to understand what magic made the Renaissance first bloom by the Arno, look here; this ancient, mysterious building is the egg from which Florence's golden age was hatched. By the quattrocento, Florentines firmly believed their baptistry was originally a Roman temple to Mars, a touchstone linking them to a legendary past. Scholarship sets its date of construction between the 6th and 9th centuries, in the darkest Dark Ages, which makes it even more remarkable; it may as well have dropped from heaven. Its distinctive dark green and white marble facing, the tidily classical pattern of arches and rectangles that deceived Brunelleschi and Alberti, was probably added around the 11th century. The masters who built it remain unknown, but their strikingly original exercise in geometry provided the model for all of Florence's great church façades. When it was new, there was nothing remotely like it in Europe; to visitors from outside the city it must have seemed almost miraculous.

Every 21 March, New Year's Day on the old Florentine calendar, all the children that had been born over the last 12 months would be brought here for a great communal baptism, a habit that helped make the baptistry not merely a religious monument but a civic symbol, in fact the oldest and fondest symbol of the republic. As such the Florentines never tired of embellishing it. Under the octagonal cupola, the glittering 13th- and 14th-century gold-ground mosaics show a strong Byzantine influence, perhaps laid by mosaicists from Venice. The decoration is divided into concentric strips: over the apse, dominated by a 28ft figure of Christ, is a *Last Judgement*, while the other bands, from the inside out, portray the *Hierarchy of Heaven*, *Story of Genesis*, *Life of Joseph*, *Life of Christ* and the *Life of St John the Baptist*, the last band believed to be the work of Cimabue. The equally beautiful mosaics over the altar and in the vault are the earliest, signed by a monk named Iacopo in the early 1200s. New lighting installed in 1999 has vastly improved visitors' view of the ceiling.

To match the mosaics, there is an intricate tessellated marble floor, decorated with signs of the Zodiac; the octagonal space in the centre was formerly occupied by the huge font. The green and white patterned walls of the interior are remarkable, combining influences from the ancient world and modern inspiration for something new, the perfect source that architects of the Middle Ages and Renaissance would strive to match. Much of the best design work is in the **galleries**, partially visible from the floor. The baptistry is hardly cluttered; besides a 13th-century Pisan-style baptismal font, only the **Tomb of Anti-Pope John XXIII** by Donatello and Michelozzo stands out. This funerary monument, with marble draperies softening its classical lines, is one of the prototypes of the Early Renaissance. But how did Anti-Pope John, deposed by the Council of Constance in 1415, earn the privilege of a tomb here? Why, it was thanks to him that Giovanni di Bicci de' Medici made a fortune as head banker to the Curia.

The Gates of Paradise

Historians used to pinpoint the beginning of the 'Renaissance' as the year 1401, when the merchants' guild, the Arte di Calimala, sponsored a competition for the

Highlights of Florence

Florence's museums, palaces and churches contain more good art than perhaps any city in Europe, and to see it all without hardship to your eyes, feet and sensibilities would take at least three weeks. If you have only a few days to spend, the highlights will easily take up all of your time – the **Cathedral** and **Baptistry**, the paintings in the **Uffizi** (preferably not all in the same day) and the sculptures in the **Bargello**, which is more worthy of your brief time than the **Accademia**, where the rubbernecks pile in to see Michelangelo's *David*. Stop in for a look at the eccentric **Orsanmichele**, and see the Arno from the **Ponte Vecchio**, taking in some of the oldest streets in the city.

If your heart leans towards the graceful lyricism of the 1400s, don't miss the **Cathedral Museum** and the Fra Angelicos in **San Marco**; if the lush virtuosity of the 1500s is your cup of tea, visit the Pitti Palace's Galleria Palatina. Two churches on the edges of the centre, **Santa Maria Novella** and **Santa Croce**, are galleries in themselves; **Santa Maria del Carmine** has the restored frescoes of Masaccio. Devotees of the Michelangelo cult won't want to miss the Medici Chapels and library at **San Lorenzo**. Or head for the oasis of the **Boboli Gardens**. Finally, climb up to **San Miniato**, for the beautiful medieval church and enchanting view over the city.

Florence's 'secondary' sights are just as interesting. You could spend a day walking around old **Fiesole**, or 15 minutes looking at Gozzoli's charming fresco in the **Palazzo Medici-Riccardi**. The **Palazzo Vecchio** has more, but less charming, Medici frescoes. You can see how a wealthy medieval Tuscan merchant lived at the **Palazzo Davanzati** (at the time of writing it is closed for restoration), while the **Museum of the History of Science** will tell you about the scientific side of the Florentine Renaissance; **Santa Trínita**, **Santo Spirito**, **Ognissanti** and the **Annunziata** all contain famous works from the Renaissance. The **Casa Buonarroti** has some early sculptures of Michelangelo; the **Archaeology Museum** has even earlier ones by the Etruscans, Greeks and Egyptians; the Pitti Palace's **Museo degli Argenti** overflows with Medicean jewellery and trinkets. Take a bus or car out to Lorenzo il Magnifico's villa at **Poggio a Caiano**, or to the Medicis' other garden villas: **La Petraia** and **Castello**, or Villa Demidoff at **Pratolino**.

There are two museums with 19th- and 20th-century collections to bring you back to the present: the recently expanded **Galleria d'Arte Moderna** in the Pitti Palace, and the **Collezione della Ragione**. There are two museums founded by Englishmen: the **Horne Museum** with Renaissance art, and the eccentric **Stibbert Museum** with everything but the kitchen sink. Strangest of all are the museums in **La Specola**, featuring stuffed animals and wax figures.

Most of the important museums, excluding the Palazzo Vecchio, are state-run and can be pre-booked. Call **t** 055 294883.

baptistry's north doors. The **South Doors** (the main entrance) had already been completed by Andrea Pisano in 1330 in the style of the day. Their 28 panels in quatrefoil frames depict scenes from the life of St John the Baptist and the seven Cardinal and Theological Virtues – formal and elegant works in the best Gothic manner.

The celebrated competition of 1401 – perhaps the first ever held in the annals of art – pitted the seven greatest sculptors of the day against one another. Judgement was based on trial panels of the Sacrifice of Isaac, and in a dead heat at the end of the day were the two by Brunelleschi and Lorenzo Ghiberti, now displayed in the Bargello. Ghiberti's more classical-style figures were eventually judged the better, and it was a serendipitous choice; he devoted nearly the rest of his life to creating the most beautiful bronze doors in the world while Brunelleschi, disgusted by his defeat, went on to build the most perfect dome. Ghiberti's first efforts, the **North Doors** (1403–24), are contained, like Pisano's, in 28 quatrefoil frames. In their scenes on the Life of Christ, the Evangelists, and the Doctors of the Church, you can trace Ghiberti's progress over the 20 years he worked in the increased depth of his compositions, not only visually but dramatically; classical backgrounds begin to fill the frames, ready to break out of their Gothic confines. Ghiberti also designed the floral frame of the doors; the three statues, of John the Baptist, the Levite and the Pharisee, by Francesco Rustici, were based on a design by Leonardo da Vinci and added in 1511.

Ghiberti's work pleased the Arte di Calimala, and they set him loose on another pair of portals, the **East Doors** (1425–52), his masterpiece and one of the most awesome achievements of the age. Here Ghiberti (perhaps under the guidance of Donatello) dispensed with the small Gothic frames and instead cast 10 large panels that depict the Old Testament in Renaissance high gear, reinterpreting the forms of antiquity with a depth and drama that have never been surpassed. Michelangelo declared them 'worthy to be the Gates of Paradise'. The doors (they're actually copies – eight of the original panels, restored after flood damage, are on display in the Museo dell' Opera del Duomo) have been cleaned and stand in gleaming contrast to the others. In 1996 copies of Andrea Sansovino's marble statues of Christ and John the Baptist (1502) and an 18th-century angel were installed over the doors. The originals had begun to fall to bits in 1974; they too are now in the Museo dell' Opera.

Ghiberti wasn't exactly slow to toot his own horn; according to himself, he planned and designed the Renaissance on his own. His unabashedly conceited *Commentarii* were the first attempt at art history and autobiography by an artist, and a work as revolutionary as his doors in its presentation of the creative God-like powers of the artist. In a typical exhibition of Florentine pride he also put busts of his friends among the prophets and sibyls that adorn the frames of the East Doors. Near the centre, the balding figure with arched eyebrows and a little smile is Ghiberti himself.

The Duomo

Open Mon–Wed and Fri 10–5, Thurs 10–3.30, Sat 10–4.45, Sun 1.30–4.45.

For all its importance and prosperity, Florence was one of the last cities to plan a great cathedral. Work began in the 1290s, with the sculptor Arnolfo di Cambio in charge, and from the beginning the Florentines attempted to make up for their delay with sheer audacity. 'It will be so magnificent in size and beauty,' said a decree of 1296, 'as to surpass anything built by the Greeks and Romans.' In response, Arnolfo planned what in its day was the largest church in Catholicism; he confidently laid the foundations for an enormous octagonal crossing 146ft in diameter, then died before working out a way to cover it, leaving behind the job of designing the biggest dome in the world.

Beyond its presumptuous size, the cathedral of Santa Maria del Fiore shows little interest in contemporary innovations and styles; a visitor from France or England in the 1400s would certainly have found it somewhat drab and architecturally primitive. Visitors today often circle confusedly around its grimy, ponderous bulk. Instead of the striped bravura of Siena or the elegant colonnades of Pisa, they behold an astonishingly eccentric green, white and red pattern of marble rectangles and flowers – like Victorian wallpaper, or as one critic expressed it, 'a cathedral wearing pyjamas'. In the sun, the cathedral under its sublime dome sports festively above the dullish dun and ochre sea of Florence; in dismal weather it sprawls morosely across its piazza like a beached whale tarted up with a lace doily front.

The fondly foolish **façade** cannot be blamed on Arnolfo. His original design, only one-quarter completed, was taken down in a late 16th-century Medici rebuilding programme that never got off the ground. The Duomo turned a blank face to the world until the present neo-Gothic extravaganza was added in 1888. Walk around to the north side to see what many consider a more fitting door, the **Porta della Mandorla** crowned with an Assumption of the Virgin in an almond-shaped frame (hence 'Mandorla'), made by Nanni di Banco in 1420.

Brunelleschi's Dome

Open Mon–Fri 8.30–7, Sat 8.30–5.40; adm.

Brunelleschi's dome, more than any landmark, makes Florence Florence. Many have noted how the dome repeats the rhythm of the surrounding hills, echoing them with its height and beauty; from those city streets fortunate enough to have a clear view, it rises among the clouds with all the confident mastery, proportions, and perfect form that characterize the highest aspirations of the Renaissance. But if it seems miraculous, it certainly isn't divine; unlike the dome of the Hagia Sophia, suspended from heaven by a golden chain, Florence's was made by man.

Losing the competition for the baptistry doors was a bitter disappointment to Filippo Brunelleschi. His reaction was typically Florentine: not content with being the second-best sculptor, he turned his talents to a field where he thought no one could beat him, launching himself into a study of architecture and engineering, visiting Rome and probably Ravenna to snatch secrets from the ancients. When proposals were solicited for the cathedral's dome in 1418, he was ready with a brilliant *tour de force*. Not only would he build the biggest, most beautiful dome of the time, but he would do it without any expensive supports while work was in progress, making use of a cantilevered system of bricks that could support itself while it ascended.

Brunelleschi studied, then surpassed the technique of the ancients. To the Florentines, who could have invented the slogan 'form follows function' for their own tastes in building, it must have come as a revelation: the most logical way of covering the space was a work of perfect beauty. Brunelleschi's dome put a crown on the achievements of Florence. After 500 years it is still the city's pride and symbol.

The best way to appreciate Brunelleschi's genius is by touring inside the two concentric shells of the dome (*see* over), but before entering, note the eight marble ribs that define its octagonal shape; hidden inside are the three huge stone chains that bind them together. Work on the balcony around the base of the dome, designed by Giuliano da Sangallo, was halted in 1515 after Michelangelo commented that it resembled a cricket's cage. As for the lantern, the Florentines were famous for their fondness and admiration for Doubting Thomas, and here they showed why. Even though they marvelled at the dome, they still doubted that Brunelleschi could construct a proper lantern, and forced him to submit to yet another competition. He died before it was begun, and it was completed to his design by Michelozzo.

The Interior

After the façade, the austerity of the Duomo interior is startling. There is plenty of room – contemporary writers mention 10,000 souls packed inside to hear Savonarola's sermons. But, the Duomo hardly seems a religious building – more a *Florentine* building, with simple arches and counterpoint of grey stone and white plaster, full of old familiar Florentine things. Near the entrance, on the right-hand side, are busts of Brunelleschi and Giotto. On the left wall, posed inconspicuously, are the two most conspicuous monuments to private individuals ever erected by the Florentine Republic. The one on the right, is to **Sir John Hawkwood**, the English *condottiere* whose name the Italians mangled to Giovanni Acuto, a commander who served Florence for many years and is perhaps best known to English speakers as the hero of *The White Company* by Sir Arthur Conan Doyle. Hawkwood had the Florentines' promise to build him an equestrian statue after his death; it was a typical Florentine trick to pinch pennies and cheat a dead man, but they hired the greatest master of perspective, Paolo Uccello, to make a fresco that looked like a statue (1436). Twenty years later, they pulled the same trick again, commissioning Andrea del Castagno to paint the non-existent equestrian statue of another *condottiere*, Niccolò da Tolentino. A little further down, Florence commemorates its own secular scripture with Michelino's well-known fresco of Dante, a vision of the poet and his *Paradiso* outside the walls of Florence. Two singular icons of Florence's fascination with science stand at opposite ends of the building: behind the west front, a bizarre clock painted by Uccello, and in the pavement of the left apse, a gnomon fixed by the astronomer Toscanelli in 1475. A beam of sunlight strikes it every year at the summer solstice.

For building the great dome, Brunelleschi was accorded a special honour – he is one of the few Florentines to be buried in the cathedral. His tomb may be seen in the **Excavations of Santa Reparata** (*the stairway descending on the right of the nave; open Mon–Sat 10–5; adm*). Arnolfo di Cambio's cathedral was constructed on the ruins of the ancient church of Santa Reparata, which lay forgotten until 1965. Excavations have revealed not only the palaeo-Christian church and its several reconstructions, but also the remains of its Roman predecessor – a rather confusing muddle of walls that have been tidied up in an ambience that resembles an archaeological shopping centre. A coloured model helps explain what is what, and glass cases display items found in the dig, including the spurs of Giovanni de' Medici, who was buried here in 1351. In the ancient crypt of Santa Reparata are 13th-century tomb slabs, and in another section there's a fine pre-Romanesque mosaic pavement.

There is surprisingly little religious art – the Florentines for reasons of their own have carted most of it off into the Cathedral Museum (*see* opposite). Under the dome are the entrances to the two sacristies, with terracotta lunettes over the doors by Luca della Robbia; the scene of the Resurrection over the north sacristy is one of his earliest and best works. He also did the bronze doors beneath it, with tiny portraits on the handles of Lorenzo il Magnifico and his brother Giuliano de' Medici, targets of the Pazzi conspiracy in 1478. In the middle apse, there is a beautiful bronze urn by Ghiberti containing relics of the Florentine St Zenobius. The only conventional religious decorations are the frescoes some 200ft up in the dome, mostly by Vasari. As you stand squinting at them, try not to think that the cupola weighs around 25,000 tons.

A door on the left aisle near the Dante fresco leads up into the **dome** (*open Mon–Fri 8.30–7 and Sat 8.30–5.40; adm*). The complicated network of stairs and walks between the inner and outer domes (not too difficult, if occasionally claustrophobic and vertiginous) was designed by Brunelleschi, and offers an insight on how thoroughly the architect thought out the problems of the dome's construction, even inserting hooks to hold up scaffolding for future cleaning or repairs; Brunelleschi installed restaurants to save workers the trouble of descending for meals. There is also no better place to get an idea of the dome's scale; the walls of the inner dome are 13ft thick, and those of the outer dome 6ft. These give the dome enough strength and support to preclude the need for further buttressing.

From the gallery of the dome you can get a good look at the lovely **stained glass** by Uccello, Donatello, Ghiberti and Castagno, in the seven circular windows, or *occhi*, made during the construction of the dome, which are being restored one by one. Further up, the views through the small windows offer tantalizing hints of the breathtaking panorama from the marble lantern at the top. The bronze ball at the very top was added by Verrocchio, and can hold almost a dozen people when open.

Giotto's Campanile

The dome steals the show, putting one of Italy's most beautiful bell towers in the shade both figuratively and literally. The dome's great size – 366ft to the bronze ball – makes the campanile look small, though 280ft is not exactly tiny. Giotto was made director of the cathedral works in 1334, and his basic design was completed after his death (1337) by Andrea Pisano and Francesco Talenti. It is difficult to say whether they were entirely faithful to the plan. Giotto was an artist, not an engineer. After he died, his successors realized the thing, then only 40ft high, was about to tumble over, a problem they overcame by doubling the thickness of the walls.

Besides its lovely form, the green, pink and white campanile's major fame rests with Pisano and Talenti's **sculptural reliefs** – a veritable encyclopaedia of the medieval world view with prophets, saints and sibyls, allegories of the planets, virtues and sacraments, the liberal arts and industries (the artist's craft is fittingly symbolized by a winged figure of Daedalus). All of these are copies of the originals now in the Cathedral Museum. If you can take another 400 steps or so, the **terrace** on top (*open daily 8.30–7.30; adm*) offers a slightly different view of Florence and of the cathedral itself.

Loggia del Bigallo

The most striking secular building on the Piazza del Duomo is the Loggia del Bigallo, south of the baptistry near the beginning of Via de' Calzaiuoli. This 14th-century porch was built for one of Florence's great charitable confraternities, the Misericordia which still has its headquarters across the street and operates the ambulances parked in front; in the 13th and 14th centuries members courageously nursed and buried victims of the plague. The Loggia itself originally served as a lost and found office for children; if unclaimed after three days they were sent to foster homes.

East of the Loggia del Bigallo is a stone bench labelled the 'Sasso di Dante' – **Dante's Stone** – where the poet would sit and take the air, observing his fellow citizens and watching the construction of the cathedral.

Museo dell'Opera del Duomo

Open Mon–Sat 9–7.30, Sun 9–1.40; adm.

The Cathedral Museum (Piazza del Duomo 9, near the central apse) is one of Florence's finest, and houses both relics from the construction of the cathedral and the masterpieces that once adorned it. It reopened in early 2000 after major restructuring to improve the layout and make it more visitor-friendly: there is now full disabled access, better information, a more logical layout, in a more or less chronological order, and greatly increased floor space. The courtyard has been covered by a glass roof and turned into an exhibition room; and there are long-term plans to incorporate a neighbouring 18th-century theatre into the museum, which has been closed for several centuries and was most recently used as a garage. Restoration work should be finished by 2007 when the museum will have doubled in size.

The entrance leads into the new ticket hall – pristine in marble and stone, the same materials used in the Duomo's construction – and past the bookshop. Just after the entrance are several fragments of Roman reliefs, then two anterooms which contain restored statues or bits of statues that once adorned the façade of the Duomo.

The first hall is devoted to the cathedral's sculptor-architect Arnolfo di Cambio and contains the statues he made to adorn it: the unusual Madonna with the glass eyes, Florence's old patron saints, Reparata and Zenobius, and nasty old Boniface VIII, who sits stiffly on his throne like an Egyptian god. There are the four Evangelists, including a St John by Donatello, and a small collection of ancient works – Roman sarcophagi and an Etruscan cippus carved with dancers. Note the 16th-century 'Libretto', a fold-out display case of saintly odds and ends. The Florentines were never enthusiastic about the worship of relics, and long ago they shipped San Girolamo's jawbone, John the Baptist's index finger and St Philip's arm across the street to this museum.

A nearby room contains a collection of altarpieces, triptyches and paintings of saints including Giovanni del Biondo's *Saint Sebastian*. Also here are a series of marble relief panels by Baccio Bandinelli from the altarpiece of the cathedral. A small room next to this contains a section (several fragments pieced together) of the door known as the 'Porta della Mandorla' on the north side of the Duomo. This is an intricately carved marble relief, including a small figure of Hercules with his stick, significant in that it was the first representation of the adult male nude and a taste of things to come, more of a statue than a relief. Also in this room are two statues known as *The Profetini*, which once stood over the door and are attributed to the young Donatello.

On the landing of the stairs, stands the *Pietà* that Michelangelo intended for his own tomb stands on the landing. The artist, increasingly cantankerous in his old age, became exasperated with this complex work and took a hammer to Christ's arm – the first known instance of an artist vandalizing his own creation. His assistant repaired the damage and finished part of the figures of Christ and Mary Magdalene. According to Vasari, the hooded figure of Nicodemus is a self-portrait.

Upstairs, the first room is dominated by the two **Cantorie**, two marble choir balconies with exquisite bas-reliefs, made in the 1430s by Luca della Robbia and Donatello. Both rank among the Renaissance's greatest works. Della Robbia's delightful horde of children dancing, singing and playing instruments is a truly angelic choir, Apollonian in its calm and beauty. It is perhaps the most charming work ever to have been inspired by the forms of antiquity. Donatello's *putti*, by contrast, dance, or rather race, through their quattrocento decorative motifs with fiendish Dionysian frenzy. Grey and weathered prophets by Donatello and others stand along the white walls. These originally adorned the façade of the campanile. According to Vasari, while carving the most famous of these, *Habbakuk* (better known as *lo Zuccone*, or 'baldy'), Donatello would mutter under his breath 'Speak, damn you. Speak!' The next room contains the original panels on the Spiritual Progress of Man from Giotto's campanile, made by Andrea Pisano.

The first thing you see as you enter the last room is Donatello's statue *Mary Magdalene*, surely one of the most jarring figures ever sculpted, ravaged by her own piety and penance, her sunken eyes fixed on a point beyond this vale of tears. This room is dedicated to works removed from the baptistry, especially the lavish silver altar (14th–15th-century), made by Florentine goldsmiths, portraying scenes from the life of the Baptist. Antonio Pollaiuolo used the same subject to design the 27 needle-work panels that once were part of the priest's vestments. There are two 12th-century Byzantine mosaic miniature masterpieces, and a St Sebastian triptych by Giovanni del Biondo that may well be the record for arrows; the poor saint looks like a hedgehog.

A ramp leads into the new part of the museum from the room containing the panels from the campanile. Cases either side display the collection of pulleys and instruments used in the construction of the cathedral. At the bottom of the ramp on the left is Brunelleschi's death mask, facing a model of the lantern, which he was never to see. A window behind this model cleverly gives a close up view of the cupola itself, which is topped by that self-same lantern.

A series of rooms off a long corridor contain bits and pieces brought out of storage, including the four carved façades, artists' models for the design of the cricket's-cage pattern round the base of the cupola. The corridor leads into a room whose walls are filled with drawings of the Duomo from the 1875 competition to design the façade.

From here, a staircase leads down into the courtyard where eight of Ghiberti's panels from the *Gates of Paradise* are on display. The plan is still to reconstruct the doors and their cornice once the latter and the last two panels are restored. It will be placed in the new space next door to the museum by 2007.

Via de' Calzaiuoli and Piazza della Repubblica

Of all the streets that radiate from the Piazza del Duomo, most people almost intuitively turn down the straight, pedestrian-only Via de' Calzaiuoli, the Roman street that became the main thoroughfare of medieval Florence, linking the city's religious centre with the Piazza della Signoria. Widening of this 'Street of the Shoemakers' in the 1840s has destroyed much of its medieval character, and the only shoe shops to be seen are designer-label. Its fate seems benign, though, compared with what happened to the Mercato Vecchio, in the fit of post-Risorgimento 'progress' that converted it into the **Piazza della Repubblica**, a block to the right along Via Speziali.

On the map, it's easy to pick out the small rectangle of narrow, straight streets around Piazza della Repubblica; these remain unchanged from the little *castrum* of Roman days. At its centre, the old forum deteriorated through the Dark Ages into a shabby market square and the Jewish ghetto, a densely populated quarter known as the Mercato Vecchio, the epitome of the picturesque for 19th-century tourists but an eyesore for the movers and shakers of the new Italy, who tore it down. They erected a triumphal arch to themselves and proudly blazoned it with the inscription 'THE ANCIENT CITY CENTRE RESTORED TO NEW LIFE FROM THE SQUALOR OF CENTURIES'. The sad result, the Piazza della Repubblica, is one of the most ghastly squares in Italy, a brash intrusion of ponderous 19th-century buildings. Just the same, it is popular with locals and tourists alike, closed to traffic and full of outdoor cafés, something of an oasis among the narrow, stern streets of medieval Florence.

From Piazza della Repubblica the natural flow of street life will sweep you down to the **Mercato Nuovo**, the old Straw Market, bustling under a beautiful loggia built by Grand Duke Cosimo in the 1500s. Nowadays vendors hawk purses, stationery, toys, clothes, umbrellas and knick-knacks. In medieval times this was the merchants' exchange, where any merchant who committed the crime of bankruptcy was publicly spanked before being carted off to prison; in times of peace it sheltered Florence's battle-stained *carroccio*. Florentines often call the market the 'Porcellino' (piglet) after the large bronze boar erected in 1612. The current boar was put in place in 1999, a copy of a copy of the ancient statue in the Uffizi. The drool spilling from the side of its mouth reminds us that Florence is no splashy city of springs and fountains. Rub the piglet's snout, and supposedly destiny will one day bring you back to Florence. The pungent aroma of the tripe sandwiches sold nearby may give you second thoughts.

Orsanmichele

Open Mon–Fri 9–12 and 4–6, Sat and Sun 9–1 and 4–6. (However, closed most of the time due to lack of staff!) Open for concerts in the summer. No information is currently available about about when it will re-open.

There is a wonderfully eccentric church on Via de' Calzaiuoli that looks like no other in the world: Orsanmichele rises up in a tall, neat three-storey rectangle. It was built on the site of ancient San Michele ad Hortum (popularly reduced to 'Orsan-michele'), a 9th-century church located near a vegetable garden, which the *comune* destroyed in 1240 to erect a grain market; after a fire in 1337 the current market building (by Francesco Talenti and others) was erected, with a loggia on the ground floor and emergency storehouses on top where grain was kept against a siege.

The original market had a pilaster with a painting of the Virgin that became increasingly celebrated for performing miracles. The area around the Virgin became known as the Oratory, and when Talenti reconstructed the market, his intention was to combine both its secular and religious functions; each pilaster of the loggia was assigned to a guild to adorn with an image of its patron saint. In 1380, when the market was relocated, the entire ground floor was given over to the functions of the church, and Francesco Talenti's son Simone was given the task of closing in the arcades with lovely Gothic windows, later bricked in.

The church is most famous as a showcase of 15th-century Florentine sculpture; displaying the stylistic innovations through the decades. Each guild sought to outdo the others by commissioning the finest artists of the day to carve their patron saints and create elaborate canopied niches to hold them. The first statue to the left of the door is one of the oldest; Ghiberti's bronze *St John the Baptist*, erected in 1416 for the Arte di Calimala, was the first life-sized Renaissance statue cast in bronze. Continuing to the left on Via de' Lamberti you can compare it with Donatello's *St Mark*, patron of the linen dealers and used-cloth merchants. Finished in 1411, it is considered the first free-standing marble statue of the Renaissance.

The niches continue around Via dell'Arte della Lana, named after the Wool Merchants' Guild, the richest after that of the Bankers. Their headquarters, the **Palazzo dell' Arte della Lana**, is linked by an overhead arch with Orsanmichele; built in 1308, it was restored in 1905 in a William Morris style of medieval picturesque. The first statue on this façade of Orsanmichele is *St Eligio*, patron of smiths, by Nanni di Banco (1415), with a niche embellished with the guild's emblem (black pincers) and a bas-relief below showing one of this rather obscure saint's miracles – apparently he shod a horse by cutting off its hoof, shoeing it, then sticking it back on the leg. The other two statues on this street are bronzes by Ghiberti, the Wool Guild's *St Stephen* (1426) and the Exchange Guild's *St Matthew* (1422), the latter an especially fine work.

On the Via Orsanmichele façade stands a copy of Donatello's famous *St George* (the original now in the Bargello) done in 1417 for the Armourers' Guild, with a dramatic predella of the saint slaying the dragon, also by Donatello, that is one of the first known works making use of perspective; next are the Stonecutters' and Carpenters' Guild's *Four Crowned Saints* (1415, by Nanni di Banco), inspired by Roman statues. Nanni also contributed the Shoemakers' *St Philip* (1415), while the next figure, *St Peter*, is commonly attributed to Donatello (1413). Around the corner on Via Calzaiuoli stands the bronze *St Luke*, patron of the Judges and Notaries, by Giambologna, a work of 1602 in a 15th-century niche, and the *Doubting of St Thomas* by Andrea del Verrocchio (1484), made not for a guild but the Tribunal of Merchandise, who like St Thomas wanted to be certain before making a judgement. In the rondels above some of the niches are terracottas of the guilds' symbols by Luca della Robbia.

Orsanmichele's dark **interior** (*closed for restoration*) is ornate and cosy, with more of the air of a guildhall than a church. It makes a picturebook medieval setting for one of the masterpieces of the trecento: Andrea Orcagna's beautiful Gothic **Tabernacle** (*open 9–12 and 4–6*), a large, exquisite work in marble, bronze and coloured glass framing a contemporary painting of the Madonna (either by Bernardo Daddi or Orcagna himself), replacing the miraculous one, lost in a fire. The Tabernacle was commissioned by survivors of the 1348 Black Death. On the walls and pilasters are faded 14th-century frescoes of saints, placed as if members of the congregation; if you look at the pilasters on the left as you enter and along the right wall you can see the old chutes used to transfer grain.

Piazza della Signoria

Now that this big medieval piazza is car-free, it serves as a great corral for tourists, endlessly snapping pictures of the Palazzo Vecchio or strutting in circles like pigeons. In the old days it would be full of Florentines, the stage set for the tempestuous life of their republic. The public assemblies met here, and at times of danger the bells would ring and the piazza fill with citizen militias, assembling under the banners of the quarters and guilds. Savonarola held his Bonfire of Vanities here, and only a few years later the disenchanted Florentines ignited their Bonfire of Savonarola on the same spot. (You can see a painting of the event at San Marco.) Today the piazza is still the favoured spot for political rallies.

The three graceful arches of the **Loggia dei Lanzi** (at the time of writing, covered in scaffolding), next to the Palazzo Vecchio, were the reviewing stand for city officials during assemblies and celebrations. Florentines often call it the Loggia dell'Orcagna, after the architect who designed it in the 1370s. In its simple classicism the Loggia anticipates the architecture of Brunelleschi and all those who came after him. The city has made it an outdoor sculpture gallery, with some of the best known works in Florence: Cellini's triumphant *Perseus,* radiant after recent restoration, and Giambologna's *Rape of the Sabines*, other works by Giambologna, and a chorus of Roman-era Vestal Virgins along the back wall. Cosimo himself stands imperiously at the centre of the piazza, a bronze equestrian statue also by Giambologna.

All the statues in the piazza are dear to the Florentines for one reason or another. Some are fine works of art; others have only historical associations. Michelangelo's *David*, a copy of which stands in front of the palazzo near the spot the artist intended for it, was meant as a symbol of republican virtue and Florentine excellence. At the opposite extreme, Florentines are taught almost from birth to ridicule the **Neptune Fountain**, a pompous monstrosity with a giant marble figure of the god. The sculptor, Ammannati, thought he would upstage Michelangelo, though the result is derisively known to all Florence as Il Biancone ('Big Whitey'). Bandinelli's statue of *Hercules and Cacus* is almost as big and just as awful; according to Cellini, it looks like a 'sack of melons'.

Palazzo Vecchio

Open Mon–Wed and Fri–Sun 9–7, Thurs 9–2; adm. The façade of the palazzo is presently covered with scaffolding which is due to stay up while they restore the building's exterior.

When Goethe made his blitz-tour of Florence, the Palazzo Vecchio (also called the Palazzo della Signoria) helped pull the wool over his eyes. 'Obviously,' thought the great poet, 'the people...enjoyed a lucky succession of good governments' – a remark which, as Mary McCarthy wrote, could make the angels in heaven weep. But none of Florence's chronic factionalism mars Arnolfo di Cambio's temple of civic aspirations, part council hall and part fortress. In many ways, the Palazzo Vecchio is the ideal of stone Florence: rugged and imposing, with a rusticated façade that was to inspire so many of the city's private palaces, yet designed according to the proportions of the Golden Section of the ancient Greeks. Its dominant feature, the 308ft tower, is a typical piece of Florentine bravado, for long the highest point in the city.

The Palazzo Vecchio occupies the site of the old Roman theatre and the medieval Palazzo dei Priori. In the 13th century this earlier palace was flattened along with the Ghibelline quarter interred under the piazza, and in 1299 the now ascendant Guelphs called upon Arnolfo di Cambio, master builder of the cathedral, to design the most impressive 'Palazzo del Popolo' (as the building was originally called) possible. The palace's unusual trapezoidal shape is often, but rather dubiously, explained as Guelph care not to have any of the building touch land once owned by Ghibellines. One doubts that even in the 13th century property realities allowed such delicacy of sentiments; nor does the theory explain why the tower has swallowtail Ghibelline crenellations, as opposed to the square Guelph ones on the palace itself. Later additions to the rear of the palace have obscured its shape even more, although the façade is essentially as Arnolfo built it, except for the bet-hedging monogram over the door hailing Christ the King of Florence, put up in the nervous days of 1529, when the Imperial army of Charles V was on its way to destroy the last Florentine republic; the inscription replaces an earlier one left by Savonarola. The room at the top of the tower was used as prison for famous people and dubbed the *alberghetto*; inmates in 'the little hotel' included Cosimo il Vecchio before his brief exile, and Savonarola, who spent his last months, between torture sessions, enjoying a superb view of the city before his execution in the piazza below.

Inside the Palazzo Vecchio

Today the Palazzo Vecchio serves as Florence's city hall, but nearly all its historical rooms are open to the public. With few exceptions, the interior decorations date from the time of Cosimo I, when he moved his Grand Ducal self from the Medici palace in 1540. To politically 'correct' its acres of walls and ceilings in the shortest amount of time, he turned to his court artist Giorgio Vasari, famed more for the speed at which he could execute a commission than for its quality. On the ground floor of the palazzo, before you buy your ticket, you can take a look at some of Vasari's more elaborate handiwork in the **Courtyard**, redone for the occasion of Francesco I's unhappy marriage to the plain and stupid Habsburg Joanna of Austria in 1565.

Vasari's suitably grand staircase ascends to the vast **Salone dei Cinquecento**, added by Savonarola for meetings of the 500-strong Consiglio Maggiore, the reformed republic's democratic assembly. Leonardo da Vinci and Michelangelo were commissioned in 1503 to paint the two long walls of the *salone* in a kind of Battle of the Brushes. Unfortunately, neither came near to completing the project; Leonardo managed to fresco a section of the wall, using the experimental techniques that were to prove the undoing of his *Last Supper* in Milan, while Michelangelo only completed the cartoons before being summoned to Rome by Julius II, who required the sculptor of the *David* to pander to his own personal megalomania.

In the 1560s Vasari removed what was left of Leonardo's efforts and refrescoed the room as a celebration of Cosimo's military triumphs over Pisa and Siena, complete with an apotheosis of the Grand Duke on the ceiling. These wall scenes are inane; big, busy, crowded with men and horses who appear to have all the substance of overcooked pasta. The sculptural groups lining the walls of this large room (the Italian parliament sat here from 1865 to 1870 when Florence was the capital) are only slightly more stimulating; even Michelangelo's *Victory*, on the wall opposite the entrance, is more virtuosity than vision: a vacuous young idiot posing with one knee atop a defeated old man still half-submerged in stone, said to be a self-portrait of the sculptor. Its neighbour, a muscle-bound *Hercules and Diomedes* by Vicenzo de' Rossi, probably was inevitable in this city obsessed by the possibilities of the male nude.

Beyond the *salone*, behind a modern glass door, is a much more intriguing room the size of a closet. This is the **Studiolo of Francesco I**, designed by Vasari in 1572 for Cosimo's melancholic and reclusive son, where he would escape to brood over his real interests in natural curiosities and alchemy. The little study, windowless and more than a little claustrophobic, has been restored to its original appearance, lined with allegorical paintings by Vasari, Bronzino and Allori, and bronze statuettes by Giambologna and Ammannati, their refined, polished, and erotic mythological subjects part of a carefully thought-out 16th-century programme on Man and Nature. The lower row of paintings conceals Francesco's secret cupboards where he kept his most precious belongings, his pearls and crystals and gold.

After the *salone* a certain fuzziness begins to set in. Cosimo I's propaganda machine in league with Vasari's fresco factory produced room after room of self-glorifying Medicean puffery. The first series of rooms, known as the **Quartiere di Leone X**, carry ancestor-worship to extremes, each chamber dedicated to a different Medici: in the first Cosimo il Vecchio returns from exile amid tumultuous acclaim; in the second Lorenzo il Magnifico receives the ambassadors in the company of a dignified giraffe; the third and fourth are dedicated to the Medici popes, while the fifth, naturally, is for Cosimo I, who gets the most elaborate treatment of all.

Upstairs the next series of rooms is known as the **Quartiere degli Elementi**, with more works of Vasari and his studio, depicting allegories of the elements. In a small room, called **Terrazzo di Giunone**, is the original of Verrocchio's boy with the dolphin, from the courtyard fountain. A balcony across the Salone dei Cinquecento leads to the **Quartiere di Eleonora di Toledo**, Mrs Cosimo I's private apartments. Her chapel is one of the masterpieces of Bronzino, who seemed to relish the opportunity to paint something besides Medici portraits. The **Sala dell' Udienza**, beyond the second chapel, has a magnificent quattrocento coffered ceiling by Benedetto and Giuliano da Maiano, and walls painted by Mannerist Francesco Salviati (1550–60).

The last room, the **Sala dei Gigli** ('of the lilies') boasts another fine ceiling by the da Maiano brothers; it contains Donatello's restored bronze *Judith and Holofernes*, a late and rather gruesome work of 1455; the warning to tyrants inscribed on its base was added when the statue was abducted from the Medici palace and placed in the Piazza della Signoria. Off the Sala dei Gigli are two small rooms of interest: the **Guardaroba**, or unique 'wardrobe' adorned with 57 maps painted by Fra Egnazio Danti in 1563, depicting all the world known at the time. The **Cancelleria** was Machiavelli's office from 1498 to 1512, when he served the republic as a secretary and diplomat. He is commemorated with a bust and a portrait. Poor Machiavelli would probably be amazed to learn that his very name had become synonymous with cunning, amoral intrigue. After losing his job upon the return of the Medici, and at one point being tortured and imprisoned on false suspicion of conspiracy, Machiavelli was forced to live in idleness in the country, where he wrote his political works and two fine plays, feverishly trying to return to favour. His concern throughout had been to advise realistically, without mincing words, the fractious and increasingly weak Italians on how to create a strong state. His evil reputation came from openly stating what rulers do, rather than what they would like other people to think they do.

The **Collezione Loeser**, a fine assortment of Renaissance art left to the city in 1928 by Charles Loeser, the Macy's department-store heir, is also housed in the Palazzo Vecchio, in the mezzanine before you exit the museum.

Collezione A Della Ragione

After the pomposity of the Palazzo Vecchio and a Campari cure at the Piazza della Signoria's Café Rivoire, you may be in the mood to reconsider the 20th century in Florence's only museum of modern art, recently moved to the renovated Complesso delle Oblate in Via Sant'Egidio 21 (*due to open some time in 2005; call* **t** *055 262 5961 for info*). There are typical still lifes by De Pisis; equally still landscapes by Carlo Carra; mysterious baths by De Chirico; Tuscan landscapes by Mario Mafai, Antonio Donghi and Ottone Rosai; a speedy Futurist horse by Fortunato Depero and a window with doves by Gino Severini; a number of richly coloured canvases by Renato Guttuso, paintings after Tintoretto by Emilio Vedova, and many others.

The Uffizi

Long queues in the summer are very common; try to arrive early. Open Tues–Sun 8.15–6.50; adm exp. Pre-book by phone, **t** *055 294883: pay at the door when you pick up your ticket.*

Florence has the most fabulous art museum in Italy, and as usual we have the Medici to thank; for the building that holds these treasures, however, credit goes to Grand Duke Cosimo's much maligned court painter. Poor Giorgio Vasari! His roosterish boastfulness and the conviction that his was the best of all possible artistic worlds, set next to his very modest talents, have made him a comic figure in most art criticism. On one of the rare occasions when he tried his hand as an architect, though, he gave Florence something to be proud of. The Uffizi ('offices') were built as Cosimo's secretariat, incorporating the old mint (producer of the first gold florins in 1252), the archives and the large church of San Pier Scheraggio, with plenty of room for the bureaucrats needed to run Cosimo's efficient, modern state. The matched pair of arcaded buildings have coldly elegant façades that conceal Vasari's surprising innovation: iron reinforcements that make the huge amount of window area possible and keep the building stable on the soft sandy ground. It was a trick that would be almost forgotten until the Crystal Palace and the first American skyscrapers. Almost from the start the Medici began to store some of their huge collection in parts of the building. There are galleries in the world with more works of art – the Uffizi counts some 1,800 – but the Uffizi overwhelms by the fact that everything in it is worth looking at.

The Uffizi has undergone major reorganization in the last couple of years. Some of this involved the restoration of remaining damage after the bomb of 1993 (all but a very few paintings are now back on display), but improvements have also been made on a practical level. Major restoration of the vaulted rooms on the ground floor has resulted in a vastly improved space; there are now three entrances (for individuals, for groups and for pre-paid tickets), bookshops, cloakrooms, video and computer facilities and information desks.

If you are particularly keen on seeing a certain painting, note that rooms may be temporarily closed when you visit; this often seems to depend on staff availability. There is a list of these closures at the ticket counters. Some works are still hung out of chronological order, and the rooms containing work by Caravaggio and Rubens are closed until further notice (although two of the Caravaggios are at present hung in Room 16 – *see* p.138).

From the ticket counter you can take the lift or sweeping grand staircase up to the second floor, where the Medici once had a huge theatre, now home to the **Cabinet of Drawings and Prints**. Although the bulk of this extensive and renowned collection is only open to scholars with special permission, a roomful of tempting samples gives a hint at what they have a chance to see.

Nowadays one thinks of the Uffizi as primarily a gallery of paintings, but when it first opened visitors came for the fine collection of Hellenistic and Roman marbles. Most of these were collected in Rome by Medici cardinals, and not a few were sources of Renaissance inspiration. The **Vestibule** at the top of the stairs contains some of the best, together with Flemish and Tuscan tapestries made for Cosimo I and his successors. **Room 1**, usually shut, contains excellent early Roman sculpture.

Rooms 2–6: 13th and 14th Centuries

The Uffizi's paintings are arranged in chronological order, the better to educate its visitors on trends in Italian art. The roots of the Early Renaissance are most strikingly revealed in **Room 2**, dedicated to the three great **Maestà** altarpieces by the masters of the 13th century. All portray the same subject of the Madonna and Child enthroned with angels. The one on the right, by Cimabue, was painted around the year 1285 and represents a breaking away from the flat, stylized Byzantine tradition. To the left is the so-called *Rucellai Madonna*, painted around the same period by the Sienese Duccio di Buoninsegna for Santa Maria Novella. It resembles Cimabue's in many ways, but with a more advanced technique for creating depth, and the bright colouring that characterizes the Sienese school. Giotto's altarpiece, painted some 25 years later, takes a great leap forward, not only in his use of perspective, but in the arrangement of the angels, standing naturally, and in the portrayal of the Virgin, gently smiling, with real fingers and breasts.

To the left, **Room 3** contains representative Sienese works of the 14th century, with a beautiful Gothic *Annunciation* (1333) by Simone Martini and the brothers Pietro and Ambrogio Lorenzetti. **Room 4** is dedicated to 14th-century Florentines: Bernardo Daddi, Nardo di Cione, and the delicately coloured *San Remigio Pietà* by Giottino. **Rooms 5 and 6** portray Italian contributions to the International Gothic school, most dazzlingly Gentile da Fabriano's *Adoration of the Magi* (1423), two good works by Lorenzo Monaco, and the *Thebaid* of Gherardo Starnina, depicting the rather unusual activities of the 4th-century monks of St Pancratius of Thebes, in Egypt.

Rooms 7–9: Early Renaissance

In the Uffizi, at least, it's but a few short steps from the superbly decorative International Gothic to the masters of the Early Renaissance. **Room 7** contains minor works by Fra Angelico, Masaccio and Masolino, and three masterpieces. Domenico Veneziano's pastel *Madonna and Child with Saints* (1448) is one of the rare pictures by this Venetian master who died a pauper in Florence. It is a new departure not only for its soft colours but for the subject matter, unifying the enthroned Virgin and saints in one panel, in what is known as a *Sacra Conversazione*. Piero della Francesca's famous *Double Portrait of the Duke Federigo da Montefeltro and his Duchess Battista Sforza of Urbino* (1465) depicts one of Italy's noblest Renaissance princes – and surely the one with the most distinctive nose. Piero's ability to create perfectly still, timeless worlds is even more evident in the allegorical 'Triumphs' of the Duke and Duchess painted on the back of their portraits. A similar stillness and fascination floats over into the surreal in Uccello's *Rout of San Romano* (1456), or at least the third of it still present (the other two panels are in the Louvre and London's National Gallery; all three once decorated the bedroom of Lorenzo il Magnifico in the Medici palace). Both Piero and Uccello were deep students of perspective, but Uccello went half-crazy; applying his principles to a violent battle scene has left us one of the most provocative works of all time – a vision of warfare in suspended animation, with pink, white and blue toy horses, robot-like knights, and rabbits bouncing in the background.

Room 8 is devoted to the works of the rascally romantic Fra Filippo Lippi, whose ethereally lovely Madonnas were modelled after his brown-eyed nun. In his *Coronation of the Virgin* (1447) she kneels in the foreground with two children, while the artist, dressed in a brown habit, looks dreamily towards her; in his celebrated *Madonna and Child with Two Angels* (1445) she plays the lead before the kind of mysterious landscape Leonardo would later perfect. Lippi taught the art of enchanting Madonnas to his student Botticelli, who has some lovely works in this room and the next; Alesso Baldovinetti, a pupil of the far more holy Fra Angelico, painted the room's beautiful *Annunciation* (1447).

Room 9 has two small scenes from the *Labours of Hercules* (1470) by Antonio Pollaiuolo, whose interest in anatomy, muscular expressiveness and violence presages a strain in Florentine art that culminated in the great Mannerists. He worked with his younger brother Piero on the refined, elegant *SS. Vincent, James and Eustace*, transferred here from San Miniato. This room also contains the Uffizi's best-known forgery: *The Young Man in a Red Hat* or self-portrait of Filippino Lippi, believed to have been the work of an 18th-century English art dealer who palmed it off on the Grand Dukes.

Botticelli: Rooms 10–14

To accommodate the bewitching art of 'Little Barrels' and his 20th-century admirers, the Uffizi converted four small rooms into one great Botticellian shrine. Although his masterpieces displayed here have become almost synonymous with the Florentine Renaissance at its most spring-like and charming, they were not publicly displayed until the beginning of the 19th century, nor given much consideration outside Florence until the early 20th century. Botticelli's best works date from his days as a darling of the Medici – family members crop up most noticeably in the *Adoration of the Magi* (1476), where you can pick out Cosimo il Vecchio, Lorenzo il Magnifico and Botticelli himself (in the right foreground, in a yellow robe, gazing at the spectator). His *Annunciation* is a graceful, cosmic dance between the Virgin and the Angel Gabriel. In the *Tondo of the Virgin of the Pomegranate* the lovely melancholy goddess who was to become his Venus makes her first appearance.

Botticelli is best known for his sublime mythological allegories, nearly all painted for the Medici and inspired by the Neoplatonic, humanistic and hermetic currents that pervaded the intelligentsia of the late 15th century. Perhaps no painting has been debated so fervently as *La Primavera* (1478). This hung for years in the Medici Villa at Castello, and it is believed that the subject of the Allegory of Spring was suggested by Marsilio Ficino, one of the great natural magicians of the Renaissance, and that the figures represent the 'beneficial' planets able to dispel sadness. *Pallas and the Centaur* has been called another subtle allegory of Medici triumph – the rings of Athena's gown are supposedly a family symbol. Other interpretations see the taming of the sorrowful centaur as a melancholy comment on reason and civilization.

Botticelli's last great mythological painting, *The Birth of Venus*, was commissioned by Lorenzo di Pierfrancesco and inspired by a poem by Poliziano, Lorenzo il Magnifico's Latin and Greek scholar, who described how Zephyr and Chloris blew the newborn goddess to shore on a scallop shell, while Hora hastened to robe her, a scene Botticelli portrays once again with dance-like rhythm and delicacy of line. Yet the goddess of love floats towards the spectator with an expression of wistfulness – perhaps reflecting the artist's own feelings of regret. For artistically, the poetic, decorative style he perfected in this painting would be disdained and forgotten in his own lifetime. Spiritually, Botticelli also turned a corner after creating this haunting, uncanny beauty – his and Florence's farewell to a road not taken. Although Vasari's biography of Botticelli portrays a prankster rather than a sensitive soul, the painter absorbed more than any other artist the *fin-de-siècle* neuroticism that beset the city with the rise of Savonarola. So thoroughly did he reject his Neoplatonism that he would only accept commissions of sacred subjects or supposedly edifying allegories like his *Calumny*, a small but rather disturbing work, and a fitting introduction to the dark side of the quattrocento psyche.

This large room also contains works by Botticelli's contemporaries. There are two paintings of the *Adoration of the Magi*, one by Ghirlandaio and one by Filippino Lippi, which show the influence of Leonardo's unfinished but radical work in pyramidal composition (in the next room); Leonardo himself got the idea from the large *Portinari Altarpiece* (1471), at the end of the room, a work by Hugo Van der Goes, brought back from Bruges by Medici agent Tommaso Portinari.

Rooms 15–24: More Renaissance

Room 15 is dedicated to the Florentine works of Leonardo da Vinci's early career. Here are works by his master Andrea Verrocchio, including the *Baptism of Christ*, in which Leonardo painted the angel on the left. Art critics believe the *Annunciation* (1475) is almost entirely by Leonardo – the soft faces, botanical details, and misty, watery background would become his trademarks. Most influential was his unfinished *Adoration of the Magi* (1481), an unconventional composition that Leonardo abandoned when he left Florence for Milan. Although at first glance it's hard to make out much more than a mass of reddish chiaroscuro, the longer you stare, the better you'll see the serene Madonna and Child surrounded by anxious, troubled humanity, with an exotic background of ruins, trees and horsemen.

Other artists in Room 15 include Leonardo's peers: Lorenzo di Credi, whose religious works have eerie garden-like backgrounds, and the nutty Piero di Cosimo, whose dreamy *Perseus Liberating Andromeda* includes an endearing mongrel of a dragon that gives even the most reserved Japanese tourist fits of giggles. Tuscan maps adorn **Room 16**, as well as scenes by Hans Memling. Temporarily housed here, away from their normal home in Room 43, are Caravaggio's *Bacchus* and *The Head of Medusa*, believed to be self-portraits. In its day the fleshy, heavy-eyed *Bacchus*, half portrait and half still life, was considered highly iconoclastic.

The octagonal **Tribuna** (Room 18) with its mother-of-pearl dome and *pietra dura* floor and table was built by Buontalenti in 1584 for Francesco I and, like the Studiolo in the Palazzo Vecchio, was designed to hold Medici treasures. For centuries the best-known of these was the *Venus de' Medici*, a 2nd-century BC Greek sculpture, farcically claimed as a copy of Praxiteles' celebrated *Aphrodite of Cnidos*, the most erotic statue in antiquity. In the 18th century, amazingly, this rather ordinary girl was considered the greatest sculpture in Florence; today most visitors walk right by without a second glance. Other antique works include the *Wrestlers* and the *Knife Grinder*, both copies of Pergamese originals, the *Dancing Faun*, the *Young Apollo*, and the *Sleeping Hermaphrodite* in the adjacent room, which is usually curtained off.

The real stars of the Tribuna are the Medici court portraits, many of them by Bronzino, who was not only able to catch the likeness of Cosimo I, Eleanor of Toledo and their children, but could also aptly portray the spirit of the day – these are people who took themselves very seriously indeed. They have for company Vasari's posthumous portrait of *Lorenzo il Magnifico* and Pontormo's *Cosimo il Vecchio*, Andrea del Sarto's *Girl with a Book by Petrarch*, and Rosso Fiorentino's *Angel Musician*, an enchanting work entirely out of place in this stodgy temple.

Two followers of Piero della Francesca, Perugino and Luca Signorelli, hold pride of place in **Room 19**; Perugino's *Portrait of a Young Man* is believed to be modelled on his pupil Raphael. Signorelli's *Tondo of the Holy Family* was to become the inspiration for Michelangelo's (*see* below). The room also contains Lorenzo di Credi's *Venus*, inspired by Botticelli. The Germans appear in **Room 20**: Dürer's earliest known work, the *Portrait of his Father* (1490), done at age 19, and *The Adoration of the Magi* (1504). Also here are Lucas Cranach's Teutonic *Adam and Eve* and his *Portrait of Martin Luther* (1543), not someone you'd necessarily expect to see in Florence. **Room 21** is dedicated to the great Venetians, most famously Bellini and his uncanny *Sacred Allegory* (1490s), the meaning of which has never been satisfactorily explained. There are two minor works by the elusive Giorgione, and a typically weird *St Dominic* by Cosmè Tura.

Later Flemish and German artists appear in **Room 22**, works by Gerard David and proto-Romantic Albrecht Altdorfer, and a portrait attributed to Hans Holbein of *Sir Thomas More*. **Room 23** is dedicated to non-Tuscans Correggio of Parma and Mantegna of the Veneto, as well as Boltraffio's strange *Narcissus*.

Rooms 25–27: Mannerism

The window-filled South Corridor, with its views over the city and its fine display of antique sculpture, marks only the halfway point in the Uffizi but nearly the end of Florence's contribution. In the first three rooms, however, local talent rallies to produce a brilliantly coloured twilight in Florentine Mannerism. By most accounts, Michelangelo's only completed oil painting, the *Tondo Doni* (1506), was the spark that ignited Mannerism's flaming orange and turquoise hues. Michelangelo was 30 when he painted this unconventional work, in a medium he disliked (sculpture and fresco being the only fit occupations for a man, he believed). It's a typical Michelangelo story that when the purchaser complained the artist was asking too much for it, Michelangelo promptly doubled the price. As shocking as the colours are the spiralling poses of the Holy Family, sharply delineated against a background of five nude, slightly out-of-focus young men of uncertain purpose (are they pagans? angels? boyfriends? or just fillers?) – an ambiguity that was to become a hallmark of Mannerism; as the *Ignudi* they later appear on the Sistine Chapel ceiling. In itself, the *Tondo Doni* is more provocative than immediately appealing; the violent canvas in Room 27, Rosso Fiorentino's *Moses Defending the Children of Jethro*, was painted some 20 years later and at least in its intention to shock the viewer puts a cap on what Michelangelo began.

Room 26 is dedicated mainly to Raphael, who was in and out of Florence in 1504–8. Raphael was the sweetheart of the High Renaissance. His Madonnas, like *The Madonna of the Goldfinch*, have a tenderness that was soon to be over-popularized by others and turned into holy cards, a cloying sentimentality added over the centuries.

It's easier, perhaps, to see Raphael's genius in non-sacred subjects, like *Leo X with Two Cardinals*, a perceptive portrait study of the first Medici pope with his nephew Giulio de' Medici, later Clement VII.

The same room contains Andrea del Sarto's most original work, the fluorescent *Madonna of the Harpies* (1517), named after the figures on the Virgin's pedestal. Of the works by Pontormo, the best is in **Room 27**, *Supper at Emmaus* (1525), a strange canvas with the Masonic symbol of the Eye of God hovering over Christ's head.

Rooms 28–45

The Uffizi fairly bristles with masterpieces from other parts of Italy and abroad. Titian's delicious nudes, especially the voluptuous *Venus of Urbino*, raise the temperature in **Room 28**; Parmigianino's hyper-elegant *Madonna with the Long Neck* (1536) in **Room 29** is a fascinating Mannerist evolutionary dead-end. **Room 31** holds Paolo Veronese's *Holy Family with St Barbara*, bathed in a golden Venetian light, with a gorgeously opulent Barbara. Sebastiano del Piombo's *Death of Adonis*, in **Room 32**, is notable for its melancholy, autumn atmosphere, and Venus's annoyed look. Tintoretto's shadowy *Leda* languidly pretends to restrain the lusty swan.

Room 41 is Flemish domain, with brand-name art by Rubens and Van Dyck; the former's *Baccanale* may be the most grotesque canvas in Florence. **Room 42**, the *Sala della Niobe*, was reopened in December 1998 after the bomb damage was repaired. A series of statues, *Niobe and her Sons* (18th-century copies of Hellenic works), are housed in the high, arched-ceilinged room, which is covered in pristine plaster and gold leaf. **Room 43** houses some striking Caravaggios.

Struggle on gamely to **Room 44**, where there are three portraits by Rembrandt including two self-portraits, and landscapes by Ruysdael. **Room 45** has some fine 18th-century works, including portraits by Chardin, Goya and Longhi, and Venetian landscapes by Guardi and Canaletto. Even more welcome by this time is the **bar**, with a summer terrace and in a superb position overlooking Piazza Signoria.

The **Contini Bonacossi** collection, once housed in the Meridiana Pavilion at Palazzo Pitti, was moved to the Uffizi in 1999. Visits are by appointment only (**t** *055 265 4321*), and there is a separate entrance in Via Lambertesca. The Uffizi ticket is also valid for this. This recent bequest includes works of Cimabue, Duccio and Giovanni Bellini, some sculpture and china, and also paintings by El Greco, Goya and Velazquez – the last represented by an exceptional work, *The Water Carrier of Seville*.

Corridoio Vasariano

*Open for very limited periods during the year. It is now open to individuals, not just groups. Hours are also very limited. Call **t** 055 265 4321 for info and bookings (obligatory); adm exp.*

In 1565, when Francesco I married Joanna of Austria, the Medici commissioned Vasari to link their new digs in the Pitti Palace with the Uffizi and the Palazzo Vecchio in such a manner that the Archdukes could make their rounds without rubbing elbows with their subjects. With a patina of 400 years, it seems that Florence wouldn't look quite right without this covered catwalk, leapfrogging on rounded arches from the back of the Uffizi, over the Ponte Vecchio, daintily skirting a medieval tower, and darting past the façade of Santa Felicità to the Pitti Palace.

The Corridoio does not only offer interesting views of Florence: it has been hung with a celebrated collection of artists' self-portraits, beginning, reasonably, with Vasari himself before continuing in chronological order, past the Gaddis and Raphael to Rembrandt, Van Dyck, Velazquez, Hogarth, Reynolds, Delacroix and Corot.

The Museum of the History of Science (Museo di Storia della Scienza)

Open summer 9.30–5, Tues and Sat 9.30–1, closed Sun;
winter 9.30–5, Tues 9.30–1, 2nd Sun of month 10–1; adm.

For all that Florence and Tuscany contributed to the birth of science, it is only fitting to have this museum in the centre of the city, behind the Uffizi in Piazza Giudici. Much of the first floor is devoted to instruments measuring time and distance: Arabian astrolabes and pocket sundials, Tuscan sundials in the shape of Platonic solids, enormous elaborate armillary spheres and a small reliquary holding the bone of Galileo's finger, erect, like a final gesture to the city that until 1737 denied him a Christian burial. Here, too, are two of his original telescopes and the lens with which he discovered the four moons of Jupiter. Other scientific instruments come from the Accademia del Cimento (of 'trial' or 'experiment'), founded in 1657 by Cardinal Leopoldo de' Medici, the world's first scientific organization, dedicated to Galileo's principle of inquiry and proof by experimentation. 'Try and try again' was its motto.

Upstairs, there's a large room filled with machines used to demonstrate principles of physics, which the women who run the museum will operate if you ask. Two unusual ones are the 18th-century automatic writer and the instrument of perpetual motion. The rooms devoted to medicine contain a collection of 18th-century wax anatomical models, designed to teach budding obstetricians about unfortunate foetal positions, as well as a fine display of surgical instruments from the period.

The Ponte Vecchio and Ponte Santa Trínita

Bent bridges seeming to strain like bows
And tremble with arrowy undertide...
Elizabeth Barrett Browning, 'Casa Guidi Windows'

Often at sunset the Arno becomes a stream of molten gold, that is, during those months when it has a respectable flow of water. But even in the torrid days of August, when the Arno shrivels into muck and spittle, its two famous bridges retain their distinctive beauty. The most famous of these, the **Ponte Vecchio** or 'Old Bridge', crosses the Arno at its narrowest point; the present bridge, with its three stone arches, was built in 1345, and replaces a wooden construction from the 970s, which in turn was the successor to a span that may well have dated back to the Romans. On this wooden bridge, at the foot of the *Marzocco*, or statue of Mars, Buondelmonte dei

Buondelmonti was murdered in 1215, setting off the wars of the Guelphs and Ghibellines. The original *Marzocco* was washed away in a 14th-century flood, and Donatello's later version has been carted off to the Bargello.

Like old London Bridge, the Ponte Vecchio is covered with shops and houses. By the 1500s it had become the street of hog butchers, though after Vasari built Cosimo's secret passage on top, the Grand Duke evicted the butchers and replaced them with goldsmiths. They have been there ever since, and shoppers from around the world descend on it each year to scrutinize the traditional Florentine talent for jewellery – not a few of the city's great artists began their careers as goldsmiths, beginning with Ghiberti and Donatello, and ending with Cellini, whose bust adorns the middle of the bridge. In the 1966 flood the shops did not prove as resilient as the Ponte Vecchio itself, and a fortune of gold was washed down the Arno.

In the summer of 1944, the river briefly became a German defensive line during the slow painful retreat across Italy. Before leaving Florence, the Nazis blew up every one of the city's bridges, saving only, on Hitler's special orders, the Ponte Vecchio, though they blasted a large number of ancient buildings on each side of the span to create piles of rubble to block the approaches. Florence's most beautiful span, the **Ponte Santa Trìnita**, was the most tragic victim. Immediately after the war the Florentines set about replacing the bridges exactly as they were: for Santa Trìnita, old quarries had to be reopened to duplicate the stone, and old methods revived to cut it (modern power saws would have done it too cleanly). The graceful curve of the three arches was a problem; they could not be constructed geometrically, and considerable speculation went on over how the architect (Ammannati, in 1567) did it. Finally, recalling that Michelangelo had advised Ammannati on the project, someone noticed that the same form of arch could be seen on the decoration of the tombs in Michelangelo's Medici Chapel, constructed most likely by pure artistic imagination. Fortune lent a hand in the reconstruction; of the original statues of the 'Four Seasons', almost all the pieces were fished out of the Arno and rebuilt. Spring's head was eventually found by divers completely by accident in 1961.

Dante's Florence

Dante would contemplate his Beatrice, the story goes, at Mass in the **Badia Fiorentina** (*entrance on Via Dante Alighieri; Cloister open Mon 3–6; church open Mon 3–6, Tues–Sat 6.30–6*), a Benedictine church on Via del Proconsolo across from the Bargello, with a lovely Gothic spire to grace this corner of the Florentine skyline. The church has undergone many rebuildings since Willa, widow of a Margrave of Tuscany, began it in around 990, but there is still a monument to Ugo, the 'Good Margrave' mentioned in Dante, and a painting of the Madonna appearing to St Bernard by Filippo Lippi.

Between the Badia and Via del Calzaiuoli, a little corner of medieval Florence has survived the changes of centuries. In these quiet, narrow streets you can visit the **Casa di Dante** (*closed for restoration work; unknown when it will re-open*), which was actually built in 1911 over the ruins of an amputated tower house, although scholars all agree that the Alighieri lived somewhere in the vicinity. Since 1960 this museum dedicated to Dante has made a game attempt to evoke Dante's life and times, in spite of neglect. Near the entrance is an edition of *The Divine Comedy*, all printed in tiny letters on a poster by a mad Milanese. Upstairs there are copies of Botticelli's beautiful line illustrations for the *Commedia*.

Nearby, the stoutly medieval **Torre del Castagna** is all that remains of the original Palazzo del Popolo, the residence of the *priori*, the governors of the city, before the construction of the Palazzo Vecchio. Dante himself was a *priore* once, and he would have spent his two-month term of office living here, as the law required.

After giving up on Beatrice, Dante married Gemma Donati, in the **Santa Margherita** church on the same block. Another church nearby, **San Martino del Vescovo** (*open Mon–Sat 10–12 and 3–5, closed Sun*), has a fine set of frescoes from the workshop of Ghirlandaio.

Museo Nazionale del Bargello

Open daily 8.15–1.50; closed 1st and 3rd Sun, and 2nd and 4th Mon of month; adm.

Across from the Badia Fiorentina looms the Bargello, a battlemented urban fortress, well proportioned yet of forbidding grace; for centuries it saw duty as Florence's prison. Today its only inmates are men of marble, gathered together to form Italy's finest collection of sculpture, a fitting complement to the paintings in the Uffizi. The Bargello is 'stone Florence' squared to the sixth degree, rugged and austere *pietra forte*, the model for the even grander Palazzo Vecchio. Even the treasures it houses are hard, definite, certain – and almost unremittingly masculine. The Bargello offers the best insight available into Florence's golden age, and it was a man's world indeed.

Completed in 1255, the Bargello was intended as Florence's Palazzo del Popolo, though by 1271 it served instead as the residence of the foreign *podestà*, or chief magistrate, installed by Guelph leader Charles of Anjou. The Medici made it the headquarters of the captain of police (the *Bargello*), the city jail and torture chamber, a function it served until 1859. In the Renaissance it was the peculiar custom to paint portraits of the condemned on the exterior walls of the fortress; Andrea del Castagno was so good at it that he was nicknamed Andrea of the Hanged Men. All of these ghoulish souvenirs have long since disappeared, as have the torture instruments – burned in 1786, when Grand Duke Peter Leopold abolished torture and the death sentence in Tuscany, only a few months after the Venetians led the way. Today the **Gothic courtyard**, former site of the gallows and chopping block, is a delightful place, owing much to an imaginative restoration in the 1860s. The encrustation of centuries of *podestà* armorial devices and plaques in a wild vocabulary of symbols, the shadowy arcades and stately stairs combine to create one of Florence's most romantic corners.

The main ground-floor gallery is dedicated to Michelangelo and his century, although it must be said that the Michelangelo of the Bargello somewhat lacks the accustomed angst and ecstasy. The real star of the room is **Benvenuto Cellini**, who was, besides many other things, an exquisite craftsman and daring innovator.

The stairway from the courtyard leads up to the shady **Loggia**, now converted into an aviary for Giambologna's charming bronze birds, made for the animal grotto at the Medici's Villa di Castello.

The **Salone del Consiglio Generale**, formerly the courtroom of the *podestà*, contains the greatest masterpieces of Early Renaissance sculpture. And when Michelangelo's maudlin self-absorption and the Mannerists' empty virtuosity begin to seem tiresome, a visit to this room will prove a welcome antidote. Donatello's originality and vision are strikingly modern – and mysterious. On the wall hang the two famous trial reliefs for the second set of baptistry doors, by Ghiberti and Brunelleschi, both depicting the Sacrifice of Isaac. The remainder of the first floor houses fascinating collections of decorative arts donated to the Bargello in the last century.

Some of the most interesting items are in the next rooms, especially the works in the **ivory collection** – Carolingian and Byzantine diptychs, an 8th-century whalebone coffer from Northumbria adorned with runes, medieval French miniatures chronicling 'The Assault on the Castle of Love', 11th-century chess pieces, and more.

A stairway from the ivory collection leads up to the **Second Floor**. It houses some of the finest enamelled terracottas of the della Robbia family workshop, a room of portrait busts, works by Antonio Pollaiuolo and Verrocchio, including his *David* and lovely *Young Lady with a Nosegay*. There is also a collection of armour, and the most important collection of small Renaissance bronzes in Italy.

Piazza San Firenze to the Duomo

The strangely shaped square that both the Badia and the Bargello call home is named after the large church of **San Firenze**, now partially used as Florence's law courts. At the corner of the square and Via Gondi, the **Palazzo Gondi** is a fine Renaissance palace built for a merchant by Giuliano da Sangallo in 1489 but completed only in 1884; it's not easy to pick out the discreet 19th-century additions. A block from the square on Via Ghibellina, the **Palazzo Borghese** (No.110) is one of the finest neoclassical buildings in the city, erected in 1822 for a party in honour of Habsburg Grand Duke Ferdinand III. The host was one of the wealthiest men of his day, the Roman prince Camillo Borghese, husband of Pauline Bonaparte and the man responsible for shipping many of Italy's art treasures off to the Louvre.

From Piazza San Firenze, Via del Proconsolo leads straight to the Piazza del Duomo, passing by way of the **Palazzo Pazzi-Quaratesi** (No.10), the 15th-century headquarters of the banking family that organized the conspiracy against Lorenzo and Giuliano de' Medici. No.12, the Palazzo Nonfinito – begun in 1593 but, as its name suggests, never completed – is now the home of the **Museo Nazionale di Antropologia ed Etnologia** (*open Mon–Wed, Fri and Sat 9–1, Tues 9–1 and 3–5; adm*), founded in 1869, the first ethnological museum in Italy, with an interesting collection of Peruvian mummies, musical instruments collected by Galileo Chini (who decorated the Liberty-style extravaganzas at Viareggio), some lovely and unusual items of Japan's Ainu and Pakistan's Kafiri, and a large number of skulls from all over the world.

Florence As It Was

Borgo degli Albizi, the fine old street passing in front of the Palazzo Nonfinito, was in ancient times the Via Cassia, linking Rome with Bologna, and it deserves a leisurely stroll for its palaces (especially No.18, the cinquecento Palazzo Valori, nicknamed 'Funny Face Palace' for its surreal, semi-relief herm-busts of Florentine immortals on three floors of the façade). If Borgo degli Albizi, too, fails to answer to the Florence you've been seeking, take Via dell'Oriuolo (just to the left at Piazza G Salvemini) for the **Museo di Firenze Com'Era** (Museum of Florence As It Was), located at the big garden at No.24 (*open Fri–Wed 9–2; adm*). The jewel of this museum is right out in front, the nearly room-sized *Pianta della Catena*, most beautiful of the early views of Florence. It is a copy; the original, made in 1490 by an unknown artist – that handsome fellow pictured in the lower right-hand corner – was lost during the last war in a Berlin museum. This fascinating painting captures Florence at the height of the Renaissance, a city of buildings in bright white, pink and tan; the great churches are without their façades, the Uffizi and Medici chapels have not yet appeared, and the Medici and Pitti palaces are without their later extensions.

The museum is not large. At present it contains only a number of plans and maps, as well as a collection of amateurish watercolours of Florence's sights from the last century, and paintings of Florence's surroundings by Ottone Rosai, a local favourite who died in 1957. Today's Florentines seem much less interested in the Renaissance than in the city of their grandparents. For some further evidence, look around the corner of Via S. Egidio, where some recent remodelling has uncovered posters over the street from 1925, announcing plans for paying the war debt and a coming visit of the *Folies Bergère*. The Florentines have restored them and put them under glass.

From Via dell'Oriuolo, Via Folco Portinari takes you to Florence's main hospital, **Santa Maria Nuova**, founded in 1286 by the father of Dante's Beatrice, Folco Portinari. A tomb in the hospital's church, Sant'Egidio, is all that remains of the family. Readers of Iris Origo's *The Merchant of Prato* will recognize it as the workplace of the good notary, Ser Lapo Mazzei. The portico, by Buontalenti, was finished in 1612.

Medieval Streets North of the Arno

Just west of Via Por S. Maria, the main street leading down to the Ponte Vecchio, you'll find some of the oldest and best-preserved lanes in Florence. Near the Mercato Nuovo at the top of the street (*see* p.129) stands the **Palazzo di Parte Guelfa**, the 13th-century headquarters of the Guelph party, and often the real seat of power in the city, paid for by property confiscated from the Ghibellines; in the 15th century Brunelleschi added a hall on the top floor and an extension. Next door is the guildhall of the silk-makers, the 14th-century **Palazzo dell' Arte della Seta** still bearing its bas-relief emblem, or *stemma*, of a closed door, the age-old guild symbol. It's worth continuing around the Guelph Palace to Via Pellicceria to see the fine ensemble of medieval buildings on the tiny square near Via delle Terme, named after the old Roman baths.

Palazzo Davanzati

The palazzo, closed for restoration since 1994, was due to reopen partially in July 2001, but timings have slipped. The ground floor and first floor rooms are due to open in 2006, the rest who knows when... Until then, you can see an exhibition on the palace on the ground floor, 8.30–1.50; closed alternate Sundays and Mondays.

To get an idea of what life was like inside these sombre palaces some 600 years ago, stroll over to nearby Via Porta Rossa, site of the elegant Palazzo Davanzati, now arranged as the **Museo della Casa Fiorentina Antica**, one of the city's most delightful museums, offering a chance to step back into domestic life of yore. Originally built in the mid-14th century for the Davizzi family, the house was purchased by merchant Bernardo Davanzati in 1578 and stayed in the family until the 1900s. Restored by an antique collector in 1904, it is the best-preserved medieval-Renaissance house in Florence.

Piazza Santa Trínita

Three old Roman roads – Via Porta Rossa, Via delle Terme and Borgo SS. Apostoli – lead into the irregularly shaped Piazza Santa Trínita. Borgo SS. Apostoli is named after one of Florence's oldest churches, the little Romanesque **Santi Apostoli** (11th century), which is located in the sunken Piazzetta del Limbo, former cemetery of unbaptized babies.

Piazza Santa Trínita itself boasts an exceptionally fine architectural ensemble, grouped around the 'Column of Justice' from the Roman Baths of Caracalla, given by Pius IV to Cosimo I, and later topped with a red statue of Justice by Francesco del Tadda. Its pale granite is set off by the palaces of the piazza: the High Renaissance-Roman **Palazzo Bartolini-Salimbeni** by Baccio d'Agnolo (1520) on the corner of Via Porta Rossa, formerly the fashionable Hôtel du Nord where Herman Melville stayed; the medieval **Palazzo Buondelmonti**, with a 1530 façade by Baccio d'Agnolo, once home to the reading room and favourite haunt of such literati in the 19th century as Dumas, Browning, Manzoni and Stendhal; and the magnificent curving **Palazzo Spini-Ferroni**, the largest medieval palace in Florence, built in 1289 and still retaining its original battlements. This is now home to the heirs of the Florentine designer Ferragamo and houses a retail outlet and a fascinating small **museum** of Ferragamo's life and work, including some of the most beautiful shoes in the world (*open Mon–Fri 9–1 and 2–6 by appt only, t 055 336 0456; free*).

Santa Trínita

Open Mon–Sat 8–12 and 4–6, Sun 4–6 only.

The church of Santa Trínita has stood here, in one form or another, since the 12th century; its unusual accent on the first syllable (from the Latin *Trínitas*) is considered proof of its ancient foundation. Although the pedestrian façade added by Buontalenti in 1593 isn't especially welcoming, step into its shadowy 14th-century interior for several artistic treats, beginning with the **Bartolini-Salimbeni Chapel** (fourth on the right), frescoed in 1422 by the Sienese Lorenzo Monaco; his marriage of the Virgin takes place in a Tuscan fantasy backdrop of pink towers. He also painted the chapel's graceful, ethereally coloured altarpiece, the *Annunciation*.

In the choir, the **Sassetti Chapel** is one of the masterpieces of Domenico Ghirlandaio, completed in 1495 for wealthy merchant Francesco Sassetti and dedicated to the Life of St Francis, but also to the life of Francesco Sassetti, the city and his Medici circle: the scene above the altar, of Francis receiving the Rule of the Order, is transferred to the Piazza della Signoria, watched by Sassetti (to the right, with the fat purse) and Lorenzo il Magnifico; on the steps stands the great Latinist Poliziano with Lorenzo's three sons. The *Death of St Francis* pays homage to Giotto's similar composition in Santa Croce. The altarpiece, the *Adoration of the Shepherds* (1485), is one of Ghirlandaio's best-known works, often described as the archetypal Renaissance painting, a contrived but charming classical treatment; the Magi arrive through a triumphal arch, a Roman sarcophagus is used as manger and a ruined temple for a stable – all matched by the sibyls on the vault; the sibyl on the outer arch is the one who supposedly announced the birth of Christ to Augustus.

Santa Trínita is a Vallombrosan church and the first chapel to the right of the altar holds the Order's holy of holies, a painted crucifix formerly in San Miniato. The story goes that on a Good Friday, a young noble named Giovanni Gualberto was on his way to Mass when he met the man who had recently murdered his brother. Rather than take his revenge, Gualberto pardoned the assassin in honour of the holy day. When he arrived at church to pray, this crucifix nodded in approval of his mercy. Giovanni was so impressed that he went on to found the Vallombrosan order in the Casentino.

The **Sanctuary** was frescoed by Alesso Baldovinetti, though only four Old Testament figures survive. In the second chapel to the left the marble *Tomb of Bishop Benozzo Federighi* (1454) is by Luca della Robbia. In the fourth chapel, a detached fresco by Neri di Bicci portrays San Giovanni Gualberto and his fellow Vallombrosan saints.

West of Piazza della Repubblica

The streets west of Piazza della Repubblica have always been the choicest district of Florence, and **Via de' Tornabuoni** the city's smartest shopping street. These days you won't find many innovations: Milan's current status as headquarters of Italy's fashion industry is a sore point with Florence.

In the bright and ambitious 1400s, however, when Florence was the centre of European high finance, Via de' Tornabuoni and its environs was the area the new merchant élite chose for their palaces. Today's bankers build great skyscrapers for the firm and settle for modest mansions for themselves; in Florence's heyday, things were reversed. Bankers and wool tycoons really owned their businesses. While their places of work were quite simple, their homes were imposing city palaces, all built in the same conservative style and competing with each other in size like some Millionaires' Row in 19th-century America.

The champion was the **Palazzo Strozzi**, a long block up Via de' Tornabuoni from Piazza Trínita. This rusticated stone cube of fearful dimensions squats in its piazza, radiating almost visible waves of megalomania. There are few architectural innovations in the Palazzo Strozzi, but here the typical Florentine palace is blown up to the level of the absurd: although three storeys like other palaces, each floor is as tall as three or four normal ones, and the rings to tie up horses could hold elephants. Like Michelangelo's *David*, Florence's other beautiful monster, it emits the unpleasant sensation of what Mary McCarthy called the 'giganticism of the human ego', the will to surpass not only antiquity but nature herself. Nowadays, at least, the Strozzi palace is moderately useful as a space to hold temporary exhibitions.

Palazzo Rucellai

There are two other exceptional palaces in the quarter. At the north end of Via de' Tornabuoni stands the beautiful golden **Palazzo Antinori** (1465, architect unknown), which has Florence's grandest Baroque façade, **San Gaetano** (1648, by Gherardo Silvani), as its equally golden companion, despite being decorated with statues that would look right at home in Rome but look like bad actors in Florence.

The second important palace, Florence's most celebrated example of domestic architecture, is the **Palazzo Rucellai**, in Via della Vigna Nuova. Its original owner, Giovanni Rucellai, was a quattrocento tycoon like Filippo Strozzi, but an intellectual as well, whose *Zibaldone*, or 'commonplace book' is one of the best sources available on the life and tastes of the educated Renaissance merchant. In 1446 Rucellai chose Leon Battista Alberti to design his palace. Actually built by Bernardo Rossellino, it follows Alberti's precepts and theories in its use of the three classical orders; instead of the usual rusticated stone, the façade has a far more delicate decoration of incised irregular blocks and a frieze, elements influential in subsequent Italian architecture – though far more noticeably in Rome than Florence itself. Originally the palace was only five bays wide, and when another two bays were added later the edge was left ragged, unfinished, a nice touch, as if the builders could return at any moment and pick up where they left off. The frieze, like that on Santa Maria Novella, portrays the devices of the Medici and the Rucellai families (Giovanni's son married a daughter of Piero de' Medici), a wedding fêted in the **Loggia dei Rucellai** across the street, also designed by Alberti.

Piazza Goldoni and Ognissanti

Before taking leave of old Florence's west end, head back to the Arno and **Piazza Goldoni**, named after the great comic playwright from Venice. The bridge here, the **Ponte alla Carraia**, is new and nondescript, but its 1304 version played a leading role in that year's most memorable disaster: a company staging a water pageant of the *Inferno*, complete with monsters, devils and tortured souls, attracted such a large crowd that the bridge collapsed under the weight, and all were drowned.

The most important building on the piazza, the **Palazzo Ricasoli**, was built in the 15th century but bears the name of one of unified Italy's first Prime Ministers, Bettino 'Iron Baron' Ricasoli. Just to the east on Lungarno Corsini looms the enormous

Palazzo Corsini, the city's most prominent piece of Roman Baroque extravagance, begun in 1650 and crowned with a bevy of statues. The Corsini, the most prominent family of 17th- and 18th-century Florence, were reputedly so wealthy that they could ride from Florence to Rome entirely on their own property. The **Galleria Corsini** (*adm by appt only,* **t** *055 218994; Mon 9–4, Tues–Fri 9–1, enter from Via Parione*), houses paintings by Giovanni Bellini, Signorelli, Filippino Lippi and Pontormo, and *Muses* from the ducal palace of Urbino, painted by Raphael's first master, Timoteo Viti. It also has the rarest of Florentine amenities: a garden, a 17th-century oasis of box hedges, Roman statues, lemon trees and tortoises. Further east on Lungarno Corsini stood the Libreria Orioli, which caused a scandal when it published the first edition of *Lady Chatterley's Lover* in 1927.

To the west of Piazza Goldoni lies the old neighbourhood of the only Florentine to have a continent named after him. Amerigo Vespucci (1451–1512) was a Medici agent in Seville, and made two voyages from there to America on the heels of Columbus. His parish church, **Ognissanti** (All Saints) (*open 8–12.30 and 5–7.30*), is set back from the river behind a Baroque façade, on property donated in 1256 by the Umiliati, a religious order that specialized in wool-working. The Vespucci family tomb is below the second altar to the right, and Amerigo himself is said to be pictured next to the Madonna in the fresco of the Madonna della Misericordia. Also buried in Ognissanti was the Filipepi family, one of whom was Botticelli.

The best art is to be found in the **Convent**, just to the left of the church at No.42 (*open Sat, Mon and Tues 9–12; you may have to ring*). Frescoed in the refectory is the great *Last Supper*, or *Cenacolo*, painted by Domenico Ghirlandaio in 1480. It's hard to think of a more serene and elegant Last Supper, alike to a garden party with its background of fruit trees and exotic birds; a peacock sits in the window, cherries and peaches litter the lovely tablecloth. On either side of the fresco are two scholarly saints moved from the church itself; Ghirlandaio's *St Jerome* and, on the right, young Botticelli's *St Augustine*.

Santa Maria Novella

Open Mon–Thurs and Sat 9.30–5; Fri, Sun and hols 1–5; adm.

As in so many other Italian cities, the two churches of the preaching orders – the Dominicans' Santa Maria Novella and the Franciscans' Santa Croce – became the largest and most prestigious in the city, where wealthy families vied to create the most beautiful chapels and tombs. In Florence, by some twitch of city planning, both of these sacred art galleries dominate broad, stale squares that do not invite you to linger; in the irregular **Piazza Santa Maria Novella** you may find yourself looking over your shoulder for the ghosts of the carriages that once raced madly around the two stout obelisks set on turtles, just as in a Roman circus, in the fashionable carriage races of the 1700s. The arcade on the south side, the **Loggia di San Paolo**, is very much like Brunelleschi's *Spedale degli Innocenti*, although it suffers somewhat from its use as a busy bus shelter; the lunette over the door, by Andrea della Robbia, is the *Meeting* *of SS. Francis and Dominic.* Santa Maria Novella redeems the anomie of its square with its stupendous black and white marble **façade**, the finest in Florence. The lower part, with its looping arcades, is Romanesque work in the typical Tuscan mode, finished before 1360. In 1456 Giovanni Rucellai commissioned Alberti to complete it, a remarkably fortunate choice. Alberti's half not only perfectly harmonizes with the original, but perfects it with geometrical harmonies to create what appears to be a kind of Renaissance Sun Temple. The original builders started it off by orienting the church to the south instead of west, so that at noon the sun streams through the 14th-century rose window. The only symbol Alberti put on the façade is a blazing sun; the unusual sundials, over the arches on the extreme right and left, were added by Cosimo I's court astronomer Egnazio Danti. The base of the façade is also the base of an equilateral triangle, with Alberti's sun at the apex. The beautiful frieze depicts the Rucellai emblem (a billowing sail), as on the Palazzo Rucellai. The wall of Gothic recesses to the right, enclosing the old cemetery, are *avelli*, or family tombs.

The **interior** is vast, lofty and more 'Gothic' in feel than any other church in Florence – no thanks to Vasari, who was set loose to remodel the church to 16th-century taste, painting over the original frescoes, removing the rood screen and Dominicans' choir from the nave, and remodelling the altars; in the 1800s restorers did their best to de-Vasari Santa Maria with neo-Gothic details. Neither party, however, could touch two of the interior's most distinctive features – the striking stone vaulting of the nave and the perspective created by the columns marching down the aisles, each pair placed a little closer together as they approach the altar.

Over the portal at the entrance is a fresco lunette by Botticelli that has recently been restored. One of Santa Maria Novella's best-known pictures has also recently been restored and is at the second altar on the left: Masaccio's *Trinita*, painted around 1425, one of the revolutionary works of the Renaissance. Masaccio's use of architectural elements and perspective gives his composition both physical and intellectual depth. The flat wall becomes a deeply recessed Brunelleschian chapel, calm and classical, enclosed in a coffered barrel vault; at the foot of the fresco a bleak skeleton decays in its tomb, bearing a favourite Tuscan reminder: 'I was that which you are, you will be that which I am.'

Above this morbid suggestion of physical death kneel the two donors; within the celestially rational inner sanctum the Virgin and St John stand at the foot of the Cross, humanity's link with the mystery of the Trinity. In the nearby pulpit, designed by Brunelleschi, Galileo was first denounced by the Inquisition for presuming to believe that the earth went around the sun.

There is little else to detain you in the aisles, but the first chapel in the left transept, the raised **Cappella Strozzi**, is one of the most evocative corners of 14th-century Florence, frescoed entirely by Nardo di Cione and his brother, Andrea Orcagna; on the vault pictures of St Thomas Aquinas and the Virtues are echoed in Andrea's lovely altarpiece *The Redeemer Donating the Keys to St Peter and the Book of Wisdom to St Thomas Aquinas*; on the left wall there's a crowded scene of Paradise, with the righteous lined up in a medieval school class photograph. On the right, Nardo painted a striking view of Dante's *Inferno*, with all of a Tuscan's special attention to precise

Santa Maria Novella

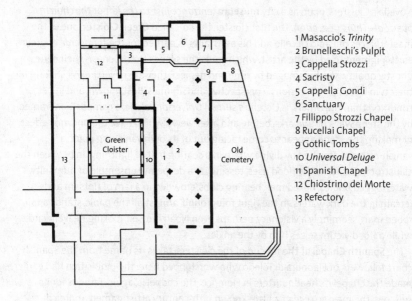

1 Masaccio's *Trinity*
2 Brunelleschi's Pulpit
3 Cappella Strozzi
4 Sacristy
5 Cappella Gondi
6 Sanctuary
7 Fillippo Strozzi Chapel
8 Rucellai Chapel
9 Gothic Tombs
10 *Universal Deluge*
11 Spanish Chapel
12 Chiostrino dei Morte
13 Refectory

map-like detail. Dramatically in the centre of the **Nave** hangs Giotto's *Crucifix* (*c.*1300), one of the artist's first works. In the **Gondi Chapel** hangs another famous *Crucifix*, carved in wood by Brunelleschi, which, according to Vasari, so astonished his friend Donatello that he dropped the eggs he was carrying in his apron for their lunch when he first saw it.

The charming fresco cycle in the **Sanctuary** (1485–90), painted by Domenico Ghirlandaio, is the *Lives of the Virgin, St John the Baptist and the Dominican Saints* portrayed in magnificent architectural settings; little Michelangelo was among the students who helped him complete it. Nearly all of the bystanders are portraits of Florentine quattrocento VIPs, including the artist himself (in the red hat, in the *Expulsion of St Joachim from the Temple*), but most prominent are the ladies and gentlemen of the Tornabuoni house. More excellent frescoes adorn the **Filippo Strozzi Chapel**, the finest work ever to come from the brush of Filippino Lippi, painted in 1502 near the end of his life; the exaggerated, dark and violent scenes portray the lives of St Philip (his crucifixion and his subduing of the dragon before the Temple of Mars, which creates such a stench that it kills the heathen prince) and of St John the Evangelist (raising Drusiana from the dead and being martyred in boiling oil). The chapel's beautifully carved tomb of Filippo Strozzi is by Benedetto da Maiano. The **Rucellai Chapel** contains a marble statue of the Madonna and Bambino by Nino Pisano and a fine bronze tomb by Ghiberti, which makes an interesting comparison with the three Gothic tombs nearby in the right transept. One of these contains the remains of the Patriarch of Constantinople, who died in here after the failure of the Council of Florence in 1439 to reunite the Western and Eastern Churches.

The Green Cloister and Spanish Chapel

More great frescoes, restored after the flood, await the visitor in Santa Maria Novella's Cloisters, open as a city museum (*entrance just to the left of the church; open Sat–Thurs 9–2; adm*). The first cloister, the so-called **Green Cloister**, one of the masterpieces of Paolo Uccello and his assistants, is named for the *terraverde* or green earth pigment used by the artist, which lends the scenes from Genesis their eerie, ghostly quality. Much damaged by time and neglect, they are nevertheless striking for their two Uccellian obsessions – perspective and animals. Best known, and in better condition than the others, is Uccello's surreal *Universal Deluge*, a composition framed by the steep walls of two arks, before and after views, which have the uncanny effect of making the scene appear to come racing out of its own vanishing point, a vanishing point touched by divine wrath in a searing bolt of lightning. In between the claustrophobic walls the flood rises, tossing up a desperate ensemble of humanity, waterlogged bodies, naked men bearing clubs, crowded in a jam of flotsam and jetsam in the dark waters. In the right foreground, amidst all the panic, stands a tall robed man, seemingly a visionary, perhaps even Noah himself, looking heavenward while a flood victim seizes him by the ankles.

The **Spanish Chapel** at the far end of the cloisters, takes its name from the Spanish court followers of Eleonora di Toledo who worshipped here; the Inquisition had earlier made the chapel its headquarters in Florence. The chapel is, again, famous for its frescoes, the masterpiece of a little-known 14th-century artist named Andrea di Buonaiuto, whose subject was the Dominican cosmology, beautifully portrayed so that even the 'Hounds of the Lord' (a pun on the Order's name, the 'Domini canes') on the right wall seem more like pets than militant bloodhounds sniffing out unorthodox beliefs. The church behind the scene with the hounds is a fairy-pink confection of what Buonaiuto imagined the Duomo would look like when finished; it may well be Arnolfo di Cambio's original conception. Famous Florentines, including Giotto, Dante, Boccaccio and Petrarch, stand to the right of the dais supporting the pope, emperor and various sour-faced hierophants. Off to the right the artist has portrayed four rather urbane Vices with dancing girls, while the Dominicans lead stray sheep back to the fold. On the left wall, St Thomas Aquinas dominates the portrayal of the Contemplative Life, surrounded by Virtues and Doctors of the Church.

The oldest part of the monastery, the **Chiostrino dei Morti** (1270s), contains some 14th-century frescoes, while the **Great Cloister** beyond is now off limits, the property of the Carabinieri, the new men in black charged with keeping the Italians orthodox. Off the Green Cloister, the **Refectory** is a striking hall with cross vaulting and frescoes by Alessandro Allori, now serving as a museum.

Around Santa Maria Novella

Just behind, but a world apart from Santa Maria Novella, another large, amorphous square detracts from one of Italy's finest modern buildings – the **Stazione Centrale**, designed by the architect Michelucci in 1935. Adorned by only a glass block canopy at the entrance (and an early model of that great Italian invention, the digital clock), the station is nevertheless remarkable for its clean lines and impeccable practicality.

Leading south from Piazza Santa Maria Novella, Via delle Belle Donne was once known for its excellent brothels. Today it is worth a short stroll to see one of the very few crossroads in Italy marked by a cross, a Celtic custom that never really caught on here. According to legend, **Croce del Trebbio** (from a corruption of 'trivium') marks the spot of a massacre of Patarene heretics in the 1240s, after the masses had been excited by a sermon given by the fire-eating Inquisitor St Peter Martyr from the pulpit of Santa Maria Novella.

San Lorenzo and the Medici Chapels

The lively quarter just east of Santa Maria Novella has been associated with the Medici ever since Giovanni di Bicci de' Medici commissioned Brunelleschi to rebuild the ancient church of San Lorenzo in 1420; subsequent members of the dynasty lavished bushels of florins on its decoration and Medici pantheon, and on several projects commissioned from Michelangelo. The mixed result of all their efforts could be held up as an archetype of the Renaissance, described by Walter Pater as 'great rather by what it designed or aspired to do, than by what it actually achieved'. San Lorenzo's façade of corrugated brick, was the most *nonfinito* of all of Michelangelo's unfinished projects; commissioned by Medici Pope Leo X in 1516, the project never got further than Michelangelo's scale model, which may be seen in the Casa Buonarroti. To complete the church's dingy aspect, the piazza in front contains a universally detested 19th-century statue of Cosimo I's dashing father, Giovanni delle Bande Nere, who died at the age of 28 of wounds received fighting against Emperor Charles V.

The **interior** was completed after Brunelleschi's death to his design, classically calm in good grey *pietra serena*. Of the artistic treasures it contains, most riveting are **Donatello's pulpits**, the sculptor's last works, completed by his pupils after his death in 1466. Cast in bronze, the pulpits were commissioned by Donatello's friend and patron Cosimo il Vecchio. Little in Donatello's previous work prepares the viewer for these scenes of Christ's passion and Resurrection with their rough and impressionistic details, their unbalanced, emotional and overcrowded compositions, more reminiscent of Rodin than anything Florentine. Off the left transept the **Old Sacristy** is a beautiful vaulted chamber with calmer sculptural decoration by Donatello.

Just beyond the Bronzino a door leads into the 15th-century **Cloister**, and from there a stair leads up to Michelangelo's **Biblioteca Laurenziana** (*open Mon–Sat 8.30–1.30*).

The Medici Chapels

Open daily 8.15–5; closed 2nd and 4th Sun and 1st, 3rd and 5th Mon of month.

San Lorenzo is most famous, however, for the Medici Chapels, which lie outside and behind the church. The entrance leads through the crypt, a dark and austere place where many of the Medici are actually buried.

Their main monument, the family obsession, is just up the steps, and has long been known as the **Chapel of the Princes**, a stupefying, costly octagon of death that, as much as the Grand Dukes fussed over it, lends their memory an unpleasant aftertaste of bric-a-brac that grew and grew. Perhaps only a genuine Medici could love its trashy opulence; all of Grand Duke Cosimo's descendants worked like beavers to finish it according to the plans left by Cosimo's illegitimate son, Giovanni de' Medici. Yet even today it is only partially completed, the *pietre dure* extending only part of the way up the walls. The 19th-century frescoes in the cupola are a poor substitute for the originally planned 'Apotheosis of the Medici' in lapis lazuli, and the two statues in gilded bronze in the niches over the sarcophagi are nothing like the intended figures to be carved in semi-precious stone. The most interesting feature is the inlaid *pietra dura* arms of Tuscan towns and the large Medici arms above, with their familiar six red boluses. (The balls probably derive from the family's origins as pharmacists (*medici*), and opponents called them 'the pills'. Medici supporters, however, made them their battle cry in street fights: 'Balls! Balls!')

A passageway leads to Michelangelo's **New Sacristy**, commissioned by Leo X to occupy an unfinished room originally built to balance Brunelleschi's Old Sacristy. Michelangelo's first idea was to turn it into a new version of his unfinished, overly ambitious Pope Julius Tomb, an idea quickly quashed by his Medici patrons, who requested instead four wall tombs. Michelangelo only worked on two of the monuments, but managed to finish the New Sacristy itself, creating a silent and gloomy mausoleum, closed in and grey, a chilly introspective cocoon calculated to depress even the most chatty tour groups.

Nor are the famous tombs guaranteed to cheer. Both honour nonentities: that of *Night and Day* belongs to Lorenzo il Magnifico's son, the Duke of Nemours, and symbolizes the Active Life, while the *Dawn and Dusk* is of Guiliano's nephew, Lorenzo, Duke of Urbino (and dedicatee of *The Prince*), who symbolizes the Contemplative Life (true to life in one respect – Lorenzo was a disappointment to Machiavelli and everyone else, passively obeying the dictates of his uncle Pope Leo X). Idealized statues of the two men, in Roman patrician gear, represent these states of mind, while draped on their sarcophagi are Michelangelo's four allegorical figures of the Times of Day, so heavy with weariness and grief they seem ready to slide off on to the floor. The most finished figure, *Night*, has always impressed the critics; she is almost a personification of despair, the mouthpiece of Michelangelo's most bitter verse:

> *Sweet to me is sleep, and even more to be like stone*
> *While wrong and shame endure;*
> *Not to see, nor to feel, is my good fortune.*
> *Therefore, do not wake me; speak softly here.*

Both statues of the dukes look towards the back wall, where a large double tomb for Lorenzo il Magnifico and his brother Giuliano was originally planned, to be decorated with river gods. The only part of this tomb ever completed is the statue of the *Madonna and Child* now in place, accompanied by the Medici patron saints, the doctors Cosmas and Damian.

In 1975, charcoal drawings were discovered on the walls of the little room off the altar (*ask at the cash desk for a permit, as only 12 people can enter at one time*). They were attributed to Michelangelo, who may have hidden here in 1530, when the Medici had regained Florence and apparently would only forgive the artist for aiding the republican defence if he would finish their tombs. But Michelangelo had had enough of their ducal pretences and went off to Rome, never to return to Florence.

Mercato Centrale and Perugino

What makes the neighbourhood around San Lorenzo so lively is its street market, which the Florentines run with an almost Neapolitan flamboyance (*open Tues–Sat, also open Mon in summer*). Stalls selling clothes and leather extend from the square up Via dell' Ariento and vicinity (nicknamed 'Shanghai') towards the **Mercato Centrale**, Florence's main food market (*open Mon–Fri 7–2; some stalls also open Sat afternoon*), a cast-iron and glass confection of the 1870s, brimful of fresh fruit and vegetables, leering boars' heads and mounds of tripe.

Beyond the market, at Via Faenza 42, is the entrance to Perugino's **Cenacolo di Foligno** fresco, housed in the ex-convent of the Tertiary Franciscans of Foligno (*open daily 9–12; ring the bell*). This 1490s Umbrian version of the Last Supper was discovered in the 1850s and has recently been restored.

Palazzo Medici-Riccardi

A block from San Lorenzo and the Piazza del Duomo stands the palace that once held Florence's unofficial court, where ambassadors would call, kings would lodge, and important decisions would be made. Built in 1444 by Michelozzo for Cosimo il Vecchio, it was the principal address of the Medici for a hundred years, until Cosimo I abandoned it for larger quarters in the Palazzo Vecchio and the Pitti Palace. In 1659 the Riccardi purchased the palace, added to it and did everything to keep it glittering until Napoleon and his debts drove them to bankruptcy in 1809. The palace is now used as the city's prefecture.

In its day, though, it was the largest private address in the city, where the family lived with the likes of Donatello's *David* and *Judith and Holofernes*, Uccello's *Battle of San Romano* and other masterpieces now in the Uffizi and Bargello. Frescoes are much harder to move, however, and the Palazzo Medici is worth visiting to see the most charming one in Italy, Benozzo Gozzoli's 1459 *Procession of the Magi*, located in the **Cappella dei Magi** upstairs (*open Thurs–Tues 9–7; adm. Only a few people allowed in at a time; in summer you can reserve, t 055 276 0340*).

Painting in a delightful, decorative manner more reminiscent of International Gothic than the awakening Renaissance style of his contemporaries, Gozzoli took a religious subject and turned it into a merry, brilliantly coloured pageant of beautifully dressed kings, knights and pages, accompanied by greyhounds and a giraffe, who travel through a springtime landscape of jewel-like trees and castles. This is a largely secular painting, representing less the original Three Kings than the annual pageant of the *Compagnia dei Magi*, Florence's richest confraternity. The scene is wrapped around three walls of the small chapel – you feel as if you had walked straight into a glowing fairytale world. Most of the faces are those of the Medici and other local celebrities; Gozzoli certainly had no qualms about putting himself among the crowd of figures on the right wall, with his name written on his red cap. In the foreground, note the black man carrying a bow. Blacks, as well as Turks, Circassians, Tartars and others, were common enough in Renaissance Florence, originally brought as slaves. By the 1400s, however, contemporary writers mention them as artisans, fencing masters, soldiers and one famous archery instructor, who may be the man pictured here. For an extraordinary contrast pop into the **gallery** (up the second set of stairs) with its 17th-century ceiling by Neapolitan Luca Giordano, showing the last, unspeakable Medici floating around in marshmallow clouds. In a small adjoining room is a lovely Madonna and Child by Filippo Lippi, placed here a couple of years ago after restoration.

San Marco

Convent open daily 8.15–1.50, Sat 8.15–6.50; closed 1st and 3rd Sun of month and 2nd and 4th Mon of month; adm. Church open 7–12 and 4–7 daily.

Despite all the others who contributed to this Dominican monastery and church, it has always been best known for the work of its most famous resident. Fra Angelico lived here from 1436 until his death in 1455, spending the time turning Michelozzo's simple **cloister** into a complete exposition of his own deep faith, expressed in bright colours and angelic pastels. Fra Angelico painted the frescoes in the corners of the cloister, and on the first floor there is a small museum of his work, collected from Florentine churches, as well as several early 15th-century portraits by Fra Bartolomeo, capturing some of the most sincere spirituality of the age. The *Last Supper* in the refectory is by Ghirlandaio. Other works by Fra Angelico include the *Life of Christ* series, in which the Saved are well-dressed Italians holding hands. The bad (mostly princes and prelates) are stripped to receive their interesting tortures.

Right at the top of the stairs to the monks' dormitory, your eyes meet the Angelic Friar's masterpiece, a miraculous *Annunciation* that offers an intriguing comparison with Leonardo's *Annunciation* in the Uffizi. The subject was a favourite with Florentine artists, not only because it was a severe test – expressing a divine revelation with a composition of strict economy – but because the Annunciation, falling near the spring equinox, was New Year's Day for Florence until the Medici adopted the Pope's calendar in the 17th century. In each of the monks' cells, Fra Angelico and students painted the *Crucifixion,* all the same but for some slight differences in pose; glancing in the cells down the corridor in turn gives the impression of a cartoon. One of the cells belonged to Savonarola, who was the prior here during his period of dominance in Florence; it has the simple furniture of the period and a portrait of Savonarola by Fra Bartolomeo. In a nearby corridor, you can see an anonymous painting of the monk and two of his followers being led to the stake on Piazza della Signoria. Michelozzo's Library, off the main corridor, is as light and airy as the cloisters below; in it is displayed a collection of choir books, one illuminated by Fra Angelico.

Near San Marco, at Via G La Pira 4, the **University of Florence** runs several small museums; nearly all the collections were begun by the indefatigable Medici. The **Geology and Palaeontology Museum** (*open winter Tues 9–1 and 2–6, Wed–Sat 9–1; summer Wed and Fri 9–1; adm*) has one of Italy's best collections of fossils, many of which were uncovered in Tuscany. The **Mineralogy and Lithology Museum** (*open Mon–Fri 9–1 and 2nd Sun of month 8–2; adm*) houses a collection of strange and beautiful rocks, especially from Elba. The **Botanical Museum** (*open on request only, t 055 275 7462 for details*) is of less interest to the casual visitor, though it houses one of the most extensive herbariums in the world; most impressive here are the exquisite wax models of plants made in the early 1800s.

Also on Via La Pira is the entrance to the University's **Giardino dei Semplici**, the botanical garden created for Cosimo I. The garden maintains its original layout, with medicinal herbs, Tuscan plants, flowers and tropical plants in its greenhouses (*open summer Wed–Fri 9–1, Tues 9–1 and 3–6; winter Mon–Fri 9–1; adm*).

Sant'Apollonia and the Scalzo

Cenacoli, or frescoes of the Last Supper, became almost *de rigueur* in monastic refectories; in several of these the Last Supper is all that remains of a convent. Until 1860, the Renaissance convent of **Sant'Apollonia**, off Piazza S. Marco at Via XXVII Aprile 1 (*open daily 8.15–1.50; closed 2nd and 4th Mon and 1st, 3rd and 5th Sun of month*) was the abode of cloistered nuns, and the *cenacolo* in their refectory was a secret. When the convent was suppressed, and the painting discovered under the whitewash, the critics believed it to be the work of Paolo Uccello, but lately have unanimously attributed it to Andrea del Castagno, painted 1445–50. The other walls have sinopie of the Crucifixion, Entombment and Resurrection by Castagno; in the vestibule there are good works by Neri di Bicci and Paolo Schiavo.

Not far away you can enter a radically different artistic world in the **Chiostro dello Scalzo**, again off Piazza S. Marco at Via Cavour 69 (*open Mon, Thurs and Sat 8.15–1.50; ring the bell*). Formerly part of the Confraternity of San Giovanni Battista, all that has survived is this cloister, frescoed (1514–24) with scenes of the life of St John the Baptist by Andrea del Sarto and his pupil Franciabigio. Del Sarto, Browning's 'perfect painter', painted these in monochrome grisaille, and while the scene of the *Baptism of Christ* is a beautiful work, some of the other panels are the most unintentionally funny things in Florence – the scene of Herod's banquet is reduced to a meagre breakfast where the king and queen look up indignantly at the man bringing in the platter of the Baptist's head as if he were a waiter who has made a mistake with their order.

The Galleria dell'Accademia

Open Tues–Sun 8.15–6.50; adm.

From Piazza San Marco, Via Ricasoli makes a beeline for the Duomo, but on most days the view is obstructed by the crowds milling around No.60; in the summer the queues are as long as those at the Uffizi, everyone anxious to get a look at

Michelangelo's *David*. Just over a hundred years ago Florence decided to take this precocious symbol of republican liberty out of the rain and install it, with much pomp, in a specially built classical exedra in this gallery.

Michelangelo completed the *David* for the city in 1504, when he was 29, and it was the work that established the overwhelming reputation he had in his own time. The monstrous block of marble – 16ft high but unusually shallow – had been quarried 40 years earlier by the Cathedral Works and spoiled by other hands. The block was offered around to several other artists, including Leonardo da Vinci, before young Michelangelo decided to take up the challenge of carving the largest statue created since Roman times. And it is the dimensions of the *David* that remain the biggest surprise in these days of endless reproductions. Certainly as a political symbol of the Republic, he is excessive – the irony of a David the size of a Goliath is disconcerting – but as a symbol of the artistic and intellectual aspirations of the Renaissance period he is unsurpassed.

And it's hard to deny, after gazing at this enormous nude, that these same Renaissance aspirations by the 1500s began snuggling uncomfortably close to the frontiers of kitsch. Disproportionate size is one symptom; the calculated intention to excite a strong emotional response is another. In the *David*, virtuosity eclipses vision, and commits the even deadlier kitsch sin of seeking the sterile empyrean of perfect beauty – most would argue that Michelangelo here achieves it, perhaps capturing his own feelings about the work in the *David*'s chillingly vain, self-satisfied expression. This is also one of the few statues to have actually injured someone. During a political disturbance in the Piazza della Signoria, its arm broke off and fell on a farmer's toe. In 1991 it was David's toe that fell victim when a madman chopped it off. Since then, the rest of his anatomy has been shielded by glass.

In the Galleria next to the *David* are Michelangelo's famous *nonfiniti*, the four *Prisoners* or *Slaves*, worked on between 1519 and 1536, sculpted for Pope Julius' tomb and left in various stages of completion, although it is endlessly argued whether this is by design or through lack of time. Whatever the case, they illustrate Michelangelo's view of sculpture as a prisoner in stone just as the soul is a prisoner of the body. When Michelangelo left them, the Medici snapped them up to decorate Buontalenti's Grotta fountain in the Boboli gardens.

The Gallery was founded by Grand Duke Pietro Leopold in 1784 to provide Academy students with examples of art from every period. The big busy Mannerist paintings around the *David* are by Michelangelo's contemporaries, among them Pontormo's *Venus and Cupid*, with a Michelangelesque Venus among theatre masks. Other rooms contain a good selection of quattrocento painting, including the *Madonna del Mare* by Botticelli, a damaged Baldovinetti, the *Thebaid* by a follower of Uccello, and Perugino's *Deposition*. The painted frontal of the **Adimari chest** shows a delightful wedding scene of the 1450s with the baptistry in the background that has been reproduced in half the books that have ever been written about the Renaissance.

The hall off to the left of the *David* was formerly the women's ward of a hospital, depicted in a greenish painting by Pontormo. Now it is used as a gallery of plaster models by 19th-century members of the Accademia.

The excellent **Collection of Old Musical Instruments** once housed in the Palazzo Vecchio has moved to the Accademia. The collection of some 150 exhibits, including several violins and cellos by Cremona greats like Stradivarius and Guarneri, are on display in a room on the ground floor, properly organized and labelled.

Piazza Santissima Annunziata

This lovely square, really the only Renaissance attempt at a unified ensemble in Florence, is surrounded on three sides by arcades. In its centre, gazing down the splendid vista of Via dei Servi towards the Duomo, stands the equestrian statue of Ferdinand I (1607) by Giambologna and his pupil Pietro Tacca, made of bronze from Turkish cannons captured during the Battle of Lepanto. More fascinating than Ferdinand are the pair of bizarre Baroque fountains, also by Tacca, that share the square. Though of a nominally marine theme, they resemble tureens of bouillabaisse that any ogre would be proud to serve, topped by grinning winged monkeys.

In the 1420s Filippo Brunelleschi struck the first blow for classical calm in this piazza when he built the celebrated **Spedale degli Innocenti** (*open Thurs–Tues 8.30–2; adm*) and its famous portico – an architectural landmark, but also a monument to Renaissance Italy's long, hard and ultimately unsuccessful struggle towards some kind of social consciousness. Even in the best of times, Florence's poor were treated like dirt; if any enlightened soul had been so bold as to propose even a modern conservative 'trickle down' theory to the Medici and the banking élite, their first thought would have been how to stop the leaks. Babies, at least, were treated a little better. The Spedale degli Innocenti was the first hospital for foundlings in Italy and the world (at the left end of the loggia you can still see the original window-wheel where babies were anonymously abandoned until 1875). Today it is a nursery school. The Spedale was Brunelleschi's first completed work and demonstrates his use of geometrical proportions adapted to traditional Tuscan Romanesque architecture. His lovely portico is adorned with the famous blue and white tondi of infants in swad-dling clothes by Andrea della Robbia, added as an appeal to charity in the 1480s after several children died of malnutrition. Brunelleschi also designed the two beautiful cloisters of the convent; the **Chiostro delle Donne**, reserved for the hospital's nurses (located up the ramp on the right at No.13), is especially fine. Upstairs, the **Museo dello Spedale** (*open Thurs–Tues 8.30–2; adm*) contains a number of detached frescoes from Ognissanti and other churches, among them an unusual series of red and orange prophets by Alessandro Allori; other works include a *Madonna and Saints* by Piero di Cosimo, a *Madonna and Child* by Luca della Robbia, and the brilliant *Adoration of the Magi* (1488) painted by Domenico Ghirlandaio for the hospital's church, a crowded, colourful composition featuring portraits of members of the Arte della Lana, who funded the Spedale.

Santissima Annunziata

To complement Brunelleschi's arches, the old church of Santissima Annunziata was rebuilt and given a broad arcaded portico by Michelozzo facing the street. Behind the portico the architect added the **Chiostrino dei Voti**, a porch decorated with a collection of early 16th-century frescoes, including two by Andrea del Sarto. The best of these, faded as it is, is a finely detailed *Nativity* by Alessio Baldovinetti, one of the quattrocento's underappreciated masters.

The church itself is the gaudiest in Florence; its freshly gilded elliptical dome, its unusual polygonal tribune around the sanctuary and megatons of *pietra dura* have helped it become the city's high-society parish, where even funerals are major social events. The huge candlelit chapel in the rear is the Tempietta, also by Michelozzo, sheltering a miraculous painting of *The Annunciation*.

Archaeology Museum

Open Mon 2–7, Tues and Thurs 8.30–7, Wed and Fri–Sun 8.30–2; adm.

From Piazza SS. Annunziata, Via della Colonna leads to Florence's **Museo Archeologico**, housed in the 17th-century Palazzo della Crocetta, originally built for Grand Duchess Maria Maddalena of Austria. Like nearly every other museum in Florence, this impressive collection was begun by the Medici, beginning with Cosimo il Vecchio and accelerating with the insatiable Cosimo I and his heirs. The Medici were especially fond of Etruscan things, while the impressive Egyptian collection was begun by Leopold II in the 1830s.

The **Etruscan collection** is on the first floor, including the famous bronze *Chimera*, a remarkable beast with the three heads of a lion, goat and snake. This 5th-century BC work, dug up near Arezzo in 1555 and immediately snatched by Cosimo I, had a great influence on Mannerist artists. There is no Mannerist fancy about its origins, though; like all such composite monsters, it is a religious icon, a calendar beast symbolizing the three seasons of the ancient Mediterranean agricultural year. In the same corridor stands the *Arringatore*, or Orator, a monumental bronze of the Hellenistic period, a civic-minded and civilized-looking gentleman, dedicated to Aulus Metellus, and the statue of *Minerva*. Also to be found in this section are other Etruscan bronzes, big and small. The cases here are full of wonderful objects, anything from tiny animals to jewellery, carved mirrors and household objects such as plates – there's even a strainer. All these show just how skilled the Etruscans were in casting bronze.

The beautifully lit **Egyptian collection**, also on the first floor, has been expanded and modernized. It includes some interesting small statuettes, mummies, canopic vases, and a unique wood-and-bone chariot, nearly completely preserved, found in a 14th-century BC tomb in Thebes.

On the second floor there is plenty of Greek art; Etruscan noble families were wont to buy up all they could afford. The beautiful Hellenistic horse's head once adorned the Palazzo Medici-Riccardi. The *Idolino*, a bronze of a young athlete, is believed to be a Roman copy of a 5th-century BC Greek original. There is an excellent *Kouros*, a young man in the archaic style from 6th-century BC Sicily. An unusual, recent find, the silver

Baratti Amphora, was made in the 4th century BC in Antioch and covered with scores of small medallions showing mythological figures. Scholars believe that the images and their arrangement may encode an entire system of belief, the secret teaching of one of the mystic-philosophical cults common in Hellenistic times, and they hope some day to decipher it. There's a vast collection of Greek pottery (including the massive *François vase* in Room 2), and large Greek, Roman and Renaissance bronzes, recently brought out of storage. There are also several fabulous Greek marble sculptures dating from *c.* 500 BC.

There is virtually nothing displayed on the ground floor now although temporary exhibitions are held there. In the garden are several reconstructed Etruscan tombs (*open to visitors on Sat 8.30–2*). The fabulous collection of precious stones, coins and, most notably, cameos (amassed by the Medici) is now permanently on display in the corridor which runs between the museum and the church of Santissima Annunziata.

Santa Maria Maddalena dei Pazzi and the Synagogue

East of the Archaeological Museum, Via della Colonna becomes one of Florence's typical straight, boring Renaissance streets. It's well worth taking a detour down Borgo Pinti, to No.58, to visit one of the city's least known but most intriguing churches, **Santa Maria Maddalena dei Pazzi** (*open Mon–Sat 9.30–12 and 5–7; Sun 9.30–11 and 5–7*), a fine example of architectural syncretism. The church itself was founded in the 13th century, rebuilt in classically Renaissance style by Giuliano da Sangallo, then given a full dose of Baroque when the church was rededicated to the Counter-Reformation saint of the Pazzi family. Inside it's all high theatre, with a gaudy trompe l'œil ceiling, paintings by Luca Giordano, florid chapels, and a wild marble chancel. From the Sacristy a door leads down into a crypt to the chapterhouse, which contains a frescoed *Crucifixion* (1496), one of Perugino's masterpieces. Despite the symmetry and quiet, contemplative grief of the five figures at the foot of the Cross and the stillness of the luminous Tuscan-Umbrian landscape, the fresco has a powerful impact, giving the viewer the uncanny sensation of being able to walk right into the scene. The fresco has never been restored; in the 1966 flood, the water came within four inches of it, and stopped.

Florence's Jewish community, although today a mere 1,200 strong, has long been one of the most important in Italy, invited to Florence by the Republic in 1430, but repeatedly exiled and readmitted until Cosimo I founded Florence's Ghetto in 1551. When the Ghetto was opened up in 1848 and demolished soon after, a new **Synagogue** (1874–82) was built in Via L C Farini: a tall, charming, Mozarabic Pre-Raphaelite hybrid inspired by the Hagia Sophia and the Transito Synagogue of Toledo (*open April, May, Sept and Oct Sun–Thurs 10–5 and Fri 10–2; June–Aug Sun–Thurs 10–6 and Fri 10–3; Nov–Feb Sun–Thurs 10–2; adm*). Although seriously damaged by the Nazis in August 1944, as well as by the Arno in 1966, it has since been lovingly restored. There's a small **Jewish Museum** upstairs (*opening hours as for Synagogue; call t 055 245252/3 for info*), which has a documentary history of Florentine Jews.

Sant'Ambrogio and the Flea Market

The streets of Sant'Ambrogio are among the most dusty and piquant in the city centre, a neighbourhood where tourists seldom tread. Life revolves around the church in **Sant'Ambrogio** and its neighbouring food market made of cast iron in 1873; the church (rebuilt in the 13th century, 19th-century façade) is of interest for its artwork: the second chapel on the right has a lovely fresco of the *Madonna Enthroned with Saints* by Orcagna (or his school) and the **Cappella del Miracolo**, just left of the high altar, contains Mino da Fiesole's celebrated marble *Tabernacle* (1481) and his own tomb. The chapel has a fresco of a procession by Cosimo Rosselli, especially interesting for its depiction of 15th-century celebrities, including Pico della Mirandola and Rosselli himself (in a black hat, in the group on the left). Andrea Verrocchio is buried in the fourth chapel on the left; on the wall by the second altar, there's a *Nativity* by Baldovinetti. The fresco of an atypical *St Sebastian* in the first chapel of the left is by Agnolo Gaddi.

From Sant'Ambrogio take Via Pietrapiana to the bustling **Piazza dei Ciompi**, named after the wool-workers' revolt of 1378. In the morning, Florence's flea market or **Mercatino** takes place here, the best place in town to buy that 1940s radio or outdated ball gown you've always wanted. One side of the square is graced with the **Loggia del Pesce**, built by Vasari in 1568 for the fishmongers of the Mercato Vecchio; when that was demolished the loggia was salvaged and re-erected here.

Casa Buonarroti

Open Wed–Mon 9.30–2; adm; look out for their temporary exhibitions.

Michelangelo never lived in this house at Via Ghibellina 70, although he purchased it in 1508. That wasn't the point, especially to an artist who had no thought for his own personal comfort, or anyone else's – he never washed, and never took off his boots, even in bed. Real estate was an obsession of his, as he struggled to restore the status of the semi-noble but impoverished Buonarroti family. His nephew Leonardo inherited the house and several works of art in 1564; later he bought the two houses next door to create a memorial to his uncle, hiring artists to paint scenes from Michelangelo's life. In the mid-19th century, the house was opened to the public as a Michelangelo museum.

The ground floor is dedicated to mostly imaginary portraits of the artist, and works of art collected by his nephew's descendants, including an eclectic Etruscan and Roman collection. The main attractions, however, are upstairs, beginning with Michelangelo's earliest known work, the beautiful bas-relief *The Madonna of the Steps* (1490–1), the precocious work of a 16-year-old influenced by Donatello and studying in the household of Lorenzo il Magnifico; the relief of a battle scene, inspired by classical models, dates from the same period. Small models and drawings of potential projects line the walls; there's the wooden model for the façade of San Lorenzo, with designs for some of the statuary Michelangelo intended to fill in its austere blank spaces – as was often the case, his ideas were far too grand for his patron's purse and patience.

The next four rooms were painted in the 17th century to illustrate Michelangelo's life, virtues and apotheosis, depicting a polite, deferential and pleasant Michelangelo hobnobbing with popes. Those who know the artist best from *The Agony and the Ecstasy* may think they painted the wrong man by mistake. One of the best sections is a frieze of famous Florentines in the library. Other exhibits include a painted wooden *Crucifix* discovered in Santo Spirito in 1963 and believed by most scholars to be a documented one by Michelangelo, long thought to be lost; the contrapposto position of the slender body, and the fact that only Michelangelo would carve a nude Christ, weigh in favour of the attribution.

Santa Croce

Open Mon–Sat 9.30–5.30, Sun 1–5.30; adm (includes museum).

No place in Florence so feeds the urge to dispute as the church of Santa Croce, Tuscany's 'Westminster Abbey', the largest Franciscan basilica in Italy, a must-see for every tour group. It was here that Stendhal gushed: 'I had attained to that supreme degree of sensibility where the divine intimations of art merge with the impassioned sensuality of emotion. As I emerged from the port of Santa Croce, I was seized with a fierce palpitation of the heart; I walked in constant fear of falling to the ground.' But don't be put off; most people manage to emerge without tripping over themselves.

The contradictions begin in the **Piazza Santa Croce**, which has its interesting points – the row of medieval houses with projecting upper storeys, supported by stone brackets; the faded bloom of dancing nymphs on the **Palazzo dell' Antella**; the curious 14th-century **Palazzo Serristori-Cocchi**, opposite the church; a grim 19th-century statue of Dante (if Dante really looked like that, it's no wonder Beatrice married someone else). Because this piazza is the lowest-lying in the city, it suffered the worst in the 1966 flood, when 20ft of oily water poured in; note the plaque marking the water line on the corner of Via Verdi.

Dominant over all is Santa Croce's neo-Gothic façade, built in 1857–63 and financed by Sir Francis Sloane, whose Sloane Square in London has more admirers than this black and white design, derived from Orcagna's Tabernacle in Orsanmichele. Yet of all the modern façades built on Italy's churches to atone for the chronic Renaissance inability to finish anything, this is one of the least offensive.

The Interior

Santa Croce was founded by St Francis himself; during repairs after the flood, vestiges of a small, early 13th-century church were discovered under the present structure. It went by the board in Florence's colossal building programme of the 1290s. The great size of the new church speaks for the immense popularity of Franciscan preaching. Arnolfo di Cambio planned it, and it was largely completed by the 1450s but, as in Santa Maria Novella, Giorgio Vasari and the blinding forces of High Renaissance mediocrity were unleashed upon the interior. Vasari never had

Santa Croce

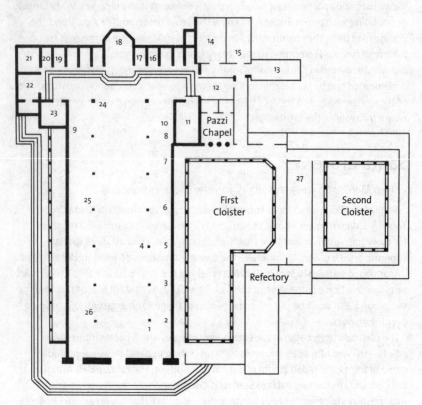

1	Madonna del Latte	15	Rinuccini Chapel
2	Tomb of Michaelangelo	16	Peruzzi Chapel
3	Monument to Dante	17	Bardi Chapel
4	Benedetto da Maiano's Pulpit	18	Sanctuary
5	Vittorio Alfieri's Tomb	19	Bardi di Libertà Chapel
6	Tomb of Machiavelli	20	Bardi di Vernio Chapel
7	Donatello's *Annunciation*	21	Niccolini Chapel
8	Tomb of Leonardo Bruni	22	Bardi Chapel
9	Tomb of Carlo Malaspini	23	Salviati Chapel
10	Tomb of Rossini	24	Monument to Alberti
11	Castellani Chapel	25	Tomb of Lorenzo Ghiberti
12	Baroncelli Chapel	26	Galileo's Tomb
13	Medici Chapel	27	Museo dell'Opera di Santa Croce
14	Sacristy		

much use for the art of Andrea Orcagna – he not only left him out of his influential *Lives of the Artists* but in Santa Croce he destroyed Orcagna's great fresco cycle that once covered the nave, replacing it with uninspired side altars.

For centuries it was the custom to install monuments to illustrious men in Santa Croce and, as you enter, you can see them lining the long aisles. Like many Franciscan churches, Santa Croce's large size, its architectural austerity and open timber roof resemble a barn, but at the end there's a lovely polygonal sanctuary, which shimmers with light and colour streaming through 14th-century stained glass. The whole interior has been treated to an overhaul, completed in 2000, including restoration of the ceiling.

Perversely, the greater the person buried in Santa Croce, the uglier their memorial. A member of the Pazzi conspiracy, Francesco Nori, is buried by the first pillar in the right aisle, and graced by one of the loveliest works of art, the *Madonna del Latte* (1478), a bas-relief by Antonio Rossellino, while the **Tomb of Michelangelo** (1570, the first in the right aisle) by Vasari is one of the least attractive. Michelangelo died in Rome in 1564, refusing for 35 years to return to Florence while alive, but agreeing to give the city his corpse. Dante has fared even worse, with an 1829 neoclassical monument that's as disappointing as the fact (to the Florentines, anyway) that Dante is buried in Ravenna, where he died in exile in 1321.

Facing the nave, Benedetto da Maiano's **marble pulpit** (1476) is one of the most beautiful the Renaissance ever produced. Behind it, the **Vittorio Alfieri Monument** (1809) was sculpted by neoclassical master Antonio Canova and paid for by his lover, the Countess of Albany. Next is the nondescript 18th-century **Monument of Niccolò Machiavelli**, and then Donatello's *Annunciation* (1430s), a tabernacle in gilded lime- stone, the angel wearing a remarkably sweet expression as he gently breaks the news to a grave, thoughtful Madonna. Bernardo Rossellino's **Tomb of Leonardo Bruni** (1447), another masterpiece of the Renaissance, is perhaps the one monument that best fits the man it honours. Bruni was a Greek scholar, a humanist, and the author of the first major historical work of the period, *The History of Florence*, a copy of which his tranquil effigy holds. The tomb, with its Brunelleschian architectural setting, proved a great inspiration to other artists, most obviously Desiderio da Settignano and his equally beautiful **Tomb of Carlo Marsuppini** (1453) directly across the nave, and the less inspired, more imitative **Monument to Rossini** crowded in to the left. The last tomb in the aisle belongs to poet and patriot Ugo Foscolo.

Santa Croce is especially rich in trecento frescoes, providing a unique opportunity to compare the work of Giotto with his followers. The south transept's **Castellani Chapel** has some of the later, more decorative compositions by Agnolo Gaddi (*Scenes from the Lives of Saints*, 1380s). The beautiful **Baroncelli Chapel** was painted with scenes from the Life of the Virgin by Agnolo's father Taddeo, Giotto's assistant in the 1330s and includes a bright, gilded altarpiece, the *Coronation of the Virgin* by Giotto and his workshop. The *Annunciation to the Shepherds* by Taddeo, seen to the left of the window, is important as it is thought to be the first nocturnal scene in the history of western art.

The next portal gives on to a **Corridor** and the **Medici Chapel** (*open for Mass at 6pm*), both designed by Michelozzo, containing one of Andrea della Robbia's finest altar-pieces and a 19th-century fake Donatello, a relief of the *Madonna and Child* that fooled the experts for decades. From the corridor a door leads to the **Sacristy**, its walls frescoed by Taddeo Gaddi (*The Crucifixion*), Spinello Aretino and Niccolò di Pietro Gerini. Behind the 14th-century grille, the **Rinuccini Chapel** was frescoed by one of Giotto's most talented followers, the Lombard Giovanni da Milano, in the 1360s.

Giotto's Chapels

The frescoes in the two chapels to the right of the sanctuary, the **Peruzzi Chapel** and the **Bardi Chapel**, were painted by the legendary Giotto in the 1330s, towards the end of his life when the artist returned from Padua and his work in the Arena chapel. The frescoes have not fared well during the subsequent 660 years. Firstly Giotto painted large parts of the walls *a secco* (on dry plaster) instead of *affresco* (on wet plaster), presenting the same kind of preservation problems that bedevil Leonardo's *Last Supper*; secondly, the 18th century thought so little of the frescoes that they were whitewashed over as eyesores. Rediscovered some 150 years later and finally restored in 1959, the frescoes now, even though fragmentary, may be seen more or less as Giotto painted them. The Peruzzi Chapel contains scenes from the Lives of St John the Evangelist and the Baptist. In the Bardi Chapel is the *Life of St Francis*, which makes an interesting comparison with the frescoes in Assisi. The contrast between Giotto's frescoes and the chapel's 13th-century altarpiece, also showing the *Life of St Francis*, is a fair yardstick for measuring the breadth of the Giottesque revolution.

Agnolo Gaddi designed the stained glass around the **Sanctuary**, as well as the fascinating series of frescoes on the *Legend of the True Cross*.

Further to the left are two more chapels frescoed by followers of Giotto: the fourth, the **Bardi di Libertà Chapel**, by Bernardo Daddi, and the last, the **Bardi di Vernio Chapel**, by Maso di Banco, one of the most innovative and mysterious artists of the trecento. The frescoes illustrate the little-known *Life of St Sylvester* – his baptism of Emperor Constantine, the resurrection of the bull, the closing of the dragon's mouth and resurrection of two sorcerers; on the other wall of the chapel are a *Dream of Constantine* and *Vision of SS. Peter and Paul*. In the corner of the transept, the richly marbled **Niccolini Chapel** offers a Mannerist-Baroque change of pace, built by Antonio Dossi in 1584 and decorated with paintings by Allori (*under restoration*). Next, the second **Bardi Chapel** houses the famous crucifix by Donatello that Brunelleschi disdainfully called 'a peasant on the Cross'. The last funeral monuments, near the door, are those of Lorenzo Ghiberti and Galileo, the latter an 18th-century work. For running foul of the Inquisition, Galileo was not permitted a Christian burial until 1737.

The Pazzi Chapel

Open Mon–Sat 9.30–5.30, Sun 1–5.30; entrance through Santa Croce; adm.

This chapel is well worth a visit. Brunelleschi, who could excel on the monumental scale of the cathedral dome, saved some of his best work for small places. Without

The Legend of the True Cross

This popular medieval story begins with Noah's son, Seth, as an old man, asking for the essence of mercy. The Angel Gabriel replies by giving Seth a branch, saying that 5,000 years must pass before mankind may know true redemption. Seth plants the branch over Adam's grave on Mount Sinai, and it grows into a magnificent tree. King Solomon orders the tree cut, but as it is too large to move, the trunk stays where it is and is used as the main beam of a bridge. The Queen of Sheba is about to cross the bridge when she has a vision that the saviour of the world will be suspended from its wood, and that his death will mark the end of the Kingdom of the Jews. She refuses to cross the bridge, and writes of her dream to Solomon, who has the beam buried deep underground. Nevertheless, it is dug up and used to make the cross of Christ.

The cross next appears in the dream of Emperor Constantine before the Battle of Milvan Bridge, when he hears a voice saying that under this sign he will conquer. When it proves true, he sends his mother Helen to find the cross in Jerusalem. There she meets Judas Cyriacus, a pious Jew who knows where Golgotha is, but won't tell until Helen has him thrown in a well and nearly starved to death. When at last he agrees to dig, a sweet scent fills the air, and Judas Cyriacus is immediately converted. To discover which of the three crosses they find is Christ's, each is held over the coffin of a youth; the True Cross brings him back to life. After all this trouble in finding it, Helen leaves the cross in Jerusalem, where it is stolen by the Persians. Their King Chosroes thinks its power will bring him a great victory, but instead he loses the battle, and Persia, to Emperor Heraclius, who decides to return the holy relic to Jerusalem. But the gate is blocked by the Angel Gabriel, who reminds the proud Heraclius that Jesus entered the city humbly, on the back of an ass. And so, in a similar manner, the emperor returns the cross to Jerusalem.

knowing the architect, and something about the austere religious tendencies of the Florentines, the Pazzi Chapel is inexplicable, a Protestant reformation in architecture unlike anything ever built before. The 'vocabulary' is essential Brunelleschi, the geometric forms emphasized by the simplicity of the decoration: *pietra serena* pilasters and rosettes on white walls, arches, 12 terracotta *tondi* of the Apostles by Luca della Robbia, coloured rondels of the Evangelists in the pendentives by Donatello, and a small, stained-glass window by Baldovinetti. Even so, that is enough. The contemplative repetition of elements makes for an aesthetic that posed a direct challenge to the International Gothic of the time.

Leaving the Pazzi Chapel (notice Luca della Robbia's terracotta decorations on the portico), a doorway on the left of the cloister leads to Brunelleschi's **Second Cloister**, designed with the same subtlety and one of the quietest spots in Florence.

The old monastic buildings off the first cloister now house the **Museo dell'Opera di Santa Croce** (*open Mon–Sat 9.30–5.30, Sun 1–5.30; adm*), where you can see Cimabue's celebrated *Crucifix*, devastated by the flood, and partly restored after one of Florence's perennial restoration controversies. The refectory wall has another fine fresco by Taddeo Gaddi, of the *Tree of the Cross and the Last Supper*; fragments of Orcagna's frescoes salvaged from Vasari's obliteration offer powerful, nightmarish vignettes of *The Triumph of Death and Hell*. Donatello's huge, gilded bronze statue *St Louis of Toulouse* (1423) – a flawed work representing a flawed character, according to Donatello – was made for the façade of Orsanmichele. The museum also contains works by Andrea della Robbia, and a painting of Mayor Bargellini with a melancholy Santa Croce submerged in the 1966 flood for a backdrop; under the colonnade there's a statue of Florence Nightingale, born in and named after the city in 1820.

Around Santa Croce: the Horne Museum

The east end of Florence, a rambling district packed with artisans and small manufacturers, traditionally served as the artists' quarter in Renaissance times. It's still one of the livelier neighbourhoods today, with a few lingering artists lodged in the upper storeys, hoping to breathe inspiration from the very stones where Michelangelo walked. It is a good place to observe the workaday Florence behind the glossy façade.

From Santa Croce, the pretty Borgo Santa Croce leads towards the Arno and the delightful **Horne Museum**, housed in a Renaissance palace, at Via de' Benci 6 (*open Mon–Sat 9–1; closed Sun and hols; adm*). Herbert Percy Horne (1844–1916) was an English art historian, biographer of Botticelli, and Florentinophile, who bequeathed his collection to the nation.

North Bank Peripheral Attractions

The Cascine

The newer sections of the city are, by and large, irredeemably dull. Much of Florence's traffic problem is channelled through its ring of avenues, or *viali*, laid out in the 1860s by Giuseppe Poggi to replace the demolished walls. On and along them are scattered points of interest, including some of the old city gates; the distances involved and danger of carbon monoxide poisoning on the *viali* make the idea of walking insane.

Bus 17C from the station or Duomo will take you through the congestion to the **Cascine**, the long (3.5km), narrow public park lining this bank of the Arno, originally used as the Medici's dairy farm, or *cascina*, and later as a Grand Ducal hunting park and theatre for public spectacles. A windy autumn day here in 1819 inspired Shelley to compose the 'Ode to the West Wind'. Three years later Shelley's drowned body was burnt on a pyre in Viareggio, by his friend Trelawny; curiously, a similar incineration took place in the Cascine in 1870 when the Maharaja of Kohlapur died in Florence. According to ritual his body had to be burned near the confluence of two rivers, in this case, the Arno and Mugnone at the far end of the park, on a spot now marked by the Maharaja's equestrian statue. Florentines come to the Cascine by day to play; it contains a riding school, race tracks, a small amusement park and zoo for the children, tennis courts, and a swimming pool. At night they come to ogle the transvestites strutting their stuff on the *viale*.

Beyond the train station, cars and buses hurtle around and around the **Fortezza da Basso**, an enormous bulk built by Antonio da Sangallo on orders from Alessandro de' Medici in 1534. It immediately became the most hated symbol of Medici tyranny. Ironically, the duke who built the Fortezza da Basso was one of very few to meet his end within its ramparts – stabbed by his relative and bosom companion 'Lorenzaccio' de' Medici. As a fortress, the place never saw any action as thrilling or vicious as the Pitti fashion shows that take place behind the walls in its 1978 aluminium exhibition hall.

Just east of the Fortezza, at the corner of Via Leone X and Viale Milton, there's an unexpected sight rising above the sleepy residential neighbourhood – the five graceful onion domes of the **Russian Church**, made even more exotic by the palm tree tickling its side. In the 19th century, Florence was a popular winter retreat for Russians who could afford it, among them Dostoevsky and Maxim Gorky. Completed by Russian architects in 1904, it is a pretty jewel box of brick and majolica decoration, open on the third Sunday of the month, when the priest comes from Nice to hold a morning service in Russian.

The Stibbert Museum

Open in summer Mon–Wed 10–2, Fri–Sun 10–6; adm.

From Piazza della Libertà, the dull Via Vittorio Emanuele heads 1km north to Via Stibbert and the Stibbert Museum (alternatively, take bus 31 or 32 from the station). Those who make the journey to see the lifetime's accumulations of Frederick Stibbert (1838–1906), who fought with Garibaldi and hobnobbed with Queen Victoria, can savour Florence's most bizarre museum, and one of the city's most pleasant small parks, laid out by Stibbert with a mouldering Egyptian temple sinking in a pond; and just try to obey the sign on the door: 'Comply with the Forbidden Admittances!'.

Stibbert's Italian mother left him a 14th-century house, which he joined to another house to create a Victorian's sumptuous version of what a medieval Florentine house should have looked like – 64 rooms to contain a pack-rat's treasure hoard of all things brilliant and useless, from an attributed Botticelli, to snuff boxes, to what a local guide intriguingly describes as 'brass and silver basins, used daily by Stibbert'.

Stibbert's serious passion, however, was armour, and he amassed a magnificent collection from all times and places. The best pieces are not arranged in dusty cases, but with a touch of Hollywood, on grim knightly mannequins ranked ready for battle.

The Oltrarno

Once over the Ponte Vecchio, a different Florence reveals itself: greener, quieter, and less burdened with traffic. The Oltrarno is not a large district: a chain of hills squeezes it against the river, and their summits afford some of the best views over the city.

Once across the Arno, the Medici's catwalk becomes part of the upper façade of **Santa Felicità**, one of Florence's most ancient churches, believed to have been founded by the Syrian Greek traders who introduced Christianity to the city, and established the first Christian cemetery in the small square in front of the church.

Rebuilt in the 18th century, there is one compelling reason to enter, for here, in the first chapel on the right, is the *ne plus ultra* of Mannerism: Pontormo's weirdly luminous *Deposition* (1528), painted in jarring pinks, oranges and blues that cut through the darkness of the little chapel. The composition itself is highly unconventional, with an effect that derives entirely from the use of figures in unusual, exaggerated poses; there is no sign of a cross, the only background is a single cloud. Sharing the chapel is Pontormo's *Annunciation* fresco, a less idiosyncratic work, as well as four tondi of the Evangelists in the cupola, partly the work of Pontormo's pupil and adopted son, Bronzino.

The Pitti Palace

As the Medici consolidated their power in Florence, they made a point of buying up the most important properties of their former rivals, especially their proud family palaces. The most spectacular example of this was Cosimo I's acquisition of the Pitti Palace, built in 1457 by a powerful banker named Luca Pitti who seems to have had vague ambitions of toppling the Medici and becoming the big boss himself. The palace, with its extensive grounds, now the Boboli Gardens, was much more pleasant than the medieval Palazzo Vecchio, and in the 1540s Cosimo I and his wife Eleanor of Toledo moved in for good.

The palace remained the residence of the Medici, and later the House of Lorraine, until 1868. The original building, said to have been designed by Brunelleschi, was only as wide as the seven central windows of the façade. Succeeding generations found it too small for their burgeoning hoards of bric-a-brac, and added several stages of symmetrical additions, resulting in a long, bulky profile, resembling a rusticated Stalinist ministry, but a landscaped one, ever since the 1996 European Summit.

There are eight separate **museums** in the Pitti; the ticket office for them all is in the far right corner of the forecourt. They are a tribute to Medici acquisitiveness in the centuries of decadence, from which, in the words of Mary McCarthy, 'flowed a torrent of bad taste that has not yet dried up...if there had been Toby jugs and Swiss weather clocks available, the Grand Dukes would certainly have collected them'. For the visitor who wants to see everything, the Pitti is pitiless; it is impossible to see all in one day.

Galleria Palatina

Open Tues–Sun 8.15–6.50; adm.

The Pitti museum most people see is the Galleria Palatina, containing the Grand Dukes' famous collection of 16th–18th-century paintings, stacked on the walls in enormous gilt frames under the berserk opulence of frescoed ceilings celebrating planets, mythology and, of course, the ubiquitous Medici. The gallery is on the first floor of the right half of the palace; the ticket office is on the ground floor, off Ammannati's exaggerated rustic courtyard, a Mannerist masterpiece.

After the entrance to the Galleria is the neoclassical **Sala Castagnoli**, with the *Tavola delle Muse* in its centre, itself an excellent introduction to the Florentine 'decorative arts'; the table, a paragon of the intricate art of *pietra dura*, was made in the 1870s. The Galleria's best paintings are in the five former reception rooms off to the left, with colourful ceilings painted in the 1640s by Pietro da Cortona, one of the most interesting Italian Baroque artists.

However, the set route takes you through the other part of the palace first, starting with the adjacent **Sala di Prometeo** containing Filippo Lippi's lovely *Tondo of the Madonna and Child* and Baldassare Peruzzi's unusual *Dance of Apollo*. Next you can peek into the **Sala di Bagni**, the Empire bathroom of Elisa Baciocchi, Napoleon's sister, who ruled the Département de l'Arno between 1809 and 1814, and seemingly spent much of those years redecorating the Pitti. Caravaggio's *Sleeping Cupid* is a couple of rooms up, in the **Sala dell'Educazione di Giove**. The next room to this is the pretty **Sala della Stufa**, frescoed with the *Four Ages of the World* by Pietro da Cortona.

The first of the reception rooms, the **Sala dell'Iliade** (frescoed in the 19th century), has some fine portraits by the Medici court painter and Rubens' friend, Justus Sustermans. Two *Assumptions* by Andrea del Sarto, *Philip II* by Titian and a Velazquez equestrian portrait of Philip IV share the room with one of the most unusual residents of the gallery, *Queen Elizabeth*, who seems uncomfortable in such company.

The **Sala di Giove**, used as the Medici throne room, contains one of Raphael's best-known portraits, the lovely and serene *Donna Velata* (1516). The small painting *The Three Ages of Man* is usually attributed to Giorgione. Salviati, Perugino, Fra Bartolomeo and Andrea del Sarto are also represented. The **Sala di Marte** has two works by Rubens, *The Four Philosophers* and the *Consequences of War*, as well as some excellent portraits by Tintoretto and Van Dyck (*Cardinal Bentivoglio*). The newly restored *Annunciation of San Godenzo*, by Andrea del Sarto, is now back in place after a long absence, and there is also Titian's rather dashing *Cardinal Ippolito de' Medici* in Hungarian costume. Ippolito, despite being destined for the Church, was one of the more high-spirited Medici.

In the **Sala di Apollo** there's more Titian – his *Portrait of a Grey-eyed Gentleman*, evoking the perfect 16th-century English gentleman, and his more sensuous than penitent *Mary Magdalene* – as well as works by Andrea del Sarto and Van Dyck. The last reception room is the **Sala di Venere**, with several works by Titian, including his early *Concert*, believed to have been partly painted by Giorgione and a powerful *Portrait of Pietro Aretino*, Titian's close and caustic friend, who complained to the artist that it was all too accurate and gave it to Cosimo I. There are two beautiful landscapes by Rubens, painted at the end of his life, and an uncanny self-portrait, *La Menzogna* ('The Falsehood') by Neapolitan Salvator Rosa. The centrepiece statue, the *Venus Italica*, was commissioned by Napoleon from neoclassical master Antonio Canova in 1812 to replace the *Venus de' Medici* which he 'centralized' off to Paris – a rare case of the itchy-fingered Corsican trying to pay for something he took.

The **Sala di Saturno**, with a newly restored ceiling, is home to several paintings from Raphael's Florence days. These include the *Maddalena and Agnolo Doni* (1506) and the *Madonna 'del Granduca'*, influenced by the paintings of Leonardo. Some 10 years later,

Raphael had found his own style, beautifully evident in his famous *Madonna della Seggiola* ('of the chair'), perhaps the most popular work he ever painted, and one that is far more complex and subtle than it appears. The rounded, intertwining figures of the Madonna and Child are seen as if through a slightly convex mirror, bulging out – one of the first examples of conscious illusionism in the Renaissance.

Some of the more interesting paintings to ferret out in the remainder of the gallery include Filippino Lippi's *Death of Lucrezia* and Raphael's *Madonna dell'Impannata*, both in the **Sala di Ulisse**.

The right half of the Pitti also contains the **State Apartments** (*included as part of the visit to the Galleria Palatina*). These were last redone in the 19th century by the Dukes of Lorraine, with touches by the Kings of Savoy.

Galleria d'Arte Moderna

Open 8.30–1.50, closed 2nd and 4th Sun and 1st, 3rd and 5th Mon of month; adm exp; tickets from main ticket office on ground floor.

On the second floor above the Galleria Palatina has been installed Florence's modern – read late 18th- to 20th-century – art museum. Though the monumental stair may leave you breathless (the Medici negotiated it with sedan chairs and strong-shouldered servants), consider a visit for some sunny painting of the Italy of your great-grandparents.

The 'Splatterers' or *Macchiaioli* (Tuscan Impressionists) illuminate **Room 16** and the rest of the museum, forming an excellent introduction to the works by Silvestro Lega, Giovanni Fattori, Nicolo Cannicci, Francesco Gioli, Federigo Zandomeneghi and Telemaco Signorini, with an interval of enormous Risorgimento battle scenes. What comes as a shock, especially if you've been touring Florence for a while now, is that the marriage between painting and sculpture that characterizes most of Italian art history seems to have resulted in a nasty divorce in the late 1800s: while the canvases radiate light, statuary becomes disturbingly kitsch, obsessed with death and beauty.

The Galleria was reopened after a major reorganization in 1999 and now consists of over 30 rooms. The most recent paintings on display are those in the last rooms, which cover the years 1900–23. There are plans eventually to open 13 more rooms covering 1923–45.

Museo degli Argenti

Open Nov–Feb daily 8.15–4.30; March daily 8.15–5.30; April, May, Sept, Oct 8.15–6.30; June–Aug 8.15–7.30; closed 1st and last Mon of month; adm (combined ticket with Boboli, Museo della Porcellana)

The ground floor on the left side of the Pitti was used as the Medici summer apartments and now contains the family's remarkable collection of jewellery, vases, trinkets and pricey curiosities. The Grand Duke's guests would be received in four of the most delightfully frescoed rooms to be found anywhere in Florence, beginning with the **Sala di Giovanni di San Giovanni**, named after the artist who painted it in the 1630s. The theme is the usual Medicean self-glorification – but nowhere does such dubious material achieve such flamboyant treatment. Here the Muses, chased from Paradise, find refuge with Lorenzo il Magnifico; Lorenzo smiles as he studies a bust of Pan by Michelangelo. His real passion, a collection of antique vases carved of semi-precious stones or crystal, is displayed in a room off to the left; the vases were dispersed with the rise of Savonarola, but Lorenzo's nephew Cardinal Giulio had no trouble in locating them, as Lorenzo had his initials LAUR.MED. deeply incised into each. The three **Reception rooms** were painted in shadowy blue trompe l'œil by two masterful Bolognese illusionists, Agostino Michele and Angelo Colonna.

The Grand Dukes' treasure hoard is up on the mezzanine. These golden toys are only a fraction of what the Medici had accumulated; despite the terms of Anna Maria's will, leaving everything to Florence, the Lorraines sold off the most valuable pieces and jewels to finance Austria's wars. Among the leftovers here, however, is a veritable apoplexy of fantastical bric-a-brac.

More Pitti Museums

The **Museum of Costumes** (*open daily 8.15–1.50; closed 2nd and 4th Sun and 1st, 3rd and 5th Mon of month*) is housed on the second floor of the Palace, near to the Galleria d'Arte Moderna; which has the reconstructed dress Eleanor of Toledo was buried in – the same one that she wears in Bronzino's famous portrait. The **Porcelain Museum** (*open same times as Museo degli Argenti*) is housed in the casino of Cosimo III, out in the Giardino del Cavaliere in the Boboli Gardens (*follow the signs*).

Boboli Gardens

Open from 9am until one hour before sunset; adm; t 055 265 1838.

Stretching back invitingly from the Pitti, the shady green of the Boboli Gardens, Florence's largest (and only) central public garden is an irresistible oasis in the middle of a stone-hard city. Originally laid out by Buontalenti, the Boboli reigns as queen of all formal Tuscan gardens, the most elaborate and theatrical, a Mannerist-Baroque co-production of Nature and Artifice laid out over a steep hill, full of shady nooks and pretty walks and beautifully kept. The park is populated by a platoon of statuary, many of them Roman works, others absurd Mannerist pieces.

There are three entrances and exits: through the main courtyard of the Pitti Palace, from Via Romana and in Porta Romana. The main, route, from the Pitti Palace, starts at the **Amphitheatre**, which ascends in regular tiers from the palace, and was designed like a small Roman circus to hold Medici court spectacles. It has a genuine obelisk, of Rameses II from Heliopolis, snatched by the ancient Romans and shipped here by the Medici branch in Rome. The granite basin, large enough to submerge an elephant, came from the Roman Baths of Caracalla. Straight up the terrace is the **Neptune Fountain**; a signposted path leads from there to the pretty **Kaffeehaus**, a boat-like pavilion with a prow and deck offering a fine view of Florence and drinks in the summer. From here the path continues up to the **Belvedere Fort** (*newly opened after restoration*). Other signs from the Neptune Fountain point the way up to the secluded **Giardino del Cavaliere** (*ticket combined with that of Galleria Palatina*), located on a bastion on Michelangelo's fortifications. Cosimo III built the casino here to escape the heat in the Pitti Palace; the view over the ancient villas, vineyards and olives is pure Tuscan enchantment. The **Porcelain Museum** here (*see* above) contains 18th- and 19th-century examples of chinawork from Sèvres, Meissen and Vienna.

At the bottom right-hand corner of the garden lies the remarkable **Grotta di Buontalenti** (*ticket combined with that of the Galeria Palatina*), one of the architect's most imaginative works, anticipating Gaudí with his dripping, stalactite-like stone, from which fantastic limestone animals struggle to emerge. Casts of Michelangelo's *nonfiniti* slaves stand in the corners, replacing the originals put there by the Medici, while back in the shadowy depths stands a luscious statue of Venus coming from her bath by Giambologna. The Grotta di Buontalenti has been restored but the fountains are not working yet due to technical problems.

Casa Guidi

In the old days the neighbourhood around the Pitti was a fashionable address, but during the 19th century rents for a furnished palace were incredibly low. Shortly after their secret marriage, the Brownings found one of these, the **Casa Guidi** at Piazza San Felice 8, the perfect place to settle; during their 13 years here they wrote their most famous poetry. The house is now owned by the Browning Institute, you can visit it at certain times (*open April–Nov Mon, Wed and Fri 3–6; closed Dec–Mar; donations expected*). Dostoevsky wrote *The Idiot* while living nearby, at No.21 Piazza Pitti.

Stuffed Animals and Wax Cadavers

Past the Pitti on Via Romana 17, is one of Florence's great oddball attractions, the **La Specola** museum (*open Mon–Wed, Fri and Sat 9–1; adm*). The **Zoological Section** has a charmingly old-fashioned collection of nearly everything that walks, flies or swims, from the humble sea worm to the rare Madagascar Aye-Aye or the swordfish, with an accessory case of different blades. The real horror show stuff, however, is kept hidden away in the **Museum of Waxes**. Dotty, prudish old Cosimo III was a hypochondriac and morbidly obsessed with diseases, which his favourite artist, a Sicilian priest named Gaetano Zumbo, was able to portray with revolting realism. His macabre anatomical models were one of the main sights for Grand Tourists in the 1700s.

Santo Spirito

Open Mon–Sat 10–12 and 4–5.30, Sun 10.30–12.

Piazza Santo Spirito, the centre of the Oltrarno, is home to a small market on Mon–Sat mornings under the plane trees as well as a quiet café or two. In the evening it changes face and the bars fill with people, who meet and chat in the piazza and on the church steps until the early hours. At the southern end, a plain 18th-century façade hides Brunelleschi's last, and perhaps greatest church. He designed Santo Spirito in 1440 and lived to see only one column erected, but subsequent architects were faithful to his elegant plan for the interior. This is done in the architect's favourite pale grey and *pietra serena* articulation, a rhythmic forest of columns with semicircular chapels is gracefully recessed into the transepts and the three arms of the crossing. The effect is somewhat spoiled by the ornate 17th-century *baldacchino*, which sits in this enchanted garden of architecture like a 19th-century bandstand.

The art in the chapels is meagre, as most of the good paintings were sold off over the years. The best include Filippino Lippi's beautiful, restored *Madonna and Saints* in the right transept and Verrocchio's jewel-like *St Monica and Nuns* in the opposite transept. To the left of the church, in the **refectory** (*open Tues–Sat 10–1.30, Sun and hols 10–12.30; adm*) of the vanished 14th-century convent, are the scanty remains of a *Last Supper* and a well-preserved, highly dramatic *Crucifixion* by Andrea Orcagna.

Santa Maria del Carmine and the Cappella Brancacci

Open 10–5 (last adm 4.45), Sun and hols 1–5; closed Tues; adm; only 30 people are admitted at a time, for 15 minutes; booking required, t 055 276 8224.

There is little to say about the surroundings, the piazza-cum-car park, the rough stone façade, or the interior of the Oltrarno's other great church, Santa Maria del Carmine, which burned in 1771 and was reconstructed shortly after. Miraculously, the **Cappella Brancacci**, one of the landmarks in Florentine art, survived both the flames and attempts by the authorities to replace it with something more fashionable. Three artists worked on the Brancacci's frescoes: Masolino, who began them in 1425, and who designed the cycle; his pupil Masaccio, who worked on them alone for a year before following his master to Rome, where he died at the age of 27; and Filippino Lippi, who finished them 50 years later. Filippino took care to imitate Masaccio as closely as possible, and the frescoes have an appearance of stylistic unity. Between 1981 and 1988 they were subject to one of Italy's most publicized restorations, cleansed of 550 years of dirt and overpainting, enabling us to see what so thrilled the painters of the Renaissance.

Masaccio in his day was a revolution and a revelation in his solid, convincing naturalism; his figures stand in space, without any fussy ornamentation or Gothic grace, very much inspired by Donatello's sculptures. Masaccio conveyed emotion with broad, quick brush strokes and with his use of light, most obvious in the *Expulsion of Adam and Eve*, one of the most memorable and harrowing images created in the Renaissance. In the *Tribute Money*, the young artist displays his mastery of artificial perspective and light effects. The three episodes in the fresco show an official demanding tribute from the city, St Peter fetching it on Christ's direction from the mouth of a fish, and lastly, his handing over of the money to the official.

Other works by 'Shabby Tom' include *St Peter Baptizing* on the upper register, and *St Peter Healing with his Shadow* and *St Peter Enthroned and Resurrecting the Son of the King of Antioch*, the right half of which was finished by Filippino Lippi. The elegant Masolino is responsible for the remainder, except for the lower register's *Release of St Peter from Prison*, *St Peter Crucified* and *St Paul Visiting St Peter in Prison*, all by Filippino Lippi, based on Masaccio's sketches.

Among the detached frescoes displayed in the cloister and refectory is a good one by Filippino's dad, Fra Filippo Lippi, who was born nearby in Via dell'Ardiglione.

A City with a View

Great Aunt Florence, with her dour complexion and severe, lined face, never was much of a looker from street level, but improves with a bit of distance, either mental or from one of her hill-top balconies: the Belvedere Fort, San Miniato, Piazzale Michelangelo, Bellosguardo, Fiesole or Settignano.

Belvedere Fort and Arcetri

One of Florence's best and closest balconies is the newly-restored **Belvedere Fort**, a graceful, six-point star designed by Buontalenti and built in 1590–5, not so much for the sake of defence but to remind any remaining Florentine republicans who was boss. Since 1958, it has been used for special exhibitions, but you can usually enjoy unforgettable views of Florence and the surrounding countryside from its ramparts. Leading up to it is one of Florence's prettiest streets, **Costa San Giorgio**, which begins in Piazza Santa Felicità, just beyond the Ponte Vecchio.

In this part of Florence, the countryside begins right at the city wall, a rolling landscape of villas and gardens, olives and cypresses. Via San Leonardo winds its way out towards Arcetri; a 10-minute walk will take you to the 11th-century **San Leonardo in Arcetri** (*usually open Sun am*). There is a wonderful 13th-century pulpit, originally built for San Pier Scheraggio, and a small rose window, made according to legend from a wheel of Fiesole's *carroccio*, captured by Florence in 1125. A half-kilometre further on, past the Viale Galileo crossroads, Via San Leonardo changes its name to Via Viviani, where it passes the **Astrophysical Observatory** and the **Torre del Gallo**. Another kilometre further on Via Viviani reaches the settlement of Pian de' Giullari, where Galileo spent the last years of his life, in the 16th-century **Villa il Gioiello**, virtually under house arrest after his encounter with the Inquisition in 1631, and where Milton is believed to have visited him.

San Miniato

Open summer daily 8–7.30, winter daily 8–12 and 3–6.

From Porta San Miniato you can walk up to San Miniato church on the stepped Via di San Salvatore al Monte, complete with the Stations of the Cross, or take the less pious bus 13 up the scenic Viale dei Colli from the station or Via de Benci, near Ponte alle Grazie. High atop its monumental steps, San Miniato's beautiful, distinctive façade can be spotted from almost anywhere in the city, although relatively few visitors take the time actually to visit what is in fact one of the finest Romanesque churches in Italy.

San Miniato was built in 1015, over an earlier church that marked the spot where the head of St Minias, a 3rd-century Roman soldier, bounced when the Romans axed it off. Despite its distance from the centre San Miniato has always been one of the churches dearest to the Florentines' hearts. The remarkable geometric pattern of green, black and white marble that adorns its façade was begun in 1090, though funds only permitted the embellishment of the lower, simpler half of the front; the upper half,

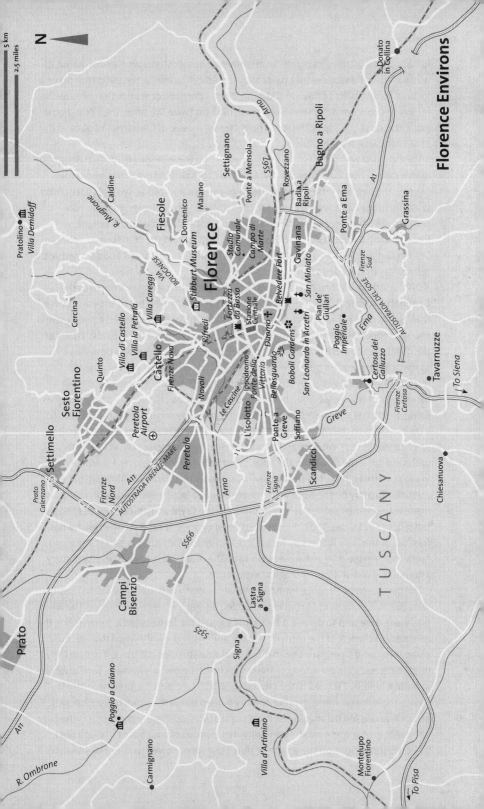

Florence Environs

5 km
2.5 miles

N

TUSCANY

Prato
Settimello
Sesto Fiorentino
Campi Bisenzio
Prato Calenzano
Firenze Nord
AUTOSTRADA FIRENZE-MARE
A11
SS66

Poggio a Caiano
Carmignano
R. Ombrone
Villa d'Artimino
Montelupo Fiorentino
To Pisa

Signa
Lastra a Signa
SS25
Arno
Firenze Signa
Scandicci
Chiesanuova

Pratolino
Villa Demidoff
Caldine
R. Mugnone
Fiesole
S. Domenico
Maiano
Settignano
Ponte a Mensola
S. Donato in Collina

Cercina
Quinto
Villa di Castello
Villa la Petraia
Villa Careggi
VIA BOLOGNESE
Stibbert Museum
Rifredi
Stadio Comunale
Campo di Marte
Rovezzano
SS67
Arno
Bagno a Ripoli

Castello
Firenze Nova
Novoli
Peretola Airport
Peretola
Le Cascine
L'Isolotto
Ponte della Vittoria
Ippodromo
Belvedere Fort
Fortezza da Basso
Stazione Centrale
Duomo
Boboli Gardens
Bellosguardo
Ponte a Greve
Sofiano
Greve
San Leonardo in Arcetri
Gavinana
San Miniato
Pian de' Giullari
Poggio Imperiale
Certosa del Galluzzo
Badia a Ripoli
Ponte a Ema
Grassina
Firenze Sud
Ema
A1
AUTOSTRADA DEL SOLE
Firenze Certosa
Tavarnuzze
To Siena

Florence

full of curious astrological symbolism (someone has written a whole book about it) was added in the 12th century, paid for by the Arte di Calimala, the guild that made a fortune buying bolts of fine wool, dyeing them a deep red or scarlet that no one else in Europe could imitate, then selling them back for twice the price; their proud gold eagle stands at the top of the roof. The glittering mosaic of Christ, the Virgin and St Minias, came slightly later.

The Calimala was also responsible for decorating the interior, an unusual design with a raised choir built over the crypt. As the Calimala became richer, so did the fittings; the delicate intarsia **marble floor** of animals and zodiac symbols dates from 1207. The lower walls were frescoed in the 14th and 15th centuries, including an enormous St Christopher. At the end of the nave stands Michelozzo's unique, free-standing **Cappella del Crocifisso**, built in 1448 to hold the crucifix that spoke to St John Gualberto (now in Santa Trínita); it is magnificently carved and adorned with terracottas by Luca della Robbia.

Off the left nave is one of Florence's Renaissance showcases, the **Chapel of the Cardinal of Portugal** (1461–6). The 25-year-old cardinal, a member of the Portuguese royal family, died in Florence at an auspicious moment, when the Medici couldn't spend enough money on publicly prominent art, and when some of the greatest artists of the quattrocento were at the height of their careers. The chapel was designed by Manetti, Brunelleschi's pupil; the ceiling exquisitely decorated with enamelled terracotta and medallions by Luca della Robbia; the Cardinal's tomb beautifully carved by Antonio Rossellino; the frescoed *Annunciation* charmingly painted by Alesso Baldovinetti; the altarpiece *Three Saints* is a copy of the original by Piero Pollaiuolo.

Up the steps of the choir more treasures await. The marble transenna and pulpit were carved in 1207, with art and a touch of medieval humour. Playful geometric patterns frame the mosaic in the apse, *Christ between the Virgin and St Minias*, made in 1297 by artists imported from Ravenna, and later restored by Baldovinetti. The colourful **Sacristy** on the right was entirely frescoed by Spinello Aretino in 1387, but made rather flat by subsequent restoration. In the **Crypt** an 11th-century altar holds the relics of St Minias; the columns are topped by ancient capitals. The **cloister** has frescoes of the Holy Fathers by Paolo Uccello, remarkable works in painstaking and fantastical perspective, rediscovered in 1925. The monks sing Gregorian chant every afternoon at about 4pm – a magical experience.

The panorama of Florence from San Miniato is lovely to behold, but such thoughts were hardly foremost in Michelangelo's mind during the Siege of Florence. The hill was vulnerable, and to defend it he hastily erected the fortress (now surrounding the cemetery to the left of the church), placed cannons in the unfinished 16th-century campanile (built to replace one that fell over), and shielded the tower from artillery with mattresses. He grew fond of the small church below San Miniato, **San Salvatore al Monte**, built by Cronaca in the late 1400s, which he called his 'pretty country lass'.

With these associations in mind, the city named the vast, square terrace car park below, **Piazzale Michelangelo**, the most popular viewpoint only because it is the only one capable of accommodating an unlimited number of tour buses (though now there are restrictions on the length of time buses are allowed to stop, the situation has improved a bit). On Sunday afternoons, crowds of Florentines habitually make a stop here during their afternoon *passeggiata*. Besides another copy of the *David* and a fun, tacky carnival atmosphere rampant with souvenirs, balloons and ice cream, the Piazzale offers views that can reach as far as Pistoia on a clear day.

Bellosguardo

Many would argue that the finest view over Florence is from Bellosguardo, located almost straight up from Porta Romana at the end of the Boboli Gardens or Piazza Torquato Tasso. Non-mountaineers may want to take a taxi; the famous viewpoint, from where you can see every church façade in the city, is just before Piazza Bellosguardo. The area is a peaceful little oasis of superb villas and houses gathered round a square – there are no shops, bars or indeed anything commercial.

Fiesole

Florence liked to regard itself as the daughter of Rome, and in its fractious heyday explained its quarrelsome nature by the fact that its population from the beginning was of mixed race, of Romans and 'that ungrateful and malignant people who of old came down from Fiesole', according to Dante. First settled in the 2nd millennium BC, it became the most important Etruscan city in the region. Yet from the start Etruscan *Faesulae*'s relationship with Rome was rocky, especially after sheltering Catiline and his conspirators in 65 BC. Its lofty position made Fiesole too difficult to capture, so the Romans built a camp below on the Arno to cut off its supplies. Eventually Fiesole was taken, and it dwindled as the camp below grew into the city of Florence, growth the Romans encouraged to spite the old Etruscans on their hill. This easily defended hill, however, ensured Fiesole's survival in the Dark Ages. When times became safer, families began to move back down to the Arno to rebuild Florence. They returned to smash up most of Fiesole after defeating it in 1125; since then the little town has remained aloof, letting Florence dominate and choke in its own juices far, far below.

But ever since the days of the *Decameron*, whose storytellers retreated to its garden villas to escape the plague, Fiesole has played the role of Florence's aristocratic suburb; its cool breezes, beautiful landscapes and belvedere views make it the perfect refuge from the torrid Florentine summers. There's no escaping the tourists, however; we foreigners have been tramping up and down Fiesole's hill since the days of Shelley. A day trip has become an obligatory part of a stay in Florence, and although Fiesole has proudly retained its status as an independent *comune*, you can make the 20-minute trip up on Florence city bus 7 from the station or Piazza San Marco. If you have the time, walk up (or perhaps better, down) the old lanes bordered with villas and gardens to absorb some of the world's most civilized scenery.

Around Piazza Mino

The long sloping stage of Piazza Mino is Fiesole's centre, with the bus stop, the local tourist office, the cafés and the **Palazzo Pretorio**, its loggia and façade emblazoned with coats of arms. The square is named after a favourite son, the quattrocento sculptor Mino da Fiesole, whom Ruskin preferred to all others. An example of his work may be seen in the **Duomo**, whose plain façade dominates the north side of the piazza. Built in 1028, it was the only building spared by the vindictive Florentines in 1125. It was subsequently enlarged and given a scouring 19th-century restoration, leaving the tall, crenellated campanile as its sole distinguishing feature. Still, the interior has an austere charm, with a raised choir over the crypt similar to San Miniato.

Up the steps to the right are two works by Mino da Fiesole: the *Tomb of Bishop Leonardo Salutati* and an altar front. The main altarpiece in the choir, of the Madonna and saints, is by Lorenzo di Bicci, from 1440. Note the two saints frescoed on the columns; it was a north Italian custom to paint holy people as if they were members of the congregation. The crypt, holding the remains of Fiesole's patron, St Romulus, is supported by columns bearing doves, spirals and other early Christian symbols.

Located on Via Dupré, the **Bandini Museum** (*open summer daily 10–7, winter Wed–Mon 10–5; adm*) contains sacred works, including della Robbia terracottas and trecento paintings by Lorenzo Monaco, Neri di Bicci and Taddeo Gaddi.

Archaeological Zone

Behind the cathedral and museum is the entrance to what remains of *Faesulae*. Because Fiesole avoided trouble in the Dark Ages, its Roman monuments have survived in much better shape than those of Florence; although hardly spectacular, the ruins are charmingly set amid olive groves and cypresses.

The small **Roman Theatre** (*open summer daily 10–7, winter Wed–Mon 9.30–6; adm*) has survived well enough to host plays and concerts in the summer; Fiesole would like to remind you that in ancient times it had the theatre and plays while Florence had the amphitheatre and wild beast shows. Close by are the rather confusing remains of two superimposed temples, the baths and an impressive stretch of Etruscan walls (best seen from Via delle Mure Etrusche, below) that proved their worth against Hannibal's siege.

The **Archaeology Museum** (*opening hours as for Roman Theatre*), in a small 20th-century Ionic temple, displays early bronze figurines with flapper wing arms, Etruscan urns and stelae, including the interesting 'stele Fiesolana' with a banquet scene.

Walking Around Fiesole

From Piazza Mino, Via S. Francesco ascends steeply (at first) to the hill that served as the Etruscan and Roman acropolis. Halfway up is a terrace with extraordinary views of Florence and the Arno sprawl, with a monument to the three *carabinieri* who gave themselves up to be shot by the Nazis in 1944 to prevent them from taking civilian reprisals. The church nearby, the **Basilica di Sant'Alessandro**, was constructed over an Etruscan/Roman temple in the 6th century, reusing its lovely *cipollino* (onion marble) columns and Ionic capitals, one still inscribed with an invocation to Venus. At the top of the hill, square on the ancient acropolis, stands the monastery of **San Francesco**, its church containing a famous early cinquecento *Annunciation* by Raffaellino del Garbo and an *Immaculate Conception* by Piero di Cosimo. A grab-bag of odds and ends collected from the four corners of the world, especially Egypt and China, is displayed in the quaint **Franciscan Missionary Museum** in the cloister (*open summer Mon–Sat 9–12 and 3–7, Sun 3–7; winter Mon–Sat 9–12 and 3–6, Sun 3–6*); it also has an Etruscan collection.

There are much longer walks to be had along the hill behind the Palazzo Pretorio. The panoramic Via Belvedere leads back to Via Adriano Mari, and in a couple of kilometres to the bucolic **Montececeri**, a wooded park where Leonardo da Vinci performed his flight experiments, and where Florentine architects once quarried their dark *pietra serena* from quarries now abandoned but open for exploration.

In Borgunto, as this part of Fiesole is called, there are two 3rd-century BC **Etruscan tombs** on Via Bargellino; east of Borgunto scenic Via Francesco Ferrucci and Via di Vincigliata pass by Fiesole's castles, the **Castel di Poggio**, site of summer concerts, and the **Castel di Vincigliata**, dating back to 1031, while further down is American critic Bernard Berenson's famous **Villa I Tatti**, which he left, along with a collection of Florentine art, to Harvard University as the Centre of Italian Renaissance Studies. The road continues down towards Ponte a Mensola (6km from Fiesole; *see p.182*) and Settignano, with buses back to Florence.

San Domenico di Fiesole

San Domenico is a pleasant walk from Fiesole towards Florence down Via Vecchia Fiesolana, a steep, narrow road that passes the **Villa Medici** (*Via Beato Angelico 2, privately owned, open Mon–Fri 9–1 though best to call first, t 055 59417, ring the bell*), built by Michelozzo for Cosimo il Vecchio; Lorenzo and his friends of the Platonic Academy would come to escape the world within its lovely gardens; it was also Iris Origo's childhood home.

San Domenico, at the bottom of the lane, is where Fra Angelico first entered his monkish world. The church of **San Domenico** (15th century) contains his *Madonna with Angels and Saints*, in a chapel on the left, and a photograph of his *Coronation of the Virgin*, which the French snapped up in 1809 and sent to the Louvre. Across the nave there's a *Crucifixion* by the school of Botticelli, an unusual composition of verticals highlighted by the cypresses in the background. In the chapterhouse of the monastery (*ring the bell at No.4*) Fra Angelico left a fine fresco *Crucifixion* and a *Madonna and Child*, which is shown with its sinopia, before moving down to Florence and San Marco.

Badia Fiesolana

The lane in front of San Domenico leads to the Badia Fiesolana (*open Mon–Fri 9–5, Sat 9–12*), Fiesole's cathedral, built in the 9th century by Fiesole's bishop, an Irishman named Donatus, with a fine view over the rolling countryside and Florence beyond. Though later enlarged, it preserves its original elegant façade, a charming example of the geometric black and white marble inlay decoration that characterizes Tuscan Romanesque churches, while the interior is adorned with *pietra serena* in the style of Brunelleschi. The ex-convent next door now houses the European University Institute.

Settignano

The least touristic hill above Florence is under the village of Settignano (bus 10 from the station or Piazza San Marco). The road passes **Ponte a Mensola**, Boccaccio's childhood home; it is believed he set scenes of the *Decameron* at the Villa Poggio Gherardo. A Scottish Benedictine named Andrew founded its church of **San Martino a Mensola** in the 9th century and was later canonized. The church was rebuilt in the 1400s, it has three trecento works: Taddeo Gaddi's *Triptych*, his son Agnolo's paintings on St Andrew's casket, and high altar triptych by the school of Orcagna. Quattrocento works include Neri di Bicci's *Madonna and Saints* and an *Annunciation* by a follower of Beato Angelico.

Settignano is one of Tuscany's great cradles of sculptors, producing Desiderio da Settignano and Antonio and Bernardo Rossellino; Michelangelo too spent his childhood here, at Villa Buonarroti. Strangely, they left behind no work as a reminder; the good art in **Santa Maria** church is by Andrea della Robbia (an enamelled terracotta *Madonna and Child*) and Buontalenti (the pulpit). However, there are more splendid views from Piazza Desiderio, and a couple of places to quaff a glass of Chianti.

Medici Villas

Like their Bourbon cousins in France, the Medici dukes liked to while their time away acquiring new palaces for themselves. In their case, however, the reason was less self-exaltation than simple property speculation; the Medici always thought several generations ahead. As a result the countryside around Florence is littered with Medici villas, most of them now privately owned, though some are at least partly open to the public.

Villa Careggi

Open Mon–Fri 9–6, Sat 9–12; but you can stroll through the grounds for free.

Perhaps the best-known is Careggi (Viale Pieraccini 17, take bus 14C from the station), originally a fortified farmhouse, but enlarged for Cosimo il Vecchio by Michelozzo in 1434. In the 1460s this villa became synonymous with the birth of humanism.

The greatest Latin and Greek scholars of the day, Ficino, Poliziano, Pico della Mirandola and Argyropoulos, would sometimes meet here with Lorenzo il Magnifico and hold philosophical discussions in imitation of a Platonic symposium, calling their informal society the Platonic Academy. It fizzled out when Lorenzo died. Cosimo il Vecchio and Piero had both died at Careggi and, when he felt the end was near, Lorenzo had himself carried out to the villa, with Poliziano and Pico della Mirandola to bear him company. After Lorenzo died, the villa was burned by Florentine republicans, though Cosimo I later had it rebuilt, and Francis Sloane had it restored.

Villa la Petraia

Open Nov–Feb 8.15–4.30, Mar and Oct until 5.30; Apr, May and Sept until 6.30; June–Aug until 7.30; adm.

Further east, amid the almost continuous conurbation of power lines and industrial landscapes that blight the Prato road, Villa la Petraia manages to remain Arcadian on its steeply sloping hill. It's very hard to reach on your own. If you don't have a car, it's best to take a taxi or, if you are adventurous, bus 28 from the station, and get off after the wastelands, by Via Reginaldo Giuliano. La Petraia was purchased by Grand Duke Ferdinando I in 1557 and rebuilt by Buontalenti, keeping the tower of the original castle intact.

Unfortunately Vittorio Emanuele II liked it as much as the Medici, and redesigned it to suit his relentlessly bad taste. Still, the interior is worthwhile for its ornate Baroque court, frescoed with a pastel history of the Medici by 17th-century masters Volterrano and Giovanni di San Giovanni; Vittorio Emanuele II added the glass roof in order to use the space as a ballroom. Of the remainder, you're most likely to remember the Chinese painting of Canton and the games room, with billiard tables as large as football fields and perhaps the world's first pinball machine, made of wood. A small room contains a most endearing statue by Giambologna, *Venus Wringing Water from Her Hair*. La Petraia's beautiful gardens and grounds, shaded by ancient cypresses, are open throughout the afternoon.

Villa di Castello

Hours as Villa la Petraia; visits to garden only; adm.

One of Tuscany's most famous gardens is just down the hill from La Petraia, at Villa di Castello (turn right at Via di Castello and walk 450 metres). The villa was bought in 1477 by Lorenzo di Pierfrancesco and Giovanni de' Medici, two cousins of Lorenzo il Magnifico who were Botticelli's best patrons, and they hung the walls of this villa with his great mythological paintings now in the Uffizi. The villa was sacked in the 1530 siege and then restored by Cosimo I; today it is the headquarters of the Accademia della Crusca, founded in 1582 and dedicated to the study of the Italian language. The garden was laid out for Cosimo I by Tribolo, who also designed the fountain in the centre, with a statue, *Hercules and Antenaeus*, by Ammannati.

Directly behind the fountain is the garden's main attraction, an artificial cavern named the **Grotto degli Animali**, filled by Ammannati and Giambologna with marvellous, true-to-life statues of every creature known to man, and lined with mosaics of pebbles and shells. The terrace above offers the best view over the garden's geometric patterns; a large statue by Ammannati of January, or *Gennaio*, emerges shivering from a pool among the trees.

A 20-minute walk north from Villa di Castello to Quinto takes you to two unusual 7th-century BC **Etruscan tombs**. Neither has any art, but the chambers under their 25ft artificial hills bear an odd relationship to ancient cultures elsewhere in the

Mediterranean – domed *tholos* tombs as in Mycenaean Greece, corbelled passages like the *navetas* of Majorca, and entrances that look like the sacred wells of Sardinia.

Sesto Fiorentino

You can change gears again by heading out a little further in the sprawl to Sesto Fiorentino, a suburb that since 1954 has been home to the famous Richard-Ginori china and porcelain firm. Founded in Doccia in 1735, the firm has opened the **Doccia Museum** on Via Pratese 31 (*signposted*) to display a neat chronological exhibition of its production of Doccia ware, including many Medici commissions (a ceramic *Venus de' Medici*), fine painted porcelain, and some pretty Art Nouveau works (*Wed–Sun 10–1 and 2–6; closed Aug; adm*).

Villa Demidoff at Pratolino

Open Mar Sun 10–6; April, Aug and Sept Thurs–Sun 10–8.30; Oct Sun 10–7; closed Nov–Feb; adm. Take bus 25 which leaves about every 20mins from the station.

The village of Pratolino lies 12km north of Florence along Via Bolognese and it was here that Duke Francesco I bought a villa in the 1568 as a gift to his mistress, the Venetian Bianca Capello. Francesco commissioned Buontalenti – artist, architect, and hydraulics engineer – to design the enormous gardens. He made Pratolino the marvel of its day, full of water tricks, ingenious automata and a famous menagerie.

Sadly, none of Buontalenti's marvels has survived, but the largest ever example of this play between art and environment has – Giambologna's massive *Apennino*, a giant rising from stone, part stalactite, part fountain himself, conquering the dragon, said to be symbolic of the Medici's origins in the Mugello just north of here. The rest of the park, made into an English garden by the Lorena family and named for Prince Paolo Demidoff who bought it in 1872 and restored Francesco's servants' quarters as his villa, is an invitingly cool refuge from a Florentine summer afternoon.

Poggio a Caiano

Open daily Nov–Feb 8.15–3.30; April, May and Sept 8.15–5.30; Mar and Oct 8.15–4.30; June–Aug 8.15–6.30; closed 2nd and 3rd Mon of month; adm. CAP buses, t 055 214637, go past every half-hour, departing from in front of McDonald's on the north side of the station.

Of all the Medici villas, Poggio a Caiano is the most evocative of the country idylls so delightfully described in the verses of Lorenzo il Magnifico; this was not only his favourite retreat, but is generally considered the very first Italian Renaissance villa. Lorenzo purchased a farmhouse here in 1480, and commissioned Giuliano da Sangallo to rebuild it in a classical style. It was Lorenzo's sole architectural commission, and its classicism matched the mythological nature poems he composed here, most famously 'L'Ambra', inspired by the stream Ombrone that flows nearby.

Sangallo designed the villa according to Alberti's description of the perfect country house in a style that presages Palladio, and added a classical frieze on the façade, sculpted with the assistance of Andrea Sansovino (now replaced with a copy). Some of the other features – the clock, the curved stair and central loggia – were later additions. In the **interior** Sangallo designed an airy, two-storey **Salone**, which the two Medici popes had frescoed by 16th-century masters Pontormo, Andrea del Sarto, Franciabigio and Allori. The subject, as usual, is Medici self-glorification, and depicts family members dressed as Romans in historical scenes that parallel events in their lives. In the right lunette, around a large circular window, Pontormo painted the lovely *Vertumnus and Pomona* (1521), a languid summer scene under a willow tree, beautifully coloured. In another room, Francesco I and Bianca Cappello his wife died in 1587, only 11 hours apart; Francesco was always messing with poisons but in fact a nasty virus was the probable killer.

In the **grounds** (*open same hours as villa*) are fine old trees and a 19th-century statue celebrating Lorenzo's 'L'Ambra'.

Carmignano and Villa Artimino

A local bus continues 5km southwest of Poggio a Caiano to the village of **Carmignano**, which possesses, in its church of **San Michele** (*open daily 7.30–5, until 6 in summer*), Pontormo's uncanny painting *The Visitation* (1530s), a masterpiece of Florentine Mannerism. There are no concessions to naturalism here – the four soulful, ethereal women, draped in Pontormo's customary startling colours, barely touch the ground, standing before a scene as substantial as a stage backdrop. The result is one of the most unforgettable images produced in the 16th century.

Also to the south, at **Comeana** (3km, signposted), is the well-preserved Etruscan **Tomba di Montefortini**, a 7th-century BC burial mound, 35ft high and 260ft in diameter, covering two chambers. A long hall leads to the vestibule and tomb chamber, both covered with false vaulting; the latter preserves a shelf most probably used for gifts for the afterlife. Nearby, the equally impressive **Tomba dei Boschetti** was seriously damaged over centuries by local farmers (*both open Mon–Sat 8–2; closed Sun*).

The Etruscan city of Artimino, 4km to the west, was destroyed by the Romans and is now the site of a small town and another Medici property, the **Villa Artimino** ('La Ferdinanda'), built as hunting lodge for Ferdinando I by Buontalenti. Its semi-fortified air with buttresses was aimed to fit its sporting purpose, but the total effect is simple and charming, with the long roofline punctuated by innumerable chimneys and a graceful stair, added in the 19th century from a drawing by the architect in the Uffizi.

There is an **Etruscan Archaeological Museum** in the basement, containing findings from the tombs; among them a unique censer with two basins and a boat, bronze vases, and a red figured krater painted with initiation scenes, found in a 3rd-century tomb (*villa open for guided tours only on Tues, t 055 871 8124; museum open Thurs–Tues 9.30–12.30; adm*). There's a convenient place for lunch in the grounds. Also in Artimino is an attractive Romanesque church, **San Leonardo**, built of stones salvaged from earlier buildings.

Poggio Imperiale and the Certosa del Galluzzo

One last villa open for visits, the **Villa di Poggio Imperiale** (*open Wed 10–12 by request, t 055 220151*), lies south of Florence, at the summit of Viale del Poggio

Imperiale, which leaves Porta Romana with a stately escort of cypress sentinels. Cosimo I grabbed this huge villa from the Salviati family in 1565, and it remained a ducal property until there were no longer any dukes to duke. Its neoclassical façade was added in 1808, and the audience chamber was decorated in the 17th century by the underrated Rutilio Manetti and others. Much of the villa is now used as a girls' school.

The **Certosa del Galluzzo** (also known as the Certosa di Firenze) lies further south, scenically located on a hill off the Siena road (*open Tues–Sun 9–11 and 3–6; closes 5pm in winter; adm by donation; take bus 36 or 37 from the station*). Founded as a Carthusian monastery by 14th-century tycoon Niccolò Acciaiuoli, the monastery has been inhabited since 1958 by Cistercians; there are 12 now living there, one of whom takes visitors around.

The Certosa has a fine 16th-century courtyard and an uninteresting church, though the crypt-chapel of the lay choir contains some impressive tombs. The Chiostro Grande, surrounded by the monks' cells, is decorated with 66 majolica tondi of prophets and saints by Giovanni della Robbia and assistants; one cell is opened for visits, and it seems almost cosy. The Gothic Palazzo degli Studi, intended by the founder as a school, contains five lunettes by Pontormo, painted while he and his pupil Bronzino hid out here from the plague in 1522.

Chianti and the Mugello

08

Chianti and the Mugello

N
10 km
5 miles

Roncobilaccio
Firenzuola
Montecarelli
Barberino di Mugello
4 Scarperia
S. Piero a Sieve
Borgo S. Lorenzo
Vaiano
M. Senario
Prato
Pratolino
Sesto Fiorentino
Campi Bisenzio
Florence
Fiesole
Signa
Scandicci
Pontassieve
Cerbaia
S. Donato in Collina
S. Casciano in Val di Pesa
S. Polo in Chianti
Mercatale in Val di Pesa
Strada in Chianti
Incisa in Val d'A.
TUSCANY
Greve in Chianti 1
Tavarnelle in Val di Pesa
S. Donato in Poggio
S. Giovanni Valdarno
Castelfranco di Sopra
Barberino Val d'Elsa
Pietrafitta
Montevarchi
Poggibonsi
Castellina in Chianti 2
Radda in Chianti
Badia Coltibuono
Colle di Val d'Elsa
Monteriggioni
Ambra
Civitella in Val Chiana
3 Cast. di Brolio
Siena

Dovadola
Predappio
Predappio Alta
Rocca San Casciano
Portico di Romagna
EMILIA-ROMAGNA
Santa Sofia
Alpe di San Benedetto
S. Godenzo
M. Falterona
Pso. d. Calla
Bagno di Romagna
Stia
Pratovecchio
Badia Prataglia
M. Secchieta
Poppi
M. Penna
Bibbiena
Pratomagno
Caprese Michelangelo
Casentino
Subbiano
Castiglion Fibocchi
Arezzo
Foce di Scopetone
Cortona

Monti del Chianti

R. Lamone
R. Bisenzio
Monti d. Calvana
R. Magnone
R. Sieve
R. Pesa
R. Greve
R. Elsa
R. Arbia
R. Arno

p.208
p.394
p.346
p.368

Highlights

1 Wine-touring around Greve in Chianti
2 The quattrocento charms of Castellina in Chianti
3 The Iron Baron's Castello di Brolio
4 Scarperia: a Florentine outpost in the Mugello

SWITZ.
FRANCE
AUSTRIA
SLOVENIA
HUNGARY
CROATIA
BOSNIA-HERZ.
YUGOSLAVIA
Corsica
ITALY
Sardinia
Sicily
TUNISIA

These two regions, Chianti to the south and the Mugello to the north of Florence, one world-famous and one obscure, are delightfully rural and endowed with every Tuscan charm. No Brunelleschi could have designed the grand stone farmhouses that crown every hill, built with an intuitive aesthetic that rarely fails, each different, offering endless variations of arches, loggias and towers, set in an equally endless variety of rolling hills, vineyards, olives and cypresses. Towns are few, monuments scattered and of minor interest, paintings and sculpture very rare. But you'll find few places more enchanting to explore – by car, by bicycle, by foot – in a day or a lifetime.

Chianti

From good Chianti, an aged wine, majestic and
imperious, that passes through my heart and chases
away without trouble every worry and grief...
Francesco Redi, *Bacchus in Tuscany*

In the 17th century, naturalist and poet Francesco Redi was the first to note the virtues of 'Florentine red' from Chianti, and since then the Italians have invested a lot of worry into defining exactly what 'Chianti' means. The name apparently derives from an Etruscan family named Clanti; geographically it refers, roughly, to the hilly region between Florence and Siena, bordered by the Florence–Siena Superstrada del Palio and the A1 from Florence to Arezzo. The part within Siena province is known as *Chianti Storico* or *Chianti Geografico*, once the territories of the Lega del Chianti, a consortium of barons formed in 1385 to protect their interests (and their wine), who adopted a black cockerel as their emblem.

But Chianti is an oenological name as well as a geographical one and, as such, first became official in 1716, when Grand Duke Cosimo III defined which parts of Tuscany could call their vintage Chianti, in effect making wine history – it was the first time that a wine had its production area delimited. The Lorraine grand dukes promoted advances in wine-making techniques and the export of Chianti. Yet the Chianti as we know it had yet to be developed, and it was largely the creation of one man – the 'Iron Baron', Bettino Ricasoli, briefly the second prime minister of unified Italy. The baron was very wealthy but not handsome, and Luigi Barzini, in *The Italians*, recounts how jealous he became when his new bride was asked to dance at a ball. Without ado, he ordered her into their carriage and told the driver to take her to the ancient family seat at Brolio in the Monti del Chianti – an isolated castle that the poor woman rarely left ever after.

To pass the time the baron began to experiment with different vines and processes, eventually hitting upon a pleasing mix of red Sangiovese and Canaiolo grapes, with a touch of white Malvasia, twice fermented in the old Tuscan manner. Meanwhile, the famous dark green flask was invented, the *strapeso*, with its straw covering woven by the local women. The end product took the Paris Exhibition of 1878 by storm; imitators soon appeared and, in 1924, the boundaries of Chianti Storico were more than doubled to create Chianti Classico, drawn by local producers to protect the wine's name, adopting the now familiar black cockerel as its symbol. In 1967 Chianti Classico, along with Tuscany's six other Chianti vinicultural zones, was given its *denominazione di origine* status, and production soared, but quality and sales declined. To improve it, the Chianti Classico Consortium was upscaled to a DOCG rating to guarantee that all wines bearing the black cockerel would be tested and approved by a panel of judges.

But it was tales of Elizabeth Barrett Browning quaffing Chianti and finding her inspiration in its ruby splendour, as well as the sunny rural elegance of the region, that attracted first the English and Dutch, then the Swiss, Americans, French and Germans, especially in the 1960s and 1970s; they form one of Italy's densest foreign colonies, wryly nicknamed 'Chianti-shire'. The newcomers brought more money than Chianti's mouldering barons and contessas had seen since the Renaissance; property prices shot to the moon. But the presence of so much money has begun to cast a shadow over the heart of this ancient, enchanting region; snobbery and pretensions threaten to poison the pleasurable plonk of yesteryear. Some vintners offer limited-edition numbered bottles; designer-label Chianti is upon us. The old vines, following the contours of the hills, are being pulled out to make room for specialized vines in geometric straight lines. And as any old-timer will tell you, the modern DOCG Chianti Classico sniffed and gurgled by wine professionals isn't anything like the joyous, spontaneous wine that made Chianti famous in the first place.

Some 800 farms and estates (only a selection of the most historic are listed below) produce wine in the 70,000 hectares of the Chianti Classico zone, and one of the chief pleasures is trying as many labels as possible – with the different mixtures of grapes, different soils and bottling methods, each should be, or at least strives to be, individual. Nor do estates limit themselves to Chianti; many produce *vinsanto*, a white wine called Bianca della Lega, and many reds, as well as Chianti's other speciality, a delicate *extra-vergine* olive oil. Before setting out, call to check hours.

Western Chianti: Florence to Tavarnelle Val di Pesa

Chianti begins 10km south of Florence, but on the way you may want to follow the sign west off SS222 just past the *autostrada*, for **Ponte a Ema** and the prettily sited 14th-century chapel of the Alberti, Santa Caterina dell'Antella (*closed Sun*) with contemporary frescoes on St Catherine's life, one of Spinello Aretino's greatest works. Further along, at Grassina, there's a turn-off to **Impruneta**, a large town on a plateau noted for its terracotta tiles (including those on Brunelleschi's dome) and pottery, very much on sale, especially during St Luke's Horse and Mule Fair in October. The fair takes place in the main piazza, in the shadow of Impruneta's pride and joy, the **Collegiata**, built to house a miraculous icon of the *Madonna and Child* attributed to St Luke, dug up by a team of oxen in the 10th century. After the Collegiata was bombed in the last war, restorers brought it back to its Renaissance appearance to match its two beautiful chapels, both designed by Michelozzo and richly decorated with enamel terracottas by Luca della Robbia. One houses the icon and the other a piece of the True Cross. In an adjacent chapel is a marble relief, the *Finding of the Icon*, by the school of Donatello; the bronze crucifix in the nave is attributed to

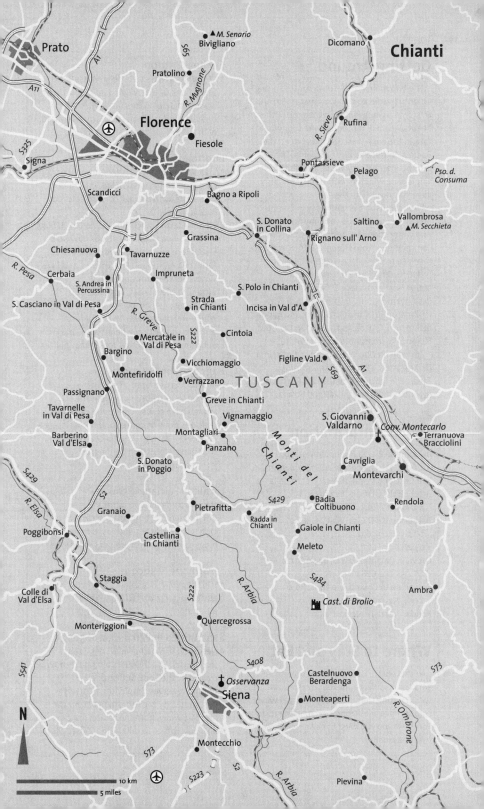

Getting Around

The two main north–south **routes** through Chianti, the old Roman Via Cassia (SS2) and the Chiantigiana (SS222), rival one another in beauty. An ideal motoring wine tour would take in the east–west SS429 between the Badia a Coltibuono and Castellina. The distances aren't very great, though the single-lane winding routes make for fairly leisurely travel.

Public transport is fairly easy in Chianti and all by **bus**, though you may not always find connections between two towns very commodious; from Florence SITA buses will take you to Greve (25km/45min), Gaiole (55km/1½hrs), Castellina in Chianti (44km/1hr), Mercatale, S. Casciano in Val di Pesa (17km/25min), Tavarnelle Val di Pesa (29km/40min), Panzano, Strada, and Radda (42km/1hr); CAP buses run frequently from Florence to Impruneta (14km/20min).

From Siena TRA-IN buses go to Castellina (20km/25min), Radda (30km/40min), Tavarnelle (38km/50min) and S. Casciano (49km/1¼hrs), Tavarnuzze and Strada.

Tourist Information

Impruneta: Piazza Buondelmonti 29, t/f 055 231 3729, *www.proimpruneta.rtd.it*.
San Casciano in Val di Pesa: Piazza della Repubblica, t/f 055 822 9558, *prosanca@ftbcc.it*.
Barberino Val D'Elsa: Via Cassia 31a, t/f 055 807 5622. *Open April–Oct*.
Greve in Chianti: Viale G. da Verrazzano 33, t/f 055 854 6287.
Castellina in Chianti: Via Feruccio 40, t 057 774 1392.
Radda: Piazza Ferucci 1, t 0577 738494.

Where to Stay and Eat

In this part of Chianti, hotels tend to be small and usually annexed to restaurants. It is worth noting that many of the larger wine estates have a few rooms or apartments to let. For these you will need to call ahead to see what's available.

Candeli ✉ 50100

★★★★★Villa la Massa, Via della Massa 6, t 055 62611, f 055 633102, *villamassa@galactica.it*, *www.villalamassa.com* (*luxury*). A large hotel, recently and spectacularly renovated, with a swimming pool and 39 rooms.

Impruneta ✉ 50023

★★★La Vallombrosina, Via Montebuoni 95, t/f 055 202 0491, *www.lavallombrosina.it* (*moderate, with bath*). A comfortable roof over your head.
B&B Benedetta Bianchi, Via Paolieri 26, t/f 055 231 2558 (*moderate*). A spacious new B&B just off the main piazza, with nicely furnished rooms and apartments, and lovely views over the surrounding hills.
I Falciani, Via Cassia 245, t 055 202 0091 (*moderate*). A rustic place full of locals, where you may dine with the TV for company on tasty *crostini ribollita* and, in autumn, on the hunters' roast meat platter.

Bagno a Ripoli ✉ 50012

Centanni, Via Centanni 7, t 055 630122 (*expensive*). Exceptionally pleasant, set among olive groves, where you can dine on a delicious array of *antipasti*, and Renaissance recipes like *brasata dei Medici*, a sweet and sour braised beef dish dating from the 17th century. *Closed Sun*.

Località I Falciani ✉ 50029

Antica Trattoria dei Cacciatori, Via Chiantigiana 22, t 055 232 6327 (*moderate*). Offers sturdy dishes, such as *rognone al ginepro*, kidneys with juniper. *Closed Wed*.

Tavarnuzze ✉ 50029

★★Gli Scopeti, Via Cassia 183, t 055 202 2008, f 055 237 3015 (*cheap*). A cheaper alternative.

Sant'Andrea in Percussina ✉ 50029

Albergaccio di Macchiavelli, t 055 828471 (*moderate*). Macchiavelli's old tavern, now owned by the Conti Serristori Wine Company, serves simple Tuscan meals – in summer, try the refreshing *panzanella* – and fine wines from the estate. You can also buy bottles to take home. *Closed Mon and Tues*.

Giambologna. The campanile dates from the 13th century, and the fine portico from 1634. Among the many terracotta shops, **Artenova** (*Via della Fonte 76, t 055 201 1060*), has creative designs and a good selection of gifts.

Macchiavelli in Exile

From the SS222 south of Florence, a byroad leads west from Tavarnuzze (8km) to **Sant'Andrea in Percussina**, long the country fief of the Macchiavelli. Here Niccolò spent his tedious exile, which he described in a letter as whiling away the day in the tavern 'playing at *cricca* and tric-trac, and this gave rise to a thousand arguments and endless exchanges of insults, most of the time there is a fight over a penny...and so surrounded by these lice, I blow the cobwebs from my brain and relieve the unkindness of my fate'. In the evening he would retire to work on *The Prince*.

His old tavern is still a tavern and his home, the Albergaccio (literally, 'nasty little inn'), contains a small museum devoted to his life. Near Chiesanuova, to the north, there's the 16th-century **Palazzo al Bosco**, attributed by some to Michelangelo, a villa built atop a 13th-century structure. The stately, theatrical 15th-century **Villa Tattoli** to the west (on the Chiesanuova–Cerbaia road) features two levels of arcades. Near Cerbaia, 5km from San Casciano, Villa Talente is the former property of the artists who built Orsanmichele in Florence (*t 055 825 9484; offers Chianti, white wine and olive oil*).

Along the Via Cassia (SS2)

Up-to-date **San Casciano in Val di Pesa**, 17km south of Florence, is the largest and busiest town in Chianti. Long an outpost of Florence, it suffered numerous vicissitudes until its walls were begun by the ill-fated Duke of Athens in 1342. Within these, near the gateway, the church of Santa Maria del Prato (1335) has retained its trecento interior and trecento art: a fine pulpit by Giovanni Balducci da Pisa, a pupil of Andrea Pisano, a crucifix attributed to Simone Martini, a triptych by Ugolino di Neri, and framed paintings on the pilasters by Giotto's pupil, Taddeo Gaddi. The recently opened **Museum of Sacred Art** (*open Sat 5–7, Sun 10.30–12 and 4–7*) includes the *Madonna and Child*, considered to be the first work by Ambrogio Lorenzetti.

In the vicinity of San Casciano, Florentine merchants and noblemen dotted the countryside with villas: the late Renaissance Fattoria Le Corti, 2km east on the Mercatale road, owned by the princely Corsini family for the past six centuries (*t 055 829 0105; own Chianti on sale*) and the 17th-century Poggio Torselli, just off the SS2, approached through a long avenue of cypresses and surrounded by a lovely garden.

Mercatale, Bargino and Barberino Val d'Elsa

Mercatale, 5km east of San Casciano, grew up around its *mercato* (market), protected in the old days by the Castle of the Florentine Bishops, now a ruin fit only to protect the odd lizard. More muscular, just east on the road to Passo dei Pecorai, is the **Castello di Greve** (*t 055 821 101; tastings and lunches with advance notice, own Chianti, Vinsanto and olive oil on sale*), bound by four round towers. The Bardi put it up in the

Where to Stay and Eat

Most of the district's lodgings are here, as well as some of Chianti's best restaurants.

Cerbaia ✉ 50026

La Tenda Rossa, Piazza del Monumento 11, **t** 055 826132 (*very expensive, but worth it*). A family-run abode of haute cuisine: pumpkin-filled *tortellini* or lettuce crêpes filled with artichoke hearts, followed by chicken with grated *porcini* mushrooms, or duck in balsamic vinegar. Save room for one of the innovative desserts. *Closed Mon lunch and Aug.*

San Casciano ✉ 50026

★★★Villa Il Poggiale, Via Empolese 69, **t** 055 828311, **f** 055 829 4296, *www.villailpoggiale.it* (*expensive*). This lovely Renaissance villa overlooking a cypress-bordered lawn has elegant rooms, decorated in pastel shades; some have four poster beds. The atmosphere is of a grand but un-stuffy private country home. Breakfasts are hearty and there is a nice pool. There are self-catering apartments too. Excellent value for money.

Nello, Via IV Novembre 66, **t** 055 820163 (*moderate*). The menu features fresh fish, plus such Tuscany staples as *ribollita pasta* with *funghi porcini*, beef braised in 'Chianti' *classico*. *Closed Wed eve and Thurs.*

★★★L'Antica Post, Piazza Zannoni 1/3, **t** 055 822313, **f** 055 822278 (*inexpensive*). Ten rooms with bath, and an excellent, persian-carpet-strewn restaurant. Try *taglierini* with razor clams and asparagus, pheasant with thyme, or rabbit in a sauce of creamed mussels; the wine list is superb. *Reservations necessary.*

Bargino ✉ 50024

★ Bargino, Via Cassia 122, **t** 055 824 9055 (*inexpensive*). Seven rooms in a garden along the old Roman road, with an excellent fish restaurant, **La Trattoria del Pesce** (*moderate*).

Mercatale ✉ 50026

★Soggiorno Paradiso, Piazza V Veneto 28, **t** 055 821327, **f** 055 821281 (*inexpensive*). Simple, but with TVs and electric kettles in the rooms.

Il Salotto del Chianti, Via Sonnino 92, **t** 055 821 8429 (*moderate*). Well-established on the local culinary scene; *ravioli con formaggio, pappardelle alla lepre* and wild boar are extraordinary. *Closed lunch and Wed.*

Tavarnelle ✉ 50028

La Gramola, Via delle Fonti 1, **t** 055 8050321 (*moderate*). A pleasantly rustic restaurant in the heart of the town, serving variations on traditional Tuscan dishes. The mixed *antipasto* plate is always tasty, ravioli stuffed with pumpkin and flavoured with local truffles are earthy. *Dinner only (except Sun); closed Tues.*

Youth Hostel, Via Roma 137, **t** 055 807 7009 (*inexpensive*). One of the pleasant Chianti hostels, with 60 beds. *Open all year.*

Barberino Val d'Elsa ✉ 50021

★★Primavera, Via della Republicca 27, **t/f** 055 805 9223 (*moderate*). A pleasant, simple hotel.

San Donato in Poggio ✉ 50028

Villa Francesca, Strada Monestiero 12, **t** 055 807 2849 (*moderate*). Tasty roasts, risotto with porcini mushrooms and *bistecca*. *Open Thurs–Sun; Thurs, Fri dinner only.*

11th century, before they moved to Florence and founded the greatest pre-Medici bank. Other villas worth visiting near Mercatale are Villa Caserotta, once property of the Strozzi, and the fortified Villa Palagio, on the Mercatale–Campoli–Montefiridolfi road, adapted from a 14th-century castle. The Mercatale–Panzano road will bring you to **La Torre a Luciana**, an unspoiled medieval hamlet once belonging to the Pitti family.

The Via Cassia, between San Casciano and Bargino, passes the ancient **Castle of Bibbione**, once residence of the Buondelmonte family, who owned much of this territory in the days when they were throwing fat on the Guelph and Ghibelline fires in Florence. Near **Bargino**, in the same bellicose spirit, is the impressive fortified hamlet of **Montefiridolfi**, just east of the Via Cassia. This road, meanwhile, rolls south through lovely hills towards **Tavarnelle Val di Pesa**, of mostly 19th-century origin, and medieval **Barberino Val d'Elsa**, with some Etruscan finds in the town hall and a good 10th-century Romanesque church, the Pieve di Sant'Appiano. From here the Via Cassia continues to **Poggibonsi** (*see* pp.349–50), with a possible detour to **La Paneretta**, a sturdy 15th-century fort amid the olive groves, with Baroque frescoes inside.

Central Chianti: Along the Chiantigiana (SS222)

From Florence the scenic Chiantigiana (SS222) passes the Ugolino Golf Course (*see* p.88) and offers its first tempting detour at Petigliolo: turn left after 4km for the ivy-covered Santo Stefano a Tizzano, a Romanesque church built by the Buondelmonti, not far from an 11th-century castle-villa, the **Castello di Tizzano** (*t 055 855 5040; offers Chianti Riserva, Vinsanto Naturale and prize-winning olive oil*). The same road continues for 2km to **San Polo in Chianti**, the centre of Tuscany's iris industry, celebrated in an Iris Festival in May. On a hill from San Polo you can see a lonely building once belonging to the Knights Templar; an equally ancient church, San Miniato in Robbiana, was reconsecrated in 1077 by the Bishop of Fiesole, according to a still legible inscription. San Polo's **Antico Toscano** is a wine shop with offerings from all over the region.

Strada, 14km from Florence along the Chiantigiana, is thought to take its odd name from an old Roman road. In the Middle Ages, the road to the south, towards the Valdarno was protected by the **Castello di Mugano**, one of the best preserved in the region, polished up by a recent restoration. The rolling countryside is the dominant feature until **Vicchiomaggio**, with a distinctive castle where Leonardo da Vinci once stayed. This is now the British-run Fattoria Castello di Vicchiomaggio (*t 055 854079; own-label Chianti, Vinsanto, olive oil, honey and upmarket accommodation*).

New Yorkers will recognize the name of nearby **Verrazzano** at once, thanks to Giovanni da Verrazzano, a captain who, in the service of François I of France, discovered New York Harbour and Manhattan island in 1524. He disappeared on his second voyage to Brazil, but surely smiles down on the bridge named in his honour. His birthplace, the **Castello di Verrazzano** (*call t 055 854243; tastings with a week's notice*), offers wines and olive oils. East of the Chiantigiana, 1.5km north of Greve, stands the 13th-century **Castello di Uzzano** (*t 055 854032; tastings with one day's notice*), built by the Bishop of Florence, which was gradually converted into one of Chianti's most impressive villa estates.

Greve in Chianti and Environs

The biggest **wine fair** in Chianti occurs in September in the medieval town of **Greve** (pop. 10,800), which is seen as the region's capital. Located on the banks of the river, it is celebrated for its charming, arcaded, funnel-shaped **Piazza del Matteotti**, studded with a statue of Verrazzano. And that's about all– its castle was burned in 1387, and its Franciscan convent became a prison in the 19th century. In the church of **Santa Croce** there's a triptych by Lorenzo di Bicci and a painting by the 'Master of Greve'.

Where to Stay

Greve ✉ 50022

★★★**Del Chianti**, Piazza Matteotti 86, t/f 055 853763, *www.albergodelchianti.it* (*expensive*). Pleasantly refurbished; near the centre, with comfortable, stylish air-conditioned rooms, and a pool and garden in the back.

★★★**Giovanni da Verrazzano**, Piazza Matteotti 28, t 055 853189, f 055 853648, *www. verrazzano.it* (*expensive*). Eleven elegant rooms overlooking the pretty main square.

Villa Vignamaggio, Via Petriolo 5, t 055 854 4840, f 055 854 4468, *www.vignamaggio.it* (*expensive*). 5 mins drive from Greve on the Panzano road. You can stay in buildings in the grounds or in the historic villa (see p.198). Tennis and a pool are available. Mona Lisa was born here in 1479, and *Much Ado About Nothing* was filmed here in 1992.

Panzano ✉ 50022

★★**Villa le Barone**, Via S. Leolino 19, t 055 852621, f 055 852277, www.villalebarone.it (*luxury half-board only*). Just south of Greve is the 16th-century villa of the della Robbia family, who still own it: it's a lovely, intimate hotel, a great base for visiting the region, or for lounging in the pretty garden by the pool (bring the children). Many rooms are decorated in della Robbia blue and white. *Open April–Oct; min stay 3 nights.*

Villa Rosa Via San Leolino 59, t 055 852577, f 055 856 0835, *www.resortvillarosa.it* (*expensive*). On the road between Panzano and Radda, Villa Rosa has a pleasant, relaxed atmosphere; there is a shady terrace at the back and a pool on the hillside, which enjoys beautiful views.

Monte S. Michele ✉ 50020

Villa San Michele, t 055 851034 (*inexpensive*). The youth hostel, with beds for 60. *Closed Nov–Mar.*

Castellina ✉ 53011

★★★★**Tenuta di Ricavo**, t 0577 740221, f 0577 741014, *www.ricavo.com* (*very expensive*). 3km north of Castellina, this is more than a hotel – it's an entire medieval hamlet of stone houses, wonderfully isolated in the pines and with a large garden and pool. Many rooms are situated in the old houses, ideal for families. *Open April–Oct.*

★★★★**Villa Casalecchi**, t 0577 740240, f 0577 741111, *www.villacasalecchi.com* (*very expensive*). A comfortable if rather sombre old house, set among trees and vineyards on a slope, with some elegant rooms full of antiques and some not so elegant, but a big pool and enchanting views over the hills. *Open April–Oct.*

★★★**Salivolpi**, Via Fiorentina, t 0577 740484, f 0577 740998, *www.hotelsalivolpi.com* (*moderate*). Two old farmhouses have been combined to create this smart establishment just outside Castellina; a garden and pool are added attractions.

Eating Out

Greve ✉ 50022

Bottega del Moro, Piazza Trieste 14r, t 055 853753 (*expensive–moderate*). Right in the heart of Greve, a simple *trattoria* where you can eat typical Tuscan dishes. *Closed Wed.*

Osteria di Passignano, Via Passignano 33, Badia a Passignano t 055 807 1278 (*expensive*). Set in the old wine cellars of a monastery on the famous Antinori wine estates just south of Florence, this is one of the best country restaurants in the area. The atmosphere is elegant rustic and the creative food is firmly rooted in Tuscan and Italian traditions. *Closed Sun and most of Jan.*

La Cantinetta di Rignana, Via Rignana, Greve. t 055 852601 (*moderate*). This *trattoria* is situated in idyllic countryside between

Greve is awash with wine, so seek out the specialized wine shops (*see* 'Wine Tasting in and around Greve', above). Meat-lovers flock to the **Macelleria Falorni** (*Piazza Matteotti 69/71, t 055 853029*), one of the region's most famous butchers, acclaimed for its cured hams and *finocchiona* salamis flavoured with fennel seeds. In a nearby hamlet, **Cintoia**, east of Chiocchio, there is the little church of

Greve and Badia in Passignano (to the south), and has a panoramic terrace ideal for long, lazy lunches. Whet the appetite with a *bruschetta* doused in local oil; pastas come with mushrooms, truffles or traditional meat sauces. *Closed Tues.*

Giovanni da Verrazzano, Piazza Matteotti 28, t 055 853189 (*moderate*). This is one of Greve's most charming restaurants, furnished with antiques and with a lovely terrace overlooking the piazza. The main meat dishes are especially good – *nana in sugo* (duck in wine sauce), turkey with olives, and a varied mixed grill. *Closed Mon.*

There are also a number of good places in the following villages close to Greve:

Montefioralle ✉ 50022

Taverna del Guerrino, Via di Montefioralle 39, t 055 853106 (*moderate*). A rustic place surrounded by a panoramic garden, offering good Tuscan home cooking, including *panzanella*, *ribollita* (Tuscan bread soup), sausage and beans *all'uccelletto* and wines from the local *fattoria*. *Closed Mon–Wed.*

Spedaluzzo ✉ 50027

La Cantinetta, on the Chiantigiana 93, t 055 857 2000 (*moderate*). Good home-made pasta and country specialities like stuffed rabbit, pigeon, stuffed artichokes and grilled meats. *Closed Mon.*

Località Lucolena ✉ 50020

Borgo Antico, t 055 851024 (*moderate*). Worth trying for tasty *Pappardelle* made with chestnut flour with wild boar or duck sauce. Porcini mushrooms in season. Also rooms for rent. *Closed Mon–Thurs in winter.*

Panzano ✉ 50022

Montagliari, Via di Montagliari 28, t 055 852184 (*moderate*). Decorated in the style of an old Tuscan farmhouse, with tables in the panoramic garden. Dishes include ravioli filled with walnuts, boar *alla cacciatora* and *pollastro Montagliari al vino bianco* (chicken with white wine and black olives). *Booking obligatory.*

Castellina ✉ 53011

Albergaccio di Castellina, Via Fiorentina 35, on the road to San Donato, t 0577 741042 (*expensive*). On the outskirts of town, this serves 'creative' fare. *Closed Sun.*

Antica Trattoria Le Torre, Piazza del Comune 1, t 0577 740236 (*moderate*). A popular, family-run place, with a cosy atmosphere and tasty dishes like risotto with mushrooms and an exceptional *fagiano alla torre*, prepared to an ancient Chianti recipe. *Closed Fri.*

Pietrafitta Ristoranti in Chianti Località Pietrafitta 41, t 0577 741123 (*moderate*). This is slightly cheaper, owned by an American with an Australian cook, offering surprisingly good regional and international dishes. Imaginative Italian–Mediterranean food. *Closed Tues.*

Wine-tasting in and around Greve

Bottega del Chianti Classico, Via Cesare Battisti 4, t 055 853631.

Castello di Querceto, just outside Greve on the Figline Val d'Arno road, t 055 85921. A lovely place offering a wide variety of wines, including Sangiovese aged in *barriques*, and olive oil (*tastings with one week's notice*).

Enoteca del Chianti Classico, Piazzetta S. Croce 8, t/f 055 853297.

Fontodi, Via S. Leolino 87, on the Chiantigiana, near Sant'Eufrosino, t 055 852005. Also has wine aged in *barriques*, Chianti, Bianco della Lega and olive oil (*tastings with one week's notice*).

Santa Maria a Cintoia which has a beautiful 15th-century panel attributed to Francesco Granacci.

The ancient village and castle of **Montefioralle**, 1km west of Greve, is where the people of Greve lived in the bad old days. Recently restored, it is an interesting place to poke around in, with its octagonal walls intact, its old tower houses, and two

Romanesque churches: Santo Stefano, housing early Florentine paintings, and the porticoed Pieve di San Cresci a Montefioralle, just outside the walls. A minor road to the west passes the ruined castle of **Montefili**, built in the 900s as the eastern outpost of one of Chianti's most powerful religious institutions, the **Badia a Passignano**, a fortified complex, converted since into a villa. You can visit the old abbey church, **San Michele**, which contains paintings by Ghirlandaio, Alessandro Allori and Domenico Cresti (better known as Passignano) and a bust of San Giovanni Gualberto, founder of the Vallombrosan Order, who arrived here in the mid-11th century. Most buildings date from the 14th century, with a few 17th- and 19th-century remodellings.

Just east of Greve, the beautiful villa **Vignamaggio** was built by the Gherardini family, whose most famous member, Lisa, was born here. She married Francesco del Giocondo before posing for the world's most famous portrait. More recently, in 1992 it was the setting for Kenneth Branagh's film, *Much Ado About Nothing*. **Panzano**, an agricultural centre 6km south of Greve on the Chiantigiana, played an important role in the Florence–Siena squabbles, but retains only part of its medieval castle. Its famous butcher, Dario Cecchini, is known for his protests when 'beef on the bone' was banned in 2001. He holds court in his shop (Via XX Luglio 11) on the outskirts of town on Sunday mornings, while playing loud music and reciting Dante. Panzano is best known for its embroidery, and for the **Pieve di San Leolino**, 1km south, with its pretty 16th-century portico on a 12th-century Romanesque structure; inside there's a triptych by Mariotto di Nardo. Another Romanesque church south of Panzano, Sant'Eufrosino, just off the SS222, enjoys especially fine views. Near Panzano is the **Fattoria Montagliari** (*sells a wide variety of its own wines, grappa, olive oil, cheese, salami, honey, etc.*). **Pietrafitta**, 9km further south and 4km from Castellina, is a lovely hamlet hidden in the woods.

Castellina in Chianti

One of Chianti's most charming hill-top villages, Castellina (pop. 2,700) was fortified by Florence as an outpost against Siena, and for centuries its fortunes depended on who was on top in their endless war. It was lost to a combined Sienese-Aragonese siege in 1478, though after the fall of Siena itself in 1555 both cities lost interest in Castellina, and today it looks much as it did in the quattrocento: the circuit of walls is almost intact, complete with houses built into and on top of them. The **Rocca**, or fortress, is in the centre, its mighty donjon now home to the mayor; and the covered walkway, Via delle Volte, is part of the 15th-century defensive works. Less historic but worth visiting is the Bottega del Vino Gallo Nero, Via della Rocca 10 (*sells wines and olive oils*). You can explore the **Ipogeo Etrusco di Montecalvario**, a recently restored 6th-century BC Etruscan tomb. West of Castellina on the SS429, **Granaio** is home to one of Chianti's most renowned wineries, the **Melini Wine House**, established in 1705.

There are many splendid old farmhouses and villas around Castellina, nearly all formerly fortifications along Chianti's medieval Maginot line, like the **Villa La Leccia** just southwest of Castellina, and the **Castello di Campalli** near **Fonterutoli**, an ancient hamlet south on the Chiantigiana. In the 13th century Florence and Siena often met here to work out peace settlements, none of which lasted long. Since 1435 the Mazzei family at the **Fattoria di Fonterutoli** (*t 0577 740476*) has produced wine in traditional oak casks, including Chianti and Bianco della Lega, as well as lavender products, honey and Tuscany's finest *extra-vergine*. Further south, **Quercegrossa**, 10km from Siena, but now practically a suburb of the city, was the birthplace of quattrocento sculptor Jacopo della Quercia. A road forks northeast for Vagliagli, site of the medieval **Fattoria della Aiola** (*t 0577 322509; with wines, grappa, olive oil, honey and vinegar*).

Monti del Chianti: Radda and Gaiole

East of Castellina lies the more rugged region of the Monti del Chianti. Here in the ancient capital of the Lega del Chianti, **Radda in Chianti** (pop. 1,650), the streets follow a medieval plan, radiating from the central piazza and its stately, heraldy-encrusted Palazzo Comunale, and a 15th-century fresco *Madonna, St Christopher and St John the Baptist* in the atrium. Just outside town is the Franciscan **Monastero,** a pretty 15th-century church. Two medieval villages are nearby: **Ama**, with its castle 8km to the south, near the attractive Romanesque church of San Giusto; and **Volpaia**, 7km to the north, with another ancient castle and walls, and an unexpected 'Brunelleschian' church, La Commenda. Also near Radda is the **Fattoria Vigna Vecchia** (*t 0577 738090, www. vignavecchia.com; offers Chianti, grappa*, vinsanto, *olive oil and tastings with 3 days' notice*).

On the way to Gaiole, 10km east of Radda, you pass the ancient **Badia a Coltibuono**, one of the gems of Chianti. Set among centuries-old trees and gardens, the abbey is believed to have been founded in 770, passing to the Vallombrosan Order in the 12th century. The Romanesque church, San Lorenzo, dates from 1049. The monastery was converted into a splendid villa, owned in the 19th century by the Poniatowski, one of Poland's greatest noble families, and now occupied by a wine estate, **Fattoria Badia a Coltibuono.** You can visit the cellars and Italianate garden (*t 0577 74481, f 0577 749235; open May–Oct, Mon–Sat, 2.30–6.30*) and restaurant (*see* 'Where to Stay and Eat', p.200).

Gaiole in Chianti (pop. 4,780) is an ancient market town: the **Agricoltori Chianti Geografico** (*Via Mulinaccio 10, t 0577 749489; sells Chianti, Vernaccia di San Gimignano, Vinsanto and olive oil*) is the headquarters of a local cooperative; the **Enoteca Montagnani**, Via B Bandinelli 9, specializes in Chianti Classico. Beside wine tasting Gaiole has little to offer, but it is a good base for visiting the impressive castles between the Arno and Siena. Just to the west are the walls and imposing donjon of the well-preserved 13th-century **Castello di Vertine**, one of the most striking sights in Chianti. To the east of Gaiole is the ancient fortified village of **Barbischio**, and 3km south on the SS408 is the impressive medieval **Castello di Meleto** with its sturdy cylindrical towers. From here the road continues 4.5km up to the mighty **Castello di Castagnoli,** guarding a fascinating little medieval town in a commanding position.

Most majestic of all is the Iron Baron's isolated **Castello di Brolio** (*open daily 9–12 and 3–sunset*) some 10km south of Gaiole along the SS484, high on a hill with views for miles around. Donated to the monks of the Badia in Florence in 1009, by Matilda of Tuscany's father Bonifacio, it passed to the Ricasoli in 1167. In 1478 the castle was

Where to Stay and Eat

Radda ✉ 53017

La Locanda, Località Montanino, Vilpaia, **t** 0577 738833, *www.locanda.it* (*luxury*). Set on a wooded hillside overlooking the hamlet of Volpaia, this little hotel, housed in a collection of restored stone farm buildings, enjoys perfect peace and the atmosphere of a private house. Rooms are rustic but stylish, views from the terraced garden are stunning, the food is good and there is a small pool.

★★★★Relais Vignale, Via Pianigiani 8, **t** 0577 738300, **f** 0577 738592, *www.vignale.it* (*very expensive*). Thirty rooms in a charming old house, with some fine views and a pool for hotter days. Their excellent restaurant is 320m down the road. *Open April–Dec.*

Podere Terreno, on road to Volpaia, **t/f** 0577 738312 (*expensive – half board*). A working wine-producing farm and *agriturismo*, 5km north of Radda. Rooms are simple, the atmosphere relaxed, with meals served at a communal table in a cluttered living room.

★Il Girarrosto, Via Roma 41, **t** 0577 738010 (*inexpensive*). In the village centre, nine simple rooms annexed to this very popular restaurant (*moderate*). Ideal if you're in the mood for a roast meat and wine debauch. *Closed Wed.*

Antica Trattoria Botteganova, Via Chianti-giana 29, **t** 0577 284230 (*very expensive*). Known for fish and meat in interesting combinations – *tortelli* with truffle and parmesan sauce, clams with aniseed, and sweet and sour pigeon. Leave space for the wonderful desserts. *Closed Mon.*

Il Vignale, Via XX Settembre 23, **t** 0577 738094 (*very expensive*). A family-run restaurant, featuring refined Tuscan home cooking, very popular locally. *Closed Thurs.*

Badia a Coltibuono, next to the old abbey of the same name between Radda and Gaiole, **t** 0577 749031 (*expensive*). Delicious *tortelloni*, *tagliatelle ai porcini*, meats roasted on a spit, and tempting desserts.

Il Carlino d'Oro, Via Brolio, San Regolo, **t** 0577 747136 (*cheap*). Enjoying an idyllic setting in the shadow of the great Castello di Brolio, this small, family-run *trattoria* is very popular, so be sure to book at weekends. Excellent *minestra di fagioli* (bean soup) or *pappardelle* with hare sauce, grilled meats and delicious deep fried chicken and rabbit. *Open lunch only, plus dinner Fri–Sun in summer. Closed Mon.*

Gaiole ✉ 53013

★★★★Castello di Spaltenna, **t** 0577 749483, **f** 0577 749269, *www.spaltenna.it* (*very expensive–expensive*). Beautifully located in an old fortified monastery in Spaltenna, just above Gaiole, with some theatrical medieval touches. The 21 delightful, comfortable bedrooms, furnished with antiques, have stunning panoramic views over the valley or courtyard. There is also an indoor pool, sauna and beauty centre. *Closed mid-Jan–Mar.* The restaurant (*very expensive*) in the ancient castle refectory serves both traditional and creative Tuscan dishes.

Castelnuovo Berardenga, Relais Borgo San Felice, Loc. Borgo San Felice, **t** 0577 359260, **f** 0577 359089, *www.relaischateaux.fr/borgofelice* (*very expensive*). A lovely renovated hilltop hamlet, entirely occupied by this hotel; beautifully furnished rooms are dotted around various buildings in the village. There is an excellent restaurant, gym, pool and tennis court. Surrounded by vines of the famous San Felice estate. *Closed Nov–Easter.*

Castello di Tornano, Loc. Lecchi, **t/f** 0577 746067, *www.castelloditornano.it* (*rooms – very expensive; apartments – moderate*). A restored, fortified farmhouse and castle with a 1,000-year-old tower commanding views of steep wooded hills. The outbuildings have been converted into self-catering apartments in rustic style sleeping 2–4. The castle and tower now house nine luxurious double rooms and suites, all furnished with original antiques; they also have use of the grand public rooms in the castle. There is a restaurant, pool and tennis court.

Brolio ✉ 53013

Castello di Brolio (*call the tourist office for contact details*). Three large apartments available in this famous site, near to Gaiole. *Reserve far in advance.*

Osteria del Castello, **t** 0577 747277 (*expensive*). This osteria has now been transformed into a delightful restaurant, serving understated, elegant food in surroundings to match. *Closed Thurs.*

bombarded for weeks by the Aragonese and Sienese, who later demolished it so the 'the walls levelled with the earth'. Florence rebuilt it, and in the mid-19th century Baron Ricasoli converted it into a splendid fortified residence, while experimenting with the modern formula for Chianti. You can sample the famous wines and olive oil and visit the cellars 10km south at the **Cantine Barone Ricasoli** (*call ahead* **t** *0577 7301*). The **Fattoria dei Pagliaresi** (*t 0577 359070; offers older wines as well as new, and olive oil*) is near Castelnuovo Berardenga, between S. Gusmé and Pianella. To the south, Castelnuovo Berardenga is an agricultural centre with the remains of a 14th-century castle, and from here it's 16km to **Monteaperti**, where Florence almost went down the tubes (to continue south, *see* 'Monte Oliveto Maggiore and Around', p.396).

The Mugello

Over the years, as their ambitions became less discreet, the Medici concocted a pretty story of how they were descended from knights of Charlemagne. In truth they came down to Florence from the Mugello, the hilly region just to the north – as did Giotto and Fra Angelico. As far back as Boccaccio's time, the Mugello was considered the loveliest region of the Florentine *contada*, and its bluish-green hills are dotted with elegant weekend and summer retreats, rather smarter than the typical stone *fattorie* of the Chianti. The Florentines come here whenever they can, and if you find

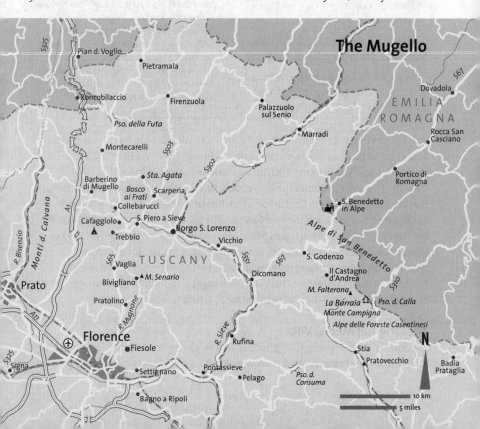

Getting Around

The Mugello lies to the east of the A1 and north of Pontassieve. It has two exits off the A1: at Barberino (28km from Florence) and Roncobilaccio (47km) near the Passo della Futa.

The two main **roads** north from Florence, the SS65 (Via Bolognese) to the Medici Villas and Passo della Futa and the SS302 to Borgo San Lorenzo (28km), are pretty drives. North of the river Sieve, mountain roads slow travelling – allow at least two hours from Florence to Firenzuola (51km), more to Marradi (64km).

You can also do a loop by **train** through the Mugello from Florence, passing through Pontassieve, Dicomano, Vicchio, Borgo San Lorenzo, San Piero a Sieve, and Vàglia. SITA **buses** are more scenic and just as infrequent; check times before setting out (most pass through the junction at San Piero). Better still, hire a car.

Tourist Information

For the Mugello: Borgo san Lorenze Via P. Togliatti 45, **t** 055 845271, **f** 055 845 6288, *wwww.mugellotoscana.it.*

Where to Stay and Eat

The Mugello has quite a few hotels, most fairly pricy and nearly all in the countryside, so you need a car to reach them.

Bivigliano ✉ 50030

★★★**Giotto Park Hotel/Giotto Park Hotel Dipendenza**, Via Roma 11, **t** 055 406608, **f** 055 406730, *www.giottoparkhotel.it* (*expensive*). This small, restful villa, along with the cheaper *dipendenza*, is a comfortable option, set in a garden with a tennis court.

Borgo San Lorenzo ✉ 50032

★★★**Locanda degli Artisti**, Piazza Romagnoli 2, **t** 055 845 5359, **f** 055 845 0116, *www. locandartisti.it* (*moderate*). In the centre and next to the excellent Ristorante degli Artisti (different owners), this neat little guest house has eight simple but pretty rooms.

Ristorante degli Artisti, Piazza Romagnoli 1, **t** 055 845 7707 (*moderate*). Elegant, serving Mugello cooking in the *centro storico* of Borgo, with a pretty courtyard terrace. Just about everything is home-made. *Closed Wed.*

Marradi ✉ 50034

Palazzo Torriani, Via Fabroni 58, **t** 055 804 2363, **f** 055 804 2835, *www.palazzotorriani.it* (*moderate*). Housed in a beautifully-restored 16th-century palazzo in the centre of the town, this '*residenza d'epoca*' consists of 3 self-catering apartments one of which can be rented as two separate bedrooms. The rooms are graced with early 20th century frescoes and are furnished with family antiques. Meals available on request.

yourself stewing with them in the traffic gridlocks approaching Piazza della Libertà, know that all you have to do is turn up the Via Bolognese or Via Faentina and in 10 minutes you'll be in a cool, enchanting world immersed in green.

North of Florence altitudes rise appreciably towards the central Appennine spine that divides Tuscany from Emilia-Romagna. Tucked in these hills lies the Mugello basin, a broad valley along the river Sieve and its tributaries, which, in the Miocene era, held a lake. Most of the towns of the Mugello are here, surrounded by a sea of vines; olive groves cover the slopes, but soon give way to deep forests of pines, chestnuts and oaks, cool and refreshing, dotted with small resorts. And like any fashion-conscious Florentine, the Mugello changes colours with the seasons, and is strikingly beautiful any time of year, a place to return to, again and again.

The Original Medici Villa

Following Via Bolognese (SS65) north, past the gardens of **Pratolino**, one of the last Medici villas (*see* **Florence**, 'Medici Villas', p.182), it's a panoramic and winding 30km to

Scarperia ✉ 50038

Hotel Cantagallo, Viale Kennedy 17, **t 055 843 0442, **f** 055 843 0443 (*moderate*). A tidy little hotel overlooking a shady garden.

Teatro dei Medici, Loc. La Torre 12, **t** 055 845 9876 (*moderate*). Set in an old house that once belonged to the Medici, this is the place to go for Mugello cooking – and everyone does – so in summer it's worth booking ahead. Country *antipasti*, good pasta dishes and wild game in season.

Locanda Senio ✉ 50035

***Palazzuolo sul Senio, Borgo dell'Ore 1, **t** 055 8046019, **f** 055 8043949, *www. locandasenio.it* (*very expensive*). The eight pretty bedrooms and suites at this hotel, which occupies a series of ancient buildings in the medieval town of Palazzuolo, are furnished with antiques. The food is excellent, there is a heated pool and a small health spa, which you can use free of charge.

Vicchio ✉ 50039

Villa Campestri, Via de Campestri 19, **t** 055 849 0107, **f** 055 849 0108, *www.villa campestri.it* (*very expensive*). On a hill south of Vicchio stands one of the most beautiful hotels in the region: an elegant Tuscan villa set in a 300-acre park, boasting a pool with a view, exquisitely furnished rooms and a good restaurant.

Antica Porta di Levante, Piazza Vittorio Veneto 5, **t** 055 840050 (*moderate*). *Closed Mon*. A young enthusiastic team run this interesting little restaurant just outside Vicchio's old eastern gate. Dishes are creative Tuscan using season ingredients (some work better than others) and there's a comprehensive wine list. There's a pretty vine-covered terrace too.

La Casa di Caccia, **t** 055 840 7629 (*moderate*). An isolated old hunting lodge, about 20mins of winding, climbing road north of Vicchio, with stunning views across the valley. Game, home-made pasta, grilled meats.

Sagginale ✉ 50032

Trattoria Sagginale, **t** 055 849 0130 (*cheap*). Between Borgo San Lorenzo and Vicchio, a family-run restaurant known locally as 'Da Giorgione' at the back of a shop, serving excellent rustic food in a simple setting – try the fabulous home-made ravioli rolled, stuffed rabbit. *Closed Thurs, and Mon–Wed lunch.*

Ponte a Vicchio ✉ 50039

Casa del Prosciutto, **t** 055 844031 (*moderate*). Part-grocer, part-*trattoria*, specializing in local dishes including good char-grilled chicken and potato-stuffed *tortelli* (takeaway as well). *Lunch only, closed Mon.*

---

two of the very first. On the way, a slight detour east (from Pratolino or Vaglia) ascends to **Monte Senario** (820m/2,680ft) where, in 1233, seven Florentine noblemen founded the mendicant Servite Order, living in grottoes and building simple cells in the woods. The Servites later built Santissima Annunziata in Florence. Rebuilt in the 16th century, the monastery here has amazing views over the Arno valley and Mugello.

North, towards San Piero a Sieve, there's a turn-off west on an untarred road for the Medici **Castello di Trebbio**, a family estate remodelled in 1461 by Michelozzo into a fortified villa with a tower. It has a formal Italian garden, which you can visit. For groups ring **t** 055 845 6230.

A bit further up looms the even grander **Villa Cafaggiolo** (*open Wed and Fri 2.30–6.30, Sat–Sun 10.30–12.30 and 2.30–6.30*), favoured by Cosimo il Vecchio and Lorenzo il Magnifico, who spent as much of the summer as possible in its cool halls. Cosimo had Michelozzo expand and transform this ancient family seat into an imposing castellated villa, its entrance protected by a bulging tower, adorned with an incongruous clock. To the east, a minor road leads up to the wooded **Bosco ai**

Deluxe Virgins

Some day, on a trip to one of the fancier Italian food shops, you may pause near the section devoted to condiments and wonder at the beautiful display of bottles of unusually dark whiskies and wines, with corks and posh, elegant labels – why, some is even DOC, though much of it is far more costly than the usual DOC vintages. A closer look reveals these precious bottles are full of nothing but olive oil. Admittedly *olio extra vergine di oliva* from Tuscany and Umbria makes a fine salad dressing – according to those in the know the oil of the Chianti brooks few rivals, Italian or otherwise. Its delicate, fruity fragrance derives from the excellent quality of the ripe olive and the low acidity extracted from the fruit without any refinements. The finest, Extra Virgin, must have less than 1 per cent acidity (the best has 0.5 per cent acidity). Other designations are Soprafino Virgin, Fine Virgin, and Virgin (each may have up to 4 per cent acidity) in descending order of quality.

As any Italian will tell you, it's good for you – and it had better be, because Tuscan or Umbrian chefs put it in nearly every dish, as they have for centuries. The only difference is that it now comes in a fancy package for a fancy price, a victim of the Italian designer label syndrome and Tuscan preciosity. Not only does the olive oil have corks, but the trend in the early 1990s was for some of the smarter restaurants to offer an olive oil list similar to a wine list – one restaurant in Tuscany even had an oil sommelier. Many of these, perhaps fortunately, seem to have gone out of business.

Frati, with a simple porticoed church also by Michelozzo; inside there's a fine crucifix by Donatello, and another attributed to Desiderio da Settignano.

Beyond Cafaggiolo, towards Barberino (about 4km from Barberino) is the huge artificial **Lago di Bilancino**. The lake, which is dammed (the dam controls the water of the Sieve river) occupies nearly five square kilometres, has a beach with sunbeds and umbrellas and is good for water sports: sailing, windsurfing, fishing and canoeing. Bars, restaurants and other leisure facilities are also being developed. There have been many problems and lots of controversy over the plans, but all is now going ahead.

To the Passo della Futa

Just off the *autostrada*, the largest town on the western rim of the Mugello basin is **Barberino di Mugello**, a market town spread under the **Castello dei Cattani**. Its 15th-century Palazzo Pretorio, like many others, is emblazoned with coats of arms; the open Loggie Medicee is another work by Michelozzo. On SS65, 5km away at Colle Barucci, is one of the grandest estates in the Mugello, the **Villa delle Maschere** ('of the masks').

Continue 14km north for the breathtaking views from the **Passo della Futa** (903m/ 2,962ft), a pass on the principal Apennine watershed; below, the whole Mugello is spread out like a relief map. In 1944, the pass was the Germans' strong point on the Gothic Line – until the allies rendered it useless by capturing Firenzuola to the north. Beyond the pass the road winds under the craggy **Sasso di Castro** (1,276m/4,185ft); at La Casetta you can turn off for Firenzuola (*see* opposite) or hotfoot it over the mountains in time for dinner in Bologna, the culinary capital of Italy.

Scarperia and Around

Standing at the major crossroads of the SS503 north and the SS551 along the Sieve, **San Piero a Sieve** is a busy little town defended by a mighty Medici citadel, the **Fortezza di San Martino**, designed by Buontalenti in 1571. Its Romanesque parish church, with a façade from 1776, contains a remarkable octagonal baptismal font in polychrome terracotta, by Luca della Robbia. From here it's 4km to **Scarperia**, the most charming town in the Mugello, perched high above the valley. Florence fortified it in 1306, and laid out its simple rectangular plan, with one long main street.

The **Palazzo dei Vicari** (*open 15 Sept–1 June: Sat–Sun and hols 10–1, 3–6.30; 1 June– 15 Sept: Wed, Thurs and Fri 3.30–7.30, Sat–Sun and hols 10–1, 3.30–7.30*), dating from 1306, is so heavily decorated with stone and ceramic coats of arms that it resembles a page from a postage stamp album. Its atrium and upper halls have 14th- and 15th-century frescoes, the earliest ones by the school of Giotto. The palazzo also houses the **Museo dei Ferri Taglienti** (*same hours as Palazzo dei Vicari*), a small museum dedicated to knife-making and cutting tools. The oratory of the **Madonna di Piazza** has an attractive Renaissance front and a cinquecento fresco of the Madonna and Child, attributed to Iacopo del Casentino; the church dedicated to Our Lady of the Earthquakes has a fresco that some attribute to Filippo Lippi.

From the 16th century, Scarperia supplied the duchy of Tuscany with knives, forks and scissors, as well as daggers and swords. By 1900 there were 46 thriving firms, though machine-made competition has reduced this. Firms still making knives, where you can buy bone- or horn-handled cutlery (at high prices) include Conaz (Via Roma 8), Saladini (Via Solferino 15), Berti (Via Roma 37) and Giglio (Via delle Oche). Scarperia is now better known for the **Autodromo Internazionale del Mugello**, a 5km track built by Florence's Auto Club in 1976, which is fairly well hidden in the hills east of town.

The Mugello's most fascinating historical relic, 4km northwest of Scarperia, is the 11th-century parish church of **Sant'Agata** (*open daily 7.30–5*), restored after an earthquake in 1919, with an unusual apse and a pulpit from 1175, decorated with white and green marble intarsia designs and animals. The chapel to the right of the altar houses Bicci di Lorenzo's painting, *The Mystical Marriage of St Catherine*. **Firenzuola** is 22km north of Scarperia and is famous for its production of 'Pietra Serena', the pale grey stone you see in buildings all over Tuscany. A small holiday resort, cool even in August, it was devastated in the Second World War and rebuilt along the lines of the original street plan between the Porta di Bologna and the Porta di Firenze. Four kilometres west, in Cornacchiaia is a church believed to date back to Carolingian times.

Borgo San Lorenzo and Vicchio

Borgo San Lorenzo (pop. 16,300) on the river Sieve is the boom town of the Mugello, partly due to its fast-train rail link to Florence. It's surrounded by new residential neighbourhoods with gardens full of little chameleons; and indeed they are fond of animals here, as evidenced by the **Statue of Fido** in honour of man's best friend, in Piazza Dante. Otherwise, the main sights are two Romanesque churches: San Lorenzo, with an unusual hexagonal campanile built in 1263, and 3km north, the parish church of San Giovanni Maggiore, with a bell tower that is square at the base but octagonal on top, and a lovely 12th-century pulpit in marble intarsia. To the north the road divides into the SS477 to **Palazzuolo sul Senio** (which has an annual festival, see p. 70) and the SS302 to **Marradi**, also small resorts; Palazzuolo has a small **Ethnographic Museum** (open Mar–June and Sept–Dec Sun 3–6; July–Aug Tues 8–11pm, Thurs, Sat, Sun 4–7) in the 14th-century Palazzo dei Capitani.

Vícchio, east of San Lorenzo, is a sleepy little town, birthplace of the Blessed Fra Angelico (Giovanni da Fiesole, 1387–1455) and often a home from home for Benvenuto Cellini. The Palazzo Pretorio contains the **Museo Comunale Beato Angelico** (t 055 844 8251; open Sat–Sun 10–12 and 4–7, also Thurs 10–12 in summer; adm), with detached frescoes, Etruscan finds from nearby Poggio alla Colla, and a 13th-century holy water stoup. Not to be outdone, the nearby hamlet of **Vespignano** was the birthplace of Giotto di Bondone (1267–1337). The simple stone cottage where the father of Renaissance painting is said to have been born has been carefully restored as the **Casa di Giotto** (open Sat–Sun 10–12 and 4–7, also Thurs 10–12 in summer; adm). According to tradition, Cimabue discovered Giotto near the old (restored) bridge over the Enza, where the young shepherd was sketching his sheep on a stone.

The Valdisieve

The lower Sieve valley is mostly industrial: **Dicomano** can boast of an interesting fresco by the school of Piero della Francesca, but little else besides a big Saturday-morning market and the junction for the SS67, which climbs east into a pretty range of mountains called the Alpi di San Benedetto. **San Godenzo**, 10km up the SS67, is the largest village, site of an 11th-century Benedictine abbey; its plain church has a raised presbytery and a polyptych by the school of Giotto.

From San Godenzo a road continues up to the birthplace of Andrea del Castagno, now called **Il Castagno d'Andrea** ('Andrew's chestnut') (1,022m/3,355ft), a small holiday village. Wind a further 18km up to **S. Benedetto in Alpe**, with a 9th-century Benedictine abbey that sheltered Dante (Inferno, Canto XVI, 94–105), and where you can hire horses to visit the enchanting Valle dell'Aquacheta with its pretty waterfall. In the old town of **Portico di Romagna** 11km further north, the Portinari family, including the beautiful Beatrice, spent their summers – their house still stands in the main street. Deeper into Romagna lie the fascinating medieval town of **Brisighella**, the ceramic city of **Faenza**, and **Ravenna**, not only filled with ravishing Byzantine mosaics from the time of Justinian but also the site of Dante's real tomb.

There is little along the lower Sieve. **Rufina**, 10km south of Dicomano, is dominated by the 16th-century Villa Poggio Reale, producing Chianti Rufina and Pomino wines. Continuing east along the SS70 beyond Pontassieve, turn left after a few kilometres for **Castello di Nipozzano** (for opening times call t 055 27141), one of the great Frescobaldi wine estates, producing prize-winning oak-aged red wines. For white wines, climb into the hills to the north and visit **Castello di Pomino**, another Frescobaldi property. **Poggio Reale** has a small wine museum (call ahead, t 055 839 5078). From **Pontassieve** the scenic SS70 leads up to the dramatic Passo della Consuma (1,022m/3,355ft) before descending into the Casentino (see pp.397–401).

The Valdarno, Prato and Pistoia

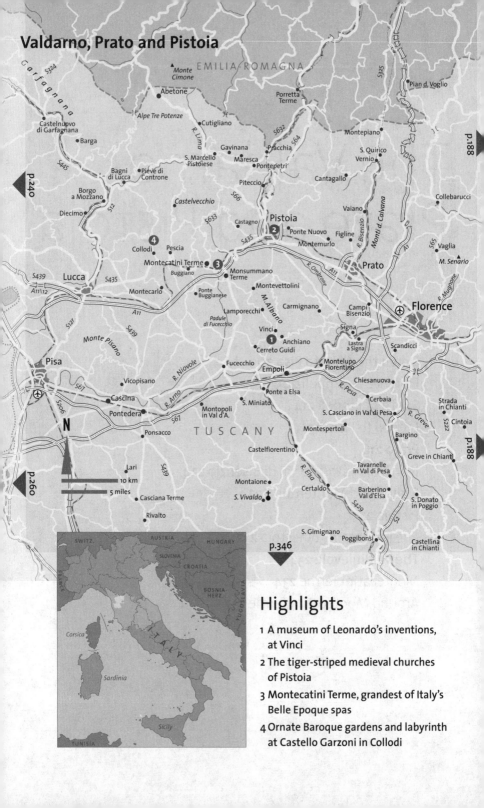

Valdarno, Prato and Pistoia

p.188

p.240

p.188

p.260

p.346

Highlights

1 A museum of Leonardo's inventions, at Vinci

2 The tiger-striped medieval churches of Pistoia

3 Montecatini Terme, grandest of Italy's Belle Epoque spas

4 Ornate Baroque gardens and labyrinth at Castello Garzoni in Collodi

Whether you travel by car, bus or train, there are two routes between Florence and Pisa. The route along the Arno, often hemmed in by the hills, has always been historically and economically the least important and carries less traffic. The large cities of Prato, Pistoia and Lucca grew up in an arc north of the Monte Albano hills, where there's more fertile land and room to grow, and the route takes in the nearby Florentine towns of Vinci, Castelfiorentino and Certaldo.

Down the Arno to Pisa

Florence to Empoli

The old Florentine satellite town of **Scandicci** (6km west), once in the business of renting villas to foreigners like Dylan Thomas and DH Lawrence (who finished *Lady Chatterley's Lover* here), has since found more profit in industry. Most towns along the Arno specialize in certain products; in **Lastra a Signa** it's straw goods, sold in numerous village shops. Lastra retains its 14th-century walls and the **Loggia di Sant'Antonio**, all that survives of the hospital founded by Florence's Silk Guild in 1411; many believe Brunelleschi was the architect, and that the work was a prototype of Florence's Spedale degli Innocenti, funded by the same guild. Just outside Lastra, the church of **San Martino a Gangalandi** has a beautiful, semicircular apse with *pietra serena* articulation designed by Alberti. In **Signa**, the next village, the Romanesque **San Lorenzo** houses a remarkable 12th-century marble pulpit and trecento frescoes.

After Signa the road and river continue 12km through a gorge before **Montelupo Fiorentino**, celebrated since the Renaissance for its terracottas and delicately painted ceramics. The town hosts a ceramics fair at the end of June, which also features Renaissance music and costumes, demonstrations and exhibitions. The **Museo Archeologico e della Ceramica**, Via Baccio Sinaldi 45 (*t 0571 51352; open Tues–Sun 10–6; adm*), has examples from nearly every period, and a display on the lower Valdarno's prehistory, while Montelupo's shops sell more recent ceramic creations. The old **castle** here was built in 1203 by the Florentines, during the wars against Pisa; the church **San Giovanni Evangelista** contains a lovely *Madonna and Saints* by Botticelli and his assistants. On the outskirts of Montelupo, you can see Buontalenti's **Villa Ambrogiana** (1587) from the outside, though you'll probably want to avoid being invited in – it's a mental hospital. From Montelupo a road leads southeast 20km to the town of San Casciano in Val di Pesa, in Chianti (*see* p.193).

Empoli

The modern market town of **Empoli**, 32km from Florence, was witness to one of the turning points in Tuscan history: in 1260, the Ghibellines of Siena, fresh from their great victory over Florence at Monteaperti, held a parliament in Empoli to decide the fate of their arch enemy. Everyone was for razing Florence to the ground once and for all, and waited for the approval of their leader, Farinata degli Uberti.

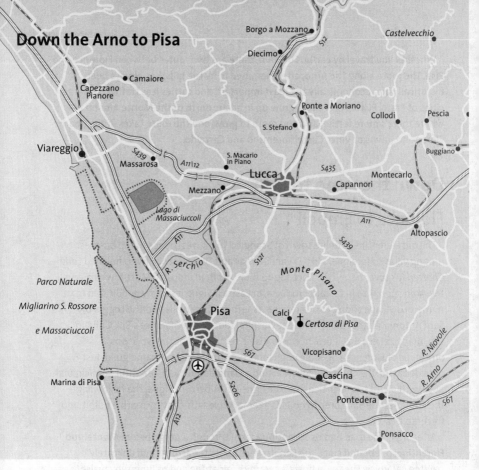

Down the Arno to Pisa

The Uberti were Florentine gangster nobles famous for their hatred of their fellow citizens, and Farinata surprised all when he announced that, even if he had to stand alone, he would defend Florence for as long as he lived. The Sienese let their captain have his way, and lost their chance of ever becoming *numero uno* in Tuscany.

The prosperous new Empoli (pop. 45,000) produces green glass and raincoats. You'll find little to recall the days of Farinata, until you reach the piazza named after him; here is the palace where the parliament convened, across from the gem of a Romanesque church, the **Collegiata Sant'Andrea**, with its green and white marble geometric façade in the style of Florence's San Miniato. The lower portion dates from 1093; the upper had to wait until the 18th century, but it harmonizes extremely well.

Museo della Collegiata

Empoli has its share of 13th- and 14th-century Florentine art, much of it now in the small but choice **Museo della Collegiata** (*open Tues–Sun 9–12 and 4–7; adm*) in the Collegiata's cloister. The most celebrated work is Masolino's *Pietà* fresco, with its poignant faces; upstairs there's an elegant relief of the *Madonna and Child* by Mino da Fiesole and his brother Antonio's painted tabernacle of St Sebastian. Lorenzo Monaco contributes a long-eyed *Madonna and Saints*; Lorenzo di Bicci's scene of San

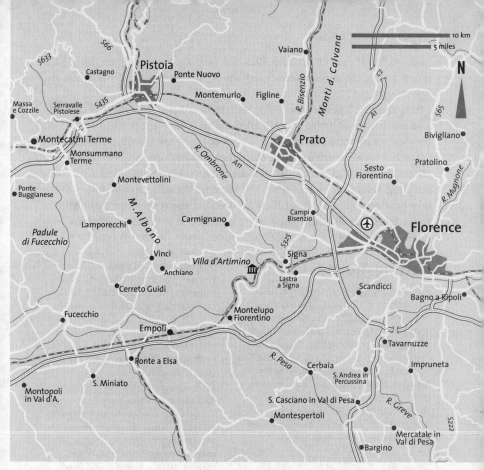

Nicola da Tolentino shielding Empoli from a rain of plague arrows is a quattrocento view of the city. There is a rare series of frescoes by Masolino's master, Starnina, as well as two saints by Pontormo, who was born nearby, and the fine *Tabernacle of the Holy Sacrament* by Francesco Botticini and his son Raffaello, with a good predella.

The upper Loggia has works by Andrea della Robbia, and the suspended wooden wings of the donkey that flies down on a wire from the church tower on *Corpus Domine* (although a papier-mâché donkey has of late replaced the original one). Empoli's **Santo Stefano** church (*open Tues–Fri 9–12 by appt – enquire at the Museo della Collegiata*), restored after damage during the Second World War, has more beautiful frescoes by Masolino and a marble *Annunciation* by Bernardo Rossellini.

Around Empoli

Northwest of Empoli, in the Monte Albano, lies the old hill townlet of **Cerreto Guidi**, former property of the Counts of Guidi, taken over by Florence in 1237. It is known these days for its *Chianti Putto*, and for the **Villa Medicea** (*open daily 9–6.30; closed 2nd and 3rd Mon of month; adm*), rebuilt for Cosimo I by Buontalenti in 1564, relatively simple as Medici villas go, but approached by the 'Medici bridges', a grand double ramp of bricks. In 1576 Cosimo I's daughter Isabella was murdered here by her husband Paolo Orsini for her infidelities; look carefully and you will see the unhappy couple among the scores of Medici portraits in the villa. From the terrace there are fine views of the Monte Albano.

From Cerreto it's 5km to **Vinci**, a tiny town most famous as the home of Leonardo, who was born in a humble house in Anchiano on 15 April 1452, the illegitimate son of the local notary and a peasant girl. In his honour, the town's landmark Conti Guidi Castle has been converted into the **Museo Leonardiano** (*open Nov–Feb daily 9.30–6; March–Oct daily 9.30–7; adm*), full of models of inventions he designed in his *Codex Atlanticus* notebooks, most of which this supreme 'Renaissance man' never had the time or attention span to build. There are descriptions in English for the hundred or so machines, including some inspired by those invented by Brunelleschi to build Florence's cathedral dome. More speculative designs include a flying machine, a

Getting Around

If you're **driving**, persist: the Florentine sprawl finally gives way at Signa and after that the Arno road (S67) becomes even scenic in stretches. LAZZI **buses** take the main route to Pisa; SITA goes directly from Florence to Castelfiorentino or Certaldo; for Vinci, COPIT. **Trains** at least once an hour follow the Arno between Florence and Pisa, and at Empoli turn off for Castelfiorentino, Certaldo, Poggibonsi and Siena. Note that San Miniato and Fucecchio share a railway station; local buses commute from there to both centres.

Tourist Information

Vinci: Via delle Torri 11, **t** 0571 568012. (Also serves Empoli.)
San Miniato: Piazza del Popolo 3, **t** 0571 42745.
Castelfiorentino: c/o the Station, Via Ridolfi, **t**/**f** 0571 629049. *Open April–Oct.*
Certaldo: Via Cavour 32, Viale Fabbiano 5, **t** 0571 656721.

Where to Stay and Eat

The lower Arno Valley isn't exactly awash with pleasure domes, but you won't starve.

Santa Maria a Marciola ✉ 50018
Fiore, Via di Marciola 112, near Scandicci, **t** 055 768678 (*moderate*). A good place to stop if it's time to eat just as you're leaving or approaching Florence, not only for its

delicious crêpes and mixed meats on the grill, game, *bistecca*, etc, but for its lovely garden setting and pine-clad slopes. *Open for dinner daily and Sun and Sat lunch.*

Vinci ✉ 50059
★★★Alexandra, Via dei Martiri 36, **t** 0571 56224, **f** 0571 567972 (*moderate*). Vinci's one hotel; quiet and comfortable.

As for restaurants, there isn't much choice.
Antica Cantina di Bacco, Piazza Leonardo da Vinci 3. **t** 0571 568041 (*cheap*). A cosy wine bar with an attractive terrace, serving the usual *enoteca* fare; toasted *crostoni* with various toppings, a few pasta dishes, cheeses, desserts and, of course, wine.

Empoli ✉ 50053
Empoli isn't a posh town by any means, but it can be an agreeable place to stay over. It also has some good places to eat.
★★★Sole, Piazza Don Minzoni, **t** 0571 73779 (*moderate*). A good bargain, by the station.
Cucina Sant' Andrea, Via Salvagnoli 43, **t** 0571 73657 (*expensive–moderate*). On the remains of the city walls, this *trattoria* run by a brother and sister serves creative versions of local dishes: pigeon terrine, courgette flan, risotto with artichokes, wild boar and game.
La Panzanella, Via dei Cappucini 10, **t** 0571 922182 (*cheap*). An old-fashioned *trattoria*, also by the station, which does an unusual artichoke soup and wonderful things with porcini mushrooms in season. Also a few fish dishes. *Closed Sun.*

paddle boat, a spring-driven mechanical car, an almost perfect modern bicycle, diving gear, a parachute and a device to walk on water. Also present are Leonardo's famous tank, machine gun and helicopter. This gentle fellow once said, 'I'll do anything for money', which must be one of the most startling quotes of the Renaissance. On the other hand, nothing could be more typical of the age than brilliance combined with immorality; while he often neglected his art, Leonardo was happy to help the bellicose princes who employed him with their military problems. We should probably be thankful that these gadgets never escaped from his note-book. Leonardo was baptized in the font in **Santa Croce**, next door to the museum.

From Vinci it's a 3km walk (or drive) southeast to **Anchiano**, where the simple stone house where Leonardo was born has been restored (*open Nov–Feb daily 9.30–6, in summer until 7; adm*).

San Miniato ✉ 56027

★★★**Miravalle**, Piazza Castello 3, **t** 0571 418075, **f** 0571 418075, *www.albergomiravalle.com* (*moderate*). Frederick II's 12th-century imperial palace, near the top of town.

Il Canapone, Piazza Bonaparte 5, **t** 0571 418121 (*moderate*). A simple place where you can try the local truffles on spaghetti, in risotto, or with veal *scaloppine*; in the spring there's risotto with asparagus. *Closed Mon.*

Certaldo ✉ 50052

★★★**Osteria del Vicario**, Via Rivellino 3, **t/f** 0571 668228 (*moderate*). A beautiful 12th-century ex-monastery with a garden, surrounded by a Romanesque courtyard. Rooms are simple, with terracotta floors, and the restaurant (*expensive*) serves creative fresh local fare. *Restaurant closed Wed.*

★★**Il Castello**, Via della Rena 6, **t/f** 0571 668250, *www.albergocastello.it* (*expensive–moderate*). One of the more interesting of the three small hotels in town.

One place in Certaldo can satisfy all your little vices at once:

Dolci Follie, Piazza Bocaccio **t** 0571 668188 (*moderate–cheap*). A fancy *pasticceria*, a wine bar and a fine little restaurant, where the cuisine (both fish and meat dishes) is more than a prelude to the exquisite desserts.

Artimino ✉ 50040

Paggeria Medicea, **t** 055 871 8081, **f** 055 871 8080, *www.artimino.com* (*very expensive*). An interesting place, located in the Medici Villa Artimino near Carmignano. A former country residence of the famous family, the stables have been converted into a very comfortable hotel with pool and tennis.

Da Delfina, **t** 055 871 8074 (*expensive*). Boasts a Michelin star and a well-deserved reputa-tion. There's Tuscan food (ravioli stuffed with potato), and a terrace for dining out.

Fucecchio ✉ 50054

Le Vedute, Via Romana-Lucchese 121, **t** 0571 297498 (*expensive*). A good inland seafood restaurant, pleasantly situated in the coun-try. Serves good meats as well, especially in autumn. In summer you can linger on the veranda. *Closed Mon.*

★★★**La Campagnola**, Viale Colombo 144, **t** 0571 260786, **f** 0571 261781 (*moderate*). 25 air-conditioned rooms.

Montopoli in Val d'Arno ✉ 56020

★★★**Quattro Gigli**, Piazza Michele 2, **t** 0571 466 878, **f** 0571 466 879, *www.quattrogigli.it* (*moderate*). In this little place across the Arno, the old town hall has been converted into an inn with 28 rooms of varying quality. The restaurant, beyond the permanent dis-play of Montopoli's painted ceramics, has a delightful terrace and features an imagina-tive menu. Some of the dishes are based on centuries-old recipes, such as tripe with eggs and saffron. Others are more creative, such as fresh tuna soufflé with artichokes, *pici* with baby squid, sea bass cooked with *aceto balsamico* or duck with dried fruit. *Closed Mon, also Sun eve in winter.*

South of Empoli

San Miniato

Just southwest of Empoli, the river Elsa flows into the Arno near **San Miniato** (pop. 23,000), a hill town that grew up at the crossroads of the Via Francigena (the main pilgrimage route from France to Rome) and the Florence–Pisa road. On a clear day the view takes in everything from Fiesole to the sea. Its strategic location made it the Tuscan residence of the Emperors, from Otto IV to Frederick II; Matilda of Tuscany was born here in 1046, and in the 12th century it was an important imperial fortress, protecting the crossroads and levying tolls on travellers and merchandise.

Of the citadel, only two towers survive: the present campanile of the cathedral and the taller 'Torrione', in the shady Prato del Duomo that crowns San Miniato, with its peculiar chimney-like structures on top. It was from the top of this tower that Frederick II's secretary and court poet Pier della Vigna, falsely accused of treason, leapt to his death, to be discovered by Dante in the forest of suicides, as described in the *Inferno* XIII. Also in the Prato del Duomo stand the 12th-century **Palazzo dei Vicari dell'Imperatore** and the **Duomo** itself, with a Romanesque brick façade, incorporating pieces of sculpted marble and 13th-century majolica that catch the light as the sun sets. Most of the art in the interior is Baroque, except for a fine 13th-century holy water stoup; most of the earlier artworks from the region have been placed in the **Museo Diocesano d'Arte Sacra**, to the left of the cathedral (*open Tues–Sun 10–12.30 and 3–6.30*). Among the prizes are the fresco of the *Maestà* by the 'Maestro degli Ordini' from Siena, a bust of Christ attributed to Verrocchio, Neri di Bicci's *Madonna con Bambino* and a *Crucifixion* by Filippo Lippi. Since 1968, the Prato del Duomo has also been the site of the **National Kite Flying Contest** (*1st Sun after Easter*).

In the Piazza del Popolo's 14th-century church of **San Domenico** you can see minor works by Masolino, Pisanello and the della Robbias. Bernardo Rossellino carved the fine 15th-century tomb of Giovanni Chiellini, the Florentine founder of San Miniato's Hospital of Poor Pilgrim Priests. The tomb is modelled after Rossellino's famous tomb of Leonardo Bruni in Florence's Santa Croce. The beautiful church of **San Francesco** has fresco fragments by a follower of Masolino. Napoleon paid a visit in 1797, to visit his relatives in the **Palazzo Bonaparte**. In the surrounding countryside are rich caches of white truffles, sought fervently in the autumn for the large market on the last Sunday in November; and many of what appear to be plain-looking Romanesque churches around San Miniato are actually tobacco-curing barns from the 1900s.

Castelfiorentino and San Vivaldo

Some 12km south along the Valdelsa from San Miniato, **Castelfiorentino** (pop. 18,000) is another old hill town, though much rebuilt after damage in the Second World War. Castelfiorentino's church of **Santa Verdiana** dates from the 18th century and houses the **Museo di Arte Sacra Santa Verdiana** (*open Sat 4–7, Sun and hols 10–12 and 4–7*), with some excellent trecento paintings, including a *Madonna* attributed to Duccio da Buoninsegna, another by Francesco Granacci, and a triptych by Taddeo Gaddi. In the **Biblioteca Comunale**, Via Tilli 41 (*open Mon, Wed and Sat 9–1; Tues and Thurs 3.30–7; adm*) are frescoes by Benozzo Gozzoli that were originally in the Tabernacle of the Madonna della Tosse 'the coughing Madonna' in a nearby village, and also from the Cappella della Visitazione.

One of the more unusual sights in Tuscany, the **Monastery of San Vivaldo**, lies to the southwest of Castelfiorentino, beyond the village of Montaione. Vivaldo, a hermit from San Gimignano, lived in a hollow chestnut tree where he was found dead in 1301, still in the attitude of prayer. A Franciscan community grew up in his footsteps, and in 1500, when the monastery was being rebuilt, one member, Fra Tommaso da Firenze, designed a 'New Jerusalem' in the monastery's wooded hills, with 34 chapels representing the sites of Christ's Passion. To render the symbolic journey more realistic for pilgrims, the 34 chapels combined polychrome terracottas by Giovanni della Robbia and other artists, set in frescoes – Pope Leo X immediately granted a fat indulgence to anyone who did the whole route. Today only 17 of the chapels survive (*Oct–Mar guided tours Sun and hols 3.30; April–Sept guided tours Sun and hols 5pm; to visit outside these hours, call* **t** *0571 699252 for an appointment*).

Certaldo

Certaldo (pop. 16,000), former seat of Florence's deputy, or Vicarate of the Valdelsa, is synonymous with Giovanni Boccaccio, who spent the last 13 years of his life up in the old town, known as Castello Aldo, which could be a set for the *Decameron* itself (don't confuse it with the ugly sprawl of the new town at the bottom of the hill). Everything here is of good, honest brick, from the pavements to the palazzi, of which the most striking is the 14th-century castellated **Palazzo Pretorio**, studded with the arms of the former Vicars. Inside it has a beautiful courtyard and museum (*open summer daily 10–7, winter Tues–Sun 10.30–4.30; adm*) containing Etruscan artefacts, frescoes and, in the annexed church and cloister, Gozzoli's *Tabernacle of the Punished*, not one of his more cheerful works. The walls of the old jail bear the forlorn graffiti of past prisoners.

The house traditionally associated with Certaldo's great author is the **Casa di Boccaccio**, on Via Boccaccio 18, which has been restored and is now the seat of the International Centre of Boccaccio Studies (*open April–Sept daily 10–7; Oct Mon, Wed–Fri 10.30–4.40, Sat and Sun 10–7; Nov–Mar Wed–Mon 10.30–4.30*). Boccaccio died here in 1375 and lies buried in **Santi Michele ed Iacopo**, under an epitaph he penned himself; a 16th-century monument erected in his honour was destroyed by prudes in 1783. Boccaccio himself, in his later years, regretted the racy frivolity of his most famous book, wishing he had spent his time on serious Latin works – not a regret too many people have ever shared. From Certaldo you can follow a pretty road to the south which leads to **San Gimignano** (*see* pp.350–5), about 13km away.

Empoli to Pisa

There is no compelling reason to stop in the lower Valdarno unless you're low on petrol. If you're spending more time here, consider a visit to **Fucecchio** for its panoramic views, or better yet for the **Padule di Fucecchio** (*open all year; guided nature tours in spring by Centro di Ricerca, Documentazione e Promozione del Padule di Fucecchio t 0573 84540*), claimed to be Italy's biggest inland swamp and certainly an excellent place for bird-watching.

Next comes **Montopoli in Val d'Arno**, a tiny medieval town dating from the 11th century on the south bank. Further down-river lies industrial **Pontedera**, where the Piaggio Company produces most of Italy's motor scooters. Here you may detour south on the SS439 to Volterra (*see* pp.355–63), by way of **Ponsacco** and the four-towered **Villa di Camugliano**, built by Alessandro and Cosimo I, an example of Medici real estate speculation. Between here and Volterra roll the Pisan Hills, some of the quietest, most rural countryside in Tuscany; the main attraction may be precisely its lack of art and history. Alternatively, from Ponsacco, you can head southwest to tiny **Lari**, with the remains of a Medici fortress, and for your rheumatism, to Casciana Terme, famous for its cures in Roman times, and rebuilt by the Pisans in the 14th century. The hamlet of **Rivalto**, 6km south of the spa, has almost perfectly preserved its medieval character.

Vicopisano, north of the Arno, defended the eastern frontier of Pisa from Lucca's ambitions, and its impressive *castello* was remodelled by Brunelleschi after the Florentine conquest of Pisa; vineyards now surround its walls and towers. Across the bridge, **Cascina** still has most of its medieval walls and Roman grid plan. It also has three churches that are worth a visit: **San Casciano**, an unusual 12th-century Roman-esque church, with blind arches and some fine sculptural details; Romanesque **San Benedetto a Settimo**, adorned with a 14th-century alabaster altarpiece of Irish origin; and **San Giovanni Evangelista**, built by the Knights of St John, with trecento Sienese frescoes, recently restored after the church was used as a barn for several centuries. Further west lies the Certosa di Pisa (8km; *see* p.282) and Pisa itself (14km; *see* p.269).

Prato

Prato is only 18km from Florence but a world away in atmosphere; this is a city that works for its living, where the population has doubled since the Second World War to 145,000, third largest in Tuscany after Florence and Livorno. And a vibrantly, joyously proletarian city it is, fond of Henry Moore, comic books, avant-garde theatre and heavy-metal bars, full of people wanting you to sign petitions or buy encyclopaedias, all proud to live in 'the Manchester of Tuscany'. Living in Florence's shadow for the past thousand years has not dampened Prato's spirits; as in the days of the famous Francesco di Marco Datini, immortalized in Iris Origo's book *The Merchant of Prato*, this city still earns its keep from the manufacture of textiles, and especially the recycling of wool and rags. In the Renaissance, Prato made enough profit from these rags to hire the greatest artists of the day to embellish its churches and palaces.

History

In the 9th century Prato was known as Borgo al Cornio. Outside the town was a meadow, or *prato*, the site of the market and fortifications, which gradually became

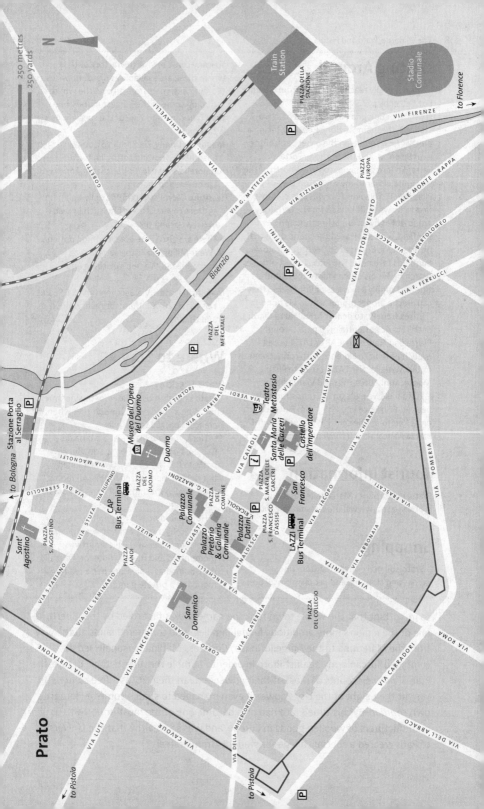

Getting Around

Prato is easily reached by **train** from Florence but better by LAZZI bus (25mins), Pistoia (25mins) or Bologna (55mins), and has two stations: the main Stazione Centrale, facing a pretty green square on the other bank of the river Bisenzio; and the Stazione Porta al Serraglio (not all trains stop), just north of the walls and closer to the centre, on the Florence–Pistoia line. This was one of Italy's first railways, built in 1848 for the Lorraine grand dukes by an Englishman, Ralph Bonfield, who so pleased the grand duke that he was made Count of St George of Prato. All Bonfields take note! The Prato tourist office is searching for his descendants, to claim the title and supply a likeness of Bonfield so they can erect a proper monument in his honour.

Buses from Prato depart from Piazza Ciardi or the Stazione Centrale; all pass through Piazza San Francesco (CAP or LAZZI buses, every half-hour to Florence with connections to the Mugello; also LAZZI buses to Pistoia, Montecatini, Lucca, Pisa and Viareggio).

Prato has two exits on the *autostrada* A11 between Florence and Pisa (from Florence get on at Peretola). The centre is closed to traffic: Piazza Mercatale is a convenient place to park.

Tourist Information

Prato: Piazza Santa Maria delle Carceri 15, t 0574 24112, *www.prato.turismo.toscana.it.*

Shopping

Prato still makes its living from fine fabrics and clothing, and people from all over Tuscany come to visit the **factory outlets** where these are available at discount prices. Clothing designers from all over the world, including some of the biggest names, buy their fabric in Prato. One of the specialities is **cashmere**.

Maglificio Denny, Zia Zarini 261, t 0574 592350. Cashmere, wool and cotton knitwear.

Anngorelle, Via Vella, t 0574 467275. For Cashmere and mohair.

Tessiture Cecchi & Cecchi, Via delle Calandre 53. Does covers, scarves and such in cashmere, wool and silk.

There are also some good **clothing** outlets:

M-Wear-Milior, Via Pistoiese 755D, t 0574 818288. Women's clothing and accessories.

Maglificio Pratesi, Via Baccheretana 83, Seano, t 055 870 5467. Clothing for men, women and children.

Where to Stay

Prato ✉ 50047

Prato's hotels mostly cater for businessmen, but can be a good bet in the summer when Florence is packed to the gills.

★★★Flora, Via Cairoli 31, near S. Maria dei Carceri, t 0574 33521, f 0574 400289, *www. prathotels.it* (*expensive*). Old-fashioned but decent modernized rooms. All rooms have a video machine and there is a small video library.

★★★Hotel Giardino, Via Magnolfi 2, t 0574 26189, f 0574 606591, *www.giardino hotel.com* (*expensive*). This smartly modernized and friendly hotel on Piazza del Duomo has a pleasant bar, a reading room and a private garage.

so important that the whole town took the name. It was first ruled by the Alberti, one of the region's more ambitious feudal families, who conquered lands all the way from the Maremma to the Mugello. In 1107 Countess Matilda personally led a combined Tuscan army against Prato in order to humble the Alberti; then, in 1140, the Pratesi rid their counts of most of their power and ran their city as a free *comune*. In 1193, at the height of the city's power, it even managed to snatch some of Florence's own *contado*. By this time Prato had also become one of the most important manufacturers of woollen goods in Europe, and was so wealthy that the University of Paris created a special college for students from Pratesi.

***Villa Santa Cristina**, Via Poggio Secco 58, t 0574 595 951, f 0574 572 623 (*expensive*). A relaxing spot with a garden, pool and most other comforts, over the river in the hills to the east of Prato.

***San Marco**, Piazza San Marco 48, t 0574 21321, f 0574 22378, *www.hotelsanmarco prato.com* (*moderate*). A pleasant place between the Stazione Centrale and the Castello, convenient if you arrive by train.

***Villa Rucellai**, Via di Canneto 16, 4km northeast of town, t 0574 460392 (*moderate*). A delightful B&B in a Renaissance villa, with pool. Despite being surrounded by Prato's industrial sprawl, its formal gardens and the wonderful atmosphere of the house (filled with the family's books, pictures and furniture) is an oasis. What's more, it's good value.

****Toscana**, Piazza Ciardi 3, t 0574 28096, f 0574 25163 (*moderate*). More economical, on a quiet square on the far side of the Stazione Porta al Serraglio.

Eating Out

One reason for staying in Prato is the food, especially if you like fish.

Osvaldo Baroncelli, Via Fra Bartolomeo 13, t 0574 23810 (*very expensive–expensive*). A small establishment with an innovative chef. The set menu is good value. A la carte options include fricassée of salt cod, Tuscan bean and spelt soup with fish and frizzled leeks, pasta with fish and artichoke hearts, and fish couscous. There is a fabulous array of Italian and French cheeses. *Closed Sun.*

Enoteca Barni, Via Ferucci 22, t 0574 607 845 (*expensive*). Has an excellent wine list; the food is good with simpler, cheaper lunch menus and more interesting choices at night, in a more elegant setting – asparagus soufflé with foie gras sauce, red mullet with basil, black olives and tomato, bean and cabbage soup with lobster, lamb in a herb crust. *Closed Sat lunch, Sun and Mon dinner; Aug.*

Il Pirana, Via Valentini 110, (south of Viale Vittorio Veneto, between the central station and Piazza San Marco), t 0574 25746 (*expensive*). Maintains a justified reputation for some of the best seafood in inland Tuscany. An elegant place, hidden behind reflecting glass windows. Try the *gran piatto* of raw marinated fish, *gnocchetti* with scampi and zucchini flowers, or fish ravioli in lobster sauce. *Closed Sat lunch and Sun.*

Maffei, Via Ricasoli 22. The distinctive bright blue bags displayed in the window of this *biscotteria* and bar contain the best *biscotti* (or *cantucci*) *di Prato* around. Don't settle for anything less.

Osteria Cibbé, Piazza Mercatale 49, t 0574 607509 (*cheap*). A small, family-run *osteria* with marble-topped tables set in a brick-vaulted room, serving delicious rustic dishes such as *pappa al pomodoro*, *garganelli* with aubergine and wild mushrooms, stock fish *in inzimino* (spicy sauce with Swiss chard), and meatballs with ricotta cheese. *Closed Sun.*

La Vecchia Cucina di Soldano, Via Pomeri 23, t 0574 34665 (*cheap*). A very gratifying *trattoria* for something less elaborate, with a traditional menu cooked and served on red-checked cloths by the Mattei family, that's full of *ribollita* and *pasta e fagioli*, stuffed celery and all the other old-fashioned soups and stews, including the house speciality, a hearty beef and onion stew known as *francesina*. *Closed Sun.*

Florence, however, could not countenance so near and ambitious a rival, and in 1350, on charges of fomenting rebellion in the Valdelsa, Florence besieged Prato. An honourable peace was made; the next year Florence cemented its hold over its neighbour by purchasing it for the sum of 17,500 florins from its nominal overlord, the Angevin Queen of Naples.

Despite the ignominy of being bought, Prato functioned more as Florence's ally than its possession, retaining a certain amount of local autonomy. The late 14th century was the day of Francesco di Marco Datini, the Merchant of Prato, one of the richest men in Europe and history's first recorded workaholic businessman. However, although he built his palace in his home town of Prato, the big profits were to be had in Florence, and Datini spent most of his time there. Under the influence of Savonarola's preaching, Prato joined Florence in rebelling against Medici rule, but was soon to play the role of whipping boy, when the Spaniards, at the instigation of the Medici Pope Leo X, besieged and sacked the city with unheard-of brutality. Since that dark day, Prato's history has followed that of its imperious neighbour, until a few years ago, at least. You can't keep a good town down forever, and Prato and its hinterlands have finally wriggled out from Florentine control and become a province in their own right – one of Italy's newest, and smallest.

Frederick's Castle

Open Wed–Sun 9–1 and 4–7; winter: mornings only; adm.

Most people, whether arriving by car, bus, or at the Stazione Centrale, approach the walled core of Prato through the Piazza San Marco, embellished with a white puffy sculpture by Henry Moore from 1974. Viale Piave continues to the defiantly Ghibelline swallowtail crenellations of the **Castello dell'Imperatore**. Built in 1237 by Frederick II, Holy Roman Emperor and heir to the Norman kingdom in southern Italy and Sicily, it marks a strange interlude in Prato's past. Frederick, unlike his grandfather Frederick Barbarossa, never spent much time in Tuscany, preferring his more civilized dominions in Apulia and Sicily, where he could discuss poetry, philosophy and falconry (in Arabic or Latin) with his court scholars. When he did come, it was in magnificent progress featuring dancing girls, elephants and the Muslim imperial bodyguard. His Tuscan taxpayers were not impressed; nor did they much appreciate Frederick's tolerant, syncretistic approach to religion. The popes excommunicated him twice. He built this castle here because he had to, not so much to defend Prato, but to defend his imperial *podestà* from the Pratesi, and perhaps impress the locals with its design – its clean lines must have seemed very sharp and modern in the 13th century.

Don't doubt for a minute that this castle is quite intentionally a work of art. The design, by a Sicilian named Riccardo da Lentini, is perfectly in tune with the south Italian works of the 'Hohenstaufen Renaissance' of Frederick's reign, a reminder of a rare age when artistically the south was keeping up with northern Italy, and often a little in advance. There isn't much inside the castle now, though the city often uses the space for special exhibitions. Usually it is possible to walk up along its walls for a bird's-eye view of Prato.

Santa Maria delle Carceri

Next to the castle stands the unfinished black and white marble façade of **Santa Maria delle Carceri**, begun in 1485 by Giuliano da Sangallo. Brunelleschian architecture was always a fragile blossom, as is clearly shown by the failure of this sole serious attempt to transplant it outside the walls of Florence. Santa Maria always merits a mention in architectural histories. It was an audacious enterprise: Sangallo, a furiously diligent student of Vitruvius and Alberti, attempted to create a building based entirely on philosophical principles. Order, simplicity and correct proportion, as in Brunelleschi's churches, were to be manifest, with few frills allowed. Sangallo, the favourite of Lorenzo il Magnifico, unfortunately proved to be a better theorist than he was an architect. Santa Maria was a clumsy tombstone for the sort of theoretical architecture that was a fad in the 1400s, one more often expressed in paintings than actual buildings. The interior is better than the exterior; a plain Greek cross in the Brunelleschian manner with a decorative frieze and *tondi* of the four Evangelists by Andrea della Robbia. The church's name – *carceri* means prisons – refers to a local miracle, a speaking image of the Virgin painted on a nearby prison wall, that occasioned the building of the church. Behind the church is Prato's grand 1820's **Teatro Metastasio**, home to some of the most innovative theatre in Italy and also to frequent concerts.

Piazza San Francesco and Datini

From Santa Maria delle Carceri you can see the apse of Prato's huge brick church of **San Francesco**, dating from the end of the 13th century, and embellished in front with white and green marble stripes. Inside, on the left wall is the Tomb of Gemignano Inghirami, one of Europe's crack lawyers of the quattrocento, the design attributed to Bernardo Rossellino (1460s); near the altar is the **tomb slab of Francesco di Marco Datini** (1330–1410) by Niccolò di Piero Lamberti. Off the elegant Renaissance cloister you'll find the entrance to the **Cappella Migliorati**, beautifully frescoed in 1395 by Niccolò di Pietro Gerini, one of the period's finest draughtsmen; here he depicts the Lives of Saints Anthony Abbot and Matthew.

Niccolò also frescoed the **Palazzo Datini**, nearby on Via Mazzei 33 (*open Mon–Sat 9–12 and 4–6*), the showplace palace built in the 1390s by the Merchant of Prato. If there were an Accountants' Hall of Fame, Francesco di Marco Datini would surely be in it; he helped invent that dismal science. Nor did he ever let anyone throw anything away, leaving to posterity 150,000 documents, ledgers (all inscribed: 'For God and Profit') and private letters that are stored in the archives in this palace; these formed the basis for Iris Origo's fascinating account of his life and times. Datini left nearly all of his indecent fortune to the Ceppo, a Pratese charity he founded in 1410 and which now has its headquarters on the first floor of this palace; in gratitude the city had the façade frescoed with scenes of his life, unfortunately now much faded.

Galleria Comunale

Currently closed. The most important works have been moved temporarily to the Museo di Pittura Murale (see p.223).

Just north lies Prato's charming civic centre, the **Piazza del Comune**, decorated with a 19th-century **statue of Datini** with bronze reliefs of the merchant's life, and a pretty fountain by Tacca nicknamed 'Il Bacchino', or Little Bacchus (1659). The city's **Palazzo Comunale**, behind the portico, retains only traces of its medieval heritage; drop in to see its **Sala di Consiglio** with its coffered ceiling, two quattrocento frescoes and portraits of the grand dukes. The rugged **Palazzo Pretorio** is entirely medieval, a relic of the days when Prato governed itself without any help from the Medici; the stair on the façade leads up to the **Galleria Comunale** with a good collection of mostly Florentine art. There's a tabernacle by Filippino Lippi, painted for his mother and later restored after damage in the war; up in the grand **Salone Udienza** with the fine wood ceiling is Bernardo Daddi's *Story of the Holy Girdle*, a predella telling the tale of Prato's most famous relic, the Virgin Mary's belt. According to tradition she gave it to Doubting Thomas, from whom it was passed down until it became part of the dowry of a woman who married Michele, a knight from Prato during the First Crusade. Michele returned to Prato and hid the precious relic under his mattress; angels lifted him off, and the girdle was given into the care of the cathedral. In the same hall are fine 14th-century works by Giovanni di Milano, Michele di Firenze, Lorenzo Monaco, and a *tondo* attributed to Luca Signorelli. In an adjoining room is *Noli me tangere* by Battistello, a follower of Caravaggio; this curious work portrays Christ wearing a fedora at a rakish angle, doing a quick dance step to evade the Magdalene's touch.

For a celebration of Prato medieval and modern textile industry visit the **Museo del Tessuto** (*open Mon and Wed–Sun 10–6*) which has a unique collection of fabrics and looms dating back to the 5th century AD. It is housed in a stunning 19th-century textile mill at Via Santa Chiara 24, where the full collection of fabrics (some 6,000 pieces, including contemporary textiles) is on display.

Cathedral of Santo Stefano

In the centre of Prato rises its cathedral, like a faded beauty who never recovered from the blow of a broken engagement. It was begun with great promise in the 13th century, and added to on and off for the next 200 years, with ever-dwindling passion and money. The best features are an exotic, almost Moorish campanile, a rather dirty Andrea della Robbia lunette of the *Madonna and St Stephen* over the door, a big clock on the half-striped façade that makes you smile when you notice it sitting where the rose window ought to be and, above all, the circular **Pulpit of the Sacred Girdle**, projecting from the corner of the façade. Perhaps no other church in Italy has such a perfectly felicitous ornament, something beautiful and special that the Pratesi look at every day as they walk through the piazza. Michelozzo designed it in 1428 and Donatello added the delightful reliefs of dancing children and *putti* along the lines of his *cantoria* in Florence's cathedral museum (the bas reliefs are only casts, but you can see the originals in the Museo dell'Opera). The Holy Girdle (*see* above) is publicly displayed here five times a year on Easter Day, 1 May, 15 August, 8 September and Christmas Day.

The Duomo's interior continues the motif of green and white stripes in its Romanesque arcades and ribs of the vaulting. The **Chapel of the Sacred Girdle**, just to the left as you enter, is protected by a screen, and the inside is covered with frescoes by Agnolo Gaddi on the legend of the girdle, and adorned with a beautiful marble statue, the *Madonna and Child*, by Giovanni Pisano. In the left aisle there's a masterful **pulpit** carved by Mino da Fiesole and Antonio Rossellino, with harpies around the base. Filippo Lippi's celebrated frescoes on the *Lives of Saints John the Baptist and Stephen* (1452–66) are undergoing restoration and work is expected to continue for several years (*to visit the chapel and see the work in progress contact the* *tourist office for a guided tour, Sat at 10, 11, 4 and 5, Sun at 10 and 11; adm*). While painting these frescoes, his first major work, Lippi fell in love with a brown-eyed novice, Lucrezia Buti, who according to tradition posed for his magnificent *Herod's Banquet*, either as the melancholy Salome herself or as the figure in the long white dress, second from the right; Fra Filippo placed himself among the mourners for St Stephen, third from right, in a red hat. The less lyrical frescoes in the next chapel are by Uccello and Andrea di Giusto. There's a lovely, almost Art Nouveau, candelabra on the high altar by Maso di Bartolomeo (1440s), closely related to his work in Pistoia cathedral.

The **Museo dell'Opera del Duomo** (*open Mon and Wed–Sat 9.30–12.30 and 3–6.30, Sun 9.30–12.30; adm*) is located next door in the cloister, one side of which retains its 12th-century geometric marble decorations and rambunctious capitals. The museum is currently undergoing long-term restoration work to enlarge it and only two rooms are open. The most important works are now at the Museo di Pittura Murale (*see* below). The tragic star of the museum is the original pulpit of the Sacred Girdle, with Donatello's merry *putti* made lepers by car exhaust. Lippi's *Death of San Girolamo* was painted to prove to the bishop that he was the man to fresco the cathedral choir. Other works include his son Filippino's *St Lucy*, blissfully ignoring the knife in her throat, and another full-length portrait, of *Fra Jacopone di Todi*, believed to be an early work by Uccello. More dancing *putti* adorn the *Reliquary of the Sacred Girdle* (1446) by Maso di Bartolomeo, which was stolen but recovered at the Todi antique fair. Also worth seeing are the saccharine *Guardian Angel* by Carlo Dolci, a sophisticated *Madonna with Saints* by the quattrocento 'Master of the Nativity of Castello', and a strange reliquary that resembles a mushroom.

Walking through Prato

Most of Prato's old streets are anonymous, self-effacing Tuscan. Sadly, some areas suffered bomb damage in the war, notably the great pear-shaped **Piazza del Mercatale** on the banks of the Bisenzio. This was long the working core of the city, surrounded entirely by porticoes and workshops; it was and is the site of Prato's big market and fairs. A few faded, peeling, porticoed buildings remain, overlooking the river that has laundered the products of Prato's principal industry for eight centuries.

Sunday is a good day to visit sturdy brick **San Domenico** on the west side of town, a large Gothic church begun in 1283 and completed by Giovanni Pisano, one side of it lined with arcades. There's not much to see inside, but the adjacent convent, the home of painter Fra Bartolomeo and Pratese address of Savonarola, holds the **Museo di Pittura Murale** (*open Mon, Wed, Thurs and Sat 9–1; Fri–Sat 9–1 and 3–6; adm*), housing a collection of detached frescoes from surrounding churches, and currently holding some of the works of Prato's other museums while they undergo reorganization. There are charming quattrocento graffiti court scenes from the Palazzo Vaj, a sinopia from the cathedral attributed to Uccello, and Niccolò di Piero Gerini's *Tabernacle of the Ceppo*. Filippo Lippi painted the *Madonna del Ceppo* for the Ceppo offices in the Palazzo Datini; it portrays the tycoon himself, with four fellow donors, who contributed less and thus get portrayed as midgets.

Just north of San Domenico, **San Fabiano**, Via del Seminario 30, has an enchanting pre-Romanesque mosaic pavement, depicting mermaids, birds and dragons biting their own tails; north of San Fabiano, 15th-century **Sant'Agostino** contains Prato's most ridiculous painting, the *Madonna della Consolazione* (attributed, naturally, to Vasari), who does her consoling by distributing belts from heaven.

Despite all its artistic treasures, Prato doesn't sit on its Renaissance laurels. In 1988 the ambitious **Centro per L'Arte Contemporanea Luigi Pecci** opened on Viale della Reppublica in the suburbs (*open Wed–Mon 9–7; adm exp*), with a collection of modern works from artists around the world. The only place to see contemporary art on this scale in Tuscany, it holds temporary exhibitions by important artists, and also summer concerts in the amphitheatre. Since the successful reception of Henry Moore's big lump by the train station in the 1970s, Prato has also accumulated outdoor abstract sculpture in a big way. Two that stand out, if only for their breathtaking pretentiousness, are Barbara Krueger's billboard *Untitled* (Viale da Vinci), and Anne and Patrick Poirier's *Monumentum Aere Perennis*, in the grounds of Centro Luigi Pecci. A regular season of concerts is held here.

North of Prato: the Val di Bisenzio

Prato's river begins some 40km up in the Apennines, and along its valley runs the SS325, a secondary highway towards Bologna. This valley was long the fiefdom of the Alberti counts, whose fortifications dot its sides. **Vaiano**, the first town on the main route, has a Romanesque abbey church and green-striped campanile as its landmark; just beyond are the ruins of the Alberti's **Rocca di Cerbaia** (12th century). The highway continues to **Vernio** and **San Quirico**, with another ruined Alberti castle up above.

From San Quirico's neighbour to the west, **Cantagallo** ('Cock's crow'), a lovely walking path leads up to the **Piano della Rasa** in little over an hour, which is a panoramic valley with an alpine refuge (*open April–Oct*). Further north on the SS325, at the small resort of **Montepiano**, the waters destined for the Tyrrhenian and Adriatic split and go their own ways. There is another ancient abbey here, the Vallombrosan **Badia di Santa Maria**, with good 13th- and 14th-century frescoes. From the abbey begins another fine walking path up to **Alpi di Cavarzano** (1,008m/3,306ft), and from there, it is another hour or so's walk up to the highest peak in the region, **Monte La Scoperta** (1,278m/4,192ft).

Figline and Montemurlo

The old road between Prato and Pistoia passes near **Figline di Prato**, a medieval village well-known for its terracotta vases. Figline has a 14th-century parish church with contemporary mural paintings, including a 'primitive' *Last Supper* and also a *St Michael* with a finely detailed background; a small parish museum contains other 'primitives'. **Montemurlo**, on its hill over the plain of Prato, is also medieval; in 1537 its castle, a stronghold of the Guidi counts, was the Alamo for the anti-Medici republican oligarchs of Florence, led by Filippo Strozzi, who were defeated here once and for all by the troops of Cosimo I. The old walled town is interesting, with an impressive and rather stylish **Rocca** for its crown, approached these days by a Mannerist ramp. The Romanesque church of 'Beheaded John' (**San Giovanni Decollato**) has a pretty campanile and some good art in its baroqued interior, including a miraculous Byzantine crucifix and a 16th-century painting by Giovanni da Prato illustrating its story.

Pistoia

You know **Pistoia** (pop. 94,000) is near when the road plunges into a Lilliputian forest of umbrella pines and cypresses, all in tidy rows. These are Italy's most extensive ornamental nurseries, a gentle craft that thrives in the rich soil at the foot of the Apennines. But Pistoia wasn't always content to cultivate its own garden peacefully;

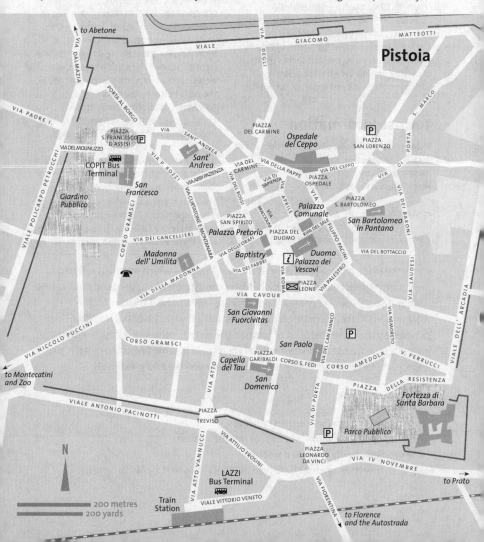

Getting Around

Pistoia lies along the A11, and at the foot of two important routes north over the Apennines, the SS64 towards Bologna and SS633 to Abetone. From the station, just south of the city walls at the end of Via XX Settembre, there are frequent **trains** along the main Florence–Lucca line. COPIT **buses** for Vinci and Empoli (37km/2hrs – a beautiful, twisting road over the Monte Albano), Cutigliano (37km/1hr 45min), Abetone (50km/2½hrs), the zoo, Montecatini (16km/30min), and other destinations in Pistoia's little province depart from Piazza San Francesco. LAZZI buses depart for Florence (35km/1hr), Prato, Lucca (43km/1½hrs), Montecatini, Viareggio and Pisa (65km/2hrs) from Viale Vittorio Veneto, near the train station. **Cars** are banned from most of the city centre (in theory, anyhow) but there's plenty of parking around the Fortezza di Santa Barbara in the southeast corner of the walls.

Tourist Information

Pistoia: Piazza del Duomo, in the bishop's palace, **t** 0573 21622, **f** 0573 34327, *www.pistoia.turismo-tuscany.it*.
Post office: Via Roma 5.

Festivals

Giostra dell'Orso (Joust of the Bear), *25 July*. The culmination of a month of concerts, fairs and exhibits. The Joust began in the 14th century, pitting 12 knights against a bear dressed in a checked cloak. The bear has been replaced by two wooden dummies, but the pageantry remains the same.

Where to Stay

Pistoia ✉ 51110

Pistoia gives the impression that it's more accustomed to lodging and feeding business travellers than pleasure-seekers. On balance, it might be better to make this city a day trip, or stay in nearby Montecatini Terme instead.

There are a couple of options if you travel a few kilometres outside town.

***Il Convento, Via S. Quirico 33, 5km east at Pontenuovo, **t** 0573 452651, **f** 0573 453578, *www.ilconventohotel.com* (*expensive*). A former convent, preserving its exterior if not all of its interior. The setting is quiet, with views over Pistoia; there's a pool and one of the city's better restaurants.

Villa Vannini, about 6km north of town, **t** 0573 42031, **f** 0573 26331, *www.volpe-uva.it* (*moderate*). Even more rural is this delightful, if slightly fading villa among the fir trees, where you can relax with wonderful hill walks on the doorstep; elegant, comfortable, good-value rooms, and a fantastic restaurant.

There are a few reasonable options if you do need somewhere in Pistoia itself.

Tenuta di Pieve a Celle, Via Pieve a Celle, **t** 0573 913087 (*expensive*). A stylish *agriturismo*

this is the place, after all, that gave us the word 'pistol' – which originally referred to the surgical knives made in the city, but later came to mean daggers, and finally guns.

Today it specializes in light rail trains (the Breda works built the cars for the Washington DC metro), mattresses, cymbals and baby trees. Although seldom sampled by the moveable feast of tourism, the historic centre of Pistoia is almost perfectly intact, and behind its medieval walls there is some fine art to be seen, part Pisan, part Florentine, reflecting its position between the two great rivals.

History

...Proud you are, envious, enemies of heaven,
Friends to your own harm and, to your own neighbour,
The simplest charity you find a labour.
  'Invective against the People of Pistoia', a sonnet by Michelangelo

right next to the zoo, this farmhouse has been converted into five guest rooms with great taste and style. The setting is lovely (the only sound that might disturb the peace is the odd animal roar) and there is a fine pool. Guests can order dinner.

***Piccolo Ritz**, Via Vannucci 67, **t** 0573 26775, **f** 0573 27798 (*moderate*). A newer place near the station – nice, but somewhat noisy.

***Leon Bianco**, Via Panciatichi 2, **t** 0573 26675, **f** 0573 26676, *www.hotelleon bianco.com* (*moderate*). A bit dated, but reasonably comfortable, with views over the campanile.

***Hotel Patria**, Via Crispi 8, **t** 0573 25187, **f** 0573 368168, *www.patriahotel.it* (*moderate*). Situated near San Domenico, this hotel has recently been revamped so is a bit more cheerful than the other hotels in town. You can even have bacon and eggs for breakfast.

****Firenze**, Via Curtatone e Montanara 42, **t/f** 0573 23141, *www.hotelfirenze.it* (*moderate*). The closest thing to inexpensive accommodation, near Piazza del Duomo, but it's a bit woebegone.

Eating Out

Pistoia has many simple *trattoria*s and pizzerias, and also several places offering delicious local cuisine.

La Bottegaia, Via del Lastrone 17, **t** 0573 365602 (*moderate*). Tucked away behind the baptistry, occupying a beautifully appointed vaulted room and a lovely terrace, this wine bar/restaurant serves snacks (selections of cheeses and meat, *bruschette* and salads) and full meals from a short, but ever-changing menu. The *menu degustazione* is excellent value and features such dishes as celery soup with pecorino cheese, leek flan, pesto lasagne, and duck breast with wild fennel. There are some 600 wines to choose from too. *Closed Sun lunch, Mon.*

San Jacopo, Via Crispi 15, **t** 0573 27786 (*cheap*). A pleasant *trattoria*, serving top quality traditional food (both fish and meat dishes) on crisp white cloths; Tuscan soups, spaghetti with clams, tripe, *baccalà*, rabbit with olives and, in season, porcini mushrooms. *Closed Tues lunch, Mon.*

Trattoria dell' Abbondanza, Via dell' Abbondanza 10, **t** 0573 368037 (*cheap*). There is an abundance of tempting dishes at this cheerful *trattoria* near the Duomo. The food is rustic and delicious: porcini soup, *gnocchi all'Abbondanza* (with tomatoes, pesto and pecorino cheese), octopus and potato stew, and roast pork spiked with rosemary and garlic. *Closed Thurs lunch, Wed.*

And outside the town itself:

Rafanelli, Via Sant'Agostino 47, Sant'Agostino, **t** 0573 532046 (*moderate*). Local dishes, including *maccheroni* with duck, game dishes and lamb, served in a pretty country villa setting, also does a great *bistecca*, grilled over a wood fire. *Closed Sun eve, Mon and Aug.*

Pistoia's fellow Tuscans have looked askance at her ever since Roman times, when the city was called *Pistoria* and saw the death struggle of the Catiline conspiracy, the famous attempted coup against the Roman Republic in 62 BC, which ended when the legions tracked down the escaped Catiline and his henchmen near Pistoia. Its position on the Via Cassia helped it prosper under the Lombards, who elevated it to a royal city. In 1158 Pistoia became a *comune*, and was seen as enough of a threat for Florence and Lucca to gang up against it twice. In the 13th century Pistoia's evil reputation gave it credit for having begun the bitter controversy between Black and White Guelphs that so obsessed Florence; Dante, himself a victim of that feud, made sure that in writing the *Divina Commedia* he never missed an opportunity to curse and condemn the fateful city. In 1306 Florence exacted revenge by capturing Pistoia, and as usual she adapted her politics to the nature of her conquest: Prato she made an ally, Pisa she held with fortresses, but Pistoia she controlled with factions. The only interlude came between 1315 and 1328, when Lucca's Castruccio Castracani held Pistoia as part of his empire; it was a short-lived respite, however: after his fall the Florentines soon returned. Pistoia, preoccupied with its own quarrels, carried on happily ever after, making a good living from its old speciality, ironworking. It proudly supplied the conspirators of Europe with fine daggers, and later, keeping up with technological advances, with pistols.

Piazza del Duomo

Pistol-Pistoia no longer packs any heat, but it packs in the heart of its 16th-century diamond-shaped walls one of the finest squares in Italy, a lesson in the subtle medieval aesthetic of urban design, an art lost with the endless theorizing and compulsive regularity of the Renaissance. The arrangement of the buildings around the L-shaped **Piazza del Duomo** seems at first to be haphazard. The design is meant to be experienced from street level; if you try walking into the piazza from a few of its surrounding streets, you'll see how from each approach the monuments reveal themselves in a different order and pattern, like the shaking of a kaleidoscope; the windows of the Palazzo del Comune echo those on the Palazzo del Podestà, and the striped decoration of the baptistry is recalled in the campanile and Duomo. The piazza provides the perfect setting for Pistoia's great annual party in July, the colourful *Giostra dell'Orso* (Joust of the Bear, *see* 'Festivals', p.70).

The **Duomo**, dedicated to San Zeno, dates from the 12th century; the Pisan arcades and stripes of its façade, combined over the geometric patterns of the Florentine Romanesque and polychrome terracotta lunette by Andrea della Robbia, strike an uneasy balance between the two architectural traditions. The outsize **Campanile**, originally a watchtower, tips the balance towards Pisa, with exotic, almost Moorish candy-striped arches at the top added in the 14th century when it was converted to church use – though you can still see the old Ghibelline crenellations on top. Inside the cathedral is a wealth of art – on the right a **Font** with quaint medieval heads, redesigned by Benedetto da Maiano, the **Tomb of Cino da Pistoia** (1337), a close friend of Dante, shown lecturing to a class of scholars, and a 13th-century painted crucifix by Coppo di Marcovaldo. The cathedral's most precious treasure is in the **chapel of St James** (*contact the sacristan to view; adm*): a fabulous altar made of nearly a ton of silver, comprising 628 figures, begun in 1287 and added to over the next two centuries; among the Pisan, Sienese and Florentine artists who contributed to this shining *tour de force* was Brunelleschi, who added the two half-figures on the left before he decided to devote all his talents to architecture. Some of the oldest art, fine medieval reliefs of the Last Supper and Gethsemane, have been relegated to the dim and ancient crypt. By the altar there's a fine painting by Caravaggio's pupil, Mattia Preti, and Maso di Bartolomeo's bronze candelabra. On the left the **chapel of the Sacrament** contains a bust of a Medici archbishop attributed to Verrocchio, who also added the statues of Faith and Hope to the weeping angels on the **tomb of Cardinal Forteguerri**, just left of the main entrance.

Next to the Duomo stands the partly striped and partly brick **Palazzo dei Vescovi**, mangled by remodellings over the centuries. The tourist information office is here, and the restorations undertaken to install it uncovered some Etruscan *cippi* (gravestones), and the foundations of Pistoia's original cathedral. The Etruscan finds, along with relics of Roman Pistoia, have been arranged in an '**Archaeological Itinerary**' in the Palazzo's basement, and the old cathedral is now included in the **Museo San Zeno** (*open Tues, Thurs–Fri plus 2nd and 4th Sun of the month, 10–1 and 3–5*), along with some paintings and a fine reliquary by Lorenzo Ghiberti.

Across from the Duomo stands Pistoia's octagonal zebra of a **baptistry** (*open Tues–Sat 10–12.30 and 3–6, Sun 9.30–12.30*), whose proper name is San Giovanni in Corte. Built over the site of a Lombard-era royal palace (the *corte*), it was finished in 1359, to a design by Andrea Pisano. It is one of the few outstanding Gothic buildings in Tuscany, embellished with fine sculptural details on the outside. The interior has a remarkable conical ceiling of brick and a beautifully decorated font dating from 1226, designed by Lanfranco da Como. In Piazza della Sala, behind the baptistry, is a medieval well, topped by a Florentine *Marzocco*.

Museo Civico

Open Tues–Sat 10–7, Sun 9.30–12.30; adm.

The Piazza del Duomo's other two palaces are civic in nature. The 14th-century **Palazzo Pretorio** on the west side has a decorated courtyard and an old stone bench where the judges once sat and where they often condemned malefactors to a unique punishment – they were ennobled. Not that Pistoia wanted to reward them; rather, to become noble meant losing one's rights as a republican citizen. The tower near here is known as the tomb of Catiline, who according to tradition was secretly buried here.

On the other side of the piazza stands the elegant **Palazzo Comunale**, begun in 1294, and prominently embellished with the usual Medici balls and the more unusual black marble head, believed to be that of a Moorish king captured by a captain from Pistoia on a freebooting expedition to Mallorca. Besides the town council and offices, the palazzo houses the **Museo Civico**, an excellent collection of great and odd paintings to suit even the most jaded of palates. Pistoiese patrons were uncommonly fond of 'Sacred Conversations' – group portraits of saints around the Madonna, and there are good ones by Mariotto de Nardo, Beccafumi, Lorenzo di Credi and Pistoia's own Gerino Gerini (1480–1529), a follower of Raphael. From the 15th-century 'Maestro delle Madonne di Marmo' there's a sweetly smiling marble relief of the Madonna and child; then two fancy St Sebastians with flowing curls, who precede the *Madonna della Pergola*, by local painter Bernardino di Antonio Detti (1498–1554), whose flaccid charwoman of a Madonna holds a child with a large housefly on his chubby arm before a crazy quilt of confusing iconography – children with dolls, the Judgement of Solomon, a child with a fruit-bowl, a floor littered with flowers, amulets, spoons and rags. On the mezzanine is the document centre of the great 20th-century Pistoiese architect Giovanni Michelucci; a comprehensive collection of models and drawings, as well as photos of his buildings and the media reaction to them. One example of his work is the large, angular Santa Maria Novella station in Florence, another is the restaurant in the Parco Collodi (*see p.237*).

Plod up another flight of stairs to see some screamingly lurid paintings from the 17th–19th centuries, with enough historical canvases of murder and mayhem to suggest the local taste for violence lingered on for some time, at least within the confines of art. There are two mythological paintings swathed in Caravaggiesque darkness by Cecco Bravo; a 17th-century *Young Woman with a Flower*, bathed in ghostly light; a sensuous, pouting St Sebastian, disdainfully plucking arrows from his chest; an absurd allegory of Medici rule in Pistoia, with *putti* scattering the family's lily symbol like flowers over the city; a Magdalene fondly patting a skull; as well as two rather nightmarish imaginary battle scenes by a 17th-century Neapolitan named Francesco Graziani.

Just off the Piazza del Duomo on Ripa del Sale, the 16th-century Palazzo Rospigliosi houses two small museums, the **Museo Rospigliosi**, with a collection of its original furniture and paintings *in situ*, the paintings mostly by a Pistoiese artist named Giacinto Gimignani, and the **Museo Diocesano** (*both open Tues, Thurs and Fri 10–1 and 4–7, Wed and Sat 10–1; joint adm*), displaying crosses and reliquaries from the early Middle Ages.

Ospedale del Ceppo and Sant'Andrea

In medieval Tuscany, it was customary to collect alms in a hollowed-out log (or *ceppo*) left in a public place, to be gathered and distributed to the poor at Christmas-time. *Ceppo* became synonymous with the word charity, as in Datini's famous foundation in Prato, and even earlier here in Pistoia, when the **Ospedale del Ceppo** (*a working hospital; call the tourist office to arrange a visit*) was founded in the 13th century. Still functioning at the same address (walk down Via Filippo Pacini from the Palazzo Comunale), the building was given a fine arcaded porch in the 1500s, in the style of the famous Spedale degli Innocenti in Florence. And, as in Florence, the della Robbias were called upon to provide the decoration, in this case the usually insipid Giovanni, who with the help of his workshop and other artists, created not only the typical della Robbian *tondi*, but a unique terracotta frieze that spans the entire loggia in resplendent Renaissance Technicolor, with scenes of the acts of mercy and theological virtues. Inside there's a small **Museo dei Ferri Chirurgici** dedicated to Pistoia's old iron industry, especially surgical knives.

A short walk west of the hospital on Via Sant'Andrea is the 12th-century church of **Sant'Andrea** (*open daily 8–12.30 and 3.30–6*), with a Pisan façade and over the door, a charming bas-relief of the Journey of the Magi, dated 1166, and a pair of ghastly, leering lions. The real jewel is inside: Giovanni Pisano's hexagonal **pulpit** (1297), exquisitely carved in stirring high relief with scenes of the Nativity, Massacre of the Innocents, Adoration of the Magi, Crucifixion and Last Judgement, with sibyls in the corners and pedestals in the forms of the four Evangelists – one of the masterpieces of Italian Gothic. Sant'Andrea contains three other crucifixions: Giovanni Pisano's wooden crucifix in the right aisle, a medieval version over the main altar, portraying Christ crowned and dressed in a kingly robe, and in the right nave, a large, rather mysterious painting of the saint crucified on a tree.

San Francesco and the Madonna dell'Umilità

Pretty striped churches circle the centre of Pistoia like zebras on a merry-go-round. The two plain ponies in the lot lie to the west. The large **San Francesco al Prato** in Piazza San Francesco d'Assisi, plain and Gothic like most Franciscan churches, has some notable 14th-century frescoes, especially in the chapel to the left of the altar, with Sienese scenes portraying the Triumph of St Augustine. On the side of the church there's an ancient olive tree and a memorial to assassinated prime minister Aldo Moro, a stark contrast with the heroic Fascist-era war monument in the piazza itself. South along Corso Gramsci is Pistoia's main theatre, the 1694 **Teatro Manzoni**; further south, on Via della Madonna, towers Pistoia's great experiment in High Renaissance geometry, the octagonal, unstriped **Basilica della Madonna dell'Umilità** begun in 1518 by local architect and pupil of Bramante, Ventura Vitoni, who graced it with an imposing barrel-vaulted vestibule. In the 1560s Giorgio Vasari was called upon to crown Vitoni's fine start; not content to limit his mischief to Florence, he added a dome so heavy that the basilica has been threatening to collapse ever since. More work to shore it up is currently underway.

San Giovanni Fuoricivitas and San Domenico

To the south of the Piazza del Duomo (Via Roma to Via Cavour) lies the tiny **Piazza San Leone**, the ancient Lombard centre of Pistoia; its stubby tower once belonged to the nastiest Pistoian of them all, a 13th-century noble thug and church robber named Vanni Fucci whom Dante found in one of the lower circles of Hell, entwined in a serpent, cursing and making obscene gestures up at God. Around the corner of Via Cavour, the 12th-century **San Giovanni Fuorcivitas** claims the honour of being the most striped church in all Christendom, its green and white flank an abstract pattern of lozenges and blind arches that out-Pisas anything in Pisa. The gloomy interior holds a dramatic pulpit (1270) by Fra Gugliemo da Pisa, a pupil of Nicola Pisano, a holy water stoup supported by caryatids by Giovanni Pisano and a white, glazed terracotta group of the Visitation by Luca or Andrea della Robbia.

Piazza Garibaldi, also to the south, is adorned with a good equestrian statue of Garibaldi, some florid street lamps, and **San Domenico**, begun in the late 13th century. In its spacious, airy interior, there's a splendid Baroque organ from 1617 and two Renaissance tombs: that of Filippo Lazzari, by the Rossellino brothers, portraying the deceased lecturing to his pupils (one of whom can't help yawning), and the other of Lorenzo da Ripafratta, with a fine effigy. In 1497, Benozzo Gozzoli died of the plague in Pistoia and is buried somewhere in the cloister of San Domenico; you can see a fresco he began of the Journey of the Magi nearby. Although the monastery is still in use, you can ring to see the frescoes in the chapter house, among them good Sienese works and a *Crucifixion* with its sinopia, dating back to the mid-13th century. Even more interesting are the frescoes across the street in the little **Cappella del Tau** (*open Mon–Sat 9–2*), so named after the blue T its priests wore on their vestments. The vividly coloured scenes of Adam and Eve and assorted saints are attributed in part to Masolino. The convent of the chapel has become the **Marino Marini centre** (*open Tues–Sat 9–1 and 3–7, Sun 9–12.30; adm*). The collection traces the career of this

Pistoiese artist, who died in 1980, in both paint and sculpture; it includes the bronze *Young Girl* which recalls the antique tradition not only in her facial features but also her truncated arms. Next to it, at No.72, note the coat of arms over the pretty window of two dancing bears, recalling the Giostra dell'Orso. There's another good Gothic façade on **San Paolo**, a block to the east, with broader stripes and a statue of St James on the very top, attributed to Orcagna.

There are more old churches in central Pistoia, but only one other worth going out of your way to visit: **San Bartolomeo in Pantano** (St Bart in the Bog), on the east side of town, built on marshy land in the 8th century and sinking gently into the ground ever since. It has an attractive, partially completed façade, and contains a carved marble lectern of 1250 by Guido da Como.

The Zoo, the Medici and some Iron

The newest stripes in Pistoia may well be on the zebras in the **Pistoia Zoo** (*open summer 9–7, winter 9–5; adm exp*), 4km northwest of the city in Via Pieve a Celle. Though the Medici always kept big menageries, modern Italians don't usually care for zoos; this is one of the best in the country, even though it's only just over 30 years old. Polar bears, kangaroos, giant turtles, reptiles, and other zoo favourites are in attendance.

Thirteen kilometres to the southeast, off the SS66, is yet another Medici villa, the **Villa della Magia in Quarrata** (*closed for restoration; call t 0573 7710 for info*), begun in 1318. Its grand hall has 18th-century frescoes, and in 1536 Charles V and Alessandro de' Medici met there. In Pistoia itself you can visit one of the city's wrought-iron 'laboratories', **Bartoletti** (*open Mon–Sat; t 0573 452784*), in Via Sestini 110.

The Mountains of Pistoia

North of Pistoia rises a fairly unspoiled stretch of the central Apennines, luxuriantly forested and endowed with some lovely mountain escape routes, deep green in the summer and ski white in the winter. Main routes include the beautiful Bologna road (SS64) known as the 'Porrettana', which follows the Bologna–Pistoia railway through the sparsely settled mountains, and the equally beautiful, parallel SS632, less encumbered with traffic. The main mountain resorts up to Abetone are along the SS66 and SS12, as easily reached from Lucca as from Pistoia.

Due north of Pistoia, 10km along a byroad towards Piteccio, is the ancient hamlet of **Castagno**, now converted into a unique open-air art gallery. Its lanes are embellished with 20th-century frescoes on the 12 months; modern statues pose in the nooks and crannies; and Castagno's ancient church and oratory dedicated to St Francis, both with interesting frescoes, have recently been restored. A 4km backtrack takes you to the main SS66; at Pontepetri (20km) the SS632 veers north to the formerly popular little mountain resort of **Pracchia**.

Most visitors continue along the SS66 for the newer summer–winter resorts by way of the lovely state forest of Teso, at the fine old villages of **Maresca** and **Gavinana**. The latter is notorious in Florentine history for the defeat of its army by the imperial

Tourist Information

San Marcello Pistoiese: Via Marconi 28,
t 0573 630145, f 0573 622120.
Cutigliano: Via Roma 25, t 0573 68029.
Abetone: Piazza Piramidi, t 0573 60231.

Where to Stay and Eat

There's nothing posh about this pretty but neglected corner of Tuscany – nearly all hotels are good bargains. In the mountains, many open only during the ski season and in July and Aug. There are some economical holiday villas near the towns and alpine refuges in the mountains nearby; the tourist office has a complete list.

San Marcello Pistoiese ✉ 50128

★★★Il Cacciatore, Via Marconi 87, t 0573 630533, f 0573 630134 (*moderate*). Pleasant, green and quiet. *Open all year.*

La Vecchia Cantina, Via Risorgimento 4, t 0573 64158 (*moderate*). Menus are seasonal and dishes are rooted in local traditions; ravioli with goat's cheese, home made pasta with courgette flowers and prosciutto, mushrooms or artichokes, boar stewed with wine and chestnuts and pork fillet with apple sauce. Good cheese and wine too. *Closed Tues in winter.*

Cutigliano ✉ 50124

★★★Hotel Miramonte, Piazza Catalina 12, t 0573 68012, f 0573 68013 (*inexpensive*). Quiet with a nice garden and restaurant.

L'Osteria, Via Roma 6, t 0573 68272 (*cheap*). Top-class mountain food in the centre of town. Hearty soups, local lamb and pecorino cheeses. *Closed Tues lunch, Mon.*

Abetone ✉ 51021

This ski resort is somewhat fancier.

★★★★Il Granduca, Via Brennero 289, t 0573 60067, f 0573 60585 (*moderate*). More elegant than most. *Open July–Aug and Dec–April.*

★★★Regina, Via Uccelleria 5, t 0573 60007, (*expensive–moderate*). On a quieter street. *Open July–mid-Sept and Dec–April.*

Ostello Renzo Bizzari, Via Brennero at Cosuma, t 0573 60117 (*cheap*). The youth hostel, with room for 92. *Open Dec–Mar and July–Aug, longer on demand.*

Da Pierone, Via Brennero 556, t 0573 60068 (*moderate*). Rustic family-run restaurant serving local dishes, veal escalope with truffles, excellent choice of wine. *Closed Thurs.*

La Capannina, Via Brennero 520, t 0573 60562 (*moderate*). Good choice: rustic décor, local dishes and a wide selection of wines. *Closed Mon and Tues outside high season.*

forces of Charles V, a battle that cost the lives of both commanders. The Florentine leader, Francesco Ferrucci, was knifed in the back, and has his own little museum in the main piazza. The SS66 continues to **San Marcello Pistoiese**, 29km from Pistoia, the 'capital' of the mountains, in a lovely setting, where since 1854 the inhabitants have launched a hot-air balloon each year on 8 September as a farewell to summer. You can walk over the 720ft **suspension bridge of Mammiano** all year round, however. **Cutigliano**, a growing winter resort 7km north, has 27km of ski trails and a cable car up to its highest peak, Doganaccia (1,175m/3,854ft). In the village itself, the **Palazzo Pretorio** fairly bristles with the coats of arms of its former governors.

Near the northern border of Tuscany, through a lush and ancient forest, lies **Abetone** (1,400m/4,592ft), one of the most famous resorts in the central Apennines. Named after a huge fir tree, it grew up in the late 18th century, when Grand Duke Pietro Leopoldo built the road to the Duchy of Modena, designing it not to pass through the detested Papal States (the modern province of Bologna). Two milestones at Abetone mark the old boundary. The closest ski resort to Florence, it is highly developed, with 35km of trails, a new cable car and 23 chairlifts; in summer its cool climate, pools and other facilities make it popular, especially at weekends. In other seasons, rain is not exactly unknown.

The Valdinievole

Montecatini Terme

West of Pistoia lies the Valdinievole, the 'Valley of Mists', a land obsessed with water, though mostly of the subterranean, curative variety, available in Italy's most glamorous thermal spa, **Montecatini** (pop. 21,500). Leonardo da Vinci's first known drawing was of a view towards Montecatini from Lamporecchio, near his home town of Vinci (*see* pp.212–13), and it is believed that his lifetime fascination with canals, locks, currents and dams and the misty, watery backgrounds of his most famous paintings come from a childhood spent in the Valdinievole. He even designed a fountain for the baths of Montecatini in one of his notebooks, which after 380 years is now being built of Carrara marble as his monument.

Even in these days of holistic medicine, preventive medicine, herbal cures and pharmaceutical paranoia, the Montecatini tourist board despair that Anglo-Saxons from both sides of the Atlantic refuse to believe that soaking in or drinking mere water can do anything as beneficial for them as imbibing a pitcher of Chianti. Unlike

Getting Around

Montecatini is easily reached by **train** from Florence (51km/1½hrs), Pistoia (16km/25mins) and Lucca (27km/45mins). The station, **t** 0572 78551, is on Via Toti, as is the LAZZI **bus** terminal, **t** 0572 911781, with hourly connections (at least until evening) to Florence, Lucca, Pisa, Viareggio and Montecatini Alto; also to Collodi via Pescia (6 daily).

Tourist Information

Montecatini: Viale G Verdi 66, **t/f** 0572 772244.

Where to Stay

Montecatini Terme ✉ 51016

Even if you don't care to take the waters, you'll have no difficulty finding a room. Italy's choicest spa has no fewer than six hotels that claim the title of 'Grand' and a half-dozen others that only decline to for discretion's sake. **Full board**, not counting breakfast, is the rule in most places; outside high season they might not require it, but ring ahead to make sure. The **APIA hotel association** on Via delle Saline 88, **t/f** 0572 72603, helps with bookings.

★★★★★**Grand Hotel Bellavista**, Viale Fedeli 2, **t** 0572 78122, **f** 0572 73352, *www.pancioli hotels.it* (*luxury*). Among the grandest, offering golf, tennis, indoor pool, luxurious rooms, sauna, health club, and an infinite number of chances for self-indulgence. *Open April–Nov.*

★★★★★**Grand Hotel & La Pace**, Corso Roma 12, **t** 0572 75801, **f** 0572 78451, *www.grandhotel lapace.it* (*luxury*). Renowned throughout the rest of Europe for its genuine *belle époque* charm, this hotel has similarly impressive luxuries as the Bellavista; and the restaurant is unquestionably elegant, if expensive. *Open April–Oct.*

★★★★**Grand Hotel Plaza e Locanda Maggiore**, Piazza del Popolo 7, **t** 0572 75831, **f** 0572 767985, *www.hotelplaza.it* (*expensive*). This was apparently Verdi's favourite; it has a pool and air-conditioned rooms. *Open all year.*

★★★**Belvedere**, Viale Fedeli 10, **t** 0572 70251, **f** 0572 70252, *www.gallinganihotels.it* (*expensive*). One of the more charming choices, featuring an indoor pool, tennis courts and friendly service, next to the Parco delle Terme. *Open April–Oct.*

Villa Pasquini, in Massa e Cozile, 8km from Montecatini, **t** 0572 72205, **f** 0572 910888, *www.villapasquini.it* (*expensive*). Charming,

so many continental enthusiasts, we defy the wisdom of the ancients – especially the Romans, who spent the plunder accumulated from conquering the world on ever more fabulous baths. But taking the waters, no matter how hot, radioactive, or chock-full of minerals, is only half the cure; the other is simply relaxation; the chance to stroll through gardens, listen to a little music, linger in a café, to indulge in a bit of the old *dolce far niente*. In Montecatini you can do just that without touching a blessed, unfermented drop, surrounded by *belle époque* nostalgia from the days when the spa seethed with dukes, politicians, literati and actresses; you may recognize it from the film *Dark Eyes* (*Oci Ciornie*), starring Marcello Mastroianni.

Parco delle Terme

Baths open May–Oct, exc the Excelsior, which stays open all year. Tickets for a day or subscriptions are available from the central office in Viale Verdi 41, t 0572 778428, f 0572 778444, www.termemontecatini. Adm – an all-day visit to Tettuccio is €12.50 in high season.

A short stroll from the station, past Montecatini's trendy boutiques, cafés, cinemas and some of its 200 hotels up to Viale Verdi, will take you to the town's mineral

friendly and old-fashioned, set in lush gardens with rooms verging on the grand (some of them have frescoes), and a good restaurant.

★★★Corallo, Viale Cavallotti 116, **t** 0572 78288, **f** 0572 79512, *www.golfhotelcorallo.it* (*moderate*). Small but refined, with a pool and garden, on a quiet side street near the park. *Open all year.*

Il Salotto di Gea, Via Talenti 2, **t** 0572 904318 (*moderate*). A small hotel (only 8 rooms) in the heart of the old town, a delightful and good-value alternative to some of the rather overblown hotels in Montecatini. Rooms are decorated with unfussy good taste. Breakfast is served on the piazza in summer. The restaurant offers tempting fish and meat dishes: warm octopus salad, spaghetti with mullet roe, aubergine ravioli with pesto, and fillet of beef with a Chianti sauce.

Eating Out

Montecatini Terme ✉ 51016

Most guests dine in their hotels, but there are some places that are well worth making the effort to leave the hotel and get there for.

Enoteca Giovanni, Via Garibaldi 25, **t** 0572 71695 (*very expensive*). Break loose at least once for the imaginative fare at this unique and much-honoured place, where game dishes – hare, venison, wild duck – and fish turn into impeccably *haute cuisine* in the hands of a master chef. *Closed Mon.*

Ristorante il Cucco, Via Salsero 3, **t** 0572 72765 (*expensive*). Elaborate Tuscan cooking, both meat and seafood, at more reasonable prices: try the spaghetti with fresh anchovies and breadcrumbs. *Closed Wed lunch, Tues.*

Cucina da Giovanni, Via Garibaldi (*moderate*). Next door to the *Enoteca da Giovanni* (*see above*), offering simple fare at more modest prices (try the wonderful *antipasti* and fabulous *maccheronicini* with duck sauce).

La Torre, Piazza Giusti, **t** 0572 70650 (*moderate–cheap*). A wine bar/restaurant, up in the old town. If you want a full meal (rather than a drink and a snack), there are soups, good pastas and simple meat dishes.

When you get tired of immersing yourself in the health-giving waters, why not dip into the vintages at a wine bar instead? Either of the following should do the trick:

Enoteca, Via Forini 13.

Antinori 'Degustazione Vini', Viale Verdi 35.

water Elysium, the immaculately groomed **Parco delle Terme**, where the high temples of the cult dot the shaded lawn. The Lorraine grand dukes, spa-soaks like their Habsburg cousins, were behind the initial development of Montecatini's springs, and many of the baths, or *terme*, are neoclassical pavilions – monumental, classical and floral architecture that lent itself nicely to the later Liberty-style embellishments of the 1920s. You can take in some of these Art Nouveau fancies in Montecatini's Municipio, on Viale Verdi opposite the park, or in the most sumptuous and ancient of its nine major bathing establishments, **Tettuccio**. In the 1370s a group of Florentines attempted to extract mineral salts from the spring and built a little roof (*tettuccio*) over it; and although they failed it was soon discovered that the water had a good effect on rotten livers – one of the first to come here was Francesco Datini, the Merchant of Prato, in 1401. By the 18th century, Tettuccio was in a state of ruin, and Grand Duke Leopold I had it splendidly rebuilt. His façade remains, while the interior was redone by Montecatini's greatest architect, Ugo Giovanozzi, in the 1920s, and embellished with paintings by Italy's Art Nouveau master, Galileo Chini, and ceramic pictures by Cascella in the drinking gallery; there's an elegant café, fountains, a reflecting pool and rotunda, writing hall, music rooms, a little city within a city – all adorned with scenes from an aquatic Golden Age of languid nymphs – surely the perfect place to sip your morning glass of liver-flushing water.

Other establishments, each with their special virtues, are nearby – the Palladian-style arcade of the **Regina** spring; the **Terme Leopoldine**, another grand ducal establishment, with mud baths housed in a temple-like building dedicated to Aesculapius, the god of health; the half-neo-Renaissance, half-modern **New Excelsior baths**; the pretty Tuscan rustic **Tamerici**, in its lush garden; the **Torretta**, with its phony medieval tower and afternoon concerts in the loggia.

During Digestion

While the water works its way through your system, you can work your way through Montecatini's diversions. The **Art Academy** consists solely of donations from Montecatini's admirers – the piano Verdi used during his annual stays in the Locanda Maggiore, where he composed *Otello*, and art by Salvador Dali, Galileo Chini, Fattori and many others. Just behind the Parco delle Terme is **Le Panteraie**, a wooded park with a swimming pool, where deer roam freely.

You can play a round at the **Montecatini Golf Course** (*t 0572 62218*), among olive groves and cypresses, or a game of tennis at the centrally-situated courts of La Toretta, (*t 0572 78161*). Alternatively you can try to win back your hotel bill at the trotting races at the **Ippodromo**. The **Kursaal**, with cinema, nightclub and games, is a popular meeting place. One of the prettiest excursions is to take the funicular up to **Montecatini Alto**, the original old hill town, with breathtaking views over the Valley of Mists and a charming little piazza with a small theatre; nearby you can visit the stalactites in the **Grotta Maona** (*open April–Oct*).

Around Montecatini Terme

Monsummano and Serravalle

Narrow lanes crisscross the Valdinievole landscape, offering a wealth of tempting excursions further afield. Approximately 5km east of Montecatini is its sister spa, **Monsummano Terme**, which as its speciality offers vapour baths in natural grottoes. The first of these was discovered by accident in 1849, when the Giusti family moved a boulder and found the entrance to a stalactite cave. The **Grotta Giusti**, which is 325ft deep, has three small lakes fed by hot springs. These caves, including the steamy **Grotta Parlanti** (*open May–Oct; info t 0572 953029*), are only open to visitors seeking serious thermal treatment.

Monsummano meanwhile hasn't rested on its vapours, but has transformed itself into one of Italy's biggest shoe-making towns; like Montecatini it has an old antecedent atop a hill, **Monsummano Alto**, today all but abandoned, but with a pretty Romanesque church, a romantically ruined castle and splendid views. Another panoramic view may be had from **Montevettolini**, 4km from Monsummano, site of a villa built by Ferdinando I in 1597.

Where to Stay and Eat

Monsummano Terme ✉ 51015
★★★★**Grotta Giusti**, Via Grotta Giusti 171, t 0572 51165, f 0572 51269, *www.grotta giustispa.com* (*luxury*). Near the vaporous grottoes, the villa of the family of the poet Giuseppe Giusti. Recently upgraded and now a very comfortable hotel filled with antiques, rich fabrics, etc. Half or full board obligatory in high season (Aug–Sept, Christmas, Easter). *Open Mar–Nov*.

Montevettolini ✉ 51015
Villa Lucia, Via dei Bronzoli 144, t 0572 617790, *www.bboftuscany.com* (*very expensive*). An English-style B&B (the *padrona* is American/Italian), in a delightful setting on a hillside, with garden and pool.
San Michele, Piazza Bargellini 80, Montevettolini, t 0572 617 547 (*cheap*). A café-bar-restaurant with a tempting array of *antipasti* (smoked salmon, caviar, *carpaccio* with truffles), followed by spaghetti with lobster, perhaps, and prawns. *Closed Mon*.

Pescia ✉ 51017
★★★**Villa delle Rose**, Via del Castellare 21, t 0572 4670, f 0572 444 003, *www.rthotels.com* (*moderate*). Just outside Pescia, with a pleasant garden and pool and comfortable, modern rooms.
Cecco, Via Forti 96/98, t 0572 477955 (*moderate*). Fine dining on seasonal dishes starring Pescia's famous asparagus, or wild mushrooms, truffles or zucchini flowers; for dessert, there's *torta di Cecco*, prepared according to an ancient recipe. *Closed Mon*.
Monte a Pescia, Via del Monte Ovest 1, Monte a Pescia, t 0572 476887 (*moderate*). A rustic restaurant in a tiny, hilltop hamlet just outside Pescia, with a terrace overlooking the Valdinievole. Home-made pasta is served with asparagus, porcini or game sauce and meat is grilled over an open fire.

Collodi ✉ 51014
All'Osteria del Gambero Rosso, Parco Collodi, t 0572 429 364 (*moderate–cheap*). Set in the grand Parco Collodi, this restaurant has made a name for its food as much as for its attractive surroundings. The building was designed by Giovanni Michelucci, arguably one of Italy's greatest 20th-century architects. Tuck into cannelloni, *tagliolini* with porcini mushrooms and prosciutto, and excellent crêpes stuffed with seafood or spinach. *Closed Mon eve and Tues*.

Continuing east, the old fortress at **Serravalle Pistoiese**, 'locks the valley' between the Apennines and Monte Albano. Its old Lombard tower and 14th-century additions saw considerable action in Tuscany's days of inter-urban hooliganism.

Pescia

To the west of Montecatini, there's another attractive old hill town, **Buggiano Castello**, and for those who imagine that frescoes went out of fashion years ago, there's San Michele in nearby **Ponte Buggianese**, freshly frescoed in stark colours by Pietro Annigoni. The colours are even more dazzling in **Pescia** (pop. 20,000), Italy's capital of flowers, a title snatched from San Remo on the Riviera. Some three million cut flowers are sent off every summer's day from Pescia's giant market; besides the gladioli, it is celebrated by gourmets for its tender asparagus and *fagioli*.

Pescia has several interesting monuments, beginning with a 14th-century church of **San Francesco**, containing Bonaventura Berlinghieri's 1235 portrait of St Francis with scenes from his life, considered to be one of the most authentic likenesses of the saint; also take a look at the *Crucifixion* by Puccio Capanna in the sacristy. The **Duomo** was rebuilt in the 1600s, but has a fine Romanesque campanile sporting a little cupola, and a late terracotta triptych by Luca della Robbia. On the long, narrow Piazza Mazzini stands the imposing **Palazzo del Vicario**; in nearby **Sant'Antonio**, from the 1360s, look up the 'Ugly Saints', a 13th-century wooden *Deposition from the Cross*.

The green, hilly region of prosperous villages north of Pescia in the upper Valdinievole is known as 'Little Switzerland'. In its cheerful core, some 12km from Pescia, stands one of Italy's most bizarre churches, the 12th-century **Pieve di Castelvecchio**, decorated with grinning and grimacing stone masks.

Collodi and Pinocchio

Just west of Pescia is **Collodi**. As a child, Florentine writer Carlo Lorenzo (1826–90) often visited his uncle who worked in the castle, and took the name Collodi as his own when he published his *Adventures of Pinocchio*. In his honour the town has built the **Parco di Pinocchio** (*open 8.30–sunset; adm*), with a bronze statue of the character by Emilio Greco and a piazza of mosaics with scenes from the book by Venturino Venturi, as well as other figures, all very much in the angular style of the late 1950s and early 60s; there's a lawn maze, a museum dedicated to the book, a playground and other amusements for the kids. Adults, meanwhile, can try to work their way through a much older labyrinth in the magnificent, recently restored hillside gardens of the **Castello Garzoni** (*gardens open mid-Nov–mid-Mar, Sun only, 9–one hour before sunset; adm*), designed in the 17th century by Ottaviano Diodati of Lucca and considered one of the finest late Italian gardens, ornate with a labyrinth, fountains and statuary. The castle 'of a hundred windows' has a few grand rooms, and the kitchen where young Carlo sat and dreamed up Pinocchio.

Lucca, the Garfagnana and Lunigiana

10

Lucca, the Garfagnana and Lunigiana

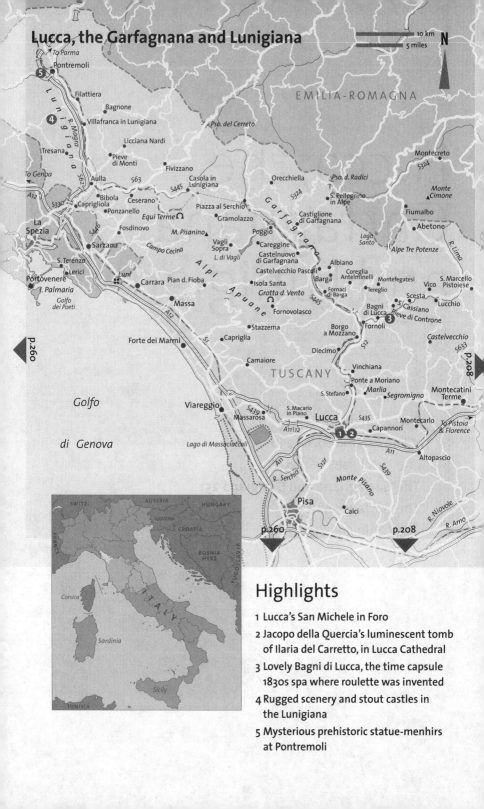

Highlights

1 Lucca's San Michele in Foro

2 Jacopo della Quercia's luminescent tomb of Ilaria del Carretto, in Lucca Cathedral

3 Lovely Bagni di Lucca, the time capsule 1830s spa where roulette was invented

4 Rugged scenery and stout castles in the Lunigiana

5 Mysterious prehistoric statue-menhirs at Pontremoli

Lucca

Nowhere in Lucca
will you see the face of a Philistine.

Heine, *Travels in Lucca*

Of all Tuscany's great cities, Lucca (pop. 92,500) is the most cosy, sane and domestic, a tidy gem of a town encased within its famous walls. Yet even these hardly seem formidable, more like garden walls than something that would keep the Florentines at bay. The old ramparts and surrounding areas, once the outworks of the fortifications, are now full of lawns and trees; on the walls, where the city's soldiers once patrolled, citizens ride their bicycles, walk their dogs, and stop to admire the view.

Like paradise, Lucca is entered by way of St Peter's Gate. Once inside you'll find tidy, well-preserved Romanesque churches and medieval towers that destroyed Ruskin's romantic notion that a medieval building had to be half-ruined to be beautiful, a revelation that initiated his study of architecture. Nor do Lucca's numerous Liberty-style shop signs show any sign of rust; even the mandatory peeling ochre paint and green shutters of the houses seem part of some great municipal housekeeping plan. Bicycles have largely replaced cars within the walls. At first glance it seems too bijou, but after its long and brave history it has earned the right to a little quiet. The hordes of tourists leave Lucca alone for the most part, though a small number of discreet visitors, many of them German and Swedish, come back every year. They don't spread the word, apparently trying to keep one of Italy's most beautiful cities to themselves.

History

Lucca's rigid grid of streets betrays its Roman origins; it was founded as a colony in 180 BC as *Luca*, and it was here in 56 BC that Caesar, Pompey and Crassus met to form the ill-fated First Triumvirate. It was converted to Christianity early on by St Peter's disciple Paulinus, who became first bishop of Lucca. The city did especially well in the Dark Ages; in late Roman times it was the administrative capital of Tuscany, and under the Goths managed to repulse the murderous Lombards; its extensive archives were begun in the 8th century, and many of its churches were founded shortly after. By the 11th and 12th centuries Lucca emerged as one of the leading trading towns of Tuscany, specializing in the production of silk, sold by colonies of merchants in the East and West, who earned enough to make sizeable loans to Mediterranean potentates. A Lucchese school of painting developed, and beautiful Romanesque churches were erected, influenced by nearby Pisa. Ghibellines and Guelphs, and then Black and White Guelphs made nuisances of themselves as they did everywhere else, and Lucca often found itself pressed to maintain its independence from Pisa and Florence.

In 1314, at the height of the city's wealth and power, the Pisans and Ghibellines finally managed to seize it. But Lucca had a trump card: a remarkable adventurer named Castruccio Castracani, an ambitious noble who lived for years in exile – part of it in England. When he heard the bad news he at once set forth to rescue his home town. Within a year he had chased the Pisans out and seized power for himself,

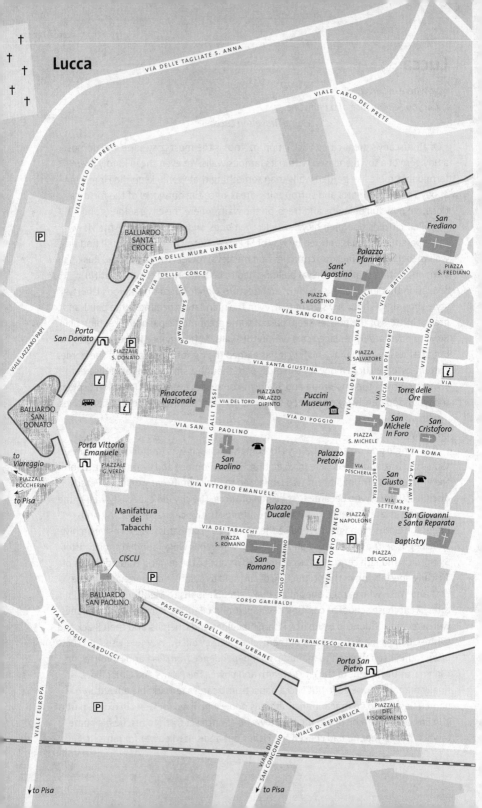

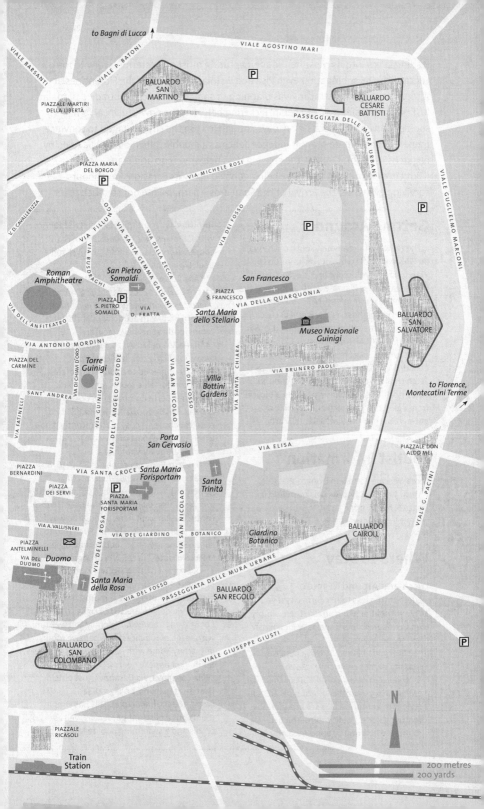

leading Lucca into its most heroic age, capturing most of western Tuscany to form a Luccan empire, subjugating even Pisa and Pistoia. After routing the Florentines at Altopascio in 1325, Castracani was planning to snatch Florence too, but died of malaria just before the siege was to begin. Bickering between the powerful local families soon put an end to Lucca's glory days, though in 1369 the city managed to convince Emperor Charles IV to grant it independence as a republic, albeit a republic ruled by oligarchs like Paolo Guinigi, the sole big boss between 1400 and 1430.

But Lucca continued to escape being gobbled up by its voracious neighbours, surviving even after the arrival of the Spaniards – perhaps due not so much to its

Getting Around

The **railway** station is just south of the walls on Piazza Ricasoli, with lots of trains on the Viareggio–Pisa–Florence line, t 0583 892021. **Buses** leave from Piazzale Verdi, just inside the walls on the western end: LAZZI buses to Florence, Pistoia, Pisa, Prato, Bagni di Lucca, Abetone, Montecatini and Viareggio (t 0583 584876); and CLAP (that's right, CLAP) buses to towns within Lucca province, including Collodi, Marlia, and Segromigno, as well as the Serchio valley (t 0583 587897). Get around Lucca itself like a Lucchese by hiring a **bicycle** from Poli (t 0583 493787) or Bizzarri (t 0583 496031), both in the Piazza Santa Maria.

Tourist Information

Lucca: Vecchia Porta San Donato, Piazzale Verdi, t 0583 583150, www.carismalucca.it.
Piazza S. Maria: t 0583 919931, www.luccaturismo.it.

Where to Stay

Lucca and Around ✉ 55100

Lucca can be less than charm city if you arrive without booking ahead; there simply aren't enough rooms (especially inexpensive ones) to meet demand.

★★★★★**Locanda l'Elisa**, Via Nova per Pisa, Massa Pisana, t 0583 379 737, www.locandalelisa.com (luxury). Part of the Relais e Chateaux group, this bright blue, French-style 18th-century villa is set in a glorious mature garden. Public rooms and bedrooms are luxuriously appointed and furnished with antiques and elegant fabrics, with canopies over the beds. There is a conservatory restaurant (expensive) and a pool. Closed Jan.

★★★★**Alla Corte degli Angeli**, Via degli Angeli 23, t 0583 469204, f 0583 991989, www.allacortedegliangeli.com (very expensive). Modern B&B with attractive, comfortable rooms; bathrooms have jacuzzis.

★★★★**Ilaria**, Via del Fosso 20, t 0583 476158, www.hotelilaria.com (very expensive). Recently upgraded to a four-star hotel, smart comfortable rooms and car park.

★★★**La Luna**, Corte Compagni 12, t 0583 493634, f 0583 490021, www.hotellaluna.com (expensive). A cosy place, recently renovated, in a quiet part of the centre, with a private garage for your car.

★★★**Universo**, Piazza Puccini, t 0583 493678, f 0583 954854, www.hoteluniverso.it (expensive). Within the walls, a slightly frayed, green-shuttered and delightful hotel, in the centre. Ruskin slept here, paving the way for nearly everyone else who followed him to Lucca. Some rooms are better than others.

★★★**Piccolo Hotel Puccini**, Via di Poggio 9, t 0583 55421, f 0583 53487, www.hotelpuccini.com (moderate). A central, small, comfortable hotel with 14 rooms.

★★**Diana** Via del Molinetto 11, t 0583 592202, f 0583 47795 (moderate). Friendly and well run, with some of the nicest inexpensive rooms in Tuscany, some with bath. Now has a more up-market annexe nearby.

★★**Villa Casanova**, Via Casanova, just outside the city at Balbano, t 0583 548429, f 0583 368955 (moderate). This has simple rooms but a pleasant garden, as well as tennis and a swimming pool to lounge by.

great walls as to its relative insignificance. Amazingly enough, after the Treaty of Câteau-Cambrésis, Lucca stood together with Venice as the only truly independent states in Italy. And, like Venice, the city was an island of relative tolerance and enlightenment during the Counter-Reformation, its walls proving stout enough to deflect the Inquisition. In 1805 Lucca's independence ended when Napoleon gave the republic to his sister Elisa Baciocchi, who ruled as its princess; it was given later to Marie Louise, Napoleon's widow, who governed well enough to become Lucca's favourite ruler and earn a statue in the main Piazza Napoleone. Her son sold it to Leopold II of Tuscany in 1847, just in time for it to join the Kingdom of Italy.

Affittacamere S. Frediano, Via degli Angeli 19, **t** 0583 469630 (*moderate*). Six spotless, nicely furnished rooms (not all with private bath) near the Anfiteatro.

Da Elisa alle Sette Arti, Via Elisa 25, **t** 0583 494539, **f** 0583 471609, *www.daelisa.com* (*inexpensive*). This good value guest house offers nine pretty and airy rooms in the centre of town with use of kitchen. Breakfast is taken at a neighbouring bar.

Locanda Buatino, Borgo Giannotti 508, **t** 0583 343207, **f** 0583 343298 (*inexpensive*). Just outside the city walls to the north, with five simple but welcoming rooms above a restaurant of the same name (*see* below).

Eating Out

Within the walls:

Il Giglio, Piazza del Giglio, **t** 0583 494058 (*expensive*). Lucca's best seafood place, in Hotel Universo – river trout is a speciality. *Closed Tues eve and Wed.*

Lal Buca di Sant'Antonio, Via della Cervia 3, **t** 0583 55881 (*moderate*). An inn since 1782, offering old recipes like smoked herring and kid on a spit, newer dishes like ravioli with ricotta and sage. *Closed Mon.*

Da Giulio in Pelleria Via Conce, **t** 0583 55948, (*moderate*). Less expensive, surprisingly sophisticated twists on 'peasant' fare. Booking advised. *Closed Sun and Mon.*

Vineria dei Santi, Vineria I Santi, Via dell'Anfiteatro 29a, **t** 0583 496124 (*moderate*). Tucked behind Piazza dell'Anfiteatro, this restaurant/wine bar has a pretty terrace. You can order a glass of good wine and snack on a selection of cheeses and salamis and hams or go for something more substantial from the daily menu: honey-glazed turkey breast or baby squid (*moscardini*) soup.

Buatino, Via Borgo Giannotti 508, **t** 0583 343207 (*cheap*). Here you can enjoy good-value, excellent meals in lively surroundings: there's *zuppa di farro*, delicious roast pork, salt cod with leeks, and more. *Closed Sun.*

Da Leo, Via Tegrinin 1 **t** 0583 492236 (*cheap*). Pretty chaotic, full of both locals and tourists. Rabbit stewed with olives, and veal with green peppers; fish only on Fridays. *Closed Sun.*

Gli Orti di Via Elisa, Via Elisa 17, **t** 0583 491241 (*cheap*). This cheerful *trattoria* is great for an inexpensive meal. Pizzas, salads, plus good pastas, etc. *Closed Thurs lunch, Wed.*

Caffé di Simo, Via Fillungo 58. Come here for a drop of java in a classic turn-of-the-century *gran caffé*.

Lucca's table service will be particularly memorable if you have the horsepower to get out to some of the villages in its immediate surroundings:

La Mora, Via Sesto di Moriano 104, Ponte a Moriano, **t** 0583 406402 (*expensive*). North of Lucca, in an old posthouse with four cosy rooms inside and dining outside under a pergola in the summer. According to the season, choose delicious ravioli flavoured with marjoram, roast lamb, pigeon or local freshwater fish.

Vipore, in nearby Pieve Santo Stefano, **t** 0583 394065 (*expensive*). Located in a 200-year-old farmhouse, with views over the fertile plain of Lucca. Top-quality prime ingredients go into fresh pasta and meat dishes. *Closed Mon.*

The Walls

Lucca's lovely bastions evoke the walled rose gardens of chivalric romance, enclosing a smaller, more perfect cosmos. They owe their charm to Renaissance advances in military technology. Prompted by the beginning of the Wars of Italy, Lucca began to construct the walls in 1500. The councillors wanted up-to-date fortifications to counter new advances in artillery, and their (unknown) architects gave them state-of-the-art examples, a model for the new style of fortification soon to transform the cities of Europe. Being Renaissance Tuscans, the architects also gave them a little more elegance than was strictly necessary. The walls were never severely tested. Today, with the outer ravelins, fosses and salients cleared away (such earthworks usually took up as much space as the city itself), Lucca's walls are just for decoration; under the peace-loving Duchess Marie-Louise they were planted with a double row of plane trees to create a 4km elevated garden boulevard, offering a continuous bird's-eye view over Lucca. They are among the best preserved in Italy. Of the gates, the most elaborate is the 16th-century **St Peter's Gate**, near the station, its portcullis still intact, with Lucca's motto of independence, LIBERTAS, inscribed over the entrance. One of the best ways to explore the walls is by bicycle; hire one (see p.244) and do a circular tour.

San Martino Cathedral

Open summer Mon–Fri 9.30–5.45, Sat 9.30–6.45, Sun 9–9.50, 11.30–11.50 and 1–5; winter Mon–Sat 9.30–5.

Through St Peter's Gate (Porta San Pietro), and then to the right, Corso Garibaldi leads to Lucca's cathedral (Duomo), perhaps the most outstanding work of the Pisan style outside Pisa, begun in the 11th century and completed only in the 15th. Above the singular porch, with three different-sized arches, are three levels of colonnades, with pillars arranged like candy sticks, while behind and on the arches are exquisite 12th- and 13th-century reliefs and sculpture – the best work Lucca has to offer. Look out especially for the *Adoration of the Magi* by Nicola Pisano, for the column carved with the Tree of Life, with Adam and Eve crouched at the bottom and Christ on top, and a host of fantastical animals and hunting scenes, the months and their occupations, mermaids and dragons (see Pienza, p.376), and a man embracing a bear, even *Roland at Roncevalles*, all by unknown masters. There is also a medieval maze on the right side of the portico, which you can trace with your finger. Walk round the back, where the splendidly ornate apse and transepts are set off by the green lawn. The crenellated **Campanile** dates from 1060 and 1261.

The dark interior offers an excellent introduction to the works of Lucca's one and only great artist, **Matteo Civitali** (1435–1501), a barber until his mid-30s, when he decided he'd much rather be a sculptor. He deserves to be better known – but may never be, since everything he made is still in Lucca. His most famous work is the octagonal **Tempietto** (1484), a marble tabernacle in the middle of the left aisle, containing Lucca's most precious holy relic, the world-weary *Volto Santo* (Holy Image), a cedar-wood crucifix said to be a true portrait of Jesus, sculpted by Nicodemus, an eye-witness to the crucifixion. Saved from the iconoclasts, it was set adrift in an empty boat and floated to Luni, where the bishop was instructed by an angel to place it in a cart drawn by two white oxen, and where the oxen should halt, there should the image remain. They lumbered to Lucca, where the *Volto Santo* has remained. Its likeness appeared on the republic's coins, and there was a devoted cult of the image in medieval England; Lucca's merchant colony in London cared for a replica in old St Thomas's, and according to William of Malmesbury, King William Rufus always swore by it, '*per sanctum vultum de Lucca*'. Long an object of pilgrimage, the image goes out for a night on the town in a candlelight procession each 13 September.

Further up the left aisle a chapel contains Fra Bartolomeo's *Virgin and Child Enthroned*. Here, too, is an altarpiece by Giambologna, *Christ with SS. Peter and Paul*. Civitali carved the cathedral's high altar, and also two tombs in the south transept. A door from the right aisle leads to the sacristy (*adm*), where you can see Lucca's real icon, the remarkable **Tomb of Ilaria del Carretto** (1408), perhaps Jacopo della Quercia's most beautiful work, a tender, effigy of the young bride of boss Paolo Guinigi, with a dog at her feet, waiting for his mistress to awaken. The city has always had a strange love–hate relationship with this lovely statue. Right after her husband was overthrown they hustled her out of the cathedral, and she didn't come back for centuries. Near the statue is a *Madonna Enthroned with Saints* by Domenico Ghirlandaio.

A side altar near the sacristy has a typically strange composition from the Venetian Tintoretto, a *Last Supper* with a nursing mother in the foreground and cherubs floating around Christ. In the centre, unfortunately often covered up, is a particularly fine section of the inlaid marble floor; on the entrance wall, a 13th-century sculpture of St Martin has been brought in from the façade.

An **Antiques Market** takes place in the cathedral's Piazza di San Martino the third Saturday and Sunday of each month. Next to the cathedral is the **Museo della Cattedrale** (*open mid-March–Oct daily 10–6, Nov–mid-March Mon–Fri 10–2, Sat and Sun 10–5; adm*). Its treasures, include the crown and garments of the *Volto Santo*, some good 13th-century reliquaries and pyxes, tapestries and paintings from Lucca's ancient cathedral, San Giovanni, and della Quercia's *St John the Evangelist*. The museum's upstairs windows afford a close-up view of some of the wonderful sculpture on the cathedral.

Across Piazza San Martino from the cathedral, **San Giovanni e Santa Reparata** (*open daily 10–6; adm*) was Lucca's original cathedral. The exterior has only parts of an 1187 portal to show for its old distinction, but inside there are some surprises. Excavations during the 1970s uncovered a series of buildings: the site of a 5th-century basilica, adjacent to it a huge, square **baptistry** from the 1300s, and under this the original Roman font – a walk-in model for total immersion baptisms – with bits of its mosaics, as well as later Romanesque pavements and a bishop's chair. San Giovanni also has a superb painted coffered ceiling and, above the main door, an attractive organ case, though the pipes have been removed. Lucca was once a city of organ builders, and many of the churches have beautifully crafted instruments with elaborate cases.

Piazza Napoleone and Piazza San Michele

San Giovanni lies on the Via del Duomo between Piazza San Martino and Lucca's shady twin squares, **Piazza del Giglio** and **Piazza Napoleone**, the focus of the Lucchesi evening *passeggiata*. The architectural hotchpotch of a palace on Piazza Napoleone, formerly seat of the republican council, has been called the **Palazzo Ducale** ever since it was used by Lucca's queen for a day, Elisa Bonaparte Baciocchi. In the 16th century, Ammannati had a go at it, and the courtyard, at least, still preserves signs of his Mannerist handiwork. One of Matteo Civitali's most beautiful works, the tomb of San Romano, is in the rarely opened church of **San Romano**, behind the Palazzo.

Via Vittorio Veneto leads from Piazza Napoleone into Piazza San Michele, with a church many people mistake for Lucca's cathedral. Built about the same time, and with a similar Pisan façade, it is almost as impressive. The full name, **San Michele in Foro** (*open daily 7.30–12 and 3–6*), stems from its location on what was Roman Lucca's forum. The ambitious façade rises high above the level of the roof, to make the building look even grander. Every column in the Pisan arcading is different; some doubled, some twisted like corkscrews, inlaid with mosaic Cosmati work, or carved with fanciful figures and beasts, exquisite work similar to the cathedral's, and recently completely restored. The whole is crowned by a giant statue of the Archangel – note the bracelet on his arm, set with real jewels. On the corner of the façade is a Madonna by Civitali; the graceful, rectangular campanile is Lucca's tallest and loveliest.

Inside, there's a glazed terracotta *Madonna and Child* attributed to Luca della Robbia, a striking 13th-century *Crucifixion* over the high altar and a painting of plague saints by Filippino Lippi. Giacomo Puccini began his musical career as a choirboy in San Michele (his father and grandfather had been organists in the cathedral) – he didn't have far to go, as he was born in Via di Poggio 30, just across the street. The house is now a little **Puccini Museum** (*entrance in Corte San Lorenzo 9; open summer Tues–Sun 10–1 and 3–7*), with manuscripts, letters, mementos, the overcoat and odds and ends of the great composer, as well as the piano he used to compose *Turandot*.

Pinacoteca Nazionale

The quarter west of San Michele is perfumed by the big state tobacco factory, which produces Toscanelli cigars, the world's vilest smokes. Via San Paolino (the Roman *decumanus major*) leads to the church of **San Paolino** where little Puccini played the organ to earn some pin-money. It contains two beautiful works: a 13th-century French *Madonna and Child* brought back by Lucchese merchants from Paris, and an anonymous quattrocento Florentine *Coronation of the Virgin*, with Mary hovering over a city of pink towers; unusually she is crowned by God the Father instead of Christ.

The **Pinacoteca Nazionale** (*open Tues–Sat 8.30–7, Sun 8.30–1; adm*) is housed in the 17th-century Palazzo Mansi, in Via Galli Tassi. Most of the art, as well as the rich furnishings, dates from the 17th century. Portraits by Pontormo and Bronzino hang in the Prima Sala after the large hall: the Salone has a dark, damaged Veronese, and a follower of Tintoretto's *Miracle of St Mark Freeing the Slave*, showing the saint dive-bombing from heaven to save the day. There is also a set of neoclassical reliefs from the Palazzo Ducale of the *Triumphs of Duchess Maria Luisa*. The 1600s frescoes are more fun than the paintings, especially the *Judgement of Paris*, which Venus wins by showing a little leg. And one can't help but wonder what rococo dreams tickled the fancy of the occupants of the amazing bedroom.

San Frediano and the Amphitheatre

East of San Michele, medieval **Via Fillungo** and its surrounding lanes make up the busy shopping district, a tidy grid of straight and narrow alleys where Lucca's contented cheerfulness seems somehow magnified. Along Via Fillungo you can trace the old loggias of 14th-century palaces, now bricked in, and the ancient **Torre delle Ore** (tower of hours) which since 1471 has striven to keep the Lucchesi on time, and perhaps now suggests that it's time for a coffee in Lucca's historic **Caffè di Simo** at Via Fillungo 58. At Via Fillungo's northern end stands the tall church and taller campanile of **San Frediano**, built in the early 1100s, and shimmering with the colours of the large mosaic on its upper façade, showing Christ and the Apostles in elegant flowing style. The 11th-century bronze Arabian falcon at the top is a copy – the original is kept in a safe. The palatial interior houses Tuscany's most remarkable baptismal font, the 12th-century *Fontana lustrale* carved with reliefs, and behind it, a lunette of the *Annunciation* by Andrea della Robbia. On the left are several chapels, one with frescoes by Aspertini. The last chapel on the left has an altarpiece and two tomb slabs by Jacopo della Quercia and his assistants. The bedecked mummy is St Zita, patroness of maids and ladies-in-waiting; even in England maids belonged to the Guild of St Zita. The Lucchesi are very fond of her, and on 26 April they bring her body out to caress.

Next to San Frediano, on Via degli Asili, the **Palazzo Pfanner** (*open Mar–Oct daily 10–6; Nov–Feb by appt only, t 340 923 3085*) has an 18th-century garden, a fine staircase, a collection of silks made in Lucca, and 17th–19th century costumes. In the other direction, skirting Via Fillungo, narrow arches lead into something most visitors miss, the **Roman Amphitheatre**. Only outlines of its arches are still traceable in the outer walls, while within the inner ring only the form remains – the marble was probably carted off to build San Michele and the cathedral – but the outline has been perfectly preserved. The foundations of the grandstands now support a perfect ellipse of medieval houses. Duchess Marie Louise cleared out the old buildings in the former arena, and now, where gladiators once slugged it out, boys play football and the less active while away the time in cafés and shops around the piazza.

The streets in this quarter have scarcely changed in the past 500 years. Along Via Sant'Andrea and narrow Via Guinigi, you'll pass a number of resolutely medieval palaces, including that of the Guinigi family. Their lofty stronghold, the **Torre Guinigi** (*mid-Sept–Feb daily 9.30–6; March 9.30–7; April 9.30–8; Summer 9–midnight; adm*), stands next to their palace and is one of Lucca's landmarks, with a tree sprouting out of its top – the best example of that quaint Italian fancy. The tower has been restored and it's worth the stiff climb up for the view over the city and the Apuan Alps.

The East Side

Roman Lucca ended near the Guinigi palace, and when a new church was built in the early 12th century it was outside the gate, hence the name of **Santa Maria Forisportam** in Via Santa Croce, a pretty church in the Pisan style with blind arcades. Inside, it not only looks but smells terribly old, and contains two paintings by the often esoteric Guercino. Beyond the church is the best-preserved gate of 1260, the **Porta San Gervasio** giving on to the former moat, now a picturesque little canal running along Via del Fosso. Just across the canal from the gate is **Santa Trinità** (*if closed, ask for the key in the convent next door*), home of Civitali's *Madonna della Tosse* (Our Lady of the Cough), a bit too syrupy sweet, but perhaps that helped the cure. Nearby on Via Elisa is the entrance to the **Villa Bottini gardens** (*open Sun–Fri 9–7*), one of the few green oases inside the city walls.

At the northern end of Via del Fosso stands a 17th-century column dedicated to another Madonna, and to the east, the church of **San Francesco**, a typical 13th-century Franciscan preaching church with the tombs of Castracani and Lucchese composer Luigi Boccherini (d. 1805) – he of the famous *minuet* – and some detached frescoes of the Florentine school. Beyond San Francesco stands the palatial brick Villa Guinigi, built in 1418 by the big boss Paolo Guinigi in his glory days. Now the **Museo Nazionale Guinigi** (*open Tues–Sat 8.30–7, Sun 8.30–1; adm*), its ground floor houses a collection of Romanesque reliefs, capitals and transennas, some of which are charmingly primitive – St Michael slaying the dragon, Samson killing the lion, a 9th-century transenna with birds and beasts, spirals and daggers. Upstairs, room XI has a lovely *Annunciation* by Civitali. The painting gallery contains intarsia panels from the cathedral, each with scenes of Lucca as seen from town windows, some trecento works by the Lucca school and a charming quattrocento *Madonna and Child* by the 'Maestro della Vita di Maria'. Other rooms contain oversized 16th-century canvases, some by Vasari.

Villas around Lucca

In 16th-century Lucca, as elsewhere in Italy, trade began to flounder, and merchants turned to the joys of property, where they could decline genteelly in a little country palace and garden. For the Lucchesi, the preferred site for such pleasure domes was in the soft, rolling country to the north and northeast of the city. Three of these villas or their grounds are open for visits. In Segromigno, 10km from Lucca towards Pescia, there's the charming, mid-16th-century but often modified **Villa Mansi** (*open summer 10–1 and 3–6, winter 10–1 and 3–5; adm*), embellished with a half-Italian (geometric) and half-English (not geometric) garden by the Sicilian architect Juvarra.

Nearby in Camigliano, the even more elaborate **Villa Torrigiani** (*villa and park open Mar–mid-Nov Wed–Mon 10–1 and 3–sunset; in winter call ahead t 0583 928041; adm exp*), also begun in the 16th century , was celebrated for its fabulous parties and entertainments. Set in a lush park of pools and trees, it has 16th–18th century furnishings. Elisa Bonaparte Baciocchi combined a villa and a summer palace to make her country retreat, now called the **Villa Pecci-Blunt ex-Villa Reale** in Marlia. Only the park and the Giardino Orsetti are open, but they are worth the trip (*tours by appt, t 0583 30108, Mar–Nov Tues–Sun at 10, 11, 12, 3, 4, 5 and 6; Dec–Feb call ahead; adm*).

The Lucchese Plain

East and west of Lucca, what was swampland in the Middle Ages has been reclaimed to form a rich agricultural plain. One of its features are its 'courts' – farm hamlets not constructed around a central piazza, but with houses in neat rows. At one time there were 1,100 such courts on the plain. Among the highlights of the area is curious **Castello di Nozzano** just to the west, built by Matilda of Tuscany on a hill, its pretty tower now incongruously topped by a large clock. To the east, one of the first villages, **Capannori**, is the head town of several courts and has a couple of interesting Romanesque churches, especially the 13th-century **Pieve San Paolo**, around which a small village incorporated itself, using the campanile for defence. The most imposing monument nearby is the 19th-century **Acquedotto del Nottolini**, which is also visible from the *autostrada*. Just south is the pretty hill-top village of **Castelvecchio**, its tall houses forming an effective circular wall. **Altopascio**, on the Lucca–Empoli road, was built around an 11th-century hospice run by an obscure chivalric order called the Hospitaller Knights of the Order of Altopascio, who originally occupied themselves with rescuing travellers from the swamps. Only the campanile of their church remains in the village today. **Montecarlo** gives its name to a very good dry white wine produced in the immediate area.

The Garfagnana and Lunigiana

The rugged northern finger of Tuscany encompasses the region's 'Alps', the tall and jagged **Alpi Apuane**, which like the real Alps wear brilliant white crowns, though not made of snow – that's marble up there, the 'tears of the stars', the purest and whitest in Italy. Historically the land is divided into two mini-regions: along the bank of the Serchio river, between the Apuan Alps and the Apennines, is the **Garfagnana**; while the region north of the village of Piazza al Serchio is the **Lunigiana**, former hinterland of the ancient Roman port of Luni.

The Garfagnana and Lunigiana are relatively undiscovered, and threaten to dispel many people's typical image of Tuscany; the mountains are too high, the valleys are too narrow, and you're more likely to find yourself amidst pine forests than vineyards and olive groves. However, a spell in this striking mountain scenery can be just what you need when the thought of cathedrals or art galleries begins to pall.

The Garfagnana

For many years the chief export of the Garfagnana has been Italians; the green hills and mountains, the narrow valley of the Serchio, between the Apennines and the Apuan Alps, the stone villages perched on slopes that look so picturesque on postcards were simply never generous enough to provide a sufficient livelihood for their inhabitants. The chief staple of the district until recently was flour made from chestnuts, and chestnut groves still cover much of the region.

Lucca to Bagni di Lucca

North of Lucca, the first tempting detour off the SS12 is to one of the many Romanesque churches in the region, **San Giorgio di Brancoli**, near Vinchiana, as

Getting Around

CLAP **buses** from Lucca connect the city to Bagni di Lucca (27km/40min), Barga (37km/1hr), and Castelnuovo di Garfagnana (50km/1½hrs). The **railway station** is just south of the walls on Piazza Ricasoli. **Trains** on the scenic Lucca–Aulla line go up the Serchio valley, though beware that the stations for Bagni di Lucca and Barga are quite a distance from their centres and don't always have buses that connect; you'd be better off taking the bus to begin with.

If you're **driving** from the south, the most convenient way into these mountains begins at Lucca; both the SS12 and SS445 routes follow the river Serchio.

Tourist Information

Bagni di Lucca: Viale Umberto I, 139, t 0583 805745 (*summer only*).
Barga: Piazza Angelo, t 0583 724745.
Castelnuovo di Garfagnana: Rocca Loggiato Porta 10, t/f 0583 641007, *www.corriere digarfagnana.com*.
The Visitors' Centre for the Parco Regionale delle Alpi Apuane is at Piazza delle Erbe 1, t 0583 644242.

Where to Stay and Eat

There's nothing exceptional in Garfagnana, but the Italians firmly believe the further north in Tuscany you go, the better the cooking, graced by the kindly influences of Liguria and Emilia-Romagna; the pasta dishes in the region are especially good. Specialities include *torte di erbe* (vegetable pies), chestnut puddings and *pattona* (chestnut biscuits).

Bagni di Lucca ✉ 55022

Bagni di Lucca is wonderfully genteel, with a score of quiet, modest Victorian hotels.
★★★Regina Park Hotel, Viale Umberto I 157, t 0583 805508, *www.coronaregina.it* (*expensive*). A smart hotel with all mod cons housed in a Renaissance palazzo in the centre of Bagni. A lovely loggia overlooks the ample grounds, which back onto the river Lima. *Closed mid-Oct–Easter.*
★★★Corona, Via Serraglia 78, t 0583 805151, *www.coronaregina.it* (*moderate*). Under the same ownership as the Regina, this is cheaper, but still very comfortable. The restaurant serves imaginative dishes such as *zucchini*, *taleggio* and truffle timbale, gnocchi with baby squid and chick peas, and duck breast cooked with blackcurrants.

notable for its lovely setting as for its 12th-century pulpit. **Diécimo**, across the river, has a name that survives from Roman times – it lies 10 Roman miles (18km) from Lucca. The town's main landmark is the mighty Romanesque campanile of the 13th-century church of **Santa Maria**, standing out starkly against the surrounding hills. **Borgo a Mozzano**, 4km further upstream, is famous for its beautiful little hump-back bridge, with arches in five different shapes and sizes, which is dedicated to the Magdalene, or to the Devil. According to legend, he built it one dark and stormy night in exchange for the first soul to cross – the clever villagers outwitted him by sending a dog over in the morning. The real builder in this case was the slighty less lethal 11th-century Countess Matilda who, besides the bridge, endowed the villages around Borgo with a number of solid Romanesque parish churches. Inside Borgo's church you can see a wooden *San Bernardino* by Civitali.

To the north, just above the confluence of the Serchio river and the Torrente Lima, lie the long and narrow riverside hamlets that make up **Bagni di Lucca**, Lucca's once-grand old spa, first mentioned in the days of Countess Matilda. In the early 1800s, under the patronage of Elisa Bonaparte Baciocchi, it enjoyed a moment in high society's favour – long enough to build one of Europe's first official gambling casinos (1837; roulette was invented here), an Anglican church in an exotic Gothic Alhambra

*Roma, Via Umberto I 110, **t/f** 0583 87278 (*inexpensive*). Toscanini, Puccini and Caruso all stayed here, a small, old-fashioned place with a shady garden at the back, also in Villa di Bagni. Most rooms have bath.

Circolo dei Forestieri, Loc Ville, **t** 0583 86038 (*moderate–cheap*). Slightly smarter, where you can eat *filetto al pepe verde* and *crêpes ai funghi*. *Closed Mon and Tues lunch.*

Da Vinicio, Via del Casino, **t** 0583 87250 (*cheap*). A chaotic and popular pizzeria a block west of Bagni's bridge, also good roast pigeon and seafood.

Barga ✉ 55051

****Il Ciocco in Castelvecchio, 6km north at Pascoli, **t** 0583 7191, **f** 0583 723197, *www. ciocco.it* (*expensive*). A huge resort hotel with some 260 rooms plus self-catering chalets. heliport, restaurant, bars, tennis court – in short, the works.

***Villa Libano, Via del Sasso 6, **t** 0583 723774, **f** 0583 724185, *www.hotelvillalibano. com* (*inexpensive*). A lovely place in a courtyard, set next to Barga's city park; there's a restaurant with tables out in the garden.

Terrazza, 5km north at Albiano, **t** 0583 766155 (*cheap*). The best restaurant, featuring the specialities of the region. *Closed Wed.*

Castelnuovo di Garfagnana ✉ 55032

***Da Carlino, Via Garibaldi 15, **t** 0583 644270 **f** 0583 62616, *www.dacarlino.it* (*moderate–cheap*). A rustic old place with an Alpine feel to it, now run by Carlino's grandson. Excellent restaurant serves home-made and organic produce, also pizzas baked in a wood oven.

La Geragetta, Capanne di Careggine, **t** 0583 667065 (*cheap*). For a rustic feast with the majestic backdrop of the Apuanian Alps, seek out this Alpine chalet-style restaurant just above Isola Santa. You will be hard-pressed to pay more than €17 for everything, from the *aperitivo* at the start to the *grappa* at the finish of your meal. In between, your digestion will be challenged by a vast range of *antipasti*, home-made pastas, game and roast meats, mushrooms in season, good solid desserts and unlimited wine. *Closed Mon.*

Osteria Vecchio Mulino, Via Vittorio Emanuele 12, **t** 0583 62192 (*cheap*). This atmospheric wine bar, just outside the city walls, is a great place for a snack accompanied by some wonderful wines. Eat cold meats and superb cheeses from wooden boards at long tables surrounded by bottles, or try one of the excellent flans, with delicious marinated picked vegetables. *Closed Mon.*

style, and an unusual 1840 suspension bridge (the **Ponte alle Catene**) – before sinking into obscurity. In Bagni's heyday, though, Byron, Browning, Shelley and Heine came to take the sulphur and saline waters, and perspire in a natural vapour bath. Heine was particularly enthusiastic: 'A true and proper sylvan paradise. I have never found a valley more enchanting,' he wrote; even the mountains are 'nobly formed' and not 'bizarre and Gothic like those in Germany'. Little has changed, and these days Bagni di Lucca is a sleepy but charming little place, with some pretty villas, elegant thermal establishments that spring into action every summer, a miniature pantheon, and a fancy Circolo dei Forestieri, or foreigners' club (now a restaurant) on the river-front.

Up the Lima Valley

From Bagni di Lucca, the SS12 leads towards San Marcello Pistoiese and the ski resort of Abetone (*see* p.233), following the lovely valley of the Lima. A byroad beginning at Bagni leads to picturesque, rugged stone hamlets like **Pieve di Controne** and **Montefegatesi** which only appear on the most detailed maps; from Montefegatesi, an unsealed road continues to the dramatic gorge of **Orrido di Botri** at the foot of the Alpe Tre Potenze (1,939m/6,363ft). As the byroad winds back towards the SS12 at

Scesta, it passes **San Cassiano**, site of a fine 13th-century Pisan-style church with a delicately carved façade, in an isolated setting. Other byroads from the SS12 lead to tiny hamlets like **Vico Pancellorum** to the north and **Lucchio** to the south.

To Barga and the Cave of the Wind

The Garfagnana proper begins where the Lima flows into the river Serchio at Fornoli. In the 14th century this area was ruled by the kinsmen of Castruccio Castracani; one of their prettiest mountain hamlets is **Tereglio**, along the scenic northeast road to the **Alpe Tre Potenze**, before it meanders on to Abetone. The Castracani had their base at **Coreglia Antelminelli**, high above the Serchio and the main SS445 (turn off at Piano di Coreglia). Coreglia's church contains a magnificent 15th-century processional cross, and there's a **Museo della Figurina** (*open summer Mon–Sat 8–1, Sun 10–1 and 4–7; winter Mon–Sat 8–1; adm*) devoted to the Garfagnana's traditional manufacture of plaster figures. To the north, the hill town of **Barga** (pop. 11,000) stands above its modern offspring, Fornaci di Barga on the main SS445. Barga was astute enough to maintain its independence until 1341, when it decided to link its fortunes with Florence. At the very top of town stands Barga's chief monument, its **cathedral**, begun in the year 1000 on a terrace, with a panoramic view over the rooftops and of surrounding hills apparently clad in green velvet, and bare mountains scoured with white marble. Built of a blonde stone called *alberese di Barga*, its square façade is discreetly decorated with a shallow pattern, charming reliefs and two leering lions; on the side the campanile is incorporated into the church; over the portal, there's a relief of a feast scene with a king and dwarfs. There's yet another dwarf inside, supporting one of the red marble pillars of the **pulpit** by the idiosyncratic 13th-century Como sculptor, Guido Bigarelli. The other pillars required a pair of lions, one grinning over a conquered dragon, one being both stroked and stabbed by a man. Less mysterious are the naive reliefs around the pulpit itself, startlingly sophisticated versions of familiar scriptural scenes. In the choir note the venerable polychrome wood statue of St Christopher (early 1100s) and a choir screen with strange medieval carvings, including a mystic mermaid (*see pp.377–8*). Around the back, the cathedral's garden has a magnificent Lebanon cedar. Next to the cathedral stands the **Palazzo Pretorio**, with a small **Museo Civico,** and 14th-century **Loggetta del Podestà**; if you go down the stairs towards the dungeon you can see Barga's old corn measures – a medieval Trading Standards Office.

The rest of Barga is a photogenic ensemble of archways and little palazzi piled on top of each other, with walls, gates and a ravine planted with kitchen gardens. Things get lively in July and August with the classes and performances of **Opera Barga** in the old Dei Differenti Theatre, founded in 1600. Between Barga and Fornaci di Barga, you can measure the showy success of the city's emigrants who returned to build modern palaces in the suburb of Giardino.

From Barga you can take a 17km potholing detour to Fornovalasco in the Apuan Alps to see Tuscany's best cave, the **Grotto del Vento** (*open daily all year; guided 1hr tours at 10, 11, 12, 2, 3, 4, 5 and 6, 2-hour tours for real cave fiends daily April–Oct; winter Sun and hols only, at 11, 3, 4 and 5pm; sometimes only part of the cave is visited; less crowded in* *the mornings; call t 0583 722 024, f 0583 722 053 for details; adm exp*), a long cavern of fat stalactites, bottomless pits and abysses, and subterranean lakes and streams, set in a barren, eerie landscape.

Castelnuovo di Garfagnana

Hanging over the Serchio, 11km north of Barga, is **Castelnuovo di Garfagnana**, the region's lively 'capital', guarded by its **Rocca**. Its most famous commander was Ludovico Ariosto, author of the epic poem of chivalry and fantasy, *Orlando Furioso*. Ariosto was employed by the Este Dukes of Ferrara to chase bandits and collect tolls here in the 1520s, but didn't take to it. 'I'm not a man to govern other men,' he wrote, 'I have too much pity, and can't deny the things they require me to deny.'

Castelnuovo makes a handy base for excursions into its often wild surroundings. Northeast, past the small resort of **Castiglione di Garfagnana**, a tortuous mountain road continues through 16km of magnificent scenery to the **Foce delle Radici** (the pass into Emilia-Romagna) and **San Pellegrino in Alpe**, with magnificent views, an ancient monastery and a good little museum, the **Museo Etnografico Campagna** (*t 0583 649072, open April–May Tues–Sun 9–12 and 2–5; June–Sept Tues–Sun 9.30–1 and 2.30–7; daily July and Aug; winter Mon–Sat 9–1 Sun 9–12 and 2–5; adm*). West of Castelnuovo a scenic road leads over the Apuan Alps to Carrara and the coast, through the desolate Turrite Secca, its sombre features relieved by the romantic oasis of **Isola Santa** (13km) – a tiny, slate-roofed village amid trees on a lake, once a hideout for medieval renegades; now it is abandoned, save for a few old folks and the sheep who lives behind the altar of the church.

North of Castelnuovo the road enters Garfagnana Alta, one of the least-known corners of Tuscany. Just north of town lies the **Parco Naturale dell'Orecchiella**, with eagles, mouflons, deer and a botanical garden, its mountains crisscrossed by paths; pick up a map at the visitor centre in Orecchiella. At Poggio, back on the Serchio, there's a turn-off for **Careggine**, a lofty old hamlet with commanding views, and the artificial **Lago di Vagli**. Creating this lake submerged the village of Fabbriche; the campanile may still be seen sticking stubbornly out of the water. There are more stunning views from **Vagli Sopra**, village of old marble quarries and an 18th-century road, deteriorated into a footpath, which leads into the Valle di Arnetola. Towering over all is **Monte Pisanino** (1,945m/6,380ft), the tallest of the Apuan Alps; the road up to the summit and the alpine refuge of Donegani, passing the lakelet of Gramolazzo, begins at **Piazza al Serchio**, leaving the Serchio and the Garfagnana behind.

The Lunigiana

Even less populous and less visited than the Garfagnana, the Lunigiana, separating Liguria and Emilia-Romagna from the rest of Tuscany, has traditionally been a tough nut for its would-be governors to crack. The Romans of Luni (founded in 180 BC to contain the fearsome Ligurians) found it a wild place; even in the 7th century, missionaries were still bashing revered ancient idols. This rugged territory of chestnut

Getting Around

If you're approaching from the north, **trains** and *autostrade* from Genoa (A12) and Parma (A15) merge near Aulla. From here there are frequent trains to Massa-Carrara, Viareggio and Pisa, Pontremoli or Lucca. From Lucca, trains to Aulla take over 2hrs (85km) and to Pontremoli 2½ hrs (108km). CAT **buses** serve the Lunigiana, with Aulla as the main depot; there are services to Massa and Carrara, and to Bagnone, Filattiera, Fivizzano, Fosdinovo, Licciana Nardi, Pontremoli and Villafranca.

Tourist Information

Fivizzano: Via Roma, t 0585 92017.
Pontremoli: Piazza della Reppublica, t 0187 833701.

Where to Stay and Eat

Equi Terme ✉ 54022

★La Posta in Via Provinciale, t 0585 97937 (*inexpensive*). Friendly little place with a bright restaurant and attractive rooms. Eat ravioli stuffed with ricotta and nettles or the house special 'La Spagnola' (a kind of cheesy strudel). *Closed Feb.*

Bagnone ✉ 54021

I Fondi, Via della Repubblica 26, t 0187 429086 (*cheap*). Up in fortified Bagnone, you can fortify yourself with good, solid country cooking – lasagne with pesto or mushrooms, ravioli filled with gorgonzola and *radicchi*, *testeroli* in pesto, duck cooked with herbs, wild boar, local sausages.

Fivizzano ✉ 54013

★★Il Giardinetto, Via Roma 151, t 0585 92060 (*moderate*). A delightful, old-fashioned place overlooking Piazza Medicea. Rooms are comfortable, and there's a little garden. The *antipasti* are especially tempting, as well as the pasta and game (try the pasta with venison sauce, polenta with mushrooms, and venison stewed with juniper). *Closed Oct.*

Pontremoli ✉ 54027

Pontremoli is rich in good restaurants, and has several hotel options.

★★★Golf Hotel, Via Pineta, t 0187 831573, f 0187 831591, *www.golfhotel.it* (*moderate*). New, out of town in a pine wood, offering a restaurant and 80 very comfortable rooms, all with bath and TV.

Da Bussé, Piazza del Duomo 31, t 0187 831371 (*moderate*). An age-old restaurant featuring Pontremoli's special *pasta testaroli* with pesto, *involtini* (little meat parcels) in tomato sauce, stuffed pigs' trotters, and a delicious Swiss chard and ricotta pie. A sign on the door announces that they don't cook mushrooms. Finish with *spongata*, a local chocolate tart. *Open lunch only Mon–Thurs, lunch and dinner Sat–Sun; closed Fri.*

Osteria Caveau del Teatro, Piazza Santa Cristina, t 0187 833328, *www.caveaudelteatro.it* (*moderate*). Elegant yet cosy cellar restaurant offering a change from rustic fare. The menu features such dishes as paté of foie gras with port, potato *tortelli* with a parmesan cream, roast pork with orange, and chocolate mousse with apricot coulis. The adjoining 17th-century tower houses 7 delightful bedrooms, beautifully furnished with antiques.

La Manganella, Via Garibaldi 20, t 0187 830653 (*moderate*). If you want mushrooms, here they do them every way under the sun: grilled, raw in salad, *trifolati* (sautéed), with pasta... *Closed Mon.*

Trattoria del Giardino da Bacciottini, Via Ricci Armani 13, t 0187 830120 (*cheap*). In the old town, you'll find *fritelle* of salt cod, marinated herrings and excellent *testaroli* with pesto and lamb.

forests is crowded with the castles of would-be rulers and other toll-collecting gangsters. In the early 1900s the Lunigiana was a stronghold of rural anarchism, and in 1944 its partisans made it one of the bigger free zones in the north. Since then life has been fairly tranquil; rocky, forested landscapes, ruined castles (many bombed in the last war) and simple Romanesque churches form the main attractions.

Piazza al Serchio to Aulla

Beyond **Piazza al Serchio**, the first town of consequence along the SS445 is fortified **Casola in Lunigiana** (20km); just beyond, a road veers south for the spa of **Equi Terme,** a tiny place where the medieval town is spectacularly perched on a rock above the new town. Equi is less known these days for its waters than for its cave, **La Buca del Cane,** or Dog's Hole (*closed to visitors*) after its relics of prehistoric man's best friend. Our ancestors also apparently socialized with bears (or ate them), judging by the bones that have been found here. **Fivizzano** to the north (on the SS63 or by road from Casola) belonged to the Malaspina of Massa until the Medici snatched it and fortified it as a grand ducal outpost. The main square, **Piazza Medicea**, has a grand fountain paid for by Cosimo III, a few Florentine-style palaces, and the 13th-century parish church with the inevitable Medici balls on the front. There are two interesting Romanesque chapels in the vicinity, **Santa Maria Assunta**, 3km towards Pognana, in a lovely isolated setting, and 12th-century **San Paolo a Vendaso** with carved capitals inside, on the SS63 towards the Passo di Cerreto.

From Ceserano, just south of the SS445, the SS446 heads southwest over the mountains to Sarzana, passing **Fosdinovo**, where the Malaspina castle that hosted Dante in 1306 is one of the most beautiful and majestic in the Lunigiana (*t 0187 68891, guided tours winter Wed–Mon 10–11 and 4–5; summer Wed–Mon 10–11 and 4–6; adm*). Inside is a collection of arms and ornaments found in local tombs.

Aulla

Aulla grew up at the Lunigiana's hotly contested crossroads, guarding access into the Magra valley. The powerful, 16th-century **Fortezza della Brunella** was built by the Genoese, who bought Aulla in 1543; Napoleon gave it to his sister Elisa in Lucca; it now contains a natural history museum (*t 01867 400252; open Tues–Sun 9–12 and 3–6, summer until 7; adm*). Nearby are the citadels of two other rivals for the town – the Bishop of Luni's **Caprigliola**, a fortified village still inaccessible to cars (6km southwest on the SS62) and the Malaspinas' fortified hamlet of **Bibola** and their romantically ruined **Ponzanello**, both due south of Aulla. The Malaspina also fortified the strategic road to the pass, to the northeast at **Licciana Nardi** (surrounded by immensely thick 11th century walls with only narrow passageways giving access to its centre), and especially at **Bastia**, 4km further on.

From Aulla you can tuck down into Liguria and the **Italian Riviera** to visit the 'Gulf of the Poets' (or, more prosaically, the Gulf of La Spezia), named after Byron, who swam across it, and Shelley, who last lived in San Terenzo near the Pisan town of **Lerici**. On the Gulf's western shore (in Liguria) lies enchanting old **Portovenere**, named after the goddess of love herself. Near Carrara are the excavations of ancient Luni (*see p.263*).

North of Aulla is **Villafranca in Lunigiana**, along the Via Francigena, the pilgrimage route from France; here you can visit the 16th-century church of **San Francesco** and an **Ethnographic Museum** (*open Tues–Sun 9–12 and 3–6, in summer until 7; adm*) devoted to rural life in the Lunigiana, especially the chestnut industry. Yet another mighty castle beckons further up at **Bagnone**, 5km to the east.

Prehistoric Mysteries

This hidden corner of Italy holds a genuine prehistoric mystery. To learn about it, climb up the narrow medieval lanes above Pontremoli to the gloomy, 14th-century Castello del Piagnaro and its **Museo delle Statue-stele della Lunigiana** (open Tues–Sun 9.30–12.30 and 2.30–6; adm). This small museum holds over a score of large, carved statue-steles of an unknown culture that flourished in the Lunigiana between the 3rd millennium BC and the 2nd century BC. The steles, rather like menhirs with personality, include stylized warriors with daggers or axes, and women with little knobbly breasts. They are displayed in semi-darkness, which adds to their mystery. The oldest (3000–2000 BC) have a U for a face and a head hardly distinguishable from the trunk; the middle period (20th–8th century BC) sport anvil heads and eyes; the last group (7th–2nd century BC) are mostly warriors, with a weapon in each hand, just as Virgil described the Gauls who invaded Lazio. They were often discovered near sources of water, and some scholars think they may have symbolized the heavens (the head), the earth (the arms and weapons) and the underworld (the lower third, buried in the ground). Similar steles turn up in southern Corsica and other places around the Mediterranean. Some of the steles had their heads knocked off, a sure sign that the pope's missionaries in the 8th century were doing their job. Curiously, in the nearby hamlet of Vignola, a folk memory survives of the destruction of idols; during the patron saint's festival they make little wooden idols strangely similar to Pontremoli's statue-steles and burn them to celebrate the triumph over the pagans.

Pontremoli

Long and low-key, stretched lazily along the river Magra and the Torrente Verdi, is **Pontremoli** (pop. 11,000), chief town of the Lunigiana and the northernmost in Tuscany. The Via Francigena passes through the middle. Pontremoli is full of wonderful belle époque details – lamp-posts, shop fronts and interiors, even the marble street names. The historical Liberty-style Caffè Fratechi Aichta in Piazza della Repubblica, with its old carved wood cabinets and counters, is well worth a visit. The town wasn't always so peaceful: in 1322 Guelph and Ghibelline quarrels led Castruccio Castracani to build a fortress, called Cacciaguerra ('drive-away war') in the town centre to keep the two parties apart until they made peace. Of this noble effort only the **Torre del Campanone** and what is now the campanile of the **Duomo** survive. The Duomo itself has a fine, ballroom interior hung with dozens of glittering chandeliers, unusual for Tuscany. Over the Torrente Verdi, the church of **San Francesco** contains a lovely polychrome relief of the Madonna and Child attributed to Agostino di Duccio. Between the centre and the station the oval 18th-century church of **Nostra Donna** is a rare example of Tuscan rococo.

In 1471 the Virgin made an appearance a mile south of Pontremoli, and to honour the spot the **church of Santissima Annunziata** was built with a lovely marble **Tempietto** by Jacopo Sansovino, a quattrocento fresco of the Annunciation by Luca Cambiaso, an elegant triptych of uncertain hand or date, and some fun trompe l'œil frescoes by a Baroque painter from Cremona named Natali.

The Tuscan Coast

11

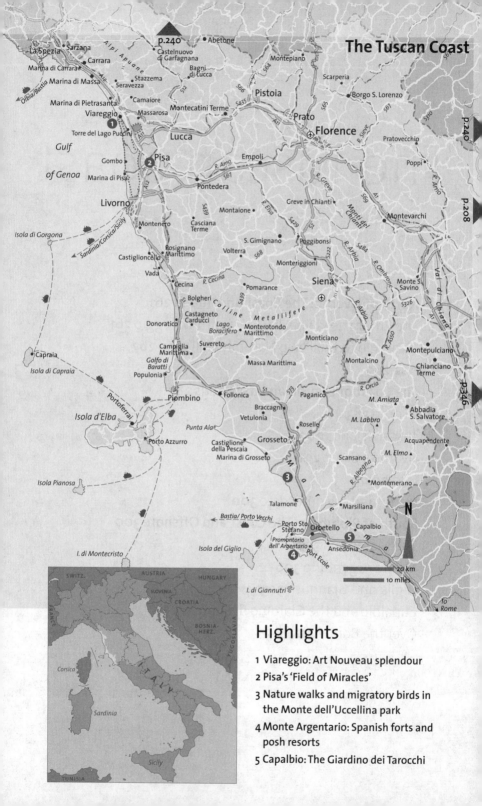

The Tuscan Coast

p.240

La Spezia
Sarzana
Marina di Carrara
Carrara
Marina di Massa
Marina di Pietrasanta
Viareggio ❶
Torre del Lago Puccini
Gombo
Marina di Pisa

Gulf

of Genoa

Alpi Apuane
Castelnuovo di Garfagnana
Bagni di Lucca
Stazzema
Seravezza
Camaiore
Massarosa
Montecatini Terme
Lucca
Pisa ❷
Pontedera
Empoli

Abetone
Montepiano
Scarperia
Borgo S. Lorenzo
Pistoia
Prato
Florence
Pratovecchio
Poppi

Isola di Gorgona

Sardinia/Corsica/Sicily

Livorno
Montenero
Casciana Terme
Rosignano Marittimo
Castiglioncello
Vada
Cecina
Bolgheri
Castagneto Carducci
Donoratico
Campiglia Marittima
Golfo di Baratti
Populonia
Piombino

R. Arno
Montaione
Volterra
Monteriggioni
Pomarance
Lago Boracifero
Monterotondo Marittimo
Suvereto
Massa Marittima

Greve in Chianti
Poggibonsi
S. Gimignano
Colline Metallifere
Monticiano
Siena
Montevarchi
Monte S. Savino
Montepulciano
Chianciano Terme

Capraia
Isola di Capraia

Portoferraio
Isola d'Elba
Porto Azzurro

Isola Pianosa

Follonica
Braccagni
Vetulonia
Roselle
Punta Ala
Castiglione della Pescaia
Marina di Grosseto
Grosseto

Paganico
M. Amiata
Abbadia S. Salvatore
Acquapendente
Scansano
M. Labbro
M. Elmo
Montemerano
Marsiliana
Talamone
Capalbio ❺
Orbetello
Ansedonia

Bastia/ Porto Vecchi

I. di Montecristo

Porto Sto. Stefano
Promontorio dell' Argentario ❹
Port Ecole
Isola del Giglio
I. di Giannutri

N

20 km
10 miles

To Rome

Highlights

1 Viareggio: Art Nouveau splendour

2 Pisa's 'Field of Miracles'

3 Nature walks and migratory birds in the Monte dell'Uccellina park

4 Monte Argentario: Spanish forts and posh resorts

5 Capalbio: The Giardino dei Tarocchi

The Etruscan Riviera, the Tyrrhenian shore, Tuscany by the sea – most of it is flat, straight, dull (apart from the incredible backdrop of marble mountains behind) and endowed with wide, usually crowded, sandy beaches. The sea isn't as clean as it might be, and the closer you get to the mouth of the Arno and Livorno, the less savoury it becomes. For a spell on the beach, you may find Tuscany's archipelago of seven islands more congenial – the sea is cleaner and the coast and beaches prettier.

Harder to escape, unless you go to the smallest islands, is Italian beach culture. Much of the shore is privately owned and you must pay for access to a veritable wall of deck chairs and beach umbrellas, packed as densely as possible; behind this there's inevitably a busy road, where the traffic is mainly vans with loudspeakers and motor-cycles; behind the busy road is another wall of hotels, and perhaps a few pine woods. As always, you'll find it more pleasant and less frenzied outside July and August.

The most beautiful and fashionable section of the Tuscan coast is the Argentario, around Porto Santo Stefano, but it's also the most expensive. Elba, the largest island, is rugged and beautiful, but a busy Euro-holiday destination. Other places are an acquired taste: Viareggio, with more character than most, and the Puccini opera festival in nearby Torre del Lago, or Livorno, one of Italy's largest ports, famous for its seafood restaurants. The mellow old city of Pisa, an ancient maritime republic long ago silted up by the Arno, needs no introduction. In Carrara you can learn about marble in the Apuan Alps, in the Maremma you can learn about Italian cowboys and discover the lovely old town of Massa Marittima.

North of Livorno: The Coast and Inland

The Riviera della Versilia: Carrara to Viareggio

Carrara

In the centre of dynamic, up-to-date **Carrara** (pop. 69,000) there's a garden square called Piazza Gramsci with an unusual fountain, consisting of a large, snow-white sphere of marble that revolves hypnotically, glistening with water, while the Apuan Alps tower in the background, streaked with the white quarries from where the sphere was 'liberated'. Carrara means marble; its name is believed to come from 'kar', the Indo-European word for stone. The Romans were the first to extract it 2,000 years ago; they drove wooden wedges soaked in water into the natural cracks in the stone, and when the wedges swelled, the marble broke off, and was rolled away on iron balls and sent to Rome to become Trajan's column or Apollo Belvedere.

The same techniques were still being used when Carrara began its revival in 1502, when Pope Julius II sent Michelangelo to find the marble for his tomb. These mountains are haunted by the memory of the 'divine' sculptor, in his old clothes and smelly goatskin boots, going to the most inaccessible corners to discover new veins of perfect, white stone. Michelangelo thought quarrying just as serious an art as sculpture; he loved to spend time here with his rock, and he claimed with his usual modesty to have 'introduced the art of quarrying' to Carrara. Marble has also made

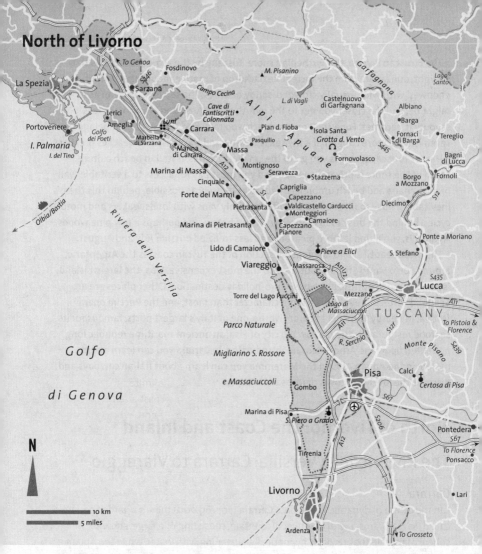

the Carraresi traditionally a breed apart – although their official past is dominated by the rule of godfatherish noble clans like the Malaspina and Cybo-Malaspina, the undercurrents were always fiercely independent, leaning strongly towards anarchism.

Some of Carrara's marble went into its one outstanding monument, the **cathedral**, a distinctive Romanesque church begun in the 11th century with marble stripes and an arch of marble animals, and later embellished with an exquisite 14th-century rose window made of marble lace, and marble art and statues inside, including a huge marble bowl in the baptistry. In the little piazza there's a bulky sculpture by the Florentine hack Bandinelli, generally known as the Giant, although it is supposed to be *Andrea Doria in the Guise of Neptune*. Next to Piazza Gramsci, on Via Roma 1, is the **Accademia delle Belle Arti**, set in a medieval castle. It was converted into a palace in the 16th century by Alberico Cybo-Malaspina, the Marchese di Massa, whose descendants ruled Massa and Carrara until they died out in 1829, when the state joined the Duchy of Modena until unification. The courtyard contains sculptures from Luni and the *Edicola dei Fantescritti*, a Roman tabernacle from the Fantescritti quarry, with bas-reliefs of Jove, Hercules and Bacchus, arm-in-arm like old chums, surrounded by graffiti by Giambologna and other sculptors who visited the quarries.

Marble Quarries and Roman Ruins

Even though Carrara exports half a million tons of different marbles a year, there is little danger of it running out soon; though they will gravely tell you that there are only a few cubic kilometres of good stone left. The **quarries** surrounding Carrara are an unforgettable sight; usually they extend straight up to the sky, a blinding white scar down the mountain with a narrow access road zigzagging perpendicularly to the top. Signs from the centre of Carrara direct you to the quarries, or *Cave di Marmo* – **Colonnata** (8km, founded as a colony of Roman slaves and famous for *lardo di Colonnata*, a fat bacon salted in marble vats), **Fantiscritti** (a Roman quarry still in use) and **Ravaccione** (with fine views over the mountains). The **Museo Civico del Marmo** on Viale XX Settembre, the main road between Carrara and the train station (*open May, June and Sept 10–6; Oct–April 9–5; July and Aug 10–8; closed Sun and hols; adm*), takes you through the history with remarkable photographs of the marble-workers of a century ago and the surreal world of the quarries; halls of polished slabs introduce the amazing variety of marbles and travertines from the area, and the rest of the world; and there's marble art and a room of modern marble to prove it's not just limited to churches.

The Apuan Alps, only a few kilometres from the sea, give this coast a certain majesty. The beach at **Marina di Carrara** is divided in two by the marble port, which sends the big blocks all over the world; in July and August the port-resort puts on a big show of marble arts and crafts. Just to the north, on the border of Liguria near Marinella, you can visit the site of Roman **Luni**, a colony built as a bulwark against the fierce Ligurians. The city survived until the Middle Ages; the power-hungry Bishop of Luni survived even longer, until 1929, when the bishopric was combined with that of La Spezia. Excavations have brought to light a sizeable amphitheatre, forum, houses, temples, etc; on the site is the **Museo Nazionale di Luni** (*open Tues–Sun 9–7 daily in summer; adm*), with an interesting collection of marble statuary, coins, jewellery, portraits and so on, as well as a display of modern archaeological techniques used in the excavation of the site, which can be toured with a guide. To the east off the SS446, 20km in the mountains, there is an extraordinary panoramic view over the marble quarries from **Campo Cecina**. The city of Carrara has an alpine refuge here, a good base for exploring the network of trails across the Apuan Alps (the tourist office can provide a map).

Massa

Massa (pop. 66,200), nearly the same size as Carrara and co-capital of the province, was the principal seat of the Cybo-Malaspina dukes. They were never great builders or patrons, except when it came to their own digs – the polychrome 17th-century **Palazzo Cybo-Malaspina**, on central Piazza degli Aranci, with its orange trees and obelisk, and the **Castello Malaspina** up the hill on Via della Rocca (*open Sept–June Sat 9–12, Sun 3.30–6; July–Aug Tues–Sun 9.30–12.30 and 5–11.30pm; adm*), an 11th-century

Getting Around

Transport is very easy along the coast, by **train** or especially by **bus**, with three companies – CAT, CLAP and LAZZI. CAT buses link the Marinas of the coast with Massa and Carrara, and the towns of the Lunigiana; CLAP links Forte dei Marmi and Viareggio with Lucca; LAZZI connects the coast with Lucca, Montecatini, Pistoia and Florence.

There are regular **trains** along the coastal rail line, which hugs the shore except at the mouth of the Arno and the Maremma. Trains to Massa or Carrara leave you between the beach and the centre, but CAT bus connections to either are frequent. The stations at Pietrasanta and Camaiore are inland, not at the marinas.

By **car** you can whip through the dull stretches on the A12, or follow the Via Aurelia (SS1), the main Roman route, though both keep their distance from the sea.

Tourist Information

Marina di Carrara: Viale Galileo Galilei, t 0585 631925, www.aptmassacarrara.it.
Marina di Massa: Viale Vespucci 24, t 0585 240063, f 0585 869015.
Forte dei Marmi: Via Franceschi 8b, t 0584 80091, f 0584 83215.
Pietrasanta: Piazza Duomo, t 0584 795560.
Marina di Pietrasanta: Via Donizetti 14, t 0584 20331.

Where to Stay and Eat

If you are planning a camping trip, there are a lot of campsites stretched out along the public beach between the marinas of Massa and Carrara.

At many hotels in coastal resorts, half board is obligatory in high season (mid-July–mid-Aug); most of the hotels have a restaurant.

Carrara ✉ 54033

***Michelangelo, Corso F Rosselli 3, t 0585 777161, f 0585 74545 (*moderate*). Considered the best hotel, with modern rooms and parking facilities.

Ostello Apuano, Viale delle Pinete 237, Marina di Massa e Carrara, t 0585 780034, f 0585 74266 (*very cheap per head, price inc. breakfast*). The youth hostel, for anyone who's game. *Open mid-Mar–Sept.*

Most of the good places to eat are outside town. Look out for Candia, the white wine eked from Carrara's mountain terraces.

Da Venanzio, amid the quarries in Colonnata, t 0585 758062 (*expensive–moderate*). Here you can try the local speciality, *lardo* – a delicately flavoured pork fat lard preserved in salt and rosemary in large marble vats. Also recommended are lasagne with mushrooms, snails in a tomato and garlic sauce, delicious *tordelli*, or pigeon in balsamic vinegar. *Closed Thurs, and Sun eve.*

Locanda Apuane, Colonnata, t 0585 768017 (*moderate*). A cheaper option, serving delicious *antipasti* and excellent *tordelli* (meat, spinach and ricotta-filled ravioli). *Closed Mon, Sun eve.*

A good town-centre option is;
Roma, Piazza Battisti, t 0585 70632 (*moderate–cheap*). A favourite for simple Tuscan cooking; also worth trying are the delicious stuffed mussels and the very good *fritto misto* of fish. *Closed Sat lunch.*

Forte dei Marmi ✉ 55042

Don't expect to find anything cheap in Forte, though many places reduce their prices

castle with Renaissance additions, including a beautiful, ornate courtyard, loggias, and frescoed rooms. From Massa there are other marble quarries to visit, near **Pasquilio** 11km east, a balcony with views over the Gulf of La Spezia; in the same area, the **Pian della Fioba**'s botanical garden features the flora of the Apuan mountains, more stunning views, and another alpine refuge open all year.

Marina di Massa, on a marsh drained in the last century, is a lively proletarian resort with lots of pine trees; its neighbour, **Cinquale**, the 'Marina' of the old hill town of Montignoso, is smaller and prettier, and between it and Forte dei Marmi there's a

greatly in June and September. For budget accommodation, look in adjacent Marina di Pietrasanta or Torre del Lago.

*****Augustus**, Viale A Morin 169, **t** 0584 787200, *augustus@versilia.toscana.it*, *www.versilia.toscana.it/augustus* (*luxury*). The best in town: a lovely old villa in extensive grounds, set back from the sea. Inside, it is elegant and luxurious. The numerous facilities include a heated pool and chic private beach.

***Hotel Mignon**, Via G Carducci 58, **t** 0584 787495, *info@hotelmignon.it*, *www.hotel mignon.it* (*expensive*). A pleasant hotel, a couple of blocks from the sea. Bright and airy rooms, a garden and private beach with a pool.

Da Lorenzo, Via Carducci 61, **t** 0585 89671 (*very expensive*). Serves beautifully and imaginatively prepared seafood: be sure to reserve. *Closed Mon*.

Pietrasanta

A busy place, full of great places to eat and one of the nicer places to stay in the area.

****Albergo Pietrasanta**, Via Garibaldi 35, **t** 0584 793727, *info@albergopietrasanta.com*, *www.albergopietrasanta.com* (*luxury*). An upmarket hotel in a 17th-century palazzo in old town pedestrian zone. Luxurious accommodation, a conservatory for cold-weather breakfasts and a pretty courtyard garden. It has a unique collection of contemporary Italian art hung throughout public rooms and bedrooms. From the top floor, you can see the sea.

***Hotel Franceschi**, Via XX Settembre 19, **t** 0584 787114, *www.hotelfranceschi.it* (*luxury*). Don't let the 3-star rating deceive: this is another upmarket hotel. A lovely villa set in a shady garden; many of the comfortable bedrooms have a balcony. The restaurant (*expensive*) is excellent; try the house speciality *pesce in pane* (whole fish baked in a bread crust). Prices are almost halved out of season.

***Palagi**, Piazza Carducci 23, **t** 0584 70249, *info@hotelpalagi.com*, *www.hotelpalagi.com* (*expensive*). Just outside the old town walls; newly decorated, with comfortable rooms, some of which have wood-beamed ceilings.

Da Sci, Vicolo Porta a Lucca 3, **t** 0584 790983 (*moderate*). A simple, traditional *trattoria* down a narrow lane, serving vegetable flans, grilled vegetables, *pappa al pomodoro*, spinach and ricotta gnocchi and stewed rabbit. *Closed Sun*.

Enoteca Marcucci, Via Garibaldi 40, **t** 0584 791962 (*moderate*). More a restaurant with a fabulous wine list than a wine bar, the Marcucci is very popular (frequented by the rich and famous), so be sure to book. If you don't want a full meal, you can sample various starters: duck terrine, fresh tuna and tomato soup, cabbage stuffed with potatoes and porcini, parmesan and pear ice cream. Then there are a few pasta dishes and grilled meats (the duck breast with herbs is delicious). *Open for dinner only, closed Mon*.

Camaiore ✉ 55043

Locanda delle Monache, Piazza XXIX Maggio 36, **t** 0584 989258 (*moderate*). An excellent hotel and restaurant housed in a former convent in the old part of Camaiore; clean and simple.

Emilio e Bona, Località Candalla, Via Lombrice 22, **t** 0584 989289 (*expensive*). Just outside Camaiore, offering excellent fare, including duck breast with herbs, or steak with almonds. *Closed Mon*.

long stretch of free beach. Near Montignoso stand the picturesque ruins of the **Castle of Aghinolfi**, a Lombard outpost built in AD 600 by King Agilufo.

Around Forte dei Marmi

Forte dei Marmi is one of the larger and smarter resorts on the coast. Full of very chic shops, bars, clubs and restaurants, it is definitely a playground for the rich and famous. Founded in 1788, when Grand Duke Leopoldo constructed the fortress and seaport to serve the marble quarried from Seravezza, its old loading pier is now used as a promenade. In the 1860s the first holiday villas were built, and today alongside the popular white sandy beach you'll find chi-chi designer boutiques and an excellent market on Piazza Marconi on Wednesday mornings. The public stretch is to the north of the town. **Marina di Pietrasanta** isn't quite so up-market, but in its **Parco della Versiliana** is the last section of the coastal forest, lush with parasol pines, holm oaks and myrtles. This was a favourite haunt of Gabriele D'Annunzio; in the summer La Versiliana arts festival features concerts, plays and ballets in its small outdoor theatre. **Lido di Camaiore**, the last resort before Viareggio, caters mainly for families, and differs from its neighbours in its elevated garden terrace along the beach front.

Inland from Forte dei Marmi is the important marble town of **Seravezza**, where Michelangelo lived in 1517 during his marble pilgrimage to Monte Altissimo, rich in statue stone known as *statuario*. Not long afterwards, Duke Cosimo I commissioned Ammannati to build the **Villa Medicea** with its Mannerist courtyard. The **cathedral** contains works by Florentine goldsmiths, including a crucifix attributed to one of the Pollaiuolo brothers; 5km away, the **Pieve alla Cappella** has a fine rose window nicknamed the 'Eye of Michelangelo'. Another pretty place is **Stazzema**, with a Roman-esque church and more stunning views. The quarries nearby produce the blue and white streaked 'flowered' marble used in the Medicis' Princes' Chapel. Among the mountains is the curious Monte Forata (1,212m/3,975ft), with a hole near its summit.

Pietrasanta

Pietrasanta, near the coast, is a mellow old town rich in marbly traditions. It has undergone something of a revolution in the past five years and is now a chic resort patronized by well-heeled Italian holiday-makers. It is also home to a permanent sub-culture of foreign artists, attracted by its proximity to one of the world's greatest sources of marble and by the facilities around it, from marble studios to bronze foundries. Bottero still lives here part of the year, Henry Moore and Mitoraj, among others, have been temporary residents, using local craftsmen for their work.

The town's walls date from 1255, though its regular street plan suggests a Roman origin. Life centres around the large central Piazza del Duomo, with its Florentine *Marzocco* on a pillar (1514) and the **Duomo di San Martino**, begun in 1256 and restored in 1630 and 1824, with a rose window carved from a single block of marble. There is more marble inside, as well as a bronze crucifix by Tacca and a 13th-century fresco by the school of Giotto. Its Renaissance campanile looks half-finished. It shares the piazza with the **Palazzo Pretorio** and **Sant'Agostino** (14th century) with an attractive minimalist Pisan façade. From here a road leads up to the citadel, or **Rocca Arrighina**, built in the 1300s by Castruccio Castracani and lit up at night, which often hosted emperors on their way to Rome. Cosmave (*t 0584 791297, f 0584 790885*) can give information about the work of local artists. Alternatively turn right from the main gate for the central market building, its parking area adorned with an erotic statue of a woman *en déshabille* pulling a young bull after her. There is often a sculpture exhibition set up in the pretty piazza or the cloisters of Sant'Agostino.

The Mountains Beyond Pietrasanta

From Pietrasanta a road heads inland towards **Valdicastello Carducci** (birthplace of the poet Giosuè Carducci) passing the 9th-century **Pieve di Santi Giovanni e Felicità**, the oldest church in the Versilia, with 14th-century frescoes. The road winds up into the mountains giving lovely views, particularly at **Capezzano** and **Capriglia**.

Camaiore (from the Roman *Campus Major*, pop. 31,000) is an industrial town on the road to Lucca, with two Romanesque churches – the **Collegiata, Santi Giovanni e Stefano** (with a stately bell tower and Roman sarcophagus for a font), and **Badia dei Santi Benedettini**, 8th century with 11th-century additions. In Via IV Novembre, the **Museo d'Arte Sacra** (*open summer Tues, Thurs and Sat 4–7.30, Sun 9–12; winter Thurs and Sat 3.30–6, Sun 10–12*) has good Flemish tapestries. A road from Camaiore leads up to **Monteggiori**, with more fine views. Other destinations include the beautiful **Valle Freddana** and Monte Magno; and **Pieve a Elici**, near Massarosa, with a fine Romanesque church, 12th-century **San Pantaleone**. From here a minor road continues up through chestnut groves to **Montigiano**, one of the best balconies in the Apuans.

Viareggio to the Parco Naturale Migliarino

Viareggio

Up until the 1820s **Viareggio** (pop. 59,000), Tuscany's biggest seaside resort, was little more than a fishing village, named after the medieval royal road, the 'Via Regia' between Migliarino and Pietrasanta. After the 14th-century battles with Pisa, Genoa and Florence, this village was the republic of Lucca's only port. Fortifications were built – Forte del Motrone (lost in 1441), the Torre del Mare and Torre Matilde near the canal (*open on request*). Lucca's beloved Duchess Maria Luisa drained the swamps, developed the shipyards and fishing and resort industries, and laid out the neat grid of streets; by the 1860s the first cabanas and beach umbrellas had arrived.

By 1900 Viareggio was booming. Playful, intricate wooden Art Nouveau buildings lined its promenade, the Passeggiata Viale Regina Margherita. A massive fire in 1917 led to major rebuilding in the 1920s; the most important buildings were designed by Galileo Chini and the eclectic Alfredo Belluomini. Chini (1873–1956) was one of the founders of Italian Art Nouveau, or the Liberty Style, and especially well known for florid ceramics. He also designed stage sets for the New York Metropolitan Opera's premières of his friend Puccini's operas: *Turandot, Manon Lescaut* and *Gianni Schicchi*, as well as the throne room of the King of Siam (1911–14). With Belluomini he produced what has become the symbol of Viareggio, the colourful, twin-towered **Gran Caffè Margherita**, in a kind of Liberty-Mannerism; as well as the **Bagna Balena** and what is now the Supercinema, all on the Passeggiata. You can compare their work with the 1900 **Negozio Martini**, the only wooden building to survive the 1917 fire. Chini and Belluomini also designed a number of hotels (*see p.268*) as well as Puccini's villa on Piazza Puccini and the buildings at Piazza D'Azeglio 15 and Viale Manin 20.

Viareggio is also famous for its **Carnival**. Begun in the 1890s, it has grown to rival the much older carnivals of Rome and Venice, and in pure frivolity has surpassed

Tourist Information

Viareggio: Viale Carducci 10, **t** 0584 962233, **f** 0584 47336, *www.versilia.turismo.toscana. it*. In season, there is an office at the station.
Torre del Lago: Viale Kennedy 1, **t** 0584 359893. Viale Margherita 1, **t** 0584 427242

Where to Stay

Viareggio ✉ 55049

Why not try a Chini–Belluomini confection?
****Grand Hotel Excelsior**, Viale Carducci 88, **t** 0584 50726, **f** 0584 50729 (*very expensive*). One of their most extravagant ventures, built in 1923. The public rooms preserve their original décor. *Open April–Oct.*
****Plaza e de Russie**, Piazza d'Azeglio 1, **t** 0584 44449, *www. plazaederussie.com* (*very expensive*). Elegant and luxurious, with marble and Murano glass in the public rooms, and a lovely roof-top breakfast room and restaurant.

Some Liberty villas survive by the seafront, and several of these are modest hotels:
***Apollo**, Viale Caeducci 76, **t** 0584 407 2823 (*moderate*). Simple and caught in a time warp. Bedrooms are spartan, but the house has original *belle époque* features: lamps, mosaic floors, painted ceilings, plaster moulding, carved wood and wrought iron. Also a garden and a restaurant (*cheap*).
***Al Piccolo Hotel**, Via Duillio 16, **t** 0584 51014 (*moderate*). An old villa a few blocks from the sea, now a modest hotel. *Closed winter.*

There are lots of hotels along the beach, especially *inexpensive* ones – you won't have trouble finding a room.

Eating Out

Viareggio has numerous good restaurants.

Very Expensive

L'Oca Bianca, Via Coppino 409, **t** 0584 388477. South of the centre, by the port, the restaurant overlooks the yacht harbour and has 180 champagnes on its wine list. Sample Mediterranean lobster (*aragosta*), all kinds of fish and other gourmet concoctions. For a cheaper meal try the Taverna dell'Oca next door. *Dinner only.*
Romano, Via Mazzini 122, **t** 0584 31382. An elegant restaurant, reputedly the best, with an interior garden. Creative cooking and delicious seafood *à la Toscana*. Book in advance. *Closed Mon.*

Moderate

Al Porto, Via Coppino 118, **t** 0584 383878. In stunning new premises, with a huge roof terrace overlooking the port. Well-known for its *carpaccio di mare* (raw seafood), lobster *alla Catalana* (steamed and served on a bed of raw vegetables), plus excellent pasta with giant prawns, scampi, mixed seafood and crab. *Closed Mon lunch and Sun.*
Piccolo Tito, Lungomolo del Greco, **t** 0584 962016. A lively and popular restaurant with a big, sunny verandah overlooking the canal, where fish stalls thrive in the mornings. The menu offers no-nonsense, reasonably-priced fish dishes; *antipasto di pesce*, big fishy salads, seafood pastas and risottos and grilled catch of the day. There are pizzas too; it's a good place for lunch.
La Darsena, Via Virgilio 154, **t** 0584 392785. Although the Darsena is no longer the Darsena it once was, it is hugely popular. Crowds flock in for an endless variety of antipasti, pasta with red mullet or with fresh anchovies, and fish baked with potatoes and black olives or a fabulous *fritto misto. Closed Sun.*
L'Imbuto, Via Fratti 308, **t** 0584 48906 (*moderate*). This informal, lively restaurant serves innovative fish dishes such as anchovy *'sformato'*, a tangy 'tartar' of grey mullet, spaghetti with scampi, baby quid and courgettes, rolled stuffed sole with caramelised onions and (a nod to carnivores) duck breast with pears and red wine. The interesting wine list lives up to the food. *Closed Mon.*

them all. At the centre of the action are large, papier-mâché floats, often lampooning public figures and politicians. If you can't make the massive parade on *Martedì Grasso* (Shrove Tuesday, and also on the four previous Sundays), you can see the floats all year round at the **Citadella del Carnivale**, Via Maria Goretti, near the Aurelia in the northwest of the town. This vast new workshop and performance space houses the carnival floats and is the setting for concerts (mostly jazz and rock) in the summer. It is closed during much of the winter while floats are being made. (*Call* **t** *0584 46 2568 to arrange a visit.*) Viareggio also has an open-air **flea market** around Piazza Manzoni on the fourth Saturday and Sunday of each month.

Torre del Lago and Puccini

Puccini spent most of his later years in his villa at **Torre del Lago**, 6km south of Viareggio along Via dei Tigli (buses from Piazza D'Azeglio). The villa, now the **Museo Pucciniano** (*open Mar–April 10–12.30 and 3–5.30; May–Oct 10–12.30 and 3–6.30; Dec–Feb 10–12.30 and 2.30–5; closed Mon and all Nov; adm*), is on the banks of Lake Massaciuccoli, where he could practise 'my second favourite instrument, my rifle' on passing coots. The villa contains its original furnishings, old photos, the piano on which Puccini composed many of his operas, his rifles and other mementos. The maestro, along with his wife and son, is buried in the adjacent chapel.

In July and August the Torre del Lago **opera festival** presents both famous and more obscure works by the great composer. The stage is built out on the lake and the audience sit on the lakeside – beware the mosquitoes. (*For tickets contact the Festival Pucciniano, Piazzale Belvedere Puccini, Torre del Lago,* **t** *0584 359322, www.puccinifestival.it.*)

Most of Lake Massaciuccoli and the *macchia* (marshlands) and beaches to the south are part of the **Parco Naturale Migliarino San Rossore Massaciuccoli** (*open Tues, Thurs, Sat and Sun 8–2; guided tours arranged, to book call* **t** *050 530101/533751.*) To get there, catch one of the boats that run from Torre del Lago, or drive to the tiny village of Massaciuccoli. The wild beaches between Viareggio and Torre del Lago, with their low dunes and scrubby pine forest, are free and undeveloped. The forest of San Rossore, dating from Roman times, is today threatened by the spray blowing in from the polluted sea nearby, which is gradually killing the pines.

Pisa

Pisa (pop. 104,000) is at once the best-known and the most mysterious of Tuscan cities. Its most celebrated attraction has become a symbol for all Italy; even the least informed recognize the 'Leaning Tower of Pizza'. Tour buses disgorge thousands of people every day into the Field of Miracles, to spend a couple of hours 'doing' the sights before leaving again for Florence, Elba or Rome. At night even the Pisani make a mass exodus into the suburbs, as if they sense that the city is too big for them, not physically, but in terms of unfulfilled ambitions, of past greatness nipped in the bud.

Yet in 1100, Pisa was 'the city of marvels', the 'city of ten thousand towers', with a population of 300,000 – or so it seemed to the awed writers of that century, who, at least outside Venice, had never before seen such an enormous, cosmopolitan city in Christian Europe since the fall of Rome. Pisan merchants travelled all over the

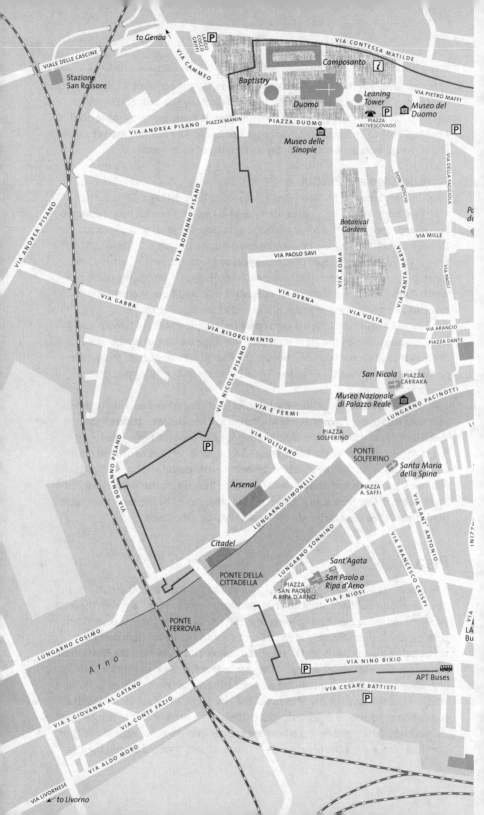

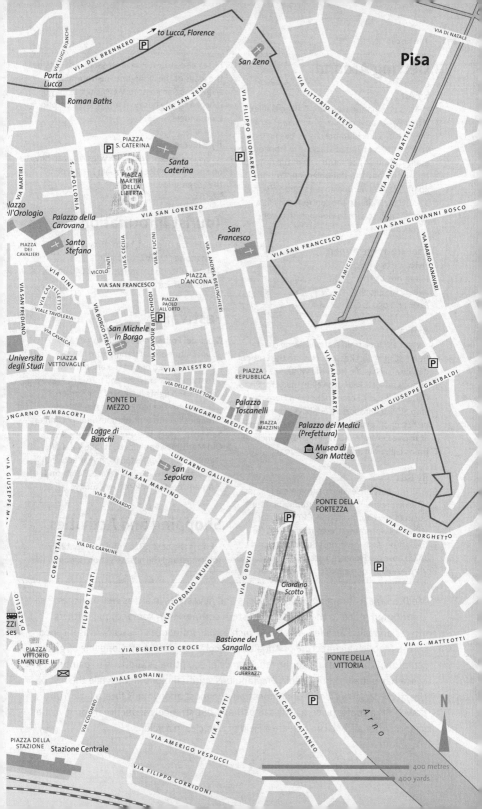

Getting Around

By Air

Pisa's international **airport**, Galileo Galilei, (*t 050 849300, www.pisa-airport.com*) 3km to the south, is linked to the city by bus no.5 which arrives at Piazza Stazione in front of the main station on the south side of the Arno – the airport and the station are only 10mins apart. The Pisa Aeroporto rail station also has a few daily trains to the centre as well as a special train service to Florence (1hr, every 1–2hrs daily).

Car Hire at the Airport

Hertz, t 050 43220.
Maggiore, t 050 42574.
Avis, t 050 42028.
Easycar, t 050 220 1219.

By Train

Pisa has three train stations: some coastal trains stop at **San Rossore**, close to the Campo dei Miracoli (visible from the window, as in the famous adverts Federico Fellini made for Pisa's Campari liquor). Some trains from Florence stop at **Pisa Aeroporto** (*see* above). You would be better off planning your trips through the **Stazione Centrale** south of the Arno, where all trains call; train information **t** 892021.

By Bus

All intercity buses depart from near Piazza Vittorio Emanuele II, the big roundabout just north of the central station: CPT buses for Volterra, Livorno and the coastal resorts (to the left on Via Nino Bixio, **t** 800 012773) and LAZZI buses to Florence, Lucca, La Spezia (on Via d'Azeglio, **t** 050 46288). Many of these buses also stop at Piazza D Manin, just outside the walls of the cathedral. The Natural Park Migliarino San Rossore Massaciuccoli may be reached by city bus no.11 from Piazza Vittorio Emmanuele.

By Bicycle

Pisa lends itself well to **bicycles**; you can hire one at **A Ruota Libera**, Via Galli Tassi 6, near the Leaning Tower.

Tourist Information

Pisa: Piazza Duomo 1, **t** 050 560464, *www.pisa.turismo.toscana.it*.
Piazza Vittorio Emanuele II 16, **t** 050 42291. Also an office at the airport.

Festivals

Gioco del Ponte, Ponte de Rezzo, *last Sun in June*. A tug-of-war dating from the 13th century, played out on the bridge, with costumes, processions and music (*see* p.305).
Regatta and lights festival of San Ranieri, *16–17 June*. The banks of the Arno glimmer magically with tens of thousands of candles.
San Sisto, *6 Aug*. Features folklore displays.
Old Maritime Republics boat race (next one 2006). Hotly contested each year between four old sea rivals: Pisa, Venice, Genoa and Amalfi; hosted by Pisa every four years.

Shopping and Activities

Pisa is the best place in Tuscany for tacky **souvenirs**, and the best selection is around the

Mediterranean, bringing back new ideas and new styles in art, as well as riches. Pisa contributed much to the rebirth of Western culture: Pisan Romanesque, with its stripes and blind arcades, which had such a wide influence in Tuscany, was inspired by the Moorish architecture of Andalucía; Nicola Pisano, first of a long line of great sculptors, is as important to the renaissance of sculpture as Giotto is to painting.

Pisa has put all its efforts into one fabulous spiritual monument, while the rest of the city wears a decidedly undemonstrative, almost anonymous face, a little run-down. It is a subtle place, a little sad perhaps, but strangely seductive if you give it a chance. After all, one can't create a Field of Miracles in a void.

Campo dei Miracoli. Light-up Leaning Towers in all sizes are an amazingly good buy; some have pens attached for the scholar, or plastic kittens for the kids' room, or naked ladies for your favourite uncle. Other specialities are medieval weapons – crossbows, cudgels, maces, whips – and plastic skulls, reptiles and insects. If it is the **boutiques** you're after head down Via Oberdan and Corso Italia.

You can go **horse-riding** at the Cooperativa Agrituristica in Via Tre Colli in Calci, **swim** in the pool in Via Andrea Pisano, or have a drink in Pisa's best cake shop and bar, Pasticceria Federico Salza in Bargo Stretto 46.

Where to Stay

Pisa ✉ 56100

Pisa isn't known for fine hotels, but there's usually enough room for the visitors who elect to stay overnight. Many of the *moderate* hotels are around the train station, south of the Arno.

Inexpensive hotels are spread throughout town and are often full of students, particularly around the start of the university term; it's always best to call ahead, or else go up to the Campo dei Miracoli.

*****Relais dell'Orologio, Via della Fagiola 12–14, **t** 050 830361, *www.hotelrelais orologio.com* (*luxury*). Housed in what was, until quite recently, the owner's 13th-century family home, the Orologio is Pisa's only five-star hotel. While it is the most comfortable place in town, the bedrooms are rather small, but the swish public rooms make up for that.

****Grand Hotel Duomo, Via S. Maria 94, **t** 050 561894, **f** 050 560418, *www.grand*

hotelduomo.it (*very expensive*). Near the Campo dei Miracoli, this is rather dreary.

***Giardino, Piazza Manin, **t** 050 562101, **f** 050 831 0392, *www.pisaonline.it/giardino* (*expensive*). This little hotel just outside the walls off Piazza dei Miracoli, has just been upgraded to a smart three-star establishment. Rooms and baths are modern and stylish and there is a pleasant terrace.

***Royal Victoria, Lungarno Pacinotti, **t** 050 940111, **f** 050 940180, *www.royalvictoria.it* (*expensive*). A hotel since 1839, overlooking the Arno and full of atmosphere. The spacious rooms (still very much in 1930s style) are sparsely furnished with heavy antiques. Dickens and Ruskin stayed here.

***Verdi, Piazza Repubblica 5, **t** 050 598947, **f** 050 598944 (*expensive*). Another good choice in this price range, in the centre, set in a well-restored historic palace.

Villa Kinzica, Piazza Arcivescovado 2, **t** 050 560419 (*expensive*). You can practically touch the Leaning Tower from the rooms of this hotel just off the Campo dei Miracoli. The bedrooms are fairly basic and rather worn at the edges, but the staff are friendly.

***Di Stefano, Via Sant'Apollonia 35, **t** 050 553559, **f** 050 556038, *www.hoteldi stefano.pisa.it* (*moderate*). Nice and central, this hotel has recently been upgraded, with TVs in all the rooms, but not all have private bath.

*Helvetia, Via Don Boschi 31, **t** 050 553084 (*moderate*). Clean and cheap. Some rooms have private bath.

Youth hostel, Via Pietrasanta 15, **t** 050 890622 (no.3 bus). As hostels go, this isn't far out: just 1km from the Campo dei Miracoli; it also provides cooking facilities.

History

Pisa used to like to claim that it began as a Greek city, founded by colonists from Elis. Most historians, however, won't accept anything earlier than around 100 BC, when a Roman veterans' colony was settled there. Records of what followed are scarce, but Pisa, like Amalfi and Venice, must have had an early start in building a navy and establishing trade connections. By the 11th century, the effort had blossomed into opulence; Pisa managed to build itself a small empire, including Corsica, Sardinia, and for a while the Balearics. Around 1060, work was begun on the great cathedral complex and many other buildings, inaugurating the Pisan Romanesque.

Eating Out

Apart from Sunday night, when it's hard to find food, at other times, walks on the wild side of the Tuscan kitchen seem more common than elsewhere – you can find eels and squid, *baccalà*, tripe, wild mushrooms, 'twice-boiled soup' and dishes that waiters cannot satisfactorily explain.

Ristoro dei Vecchi Macelli, Via Volturno 49, t 050 20424 (*expensive*). A gourmet stronghold on the north bank of the Arno, near Ponte Solferino, with highly imaginative dishes based on coastal Tuscan traditions. *Closed Wed.*

Cagliostro, Via del Castelletto 26–30, t 050 575413 (*moderate*). It's hard to believe that you are in Italy at this extraordinary restaurant /*caffè*/*enoteca*/art gallery/night club and general trendy hang-out; the cooking is 'Tuscan Creative' but throws in other dishes from all over Italy. Lunch is a somewhat more modest (and cheaper) affair. *Closed Tues.*

Osteria dei Cavalieri, Via San Frediano 16, t 050 580858 (*moderate*). Offers several fixed-price menus featuring seafood, meat and vegetarian dishes, and good game dishes such as rabbit with thyme, gnocchi with courgette flowers and pistachios and rabbit with oregano, plus an excellent wine list. *Closed Sun and sat lunch.*

Pisa has plenty of unpretentious *trattorias*, which are popular with its student population; many are in the area near the university.

Il Nuraghe, Via Mazzini 58, t 050 44368 (*moderate*). Offers specialities such as ricotta ravioli and snails. The chef is Sardinian, so Tuscan and Sarde specialities rub shoulders. *Closed Mon.*

La Mescita, Via D Cavalca 2, t 050 554294 (*moderate*). In the heart of the Vettovaglie market area, this has a huge wine list but unfortunately, the food is inconsistent in quality. *Open Tues–Sun for dinner, Fri–Sun for lunch as well.*

Osteria La Grotta, Via San Francesco 103, t 050 578105 (*moderate*). A cosy place with a simulated grotto and comforting, traditional dishes, imaginatively prepared and without pretensions. Meat-lovers are well catered for. Menu changes regularly. *Closed Sun.*

Re di Puglia, Via Aurelia Sud 7, Loc Mortellini, t 050 960157 (*moderate*). Occupying a converted farmhouse, 1km from the Pisa Sud *auto-strada* exit, this restaurant is famous for its local organic meat, much of which is cooked over an open grill. The speciality is home-reared mutton, but there is beef, too. *Dinner only, also lunch on Sun. Closed Mon and Tues.*

Pasticceria Salza, Borgo Stretto 46, t 050 580144 (*moderate*). Pisa's most elegant bar/pasticceria has tables under Borgo Stretto's portico, an excellent vantage point to watch the world go by. Come for morning coffee, a light lunch, delicious afternoon pastry or an evening aperitif. *Closed Mon.*

Trattoria S. Omobono, Piazza S. Omobono 6, t 050 540847 (*cheap*). A simple, rustic *trattoria* in a little square just off the main market place. Sample risotto with porcini, spaghetti *alla marinara*, *stoccafisso* (stockfish) with potatoes, and a wonderful fish *fritto misto*. *Closed Sun.*

Vineria di Piazza, Piazza delle Vettovaglie 13 (no telephone) (*cheap*). The food here is simple and very tasty; bean soup with *pioppini* mushrooms, fish soup, risotto with radicchio and gorgonzola. Tables right in the market. *Closed Sun.*

In 1135 Pisa captured and sacked Amalfi, its greatest rival. The First Crusade, when Pisa's archbishop led the entire fleet in support of the Christian knights, turned out to be an economic windfall for the city. And when the Pisans weren't fighting the Muslims of Spain and Africa, they were learning from them: much of medieval Arab science, philosophy and architecture came into Europe through Pisa. Pisa's architecture, the highest development of the Romanesque in Italy, saw its influence spread from Sardinia to Puglia in southern Italy; when Gothic arrived in Italy Pisa was one of the few cities to take it seriously, and the city's accomplishments in that style rank with Siena's. In science, Pisa contributed a great if shadowy figure, the mathematician Leonardo Fibonacci, who either rediscovered the principle of the Golden Section or learned it from the Arabs, and also introduced Arabic numerals to Europe. Pisa's scholarly tradition was crowned in the 1600s by its most famous son, Galileo Galilei.

Pisa was always a Ghibelline city, the greatest ally of the emperors in Tuscany if only for expediency's sake. But the real threat eventually came from the rising mercantile port of Genoa. After years of constant warfare, the Genoese devastated the Pisan navy at the Battle of Meloria (an islet off Livorno) in 1284. All chance of recovery was quashed by an even more implacable enemy: the Arno. Pisa's port was gradually silting up, and when the cost of dredging became greater than the traffic could bear, the city's fate was sealed. The Visconti of Milan seized the economically enfeebled city in 1396, and nine years later Florence snatched it from them.

Excepting the period 1494–1505, when the city rebelled and kept the Florentines out despite an almost constant siege of 15 years, Pisa's history as a key locale was ended. The Medici dukes did the city one big favour, in supporting the university and even removing Florence's own university to Pisa. In the last 500 years of Pisa's pleasant twilight, this institution has helped the city stay alive and vital, and in touch with the modern world; one of its students was the nuclear physicist Enrico Fermi.

The Field of Miracles

For the museums and monuments on the Field of Miracles, you can save by getting the joint ticket (€10.50); this doesn't include the Leaning Tower (adm €15).

Almost from the time of its conception, this was the nickname given to medieval Italy's most ambitious building programme. Too many changes were made over two centuries of work to tell exactly what the original intentions were, but of all the unique things about this complex, the location is most striking. Whether their reasons had to do with aesthetics or land values, the Pisans built their cathedral on a broad expanse of green lawn at the northern edge of town, just inside the walls. The cathedral was begun in 1063, the famous Leaning Tower and the baptistry in the middle 1100s, at the height of Pisa's fortunes, and the Campo Santo in 1278.

The Baptistry

Open April–Sept daily 8–8; Oct daily 9–7; Nov–Feb daily 10–5; Mar daily 9–6; adm.

The biggest of its kind in Italy; those of many other cities would fit neatly inside. The original architect, Master Diotisalvi ('God save you'), saw the lower half done in the Pisan-style stripes-and-arcades. A second colonnade was intended, but as the Genoese gradually muscled Pisa out of trade routes, funds ran short. In the 1260s, Nicola and Giovanni Pisano redesigned and completed the upper half in a harmonious Gothic crown of gables and pinnacles. The Pisanos also added the dome over Diotisalvi's original prismatic dome, still visible from the inside. Both domes were impressive for their time, among the largest attempted in the Middle Ages.

Inside, the austerity of the simple, striped walls and heavy columns of grey Elban granite is broken by two superb works of art. The great **baptismal font** is the work of Guido Bigarelli, the 13th-century Como sculptor who made the crazy pulpit in

Barga. Its 16 exquisite marble panels are finely carved in floral and geometrical patterns of inlaid stones, an almost monochrome variant on the Cosmati work of medieval Rome and Campania. Nicola Pisano's **pulpit** (1260) was one of that family's first, and established the form for their later pulpits, the columns resting on fierce lions, the relief panels crowded with intricately carved figures in New Testament episodes – a style that seems to owe much to the reliefs on Roman triumphal arches and columns. The baptistry is famous for its uncanny acoustics; if you have it to yourself, try singing a few notes from as near the centre as they will allow you to go. If there's a crowd the guards will just be waiting for someone to bribe them to do it.

The Cathedral

Open April–Sept Mon–Sat 10–8, Sun 1–8; Oct Mon–Sat 9–7, Sun 1–7; Nov–Feb Mon–Sat 10–5, Sun 1–5; March Mon–Sat 9–6, Sun 1–6.

One of the first and finest works of the Pisan Romanesque, the cathedral façade, with four levels of colonnades, is a little more ornate than Buscheto, the architect, planned back in 1063. These columns, with similar colonnades around the apse and the Gothic frills later added around the unique elliptical dome, are the only showy features on the calm, restrained exterior. On the south transept, the late 12th-century **Porte San Ranieri** has a fine pair of bronze doors by Bonanno, one of the architects of the Leaning Tower. The biblical scenes are enacted among real palms and acacia trees; the well-travelled Pisans would have known what they looked like.

On the inside, little of the original art survived a fire in 1595, and a coffered Baroque ceiling and some poor painting were added during the reconstruction. Some fine works remain: a few patches of the Cosmati pavement; the great mosaic of Christ Pantocrator in the apse by Cimabue; and some portraits of the saints by Andrea del Sarto in the choir and his *Madonna della Grazia* in the right nave.

The **pulpit** (*c.* 1300), by Giovanni Pisano, is that family's acknowledged masterpiece, and one of the greatest achievements of Pisan sculpture. After the 1595 fire it was left unassembled in crates until the 20th century. It show a startling mix of classical and Christian elements as never before. St Michael, as a telamon, supports the pulpit with Hercules and the Fates, while prophets, saints and sibyls look on. The relief panels, full of expressive faces, are equal to the best work of the Renaissance. Notice particularly the Nativity, the Massacre of the Innocents, the Flight into Egypt, and the Last Judgement.

The Leaning Tower

Open April–Sept daily 8.30–8.30 (until 11pm mid-June–mid-Sept); Oct daily 8.30–7.30; Nov–Feb daily 9.30–5; Mar daily 9–6. A maximum of 30 people are allowed up at a time, accompanied by a guide. Book well in advance on www.opapisa.it. Children under 8 not permitted, 8–12 year-olds must be hand-held by an adult, 12–18 year-olds must be accompanied by an adult. There are 300 steps to the top. Adm.

The stories claiming the tilt was accidental were most likely pure fabrications, to account for what must have seemed a great civic embarrassment. The argument isn't very convincing. It seems hard to believe that the tower would start to lean when only 33ft tall; much of the weight would still be in the foundations. The argument then insists that the Pisans doggedly kept building it after the lean commenced. The architects who measured the stones in the last century concluded that the tower's lean was intentional when it was begun in 1173. Mention this to a Pisan, and he will be as offended as if you had suggested lunacy is a problem in his family.

The leaning campanile is not the only strange thing in the Field of Miracles. The more time you spend here, the more you will notice: little monster-griffins, dragons and such, peeking out of every corner of the oldest sculptural work, skilfully hidden, or the big bronze griffin sitting on a column atop the cathedral apse (a copy) and a rhinoceros by the door, Muslim arabesques in the Campo Santo, perfectly classical Corinthian capitals in the cathedral nave and pagan images on the pulpit. The elliptical cathedral dome, in its time the only one in Europe, shows that the Pisans had not only the audacity but the mathematical skills to back it up. You may have noticed that the baptistry too is leaning – about 5ft, in the opposite direction. And the cathedral façade leans outwards about a foot, hard to notice but disconcerting if you see it from the right angle. This could hardly be accidental. So much in the Field of Miracles gives evidence of a very sophisticated, strangely modern taste for the outlandish. Perhaps the medieval master masons in charge here simply thought that plain perpendicular buildings were becoming just a little trite.

Whatever, the campanile is a unique and beautiful building – also a very expensive bit of whimsy, with some 190 marble and granite columns. It has also been expensive to the local and national governments who have tried to shore up the tower – $80 million since 1990, when rescue operations began. In the first phase counterweights (800 tons of lead ingots) were stacked at the base of the tower's leaning side, supporting the tilt. Then the lead ingots were replaced by an underground support: a ring of cement was laid around the foundations and anchored to 10 steel cables attached to the bedrock 164ft underground. But digging under the 14,000-ton tower is perilous; in September 1995, while workers were freezing the ground to mute vibrations, they found a ring of cement from the last century, when suddenly to their horror the tower groaned and tipped another tenth of an inch.

To prevent similar scares, in 1998 the tower was given a girdle of plastic-coated steel braces, attached by a pair of 72ft steel cables to a counterweight system hidden among the buildings on the north end of the Campo dei Miracoli. The final stage involved removing soil from under the north, east and west sides of the tower from a depth of about 20ft below ground level. This seems to have worked; the tower is not only stable but has actually righted itself about 16 inches (to a lean of about 15ft). It was finally re-opened to the public in December 2001.

Campo Santo

Open hours as Baptistry; adm.

If one more marvel in the Campo dei Miracoli is not excessive, then there is this remarkable cloister, as unique in its way as the Leaning Tower. Basically, the cemetery is a rectangle of gleaming white marble, unadorned save for the blind arcading around the façade and the beautiful Gothic tabernacle of the enthroned Virgin Mary over the entrance. With its uncluttered, simple lines, the Campo Santo seems more like a work of our own century than the 1300s.

The cemetery began, according to legend, when the battling Archbishop Lanfranchi, who led the Pisan fleet into the Crusades, came back with boatloads of soil from the Holy Land for extra-blessed burials. Over the centuries an exceptional hoard of frescoes and sculpture accumulated here. Much of it went up in flames on a terrible night in July 1944, when an Allied incendiary bomb hit the roof and set it on fire. Many priceless works of art were destroyed and others, including most of the frescoes, were damaged beyond hope of ever being perfectly restored. The biggest loss, perhaps, was the set of frescoes by Benozzo Gozzoli – including the *Tower of Babylon*, *Solomon and Sheba*, *Life of Moses* and the *Grape Harvest*; in their original state they must have been as fresh and colourful as his famous frescoes in Florence's Medici Palace. Even better known, and better preserved, are two 14th-century frescoes of the Triumph of Death and the Last Judgement by an un-known artist (perhaps Buffalmacco, who is described by Boccaccio in the *Decameron*) whose failure to sign his work unfortunately passed him down to posterity with the Hallowe'en name, 'Master of the Triumph of Death'. In this memento of the century of plagues and trouble, Death (in Italian, feminine: *La Morte*) swoops down on frol-icking nobles, while in the *Last Judgement* (which has very little heaven, but plenty of hell) the damned are variously cooked, wrapped up in snakes, poked, disembowelled, banged up and chewed on; still, they are some of the best paintings of the trecento, and somehow seem less gruesome and paranoid than similar works of centuries to come (though good enough to have inspired that pop classic, Lizst's *Totentanz*).

Another curiosity is the *Theological Cosmography* of Piero di Puccio, a vertiginous diagram of 22 spheres of the planets and stars, angels, archangels, thrones and dominations, cherubim and seraphim, etc; in the centre, the small circle trisected by a T-shape was a common medieval map pattern for the known earth. The three sides represent Asia, Europe and Africa, and the three lines the Mediterranean, the Black Sea and the Nile. Among the sculpture in the Campo Santo, there are sarcophagi and Roman bath tubs and, in the gallery of pre-war photographs of the lost frescoes, a famous Hellenistic marble vase with bas-reliefs.

Museo delle Sinopie and Museo del Duomo

Opening hours are the same as the Baptistry; adm.

There are two museums around the Campo dei Miracoli. Opposite the cathedral, the **Museo delle Sinopie** contains the pre-painting sketches on plaster of the frescoes lost in the Campo Santo fire. Many of these are works of art in their own right, which, though faint, help to give an idea of how the frescoes once looked. The **Museo del Duomo**, near the Leaning Tower in Piazza Arcivescovado, has been arranged in the old chapterhouse, with descriptions in English available for each room. The first rooms contain the oldest works – beautiful fragments from the cathedral façade and altar; two Islamic works, the very strange, original bronze **Griffin** from the top of the cathedral, believed to have come from Egypt in the 11th century, and a 12th-century bronze basin with an intricate decoration. Statues by the Pisanos from the baptistry were brought in from the elements too late; worn and bleached, they resemble a convention of mummies.

Other sculptures in the next room survived better: Giovanni Pisano's grotesque faces, his gaunt but noble *St John the Baptist* and the lovely *Madonna del Colloquio*, so named because she speaks to her child with her eyes; and in the next room are fine works by Tino di Camaino, including the tomb of San Ranieri and his sculptures from the tomb of Emperor Henry VII, sitting among his court like some exotic oriental potentate. In Room 9 are works by Nino Pisano, and in Rooms 11–12, the Cathedral Treasure. Giovanni Pisano's lovely ivory *Madonna and Child* steals the show, curving to the shape of the elephant's tusk; there's an ivory coffer and the cross that led the Pisans on the First Crusade. Upstairs are some extremely large angels used as candlesticks, intarsia and two rare illuminated 12th- and 13th-century scrolls (called exultet rolls), perhaps the original visual aids; the deacon would unroll them from the pulpit as he read so the congregation could follow the story with the pictures. The remaining rooms have some Etruscan and Roman odds and ends (including a good bust of Caesar) and prints and engravings of the original Campo Santo frescoes made in the 19th century. The courtyard has a unique view of the Leaning Tower, which seems to be bending over to spy inside.

North Pisa

With the cathedral on the very edge of town, Pisa has no real centre. Still, the Pisans are very conscious of the division made by the Arno; every year in June the neighbourhoods on either side of the river fight it out on the Ponte di Mezzo in the *Gioco del Ponte*, a medieval tug-of-war where the opponents try to push a big decorated cart over each other. From the Field of Miracles, Via Cardinale Pietro Maffi leads east to the ruins of some **Roman Baths** near the Lucca Gate; two interesting churches in the neighbourhood are **San Zeno**, in a corner of the walls, with some parts as old as the 5th century, and **Santa Caterina**, a Dominican church with a beautiful, typically Pisan façade. Inside there is an *Annunciation* and a sculpted Saltarelli tomb by Nino Pisano, and a large painting from the 1340s of the *Apotheosis of St Thomas Aquinas*, with Plato and Aristotle in attendance and defeated infidel philosopher Averroes below, attributed to Francesco Traini.

One long street near the Campo dei Miracoli begins as Via della Faggiola, leading into the **Piazza dei Cavalieri**. Duke Cosimo I started what was probably the last crusading order of knights, the Cavalieri di Santo Stefano, in 1562. The crusading urge had ended long before, but the duke found the knights a useful tool for placating the anachronistic fantasies of the Tuscan nobility – most of them newly titled bankers – and for licensing out freebooting expeditions against the Turks. Cosimo had Vasari build the **Palazzo della Carovana** for the order, conveniently demolishing the old Palazzo del Popolo, the symbol of Pisa's lost independence. Vasari gave the palace an outlandishly ornate *graffito* façade; the building now holds the Scuola Normale Superiore, founded by Napoleon in 1810. Next door, **Santo Stefano**, the order's church, is also by Vasari, though the façade was designed by a young Medici dilettante; inside are some war pennants which the order's pirates captured from the Muslims in North Africa. Also on the piazza, the **Palazzo dell'Orologio** was built around the 'Hunger Tower' (right of the big clock), famous from Dante's story in the *Inferno* of Ugolino della Gherardesca, the Pisan commander who was walled in here with his sons and grandsons after his fickle city began to suspect him of intrigues with the Genoese. The **University**, founded by his family in 1330 and still one of Italy's most important, is just south of here, while Via dei Mille leads west to the **Botanical Gardens**, created by Ferdinando I de' Medici for the university in 1595; the institute, in the grounds, has an extraordinary façade entirely covered with shells and mother-of-pearl (*closed for renovation until early summer 2005*).

From Piazza dei Cavalieri, Via Dini takes you south into the twisting alleys of the lively market area, around **Piazza Vettovaglie** ('victuals square') where every morning except Sunday the city's ancient mercantile traditions are renewed. Tucked in the main street, old arcaded **Borgo Stretto**, you'll see one of the most gorgeous façades in the city, belonging to **San Michele in Borgo**, a 10th-century church redone in the 14th century, with three tiers of arcades. Much of the interior collapsed during the bombing raids of 1944. Off to the west, Via S. Francesco leads to the church of **San Francesco**: Gothic, with a plain marble façade, but containing some good paintings – a polyptych over the altar by Tommaso Pisano, frescoes by Taddeo Gaddi, Niccolò di Pietro Gerini (in the chapterhouse) and in the sacristy, *Stories of the Virgin* by Taddeo di Bartolo (1397). The unfortunate Count Ugo and sons are buried in a chapel near the altar.

Museo Nazionale di San Matteo

Open Tues–Sat 8.30–7.30, Sun 8.30–1.30; closed Mon; adm.

On the Lungarno Mediceo, an old convent which once also served as a prison, now immures much of the best Pisan art from the Middle Ages and Renaissance. It has works by Giunta Pisano, believed to be the first artist ever to sign his work (early 1200s), and an excellent and well-arranged collection of 1300s paintings by Pisans and other schools gathered from the city's churches; a polyptych by Simone Martini, paintings by Francesco Traini, Taddeo di Bartolo, Agnolo Gaddi, Antonio Veneziano and Turino Vanni; some sculptures by the Pisanos (especially the *Madonna del Latte* by Andrea and Nino); and medieval ceramics from the Middle East, brought home by old Pisan sea dogs. In Room 7, after all the trecento works, the Early Renaissance comes as a startling revelation, as it must have been for the people of the 15th century: here is Neri di Bicci's wonderfully festive *Coronation of St Catherine* bright with ribbons, a *Madonna* from the decorative Gentile da Fabriano, a sorrowful *St Paul* by Masaccio, with softly moulded features and draperies, an anonymous *Madonna with Angel Musicians*, and a beautifully coloured *Crucifixion* by Gozzoli that looks more like a party than an execution. The last great work is Donatello's gilded bronze reliquary bust of *San Lussorio*, who could pass for Don Quixote.

Along the Lungarno

Take time to head up the Lungarno Mediceo, where Pisa's **Prefettura** is housed in the lovely 13th-century stone, brick and marble Palazzo Medici, once a favoured residence of the magnificent Lorenzo. Nearby is the beautiful 16th-century **Palazzo Toscanelli** (which was once attributed to Michelangelo), where Byron lived from 1821–2 and wrote six cantos of *Don Giovanni*. Behind it, picturesque **Via delle Belle Torri** is lined with houses from the 12th and 13th centuries, which rub shoulders with a lot of new constructions that fill in the gaps left by bombs.

Further down the Lungarno is the former Palazzo Reale, begun in 1559 by Cosimo I, which has recently found a new life as the **Museo Nazionale di Palazzo Reale** (*entrance at Lunargno Pacinotti 46; open Mon–Fri 9–3, Sat 9–2; adm*), an annexe to the Museo di San Matteo, housing a collection of old armour which gets dusted off every June for the *Gioco del Ponte*, as well as some 900 other pieces from the 15th–17th centuries. A new section is planned to concentrate paintings, sculptures and collectables (mostly from the 15th–18th centuries) from the Medici and Lorraine archducal hoards.

Just behind the Palazzo Reale, look at Pisa's other famous bell tower, belonging to the 12th-century church of **San Nicola**: cylindrical at the bottom, octagonal in the middle, and hexagonal on top. Designed by Nicolò Pisano, it has exactly the same kind of tilt as the Leaning Tower itself, built to lean forward before curving back again towards the perpendicular. Ask the sacristan to show you the famous spiral stair inside, claimed by Vasari to have inspired Bramante's Belvedere stair in the Vatican. The church contains a fine *Madonna* by Traini, a wooden sculpture, also of the Madonna, by Nino Pisano, and a painting from the quattrocento of St Nicholas of Tolentino shielding Pisa from the plague (in the fourth chapel on the right).

South of the Arno

After the Campo dei Miracoli, the thing that has most impressed Pisa's visitors is its languidly curving stretch of the Arno, an exercise in Tuscan gravity, the river lined with two mirror-image lines of blank-faced yellow and tan buildings, all the same height, with no remarkable bridges or any of the picturesque quality of Florence. Its uncanny monotony is broken by only one landmark, but it is something special.

Opposite the Palazzo Reale, **Santa Maria della Spina** sits on the bank like a precious Gothic jewel box. Although its placement on the Lungarno Gambacorti is perfect, it was built at the mouth of the Arno, where it suffered so many floods that it was on the point of vanishing in 1871, when it was dismantled and rebuilt by the city on this new site. Although it's an outstanding achievement of Italian Gothic, it wasn't originally Gothic at all. Partially rebuilt in 1323, its new architect – perhaps one of the Pisanos – turned it into an extravaganza of pointed gables and blooming pinnacles. All of the sculptural work is first class, especially the figures of Christ and the Apostles in the 13 niches facing the streets. The chapel takes its name from a thorn of Christ's crown of thorns, a relic brought back from the Crusades. Inside the luminous zebra interior, the statues of the Madonna and Child, St Peter and St John are by Andrea and Nino Pisano. A few blocks west, near the walls where the famous 'Golden Gate' – medieval Pisa's door to the sea – once stood, remains of the old brick Citadel and Arsenal are still visible across the river. Just down from Santa Maria della Spina, the church of **San Paolo a Ripa del Arno** has a beautiful 12th-century façade similar to that of the cathedral. San Paolo stands in a small park, and is believed to have been built over the site of Pisa's original cathedral; perhaps building cathedrals in open fields was an old custom. Behind it, the unusual and very small 12th-century chapel of **Sant'Agata** has eight sides and an eight-sided prismatic roof like an Ottoman tomb.

Down the Arno, the monotony is briefly broken again by the arches of the 17th-century **Logge di Banchi**, the old silk and wool market, at the Ponte di Mezzo and at the head of Pisa's main shopping street, the Corso Italia. A bit further down is another octagonal church, **San Sepolcro**, built for the Knights Templar by Diotisalvi.

Behind it, picturesque **Via San Martino** was Pisa's old casbah, the main street of the Chinizica, the medieval quarter of Arab and Turkish merchants. At No.19 a Roman relief was incorporated into the building, known since the Middle Ages as Kinzica, after a maiden who saved Pisa when the Saracens sailed up to the Golden Gate. At the east end of the Lungarno, there's a shady park, **Giardino Scotto**, in the former Bastion Sangallo. Shelley lived nearby, in the Palazzo Scotto (1820–22), where he wrote *Adonais* and *Epipsychidion*.

Around Pisa

A couple of kilometres up river to the east stands 'Pisa's second leaning tower', the campanile of the Romanesque **San Michele dei Scalzi**. Under the slopes of Monte Pisano, **Calci** has a good 11th-century church and an eroded giant of a campanile; 11km from here, in a prominent site overlooking the Arno, is the ornate **Certosa di Pisa** (*open Tues–Sat 8.30–6.30, Sun 8.30–12.30; adm*), founded in 1366, but then completely Baroqued in the 18th century, in a kind of 1920s Spanish-California exhibition style with three fine cloisters. There are some lavish pastel frescoes by Florentine Baroque artist Bernardo Poccetti and his school, and a giraffe skeleton, some stuffed penguins, Tuscan minerals, even wax intestines – all part of the university's **Natural History Collections**, founded originally by the Medici and housed in the Certosa since 1981 (*open Winter Tues–Sat 9–5, Sun and hols 10–6; Summer Tues–Fri 10–7, Sat– Sun and hols 4–midnight; adm*).

Towards the coast, 6km from Pisa, is the beautifully isolated basilica of **San Piero a Grado**. According to tradition it was founded in the first century by St Peter himself, and in the Middle Ages it was a very popular pilgrimage destination. Although first documented in the 8th century, the current buildings are 11th century, embellished with blind arcades and ceramic *tondi*. Like many early churches and basilicas, it has an apse on either end, though of different sizes; the columns were brought in from a variety of ancient buildings. The altar stone, believed to have been set there by St Peter, was found in recent excavations that uncovered the remains of several previous churches. Frescoes in the nave by a 14th-century Lucchese, Deodato Orlandi, tell the *Story of St Peter* with effigies of the popes up to the turn of the first millennium AD (John XVIII) and a view of heaven.

In 1822, a strange ceremony took place on the wide, sandy beach of **Gombo**, near the mouth of the Arno, described in morbid detail by Edward Trelawny: 'the brains literally seethed, bubbled, and boiled as in a cauldron, for a very long time. Byron could not face this scene, he withdrew to the beach and swam off to the *Bolivar*.' Such was Shelley's fiery end, after he drowned sailing from Livorno.

Gombo, and Pisa's other beaches, the **Marina di Pisa** and **Tirrenia**, are often plagued by pollution, although Marina di Pisa makes a pretty place to stroll, with its Liberty-style homes and pine forests.

The Coast of Livorno and its Islands

Livorno

...There is plenty of space; it is a fully registered cemetery with an attendant keeper. So, if any of you have the intention of retiring to this very interesting part of Tuscany you will be well taken care of!

Horace A. Hayward, on the British cemetery in Livorno

Right from its founding in 1577, the English spent so much time in this city and grew so fond of it that they decided to rename it. It's time that the bizarre anglicization, *Leghorn*, be put to sleep. The city that Duke Cosimo founded to replace Pisa's silted-up harbour is named **Livorno**. It hasn't much in common with the other Tuscan cities – full of sailors and African pedlars, blissfully unafflicted with architecture and art, as picturesque and romantic as Buffalo, New York. Instead of frescoes, Livorno has perhaps the best seafood on the Tyrrhenian coast. Instead of rusticated palazzi and marble temples, it has canals, docks and a very lively citizenry famous for freethinking and tolerance. And instead of winding country lanes, there are big white ferries to carry you off to the Tuscan Islands, Corsica or Sardinia.

History

The site had always been a safe harbour, and in the Middle Ages there was a small fortress here. It's odd no one thought of making a port here long before Cosimo. The Pisani considered it briefly in the 1300s, when it was becoming clear that Pisa's own port would ultimately fill up with the sands of the Arno. Eventually the fortress fell into the grasp of the Genoese, who sold it to Florence in 1421. Cosimo I, in his attempts to build Tuscany into a modern state, first saw the advantage of having a good port to avoid trading at the mercy of the Spaniards and Genoese. Cosimo expanded the fortress, but it was not until the reign of his successors, Francesco and Ferdinando, that Livorno really got off the ground. The first stone was laid on 28 March 1577, and a regular gridiron city soon appeared, designed by Buontalenti, and surrounded by fortresses and canals.

Almost from the beginning there was an English connection. Sir Robert Dudley, Queen Elizabeth's favourite, and illegitimate son of the Earl of Leicester, left England in 1605 after failing to prove his legitimacy in the Star Chamber court. (Perhaps he had other reasons; immediately upon arrival he converted to Catholicism and obtained a papal divorce from the wife he had abandoned back home.) Dudley built warships for the grand dukes, fortified the port of Livorno and drained the coastal swamps, making the region healthy and inhabitable for the first time.

In 1618, Livorno was declared a free port, free not only for trade but for the practice of any faith and for men of whatever nationality. It was a brilliant stroke, designed to fill out the population of this very rough and dangerous new town, and it is, to the eternal credit of the Medici dukes, an act of tolerance almost unthinkable in the Catholic Mediterranean of the 1600s. Before long, Livorno was full of persecuted Jews, Greeks, English Catholics, Spanish Muslims and loose ends from around Europe. As the only safe trading port in a sea full of Spaniards, the port acquired thriving communities of English and Dutch merchants. In the 1700s progressive, tolerant Livorno was a substantial city, a breath of fresh air in the decadent Mediterranean and a home away from home for British travellers. Shelley wrote *The Cenci* here, as well as 'To a Skylark'; he bought his fatal sailing boat in Livorno's port.

Livorno declined a little once the same low tariffs and trading advantages became available in other Mediterranean ports. The Austrian dukes, especially Leopold II, helped keep Livorno ahead of its rivals; nevertheless, true to its traditions, the city contributed greatly to the mid-century revolutionary movements and the wars of the Risorgimento. After unification it was still a lively place, full of men of many nations; it also began to make its first cultural contributions to the new Italy – the operatic composer Mascagni, the painter Modigliani, and several other artists of the Macchiaioli school. The Second World War and its bombers hit Livorno harder than anywhere in Tuscany, but the city rebuilt itself quickly. Long before other ports, Livorno realized the importance of container shipping. As the Mediterranean's first big container port, Livorno today has become the second city of Tuscany, and Italy's second-largest port after Genoa.

Four Moors, Inigo Jones and the American Market

There isn't a lot to see in Livorno. You may enjoy the place and stay for a day or two, or you may be ready to bolt after five minutes. Though the streets are usually brimming, a combination of the prevailing north Tuscan austerity and an excess of dreary architecture make Livorno a disconcertingly anonymous city. It would have been a perfect setting for a German expressionist film of the 1920s; unfortunately, such

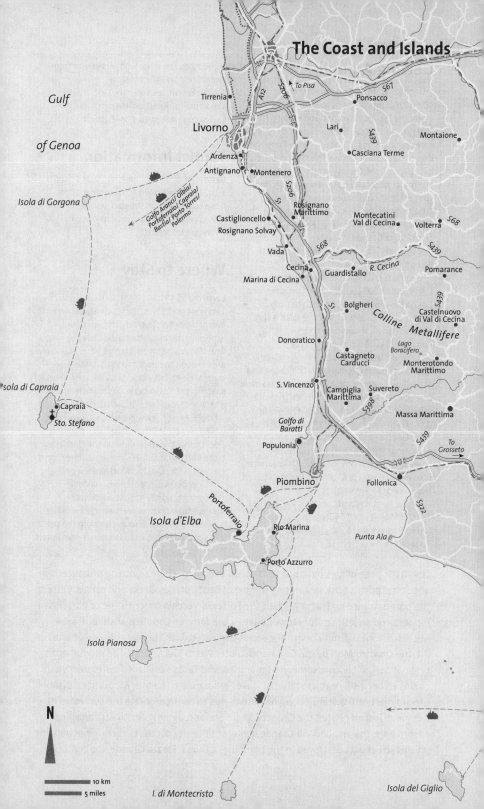

The Coast and Islands

Gulf

of Genoa

To Pisa

Tirrenia

Ponsacco

Livorno

Lari

Montaione

Ardenza

Casciana Terme

Antignano

Montenero

Isola di Gorgona

Golfo Aranci/ Olbia/
Portoferraio/ Capraia/
Bastia/ Porto Torres/
Palermo

Castiglioncello

Rosignano
Marittimo

Montecatini
Val di Cecina

Volterra

Rosignano Solvay

Vada

Pomarance

Cecina

Guardistallo

R. Cecina

Marina di Cecina

Bolgheri

Castelnuovo
di Val di Cecina

Colline

*Lago
Boracifero*

Metallifere

Donoratico

Castagneto
Carducci

Monterotondo
Marittimo

S. Vincenzo

Campiglia
Marittima

Suvereto

Isola di Capraia

Massa Marittima

Capraia

Sto. Stefano

*Golfo di
Baratti*

To
Grosseto

Populonia

Follonica

Piombino

Rio Marina

Isola d'Elba

Portoferraio

Punta Ala

Porto Azzurro

Isola Pianosa

N

10 km

5 miles

I. di Montecristo

Isola del Giglio

Getting Around

Livorno's **train** station is on the edge of the city, with plenty of trains to Pisa, Florence and along the Tyrrhenian coast. Some trains to Pisa go on to Lucca–Pistoia–Florence. There are some connections to Volterra, with a change down the coast at Cecina. The station is well over a mile from the city centre; take the no.1 bus (most other city buses also pass through the centre, though routes are circuitous).

Buses for all villages in Livorno province (the strip of coast down as far as Follonica) leave from Piazza Grande. LAZZI buses for Florence depart from Scali A Saffi, on the Fosse Reale, just off Piazza Cavour.

Livorno is the main port for **ferries** to Corsica, with daily departures (Corsica Ferries, **t** 0586 881380) from late March to early November; it's a 4-hour trip to Bastia, a very pleasant town; some Corsica Ferries call at Porto Vecchio and Elba on the way.

Compagnia Sarda Navigazione/Linea dei Golfi, **t** 0586 409925, has daily ferries to Olbia in Sardinia (a depressing town on a wonderful island) from April until September. There are other departures on the Sardinia Ferries line (**t** 0586 881380) from Easter to October; these go to Golfo Aranci on the Costa Smeralda. A newcomer, with its striking, psychedelic-painted ships, is Moby Lines, which in summer take you to Bastia or Olbia (Via Veneto 24, Livorno, **t** 0586 899950).

For the Tuscan Islands, services are handled by TOREMAR (**t** 0586 896113): they do a daily trip to Capraia, and a daily afternoon run to Portoferraio, Elba, from 16 June until 30 September. The main Elba services go from Piombino down the coast.

All ticket offices are in the port area. For departure information in a pinch, call the Capitaneria del Porto, **t** 0586 826011.

Tourist Information

Livorno: Piazza Cavour 6 (2nd floor), **t** 0586 204611, **f** 0586 896173; in summer, there are two booths in the port, on the Porto Mediceo, **t** 0586 895320, *www.livorno. turismo.toscana.it.*

Where to Stay

Livorno ✉ 57100

As it's a port town, there's an abundance of inexpensive hotels. Many, though none especially distinguished, are across the piazza from the train station. Dozens more crowd the area around the port and Via Grande. Some are real dives, but Corso Mazzini, a few blocks south of the Fosso Reale, has some nice ones.

★★★**Gran Duca**, Piazza Micheli 16, **t** 0586 891024, **f** 0586 891153, *www.granduca.it* (*expensive*). Livorno's most interesting hotel, built into a section of the walls right on the Piazza near the harbour. Inside it's modern; some rooms overlook the Quattro Mori and the port.

★★★**La Vedetta di Montenero**, Via della Leccetta 5, **t** 0586 579957, *www.hotel lavedetta.it* (*expensive*). A new hotel in the suburb of Montenero, overlooking the sea. It is a good alternative to the rather grim hotels

cinematic possibilities have not so far been exploited. There's nothing disconcerting about the **port**, a busy, fascinating jumble of boats, cranes, docks and canals. Close to the port entrance on Piazza Micheli, the **Fortezza Vecchia** conceals the original Pisan fortress and an 11th-century tower built by the famous Countess Matilda. Piazza Micheli, Livorno's front door to the sea, is decorated with Livorno's only great work of art, the **Quattro Mori** by the Carraran sculptor Pietro Tacca (1623). The monument's original design became somewhat mangled, and Tacca's brilliant figures now sit in chains under a silly earlier statue of Duke Ferdinando I. The four Moors are a symbol of Sardinia, but the statue's original intent was to commemorate the successes of the great Tuscan pirates, the Order of Santo Stefano, against North African shipping.

From here, the arcaded **Via Grande** leads into the city centre; every original building on this street was destroyed in the bombings of 1944. **Piazza Grande**, the centre of

in the town centre and has comfortable rooms (many with sea views) and a restaurant ★★**Giardino**, Piazza Mazzini 85, **t/f** 0586 806330 (*moderate*). Near the port.

Eating Out

The main purpose of a trip to Livorno is to eat seafood. The Livornese have their own ways of preparing it, now much copied throughout Tuscany, and restaurants usually prove easier on your budget than elsewhere. Besides lobster and grilled fish, pasta dishes with seafood figure on all the local menus, as does the Livornese dish, *cacciucco*, the famous fish stew.

After a rich meal, try a *bomba livornese*: the local answer to Irish coffee is made with equal quantities of coffee and rum served hot.

Ciglieri, Via Franchini 38, Ardenza, **t** 0586 508194 (*very expensive*). This highly regarded restaurant – elegant, with soft lighting and only a few tables – serves high quality fish dishes such as scampi ravioli, tagliatelle with lobsters, broad beans and deep fried parsley, sea bass with artichokes or giant prawns in a citrus sauce, and boasts a comprehensive wine list. *Closed Wed.*

La Barcarola, Viale Carducci 39, **t** 0586 402367 (*expensive*). A big, noisy place towards the train station, serving up *zuppa di pesce*, penne with scampi, and everything else the Tyrrhenian has to offer, all in the old Livornese style. Try the *Pesce alla Nonna Virginia* (Aunt Virginia's Fish), baked in the oven with vegetables. *Closed Sun and Aug.*

La Chiave, Scali della Cantine 52, **t** 0586 888609 (*moderate*). One of Livorno's better restaurants, serving elegant fish dishes: spaghetti with clams, smoked mullet roe and courgettes, oysters, caviar, risotto with crustacea flavoured with gin and meat dishes, such as quails stuffed with figs and rice. *Eves only, closed Wed.*

Da Motorino, Via Oberdan 30, **t** 0586 896485 (*moderate*). Don't be put off by the rather spartan appearance of this *trattoria* and the brusqueness of the owner; this is one of the best places to eat *cacciucco* in town. Booking is essential.

Vecchia Livorno, Via Scali delle Cantine 34, **t** 0586 884048 (*moderate*). In the *centro storico*, this lively *trattoria* serves interesting variations on traditional dishes; *linguine* with salt cod and leeks, penne with *zucchini* flowers, red mullet and saffron, stuffed mussels and a delicious *fritto misto*. If you want to try their *cacciucco* (thick, spicy fish soup) order it in advance. *Closed Tues.*

Cantina Nardi, Via L. Cambini 6, **t** 0586 808006 (*cheap*). This wine bar is a pleasant surprise for lunch when a few tables are laid, surrounded by wine bottles – who could want better company? The day's menu is written on a blackboard. *Closed eves and Sun.*

Many of the best restaurants are to the south in the seaside suburb of Ardenza.

Da Oscar, Via Franchini 78, **t** 0586 501258 (*expensive–moderate*). A favourite for decades, with a good selection of wines to accompany *linguine* and clams, risottos, and grilled *triglie* and *orate*. *Closed Mon.*

Livorno, features the **cathedral**, designed on a bad day by Inigo Jones in 1605; the present building is a complete post-war reconstruction. Jones spent some time in Tuscany as a student of Buontalenti, and he took a little bit of Livorno home with him. His plan for Covent Garden (originally arcaded all round, without the market) is a simple copy of this piazza, with St Paul's in place of the cathedral. Via Grande continues on to **Piazza della Repubblica**, contender for the title of the most ghastly square in Italy. There are no trees on it, because the piazza is really a paved-over section of the **Fosso Reale**, the curving canal that surrounded the original city of Livorno. Just off to the north, the sprawling, brick **Fortezza Nuova** stands on an island in the canal, now landscaped as a park and a popular resort for the Livornese on Sundays. Nearby, on Via della Madonna, three adjacent churches (now recycled for other uses) make a fitting memorial of Livorno's career as a truly free city. The first is

Greek Orthodox, the second Catholic, and the next Armenian. On the other side of Piazza della Repubblica, Piazza XX Settembre is the site of the Saturday **American Market**, so called for the vast stores of GI surplus sold here after the war, and still Livorno's street market for clothes and odd items.

Little Venice and the Museo Civico

By now, you may be entirely despairing of finding anything really uplifting in Livorno. But just off Piazza della Repubblica is a neighbourhood unlike anything outside Venice. In fact, they call it 'Nuova Venezia', or 'Piccola Venezia', and for picturesque tranquillity it may outdo its famous precursor. **Little Venice** is a quarter only a few blocks square, laced with quiet canals that flow between the Fortezza Nuova and the port, lined with sun-bleached tenements hung with the week's wash. The pseudo-Baroque **Santa Caterina** church is typical of the ungainly, functional buildings of early Livorno. If you're here in late July or August you'll find a livelier Little Venice than usual as the restaurants stay open late for the *Effetto Venezia*, a 10-day summer festival featuring evening shows and concerts and foodstalls selling *cacciucco*, the hearty, locally made fish soup.

Leading out eastwards from the Piazza della Repubblica, Viale Carducci is Livorno's *grand boulevard*, heading towards the railway station. Along the way it passes the **Cisternone**, a neoclassical palace built to house the water works Leopold II had constructed in the 1830s. Just next to this is the **Parterre**, a city park with a rather sad zoological garden.

Along the coast south of the centre, Viale Italia leads past the **Terrazza Mascagni**, a grandiose overlook on the sea. A few streets inland, in a park called the Villa Mimbelli, Livorno has just completed a new building for the **Museo Civico Giovanni Fattori** (*open Tues–Sun 10–1 and 4–7; adm*). This contains a good collection of works by the Macchiaioli, Italy's late 19th-century Impressionists. The museum is on the third floor of the city library, housing a small collection that includes only one work by Modigliani, but a wealth of paintings that lead up to his art. The painters represented include Ulivi Liegi, Mario Puccini, that rare blossom Lodovico Tommasi and Livorno's own Giovanni Fattori, one of the leading figures of the Macchiaioli. Together, they make a natural progression from the Biedermeier art of the 1860s – including stirring scenes of Italian volunteers leaving for the front – to the sweet haziness of the *belle époque* 1890s.

South of Terrazza Mascagni, Viale Italia continues past the **Italian Naval Academy** (where you might just get a glimpse of one of the exquisite old sailing ships the Navy uses for training), and then through some neighbourhoods full of surprisingly blatant neo-Gothic and Art Nouveau villas dating from the 1890s, on the way to **Ardenza**, with its seafront park and marina.

The English Cemeteries and Montenero

For a sentimental journey into Livorno's cosmopolitan past, pay a visit to the **English Cemeteries** on Via Pisa and Via Adua, situated next to the Anglican Church (*ask at Via Adua's Archiconfraternità della Misericordia*). Crotchety old Tobias Smollett, who never stopped crabbing about Italy and never quite got around to leaving it, is interred here, along with numerous members of the British trading community and quite a few Americans. Many of the tombs (dating back to 1670) are truly monumental, some with inscriptions from Scripture or Shakespeare; some are charmingly original. Many of those among the British community, including Byron and Shelley, chose to pass their time not in Livorno itself, but up on the suburban hill of **Montenero** to the south. Byron and Shelley spent six weeks in 1822 at Villa delle Rose (*open by request of the owner, Signor Varvaro di Valentina at No.57*), a fascinating romantic ruin of a place. There is a charming, old-fashioned funicular railway to take you to the top, where there has been a sanctuary and pilgrimage site since an apparition of the Virgin Mary there in the 1300s. The present church, full of *ex votos*, is the work of an 18th-century architect named Giovanni del Fantasia; there are also a small museum, an ancient pharmacy and a number of caves, the Grotte del Montenero.

Tuscan Islands

The Tuscan Archipelago is a broad arch of islets stretching from Livorno to Monte Argentario and enclosing Elba, the only large and heavily populated member of the group. Fate has not been kind to these islands: what with deforestation, Saracen and Turkish pirates, and finally the Italian government, not much is left. Two of the islands are still prison camps, while another is a nature reserve where no one is allowed to stay overnight. Gorgona and Capraia get a daily boat from Livorno – and are in fact administratively part of Livorno. The others will be dealt with later (*see* pp.292–300 and 309–10). Elba is most conveniently reached from Piombino; Giglio and Giannutri from Porto Santo Stefano.

Gorgona

To see **Gorgona**, 37km from Livorno, you'll either have to get permission from the Ministero di Grazia e Giustizia in Rome (quite difficult) or else punch a *carabiniere*. Gorgona, a hilly, rectangular square mile, was first used as a prison by Pope Gregory the Great, 15 centuries ago. A later Carthusian monastery lasted until the new Italian state expropriated the entire island in 1869; it was to be a 'model prison' with workshops and vineyards, but it soon deteriorated into just another lock-up. There's nothing to see on Gorgona, except maquis and a handful of olive trees, and you'll have to be content with the view from the boat, which stops daily on the way to Capraia to drop off new cons and supplies. Ambitious plans are afoot to close the prison and turn Gorgona into a wildlife reserve, but so far nothing has been decided.

Capraia

Capraia, 65km from Livorno, is the third largest of the islands, after Elba and Giglio. It measures about 10km by 5km, and has some 400 inhabitants. Like Elba, it is mountainous, but has fewer trees; most of the island is covered with scrubby *macchia*.

Tourist Information

Capraia Isola: Pro Loco, Via Roma 2,
  t 0586 905138.
Castiglioncello: Via Aurelia 967, t 0586 754890.
San Vincenzo: Via Aliata, t 0565 701533.
Piombino: Via Ferruccio, t 0565 225639.
  Open summer only.
Suvereto: Piazza dei Giudici 3, t 0565 829304.

Where to Stay and Eat

San Vincenzo ✉ 57027
Gambero Rosso, Piazza della Vittoria 13,
  t 0565 701021 (*very expensive*). Widely
  considered to be one of Italy's top restaurants. It's earned its name not only for its
  fish, but also for serving devilishly perfect
  and delicate crustacea, pasta, pheasant and
  pigeon with foie gras; there's an equally
  thorough wine list. If you can't decide, take
  the easy way out and order the *menu degus-*
  tazione. The restaurant overlooks the sea, so
  it's a wonderful place to eat and watch the
  sun go down. *Closed Mon, Tues.*

Bibbona ✉ 57020
Podere Le Mezzelune, Località Mezzelune 126
  t 0586 670266, *www.lemezzelune.it*
  (*expensive*). This four-roomed B&B between
  Livorno and Piombino has charming Italian
  owners. There are antique furnishings, a
  welcoming open fire for colder weather and
  a shady terrace for hot days. There's no
  restaurant, which is a good excuse for a
  meal at the Gambero Rosso in Vicenzo.

Donoratico ✉ 57022
Enoteca Maestrini, Via Aurelia 1 (on the SS1),
  near Castagneto Carducci. A wine bar
  serving Tuscany's best, along with light
  dinners, local cheeses and home-made
  desserts. *Closed Mon and Sept.*

In Roman times Capraia seems to have been a private estate, and the ruins of an extensive villa can be seen. In the days of the Empire, the island was occupied by a colony of Christian monks. Such a setting was perfect for the Christian ideal of withdrawal and contemplation, but it also prevented the Church authorities from keeping a close watch on the colony, and the monks slipped into unorthodoxy and loose behaviour; an armed mission from Pope Gregory the Great was needed to force them back in line in the late 6th century.

When Saracen pirates began to infest the Tyrrhenian Sea, Capraia, like most of the group, became deserted. The Pisans thought it important enough to repopulate and fortify in the 11th century. Genoa eventually gained control, as she did in Corsica only 32km away. This proximity gave Capraia its one big moment in history; in 1767 the revolutionary forces of the Corsican nationalist leader, Pasquale Paoli, and the weakness of the Genoese, resulted in, of all things, an independent Capraia, which soon learned to support itself by piracy. However, French occupation put an end to that four years later.

A decade or so ago tourist accommodation on Capraia consisted of one hotel and two tiny *pensioni*. Today, by a miracle of 21st-century Eurotourism, these have all grown into three-star hotels, and two more have sprouted to join them. It helps that Capraia is an island, and a pretty one, but its real attraction is its natural setting, its deep-sea diving and marine grottoes. In the last century the northern quarter of the island was put to use as an agricultural penal colony, which is what it is today. The civilian population is almost entirely concentrated in the port and only town, **Capraia Isola**.

The port is actually 500m from the town, connected by the island's only tarmac road. In the town are the Baroque church and convent of **Sant'Antonio**. Used as a barracks in the last century, it is now crumbling and abandoned. On the outskirts are the ruins of the **Roman villa**, apocryphally the abode of Augustus' profligate daughter Julia, and an 11th-century Pisan chapel dedicated to the **Vergine Assunta**. Overlooking it all is the large and impressive fortress of **San Giorgio**, begun by the Pisans and completed by the Genoese. The well-preserved **watch-tower** at the port was built by the Genoese Bank of St George.

On the eastern side of town there is a beach under the cliffs with an interesting tower, built by the Pisans, and connected to the cliff by a natural bridge. A visiting Californian at the turn of the century was so struck by it that he built a copy of it on a beach near San Diego.

From Capraia Isola a road leads southwest across the island, passing another Pisan church, that of **Santo Stefano**, built on the ruins of a 5th-century church used by the early monks and destroyed by the Saracen pirates. Near Monte Pontica is a cave, the **Grotta di Parino**, a sacred spot used as a place of meditation by the monks. The road ends at a lighthouse on the western coast. Just south is a sea cave, the **Grotta della Foca**, where Mediterranean seals are still reported to live. At the southern tip of the island is another Genoese watchtower, the **Torre dello Zenobito**.

Livorno's Coast

Livorno's clever tourist office has taken to calling this shore the 'Etruscan Riviera', conjuring up the irresistible idea of Etruscans lounging in beach chairs the way they do on their funerary urns. Beyond Antignano, the shoreline becomes jagged and twisting, dotted with beaches that are usually more than well exploited. **Castiglioncello** is a pretty corner of the coast, but the beaches are narrow and packed with Italians throughout the summer. Nearby **Rosignano** is a similar resort, graced with a gargantuan chemical plant. **Vada** and **Marina di Cecina** are a little better; both at least have stretches of free beach. Marina di Cecina, 36km from Livorno, is a suburb of Tuscany's newest city, **Cecina**, founded only a century ago, now an unkempt town populated by dissipated factory hands and motorcycle-heads. **San Vincenzo** is a booming, awful resort, but it has miles of good beaches on either side, perhaps your best chance on this strip of coast for a little seaside peace and quiet.

Next is the half-moon **Golfo di Baratti**, with more tranquil beaches and some Etruscan tombs from the once mighty town of **Populonia**. Modern Populonia has an impressive medieval castle and a small archaeological museum; ask there about visiting the ruins of the Etruscan city and tombs, which include a so-called 'arsenal' where the Etruscans turned Elban iron into armaments (**t** *0565 29436*). **Piombino**, at the tip of this stubby peninsula, is Tuscany's Steel City, mercilessly flattened during the war, and mercilessly rebuilt afterwards. The government might close the obsolete steelworks at any time, but Piombino will at least remain the major port for Elba. Towns of interest up in the hills include **Bolgheri**, near Cecina, centre of a DOC wine area (Bolgheri is a little-known dry white wine); **Castagneto Carducci**, a pretty town where strawberries are grown; and finally **Suvereto**, a seldom-visited medieval village with an arcaded Palazzo Comunale and the 12th-century Pisan church of San Giusto.

Elba

When the government closed the steel mills on **Elba** after the war, the national and local governments sought to make up the lost income by promoting tourism on the island. They have been singularly successful: Elba has become one of Europe's most popular holiday playgrounds, and with tourists approaching some two million every year, prosperity has returned to its 30,000 inhabitants.

Tourist Elba, however, is no glamour-puss. It is a comfortable place attracting mainly families. Germans in particular are fond of the island; they have bought up most of the southern coast, and many of them return every year. There is no single big, crowded tourist ghetto, as on some other Mediterranean islands, but plenty of quiet, small resorts all around the coast. The lives of the Elbans themselves have adjusted to the cyclical rhythms of tourist migrations. In winter the island seems empty; much of the population stays only to work during the season. Other activities do exist to supplement tourism, such as fishing and mining, but the old iron mines have finally given out after thousands of years. The last of them closed in 1984.

In an unspectacular way, Elba is beautiful. Pink and green predominate – pink for the granite outcrops and houses, green because the island is heavily forested. Like its neighbour Corsica, it is a chain of mountains rising out of the sea, the tallest of which are to the west, grouped around Monte Capanne (1,080m/3,546ft). For a mineralogist, Elba is a holiday dream – besides iron ore, dozens of common and rare minerals are found there, everything from andalusite to zircon. For most people, however, Elba's greatest attraction is its wealth of beaches and particularly mild climate – it hardly ever rains. The coastline, all bays and peninsulas, is over 150km in length, and there are beaches everywhere, large and small, sand or pebbles. Even in the crush of August, there's plenty of Elba-room for all, and if you look carefully, you just might find a beach that's not too crowded.

History

Able was I ere I saw Elba
       The Napoleonic palindrome

Elba is close enough to the Italian mainland to have been inhabited from the earliest times. When Neanderthal Man was tramping through the neighbourhood about 50,000 years ago, Elba may still have been linked to the peninsula. Later peoples, a seemingly unending parade of them, colonized the island after 3000 BC, drawn by Elba's treasure hoard of metals. In the Copper Age they mined its copper; in the Bronze Age they alloyed the copper into bronze. The copper gave out just in time for the Iron Age, and Elba, conveniently, had vast deposits of this as well.

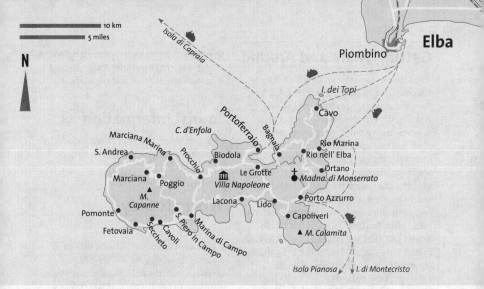

Competition was fierce: the Etruscans and Greeks fought over the island and established colonies of miners to extract the iron, but archaeologists have not been able to find evidence of any permanent settlements.

For Rome, which was expanding across the Italian peninsula in the 4th century BC, Elba was seen as an important prize. After conquering the island at the end of the century, the Romans founded towns to consolidate their hold on it. From then on, whenever the Roman legions ran their swords through Teutons, Persians, Gauls, Carthaginians or each other, those swords were usually made from Elban iron. The mines and forges, then as now, were concentrated on the eastern third of the island, while the beautiful beaches in the rest of the island became a holiday spot for wealthy Romans, as demonstrated by the archaeological remains of large villas discovered near Portoferraio.

The fall of Rome brought invasions, disorder, depopulation and pirates to Elba; the Lombards in the 6th century, under the murderous Gummarith, subjugated the island with their usual bloodshed; Saracens and adventurous barons from Italy fought for the scraps. By the 11th century Pisa had assumed complete control, as the island lay across its most important trade route. It held Elba for almost 500 years, constructing fortresses at Luceri and Volterraio and exploiting the mineral resources. At the time the capital was called *Ferraia*, of which the modern capital of Portoferraio was only the port. Nowadays not a trace remains of the medieval city, and archaeologists are still trying to locate its site.

From the 13th century on, Genoa contested Pisa's possession of the island. In the 16th century, Duke Cosimo I saw his opportunity and seized it for Florence. He built Portoferraio and the walls around it, but soon had to contend with the growing power of Spain in the western Mediterranean, and after some inconclusive skirmishes, Elba was partitioned between Tuscany and Spain. Spain built the town and fortress of Porto Azzurro as a counter to Portoferraio, an arrangement that lasted throughout the 18th century, despite French efforts to grab the island.

Getting There and Around

You'll never have to wait long for a **ferry** to Elba, especially during the summer. Apart from the scant services from Livorno (*see* p.286), gritty Piombino is the point of departure. Any train going down the Tyrrhenian coast will take you as far as the station called Campiglia Marittima; from there the FS operates a regular shuttle train to Piombino (don't get off at the central station; the train has a short stop there and continues to the port). Two companies run services to Elba: TOREMAR (head office: Via Calafati 6, Livorno, t 0586 896113; on Elba, Calata Italia 23, t 0565 918080; in Piombino, Piazzale Premuda, t 0565 31100); NAVARMA (head office: Piazzale Premuda, Piombino, t 0565 221212).

The most frequent passage is the 1hr Piombino–Cavo–Portoferraio trip, and there are also TOREMAR hydrofoils that go from Piombino to Rio Marina and then to Porto Azzurro (2hrs). Services to Elba can be as frequent as every half-hour in July, down to two or three a day in winter. TOREMAR also has a daily Livorno–Portoferraio run (5hrs) by way of Gorgona and Capraia in the summer. Note that the NAVARMA service in summer carries on from Portoferraio to Bastia, in Corsica. To keep up with demand in the summer, Elba Ferries runs hydrofoils from Piombino to Portoferraio; these only take 25mins, but are more expensive.

Elba has just room enough for an **airport** (t 0565 976011), and there are plenty of flights in the summer – mainly to Germany, Switzerland and Austria, with an infrequent service to Pisa, Florence and Milan.

Elba has an efficient **bus** service to every corner of the island and buses depart frequently. Portoferraio is the hub of the system, with buses leaving and returning to the terminal by the Grattacielo, facing the harbour.

There are plenty of **car hire** agencies on the island, in all the principal towns; you can hire scooters and bicycles everywhere too, and the tourist office has itineraries for bicycle and mountain bike trips around the island.

Tourist Information

Elba: Grattacielo building, Calata Italia 26, Portoferraio, across from the ferry dock, t 0565 914671/2.

Where to Stay

Elba ✉ 57037

With more than 150 hotels on the island, Elba has something for everyone. The emphasis is on the not-too-expensive resort, attractive to family holiday-makers. Many hotels stay open all year, with substantial off-season discounts. Beware, however: Elba is a big package-tour destination, and despite its scores of lodgings, you'll need to book ahead. Note that many hotels require half-board in high season (mid-June–mid-Sept). For a wide choice of self-catering accomodation across the island, visit *www.charmingvillas.com*

★★★★**Villa Ottone**, at Ottone, t 0565 933042 (*expensive*). A 19th-century villa on the beach, brought up to date, with a shady garden and tennis court.

The Hermitage, Località Biodola, Portoferraio, t 0565 9740 (*expensive*). This sprawling resort hotel sits back forma white sandy beach and, having lots of facilities, it is popular with families. Rooms are quite luxurious. *Closed mid-Oct–Easter.*

★★**L'Ape Elbana**, Salità de' Medici 2, t/f 0565 914245 (*moderate*). In Portoferraio, one interesting possibility is the 'Elban Bee', the oldest hotel on the island; it entertained Napoleon's guests.

The resorts begin where Portoferraio's suburbs end. Some areas within a few km offer good value in lovely settings.

Portoferraio

Portoferraio (pop. 11,000) is the capital and indeed the only city of Elba. The massive walls built by Duke Cosimo remain, though Portoferraio has spilled out west along the bay. Here the ferries dock at the Calata Italia, where the visitor's introduction to Elba is the **Grattacielo** (skyscraper), a 10-storey pile of peeling paint built in the 1950s,

Tirrena, also at Magazzini, t 0565 933002, f 0565 933452, *www.elbahotelelba.com* (*moderate*).

At Cavo, on the east coast, prices tend to be slightly lower, and there are plenty of campsites and holiday apartments. The same is true of most beaches on the southeastern peninsula around Capoliveri.

La Conchiglia, Cavoli, t 0565 987010, *www.laconchigliacavoli.it* (*moderate – half-board only*). Small, with air-conditioning.

La Voce del Mare, Naregno beach, t 0565 968455 (*moderate – half-board only*). One of many nice hotels on the beach. The best beach may be at Cavoli, west of Campo nell'Elba.

Among the resorts to the west, there are some smart places near Procchio, more modest hotels at Sant'Andrea and Pomonte, and a few that are blissfully out of the way.

***Hotel Ilio**, Capo Sant' Andrea 24, t 0565 908018, *www.ilio.it* (*very expensive – half board obligatory April-mid Oct*). With only 19 rooms, in a modern white-washed villa and its outbuildings, this has an intimate feel. The pretty bedrooms are pretty with rattan furniture. Breakfasts are huge and the obligatory evening meals are excellent.

Eating Out

There are many restaurants on Elba, but few that really stand out. Elba's DOC wines, *Elba rosso* and *Elba bianco*, complement any meal.

Piombino (Mainland)

Ristorante Terrazza, Piazza Premuda, t 0565 226135 (*moderate*). Somewhere to wait for the ferry, above the bar in the port, with delicious *spaghetti alle vongole* and a picture window with a good view of Piombino's steel mills.

Portoferraio

La Barca, Via D. Guerrazzi, t 0565 918036 (*moderate*). A good honest *trattoria* a few steps from Piazza della Repubblica, with all sorts of seafood *antipasti* and pastas galore. Friendly service. *Closed Wed*.

La Ferrigna, Piazza della Repubblica 22, t 0565 914129 (*moderate*). One of the most popular places in Portoferraio, offering extravagant seafood *antipasti*, stuffed roast fish, and an Elban version of *Livornese cacciucco*, at tables on the convivial piazza. *Closed Tues*.

Porto Azzurro

Tavernetta, Lungomare Vitaliani 42, t 0565 95110 (*cheap*). One of many seafood places on the beach in southern Elba, built over the sea for a fine view. *Closed Thurs*.

Capoliveri

Chiasso, Via Nazario Sauro 20, t 0565 968709 (*expensive*). Offers a local dish – stuffed fresh anchovy spaghetti with fish roe and an Elban favourite, *risotto al nero di seppia* (with cuttlefish in its own ink). *Closed Tues*.

Solemar, outside Capoliveri at Loc Lacona, t 0565 964248 (*cheap*). Nice *trattoria* with the best pizzas on Elba. *Closed Mon in winter*.

Poggio

Osteria del Noce, Via della Madonna 27, Marciana Alta, t 0565 901284 (*moderate*). Beautifully situated in the hilltop village of Marciana Alta with fabulous views to the sea. Sit at tables carved from old wine barrels for dishes with flavours of Elba, Liguria and Sardinia; bean and mussel soup, pasta with clams and courgettes or fresh tuna and rocket, grilled tuna steaks and the catch of the day baked on a bed of potatoes and black olives. Booking is essential.

Marciana Marina

Rendezvous, Piazza della Vittoria, t 0565 99251 (*very expensive*). Famous for a curious dish of baked potato stuffed with seafood, but the crustacea and mollusc soup is also excellent. *Closed Wed in winter*.

which is surely one of the most endearingly hideous buildings in the Mediterranean. It contains tourist information, most of the ferry offices, and the Portoferraio bus terminal at the back, the hub of connections to all the towns and resorts on the island.

Follow Calata Italia and its various pseudonyms under the walls, next to the old U-shaped harbour. On the far side rises the **Torre del Martello**, from which in the old days a chain was stretched across the harbour in times of danger. The main gate of the city is the **Porta a Mare** at the base of the U, over which can be seen the inscription of Duke Cosimo reminding us with the usual Medicean vanity how he built the whole town 'from the foundations upwards'; the new town had originally been dubbed Cosmopolis.

Directly inside the Porta a Mare is **Piazza Cavour**. Portoferraio is a big natural amphitheatre; from the piazza the town slopes upwards in all directions towards the walls on the high cliffs. North of the piazza, Via Garibaldi leads up to the main attraction, Napoleon's house, the **Villa dei Mulini** (*open Wed–Mon 9–7; joint adm with the Villa di San Martino, see below*), yellowing, unloved, unchanged since Napoleon had it built according to his own simple tastes; inside you can see his furnishings, books

Napoleon on Elba

During the Napoleonic wars Elba was occupied for a time by the English, and Portoferraio was unsuccessfully besieged for over a year by Napoleon's troops in 1799. Napoleon finally annexed it in 1802, with no premonitions that the 1814 Treaty of Fontainebleau would put a temporary end to the First Empire and send him there.

Napoleon himself chose Elba, from the variety of small Mediterranean outposts offered him, for 'the gentleness of its climate and its inhabitants'. Also, perhaps because on clear days he could see his own island of Corsica. No one, however, seems to have consulted the Elbans themselves on the matter, and they can be excused for the cold indifference with which they received their new ruler.

On 4 May 1814, he arrived at Portoferraio with some 500 of his most loyal officers and soldiers and a British Commissioner charged with keeping an eye on him. But Napoleon soon won over the hearts of the Elbans by being the best governor they had ever had. New systems of law and education were established, the last vestiges of feudalism abolished, and what would today be called economic planning was begun; he reorganized the iron mines and started work on Elba's modern network of roads.

Not that Napoleon ever really took his stewardship seriously. Remaking nations and institutions was a reflex by then, after doing it all across Europe for 20 years. It was the return to France that occupied his attention. The atmosphere was thick with intrigues and rumours, and secret communications flowed incessantly between Napoleon and his partisans on the Continent. On 20 February 1815, just nine months after his arrival, the Elbans and the embarrassed British watchdog awakened to find the emperor missing. The 'Hundred Days' had begun. Later, after Waterloo, a smaller, gloomier and more distant island would be found to keep Napoleon out of trouble.

Elba was returned to Tuscany, and soon after it joined the new Kingdom of Italy. It was hit hard by the Second World War; Portoferraio and its environs were bombed in 1943–4, first by the Allies, and then by the Germans. In 1944, in one of the more disgraceful episodes of the war, Elba was 'liberated' by Free French and African troops, with more murder, pillage and rape than had been seen in the Mediterranean since the days of the pirates.

and other paraphernalia, including the flag with three golden bees that he bestowed on the Elbans. It's worth the trip just to see the contemporary political cartoons mocking him. The gardens, equally uncared for, offer fine views over the city walls. On either side you can see the two Medici fortresses dominating the highest points in the city: **Forte Falcone** to the west (*open daily Easter–Sept 9–6, July–Aug 9–midnight; adm*), which you can visit, and **Forte Stella** to the east, now used as housing.

On the way down Via Garibaldi are two parish churches: the **Holy Sacrament**, which has a copy of Napoleon's death mask, or the **Misericordia**, which on 5 May holds a procession to commemorate Napoleon's death, complete with a replica of his coffin. The **Town Hall**, originally a bakery for Cosimo's troops, was the boyhood home of Victor Hugo, whose father was the French military commander in Elba. There's a Roman altar in the courtyard; inside, the **Biblioteca Foresiana** (*closed for renovation; call t 0565 937111 for information*) has a library of books about Elba and a small picture collection.

Two blocks west is the tiny but surprisingly grand **Teatro dei Vigilanti**, rebuilt by Napoleon from an abandoned church, while east of Via Garibaldi lies the **Piazza della Repubblica**, the throbbing heart of Portoferraio, with its crowded cafés, 18th-century **cathedral** (not really a cathedral at all these days) and the nearby market. Outside the walls, on the eastern side of the port, an salt warehouse has been converted into the **Museo Civico Archeologico** (*Tues–Sun 10–1 and 4–7.40, afternoon hours vary in winter; adm*), with items from the Roman patrician villas, one of which was discovered here.

Around Portoferraio

Most of Portoferraio's hotels and restaurants are in the modern extension outside the city walls. There's a pebble beach, **Le Ghiaie**, on the north side, and another, **Le Viste**, under the walls near Forte Falcone. One of the two roads from the capital leads along the northern coast to the small resorts of **Acquaviva** and **Viticcio**, and to **Capo d'Enfola**, a lovely headland rising sheer out of the sea, barely connected to the rest of the island.

The second road runs south to the junction of **Bivio Boni**, where it branches to the east and west. Nearby is a thermal spa at **San Giovanni**, and the ruins of a Roman villa at **Le Grotte**, on the south shore of the Gulf of Portoferraio, more interesting for its view than its scant remains. There are beaches here at Ottone, Magazzini and **Bagnaia**, the latter the site of the simple, beautiful 12th-century **church of Santo Stefano**, the best Pisan monument in the archipelago. At **Acquabona** you can shoot some bogeys at one of Elba's two golf courses (nine holes), or continue west from Bivio Boni to the resort at **Biodola Bay** and the **Villa Napoleone di San Martino** (*same hours as Villa dei Mulini in Portoferraio but closed Mon; joint adm*). The emperor soon tired of life in Portoferraio and built this house as his country retreat. In later years the husband of his niece (daughter of Jérome) purchased the place and added a pretentious neoclassical façade with big Ns pasted everywhere; it's now another Napoleonic museum, with a little art gallery including a *Galatea* by Canova.

Eastern Elba

Rio nell'Elba is the old mining centre, though it's not what one would expect – it's as pleasant and pastel as any other Elban town, set in the hills overlooking the eastern coast. Archaeological sites, the scanty remains of mines and Etruscan mining camps dot the neighbourhood. There are many undeveloped beaches on the western side of Rio's peninsula, including Nisporto and Nisportino. The road between Portoferraio and Rio passes the steep hill of **Volterraio**, where you can make the long climb to the 11th-century Pisan castle perched on the summit. **Rio Marina**, as its name implies, is the port for Rio nell'Elba. Here, the **Mineralogical Museum** (*open 15 Mar–15 Oct daily 9.30–12.30 and 3.30–6.30. Hours are likely to vary in high summer; adm*) in the Palazzo Comunale has displays of the island's unusual rocks and minerals – few places on earth have such a variety. Devoted rock hounds will continue on to the **Parco Minerario** (*Visits at 6pm in summer. For guided visit, call **t** 0565 962088*) in an old mine. Rio Marina has a busy harbour, its many small fishing boats under the vigilant eye of an octagonal Pisan watchtower. The eastern side of this peninsula, like the western side, has some fine beaches where you can sometimes escape the crowds – Ortano, Porticciolo, Barbarossa among others. On the northern tip stands **Cavo**, an older resort town on a tiny port.

Porto Azzurro and Capoliveri

South of Rio, the road passes through some difficult terrain towards **Porto Azzurro**, built by the Spaniards and now a large holiday town. Until 1947 it was called *Porto Longone*. The fortress, built in 1603 to withstand the Austrians and French, was later converted into a famous Italian calaboose that hosted many political prisoners and criminal celebrities.

Besides the town beach, there are several others nearby, including a bizarre one at **Terrenere**, where a yellow-green sulphurous pond festers near the blue sea in a landscape of pebble beach and ancient mine debris – for those jaded travellers seeking something beyond Elba's mass tourism. During the season, day excursions run from Porto Azzurro to the island of Montecristo.

Just north of Porto Azzurro is the **Sanctuary of Monserrato**, a famous shrine with an icon known as the 'Black Madonna'. The Spanish governor built this here in 1606 because the mountain (Monte Castello) reminded him of the peculiar mountain of Monserrat near Barcelona. Similar Black Madonnas are revered from Portugal to Poland; over the centuries the oxidization of yellow paint has darkened them. South of Porto Azzurro is another Spanish fortress at **Capo Focardo**, on a large oval-shaped peninsula consisting of Monte Calamita and the rough hill country around it.

On this peninsula is **Capoliveri**, one of the oldest inhabited sites on the island. The town takes its name from the Roman *Caput Liberi*, which may refer either to the worship of Liber, an Italian equivalent of Dionysus (this has always been a winegrowing area) or to the free men (*liberi*) who lived there. In Roman times Capoliveri was a refuge for any man who could escape to it. It has had a reputation for independence ever since, giving a bad time to the Pisans, the Spanish, and even Napoleon. Today it is peaceful, with fine views from its hilltop over the surrounding countryside and sea, though much of its scenic coast is privately owned. South of Capoliveri, near the coast, is the **Sanctuary of the Madonna delle Grazie**, with a painting of the Madonna and Child by the school of Raphael, miraculously saved from a shipwreck. The coast west of Capoliveri is marked by two lovely broad gulfs, **Golfo Stella** and **Golfo di Lacona**, separated by a steep, narrow tongue of land. Both are developed resort areas, with centres at Lacona and Lido Margidore.

Western Elba

Beyond Biodola, the scenic corniche road west from Portoferraio passes through the adjacent resorts of **Prócchio** and **Campo all'Aia**; the former is larger and one of the more expensive resorts on Elba. **Marciana Marina**, 7km west, is another popular resort, with a 15th-century Pisan watchtower, the **Torre Saracena**. This is the port for **Marciana**, the oldest continuously inhabited town on Elba.

In the 14th and 15th centuries, when life near the coast wasn't safe, Marciana was the 'capital' of the feudal Appiani barons, the most powerful family on the island. Today, high in the forests on the slopes of Monte Capanne, it is surprisingly beautiful, characterized by narrow streets, stone stairs, archways and belvederes. Sections of the old city wall and gate are still intact, and the old Pisan **fortress** hangs over the town (*opening hours vary – usually mornings, and evenings 6–11pm; closed Nov–Easter; t 0565 901215; adm, joint ticket with Archaeology Museum*). The palace of the Appiani may be seen on a narrow *vicolo* in the oldest part of town. Marciana's **Archaeology Museum** (*opening hours as for fortress, above*) has a small collection of prehistoric and Roman objects found in the area. In season, a cable lift (*departs daily April–Oct at 10, 12, 2.45 and 5; fare exp*) climbs to the summit of Elba's highest peak, **Monte Capanne** (1,019m/3,342ft), with stupendous views over Corsica, the Tuscan archipelago and the mountains of Tuscany itself.

Three churches outside Marciana are of interest: the ruined Pisan **San Lorenzo**, the **Sanctuary of San Cerbone**, who escaped here from the troublesome Lombards (later his body was buried in a rainstorm, so they wouldn't see), and the **Sanctuary of the Madonna del Monte**, dating from the 11th century and one of the island's most important shrines, with a Madonna painted on a lump of granite. Pagan Elbans may have worshipped on this site as well, as did Napoleon for two weeks, after a fashion, with his Polish mistress, Maria Walewska. Another mountain village is **Poggio**, just to the east, with a natural spring where the Elbans bottle their *acqua minerale* – called Napoleone, of course. It's very good, but the Elbans keep it all to themselves.

On the rugged coast to the west and south of Marciana, there are more beaches and resorts: **Sant'Andrea**, **Patresi**, **Chiessi**, **Pomonte**, **Fetovaia** (a lovely stretch, protected by a rocky promontory), **Seccheto** and **Cavoli**. Seccheto has ancient granite quarries from which the stone was cut for the Pantheon in Rome.

Elba's pocket-sized plain, the **Campo nell'Elba**, stretches 7km east of Marciana, extending from Procchio to Marina di Campo and separating the western mountains from the central range. Elba's airport is here – the only place they could put it. Two old towns lie on the edge of the plain: **Sant'Ilario in Campo** and **San Piero in Campo**. San Piero's parish church of San Niccolò has interesting frescoes; it was built on the ruins of an ancient temple to Glaucus. Halfway between the towns are the ruins of the Pisan church of **San Giovanni**, along with a watchtower (*closed; may be viewed from outside*). On the coast is **Marina di Campo**, Elba's first, perhaps largest resort, with the largest beach. The harbour watchtower was built by the Medici.

Pianosa and Montecristo

Two other members of the Tuscan archipelago are included in Livorno province: one you won't want to visit, and the other you usually can't. **Pianosa** is the black sheep of the chain. Its name, taken from the Roman *Planasia*, explains why – it's as flat as a pool table. Like Gorgona, Pianosa's unhappy fate was to serve as a prison island, although it has been closed for many years. There are some substantial ruins of a Roman villa, from the days when Pianosa was the playground of Cornelius Agrippa, Emperor Augustus' great general, but to see them you'll need special permission from the prison authorities in Rome.

Likewise, don't count on visiting **Montecristo**, which lies 40km south of Elba. Once the hunting preserve of King Vittorio Emanuele III, the tiny island, in fact the tip of an ancient volcano, has now been declared a nature reserve. Private boats and day trips organized from Porto Azzurro on Elba may dock at Cala Maestra, but visitors are only allowed to stay on the cove and its beach; the mountain, ruins of a medieval monastery and royal villa (now the custodian's house) are out of bounds. In Roman times this was an important religious site, *Mons Jovis*, with a famous temple of Jupiter; not a trace remains. The early Church wasted no time Christianizing the place, renaming it Montecristo. The first monastic community was founded in the 6th century by San Mamiliano (*see* pp.310–11), who reportedly killed a dragon upon arrival. None of *The Count of Monte Cristo* is really set here; like the Count himself, seeing the place on a map is probably as close to it as Alexandre Dumas ever got.

South of Piombino: The Coast and Offshore

The Maremma

In a sense, this flat, lonely stretch of coast really belongs to Italy's south. History has been unkind to the Maremma, domain first of the Etruscans, later of the anopheles mosquito. Like many southern coastal regions, the Maremma was a prosperous agricultural region until Roman times. The Romans gave it its name: the 'maritime' zone (as names such as Massa Marittima), gradually mangled into Maremma.

Historians sometimes give the Romans too much credit for capable governance; on the contrary, their grasping, bureaucratic state slowly corroded and eventually destroyed the Italian economy. Many centuries of Roman misgovernment – impossible taxes, cheap imported grain and especially, in this case, neglect of the Etruscans' system of drainage canals – doomed the Maremma to a slow death.

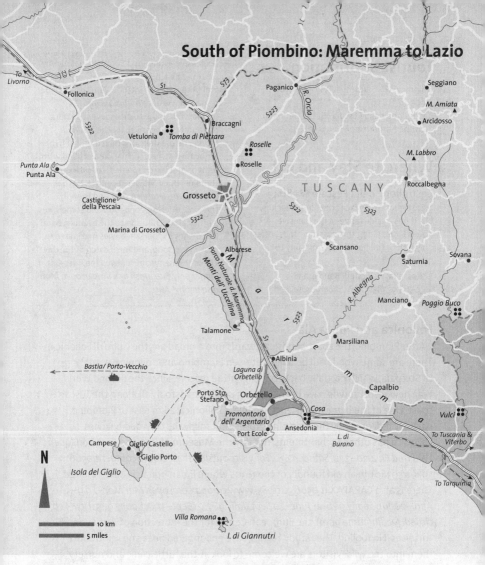

When the drainage canals failed, much of the land was abandoned and reverted to swamps, breeding the malarial mosquitoes that made the Maremma of the Middle Ages a place of suffering and death, inhabitable only by the *butteri*, tough Tuscan cowboys who tended the herds in the abandoned marshy pastures. A considerable body of folklore has grown up around the *butteri*, and the Maremma's proudest moment came in the last century when some of them went to Rome and defeated Buffalo Bill and his travelling Wild West show in a test of cowboy know-how. The first work of reclamation began with the Austrian Grand Dukes. The Italian Kingdom that followed them forgot all about the Maremma, and it was not until after the Second World War that the task was completed. The Maremma today is back on its feet, a new region and a little rough around the edges, but prosperous once more.

Tourist Information

Follonica: Via Giacomelli II, **t** 0566 52012, **f** 0566 53833.

Castiglione della Pescaia: Piazza Garibaldi, on the harbour, **t** 0564 933678.

Where to Stay and Eat

Castiglione della Pescaia ✉ 58043

Castiglione may lack appealing beaches, but it has a wide range of inexpensive hotels – rare along this coastline. Most offer only half or full board from mid-July to mid-Sept.

★★Rossella, Via Fratelli Bandiera 18, **t** 0564 933832, *www.albergorosella.it* (*expensive* – June–mid-Sept half-board only). Near the beaches.

Hotel Miramare, Via Vittorio Veneto 27, **t** 0564 933524, *www.hotelmiramare.info* (*moderate*). Home to an excellent seafood restaurant (*expensive*). Try the *tesoro di Montecristo*, a delicious mixed grill of fish. Innovative dishes, such as crêpes filled with prawns and baked *spaghetti al cartoccio*.

Osteria nel Buco, Via del Recinto 11. **t** 0564 934460 (*moderate*). A cosy and friendly *trattoria*, offering good food and sometimes a musical contribution to the evening. Local fish dishes include anchovies marinated in pesto, crab soup, and fresh catch of the day. There are meaty alternatives too. *Tues–Sat dinner only, Sun lunch and dinner; open Mon also in July–Aug.*

Follonica and Punta Ala

After Piombino, the coast bends eastwards into a broad arc, the Golfo di Follonica. There are some wonderful beaches between Piombino and Follonica, notably La Sterpaia, which partially backs on to a nature reserve. Since the Second World War, new resort towns have been popping up like toadstools all along the Tuscan coast. One of the biggest and least likeable is **Follonica**, 21km east of Piombino, partially redeemed by the long pine groves that follow its crowded beaches. Follonica has other enchantments, notably the **Museum of Iron and Cast Iron** (*open Wed and Fri 4.30–7.30, Sat 10–12.30. For visits outside these hours, contact **t** 0566 59391/59380*), in an old foundry of the 1830s where Elban iron was once smelted. There is also **CARAPAX** (**t** *0566 940083, www.carapax.org; open Mar Mon–Fri 9–5; April–20 June daily 9–6; 21 June–20 Sept daily 9–7; 21 Sept–31 Oct daily 9–5; Nov–Feb closed; feeding time 9am*), the European Centre for the Protection of Turtles and Tortoises. No fooling. They study turtles, save endangered ones and reintroduce them into the wild. Visitors are welcome to look at the turtle clinic and nursery, and see exotic species from as far as the Amazon and the Sahel. The centre is also working to reintroduce the stork to Italy, and has a colony of them in Italy's biggest aviary.

On the promontory that closes the gulf, 14km to the south, **Punta Ala** is a new, entirely synthetic resort, built in the suburban style of the Costa Smeralda. It's an attractive location, with a fine sandy beach and views around the gulf, and it attracts a very well-heeled clientele with unusual (for Tuscany) diversions like golf (*at the Golf Hotel, Via del Gualdo*) and polo (*Polo Club*).

Castiglione della Pescaia, to the south, is just the opposite: much less exclusive, attached to an attractive, ancient fishing village. The beach isn't great, but the town on its hill, with trees and ivy-covered walls, is one of the more pleasant detours on this coast. The Spanish left a 16th-century castle, the Rocca Aragonese, and the church of

San Giovanni has an interesting tower that could pass for a minaret. From the harbour, Navimaremma offers summer island cruises; the tourist office has details.

Grosseto

For the original edition of this book, years ago, we enjoyed writing the following:

When Duke Cosimo I gobbled up Grosseto in 1559, along with the rest of the Sienese republic, he resolved to make it into a fortress town, guarding his southern borders against Spain and the pope. Following the manic geometry of the age, Cosimo's architects enclosed Grosseto in a nearly perfect hexagon of walls. But as any good Chinese geomancer (or reader of Doris Lessing's Shikasta*) could have told the Duke, one can't take such matters lightly. Maybe it was the wrong polygon for the prevailing telluric forces, but Grosseto (pop. 70,000) has certainly been suffering from some strange vibrations. Come to Grosseto, and you will find a city of Art Nouveau buildings and perverse teenagers, a city conducive to hallucinations, its streets alive with swirls of dust and flying plastic bags. Its citizens have a penchant for punk music and American football (the Grosseto 61ers), also, so they claim, the highest rate of drug addiction in Italy. It is the only city in Italy, outside Calabria, where you cannot buy a decent slice of pizza.*

God knows where the flying bags, the hallucinations and the 61ers have gone, and today the teenagers look no more perverse than anywhere else in Europe. Under the prevailing prosperity, the natural Tuscan sense of order and propriety has slowly been asserting itself here. Instead of punk music, there is a busy *assessorato della cultura* in the town hall laying on dance and chamber music concerts and scholarly conferences. Italy's Most Improved Town, always a likeable place, grows steadily more normal, even pleasant – though the *pizza a taglio* situation still needs some work.

Around La Vasca

Via Carducci leads you from the station towards the fearful hexagon, passing Mussolini's contribution to the city, the circular Piazza Fratelli Rosselli that is really known to one and all as **La Vasca** (which can mean 'tub' or 'toilet bowl'); here the starring role is played by an exuberant Mussolini **post office**, with heroic statuary in travertine. The main gate is only a block away. Cosimo's walls are perfectly preserved, done in tidy, reddish brick festooned with Medici balls. Much of the old city looks very Spanish; the Art Nouveau pharmacies and shoe shops along the main street, Corso Carducci, contribute to the effect, as does the arcaded Piazza del Duomo, very like a Spanish *Plaza Mayor*. The **Duomo**, built 1190–1250, suffered grievously from over-ambitious restoration in the 1840s; the façade looks more like a Hollywood prop than a genuine cathedral. Have a look inside for a genuinely lovely painting, Matteo di Giovanni's *Madonna delle Grazie* (1470). Around the side of the Duomo there is an interesting sundial, and in the piazza an allegorical monument to the Maremma's benefactor, the Lorraine Grand Duke Leopold II; the woman he is raising up represents the suffering Maremma, and the snake he's crushing is Malaria.

Around the corner in Piazza Baccarini, two museums, collectively called the **Museo Archaeologica e d'Aste della Maremma** (*t 0564 488750; open summer Tues–Sun 10–1*

Getting Around

Trains depart regularly for Siena, via Roccastrada and Buonconvento (seven a day, some of which continue on to Florence), and on the coastal line for Livorno, or Orbetello and Rome. RAMA buses (t 0564 25215) have connections to Siena (seven a day) and every town in Grosseto province, including Massa Marittima (twice daily, see **Hill Towns West of Siena**, p.389), Arcidosso and Pitigliano (five daily, see **Southern Tuscany**, pp.414 and 418). Everything leaves from the train station.

Tourist Information

Grosseto: Viale Monterosa 206, t 0564 462611, www.lamaremma.info.

Where to Stay and Eat

Grosseto ✉ 58100

Hotels here tend to be simple. In the unlikely event that you can't find anywhere, the city's *Consorzio Albergatori* might be able to help (t 0564 415446).

★★★★**Bastiani Grand Hotel**, Via Gioberti 64, t 0564 20047, f 0564 29321, www.hotel bastiani.com (*expensive*). One exception to the rule is this city-centre hotel, housed in a gracious 1890s palazzo.

★★★**Leon d'Oro**, Via San Martino 46, t 0564 22128, f 0564 22578 (*moderate*). Offers double rooms with bath, and the restaurant's not bad either. *Closed Sun.*

Buca di San Lorenzo, Via Manetti 1, t 0564 25142 (*moderate*). Dug into the Medicean walls. Menus depend on what is available at the market; only the freshest fish is used. All pasta is home-made. *Closed Sun.*

Il Canto del Gallo, Via Mazzini 29, t 0564 414589 (*moderate*). A tiny *trattoria* in the centre of the old town. The owner will advise you on what to eat and then prepare it personally. Home-made pasta with wild boar, spelt soup, wild boar stew and other local specialities; fish if you order in advance. Booking essential. *Closed lunch and Sun.*

Da Remo, Rispescia Stazione, t 0564 405014 (*moderate*). A few km south of Grosseto, just off the Aurelia. Mixed *antipasti* include a superb *insalata di mare* and grilled oysters while the sea bass cooked *al cartoccio* (in foil) with mussels, clams and local herbs is sublime. *Closed Wed.*

La Taverna Etrusca, Vetulonia (*cheap*). If you're going up to visit Vetulonia, try this good inexpensive *trattoria* at the top of town; it also has some reasonably priced rooms.

and 5–8; Nov–Feb Tues–Fri 9–1, Sat–Sun 9.30–1 and 4.30–7; Nov and April Tues–Sun 9.30–1 and 4.30–7) want to show you something of life in this region before there ever was a Grosseto. Some parts of the this coastline just can't stand still. Thousands of years ago, Grosseto and most of its surrounding plain were under water; by the time of the Etruscans, the sea had receded, leaving a large lake on the plain. Two wealthy Etruscan cities, *Vetulonia* and *Roselle* (*see* below), stood on the hills above the lake, and they contributed most of the items here: cinerary urns with scenes from Homer, architectural fragments and delicate terracottas, some preserving bits of their original paint. The collection is not a rich one, though well organized and relentlessly didactic. Up on the third floor, the city **Pinacoteca** (*recently reopened after restoration, same opening hours as the Archaeology Museum*) houses some good Sienese art, including an amazing, very Byzantine *Last Judgement* by the 13th-century artist Guido da Siena.

Just north of the museum, the church of San Francesco has an early work by Duccio di Buoninsegna, the crucifix above the high altar, and also some good 13th-century frescoes. From here, you can start a walk around the Medicean walls. After Italian unification, the bastions were landscaped into beautiful semi-tropical gardens; some are still well kept, while others have decayed into spooky jungles. The liveliest parts of Grosseto are the shopping streets around Piazza del Mercato; nearby, just outside the walls, mornings see a large, almost picturesque street market.

Roselle and Vetulonia

You can learn more about these two Etruscan towns from the Grosseto museum than from visiting the ruins, although this can be fun. **Roselle**, 7km north of the city, is the mother city of Grosseto. It survived Roman rule better than many other Etruscan cities, but by the 5th century it was almost abandoned. Nevertheless, the bishops of Roselle hung on until 1178, when the seat was transferred to Grosseto.

Like many other Etruscan towns, Roselle stands atop a high plateau and is surrounded by over 3km of walls. A Roman road leads up to the complex where there are still a few building foundations, remains of the baths, the imperial forum and the outline of the Roman amphitheatre, a medieval tower, and necropolises. North of the site are the ruins of a **Roman villa** (*open daily 9–dusk*) with parts of its original mosaic floor paving. The last occupant operated a forge here to melt down bronze statues.

Vetulonia, 17km from Grosseto, above the Via Aurelia west of Braccagni, lives on in its worthy successor, Massa Marittima (*see* pp.363–5). On the site itself, a miniature hill town survives, set in rugged but lovely countryside with occasional views over the Tyrrhenian and the islands. Like Roselle, it lasted until the Middle Ages, and was probably destroyed in a 14th-century revolt against its Pisan overlords.

Bits of old Vetulonia can be seen in the **Aree Archeologiche** (signposted) and the nearby **museum** (*open daily winter 9–5; summer 9–7.30; joint adm for both*). The scanty ruins are more Roman and medieval than Etruscan, but on the periphery are some interesting tombs (also signed): the massive **Tomba della Pietrera** and the unique **Il Diavolino** (7th century BC). Both have a long corridor under a tumulus, with an arched burial chamber in the centre; the Diavolino has a window to the sky.

Monti dell'Uccellina: The Maremma Nature Park

Open daily from 8 until 1 hour before sunset; adm. The visitors' centre is at Alberese, west of the coastal Via Aurelia/SS1; park and take the regular shuttle service into the park. During the summer some areas can only be visited by guided tour. Adm limited; during busiest times – Easter, 29 April–1 May, July and August – it's best to call ahead, **t** *0564 407098; ask about guided tours in English during the summer.*

One effect of the Maremma's history of abandonment is a beautiful, unspoiled coast. In the 1950s and 1960s developers followed the DDT wherever they could, but the government managed to set aside a few of the best parts. The **Monti dell'Uccellina**, a ragged chain of hills south of Grosseto, largely covered with umbrella pines, is an important pit stop for migratory birds between Europe and Africa, hence the name.

The park has some pretty strict rules. Only 500 people a day, and no cars and no dogs, are allowed to enter. Nine walks have been laid out, lasting 2–6 hours, and visitors are expected to keep to them. Note that one of the walks begins from a separate park entrance at Talamone, further south, but it doesn't connect to the others. The visitors' centre recommends you bring good shoes and some water, and if you like they can book you an experienced guide for about €12 an hour.

For such a small area (roughly 5km by 15km), the park has a lot to see: nine old defence towers, dozens of caves and the ruins of an 11th-century monastery, **San Rabano**, that belonged to the Knights of Malta. It retains its campanile and some early medieval stone-carving. Where the park meets the sea there is a strip of fabulous beaches. Despite the park status, some people still make their living here, herding cattle, cutting cork oak and gathering pine nuts for Italy's pastry cooks.

The park's landscape ranges from swamps to heather and scented *macchia* (mixed Mediterranean scrub) to pine groves, and includes among its fauna wild horses, deer and boar, along with the *uccellini* themselves – herons, eagles and falcons, ospreys and kingfishers, every sort of duck, and that most overdressed of all waterfowl, the *cavaliere d'Italia*. Some peripheral areas can be toured on horseback, and Il Rialto at Albarese (**t** *0564 407 1020*) can fix you up with a steed; they also rent bikes and canoes.

Talamone

The Sienese Republic never really had a port, gravely hampering its foreign trade. Now and then, it tried to make one out of **Talamone**, a fishing village at the tip of the Monti dell'Uccellina. Unfortunately, the little harbour couldn't be kept clear, a continuing embarrassment for the republic; even Dante dropped a jibe about foolishly 'hoping from Talamone'. Garibaldi had better luck: when in 1860 he and his 'Thousand' chose to stop here rather than Sardinia, they avoided the orders for their arrest that had been sent by the treacherous Count Cavour; Garibaldi also found a cache of weapons in Orbetello, which came in handy during the conquest of Sicily.

Today the walled village on its rock has become a discreet, laid-back resort with a small marina. Above, a 16th-century Spanish castle sits like an abstract modern sculpture, set to house a new museum devoted to nature in the Monti dell'Uccellina.

Monte Argentario

In the last decade or so, this curiosity of the Tuscan coast has grown popular. It has much going for it: some attractive old towns, a genuine Mediterranean feeling and matching scenery, a noticeable attraction on the humdrum Tuscan coast. Once, long ago, Argentario was an island, the member of the Tuscan archipelago closest to the shore. No one seems able to explain how it happened, but the Tyrrhenian currents gradually built up two symmetrical sand bars, connecting the rugged, mountainous island to the mainland. In between, there was a peninsula with the Etruscan, then Roman city of Orbetello; the Romans built a causeway on to Argentario that split the natural lagoon in half. It is said that sailors named the Argentario in classical times, noticing the bright flashes of silver from the olive trees that still cover its slopes.

Most books describe Porto Santo Stefano and Porto Ercole as 'exclusive', even 'posh'. Not true. The Argentario attracts its share of the high life, particularly the yachting crowd from Rome, and it's a bit pricier than other resorts. But the peninsula has not become an overcrowded beach Babylon like Elba. The beaches are not special, and Tuscany's art and other attractions are far away, but on balance, if you're after the best place for a seaside holiday in the region, the Argentario presents a strong case.

Orbetello

Go to the northern tip of **Orbetello**'s peninsula, near the causeway, and look over the water; below the modern breakwater, you can see bits of ancient wall in huge irregular blocks. These are the sole remnants of Etruscan Orbetello, probably the biggest port on the Etruscan coast, and defensible enough to give the city a minor historical role over the centuries. The Byzantines held out longer here than anywhere else on this coast; the city then fell into the hands of the Three Fountains Abbey in Rome, who handed it to the Pope – until 1980 the pope was also bishop of Orbetello. After the treaty of Câteau-Cambrésis in 1559, Orbetello became capital of a new province – the Spanish military *Presidio*, from which imperialist Spain could menace both Tuscany and the Pope, ruled by a viceroy directly responsible to the King.

The Spanish Presidio lasted only until 1707, but it had a strong impact on the area's buildings and its people. Orbetello was briefly something of a resort, but passed this role on to Porto Ercole and Porto Santo Stefano, and its most recent flash of glory came in the 1930s when Mussolini made it Italy's main seaplane base. Fascist hero Italo Balbo began his famous transatlantic flight from the lagoon in 1933, landing at the opening of the Chicago World's Fair.

Confined on its peninsula, with its palm trees and sun-bleached Spanish walls, Orbetello (pop. 13,500) is a charming town, where buses barely squeeze through the main gate. Viale Italia, the main street, runs down the centre of the peninsula; just north on Piazza della Repubblica, the **cathedral**'s façade has a sculpted portal and rose window from 1376, though its interior was rebuilt in the 1600s.

Orbetello's **lagoons**, on average about 3ft deep, are partially used for fish farms, but most of the northern half has been declared a nature reserve, run by the World Wild Fund for Nature. Like the Monti dell'Uccellina, the area is a breeding ground for marine birds, and also storks and a species of eagle, not to mention the stilt plover, the bee-eater and the lesser hen harrier. Their nesting period lasts from April to October, and from May to September the reserve is closed to humans. The **visitors' centre** is on the coast road between Orbetello and Albinia (*open Oct–April for guided tours, Thurs, Sat and Sun, 10 and 3;* **t** *0564 820297 for info; adm*).

Porto Ercole and Porto Santo Stefano

Over the causeway from Orbetello on to Monte Argentario, you can go either north or south to begin the *gita panoramica*, the 24km road that circles the island (it offers some exceptional views, but it's not surfaced the whole way and you won't get round unless you have a jeep). To the south, **Porto Ercole** wraps itself around a yacht-filled harbour, guarded on either side by Spanish fortresses. Forte Stella and Forte San Filippo were probably the last word in 16th-century military architecture, with low, sloping walls and pointed bastions draped over the cliffs; today they are an ominous, surreal sight. San Filippo is the most interesting, though you can't visit – it has been

Getting Around

Orbetello is the centre for public transport around the Argentario, with a bus station just off Piazza della Repubblica. There are regular **buses** for Porto Ercole, Porto S. Stefano, Grosseto, and the **railway station**, about 2km east of town, on the Grosseto–Rome coastal line, plus daily buses to Capalbio and Pitigliano.

Tourist Information

Orbetello: Piazza della Reppublica, t 0564 860447.
Porto Santo Stefano: Corso Umberto 55, t 0564 814208.
Capalbio: Capalbio Scalo, t 0564 8638.

Where to Stay and Eat

Orbetello ✉ 58035

★★★San Biagio Relais, Via Dante 34, t 0564 860543, f 0564 867787, www.sanbiago relais.com (very expensive) Another good choice in the centre of town; this new, classy hotel (housed in an elegant palazzo) has 17 comfortable, individually furnished rooms and suites decorated in warm colours and furnished with antiques.

★★★Hotel Relais Presidi, Via Mura di Levante 34, t 0564 867601, f 0564 860432, www.ipresidi.com (expensive). The best in Orbetello, with lagoon views and a restaurant. Most rooms have balconies.

★Piccolo Parigi, Corso Italia 169, t 0564 867233 (inexpensive). Delightful, very friendly and very Mediterranean, in the middle of town, ideal if you're travelling on a budget.

Osteria del Lupacante, Corso Italia 103, t 0564 867618 (moderate). Wonderful fresh seafood, from octopus and potato salad to spaghetti with sea urchin or zucchini flowers stuffed with baby squid. Closed Tues in winter.

I Pescatori, Via Leopardi 9, t 0564 860611 (cheap). Opened by the local fisherman's co-op, and featuring only fish caught in the lagoon, this simple restaurant (where you eat off plastic plates) is delightful. Housed in a former warehouse on the lagoon, you select your fish and pay at the cash desk then sit down to smoked mullet roe, pasta with John Dory or mullet, roast catch of the day or eel. The local wine is cold and cheap. Open daily for dinner mid-June–mid Sept, Fri–Sun for dinner in winter.

Porto Ercole ✉ 58018

★★★★Il Pellicano, Cala dei Santi, a cove near Porto Ercole, t 0564 858111, f 0564 833418,

converted into holiday flats. Above the souvenir shops and seafood restaurants of the harbour, there is a fine old town, entered through a Gothic gate constructed by the Sienese. Little Piazza Santa Barbara is the centre, with the dignified 17th-century palace of the Spanish governor, and a view over the harbour below. Caravaggio was buried in the church of Sant'Erasmo in 1609 after dying of malaria in a tavern nearby; the artist was on his way back from Malta to Rome, where he had hoped the Pope would pardon him for a tennis-court murder committed years before. Beyond Porto Ercole, the coast road twists and turns under the slopes of Il Telegrafo, Argentario's highest peak (635m/2,083ft). One feature of the gita panoramica is the many defence towers, some built by the Sienese, others by the Spaniards.

On the northern side of the Argentario, **Porto Santo Stefano** makes a matching bookend for Porto Ercole. Larger than its sister town, this one also began as a sleepy fishing village. Now the fishing boats are elbowed off to the side of the port by speedboats, big shiny yachts and the Giglio ferries, and the old town has become lost in the agglomeration of hotels and villas on the surrounding hills. However, it remains less exclusive than Porto Ercole and more of a real community than an exclusive yachting port. There are really two harbours: the first, larger one has the

www.pellicanohotel.com (*luxury – half-board obligatory mid-June–Sept*). If you've bushels of money and like swilling gin with yachtsmen and Italian TV stars, this Relais et Châteaux hotel provides every imaginable amenity. There's a beach, a pool, windsurfing and every other water sport, plus tennis – not to mention a first-class restaurant.

★★★★Torre di Calapiccola, t 0564 825111, f 0564 825235, www.torredicalapiccola.com (*luxury*). An apartment complex spectacularly set high above the sea, with a beach and activities, or for peace and quiet on the western tip of the peninsula.

★★★Don Pedro, Via Panoramica, t 0564 833914, f 0564 883129, www.hoteldonpedro.it (*very expensive*). Above the town, but some way from the nearest beach.

★La Conchiglia, Via della Marina, t 0564 833134 (*moderate*). One of the few moderate places on Argentario proper.

Osteria I Nobili Santi, Via dell'Ospizio 8, t 0564 833015 (*moderate*). This excellent little fish restaurant serves up elegant dishes of the freshest of fish (and only fish) in an elegant setting. The mixed *antipasto* (comprising at least ten dishes) is superb as is the pasta – try sea bass ravioli or gnocchi with a scampi cream. Follow this with a tasty 'fritto misto' or baked fish with potatoes and black olives. *Open Tues–Sun; closed for lunch in summer.*

Porto Santo Stefano ✉ **58019**

★★★Filippo II, t 0564 811611, www.filippo secondo.it (*expensive*). Recently refurbished, this is doubtless the best in town; close to the beaches at Poggio Calvella.

★★★La Caletta, Via Civinni 10, t 0564 812939, f 0564 817506, www.hotelcaletta.it (*expensive*). Pleasant rooms overlooking the sea.

★★Alfiero, Via Cuniberti 12, t 0564 814067 (*moderate*). A simple, less expensive hotel at the centre of the action around the harbour.

Dal Greco, Via del Molo 1, t 0564 814885 (*expensive*). An elegant establishment on the yacht harbour, pricy but worth it. *Terrina di pesce* with vegetables, and lobster, are the star attractions. *Closed Tues.*

I Due Pini, Loc La Soda, t 0564 814012 (*expensive*). A wood-panelled restaurant in a stunning beachside setting, on the coast road into Porto Santo Stefano. The food is good (although pricy) too; a fabulous array of *antipasti*, pasta with lobster or clams, and fish and crustacea.

Orlando, Via Breschi 3, t 0564 812788 (*moderate*). Popular and lively, with a terrace overlooking the sea. The mixed seafood *antipasto* is generous, 'Pirates' spaghetti is delicious, as are the sautéed prawns. Honest prices and a relaxed atmosphere. *Closed Wed.*

ferries and the fish markets; the yachts – and some real dreadnoughts they are – call at the western harbour, at the other side of a small promontory.

The two spits of land joining Argentario to the mainland are made up of two long beaches, the Giannella and the Feniglia. The latter is backed by a beautiful protected pine forest (a nature reserve) with a path running right along it. You can hire bikes and ride the 7km of its length, branching on to the beach at various points. The Giannella is backed by the main road, but faces west so you get lovely sunsets.

Giglio and Giannutri

Giglio

Giglio is the largest of the Tuscan islands after Elba, measuring about 21km by 8km. It is also second in population, with about 1,600 souls, almost all in its three little villages: Giglio Porto, Giglio Castello and Giglio Campese. Like many Italian islands, Giglio suffered grievously from deforestation and abandonment of the land in the 18th and 19th centuries. Though much of it remains green and pretty, large expanses

Getting There and Around

Porto S. Stefano is the **port** for Giglio, a one-hour run; the ferry service is shared by the TOREMAR line (**t** 0564 810803) and Mareggiglio, (**t** 0564 812920), both in Porto S. Stefano; boats run at least twice daily, and more frequently in the summer.

The **railway station** for Porto S.Stefano, along the main Livorno–Rome line, is Orbetello Scalo; buses meet the trains to carry passengers to the port. Giannutri can be reached regularly only in July and August, on a daily boat from Porto S. Stefano. On Giglio, buses run fairly regularly from the ferry dock to Giglio Castello and Giglio Campese.

Tourist Information

Giglio Porto: Via Umberto I 48, **t** 0564 809400 (*summer only*).

Where to Stay and Eat

Giglio ✉ 58012

The number of tourists, and hotels (12) on Giglio seems to have stabilized, leaving it not entirely overcrowded even in the summer.

★★★**Arenella**, Via Arenella 5, **t** 0564 809340, **f** 0564 809443 (*expensive*). Persevere until you leave the Porto to enjoy something rather more serene; this is near the beach, with a pretty garden and a good restaurant.

★★★**Demo's**, Via Thaon De Revel, **t** 0564 809235, **f** 0564 809319, *www.hoteldemos.com* (*expensive*). Right in the port, in the 1960s Miami Beach style.

★★**La Pergola**, next door, **t** 0564 809051 (*moderate*). Smaller and cosier.

If you really want to get away from it all, your best chance is in Cala degli Alberi:

★★**Pardini's Hermitage**, Cala degli Alberi, **t** 0564 809034, **f** 0564 809177 (*luxury – full board*). In its quiet cove, this can only be reached by boat (ask at the Giglio Sub shop on the port, but with only 11 rooms it's best to book). Sports and nature activities if you want, or just enjoy the sea and mountains. Only full or half board in the summer.

Giglio Campese ✉ 58012

★★★**Campese**, Via della Torre 18, **t** 0564 804003, **f** 0564 804093, *www.hotel campese.com* (*very expensive* – half board). A good, modern beach hotel.

Giglio Porto

La Margherita, **t** 0564 809237 (*moderate*). One of the most popular of the seafood restaurants around the harbour; good fish and a terrace on the beach. *Closed Mon.*

Giglio Castello

Da Maria, Via Casamatta 12, **t** 0564 806062 (*very expensive*). A real find, with good seafood (stuffed squid or lobster flambé) and game dishes like the house speciality, wild rabbit *alla cacciatora*. *Closed Wed.*

Da Santi, Via Marconi 20, **t** 0564 806188 (*expensive*). Those 'in the know' go to Santi's in the old town. An ex-ship's cook, he cooks good fresh food in his simple old-fashioned restaurant. Specialities include sea bass ravioli and game. Sample, too, the local white wine, which is rarely on sale. *Closed Mon off season.*

are now almost barren. Recently, however, a remarkable change in Giglian environmental consciousness seems to have occurred; if the big signs all over the harbour are any indication, they've gone to the opposite extreme – no camping, no noise, no riding over the wild flowers (and no collecting rocks – they're part of the island too).

The word *Giglio* means lily, and the lily has become the island's symbol, although it has in fact nothing to do with its name. The Romans called it *Aegilium* or *Gilium*. Under them, Giglio like most of the other Italian islands was a resort for the very wealthy. Pisa, Aragon and various feudal families held the island in the Middle Ages. Duke Cosimo seized it for Tuscany in the 16th century, but did little to protect it against its greatest danger, pirates. Fortunately, the Giglians had the holy right arm of San Mamiliano to protect them. This 6th-century Sicilian bishop, fleeing from the

Arian heretics, became a hermit on Montecristo. When he died, a divine signal alerted fishermen from Elba, Giglio and even Genoa, who arrived at the same time and began to fight over the remains. In the true tradition of Christian brotherhood, they struck a deal and cut Mamiliano in three pieces. Giglio got the arm, which proved its worth by chasing away Turkish pirates in 1799. On other occasions it wasn't so helpful. The redoubtable pirate Barbarossa carried off most of the population in 1534, and his understudy Dragut came back for the rest in 1550.

Giglio Porto, the island's metropolis, is a colourful place, with red and green light-houses to welcome the ferries, and pink and beige houses straggling up the hills. There are two beaches south of the town, at **Cala delle Canelle** and **Cala delle Caldane**, one to the north at **Punta Aranella**, all more or less developed, and in the town itself, the world's smallest beach, tucked behind the houses on the left side of the port. From Giglio Porto a difficult mountain road leads up to **Giglio Castello**, the only secure refuge in pirate days, and until recently the only real town. The fortress itself was begun by the Pisans and completed under the grand dukes. The picturesque town inside, all medieval alleys and overhanging arches, has plenty of gulls and swallows, a few German tourists, and a small Baroque church with an odd tower and the famous arm of San Mamiliano.

From Giglio Castello, a road leads southwards past **Poggio della Pagana**, the island's highest peak (498m/1,633ft), through land largely reforested with pines to Punta del Capel Rosso, at the southern tip, then back along the coast to Giglio Porto. The main road from Giglio Castello continues on to **Giglio Campese**, a growing resort area with an old watchtower and a large sandy beach.

Giannutri

Giannutri, the southernmost island of the Tuscan archipelago, is a rocky crescent about 5km long, with little water and no fertile ground, and little history to speak of. The ancient Greeks knew it as *Artemisia*, and the Romans as *Dianium*; perhaps the associations with the moon goddess came from the island's crescent shape. In Roman times it was an estate of the noble Ahenobarbus family, and there are the substantial ruins of a **Roman Villa** (1st century AD) near Cala Maestra, which are a popular destination for daytrippers from Porto Santo Stefano in the summer months. Though Giannutri has no permanent population, there is a tourist village and some holiday cottages near the well-protected bay, **Cala Spalmatoio**, on the eastern coast.

Capalbio and the Giardino dei Tarocchi

Back on the coast south of Orbetello, almost nothing is left of **Ansedonia**, destroyed by the Sienese in 1330. There's a beach, a few hotels, and an unusual Etruscan attempt to stop Cosa's harbour from silting up: deep channels hewn from the solid rock. For ruins you must climb up to **Cosa**, settled by Romans in the 3rd century BC to keep an eye on the restless Etruscan cities – and maybe accelerate their decline by draining off trade. Cosa was sacked by Visigoths in the 5th century, but the ruins give a fair idea of the Roman city: a typical rectangular circuit of walls with three gates, a strict street grid, a 'Capitoline' temple, and cisterns for rainwater. Remains of the port are visible from Ansedonia harbour and there is also a small museum on the site.

Before the Via Aurelia (SS1) passes from Tuscany into Lazio, it skirts another World Wild Fund for Nature project, a nature reserve at the **Lago di Burano** (*tours Sept–April Sun at 10 and 3; in summer you can book, t 0564 898829; adm*). Though small, the lagoon attracts all the same birds as the Monti dell'Uccellina and Orbetello lagoons; including, in summer, perhaps the only cranes left on the Italian mainland.

Capalbio, 6km inland, is one of the loveliest villages in southern Tuscany. It's a circular, hill-top enclave built around a castle, with a pretty 12th-century church. Head a few kilometres east, though, by the Lazio border, for a sneak preview of what may some day be one of Tuscany's best-known sights. They don't want any publicity, and it isn't signed, but if you turn off the SS1 to Capalbio, and turn right just before the first petrol station, you'll get a surprise. The **Giardino dei Tarocchi** (*open mid-May–late Oct daily 12.30–7.30; adm exp; winter 1st Sat of each month for group visits, min 15 people, adm free, request by fax f 0564 895700 or email tarotg@tin.it*) is the project of French artist Niki de Saint-Phalle (who died in 2002), known for her works at the Pompidou Centre and the Bastille Opera in Paris, and for the colossal, humorous figures she calls 'nanas' scattered over Europe. In this garden, created for abstruse meditation, monumental sculptures represent each of the 22 key arcana of the Tarot deck: mad, brilliant works in concrete, bright ceramics and mirrors that hark back to Antonio Gaudi. A few are over 50ft tall, glittering over the Maremma coast like some interplanetary Lunar Park. Their symbolism is often obscure, but some, like the broken *Tower*, are unmistakable.

Over the Border

If you're bound for Rome, there are a few attractions in Lazio to distract you along the way. The wealthiest Etruscan cities were here rather than Tuscany, and so the finest painted tombs are on the north Lazio coast at **Tarquinia** and **Cervetri**. Inland are the remains of the Etruscan town of **Vulci**, the fortress of Castello dell'Abbadia holds an Etruscan museum, and an Etruscan bridge spans the gorge. Not much has happened here since Etruscan times, but **Tuscania** has two extremely unusual early medieval churches in the style of medieval southern Italy. Further inland is a chain of lakes, including tranquil **Lake Vico**, and the city of **Viterbo**, once home to the popes.

Siena

12

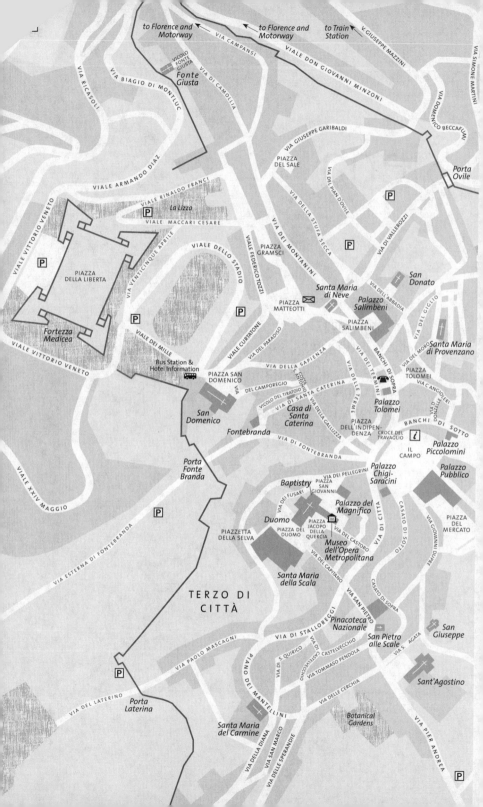

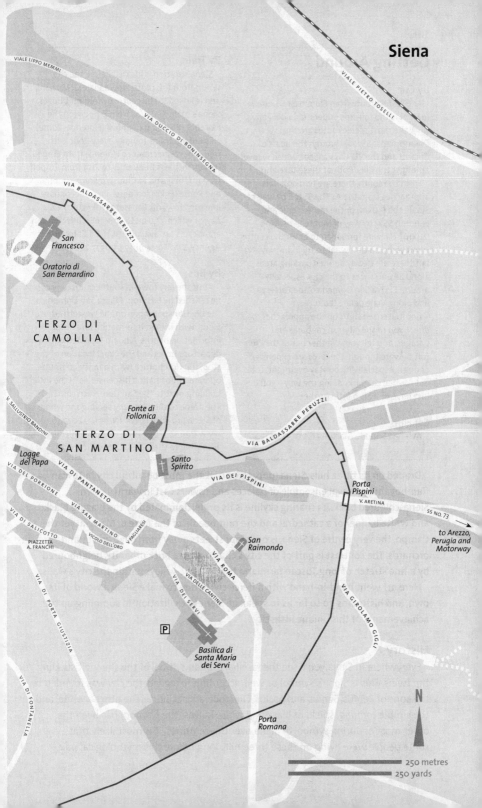

Siena

VIALE LIPPO MEMMI

VIA DUCCIO DI BONINSEGNA

VIALE PIETRO TOSELLI

VIA BALDASSARRE PERUZZI

San Francesco

Oratorio di San Bernardino

TERZO DI CAMOLLIA

Fonte di Follonica

V. SALLUSTRIO BANDINI

TERZO DI SAN MARTINO

Logge del Papa

VIA DEL PORRIONE

VIA DI PANTANETO

Santo Spirito

VIA DEI PISPINI

VIA BALDASSARRE PERUZZI

Porta Pispini

V. ARETINA

SS NO. 73

to Arezzo, Perugia and Motorway

VIA DI SALICOTTO

VIA SAN MARTINO

VICOLO DELL'ORO

V. PAGLIARESI

PIAZZETTA A. FRANCHI

San Raimondo

VIA ROMA

VIA GIROLAMO GIGLI

VIA DI PORTA GIUSTIZIA

VIA DELLE CANTINE

VIA DEI SERVI

P

Basilica di Santa Maria dei Servi

VIA DI FONTANELLA

Porta Romana

N

250 metres
250 yards

Getting Around

By Car

The fastest route from Florence to Siena (68km) is the toll-free Superstrada del Palio (1hr); the most scenic routes are the Chiantigiana (SS222) through the heart of Chianti and the Via Cassia (SS2), which weave amongst the hills. Both of these take 2hrs.

From the south, there are two possible approaches from the A1: the SS326 by way of Sinalunga (50km) or the more scenic and winding SS73 by way of Monte Sansovino (44km). Cars are forbidden to enter the centre – and you wouldn't want to try it anyway – but there are clearly defined **parking areas** along all entrances to the city, especially around Piazza San Domenico, the Fortezza and along Viale dello Stadio.

Computerized signs on the approaches direct you to the city-run car parks and garages, and tell you whether or not they're full. Beware though: the rates are expensive enough, especially if you stay overnight. Look out for free car parks along the way – you'll just have to walk a little further.

Car Hire

Avis, Via Simone Martini 36, **t** 0577 270305.

By Train

Siena's station is located below the city, 1½km from the centre down Viale G. Mazzini, and is linked to the centre by frequent buses. Siena's main line runs from Empoli (on the Florence–Pisa line) to Chiusi (Florence–Rome).

There are trains roughly every hour, with frequent connections to Florence from Empoli (97km/1hr), less frequently to Pisa from Empoli (125km/2hrs), and to Chiusi towards Umbria and Rome (65km to Chiusi, 1hr). A secondary line runs towards Grosseto (70km/1hr) – 8 a day, of which 3 go on to Orbetello. Information and tickets are available at the **Il Caroccio Agency**, Via Mortanini 73, **t** 0577 226964.

By Bus

Almost every town in southern Tuscany can be reached by bus from **Piazza San Domenico**, the big transport node on the western edge of Siena, with tourist information and hotel information booths. A board is posted with all departure times and the exact location of the stop; the ticket office (with a fancy, computer-operated information dispenser) is in the little building next to the San Domenico church. The name of the company serving the whole of Siena province is TRA-IN, **t** 0577 204246, *www.trainspa.it*, causing endless difficulties, according to the local tourist office, with

---

Draped on its three hills, Siena (pop. 59,000) is the most beautiful city in Tuscany, a flamboyant medieval ensemble of palaces and towers cast in warm, brown, Siena-coloured brick. Its soaring skyline is its pride, dominated by the blazing black and white banner of a cathedral and the taut needle of the Torre di Mangia; yet the Campo, the very centre of Siena, is only four streets away from olive groves and orchards. The contrast is part of the city's charm: dense brick urbanity, neighboured by a fine stretch of long Tuscan farmland that fills the valleys within the city's walls.

Here art went hand-in-hand with a fierce civic pride to make Siena a world of its own, and historians go so far as to speak of 'Sienese civilization' in summing up the achievements of this unique little city.

History

Everywhere in Siena you'll see the familiar Roman symbol of the she-wolf suckling the twins. This is Siena's symbol as well; according to legend, the city was founded by the sons of Remus, Senius and Ascius. One rode a black horse, the other a white, and the simple *comunal* shield of black and white halves (the *balzana*) has been the other most enduring symbol of Siena over the centuries. It is most likely that some people were living on these three hills long before this mythological pair;

English tourists looking for TRA-INs in the train station; for some of the closer villages, look for TRA-INs on Viale F. Tozzi, just north of San Domenico.

Other companies depart for other cities like Florence (SITA, about once every hour, also to Rome, Perugia, Pisa, etc.), but all leave from San Domenico. Within the walls, there is now a bus service run by the TRA-IN, using what they call the *pollicini* or Tom Thumbs: little buses designed to get around narrow streets. Regular buses to the **train station** and everywhere else in the modern suburbs depart from **Piazza Matteotti**, north of the Campo.

Tourist Information

Siena: Piazza del Campo 56, **t** 0577 280551, **f** 0577 270676, *aptsiena@siena. turismo.toscana.it*; *www.siena. turismo.toscana.it www.terresiena.it*
Post office: Piazza Matteotti 37.

Shopping

Siena, with its population of only 60,000, is blissfully short of designer boutiques; even the usual tourist trinkets seem to be lacking – illuminated plastic models of the cathedral are harder to find every year. Nevertheless, a thorough search of the back streets will turn up plenty of unpretentious artisan workshops – almost all of which are so unconcerned with the tourist industry that they don't even bother hanging out a sign. The following are just some examples.

Stained glass:Vetrate Artistiche Toscane, Via Galuzza 5, just off Piazza Indipendenza, *www.glassisland.com*. Creations (most of them portable) in a distinctive modern style. The artist is also available to give informal talks about his work.

Ceramics: Via di Città 94. Selling a range of interesting pieces.

Libreria Senese, Via di Città 62–64. Siena's best bookshop, just down the street.

Antica Drogheria Manganelli, Via di Città 71–73, **t** 0577 280002. One hundred-year-old original wooden shelving lines the walls of this gourmet's treasure trove, jammed full of delicious regional foods and wines. Worth a visit.

Morbidi, Via Banchi di Sopra 73/75. For delicious picnic treats; a multitude of cheeses, hams, salamis, prepared dishes, wines and breads.

La Fattoria Toscano, Via di Cittè 51. Those gastronomic goodies.

excavations have found traces of Etruscan and even Celtic habitation. The almost impregnable site, dominating most of southern Tuscany, would always have been of interest. Roman-era *Sena Julia*, refounded by Augustus as a colony for his veterans, never achieved much importance, and we know little about the place until the early 12th century, when the emerging *comune* began keeping written records. In 1125, an increasingly independent Siena elected its first consuls. By 1169, the *comune* had wrested political control away from the bishop, and some 10 years later, Siena developed its own written constitution.

The political development of the city is complex, and with good reason. Twelfth-century Siena was a booming new city: having control over its rich countryside, supplying some of the best wool in Italy, helped start an important cloth industry, and a small silver mine, acquired from Volterra in the 1160s, provided seed capital for what was to become one of the leading banking towns of Europe. Like so many other Italian cities, Siena was able early on to force its troublesome rural nobles to live within its walls, where they built scores of tall defence towers, fought pitched battles in the streets and usually kept the city divided into armed camps; in the narrowest part of the city, the *comune* once had to lay out new streets parallel to Via Camollia because of one particularly boisterous nobleman whose palace most

Market Days

Markets are held around the Fortezza and Via XXV Aprile. *Wed.*

Where to Stay

Siena ✉ 53100

Until the opening of the luxurious Grand Hotel Continentale a few years ago, Siena's finest and most interesting hotels were all outside the walls, in the countryside or near the city gates. With the exception of the Continentale, what's left in the centre is simple but comfortable enough. In summer, rooms are in short supply and it's best to book ahead. If you come without a reservation, it is worth contacting the following organizations: **Hotel Information Centre**, Piazza San Domenico, **t** 0577 288084, **f** 0577 280290, *www.hotel siena.com*. Make this your first stop. Run by the city's innkeepers, it's conveniently located at the terminus of all intercity bus routes. If you arrive by train, take the city bus up from the station to Piazza Matteotti and walk a block down Via Curtatone. Even at busy times, they should be able to find you something – except during the Palio when you should book several months in advance. *Open Mon–Sat 9–7, until 8 in summer.*

Luxury

If you have a car, there are a number of hotels outside the walls that offer rural Tuscan charm and views of the city that more than make up for the slight inconvenience of getting there.
★★★★★La Certosa di Maggiano, 1km southeast of the city, near the Porta Romana, **t** 0577 288180, **f** 0577 288189, *www.certosadi maggiano.com*. This must be one of the most remarkable establishments in Italy, set in a restored 14th-century Carthusian monastery. There are 18 rooms, a heated pool, air conditioning that works, a quiet chapel and cloister, a salon where guests can play backgammon and chess, tennis courts, an excellent restaurant and a library fit to feature in any antiquarian's dream. It doesn't come cheap, but it is lovely.
★★★★★Continentale, Via Banchi di Sopra 85, **t** 0577 56011/44204, **f** 0577 560 1555, *www. grandhotelcontinentalesiena.it*. Over 50 rooms, all furnished with fine fabrics and antiques.
★★★★Villa Scacciapensieri, on Strada Scacciapensieri 10, 3km north of the city, **t** 0577 41441, **f** 0577 270854, *www.villa scacciapensieri.it*. Come here to marvel at glorious sunset views over Siena. This is a quiet country house divided into 28 spacious rooms; besides the view, it has a pool and a good restaurant with an outdoor terrace.

Sienese were afraid to pass. Yet Siena was never completely able to bring its titled hoodlums under control. The businessmen made the money, and gradually formed their city into a sophisticated self-governing republic, but the nobles held on to many of their privileges for centuries, giving an anachronistically feudal tinge to Siena's life and art.

Like its brawling neighbours, medieval Siena enjoyed looking for trouble; in the endless wars of the 13th century, they never had to look very far. Originally a Guelph town, Siena changed sides early to avoid being in the same camp with arch-rival Florence. Along with Pisa, Siena carried the Ghibelline banner through the Tuscan wars with varying fortunes. Its finest hour came in 1260, when a Florentine herald arrived with the arrogant demand that Siena demolish its walls and deliver up its large population of Ghibelline exiles from Florence. If not, the armies of Florence and the entire Guelph League – some 40,000 men – were waiting outside to raze the city to the ground. Despite the overwhelming odds, the Sienese determined to resist. They threw the keys of the city on the altar of the as yet unfinished new cathedral, dedicating Siena to the Virgin Mary (a custom they have repeated ever since when the city is endangered, most recently just before the battle for liberation in 1944). In

Very Expensive

★★★Park Hotel, Via Marciano 18, **t** 0577 44803, **f** 0577 49020, *www.parkhotelsiena.it*. A 16th-century building designed by Peruzzi, on the hill that dominates Siena, with great views.

Hotel Garden Via Custoza 2, **t** 0577 47056, *www.gardenhotel.it*. This renovated 18th-century villa stands about 1km from town in a big garden. Rooms are in the main villa (where there are antiques and original frescoes) or in one of three annexes. There is a pool, a good restaurant and the staff are helpful.

Expensive

★★★Antica Torre, Via di Fieravecchia 7, **t/f** 0577 222255. Siena's most popular small (only eight rooms) hotel; a restored 16th-century tower, with marble floors, antiques and beamed ceilings.

★★★Duomo, Via Stalloreggi 34, **t** 0577 289088, **f** 0577 43043, *www.hotelduomo.it*. A friendly, comfortably old-fashioned place south of the Duomo. Rooms are a bit stark but clean.

★★★Palazzo Ravizza, Pian dei Mantellini 34, near the Porta Laterina, just inside the walls, **t** 0577 280462, **f** 0577 221597, *www.palazzoravizza.it*. An elegant 19th-century palazzo with up-market rooms furnished with antiques. There is a lovely garden at the back and a restaurant, too.

★★Il Giardino, Via Baldassare Peruzzi 35, **t** 0577 285290, **f** 0577 221197, *www.hotelil giardino.it*. Highly recommended in readers' letters, near the Porta Pispini, with views and a swimming pool.

★★Piccolo Hotel Il Palio, Piazza del Sale 19, **t** 0577 281131, **f** 0577 281142, *www.piccolo hotelilpalio.it*. A little way from the centre, but it has the advantages of a quiet location and a friendly, English-speaking owner.

Villa Liberty, Viale V. Veneto 11, **t** 0577 44966, **f** 0577 44770, *www.villaliberty.it*. A pleasant and elegant 'Liberty-style' villa near San Domenico and set in a garden. Rooms are well-furnished; two have private terraces.

Moderate

Many of Siena's two- and three-star hotels are around the entrances to the city, but there are also a number of options closer to the centre.

★★Canon d'Oro, Via Montanini 28, **t** 0577 44321, **f** 0577 280868. Near the bus station; Nice, friendly and good value. Rooms have all been renovated in the last couple of years.

★★Centrale, Via Angolieri 26, **t** 0577 280379, **f** 0577 42152. Very near to the Campo. The seven rooms are spacious and comfortable.

★★Piccolo Hotel Etruria, Via delle Donzelle 3, **t** 0577 288088, **f** 0577 288461. Friendly, clean

the morning, they marched out to the **Battle of Monteaperti** and beat the Florentines so badly that they captured their *carroccio*.

After the battle, Siena had Florence entirely at her mercy and, naturally, was anxious to level the city and scatter the ground with salt. One of the famous episodes in the *Inferno* relates how the Florentine exiles, who made up a substantial part of the Sienese forces, refused to allow it. Unfortunately for Siena, within a few years Florence and the Tuscan Guelphs had the situation back under control and Siena was never again to come so close to dominating Tuscan affairs. Nevertheless the city would be a constant headache to Florence for the next three centuries.

When things were quiet at the front, the Sienese had to settle for bashing each other. The constant stream of anti-Siena propaganda in Dante isn't just Florentine bile; medieval Siena thoroughly earned its reputation for violence and contentiousness. The impressive forms and rituals of the Sienese Republic were merely a façade concealing endless, pointless struggles between the various factions of the élite. Early on, Siena's merchants and nobles divided themselves into five *monti*, syndicates of self-interest that worked like political parties only without any pretence of principle. At one point, this Tuscan banana republic had

and a good bargain. Four rooms in the annexe opposite. Restaurant (*cheap*) next door also owned by the hotel.

Eating Out

Sitting between three of Italy's greatest wine- producing areas, the Chianti, the Brunello of Montalcino and the Vino Nobile of Montepulciano, Siena always has something to wash down the simple dishes of its table. This city's real speciality is sweets, and visitors often find they have no room for a meal after repeated slices of *panforte*, a heavy but indecently tasty cake laced with fruits, nuts, orange peel and secret Sienese ingredients or *panpepato*, similar but containing pepper.

They are all artists – shop windows flaunt gargantuan creations of cake and crystallized fruit, several feet high and as colourful as a Lorenzetti fresco, set out proudly for all to see before they are carted off to a wedding party.

The *Enoteca* inside the Medici fortress (*see* p.343) is another distraction; at times, special tastings are organized, concentrating on a particular region of Italy.

As a university town, Siena is never short on snacks and fast food; try *cioccina*, their special variation on pizza; or *pici* (thick south Tuscan spaghetti) with a sauce prepared from ground pork, *pancetta*, sausages and chicken breasts, added to tomatoes cooked with Brunello wine, which is the city's favourite pasta dish.

Expensive

Antica Trattoria Botteganova, Via Chiantigiana 29, t 0577 284230. A few km northeast of Siena on the SS408 to Montevarchi. Meats such as the stuffed rabbit are earthy, or try the more delicate fish choices such as the tomato flan with basil-flavoured sturgeon fillets. *Closed Sun.*

Certosa di Maggiano, Via di Certosa 82, t 0577 288180. In an exquisite setting: part of a luxury hotel housed ina former Carthusian monastery, with 14th-century cloisters. Modern, *haute cuisine* dishes served with some pomp.

Compagnia dei Vinattieri,Via delle Terme, t 0577 236568. The many wines on offer in this basement restaurant/*enoteca* are stored in a 14th-century cellar – ask to have a look before you leave. You can pop in for just a drink and a snack, but that would mean missing out on excellent dishes, such as ravioli with a mild goat's cheese and basil sauce, stuffed chicken neck (!) with a pungent 'salsa verde', rabbit stewed with black olives and chocolate and coffee mousse.

10 constitutions in 27 years, and more often than not, its political affairs were settled in the streets. Before the Palio was invented, Siena's favourite civic sport was the *Gioco del Pugno*, a general, 300-a-side fist fight in the Campo. Sometimes tempers flared and the boys would bring out the axes and crossbows.

Siena's Golden Age

The historical record leaves us with a glaring paradox. For all its troubles and bad intentions, Siena often managed to run city business disinterestedly and with intelligence. An intangible factor of civic pride always made the Sienese do the right thing when something important was at hand, like battling with the Florentines or selecting a new artist to work on the cathedral. The Battle of Monteaperti may have proved a disappointment in terms of territorial ambitions, but it inaugurated the most brilliant period of Sienese culture, and saw the transformation of the hilltop fortress town into the beautiful city we see today. In 1287, under pressure from the Guelphs and their Angevin protectors, Siena actually allied itself with Florence and instituted a new form of government: the '**Council of the Nine**'. Excluding nobles from office, as Florence would do six years later, the rule of the Nine was to last until 1355, and it gave Siena a more stable regime than it knew at any other period.

Da Enzo, Via Camollia 49, **t** 0577 281277.
A traditional restaurant with a long, varied menu, offering plenty of choice between fish and meat. The cutlets of wild boar in a sweet and sour sauce and fish baked in a potato crust are delicious. *Closed Sun.*

Ai Marsili, Via del Castoro 3, **t** 0577 47154.
An elegant setting and a wide choice of excellent Sienese dishes. Among them, Catherine de'Medici's famous dish, *faraona alla Medici*, guinea fowl roasted with pine nuts, almonds and plums. *Closed Mon.*

Osteria Le Logge, Via del Porrione 33, **t** 0577 48013. The high-ceilinged and airy main room of this restaurant must be one of the most pleasant places to eat in Siena. A tempting choice of *antipasti* precede such dishes as wild boar with juniper berries and lasagne with turbot, mozzarella and pesto. *Closed Sun.*

Moderate

Guido, Vicolo Pier Pettinato 7, **t** 0577 280042.
A central, traditional Sienese restaurant with a somewhat medieval feel. The grilled lamb, veal and *bistecca* are excellent.

Osteria di Castelvecchio, Via Castelvecchio 65, **t** 0577 49586. The décor here is original and modern, but this building was once the stable block of one of Siena's oldest *palazzi*. Traditional recipes (penne with *salsiccia* and peppers, risotto with fresh herbs) with an emphasis on vegetarian dishes. The *menu degustazione* is good value. *Closed Tues.*

Osteria di Ficomezzo, Via dei Termini 71, **t** 0577 222384. Lunch is a simple affair here. In the evenings there are more inventive dishes, such as guinea fowl cooked with tarragon, served alongside the more traditional *pici*, hearty soups and stews. *Closed Sun.*

Cheap

Il Grattacielo, Via dei Pontani 8, **t** 0577 289326.
Another popular student hangout. The simple dishes are good value for money and the wine flows freely. *Closed Sun.*

Osteria La Chiacchiera, Via Costa di Sant' Antonio 4, **t** 0577 280631. This friendly, highly recommended little *trattoria* serves excellent local dishes: *pici*, *ribollita*, kidneys, cockscombs (*cibreo*), stews or a simple *bistecca*. There are outdoor tables for summer dining.

Pizzeria Carlo e Franca, Via Pantaneto 138, **t** 0577 284385. *Antipasti* and pizzas at reasonable prices, and not far from the centre. *Closed Wed.*

La Torre, Via Salicotto 17, **t** 0577 287548.
A fun, lively place; popular with students. *Closed Thurs.*

Business was better than ever. The city's bankers came to rival Florence's, with offices in all the trading centres and capitals of Europe. A sustained peace, and increasing cultural contacts with France and Naples, brought new ideas and influences into Siena's art and architecture, just in time to embellish massive new building programmes like the **cathedral** (begun in 1186, but not substantially completed until the 1380s) and the **Palazzo Pubblico** (1295–1310). Beginning with Duccio di Buoninsegna (1260–1319), Sienese artists took the lead in exploring new concepts in painting and sculpture and, throughout the 1300s, contributed as much as or more than the Florentines in laying the foundations for the Renaissance. Contemporary records betray an obsessive concern on the part of bankers and merchants for decorating Siena and impressing outsiders. At the height of its fortunes, in the early 14th century, Siena ruled most of southern Tuscany. Its bankers were known in London, in the Baltic and in Constantinople, and its reputation for beauty and culture was matched by few cities in Europe.

The very pinnacle of civic pride and ambition came in 1339, with the fantastical plan to expand the still-unfinished cathedral into the largest in all Christendom. The walls of that effort, a nave that would have been longer than St Peter's in Rome, stand today as a monument to the dramatic event that snapped off Siena's career in

Ancient Rivals

Few rivalries have been more enduring than that between Florence and Siena; to understand Tuscany, take a moment to compare the two. Long ago, while Florence was off at university busily studying her optics and geometry, Lady Siena spent her time dancing and dropping her scarf for knights at the tournament. Florence thought she had the last laugh in 1555, when Duke Cosimo and his black-hearted Spanish pals wiped out the Sienese Republic and put this proud maiden in chains. It's frustrating enough today, though, when Florence looks up in the hills and sees Siena, an unfaded beauty with a faraway smile, sitting in her tower like the Lady of Shalott.

For two towns built by bankers and wool tycoons, they could not have less in common. Siena may not possess an Uffizi or a David, but neither does it have to bear the marble antimacassars and general stuffiness of its sister on the Arno, nor her smog, traffic, tourist hordes and suburban squalor. Florence never goes over the top. Siena loves to, especially in the week around the race of the Palio, the wildest party in Tuscany, a worthy successor to the fabulous masques and carnivals, the bullfights and bloody free-for-alls of the Sienese Middle Ages. In fact, Florence has been clicking its tongue at Siena since the time of Dante, who refers sarcastically in his *Inferno* to a famous club called the *Brigata*, made up of 12 noble Sienese youths who put up 250,000 florins for a year of nightly feasting; every night they had three sumptuously laid tables, one for eating, one for drinking and the third to throw out the window.

But there's more to Siena than that. This is a city with its own artistic tradition (*see* **Art and Architecture**, p.14); in the 1300s, Sienese painters were giving lessons to the Florentines. Always more decorative, less intellectual than Florence, Siena fell behind in the quattrocento. By then, fortunately, the greatest achievement of Sienese art was already nearing completion – Siena herself.

full bloom. The **Black Death** of 1348 carried off one-third of the population – a death toll perhaps no greater than in some other Italian cities, but it struck Siena at a moment when its economy was particularly vulnerable, and started a slow but irreversible decline that was to continue for centuries. Economic strife led to political instability, and in 1355 a revolt of the nobles, egged on by Emperor Charles IV who was then in Tuscany, overthrew the Council of the Nine. Then in 1371, seven years before the Ciompi revolt in Florence, the wool workers staged a genuine revolution. Organized as a trade union of sorts, the **Compagnia del Bruco**, seized the Palazzo Pubblico and instituted a government with greater popular representation.

The decades that followed saw Siena devote more and more of its diminishing resources to buying off the marauding mercenary companies that infested much of Italy at this time. By 1399 the city was in such dire straits that it surrendered its independence to **Giangaleazzo Visconti**, the tyrant of Milan, who was then attempting to surround and conquer Florence. After his death, Siena reclaimed its freedom. Political confusion continued throughout the century, with only two periods of relative stability. One came with the pontificate (1458–63) of Pius II, the great Sienese scholar **Aeneas Silvius Piccolomini**, who exerted a dominating influence over his native city while he ruled at Rome. In 1487, a nobleman named **Pandolfo Petrucci** took over the government; as an honest broker, regulating the often murderous ambitions of the *monti*, he and his sons kept control of the republic until 1524.

The Fall of the Republic

Florence was always waiting in the wings to swallow up Siena and finally had its chance in the 1500s. The real villain of the piece, however, was not Florence but that most imperious Emperor, **Charles V**. After the fall of the Petrucci, the factional struggles resumed immediately, with frequent assassinations and riots, and constitutions changing with the spring fashions. Charles, who had bigger prey in his sights, cared little for the fate of the perverse little republic; he feared, though, that its disorders, religious toleration, and wretched financial condition were diseases that might spread beyond its borders. In 1530, he took advantage of riots in the city to install an imperial garrison. Yet even the emperor's representatives, usually Spaniards, could not keep Siena from sliding further into anarchy and bankruptcy on several occasions, largely thanks to Charles's war taxes. Cultural life was stifled as the Spaniards introduced the Inquisition and the Index. Scholars and artists fled, while poverty and political disruptions meant that Siena's once proud university ceased to function.

In 1550, Charles announced that he was going to build a fortress within the city walls, for which the Sienese were going to pay. Realizing that the trifling liberty still left to them would soon be extinguished, the Sienese ruling class began intrigues with Charles' great enemy, France. A French army, led by a Piccolomini, arrived in July 1552. Inside the walls the people revolted and locked the Spanish garrison up in its own new fortress. The empire was slow to react but, inevitably, in late 1554, a huge force of imperial troops, along with those of Florence, entered Sienese territory. The siege was prosecuted with remarkable brutality by Charles's commander, the **Marquis of Marignano**, who laid waste much of the Sienese countryside (which did not entirely recover until this century), tortured prisoners and even hired agents to start fires inside the walls. After a brave resistance, led by a republican Florentine exile named **Piero Strozzi** and assisted by France, Siena was starved into surrendering in April 1555. Two years later, Charles's son Philip II sold Siena to Duke Cosimo of Florence and the republic was consumed by the new Grand Duchy of Tuscany.

If nothing else, Siena went out with a flourish. After the capture of the city, some 2,000 republican bitter-enders escaped to make a last stand at Montalcino. Declaring 'Where the *Comune* is, there is the City', they established what must be the world's first republican government-in-exile. With control over much of the old Sienese territory, the '**Republic of Siena at Montalcino**' held out against the Medici for another four years.

With its independence lost and its economy irrevocably ruined, Siena withdrew into itself. For centuries there was to be no recovery, little art or scholarship, and no movements towards reform. The Sienese aristocracy, already decayed into a parasitic *rentier* class, made its peace with the Medici dukes early on; in return for their support, the Medici allowed them to keep much of their power and privileges. The once-great capital of trade and finance shrank rapidly into an overbuilt farmers' market, its population dropping from a 14th-century high of 60–80,000 to around a mere 15,000 by the year 1700. This explains largely why medieval and Renaissance Siena is so well preserved – for better or worse, nothing ever happened to change it.

By the Age of Enlightenment, with its disparaging of everything medieval, the Sienese seem to have quite forgotten their own history and art, so it is no surprise that the rest of Europe forgot them too. During the first years of the Grand Tour, no self-respecting northern European considered visiting Siena. Few had probably ever heard of it and those who stopped overnight on the way to Rome were usually dismayed at the 'inelegance' of its medieval buildings and art.

It was not until the 1830s that Siena was rediscovered, with the help of *literati* like the Brownings, who spent several summers here, and later that truly Gothic American, Henry James. The Sienese were not far behind in rediscovering it themselves. The old civic pride that had lain dormant for centuries yawned and stretched like Sleeping Beauty and went diligently back to work.

Before the 19th century was out, everything that could still be salvaged of the city's ancient glory was refurbished and restored. More than ever fascinated by its own image and eccentricities, and more than ever without any kind of economic base, Siena was ready for its present career as a cultural attraction, a tourist town.

Orientation: *Terzi* and the *Contrade*

The centre of Siena, the site of the Palio and, importantly to the Sienese, the 'farthest point from the world outside', is the piazza called **Il Campo**. The city unfolds from it like a three-petalled flower along three ridges. It has been a natural division since medieval times, with the oldest quarter, the **Terzo di Città**, to the southwest; the **Terzo di San Martino**, to the southeast; and the **Terzo di Camollia**, to the north.

Siena is tiny, barely over a square mile in size. The density, and especially the hills, make it seem much bigger when you're walking. There are no short cuts across the valleys between the three *terzi*. Although there are few cars in the centre, taxis and motorbikes will occasionally try to run you down.

Contrade

The Sienese have taken the *contrade* for granted for so long that their history is almost impossible to trace. Basically, the word denotes the 17 neighbourhoods into which Siena is divided. Like the *rioni* of Rome, they were once the original wards of the ancient city – not merely geographical boundaries but self-governing entities; the ancients with their long racial memories often referred to them as the city's 'tribes'. In Siena, the *contrade* survived and prospered all through classical times and the Middle Ages. More than anything else, they maintained the city's traditions and sense of identity through the dark years after 1552. Incredibly enough, they're still there now, unique in Italy and perhaps all Europe. Once Siena counted over 60 *contrade*. Now there are 17, each with a sort of totem animal for its symbol:

The Palio

The thousands of tourists who come twice a year to see the Palio, Siena's famous horse race around the Campo, probably think the Sienese are doing it purely for their benefit. Yet, like the *contrade* which contest it, the Palio is an essential aspect of Sienese culture, as significant to the city today as it was centuries ago. Here are the plain facts on Italy's best-known annual festival.

The oldest recorded Palio was run in 1283, though no one knows how far the custom goes back. During the Middle Ages, besides the horse races there were violent street battles, bloody games of primeval rugby and even bullfights. (Bullfights were also common in Rome and there's an argument to be made that Italy is actually the place where the Spaniards got the idea, back in the 16th and 17th centuries when Spain's own medieval passion for such things was all but forgotten.) At present, the course comprises three laps around the periphery of the Campo, although in the past the race has been known to take in some of the city's main streets.

The *palio* (Latin *pallium*) is an embroidered banner offered as a prize to the winning *contrade*. Two races are held each year, on 2 July and 16 August, and the *palio* of each one is decorated with an image of the Virgin Mary; after political violence, the city's greatest passion has always been Mariolatry. The course has room for only 10 horses in each race, so some of the 17 *contrade* are chosen by lot each race to ensure that they all have a fair chance. The horses, too, are selected by lot, but the *contrade* are free to select their own jockeys.

Although the race itself lasts only a minute and a half, there's a good hour or two of pageantry preceding it; the famous flag-throwers or *alfieri* of each participating *contrada* put on a dazzling show, while the medieval *carroccio*, drawn by a yoke of white oxen, is pressed into service to circle the Campo, bearing the prized *palio* itself.

The Palio is no joke; baskets of money ride on each race, not to mention the sacred honour of the district. To obtain divine favour, each *contrada* brings its horse into its chapel on race morning for a special blessing (and if a little horse manure drops during the ceremony, it's taken as a sign of good luck). The only rule stipulates that you can't seize the reins of an opponent. There are no rules against bribing opposing jockeys, making alliances with other *contrade* or ambushing jockeys before the race.

The course around the Campo has two right angles. Anything can happen; recent Palii have featured not only jockeys but *horses* flying through the air at the turns. The Sienese say no one has ever been killed at a Palio. There's no reason to believe them. They wouldn't believe it themselves, but it is an article of faith among the Sienese that fatalities are prevented by special intervention of the Virgin Mary. The post-Palio carousing, while not up to medieval standards, is still impressive; in the winning *contrada* the party might go on for days on end, while the losers shed bitter tears.

No event in Italy is as infectiously exhilarating as the Palio. There are two ways to see it, either from the centre of the Campo, packed tight and always very hot, or from an expensive (€130–260) seat in a viewing stand, but book well in advance if you want one of these. Several travel agencies offer special Palio tours (*see* **Travel**, pp.59–62); otherwise make sure you book by April.

Aquila (Eagle), *Onda* (Dolphin), *Tartaruga* (Turtle), *Pantera* (Panther), *Selva* (Rhinoceros) and *Chiocciola* (Snail): all southwest of the Campo in Terzo di Città.

Leocorno (Unicorn), *Torre* (Elephant), *Civetta* (Owl), *Nicchio* (Mussel shell) and *Valdimontone* (Ram): in Terzo di San Martino southeast of the Campo.

Oca (Goose), *Drago* (Dragon), *Giraffa* (Giraffe), *Lupa* (Wolf), *Bruco* (Caterpillar) and *Istrice* (Porcupine): all in the north in the Terzo di Camollia.

Sienese and Italian law recognize each of these as legally chartered communities; today a *contrada* functions as a combination of social-and-dining club, neighbourhood improvement organization, religious confraternity and mutual assistance fund. Each elects its own officials annually in May. Each has its own chapel, museum and fountain, its own flag and colours, and its own patron saint who pulls all the strings he can in Heaven twice a year to help his beloved district win the Palio.

Sociologists, and not only in Italy, are becoming ever more intrigued with this ancient yet very useful system, with its built-in community solidarity and tacit social control. (Siena has almost no crime and no social problems, except of course for a lack of jobs.) The *contrade* probably function much as they did in Roman or medieval times, but it's surprising just what up-to-date, progressive and adaptable institutions they can be, and they are still changing today. Anyone born in a *contrada* area, for example, is automatically a member; besides their baptism into the Church, they also receive a sort of 'baptism' into the *contrada*. This ritual isn't very old and it is conducted in the pretty new fountains the *contrade* have constructed all over Siena in recent years as centrepieces for their neighbourhoods.

To learn more about the *contrade*, the best place to go is one of the 17 little *contrada* museums. The tourist office can give you a list of addresses. One of the best is that of the Goose in the Terzo di Camollia. Though the caretakers usually live close by, most of them ask visitors to contact them a week in advance. The tourist office also has details on the dates of the annual *contrada* festivals and the other shows and dinners they are wont to put on; visitors are always very welcome.

Walking in Siena

If you keep your eyes open while walking the back streets of Siena, you'll see the city's entire history laid out for you in signs, symbols and a hundred other clues. You usually won't have trouble guessing which *contrada* you're in. Little ceramic plaques with the *contrada* symbol appear on buildings and street corners, not to mention flags in the neighbourhood colours, bumper stickers on cars and the fountains, each with a modern sculptural work, usually representing the *contrada*'s animal.

Look for noblemen's coats of arms above the doorways; aristocratic, archaic Siena will show you more of these than almost any Italian city. In many cases, they are still the homes of the original families, and often the same device is on a dozen houses on one block, a reminder of how medieval Siena was largely divided into separate compounds, each under the protection (or intimidation) of a noble family. One common symbol is formed from the letters IHS in a radiant sun. Siena's famous 15th-century preacher, San Bernardino, was always pestering the nobles to forget their contentiousness and enormous vanity; he proposed that they replace their heraldic symbols with the monogram of Christ. The limited success his idealism met with can be read on the buildings of Siena today.

They don't take down their old signs in Siena. One, dated 1641, informs prostitutes that the Most Serene Prince Matthias (the Florentine governor) forbids them to live on his street (Via di Salicotto). Another, a huge 19th-century marble plaque on the Banchi di Sotto, reminds passers-by that 'in this house, before modern restorations reclaimed it from squalidness, was born Giovanni Caselli, inventor of the pantograph'. A favourite, to be found on Via del Giglio, announces a stroke of the rope and a 16-lira fine for anyone throwing trash in the street, with proceeds to go to the accuser.

The Campo

There is no lovelier square in Tuscany and none more beloved by its city. The Forum of ancient *Sena Julia* was on this spot, and in the Middle Ages it evolved into its present fan shape, rather like a scallop shell or classical theatre. The Campo was paved with brick as early as 1340; the nine sections into which the fan is divided are in honour of the Council of the Nine, rulers of the city at the time. Thousands crowd over the bricks every year to see the Palio run on the periphery.

For a worthy embellishment to their Campo, the Sienese commissioned for its curved north end the **Fonte Gaia** from Jacopo della Quercia, their greatest sculptor, though what you see now is an uninspired copy from 1868. He worked on it from 1408 to 1419, creating the broad rectangle of marble with reliefs of Adam and Eve and allegorical virtues. It was to be the opening salvo of Siena's Renaissance, an answer to the baptistry doors of Ghiberti in Florence (for which della Quercia himself had been one of the contestants). Perhaps it was a poor choice of stone, but the years have been incredibly unkind to this fountain; the badly eroded remains of the original can be seen up on the loggia of the Palazzo Pubblico.

No one can spend much time in Siena without noticing its fountains. The republic always made sure each part of the city had access to good water; medieval Siena created the most elaborate engineering works since ancient Rome to bring the water in. Fonte Gaia, and others such as Fontebranda, are fed by underground aqueducts that stretch for miles across the Tuscan countryside. Charles V, when he visited the city, is reported to have said that Siena is 'even more marvellous underground than it is on the surface'.

The original Fonte Gaia was completed in the early 1300s; there's a story that soon afterwards some Sienese citizens dug up a beautiful Greek statue of Venus signed by Praxiteles himself. The delighted Sienese carried it in procession through the city and installed it on top of their new fountain. With the devastation of the Black Death, however, the preachers were quick to blame God's wrath on the indecent pagan on the Fonte Gaia. Throughout history, the Sienese have always been ready to be shocked by their own sins; in this case, with their neighbours dropping like flies around them, they proved only too eager to make poor Venus the scapegoat. They chopped her into little bits, and a party of Sienese disguised as peasants smuggled the pieces over the border and buried them in Florentine territory to pass the bad luck on to their enemies.

Palazzo Pubblico

If the Campo is like a Roman theatre, the main attraction on stage since 1310 has been this brick and stone palace, the enduring symbol of the Sienese Republic and still the town hall today. Its façade is the face of Siena's history, with the she-wolf of Senius and Ascanius, Medici balls, the IHS of San Bernardino, and squared Guelph crenellations, all in the shadow of the tremendous **Torre di Mangia** (*open daily, Nov–mid-Mar 10–4; mid-Mar–Oct 10–7; July–Aug 10am–11pm; adm €6 (€5 if you pre-book)*), the graceful, needle-like tower that Henry James called 'Siena's Declaration of Independence'. At 332ft, the tower was the second-tallest ever raised in medieval Italy (only the campanile in Cremona beats it). At the time, the cathedral tower up on its hill completely dominated Siena's skyline; the Council of the Nine wouldn't accept that the symbol of religious authority or any of the nobility's fortress-skyscrapers should be taller than the symbol of the republic, so its Perugian architects, Muccio and Francesco di Rinaldo, made sure it would be hard to beat.

There was a practical side to it, too. At the top hung the *comune*'s great bell, which had to be heard in every corner of the city tolling the hours and announcing the curfew, or calling the citizens to assemble in case of war or emergency. One of the first men to hold the job of bell-ringer gave the tower its name, a fat, sleepy fellow named *Mangiaguadagni* (eat the profits) or just Mangia for short; there is a statue of him in one of the courtyards. Climb the tower's endless staircase for the definitive view of Siena – on the clearest days, you'll also be able to see about half of the medieval republic's territory, a view that is absolutely, positively worth the slight risk of cardiac arrest. At the foot of the tower, the marble **Cappella della Piazza**, with its graceful rounded arches, stands out clearly from the Gothic earnestness of the rest of the building. It was begun in 1352, in thanks for deliverance from the Black Death, but not completed until the mid-15th century.

Most of the Palazzo Pubblico's ground floor is still used for city offices, but the upper floors have been made into the city's **museum** (*open Nov–mid-Mar 10–6.30, mid-Mar–Oct 10–7; adm*).

Here the main attraction is the series of state rooms done in frescoes, a sampling of the best of Sienese art throughout the centuries. First, though, come the historical frescoes in the **Sala del Risorgimento**, done by an artist named A.G. Cassioli in 1886: the meeting of Vittorio Emanuele II with Garibaldi, his coronation, portraits, epigrams of past patriots and an 'allegory of Italian Liberty', all in a colourful and photographically precise style.

Next, on the same floor is the **Sala di Balia** with frescoes depicting the life of Alessandro VII and some vigorous battle scenes by the Sienese Spinello Aretino (1300s) and the *Sixteen Virtues* by Martino di Bartolomeo. The adjoining **Anticamera del Concistoro** has a lovely *Madonna and Child* by Matteo di Giovanni. In the **Sala del Concistoro**, Gobelin tapestries adorn the walls while the great Sienese Mannerist

Beccafumi contributed a ceiling of frescoes in the 1530s celebrating the political virtues of antiquity; that theme is continued in the **vestibule to the chapel**, with portraits of ancient heroes from Cicero to Judas Maccabeus, all by Taddeo di Bartolo. These portrayals, along with more portraits of the classical gods and goddesses and an interesting view of ancient Rome, clearly show the extent of a real fascination with antiquity even in the 1300s.

Intruding among the classical crew, there's also a king-sized St Christopher covering an entire wall. Before setting out on a journey, it was good luck to catch a glimpse of this saint, and in Italy and Spain, he is often painted extra large so you won't miss him. In a display case in the hall, some of the oldest treasures of the Sienese Republic are kept: the war helmet of the Captain of the People, and a delicate **golden rose**, a gift to the city from the Sienese Pope, Pius II.

The chapel (**Cappella del Consiglio**) is surrounded by a lovely wrought-iron grille designed by Jacopo della Quercia; when it is open, you can see more frescoes by Taddeo di Bartolo, an altarpiece by Il Sodoma and some exceptional carved wood seats by Domenico di Nicolò (*c.* 1415–28). In the adjacent chamber (**Sala del Mappamondo**), only the outline is left of Lorenzetti's cosmological fresco, a diagram of the universe including all the celestial and angelic spheres, much like the one in the Campo Santo at Pisa. Above it, there is a very famous fresco by Simone Martini (*c.* 1330), showing the redoubtable *condottiere* **Guidoriccio da Fogliano** on his way to attack the castle of Montemassi, during a revolt against Siena. Also by Martini is an enthroned Virgin or *Maestà*, believed to be his earliest work (1315).

The Allegories of Good and Bad Government

When you enter the **Sala dei Nove** (or Sala della Pace), meeting room of the Council of the Nine, you'll understand at a glance why they ruled Siena so well. Whenever one of the councillors had the temptation to skim some cream off the top, or pass a fat contract over to his brother-in-law the paving contractor, or tighten the screws on the poor by raising the salt tax, he had only to look up at Ambrogio Lorenzetti's great frescoes to really feel like a worm. There are two complementary sets, with scenes of Siena under good government and bad, and allegorical councils of virtues or vices for each. Enthroned Justice rules the good Siena, with such counsellors as Peace, Prudence and Magnanimity; bad Siena groans under the thumb of one nasty piece of work, sneering, fanged Tyranny and his cronies: Pride, Vainglory, Avarice and Wrath, among others. The good Siena is a happy place, with buildings in good repair, well-dressed folk who are dancing in the streets, and well-stocked shops where the merchants appear to be making a nice profit. Bad Siena is almost a mirror image, only the effects of the Tyrant's rule are plain to see: urban blight, crime in broad daylight, buildings crumbling and abandoned, and business bad for everybody – a landscape which for many of us modern city dwellers will seem all too familiar.

Lorenzetti finished his work around 1338, probably the most ambitious secular painting ever attempted up to that time. The work has been recently cleaned and restored; fittingly, Good Government has survived more or less intact, while Bad Government has not aged so well and parts have been lost. In the next room is

Guido da Siena's large *Madonna and Child* (mid-1200s), the earliest masterpiece of the Sienese school. If you're not up to climbing the tower, at least take the long, unmarked stairway by the Sala del Risorgimento, leading up to the **loggia**, with the second-best view over Siena and disassembled pieces of della Quercia's reliefs from the Fonte Gaia, not particularly impressive in their worn and damaged state.

Around the Campo

Part of the Campo's beauty lies in the element of surprise; one usually enters from narrow arcades between the medieval palaces that give no hint of what lies on the other side. Two of Siena's three main streets form a graceful curve around the back of the Campo; where they meet the third, behind the Fonte Gaia, is the corner the Sienese call the **Croce del Travaglio** (a mysterious nickname: the 'Cross of Affliction').

Here, the three-arched **Loggia della Mercanzia**, in a sense Siena's Royal Exchange, was where the republic's merchants made their deals and settled their differences before the city's famed commercial tribunal. The Loggia marks the transition from Sienese-Gothic to early Renaissance style – begun in 1417, it was probably influenced by Florence's Loggia dei Lanzi. The five statues of saints on the columns are the work of Antonio Federighi and Vecchietta, the leading Sienese sculptors after della Quercia.

The three streets that meet here lead directly into the three *terzi* of Siena. All three are among the city's most beautiful, in particular the gracefully curving **Banchi di Sotto**, main artery of the Terzo di San Martino. Just beyond the Campo, this street passes Siena's most imposing *palazzo privato*, the **Palazzo Piccolomini** (*Library open (to view the* Tavolette della Biccherna) *Mon–Sat with entrance at 9.30, 10.30 or 11.30am*), done in the Florentine style by Rossellino in the 1460s. This palace now houses the old Sienese state archive – not a place you might consider visiting but for the presence of the famous *Tavolette della Biccherna* (the account books of the *Biccherna* or state treasury). Beginning in the 1200s, the republic's custom was to commission the best local artists to decorate the covers of the *tavolette*, portraying such prosaic subjects as medieval citizens coming to pay their taxes, city employees counting their pay and earnest monks trying to make the figures square – all are Cistercians from San Galgano (*see* pp.365–6), the only people medieval Siena trusted to do the job. Among other manuscripts and documents you'll find Boccaccio's will.

Terzo di Città

Southwest from the Croce del Travaglio, Via di Città climbs up to the highest and oldest part of Siena, the natural fortress of the Terzo di Città. Among the palaces it passes is the grandiose **Palazzo Chigi-Saracini**, with a wretched old tree, barely surviving, hanging over the street from its stony courtyard. The palace contains an internationally important music school, the Accademia Musicale Chigiana, and a large collection of Sienese and Florentine art (*open to the public for limited periods of the year. Call **t** 0577 246928 for information*). Next door is yet another reminder of the Piccolomini, the **Palazzo delle Papesse**. The family, along with the Colonna of Rome and the Correr of Venice, was one of the first to really exploit the fiscal possibilities of the papacy; Aeneas Silvius (Pius II) built this palace, also designed by Rossellino, for his sister, Caterina Piccolomini.

The Duomo

All approaches from Via di Città to Siena's glorious **cathedral**, spilling over the highest point in the city, are somewhat oblique. Easiest, perhaps, is Via dei Pellegrini, which winds around the back, past the unusual crypt-baptistry tucked underneath (*see* pp.336–7), up the steps to the Piazza del Duomo, and through a portal in a huge, free-standing wall of striped marble arches, a memorial to that incredible ill-starred 1339 rebuilding plan confounded by the plague. The cathedral the Sienese had to settle for may not be a transcendent expression of faith, and it may not be a great landmark in architecture, but it is certainly one of the most delightful, decorative ornaments in Christendom.

Begun around 1200, one of the first Gothic cathedrals in central Italy, it started in the good medieval tradition as a communal effort, not really a project of the Church. There doesn't seem to have been much voluntary labour – even in the Middle Ages, Italians were a little too blasé for that – but every citizen with a cart was expected to bring in two loads of marble from the quarries each year, earning him a special indulgence from the bishop. One load must have been white and the other black for, under the influence of Pisa, the Sienese built themselves one thoroughly striped cathedral – stripes darker and bolder than Pisa's or even Pistoia's. The campanile, with its distinctive fenestration, narrowing in size down six levels, rises over the city like a giant ice cream parfait. Most of the body of the church was finished by 1270, and 14 years later, Giovanni Pisano was called in to create the sculpture for the lavish **façade**, with statues of biblical prophets and pagan philosophers. The upper half was not begun until the 1390s and the glittering mosaics in the gables are, like Orvieto's, the work of Venetian artists of the late 19th century.

The Cathedral Interior: the Marble Pavement

Open winter Mon–Sat 10.30–6.30, Sun and hols 1.30–5.30;
summer Mon–Sat 10.30–7.30, Sun and hols 1.30–6.30.

This is a virtual treasure box, fit to keep a serious sightseer busy for an entire day. Upon entering the main portal, the ferociously striped pilasters and the Gothic vaulting, a blue firmament painted with golden stars, inevitably draw the eye upwards. The most spectacular feature, though, is at your feet – the marble pavement, where the first peculiar figure smiling up at you is **Hermes Trismegistus** (*see* p.334), the legendary Egyptian father of alchemy, depicted in elegant *sgraffito* work of white and coloured marble. In fact, the entire floor of the cathedral is covered with almost 12,000 square metres of virtuoso *sgraffito* in 56 scenes, including portraits, mystical allegories and Old Testament scenes. Like the Biccherna covers in the Palazzo Piccolomini, they were a tradition carried on over centuries. Many of Siena's best artists worked on them, beginning in 1369 and continuing into the 1600s; Giorgio

Siena Cathedral

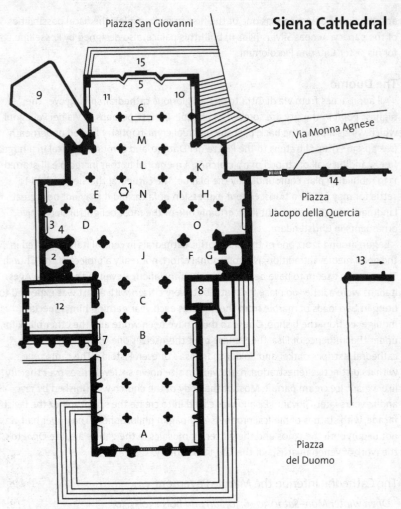

Piazza San Giovanni

Via Monna Agnese

Piazza
Jacopo della Quercia

Piazza
del Duomo

1 Pisano's Pulpit
2 Chapel of San Giovanni Battista
3 Tomb of Cardinal Pecci (Donatello)
4 Tomb of Cardinal Petroni (Tino da Camaino)
5 Stained Glass of Duccio
6 High Altar
7 Piccolomini Altar (della Quercia, Michelangelo)
8 Campanile
9 Sacristy
10 Cantorie
11 Choir
12 Piccolomini Library
13 To Cathedral Museum
14 Cathedral Extension
15 Baptistry (lower level)

A *Hermes Trismegistus*
B *Allegory of Virtue*
C *Wheel of Fortune*
D *Massacre of the Innocents*
E *Judith Liberating Bethulia*
F *Seven Ages of Man*
G *Allegories of Faith, Hope and Charity*
H *Story of Absalom*
I *Emperor Sigismund on his Throne*
J *Sacrifice of Elias, Execution of the False Prophets*
K *Samson and the Philistines*
L *David the Psalmist*
M *Sacrifice of Abraham*
N *Moses Receives the Commandments*
O *Story of Jephta*

Vasari claimed that Duccio di Buoninsegna himself first worked in this medium, though he has none among the pictures here.

Even in a building with so many marvels – the Piccolomini Library, Nicola Pisano's pulpit, Duccio's stained glass, works by Donatello, della Quercia, Pinturicchio, Michelangelo, Bernini and many others – this pavement perhaps takes pride of place. The greatest limitation of Sienese art was always the conservatism of its patrons, accustomed to demanding the same old images in the same old styles. Commissions from the Office of Cathedral Works, controlled by the state, were usually more liberal, allowing the artists to create such unique, and in some cases startling images, one of the greatest achievements of Renaissance Siena.

The Hermes on the cathedral pavement, by Giovanni di Stefano, was completed in the 1480s, a decade after Ficino's translation; he is shown with Moses, holding a book with the inscription 'Take up thy letters and laws, O Egyptians'. On either side, all 10 prophetic *Sibyls*, done by various artists at the same time, decorate the aisles. Nor are Hermes and the sibyls the only peculiar thing on this floor. Directly behind him begins a series of large scenes, including a *Wheel of Fortune*, with men hanging on to it for dear life, another wheel of uncertain symbolism, and emblems of Siena and other Tuscan and Latin cities. Oddest of all is a work by Pinturicchio, variously titled the *Allegory of Virtue* or the *Allegory of Fortune*; on a rocky island full of serpents, a party of well-dressed people has just embarked, climbing to the summit where a figure of 'Socrates' accepts a pen from a seated female figure, and another, 'Crates', empties a basket of gold and jewels into the sea. Below, a naked woman with a gonfalon stands with one foot in a boat and another on land.

Unfortunately, many of the best scenes, under the crossing and transepts, are covered to protect them. You'll need to come in the peak tourist season to see the visionary works of Alessandro Franchi – the *Triumph of Elias* and other events in that prophet's life – and Domenico Beccafumi's *Sacrifice of Elias* and the *Execution of the False Prophets of Baal*, which are usually uncovered for a couple of months in late summer (*Sept–Oct; call tourist office for confirmation*) Other works that are uncovered all year include *The Seven Ages of Man* by Antonio Federighi, *Scenes From the Life of Moses* by Beccafumi, Matteo di Giovanni's *Massacre of the Innocents* (always a favourite subject in Sienese art), and, best of all, the beautifully drawn *Judith Liberating the City of Bethulia*, a collaboration of Federighi, Matteo di Giovanni and Urbano da Cortona.

Elsewhere in the Cathedral

Perhaps the greatest attraction above floor level is the great Carrara marble **pulpit** done by Nicola Pisano in the 1280s. Pisano started on it directly after finishing the one in Pisa; one of the assistants he brought here to help with the work was the young Arnolfo di Cambio. The typical Pisano conception is held up by allegorical figures of the seven liberal arts – more sibyls, prophets, Christian virtues and saints tucked away in the odd corners, and vigorous, crowded relief panels from the Passion as good as the ones in Pisa. Nearby, in the left transept, the **chapel of San Giovanni Battista** has frescoes by Pinturicchio and a bronze statue of St John the

Hermes Trismegistus

Hermes Trismegistus is someone rarely seen in art, though he is a mysterious protagonist in a great undercurrent of Renaissance thought. 'Thrice-great Hermes', mythical author of a series of mystic philosophical dialogues from the 2nd century AD, had a profound influence on Greek and Arabic thought, gradually becoming associated (correctly or not) with the Egyptian god Thoth, inventor of writing and father of a deep mystical tradition that continues up to this day.

In the 1400s, the Hermetic writings were introduced in the West, thanks largely to the work of Greek scholars fleeing the Ottoman conquest of Constantinople and Trebizond. These writings made quite a splash, prompting a number of key figures to take action. So great was its impact that Marsilio Ficino, the Florentine Humanist and friend of Cosimo de' Medici, completed the first Latin translation of the Hermetic books in 1471 – Cosimo specifically asked him to put off his translations of Plato to get this more important work finished!

To the men of the Renaissance, Hermes was a real person, an Egyptian prophet, who lived in the time of Moses and may perhaps have been his teacher. They saw, revealed in the Hermetic books, an ancient, natural religion, prefiguring Christianity and complementary to it – and, in fact, much more fun than Christianity, for the magical elements in it were entirely to the taste of neo-Platonists like Ficino. From a contemporary point of view, the recovery of Hermes Trismegistus was one of the main intellectual events of the century, one that witnessed a tremendous revival of natural magic, alchemy and astrology.

The memorable Hermes in Siena is depicted surrounded by a bevy of 10 Sibyls: those of Cumae and Tivoli (the Italian contingent), Delphi, Libya, the Hellespont, Phrygia and others. These ladies, part of a pan-Mediterranean religious tradition even older than Hermes Trismegistus, are far more common in Tuscan religious iconography (as seen in the Baptistry and Santa Trinità in Florence, or most famously, on Michelangelo's Sistine Chapel ceiling), for the belief that they all in some way foretold the birth of Christ.

Baptist by Donatello, who also contributed the **Tomb of Giovanni Pecci**, a 1400s Sienese bishop. Another tomb worth a look is that of Cardinal Petroni, an influential early Renaissance design from 1310 by Tino di Camaino.

Some of the **stained glass** in the cathedral is excellent, especially the earliest windows, in the apse, designed by Duccio, and the rose window with its cornucopia. Over the high altar is a bronze **baldachin** by Vecchietta, and in the north aisle the **Piccolomini Altar** includes four early statues of saints by Michelangelo, and one by Torrigiano, the fellow who broke Michelangelo's nose and ended up in exile, working in Westminster Abbey. There is also a *Madonna* by Jacopo della Quercia. Throughout the cathedral, as everywhere else in Siena, be sure to keep an eye out for details – like the tiny, exquisite heads of the popes that decorate the clerestory wall. The Office of Works never settled for anything less than the best, and even such trifles as the holy water fonts, the choir stalls, the iron grilles and the candlesticks are works of genuine artistic merit.

Piccolomini Library

Open winter Mon–Sat 10.30–6.30, Sun and hols 1.30–5.30;
summer Mon–Sat 10.30–7.30.30, Sun and hols 1.30–6.30; adm.

This is the room with the famous frescoes by Pinturicchio, built to hold the library of Aeneas Silvius, the greatest member of Siena's greatest noble family. The entrance is off the left aisle, near the Piccolomini altar.

Aeneas Silvius Piccolomini, eventually to become Pope Pius II, was the very definition of a Renaissance man. He was probably the greatest geographer of his age: his works were studied closely by Columbus. Beyond that, and his activities as a poet, diplomat and historian, founder of Pienza and an important patron of artists and humanist scholars, he had, of course, a busy clerical-political career, working fitfully to reform the Church of Rome and the constitution of his native city. In 1495, 31 years after his death, Cardinal Francesco Piccolomini, the man who would become Pope Pius III, decided his celebrated uncle's life would make a fine subject for a series of frescoes. He gave the job to Pinturicchio, his last major commission; among his assistants was the young, still impressionable Raphael – anyone who knows his *Betrothal of the Virgin* will find these paintings eerily familiar.

The 10 scenes include Aeneas Silvius' attendance at the court of James I in Scotland – a Scotland with a Tuscan fantasy landscape – where he served with an embassy. Later he is shown accepting a poet laureate's crown from his friend Emperor Frederick III and presiding over the meeting of Frederick and his bride-to-be, Eleanor of Aragon. Another fresco depicts him canonizing St Catherine of Siena. The last, poignant one portrays a view of Ancona, and its cathedral up on Monte Guasco, where Pius II went in 1464, planning a crusade against the Turks. While waiting for the help promised by the European powers, help that never came, he fell ill and died.

Art historians and critics, following the sniping biography of the artist by Vasari, are not always kind to Pinturicchio. As with Gozzoli's frescoes for the Medici Palace in Florence, the consensus seems to be that this is a less challenging sort of art or perhaps just a very elevated approach to interior decoration. Certainly Pinturicchio seems extremely concerned with the latest styles in court dress and coiffure. However, the incandescent colour, fairytale backgrounds and beautifully drawn figures prove irresistible. These are among the brightest and best-preserved of all quattrocento frescoes; the total effect is that of a serenely confident art, concerned above all with beauty for beauty's sake, even when chronicling the life of a pope. Aeneas Silvius' books have all been carted away somewhere but one of his favourite things remains, a marble statue of the *Three Graces*, a copy of the work by Praxiteles that was much studied by the artists of the 1400s.

Museo dell'Opera Metropolitana

Open daily Nov–mid Mar 9–1.30, summer 9–7.30, Oct 9–6; adm.

Around the side of the cathedral, off the right transept, Piazza Jacopo della Quercia is the name the Sienese have given to the doomed nave of their 1330s **cathedral extension**. All around this square, heroic pilasters and arches rise, some incorporated into the walls of later buildings. Beyond the big, blank façade, a little door on the right allows entrance to the **Museo Metropolitana**, built into what would have been one of the cathedral transepts. This is the place to go to inspect the cathedral façade at close range. Most of the statues on the façade today are modern copies, replacing the works of great sculptors like Nicola Pisano, Urbano da Cortona and Jacopo della Quercia. The originals have been moved to the museum for better preservation and you can look the cathedral's marble saints right in the eye – if you care to; many of these remarkable statues, fairly alive with early Renaissance *prontezza* (alertness), seem ready to hop off their pedestals and start declaiming if they suspect for a minute you've been skipping Sunday Mass.

Besides these, there are architectural fragments and leftover pinnacles, as well as some bits of the marble pavement that had to be replaced. On the first floor, a collection of Sienese paintings includes Duccio di Buoninsegna's masterpiece, the *Maestà* that hung behind the cathedral's high altar from 1311 until 1505. Painted on both sides, the main composition is a familiar Sienese favourite, the enthroned Virgin flanked by neat rows of adoring saints – with expressive faces and fancy clothes set against a glittering gold background. Among the other paintings and sculptures are works by Pietro and Ambrogio Lorenzetti, Simone Martini, Beccafumi and Vecchietta.

Among the works on the top floor is the *Madonna dagli Occhi Grossi* ('of the Big Eyes') by an anonymous artist of the 1210s, a landmark in the development of Sienese painting and the original cathedral altarpiece. There's a hoard of golden croziers, reliquaries and crucifixes from the cathedral treasure, including another lovely golden rose from the Vatican – probably a gift from Aeneas Silvius. A stairway from here leads up to the top of the **Facciatone**, the 'big façade' of the unfinished nave, where you can contemplate vain ambitions and enjoy a view over the city.

Baptistry

Open summer daily 9–7.30; Oct daily 9–6; winter daily 10.30–1 and 2–5; adm.

Outside the unfinished cathedral nave, a long, steep set of stairs leads down around the back of the church to Piazza San Giovanni. In this lower but prominent setting, the Office of Works architects squeezed in a baptistry, perhaps the only one in Italy situated directly under a cathedral apse. Behind its unfinished 1390s Gothic façade, this baptistry contains yet another impressive hoard of art. It's hard to see anything in this gloomy cellar, though; bring plenty of coins for the lighting machines. Frescoes by Vecchietta, restored to death in the 19th century, decorate much of the interior. The crown jewel, however, is the **baptismal font**, a king-sized work embellished with some of the finest sculpture of the quattrocento. Of the gilded reliefs around the sides, *Herod's Feast* is by Donatello, and the *Baptism of Christ* and *St John in Prison* by Ghiberti. The first relief, with the *Annunciation of the Baptist's Birth*, is the work of Jacopo della Quercia, who also added the five statues of prophets above. Two of the statues at the corners of the font, the ones representing the virtues Hope and Charity, are also by Donatello.

Just across the street from the baptistry, the Renaissance **Palazzo del Magnifico** was the family headquarters of the Petrucci, Sienese power-brokers (and perhaps would-be tyrants) in the late 15th and early 16th centuries.

Ospedale di Santa Maria della Scala

Open Mar–Oct daily 10.30–6.30, Nov–Feb daily 10.30–4.30; adm.

Opposite the old cathedral façade, one entire side of the piazza is occupied by the great **Ospedale di Santa Maria della Scala**. Believed to have been founded in the 9th century and for centuries one of the largest and finest hospitals in the world, it is now an exciting museum project. According to legend, the hospital had its beginnings with a pious cobbler named Sorore, who opened a hostel and infirmary for pilgrims on their way to Rome. (Siena was an important stop on medieval Europe's busiest pilgrimage route, the Via Francigiana). Sorore's mother, it is said, later had a vision here – of babies ascending a ladder (*la scala*) into heaven and being received into the arms of the Virgin Mary – and consequently a foundling hospital was soon added. A meticulous attention to the health of its citizens was always one of the most praiseworthy features of Siena; even in the decadence of the 1700s, advances in such things as inoculation were being made here. In the 14th century, it insisted on such revolutionary practices as the washing of hands by doctors and nurses, meals adapted to each patient's illness, and the use of iron beds (to prevent the spread of bed bugs). To encourage donations, laws were passed allowing wealthy Sienese to deduct gifts from their taxes (remember, this was the 14th century) and not a few left huge sums in their wills; after the plague of 1348, the hospital was up to its ears in gold.

In recent years, the hospital functions have been gradually moved out to more accessible locations (one of the last to die here was novelist and folktale compiler Italo Calvino). As the place closed up, there was talk of converting it into a museum. Now they're doing it, and in a big way. The Sienese say that their new museum, dedicated to all the arts and the city's history, will be one of the largest in the world, with three times the exhibition space of the Pompidou Centre. Don't ask when it will be finished; the point of this innovative exercise is that it will *never* be finished. An international competition was held to plan the new complex; the winner, Professor Guido Canali of Parma, came up with the idea of a *cantiere didattico*, a kind of 'educational construction site', where the process of museum-building itself is part of the attraction. They should have many of the permanent exhibits in place in 10 years or so, along with shops, temporary exhibits and restoration workshops. In a typical gesture of Sienese pride, the *comune* declined to ask for state help in completing this project; they mean to keep control by paying the whole bill themselves.

For now, it's definitely worth the price of admission just to see the big frescoes in the **Sala dei Pellegrini**, the hospital's main reception hall. Another pioneering fresco-cycle devoted to a secular subject, like those in the Palazzo Pubblico, this is a tribute to old Siena's advanced, humanistic outlook; all the scenes are devoted to the history of the hospital, including the vision of Sorore's mother and everyday views of the hospital's activities. In the best of them, Domenico di Bartolo shows how Sienese art was still keeping up with the Florentines in 1441 with his *Reception, Education and Marriage of a Daughter of the Hospital*; care of abandoned children, the *getatelli* (literally, 'little ones thrown away'), was one of the hospital's important functions. Other frescoes, by different Sienese artists, portray in loving detail the caring for the sick, the distribution of alms to the poor, and the paying of the wet-nurses of the *getatelli*. All are lively, crowded scenes of life in a unique institution, and an insight into a side of old Siena you might not have thought existed.

Already, there is plenty to see, including a collection of precious golden reliquaries and other church paraphernalia, some of it from medieval Constantinople, in refurbished chambers cheerfully marked *isolamento dei contagiosi*. Some other original features of the hospital include the **Cappella del Sacro Chiodo**, with damaged frescoes by Vecchietta, the elaborate **Cappella SS. Annunziata**, and the thoroughly spooky **Cappella di Santa Caterina**, which begins with a leering skull and ends with an altarpiece by Taddeo di Bartolo. Old views and relics of the hospital are displayed in many of the long hallways; in some of the oldest, you can see how the façade was originally covered with frescoes (by Pietro and Ambrogio Lorenzetti), a colourful counterpoint to the cathedral façade across the way. Another part of the complex now houses the **Museo Archeologico** (*open daily winter 10.30–4.30, summer 10–6, joint adm with Santa Maria della Scala*) with an Etruscan and Roman collection.

The Pinacoteca

The ancient quarter of steep narrow streets north of the cathedral is the *contrada* of the *Selva* (forest) – Rhinoceros country. In its heart, Piazza della Selva, one of the most charming of the new *contrada* fountains has a bronze statue of the neighbourhood's Rhinoceros symbol. Leaving the cathedral in the opposite direction, south down Via del Capitano, will lead you into the haunts of the Dolphin and Turtle (*Onda* and *Tartaruga*). Where the street meets Via di Città, it changes its name to Via San Pietro, passing the 14th-century Palazzo Buonsignori, one of the most harmonious of the city's noble palaces, now restored as the home of the **Pinacoteca Nazionale** (*open Mon 8.30–1.30, Tues–Sat 8.15–7.15, Sun and hols 8.15–1.30; adm*).

This is the temple of Sienese art, a representative sampling of this inimitable city's style; many of the works have been recently restored. The collection is arranged roughly chronologically, beginning on the top floor with Guido da Siena and his school in the mid-13th century (Room 2), continuing through an entire room of delicate, melancholy Virgins by Duccio and his followers, before reaching a climax with Duccio's luminous though damaged *Madonna dei Francescani* in Room 4. Madonnas and saints fill room after room, including important works by Siena's greatest 14th-century artists. One of the most famous is Simone Martini's *Madonna and Child*; the story goes that this Madonna was a great Palio fan. When everyone had gathered in the Campo for the event, she would wander out in the empty streets and tiptoe over for a look. One day, she lingered too long in the Campo and had to run back home, losing her veil in her haste. She has yet to find it, and according to the Sienese, she weeps sweetly during the Palio, probably because she can't get through the Pinacoteca's security system. Other Madonnas that stand out are those of Pietro and Ambrogio Lorenzetti (*Madonna Enthroned* and the *Annunciation*, both in Room 7) and Taddeo di Bartolo (*Triptych*, in Room 11), with their rosy blooming faces and brilliant colour, a remarkable counterpoint to the relative austerity of contemporary painting in Florence. One element that is clearly evident in many of these paintings is Sienese civic pride; the artists take obvious delight in including the city's skyline and landmarks in the background of their works – even in Nativities.

Sienese Renaissance painters are well represented, often betraying the essential conservatism of their art and resisting the new approaches of Florence: Domenico di Bartolo's 1433 *Madonna* in Room 9; Nerocchio and Matteo di Giovanni of the 1470s (Room 14); Sano di Pietro, the leading painter of the 1440s (Rooms 16–17). The first floor displays some of Il Sodoma's most important works, especially the great *Scourging of Christ* in Room 31 (1514); in Room 37 the *Descent into Hell* is one of the finest works by Siena's greatest Mannerist, Beccafumi.

Around the Terzo di Città

Next to the Pinacoteca, the church of **San Pietro alle Scale** contains *The Flight into Egypt*, an altarpiece by Rutilio Manetti, the only significant Sienese painter of the Baroque era, a follower of Caravaggio. **San Giuseppe**, at the end of Via San Pietro, marks Siena's uneasy compromise with the new world of the 1600s. One of the city's first Baroque churches, it was nevertheless built not in Baroque marble or travertine but good Siena brown brick. This is the church of the *Onda* (Dolphin) district; the *contrada*'s fountain is in front. Just around the corner, the gloomy bulk of **Sant'Agostino** conceals a happier rococo interior of the 1740s by Vanvitelli, the Dutchman (born Van Wittel) who was chief architect for the Kings of Naples. Most of the building dates back to the 13th century, however, and there are surviving bits of trecento frescoes and altarpieces all around. In the north aisle, the Piccolomini chapel (*usually shut*) has a fine painting by Il Sodoma, an *Epiphany* and a *Massacre of the Innocents* by Matteo di Giovanni.

Via Piero Andrea Mattioli leads from here to the city walls and the Porta Tufi, passing along the way a path that leads to Siena's small **Botanical Gardens** (*open Mon–Fri 8–12.30 and 2.30–5.30, Sat 8–12; book in advance for guided tours, t 0577 232874*). Further west, the *contrada* of the *Chiocciola* (Snail) is centred on the church of **Santa Maria del Carmine**, a 14th-century church remodelled by Baldassare Peruzzi in 1517; inside there is a painting of *St Michael* by Beccafumi and a rather grimly Caravaggiesque *Last Judgement* by an anonymous 16th-century artist.

Terzo di San Martino

Beginning again at the Croce del Travaglio and the Palazzo Piccolomini (*see p.330*), Banchi di Sotto leads into the quiet eastern third of the city, passing the **Loggia del Papa**, a Renaissance ornament given to Siena by Aeneas Silvius Piccolomini in 1462.

The most intriguing parts of this neighbourhood are found on the hillside behind Piazza del Mercato, old streets on slopes and stairs in the *contrada* of the *Torre* (Elephant) – one of the 'unlucky' *contrade* that hasn't won a Palio in decades. Nevertheless they have a fine fountain with their elephant-and-tower emblem on pretty Piazzetta Franchi. One of the more characteristic streets in this part of town is **Via dell'Oro**, an alley of overhanging medieval houses, much like the ones in the Palazzo Pubblico's frescoes of Good and Bad Government (*see* p.329). For a change, **Via Porta Giustizia** will lead you on a country ramble within the city's walls, along the valley that separates Terzo San Martino and Terzo di Città.

Among the noteworthy churches in this Terzo are **Santo Spirito** on Via dei Pispini, with further frescoes by Il Sodoma in the first chapel on the right; and **Santa Maria dei Servi**, to the south on Via dei Servi in the *contrada* of *Valdimontone* (Ram). Here, in the north transept, is one of the earliest and finest Sienese nativities, the altarpiece in the second north chapel, by Taddeo di Bartolo. Good paintings include a *Madonna* by Coppo di Marcovaldo and the *Madonna del Popolo* by Lippo Memmi. An interesting comparison can be made between two versions of that favourite Sienese subject, the *Massacre of the Innocents*: one from the early trecento by Pietro Lorenzetti, and another from 1491 by Matteo di Giovanni.

Nearby at Via Roma 7, the *Società Esecutori Pie Disposizioni* keeps an **oratory** and a small but good collection of Sienese art (*call ahead, t 0577 284300; open Mon and Fri 9–1, Tues and Thurs 3–5.30*). This Terzo also has two of the best surviving city gates, the **Porta Romana** at the end of Via Roma, and the elegant **Porta Pispini** on the road to Perugia. The latter was once embellished with a *Nativity* by Sodoma, of which only traces are still visible.

Terzo di Camollia

Leading north from the Campo, the **Via Banchi di Sopra** is a most aristocratic thoroughfare, lined with the palaces of the medieval Sienese élite. It forms the spine of this largest and most populous of the *terzi*. The first important palace is also one of the oldest, that of the Tolomei family, a proud clan of noble bankers who liked to trace their ancestry back to the Greek Ptolemies of Hellenistic-era Egypt. The **Palazzo Tolomei**, begun in 1208, is the very soul of Sienese Gothic; it gave its name to Piazza Tolomei in front, the space used by the republic for its assembly meetings before the construction of the Palazzo Pubblico.

Just a few blocks down Banchi di Sopra, **Palazzo Salimbeni** on Piazza Salimbeni was the compound of the Tolomeis' mortal enemies; their centuries-long vendetta dragged Sienese politics into chaos on more than a few occasions. Together with the two adjacent palaces on the square, the Salimbeni is now the home of the *Monte dei Paschi di Siena*, founded by the city as a pawnshop in 1472, now a remarkable savings bank with a medieval air about it that has a tremendous influence over everything that happens in southern Tuscany, and branches as far away as Australia – they also have a good art collection, sometimes open to the public along with special exhibitions. The national government is currently trying to privatize the Monte dei Paschi, which makes the Sienese hopping mad. A little further up the street, the plain brick **Oratory of Santa Maria di Nevi** is almost always locked up; if you should chance to see it open, stop in to see the altarpiece, the finest work of the late 1400s painter Matteo di Giovanni.

East of these palaces, in the neighbourhood of the *Giraffa* (Giraffe), is one of the last important churches built in Siena, the proto-Baroque **Santa Maria di Provenzano** (1594), at the end of Via del Moro. This particular Virgin Mary, a terracotta image said to have been left by St Catherine (*see* below), has had one of the most popular devotional cults in Siena since the 1590s; the annual Palio is in her honour. The quiet streets behind the church, Siena's red-light district in Renaissance times, lead to **San Francesco**, begun in 1326, one of the city's largest churches. It's a sad tale; after a big fire in the 17th century, this great Franciscan barn was used for centuries as a warehouse and barracks. Restorations began in the 1880s and the 'medieval' brick façade was completed only in 1913. The interior is still one of the most impressive in Siena, a monolithic rectangle with vivid stained glass (especially in late afternoon) and good transept chapels in the Florentine manner. A little artwork has survived, including traces of frescoes by both the Lorenzettis in the north transept. To the right is the fine Renaissance cloister.

Next to San Francesco is the equally simple **Oratorio di San Bernardino** (*open mid-Mar–Oct daily 10.30–1.30 and 3–5.30; adm*), begun in the late 1400s in honour of Siena's famous preacher and graced with the preacher's heart. Its upper chapel, a monument of the Sienese Renaissance, contains frescoes by Beccafumi, Il Sodoma and the almost forgotten High Renaissance master Girolamo del Pacchia, few of whose works survive. The areas west of San Francesco, traditionally a solid working-class quarter, make up the *contrada* of *Bruco* (Caterpillar); their fountain is under the steps on Via dei Rossi. On the wall of the house opposite is a curious marble relief of a woman at a window peering at a pomegranate from behind half-closed curtains. Caterpillars are everywhere.

Bruco's name recalls the Compagnìa del Bruco, the trade union that initiated the revolt of 1371, temporarily reforming Siena's faction-ridden government. The workers paid a terrible price for it; while the revolution was under way, some young noble *provocateurs* started a fire that consumed almost the entire *contrada*. Today *Bruco* fares worst of the 'unlucky' neighbourhoods; it hasn't won a Palio since 1955.

St Catherine, St Dominic and the Goose

Unlike the poor caterpillar, the equally proletarian *Oca* (Goose) seems the best organized and most successful *contrada*. On occasion during the Napoleonic Wars, with Tuscan and city governments in disarray, the *Oca*'s men took charge of the city.

The goose's most famous daughter, Caterina Benincasa, was born here on Vicolo del Tiratoio in 1347. She was the last but one of 25 children born into the family of a wool-dyer. At an early age the visions started. By her teens, she had turned her room at home into a cell and, while she never became a nun, she lived like a hermit, a solitary ascetic in her own house, sleeping with a stone for a pillow. After she received the stigmata, like St Francis, her reputation as a holy woman spread across Tuscany; popes and kings corresponded with her, and towns would send for her to settle their disputes. In 1378 Florence was under a papal interdict, and the city asked Catherine to plead its case at the papal court at Avignon. She went, but with an agenda of her own – convincing Pope Gregory XI to move the papacy back to Rome where it belonged. As a woman, and a holy woman to boot, she was able to tell the pope to his face what a corrupt and worldly Church he was running, without ending up dangling from the top of a palace wall.

Talking the pope (a French pope, mind you) into leaving the civilized life in Provence for turbulent, barbaric 14th-century Rome is only one of the miracles with which Catherine was credited. Political expediency probably helped more than divine intervention – much of Italy, including anathemized Florence, was in revolt against the absentee popes. She followed them back and died in Rome in 1380, aged only 33.

Canonization came in 1460, and in the 19th century, she was declared co-patron of Italy (along with St Francis) and one of the Doctors of the Church. She and St Teresa of Avila are the only women to hold this honour – given in acknowledgement of their inspired devotional writings and their practical, incisive letters encouraging church reform.

The *contrada* of the Goose stretches down steeply from Banchi di Sopra to the western city walls. At its centre, on Vicolo di Tiratoio, St Catherine's house is preserved as a shrine; the **Santuario e Casa di Santa Caterina** (*open daily 9–12.30 and 3–6*) includes the whole of the Benincasa home and the dyer's workshop, each room converted into a chapel, many with frescoes by 15th- and 16th-century Sienese artists. The adjacent oratory is now the *Oca*'s *contrada* chapel (note the goose in the detail of the façade).

Via Santa Caterina, the main street of the *Oca*, slopes down towards the city walls and **Fontebranda**, a simple pointed-arched fountain of the 13th century. It doesn't seem much now, but medieval and Renaissance travellers always remarked on it, and it was an important part of Siena's advanced system of fountains and aqueducts. The church of **San Domenico**, on the hill above Fontebranda, similarly fails to impress, at least when you see it close up from the bus depot on Piazza San Domenico. From Fontebranda, however, the bold Gothic lines of the apse and transepts give a great insight into the straightforward, strangely modern character of much Sienese religious architecture. It's a long climb up to the church from here. Inside, the church is as big and empty as San Francesco; among the relatively few works of art is the only existing portrait of St Catherine, on the west wall, painted by her friend, the artist Andrea Vanni. In this church, scene of so many incidents from the saint's life, you can see her head in a golden reliquary, though the real attraction is the wonderfully hysterical set of murals by Il Sodoma in the **Cappella Santa Caterina**, representing the girl in various states of serious exaltation.

The open, relatively modern quarter around San Domenico offers a welcome change from the dark and treeless streets of this brick city, in a shady park called **La Lizza** and the green spaces around the **Fortezza Medicea**. Though the site is the same, this is not the hated fortress Charles V compelled the Sienese to build in 1552;

as soon as the Sienese chased the imperial troops out, they razed it to the ground. Cosimo I forced its rebuilding after annexing Siena, but to make the bitter pill easier to swallow, he employed a Sienese architect, Baldassare Lanci, and let him create what must be the most elegant and civilized, least threatening fortress in Italy. The Fortezza, a long, low rectangle of Siena brick profusely decorated with Medici balls, seems more like a setting for garden parties or summer opera than anything designed to intimidate a sullen populace.

The Sienese weren't completely won over; right after the Italian reunification, they renamed the central space of the fortress **Piazza della Libertà**. The grounds are now a city park, and the vaults of the munition cellars have become the **Enoteca Nazionale** (*open Tues–Sat 12pm–1am, Mon 12pm–8pm, closed Sun; adm?*), the 'Permanent Exhibition of Italian Wines'. Almost every variety of wine Italy produces can be bought here, by the glass or by the bottle. The Enoteca's purpose is to promote Italian wines – it ships thousands of bottles overseas each year and hosts an annual *Settimana dei Vini* featuring regional wines in the first half of June.

East of the fortress, beyond the Lizza and the city stadium, lie the twin centres of modern Siena, **Piazza Gramsci**, terminus for most city bus lines, and **Piazza Matteotti**. Continuing northwards towards the Camollia Gate, you pass the little Renaissance church of **Fonte Giusta**, just off Via di Camollia on Vicolo Fontegiusta. Designed in 1482 by Urbano da Cortona, this church contains a fresco by Peruzzi (another sibyl) and a magnificent tabernacle over the main altar; there is also a whalebone, left here, according to local legend, by Christopher Columbus. The **Porta Camollia**, in the northernmost corner of Siena, underwent the Baroque treatment in the 1600s. Here you will see the famous inscription 'Wider than her gates Siena opens her heart to you'. Old Siena was never that sentimental. The whole thing was added in 1604 – undoubtedly under the orders of the Florentine governor – to mark the visit of Grand Duke Francesco I, who wasn't really welcome at all.

Peripheral Attractions

From Porta Camollia, Viale Vittorio Emanuele leads through some of the modern quarters outside the walls. Beyond the gate it passes a column commemorating the meeting of Emperor Frederick III and his bride-to-be Eleanor of Aragon in 1451 – the event captured in one of the Pinturicchio frescoes in the Piccolomini Library. Next looms a great defence tower, the **Antiporto**, erected just before the Siege of Siena and rebuilt in 1675. Further down, the **Palazzo dei Diavoli** (1460) was the headquarters of the Marquis of Marignano during the siege.

There isn't much on the outskirts of the city – thanks largely to Marignano, who laid waste lovely and productive lands for miles around. Some 2km east (take Via Simone Martini from the Porta Ovile), in the hills above the railway station, the basilica and monastery of **L'Osservanza** has been carefully restored after serious damage in the last war. Begun in 1422, a foundation of San Bernardino, the monastery retains much of its collection of 13th-and 14th-century Sienese art.

To the west of the city, the road to Massa Marittima passes through the hills of the Montagnola Sienese, an important centre of monasticism in the Middle Ages (*see* San Galgano, pp.365–6). Near **Montecchio** (6km), the hermitage of **Lecceto**, one of the oldest in Tuscany, has been much changed, but still has some Renaissance frescoes in the church and a 12th-century cloister; nearby, the hermitage of **San Leonardo al Lago** is mostly in ruins but the 14th-century church survives, with masterly frescoes (*c.* 1360) by Pietro Lorenzetti's star pupil, Lippo Vanni. Just outside the village of **Sovicille** (13km), there is a 12th-century Romanesque church, the **Pieve di Ponte alla Spina**.

The village of **Rosia** (17km) has another Romanesque church, and just south is the Vallombrosan **Abbey of Torri** (*open Mon–Fri 3.30–6*), with much from its original foundation in the 1200s; it has a rare three-storey cloister, with three types of columns.

Hill Towns
West of Siena

13

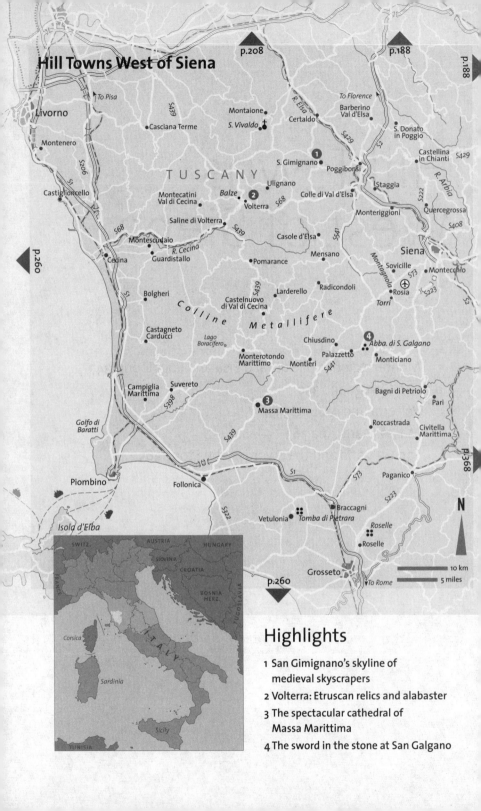

To Pisa

Livorno

S439

Montaione

S. Vivaldo ✝

Casciana Terme

Certaldo

To Florence

Barberino
Val d'Elsa

S. Donato
in Poggio

Castellina
in Chianti

S429

R. Arbia

Montenero

S206

S. Gimignano ①

Poggibonsi

T U S C A N Y

Ulignano

Staggia

S2

S222

Castiglioncello

S5

Montecatini
Val di Cecina

Balze ②

Volterra

S68

Colle di Val d'Elsa

Monteriggioni

Quercegrossa

S408

Saline di Volterra

S439

Casole d'Elsa

S541

Siena

p.260

Montescudaio

R. Cecina

Guardistallo

Cecina

S68

Pomarance

Mensano

Montagnola

Sovicille

S73

Montecchio

S2

Bolgheri

S1

Colline

S439

Larderello

Radicondoli

Rosia

S223

Metallifere

Torri

Castagneto
Carducci

Castelnuovo
di Val di Cecina

Lago
Boracifero

Chiusdino

Palazzetto

Abba. di S. Galgano ④

Monticiano

Monterotondo
Marittima

Montieri

S441

Campiglia
Marittima

Suvereto

S998

Massa Marittima ③

Bagni di Petriolo

Pari

Golfo di
Baratti

S439

Roccastrada

Civitella
Marittima

p.368

Piombino

Follonica

S1

S73

Paganico

S223

N

S322

Braccagni

S223

Vetulonia

Tomba di Pietrara

Roselle

Isola d'Elba

Roselle

Grosseto

p.260

To Rome

10 km

5 miles

SWITZ.

AUSTRIA

HUNGARY

FRANCE

SLOVENIA

CROATIA

BOSNIA
HERZ.

YUGOSLAVIA

Corsica

ITALY

Sardinia

Sicily

TUNISIA

Highlights

1 San Gimignano's skyline of
medieval skyscrapers

2 Volterra: Etruscan relics and alabaster

3 The spectacular cathedral of
Massa Marittima

4 The sword in the stone at San Galgano

In the late Middle Ages, this dramatically diverse, often rugged countryside was a border region, both culturally and politically, its people alternately subject to the strong pull of Florence and Siena. Its towns do not have that much in common: Poggibonsi is almost all new, while Volterra goes back to the Etruscans. San Gimignano presents its famous skyline of medieval skyscrapers, while parts of the Metal Hills show outlandish silhouettes of cooling towers from the ubiquitous geothermal power plants. San Gimignano and Volterra are the main attractions, both beautiful cities containing some remarkable works of art. Massa Marittima, often overlooked, has one of the finest cathedrals in Italy.

Beyond that there is a doll-sized walled city, bubbling sulphurous pits, alabaster souvenirs, a Roman theatre, lonely moors and a sword in a stone (not King Arthur's but someone else's).

Monteriggioni, Colle di Val d'Elsa and Poggibonsi

Monteriggioni

The SS2 passes a genuine curiosity 11km north of Siena, the tiny fortified town of **Monteriggioni**. For much of Siena's history, this was its northernmost bastion, often in the frontlines in the wars with Florence after its construction in 1219. Now it sits like a crown on its roundish hill, a neat circle of walls with 14 towers, with just enough room inside for two oversized piazzas, a few houses and their gardens, and the inevitable bars and restaurants. In late July, the town hosts a medieval festival – a re-enactment of medieval life with food, drink, music and dancing – the highlight is the third weekend in July. Some 3km further towards Colle di Val d'Elsa, there is a turn-off to the left for the 12th-century Abbey of Santi Salvatore and Cirino, better known as the **Abbadia dell'Isola**. The Cistercians began it in 1101 on an 'island' among the marshes, hence the name. Inside this stark Romanesque building is a restored fresco by Taddeo di Bartolo and a Renaissance altarpiece.

Colle di Val d'Elsa

Colle di Val d'Elsa (pop. 16,300), a striking, ancient town up on a steep hill, presents an impressive silhouette if you see it from the right angle – it's long enough but at most only three blocks wide. Though probably as old as the Etruscans, Colle first became prominent in the 12th century, a safe, fortified stronghold that attracted many migrants from the surrounding plains. In later centuries, it was known for the manufacture of wool, paper and ceramics; today, Colle is Italy's largest producer of fine glass and crystal, and there are lots of shops selling it. There is also a new museum, the **Museo Del Cristallo** (*Via dei Fossi, t 0577 924135; open April–Oct Tues–Sun 10–12 and 4–7.30; Nov–Mar Tues–Fri 3–7, Sat–Sun 10–12 and 3-7; adm*) in a 19th-century crystal factory in the 'new' town (down the hill). The Collegiani will never allow the world to forget that their town was the birthplace of Arnolfo di Cambio, the great architect who built Florence's Palazzo Vecchio and began its cathedral.

Getting Around

The main routes between Florence and Siena – the Via Cassia (SS2) or the parallel Superstrada del Palio – have exits for Colle di Val d'Elsa (27km/35mins from Siena, 49km/1hr from Florence) and Poggibonsi, 7km further north on SS68.

Poggibonsi is a major **bus** junction in south Tuscany, with easy connections to Florence, Siena, San Gimignano, Volterra and Colle di Val d'Elsa (TRA-IN buses if you're coming from Siena, SITA from Florence). Poggibonsi is also on the Empoli–Siena **railway** line, with a branch or bus beyond to Colle in 15mins.

Tourist Information

Monteriggioni: Largo Fontebianda 5, t/f 0577 304810.

Colle di Val d'Elsa: Via Campana 43, t 0577 922791, f 0577 922621.

Where to Stay and Eat

Monteriggioni ✉ 53035

If you're heading from Florence to Siena, or from Siena out to the west, a good place to stop for lunch is the little castle village of Monteriggioni.

Il Pozzo, Piazza Roma 2, t 0577 304127 (*expensive*). Here they do some of the simpler dishes very well – bean soup and roast meats – but their real forte is fancy desserts (they even serve *crêpes Suzette*). *Closed Sun eve and Mon*.

Hotel Monteriggioni, t 0577 305009, f 0577 305011, *www.monteriggioni.net* (*very expensive*). If you want to keep within the walls, you can have a very comfortable stay at the Monteriggioni, made up of two old stone houses, a garden and even a tiny pool.

Colle di Val d'Elsa ✉ 53034

★★★**Villa Belvedere**, Località Belvedere, t 0577 920966, f 0577 924128, *www.villabelvedere.com* (*expensive*). Located 1km or so east of the town, near the Siena highway, this pretty, old villa has a good restaurant, a big garden, swimming pool and 15 simple rooms.

★★★**Arnolfo**, in the Borgo at Via Campana 8, t 0577 922020, f 0577 922324, *www.hotel arnolfo.it* (*moderate*). Simple and comfortable, in the town itself.

Arnolfo Restaurant, Via XX Settembre 52, t 0577 920549 (*expensive*). This occupies a Renaissance palace, the perfect setting for what is widely considered one of the top restaurants in all Italy. Menus change with the seasons, but you can always choose from two *menu degustazioni* – one 'traditional', one 'creative'. *Closed Tues and Wed*.

Osteria di Sapia, Via del Castello 4, t 0577 921453 (*moderate*). The décor in this elegant osteria (yellow and blue walls and lots of ethnic bits and pieces) situated in the old town is a refreshingly far cry from typical Tuscan rustic. The food, too, is a bit different. Creative variations on the Tuscan theme include vegetarian lasagne and pork tenderloin cooked with peaches and *vin santo*. The two set menus are good value and there is a lovely terrace. *Closed Mon, lunch Nov–Feb*.

Fattoria di Mugnano, 7km along the Colle–Volterra road, t 0577 959023 (*cheap*). An old farm, now a thriving business, out among the olive groves in the nearby hamlet of Mugnano. The delightful restaurant offers local and Sicilian cuisine; they'll sell you some of the wine and olive oil. They also offer a few spartan rooms (*inexpensive*). *Closed Thurs*.

L'Oste di Borgo, Via Gracco del Secco 58, t 0577 922499 (*cheap*). A nice little *osteria* with a terrace and a few marble-topped tables in a wood-panelled room and background jazz. You can eat a light meal (choose from an interesting selection of pastas and salads), or snack on *bruschette*, local cheeses, hams and salamis. *Closed Wed*.

Poggibonsi ✉ 53036

★★★**Alcide**, Via Marconi 67a, t 0577 937501, f 0577 981729 (*moderate*). If you're spending time in Poggibonsi this offers doubles with air conditioning. Their restaurant (*expensive*) is one of the better places for seafood in this landlocked province, featuring dishes with a South Italian slant, like Apulian *orecchiette* in a sauce with cuttlefish and several varieties of maritime risotto. *Closed Sun eve, Mon*.

Down on the plain below the citadel, the modern part of the town surrounds the arcaded **Piazza Arnolfo di Cambio**. Via Garibaldi or Via San Sebastiano will take you up to old Colle – but for a proper introduction you'll need to come on the road from Volterra, passing through a grim Renaissance bastion called the **Porta Nuova**, designed by Giuliano da Sangallo, and then across the medieval-Renaissance suburb known as the **Borgo**. Between the Borgo and the old town, called the **Castello**, there is a picturesque narrow bridge and the **Palazzo di Campana** (1539, by Giovanni di Baccio d'Agnolo); the arch in its centre is the elegant gateway to the town.

Via del Castello runs straight up the centre, with narrow medieval alleys on both sides. Here you'll find the **cathedral**, built in 1603 (Colle only got its own bishop in 1592) with a Victorian-era façade, a few Renaissance palaces, and some museums. Beside the cathedral, in the Palazzo Pretorio, a small **Museo Archeologico** (*open Oct–April Tues–Fri 3.30–5.30, Sat, Sun and hols 10–12 and 3.30–6.30; May–Sept Tues–Sun 10–12 and 4.30–7.30; adm*) displays Etruscan objects; there is a small picture collection in the nearby **Museo Civico** (*same hours as Museo Archeologico; adm*). The best is the **Museo d'Arte Sacra** (*same hours as Museo Archeologico; adm*) in the old episcopal palace, with a few Sienese and Florentine paintings and the frescoes commissioned by some jolly 14th-century bishop – scenes of the hunt and from the Crusades, believed to be the work of Ambrogio Lorenzetti.

Near the end of Via del Castello, the Collegiani claim an old tower-fortress as the **House of Arnolfo di Cambio**. Arnolfo's father, a gentleman and an architect, probably came to Colle di Val d'Elsa from Lombardy in the 1230s, bringing the great tradition of the Lombard master masons into Tuscany. He may have received his initiation into the new (for Italy) Gothic style from studying works in Siena or the new Cistercian abbey at San Galgano. He worked for Nicola Pisano on the Siena cathedral pulpit, and for Giovanni Pisano on the Fonte Maggiore in Perugia, and probably moved to Florence in the 1270s.

South of Colle, many of the villages in the hills retain their simple Romanesque churches from the 11th–12th centuries, beginning with the isolated **Badia a Coneo**, a Vallombrosan foundation of the 1120s (5km from Colle on an unpaved lane off the road to Casole). At **Casole d'Elsa** (15km south, local bus), a town that took hard knocks in the last war, there is an interesting **Collegiata** church begun in the 12th century, with Sienese frescoes, two fine, late 14th-century sepulchres by Gano da Siena, and terracottas by Giovanni della Robbia. Casole's Sienese **Rocca** held out into the 16th century, long after the rest of the Valdelsa flew the Florentine flag. South from Casole, the road winds through pleasant, green countryside leading up to the Colline Metallifere, the 'metal hills', and you can seek out more Romanesque churches in **Mensano** (7km) and **Radicondoli** (15km, the church of **San Simone**).

Poggibonsi

If you spend enough time in Tuscany, sooner or later you are bound to pass through **Poggibonsi** (pop. 25,700), a major knot on the SS2, SS429 and Superstrada del Palio roads linking Siena to Florence and Pisa. These days, residents of the pretty tourist towns of central Tuscany are not above having a laugh at the expense of this homely, hard-working industrial centre. Poor Poggibonsi! Founded only in 1156, the original *Poggiobonizzo* grew rapidly. By 1220, it was probably one of the largest cities in Tuscany, with a population of some 15,000; in that year, Emperor Frederick II declared it a *Città Imperiale* with special rights and privileges. Ghibelline politics and its imperial favour, however, were to prove Poggiobonizzo's undoing. In 1270, San Gimignano and Colle di Val d'Elsa, along with the Florentines and the troops of Charles of Anjou, besieged and conquered the city, then razed it to the ground. Some of the poorer citizens stayed behind, refounding the town as a market village on the plain. Poggibonsi was thoroughly wrecked again during the battles of 1944, but has grown tremendously since to become the biggest town between Florence and Siena.

There isn't much to see; the 14th-century Palazzo Pretorio and the collegiate church on the main street recall something of the appearance of pre-war Poggibonsi. Close by, the **Castello della Magione** is a small complex from the 1100s; the Romanesque chapel and outbuildings form a little closed square, a fortified pilgrims' hospice said to have been built by the Templars. Above the town, an unfinished fortress begun by Lorenzo de' Medici covers much of the original city of Poggiobonizzo.

Just 2km south of town near the SS2, is the austerely Franciscan **Basilica of San Lucchese**; inside are some good frescoes, including works by Taddeo Gaddi and Bartolo di Fredi. Not surprisingly, this strategically important corner of Tuscany is scattered with castles, including the 13th-century **Castello della Rochetta**, once the home of the famous *condottiere* Sir John Hawkwood, and the romantically ruined **Rocca di Staggia** (5km south of Poggibonsi on the SS2), built by the Florentines in the 1430s – a counterpart to Sienese Monteriggioni, just a few kilometres further on.

San Gimignano

In the miniaturist landscape of this corner of Tuscany, **San Gimignano**, Italy's best-preserved medieval city, is an almost fantastic landmark. Seen from Poggibonsi or the Volterra road its medieval towers, some of them over 50m tall, loom over the surrounding hills. Once, almost every city in central Italy looked like this; more than just defensive strongholds in the incessant family feuds, these towers served as status symbols for the families and the cities themselves, a visible measure of a town's power and prosperity. By the 16th century, most of Italy's towers had succumbed to age, decay and the efforts of the urban *comuni*, which pruned and destroyed these symbols of truculent nobility at every opportunity. Oddly, this did not happen in San Gimignano, famous even in the 1300s as the '*città delle belle torri*'. Originally there were at least 70 towers (in a town one-eighth of a square mile in size). Only 15 remain, but in conjunction with the beautiful streets, churches and public buildings, they are enough to give you the impression that the town has been hermetically sealed in a time-capsule since the Middle Ages.

History

According to legend, the town was originally called Castel della Selva. When the Gothic army of Totila passed through in the 550s, the townsfolk for some reason chose to pray to an obscure saint named Gimignano, a martyred bishop of Modena,

Getting Around

The railway station is 11km away and is an infrequent stop on the Empoli–Siena line. Buses to the town *usually* coincide with the **trains**, but from either Siena or Florence you'll be better off taking the bus, which leaves you right at the Porta San Giovanni, the main entrance to the town.

TRA-IN **buses** from Siena (38km/45mins – the same bus that goes to Colle di Val d'Elsa) are very frequent, though for most, you will need to change in Poggibonsi. Several daily SITA buses arrive from Florence (54km/1hr 15mins) and there are four buses a day to nearby Certaldo.

If you're **driving**, San Gimignano is 11km west of Poggibonsi, 13km south of Certaldo or 14km from Colle di Val d'Elsa, each route more scenic than the last. Within the walls, San Gimignano is usually closed to traffic; the main car park is outside Porta San Giovanni. Get a pass from the police to park at one of the hotels inside.

Tourist Information

San Gimignano: Piazza del Duomo 1, **t** 0577 940008, **f** 0577 940903, *www.sangimignano.com*

Admission

If you plan to visit all the key sights, it is worth buying the cheaper joint ticket (*biglietto cumulativo* €7.50) which covers the four museums, the tower of Palazzo del Popolo and the Capella di Santa Fina, but not the Collegiata.

Shopping

There isn't any particular artisan tradition here, but so many tourists visit that enterprising shop owners have assembled a host of interesting things – the town hasn't quite turned into a great trinket bazaar, but it's getting there.

Linea Oro, Via San Giovanni. Among the good buys are pretty things in alabaster from nearby Volterra.

Via San Matteo 85, north of Piazza del Duomo. One of the best shops for alabaster is here.

La Stamperia, Via San Matteo 88. Sells original prints including views of Tuscan towns and countryside.

Ceramics are everywhere; some of the local work is quite good and inexpensive.

Just within Porta San Giovanni is a 13th-century church now converted to a shop for local wine, olive oil and other farm products.

San Gimignano's other specialities are a formidable white wine called Vernaccia (*see* p.354) and a sweet called *mandorlato*, very like the *panforte* of Siena. Many local vineyards would be glad to sell you a bottle of *Vernaccia*. One such is **Cantine Baroncini**, Casale, **t** 0577 940600.

Activities

If you want to explore the surrounding countryside on horseback, there is a riding centre close by.

Vecchio Maneggio, Sant'Andrea 22, Ulignano, **t** 0577 950232, 5km along the road to Certaldo. Also an *agriturismo* offering rooms (*moderate*).

for their salvation from a near-guaranteed sacking. Gimignano came through in style, looming down from the clouds in golden armour to scare away the besiegers.

Although it must have been an important and prosperous place, San Gimignano does not cut much of a figure in the medieval chronicles. The city was an independent republic from the early 1100s until 1353, when it came under the rule of Florence. It certainly participated in the Guelph–Ghibelline strife, and in all the other troubles of the period, though today it is probably best remembered as the home town of the poet Folgore of San Gimignano (c. 1250), famous for his lovely sonnets to the months of the year. San Gimignano has the air of a false start, a free *comune* that could build a wall and defend itself, yet lacked the will or the money to make itself into a Siena

Where to Stay

San Gimignano ✉ 53037

In the summer, you may want a hand finding a place to sleep.

Hotel Association, just inside the gate on Via S. Giovanni, t/f 0577 940809.

★★★Antico Pozzo, Via San Matteo 87, **t** 0577 942014, **f** 0577 942117, *www.l'anticopozzo.com* (*expensive*). Next to the main square, this is a stylish hotel with wonderful views from rooms at the top of the house. The building dates from the 1500s – several of the rooms even have delicately frescoed ceilings.

★★★Le Renaie, Loc Pancole, about 7km towards Certaldo, **t** 0577 955044, **f** 0577 955126, *www.hotellerenaie.com* (*expensive*). If you prefer the tranquillity of the very lovely Tuscan countryside, head north of town to find this attractive modern building, with a garden, pool and tennis court.

★★★La Cisterna, **t** 0577 940328, **f** 0577 942080, *www.hotelcisterna.it* (*expensive*). If the Leon Bianco is full, this is in the same square and also comes highly recommended.

★★★Leon Bianco, Piazza della Cisterna, **t** 0577 941294, **f** 0577 942123, *www.leon blanco.com* (*moderate*). An excellent hotel with modern rooms.

To fill the vacuum of inexpensive accommodation, a score of San Gimignese rent out rooms. The tourist office can give you a list.

Eating Out

San Gimignano may entertain a good many visitors, but it makes a fine host.

Dorando, Vicolo del Oro 2, **t** 0577 941862 (*expensive*). For the more adventurous. The chef attempts to recreate authentic Renaissance and Medieval cuisine – *cibreo* (a chicken liver pâté so rich Caterina de' Medici nearly died from a surfeit of it), boned guinea fowl with honey and black sesame seeds, maccheroni with duck and mushroom sauce and a truffle glaze, crème caramel flavoured with coriander, and things stranger still. Readers have praised it highly. *Closed Mon in winter.*

Le Terrazze, in Hotel La Cisterna (*see left*), **t** 0577 940328 (*moderate*). Popular for its panoramic views as well as the cuisine. The *medaglione al vin santo* is a surprise treat or else the *ossobuco alla Toscana* following old house specialities like *zuppa sangimignese* and *pappardelle alla lepre* (wide noodles with hare sauce). *Closed Wed lunch, Tues.*

Osteria delle Catene, Via Mainardi 18, **t** 0577 941966 (*moderate*). Good regional food. *Closed Wed.*

Osteria del Carcere, Via del Castello 13, **t** 0577 941905 (*moderate–cheap*). A tiny restaurant that serves unusual cold cuts and terrines, a delicious saffron-flavoured goats' cheese mousse, soups, roast guinea fowl with chestnuts and lamb with pecorino cheese. *Closed Thurs lunch, Wed.*

Enoteca Gustavo, Via San Matteo 29, **t** 0577 940057 (*cheap*). A good choice for a glass of local Vernaccia and a snack, this wine bar serves all sorts of sandwiches and *crostoni* (a rustic toasted open sandwich), cheeses and meats. *Closed Tues.*

Gelateria di Piazza, Piazza della Cisterna, **t** 0577 942244. Truly wonderful ice cream in a myriad of flavours. *Closed Nov–Feb.*

or a Florence. When it lost the wealth or the fierceness that briefly made it an important player on the Tuscan stage, the city crystallized into its medieval form, a perfect preparation for its role as a tourist town. Today San Gimignano has a population of some 7,700. On a good day in July or August, it may see several times that in day-trippers. Even during the Renaissance, the town was a resort for the Florentines: Dante, Machiavelli and Savonarola all spent time here, and artists like Ghirlandaio and Gozzoli were happy to come up for a small commission. Don't let the prospect of crowds keep you from visiting. San Gimignano handles them gracefully; its fine art, elegant medieval cityscapes and the verdant rolling countryside right outside its gates make this one of the smaller towns of Tuscany most worth seeing.

Piazza del Duomo and the Palazzo del Popolo

From the southern gate, Porta San Giovanni, the street of the same name leads towards the town centre, passing the little churches of **San Giovanni**, built by the Knights Templar, and **San Francesco**, with a good Pisan-Romanesque façade, now deconsecrated and converted into a wine shop. Another ancient gate, the Arco dei Bacci, leads into the triangular **Piazza della Cisterna** and the adjacent **Piazza del Duomo** – a superbly beautiful example of asymmetrical, medieval town design. Piazza della Cisterna contains the town's well and some of its towers.

On Piazza del Duomo, two stout, Gothic public buildings with Guelph crenellations and lofty towers compete with the Collegiata church for your attention. The **Palazzo del Podestà**, with its vaulted *loggia*, was begun in the 1230s by Emperor Frederick II at the height of imperial power. Above it stands the Torre della Rognosa, with a small cupola; at 167ft it once marked the height limit for private towers – the *podestà* didn't want anyone putting him in the shade. Later, when the *comune* was able to wrest effective self-government from the emperors, it built an even taller tower for the **Palazzo del Popolo** across the piazza; the 177ft Torre Grossa was completed about 1300 and the rest of the Palazzo about 20 years later.

Underneath this tower, an archway leads into the charming, thoroughly medieval **Cortile**, or courtyard, with bits of frescoes (one by Il Sodoma) and the painted coats of arms of Florentine governors from after 1353. A stairway leads up to the **Museo Civico** (*open Mar–Oct daily 9.30–7; Nov–Feb daily 10–5; adm*), with an excellent collection of art from both Florentine and Sienese masters. One of the oldest works is a remarkable painted crucifix by Coppo di Marcovaldo (*c.* 1270) that predates (and some might say surpasses) the similar, more famous crucifixes of Giotto. There are also two sweet Madonnas by Benozzo Gozzoli, a pair of *tondi* by Filippino Lippi portraying the Annunciation, and a big, colourful enthroned Virgin by Pinturicchio, famous for the Piccolomini chapel in Siena. Taddeo di Bartolo's paintings depict the story of San Gimignano; he is pictured calming the sea, exorcizing a devil who had been inhabiting the daughter of Emperor Jovian, and succumbing to the flesh while saying Mass (he has to pee, but on sneaking out of the church, a winged devil attacks him; fortunately, he has a crucifix to hand, and drives it away).

To the San Gimignanese, the biggest attraction of the museum is the Sala del Consiglio, or **Sala di Dante**, where the poet spoke in 1299 as an ambassador of Florence, seeking to convince the *comune* to join the Guelph League. The frescoes on its walls include more works by Gozzoli, a glittering company of angels and saints in the *Maestà* of the Sienese artist Lippo Memmi, and some trecento scenes of hunting and tournaments. After this, contemplate a climb up the **Torre Grosso** (*same hours as Museo Civico; adm*) – several hundred steps, but the view is worth the effort.

The Collegiata

The name Piazza del Duomo is misleading: San Gimignano no longer has a cathedral, but a **Collegiata**, begun in the 12th century and enlarged in the 15th, which would make an impressive seat for any bishop. It turns a blank brick façade to the world, but the interior is a lavish imitation of Siena Cathedral, with its tiger-striped arches and

Local Wine

San Gimignano has its own wine, *La Vernaccia di San Gimignano* (makes one think of varnish), a dry, light yellow white, with a pungent bouquet and a slightly bitter aftertaste. It is generally drunk with fish dishes and as an apéritif, but it's also good to try with typical San Gimignano dishes such as liver, tripe, rabbit and *panzanella*.

The wine is made only from the hills around San Gimignano and has been around since antiquity. It gets a mention in Dante's *Purgatory*: Pope Martin IV apparently drowned eels in Vernaccia before roasting them over a charcoal fire. It has recently been awarded the DOCG.

vaults painted with golden stars. Its walls, however, outshine the larger cathedral with first-class frescoes of the 14th and 15th centuries, mostly by artists from Siena.

In the north aisle, Bartolo di Fredi painted the Old Testament scenes in the 1360s. Note *Noah with the Animals* and *The Torments of Job* (also how each scene is accompanied by a neat explanation in simple Italian, a fascinating example of the artists and the Church coming to terms with a newly literate public). Some of Bartolo's best work is in the lunettes off the north aisle: a medieval cosmography of the Creation, scenes of Adam naming the animals and a graphic view of the creation of Eve. New Testament pictures by Barna da Siena (about 1380) cover the south wall; his *Crucifixion* is an exceedingly fine work. On the west wall, over the entrance, is a well-punctured *Saint Sebastian* by Gozzoli and the most perverse *Last Judgement* in Italy. What moved Taddeo di Bartolo – a painter of rosy Sienese Virgins – to this madness isn't recorded. You may think you have seen the damned suffering interesting tortures and indignities before; Italy has plenty of such scenes. This is the first time that delicacy forbids us to describe one. It's a little faded, unfortunately, but you'll find it near two wooden figures depicting an *Annunciation* by Jacopo della Quercia.

Off the south aisle, the **Chapel of Santa Fina** (*open 1–20 Jan and Mar Mon–Sat 9.30–5, Sun and hols 12.30–5; April–Oct Mon–Fri 9.30–7, Sat 9.30–5, Sun 12.30–5; 21 Jan–28 Feb open only for religious functions; adm*) offers a delightful introduction to one of the most irritating hagiographies in Christendom. Little Fina was going to the well for water, when she accepted an orange from a young swain. Upon returning home, her mother told her how wicked she was to take it, whereupon the poor girl became so mortified over her great sin that she lay down on the kitchen table and prayed for forgiveness without ceasing for the next five years. Finally, St Anthony came to call her soul up into heaven, and the kitchen table and all the towers of San Gimignano burst into bloom with violets. Domenico Ghirlandaio got the commission to paint all this; he did a splendid job (1475) in the brightest springtime colours. In the last scene, note San Gimignano's famous towers in the background.

Just to the left of the Collegiata there is a lovely small courtyard where musicians sometimes play on summer weekends. Here, on the wall of the baptistry, you will see another fine fresco by Ghirlandaio, an *Annunciation* that has survived reasonably well for being outside for 500 years. The town's two other museums are housed here, in the same building as the **Museo Archeologico**: the **Museo Etrusco** has a small collection of local archaeological finds and the **Museo d'Arte Sacra** has some good painted wood statues from the late Middle Ages (*open March and Nov–20 Jan Mon–Sat 9.30–5, Sun 12.30–5; April–Oct Mon–Fri 9.30–7, Sat 9.30–5; Sun 12.30–5; closed Jan–Feb; adm*).

Around the Town

From Piazza del Duomo, it's not too difficult a climb up to the **Rocca**, a ruined fortress of the 1350s, offering one of the best views of this towered town. In the summer, it's the site of an outdoor cinema. Down Via di Castello, at the eastern end of town, the **Oratory of San Lorenzo in Ponte**, now unused, has quattrocento Florentine frescoes and an exhibition of finds from the pharmacy of the Hospital of Santa Fina in the 16th–18th centuries. The busiest and finest street of San Gimignano heads north from Piazza del Duomo: Via San Matteo, lined with shops and modest Renaissance palaces. It begins by passing the three truncated **Salvucci Towers**, once the fortified compound of the Ghibelline Salvucci, one of the town's most powerful families (the towers of their enemies, the Guelph Ardinghelli, are the ones on the west side of Piazza della Cisterna).

In the quiet streets on the north side of town is the church of **Sant'Agostino**, famous for a merry series of frescoes by Gozzoli on the *Life of St Augustine*. Many of the frescoes are faded and damaged, but not the charming panel where the master of grammar drags sullen little Augustine off to school. Another well-preserved scene shows the saint in Rome, with most of the city's ancient landmarks visible in the background. Gozzoli also painted the *St Sebastian* on the left aisle. There is a haunting altarpiece (1483) by Piero Pollaiuolo, with an anticipatory touch of the El Greco to it, and some good trecento Sienese painting in a chapel off to the right. Across the piazza from Sant'Agostino, the little church of **San Pietro** has more trecento Sienese painting. Via Folgore di San Gimignano leads to the northeast corner of the town; **San Jacopo** stands under the town wall, another simple but interesting building left by the Templars.

Around much of San Gimignano, the countryside begins right outside the town's wall. Pleasant walks or picnics can be had in any direction, with a few landmarks to visit along the way: the **Fonti**, arched, medieval well-houses much like Siena's, are just outside the Porta dei Fonti, south of San Jacopo. Further away, there is the **Pieve di Cellole,** a pretty 12th-century church in a pleasant, peaceful setting, 4km west of the Porta San Matteo; its harmonious serenity amid the cypresses inspired Puccini's opera *Suor Angelica*. There are a number of ruined castles and monasteries around the town, each offering a different view of San Gimignano's remarkable skyline.

Volterra and Around

On a good day in spring or summer, the sunshine illuminates Volterra's elegant streets and *piazze* full of locals, and bouncing holiday-makers come to buy alabaster cups and lampshades. A cloudy, windy day may remind you of fate and of the Etruscans, who arrived here some 2,700 years ago. Like so many of their other cities, the Etruscans founded Volterra on top of a steep hill with a flat top; from afar, you see only a silhouette looming over an eerie, empty landscape. The soil around

Getting Around

Volterra lies 81km/2½hrs southwest of Florence by way of Colle di Val d'Elsa and the winding SS68; it's 50km/1½hrs west from Siena; and 61km/2hrs southeast of Pisa by way of Cascina and the SS439. It isn't the easiest town to reach if you don't have a car.

The only **train** service gets as far as Saline di Volterra, 10km southwest of the city. This is an infrequent branch line that goes to Cecina, 30km to the west on the coast south of Livorno. Some trains continue on from Cecina to Pisa. (It wasn't like this in the old days: as late as the 1920s, a little steam train used to climb right up to the town.) Buses connect the Saline station with Volterra, but not always when you need them.

All **buses** leave from Piazza Martini della Libertà, which is just inside the walls. You can get information, timetables and buy tickets from the tourist office. There are plenty of buses which go direct to Pisa and Montecatini Terme, four a day to Florence and Siena via Colle Val d'Elsa, and a few to Poggibonsi and San Gimignano; three a day go to Livorno via Cecina; there are also two to Massa Marittima (usually with a change at Monterotondo).

Cars aren't allowed within Volterra's walls, but lots of parking space is provided all around the walls and at the gates. Strangely enough there are also some street parking spaces inside, and you can usually sneak your car into one that's near your hotel in the evening; it's best to check out the situation on foot beforehand.

Tourist Information

Volterra: Via Turazza 2, t 0588 86150, f 0588 90350, *www.provolterra.it*. Palazzo dei Priori 19–20, t/f 0588 87257, *www.volterratur.it*.

Alabaster

Archaeological evidence has the Villanovan culture in Tuscany finding creative uses for the *pietra candida*, alias $CaSO_4 2H_2O$, as early as 800 BC. The Etruscans made good use of this luminous, easily worked mineral in their funeral urns and everyday objects. It appears that the locals forgot all about it during the Dark Ages, though now and then, some artist would turn a chunk into a vase or cup (the Medici, with their insatiable lust for dust magnets, bought quite a few). The craft of carving alabaster revived dramatically in the last two centuries. Volterra today is full of small workshops, and even a few large firms that turn the stone into vases, figurines, ashtrays and everything else that's serviceable or collectable.

Many of the alabaster-workers are genuine artists, turning out one-of-a-kind pieces at high prices; the city runs a contest each year for the best. Others produce vast numbers of attractive little baubles from €3 and up.

There are shops selling alabaster in every corner of Volterra; it's best to seek these out, and avoid the temptations of the big glossy establishments in the most prominent places.

Via Porta all'Arco 45. The shop of Paulo Sabatini, who has won several prizes in the annual competition, with some of the most original creations in town.

Via Porta all'Arco 26. Stocks some more unusual alabaster miniatures.

More can be found along Via di Sotto.

Via di Sotto 2. Simple, elegant vases and lamps.

'**Come una Volta**', Via di Sotto 6.

Via Antonio Gramsci Nos.20 and 53. Two of the more interesting shops among many.

Via Guarnacci 26. More avant-garde, with some splashy modern work in coloured alabaster.

Volterra (pop. 12,796) is a thin clay, not much good for vines or olives. Few trees grow here. It makes good pasture land – not as barren as it looks, but disconcerting enough among the green woods and well-tended gardens of this part of Tuscany.

History

Etruscan **Velathri**, one of the largest and most powerful cities of the Dodecapolis, grew up in the 9th or 8th century BC from an even earlier settlement of the

City Artisans' Cooperative, Piazza dei Priori.

For really serious alabaster – say, complete bathrooms or life-size copies of the Trevi Fountain – try the big shops with big car parks around the outskirts of town.

If Auro Bongini's workshop on **Via Don Minzoni 54** is open, it's well worth taking a look. He makes doll's house furniture from local olive wood in 19th-century style. His exhibition work fills the small workshop, but there are also a few individual pieces for sale. If you are interested, you can call in advance to make an appointment, **t** 0588 88040.

Where to Stay and Eat

Volterra ✉ 56048

Volterra does not see as many tourists as San Gimignano, but is nevertheless just as expensive – at least, inexpensive rooms are hard to find.

L'Etrusca, Via Porta all'Arco 37, **t/f** 0588 84073 (*moderate*). This has small apartments with kitchenettes just off Piazza del Popolo. Guests may use the pool at the sister hotel/restaurant **Sant'Elisa** (*see* right).

★★★Villa Nencini, Borgo S. Stefano, **t** 0588 86386, **f** 0588 80601, *www.villanencini.it* (*moderate*). A 16th-century house with beautiful views, located just north of the city centre.

★★★Nazionale, Via dei Marchesi 11, **t** 0588 86284, **f** 0588 84097, *www.albergo nazionalevolterra.it* (*moderate*). A pleasant old hotel, situated within the walls of the town.

★★★★San Lino, Via San Lino 26, near Porta San Francesco, **t** 0588 88053, **f** 0588 80620, *www.hotelsanlino.com* (*moderate*). More upscale, with tastefully remodelled rooms in an old cloister, standing out only for being the only place with parking.

Ostello della Gioventù, Via Don Minzoni, **t** 0588 887257. Students aren't entirely out of luck: there's the youth hostel, providing an institutional atmosphere but at rock-bottom rates.

Many restaurants in Volterra specialize in roast boar and the like, medieval cuisine entirely in keeping with the spirit of the place.

Del Duca, Via di Castello 2, **t** 0588 81510 (*expensive*). Volterra is distinctly lacking in good restaurants, but this new one stands out. The set *menu degustazione* is good value, or choose from the full menu: rabbit with black olives cooked in Vernaccia, duck breast or *foie gras*, and a delicious chocolate soufflé to finish. *Closed Tues*.

Il Porcellino, Vicollo delle Prigioni 16, **t** 0588 86392 (*moderate*). Lots of different set menus, combining seafood and familiar Tuscan favourites with local treats like roast pigeon and boar with olives. *Closed Oct–Mar*.

Il Sacco Fiorentino (the name refers to Lorenzo de' Medici's massacre of the citizens of Volterra in 1472), Piazza XX Settembre 18, **t** 0588 88537 (*cheap*). Combines a vast range of *crostini*, gnocchi with baby vegetables, penne with Tuscan cheeses, roast pork with black olives, rabbit cooked in garlic and *vin santo* and pigeon with red radicchio and *vin santo*, an imaginative menu that changes with the seasons. *Closed Wed*.

Sant' Elisa, about 3km away on the SS68, **t** 0588 80034, **f** 0588 87284 (*cheap*). One of the restaurants most popular with the Volterrans. Superb simple, homecooked food; it serves lots of game, such as *pappardelle* with wild boar or deer sauce, or wild boar stew with black olives. Also a 3-star hotel with pool. *Closed Tues*.

Taverna dei Priori, Via G. Matteotti 19, **t** 0588 86180 (*cheap*). Good for a quick bite: it's essentially a *tavola calda*, serving sandwiches, salads and cooked food. *Closed Wed*.

Villanovan culture; it is undoubtedly one of Italy's oldest cities. The attraction that has kept this hill continuously occupied for so many centuries is easily explained – sulphur, alum, salt, alabaster, lead and tin; the town is at the centre of one of the richest mining regions in Italy. In Etruscan days, there was iron, too, and the people of Velathri did a thriving trade with the Greeks and Carthaginians.

Velathri reached the height of its prosperity in the 5th and 4th centuries BC, leaving as testimony three great circuits of walls; the largest is over 8km in length, enclosing an area three times the size of the present city. The Romans captured it sometime in the 3rd century and Velathri began to decline. Along with most of Etruria, the city chose the populist side in the Social Wars, and was punished with a siege and sacking by Sulla in about 80 BC. Yet Roman *Velaterrae* remained an important town. It was the home of Saint Linus, successor to St Peter and the second pope.

Even though many of the mines were giving out, Volterra managed to survive the Dark Ages intact. The Lombards favoured it, and for a time it served as their capital. Medieval Volterra was ruled by its bishops, who were increasingly finding themselves in conflict with the rising middle class. An independent *comune* was established late in the 12th century, a good Ghibelline town that participated in most of the factional wars of the period, before finally coming under the nominal control of Florence in 1361.

The Florentines were content with an annual tribute until the 'affair of the alum' in the 1470s, that wonderfully Italian ruckus that caused Pope Sixtus IV to plot the murder of Lorenzo de' Medici, excommunicate him and finally declare war on him. Lorenzo had taken over a syndicate to mine here for alum, a key material used in dyeing cloth, on which the popes had a monopoly from their mines at Tolfa. Besides alarming the pope, Lorenzo also caused the Volterrans to revolt when they realized that he wanted to keep production down and prices high without letting any profit trickle down to them (the Medici Bank, not surprisingly, also controlled the sale of the pope's alum). Lorenzo eluded the pope with some difficulty (*see* **Florence**, History, pp.112–113) and then hired the mercenary captain Federico da Montefeltro – none other than the famous broken-nosed Duke of Urbino, patron of artists and scholars – to subdue the Volterrans. This he did with a brutality quite unbecoming to the 'ideal Renaissance prince'. Lorenzo wept some crocodile tears over Volterra; after extinguishing the city's independence once and for all, he offered it the magnificent sum of 2,000 florins in damages.

Fortunately for the Volterrans, the mining business was picking up again. Between 1400 and 1800, many pits that had been abandoned since Roman times were reopened. In particular, Volterra became Europe's largest centre for the mining and working of alabaster, a craft tradition that is still the city's biggest business today.

A Little Archaeology

Coming from Florence or Siena, the entrance to Volterra will be the eastern gate, the **Porta a Selci**, with a moving tribute to the *partigiani* of Volterra killed in 1944–5. Inside the gate, Via Don Minzoni leads towards the bus terminal at Piazza XX Settembre, passing along the way at No.15 the **Museo Etrusco Guarnacci** (*open mid-Mar–Oct daily 9–7; 5 Nov–15 Mar daily 9–2; adm exp, a joint ticket covers Volterra's other museums*), the repository for finds from the Velathri necropolises. Over 600 sculpted alabaster, travertine or terracotta cinerary urns make up the core of the collection. Exhibits are arranged in chronological order, except for the original Guarnacci collection which is grouped by subject matter. These tend to be conventional – an Etruscan family would ask the artist for a scene from Greek mythology, from the Trojan War perhaps, or something like the death of Actaeon, or a daemon conducting the souls of the dead down to the underworld. Perhaps the artist already had one in stock. One rule of Etruscan art is its lack of rules. Expect anything: some of the reclining figures of the dead atop the urns are brilliant portraiture, while others could be the first attempts of a third-grade craft class. All, holding the little cups or dishes they carry down into Hades, look as serene and happy as only a defunct Etruscan can.

As always, the Etruscans do their best to make you laugh. One terracotta, the *Urna degli Sposi*, portrays a hilariously caricatured couple who look as if they are about to start arguing over whose turn it is to do the dishes. Another Etruscan joke is the *Ombra della Sera* (evening shadow), quite a celebrity around Volterra, a small, carefully detailed bronze of a man with a quizzical expression and spidery, grotesquely elongated arms and legs. There are also prehistoric finds, Roman mosaics from the baths, artefacts discovered in the theatre, and some fine pieces of Etruscan jewellery.

The museum lies a stone's throw from Piazza XX Settembre, the bus terminal; from here Via Gramsci leads towards the town centre. Climb any of the alleys to the south of the museum, however, and you'll reach Volterra's **Parco Archeologico** (*open Nov–mid-March Sat 10.30–4, Sun 10.30–5; summer daily 10.30–5.30*) just inside the walls. There isn't much that's archaeological about it – some Etruscan foundations and a huge ancient cistern called the *Piscina Romana* – but the park is a marvel, a lush English garden of manicured lawns and shady groves unlike anything else in Tuscany. Above the park stretches an exceptionally long and elegant castle, the **Fortezza Medicea**, begun in 1343 and completed by Lorenzo de' Medici in 1472. You can't get in; it has been a prison almost from the day it was built, perhaps the fanciest in this nation of fancy calabooses.

Piazza dei Priori

This is a fine little republican piazza, surrounded by plain, erect *palazzi* that discreetly call your attention to the sober dignity of the *comune*. The **Palazzo dei Priori**, of 1208, is said to be the oldest such building in Tuscany, the model for Florence's Palazzo Vecchio and many others. Its tower has long been closed, but if you ever find it reopened, climb up for a view that literally takes in all of Tuscany; on a clear day, you'll see Monte Amiata, all the coast from La Spezia to the Argentario, and Corsica and Elba as well.

Across the square, the simple **Palazzo Pretorio** is almost as old. Next to it, the rakishly leaning **Porcellino Tower** takes its name from the little pig sculpted in relief near the base, just barely visible after seven centuries.

The Cathedral and the Etruscan Arch

Just to the right of the Palazzo dei Priori, a bit of green and white striped marble façade peeks out between the palaces. This is the back of the Archiepiscopal Palace, located around the corner in the **Piazza del Duomo**. Quiet and dowdy, the contrast of this square with the well-built Piazza dei Priori is striking, a lasting memory of the defeat of Volterra's medieval bishops by the *comune*. Its octagonal **baptistry**, begun in 1283, has its marble facing completed only on one side. Within, there is a fine baptismal font sculpted by Andrea Sansovino in the early 1500s, an altar by Mino da Fiesole, and a holy water dish carved out of an Etruscan boundary stone.

The plain **cathedral** façade has a good marble doorway. This forlorn mongrel of a building was begun in the Pisan-Romanesque style in the 1200s, and worked on fitfully for the next two centuries. The campanile went up in 1493, and the interior was entirely redone in the 1580s when the blatant Medici coat of arms was placed over the high altar. Do not pass this old Duomo by; the works of art inside are few in number, but of an exceptionally high quality. Fittingly, as this is Volterra, some of the windows are made of thin-sliced alabaster, a stone that was also used in the intricate, Renaissance **tabernacle** by Mino da Fiesole over the high altar.

The chapels on either side have excellent examples of Tuscan woodcarving: a 15th-century piece attributed to a local artist named Francesco di Domenico Valdambrino off to the left, the *Madonna dei Chierici*, and to the right, a poly-chromed *Deposition* with five separate, full-sized figures, certainly ranked among the best of 13th-century Pisan sculpture, shining immaculately after a recent restoration. Another chapel off to the right contains fragments of unusually good anonymous trecento frescoes of the *Passion of Christ*, very much ahead of their time in composition, in the figures and the folds of the draperies – even Giorgio Vasari might have liked them.

In the left aisle, the ***pergamo*** (pulpit) is one of the lesser-known works of the Pisani, less spectacular than the ones in Pisa, Siena and Pistoia, but still showing something of the vividness and electric immediacy seen in the best Pisan sculpture. Guglielmo Pisano did the fine relief of the *Last Supper* (note the faces of the Apostles and the sly metaphorical monster sneaking under the table). The pulpit's supporting columns rest on two lions, a bull and one unclassifiable beast, all by Bonamico Pisano. In the oratory, off the left aisle near the entrance, behind a 16th-century wooden statue group of the *Adoration of the Magi*, is a small fresco said to be by Benozzo Gozzoli, though perhaps because of its deterioration or early date, it lacks Gozzoli's usual charm.Close by in the Archiepiscopal Palace, a small **Museo d'Arte Sacra** (*open mid-Mar–Oct 9–7; 5 Nov–15 Mar 9–2; adm exp*) displays sculpture and architectural fragments, and a della Robbia terracotta of St Linus, Volterra's patron.

From the Duomo, if you retrace your steps back towards Piazza dei Priori and turn down Via Porta all'Arco, you'll find the quaintest old relic in Volterra, the **Arco Etrusco**. The Etruscans built the columns at least, though the arch above them was rebuilt in Roman times. Set into this arch are three primeval black basalt sculpted heads from the original gate, *c.* 600 BC, believed to represent the Etruscan gods Tinia (Jupiter), Uni (Juno) and Menvra (Minerva). Some of the features of Juno are barely traceable; 2,700 years of wind and rain have worn all three into great black knobs – carved out of the voussoirs, they resemble nothing so much as garden slugs.

The Pinacoteca

Open mid-Mar–Oct daily 9–7, 5 Nov–15 Mar daily 9–2; adm exp, joint ticket valid 1 year covers Volterra's other museums, no single tickets.

Just off Piazza dei Priori, the intersection of Via Roma and Via Buonparenti is one of the most picturesque corners of Volterra, with venerable stone arches and tower houses such as the 13th-century Casa Buonparenti. Via Buonparenti leads into Via dei Sarti; the elder Antonio da Sangallo's Palazzo Solaini (note the elegant arcaded courtyard) has been restored to hold Volterra's **Pinacoteca**, another small but choice collection. Trecento Sienese painting is well represented, including a glorious altarpiece of the *Madonna and Child* by Taddeo di Bartolo. To complement the remarkable 14th-century wood sculptures in the Duomo, the Pinacoteca has two figures portraying the *Annunciation* by Francesco di Valdambrino. Neri di Bicci was a quattrocento Florentine, but his *St Sebastian* here looks entirely Sienese – probably at the request of the customer. Among other Tuscan works, there is a shiny altarpiece by Ghirlandaio, and two by Luca Signorelli (or his workshop): a *Madonna and Saints* and an *Annunciation*. Only tantalizing fragments are left of another altarpiece by Giuliano Bugiardini (1475–1554), a little-known Florentine with a very distinctive style.

For all that, the prize of the collection is the Rosso Fiorentino *Deposition*, dated 1521 and perhaps his greatest work in all Italy. Even out in the boondocks of Volterra, it attracts considerable attention from the art scholars, being a seminal work and one of the thresholds from the Renaissance into Mannerism, with all the precision and clarity of the best quattrocento work, yet also possessing an intensity that few works had ever achieved. The *Descent from the Cross* is a starkly emotional subject; in Rosso's work it is terror and disarray, a greenish Christ and a small, nearly hysterical crowd dramatically illuminated against a darkening deep blue sky. You'll find little that this painting has in common with Rosso's contemporaries, not even with his fellow madman Pontormo (who did his own, quite different, *Deposition* in Florence's Santa Felicità) – but oddly enough, it could almost be mistaken for a work of Goya. Many of the best paintings are currently covered with little bits of what looks like sticking plaster, the result of a blunder by the administration who, it is said, turned the heating up too high. As a result the paint bubbled on the canvases and they are being restored.

San Francesco and the Roman Theatre

On the corner east of the Pinacoteca, the church of **San Michele** has a Pisan Romanesque façade. In the other direction, towards the Porta San Francesco on the western edge of town, you pass through back streets dusty with alabaster workshops, before finally arriving at the church of **San Francesco** on Via San Lino. Here the attraction is off to the right of the altar, the **chapel of the Holy Cross**, completely frescoed in 1410 by a Florentine artist whose name seems to be Cenni di Francesco di Ser Cenni – a rare soul, indeed, with a sophisticated, wonderfully reactionary, medieval sense of composition and his own ideas about Christian iconography, done in a bold style that in places almost seems like modern poster art. The *Legend of the Cross* frescoes generally follow those of Gaddi at Santa Croce in Florence (*see* pp.165 and 165), and there are also scenes of *St Francis*, the *Passion*, and the *Massacre of the Innocents*, many with fantasy city backgrounds. Note the *Dream of Constantine* (or of Heraclius), in his tent adorned with the imperial eagle; naturally the artist had never seen a Roman eagle, but he painted a very nice medieval German one instead.

Just to the right of San Francesco, a pedestrian passage under the walls takes you out to Viale Francesco Ferrucci, home to a lively outdoor **market** on Saturday mornings. Beneath the walls, ancient Velaterrae's large **Roman theatre** (*open Nov–mid-Mar Sat 10.30–4, Sun 10.30–5; summer daily 10.30–5.30*) has been excavated. Enough marble slabs and columns have survived for the archaeologists to reconstruct part of the stage building, an impressive testimony to the past importance of the city. Behind the theatre are ruins of baths and a large rectangular *palaestra*, a yard for exercise and gymnastics.

The *Balze*

Leaving Volterra from San Francesco Gate, you pass the Borgo San Giusto and its ruins of the 12th-century Pisan-Romanesque church of **Santo Stefano**. The road to Pisa exits through the outer **Etruscan walls**; though barely more than foundations, they are traceable for most of their length around the city and easily visible here.

Some 2km beyond, decorating the moors, are the *balze*: barren clay-walled gullies that may have begun as Etruscan mining cuts. They've a life of their own; medieval chronicles report them gobbling up farms and churches around the city, and no one has yet found a way to stop their inexorable growth. In the 1700s they tried to atone for their appetite, revealing some of the most important Etruscan necropolises yet discovered, and contributing urns to the Guarnacci Museum. Now even the necropolises are all but gone, though on the edge of one cliff you can see the **Badia**, an 11th-century Camaldolensian abbey, now half-devoured.

The Val di Cecina and the Metal Hills

There are few attractions in the romantic emptiness of the Volterran Hills. If you take the SS68 west from Volterra along the Cecina Valley to Guardistallo, you reach a rolling valley with pines and cypresses in just the right places – a suitable Tuscan backdrop for any Renaissance painting. **Montecatini Val di Cecina**, in the hills to the north, is quiet and medieval, with a 12th-century castle. Further west, a big wine area extends around **Montescudaio** (Montescudaio, red and white, is a distinguished though lesser-known dry variety with a DOC label).

The most unusual road from Volterra, the SS439, leads south over the Colline Metallifere towards Massa Marittima and the coast. These 'metal hills', along with the iron mines of Elba, did much to finance the gilded existence of the Etruscans. Several mines operate today, though driving through the hills you may see little but oak forests and olive groves. **Pomarance** holds few surprises, but wait for **Larderello**, the self-proclaimed 'World Centre of Geothermal Energy'. This is the north boundary of volcanic Italy; that extinct volcano, Monte Amiata, and the ancient crater lakes of Umbria and Lazio are not far away. This far north, the only manifestations of a subterranean nature are benign little geysers and gurgling pools of sulphurous mud. Larderello is a growing town; huge ugly cooling towers of the type that signify a nuclear power plant anywhere else can be spotted wherever there is a geothermal source worth tapping. Near the centre, there is a strange, postmodernist church designed in the 1950s by Michelucci, the architect of Florence's rail station, and the **Museo della Geotermia** (*t 0588 07724, open daily 8–12.30 and 1.30–5.30; closed Sat in winter; adm*), which may explain something of this overheated little town's career.

After Larderello, and almost as far as Monterotondo, the landscape is downright uncanny. It smells bad, too; geysers and steam vents (*soffioni*) whistle and puff by the roadside, while murky pits bubble up boric salts amidst yellow and grey slag piles. Follow the yellow signs of the *'itinerario dei soffioni'* to see the best of it. Despite the sulphur and borax, the cooling towers and occasional rusting hulks of old mining equipment, the Metal Hills are quite winsome, especially south of Larderello (still on the SS439) around the medieval village of Castelnuovo di Val di Cecina, surrounded by chestnuts and the Ala dei Diavoli (Devils' Wing) pass at the crest of the hills. Monterotondo Marittimo, further south, has more than its fair share of subsurface curiosities; nearby Lago Boracifero is Italy's centre for borax mining. In some places, the ground is covered with strange webs of steam pipes, built since the *comune* discovered its unique resource could power almost everything in town for free.

Massa Marittima

This lovely, rugged area is part of the coastal Maremma district only in name; even in Roman times it was considered part of the 'maritime' province. And for just as long, **Massa Marittima** has been making its living from the mines, though today its 10,000 people are not enough to fill the space within its medieval walls. Albeit small, its brief prosperity left it beautiful, and well worth visiting: firstly, to see the second city of the Sienese Republic, a lesson in urban refinement within a small place; and secondly, to see its exquisite cathedral, one of Tuscany's great medieval monuments.

This town appeared as a free *comune*, the *Repubblica Massetana*, around 1225, just coinciding with a dizzying period of prosperity owing to its discovery of new silver and copper deposits nearby. Unfortunately, this wealth proved fatally attractive to Massa's bigger neighbours. Pisa and Siena fought over it for a century and it finally fell to the latter in 1337. Soon after, the mines gave out, putting Massa into centuries of decline. Malaria was a problem from the 1500s, and not until the Lorraine dukes drained the wet places and reopened some of the mines, did things start looking up.

The Duomo

It's quite a sight, rising incongruously on its pedestal, its effect heightened by its setting above and at an angle to Massa's **Piazza Garibaldi**, a true *tour de force* of medieval town design. Reconstruction of an earlier cathedral began around 1200 and finished in 1250, though some additions were made; note the contrast between the original Pisan-Romanesque style, with blind arches and lozenges, and the Sienese campanile, added about 1400. Its best features include Gothic windows, capitals and the carvings of animals protecting humans on the façade and the left side.

Getting Around

Massa is only 22km off the coastal Via Aurelia at Follonica, absolutely worth the diversion if you are passing that way; direct from Siena it's a not particularly captivating 65km/1hr 20mins **drive** on the SS73 (passing by San Galgano) and the SS441.

There are three or four **buses** a day from Volterra (change at Monterotondo), five to nearby Follonica, and frequent buses and **trains** from there to Grosseto (Massa is in Grosseto province); also two a day to Florence and Siena, and one direct to Grosseto. Information and tickets from *Agenzia Massa Veterensis* opposite the Duomo. Most buses stop on Via Corridoni, behind and a little downhill from the Duomo.

Tourist Information

Massa: Via Todini 3/5, **t** 0566 902756, **f** 0566 940095.

Where to Stay and Eat

Massa Marittima ✉ 58024

Massa becomes ever more popular and its room capacity is often stretched to the limit.

★★Duca del Mare, Via D. Alighieri 1/2, **t** 0566 902284, **f** 0566 901905, *www.ducadelmare.it* (*moderate*). One of the town's three hotels, just below the town centre on the Via Massetana, in a lovely setting with a garden and views over the countryside (Massa lies on a rather steep hill); it's set in a modern building and has a simple *trattoria*. Pool, too!

★★Girifalco, Via Massentana, **t**/**f** 0566 902177, *www.ilgirifalco.com* (*inexpensive*). Offers similar amenities (but no pool) and the same views as Duca del Mare, but cheaper.

Dining in Massa is uncomplicated.

Da Bracoli, Località Ghirlanda, **t** 0566 902318 (*very expensive*). Offers *haute cuisine* variations on local dishes and a formidable wine list in an elegant setting. *Closed Mon and Tues.*

Taverna del Vecchio Borgo, **t** 0566 903950 (*expensive*). This comes highly recommended, not only for its food – game dishes including pheasant, boar and venison – but for its long list of grappas. *Closed Sun eve and Mon.*

Da Tronca, Vicolo Porta 5, **t** 0566 901991 (*cheap*). This rustic *trattoria* with its rough stone walls and arches has something of a medieval atmosphere. The food is local and delicious; anchovies in pesto, *tortelli Maremmani* (stuffed with chard and ricotta), pasta with courgettes and ricotta, mushroom soup, wild boar, rabbit and tripe. *Closed Wed and lunch.*

The interior, under massive columns with delicate capitals, each one different, has a few trecento and quattrocento frescoes, including one of St Julian tending the sick near the main entrance. On the left, there is a luminous *Madonna* by Duccio (1318) and unique reliefs from the original 11th-century church: staring priests and apostles in vigorous, cartoon-like style. On the right hangs the *Nativity of Mary* by that most peculiar Sienese artist, Rutilio Manetti (d. 1639): woebegone ladies and a jellicle cat attend a pug-nosed, thumb-sucking, very unbeatific baby Mary. Nearby is a fine font with reliefs by Giraldo da Como (*c.* 1250) and a Renaissance tabernacle added in 1447. A wooden crucifix by Giovanni Pisano hangs over the high altar; in the Gothic apse is the *Ark of San Cerbone* with more reliefs (1324) on the life of Massa's patron saint.

Up and Down Massa

Next to the cathedral on Piazza Garibaldi, the 1230 **Palazzo del Podestà** holds Massa's **Museo Archeologico** (*open Nov–Mar Tues–Sun 10–12.30 and 3–5; April–mid-July Tues–Sun 10–12.30 and 3.30–7; 21 July–31 Aug Tues–Sun 10–1 and 4–10; Sept–Oct Tues–Sun 10–12.30 and 3.30–7; adm*), with a well-organized if a little uninspiring archaeological collection – the Medici dukes carried the best finds to Florence. The museum also houses the offices of La Coop Colline Metallifere (*t 0566 902289*), which runs all Massa's museums.

In the small Pinacoteca, the best work is a *Maestà* by Ambrogio Lorenzetti, aglow with rosy faces, flowers and golden trim. Note the angel with the distaff and spindle in the centre – a sure sign that the local wool guild paid for the painting. Today the city offices are in the **Palazzo Comunale** across the square, formed from a group of connected tower-houses from the 13th and 14th centuries. Note the inscription above the door of another old building there: MASSA VETERNENSIS CELEBRIS VETULONIA QUONDAM (Massa was once famed Vetulonia).

Just as Grosseto sees itself as successor to Etruscan *Roselle*, Massa is heir to lost Vetulonia, the once-great city of the Dodecapolis near the coast (*see* p.305). Piazza Garibaldi is lively, often crowded with Teutons perching on the steps of the Duomo or swilling beer in the café-pizzerias. Via Libertà leads into the older quarter, a nest of arches and alleys barely changed over centuries. Like Siena, Massa is divided into three *terzi*; this is the *terzo* of Civitavecchia. Via Moncini climbs to the **Città Nuova**, a 14th-century suburb behind unusual Sienese fortifications; the street ends at Piazza Matteotti, with the 1330 **Torre del Candaliere** (Torre dell'Orologio), linked to the fortifications by the **Sienese Arch**, a slender walkway; it's a beautiful ensemble, more for show than any military consideration (*open Nov–Mar Tues–Sun 11–1 and 2.30–4.30; April–Oct Tues–Sun 10–1 and 3–6; adm*). Up Corso Diaz, **Sant'Agostino** church (completed 1313), has works by Rutilio Manetti.

Finally, no visit to Massa is complete without a trip to a mining museum (ask politely at the city library and they may show you the city's treasure, the 1310 *Codice Minerario Massetano*, modern Europe's first code of laws concerning mining rights). The **Museo di Arte e di Storia della Miniera** on Piazza Matteotti (*open April–Sept Tues–Sun 3–5.30; closed Oct–Mar; adm*) is very small, but there's another one, the **Museo della Miniera** on Via Corridoni (*open for guided tours only, leaving regularly: in summer between 10.15 and 5.45; in winter between 10.15 and 4.15; closed Mon; call t 0566 902289 for exact times. Visits in English on request; adm*). Here the entrance leads into nearly half a mile of tunnels, with exhibits to show how the job was done from medieval days to the present.

San Galgano and the Sword in the Stone

The SS73 east from Massa to Siena skirts the southern Colline Metallifere, through lands that saw a great medieval flowering of monasticism. The monks are mostly long gone, but they left one of the most unusual, least-visited sights in Tuscany – the ruined Cistercian **Abbey of San Galgano** (*open daily 8am–11pm*), some 2km north of Palazzetto. In some of the older paintings in Siena's Pinacoteca, you will see the oddly Arthurian figure of a man apparently drawing a sword from a stone. This is San Galgano and, in fact, he is putting the sword in.

Galgano Guidotti, from nearby Chiusdino, was a dissolute soldier who one day had a vision of St Michael on the slopes of Montesiepi, ordering him to change his ways.

Thrusting his sword into a rock to symbolize his new life, Galgano became a holy hermit; an ensuing career of miracles ensured his rapid canonization in 1181.

Almost from the start, the community he founded here was associated with the Cistercian Order, attracting monks from France as well as from around Siena. For centuries they played a vital role in the community, draining swamps, building mills and starting up a small textile industry. The Republic of Siena found them indispensable as architects, administrators – and as accountants. Many of the *Biccherna* covers in the Siena archives show Cistercians puzzling over the books or handing out pay. With its immense wealth, and its French architects eager to initiate the backward Italians in the glories of the new Gothic style, the order began its great **Abbey Church** in 1218. The Cistercians were already in a bad way when the abbey was dissolved in 1600; soon after their departure the roof, the façade and the campanile collapsed, leaving the grandest French-Gothic building in Tuscany a ruin. Its beautiful travertine columns and pointed arches remain, with the sky as roof and green lawns as carpet. Parts of the monastery survive, now in the care of Olivetan nuns.

After Galgano's death, St Michael appeared again on a hill above the abbey to command his followers to build the **Cappella di Montesiepi** over the sword in the stone. The curious round chapel, one of very few in Italy, was begun in 1185. The sword is still there, protruding from its rock right in the centre. As with all the sites associated with St Michael, it is a reminder of a branch of medieval mysticism that, while not entirely lost, is hardly well understood. It's a very curious place – during a recent visit, a beautiful woman in black entered, carrying a gleaming silver sword, and went off to a side room with the caretaker (we didn't ask). Note the pair of human hands in a glass box, with a card explaining how they were bitten off by wolves. The altar has a cross of the type often seen on buildings of the Knights Templar, and the ceiling dome, patterned in 22 concentric stripes, may be a representation of the heavenly spheres of medieval cosmology (as in the famous fresco in Pisa's Campo Santo). In a side chamber is a series of frescoes by Ambrogio Lorenzetti on the life of the saint, an *Annunciation* and a *Coronation of the Virgin*.

In the silent countryside around town, possible detours include **Chiusdino** (8km west), the dense, sleepy birthplace of San Galgano, or the aged **Monticiano**, south on the SS73, where a Romanesque church has trecento frescoes by Bartolo di Fredi.

South Along Route 223

Possibly the least interesting route south from Siena leads to Grosseto, passing through the fertile, but nearly empty, valley of the River Merse. Once into Grosseto province it becomes even emptier, though there are a few towns worth a visit: old, walled **Bagni di Petriolo**, with thermal springs to relieve your gout; **Civitella Marittima**, a hill town with the Romanesque church of San Lorenzo al Lanzo, and **Paganico**, a charming village retaining its Sienese walls. Its church, San Michele, has well-preserved frescoes by trecento and quattrocento Sienese artists.

Southern Tuscany

14

Southern Tuscany

p.394

To Arezzo

Siena

Monteaperti · Monte S. Savino · Castiglion Fiorentino · Cortona

Montecchio · Rapolano Terme · Lucignano · Tuoro sul Trasimeno

Pievina · S326 · Sinalunga

Ponte a Tressa · Asciano

Lucignano d'Arbia · Fatt. d'Amorosa · Bettolle · Lago Trasimeno

1 Abbazia di M. Oliveto Maggiore · Trequanda · Torrita di Siena · Castiglione del Lago

Murlo · S. Giovanni d'Asso · Montisi · Castiglione del Lago

Buonconvento · Montefollonico · S146 · Montepulciano · Macchie

Pari · Montalcino · **2** S. Biagio **3** · L. di Montepulciano · L. di Chiusi · Paciano

Pienza · Pieve di Corsignano · Monticchiello · Chianciano · **4**

S. Quirico d'Orcia · Chianciano Terme · Chiusi

Bagno Vignoni · Sarteano · Città della Pieve

S. Antimo · Ripa d'Orcia · Cetona · UMBRIA

S. Angelo in Colle · Castiglione d'Orcia

Civitella Marittima · R. Orcia · S323 · Campiglia d'Orcia · Fabro

Paganico · Seggiano · Vivo d'Orcia · Bagni S. Filippo · S. Casciano dei Bagni

TUSCANY · M. Amiata · S478 · Radicofani · To Rome

Roselle · Castel d. Piano · Arcisossо · Abbadia S. Salvatore · Orvieto

Grosseto · M. Labbro · Piancastagnaio

Roccalbegna · Sta. Fiora · Castell' Azzara · LAZIO

S322 · S323 · Semproniano · Monti Volsini

Scansano · M. Elmo · Sovana · Sorano · Bolsena

Saturnia · Lago di Bolsena

Magliano in Toscana · Montemerano · Manciano · Pitigliano

S. Bruzio · Poggio Buco

Talamone · Marsiliana

Albinia · Capalbio

Laguna di Orbetello · Orbetello · To Rome

10 km / 5 miles · **N**

p.346 · **pp.442–3** · **p.522** · **p.260**

Highlights

1 Monte Oliveto Maggiore: Siena's élite Renaissance hermitage
2 Pienza: Pope Pius II's Renaissance city
3 Montepulciano: Vino Nobile and fine art
4 Chiusi: underground Etruscan mysteries

Not counting the coastal Maremma around Grosseto, the old territories of the Sienese Republic make a complete and coherent landscape, rolling hills mostly given over to serious farming and pastureland. It isn't as garden-like as some other parts of Tuscany, though tidy vineyards and avenues of cypresses are not lacking. Hill towns, ready landmarks, poke above the horizon – Montepulciano off to the east, Pienza a bit to the left, while that castle on the left of the road must be Castiglione d'Orcia. At times, it seems the whole region is laid out before you, bounded on one side by the hills around Siena, on the other by the cones of Monte Amiata and Radicofani.

In the little tourist offices in these towns, they remark that not too many English or Americans pass through, which is a pity. It's beautiful countryside, the food and wine are among the best in Tuscany, and there are delightful towns with souvenirs from the Renaissance and Middle Ages.

Asciano and the *Crete*

The SS326 from Siena heads east; its main purpose is to get you out to Cortona (*see* pp.416-20) and then to Umbria. Before it leaves Siena province, the road passes the village of **Monteaperti**, where the Sienese won their famous victory over Florence in 1260, and **Rapolano Terme** (27km), a small spa that retains some of its medieval walls. Besides the hot springs there is a surplus of natural gas in the area, some of it pumped out from wells, and some just leaking out of the ground – don't drop any matches. **Asciano**, 10km south of Rapolano, has walls built by the Sienese in 1351 and a good collection of Sienese art. The **Museo d'Arte Sacra** and the **Museo Etrusco** are now united in the same building, Palazzo Corboli at Corso Matteotti 122 (*open Mar–Oct Tues–Sun 10–1 and 3–7; Nov–Feb Thurs–Sat 10–1 and 3–5.30, Sun 10–1 and 2.30–6*). In a house at Via del Canto 11, there are some recently discovered Roman mosaics; ask at the pharmacy on Corso Matteotti to arrange a visit.

Southeast of Siena, the valleys of the Ombrone and the Asso enclose the country of the *crete*. Like the *balze* of Volterra, the *crete* are uncanny monuments to the power of erosion. The countryside around Asciano is dotted with them, exposing chalk cliffs where the soil above has eroded; they often appear in the backgrounds of 14th- and 15th-century Sienese and Florentine paintings (similar eroded chalk hills are called *biancane*). This is sheep country and it suffered a great deal after the Second World War, when many of the local men left the area to seek work in the cities. Today, immigrants from Sardinia make up a sizeable minority of the population, born shepherds who are trying to get the business back on its feet.

Old **Sinalunga**, up on its hill, is next (22km west), but offers little to detain you; the main square is named after Garibaldi, to commemorate his arrest here in 1867 on the orders of King Vittorio Emanuele, who was afraid his volunteers were about to attack Rome. **Torrita di Siena**, an old Sienese border fortress 6km southwest of the junction with the A1 from Florence to Rome, owes its name to the tall towers of its walls, some of which remain.

Tourist Information

Rapolano Terme: Piazza Matteotti 9,
t 0577 724079.
Asciano: Corso Matteotti 18, t 0577 719510.
Buonconvento: Via Soccini 32, t 0577 807181.
San Giovanni d'Asso: Via Piazza Gramsci 1,
t 0577 803101.
Trequanda: Via Roma 4, t 0577 662296.

Where to Stay and Eat

Accommodation isn't always easy to find in this quiet corner of Tuscany. Villages may only have one real hotel, or none. However, there are plenty of rooms in the various *agriturismo* farmhouses dotted around; either follow signs on the road, or ask at the local tourist office. Some restaurants, too, have rooms to rent and there are always a few private homes with rooms to rent that don't advertise. Don't be shy; ask around and you'll find something.

Asciano ✉ 53041

Da Miretta, near Asciano at Loc La Pievina on the Laurentana road, t 0577 718368 (*expensive*). A very friendly place, serving regional dishes and seafood – save some room for the homemade desserts. The enormous set meal (€35–45 for the fish meal; meat costs less at €35) involves at least three hours, delicious dishes (including *antipasti* and up to six desserts) and local wine. *Closed Mon, Tues. Only open for dinner plus Sunday lunch.*

Buonconvento ✉ 53022

★★Albergo Ristorante Roma, Via Soccini 14, t 0577 806021, f 0577 807284 (*inexpensive*). The closest rooms to Monte Oliveto Maggiore are in Buonconvento, on the main street of the old town. Simple and old-fashioned, the Roma also has a very good restaurant, a nice place to have a snack after visiting Monte Oliveto Maggiore.

Sinalunga ✉ 53048

★★★★Locanda dell'Amorosa, 2km south of Sinalunga at Loc L'Amorosa, t 0577 677211, f 0577 678216, *www.amorosa.it* (*luxury*). This is something really special, though you need to reserve long in advance. It is an entire medieval hamlet, complete with a manor house and frescoed church. There are 16 beautiful rooms and a swimming pool. The restaurant (*very expensive*) gets mixed reviews. The seasonal menu usually includes some freshwater fish dishes (Lake Trasimeno isn't far away) such as *ravioli di pesce*; for seconds, try stuffed pigeon or the big Florentine steaks. *Closed Tues lunch, Mon.*

Monte Oliveto Maggiore and Around

South of Siena, the SS2 wends towards Rome, roughly following the Roman Via Cassia and the medieval pilgrims' path to Rome, the *Via Francigena*. Along the way, it passes **Lucignano d'Arbia** (16km), a charming, tiny village with a medieval church, and **Buonconvento** (27km), a gritty industrial town that hides a miniature walled medieval centre – it would make a pretty hill town, if it only had a hill. The walls, no longer very proper or military, are peppered with windows of the houses that have been built against them. There are two fine gates at either end of the main street, and in the middle, the 14th-century parish church with an altarpiece by Matteo di Giovanni.

In the broken, jumbled hills south of Asciano, austere green meadows alternate with ragged gullies and bare white cliffs. At the centre of these *crete*, in the bleakest and most barren part, there is a grove of tall, black cypresses around the monastery of **Monte Oliveto Maggiore** (*open daily but times are not reliable. It is advisable to call to check, on t 0577 707611*), 9km from Buonconvento on the SS451. Gentlemen from Siena's merchant élite founded Monte Oliveto, including Giovanni Tolomei and Ambrogio Piccolomini, both jaded merchants and sincere Christians who retired here in 1313 to escape the fatal sophistication of the medieval city. Their new Olivetan Order was approved by the pope only six years later. With such wealthy backers, the monastery became a sort of élite hermitage for central Tuscany. An ambitious building programme in the 1400s made it a marvel of Renaissance clarity and rationality, expressed in simple structures and good Siena brick. The beautiful, asymmetrical **gatehouse**, decorated with a della Robbia terracotta, makes a fitting introduction to the complex. Inside, the well-proportioned brick **Abbey Church** (finished in 1417) has an exceptional set of wooden intarsia **choir stalls** by the master of the genre, Fra Giovanni da Verona, among the best work of this kind in all Italy. Note also the unusual dome with an octagon of interlocking arches, an Islamic Andalucian design that made its way here via Spanish Christian churches and the chapel of the Castel Nuovo in Naples.

The monastery's greatest treasure, however, is the **Great Cloister**, embellished with 36 frescoes of scenes from the life of St Benedict (whose original rule Tolomei and the Olivetans were trying to restore). All 36 are currently undergoing restoration; the first nine are by Luca Signorelli, with formidable ladies and bulky, white-robed monks in the artist's distinctive balloonish forms and sparing use of colour. All the rest are the work of Il Sodoma (1505–8) – some of his best painting, ethereal scenes of Pre-Raphaelite ladies and mandarin monks, with blue and purple backgrounds of ideal landscapes and cities. If you are of the persuasion, popular enough a century ago, that it was with Raphael and Michelangelo that the Renaissance started to go wrong, you should visit here. Il Sodoma, not a Florentine nor really even a Sienese (he was from Vercelli in the north), wrote the last word to the mainstream tendency of Tuscan painting before the excesses of Mannerism. Mr Sodomite himself appears in the scene *'Come Benedetto risaldò lo capistero che era rotta'* ('How Benedict repaired the broken sieve'); he's the dissipated fellow on the left with the white gloves. Look carefully – not only did Sodoma paint himself in, but also his pet badgers, of which he was very fond. They and others of Sodoma's many pets appear in various other frescoes.

Unlike so many great Tuscan art shrines, Monte Oliveto, isolated here in the Sienese hills, retains something of its original aloof dignity. Although Napoleon himself suppressed the monastery in 1810, a group of talented brothers still works here, specializing in the restoration of old books. They won't be telling you much about the place – they're vowed to silence – but there is a monkish gift shop outside that sells home-made wine and honey, as well as other products from the monasteries around Tuscany.

In the *crete* around Monte Oliveto, the village of **San Giovanni d'Asso** (8km southeast) is built around a Sienese fortress; the church of San Pietro in Villore is from the 12th century, with an ambitious, unusual façade. From here, unsignposted byroads lead east to **Montisi** (7km) and **Trequanda** (12km), two fine villages, seldom visited because they're hard to find; the latter has a 13th-century castle and a Romanesque church. You might even find **Sant'Anna in Camprena**, between Montisi and Pienza, an ambitious medieval monastery complex that time forgot – until the location scouts from *The English Patient* arrived. The place is now being fitfully restored, and if you liked Sodoma's work in Monte Oliveto, stop in here to see another of his frescoes, portraying Christ with children, small dogs and fantasy Roman monuments.

Montalcino and Around

Situated on a lofty hill inhabited since Etruscan times, swathed in vineyards and olive groves, the walled village of **Montalcino** (pop. 5,400) dominates the serene countryside 14km south of Buonconvento. Its major attraction is liquid – Brunello di Montalcino, a dark pungent red proudly holding its own among Italy's finest wines.

Every year at the Palio in Siena, there is a procession of representatives from all the towns that once were part of the republic. The honour of leading the parade belongs to Montalcino, for its loyalty and for the great service it rendered in 1555 after the fall of Siena (*see* **Siena**, History, p.323). During the siege, diehard republicans escaped from Siena to the impregnable fortress of Montalcino, where they established the 'Republic of Siena at Montalcino', holding out against the Medici until 1559. Today, Montalcino tries hard to be up to date (it was the first town in Tuscany to declare itself a 'denuclearized zone'); in reality, it's a friendly, resolutely sleepy town.

Within the Walls

Right on Piazza Cavour is one of Montalcino's modest museums: the small **Archaeology Museum**, set in a former hospital pharmacy with detached frescoes by a student of Il Sodoma. Via Mazzini leads west to the Piazza del Popolo, and the attractive **Palazzo Comunale**, begun in the late 13th century, with a slender tower that apes the Torre di Mangia in Siena. Nearby, **Sant'Agostino** is a simple Sienese church, preserving some original frescoes from the 1300s. The **Diocesan and Civic Museum** around the corner (*open Tues–Sun 10–1 and 2–5.30; adm*), has a collection of Sienese painting and polychromed wood statues, including Madonnas by three great Sienese artists (Martini, Pietro Lorenzetti and Il Vecchietta), and some of the earliest successes of Sienese art, an illuminated Bible and painted crucifix, both from the 12th century. Besides some minor works of the 14th–15th-century Sienese masters, there is a collection of locally produced majolica from the same period.

Just down Via Ricasoli, at the east end of Montalcino, the impressive 14th-century **Rocca** (*open daily summer 9–8, winter 9–6; free, but adm to go up on the walls*) was the centre of the fortifications that kept the Spaniards and Florentines at bay. This citadel means a lot to Italian patriots; it was the last stronghold of the Sienese and a symbol of all the medieval freedoms of the Italian cities blotted out in the reactionary 1500s. Near the entrance is a plaque with a poem from the 'Piedmontese Volunteers of Liberty', extolling Montalcino's bravery in 'refusing the Medici thief'. Now a city park, the Rocca contains the last battle standard of the Sienese Republic and an **Enoteca**, where you can become better acquainted with Montalcino's venerable Brunello and other local wines, such as Moscadello and Rosso di Montalcino.

Following the town walls on the north side, you pass through neighbourhoods largely made up of orchards and gardens – Montalcino isn't nearly as busy a place as it was in the 1400s. The **cathedral**, on Via Spagni, was mostly rebuilt in the 1700s. Follow that street past the Baroque church of the Madonna del Soccorso, and you come to the city park, the 'Balcony of Tuscany', with views over Siena and beyond.

Getting Around

There are regular **buses** from Siena (41km/1hr), a few of which involve a change at Buonconvento, near the SS2 crossroads for Montalcino. Buses stop at Piazza Cavour at the eastern end of town; you can obtain tickets and perhaps information at the bar on the piazza. Unfortunately, there are no convenient buses to take you to Sant'Antimo.

Besides wine, Montalcino is known for its honey and in early September hosts the **National Honey Fair**.

Tourist Information

Montalcino: Costa del Municipio 8, t/f 0577 849331.

Where to Stay and Eat

Montalcino ✉ 53024

★★★★La Vecchia Oliviera, Porta Cerbaia, t 0577 846028, f 0577 846029, *www.vecchiaoliviera. com* (*very expensive*). As the name suggests, this hotel occupies what was once an olive press. Offering the most luxurious accommodation in Montalcino, it is situated by the old gate into the town. The 13 comfortable and elegant rooms are prettily decorated; the swimming pool has a jacuzzi.

★★★Dei Capitani, Via Lapini 6, t/f 0577 847227, *www.deicapitani.it* (*expensive*). This old palazzo is your best bet in the centre. It has wonderful views, a small pool and (a rarity here) a car park.

★★★Il Giglio, Via Soccorso Saloni 5, t/f 0577 848167, *www.gigliohotel.com* (*moderate*). Similarly central.

★★★Bellaria, Via Osticcio 19, t 0577 849326, f 0577 848668, *www.hotelbellaria montalcino.com* (*moderate*). A farmhouse hotel, a short walk through a pine wood to town. Some rooms, and the pool, have fabulous views.

Boccon Divino, Loc Colombaio Tozzi, t 0577 848233 (*expensive*).Sit on the terrace and enjoy some of the best food in the area, such as saffron ravioli with black truffles, *gnocchetti* with truffles, meat roasted *sotto sale* (in a salt crust) with a delicious lettuce sauce and marvellous *bistecca alla Fiorentina. Closed Tues.*

Osteria Osticcio, Via Matteotti 23, t 0577 848271 (*moderate–cheap*). Magnificent views from the back of this pleasant wine bar. Good for a glass of wine and a snack: meats, cheeses *crostini* and salads. *Closed Tues.*

Locanda Sant'Antimo, near the church in Sant'Antimo. A good pizzeria which also has rooms (*inexpensive*).

Il Pozzo, Piazza del Pozzo, Loc S. Angelo in Colle, t 0577 844015 (*cheap*). Worth the detour for a cheap, traditional meal. *Closed Tues.*

Sant'Antimo

Open daily 6am–9pm; adm.

A few of the vineyards that produce the famous Brunello di Montalcino are on the road south for **Sant'Antimo**. Two of them welcome visitors (*call before visiting*): the **Azienda Agricola Greppo** (*t 0577 848087*) and the **Cantine dei Barbi** (*t 0577 841111*). Sant'Antimo itself, about 10km south of Montalcino, is worth the detour. One of the finest Romanesque churches in Tuscany, it originally formed part of a 9th-century Benedictine monastery founded, according to legend, by Charlemagne himself. The present building, begun in 1118, incorporates parts of the Carolingian works, including the crypt. This half-ruined complex, reached by a long, winding avenue of cypresses, could easily serve as the set for *The Name of the Rose*. An important monastic community once flourished here, and there are still some monks about; they'll sell you a CD of their Gregorian chant, which you can hear them sing at Mass (*Mon–Sat 9.15am and 7pm, Sun 11am and 6.30pm*). The church is exquisite, with its elegant tower and rounded apse. Some of the stone inside, on the capitals and elsewhere, is luminous alabaster from Volterra. The sophistication of the architecture is impressive – in particular, the Byzantine-style women's gallery, and the ambulatory behind the apse with its radiating chapels.

The Val d'Orcia

San Quirico d'Orcia, a humble little agricultural centre where the SS146 from Pienza joins the SS2, still has some of its medieval walls. Once on the pilgrim route of the Via Francigena, the town was endowed with hospices and hospitals built to accommodate pilgrims en route to Rome. The magnificent **Collegiata**, rebuilt in the 12th century over an earlier 8th-century church, has an exceptional façade built from local travertine and three portals from the 1200s, sculpted with lions and telamons, the finest of their kind in the area. Just behind it is the newly-restored and somewhat forbidding 17th-century **Palazzo Chigi** – a surprisingly grand presence for such a tiny town. Since its restoration, the frescoed rooms are open to visitors (*open daily 8–6.30; adm*). There are a couple more attractive churches in the town: **Santa Maria di Vitaleta**, with a Gothic façade and an enamel *Annunciation* by Andrea della Robbia on the high altar, and the pretty little 11th-century **Santa Maria Assunta**. You

Tourist Information

San Quirico: Via Dante Aligheri 33, **t** 0577 897211. *Closed Oct–Easter.*
Castiglione d'Orcia: Viale G. Marconi 13, **t** 0577 887363.
Radicofani: Via R. Magi 57, **t** 0578 55684.

Festivals

'**Incontri in Terra di Siena**': **t** 0578 69101, *www.lafoce.com* for details, *late July*. A chamber music festival based at *La Foce*, home of the writer Iris Origo, on the Monte Amiata road from Chianciano.
Festival del Val d'Orcia: *late July–August*. A month of music, theatre and dance.

Where to Stay and Eat

Bagno Vignoni ✉ **53027**
Hotel Posta Marcucci, Via Ara Urcea, **t** 0577 887112, **f** 0577 887119, *www.hotelposta marcucci.it* (*expensive*). On a hillside, with a thermal pool and terraces enjoying stunning views over the Val d'Orcia. The restaurant serves rather dismal food though.

La Locanda del Loggiato, Piazza del Maretto 30, **t** 0577 888925, **f** 0577 888370, *www.loggiato. it* (*expensive*). A B&B on the main square. Its six rooms occupy the first floor of a lovely medieval house. Eat in the wine bar that takes over the breakfast room in the evening.
Osteria del Leone, Via dei Mulini 4, **t** 0577 887300 (*moderate*). A very good restaurant. Specialities include traditional *bruschetta*, *pici*, *tagliata* (steak) topped with rocket, vegetarian options and fish, too. *Closed Mon*.

San Quirico d'Orcia ✉ **53027**
Hotel Palazzo del Capitano, Via Poliziano 18, **t** 0577 89028, *www.palazzodelcapitano.com* (*very expensive*). This elegant 15th-century palazzo is in the medieval heart of town. The 11 rooms are tastefully done in pastel colours with linen fabrics and some romantic four-posters. There is a pretty terrace and garden and an excellent restaurant in the old bakery.

Radicofani ✉ **53040**
La Palazzina, Loc Le Vigne, **t** 0578 55771, *www.fattorialapalazzina.com* (*moderate*). A 200-year-old villa located just outside the village, with a few rooms and a pool. Set in lovely grounds. Min 3 nights in high season.

can also visit the **Horti Leonini** (*open daily, dawn to sunset*), a lovely garden designed in the late 15th century by Diomede Lioni as a resting place for pilgrims.

There are a couple of points of interest nearby: **Ripa d'Orcia**, a hamlet with a stately castle of its own (*now a hotel, call* **t** *0577 897376, www.castelloripadorcia.com*), 7km to the south, and **Bagno Vignoni**, a small spa town just south off the SS2, where the piazza has a '*vasca termale*' built by Lorenzo de' Medici, who came for the waters. There used to be three of these pools – one for men, one for women and one for horses. The one pool that remained was fed by a spring that has dried up. Once this pool has been cleaned and restored, water from a new spring will be redirected to it. If you long for a bathe, it is possible to buy day tickets for the hot springs at the Hotel Posta Marcucci (*see* 'Where to Stay and Eat', opposite).

Before the modern SS2 was built, the old Via Francigena traversed the valley of the Orcia, passing a patch of castles and fortified towns that began in the early Middle Ages. **Castiglione d'Orcia** (9km south of San Quirico) is as medieval-looking a town as you could ask for (though its cobbled piazza and fountain are from the 1600s) with two parish churches. The ruined fortress overlooking the town was built by the Aldobrandeschi family, who controlled much of southern Tuscany as late as the 1200s. Just outside to the north a pretty road winds up through olive groves to **Rocca d'Orcia**, another well-preserved medieval village clustered below its impressive castle, the **Rocca di Tentatenno**, which is open to visitors and used for art exhibitions. Another 15km south of Castiglione is the village of **Vivo d'Orcia**, which began as a Camaldolensian monastery in 1003; when the monastery withered the village grew instead, leaving only the pretty Romanesque **Cappella dell'Ermicciolo** in the woods above the town.

Bagni San Filippo, some 8km east of Vivo, circling back towards the SS2, may go into the books as the world's smallest thermal spa – a telephone booth, a few old houses and one small hotel. It takes its name from San Filippo Benizi, a holy hermit of the Middle Ages who hid here when he heard there was a movement to elect him pope. Gouty old Lorenzo Il Magnifico used to come here, too, though he didn't leave any embellishments like the piazza in Bagno Vignoni. You can stop here for a swim in the natural terraced pools of the **Fosso Bianco**, a glistening limestone formation – a sort of stone waterfall – created by the flowing sulphurous waters.

Radicofani

Some wonderfully rugged countryside lies in the valley of the Orcia, east of this chain of villages, especially along the roads approaching **Radicofani**, a landmark of southern Tuscany, with its surreal, muffin-shaped hill topped by a lofty tower. The ruined fortress around it, originally built by Pope Adrian IV (the Englishman Nicholas Breakspear), served in the 1300s as headquarters for the legendary bandit Ghino di Tacco, solid citizen of Dante's *Inferno* and subject of a story in the *Decameron* (Day 10, Number 2), about how he imprisoned the Abbot of Cluny in this tower. The elegant loggias on the highway, just outside town, belong to the 17th-century Palazzo La Posta, once the only good hotel between Siena and Rome; most of the famous on the Grand Tour stopped on their way through.

Pienza

Some 50km south of Siena on the SS2, you'll come across a perfect, tiny core of Renaissance order and urbanity, surrounded by a village of about 2,500 souls. **Pienza** is a delightful place, even if it does get more than its share of tourists. Like Monte Oliveto Maggiore, it is a small dose of the best of the Renaissance, a jewel set among some of the most glorious and archetypal of Tuscan landscapes.

During a period of political troubles, common enough in Renaissance Siena, the great family of the Piccolomini chose to exile itself temporarily in one of its possessions, the village of Corsignano. Aeneas Silvius Piccolomini (*see p.335*) was born there in 1405; later, as Pope Pius II, he became determined to raise his country birthplace into a city. No historian has ever discovered any compelling economic or military reason for a new town here. Architect Bernardo Rossellino designed it, with some help from Pius, the pennies of the faithful paid for it, and Pius named it after himself: Pienza. Perhaps fortunately, after the first wave of papal patronage Pienza was nearly forgotten. The strict grid of streets that was to extend over the Tuscan hills never materialized, and only the central piazza with a new cathedral and a Piccolomini palace was ever completed – enough to reveal something of the original intention.

Pienza's Piazza Pio II

Piazza Pio II, the heart of Rossellino's design scheme, is simple and decorous; it displays the chief buildings of the town without any of the monumental symmetry of the later Renaissance, relying on proportion alone to tie it all together. Such a square shows how, despite all its paintings of ideal buildings and streetscapes, the Early Renaissance still followed the 'picturesque' urban design of the Middle Ages; Piazza Pio was made to be a stage set for daily life or the background of a painting.

Rossellino designed a truly elegant façade for the **cathedral** (1462), capturing the spirit of the times by omission – there is no hint anywhere that it belongs to a Christian building, though the arms of the Piccolomini and the papal keys are carved on the pediment. The interior, though equally elegant, is surprisingly tame Gothic – as if this bold Renaissance architect were a slightly embarrassed humanist who believed that only Gothic truly suited a church. Rossellino also carved a marble altar and baptismal font in the lower church; there are also altarpieces by other leading Sienese artists: Sano di Pietro, Matteo di Giovanni, Vecchietta and Giovanni di Paolo. Nothing in this cathedral has been changed, or even moved, since the day it was completed; Pius' papal bull of 1462 expressly forbade it. See it while it lasts: the cathedral, built on the edge of a slight cliff, has been subsiding almost since it was built. Occasionally sulphurous fumes seep from the floor. If you walk around the left side of the building, there is a fine view over the countryside, and also a glimpse of the fearfully large cracks that have been developing in the apse. No one has yet discovered a way to shore it up permanently, and even though restoration work has been done it could still collapse, at least partially, at any time. This collection has been rehoused in the **Museo Diocesano** (*see opposite*).

Next to the cathedral, the columned **well**, a favourite sort of Renaissance urban decoration, is also by Rossellino. So is the newly restored **Palazzo Piccolomini**, a rehash

Tourist Information

Pienza: Pro Loco, Piazza Pio II, **t** 0578 749 071.
Offers occasional guided tours of town.

Shopping

Corso Rossellino leads from the centre of the village to Porta Murello and the bus terminus, passing trendy artisan shops selling ceramics and leatherwork, antique shops and health food stores. Pienza for some reason has dozens of these, offering among other things the very good, locally made honey and preserves. And if Renaissance architecture leaves you cold, you can at least come for the sheep's cheese, maybe Italy's best. Pienza's variety of pecorino has a delicate taste, available in different strengths depending on how long it has been aged. This 'capital of sheep's cheese' has been making it at least since the time of the Etruscans.

Where to Stay and Eat

Pienza ✉ **53026**

If you are on a low budget, a number of private houses in the town offer rooms for rent; the tourist office has a full list.

★★★Il Chiostro, Corso Il Rossellino 26, **t** 0578 748400, **f** 0578 748440, *www.relaisilchiostro dipienza.com* (*very expensive*). As the name

implies this is an old cloister, in the centre just off Piazza Pio II; modernized rooms have been stylishly restored with all the amenities, beautiful gardens, a small pool, and a good restaurant.

La Saracina, about 7km from Pienza on the road to Montepulciano, **t** 0578 748022, *www.lasaracina.it* (*expensive*). Five suites and rooms in an old farmhouse with beautiful gardens, pool and tennis, out in the countryside.

★★★Corsignano, Via della Madonnina 9, **t** 0578 748501, **f** 0578 748166 (*moderate*). Modern and comfortable.

Latte di Luna, Via S. Carlo 2/4, **t** 0578 748606 (*moderate*). Popular with the locals, serving homemade pasta with truffles, duck with olives, wild boar and local *grappa. Closed Tues.*

La Pergola, Via dell'Acero 2, **t** 0578 748051. (*moderate*). The building (just outside town on the road to San Quirico) that houses this excellent restaurant may be uninspiring, but the food is anything but that and prices are reasonable. Carefully prepared versions of local dishes are served up plus the odd surprise; an amazing olive oil ice cream, for example. There is a fine selection of cheeses and an interesting wine list, too.

Sperone Nudo, Via G. Marconi, **t** 0578 748641. (*cheap*). This is a great stop for lunch, where you can get a glass of wine and *bruschette*, sandwiches or other snacks. *Closed Mon.*

of the more famous Palazzo Rucellai in Florence, whose design follows Alberti. The best bit is at the rear, where a three-storey loggia overlooks a 'hanging garden' on the cliff edge. The interior of the palace and gardens are open to visitors (*open winter Tues–Sun 10–12.30 and 4–7; summer Tues–Sun 10–12.30 and 3–6; adm*). Other buildings on the piazza include the **Archbishop's Palace** and the Gothic **Palazzo Comunale**. Behind the Palazzo Piccolomini, the church of **San Francesco** predates the founding of Pienza; there are some 14th–15th-century frescoes inside including one attributed to Luca Signorelli. The **Museo Diocesano di Pienza** (*open Wed–Mon 10–1 and 3–6.30; Nov–Mar Sat, Sun and hols 10–1 and 3–6, or by pre-booking t 0578 749905; adm*), in the sumptuously restored 15th-century Palazza Borgia in Corso Rossellino, boasts a collection of objects from nearby churches, several paintings (some by Signorelli), as well as Flemish tapestries.

Few people visit the 11th-century **Pieve** of old Corsignano, 1km west of the town (signposted from the car park/piazza at the entrance to the central pedestrian zone). This unusual church, where Aeneas Silvius was baptized, has some even more peculiar carvings over its entrance. Mermaids, or sirens, turn up with some frequency in Romanesque *tympana* and capitals, in Tuscany and Apulia especially, as well as many other places in Italy and France. Here there are several – one spreading its forked tail to display the entrance to the womb, flanked by others, and a dancer and a musician, with dragons whispering into their ears. Such symbols are steeped in medieval mysticism, not entirely inaccessible to the modern imagination. One scholar interprets this scene as a cosmic process: the sirens, representing desire, as the intermediary by which nature's energy and inspiration (the dragons) are conducted into the conscious world. It has been claimed that they betray the existence of an ecstatic cult, based on music and dance and descended from the ancient Dionysian rituals.

Montepulciano

Another graceful hill town lingers south of Siena, also with a distinguished past and best known for wine. **Montepulciano** is larger (pop. 14,500) and livelier than Montalcino, with some fine buildings and works of art. Old Montalcino was a home from home for the Sienese, while Montepulciano usually allied itself with Florence. Its Vino Nobile di Montepulciano, while perhaps not as celebrated as Montalcino's Brunello, was praised by connoisseurs over 200 years ago, and can certainly contend with Italy's best today.

Inhabitants of Montepulciano, which began as the Roman *Mons Politianus*, are called *Poliziani*, and that is the name of its most famous son – Angelo Ambrogini, or Poliziano, was one of the first Renaissance Greek scholars, an accomplished poet and critic and scholar at the court of Lorenzo de' Medici and tutor to his children. Botticelli's mythological paintings may have been inspired by his *Stanze per la Giostra*. Today's Poliziani are a genteel and cultured lot, still capable of poetic extemporization and singing. The *Bruscello*, a partly improvised play on medieval and Renaissance themes in music and verse, acted by the townspeople in the Piazza Grande each August, is the town's biggest festival. A second August festival, the *Bravio delle Botti*, requires no poetry but plenty of sweat, when neighbourhood teams race up the steep main street pushing huge barrels.

Palazzi and Pulcinella

Entering the city through the **Porta al Prato**, you will first encounter a stone column bearing the *marzocco*, a symbol of Montepulciano's long attachment to Florence. Though nominally under Florentine control, the city was allowed a sort of independence up to the days of Cosimo I. The main street, called here Via di Gracciano del Corso, climbs and winds in a circle up to the top of the city (if you follow it all the way, you'll walk twice as far as you need to, and end up thinking Montepulciano is a major metropolis). This stretch is lined with noble palaces: those at No.91 and No.82 are both the work of the late Renaissance architect Vignola, famous for his Villa Giulia in Rome and the Farnese Palace in Caprarola (Lazio). Up at No.73, **Palazzo Bucelli** has the most unusual foundation in Italy – made almost entirely of Etruscan cinerary urns, filled with cement and stacked like bricks, many still retaining their sculpted reliefs. Montepulciano was once Etruscan, though the urns probably came from Chiusi.

Piazza Michelozzo, where the street begins to ascend, is named after the Florentine architect of **Sant'Agostino** church, with an excellent, restrained Renaissance façade, similar to the cathedral in Pienza though more skilfully handled. Michelozzo also contributed the terracotta reliefs over the portal. Across the piazza, note the figure atop the old **Torre del Pulcinello**. To anyone familiar with Naples, the white *Commedia dell'Arte* clown banging the hours on the town bell will be an old friend. It is said that a Neapolitan bishop was once exiled here for indiscretions back home, and when he returned, he left this bit of Parthenopean culture as a souvenir to thank the Poliziani.

Continuing along the main street, you pass a dozen or so more palaces, reminders of the city's aristocratic past. There is one florid Baroque interior, in the **Gesù Church** by Andrea Pozzo. Further down, the street curves around the medieval **Fortezza**, now partly residential, within the oldest part of town, a fascinating quarter of ancient alleys.

Piazza Grande

These days, when even the stalwart citizens of hill towns are a little too spoiled to walk up hills, the old centres of towns sometimes become quiet and out-of-the-way. So it is in Montepulciano, where the **Piazza Grande** is city's highest point. On one side, Michelozzo added a rusticated stone front and tower to the 13th-century **Palazzo Comunale** to create a lesser copy of Florence's Palazzo Vecchio. Opposite, a Renaissance well stands in front of the **Palazzo Contucci**, built by the elder Antonio da Sangallo. On the west side, a tremendous pile of bricks, a sort of tenement for pigeons, proclaims the agonizing unfinishability of the **cathedral**, sad victim of a doomed rebuilding project begun in 1592. Like the toad, believed by medieval scholars to conceal a precious jewel in its brain, this preposterous building hides within its bulk a single transcendent work of art. Atop a marble Renaissance altar adorned with *putti* stands an *Assumption of the Virgin* by Taddeo di Bartolo, one of the greatest of all 14th-century Sienese paintings. Set in glowing, discordant colours – pink, orange, purple and gold – this is a very spiritual Madonna, attended by a court of angel musicians. Don't miss the predella panels beneath; each is a serious, inspired image from the Passion, including one panel of the *Resurrection* that can be compared to Piero della Francesca's more famous version in Sansepolcro.

The **Museo Civico**, holding the **Pinacoteca Crociani** just down Via Ricci (*open Tues–Sun 10–1 and 3–6; in summer until 8; Dec–Mar Sat–Sun 10–1 and 3–6; adm*), houses several collections under one roof. On the first and second floors are some della Robbia terracottas from the dissolved convent that was once downstairs, and the Crociani collection of paintings. The old collection, with a *Crucifixion* from Filippino Lippi's workshop, an *Assumption* by the Sienese Jacopo di Mino, an odd work by Girolamo di Benvenuto – baby Jesus as an *objet d'art* – and, even more peculiar, an inexplicable *Allegory of the Immaculate Conception* by one Giovanni Antonio Lappoli (d. 1552), has gained additions from other collections in Montepulciano. However, the key improvement is the archaeological section on ground level, now rearranged to include the contents of five locally discovered Etruscan tombs previously housed in the Uffizi. Artefacts include Bucchero ware, ceramics and bronzes dating from the 5th to the 2nd century BC.

Continue down Via Ricci and you will find the church of **Santa Lucia**, with a small *Madonna* by Luca Signorelli in a chapel off to the right.

Antonio da Sangallo's San Biagio

One of the set pieces of Renaissance architecture was the isolated temple, a chance to create an ideal building in an uncluttered setting, often on the edge of a city. Giuliano da Sangallo's Santa Maria delle Carceri in Prato was the first and worst, followed by Bramante's San Pietro in Montorio in Rome and the Tempio della Consolazione in Todi (Umbria). Montepulciano's example of this genre lies south of the city (a lengthy walk downhill and back, if you don't have a car) near the road junction for Chianciano; a stately avenue of cypresses, each over a small marker commemorating a local soldier who died in the First World War, leads to the site.

Antonio da Sangallo, long in the shadow of his less talented brother Giuliano, left his masterpiece here. **San Biagio** stands in a small park, a central, Greek cross church of creamy travertine. As with so many other Renaissance churches, there is more

Getting There and Around

Montepulciano is situated 12½km/20mins east of Pienza on the SS146, 66km/1½hrs from Siena, and 16km/30mins west of the Chiusi exit on the A1.

The **train** station (Florence–Rome line) is way out in the countryside, irregularly served by buses to town, and it tends to be only local trains that stop; a better possibility is to use the station at Chiusi-Chianciano, which has bus connections up to Chiusi town, to Chianciano Terme, Montepulciano and occasionally Pienza.

The **bus** station in Montepulciano is just outside the Porta al Prato, the main gate into the city. There are very regular buses to Chianciano Terme–Chiusi–Chiusi station; slightly fewer to Pienza; one each in the morning and afternoon for Siena (via Pienza and San Quirico), also daily connections to Abbadia San Salvatore, Montalcino, Perugia and Arezzo.

There is an LFI bus information booth inside the train station at Chiusi; outside, besides the buses mentioned above, there are rather infrequent LFI connections to Cortona, Arezzo, Perugia, Orvieto and Città della Pieve.

If you aren't up to climbing up to the top of Montepulciano, the LFI runs a handy **minibus** service up the Corso to Piazza Grande.

Tourist Information

Montepulciano: Via Gracciano nel Corso 59a, off Piazza Grande, t 0578 757341. Open daily 9–12.30 and 3–6.

Where to Stay and Eat

Montepulciano ✉ 53045

Montepulciano puts out the welcome mat at a few very amiable hotels.

★★★**Marzocco**, Via G. Savonarola 18, t 0578 757262, f 0578 757530, *www.albergo marzocco.it* (*moderate*). An airy, serendipitous establishment, family-run, and located next to the *Marzocco* itself, just inside the main gate.

★★★**Borghetto**, Borgo Buio t 0578 757535, *www.ilborghetto.it* (*expensive*). Just around the corner, with pleasant rooms, some of which have great views over the edge of the town.

★★★**Il Riccio**, Via Talosa 21, t/f 0578 757713, *www.ilriccio.net* (*moderate*). Tastefully furnished rooms in a renovated medieval palazzo, with a pleasant rooftop terrace for catching the sun.

If you can't find a room in the town, there are lots of *agriturismo* places in the surrounding countryside, and hundreds of rooms just a few km south at Chianciano

architecture than Christianity in the design, a consciously classical composition, using an adaptation of the 'Tuscan' order on the ground level, Ionic on the second and Corinthian on the upper storeys of the campanile, gracefully fitted into one of the corners of the Greek cross. The interior, finished in marble and other expensive stone, is equally symmetrical, rational and impressive. Over the handsome altar, a Latin inscription proclaims, '*Hinc deus homo et home Deus. Immensum Concept – Aeternum Genuit*' (Hence God is Man, and for humanity, the created Eternity). The beautiful **Canon's House**, with its double *loggia*, is also the work of Sangallo.

Around Montepulciano

Among some beautiful villages on the hills around Montepulciano, **Montefollonico** (8km northwest), has a frescoed church and Palazzo Comunale, both 13th-century. **Monticchiello**, 7km southwest on a back road towards Pienza, hangs languorously on its hilltop; it too has a 13th-century church, with a rose window, an altarpiece by Pietro Lorenzetti and Sienese frescoes (late 14th century).

Terme (*see* p.382). If you go to Sant'Albano, 3km from Montepulciano, you'll find seven more hotels, all in the inexpensive range, stuck in the middle of nowhere – presumably because there are more thermal baths nearby.

The best restaurants are outside town.

La Chiusa, Via Madonnina, Montefollonico, **t** 0577 669668, *www.ristorantelachiusa.it* (*very expensive*). Located in an old *frantoio* or olive press, on the edge of the village of Montefollonico, with panoramic views back towards Montepulciano. La Chiusa has been acclaimed as the best restaurant in southern Tuscany, and though its reputation has wobbled slightly in recent years, you're guaranteed at the very least an incredible seven-course *menu degustazione* and an exhaustive wine list. It also has some very luxurious suites and rooms. *Closed Tues.*

La Grotta, **t** 0578 757607 (*expensive*). In the shadow of the dramatic San Biagio, serving traditional Tuscan dishes with a creative twist, with the likes of smoked goose breast, ravioli stuffed with pigeon and saffron, pigeon stuffed with truffles or duck breast with juniper berries and orange peel. *Closed Wed.*

Osteria Borgo Buio, Via di Borgo Buio 10, **t** 0578 717497 (*moderate*). This excellent *osteria* not only offers local dishes such as *pici* and other homemade pasta dishes,

but also historical dishes such as *pepposo*, a peppery beef stew cooked in *vino nobile*. *Closed Thurs.*

Caffé Poliziano, on the Corso. Montepulciano's old-fashioned *gran caffé*; worth visiting at least for a cup of coffee.

Alternatively, why not have a picnic? Stock up on some of the fine local products – honey and preserves, pecorino cheese, ham or boar salami and a case of *vino nobile*; any of the back roads off the SS146 will lead you at some point to an ideal spot.

Monticchiello ✉ 53020

L'Olmo, **t** 0578 755133, **f** 0578 755124, *www. olmopienza.it* (*luxury*). Just below Montichiello is an elegant guesthouse in a beautifully restored stone post-house, with gardens and a pool overlooking the Val d'Orcia. Bedrooms are supremely comfortable and decorated in sophisticated rustic style; dinner is available on request. *Closed mid-Nov–Easter.*

La Porta, Via del Piano 1, **t** 0578 755163. An excellent *osteria/enoteca*, with wonderful views over Pienza and the valley from its panoramic terrace. Here you can have anything from a sandwich or a plate of local cheeses with a glass of wine, to a pasta dish or a succulent *tagliata* of tender steak topped with rocket leaves. *Closed Thurs.*

Vino Nobile and Other Delights

Montepulciano and its environs are full of *cantine*, and each of these is full of people ready for long discussions on the virtues of this famous wine.

After two years, it carries the bouquet of unknown autumn blooms, a perfume that confounds melancholy; its colour is a mystery of faith. Certain writers are known to be very fond of it. A wine tour of Montepulciano should begin with the **Cantine Cantucci**, on the Piazza Grande, where they might show you the salon with frescoes by Baroque artist Andrea Pozzo. The **Cantina Gattavecchia**, next to the church of Santa Maria at the southern end of town, has a *cantina* dating back to the 1500s; don't neglect the venerable cellar built into the embankment beneath Piazza Grande, next to the Teatro Poliziano.

Vino Nobile isn't the only variety of wine made in these parts. There is a version of Chianti – Chianti Colli Senesi, a creditable white Valdichiana and a sweet dessert Vinsanto. And on those evenings when quantity means more than quality, try any of the mass-produced Montepulciano reds; more honourable plonk is hard to find.

Besides wine, Montepulciano has some local surprises to offer – jams, preserves, honey and other farm specialities have all recently become prominent in this corner of Tuscany, where the ideology of natural food has become just as popular as in the trendiest neighbourhoods of New York. You'll find them in almost any grocer's. Montepulciano has some very good antique stores on its back streets, and a sound crafts tradition, especially in woodcarving. On Piazza Grande, there is a School of Mosaics; take a peek at the mosaic fountain in the courtyard.

Chianciano Terme

'*Chianciano – Fegato Sano*' – this is the slogan you see everywhere in **Chianciano Terme** (pop. 7,500): on the signs that welcome you, on the municipal buildings, even on the garbage trucks: 'Chianciano, for a healthy liver'. And after rotting yours on too much Montepulciano wine, how convenient to have a spa close at hand to flush it out and get it pumping again. The waters here were known to the Etruscans, but have only been exploited in a big way in the last 50 years. There is an old walled town, Chianciano Vecchio, with a medieval clock tower and a Museo d'Arte Sacra; at the gate is the bus station and information booth. Just outside the old town, the **Museo Civico Archeologico delle Acque** (*open April–Oct Tues–Sun 10–1 and 4–7; Nov–Mar Sat and Sun 10–1 and 4–7; other days by appt only, call t 0578 30471; adm*) occupies an old granary, displaying mainly Etruscan and Roman exhibits excavated locally since 1986. Among the usual bronzes and ceramics are finds from Poggio Bacherina, an Etruscan farm uncovered between 1986 and 1989. The newest display has reconstructions of tombs, built in the hollows that were originally carved out to hold wine barrels in the granary. These 'tombs' contain finds from the excavation of the Tolle Necropoli at neaby La Foce, arranged more or less as they were found at the site.

Beyond, modern Chianciano stretches for miles down Viale della Libertà, passing hundreds of hotels, gardens with clipped lawns, and bathhouses in a clean, modern style from the 1950s. Besides repairing your liver, Chianciano has mineral mud packs for your acne, hot aerosol douches and plenty of other medically respected treatments for your every ailment. They'll lock you in a room full of gas for a collective dry nebulization, throw you in the hydro-gaseous bath and then hand you over to the *masseuses* (this for patients suffering from trauma), or put you face-to-face with the sulphurous sonic aerosol spray. 'Ah,' said the despairing Italians, 'the English never come. They simply do not understand the baths...'

Around Chianciano: La Foce and Castelluccio

Southwest of Chianciano lies **La Foce**, a large estate on the hills overlooking the Val d'Orcia. Its strategic position on the Via Francigena has long attracted settlers; recent excavations brought to light a burial place from the 7th century BC.

Antonio and Iris Origo bought the property in 1924 when it was barren and poverty-ridden, working throughout their lives to regenerate the area; they set up a school, a day clinic and a nursery, also an orphanage during the war. Iris Origo's autobiographical books *Images and Shadows* and *War in the Val d'Orcia* make fascinating reading: the former covers the estate's development, while the latter focuses on the war years.

The villa was built in the late 15th century as a hostel for pilgrims and merchants, and restored by the Origos under the guidance of English landscape architect Cecil Pinsent, who designed the delightful gardens (*gardens only open Wed 3pm–dusk; t 0578 69101*). Nearby, on the road to Montepulciano, is the medieval **Castelluccio**, also part of the estate and open to visitors. As well as exhibitions, it holds concerts in the summer, as a venue for the **Incontri in Terra di Siena** music festival (*see* p.374).

Tourist Information

Chianciano Terme: Piazza Italia 67, t 0578 671122.

Where to Stay and Eat

Chianciano Terme ✉ 53042

Whether or not you feel ready to entrust yourself to the thermal torture of the spa, Chianciano can be useful in the summer when hotels are booked solid everywhere else. **Azienda Autonima di Cura**, Viale Roma 67. Offers help with accommodation.

Most of Chianciano's hotels were built in the last 30 years – nothing is outstanding, but you will find a fair amount of choice within every price range. As in most spa towns, people tend to dine in their hotels, but a few restaurants have cropped up, too.

La Foce, Casella Postale 55, t 0578 69101, *www.lafoce.com* (*luxury–expensive*). Several of the farmhouses on this estate have been turned into up-market self-catering apartments, sleeping 2–14 guests. Furnishings are elegant rustic in style, with plenty of antiques, and each house has use of a pool and private garden. Meals available on request.

L'Oasi, Loc La Foce, t 0578 755 077 (*moderate*). A useful stop-off just below La Foce on the road to Monte Amiata, this is a rustic, family-run bar/restaurant, serving *panini* with slabs of the local pecorino or heartier fare, such as *pici* and wild boar.

La Rosa del Trinoro, on the road between La Foce and Sarteano, at Castriglioncello del Trinoro, t 0578 265 529, *www.larosadel trinoro.it* (*expensive*). It's worth climbing the 11km of 'white road' from La Foce (turn left just after the villa towards Chiarentana) for the view alone, but also for the 'other worldliness' of this tiny hamlet. The menu features creative and elegant versions of local and not-so-local dishes; there are also nine pleasant rooms (*moderate*).

Chiusi and Around

If anyone ever read you Macaulay's rouser *Horatio at the Bridge*, you will remember the fateful Lars Porsena of Clusium, leading the Etruscan confederation and their Umbrian allies to attack Rome in brave days of old. Thanks to Horatio, Rome survived and made a name for itself; here you can see what happened to Clusium – or *Camars*, as the Etruscans called it. Most of its 9,500 citizens live in the new districts by the railway station, but the hill town on the site of Lars Porsena's capital still thrives.

Archaeological Museum

Open daily 9–8; adm.

From those brave days of old, Chiusi retains at least an excellent **Archaeological Museum**, beautifully laid out and well-labelled. As with so many Etruscan collections, the main attraction is the large number of cinerary urns, and as usual, the Etruscans are able to produce a bewildering variety of styles and themes. Large urns with thoughtful, reclining figures are common, as well as mythological battle scenes with

Tourist Information

Chiusi: Pro Loco, Via Porsenna 67,
  t 0578 227 667.

Where to Stay and Eat

Chiusi ✉ 53043

Most of the hotels are down by the railway station in Chiusi Scalo, and unremarkable.
★★★**Centrale**, Piazza Dante 3, t 0578 20118 (*moderate*). A typical offering, with several modern rooms.
There are a couple of options out of town.
Le Anfore, Via Chiusi 30, just outside town on the road to Sarteano, t/f 0578 265521, *www.balzarini.it* (*moderate*). An attractive and beautifully restored farmhouse providing good value family accommodation with pool, tennis and riding – there's even a restaurant.
★★★**La Fattoria**, Conciarese al Lago, t 0578 21407, *www.la-fattoria.it* (*moderate*). An old farmhouse with views over the lake; there are eight nice rooms and a very good restaurant specializing in fresh fish from the lake, plus every sort of roast and pasta dish made with porcini mushrooms. *Closed Mon.*
Zaira, Via Arunte 12, t 0578 20260 (*moderate*). Italians in the know make the detour off the

Rome–Florence *autostrada* up to the oldest part of Chiusi, heading for this restaurant with its speculative 'Etruscan cuisine'. Every restaurant that tries to reconstruct an Etruscan menu comes up with something different. No matter; it's a harmless fancy, and with dishes such as *pasta del lucumone* (with ham and three different cheeses), duck cooked in *vino nobile* and guinea fowl *al cartoccio*, it's hard to complain. Zaira takes special pride in the wine list, having one of Tuscany's largest cellars. It's good value, too. *Closed Mon in winter.*
La Solita Zuppa, Via Porsenna 21, t 0578 21006 (*moderate*). The name is too modest – not really the 'same old soup', but their speciality: four or five different kinds on any given day, along with homemade *pici* and good meat dishes; in a warm, old-fashioned *osteria* atmosphere up in the Old Town. *Closed Tues.*
Da Gino, Via Cabina Lago 42, t 0578 21408 (*moderate*). On the shores of the Lago di Chiusi. The speciality is fresh lake fish, grilled over bamboo fire (also from the lake) and *Tegamaccio* (fish soup) and eel. *Closed Wed.*

Sarteano ✉ 53047

Residenza Santa Chiara, Piazza S. Chiara, t 0578 265412, f 0578 266849, *www. conventosantachiara.it* (*expensive*). Nice old

winged gods. Not all the tombs contained the well-known rectangular urns; some Etruscans chose to be buried in 'canopic' jars, surmounted by a terracotta bust of the deceased. Camars was a wealthy town, and the excavations at its necropolises unearthed a large amount of Greek pottery – note the urn with Achilles and Ajax playing at dice, and the Dionysian scenes with sexy maenads and leering satyrs. Many Etruscan imitation vases are on display; it's easy to believe the local talent could have done as well as the Greeks, had they only possessed thinner paintbrushes. To end the collection, there is a glittering hoard of nice barbaric trinkets from some 6th–7th-century Lombard tombs on the Arusa hill just outside town.

Etruscan Tombs and Tunnels

If you're interested in seeing some of the Etruscan tombs (5th–3rd century BC) where these items were discovered, mention it to the museum guards, who arrange guided tours – in fact, they'll probably ask you first. These are the only good painted tombs in Tuscany; the best one, the **Tomba della Scimmia**, contains paintings of wrestlers and warriors, in addition to the monkey that gives the tomb its name.

building at the top of the town with a cool, shady garden, simple but perfectly adequate rooms, and an excellent restaurant.

La Giara, Viale Europa 2 (6km southwest of Chiusi), t 0578 265511 (*expensive*). Usually crowded with Sartanese, and with good reason, lured in by the homemade pasta, pizza, roast duck and lamb chops. *Closed Mon.*

Osteria Da Gagliano, Via Roma 5, t 0578 268022 (*moderate*). A simple *osteria* with wooden tables and benches. Excellent local dishes include gnocchi (on Thursdays), tripe or pecorino *al forno. Closed Tues.*

Cetona ✉ 53040

****La Frateria**, Convento di San Francesco, t 0578 238015, *www.mondox.it* (*very expensive*). The most unusual hotel in the area, in the buildings of a 13th-century monastery founded originally by St Francis. It's now run by a community of young people who have managed to preserve a feeling of peace and tranquillity in keeping with the setting, despite the lavish physical comforts on offer. Among the luxuries is an excellent, if somewhat overpriced, restaurant. *Closed Jan.*

La Locanda di Anita, Piazza Balestrieri 5, t 0578 237075, *www.lalocandadianita.it* (*expensive*). A tiny *locanda* with four beautiful rooms and a suite, and a pretty breakfast terrace. You can enjoy good, homecooked food in

the nearby **L'Osteria Vecchia**, under the same management.

San Casciano dei Bagni ✉ 53040

****Fonteverde**, Loc Terme 1, t 0578 58023, f 0578 58013, *www.fonteverdespa.com* (*luxury*). A new luxury spa hotel built in and around a Medici villa with extensive gardens on the site of the restored thermal baths. B&B or a package including full-board and a huge range of beauty therapies and treatments.

****Sette Querce**, Viale Manciati 2, t 0578 58174, f 0578 58172, *www.settequerce.it* (*expensive, suites very expensive*). A delightful hotel furnished in a riot of colour. Comfortable rooms have their own sitting area and some have kitchenette. Breakfast is served in your room, other meals are available at **Da Daniela** (*see* below).

La Fontanella, Via Roma 6, t 0578 58300, *www.albergolafontanella.com* (*expensive*). Good value, and with an excellent restaurant (*moderate–cheap*).

Da Daniela, Piazza Matteotti 7, t 0578 58041 (*moderate*). Serves interesting variations on local themes in a lovely, brick-vaulted room. Sample bean soup, ravioli stuffed with pigeon, fricassee of lamb with artichokes or rich, bubbling pecorino with truffles. Leave room for *mousse di marrons glacées* topped with forest fruits. *Closed Wed in winter.*

The **Tomba della Pellegrina** and the **Tomba del Granduca** are also interesting, as is the **Tomba Bonci Casuccini**, in a different necropolis east of town.

The Cathedral

Across the street from the museum, Chiusi's cathedral is the oldest in Tuscany. Only parts of it – the recycled Roman columns in the nave – go back to the original 6th-century building. The cathedral was rebuilt in the 12th century and again in the 19th. Have a look at the mosaics that cover the walls inside. At first glance, they seem astounding, an unknown chapter in early Christian art. Then you'll notice they have a touch of Art Nouveau about them – and finally, you realize they aren't mosaics at all, but skilfully sponged-on squares of paint, a crazy masterpiece of mimicry completed in 1915. The small **cathedral museum** (*open 15 June–Sept Mon–Fri 9.30–12.45 and 4–7; Oct–14 June 9.30–12.45 only; adm*) contains Roman fragments and some beautiful 15th-century illuminated choir books. The best part, though, is that your admission includes a climb up the campanile, and a descent into the mysterious network of tunnels and galleries underlying the town, bits of which go back to the time of the Etruscans. Whatever their original purpose, some were converted into catacombs by early Christian communities; there's also an underground cistern from Roman times.

Around Chiusi: Lakes, Sarteano and More *Crete*

Just northeast of Chiusi, the **Lago di Chiusi** and the **Lago di Montepulciano** are pretty patches of blue on the border between Tuscany and Umbria, smallest in the chain of lakes that begins with Lago Trasimeno. Lago di Chiusi, in particular, is nice for a picnic, close to the *autostrada* if you're headed from Florence to Rome or Orvieto.

Sarteano is a smaller resort spa, 9km south of Chianciano or Chiusi, attached to a fine old hill town with some Renaissance palaces, a squarish medieval fortress, and the church of **San Martino in Foro**, with an *Annunciation* that is one of the best works of the Sienese Mannerist Beccafumi. A small and delightful Etruscan museum – the **Museo Civico Archeologico** – has opened in the impressive Palazzo Gabrielli, containing some wonderful funerary accoutrements. Most striking of all are the magnificent urns containing bones and other anthropomorphic paraphernalia.

Another 6km south of Sarteano, off the ruggedly scenic SS321, lies **Cetona**, a small, untouristic gem, with a growing population of discerning foreign residents who have rejected Chianti country and all that it implies. The Palazzo Comunale has a **Museo Civico per la Preistoria del Monte Cetona**, documenting archaeological discoveries since the 1920s, including a massive bear some believe to be 50,000 years old.

Take the road to Sarteano, and after 6km or so you'll reach the **Parco Archeologico Naturalistico di Belvedere**, with remains from one of the most important Bronze Age sites in Italy. On the approach to Sarteano, you can visit the 14th-century ex-convent of Santa Maria a Belvedere, now inhabited by the same community who run the up-market La Frateria di Padre Egidio (*see* 'Where to Stay and Eat', p.385), but also housing frescoes attributed to Petruccioli and Andrea di Giovanni.

The SS478 from Sarteano towards Monte Amiata passes one of the loneliest, most barren regions of *crete* en route to the Val d'Orcia (*see* p.374), while the road south from Cetona takes you on a beautiful, winding drive skirting Monte Cetona, punctuated with dramatic views as you pass through woods and olive groves towards **San Casciano dei Bagni**, a pretty spa town on the borders of Umbria and Lazio. There are a couple of ancient churches and a castle; the hot springs are just outside to the south. The resort's heyday was in the Renaissance, when Grand Duke Ferdinand built a villa there and developed the spa; the baths have been restored and the Medici villa transformed into a luxury hotel (*see* 'Where to Stay and Eat', p.385).

Monte Amiata and Around

Monte Amiata, the rooftop of southern Tuscany, is an extinct volcanic massif with a central peak over a mile high (1,722m/5,649ft). With no real competition close by, it has become a skiing and hiking centre – the closest to Rome, and as such, popular in both summer and winter. The presence of Europe's second-largest mercury mine (a complex that has been putting dinner on the table for Abbadia San Salvatore since the Middle Ages) does not detract from area's natural beauty. The lower, uncultivated slopes are covered in chestnut and beech trees. Higher up, there are beautiful mature forests, where the leaves catch the early frosts and change colour marvellously in the autumn.

Abbadia San Salvatore

A thousand years ago, you might have heard of this town, home of the most important monastic centre in Tuscany and a fair-sized city in its own right. History passed by **Abbadia San Salvatore** a long time ago; today it makes a modest living as a mountain resort, the gateway to Monte Amiata. Abbadia (pop. 7,900) appears modern at first, but just behind Viale Roma, a narrow gateway leads into the grey, quiet streets of the **medieval centre**. It isn't very large, and there are no buildings of particular interest, but it is as complete and unchanged as any medieval quarter in Tuscany. Note the symbols carved into many of the doorways: coats of arms, odd religious symbols (a snake, for example) or signs like a pair of scissors that declare the original owner was a tailor.

The **abbey church** is outside the centre, a few blocks north in Via del Monastero; in the Middle Ages it must have been open countryside. According to legend – there's even a document telling the story, dated the Ides of March, 742 – the Lombard King Rachis was on his way to attack Perugia when a vision of the Saviour appeared to him. Rachis not only founded the monastery, but retired to it as a monk. Historians consider the whole business a convenient fabrication, but by 1000, the abbey had achieved considerable wealth and influence, ruling over a large piece of territory and waging occasional wars with the Bishop of Chiusi. In 1036, the present church was begun, an excellent Romanesque work that may seem plain to us, but was undoubtedly one of the grandest sights in Tuscany when it was new.

Getting Around

Don't try to get to Amiata by **train**; there's a 'Monte Amiata station' on an infrequent branch line from Siena, but it's really some 40km on the northern side of the massif, near Castiglione d'Orcia. It's much easier to get a **bus** from Siena, Chiusi or Grosseto. Buses stop on Viale Roma in the centre of Abbadia San Salvatore (tickets and timetables in the toy store behind the information booth); a few go daily to Buonconvento and Siena (79km/ 2½hrs), Montepulciano–Chiusi (48km/1½hrs); nine a day go from Abbadia to Arcidosso (25km/1hr) and Castel del Piano on the western side of Amiata.

Note that Arcidosso and the other towns on the west slope are in Grosseto province; almost all the buses there go on to Grosseto. There are also at least two daily ACOTRAL or SIRA buses that run through Castel del Piano, Arcidosso and Abbadia San Salvatore to Viterbo and on to Rome.

Tourist Information

Abbadia San Salvatore: Via Adua 25, t 0577 775811, *info@amiata.turismo. toscana.it.*

Castel del Piano: Via G. Marconi 2, t 0564 951026.
Arcidosso: Piazza Castello 1, t 0564 968010.

Sports and Activities

As one of the few good **skiing** areas close to Rome, Monte Amiata can be a busy place. The pistes begin almost at the summit; there are two chair lifts and 13 ski lifts. The 15 runs (the longest is 1,500m/4,900ft) are connected by paths through the forest. There are also ski schools (t 0577 789740 and t 0564 959004).

It's also perfect for **cross-country skiing** and **hiking**. A network of hiking trails has been marked as far as Castiglione d'Orcia. The tourist offices can give you a map: ask for the *Cartografia dei Sentieri.*

For snow news and information, call the tourist office in Abbadia San Salvatore, t 0577 775811.

Where to Stay and Eat

Monte Amiata ✉ 53021
For skiing, there are pleasant facilities near the summit.
★★★Rifugio Cantore, at '*Secondo Rifugio 10*', along the road from Abbadia, t 0577 789704

Behind the twin-steepled façade, the church is surprisingly long; the eastern end has a raised chancel, leading to a series of arches over the altar and choir. Here frescoes by Nasino, an early 1700s artist, tell the story of King Rachis. His **crypt**, under the chancel, was the original 8th-century church. The proportions are thoroughly Byzantine, with stone vaulting and oddly carved columns and capitals, no two alike.

South of Abbadia San Salvatore, **Piancastagnaio** is a smaller mountain resort. It has a **castle** of the Aldobrandeschi, housing a small museum, a 17th-century palace and, as its name implies, lots of chestnut trees. Chestnuts and chestnut flour were once the staple food around Amiata; restaurants still occasionally offer chestnut polenta.

Around Amiata

On the panoramic route around Amiata is **Seggiano**, 20km northwest of Abbadia, with its unusual 16th-century church with a square cupola, the Madonna della Carità. South another 7km is **Castel del Piano**, with an old centre, laid out in *belle époque* parks and boulevards. **Arcidosso**, another 4km south, is the largest town (pop. 4,500) on the Grosseto side of Amiata, with a stately Aldobrandeschi fortress, and one church outside the town, the triple-apsed Santa Maria in Lamula, begun in the 900s and redone in the 12th century.

(*moderate*). Stays open all year to cater for summer mountaineering.

***La Capannina**, Vette Amiata, **t** 0577 789713, **f** 0577 789777 (*moderate*). A cosy place, a little further up. The hotel restaurant is one of the best in the area; lots of dishes with mushrooms (including polenta, that northern Italian alternative to pasta that is also popular around here) and also stuffed pigeon. *Open 15 Dec–Easter, also June–mid Sept and Oct weekends.*

Abbadia San Salvatore ✉ 53021

Abbadia San Salvatore is popular, not just for winter skiing, but also as a cool summer retreat. There are a dozen or so hotels in town.

***Adriana**, Via Serdini 76, **t** 0577 778116, (*moderate*). A few blocks north of the centre.

Relais San Lorenzo, Loc San Lorenzo, **t** 0577 785003 (*moderate*). A new hotel/restaurant in an old building on the slopes of Monte Amiata in a wonderful setting, with ample grounds. Eighteen rooms and apartments, all comfortably furnished and with fridges, plus the usual 3-star amenities. The restaurant serves excellent local food.

****San Marco**, Via Matteotti 19, **t/f** 0577 778089 (*moderate–inexpensive*). Newer, with a restaurant serving a *menu fisso* (*cheap*).

Arcidosso ✉ 58031

An excellent base for Amiata; there are several good modern hotels, many at bargain rates.

***Aiuole**, Loc Aiuole, **t** 0564 967300 (*moderate*). The restaurant here specializes in porcini mushroom soup, but also other sturdy dishes and excellent local cheeses. *Closed Mon in winter.*

Castel del Piano ✉ 58033

There are a couple of further options a few kilometres from Arcidosso.

***Contessa**, at Prato della Contessa, **t** 0564 959000, *www.hotelcontessa.it* (*moderate*). This hotel is in a lovely setting above town on the slopes of Monte Amiata and organizes nature walks, cultural tours and more. The restaurant, which is also good, lays on special seasonal menus.

Albergo Ristorante Silene, Località Pescina 9, **t** 0564 950805 (*expensive*). Silene has been serving food (and providing a bed – six nice rooms, *moderate*) since 1830. The regularly changing menu features seasonal local produce, offering dishes such as *taglierini* with wild asparagus, *gnocchetti* with truffles and wild boar stew spiked with juniper. The hot chocolate soufflé is divine.

The town is best known, however, for the strange career of David Lazzaretti, a millenarian prophet gunned down by the Carabinieri during a disturbance in 1878. People in this area still talk about Lazzaretti; his movement, combining reformed religion and plain rural socialism (in an age when land reform was Italy's biggest social issue), spread widely in southern Tuscany. Before Lazzaretti's murder, his followers had started to create a sort of commune on **Monte Labbro**, 10km to the south. The tower, bits of buildings and remains of the church they built on Monte Labbro still stand, and a few of the faithful occasionally hold 'Giurisdavidical' services there.

Roccalbegna, 20km south on the SS323, has another Aldobrandeschi castle, and some Sienese art in SS. Pietro e Paolo and the nearby Oratorio del Crocifisso. For a landmark Roccalbegna has one very conspicuous rock, a bizarre conical mass looming over the village called simply 'La Pietra'. The Aldobrandeschi also built at **Santa Fiora**, a pleasant town 7.5km south, with della Robbia terracottas in its three churches. Just south of Arcidosso, on the northern slopes of Monte Labbro, is a nature reserve, the **Parco Faunistico del Monte Amiata** (*open Tues–Sun dawn–sunset;* **t** *0564 966867*). Hiking trails offer a look at various kinds of deer, mountain goats, and maybe wolves – there is a project to reintroduce these here.

Amiata's summit, decorated with the obligatory iron crucifix (made in the Victorian foundries of Follonica, like the bandstands and even some of the fountains you will see locally), lies about halfway between Abbadia and Arcidosso; roads reach almost to the top. The skiing area is here, too, at the point called **Vetta Amiata**.

The Lost Corner of Tuscany

Only a true connoisseur of regional obscurity would appreciate the inland reaches of Grosseto province, the largest stretch of territory in Italy north of the Abruzzo without a single well-known attraction. Once part of the Etruscan heartland, these towns have been poor and usually misgoverned ever since – by the Romans, the noble Aldobrandeschi, the popes and the Tuscan dukes. Some don't even consider the area part of Tuscany, and it's true that in many ways, it has more in common with the haunted, empty expanses of northern Lazio across the border.

Sorano

Southeast 20km from Santa Fiora, **Castell'Azzara** takes its name from a medieval game of dice (the word similar to our *hazard*); one of the Aldobrandeschi won it in a crap shoot. **Sorano**, a grim, grey town to the south, clings tenaciously to its rock, almost hidden between two deep and lovely wooded canyons. Bits of the town have been crumbling down into the surrounding valleys for centuries; many houses were destroyed in a landslide 80 years ago. It is still inhabited, though more houses have been abandoned as younger people move away to find work. Sorano is dominated by two equally grim castles; the larger is the 15th-century **Rocca degli Orsini**. Outside town on the road to Sovana is a strange natural rock formation called the **Mano di Orlando**, the 'Hand of Roland'.

Sovana and the Vie Cave

Sovana, 10km to the west, with a population of about 190, is another medieval time capsule, a town almost perfectly preserved in its 13th- or 14th-century appearance, perched dramatically on a ridge overlooking the surrounding countryside. Sovana was an important Etruscan city, and in the 11th century it thrived as the family headquarters of the Aldobrandeschi. This powerful clan, controlling much of southern Tuscany and northern Lazio, had a political role on a European level. The zenith of its influence came with the election to the papacy of one of its members in 1073. Gregory VII (his common name *Hildebrand* betrays the Aldobrandeschis' Teutonic origins) made a great reforming pope, but he also took care of the family interests.

On Sovana's humble main street, the Via di Mezzo, you can see the 13th-century Palazzo del Pretorio, with only a clock and *bifore* windows to betray its civic dignity. There is some interesting early Christian and medieval sculpture preserved in the 12th-century church of **Santa Maria** in the village centre, including a remarkable 9th-century *ciborium* in bold barbaric arabesques and floral motifs, along with Renaissance frescoes. The **Duomo**, just outside the village, has an octagonal dome

Tourist Information

Sorano: Piazza Busatti 8, **t/f** 0564 633099.
Pitigliano: Piazza Garibaldi 51, off the main piazza, **t/f** 0564 617111.
Saturnia: in the old town, Piazza Vittorio Veneto 8, **t** 0564 601280, **f** 0564 601257.
Manciano: Via Marsala, **t** 0564 620532, **f** 0564 621877. *Winter open Fri–Sun only*.

Where to Stay and Eat

Real pioneers will be able to find reasonable accommodation and good food throughout. The region produces some good but little-known wines, notably Morellino di Scansano, a severe dry variety with a beautiful deep red colour, and also a delicious, crisp Bianco di Pitigliano.

Pitigliano ✉ 58017

Guastini on Piazza Petruccioli 4, **t 0564 616065, **f** 0564 616652 (*moderate–inexpensive*). Central, with a restaurant (*inexpensive*) specializing in homemade pasta, Bianco di Pitigliano wine and 'Etruscan-style' dishes like *biglione d'agnello*; well worth the price.
Corano, Loc Corano on the SS74, **t/f 0564 616112 (*moderate*). Just outside Pitigliano, with 35 modern rooms and also a swimming pool.
Il Tufo Allegro, Vicolo della Costituzione, **t** 0564 616192 (*moderate*). A wonderful restaurant in a great setting carved out of tufa. The menu is seasonal: in winter hearty dishes include rabbit stewed in locally made Morellino or *pappardelle* with lamb and artichoke sauce; in summer *tagliolini* with marinated vegetables. There's a good wine list, too. *Closed Tues*.
Trattoria dell'Orso, Piazza San Gregorio, **t** 0564 614273 (*cheap*). Offers a wide range of the local *cucina tipica*: tagliatelle with truffles, boar *alla cacciatore*, and plenty of roast meats and an excellent-value menu, well within the cheap range for *à la carte*.

Sovana ✉ 58010

***Taverna Etrusca, Piazza Pretorio, **t** 0564 616183, **f** 0564 614193 (*moderate*). Soak up the ambience of the Dark Ages in this square, sampling roast boar and the other south Tuscan favourites. Seven newly renovated rooms upstairs.
Hotel della Fortezza, Piazza Cairoli, **t** 0564 632010, **f** 0564 632012, *www.fortezzahotel.it* (*moderate*). Partly occupies the 11th-century Orsini fortress on the edge of the town. Antique-filled rooms with fabulous views.
*Scilla, Via del Duomo 5, **t** 0564 616531, **f** 0564 614329 (*moderate*). Also a restaurant (*moderate*) with terrace, serving ravioli with ricotta and asparagus, pork with porcini mushrooms and thyme, and delicious local cheeses. *Closed Tues*.

Saturnia ✉ 58050

Saturnia has plenty of accommodation.
****Hotel Terme di Saturnia, Strada Provinale della Follonato, **t** 0564 601061, **f** 0564 601266 (*luxury*). The best in town, and very popular. The restaurant (*moderate*) merits a visit with fresh seafood, including a good *risotto marinaro*, besides game dishes like quail with olives.
Villa Clodia, Via Italia 43, **t** 0564 601212, **f** 0564 620013, *www.laltramaremma.it* (*moderate*). A friendly little place with its pleasant rooms and great views.
Locanda Laudomia, Poderi di Montemerano, 7km south of Saturnia, **t** 0564 620062, **f** 0564 620013 (*inexpensive*). Peace and quiet in the countryside, with 12 pretty bedrooms offering lovely views. Its restaurant, over the road, is good.

Montemerano ✉ 58050

Da Caino, Via Canonica 3, **t** 0564 602817, **f** 0564 602807 (*very expensive*). An elegant restaurant for a small village, where the menu varies regularly according to the availability of fresh ingredients. *Closed Thurs lunch and Wed in winter; open daily in summer*.

from the 900s, a crypt 200 years older, and some sculptural work on the façade that may have been recycled from a pagan temple.

The **Vie Cave**, which you will see signposted all around this area, are sacred ways of the Etruscans, carved for part of their length out of the *tufa* and often lined with tombs. In many cases, they follow modern roads, as with the pretty road from Sovana to Saturnia. Here you can stop to see the **Tomba della Sirena**, where the pediment is carved with a much-eroded fork-tailed mermaid – possibly the original of the mermaids on the Pieve di Corsignano and elsewhere around Tuscany.

Not far from here is the 3rd-century BC **Tomba Ildebranda**. This elaborate tomb once had the façade of a Greek temple, though little of the colonnade survives. It resembles the rock-cut tombs of the same era common in Lycia, on the south coast of Turkey, built by people who may have been the Etruscans' cultural cousins.

Pitigliano

Just 8km away is **Pitigliano**, another ominous-looking place that could be Sorano's twin. It makes a memorable sight, perched along the edges of the cliffs; underneath are countless holes in the cliff faces that were once Etruscan tombs, now used as stables or storehouses. Once inside, you'll find the hill town itself as attractive as any of the better-known ones further north. Piazza della Repubblica has a big fountain and the 14th-century **Palazzo Orsini**, stronghold of the powerful Roman family that aced the Aldobrandeschi out of many of their holdings in south Tuscany. The castle has a small **museum** of Etruscan finds, and an analemmic sundial with a Latin inscription reminding us the hours are 'for work, not for play'.

Pitigliano has a picturesque medieval centre, and a 16th-century **aqueduct**, running across Via Cavour. The alleys around Vicolo Manin, where parts of **synagogue** still stand, were once Pitigliano's **Jewish ghetto** (*open summer Sun–Fri 10–12 and 4–6.30, winter mornings and some afternoons, check with tourist office*); the centuries-old Jewish community was decimated in 1945. Other Jewish relics can be visited on the International Day of Jewish Culture, usually the first Sunday in September. On the cliffs underneath the town, along the road for Sovana, is a Christian **cave chapel** (*c.* 400 AD). They claim it's the oldest in Italy.

Saturnia

Little **Saturnia**, 25km west of Sovana, sits all alone above the Val d'Albegna. One of the most ancient centres in Italy, it claims to be the first city ever founded there – by the god Saturn himself, in the Golden Age. This attractive hill town, was originally Roman, but fragments of pre-Etruscan walls can be seen, and aerial photography has discerned traces of an older city beneath the Roman level. There are hot springs in the neighbourhood, still in use; ruins are everywhere, including an Etruscan necropolis to the north, and **Poggio Buco** on the road to Pitigliano.

To the west on SS323, the walled city of **Magliano in Toscana** has a Sienese-style Palazzo dei Priori, and the church of San Giovanni Battista, with a Renaissance façade. Its best-known attraction is the **Ulivo della Strega** (the witches' olive), a gnarled tree over 1,000 years old, said to be the site of ritual dances in pagan days, and still haunted today. The tree is just outside the Porta San Giovanni, near the Romanesque **Annunziata** church, containing Sienese frescoes. About 2km southeast, on the Marsiliana road, are the ruins of the 12th-century abbey of **San Bruzio**.

Arezzo and its Province

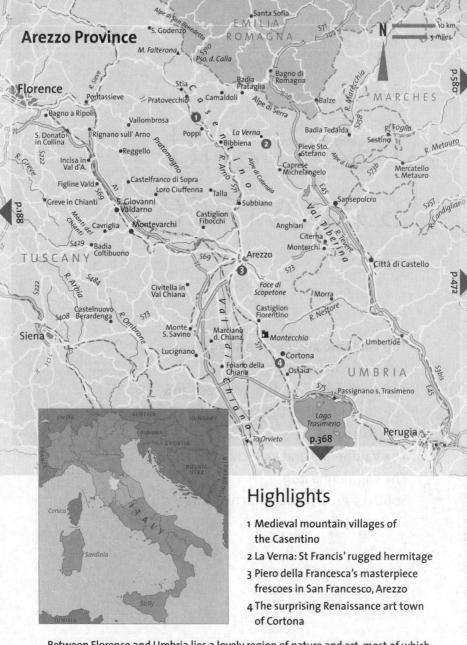

Arezzo Province

p.580

p.188

p.472

Highlights

1 Medieval mountain villages of the Casentino
2 La Verna: St Francis' rugged hermitage
3 Piero della Francesca's masterpiece frescoes in San Francesco, Arezzo
4 The surprising Renaissance art town of Cortona

Between Florence and Umbria lies a lovely region of nature and art, most of which is included in the province of Arezzo. Watered by the newly born Arno and Tiber rivers (which at one point flow within a mere 15 kilometres of each other), it occupies a keystone position in Italy, not only geographically but as amazingly fertile ground for 'key' Italians: Masaccio and Cosimo Il Vecchio's humanist Greek scholar and magician, Marsilio Ficino, were born in the Arno Valley; Petrarch, Michelangelo,

Piero della Francesca, Paolo Uccello, Luca Signorelli, Andrea Sansovino, Vasari, the great satirist Aretino, Guido Monaco (inventor of the musical scale), Pietro da Cortona and the Futurist Gino Severini were born in Arezzo or its province. Because of its strategic location battlefields and castles dot the countryside, yet here, too, is St Francis' holy mountain of La Verna, where he received the stigmata.

There are two possible routes between Florence and Arezzo: the quick one, following the trains and Autostrada del Sole down the Valdarno, or the scenic route, through the Passo della Consuma or Vallombrosa, taking in the beautifully forested areas of Pratomagno and the Casentino.

The Valdarno and Casentino

Florence to Arezzo

If a Tuscan caveman ever yearned for the ideal Neolithic home, he would have wanted to live in what is now the Arno Valley. In the Pliocene Age, the valley was a lake, a popular resort of ancient elephants, and farmers are not surprised when their ploughs collide with fossils. The typically Tuscan towns of the Valdarno, however, are hardly fossilized. On the contrary, it is a highly industrialized region: lignite and felt hats are stand out in particular, but new factories and power lines seem to be going up all the time.

Besides the *autostrada*, the main valley routes are the old SS69, and the beautiful 'Strada dei Sette Ponti', following the old Etruscan road of 'Seven Bridges' from Saltino by Vallombrosa to Castiglion Fibocchi, along what was once the upper shore of the ancient lake, between the Valdarno and the Pratomagno ridge. Along it are areas strikingly eroded into pyramids, around Pian di Scò and Castelfranco. By public transport the Valdarno's peripheral attractions are harder to reach; buses from Arezzo to Loro Ciuffenna and Castelfranco di Sopra take in much of the Strada dei Sette Ponti.

The most scenic route from Florence to the Valdarno follows the A1 down to Incisa (23km), although it's worth turning west at Torre a Cona for **Rignano sull'Arno**, with sculptures by Mino da Fiesole and Bernardino Rossellino in the church of San Clemente, and for **Sanmezzano** (2km across the Arno). Here a medieval castle was converted into a Medici villa and in the 19th century purchased by the Ximenes d'Aragona family, who gave it a Spanish-Moorish fantasy facelift. Down river, at **Incisa Valdarno**, Petrarch spent his childhood. There's an old bridge off which, the Italians claim, Lucrezia Borgia jumped in 1529, fleeing the Prince of Orange, despite the fact that she had died in childbirth 10 years earlier.

Figline Valdarno (pop. 15,000), 5km south, was in 1439, the birthplace of Ficino. The historic centre has preserved much of its character: the loggia of the old Serristori Hospital, the Palazzo Pretorio, and the **Collegiata di Santa Maria**, containing among its works of art a beautiful painting of the *Madonna with Child and Angels* by the 14th-century 'Maestro di Figline' and a fresco by the school of Botticelli.

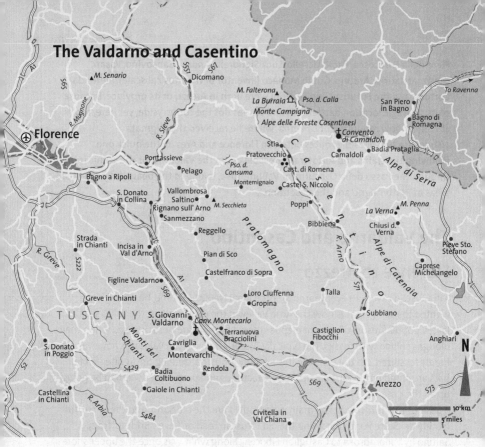

The Valdarno and Casentino

San Giovanni Valdarno

If you're only planning one stop within the Valdarno, **San Giovanni** (pop. 19,500), although one of the most industrial towns in the region, is also one of the most interesting. The Florentines fortified it in the 13th century against the warlike Aretini and sent Arnolfo di Cambio to lay out the streets and fortifications, and to design the handsome arcaded **Palazzo Comunale**; its arches are echoed by the buildings on to the piazza and are covered with escutcheons left by Florentine governors.

The oft-restored **Basilica di Santa Maria delle Grazie** (1486) has a rich 17th-century interior, though most paintings have been removed to the adjacent **Museo della Basilica** (*open summer 10.30–12.30 and 4–7; winter 10.30–12.30 and 3.30–6.30; closed Sun am and Wed; adm*): a *Madonna, Child and Four Saints*, attributed to Masaccio (1401–28), an *Annunciation* by Jacopo di Sellaio, Baroque paintings by Giovanni di San Giovanni (born here, 1592–1636), and a fresco of a local miracle, in which a grandmother is suddenly able to give milk to her starving grandchild (14th century). Best of all is Fra Angelico's *Annunciation*, in deep, rich colours, seemingly a model for the *Annunciation* in Florence's San Marco, though here Adam and Eve are off to the left, fleeing the Garden of Eden. Earlier frescoes adorn the Gothic church of **San Lorenzo**.

Some 2.5km south of San Giovanni is the Renaissance **Convento di Montecarlo**. From here the road continues up to the Monti del Chianti by way of **Cavriglia**; the hills around are scarred with open lignite mines. Cavriglia is also a natural park, where modern deer and buffalo roam with other animals from around the world.

The Valdarno also offers a look at older species of animal, especially the *elephas meridionalis* in the **Museo Paleontologico** (*open Tues–Sat 9–12.30 and 4–6, Sun 10–12; adm*) in **Montevarchi**. Montevarchi is a major marketing centre of the region, famous for hats and chickens; in its ancient core, you can trace the oval medieval street plan. In the centre stands the old **Collegiata di San Lorenzo**, which had a complete facelift in the 18th century. Within it is an unusual reliquary 'of the holy milk', brought from a cave in the Holy Land where the Holy Family is said to have rested and where a fountain of milky water flows; a small museum holds a quattrocento **Tempietto** covered inside and out with Andrea della Robbia's cherub friezes. Across the Arno, **Terranuova Bracciolini** is an old Aretine fortress town, its walls still standing.

Tourist Information

San Giovanni Valdarno: Palazzo d'Arnolfo, Piazza Cavour 1, **t** 055 9121123.

Where to Stay and Eat

Figline Valdarno ✉ 50063
★★★Hotel Masaccio, **t** 055 954 4851, **f** 055 954 4322, *www.hotelmasaccio.it* (*inexpensive*). Changed hands and totally refurbished in April 2004. Thirteen rooms and a garden cater for a comfortable stay.

San Giovanni Valdarno ✉ 52027
★★★La Bianca, Viale Don Minzoni 38, **t** 055 912 3402 (*moderate*). San Giovanni doesn't get many tourists, so accommodation is limited. However this will provide an agreeable stay.
Adriano, Piazza Masaccio 15, **t** 055 912 2470 (*moderate*). A tiny place where you can dine well on the local stew, called *stufato alla sangiovannese*, or homegrown roast chicken, homemade desserts, and wines from across Tuscany.
Da Giovanni, Piazza della Libertà 24, **t** 055 912 2726 (*cheap*). A family-run place with typical Tuscan fare. *Closed Wed.*

Montevarchi ✉ 52025
L'Osteria di Rendola, Via di Rendola, Loc Rendola, **t** 055 970 7491 (*expensive*). A wonderful restaurant, serving creative Tuscan dishes such as marinated salmon with fennel risotto with pumpkin and

saffron and scampi chicken stuffed with artichokes. There is also an interesting wine list. The *agriturismo* next door offers horse-riding. *Closed Thurs lunch, Wed.*
★★★Delta, Via Diaz 137, **t** 055 901213, **f** 055 901727, *www.hoteldelta.it* (*moderate*). The best that Montevarchi has to offer, complete with a garage, air conditioning and TV in all the bedrooms.

Terranuova Bracciolini ✉ 52028
Il Canto del Maggio, Loc Penna Alta, near Loro Ciuffenna, **t** 055 970 5147 (*moderate*). This delightful restaurant occupies a stone village house with a pretty garden, in the tiny hamlet of Penna Alta. Adjacent buildings house a number of apartments to let and a wine bar. The menu is based on local dishes using fresh ingredients; *gnudi* (spinach and ricotta gnocchi) with truffles, *papardelle* with hare sauce, wild boar stew and good, local steaks. Desserts are delicious, too. Meals are served under the olive trees in summer. *Closed Mon; Oct–May also Tues. Open for dinner Tues–Sat, Sun also lunch.*
Hosteria Costachiara, Via Santa Maria 129, **t** 055 944318 (*moderate*). Follow the signs from the Valdarno *autostrada* exit, and you will come upon this wonderful, family-run country restaurant, well worth the detour. A table laden with help-yourself *antipasti* provides a tempting start to any meal, but so do the *pici* with guinea fowl sauce or *papardelle* with wild boar. Follow this with roast meats or quail cooked in wine. There are also a few pleasant rooms for rent. *Closed Mon eve and Tues.*

Along the Road of Seven Bridges

East of the Arno, the panoramic Strada dei Sette Ponti passes several medieval towns en route to Arezzo. **Reggello** (8km east of Sanmezzano) stands amid its famous olive groves; some streets retain their medieval arcades, and the 12th-century parish church of **San Pietro a Cascia** has good, early Romanesque columns with carved capitals depicting lively scenes. **Castelfranco di Sopra**, 12km south, was another Florentine military town laid out by Arnolfo di Cambio, and to the north at **Pulicciano** the landscape is eroded into pyramidical forms, or *balze*, like those at Volterra. **Loro Ciuffenna** offers some picturesque medieval corners, a Romanesque bridge and tower, and a triptych by Lorenzo di Bicci in **Santa Maria Assunta**.

Best of all is the tiny 12th-century parish church of **Gropina** (from the Etruscan *Kropina*), 2km away, an excellent example of rural Romanesque. Although it was referred to in the 8th century, the current church was built in the early 1200s. Dominated by its huge campanile, the façade is simplicity itself, while the three naves and little semicircular apse have never been altered. The columns are carved with primitive tigers, eagles, etc., while the round marble **pulpit** is a bizarre relic of the Dark Ages, carved with archaic figures raising their arms over a marble knot; over them is a kind of totem pole, geometrical and floral decorations, and a sexy siren with a snake whispering in her ear. **Castiglion Fibocchi**, 13km from Arezzo, is another typical town where little has changed, except for the industry on its outskirts.

The Pratomagno and Vallombrosa

The Strada dei Sette Ponti skirts the west of the **Pratomagno**, a wrinkled, forested mountain ridge. Its highest peak, Croce di Pratomagno (1,592m/5,222ft), is due north of Loro Ciuffenna; winding roads from Loro go through tiny mountain hamlets, while the Loro–Talla route crosses over into the Casentino.

Further to the north, the two routes from Florence into the Casentino, both take in fine, wooded scenery. The SS70 over the **Passo della Consuma** (1,025m/3,362ft) is a favourite Italian rest stop; the secondary route passes through **Vallombrosa**, famous for its abbey founded by San Giovanni Gualberto of Florence, and headquarters of his Vallombrosan order. The abbey has undergone several remodellings in the 15th and 17th centuries and is mainly of interest for its splendid position. **Saltino**, 1km away, is a small summer resort, an excellent base for a walk or a drive. One of the most beautiful routes leads up to the Monte Secchieta (1,449m/4,753ft), with views over most of north-central Italy; in the winter, the skiing facilities spring into action. For a longer outing, follow the **Panoramica del Pratomagno**, which crosses nearly the entire Pratomagno to join the Strada dei Sette Ponti near Castiglion Fibocchi.

The Casentino: North to South

The Casentino's blue mountains, pastoral meadows and velvet valleys have long been Tuscany's spiritual refuge. Since the 18th century, travellers have trickled into the area, attracted initially by its famous monasteries, then charmed by one of the loveliest and most peaceful regions in Tuscany.

The Arno, such a turgid, unmannerly creature in its lower reaches ('the emblem of Despair', Norman Douglas once called it), is a fair, sparkling youth near its source at

Getting Around

A **car** is the only way of conveniently seeing the sights, but in the Casentino you might enjoy getting around on the LFI narrow-gauge **rail** line that passes through Stia, Poppi and Bibbiena on its way to Arezzo.

Tourist Information

Stia: Pro Loco, Piazza Tanucci 65, t 0575 504106 f 0575 581122.
Badia Prataglia: Piazza 13 Aprile, t 0575 559054.
Bibbiena: Via Berni 25, t 0575 593098.

Where to Stay and Eat

Stia ✉ 52017
*** Albergo Falterona , Piazza Tanucci 85, t 0575 504982, www.casentino.net /falterona (*moderate*). In the *centro storico*, recently renovated in an upmarket rustic style; 15 rooms, one adorned with pretty frescoes.
**La Foresta, Via Roma 27, t 0575 504650 (*inexpensive*). Basic but comfortable.
Ristorante Filetto, Piazza Tanucci 28, t 0575 583631 (*cheap*). Offers *pappardelle* with wild boar and other hearty fare.

Poppi ✉ 52010
***Casentino, Piazza Repubblica, t 0575 529090, www.albergocasentino.it (*moderate*). Recently revamped and upgraded, and right opposite the castle. The popular restaurant offers tortellini, ravioli, game, truffles and mushrooms.
**Campaldino, Via Roma 95, t 0575 529008, f 0575 529032 (*moderate–inexpensive*). An inn at Ponte a Poppi, established in 1800, offering 10 simple guest rooms. The restaurant (*cheap*) offers tasty local prosciutto, ravioli stuffed with vegetables and ricotta, or succulent lamb and

chicken, and for dessert, homemade *semifreddi* and *biscotti*.
***Il Rustichello, Via del Corniolo 14, t/f 0575 556 046 (*moderate–inexpensive*). A small modern resort hotel, a great place to bring the kids. with tennis, mini golf and walks in the woods. The restaurant (*moderate*) serves great pasta dishes from Emilia-Romagna, grilled meats and Casentino cheeses.

Pratovecchio ✉ 52015
La Tana Degli Orsi, Via Roma 1, t 0575 583377 (*moderate*). This restaurant/*enoteca* (The Bears' Den) is one of the more interesting places to eat and drink in this remote area. You can enjoy a bottle of wine (chosen from some 600 labels from all over Italy) and a snack, or pick from the restaurant menu, where imaginative variations on local dishes are on offer: pear and pecorino flan, potato *tortelli* with black truffles, venison or rabbit cooked with blackcurrants and porcini. Leave room for delicious homemade desserts. *Closed lunch and Wed*.

Camaldoli ✉ 52010
*La Foresta, t 0575 556015 (*moderate*). This simple hotel/restaurant is stuck in a time warp. The spartan bedrooms have their original wood-panelled ceilings and rustic wood floors while the furniture is of rickety 1930s vintage. The restaurant serves up wholesome local food. Half board only.

Passo della Consuma
***Miramonti, t 055 830 6566 (*inexpensive*). This modern hotel enjoys a spectacular setting and long views at the top of the Passo della Consuma (1,058m/3,480ft above sea level). Bedrooms are functional, but the grounds are lovely and there is a tennis court. The restaurant (*moderate*) is a popular truck stop, serving vast portions of local fare such as *pappardelle* with venison sauce and huge steaks.

Monte Falterona (1,658m/5,438ft); one of the classic excursions is to take the trail up and spend the night, to witness the sunset over the Tyrrhenian Sea and dawn over the Adriatic. **Stia** (pop. 3,000), the first town the Arno meets, is pretty and medieval, centred about large porticoed Piazza Tanucci and **Santa Maria Assunta**. The 17th-century façade hides a fine Romanesque interior, with some curious primitive capitals, a triptych by Lorenzo di Bicci and a Madonna by Andrea della Robbia. Wool – the thick, heavy, brightly coloured *lana del Casentino* – is the main industry; in the old days, Stia was the market for the Guidi counts, whose ruined **Castello di Porciano** (*open mid-May–mid-Oct Sun 10–12 and 4–7; call **t** 0575 582626 to visit out of season; adm*) guarded the narrow Arno Valley from the 10th century. Near this (4km north of Stia) is the **Sanctuary of Santa Maria delle Grazie**, a 14th-century church containing frescoes, works attributed to Luca della Robbia, and a painting by Lorenzo di Niccolò Gerini. This road continues into the Mugello (*see* p.201), while the SS310 from Stia skirts Monte Falterona towards the **Passo la Calla** and Emilia-Romagna. Near the pass, the Alpine pasture **Burraia** (15km from Stia) is ideal for a cool summer picnic.

Down the Arno, **Pratovecchio** was the birthplace of Paolo Uccello in 1397 and he would still recognize its narrow, porticoed lanes. Just 2km from the centre is the most beautiful Romanesque church of the Casentino, **Pieve di Romena**, founded in 1152, which has retained its original lines in spite of several earthquakes and subsequent repairs (*to visit, call the custodian in advance **t** 0575 583725*). The façade is plain, but the apse has two tiers of blind arcades, pierced by narrow windows. Inside, the capitals are decorated with a medieval ménagerie. Among the works of art, dating back to the 1200s, is a Madonna by the Maestro di Varlungo. Nearby, the Guidis' **Castello di Romena** was one of the most powerful in the Casentino, with three sets of walls and 14 towers (now reduced to three), and wide-ranging views. It now houses a small archaeological museum and armour collection (*to visit, call **t** 0575 582520; adm*). Dante mentioned it in the *Inferno*, and the **Fonte Branda**, the ruins of which are close by.

Dante knew this region well; at 24, he fought with the Guelphs against the Ghibellines of Arezzo and their allies at the **Battle of Campaldino** (1289), just south of Pratovecchio. The victory made Florence the leading power in Tuscany, and from there, she went on to conquer Pisa and Arezzo. A column commemorating the battle was erected near the crossroads in 1921. At the head of the plain, just off the SS70, Countess Matilda's **Castel San Nicolò**, the wee medieval hamlet of **Strada** and its little Romanesque church form a picturesque ensemble in the wooded hills.

Poppi and Camaldoli

Between 1000 and 1440, the Casentino was ruled by the Counts Guidi, whose headquarters were at **Poppi** (pop. 5,700). From miles around, you can see their stalwart **Castello** (*open Nov–mid-Mar Thurs–Sun 10–5; mid Mar–June daily 10–6; July–Oct daily 10–7; adm*), modelled on the Palazzo Vecchio in Florence. The best-preserved medieval castle in the region, it has a magnificent courtyard and stairs that zigzag to and fro with a touch of Piranesi. If you ask, the custodian will show you the grand hall with Florentine frescoes of the 1400s, the chapel with frescoes by Taddeo Gaddi, restored about 10 years ago, and the commanding views from the tower.

The centre of Poppi has ancient porticoed lanes, winding around a small domed chapel; at the end of the main street is the Romanesque church of **San Fedele**, with a 13th-century *Madonna and Child*. Shops selling locally made copperware line the main street of lower Poppi, and there's the little **Zoo Fauna Europea** for the kids.

A beautiful road runs northeast through the Forest of Camaldoli, part of the Parco Nazionale delle Foreste Castentinesi, with a huge variety of trees, wild deer and ideal for walking. The road leads to the hermitage and monastery of **Camaldoli**, founded in 1012 by St Romualdo, a Benedictine monk. He was given this forest by Count Maldolo (hence 'Camaldoli') to found a community of hermits, similar to those of the early Christians. A conflict soon arose, for the piety of the hermits soon attracted pilgrims and visitors who interfered with their solitary meditations. Romualdo's solution was ingenious: he founded another monastery lower down, with a more relaxed rule, to entertain visitors and care for the forest domains. The Camaldolese are self-sufficient vegetarians whose rule orders them to plant at least 5,000 new trees every year. Little remains of San Romualdo's original foundation, except for portions of the 11th-century cloister, the rich library and the 16th-century pharmacy, where the monks sell their balsams, herbal remedies and liqueurs. Part of the monastery is now a *foresteria*, providing accommodation in simple rooms; you can also eat here (*call **t** 0575 556013 for information*). Some 3km further up, a beautiful hour's walk, is the **Eremo**, with its 20 cottages set in an amphitheatre of pines, each with its own chapel and walled kitchen garden, where the hermits live in silence and solitude, meeting only on certain feast days and in the church, which was decorated inside by Vasari and has two marble tabernacles by Desiderio da Settignano. The church and St Romualdo's cell are open to visitors, but you may not go past the gate to the hermits' cottages.

Badia Prataglia, 10km from Camaldoli, is the region's most popular secular retreat, a summer resort spread out among the trees and hills, with beautiful walks along streams and waterfalls leading off in all directions.

Bibbiena and La Verna

As chief town of the modern Casentino, **Bibbiena** has been enveloped in sprawl and lacks Poppi's quaint charm, though in its heart it retains its old Tuscan feel. Few buildings stand out – a good Renaissance palace, **Palazzo Dovizi**, and the church of **San Lorenzo**, where there are some excellent polychrome terracottas by Andrea della Robbia. From Bibbiena, the S208 crosses east over into a range of hills bravely called the Alpe di Catenaia, which divides the Arno from the Tiber Valley, to the famous Franciscan monastery of **La Verna**, high up on a bizarre rocky outcrop, which, according to one of St Francis's visions, had been rent and blasted into its wild shape at the moment of the Crucifixion. The land was given to Francis in 1213 by another pious nobleman, Count Orlando, and the saint at once built some mud huts here for a select group of his followers. He found La Verna a perfect spot for meditation and came to his holy mountain on six occasions. During the last, on 14 September 1224, he became the first person ever to receive the stigmata – an event pictured in the frescoes of Assisi and elsewhere – after which he could only walk in extreme pain.

The churches, chapels and convent at La Verna are simple and rustic, though the main church, the chapel of Stigmata and St Francis's tiny church of **Santa Maria degli Angeli** are decorated by the most transcendently beautiful blue, green and white terracottas that Andrea della Robbia ever made, especially the *Annunciation*. You can also visit the **Sasso Spicco**, Francis's favourite retreat under a huge boulder, and **La Penna** (1,283m/4,208ft), on a sheer precipice, with views of the Arno and Tiber valleys.

Arezzo

Strategically located on a hill at the convergence of the Valdarno, Casentino and the Valdichiana valleys, ancient **Arezzo** (pop. 92,000) was one of the richest cities of the Etruscan Dodecapolis. Nor is modern Arezzo a loser in the money game – it has one of the biggest jewellery industries in Europe, with hundreds of small firms stamping out gold chains and rings, and bank vaults full of ingots. Its second most notable industry, one that fills the shops around its main Piazza Grande, is furniture-making and marketing antiques; on the first weekend of each month, the entire square becomes an enormous antique curiosity shop.

Arezzo is a bit of a curiosity shop itself. It had only a brief, though remarkable, bask in the Renaissance sunshine, although in the Middle Ages, it was a typical free *comune*, a Ghibelline rival to Florence and a city of great cultural distinction. Around

the year 1000, it gave birth to Guido Monaco (or Guido d'Arezzo), inventor of musical notation and the musical scale; in the 13th century, it produced Margarito, or Margaritone, an important painter in the transition from the Byzantine to the Italian styles. In 1304 Petrarch, the 'first modern man', was born here into a banished Florentine Black Guelph family; his Arezzo contemporary was Spinello Aretino, one of Tuscany's trecento masters. Arezzo was at its most powerful in the early 1300s, when it was ruled by a remarkable series of warrior bishops. One died in the Battle of Campaldino; another, the fierce Guido Tarlati, ruled the city from 1312 to 1327. He expanded its territory, built new walls, settled internal bickerings, renewed warfare with Florence and Siena, and was excommunicated. After Bishop Guido came the deluge – his brother sold the city for a brief period to Florence, family rivalries exploded, the plague carried away half the population and, to top it all, in 1384 the French troops of Louis d'Anjou sacked the city and brought it to its knees, refusing to move on until Arezzo paid 40,000 florins. Florence came up with the ransom money, and in effect purchased Arezzo's independence. Although henceforth an economic backwater, on the fringe of the Renaissance, it managed to produce two leading personalities: Giorgio Vasari and Pietro Aretino, the uninhibited writer and poet whose celebrated poison pen allowed him to make a fortune by *not* writing about contemporary princes and popes – the most genteel extortionist of all time.

San Francesco

If you arrive by train or bus, Via Guido Monaco leads up to the old centre of Arezzo by way of a stern statue of musical monk Guido, and passes on the left one of Italy's prettiest post offices, with an ornate ceiling, before ending in Piazza San Francesco, site of **San Francesco** (*call t 0575 900404 or see www.pierodellafrancesca.it for details; open winter Mon–Fri 9–5.30, Sat 9–5, Sun 1–5.30; summer Mon–Fri 9–7, Sat 9–6, Sun 1–6*). This dowdy barn of a Franciscan church contains Arezzo's star attraction: Piero della Francesca's frescoes on the popular pseudo-classical/Christian subject of the Legend of the True Cross (*see* **Florence**, p.167), the most riveting cycle of frescoes of the 1400s and the gospel of Renaissance painting. Piero literally wrote the book on the new science of artificial perspective, and yet as strictly as these frescoes obey the dictates of the vanishing point they make no concessions to realism; simplified and drawn with geometrical perfection, Piero's beings are purely spiritual creatures. It is intriguing that Piero and Uccello, the two artists most obsessed with perspective and space, should have created the most transcendent art; few compositions are as haunting as Piero's *Dream of Constantine*, a virtuoso demonstration of lighting, colouring and perspective, the angel swooping down from the upper left-front of the scene – and yet all is uncannily still; the soldiers stand guard, woodenly unaware; the sleeping emperor's attendant gazes out with a bored expression. Note, too, the *Annunciation* in which Gabriel announces both the birth and death of her son to Mary.

The fact that the frescoes exist at all is nothing short of a miracle. The walls have been damaged by an earthquake, struck by lightning, burned twice and shot at by Napoleon's troops, who also scratched the eyes of the figures. To keep the church standing after so much abuse, the first restorers injected tons of cement into the

Getting Around

From Florence (75km/1½hrs), Perugia (73km/1½hrs), and Cortona (32km/45mins), the **train** is the easiest way to reach Arezzo; the station is at the southern end of town, where Via Guido Monaco meets the old city walls.

The LFI light-gauge rail line from Arezzo to the Casentino gives a picturesque ride up to Subbieno, Bibbiena, Poppi and Stia (about 17 daily); another LFI line heads south for Monte San Savino, Lucignano and Sinalunga, with connections to Chiusi and Siena. **Buses** for Cortona and other towns in Arezzo province, as well as for Siena (7 a day) and Florence (4 a day), leave from the station directly opposite on Viale Piero della Francesca, **t** 0575 382647/382651.

Tourist Information

Arezzo: Piazza della Repubblica, in front of the train station, **t** 0575 377678, **f** 0575 20839, *www.apt.arezzo.it*; *info@arezzo.turismo. toscana.it*.

Where to Stay

Arezzo ✉ 52100

No hotels in Arezzo really stand out – the forces of tourism have yet to convert old villas into modern accommodation. What the city does have is comfortable and up-to-date.

★★★★**Hotel Patio**, Via Cavour 23, **t** 0575 401962, *www.hotelpatio.it* (*very expensive*). This new hotel, just a few steps from San Francesco, is a bit like a tasteful theme park. The seven rooms are each decorated in the style of a country visited by Bruce Chatwin, so if you were to stay a week, you could sleep in China, India, Africa, Morocco and so on. It's stylish and fun and there is an American-style bar/restaurant in the basement.

★★★★**Minerva**, Via Fiorentina 4, **t** 0575 370390, **f** 0575 302415, *www.hotel-minerva.it* (*expensive*). Convenient if you're travelling by car. A few blocks west of the city walls in ugly modern suburbs, but with pleasant rooms, TV, air conditioning and parking places. It also has an excellent restaurant (*moderate*).

In town, most rooms are close to the station.

★★★**Continentale**, Piazza Guido Monaco 7, **t** 0575 20251, **f** 0575 350485, *www.hotel continentale.com* (*expensive–moderate*). A fine, older hotel, with a lovely roof terrace.

★★**Truciolini**, Via G. Ferraris 29, **t** 0575 984104, **f** 0575 984137, *www.truciolini.it* (*moderate*). Less expensive, with parking and air con.

★★★**Casa Volpi**, Via Simone Martini 2, **t** 0575 354364, *www.casavolpi.it* (*moderate*). A few kilometres to the southeast of the city, Casa Volpi is a pleasant old villa set above the road in a large garden. The comfortable bedrooms are furnished with antiques and

walls, which, combined with humidity, nearly ruined the frescoes once and for all. Although the frescoes were cleaned in the 1960s, no attempt was made to protect them from further damage. Now, after 15 years of painstaking and complex work, they have at last been fully restored and, hopefully, saved.

During the restoration, it was discovered that the 'night' the art historians always referred to in Piero's *Dream of Constantine* is not actually night after all. After removing layers of dirt, it became obvious that the artist had portrayed a magnificent dawn. So much for the most famous nighttime painting in the history of art.

Piazza Grande

Few *piazze* in Italy have the eclectic charm of Arezzo's **Piazza Grande**, the perfect backdrop for both the *Giostra del Saracino* in early September and the monthly antiques fair. On this occasion, the town sports from the four quarters of Arezzo don 13th-century costume to re-enact an event first documented in 1593, a celebration of

have lots of character. There is an excellent restaurant (*evenings only*), which serves a range of local dishes, homemade from prime ingredients.

La Foresteria, Via Bicchieraia 32, t 0575 370474, f 0575 324219 (*inexpensive*). This must be Arezzo's best bargain. Twelve simple rooms are housed in a 14th-century ex-Benedictine convent, which you approach through a marvellous cloister. Most of the rooms have beautiful frescoes and, although simple, they are not without style. Meals are served in the refectory.

Budget hotels do exist out of the centre. The following are near Porta San Lorentino.

*Toscana, Via Pirennio 56, t 0575 21692 (*inexpensive*).

Ostello Villa Severi, Via Francesco Redi 13, t 0575 299047. The local youth hostel. Take bus number 4 from the station. *Open all year*.

Eating Out

Buca di San Francesco, Via S. Francesco 1, t 0575 23271 (*moderate*). This is a tourist favourite, but it has an honest-to-goodness medieval atmosphere and tasty Tuscan fare, if adapted for the uninitiated. *Closed Mon eve and Tues, also July.*

Vino Divino, Corso Italia 53, t 0575 299598 (*moderate*). On the first floor of a 14th-century palazzo, this restaurant offers an interesting menu of local and not-so-local dishes: *taglierini* with truffles or with prawns and cherry tomatoes, wild boar with prunes. Cheeses come from all over Europe while excellent wines come from the *enoteca* (same owners) round the corner. *Closed Mon.*

Osteria La Capannaccia, Loc Campriano 51c, t 0575 361759 (*moderate–cheap*). One of the best, serving specialities of the Aretine countryside – *minestra di pane*, roast meats, including an excellent *bistecca alla Fiorentina* and Colli Aretini wines. *Closed Sun eve and Mon.*

Da Guido, Via Madonna del Prato 85, t 0575 23760 (*moderate–cheap*). A cosy *trattoria* not far from the station, serving *pappardelle* with hare sauce, *orechiette* with courgettes, duck wrapped in roast pork and rabbit with baby onions and white grapes.

Torre di Gnicchi, Piaggia San Martino 8, near Piazza Grande, t 0575 352035 (*cheap*). A tiny wine bar facing out on to Piazza Vasari, where you can enjoy a glass of wine from an interesting list, plus snacks or dishes of the day; there's no formal menu. The onion soup is excellent or you can be adventurous and go for tripe or *baccalà* (salt cod). *Closed Wed.*

Antica Osteria Agania, Via Mazzini 10, t 0575 295381 (*cheap*). Rustic, popular and excellent value. Try tripe, *baccalà*, rabbit, duck or fried eggs with truffle shavings.

the feats of arms against Saracen pirates who menaced the Tyrrhenian coast in the 16th century and penetrated inland as far as Arezzo. Revived in 1932, the festival begins with a parade of costumes and flag-tossing by the *sbandieratori*, and is followed by a test of individual prowess between eight knights, two representing each quarter, who tilt against a wooden figure named 'Buratto, King of the Indies' for the prize of a golden lance.

The **Fiera Antiquaria** attracts hundreds of vendors from all over the country, selling everything from Renaissance ceramics to 1950s junk; it takes place on the first Saturday and Sunday of each month (Sunday is the big day), but ring the tourist office in advance to make sure. The piazza and surrounding streets are also lined with antique shops. On one side of the piazza is the **Loggia del Vasari**, a large building Vasari designed for his home town in 1573, with the idea of replicating a Greek stoa, with little shops, workshops, expensive bars and restaurants under the portico. Vasari also designed the clock tower of the **Palazzetto della Fraternità dei Laici**, an ornate building, half Gothic and half by Renaissance master Bernardo

Rossellino. Although it looks like a town hall, the palazzo is really the home of a lay brotherhood founded in the 1200s. The old Palazzo del Popolo exists only in ruins, behind Vasari's loggia on Via dei Pileati. Like Pisa's, it was destroyed by the Florentines after they captured the city.

Santa Maria della Pieve

Perhaps most impressive on Piazza Grande is the round, Romanesque arcaded apse of Arezzo's great 12th-century church of **Santa Maria della Pieve**; it turns its back on the piazza, while directing its unusual Pisan-Lucchese façade towards narrow Via dei Pileati, where it's hard to see well. Each tier of arches is successively narrower, in a unique rustic style with no two columns or capitals alike. The campanile 'of a hundred holes' has so many neat rows of double-mullioned windows that it resembles a primitive skyscraper. Under the arch of the front portal, note the restored early medieval *Reliefs of the Twelve Months*: April with her flowers, February with his pruning hook and the pagan two-headed god Janus for January. The dim interior has an early Romanesque relief of the *Three Magi* on the entrance wall and decorated capitals in the nave. Like many early churches, the presbytery is raised above the low crypt, the most ancient part of the church, with primitive capitals – human faces mingling with rams, bulls and dragons. On the left wall there's another primitive relief of the *Nativity* and *Christ's Baptism*, while above in the choir is a beautiful polyptych by Pietro Lorenzetti (1320), featuring the *Madonna and Saints* modelling the latest Tuscan fashions and fabrics.

Below Santa Maria descends Corso Italia, Arezzo's main evening parade, while above, Via dei Pileati continues into the oldest quarter of the city, passing by way of **Petrarch's House** (*open Mon–Fri 10–12 and 3–5; Sat 10–12; adm*), a replacement for the original bombed in the last war; it stands near the picturesque 14th-century Palazzo del Pretorio, decked with coats of arms of imperial and Florentine governors.

The Duomo

From the Piazza Grande, narrow streets lead up to the **Passeggio del Prato**, an English-style park with lawns, trees, a café and a big white elephant of a Fascist monument to Petrarch. All of Arezzo slopes gradually upwards from the railway station, ending abruptly here; from the cliffs on the edge of the Prato there is a memorable view over the mountains towards Florence and Urbino. Overlooking the park is a half-ruined Medici fortress of the 1500s and at the other end is the back of the **Duomo**, with a lovely Gothic bell tower from the 19th century.

The cathedral, built in bits and pieces over two and a half centuries (1276–1510), has a nondescript façade but several great works of art in its dimly lit Gothic naves. Its stained glass **windows**, created by the greatest 16th-century master, Frenchman Guillaume de Marcillat, seem almost like illuminated frescoes by Gozzoli or Luca Signorelli. The magnificent marble Gothic High Altar is dedicated to San Donato and there are impressive tombs – the first is of Pope Gregory X (1205–76) with a canopy and 4th-century sarcophagus, holding the mortal dust of the pope who holds the record for taking the longest to be elected; the enclave, in Viterbo, lasted from 1268 to 1271, and only ended when the Viterbans starved the cardinals into deciding. The second, even more impressive, is the 1327 **Tomb of Bishop Guido Tarlati**, an early predecessor of the heroic sculptural tombs of the Renaissance, perhaps designed by Giotto. The tomb is divided into three sections, with a relief resembling a miniature theatre and a Ghibelline eagle on top; below lies the battling bishop's effigy; and below that, 16 fine relief panels that tell the story of his life, his battles and his good works. Beside it is Piero della Francesca's fresco of the Magdalene holding a crystal pot of ointment. The **Museo del Duomo** (*open Thurs–Sat 10–12; adm*) contains detached frescoes by Spinello Aretino and his son Parri di Spinello, a terracotta depicting the *Annunciation* by Bernardo Rossellino and paintings by 13th-century master Margarito d'Arezzo, Signorelli and Vasari.

Museo d'Arte

Open Tues–Sun 8.30–7.30; adm.

Diagonally opposite the cathedral stands Arezzo's Ghibelline **Palazzo del Comune** with its distinctive tower; from here Via Ricasoli descends past the birthplace of Guido Monaco (with a plaque of Guido's do-re-mi), to the **Museo d'Arte Medioevale e Moderna**, where you can get to know some local medieval and Renaissance artists not often seen elsewhere. The collection is housed in a medieval palace, remodelled in the Renaissance, perhaps by Bernardo Rossellino, and later used as a customs house. All is arranged chronologically: the attractive courtyard contains medieval columns and capitals, a fine sculpted horse's head and gargoyles, while the two rooms on the ground floor contain sculptural details from the cathedral façade and a fine 10th-century *pluteo* carved with peacocks.

Among the works on the first floor are a stylized Byzantine *St Francis* by Margarito d'Arezzo, painted just after the saint's death and an *Enthroned Virgin* by Guido da Siena, studded with chunky, plasticky gems. Next you'll find detached frescoes by Spinello Aretino, the city's greatest trecento artist, and by his son Parri di Spinello (1387–1453), whose ghostly battle scene *Sconfitta di Massenzio* was discovered in the Badia after the war; the museum also has one of his beautifully dressed Madonnas. Another native of Arezzo, Bartolomeo della Gatta, painted the plague saint Rocco praying to liberate the city from the Black Death. Also on the first floor is a fresco attributed to Signorelli; a huge busy canvas by Vasari of *Esther's Wedding Banquet*; a collection of small Renaissance bronzes, including a bear with a monkey on his head; beautiful ceramics from Urbino, Deruta and Montelupo; and a plate by Master Giorgio of Gubbio with his secret red. On the second floor, there's a strange painting by Angelo Cacoselli (d. 1652) called the *Maga*, of an enchantress with her animals, a small room of 18th-century Neapolitan *presepi* figurines, and some splashy Mannerist canvases by Vasari, Allori and the great Rosso Fiorentino.

Vasari, Cimabue and More Vasari

Around the corner, at Via 20 Settembre 55, is the **Casa del Giorgio Vasari** (*open Mon and Wed–Sat 8.30–7.30, Sun 8.30–1; adm*). Vasari was so fond of his own brand of spineless Mannerism that he wasn't about to leave it all for Duke Cosimo, but decorated his own house with the same fluff. Mediocrity attracts mediocrity; besides the frescoes there are several rooms of nondescript paintings, of which three stand out: the most repugnant St Sebastian ever committed to canvas, a terracotta portrait of Galba, one of Rome's ugliest mugs, by Sansovino, and a painting by a follower of Santi di Tito, of Christ and the Apostles dining in the 17th-century equivalent of a greasy spoon.

From Vasari's house, Via San Domenico will take you to the 13th-century church of **San Domenico**, with a simple asymmetrical exterior and a fine stone Gothic chapel (1360s) on the right wall, while the rest of the walls are covered with frescoes that overlap like pages on the bottom of a canary cage. The main altar has a crucifix by Cimabue (c. 1265); the chapel to the left contains a fine triptych of the Archangel Michael by the 'Maestro del Vescovado'.

Via Garibaldi from the art museum returns to the centre by way of **Santissima Annunziata**, Arezzo's late response to the Florentine Brunelleschi, begun by Bartolomeo della Gatta in the 1490s and completed by Antonio da Sangallo; the fourth altar has a painting by Pietro da Cortona and in the choir there's a stained glass window by Marcillat. Further up, off Via Porta Buia, stands **Santissime Flora e Lucilla in Badia**, a 13th-century church with an unusual interior remodelled by Vasari. He also designed the two-sided altar, with reliefs from the Gospel of St Matthew on the front and St George slaying the dragon on the back. Over the presbytery the impressive cupola is a masterful fake by 17th-century *trompe-l'œil* master Andrea Pozzo. At the entrance there's a good fresco of St Lawrence by della Gatta; the fine cloister is by Giuliano da Maiano, a student of Brunelleschi (entrance No.2, Piazza della Badia).

On the southern edge of Arezzo, near the station on Via Margaritone, the remains of a small **Roman amphitheatre** have become a quiet city park. The former Olivetan monastery, built on a curve over the amphitheatre's foundations, has been restored to house the **Museo Archeologico** (*open daily 8.30–7.30; adm*). Not much has survived of the thriving Etruscan and Roman city of *Arretium*, but there are some mosaics and sarcophagi, Etruscan urns and Greek vases, examples of the Roman era red *corallino* vases and an excellent portrait of a rather jaded-looking, middle-aged Roman worked in gold.

Santa Maria delle Grazie

Finally, you can take a 15-minute walk from Via le Mecenate out through Arezzo's auto-clogged southern suburbs to see a simple but exceptionally pretty Renaissance church, **Santa Maria delle Grazie**, finished in 1444 and given a jewel of a porch by Benedetto da Maiano, in 1482. With its subdued, delicate decoration, and round arches braced with slender iron bars, this could be the archetypal creation of early Renaissance architecture – certainly it will call to mind the backgrounds of any number of Tuscan paintings. The interior has an early Renaissance delight to match, a colourful terracotta altarpiece full of coloured fruit and *putti* by Andrea della Robbia, surrounding Parri di Spinello's *Madonna della Misericordia* (1430).

The Valtiberina and the Valdichiana

The Valtiberina

The Valtiberina, or upper valley of the Tiber, is a luminous patchwork of glowing pasturelands and pine and beech woodlands, birthplace of Michelangelo and Piero della Francesca.

Arezzo to Sansepolcro

While Michelangelo took fresh air and stone-flavoured milk from his native place, Piero della Francesca carried the light and luminous landscape along the Tuscan-Umbrian frontier with him throughout his career, and left more behind in his native haunts than Michelangelo.

From Arezzo, it's a pretty 41km drive to Sansepolcro, especially along the SS73, which ascends through the Foce di Scopetone (with panoramic views back towards the city) then continues another 17km to the short turn-off for **Monterchi**. Dedicated to Hercules in Roman times, the town is a tiny medieval triangle; while strolling its lanes, don't miss the curious underground passageway around the apse of the parish church, dating back to the Middle Ages but of uncertain purpose. Monterchi is most famous, however, for Piero della Francesca's extraordinary fresco in the little chapel at the cemetery. The *Madonna del Parto* (1445) is perhaps the first (and last?) portrayal of the Virgin in the ninth month of her pregnancy, a mystery revealed by twin angels who pull back the flaps of a tent that is empty but for Mary, who is weary and melancholy, one eyelid drooping, one hand on her hip, the other on her swollen belly, almost painful to see. It is now housed in a former school building on Via della Reglia, well signposted from all directions (*open Tues–Sun 9–1 and 2–7, until 6 in winter; adm*). Details of its restoration are exhibited with the painting.

Anghiari (pop. 6,200), between Monterchi and Sansepolcro, is a fine old town located on a balcony over the Valtiberina. Once a property of Camaldoli and later of the Tarlati family, it was the site of a 1440 victory of the Florentines over the Milanese, a decisive victory in corking up Visconti ambitions over Tuscany and the rest of Italy – also a nearly bloodless one, the epitome of Renaissance Italy's civilized chessboard wars; only one man died at Anghiari and that was an accident. Leonardo da Vinci chose it as his subject matter in the Battle of the Frescoes in Florence's Palazzo Vecchio – one of the Renaissance's greatest unhappenings, though the cartoons left behind by the master were often copied and became one of the inspirations of Florentine Mannerism. In Anghiari's Renaissance Palazzo Taglieschi at Via Mameli 16, the **Museo delle Arti e Tradizioni Popolari dell'Alta Valle del Tevere** (*open Tues–Sat 8.30–7, Sun 9–1; adm*) has exhibits relating to traditional crafts of the Upper Tiber Valley. Just over 1km to the southwest, there's the pretty Romanesque **Pieve di Sovara**, and on the Sansepolcro road, you can still make out the 8th-century Byzantine origins of **Santo Stefano**.

The Valtiberina and Valdichiana

Sansepolcro

Sansepolcro (pop. 15,500) is the largest town of the Valtiberina, famous for lace, pasta (the Buitoni spaghetti works are just outside the city) and Piero della Francesca. The painter was born here c.1410–1420 and given his mother's name as his father died before his birth. Although he worked in the Marches, Arezzo and Rome, he spent most of his life in Sansepolcro, painting and writing books on geometry and perspective until he went blind at the age of 60. Piero may have had a chance to discuss his theories with a younger son of Sansepolcro, the great mathematician Luca Pacioli (born 1440), who wrote his *Divina Proporzione* with some help from Leonardo da Vinci (he also gets credit for the first book on accounting).

Sansepolcro was founded around the year 1000, and like Anghiari, belonged to the monks of Camaldoli until the 13th century. The historic centre, with its crew-cut

Getting Around

CAT **buses** from Arezzo serve this area efficiently if not especially frequently. Sansepolcro is the terminus of Umbria's FCU light **rail** line, which slowly trundles you down to Città di Castello (16km/25mins), Umbertide, Perugia, Todi and Terni. Buses from Sansepolcro (station just outside the walls) go to Città di Castello, Caprese Michelangelo (26km/45mins), Arezzo (38km/1hr), Florence and Pieve Santo Stefano.

Tourist Information

Anghiari: Corso Matteotti 103, t 0575 749279.
Sansepolcro: Piazza Garibaldi 2,
t/f 0575 740536.

Where to Stay and Eat

Anghiari ✉ 52031

Locanda al Castello di Sorci, near Anghiari at San Lorenzo, t 0575 789066 (*cheap*). A country beanery in a former tobacco barn, in a beautiful setting. You can only eat a set menu, but it's incredible value and includes wine: the fare is simple, rustic and plentiful much of it (wine and meats) coming from the farm annexe. *Closed Mon.*

Sansepolcro ✉ 52037

****La Balestra, Via del Montefeltro 29, t 0575 735151, f 0575 740370, *www. labalestra.it* (*moderate*). Pleasant, with modern, comfortable rooms, parking and a good restaurant, with delicious homemade pasta; for seconds, try the lamb chops with courgette flowers.
***Fiorentino, Via L. Pacioli 60, t 0575 740350, f 0575 740370, *www.albergofiorentino.com* (*moderate*). Situated near the main gate, this has been the town inn since the 1820s; rooms provide all the basics and there's a garage. The restaurant is Sansepolcro's best;

it's a good place to try Italian onion soup and other local specialities, and there's a wide assortment of local cheese. *Closed Fri.*
Il Convivio, Via Traversari 1, t 0575 736543 (*moderate*). In a Renaissance palazzo, this restaurant offers interesting dishes from the Valtiberina. Try the tortelloni flavoured with lemon peel, onion soup, saddle of lamb, veal flavoured with tarragon and porcini mushrooms and truffles. *Closed Tues.*
Locanda La Pergola, Via Tiberina, Pieve Santo Stefano, t 0575 797053 (*inexpensive*). 16km north of Sansepolcro on the La Verna road, this inn has recently changed hands and been restored in classy country style with rustic antiques throughout. The restaurant (*cheap*) serves superbly cooked country food including ravioli, freshly made daily with local ricotta.
**Orfeo, Viale Diaz, t 0575 742061 (*inexpensive*). Around the corner from the Fiorentino, this will do if the others are full.
Enoteca Guidi, Via Pacioli 44, t 0575 736587 (*cheap*). A cosy wine bar with a small room lined with bottles in front and a larger dining room at the back, this is a good place for a light meal or glass of wine (from a vast choice) and a snack. Choose between various kinds of ravioli or *carpacci*, a selection of cheeses, salads and desserts. *Closed Sun lunch, Wed and Sat.*

Caprese Michelangelo ✉ 52033

***Il Faggeto, t 0575 793925 (*moderate–inexpensive*). Up in the Alpe Faggeto, above Caprese Michelangelo, this pleasant little mountain hotel and restaurant is set in a lovely forested landscape. The hotel has simple rooms; its restaurant, the **Fonte Galletta** (*moderate*), uses the freshest local ingredients – chestnuts, wild mushrooms, truffles, game, mountain hams – to create tasty dishes. The pasta is excellent, as are the homemade *semifreddi. Closed Tues and Wed Easter– Christmas; in winter open weekends only.*

towers, has plenty of character, though it's a bit dusty and plain after several earthquakes and rebuildings. It is enclosed within well-preserved walls, built by the Tarlati and given a Renaissance facelift by Giuliano da Sangallo. **Piazza Torre di Berta** is the centre of town, where on the second Sunday of September crossbow-men from Gubbio challenge the home archers in the *Palio della Balestra*, an ancient rivalry. Along Via Matteotti are many of the city's surviving 14th–16th-century palaces, most notably the Palazzo delle Laudi and the 14th-century palace housing the **Museo Civico** (*open daily 9.30–1 and 2.30–6; until 7.30 in summer; adm exp*). Here you can see Piero's masterpiece, the *Resurrection*, an intense, almost eerie depiction of the solemnly triumphant Christ stepping out of his tomb surrounded by sleeping soldiers and a land, more autumnal than springlike, as well as two of Piero's early works, the *Misericordia Polyptych*, a gold-background altarpiece dominated by a serene, giant goddess of a Madonna, sheltering under her cloak members of the confraternity (note the black hood on one) who commissioned the picture, and a damaged fresco of San Giuliano.

Other works are by his greatest pupil, Luca Signorelli (a *Crucifixion* with two saints on the back), Pontormo (*Martyrdom of San Quintino*), Santi di Tito, Mannerist Raffaellino del Colle, and the 16th-century Giovanni de' Vecchi, also of Sansepolcro, whose *Presentation of the Virgin* is interesting for its unusual vertical rhythms. You can see a 16th-century scene of Sansepolcro in the *Pilgrimage of the Company of the Crucifix of Loreto*, a relic of the days of the Black Death, as are the wooden panels of *Death* (one showing a fine strutting skeleton). Downstairs, a room contains sculptural fragments gathered from the town, including a rather mysterious 12th-century frieze of knights; upstairs there's a collection of detached frescoes.

Sansepolcro also has a couple of pretty churches: near the museum is the Gothic church of **San Francesco**, with a fine rose window and portal. The **Duomo** is on Via Matteotti; it was built in the 11th century but has been much restored since. Among the art inside is a fresco by Bartolomeo della Gatta and a polyptych by Matteo di Giovanni; note the huge rose window made of alabaster. Another church, **San Lorenzo**, has a *Deposizione* by Rosso Fiorentino.

Up the Tiber: Caprese Michelangelo

Signor Buonarroti, a minor noble of Florence, was *podestà* in the tiny town of Caprese, 26km northwest of Sansepolcro, when his wife gave birth to little Michelangelo. As was the custom in those days, the baby was sent into the countryside to be nursed by a mason's wife. 'If my brains are any good at all, it's because I was born in the pure air of your Arezzo countryside,' Michelangelo later told Vasari. 'Just as with my mother's milk, I sucked in the hammer and chisels I use for my statues.' Although he only returned once to the Valtiberina, to select sturdy firs to float down the Tiber for the scaffolding in the Sistine Chapel, Caprese does not let any opportunity slip by to remind us of its most famous son, even changing its name to **Caprese Michelangelo**. The artist's purported birthplace, the 14th-century **Casa del Podestà** (*open Nov–Mar Mon–Fri 11–5, Sat–Sun 11–6; April, May and Oct Mon–Fri 10–30–5.30, Sat–Sun until 6.30; June–July Mon–Fri 9.30–6.30, Sat–Sun until 7.30; Aug daily 9.30–7.30; Sept Mon–Fri 9.30–6.30, Sat–Sun until 7.30; adm*), has been restored and now houses a museum, with photographs and reproductions of his works. Caprese's medieval castle contains questionable tributes from modern sculptors. From here it's not far into the Alpe di Catenaia and La Verna (*see* pp.401–2).

Caprese to Sestino

East of Caprese the countryside is the biggest attraction; between **Pieve Santo Stefano** (Roman *Sulpitia*, mostly rebuilt after the Second World War) and **Badia Tedalda** (a small resort) lie the rolling Alpe della Luna, the Mountains of the Moon.

Sestino (from the Roman woodland god Sextius), Tuscany's easternmost *comune* on the border of the Marches, was ruled by the Montefeltro dukes of Urbino until 1516. It has been the area's agricultural centre since antiquity and has many medieval buildings. Near its little Romanesque parish church, the **Antiquarium** (*open daily 9.30– 12 and 3.30–6*) will show you the headless *Venus of Sestino* and other local finds. The 8th-century church shows the influence of Ravenna, Byzantine capital of the west; its 13th-century altar sits on a Roman boundary stone. Sestino is Tuscany's easternmost village; if you like this area, you may wish to cross the border into the Marches – specifically, into the lovely upland region called the Montefeltro above the Renaissance city of Urbino.

South of Arezzo: the Valdichiana

The flat Valdichiana south of Arezzo is the largest, broadest valley in the Apennines, surrounded by hills and old towns. The Etruscans, headquartered at Cortona, were the first to drain its marshlands, making it their bread-basket, so rich, it is said, that even after Hannibal's troops pillaged on their way to Lake Trasimeno, there was still more than enough to feed the army and its elephants. By the Middle Ages, however, the valley had reverted to a swamp, forcing the inhabitants back into the hills. And so it stayed, until the beginning of the 19th century, when the Lorraine Grand Dukes initiated a major land reclamation scheme. Now, once again, prosperous farms are the main feature of the Valdichiana. The equally prosperous-looking cattle are a prized breed called the Chianina, descendants of the primal herds whose fossils were discovered in the vicinity.

Monte San Savino and Lucignano

But there is more to the Valdichiana than farms and *bistecca alla fiorentina* on the hoof. On both sides of the valley are some of the most beautiful villages in this part of Tuscany. Cortona is the most famous, but there are others, like **Monte San Savino** (21km from Arezzo, on the west side of the valley), the birthplace of Andrea Contucci, better known as Andrea Sansovino (1460–1529), artistic emissary of Lorenzo de' Medici to Portugal and one of the heralds of the High Renaissance; his Florentine pupil Jacopo adopted his surname and went on to become chief sculptor and architect in Venice in its Golden Age. Monte San Savino, spread out on a low hill, is an attractive town with a *mélange* of late medieval and fine Renaissance palaces. Andrea Sansovino left several works to his hometown: an attractive portal on the

Tourist Information

Monte San Savino: c/o Corso San Gallo 2,
t 0575 849418.
Castiglion Fiorentino: Corso Italia 111,
t/f 0575 658278.

Where to Stay and Eat

Monte San Savino ✉ 52048

★★★★**Castello dei Gargonza**, an entire walled
village 8km from Monte San Savino, just off
the SS73, t 0575 847021, f 0575 847054,
www.gargonza.it (*expensive*). King of the
Valdichiana for a quiet and medieval
atmosphere, with 7 rooms and 25 self-
catering apartments/houses and a pool, all
surrounded by forest; local specialities are
served at the popular restaurant (*moderate*),
boasting a choice wine list. *Closed Tues.*
★★★**Sangallo**, Piazza Vittorio Veneto 16,
t 0575 810049, f 0575 810220, *www.hotel
sangallo.it* (*moderate*). A fine provincial hotel
in the town; no restaurant.

Castiglion Fiorentino ✉ 52043

Relais San Pietro in Polvano, Località Polvano 3,
t 0575 650100 (*very expensive*). The fabulous,
panoramic terrace, where meals are served is
one of this family-run hotel's great assets;
that and the peace and quiet of its hillside
setting. There are no TVs and small children
are discouraged; uncluttered rustic elegance
reigns throughout.
★★★**Park**, on the main Via Umbro-Casentinese
88, t 0575 680288, f 0575 680008,
www.parkhotelarezzo.com (*moderate*). A big,
modern hotel with a pool; not the most
picturesque, but it's fine for a night or two.
Antica Trattoria la Foce, Via della Foce 30,
t 0575 658187 (*cheap*). Just outside the centre,
this doesn't look much, but it serves lovely
authentic local food. Choose from pasta with
boar, hare, duck or goose, and Valdichiana
beef as a classic *secondo*; they also do a
mean pizza. *Closed Mon and weekday lunch.*

Lucignano ✉ 52046

La Rocca, Via Giacomo Matteotti 15, t 0575
836775 (*moderate*). In the delightful *centro
storico* of Lucignano, La Rocca has been
serving food since 1903. Delicious traditional
dishes such as *pici* with *sugo di nana* (duck),
tagliatelle with mushrooms or truffles, fillet
of pork with wild fennel and fantastic local
bistecca. *Closed Tues.*

church of **San Giovanni**, terracottas (along with others by the della Robbias) in the
little church of **Santa Chiara** in Piazza Jalta, and the lovely cloister of **Sant'Agostino**
(13th-century, with a small rose window by Guillaume de Marcillat). Sansovino, or
Antonio da Sangallo the Elder, designed the beautiful and harmonious **Loggia dei
Mercanti**, with its grey Corinthian capitals in the early 1500s, while Antonio da
Sangallo gets credit for the simple, partly rusticated **Palazzo Comunale**, originally
the home of the Del Monte family, whose money paid for most of Monte San
Savino's Renaissance ornaments. Foremost among the medieval monuments, the
Palazzo Pretorio was built by the Perugians, while the city walls are the work of
the Sienese.

On a cypress-clad hill 2km east, **Santa Maria della Vertighe** was built in the 12th
century and restored in the 16th; it houses a rare 13th-century triptych by Margarito
d'Arezzo and 14th-century works by Lorenzo Monaco. Some 7km west there's the
pretty **Gargonza**, with its mighty tower dominating a tight cluster of houses on a
wart of a hill, the whole of which is now a hotel (*see* 'Where to Stay and Eat', above).

Best of all, perhaps, is cheerful little **Lucignano**, south of Monte San Savino, unique
among Italian hill towns for its street plan – it is laid out in four concentric ellipses,
like a kind of maze, with four picturesque little *piazze* in the centre. One piazza is

dominated by the Collegiata with a theatrical circular stair, another by the 14th-century **Palazzo Comunale**, now the Museo Civico, containing a good collection of 13th–15th-century Sienese works, a *Madonna* by Signorelli and, most famously, a 14th-century masterpiece of Aretine goldsmiths, the delicate reliquary *Albero di Lucignano*. There are more good Sienese paintings in the church of **San Francesco**. Outside the centre there's a 16th-century Medici fortress and the **Madonna delle Querce**, a Renaissance temple sometimes attributed to Vasari, with a Doric interior.

Marciano della Chiana, 6km northeast of Lucignano, is another old fortified village with an impressive main gate, which also does time as clock and bell tower. **Foiano della Chiana**, just to the south, is encompassed by newer buildings, but in its **Collegiata** has a good *Coronation of the Virgin* by Signorelli and a terracotta by Andrea della Robbia. Between Marciano and Foiano, keep an eye open for the curious octagonal church of **Santa Vittoria**, built by Ammannati for Cosimo I.

Castiglion Fiorentino

To the east, on the last hill overlooking the Valdichiana plain, fortified **Castiglion Fiorentino** was Castiglion Aretino until the Florentines snatched it in 1384. Another old Etruscan settlement, with medieval streets, it nevertheless had more than a nodding acquaintance with the Renaissance. Like many a larger town (*see* Cortona, p.416), it built an ornamental geometric temple below the walls, the octagonal **Madonna della Consolazione**, untampered with since 1607. Then there's the 16th-century **Loggiato Vasariano**, overlooking the countryside from the old market square, and opposite, the **Palazzo Comunale**. The 1860 plebiscite that brought Tuscany into the kingdom of Italy made a big impression here: the Palazzo Comunale has a marble plaque recording not only the precise vote, but the exact day, hour and minute of the count. The façade also fits in a computerized tourist information screen.

Just behind and above the Palazzo Comunale, Castiglion's ancient heart is known as the Cassero (from the Roman *castrum*): here, you'll find the Palazzo Pretorio and the church of Sant'Angelo, the latter housing a small **Pinacoteca Civica** (*open Tues–Sun 10–12.30 and 4–6.30; adm*). The prizes are a French Renaissance gilded silver reliquary bust of Sant'Orsola, a pair of 13th-century crucifixes, the *Stigmata of St Francis* by Bartolomeo della Gatta, a *Portrait of St Francis* (1280) by the workshop of Margaritone di Arezzo, and the 15th-century *Probatica Piscina*, an uncommon subject (of Jerusalem's sheep pond, with curative waters) by Jacopo de Sellaio. The **Collegiata**, completely rebuilt in the 19th century, has kept its art: *Enthroned Madonnas* by Della Gatta, an *Adorazione* by Lorenzo di Credi, and in the adjacent Pieve Vecchia, Signorelli's fresco of the *Deposition*. The Gothic 13th-century church of **San Francesco** has a cloister, some frescoes and a wooden *Crucifixion* sculpted by Giambologna.

Dilapidated castles are all around Castiglion, most impressively at **Montecchio**, 4km south, with its tall honey-coloured tower and walls, a landmark visible all over the Valdichiana. For a while in the 1400s it was the stronghold of the *condottiere* Sir John Hawkwood, he of the famous 'monument' by Uccello in Florence cathedral.

Getting Around

Cortona is just off the main Florence–Arezzo–Rome **railway** line; the nearest station is Camucia, 5km west; if you're coming up from Umbria, the station is Terontola, 10km south. Both stations have frequent LFI **buses** up to Cortona. There are also LFI train connections to Arezzo (34km/50mins), Castiglion Fiorentino, Foiano della Chiana and Castiglione del Lago on Lake Trasimeno (22km/30mins); schedules for both buses and trains, and tickets for the former, are posted in the office in Via Nazionale, near the bus terminus and car park in panoramic Piazzale Garibaldi, or call **t** 0575 398813.

Tourist Information

Cortona: Via Nazionale 42, **t** 0575 630353, **f** 0575 630656, *www.apt.arezzo.it.*

Events and Activities

Antique furniture market, *Aug–Sept.* Antiques are the big business in Cortona; besides the offerings in the town's shops, it hosts the national antique furniture market.

Copperware show and market, *April.* A showcase for another local handmade speciality.

Umbria Jazz Festival, *July.* Concerts are held throughout the month in the public gardens as part of the festival.

Sagra di Bistecca (festival of the beefsteak), *15 August.* Featuring a huge outdoor grilling of the Valdichiana's chief product.

Swimming: Just off the mountain road above Torreone, set amongst the chestnut woods at Tornia is a pool called the 'Priest's Hole', which is both prettier and more tranquil than the public pool at Il Sodo (no set fee, but they ask for a donation).

Horse riding: Horses can be hired from Unione Popolare Sport Equestre, Loc Ossaia, Montanino di Cortona, **t** 0575 67500.

Under the Tuscan Sun Festival: Writer Frances Mayes is the co-artistic director of this mainly music festival, which attracts an international line-up of performers. Based in Cortona, it also includes food and wine events, films, talks and seminars.

Where to Stay

Cortona ✉ 52044

In Cortona, available lodgings have yet to catch up with demand, especially since the town is the site of both a language school and a University of Georgia art programme operative beween June and October.

★★★★**Il Falconiere**, San Martino a Bocena, 3km away, **t** 0575 612679, **f** 0575 612927, *www.ilfalconiere.com* (*luxury*). Outside the centre; refined, frescoed and furnished with antiques and canopied beds, it also has two pools, immaculate grounds, and a first-class restaurant (*expensive*) serving creative and refined meat and fish dishes, such as duck *tortelli* in an onion and orange sauce. Also runs cookery courses. *Closed Wed in winter.*

★★★★**San Michele**, Via Guelfa 15, **t** 0575 604348, **f** 0575 630147, *www.hotelsanmichele. net* (*expensive*). In an elegant Renaissance palace with painted friezes, ancient fireplaces and old waxed floors. Private garage.

★★★★**Residence Borgo San Pietro**, Loc San Pietro a Cegliolo, **t** 0575 604348, **f** 0575 630147, *www.borgosanpietro.com* (*moderate*).

Cortona

High above the Valdichiana plain on terraced slopes of olives and vines, **Cortona** (pop. 27,000) is one of the crown jewels of Tuscan hill towns. Some 2,000ft above sea level, sweeping down a spur of Monte Sant'Egidio, its crooked, cobbled streets climb precipitously to the Medici fortress – even halfway up, between the houses, you can see Lake Trasimeno in Umbria and Mounts Amiata and Cetona near Siena. Three Cortonese became celebrated artists: Luca Signorelli (1441/50–1523); Baroque painter Pietro Berrettini (1596–1669), better known as Pietro da Cortona, master of the

Under the same ownership as the San Michele and 4km north. Upmarket, with pool, in a lovely 17th-century farmhouse and outbuildings, that are beautifully furnished. Well-equipped self-catering apartments sleep 2–4; minimum 3-night stay Nov–Mar and minimum one week for the rest of the year. *Closed early Jan–early Mar.*

Locanda del Molino, Località Montanare, t 0575 614192, *www.locandadelmolino.com* (*moderate*). This converted stone mill house accomodates 12 rustically romantic little rooms overlooking a brook. The excellent restaurant offers homemade local dishes.

★★★Oasi Neumann, Via Contesse 1, t 0575 630354, f 0575 630477, *www.oasi neumann.com* (*moderate*). One of the nicest places to stay, with rooms in an old mansion, lovely gardens and a very warm welcome. *Open Easter–Oct.*

★★★San Luca, Piazza Garibaldi 2, t 0575 630460, f 0575 630105, *www.sanluca cortona.com* (*moderate*). Simple but comfortable; many of the rooms (especially the breakfast room) enjoy wonderful views.

★Athens, Via S. Antonio 12, t 0575 630508 f 0575 604457 (*inexpensive*). A good budget choice high up in the old town, with spacious rooms in an old building and a pretty walled garden. Only two rooms have private bath. *Open June–Nov.*

Istituto Santa Margherita, Via C. Battisti 15, t 0575 630336, f 0575 630549 (*inexpensive*). Rooms available with or without bath.

Ostello San Marco, Via Maffei 57, t 0575 601392, *www.cortonahostel.com* (*inexpensive, budget meals; IYHA card required*). One of Italy's more pleasant youth hostels, a 3km walk up from Piazza Garibaldi. *Open Mar–Oct.*

Eating Out

Cortona's restaurants are not fancy, but make a point of using local ingredients – homemade pasta, *salumeria* and beef steaks from the Valdichiana, mushrooms and truffles in season, and the local white wines called *bianchi vergini* (the white virgins).

Da Tonino, Piazza Garibaldi, t 0575 630500 (*expensive–moderate*). This is Cortona's most elegant restaurant, serving wonderful *antipasti, gnocchi di zucca* (pumpkin) with truffles and parmesan, pasta made with chestnut flour with porcini, chicken breasts with cognac and porcini. There is a cheaper lunch menu. *Closed Mon eve and Tues.*

La Grotta, Piazzetta Baldelli 3, t 0575 630271 (*moderate*). A friendly but intimate restaurant that the locals would like to keep secret. Tables are laid in a pretty courtyard. *Closed Tues.*

Miravalle, Frazione Torreone 6, t 0575 62232 (*moderate*). On the edge of town and aptly named for its stuning views out over the valley. The food's not bad either.

Osteria del Teatro, Via Maffei 3, t 0575 630556 (*moderate*). In a 15th-century palazzo with old terracotta floors, beamed ceilings and a little terrace. Nice. *Closed Wed.*

Dardano, Via Dardano 24, t 0575 601944 (*cheap*). A simple *trattoria* with an elegant vaulted ceiling. It's popular with the locals, so can be noisy and busy, but the food is good, especially the homemade *pici* with mushroom sauce. *Closed Wed.*

La Saletta, Via Nazionale 26/28, t 0575 603366, *www.cortona-lasaletta.com*. Down some Tuscan wines with regional snacks at this little wine bar near the centre. They also serve the odd pasta dish and soups and excellent sandwiches.

rooms in the Pitti Palace; and Futurist-Impressionist mosaicist Gino Severini (1883–1966), all of whom left works in their hometown.

According to Virgil and popular tradition, Cortona is nothing less than the 'Mother of Troy and Grandmother of Rome' – founded by Dardanus who, according to legend, was fighting against a neighbouring tribe when he lost his helmet (*corythos*) on the hill, thus giving the name *Corito* to the city that grew up on the spot. He later went to Asia to found Troy and give his name to the Dardanelles. There may be a grain of truth in this myth. The Etruscans claimed to have come from Western Anatolia (around 900 BC), and inscriptions very similar to Etruscan have been found on the Greek island of Lemnos, near Troy; artefacts from the Iron Age found in Anatolia and Tuscany suggest cultural affinities. Cortona was an important Etruscan city, one of the Dodecapolis and one of the largest in the north; ragged Etruscan stonework is still visible in the foundations of its walls. These stretch over 3km of the perimeter, but still cover only two-thirds of the area of the original Etruscan fortifications.

As a medieval *comune*, Cortona held its own against Perugia, Arezzo and Siena, while internally, its Ghibellines and Guelphs battled until the Ghibellines won out. When that fight was settled the ruling family, the Casali, spent the 14th century bumping each other off. This feast of self-destruction ended in 1409, when King Ladislas of Naples captured the city, selling it to Florence at a handsome profit.

Palazzo Casali – Museo dell'Accademia Etrusca

Open April–Oct Tues–Sun 10–7, Nov–Mar Tues–Sun 10–5; adm.

The heart of Cortona, the **Piazza della Repubblica**, is a striking asymmetrical square. Dominant here is the **Palazzo Comunale** (13th century), with a tower from 1503 and monumental steps. Just behind is the impressive 13th-century **Palazzo Casali**, home of the city's murderous lordlings and now the seat of the Etruscan Academy, a cultural organization founded in the 17th century by the local nobility.

Through the palazzo's attractive courtyard awaits the **Museo dell'Accademia Etrusca**, a fascinating collection begun by the Academy in 1727, encompassing bronzes (note the two-faced god Selvans); Greek vases, attesting to the city's wealth and trading contacts of long ago; Egyptian mummies and a doll-like Egyptian funeral barque; and Cortona's most famous relic, an Etruscan bronze chandelier with 16 lamps dating back to the 5th century BC, found in a nearby field. Each lamp is a grotesque squatting figure, uncircling a ring of stylized waves and dolphins, and in the centre, an archaic gorgon.

There is a fine collection of paintings, the oldest being a Roman portrait of the Muse Polyhymnia. Others include paintings by Pietro da Cortona, *Two Saints* by Niccolò di Pietro Gerini, a 12th-century Tuscan mosaic of the Madonna, a fine polyptych by Bicci di Lorenzo, a Madonna by Pinturicchio, and another by Signorelli, who portrays her in the company of the saintly protectors of Cortona, with a nasty-looking devil squirming at their feet. One room is dedicated to Francesco Laperelli (1521–70) from Cortona, who built the walls of Valletta for the Knights of Malta; also ivories, globes of the earth and sky from 1714, costumes, the library founded by the Etruscan Academy in 1727, ceramics and a fine Roman alabaster Hecate, the queen of the night. The latest permanent exhibition is a recreation of the inside of the Etruscan tumulus, the Secondo Melone di Sodo, excavated in 1991 (*see* p.420). Part of the tumulus' unique platform altar, sculpted with a man stabbing a lion while it bites off his head, is on display as well.

Museo Diocesano

Open Nov–Mar Tues–Sun 10–5; April–Oct Tues–Sun 10–7; adm.

Behind the civic museum signs point the way back to the **Duomo**, an 11th-century church unimaginatively rebuilt in 1560, probably by Giuliano da Sangallo; inside there's a mosaic by Gino Severini. However, across the piazza in the deconsecrated church of Gesù there's the excellent **Museo Diocesano** with two masterpieces: Luca Signorelli's *Deposition*, with scenes of the Crucifixion and Resurrection (the latter composition inspired by his master Piero della Francesca) with an excellent predella, and a beautiful, luminous *Annunciation* by Beato Angelico, who came to Cortona to paint this solemn angel gently whispering his tremendous message; it has another exceptional predella. Note how the frame echoes the Corinthian columns of the loggia. Other works in the collection include a 14th-century crucifix by Pietro Lorenzetti, a triptych by Il Sassetta, a fine Sienese *Madonna* by the school of Duccio di Buoninsegna, and a 2nd-century AD Roman sarcophagus with reliefs of the Battle of Lapiths and Centaurs that was closely studied by Donatello and Brunelleschi. Don't miss the fine coffered wooden ceiling of the church itself. Below the Piazza del Duomo is one of Cortona's most picturesque lanes, the medieval Via Jannelli (or del Gesù), where some houses have *porte del morto* (doors of the dead), more common in medieval Umbria than in Tuscany. Other picturesque streets to look out for are Via Ghibellina, Via Guelfa and Via Maffei, with its town palaces.

Up and Down Cortona

You'll need your climbing shoes to see the other monuments of Cortona, although **San Francesco** is only a short walk up from Piazza della Repubblica. St Francis's controversial lieutenant Brother Elias was a native of Cortona and founded this little church at an interesting angle in 1245; it still retains its original façade and one side. Both Brother Elias and Luca Signorelli are buried here and on the left wall is a fine fresco of the *Annunciation*, the last work of Pietro da Cortona. On the high altar is a slice of the Holy Cross brought back from Constantinople by Brother Elias, housed in an ivory reliquary that Byzantine emperor Nicephoras Phocas carried into battle against the Saracens in the 960s, as described in the Greek inscription on the back. From here handsome Via Berrettini continues up to Piazza Pozzo and Piazza Pescaia and the medieval neighbourhood around **San Nicolò**. This handsome little Romanesque church, built by an anachronistic architect in the 1440s, was the seat of San Bernardino da Siena's Company of St Nicholas, for whom Luca Signorelli painted a magnificent standard of the *Deposition* still hanging by the altar.

You can reach the loftiest church of them all, the **Santuario di Santa Margherita**, from San Nicolò. The views become increasingly magnificent, until you reach the pretty 19th-century neo-Romanesque sanctuary. The original church was built by Santa Margherita (1247–97), a beautiful farmer's daughter and mistress of a young nobleman; upon his sudden death, she got religion, became a Franciscan tertiary and founded a convent and hospital where she cared for the sick. Her remains are in a silver urn on the altar; her fine but empty Gothic sarcophagus on the left wall is by Angelo and Francesco di Pietro. To the right of the altar are standards and lanterns captured from the Turks in 18th-century sea battles, donated by a local commander. Just above, the overgrown **Medici Fortress** of 1556 occupies the site of the old Etruscan acropolis. Descend from Santa Margherita to the centre by way of Via Santa Margherita and the **Via Crucis**, made up of mosaic shrines by Gino Severini, commissioned in 1947 by the people of Cortona to thank their patron saint for sparing their city from the war.

As in many Etruscan and Roman towns, Cortona's gates are orientated to the four points of the compass. The northern **Porta Colonia** has an Etrusco-Roman arch and is near some well-preserved remains of the Etruscan walls; from here, it's a 15-minute walk to the late, tall Renaissance church of **Santa Maria Nuova**, partly by Vasari and one of the more serene works to come out of the Counter Reformation, designed in a Greek cross and crowned by a dome. Outside the southern **Porta Berarda**, at the end of Via Nazionale, the Gothic church of **San Domenico** has an elegant interior, presided over by a grand triptych by Lorenzo di Niccolò Gerini (1402) given to the Dominicans by Lorenzo de' Medici; and in the apse there's a *Madonna with Angels* by Signorelli. Nearby is a good stretch of Etruscan wall and the beginning of the Passeggiata Pubblica through Cortona's shady public gardens, the **Parterre**, with more grandstand views over the Valdichiana.

Around Cortona

In the Renaissance, it was fashionable in Tuscany and Umbria to decorate the outskirts of a town with a perfectly symmetrical church, exercises in geometry and divine order visible from all four sides – something, by the 16th century, impossible to do in the built-up town centres. Cortona has one of most graceful of these ornamental set pieces, **Santa Maria delle Grazie al Calcinaio**, isolated 3km down the road to Camucia. Built between 1485–1513 by Sienese architect Francesco di Giorgio Martini, this Latin cross topped with an octagonal drum has a harmonious interior, done in Brunelleschian dark and light accents, luminous and airy and pure, with accents in colour provided by fine stained glass by Guillaume de Marcillat. Unfortunately, it's rarely open but ask at the tourist office.

Ancient tombs dot the plain below. One of the most evocative, the Hellenistic **Tanella di Pitagora**, is signposted from the crossroads near Santa Maria delle Grazie (*call ahead to visit,* **t** *0575 630415*). Named after Pythagoras – apparently the ancients confused Cortona with Croton in Calabria, where the philosopher lived – the 3rd-century BC *hypogeum* is prettily surrounded by cypress trees and has an unusual vault over its rectangular funeral chamber. Northwest of Cortona, near the Camucia station, there's the 7th-century BC **Melone di Camucia**, an Etruscan *tumulus* containing two large chambers and corridors; and nearby, at Il Sodo (the hard-boiled egg), are two large 6th-century BC *tumuli* with massive walls, the **Meloni del Sodo** (*to visit tumulo I, call one day in advance,* **t** *0575 630415; guided tours available; adm*), 200m in perimeter. The keeper will take you around *tumulo* I; *tumulo* II, with its five mortuary chambers, yielded the treasures and altar in Cortona's museum and is still being excavated.

Beyond Santa Maria Nuova, the road continues another 3.5km along the slopes of Monte Sant'Egidio to the **Convento delle Celle**, founded by St Francis in 1211 in a beautiful setting. Little has changed; its simple rustic buildings have preserved their Franciscan spirit better than many others – the humble founder's cell retains the saint's stone bed.

Perugia,
Lake Trasimeno
and Assisi

To Arezzo

p.472

421

Umbertide

Cortona

Ossaia

Preggio

V a l   d i   C h i a n a

To Arezzo

A1

Sanguineto

Terontola

Tuoro sul Trasimeno

Passignano s. Trasimeno

Castel Rigone

TUSCANY

Isola Maggiore

Monte del Lago

S75

Corciano

Petrignano di Lago

Lago Trasimeno

Magione

Castiglione del Lago

2

I. Polvese

S. Feliciano

S. Savino

p.368

L. di Montepulciano

L. di Chiusi

S. Arcangelo

Chianciano

Panicarola

Macchie

UMBRIA

Fontignano

Chiusi

S71

Paciano

Tavernelle

Sarteano

Cetona

N

Città della Pieve

4

Montegabbione

10 km

5 miles

A1

To Orvieto   p.522

Perugia, the capital of Umbria, is one of Italy's greatest art cities, an intensely atmospheric place sheltering some of the most authentic medieval streets in all Europe. What's more, the Perugians have their own 'riviera' just a hop and skip to the west, on the gentle shores of Lake Trasimeno, with its bijou islands and mighty castles; Perugino was born just to the south of the lake in Città della Pieve and made these bluish-green landscapes his own. To the east, in view from Perugia's balconies, there's lovely cream- and pink-coloured Assisi, the home of St Francis, and Italy's finest collection of trecento painting.

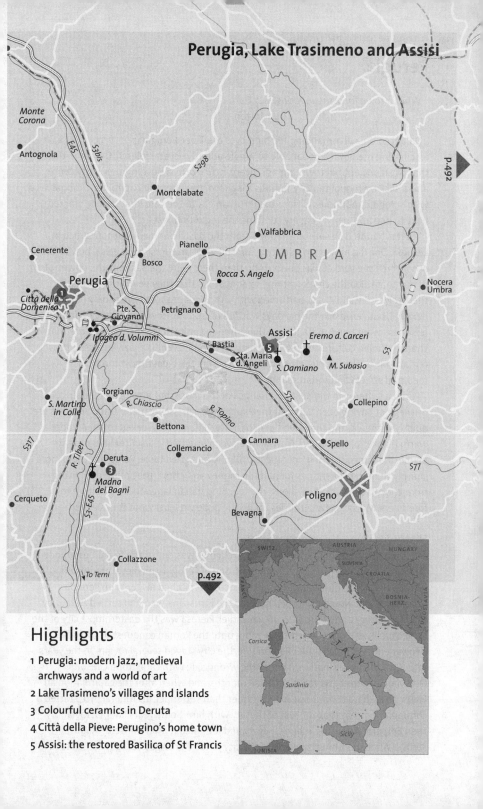

Perugia, Lake Trasimeno and Assisi

p.492

Monte Corona

Antognola

S298

Montelabate

Valfabbrica

U M B R I A

Cenerente

Pianello

Bosco

Rocca S. Angelo

Nocera Umbra

Perugia

Città della Domenica

Pte. S. Giovanni

Petrignano

Assisi

Eremo d. Carceri

Ipogeo d. Volumni

Bastia

Sta. Maria d. Angeli

S. Damiano

M. Subasio

Torgiano

R. Chiascio

Collepino

S. Martino in Colle

R. Tiber

Bettona

R. Topino

Collemancio

Cannara

Spello

Deruta

Madna dei Bagni

Bevagna

Foligno

Cerqueto

Collazzone

→*To Terni*

p.492

S317 *S3-E45* *S75* *S77* *E45* *S3bis* *S3*

Highlights

1 **Perugia:** modern jazz, medieval archways and a world of art
2 **Lake Trasimeno's** villages and islands
3 **Colourful ceramics** in Deruta
4 **Città della Pieve:** Perugino's home town
5 **Assisi:** the restored Basilica of St Francis

Perugia

What a town for assassinations!

H. V. Morton

Balanced on a commanding hill high over the Tiber, **Perugia** (pop. 155,000) is a fascinating medieval acrobat able to juggle adroitly several roles at the same time: that of an ancient hill town, a magnificent *città d'arte*, a bustling university centre and a slick cosmopolitan city, famous for chocolates. It is a fit capital for Umbria, with splendid monuments from the Etruscan era to the Late Renaissance stacked next to one another; its gallery contains the region's finest art.

Yet it is haunted by sinister shadows from the past. Four medieval popes died in Perugia. One did himself in – stuffing himself with Lake Trasimeno eels – but for the other three the verdict was poison. And then there were the Baglioni, the powerful family that ruled the city for a time; so dangerous that they nearly exterminated themselves. Blissful Assisi, perfumed with the odour of sanctity, may only be over the next hill, but Perugia in the old days was full of trouble. However, creativity and feistiness went hand-in-hand, and the Umbrian capital has contributed more than its share to Italian culture and art. Their biggest annual event is a jazz festival. Just as remarkable as the people is the stage they act on: the oldest, most romantically medieval streets and squares in Italy.

Perugia suffered in the political changes of the 1500s, but also claims the singular privilege of having been a part of the Papal States. Art, scholarship, trade and civic life quickly withered, and the town's penchant for violence was rocked to sleep under a warm blanket of Hail Marys. Now, a little over a hundred years after liberation, its people are famed for their politeness, urbanity and good taste; Perugians dress more sharply than the Florentines for half the money and effort. They make their living from chocolates and ladies' shoes, and teaching Italian language and culture to foreigners. Maybe a few centuries under the pope was just what they needed.

History

Gubbio, Perugia's longtime rival, liked to claim it was one of the first cities founded by Noah's sons after the flood. To top that, one of Perugia's medieval chroniclers records that Noah himself, at the age of 500 or so, pitched his tents on Perugia's mountain. That would have been news to the Etruscans, who had settled *Pieresa* by the 5th century BC and probably much earlier. Pieresa was the easternmost city of the Dodecapolis, and maintained its freedom until the Roman conquest of 309 BC.

Never entirely happy under Roman rule, the city staged several revolts. In the years after Caesar's assassination, it chose the wrong side with catastrophic results; Octavian's troops besieged it for seven months, and when after the capitulation an Etruscan diehard committed suicide rather than surrender, his funeral pyre started a conflagration that took the rest of the city with him. Some years later, Octavian, by then **Emperor Augustus**, rebuilt the city and renamed it after himself – *Augusta Perusia*. Almost nothing is known of the city in the Dark Ages. Totila the Goth took it

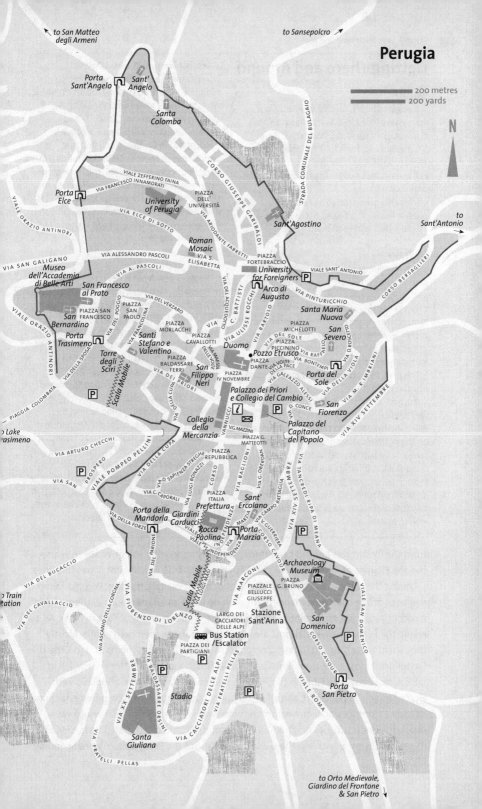

Perugia

to San Matteo
degli Armeni

to Sansepolcro

200 metres
200 yards

N

to Sant'Antonio

Porta
Sant'Angelo

Sant'
Angelo

Santa
Colomba

VIALE ZEFFERINO FAINA

VIA FRANCESCO INNAMORATI

CORSO GIUSEPPE GARIBALDI

STRADA COMUNALE DEL BULAGAIO

Porta
Elce

University
of Perugia

PIAZZA
DELL'
UNIVERSITÀ

VIA ELCE DI SOTTO

VIA ARIODANTE FABRETTI

Sant'Agostino

VIALE ORAZIO ANTINORI

VIA SAN GALIGANO

VIA ALESSANDRO PASCOLI

Roman
Mosaic

VIA S.
ELISABETTA

PIAZZA
FORTEBRACCIO

University
for Foreigners

P

VIALE SANT'ANTONIO

CORSO BERSAGLIERI

Museo
dell'Accademia
di Belle Arti

VIA A. PASCOLI

San Francesco
al Prato

PIAZZA SAN
FRANCESCO

VIA DEL POGGIO

PIAZZA
SAN
PAOLO

VIA DEL VERZARO

VIA DEL POGGIO

VIA DEL'ACQUEDOTTO

Arco di
Augusto

VIA PINTURICCHIO

Santa Maria
Nuova

San
Severo

San
Bernardino

Porta
Trasimeno

Torre
degli
Sciri

Santi
Stefano e
Valentino

PIAZZA
MORLACCHI

PIAZZA
CAVALLOTTI

Duomo

Pozzo Etrusco

VIA ULISSE ROCCHI

VIA C. BATTISTI

VIA DEL BARTOLO

PIAZZA
MICHELOTTI

VIA DEL SOLE

PIAZZA
PICCININO

VIA BONTEMPI

Porta del
Sole

VIA M. R. IMBRIANI

Scala Mobile

VIA DELLA SPOSA

VIA FRANCOLINA

VIA BALDASSARE
FERRI

San
Filippo
Neri

PIAZZA
IV NOVEMBRE

PIAZZA
DANTE

VIA DELLE
VOLTE
DELLA PACE

VIA GALEAZZO ALESSI

San
Fiorenzo

VIA XIV SETTEMBRE

PIAGGIA COLOMBATA

VIA DELLA CUPA

VIA DEI PRIORI

Palazzo dei Priori
e Collegio del Cambio

i

VANNUCCI

P

D. CONCE

Palazzo del
Capitano
del Popolo

VIA TANCREDI RIPA DI MEANA

to Lake
Trasimeno

VIA ARTURO CHECCHI

Collegio
della
Mercanzia

VANNUCCI

V.G. MAZZINI

VIA G.
MATTEOTTI

PIAZZA
MATTEOTTI

VIA SAN

VIALE POMPEO PELLINI

VIA D. SAPIENZA STREGHE

PIAZZA
REPUBBLICA

CORSO

VIA BAGLIONI

VIA G. OBERDAN

P

PROSPERO

VIA C. CAPORALI

VIA LUIGI BONAZZI

VIA XIV SETTEMBRE

Porta della
Mandorla

Giardini
Carducci

VIA DELLA FORZE

Prefettura

Rocca
Paolina

VIALE INDIPENDENZA

PIAZZA
ITALIA

Sant'
Ercolano

Porta
Marzia

VIA V. GUERRIERA

CORSO CAVOUR

VIA V. CAMPO BATTAGLIA

VIA DEL BUCACCIO

VIA DEL CAVALLACCIO

VIA ASCANIO DELLA CORGNA

VIA FIORENZO DI LORENZO

Scala Mobile

VIA MARCONI

PIAZZALE
BELLUCCI
GIUSEPPE

Archaeology
Museum

M

PIAZZA
G. BRUNO

San
Domenico

VIALE SAN DOMENICO

to Train
Station

LARGO DEI
CACCIATORI
DELLE ALPI

Stazione
Sant'Anna

Bus Station
/Escalator

PIAZZA DEI
PARTIGIANI

CORSO CAVOUR

P

P

VIA BALDASSARRE ORSINI

VIA XX SETTEMBRE

Stadio

VIA CACCIATORI DELLE ALPI

VIA FRATELLI PELLAS

P

VIALE ROMA

Porta
San Pietro

Santa
Giuliana

VIA FRATELLI PELLAS

to Orto Medievale,
Giardino del Frontone
& San Pietro

Getting There and Around

By Air

Perugia's airport, Sant'Egidio-Perugia, is 12km east of the city towards Assisi and has connections with Milan (Malpensa), Rome (Fiumicino) and, from June to September, with Alghero and Olbia in Sardinia; for information, call t 075 592141, f 075 692 9562, *www.airport. umbria.it.*

All flights are operated by Alitalia.
Alitalia: Via Fani 14, t 8488 65641 (national), t 8488 65642 (international).

By Train

Because Perugia is up on a hill, its two train stations are both some distance from the centre. Regular city buses (nos.6, 7, 8 and 9) connect the FS station with Piazza G. Matteotti or Piazza Italia in the centre; the more convenient FCU station (S. Anna t 075 575 4038) is a short walk from Piazza dei Partigiani and the escalators up to the centre.

The main **FS station**, on Piazza V. Veneto, lies about 3km from the centre in the lower suburb of Fontivegge; it has connections for Florence (154km/2½hrs) and Arezzo (78km/1½hrs), both via the Terontola junction on the northern shore of Lake Trasimeno; for Siena (147km/3½hrs) another change is required, at Chiusi (a big pain – the FS has replaced several routes with direct buses).

For information, call Trenitalia freeline t 892021 or you can check all timetables at *www.trenitalia.com.*

Another line passes through Assisi (26km/25mins), Spoleto (47km/70mins), Foligno and Terni on the way to Rome (3hrs), while the route to Ancona (3hrs) via Foligno stops at Nocera Umbra, Gualdo Tadino, Gubbio, Genga and Fabriano. For other destinations in Umbria, you'll find the narrow-gauge **Ferrovia Centrale Umbria (FCU)** handy, t 075 575401, *www.fcu.it.* Its main station in Perugia is Stazione Sant'Anna, halfway up the hill, just off Piazza dei Partigiani. The FCU goes north to Città di Castello (45km/1hr) and Sansepolcro (60km/1½hrs) and south to Todi (41km/1hr) and Terni.

By Bus

Perugia's **bus depot** is near the FCU station in Piazza dei Partigiani, linked to Piazza Italia by a system of steps and escalators (called *scala mobile*). APM buses, t 075 573 1707 *www.apmperugia.it,* serve the villages in Perugia province (roughly the northern two-thirds of Umbria). There are about a dozen a day to Santa Maria degli Angeli (for Assisi), with five continuing on to Spello and Foligno; others to Deruta and Todi; Torgiano and Bettona; Gubbio; Gualdo Tadino; the towns of Lake Trasimeno; one to Orvieto; and five a day to Città della Pieve and Chiusi, that important rail stop on the Florence–Rome line.

SSIT (same phone as APM, *www.spoletina. com*) has one or more buses a day to Nocera Umbra, Spoleto, and Norcia and Cascia. SULGA (t 075 5009641, *www.sulga.it*) provides direct links to Rome and Fumicino airport;

from the Byzantines around 545, after a (probably apocryphal) siege of seven years, but the Exarchs of Ravenna were still, with the Lombards, fighting for it 50 years later.

Among the constantly changing alliances of medieval Italian states, Perugia found itself out of the turbulent mainstream, with no large and dangerous neighbours and a potential ally (when it suited Perugia) of pope, emperor or any of Tuscan cities. As a result, the Perugians were almost always able to manage their own affairs. Mostly they spent their time subjugating neighbours: Lake Trasimeno towns in 1130, Città di Castello not long after, then Assisi and Spello. Foligno, another bitter enemy, fell in 1282. Almost always a Guelph city, Perugia maintained a special relationship with Florence and the popes – it had allies, certainly, but friends, never. Even fierce, factional cities like Florence and Siena were careful to walk wide of this wildcat which was constantly molesting its neighbours when not itself convulsed in civil wars. Siena had its annual festive punch-up, the *Gioco del Pugno*, but the Perugians enjoyed spending

SENA (**t** 800 930 960) go to Siena, Ascoli Picero and the coast of the Marches; CONTRAM (**t** 0737 632402) to Macerata and Civitanova Marche, and Freccia dell'Appennino (**t** 800 943 0960) go down the coast of the Marches to San Benedetto del Tronto and Porto Ascoli.

By Taxi
Radio taxi: **t** 075 500 4888.

By Car
Parking in Perugia is a headache; most of the city is closed to traffic, and peripheral garages and **car parks** are few and usually charge by the hour. Car parks nearest the centre are at Piazza Italia, Piazza Pellini, the Mercato Coperto and Piazza dei Partigiani; they are all connected to the centre by elevator or escalator.

Car Hire
AVIS, at the airport, **t** 075 692 9346, **f** 075 692 9796. *Open Mon–Sat 8–1 and 3–7.30, Sun open on request*; at the railway station, **t** 075 500 0395. *Open Mon–Fri 8.30–1 and 3.30–7, Sat 8.30–1, Sat pm and Sun on request.*
Hertz, at the railway station, **t** 075 500 2439; at the airport **t** 075 592 8590, **f** 075 592 6266. *Open Mon–Fri 8.30–12.30 and 3–7, Sat 8.30–12.30.*
Maggiore, at the railway station, **t** 075 500 7499, **f** 075 501 6511; service at the airport can be provided on request, **t** 075 692 9276. *Open Mon–Fri 8.30–1 and 3.30–7, Sat 8.30–7.*

Europcar, at Via Ruggero d'Andreotto 7, **t** 075 573 1704, **f** 075 573 4201; at the airport: **t** 075 692 0615, **f** 075 573 1704. *Open Mon–Fri 8.30–12.30 and 2.30–6.30, Sat 8.30–12.30.*

There are numerous small local car hire firms, which may give better rates, although they tend not to be as flexible over pick-ups and drop-offs.

On Foot
Walking in Perugia is a delight, though you'll often find yourself out of breath. In the oldest parts, densely packed and half-covered with arches and passageways, Perugia often seems like one big building. Its difficult topography has been mastered with some cleverness – there always seem to be stairs, elevators or escalators to carry you from one part to another. Many of these are on the edges, where some truly beautiful parks have been strung along the cliffs to take advantage of unusable land – Perugia has one of the highest densities of green areas in Italy. Enjoy the street names: Via Curiosa (Curious Street); Via Perduta (Lost Street); Via Piacevole (Pleasant Street); Via Pericolosa (Dangerous Street), among many others. And look for medieval details – carved symbols and coats of arms. One local peculiarity is the narrow Porta del Morte, 'Death's Door', used only to carry out the dead, and bricked up the rest of the time – where death has once passed, the superstition went, he might pass again. Or so the story goes; in most houses these doors were the only access to the upper floors, with

their holidays at the *Battaglia de' Sassi*, the 'Battle of Stones' in the Piazza del Duomo, usually causing a dozen or so fatalities each year. In religion, besides being a graveyard for popes, Perugia gave a cold shoulder to most of the early reformers. Even St Francis, who before he became a preacher spent a year in a Perugian dungeon, couldn't make the city mend its ways. However, the medieval mass psychosis of the **Flagellants** began with the hallucinations of a monk here in 1265.

Perugia belonged to the papal dominions from the days of Charlemagne. Few popes, though, were able to exercise much control over such a volatile city. After 1303, the Priors of the 10 major guilds established their rule, although noble families like the **Oddi** and the **Baglioni** remained extremely influential. In the 1360s and 70s, when **Cardinal Albornoz** was raising armies and building castles to reassert papal authority over central Italy, Perugia revolted. Pope Urban VI paid a visit in 1387 to make up – a wild dove perched on his shoulder as he entered, which was taken to be a good omen.

ladders inside that could be pulled up in emergencies.

Tourist Information

Perugia: Piazza IV Novembre 3, **t** 075 573 6458, **f** 075 577 2686, or Via Mazzini 6, **t** 075 572 8937, **f** 075 573 9386. Check out the website on *www.umbria 2000.it* or there's the **Digiplan** computer, which (when it's working) is always right. Look for it on the *scala mobile*, up from the Piazza dei Partigiani; it prints out details on nearly any hotel, restaurant or sight in town.
Post office: Piazza Matteotti.
Churches: Unless otherwise noted, all churches in Perugia are open 8–12 and 4pm–sunset.

Festivals

Every year brings a new rash of summer events. Check the monthly *Viva Perugia: What Where When* for details.
Umbria Jazz Festival, *July*. Tickets available from the booth in Piazza della Repubblica (*www.umbriajazz.com*). An excellent festival, ever-growing in renown, which has drawn such luminaries as the late Stan Getz and Wynton Marsalis to Perugia.
Teatro in Piazza festival, *July and Aug*. Performances take place in the city's cloisters and squares.

Tenera e la notte, *July–Aug*. Music in and around the city.
Sagra Musicale Umbra, *Sept*. Featuring sacred music in Perugia's churches.
Marcia della Pace, *2nd Sun in October*. Since 1963, thousands of Italians have walked the 10km from Perugia to Assisi on this day in the name of peace; in 2001, over 250,000 came, breaking all records.
Fiera dei Morti, Pian di Massiano, *1st week in Nov*. The oldest surviving fair in Central Italy.

In addition, the large student population attracts numerous performances, including concerts and films, outdoors in summer.
Il Contrappunto, Via Scortici 4/a, near the University for Foreigners and Piazza Grimana, **t** 075 573 3667, *www.contrappunto. com*. Music, usually live and in every possible shade from jazz to traditional Turkish and tango, is regularly on tap. *Tues, Thurs and Sat*.

If you're travelling with children, Perugia has a large funfair and also Umbria's modest but sincerely meant answer to Disneyland: **Città della Domenica**, just west of the city, **t** 075 505 4941 (*open daily April–Sept 10–7, weekends only Oct–Mar*). Features a miniature Africa, serpentarium and bumper cars.

Shopping, Activities and Entertainment

The monthly *Viva Perugia: What Where When* (*see* opposite) lists all the exhibitions

---

Unfortunately, the rebellion only took the lid off a cauldron of conflicting ambitions that was ready to boil over, and Perugia's three big factions – the nobles, the *raspanti* (the wealthy merchant class) and the commoners – leapt at each other's throats. In 1393, with the connivance of the pope, a noble named **Biondo Michelotti** seized power. Five years later (again the pope was involved), Michelotti was murdered on his wedding day by the Abbot of San Pietro. In the resulting confusion, Giangaleazzo Visconti of Milan was able to grab the city for a time (1400–2), followed by a period under the rule of King Ladislas of Naples (1408–14). After Ladislas, celebrated Perugian *condottiere* **Braccio Fortebraccio** (Arm Strongarm, the Popeye of the Renaissance, whose arms picture a bouquet of spinach and a helmet), won the city by defeating another *condottiere*, Carlo Malatesta of Rimini, at the Battle of Sant'Egidio. Fortebraccio, soon master of all Umbria and 'Prince of Capua', had king-sized ambitions and potent friends – according to contemporary gossip he owned a crystal

and events happening in the city. Nonetheless, the principal Perugian occupation in the evening remains the *passeggiata* down Corso Vannucci, with a stop for a tantalizing bite at the **Bar Ferrari** (No.43), full of Perugia's famous chocolate Baci and other confections, or perhaps a refreshing ice cream at the **Gelateria Veneta** (No.20), before loitering in Piazza IV Novembre.

Market Days

Mercato della Terrazza, near the Kennedy escalator, off Piazza Matteotti. The city's daily market with a view, selling a range of clothes and shoes.

Food market, Pian di Massiano, *Sat am*.

Where to Stay

Perugia ✉ 06100

Luxury

★★★★★**Brufani Palace**, Piazza Italia 12, **t** 075 573 2541, **f** 075 572 0210, *www.sinahotels.com*. A renovated, traditional 19th-century hotel which has recently doubled in size to provide some 80 rooms. There are fine views over the countryside, luxurious fittings, air conditioning, an attractive central courtyard and a private garage.

Very Expensive

★★★★**Locanda della Posta**, Corso Vannucci 97, **t** 075 572 8925, **f** 075 573 2562, *novelbet@*

tin.it. Once host to Goethe, this old place has an ornate exterior, pleasant, renovated rooms and a garage.

★★★★**Perugia Plaza**, Via Palermo 88, **t** 075 34643, **f** 075 30863,*www.umbriahotels.com*. A prestigious hotel set in greenery at the foot of the city. It's big and comfortable, with a pool, a sauna and an excellent restaurant, the **Fortebraccio** (*moderate*), with very reasonable fixed-price menus. *Closed Mon*.

Expensive

★★★★**La Rosetta**, Piazza Italia 19, **t/f** 075 572 0841, *www.perugiaonline.com/rosetta*. Older and deservedly popular, with a variety of rooms from different periods and remodellings. It boasts a celebrated restaurant and dining in the garden in summer; the rooms, either modern or furnished with antiques, are cosy and quiet.

★★★**Fortuna**, Via Bonazzi 19, **t** 075 572 2845, **f** 075 573 5040, *www.umbriahotels.com*. This has a good location just off Corso Vannucci, and more comfort than charm; all rooms have bath and TV, and there's a garage.

★★★★**Giò Arte e Vini**, Via R. d'Andreotto 19, **t/f** 075 573 1100, *www.hotelgio.it*. It is well worth the short drive to experience this memorable hotel, dedicated to the noble art of wine-drinking. Each room is furnished with rustic Umbrian furniture, including a display case filled with bottles of wine. Guests are encouraged to taste them and buy from the amply stocked cellars on departure. The restaurant is

---

with a genie inside who gave him good advice. After conquering most of the Marches, Fortebraccio had dreams of ruling a united Italy, but his luck ran out in 1424, when he died at the hands of another Perugian during the siege of L'Aquila in Abruzzo.

In the aftermath, Pope Martin V took control of Perugia though he wasn't able to stop the increasingly bloody fighting between the noble clans. In 1488 the Oddi were exiled and the Baglioni became rulers of Perugia. This family, with their good looks, pet lions and tendency towards fratricide, blazed through Perugia's history. In 1520 the Medici Pope Leo X, tricked **Gianpaolo Baglioni**, the last family tyrant of Perugia, into coming to Rome, where he was imprisoned and murdered. The remaining Baglioni found employment as *condottieri* around Italy. One, Malatesta Baglioni, distinguished himself by betraying Florence to the Medici and Charles V in the siege of 1530. Another, Rodolfo, murdered a papal legate to avenge the death of his uncle Gianpaolo, giving **Pope Paul III** an excuse to intervene. Over time it had become

another treat: every evening, the *sommelier* chooses three different wines and, for a surprisingly modest fee, diners can quaff to their heart's content. Dishes include wild boar bites with olives and gnocchi with truffle *au gratin*.

Moderate
Priori, Via Vermiglioli 3, **t 075 572 3378, **f** 075 572 9155, *www.hotelpriori.it*. Occupies an old building in the historic centre that has now been refurbished; bear in mind that some of the more elaborate rooms fall into the *expensive* category.

Aurora, Viale Indipendenza 21, **t/f 075 572 4819. Conveniently situated only a minute's walk from Piazza Italia, on the main road up from the station. Rooms are rather spartan, but comfortable enough for a short stay, the service is friendly and prices hover near the bottom of this category.

Inexpensive
*Etruria, Via della Luna 21, **t** 075 572 3730. A simple place just off Corso Vannucci, only a few rooms have private bath; dogs allowed.

The following are similar in style and amenites and equally central:
*Paola, Via della Canapina 5, **t** 075 572 3816.
Centro Internazionale Accoglienza per la Gioventù, Via Bontempi 13, **t** 075 572 2880, **f** 075 573 9449. With bunk beds, located by the Duomo; and you don't need a youth hostel card.

The tourist office can also provide a list of rooms to rent, B&B and *agriturismo* nearby.

Outside Perugia
There are a number of comfortable hotels in Perugia's environs for those who are driving. Two are particularly attractive:

Cenerente ✉ 06070
****Castello dell'Oscano, 9km northwest of Perugia, **t** 075 584371, **f** 075 690666, *www. oscano.com* (*luxury–very expensive*). Neo-Renaissance style, with 20 antique-furnished rooms, satellite TV and a pool in a large park.

Bosco ✉ 06080
****Relais San Clemente, Passo dell'Acqua, Loc Bosco, 10km east on the road to Gubbio, **t** 075 591 5100, **f** 075 591 5001, *www.relais.it* (*very expensive*). This occupies a former 14th-century Benedictine abbey and has lovely grounds, with a pool, tennis courts and luxurious, stylish rooms; it also has a choice restaurant.

Eating Out

Some of the best restaurants are in the hotels listed, particularly **Perugia Plaza**, **La Rosetta** and **Giò Arte e Vini**.

Very Expensive
Osteria del Bartolo, Via Bartolo 30, **t** 075 573 1561. Here you can sample a little of ancient Umbria, with inventive and

customary for popes reasserting their authority to make a formal visit to Perugia; contemporaries record Paul, father of the Inquisition and one of the kinkiest, most corrupt of all popes, requiring all nuns in the city to queue up and kiss his feet.

As part of his campaign to put an end to Perugia's independence, Paul raised the salt tax in 1538, a year after promising not to. The Perugians revolted again, initiating the '**Salt War**', but were crushed by a huge papal force of mercenaries and Spaniards. Government was handed over to officials entitled Preservers of Ecclesiastical Obedience; its trade ruined and its streets full of monks, nuns and Jesuits, Perugia began a precipitous economic decline not be reversed until the Risorgimento. To this day, Perugians, and indeed all Umbrians, eat bread made without salt, an unappetising hangover from the salt rebellion (though Umbrians swear it tastes better).

The next major event in the conquered city was the Napoleonic occupation: the emperor's troops sent the hordes of monks and nuns packing, but also packed much

beautifully prepared dishes created from old recipes that you won't see anywhere else. *Closed Wed lunch, Sun.*

Moderate

Porta del Sole, Via delle Prome 11 (the extension of Via del Sole), **t** 075 572 0938. Good pizzas and wood-oven cuisine. *Eves only, closed Mon.*

Il Falchetto, Via Bartolo 20, **t** 075 573 1775. Also near the cathedral, this reeks of medieval atmosphere and serves Umbrian specialities – *salumeria*, *crostini* (pâté on toast), tagliatelle with truffles, *pasta e fagioli* (pasta with beans), grilled lamb and trout, all well prepared and followed by tasty desserts. *Closed Mon and 15–30 Jan.*

La Bocca Mia, Via V. Rocchi 36, **t** 075 572 3873. Despite Perugia's landlocked state, there's some fine seafood to be had; this is one of the best places to come, near the Etruscan Arch. They have a reputation for desserts, not usually an Umbrian forte. *Closed Sun, Mon lunch, 1–25 Aug.*

Da Cesarino, Piazza IV Novembre 4/5, **t** 075 572 8974. An old favourite, serving reliable homemade pasta and quality traditional meat dishes. *Closed Wed and 6 Jan–6 Feb.*

Osteria del Gufo, Via della Viola 18, **t** 075 573 4126. Right by San Fiorenzo, with a seasonal menu that never lacks flair. Their specialities are *fois gras* terrine, duck breast in red wine, thyme and honey sauce and, unusually for the region,

homemade desserts. *Eves only, closed Sun, Mon and Aug.*

Cheap

Il Cantinone, Via Ritorto 6, **t** 075 573 4430. Located just to the left of the cathedral, with generally simple offerings, such as *spaghetti all'amatriciana*, beans and sausage, and also *filetto tartufato* – fillet of steak smothered with a black truffle sauce. *Closed Tues.*

Ceccarani, Piazza Matteotti 16. Well worth knowing if you fancy a feast *al fresco*. This bakery boasts a wonderful array of Perugia's best bread, baked in some 30 different ways. you'll be spoilt for choice for your picnic.

Osteria Del Gambero, Via Baldeschi 17, **t** 075 573 5461. The chef at this quattrocento palazzo offers good variations on the usual Umbrian themes, including an excellent *coscio di agnello alle olive* (leg of lamb cooked with olives); choose wine from their well-stocked cellar. *Eves only, closed Sun, and part of Jan and June.*

Il Paiolo, Via Angusta 11, **t** 075 572 5611. Good value tasty food, though the pizzas are probably their forte, served in a Renaissance palazzo. *Closed Wed, and first half of Aug.*

Sandri, Corso Vannucci. This must be one of the prettiest pastry shops in Italy, with its frescoed ceiling and divinely artistic confections; their window is always ablaze with colour, set to rival even the *pinacoteca* across the street.

of Perugia's art – some of the best Peruginos included – back to the Louvre. In 1859, during the disturbances of the Risorgimento, Perugia rebelled once more against the pope. Pius IX sent his **Swiss Guard** to quell them – some 2,000 Switzers forced the city, burning, looting and butchering citizens in the streets. The final liberation a year later was greeted with delirium. King Vittorio Emanuele's army had to protect the retiring Swiss Guards from massacre by the Perugians.

Piazza IV Novembre

Magnificent, time-worn Piazza IV Novembre, once the setting for the 'War of the Stones' and countless riots and street battles, remains the heart and soul of Perugia. The old town hall, symbol of the *comune*, entirely upstages the cathedral and the two stare at each other over Italy's most beautiful medieval fountain, the 24-sided polygonal pink and white **Fontana Maggiore**, designed in the 1270s by Fra Bevignate.

The occasion was the construction of Perugia's first aqueduct since Roman times, and the Priors commissioned Nicola Pisano and his son Giovanni to sculpt the 48 double relief panels around the lower basin. Twelve of these portray that favourite medieval conceit, the *Labours of the Months*, each accompanied by its zodiacal sign; in between are scenes from Roman legend, Aesop's fables, and saints' lives, personifications of the sciences and arts – altogether a complete, circular image of the medieval world. Above them, the twelve-sided upper basin has concave panels filled with 24 saints and figures from Perugia's history, most of them by Giovanni Pisano, with three water nymphs to keep them company. The more you look, the more you realize the subtlety and dynamism of Fra Bevignate's design, particularly the way in which the panels of the lower basin are never congruent, but pull the eye along.

Surveying the piazza, high up on the wall of the **Palazzo dei Priori**, perch a Guelph lion and Perugia's totem, the famous brass griffin, an emblem visible at least once on every street. The scrap iron dangling beneath it is said to be chains and bolts from the gates of Siena, captured after a famous victory at Torrita in 1358 (this isn't true – the real war trophies, whatever they were, disappeared two centuries ago; these chains simply held them up). This stern, Gothic, asymmetrical complex, crowned with toothsome crenellations and pierced by beautiful, narrowly spaced windows, has been cleaned to look as new as when it was begun in 1297. Two later building phases left an elegant, slightly curved, elongated building, housing Perugia's finest art and also the Collegio del Cambio (*see* p.435) and the Collegio della Mercanzia (*see* p.435).

The whole first floor of the Piazza IV Novembre section is occupied by the **Sala dei Notari** (*open 9–1 and 3–7; closed Mon except June–Sept*), a remarkable room divided into bays by huge round arches, with interesting early 13th-century frescoes of Old Testament scenes along the top by a student of Pietro Cavallini. The other frescoes, painted in the 19th century, are the coats of arms of all the *podestà* and *capitani del popolo* who served Perugia from 1293 to 1443.

The Cathedral of San Lorenzo

t 075 572 3832; open Mon–Sat 9–12.45 and 4–5.15, Sun and hols 4–5.45; adm.

For all the attention they lavished on their Palazzo dei Priori, the Perugians never seemed much interested in their cathedral. After laying the cornerstone in 1345, they didn't add another stone for a decade. A century later, when the building was substantially completed, a papal legate tore part of it down to use the stone for his own palace. For the façade, they once stole half a marble facing destined for the cathedral at Arezzo, but not long after, the Aretini whipped them in battle and made them give it back. The cathedral's finest hour, perhaps, came during a fit of civic strife in 1488, when the Baglioni, fighting the Oddi, seized the building, turning it into a fortress, complete with cannon protruding from its Gothic windows. So much blood was spilled that the cathedral had to be washed out with wine and reconsecrated.

Despite its lack of a proper façade, this building seems just right for its post on lovely Piazza IV Novembre. The side facing the Fontana Maggiore has a geometrical pattern, employing the warm pink marble quarried near Assisi. Next to it a bronze statue commemorates the pleasure-loving Julius III, the only pope the Perugians ever liked. The unfinished pulpit on the façade was especially built for the charismatic revivalist San Bernardino of Siena, who preached to vast crowds in the piazza, finally persuading them to stop the *Battaglia de' Sassi* in 1425; Perugia, he claimed, was his favourite town, and judging by the church the Perugians gave him (*see* p.341), he was their favourite saint. The best feature of the façade, however, is the elegant travertine **Loggia di Braccio Fortebraccio**, added by the *condottiere* in 1423.

The Duomo's Baroqued interior is determinedly unimpressive, supported by columns badly painted to simulate marble. However, there are a few things worth picking out. In the first chapel on the right, the tomb of Bishop Baglioni (d. 1451) by Urbano da Cortona, stands across from a saccharine *Descent from the Cross* by the 16th-century painter Federico Barocci of Urbino. In the **Cappella del Sacramento**, designed by Galeazzo Alessi, Perugia's top 16th-century architect, hangs Luca Signorelli's luminous and recently restored *Pala di Sant'Onofrio* (1484), one of his earliest and best works, showing the Madonna enthroned with saints and a pot-bellied angel tuning a lute. The presbytery has beautiful intarsia choir stalls by Gianiano da Mairano and Domenico del Taso (1486–91).

On the left side, near reliefs of the *Eternal Father* and *Pietà* by Agostino di Duccio, is the **Cappella del Santo Anello**, housing the Perugians' most prized relic – the wedding ring of the Virgin Mary. Many stories have grown up around this big onyx stone that, like a 1970s mood ring, changes colour according to the moral character of the wearer. A Perugian woman stole the ring from Chiusi in the Middle Ages and the townspeople have never stopped worrying that the Chiusini might try to get it back: they keep it in 15 nested cases under 15 locks, spread the keys out among 15 notable and trustworthy citizens, and only take it out of the box on 29–30 July. The relic indirectly inspired Raphael's famous *Betrothal of the Virgin*; Raphael picked up the idea from a painting by Perugino that hung in this chapel before Napoleon spirited it off to France (now in the museum in Caen) – the emperor always had a weakness for doe-eyed Virgins and Perugino was one of his favourite painters.

Behind the cathedral, the cloister of the Canonica witnessed five conclaves of cardinals between 1124 and 1305. Among the popes elected here was Frenchman Clement V, who began the 'Babylonian Captivity' by moving the papacy to Avignon. The cloister contains the **Museo Capitolare della Cattedrale** (*t/f 075 572 3832; open Mon–Fri 10–1, Sat–Sun and hols 10–1 and 4–6; adm*), with a little art, some reliquaries and hymnals. If it's noon, the campanile bells above you will make sure you know it.

Galleria Nazionale dell'Umbria

t 075 075 57411; lift to the 3rd floor; open daily 8.30–7.30, 16 June–15 Sept Sat 8.30–11; closed 1st Mon of month; adm; ticket office on ground floor.

The elaborate **main door** (1326) of the Palazzo dei Priori is around the corner in Corso Vannucci, its lunette featuring statues of Perugia's patron saints, Louis of Toulouse, Lawrence and Ercolanus. Through this and up the lift, the Galleria Nazionale has the finest, largest collection of Umbrian (and many other) paintings anywhere, displayed with explanations in English. The mezzanine floor was left unsound by the earthquake, but the masterpieces are all accessible, displayed chronologically and thematically. The first rooms contain some striking early works, among them sculptures for a public fountain by **Arnolfo di Cambio** (1281) and others from the Fontana Maggiore by **Nicola and Giovanni Pisano**, which were replaced by copies. There's a pre-Giotto *Crucifixion* and other works of the **Maestro di San Francesco** from the 1270s. Nor are all the best works Umbrian – the Sienese, in particular, are well represented, with a fine polyptych by Vigoroso da Siena (*c.* 1290) and a sweet *Madonna* by **Duccio di Buoninsegna**.

Mesmerizing rooms of trecento and early quattrocento gold-ground Madonnas and Annunciations (by Ambrogia Maitani, Meo di Guido da Siena, Ottaviano Nelli, Peccio Capanna) culminate in **Beato Angelico**'s *Guidalotti Polyptych*, his pupil **Benozzo Gozzoli**'s *Pala della Sapienza Nuova* and **Piero della Francesca**'s *Polyptych of Sant'Antonio* (1465–70), painted for a Franciscan convent. Piero himself assembled works from two distinct periods to fulfil the wishes of the buyers, who thought the project was dragging on a bit. The *Annunciation* shows the painter at the height of his powers, creating an eerie stillness out of mathematical purity – on either side of Gabriel and the Virgin rows of arches recede into a blank wall. From the International Gothic wizards of the Marches come two works: **Gentile da Fabriano**'s *Virgin and Child* (1408), painted for Perugia's San Domenico – note how the wood of the Virgin's throne is alive and budding – and a *Madonna del Pergulato* (1445) by **Giovanni Boccati da Camerino**, master of angelic choirs, *putti*, flowers and perspective tricks.

The best Perugians of the same period, **Benedetto Bonfigli** and **Bartolomeo Caporali**, show perhaps less spirituality, but fancier clothes and a lilting lyricism. Bonfigli also contributes the sharp and meticulously drawn **Cappella dei Priori** frescoes (1454–80). These are dedicated to two of Perugia's three patrons: the older frescoes, late Gothic in style, are on the life of St Louis of Toulouse, while the unfinished later frescoes on the life of St Ercolanus show a more mature, Renaissance handling of space. They also feature the best portraits of Perugia itself, bristling with towers – at the time it had around 500, astonishing even for such a belligerent city. Also beautiful are a bronze relief of the *Scourging of Christ*, by **Francesco di Giorgio Martini**, and some terracotta reliefs by **Agostino di Duccio**.

The next section features two Perugian painters of the next generation, **Pinturicchio** and **Perugino**. Both, when young, worked on the *Miracles of San Bernardino of Siena* (1473), a series of eight small panels with charming imaginary town settings. Although he refused to participate in the High Renaissance, Pinturicchio rarely fails to charm; his nickname, 'Rich Painter', derives from his use of gold and gorgeous colours, seen here in his *Pala di Santa Maria dei Fossi*. Perugino always maintained an ideal classical vision, touched with the 'sweetness' mastered by Raphael. At his worst, Perugino can be painfully unconvincing ('I'll give them their Virgin and Saints,' you can imagine him grumbling as he dabbed on another rolling eyeball). The gallery has about a dozen of these, many almost entirely by his assistants; there's an *Adorazione* featuring the most disdainful Magi ever, as well as Perugino at his finest, in the *Polyptych of Sant'Agostino*.

The mezzanine floor, up a spiral staircase, displays long galleries of numb gigantic canvasses from the 16th to 18th centuries (a particularly good one is by **Pietro da Cortona**, the ultimate idealized *Nativity*). The wooden horse was a model for an equestrian monument to Orazio Baglioni. On the first floor, you can look through the glass door to the **Sala del Malconsiglio** (Bad Counsel), so-called because in the 1360s the Priors decided here to release some prisoners – English mercenaries from Sir John Hawkwood's company. The next year, Hawkwood's men defeated Perugia at the Battle of Ponte San Giovanni. The Perugians learned their lesson; they were never nice to anyone again. It contains the original bronze lion and griffin from the façade of the palace; over the door (on the inside) there's an early lunette by Pinturicchio.

Corso Vannucci and the Collegio del Cambio

To complement the excellent Piazza IV Novembre, Perugia has a truly noble main street. The **Corso Vannucci** is named after Pietro Vannucci, who, after all, was named Perugino after Perugia; it is always closed to traffic and the citizens stroll along it every evening in central Italy's liveliest *passeggiata*.

At Corso Vannucci 25, in the third and final annexe to the enormous Palazzo dei Priori (1443), Perugino received a major commission in 1499 to decorate the **Collegio del Cambio** (*t 075 572 8599; open Mon–Sat 9–12.30 and 2.30–5,30, Sun 9–1; joint adm with Capella di San Giovanni Battista and Collegio della Mercanzia, see below*), headquarters of Perugia's moneychangers' guild. Money-changing, or banking, was not quite reputable owing to biblical injunctions against usury and the first challenge was to come up with an appropriate decorative scheme. The city's leading humanist, Francesco Maturanzio, proposed an array of Christian, Classical and secular virtues for the walls and planetary gods for the ceiling. Perugino dressed them in the *haute couture* of the time, creating one of the finest pure Renaissance rooms in all Italy. Among these beautiful figures, Perugino painted an unflattering self-portrait in the middle of the left wall, tight-lipped and stern and sceptical, over an inscription added by the grateful Perugini 'If the art of of painting had been lost, he would have rediscovered it. If it had never been invented, he would have done so.' A tradition now scoffed at by scholars has it that Perugino's pupil Raphael, then 17, contributed the figure of *Fortitude*; more probably is the legend that he served as the model for the figure of the *Prophet Daniel*. The ceiling was later decorated with grotesques, not long after Raphael set the fashion for them in Rome with the discovery of Nero's Golden House; the magnificent woodwork is by Domenico del Tasso and Antonio Bencivenni da Mercatello (1493–1508), and the gilded terracotta statue of *Justice* (the moneychangers' guild arbitrated in financial disputes) is by Benedetto da Maiano.

The frescoes on the *Life of St John the Baptist* in the Bankers' chapel, the **Cappella di San Giovanni Battista**, are by another of Perugino's students, Giannicola di Paolo (*t 075 572 8599; open Mon–Sat 9–12.30 and 2.30–5,30, Sun 9–1; joint adm with Collegio del Cambio, see above, and Collegio della Mercanzia*). Nor is that all; the adjacent **Collegio della Mercanzia** (*t 075 573 0366, open Mar–Oct and 20 Dec–6 Jan Tues–Sat 9–1 and 2.30–5.30, Sun 9–1; 1 Nov–19 Dec and 7 Jan –28 Feb Tues, Thurs and*

Fri 8–2, Wed and Sat 8– 4.30, Sun 9–1; joint adm with Collegio del Cambio, see p.435)
at No.15bis, was the seat of the merchants' guild, one of the oldest and most
important in Perugia; the Sala di Udienza is richly decorated with 15th-century
carvings, panelling and inlays, perhaps by craftsmen from northern Europe.

A Vanished Fortress and Underground Perugia

Continuing down the Corso Vannucci, past the hotels and formidable Perugian
pastry shops, you pass from the Middle Ages to 19th-century neoclassical in the blink
of an eye at **Piazza Italia**, dominated by the bulky, 1870s **Prefettura**, emblazoned with
another griffin; behind it, the balustrades of the **Giardini Carducci** offer a splendid
view over the Perugian suburbs and the distant countryside.

To find out why there are no old buildings on this piazza, take the unobtrusive
down escalator under the colonnades of the Prefettura, into a Perugia that for over
300 years was lost to view and almost forgotten. Only days after the end of the Salt
War, Paul III found a way to intimidate the Perugians into obedience until Judgement
Day while obliterating the Baglioni family at the same stroke. The quarter of town
he demolished for his famous **Rocca Paolina** was the stronghold of the Baglioni,
including all of their palaces, 138 houses that they owned and seven churches. Most
buildings were not completely razed, however, because Paul's architect, Antonio da
Sangallo the Younger, needed them to give the new fortress a level foundation.

The 16th century may have been the age of the Renaissance, but in Italy it was also
the era of grudges; Paul III came to Perugia seven times over the next three years to
make sure the fortress was sufficiently repressive, and to crown it off, he had the
Rocca inscribed with large letters: *Ad repellandam Perusinorum audaciam* (To curb
the audacity of the Perugians). From the beginning, the Perugians looked upon it as
a loathsome symbol of oppression, of the grisly terror that came to Italy in the
1500s. No enemy ever attacked it, and throughout the centuries of papal rule, its only
real use was as a prison – a prison from which few ever found their way out again. In
the general revolutionary year of 1848, a pick was ceremoniously handed to Count
Benedetto Baglioni to begin its longed-for demolition. This was far from complete
when the papal forces returned, but as soon as Perugia was liberated from the Swiss
Guard in 1860, the Piemontese General Pepoli signed a decree giving the Rocca to
the Perugians and they gleefully tore down the rest; the workmen, with their
dynamite, were joined by the entire populace, including women and children, some
armed with pickaxes, some with their bare hands.

In a way, it's a pity the Rocca Paolina no longer stands. The old paintings and prints
in the Palazzo dei Priori depict a startlingly modern building, designed by one of the
best Renaissance architects. After demolishing it, the Perugians built the neoclassical
Piazza Italia and the Carducci Gardens to replace it; few even knew about the
medieval streets underneath, until the city made use of them to create a quick
pedestrian passage down to Piazza dei Partigiani – one of the most fascinating
things to visit in Perugia. At the bottom of the first escalator, you'll be at the
medieval street level, among the brick palaces of the Baglioni, all roofed over by the
arches and vaults of Sangallo. There are many interesting corners to explore,

including stretches of the **Rocca Paolina bastions** (*open 8–7*), where you can peek out through the pope's gun slits to look over the peaceful Viale Indipendenza below.

The entrance to the bastions from the outside is on Via Marzia, where you can also see the **Porta Marzia**, the best surviving piece of Etruscan architecture anywhere that isn't a tomb. Antonio da Sangallo carefully reassembled it here after destroying Perugia's original walls. The five sculpted panels, now almost completely eroded, probably represented five gods, although the Perugians have a strange old story that they are a Roman family who died from eating poisonous mushrooms.

Perugia's West End: Down Via dei Priori

On the Corso Vannucci side of the Palazzo dei Priori, a little archway leads into Via dei Priori and Perugia's west end, a quiet and lovely part of the city. The first sight you'll encounter is the church of **San Filippo Neri**, rebuilt by Roman architect Paolo Marucelli from an earlier church in the 1630s, with façade awkwardly squeezed and only visible in its entirety from across the small square. Perugians still call this impressive pile the *Chiesa Nuova*, surely the showiest Baroque building in Umbria; its interior, full of florid paintings, seems to be made of dirty ice cream, an echo of Rome out in the provinces. The exterior is still being repaired after earthquake damage, but inside you can see its high altarpiece of the *Immaculate Conception*, completed by Pietro da Cortona. The medieval Via della Cupa descends from here under a series of arches to the Etruscan walls and gateway, the **Porta della Mandorla**.

Further down Via dei Priori is the charming **Santi Stefano e Valentino**, a vaulted medieval church almost hidden among the houses: the altarpiece is a fine *Madonna* by the 16th-century Perugian Domenico Alfani. Next, in the shadow of the 150ft **Torre degli Sciri** (13th century), Perugia's tallest surviving tower fortress, the huge **Santa Teresa degli Scalzi** (*always locked*) was an ambitious Baroque project that was never finished. In the little piazza by the **Porta Trasimena**, built in the Middle Ages on Etruscan foundations, the church of the **Madonna della Luce** has a good Renaissance façade, a round fresco of *God the Father* by Giovanni Battista Caporali and another of the *Madonna and Saints* by Tiberio d'Assisi. The church commemorates a miracle: a barber, playing cards by his shop, swore so hard after losing a hand that a wooden Madonna in a nearby shrine shut her eyes and didn't open them for four days.

Piazza San Francesco

Turning right at the Madonna della Luce, the street opens into the green lawn of Piazza San Francesco, originally outside the walls. **San Francesco al Prato** (1230), once the finest and most richly decorated church in Perugia, suffered a partial collapse in a mudslide in 1737 and a thorough looting by Napoleon's soldiers; the elegant façade remains, in patterns of pink and white stone. Part of it is now open to the elements.

Next door, the **Oratorio di San Bernardino** commemorates the 15th-century Franciscan from Siena who made such an impression on the Perugians. 'Little St Bernard' must have been a crafty preacher to affect these pirates. The oratory was begun in 1461, the year after the saint's canonization, and placed on this site because Bernardino always stayed at the convent of San Francesco during his visits.

Agostino di Duccio (1418–81), that rare Florentine sculptor who decorated the Malatesta Temple of Rimini, was commissioned to do the façade, and he turned the little chapel into Umbria's greatest temple of pure Renaissance art. Framed in rich pink and green marbles, Agostino's reliefs are exquisite: beatific angel musicians, scenes of miracles from the life of the saint and allegorical virtues: Mercy, Holiness and Purity on the left; Religion, Mortification and Penance on the right. One of the panels on the lower frieze portrays the original Bonfire of Vanities, held in front of the cathedral after a particularly stirring sermon from Bernardino – which may have given Savonarola in Florence the idea.

Inside, the chapel's altar is a late Roman sarcophagus, perhaps that of a Christian; it seems to tell the story of Jonah and the whale and was the tomb of the Beato Egidio of Assisi (d. 1262), the third person to follow St Francis. The Oratory also has two works from the church of San Francesco: one of Benedetto Bonfigli's gonfalons, depicting the Madonna sheltering Perugia from the plague (1464), and a copy of Raphael's *Deposition,* now in Rome's Galleria Borghese.

Just behind, the convent of San Francesco holds the **Museo dell'Accademia di Belle Arti** (*closed since earthquake and undergoing restoration*) displaying a huge collection of plaster models, starring Canova's *Three Graces*; there are also prints, and typically, academic 18th- and 19th-century paintings.

Old Streets Around the Cathedral

Walk around the back of Perugia's cathedral, and you'll find yourself transported back to the Middle Ages, a half-vertical cityscape of dark, grim buildings and overhanging arches, some incorporating bits of Gothic palaces and Etruscan walls, a set no film director could possibly improve upon. And they are as old as they look. Many of the arches originally supported buildings over the street; medieval Perugia must have seemed like one continuous building, all linked by arches and passageways.

An Etruscan Well and the Arch of Augustus

At Piazza Dante 18, behind the cathedral, you can marvel at an example of ancient engineering, the 3rd-century BC **Pozzo Etrusco** (*t 075 573 3669 or infoline t 199114; open April–Oct 10–1.30 and 2.30–6.30; Nov–Mar 10.30–1.30 and 2.30–5; closed Tues except April and Aug; adm; ticket valid for Pozzo Etrusco, Cappella di San Severo and the Torre Panoramica of Porta Sant'Angelo, see p.440*), a monumental 116ft-deep well and cistern; if the debris at the bottom is ever excavated, it may prove deeper. According to estimates, it held 95,000 gallons of water, enough to supply all of Etruscan *Perusia*. Via Ulisse Rocchi, leading down steeply to the northern gate, used to be called Via Vecchia, and is the oldest street in town; Perugians have been treading it for at least 2,500 years.

The old north gate just happens to be formed of another fabulous relic of the city's past, the **Arco di Augusto**. The huge stones of the lower levels are Etruscan; above them rises a perfectly preserved Roman arch built during the emperor's refounding of Augusta Perusia. The city's new name is inscribed with typical Imperial modesty:

'Augusta' in very large letters, 'Perusia' in tiny ones. The portico atop the Roman
bastion, making this gate one of the most beautiful in Italy, was added in the
16th century. The arch faces Piazza Fortebraccio and the 18th-century Palazzo
Gallenga Stuart, now home of the **Universita per Stranieri** (University for Foreigners),
founded in 1921 for the study of Italian language and culture and attended by
students from all over the world (*see* **Travel**, p.60).

Another little walk, beginning back in Piazza IV Novembre, is down **Via Maestà
delle Volte**, one of the most picturesque medieval streets in Perugia, covered with
arches that once supported a large Gothic hall. It leads down to **Piazza Cavallotti**,
where Roman houses and a road have been discovered just under the pavement.

The University and Borgo Sant'Angelo

Another itinerary through this ancient district would begin west from behind the
cathedral down into a jumble of interwoven medieval arches and asymmetrical
vaults that lead down to Via Battisti. Near Via Battisti, a long stairway descends
through the Roman-Etruscan walls into the **Borgo Sant'Angelo**, Perugia's medieval
suburb that was once a proletarian quarter, the centre of popular resistance to the
Baglioni and the popes, and now site of the city's famous university. Walk over the
Acquedotto, which in the Middle Ages supplied water from Monte Pacciano to the
Fontana Maggiore; much later, it was converted into a long stone footbridge over the
housetops to the precincts of the **university**, founded in 1307 and still one of the
most prestigious in Italy. The central university buildings are now on Via Ariodante
Fabretti, in an Olivetan monastery liquidated by Napoleon in 1801. In the **Institute of
Chemistry** on Via Pascoli (*open Mon–Fri 8am–7pm, closed Sat, Sun and hols*), you can
see a 2nd-century **Roman mosaic**, discovered during recent construction. The scene
represents Orpheus charming the wild animals with his lyre.

Beyond the university quarters, Corso Garibaldi runs northwards through Borgo
Sant'Angelo, passing the bulky pink and white checked church of **Sant'Agostino**
(*t 075 572 2624*), with its set of extravagantly carved choir stalls by Baccio d'Agnolo,
from designs by Perugino. The fresco over the altar is by Giannicola di Paolo, a
student of Perugino, but the real prize, a five-part altarpiece by the master himself,
was looted by Napoleon. Its panels are now scattered across France, except for the
Madonna herself, who took a cannonball on the nose in Strasbourg during the
Franco-Prussian war. Further up Corso Garibaldi is a plaque commemorating the
meeting of St Francis and St Dominic, founders of the two great preaching orders
of the Middle Ages, both in Perugia to visit Pope Honorius III; contemporary
accounts say they embraced and went their separate ways, without more than a
word or two.

One of the many convents in this area is **Santa Colomba** at Corso Garibaldi 191
(*ring the bell*) whose most famous nun, the Blessed Colomba of Rieti (1467–1501),
was so wise that the magistrates of Perugia often consulted her; her cell has a lovely
painting of *Christ Carrying the Cross* by Lo Spagno and mementoes of her life. At the
end of Corso Garibaldi, one of the highest points in the city was graced in ancient
times by a circular temple, dedicated to either Venus or Vulcan. Christians converted

it into a church, still known as the **Tempio di San Michele Archangelo** (*t 075 572 2624; open daily 10–12 and 4–6*) in the 5th century, replacing the outer circle of columns with a plain stone wall. Many legends grew up around this singular church in the Middle Ages – some writers referred to it as the 'pavilion of Roland'. Today, with tons of Baroque frippery cleared away in a recent remodelling, the church has returned to something like its original appearance. Some scholars doubt there really was a temple here: the 16 beautiful Corinthian columns do come in a wild variety of styles and heights and some were undoubtedly brought from other buildings. Still, this oldest church in Umbria casts its quiet spell.

The tall **Porta Sant'Angelo** (*t 075 573 3669; open April–Oct daily 11–1.30 and 3–6.30; Nov–Mar 11–1.30 and 3–5; closed Tues except April and Aug*) behind the church, a key point in Perugia's medieval defences, was built by Lorenzo Maitani in 1326 next to a castle tower added by Braccio Fortebraccio. Beyond it, enjoy a rare patch of countryside that has remained unchanged over the centuries; here the church of **San Matteo degli Armeni** has good, recently restored 13th-century frescoes.

On Perusia's Acropolis

Yet another excursion from the cathedral and Piazza Dante would be up Via del Sole, through another ancient part of the city to **Piazza Michelotti**, an attractive spot and the highest point in Perugia. Long before the Rocca Paolina, the popes built their fortress here; and, like the work of Paul III, this castle, too, was destroyed by the Perugians. In the rebellion of 1375, the people besieged it; after bribing off Sir John Hawkwood, the paid protector of the papal legate, they knocked down the walls with the aid of a fearsome homemade catapult called the *cacciaprete* (priest-chaser). Today it is surrounded by peaceful 17th-century houses.

From here, an arched lane leads to **San Severo** (*t 075 573 3864; open April–Oct daily 10–1.30 and 2.30–6.30; Nov–Mar 10.30–1.30 and 2.30–5; closed Tues except April and Aug; adm*), founded in 1007 by Camaldolese monks; the story goes that this high ground was ancient *Augusta Perusia*'s acropolis, and the church was built over the ruins of a Temple of the Sun. One chapel survives the Baroque remodelling of the 1750s and contains a celebrated fresco of the *Holy Trinity and Saints*, one of Raphael's very first solo efforts; underneath are more saints by his master Perugino, ironically painted a couple of years after Raphael's premature death when Perugino was in a noticeable artistic decline.

Via Bontempi leads around to another Etruscan gate, the **Porta del Sole**. Two churches near here, **San Fiorenzo** in Via Alessi and the 14th-century **Santa Maria Nuova** on Via Pinturicchio (at the bottom of Via Roscetto), both have one of Benedetto Bonfigli's bizarre gonfalons; these painted banners were intended to be carried during mournful *misericordia* processions in the streets, invoking God's mercy during plagues, famines or the frequent attacks of communal guilt to which the Perugians were always subject. The one in Santa Maria Nuova (1472) is badly damaged but shows a vengeful Christ raining down thunderbolts of plague on sinful Perugia, while the Virgin, SS. Benedict and Scholastica, and the Blessed Paolo Bigazzini try to placate his wrath.

East of Santa Maria Nuova, Corso Bersaglieri continues out to the gate of Porta Sant'Antonio, where the church of **Sant'Antonio** has a frescoed *Crucifixion* recently attributed to Raphael.

To San Domenico

The streets to the southeast of the cathedral, while not quite as dramatic, are just as ancient and intractable as those to the north and west. If you care to climb a bit, a tour of this area will take you to such sights as the **Via delle Volte della Pace**, an ancient vaulted tunnel of a street just east of the cathedral, where the Perugians signed their peace treaties (with fingers crossed behind their backs). One of the few breathing spaces in the crowded district is the elongated **Piazza Matteotti**, the former marketplace and field for burning witches, parallel to and below Corso Vannucci. In the old days, it was called Piazza Sopramura, being actually built on top of a section of the Etruscan-Roman walls. The west side of the piazza is shared by the post office and an old Perugian institution, a brightly decorated kiosk with an eccentric owner who sells nothing but bananas. Opposite them stand the 17th-century Gesù church and two splendid 15th-century buildings: the **Palazzo del Capitano del Popolo** and, next to it, the **Palazzo dell'Università Vecchia**, built between 1453 and 1515 and used as the quarters of the university until 1811.

From Piazza Matteotti, Via Oberdan descends to Perugia's oddest church, **Sant'Ercolano** (1326), a tall octagon built on the old walls with a gigantic pointed arch in each facet, a double Baroque stair, a train station clock and lace curtains in the upstairs window; the interior, in good if rotting Baroque, has a Roman sarcophagus for its altar. From here, the city extends along a narrow ridge, following Corso Cavour to another colossal, ambitious, woefully unfinished church, **San Domenico** (*open church hours*). Designed by Giovanni Pisano, it was rebuilt in 1632 by Carlo Maderno when the vaulting caved in, although one wall and the apse are original; the latter has the second largest stained glass window in Italy after Milan cathedral, dated 1411. The light streaming through this colourful glass is the main feature of the interior, but there is also the fine *Tomb of Pope Benedict XI* by a student of Arnolfo di Cambio. Poisoned figs did Benedict in a year after his election, during a visit in 1304, but surprisingly, the Perugians had nothing to do with it; prime suspects after the nun who served them to him included the Florentines and King Philip the Fair of France. The fourth chapel on the right holds a beautiful marble and terracotta dossal (1459) by Agostino di Duccio.

The Museo Archeologico Nazionale dell'Umbria

t 075 572 7141; open Tues–Sun 8.30–7.30, last admission 7pm, closed Mon am; adm.

This is housed behind San Domenico, in an equally grandiose yet unfinished convent, displaying excellent material from prehistoric and Etruscan Umbria. The prehistoric collection will get you in touch with Palaeolithic, Neolithic and Bronze Age Umbria, while a large part of the historic collection comes from the Etruscan cemeteries around Perugia: an incised bronze mirror (an Etruscan speciality, 3rd century BC); intricate gold filigree jewellery; sarcophagi; a famous stone marker called the *Cippus Perusinus*, with one of the longest Etruscan inscriptions ever found (151 words); and bronzes, armour and weapons. Among the funeral vases and urns there is one portraying a hero who looks like a dentist about to examine a monster's teeth; another shows a procession, perhaps of a victor. An impressive Roman piece, a bronze statue of Germanicus, father of Caligula, found in Amelia in 1963, has been loaned back to Amelia's own Archaeological Museum (*see* p.547) after a long battle. Other Roman finds include inscriptions in honour of Augustus, the rebuilder of Perugia, and a beautiful sarcophagus sculpted with the myth of Meleager.

San Pietro

From San Domenico, Corso Cavour leaves the city at the elegant **Porta San Pietro** (1473), designed by Agostino di Duccio with help from Polidoro di Stefano. Changing its name to Borgo XX Giugno, the street continues to the end of the ridge, past the university's **Orto Medievale** at No.74 (*t 075 32643 or t 075 585 6422, ortobot@unipg.it; open Mon–Fri 9–5, until 6 in summer*), a botanical garden where each plant has a symbolic meaning, to an 18th-century park, the **Giardino del Frontone**.

Facing it is the Benedictine church of **San Pietro**, founded in the 10th century and still retaining substantial parts of its original structure. This is the most gloriously decorated church in Perugia, nearly every square inch inside covered with frescoes and canvases. During the sack by the Swiss Guards in 1859, the monks of San Pietro shielded the leaders of the revolt from the papal bloodhounds – the story goes that they cut down their bell ropes by night, and used them to lower the fugitives down the cliffs to safety. The twelve-sided bell tower is one of Perugia's landmarks. The façade has a rare fresco of the Trinity, which is a feminine word in Italian and here represented by a three-headed woman.

The basilican interior dates from the early 1500s and has a carved, gilded ceiling. Among the acres of painting are the large canvases in the nave by a Greek student of Veronese called L'Alisense. Two paintings in the right aisle have been attributed to Perugino's pupil Eusebio da San Giorgio, a Madonna and Two Saints and a St Benedict. The Cappella di San Giuseppe has fine 16th-century works, while the sacristy has paintings of Five Saints by Perugino, all that remains of yet another altarpiece looted by Napoleon, as well as a Portrait of Christ by Dosso Dossi, and a bronze crucifix by Algardi. The best works in the whole church, however, have to be the extraordinary choir stalls from the 1520s, sculpted and inlaid by Benardino Antonibi of Perugia, Nicola di Stefano of Bologna and Stefano Zambelli of Bergamo. A pretty door in the choir gives on to a little balcony with a memorable view over Assisi and Spello.

The left aisle has a *Pietà* by Fiorenzo di Lorenzo. There's a tabernacle attributed to Mino da Fiesole in the Cappella Vibi; the nearby Cappella Ranieri has a *Christ on the Mount* by Guido Reni, *St Peter and St Paul* attributed to Guercino, and a *Judith* by Sassoferrato, who was also responsible for the several Raphael and Perugino copies in the church. Beyond the Cappella del Sacramento, with paintings by Vasari, is an *Adoration of the Magi* in the nave by Eusebio da San Giorgio and a *Pietà* by Perugino.

Santa Giuliana

t 075 575051; currently closed.

Leaving Perugia, Via XX Settembre, the boulevard down to the train station, passes the 13th-century church of **Santa Giuliana**, with a delicate pink and white façade and beautiful campanile, one of Perugia's landmarks. Attributed to Gattapone, it is one of the few medieval churches in Perugia to survive essentially intact, with frescoes from the 1200s and 1300s and a cloister from 1375, now a military hospital.

Ipogeo dei Volumni

t 075 393329, www.archeologia.beniculturali.it; open daily 9–1.30 and 3.30–6.30; July–Aug 9–12.30 and 4.30–7; adm; visits are limited to a maximum of seven people at a time for a maximum of five minutes.

Near Ponte San Giovanni, east of Perugia, signs lead to one of the best preserved Etruscan tombs anywhere, sheltered by a modern yellow building next to a gritty bypass and train tracks; the way can be confusing and is most painlessly done from Perugia by taxi. Dating from the 2nd century BC, the hypogeum is characteristically shaped like an Etruscan house, with an underground *'atrium'* under a high gabled roof carved in the rock, surrounded by small rooms, the main one holding the travertine urns containing the ashes of four generations of the family. The oldest one, that of a man named Arnth, is a typical Etruscan tomb with a representation of the deceased on the lid, while that of his descendant, the 1st-century AD Pulius Voluminius, demonstrates Perugia's rapid Romanization. Unlike most Etruscan tombs, the Volumni has unusual high reliefs in stucco, rather than paintings.

Around Perugia: Torgiano, Deruta and Corciano

Torgiano

Traditionally under Perugia's influence, **Torgiano** lies 15km south of the capital. It is practically synonymous with wine and the Lungarotti family; from the late 1970s, Dr Giorgio Lungarotti has made this minute DOC growing area internationally famous. The Lungarotti foundation runs an excellent **wine museum** (*t 075 988 0200, www.lungarotti.it; open daily 9–1 and 3–6, in summer until 7; adm*), housed in the cellars of the 17th-century Palazzo Baglioni in Corso Vittorio Emanuele. Displays labelled in English trace the history of wine, techniques, rules and regulations; it also has a history of wine jars and vessels, a beautiful display of majolica, from Deruta, Faenza and Montelupo, and a wine library, with books going back to the Renaissance. You can also visit the Cantina by appointment (*t 075 988661*).

Deruta

If there's room in your suitcase, buy a plate in the tiny hill town of **Deruta** (pop. 7,500), 5km south of Torgiano. Along with Gubbio, Deruta has been Umbria's centre for ceramics and majolica since the 13th century, and still has 200 ceramic

Tourist Information

Deruta: Piazza dei Consoli 4, **t** 075 971 11559
Open Mar–Nov 9.15–12.15 and 3–6,30;
Nov–Mar 9–12 and 3–5; Closed Sun afternoon.

Where to Stay and Eat

Torgiano ✉ 06089
★★★★★**Le Tre Vaselle**, Corso Garibaldi 48,
t 075 988 0447, **f** 075 988 0214,

www.3vaselle.it (*very expensive*).
A luxurious hotel in an old palazzo and next door to houses, on the edge of the village, surrounded by vineyards and olive groves. It offers air conditioning, minibars, a baby-sitting service, pool, whirlpool, sauna, fitness suite...the list goes on. The restaurant (*expensive*) is ranked among the top in Umbria, although standards are not always consistent.

workshops. Deruta's location, on the fringe of Perugia's *contado*, brought it some hard knocks from Perugia's enemies over the centuries. During the height of its fame in the 1500s, Deruta was sacked twice, by Cesare Borgia and Braccio Baglioni, but it picked itself up and carried on making ceramics. There are dozens of ceramics shops, particularly in the lower part of town. One of the biggest is **Maioliche Sberna** (*t 075 971206*), where you can watch ceramics being made and painted in the workshop.

You can admire works of past artisans in the **Museo Regionale della Ceramica** (*t 075 971 1000, www.museoceramicaderuta.it; open Oct–Mar Wed–Mon 10.30–1 and 2.30–5; April–June daily 10.30–1 and 3–6; July–Sept daily 10–1 and 3.30–7; adm*), in a former convent on Largo San Francesco. There are examples from Deruta's golden age in the early 1500s, church floor tiles, devotional plaques and a majolica font. In Piazza dei Consoli (note the miniature copy of Perugia's Fontana Maggiore, minus the reliefs), the 14th-century church of **San Francesco** has patches of Sienese and Umbrian frescoes, while the medieval Palazzo Comunale holds a **Pinacoteca** (*t 075 971 1143; closed for refurbishment, due to reopen spring 2005*) with paintings and a gonfalon by Nicolò Alunno, painted on both sides. There's also a detached fresco by Fiorenzo di Lorenzo, one of his best works, of the *Plague Saints Rocco and Romano standing over Deruta* (1478). Another church, **Sant'Antonio Abate**, has a fresco by Bartolomeo Caporali of the *All-Protecting Virgin*, who also features in the church of the **Madonna dei Bagni** (*visits by request, call t 075 973455*), 3km south along the SS3bis in Frazione Casalina. This is full of quaint ceramic votive plaques made in the 17th and 18th centuries, showing pratfalls, sinking ships and exorcisms, all with happy endings thanks to the Madonna. Closer to Perugia, to the west of the Tiber, a country chapel outside **San Martino in Colle** has a fresco of the *Madonna and Child*, restored and attributed to Pinturicchio.

Corciano

To visit museums in Corciano, call the Comune di Corciano several days in advance, t 075 518 8254/5.

On its hill midway to Lake Trasimeno, pretty **Corciano** is protected by nearly intact 13th-century walls and castle. Controlled by Perugia into the 15th century, it has small scale versions of all the essential buildings of a *comune*, all neatly labelled with a ceramic plaque, which gives it a slight museumish air, but Corciano doesn't care. There's a car park outside the walls near the pink and white striped church of **San Francesco**; this was founded after St Francis' visit in 1211 (the Corcianese had no doubt that he was going to be canonized, so they got a headstart on his church). Perugino left one of his finest late works, the *Assumption* altarpiece (1513) in the 13th-century church of **Santa Maria**; the church also has one of Bonfigli's strange gonfalons, dedicated to the *Madonna della Misericordia*, here defending Corciano.

The big castle just north of Corciano at **Pieve del Vescovo** (*t 075 505 8611, open for pre-booked visits on the last Friday of every month*) was restored in the late 1500s by Galeazzo Alessi as a residence, but there's an even more impressive work by the same architect just north of the main road, the **Villa del Cardinale**, built for Cardinal Fulvio Della Corgna. Now owned by the state, plans are to open it to the public; it has a very imposing gate and a lovely Renaissance garden.

Lake Trasimeno

The fourth largest lake in Italy, **Trasimeno** (45km in circumference) has a subtle charm, sleepy, placid and shallow, almost marshy in places; large enough to create its own soft micro-climate, it shimmers like a mirror embedded in gentle rolling hills covered with olives and vineyards. The Etruscans of *Camars* (Chiusi) coveted the lake for its fish and the fertility of its shores, and around the time of their famous king Lars Porsena, the bad guy in Macaulay's *Horatio at the Bridge,* they founded Perugia to control it. In the 12th and 13th century, wars were fought for its eels. Napoleon took one look at it and wondered how to drain it.

Hans Christian Andersen, drawing on his own travels, put Trasimeno in one of his fairytales, *The Galoshes of Fortune* – how beautiful it was, but how poor the people were (in the 1830s), and how wretched their lives among the swarms of biting flies, mosquitoes and malaria. A postwar dose of American DDT wiped out the latter and the lake has since become a modest resort – the Umbrian Riviera. Never one to fully cooperate with humanity, Trasimeno, once prone to flooding, is now doing its best to become a peat bog. A few fishermen skim over its waters, seeking eels, tench, shad and carp. Ducks, cormorants and kingfishers love it, water lilies float among the reeds, and, as the tourist office reminds visitors, some 20 per cent of the world's artistic heritage listed by UNESCO lies within two hours of its quiet shores.

Magione and Trasimeno's East Shore

From Perugia it's 30km to Trasimeno; if you snub the company of the *autostrada,* you can visit **Magione**, a little industrial centre known for its copper- and brassware. Like any place within Perugia's radius, it spent much of the Middle Ages fighting: there's a ruined 13th-century **Torre dei Lombardi** on top of town, and on the edge stands a striking **Castello dei Cavalieri di Malta** of 1420 (*t 075 843547; open in summer for guided tours*), built by the Bolognese architect Fieravante Fieravanti and still owned by the Knights of Malta, now based in Rome. The knights had inherited

Getting Around

Lake Trasimeno lies 37km south of Arezzo, 13km south of Cortona, 69km east of Siena, and 30km west of Perugia.

By **car**, you can approach it along the A1 from the north; take the Val di Chiana exit for the spur of the *autostrada* that skirts the northern shore en route to Perugia; coming from the south, taking the Chiusi exit off the A1 will bring you out near the SS71 to Castiglione del Lago.

Train travel can be a bit awkward: Castiglione del Lago is a stop on the main Florence–Rome line, but not for the fast trains (Intercity and Eurostar), so check before setting out. Also on the main Florence–Rome line, you can change at Terontola for Perugia and the north-shore towns of Tuoro sul Trasimeno and Passignano; coming from Siena, change at Chiusi for Castiglione.

Perugia is the main **bus** terminus for the area; connections from Cortona and Siena are less frequent. A fairly frequent bus service runs around the north shore (Tuoro–Passignano–Magione–San Feliciano–San Savino–Perugia) and around the southern shore (Perugia–Magione–S. Arcangelo–Panicarola–Macchie–Castiglione del Lago). Contact APM buses, **t** 075 506781, freephone **t** 800 512141, *www.apmperugia.it*.

Alternatively, get there on your own two wheels: you can **hire bicycles** in Castiglione from Marinelli, Via B. Buozzi, **t** 075 953126, or in Passignano from Eta Beta Modelismo, Via della Vittoria 58, **t** 075 829401, or in Tuoro from Balneazione Tuoro, Loc Punta Navaccio, **t** 328 454 9766 (mobile), open April–Sept, or from Marzano, Via Console Flaminio 59, **t** 075 826269.

Castiglione, Tuoro and Passignano, the lake's ports, are linked by **boat** to one another as well as to Isola Maggiore and Isola Polvese. Connections are frequent in the summer, but only one or two daily in winters; for times, call **t** 075 827157 or ask at the Tourist Office.

Tourist Information

Castiglione del Lago: Piazza Mazzini 10, **t** 075 965 2484, **f** 075 965 2763, *www.lago trasimeno.net*, for information on the whole lake area; *info@castiglione-del-lago-pg.it* for information on Castiglione.

Tuoro Pro-Loco, Via Ritorta 1, **t** 075 825220, *www.prolocotuorosutrasimeno.it*. Summer offices at Isola Maggiore, Magione, Rossignano and San Feliciano.

Market Day

Castiglione del Lago: *Wed.*

Activities

Lake Trasimeno's shoreline is dotted with little ports, making it popular for watersports.

Sailing

Club Velistico, Viale Brigata Garibaldi 3a, Castiglione del Lago, **t** 075 953035. Loc Darsena, Passignano, **t** 075 829 6021.

Water-skiing

Scuola Federale Sci Nautica, Punta Navaccia, Via Navaccia 4, Tuoro sul Trasimeno, **t** 075 826357. *Open Mar–Oct.*
Sci Club Trasimeno, Castiglione del Lago, **t** 075 965 2836.

Where to Stay and Eat

Not many Italians think of Trasimeno as a beach resort: the shallow water is warm and muddy. There are several modest holiday hotels around Castiglione, Passignano and Magione, and plenty of *agriturismi* (the local tourist offices can send you complete lists).

Medieval Perugians were so fond of fish from Trasimeno that Nicola Pisano jokingly sculpted some on his famous fountain in front of their cathedral. Today, the catch isn't really

an 11th-century Templar hospital here, of which a few traces remain. Their church, **San Giovanni,** was damaged in the last war, and was rebuilt and frescoed in a traditional manner by the Perugian futurist Gherardo Dottori in 1947. On the main road, the little 13th-century church of the **Madonna delle Grazie** has a lovely fresco of the *Madonna Enthroned* by Andrea di Giovanni da Orvieto.

big enough to send far outside the lake area, and it tastes pretty muddy, but you can try some at the restaurants by the lake, most of them unpretentious places with reasonable prices.

Isola Maggiore ✉ 06060

***Da Sauro**, Via Guglielmi, **t** 075 826168, **f** 075 825130 (*moderate*). This is perhaps the most unusual possibility – it's certainly the best place in Umbria to get away from it all. Gracious and uncomplicated with just 12 rooms, it's the island's only hotel. It has a brilliant restaurant, specializing in fish from the lake: eels, carp and more, along with traditional Umbrian dishes.

San Feliciano ✉ 06060

*****Da Settimio**, Via Lungalago Alicato 1, **t** 075 847 6000, **f** 075 847 6275 (*moderate*). In a lakeside hamlet, 7km south of Magione, with peaceful rooms and a simple restaurant.
Rosso di Sera, Via Fratelli Papini 79, **t** 075 847 6277 (*moderate*). Watch the sunsets from the tables at this new *osteria* where the lake fish, especially in the classic *tegamaccio*, is delicious; they serve land dishes, too. *Mon–Sat eves only, Sun all day; closed Tues and 20 days in Jan.*

Castel Rigone ✉ 06060

****Relais La Fattoria**, Via Rigone 1, **t** 075 845322, **f** 075 845197, *www.relais lafattoria.com* (*expensive*). A pretty hotel, converted from 17th-century farm buildings, with a pool, 30 luxurious rooms and a good restaurant, **La Corte** (*closed 3 weeks in Jan*), serving specialities such as *filetto di persico* (perch) and *spaghetti al sugo di Trasimeno* (with a sauce of mixed lake fish).

Passignano sul Trasimeno ✉ 06065

***Lido**, Via Roma 1, **t** 075 827219, **f** 075 827251, *www.umbriahotels.com* (*expensive*). Right on the water and a little cheaper, with well-equipped rooms, and a garden to sit

and watch the ferries sailing to and fro. *Open April–Nov.*
***Villa Paradiso**, Via Fratelli Rosselli 5, **t** 075 829191, **f** 075 828118, *www.bluhotels.it* (*expensive*). Large but comfortable, with a rustic feel and a pool.
***Florida**, Via 2 Giugno 2, **t** 075 827228, (*inexpensive*). Good, with simple rooms and a welcoming atmosphere.
***Del Pescatore**, Via San Bernadino 5, **t** 075 829 6063, **f** 075 829201, *www.delpescatore.com* (*inexpensive*). Holiday apartments available here, but the main business is food, especially lake fish, served in the attractive *trattoria*. *Closed Tues.*
Cacciatori, Via Nazionale 14, **t** 075 827210 (*expensive*). A lakeside restaurant with slightly higher pretensions and excellent fish, but the prices tend to be a bit steep. *Closed Wed, and 3 weeks in Jan.*
Il Fischio del Merlo, San Donato 17a, **t** 075 829283 (*expensive*). Creative cuisine based on sea fish, as well as Chianina meat. *Closed Tues and 3 weeks in Nov.*

Castiglione del Lago ✉ 06061

***Duca della Corgna**, Via Buozzi 143, **t** 075 953238, **f** 075 965 2446, *hotelcorgna@ trasinet.com* (*moderate*). Comfortable and relaxing, in a quiet wood; the restaurant only opens in the summer.
***Miralago**, Piazza Mazzini 5, **t** 075 951157, **f** 075 951924, *www.hotelmiralago.com* (*moderate*). Small, with pretty lake views. *Closed Jan and Feb.*
***Trasimeno**, Via Roma 174, **t** 075 965 2494, **f** 075 952 5258 (*inexpensive*). Has a pool to make up for the lake's indifferent waters. *Open July and Aug only.*
La Cantina, Via Vittorio Emanuele 69, **t** 075 965 2463 (*cheap*). In the historic centre, serving smoked eel fillets, risotto of lake fish or carp wrapped in *porchetta* (a typical Trasimeno dish). *Closed Mon.*

Long before the knights, this was the birthplace of the early missionary, Fra Giovanni di Pian di Carpine ('of the hornbeam plain', as the area under Magione was known), who was sent in 1245 by Innocent IV to convert the Mongols; although his preaching failed to make much of an impact, he returned from Karakorum after 20 years and wrote the *Historia Mongolorum*, the first eyewitness account of China and the Far East, much studied by later missionaries and Marco Polo. (Some scholars suspect the Venetian merchant never visited Kubla Khan but cribbed much of his *Travels* from Fra Giovanni. Needless to say, this doesn't go down too well in Venice.)

Three of Trasimeno's prettiest beaches are spread between Magione's lakeside *frazioni*. One of these *frazioni*, **Montecolognola**, high on a hill blanketed with olives, has another castle built in the late 13th century by the beleaguered residents of Magione and has lovely views over the lake. Montecolognola's parish church has 14th- to 16th-century frescoes, another one of 1947 by Gherardo Dottori and a pretty majolica altarpiece made in Deruta. Further south are picturesque **Monte del Lago**, near the impressive but ruined **Castello di Zocco** (1400) with its five towers and **San Feliciano**. The latter village has a fascinating little **Museo della Pesca**, dedicated to the lake's fishermen, and enjoys magical sunsets over the water and Isola Polvese.

Isola Polvese, the largest of Trasimeno's three islands, is linked in the summer by boats from San Feliciano. The large village that once stood here was abandoned in the 17th century because of malaria; today, only the 14th-century castle and an older monastery still stand. Now owned by the province, Polvese has olive groves, lush vegetation and hundreds of nesting birds; a path encircles it and takes about an hour to walk, and there's a little beach and summer snack bar.

South of San Feliciano, the **Oasi delle Valle** (*t 075 847 6007; open June–Sept Tues– Sun 9–1 and 4–8; Oct–May Tues–Sun 9–1 and 3–6; guided tours for a minimum of six people, book in advance; adm*), run by the environmental group Legambiente, is the most important bird-watching area on Trasimeno, hosting an impressive number of migratory visitors, especially in spring. It is here that the Romans dug a 7km underground emissary to drain the lake when water levels reached the flood stage, diverting it through several streams and into the Tiber; a second emissary was built in 1423 by Braccio Fortebraccio. Leonardo da Vinci, who visited in 1503, suggested diverting its flow into the Tiber, Arno and Chiana rivers. As the shore grew swampier, Leonardo's proposal received serious consideration, until yet another emissary was dug here in 1896. You can walk along it and visit a museum on the site which tells the whole soggy story.

The North Shore: Castel Rigone, Passignano and Isola Maggiore

North of Magione, a road ascends to **Castel Rigone**, a dramatically poised fortress hill town founded in 543 by Rigone, lieutenant of Totila the Goth. It has spectacular views over the lake and a delightful Renaissance church, the recently restored **Madonna dei Miracoli**, built in 1494 by Perugia as a votive for the Virgin who spared the city from a plague. Built in the form of a Latin cross, it has a doorway with a relief by a student of Michelangelo, Domenico Bertini da Settignano (who, like most Renaissance artists, had a nickname – Topolino or 'Mousey' – the same as Italian for Mickey Mouse). The church has a fine interior and a gilded high altar by Bernardino di Lazzaro, a chapel with *ex votos* dedicated to the miraculous Madonna, and a sweet statue of St Anthony Abbot and his pet pig.

The lake's busiest resort, **Passignano sul Trasimeno** (from the Roman *Passum Jani*) enjoys a favoured position on its own promontory, midway between Perugia and

Cortona. In the 1930s this was the headquarters of the Società Aeronautica Italiana, which made zippy sea planes and boats, until it was bombed in the war. Within Passignano's walls is an attractive old quarter around the 14th-century castle; below lies a beach hiring out windsurfers. The art is outside the centre: near the cemetery, the **Pieve di San Cristoforo** dates from the 11th century and has recently restored frescoes from the 1300s, while 1.5km northeast, the **Madonna dell'Olivo** is an elegant Renaissance church with a beautiful high altar and a fresco attributed to Bartolomeo Caporali. The town is at its liveliest for the *Palio delle Barche* on the third Sunday of July, when young Passignanesi dressed in medieval costume carry their boats shoulder-high through the streets and launch them on to the lake for a race.

Passignano is the nearest port to **Isola Maggiore** (20mins), Trasimeno's second-largest island, with a charming 15th-century village inhabited by fishermen and women famous for their lace-making. In 1211, St Francis came to the then-deserted island to spend Lent alone. He made a lasting impression by throwing back a pike a fisherman had given him, only to be followed doggedly across the lake by his grateful 'Brother Fish' until the saint blessed him. Francis took only two loaves of bread to sustain himself, and when the fisherman returned to the island to pick him up, he was amazed to see that only one loaf had been half eaten in 40 days.

A footpath encircles the island, passing by the Franciscan convent, which was built to commemorate the saint's visit and converted in the late 19th century into a neo-Gothic folly by Senator Giacinto Guglielmi from Rome, now crumbling gently into a romantic ruin (shown by a village custodian). The 13th-century church of **San Michele Arcangelo** has frescoes and an excellent *Crucifixion* by Bartolomeo Caporali (*c.* 1460).

Tuoro sul Trasimeno

To the west of Passignano, **Tuoro sul Trasimeno** grew up in the late Middle Ages near the **Castello di Montegualandro**, a haven for citizens while their town was attacked by every army crossing the Italian peninsula or heading south to Rome.

You can visit the battlefield by car or foot, along the signposted **Percorso Storico Archeologico della Battaglia**, dotted with viewing platforms; explanatory notes along the way and maps help to bring the Roman disaster to life. Near the first platform, note the pretty portal of the Romanesque **Pieve di Confini**. Recently, Tuoro has decorated its lake shore with something unexpected: Pietro Cascella's **Campo del Sole** (1985–89), a contemporary 'solar temple' garden of 27 pillars in locally quarried sandstone, each about 12ft high and sculpted by a different artist, arranged in a wide spiral like a forest of idols to a preposterous god. **La Dogana** near here was the Customs House between the Papal States and the Grand Duchy of Tuscany, and has plaques to the many famous folk who passed this way.

Castiglione del Lago

Among the silvery olive groves that soften the west shore of Trasimeno juts the picturesque promontory of **Castiglione del Lago** (pop. 13,500), the setting for the lake's biggest town, a cheerful and mostly modern place that goes back to the

The Battle of Trasimeno

Tuoro's first battle was the worst. Two years into the Second Punic War, Hannibal was on a winning streak, having defeated the Romans twice, on the rivers Ticino and Trebbia, victories that had rallied the local Gaulish and Ligurian tribes to his banner. As it made its way south towards Rome, this swollen army got bogged down in the disease-ridden marshland of the Arno, at the cost of thousands of troops and all of the exasperated elephants who had survived the march over the Pyrenees and Alps. Meanwhile, the Roman Senate sent Consul Gaius Flaminius, a bold populist politician (builder of the Via Flaminia), and an army of 25,000 to destroy the Carthaginians once and for all. With Flaminius in pursuit through the Valdichiana, Hannibal led his army, now reduced to 40,000, to Trasimeno. Finding a perfect place for an ambush just west of Tuoro, in a natural amphitheatre closed off by the lake (the water level was considerably higher back then), he arranged his troops in the hills, determined to risk all in order to defeat the Romans and convince the restive Etruscan cities to join him.

Believing that Hannibal was at least a day's march in front, Flaminius failed to send scouts ahead; the morning of 24 June 217 BC was foggy and, according to the chroniclers, he ignored a number of auguries pointed out by his Etruscan soothsayers (he fell off his horse and the sacred chickens were off their feed). He marched straight into Hannibal's trap, along the narrow shore passage at Malpasso. In a panic, unable to get into battle formations, 15–16,000 legionaries (including Flaminius) were drowned or slaughtered within a few hours, while those who got away found a safe haven in Perugia. The blood of the dead, that legend says ran in a river for three days, is recalled in the name of the hamlet Sanguineto, their whitened bones in the hamlet of Ossaia (from *ossa*, bones). Hannibal slew all of the Roman prisoners, but freed all members of the various Italic tribes, hoping to gather support.

After Trasimeno, the Roman military machine grimly threw even more legions to their death against Hannibal at Cannae, before changing strategy and giving the Carthaginians the run of southern Italy for 15 years, harassing Hannibal while refusing to fight him before ultimately defeating him in Africa. The long-term effects of the war are felt in Italy to this day: as small farmers fled, they lost their source of income and had to sell their land to pay their debts. Snapped up cheap by a few rich men, it marked the beginning of the feudal *latifondo* system that condemned the once prosperous south of Italy to grinding poverty.

Etruscans. Emperor Frederick II destroyed Castiglione for being an ally of Guelph Perugia, then ordered Fra Elia Coppi to lay out a new town, neatly in six streets, served by three gates and three squares. Afterwards, the town kept siding with Cortona, causing no end of friction with Perugia until 1490, when it came once and for all under the Baglioni family, who during their brief period of glory hosted here such luminaries as Machiavelli and Leonardo da Vinci.

Eventually the town was recovered by the popes, one of whom, Julius III, gave it to his sister. In 1550, her son, the celebrated *condottiere* Ascanio della Corgna and husband of Giovanna Baglioni, became the first in a series of dukes who ruled the lake as an independent duchy; this lasted until 1648, when it passed into the Grand Duchy of Tuscany before returning to the popes the next century.

During Castiglione's ruritanian interlude, the great architect Vignola designed the ducal Palazzo della Corgna or **Palazzo Ducale** (*open May–June 9.30–1 and 4–7.30; July–Aug 9.30–1 and 4.30–8; Sept–Oct 9.30–1 and 3.30–7; Nov–Feb 9.30–4.30; adm*). Many rooms retain their fetching late Renaissance frescoes by Niccolò Pomarancio and the Roman school; one scene shows the Battle of Trasimeno, and another the Battle of Lepanto, in which Ascanio distinguished himself. Like the great *condottiere* Federico da Montefeltro (*see* 'Gubbio', p.480), Ascanio was something of a humanist and so he had his study decorated with frescoes on the Life of Caesar. From the palace, a covered walkway, fortified in case of surprise attack, allowed direct access to the mightiest of all the castles on the lake, the pentagonal Rocca del Leone designed in 1247 by Friar Elia Coppi with a sturdy triangular keep and four outer towers. Also worth seeing in Castiglione, in the 19th-century church of the Maddalena, is a lovely painting of the *Madonna and Child with SS. Anthony Abbot and Mary Magdalene* (1500), by Eusebio da San Giorgio.

The South Shore

Much of the south shore of the lake is patterned by vines which produce the grapes that go into Colli del Trasimeno, a local DOC wine. In **Panicarola**, the most famous producer was Ferruccio Lamborghini, who declared an ambitious intention to make wines as fine as his sports cars – his father had been a farmer, and the first motors young Ferruccio built were for his tractors. He died in 1993, before quite succeeding, but you can still buy a Lamborghini to call your own.

South of Lake Trasimeno

These hills and their towns are known for two things: their magical views over Lake Trasimeno and their souvenirs of Perugino, who made this loveliness part of his artistic vocabulary. Italian writers have often commented that Città della Pieve looks more like a Sienese town than an Umbrian one; if so, it's no great surprise – the Tuscan border and interesting towns such as Chiusi and Montepulciano are only a few miles away.

Città della Pieve

From Castiglione del Lago, it's 27km to the handsome red brick town of **Città della Pieve** (pop. 6,500). The Etruscans and Romans were here, and in the Middle Ages, it became *Castrum Plebis*, then *Castel della Pieve*. Perugia considered it within the western borders of its turf, and in the 1320s built the imposing square fortress to defend it. In 1503, Cesare Borgia sacked the town and then, typically, had two of his colleagues, the Duke of Gavina and Piero Orsini, strangled for conspiring against him. Later the town was ruled by Ascanio della Corgna and his heirs until 1601, when the Church picked it up and Clement VIII made it a bishopric and changed its name to Città della Pieve.

But Città della Pieve is best known as the birthplace of **Perugino** (Pietro Vannucci, c. 1446–1523). To Giorgio Vasari, he committed the unpardonable sin of not being born in Tuscany; if there is anything to the rather unflattering biography in Vasari's *Lives of the Artists*, Perugino was perhaps the most bitter artist of the Renaissance. Born into a desperately poor family, success turned him an untrusting miser: 'he would have gone to any lengths for money', it was said, riding out from job to job with saddle bags full of the money he was afraid to leave anywhere else. About midpoint in his career, he became an atheist; even so, he cranked out two more decades of richly rewarded, if often vacuous, Madonnas and religious scenes with lyrical soft-tinted Trasimeno backgrounds, before dying, stubbornly unconfessed and unabsolved – an extremely rare event in the 16th century – rejecting any future with the sweet angels he depicted for others.

Perugino did leave several paintings in his home town, of which the greatest is a lovely fresco of *The Adoration of the Magi* (1504), painted originally for a charitable confraternity in the **Oratorio di Santa Maria dei Bianchi** (*open June–Sept daily 10.30–12.30 and 4–7; Oct–May Fri–Sun 10–12.30 and 3.30–6*), just within the city walls. It portrays the birth of the Saviour in an Arcadian springtime, with the view from Città della Pieve towards Lake Trasimeno in the background and members of an elegant Renaissance garden party in attendance – a world that seems hardly to need a redeemer at all. The two letters from Perugino on display show that although he demanded 200 florins for his work here, he settled for much less, partly because he was painting for his fellow citizens.

Via Vannucci leads uphill to the town's cluster of monuments in Piazza Plebiscito. The rather undistinguished **Duomo** (*open daily 9.30–7*) was built in the 17th century to replace the far older church of **SS. Gervasio e Protasio**, the *pieve* (parish church) that gave the town its name; pieces of 9th-century sculptural work are embedded

Tourist Information

Città della Pieve: Piazza del Plebiscito 1, t 0578 299 375 (*open 10.30–12.30 and 4–7*).
Panicale: Piazza Umberto I, t 075 8378017. Contact them for information about visits to San Sebastiano and also the Teatro Cesare Caporali.
Paciano: Summer office only, t 075 830186.

Market Day

Città della Pieve: *Sat*.

Where to Stay and Eat

Città della Pieve ✉ 06062
There's nothing fancy in Città della Pieve, but you won't be left out in the cold.

***Al Poggio dei Papi, Loc San Litardo, t 0578 297030, f 0578 297056, *www.alpoggio deipapi.com* (*moderate*). Just outside town, comfortable, modern hotel with restaurant, olympic-size pool, gym and tennis.
Da Bruno, Via Pietro Vannucci 90–92, t 0578 298108 (*cheap*). Serves fine, unpretentious fare. *Closed Mon.*

Panicale ✉ 06064
***Le Grotte di Boldrino, Via V. Ceppari 43, t 075 837161, f 075 837166, *www.grottedi boldrino.com* (*inexpensive*). Sweet little hotel, decorated with 19th-century furnishings, and home to Panicale's best restaurant.
**Vannucci, Via Icilio Vanni 1, t 0578 299572, f 0578 298063, *www.umbriatravel.com* (*inexpensive*). Named after the town's most famous son, this is perfectly adequate.

in the façade. There are some more works by Perugino (the *Baptism of Christ* in the Cappella del Rosario and the *Madonna in Glory* in the apse), as well a crucifix in the first chapel on the right, attributed to Pietro Tacca. The second chapel contains one of the finest works by Domenico Alfani, the *Madonna and Child and Saints*.

Standing next to the Duomo is the lofty **Torre del Pubblico**, built in the 12th century but heightened in 1471; in the same piazza are the trecento **Palazzo dei Priori** and the **Palazzo della Corgna** (*t 075 965 8210; open daily Mar–April 9.30–1 and 3.30–7; May–June 10–1.30 and 4–7.30; July–Aug 10–1.30 and 4.30–8; Sept–Oct 10-1.30 and 3.30–7; Nov–Feb Sat–Sun 9.30–4.30; adm*), designed in 1551 by the Perugian architect Galeazzo Alessi; inside there are some good 16th-century frescoes by Pomarancio and Salvio Savini and a little sandstone obelisk, brought here from the convent of San Francesco. Near the piazza is what locals claim is the narrowest lane in Italy (there are several contenders for the title), **Vicolo Bacciadonne** – Kiss-the-Women Lane – you're almost compelled to do so, just to get past.

Just off the Piazza Pretorio in Via Roma stands the brick **Palazzo Bandini**, remodelled in the 16th century by Galeazzo Alessi; if you carry on, you'll come to the Porta Romana and **Santa Maria dei Servi** (*the church is often locked; the custodian at Santa Maria dei Bianchi has the key*), frescoed by Perugino with a famous *Deposition* of 1517, although it was sadly damaged when the monks erected a *cantoria* in front of it. The Porta Romana is linked by walls to the Perugian **Rocca**, built by Ambrogio and Lorenzo Maitani in 1326. Just opposite is the 13th-century church of **San Francesco**, which was completely redone in the 18th century and is now a popular shrine to Fatima. It housed two good paintings, Domenico Alfani's *Virgin and Saints* and a *Pentecost* by Niccolò Pomarancio. Next door to the right, the **Oratorio di San Bartolomeo** (*open 10–12 and 4–7*) has a large fresco of the *Crucifixion* (1342) by the Sienese painter Jacopo di Mino del Pellicciaio, surrounded by weeping angels, hence its nickname, the *Pianto degli Angeli*.

Panicale and Around

Panicale is famous for its enchanting, and strategic, view over Lake Trasimeno, which in the Middle Ages made it a prize sought by Chiusi and Perugia; even so, in 1037, Panicale became an independent *comune*, one of the first in Italy. In the 14th century, it produced the sweet early Renaissance master Tommaso Fini, otherwise known as Masolino da Panicale, who painted with Masaccio in Florence; it also produced Giacomo Paneri, a fierce and brutal *condottiere* known as Boldrino di Panicale, who was briefly lord of the town. Another native, who tips the balance on the side of art, was the poet Cesare Caporali, born in 1530.

An old walled town built on a natural terrace 'in a spiral', Panicale has several pretty squares, beginning with the asymmetrical Piazza Umberto I, home to a charming fountain of 1473 and the 14th-century **Palazzo Pretorio**, decorated with some peculiar carvings and coats of arms. Near here is the stuccoed **Teatro Cesare Caporali** (*tours of the Teatro and San Sebastiano (see p.454) arranged by the tourist office, t 075 837183, 10.40–11.10, 11.50–12.20, 4.10–4.50 and 5.30–6.10*), from the late 18th century and restored in 1991. Further up, the handsome semi-fortified Baroque **Collegiata di San Michele** has an *Adoration of the Shepherds* by Gian Battista Caporali (1519).

Panicale's most important treasure is in the church of **San Sebastiano** *(tours as for the Teatro,* see p.453*)*, which is located just outside the walls. Here Perugino left one of his finest frescoes: a formal, dream-like *Martyrdom of St Sebastian* (1505), a geometrical composition laden with antique ornamentation, where four superbly costumed and cod-pieced archers stand powerfully poised to shoot the saint, while in the background is a faithful rendition of Panicale's beautiful view over Lake Trasimeno. The same church also contains Perugino's *Madonna*, a detached fresco from the church of Sant'Agostino.

Just to the west of Panicale, **Paciano** is a well-preserved medieval village on a spur of Monte Petrarvella, wrapped in its 14th-century walls, towers and gates. The **Confraternità del Santissimo Sacramento**, now a museum (*t 075 830120, ask over the road at No.12 to be let in*), has a fresco of the *Crucifixion* (1425) by the first reputed teacher of Perugino, Francesco di Castel della Pieve. Another church, **San Giuseppe**, keeps the communal gonfalon from the workshop of Benedetto Bonfigli (*c.* 1480). Outside the walls, the **Madonna della Stella** (1574) is a simple Renaissance church with frescoes by Scilla Pecennini.

The lignite-mining village of **Tavernelle**, just off the SS220, has a pretty main piazza. Near here, the tiny *frazione* of **Mongiovino Vecchio** has a well-preserved castle overlooking a stately domed Renaissance temple, the **Sanctuario di Mongiovino**. This was begun in 1513, an early but characteristic shrine to Mary. This one, with its fine octagonal cupola, has been dubiously attributed to Michelangelo or Bramante, but a more likely candidate is Rocco di Tommaso from Vicenza, who made the two finely sculpted doorways. Inside are cinquecento frescoes by Niccolò Pomarancio and the Flemish painter Heinrich van den Broek (aka Arrigo Fiammingo).

Perugino died of the plague in nearby **Fontignano** in 1523; his tomb, and the fresco he was working on when he died, an almost primitive *Madonna and Child*, can be seen in the parish church, the **Annunziata** (*contact the tourist office for guided tours, t 075 600276*). There is a photograph of another fresco he made for the church, of the *Adoration of the Shepherds*, which is now in the National Gallery in London.

Assisi

Less than half an hour east of Perugia, and visible for miles around, **Assisi** (pop. 26,000) sweeps the flanks of Monte Subasio in a broad curve, like a pink ship sailing over the green sea of a valley below. This is Umbria's most famous town and one of its loveliest, but there's more to it than St Francis. Occupied from the Iron Age, Assisi emerged as an ancient Umbrian town in the 6th century BC, one that maintained its cultural distinction into the 1st century BC. As wealthy Roman *Asisium*, it produced the poet Sextus Propertius and first heard of Christianity from St Rufino in 238. Part of the Lombard Duchy of Spoleto, the city came into prominence again in the Middle Ages as another of Umbria's battling *comuni*, one firmly on the side of the

Ghibellines, although in 1198 it rebelled against the Duke of Spoleto and defied its nominal lord, Emperor Frederick Barbarossa.

But Assisi saved most of its bile for incessant wars with arch-rival Perugia; St Francis in his chivalry-obsessed youth had joined in the fighting. The 13th century, which saw his great religious revival, was also the time of Assisi's greatest power and prosperity, leaving behind a collection of beautiful buildings any Italian city could be proud of, and one of Europe's greatest hordes of 13th- and 14th-century frescoes in the Basilica di San Francesco. Although Cardinal Albornoz nominally put Assisi under the Church's thumb and rebuilt the Rocca Maggiore to keep it there, the city was controlled by various *signori* until the early 16th century when the papal pall descended like a curtain at the end of a play. Even pilgrimages declined dramatically after the Council of Trent began the Counter Reformation.

Another pall that fell over Assisi was taste. In 1786, Goethe, on his way to view the Temple of Minerva, walked past the Basilica of St Francis, dismissing it as 'a Babylonian tower'.

Nevertheless, it was Francis who in the long term would make all the difference to Assisi (*see* pp.34–37). Pilgrimages began again in the 19th century with the revival of interest both in the saint and in the artists who decorated his shrine – Ruskin, who went into ecstatic overdrive at the medieval purity of the frescoes and used to dream that he was a Franciscan friar, was the locomotive drawing the first train of English-speakers. Five million pilgrims and tourists crowded Assisi's narrow streets for Francis' 800th birthday year in 1982 and, although now surpassed by the new shrine of the miracle-working Padre Pio in Puglia, Assisi remains the third most visited pilgrimage site in Italy. On any given summer day, you'll see coachloads of tourists and stands peddling ceramic friars and plastic medieval torture instruments, intermingled with flocks of serene Franciscans and enthusiastic, almost bouncy nuns from Africa or Missouri or Bavaria, having the time of their lives visiting a place that, much more than Rome, is the symbol of a living faith. And it's true that something simple and good and joyful has survived in Assisi in spite of the odds.

In recent years, the city has hosted unusual demonstrations that could never have happened in Rome or anywhere else – in 1986, when Pope John Paul II hosted his interfaith World Day of Prayer, complete with Tibetan lamas, Zoroastrians and American Indian medicine men, and in the 1988 Umbria Jazz Festival, when gospel choirs from New Orleans sang in the upper church of San Francesco. The friars would only let them sing for 15 minutes at a time, fearing that the rhythm might bring down the roof and Giotto's frescoes along with it. Providence saw that the building came to no harm, and by the end, the Franciscans were clapping and stomping along with everyone else.

Tragically, where gospel singing failed, the earthquakes succeeded. In September 1997, they brought the roof down, killing two friars and two journalists who were examining the damage caused by the first shock of the day. The original medieval builders had given the basilica the flexibility to withstand earthquakes, but restorers over the centuries had been too lazy to haul out all the rubble they had created,

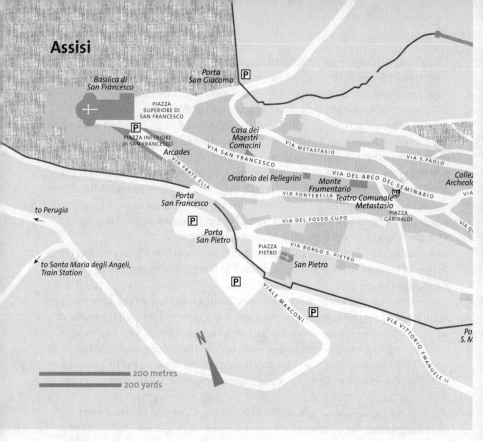

Assisi

Basilica di San Francesco

Porta San Giacomo

PIAZZA SUPERIORE DI SAN FRANCESCO

PIAZZA INFERIORE DI SAN FRANCESCO
Arcades

Casa dei Maestri Comacini

VIA SAN FRANCESCO

VIA METASTASIO

VIA S.PAOLO

Oratorio dei Pellegrini

Monte Frumentario

VIA DEL ARCO DEL SEMINARIO

Collez Archeolo

VIA

VIA FRATE ELIA

Porta San Francesco

VIA FONTEBELLA

Teatro Comunale Metastasio

to Perugia

Porta San Pietro

VIA DEL FOSSO CUPO

PIAZZA GARIBALDI

VIA Q

to Santa Maria degli Angeli, Train Station

PIAZZA PIETRO

VIA BORGO S. PIETRO

San Pietro

VIALE MARCONI

VIA VITTORIO EMANUELE II

Po S. N

N

200 metres
200 yards

and it accumulated, tons and tons of it, in the essential breathing space between the priceslessly frescoed ceiling vaults and the walls; ultimately, the weight proved too great.

The upper church reopened in November 1999 after extensive restoration and structural reinforcements. To ensure that a similar disaster never happens again, (can you ever be sure of such things?) the foundations have been reinforced to withstand earth tremors of 12 on the Richter Scale. The two arches that collapsed (over the nave and over the main door – the former killed the people standing under it) have been repaired, but are blank. Technicians are still working on the painstaking task of piecing the frescoes back together; much of what they are working with is just fine rubble. However, two of these are now back in place, the other frescoes in the nave were virtually unscathed and the façade has been beautifully restored.

The *palazzi* on the east side of Piazza del Comune were all badly damaged and many are still covered in scaffolding. Piazza S. Ruffino and around are practically invisible beneath scaffolding and tarpaulin and the Rucca is still undergoing restoration – the Assisi skyline is dotted with cranes. In fact, visitors to Assisi in the next few years will see the city, and to a lesser extent the whole region, in better condition than ever before. As a result of the quake, even buildings which were not actually damaged have been restored, as it was deemed a good time to do the work and the funds were there. It's an ill wind...?

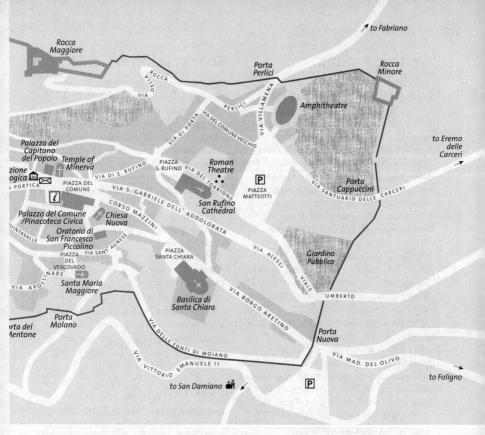

The social effects of the earthquake have not been addressed with such vigour, however, and many feel that for the sake of tourism, art has been given precedence over people (*see* **Topics**, pp.39–40).

The Basilica of San Francesco

t *075 819001, www.sanfrancescoassisi.org; open Easter–Nov Mon–Sat 6am–6.45pm, Sun and hols 6am–7.30pm; Nov–Easter daily 6am–6pm; upper basilica 8.30–6. No shorts or bare shoulders in the basilica.*

I would give all the churches in Rome for this cave.
Hippolyte Taine (19th-century French critic)

Although the medieval popes were mistrustful of the spontaneous, personal approach to faith preached by Francis and his followers, they soon realized that this powerful movement would be better off within the Church than outside it. In transforming the Franciscans into a respectable, doctrinally safe arm of Catholicism they had the invaluable aid of Francis's successor, Brother Elias, Vicar-General of the Order, a worldly, businesslike, organization man, an epicurean and a friend of Emperor Frederick II. Elias's methods caused the first split within the

Getting Around

Assisi is a 23km/30min **train** ride from Perugia or Foligno, where you'll have to change from Rome (177km/2½hrs) or Terni; for information, call **t** 075 804 0272 or freephone **t** 199 166177. The station is on the plain, a block from the suburban Basilica of Santa Maria degli Angeli, and there are regular connecting **buses** every 20mins to Piazza Unità d'Italia.

There are also convenient **buses** direct from Perugia, Bettona and Gualdo Tadino (APM, **t** 075 573 1707, freephone **t** 800 512141, *www.apmperugia.it*); Rome and Florence (SULGA, **t** 075 30799); one a day from Norcia and Cascia (SSIT); and several from Bevagna, Montefalco, Foligno and Spello (APM or SSIT). The bus stops are in Piazza Matteotti, Largo Properzio, Piazzale Unità d'Italia, S. Maria degli Angeli and Piazza Garibaldi.

If you're driving, use one of the three **car parks** out on the fringes of town: in the Piazza Unità d'Italia below the Basilica of San Francesco, at the Porta Nuova at the east end of town, and in the underground lot at Piazza Matteotti, by the Duomo. A series of little buses, the A and B, do the run between Piazza del Comune and Piazza Matteotti every 20mins or so (tickets are obtainable from newsstands, bars and tobacconists).

Car and Bike Hire

Car hire: Hertz, Via V. Veneto 4, Perugia, **t** 075 500 2439.
Bike hire: Angelucci Cicli, Via Becchetti 31, Perugia, **t** 075 804 2550, *www.angeluccicicli*.

Tourist Information

Assisi: Piazza del Comune 12, **t** 075 812534, **f** 075 813727, *info@iat.assisi.pg.it*, *www. umbria2000.it*. *Open winter Mon–Sat 8–2 and 3–6, Sun 9–1; summer Mon–Fri 8–2 and 3.30–6.30, Sat 9–1. and 3.30–6.30. Mon–Sat 8–6.30, Sun 9–1 and 2–7.* Seasonal office (*Easter–Oct*), Largo Properzio, **t** 075 816766, *open Thurs–Tues 10–7*.
Post office: Largo Properzio 4, **t** 075 813114.
Information Office of the Basilica, Piazza San Francesco, **t** 075 819 0084, **f** 075 819 0035. *Open Mon–Sat 9–12 and 2–5.30, Sun 2–5.*
Hotel booking service: Via Cristofani, **t** 075 816566, **f** 075 812315, *caa@krenet.it. Open Mon–Fri 9.30–12.30.*
Churches: Unless otherwise stated, all churches are open daily 7–12 and 2–sunset.

All the churches and major sights are now open following the earthquake, but the slow work of restoring frescoes continues and many buildings are still clad in scaffolding.

Festivals

Calendimaggio, *1st Thurs, Fri and Sat in May*. Assisi's medieval May Day celebrations, commemorating Francis's troubadour past with song, dance, torchlight parades, beautiful costumes and competitions between Lower and Upper Assisi.
Easter week. Religious celebrations take place all week. Regular features include: *Holy Thursday*: A mystery play on the

Franciscans, between those who enjoyed the growing opulence of the new dispensation and those who tried to keep to the poverty preached by their founder.

This monumental building complex, begun the day after Francis's canonization in 1228 when Pope Gregory IX laid the cornerstone, was one of the biggest causes of contention. Nothing could have been further removed from the philosophy and intentions of Francis himself; on the other hand, nothing could have been more successful in perpetuating his memory and his teaching than this great treasure-house of art.

The popes paid for it with a great sale of special indulgences across Europe and the basilica belongs to the Vatican (although thanks to a clause in the Lateran Treaty of 1929, and renewed in 1989, the Italian State is responsible for the upkeep – including all the earthquake repairs). There's a story that Brother Elias supplied the design – the

Deposition from the Cross. *Good Friday* and *Easter Sunday*: Processions through the town.

Antiques fair, *April–May*.

Festa del Perdono (Feast of Forgiveness), Porziuncola, *1–2 August*. Begun by St Francis, who once had a vision of Christ asking him what would be most helpful for the soul. Francis suggested offering forgiveness to anyone who crossed the threshold of the chapel; indulgences are given out on the day.

St Francis's Day, *3–4 October*. Religious ceremonies, singing and dancing.

Marcia della Pace, *2nd Sun in October*. A peace walk, begun in 1963, from Perugia to Assisi; in 2001, over 250,000 came, breaking all records. It's the one day *not* to come sightseeing.

Shopping

Assisi is overflowing with little ceramic friars, crossbows, local ceramics and glass, textiles and serious art galleries.

Enoteca Hispellum, Corso Cavour 35, **t** 0742 651766 (*open daily winter 9–1 and 2.30–8, summer 9–1 and 2.30–11*). Sample and buy a vast selection of local cheeses, wines, biscuits, honeys, jams, sauces and spreads.

Market Dayo
Piazza Matteotti, *Sat.*

Where to Stay

Assisi ✉ 06081

There are plenty of rooms in Assisi, but still nowhere near enough for Calendimaggio, Easter, July and August, when you should book in advance.

Very Expensive

★★★★**Le Silve**, 10km from the centre on Monte Subasio, at Armenano, **t** 075 801 9000, **f** 075 801 9005, *www.lesilve.it*. A 10th-century hostel which has been smartly fixed up for 20th-century guests, with antique furnishings and a pool and sauna. *Open Mar–Oct.*

★★★★**Subasio**, Via Frate Elia 2, **t** 075 812206, **f** 075 816691, *www.hotelsubasio.com*. This traditional, formal hotel has long been Assisi's finest and is linked to the Basilica of St Francis by a portico. Many of the rooms have views out over the countryside from vine-shaded terraces. It also has a private garage and an attractive medieval-vaulted restaurant. St Francis never slept here, but the king of Belgium and Charlie Chaplin did.

Expensive

★★★**Fontebella**, Via Fontebella 25, **t** 075 812883, **f** 075 812941, *wwwfontebella.com*. A 17th-century palazzo a bit nearer the centre. Rooms are comfortable, public rooms are elegant and a garden and garage add to the appeal.

★★★**Giotto**, Via Fontebella 41, **t** 075 812209, **f** 075 816479, *www.hotelgiottoassisi.it*. Very pleasant, modern rooms, located near the basilica. They also have a garage as well as garden terraces for relaxing in the sun.

★★★**Dei Priori**, Corso Mazzini 15, **t** 075 812237, **f** 075 816804. In a gracious, well-restored 18th-century palazzo, off the main piazza.

---

lower basilica does have an amateurish, clumsy form. The beautiful campanile dates from 1239; the completed basilica was consecrated by Innocent IV in 1253. Behind it, visible for miles around, on huge buttressed vaults, is the enormous convent built by Sixtus IV in the 15th century. Now a missionary college, it, too, was damaged by the earthquake, although a part of it is being used as a fresco hospital.

The Lower Church

With its low dark vaults, it seems at first to be a simple crypt, although once your eyes adjust to the light, you can see they are covered with magnificent 13th- and 14th-century frescoes (bring plenty of coins and a torch to illuminate them). The first chapel to the left of the frescoed nave contains magnificent frescoes, stained glass and other decorations on the *Life of St Martin* by Simone Martini, painted around 1322,

Moderate

★★★Il Palazzo, Via San Francesco 8, **t** 075 816841, **f** 075 812370, *hotel.ilpalazzo@ edisons.it*. Occupies a 13th-century building in the centre. Its 12 rooms are simple but furnished with antiques.

Brigolante Guest Apartments, 6km from the centre of Assisi at the foot of Monte Subasio, at Costa di Trex 31, **t** 075 802250, *www. brigolante.com*. If you plan to stay for a longer stretch, try this 16th-century farmhouse on a working farm, which has been converted into three self-catering apartments, each sleeping 2–4. Fine views over Subasio, as well as the chance to experience rural life and purchase fresh meat, vegetables, eggs and cheese from the premises.

★★★Umbra, Via degli Archi 6, **t** 075 812240, **f** 075 813653, *www.hotelumbra.it*. A charming family-run inn near Piazza del Comune; it's quiet, sunny and friendly with a walled garden. Rooms can be small, but many have balconies (some *expensive*). The restaurant (*closed Sun*) serves the best of regional cuisine, such as risotto with white truffles, and a cellar of excellent wine. Parking can be problematic – the nearest car park is by Santa Chiara.

★★Ideale per Turisti, Piazza Matteotti 1, **t** 075 813570, **f** 075 813020, *www.hotelideale.it*. A fine, small hotel with a garden, near the amphitheatre.

★★Country House, Via di Valecchie 41, **t** 075 816363, **f** 075 816155, *www.country housetreesse.com*.This this old stone building, in a country setting is 1km or a 10min walk to the west gate of Assisi. Lovely rooms are furnished with antiques. There is no restaurant, but the *signora* prepares a substantial, reasonably priced evening meal for guests in her kitchen (ask in the morning).

Inexpensive

★★Pallotta, Via S. Rufino 4, **t/f** 075 812307, *www.pallottaassis.it*. Small with a good, traditional eaterie.

★★San Giacomo, Via San Giacomo 6, **t** 075 816778, **f** 075 816779. Reliable and welcoming, in the historic centre.

★★Sole, Corso Mazzini 35, **t** 075 812373, **f** 075 813706, *www.assis-hotel.com*. A large place with a good restaurant, the **Ceppo della Catena**. *Closed Wed.*

★Anfiteatro Romano, Via Anfiteatro Romano 4, **t** 075 813025, **f** 075 815110. A good quiet choice near Piazza Matteotti, with only seven rooms, some with private bath.

Il Morino, Via Spoleto 8, Bastia Umbria, Perugia, **t/f** 075 8002099, *www.ilmorino. com*. 2km west of town, this attractive guest house/restaurant is housed in a converted stone building on a working farm. Two of the bedrooms have balconies with views up to the town. There is a pleasant garden and bikes are available for guests' use; reasonably priced evening meals are served too.

If everything is full, try the large pilgrimage houses in Santa Maria degli Angeli and Assisi proper.

---

while the third chapel on the right contains frescoes on the *Life of Mary Magdalene*, attributed to Giotto (1314). The Italians are convinced that the frescoes in the lower and upper churches are the climax of Giotto's early career, while most foreign scholars believe Giotto never painted them. Whatever the case, Martini's 'International Gothic-style' poses are a serious artistic challenge to the great precursor of the Renaissance. This master of line and colour creates a wonderful narrative of St Martin's life; the Gaulish soldier and wastrel who ended up as a bishop and gave half his cloak to a beggar seems a perfect foreshadowing of St Francis.

Giotto is also credited with the four beautiful allegorical frescoes over the high altar, depicting *Poverty*, *Chastity*, *Obedience* and the *Glory of St Francis*. Note the striking *Marriage of St Francis with Lady Poverty*. In the left transept are frescoes by Pietro Lorenzetti of Siena, among the best in the basilica, especially the lovely *Madonna*

★★Cenacolo Francescano, Via Piazza d'Italia 70, t 075 804 1083, f 075 804 0552, *www.hotel cenacolo.com*. One of the best, with 130 basic rooms, all with private bath, a short walk from the train station.

Alternatively, the tourist office has a long list of rooms in religious or private houses.

Sant'Antonio's Guest House, Via G. Alessi 10, t 075 812542, f 075 813723. One of the nicest, run by American sisters, offering pleasant rooms in a 12th-century villa. Guests who sign can also have a good cheap lunch here, but no dinner; beware the early curfew.

There are three hostels outside the centre: **Victor**, Via Sacro Tugurio, Rivotorto, f 075 806 5562. 3km south of Assisi.
Della Pace, Via di Valecchie 177, t/f 075 816767. New, 1km out of Porta San Pietro.
Fontemaggio, Via S. Ruffino Campagna, t 075 813636, f 075 813749. 3km east of Assisi.

San Gregorio ✉ 06086
★★★Castel San Gregorio, Via S. Gregorio 16, t 075 803 8009, f 075 803 8904 (*moderate*). Rooms in a romantic, restored 13th-century castle, in a garden, 12km northwest of Assisi.

Eating Out

Moderate
San Francesco, Via S. Francesco 52, t 075 812329. Defying the Italian rule that places with views serve food for dogs, the veranda here overlooks the basilica: fine cuisine matches the wine list. *Closed Wed and 1–15 July*.
Buca di San Francesco, Via Brizi 1, t 075 812204. Also well-known, in a cavernous medieval cellar. Try delicious cannelloni, homemade pasta with meat and porcini mushrooms, pigeon Assisi-style, or *filetto al Rubesco* (steak cooked in red Umbrian wine), accompanied by good wines. *Closed Mon, 10 Jan–Feb and most of July*.
Il Medio Evo, Via Arco dei Priori 4, t 075 813 068. Another venerable choice with an elegant medieval atmosphere and tasty *antipasti* with Umbrian *prosciutto*, pasta with truffles and *faraone all'uva* (guinea fowl with grapes). *Closed Wed, Jan*.
La Fortezza, Vicolo della Fortezza (near Piazza del Comune), t 075 812418. Delicious ricotta and spinach ravioli with basil and pine nut sauce, *parpadelle* with lamb ragù and truffled guinea fowl. *Closed Thurs and Feb*.

Cheap
La Stalla, Via Eremo delle Carceri 8, at Fontemaggio, t 075 812317. A typical country *trattoria*, converted from an old barn; it's a lovely stop on the way to the breathtaking sanctuary of Eremo delle Carceri. Good hearty fare, at very reasonable prices, washed down with local wine. *Closed Mon except at Easter and in summer*.

Don't neglect the rich strudels or chocolate and nut breads at the bakery in Piazza del Comune, near the Temple of Minerva, or at **La Bottega della Pasticceria**, Via Portica 9.

---

della Tramontana (of the sunset) *with St Francis and St John*, a *Crucifixion* (now badly damaged) and a *Descent from the Cross*. In the right transept is a work considered Cimabue's masterpiece, the *Madonna and Saints*, with a portrait of St Francis (1280), believed to be an accurate likeness; the serious-looking female saint nearby, by Simone Martini, is believed to be St Clare.

In the **crypt** lie the bones of St Francis and four of his closest followers, discovered only in 1818. Brother Elias, worried that the Perugians would come to steal the saint's body, hid it behind tonnes of stone. His fears were not unfounded; when Francis was coming back from La Verna to die, the Perugians were waiting to kidnap him along the road; Brother Elias had the foresight to direct Francis on a longer route. From the transepts, stairs lead up to a terrace and the **Museo-Tesoro della Basilica** (*open April–Oct Mon–Sat 9.30–5.30; Nov–Mar by appointment; adm*), containing anything not pillaged or pinched from the Treasury through the centuries – a beautiful Venetian cross, a French ivory Madonna from the 13th century, a Flemish tapestry with St Francis, and more. In 1995 the contents of the former 'secret sacristy' were put on display in another room: Pope Honorius III's Bull approving the Order's Rule (1223), the saint's tunic, cowl, girdle and sandals, an ivory horn given to Francis by the Sultan of Egypt which he blew to assemble his followers, the 'Laud to the Creator' and 'Benediction of Brother Leone' on parchment, in the saint's own hand, and a chalice and paten used by Francis and his followers.

The Upper Church

The **Upper Church** on its emerald-green lawn is strikingly bright and airy and vibrant with colour. It contains two major series of medieval frescoes; the earthquake left them cracked and broken in places, but more or less intact. Most of the cracks are no longer visible, and work continues on the fragmented parts. The lower set of 28 panels on the *Life of St Francis* is by Giotto or his school, while the upper, with *Old and New Testament Scenes*, is usually attributed to Cimabue's followers and Roman painters Pietro Cavallini and Jacopo Torriti. Giotto amazed his contemporaries with his ability to illustrate the physical and spiritual essentials of a scene with simplicity and

Lower Church Key

1 Cerchi Tomb with big porphyry vase (13th century)
2 Cappella di San Sebastiano, frescoes by Girolamo Martelli (1646) and the *Madonna della Salute*, the only known work by the 15th-century painter Ceccolo di Giovanni
3 *Madonna with Saints* by Ottaviano Nelli (1422)
4 Tomb of John Brienne, Latin Emperor of Constantinople (and friend of St Francis)
5 Cappella del Sacramento, with two 14th-century tombs
6 Cemetery cloister
7 Cappella di Santa Caterina, frescoes by Andrea de' Bartoli of Bologna (1360s)
8 Cappella di Santo Stefano, frescoes by Dono Doni (1574)
9 Cappella di San Martino by Simone Martini (*c.* 1320)
10 Cappella di San Lorenzo, frescoes by Andrea de' Bartoli
11 Stairs to the crypt
12 Cappella di Sant'Antonio di Padova, frescoes by Cesare Sermi (1610), early 14th-century stained glass
13 Cappella di San Valentino, with a pavement tomb of Friar Ugo of Hartlepool, one of the first English Franciscans (d. 1302)
14 Cappella della Maddalena, frescoes by Giotto and assistants (*c.* 1309)
15 *Coronation of the Virgin* by Puccio Capanna (1337), over a Cosmati work pulpit
16 The *Quattro Vele* (*Poverty, Chastity, Obedience* and the *Glory of St Francis*)
17 *The Last Judgement* by Cesare Sermei (1623)
18 Frescoes of the Passion by Pietro Lorenzetti (*c.* 1320)
19 Cappella di San Giovanni Battista, triptych by Lorenzetti (*c.* 1320-30)
20 Frescoes by Cimabue, Giotto, Martini and Lorenzetti
21 Cappella di San Nicola, frescoes by Giotto and assistants
22 Steps to the chapterhouse
23 Stairs to terrace and treasury

The Basilica of San Francesco

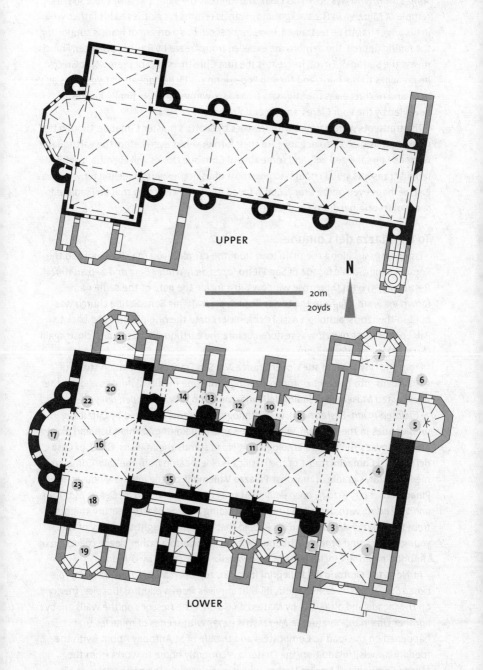

UPPER

N

20m
20yds

LOWER

drama, cutting directly to the core. The scenes begin with *St Francis Honoured by the Simple Man*, who lays down his cloak and foretells the saint's destiny (note Assisi's Temple of Minerva in the background); Francis returns his clothes to his father, who in his anger has to be restrained; Pope Innocent III has a dream of Francis supporting the falling Church; the demons are expelled from Arezzo by Brother Sylvester; Francis meets the Sultan of Egypt; he creates the first Christmas crib, or *presepio*, at Greccio; he preaches to the birds, and then to Pope Honorius III; he appears in two places at once and next receives the stigmata from a six-winged cherub; finally, he dies, bewailed by the Poor Clares, and is canonized.

The transepts were painted with frescoes by Giotto's master, Cimabue, though the works had oxidized into negatives of their former selves even before the earthquake; what can be salvaged will, and some kind of Cimabue clones will eventually refill the rebuilt transepts, good enough to give most of us non-experts a feeling for what was lost, perhaps even of the *Crucifixion*, a faded masterpiece of 1277 that still radiated some of its original drama and feeling.

To the Piazza del Comune

Entering Assisi along the main road from the car park, you may have noticed the Romanesque-Gothic façade of **San Pietro** (*open daily winter 8–12 and 2–6, summer 8–12 and 3–5*) with three rose windows, just inside the gate of the same name (down Via Frate Elia from the Lower Church piazza). This Benedictine church was built in the 1200s, although Assisi's chroniclers date the original building back to Palaeochristian times. It was restored before the earthquake, but had to close again (*t 075 812311 for information*).

From the tidy lawn of the Upper Church, Via San Francesco, the main street of Assisi, leads into the *centro storico*, passing some fine medieval houses and a rather unexpected **Museo degli Indios dell'Amazzonia** (*t 075 812280; open daily 10–12 and 3–6, closed 15 Jan–Easter; adm*), with ethnographic items collected by Capuchin missionaries in the Amazon, while in the same building Amazonian fish and plants are on show as the **Mostra Etnologica**. At No.14 stands the Masons' Guild, or **Casa dei Maestri Comacini** (most of the basilica builders came from the Lake Como area, medieval Italy's cradle of masons). **Palazzo Vallemani**, on the left, now houses the **Pinacoteca** (*t 075 812033; open daily 16 Mar–15 Oct 10–1 and 2–6; 16 Oct–15 Mar 10–1 and 2–5; adm*), with detached frescoes, including a scene of 13th-century knights from the Palazzo del Capitano del Popolo that probably caught the fancy of the young Francis, and others by Tiberio d'Assisi; there's also a rather sleepy collection of Umbrian paintings, including a *Madonna della Misericordia* by L'Alunno.

At No.11, the **Oratorio dei Pellegrini** (*t 075 812267; open Mon–Sat 10–12 and 4–6; closed Sun*) is a 15th-century gem, all that survives from a pilgrims' hospice, frescoed on the façade and altar wall by Matteo da Gualdo. The frescoes on the walls are by another Umbrian, Pierantonio Mezzastris (1477), with scenes of miracles that happened on the road to Compostela and the life of St Anthony Abbot (with the friendly camels). In addition, the Oratorio is currently home to works from the **Museo Comunale di Nocera Umbra**, which was closed by the earthquake. At No.3, the portico belonged to **Monte Frumentario**, which was built in the 13th-century as a hospital, one of the first in Italy, and was later converted into a granary. Next to it, a 16th-century **fountain** still bears the warning that the penalty for washing clothes here is one *scudo* and confiscation of laundry. Via San Francesco then passes through an archway from the city's Roman walls and continues as the Via del Arco del Seminario, named for the former missionary college on the left. Further up is the 19th-century **Teatro Comunale Metastasio**, now used as a cinema.

Near here, at Via Portica 1, is the **Museo e Foro Romano** (*t 075 813053; open daily 16 Mar–15 Oct 10.30–1 and 3–7; 16 Oct–15 Mar 10–1 and 2–7; adm*), located in the crypt of the now-vanished church of San Niccolò (1097); it has a small collection of urns, statues and bits of Roman frescoes. The collection was founded in 1793 by the local Accademia Properziano del Subasio and hasn't changed much since. A passage leads from the museum into the ancient **Roman forum** (or the sacred area of *Asisium*), excavated in the 19th century, directly under the modern Piazza del Comune. Here you can see bases of statues, a platform that may have been an altar, an inscription to the Dioscuri, steps to the temple of Minerva and the remains of a fountain.

Piazza del Comune

The long Piazza del Comune, the medieval centre of Assisi, is embellished with 13th-century buildings of the old *comune*: the lofty **Torre del Popolo** and the **Palazzo del Capitano del Popolo**, the **Palazzo del Podestà** (now the **Palazzo del Comune**) and a genuine Roman **Temple of Minerva** (*t 075 812268; open daily 7–7*) from around the 1st century BC, with Corinthian columns and travertine steps. When Goethe came to Assisi it was to see this – and nothing else. It has the best-surviving Roman temple front on the Italian peninsula, as good as any ruin in Rome for helping your imagination conjure up the classical world. But only the pronaos and façade remain; inside is some eccentric Baroque belonging to the church of Santa Maria della Minerva.

To the left of the palazzo, the **Chiesa Nuova** (*t 075 812339; open daily summer 6.30–12 and 2.30–5; winter 6.30–12 and 2.30–6*) was built in 1615 by Philip III of Spain on property owned by St Francis's father. In an adjacent alley, the **Oratorio di San Francesco Piccolino** is believed to mark the saint's birthplace.

Upper Assisi: the Cathedral, the Castle and Around

Most visitors labour under the impression that the Basilica of St Francis is Assisi's cathedral and never find their way up Via di San Rufino from Piazza del Comune to the real **Cattedrale di San Rufino** (*t 075 812283; open daily Sept–July 7–1 and 2.30–6; Aug 7–6*). Set over a piazza (another candidate for the Roman forum), this has a huge campanile and the finest Romanesque façade in Umbria (*restored since the earthquake*), designed by Giovanni da Gubbio in 1140 and adorned with fine rose windows and the robust medieval carvings of animals and saints that Goethe so disdained. In the central lunette, God the Father sits enthroned in the circle with San Rufino on the right and Mary, nursing the infant Christ, on the left. The three monumental figures in the rectangular niche above appear literally to hold up the church.

Inside the cathedral is the porphyry font where both Saint Francis and Saint Clare were baptized, as well as Emperor Frederick II, who was born nearby in Jesi, in the Marches. It is an amazing coincidence that these two major protagonists of the 13th century should have been baptized in the same place: the holy water must have had a special essence in it. Both Francis and Frederick were profoundly influenced by the East and were among the first poets to write in vernacular Italian, rather than Latin.

San Rufino's interior was restored in the 16th century, when the beautiful carved wooden choir was added. Off the right nave, there's a small **Museo Capitolare** (*t* 075 812712; open daily 16 Mar–15 Nov 10–1 and 3–6, 16 Nov–15 Mar 10–1 and 2.30–5.30; adm), with Romanesque capitals, codices, frescoes, paintings by Matteo da Gualdo and a beautiful triptych by L'Alunno (1470). You can explore the ancient **crypt** (*same hours as Museo Capitolare, above*), dating from an earlier, 11th-century church, with a few frescoes and a 3rd-century Roman sarcophagus decorated with reliefs of the myth of Endymion, where St Rufino was buried. Don't miss the barrel-vaulted Roman cistern under the campanile, with an inscription in the Umbrian dialect. The Umbrii worshipped springs, and this is believed to have been a sacred fountain. The inscription names the *marones*, or officials who were in charge of building projects, not unlike the Roman *aediles*.

From the cathedral, it's a bracing walk up to the **Rocca Maggiore** (*t* 075 815292; open daily 10–sunset, Aug 9–sunset; adm), Assisi's well-preserved castle, built in 1174 and used by Conrad von Luetzen (who cared for the little orphan Emperor Frederick II). It was then destroyed and rebuilt on several occasions, once by Cardinal Albornoz. The Rocca offers excellent views of Assisi, the Valle Umbra, a second, inaccessible fortress built by Albornoz called the Rocciciola, and the surrounding countryside.

East of the cathedral, you can visit more of Roman Asisium – the **theatre** in Via del Torrione, by the cathedral, and the remains of the **amphitheatre**, off Piazza Matteotti and Via Villamena. The **Porta Perlici** near the amphitheatre dates from 1199 and there are some well-preserved 13th-century houses on the Via del Comune Vecchio. The **Giardino Pubblico**, with its pavilions and goldfish ponds, is a pretty park, a fine place to have a picnic. Asisium had up-to-date plumbing; you might be able to pick out the Roman drain between the amphitheatre and the Giardino Pubblico, built to carry off water after the amphitheatre was flooded for mock sea battles.

Basilica di Santa Chiara

t 075 812282; open daily 6.30–12 and 2–6, summer until 7.

Born in 1194, Chiara Offreduccio was 17 when she ran away from her wealthy, noble family to become a disciple of St Francis at the Porziuncola. By 1215, she was the abbess of a Franciscan Second Order, the Poor Clares or Clarisse, based on the primitive rule of St Francis. Whatever the later church mythology, rumours were never lacking that there was more to her relationship with Francis than practical piety. Gentle and humble, she once had a vision of a Christmas service in the Basilica of St Francis while at San Damiano, over 1km away, a feat that led Pope Pius XII in 1958 to declare her the Patron Saint of Television. (Unfortunately, the plastic, reception-guaranteeing statues of St Clare, with two holes in the back for your TV antenna, are now impossible to find in

Assisi's souvenir shops). Like Francis, she lived on alms and is reputed to have twice saved Assisi from the army of Frederick II. Her rule of poverty was only confirmed by Pope Innocent IV while she lay on her deathbed, two days before she died in 1253. She was canonized two years later but, as in the case of Francis, her desire for her followers to live in absolute poverty was denied when Pope Urban IV approved a new Rule for her Order (1264). Still, it did offer something of an alternative for women in an age where many were forced into arranged marriages or convents if there wasn't enough dowry to go around; two Umbrian women who followed in Clare's footsteps were the great 13th-century mystics, the Blessed Angela of Foligno and St Clare of Montefalco.

Her **basilica**, built in 1265 below the Piazza del Comune by way of Corso Mazzini, is a pink and white striped beauty with a lovely rose window, supported by huge flying buttresses added a century later that not only keep it from falling over but create a memorable architectural space below. The church stands on the site of the old church of San Giorgio, where Francis attended school and where his body lay for two years awaiting the completion of his own basilica.

The shadowy **interior** has frescoes in the transepts by followers of Giotto, though they are damaged and hard to see; by the altar are scenes from her life by the late 13th-century Maestro di Santa Chiara. On the right, the **Oratorio del Crocifisso** contains the famous *Crucifix of San Damiano (see* p.468), a 13th-century triptych by Rinaldo di Ranuccio and reliquaries of St Clare, containing some of her garments and golden curls. The adjacent **Cappella del Sacramento** has fine Sienese frescoes; these two chapels were part of San Giorgio. Clare's body, rediscovered in 1850 under the high altar, shrivelled and darkened with age, lies like a never-kissed Snow White in a crystal coffin, down in the neo-Gothic crypt.

Piazza Vescovado and Around

From Santa Chiara, Via Sant'Agnese leads down to Piazza Vescovado and the church of **Santa Maria Maggiore** (*t 075 813085; open Easter–Nov 8–7, Nov–Easter 8–6*) (1163), with a pink and white checked façade. This was Assisi's first cathedral, built on the site of the Roman Temple of Apollo, traces of which are still visible in the 9th-century crypt. Nearby, the reputed **house of Sextus Propertius**, the Roman poet of love (46 BC–AD 14), was discovered, complete with wall paintings (*visitors need permission from the Soprintendenza Archeologica in Perugia*). Running between here and Piazza Unità d'Italia, the Via Fontebella has wrought-iron dragons and a pretty fountain.

Around Assisi

San Damiano

t 075 812273; sanctuary open daily winter 10–12 and 2–4.30 (vespers at 5pm); summer 10–12 and 2–6 (vespers at 7pm).

Many of the key events of Francis's life took place in the countryside around Assisi. **San Damiano** is a short drive or a pleasant 2km walk from Santa Chiara down Via

Borgo Aretino, through the Porta Nuova and down along the signposted route. It was in this simple, asymmetrical Benedictine priory (1030) surrounded by olives and cypress trees that the Crucifix bowed and spoke to Francis in 1205, commanding him to 'rebuild my church'. Francis took the injunction literally, and sold his father's horse and cloth to raise the money – which the priest at San Damiano refused to take, so Francis threw it out of the window and returned to restore the church with his own hands. He brought Clare to San Damiano in 1212, when restoration was complete, and here she and her followers passed their frugal, contemplative lives (forbidden to beg, they nearly starved). Sitting in the garden on one of his visits, Francis composed his superb *Cantico della creature*, the 'Canticle of All Things Created', in 1224.

The church is entered through the Cappella di San Girolamo, with a fine fresco by Tiberio d'Assisi of the *Madonna and Child, with SS. Francis, Clare, Bernardino and Jerome* (1517); the next chapel contains a large wooden crucifix of 1637 by Fra Innocenzo da Palermo. Frescoes in the church record the events that happened here (one shows the saint's father chasing him with a stick when he found out that he had sold his property). The crucifix over the altar is a copy of the original one, now in Santa Chiara. In the convent there's a fresco of the *Crucifixion* by Mezzastris, the room where St Clare died in 1253, and the tiny cloister with frescoes by Eusebio da San Giorgio (1507) of the *Annunciation* and *St Francis Receiving the Stigmata*.

San Damiano owes its preservation to the forethought of an English traveller. In 1870, when the Papal States were united to the new Kingdom of Italy, Lord Ripon, a Catholic convert, bought San Damiano to prevent it becoming state property – the fate of all the state's monastic institutions – and he let it to the friars on the sole condition that they did nothing to restore it. Lord Lothian, who inherited it, returned it to the Franciscans in 1983.

The Eremo delle Carceri and Monte Subasio

Another Franciscan shrine more true to the spirit of the saint than the great art-filled basilicas is the peaceful **Eremo delle Carceri** (*t* 075 812301; open daily Easter–Nov 6.30am–7.15pm, Nov–Easter 6.30–sunset; guided tours at 9, 11.30, 2.30 and 5.30), located in a beautiful setting on the edge of a ravine, deep in the woods along the road up Monte Subasio, a spectacular walk or drive 4km east of Assisi (leave via the Porta dei Cappuccini). This 'Hermitage of the Prison' was Francis's retreat, where he and his followers strove to live like the first Umbrian saints, walking through the woods and meditating. Bernardino of Siena founded the small convent here in 1426, where a handful of friars still live a traditional Franciscan existence on the alms they receive.

By the little triangular courtyard there are two small chapels to visit, the **Cappella di San Bernardino**, with tiny stained glass windows, and the **Cappella di Santa Maria delle Carceri**, with a fresco of the *Madonna and Child and St Francis* by Tiberio d'Assisi. A steep stair leads down to the **Grotto di San Francesco**, with one of the saint's beds hollowed from the rock, and the very old ilex down in the ravine, where the birds are said to have flocked to hear him preach, as a faded fresco on the cave recounts.

From the Eremo delle Carceri, it's 7.5km up the Collepino road to the distinctive bald summit of **Monte Subasio** (1,289m/4,229ft), now centre of a regional park, with superb views over the high Apennines to the east and a network of walking paths. In the summer, you can continue a further spectacular 10km over the mountains on an unpaved road to the medieval village of **Collepino**, above Spello (*see* p.496).

Santa Maria degli Angeli

The real centre of early Franciscanism was the oratory called the Porziuncola ('the little portion'), where angels were wont to appear, down on the plain near the train station. Francis, in return for the use of the oratory, owed a yearly basket of carp from the River Tescio to the Benedictines, still faithfully paid by the Franciscans. In 1569, a monumental basilica, **Santa Maria degli Angeli** (*t 075 80511; open daily 6.15am–8pm, August 6.30am–8pm and 9–11pm*), designed by Galeazzo Alessi, was begun to shelter the Porziuncola. Only completed in 1684, it is an excellent piece of nostalgic Baroque, though mostly rebuilt after an 1832 earthquake; the grandiose façade was only added in 1927.

Within the austere interior, the Porziuncola stands out, with frescoes touched up in the 19th century. The rugged stone of the original chapel can be seen inside (it may be as old as the 6th century), along with some darkened 1393 frescoes of St Francis's life by Ilario da Viterbo, this artist's only known work. Remains of the original Franciscan monastery have been partially excavated under the high altar; here St Clare took her vows of poverty as the spiritual daughter of Francis. St Francis died 'naked on the bare earth' in the convent's infirmary, now the **Cappella del Transito**, with some unusual frescoes by the Umbrian painter Lo Spagna, along with a statue of St Francis by Andrea della Robbia. The garden contains the roses that Francis is said to have thrown himself upon while wrestling with severe temptation, staining their leaves red with blood, only to find that they lost their thorns on contact with his body. Still thornless today, they bloom every May. Francis's cell has been covered with the frescoed Cappella del Roseto; there's also an old pharmacy and a **museum** (*t 075 805 1430; open April–Oct daily 9–12 and 3–6; closed Nov–Mar*) which has a portrait of St Francis by an unknown 13th-century master, another attributed to Cimabue, and a Crucifix (1236) by Giunta Pisano; there's also a **Museo Etnografico Universale** (*open Mon–Fri 9–12 and 3–6, Sat 9–12*) in Via de Gasperi, with items relating to Franciscan missionary work.

West of Assisi

Bastia Umbria and Around

APM buses from Assisi descend to **Bastia Umbria**, with several hotels that may be handy when Assisi is full. A prosperous industrial centre, Bastia began as an island, the *Insula Romana*, before the valley was drained. Once surrounded by walls, it was a hot potato contested by Perugia and Assisi. Its unattractive environs fend off most

Where to Stay and Eat

Bettona ✉ 06084

Relais La Corte Di Bettona, Via Caterina 2, t 075 987114, f 075 986 9130, *www. relaisbettona.com* (*very expensive*). A brand-new hotel, adding a totally unexpected corner of contemporary style to sleepy Bettona. Situated in an old stone building which has been in turn a hospital, an *oratorio* and an oil press, the 19 rooms are beautifully furnished in simple, good taste. There is a good restaurant, **Taverna Del Giullare** (*moderate*), serving Umbrian dishes with the odd twist.

visitors, but the *centro storico* has a pretty 14th-century church with a triptych by L'Alunno and frescoes by Tiberio d'Assisi and students of Bartolomeo Caporali.

North of Bastia and the village of **Petrignano** (famous for its animated *presepio* at Christmas), the valley of the Chiascio is guarded by the splendidly sited **Rocca Sant'Angelo**; nearby, the **Convento di Santa Maria della Rocchicciola** has frescoes by Bartolomeo Caporali and Lo Spagna, and a crucifix by Matteo da Gualdo. Ring the bell next to the church and the sisters will let you in.

Bettona

Southwest of Assisi, **Bettona** is a compact, nearly elliptical hill town wrapped in olive groves. It was big enough to have a long history as *Vettona*, an Etruscan city – it is the only Umbrian town east of the Tiber to have Etruscan origins – and later as a Roman *municipium*. At the northern end of the walls, the huge golden stones of the original Etruscan fortifications (4th century BC) are visible, and 1km west there's a simple, barrel-vaulted **Ipogeo Etrusco** (*collect the key from the Vigili Urbani at the Municipio in Piazza Cavour*) from the 2nd century BC, with funerary urns *in situ*.

Up in Bettona itself, central Piazza Cavour has a fountain and the 14th-century **Palazzo del Podestà**. Within this and an adjoining palazzo is the **Pinacoteca Comunale** (*t 075 987306; open Nov–Feb Tues–Sun 10.30–1 and 2.30–5; Mar–May and Sept–Oct daily 10.30–1 and 2–6; June–July daily 10.30–1 and 3–7; Aug daily 10.30–1 and 3–7; adm*) with two minor paintings by Perugino, detached frescoes by Fiorenzo di Lorenzo and Tiberio d'Assisi, Dono Doni (*Adoration of the Shepherds* with a predella on the *Life of San Crispolto*, the first Bishop of Bettona), ceramics from Deruta and wooden chests. In 1987, the most important works were stolen and found their way to Jamaica where they were recovered; they came back to Bettona in 1990. A small archaeological museum containing local finds (Etruscan onwards) has been planned for the same building, but there's no sign of it yet. At the museum, ask to visit the **Oratorio di Sant'Andrea** in the same piazza, decorated with a recently discovered fresco of the *Passion* by Giotto's school; opposite, the church of **Santa Maria Maggiore** has a gonfalon by Perugino and works by L'Alunno (*currently in museum while church is being restored; call t 075 987306 for information*).

Northern Umbria

17

Northern Umbria

To Ravenna

To Fano

Cagli

Pergola

THE MARCHES

10 km
5 miles

N

1 S. Giustino

Pitigliano

M. Petrano

Eremo di Fonte Avellana ✝

Arcevia

Fraccano

Citerna

Monterchi

Belvedere

Terme di Fontecchio

Badia di Sitria ✝

Sassoferrato

Genga

To Ancona

Citta di Castello

Pietralunga

Scheggia

3 M. Cucco

Monte Sta. Maria Tiberina

Garavelle

S. Ubaldo ✝

2 Gubbio

Costacciaro

Fabriano

p.580

Morra

R. Nestore

Montone

UMBRIA

Sigillo

Fossato di Vico

Esanatoglia

Civitella Ranieri

Umbertide

Badia S. Salvatore

Monte Corona

Abba. di Vallingegno ✝

S. Pellegrino

Valsorda

Serra Santa
Gualdo Tadino

Fiuminata

Preggio

Antognola

Tuoro sul Trasimeno

To Arezzo

Passignano s. Trasimeno

Lago Trasimeno

Montelabate

Perugia

Valfabbrica

Nocera Umbria
Bagnara

M. Pennino

p.394

pp.422–3

Assisi

To Foligno

p.492

SWITZ. AUSTRIA HUNGARY

SLOVENIA

CROATIA

BOSNIA-HERZ.

YUGOSLAVIA

Corsica

ITALY

Sardinia

Sicily

TUNISIA

Highlights

1 San Giustino: Renaissance gardens of the Castello Bufalini
2 Gubbio: the 'race of the candles'
3 Parco Naturale del Monte Cucco: mountain meadows and beech forests

Route SS3bis and Umbria's private railway, the FCU, follow the Upper Tiber Valley into a green landscape of tobacco farms, olive groves and rolling hills, enclosed by large stretches of forest and mountains – some of the most underpopulated countryside in Italy. To the west near Tuscany, arty Città di Castello is full of surprises, while to the east is stern, grey Gubbio, a drop of pure Umbrian essence up in the rugged mountains. In between are frescoes by Signorelli at Morra, a garden maze at Castello Bufalini in San Giustino, and beautiful hill towns such as Monte Santa Maria Tiberina, Citerna and Montone. The mountains along the border of the Marches form one of Umbria's beautiful natural parks, although the main towns here, Gualdo Tadino and Nocera Umbra, were the worst hit by the 1997 earthquake.

Umbertide and Around

Approaching Umbertide from Perugia, the SS3bis is fairly straight and fairly dull, but there are a couple of possible detours into the villages between it and the road to Gubbio. The most important town is **Montelabate**, where the large church of Santa Maria (1325) has an 11th-century crypt and some good frescoes, a *Madonna and Saints* by Bartolomeo Caporali and a *Crucifixion* by Fiorenzo di Lorenzo. It also has a pretty cloister from an earlier church. You might also stop in **Civitella Benazzone**, where the medieval Abbazia Celestina has been restored, and where the parish church has paintings by Benedetto Bonfigli and Domenico Alfani.

Midway between Perugia and Città di Castello, **Umbertide** (pop. 14,000) is on the Tiber, originally a trading post for the Etruscans and Umbrians. Known as *Pitulum* by the Romans, then Fratta until 1863, it changed its name in its enthusiasm for the new Kingdom of Italy, in honour of Umberto, son of Vittorio Emanuele II. Today it is sprawling and industrial, with a small *centro storico* somehow survived the allied bombs that destroyed the rest of town; Piazza 25 Aprile commemorates that day.

The main landmark, the **Rocca**, a castle with fat round crenellated towers, was built by the Perugians in the 1300s and is now the **Centro per L'Arte Contemporanea** (*open winter Tues–Sun 10.30–12.30 and 4–7; summer Tues–Sun 10.30–12.30 and 4.30–7.30; adm*), with temporary exhibitions. There are three churches in Piazza San Francesco, through the main square and over the train tracks, outside the original city walls. **Santa Croce** is now a small museum (*t 075 941 7099; open April–Sept Fri–Sun 10.30–1 and 3.30–6; Oct–Mar Sat–Sun 10.30–1 and 3–5.30; adm*), containing an excellent *Deposition* (1515) by Luca Signorelli, as well as Niccolò Pomarancio's *Madonna and Child and Angels* (1577). Its neighbour, **San Francesco**, has good, if damaged 17th-century frescoes. And, like so many Umbrian towns, Umbertide has a geometrical Renaissance temple dedicated to Mary outside the walls, the octagonal **Santa Maria della Reggia**, begun in 1559.

Tourist Information

Umbertide: Piazza Caditi del Lavoro 23, t 075 941 7099, in the car park below the Rocca.
Montone: Pro Loco, Via San Francesco 1, t 075 930 6427, f 075 930 7121

Where to Stay and Eat

Umbertide ✉ 06019

There are a pair of comfortable choices along the SS. Tiberina 3bis:

★★★Rio, t 075 941 5033, f 075 941 7029, *info@hotelrio.org, www.hotelrio.org* (*moderate*). Comfortable rooms in a modern hotel with classy restaurant and landscaped grounds.

★★Moderno, t/f 075 941 3759 (*moderate*). Slightly cheaper option.

In the centre of Umbertide:

★★Capponi, Piazza 25 Aprile 19, t 075 941 2662, f 075 941 3803, *www.hotelcapponi.com* (*inexpensive*). A simple hotel with an equally simple restaurant (t 075 941 3256, *closed Sun*), with good-quality dishes at very reasonable prices.

Montone ✉ 06060

Ristorante Erba Luna, Piazza Fortebraccio 5/6, t 075 930 6405 (*moderate*). A brand-new restaurant on Montone's main square, with views out over the valley. Serves a sophisticated version of traditional Umbrian cuisine. *Closed Tues.*

Just east of Umbertide, the magnificent 15th-century castle **Civitella Ranieri** lords it high over a wooded park; it is privately owned but occasionally open in the summer. At the foot of **Monte Corona** (693m/2,273ft), 3km south of town, the **Badia di San Salvatore** was founded by the wandering hermit saint Romualdo in 1008 for his Camaldolesian monks. Remodelled in the 18th century, and partly un-remodelled recently, it has an unusual campanile that doubled as a defensive tower. The bare stone interior has traces of 14th-century frescoes and the nave is supported by an interesting hotchpotch of capitals and columns. The 8th-century stone *ciborium* was brought here from another church. The scenery from here towards Lake Trasimeno is lovely, especially around the medieval village of **Preggio**.

Montone

Northeast of Umbertide is fortified hilltop **Montone**. Founded in the 9th century, its strategic position high over the Tiber Valley meant it was fought over by Perugia, Città di Castello and Gubbio. It's worth trudging up to the top of the village, where one of the towers of the citadel makes a fantastic belvedere over the region.

Montone's Gothic church of **San Francesco** (1305) and its convent have recently been arranged as a **Museo Comunale** (*t 075 930 6535; open April–Sept Fri–Sun 10.30–1 and 3.30–6; Oct–May Sat and Sun 10.30–1 and 3–5.30*). The church has fine frescoes, including a *St Anthony Abbot* by Bartolomeo Caporali and a damaged cycle on the *Life of St Francis*. Among the paintings in the convent there's Caporali's *Madonna del Soccorso*, with a charming scene of Montone, and paintings by local 16th-century artist Vittorio Cirelli, who let his imagination run wild in a fantastical *Immaculate Conception*, and a remarkable life-sized wooden sculptural group of the *Deposition of the Cross* from the 1200s. On the ground floor, the **Museo Etnografico** has a fascinating display of artefacts from East Africa, collected by a local resident.

Further up the valley, the *condottiere* Braccio Fortebraccio's castle, the magnificent **Rocca d'Aries**, has recently been restored. Further up the narrow road to the northeast is **Pietralunga**, a remote medieval village and a good base for exploring the mountains and forests, and for communing with the boars, foxes and other wildlife.

Morra

Tobacco is king west of the Tiber, where **Morra**, on the banks of the torrential Nestore, is the one village in particular to aim for. The story goes that Luca Signorelli, a native of nearby Cortona, happened to be passing through in 1508 when he fell in love with a pretty girl and decided to stay awhile. He picked up the commission to fresco the 15th-century **Oratorio di San Crescentino**, located on a hill outside Morra (*open daily 9–2.30 and 3–6.30; the custodian, who lives in the modern house next door, will let you in*). Signorelli worked with his assistants, but the master's hand is easily identifiable in the *Flagellation*, *Crucifixion* and *Christ between Two Angels* (look out for the trademark Signorelli bottoms). Unfortunately, most of the other frescoes aren't as well-preserved (they were restored in the 1970s) but they are beautiful; don't miss the older Gothic frescoes in the 13th-century sacristy.

Città di Castello

Set on a plateau overlooking the Tiber Valley, **Città di Castello** (pop. 38,000) is the most important city in northern Umbria. It started as *Tifernum*, and prospered under the early Roman Empire, when as *Tifernum Tiberinum* it controlled much of the trade in the upper Tiber Valley. Totila and his Goths knocked it flat, before the early Christian bishops rebuilt it into a fortress town and called it *Castrum Felicitatis* (Happy Castle). In the 1400s and 1500s, under the enlightened tyranny of the Vitelli family, the city hired some of the best Renaissance artists (Raphael among them). In the 20th century, it was the birthplace of one of Italy's best-known postwar artists, Alberto Burri, who has left the city an impressive collection of his works. Although bombed in war, Città di Castello has recovered well, and today, the Tifernati make their living from textiles, printing and tobacco.

Getting There and Around

Città di Castello has a station on the FCU Sansepolcro–Terni **train** or take the FS train to Arezzo and then the bus. There are also daily **buses** to Urbino, Gubbio and Perugia.

Parking within the city walls can be a nightmare; there are some car parks outside the walls – the free one to the north on Viale Nazario Sauro (Parcheggio Enrico Ferri) is close to an escalator taking you up into the town.

Tourist Information

Città di Castello: Via Sant'Antonio 1, **t** 075 855 4817, **f** 075 855 2100, *www. umbria2000.it*.
Piazza Matteotti, **t** 075 855 4922.

Entrance to any museum gets you a discount on others – keep your ticket.

Market Days

Food and general market, Piazza Gabriotti. *Thurs and Sat*.
Flea market, Piazza Matteotti and surrounding streets. Huge 'retro' market. *Third Sun each month*.

Where to Stay and Eat

Città di Castello ✉ 06012
★★★★**Tiferno**, Piazza R. Sanzio 13, **t** 075 855 0331, **f** 075 852 1196, *www.hoteltiferno.it* (*expensive*). The best place in the centre; a 17th-century palace with good comfortable rooms, a garage, and one of the best restaurants, with dishes like ravioli with shrimp in orange sauce or pigeon with grapes.
★★★**Hotel delle Terme**, at Fontecchio, **t** 075 852 0614, **f** 075 855 7236, *www.termedi fontecchio.it* (*moderate*). A large, pleasant hotel. Take thermal treatments or just make do with the fine open-air pool.

There are other cheaper choices in the town:
★★**Europa**, Via V.E. Orlando 2, **t** 075 855 0551, **f** 075 852 0765, *www.citta.it* (*inexpensive*).
★★**Umbria**, Via dei Galanti, **t** 075 855 4925, **f** 075 852 0911, *www.hotelumbria.net* (*inexpensive*).

Città di Castello is one place in Umbria where you can find good bread, especially the *pane nociato* with walnuts.

Il Bersaglio, Via V.E. Orlando 14, **t** 075 855 5534 (*moderate*). Just outside the city walls, it offers pasta, and well-prepared meat and game, as well as truffles and mushrooms; try the local Colli Altotiberini wines. *Closed Wed*.
Amici Miei, Via del Monte 2, **t** 075 855 9904 (*cheap*). Home cooking using seasonal ingredients: *strangozzi* with goose sauce, calves' kidneys, roast lamb and duck. *Closed Wed and two wks Nov*.
Ristorante da Meo, at Fraccano, on the SS257, 10km east of Città di Castello, **t** 075 855 3870 (*cheap*). A small restaurant of the kind fast disappearing from Italy: choose from a limited but excellent menu of the day – usually a pasta dish followed by meat grilled over the fire in front of you – and be pleasantly surprised by the bill. *Closed Wed*.

The Duomo and its Museum

Within its Renaissance walls, Città di Castello is a neat rectangle, still roughly following the street plan of ancient *Tifernum*. The **Duomo**, with exactly one half of a harmonious Baroque façade, was rebuilt in 580. After several other rebuildings, much of what you see comes from the 1400s, although parts of the original Romanesque cathedral remain – especially the 11th-century round campanile, inspired by the ancient towers of Ravenna (and just as tilted). Two handsome Gothic reliefs decorate the north portal. Inside, the single nave has a panelled wooden ceiling: the best painting is a mystical, dramatic altarpiece of the *Transfiguration* in the fourth chapel by the Florentine mannerist Rosso Fiorentino, who took refuge here when he fled the sack of Rome in 1527. Much of the rest of the decoration is by local artists: one, the 17th-century Giovanni Battista Pacetti (better known as Lo Sguazzino or 'Splashy') painted a view of his hometown in the third chapel. The lower church was the ancient crypt and contains the bodies of Città's patrons, SS. Florido and Amanzio.

The adjacent and excellent **Museo del Duomo**'s (*t 075 855 4705; open April–Sept Tues–Sun 10.30–1 and 3–6; Oct–Mar Tues–Sun 10.30–1 and 3–7.30; adm*) rarest prize is the **Treasure of Canoscio** – beautiful 6th-century liturgical silver, probably hidden by the priest when Totila and the Goths came and found again 1,400 years later in 1932. The enamelled and gilded 12th-century altar frontal, showing Christ, the Evangelists and scenes from the Life of Christ, is said to have been donated by Pope Celestine II. There's a beautifully worked 14th-century crozier and 15th-century paintings, including a *Madonna* by a follower of Signorelli; a rich collection of liturgical items, two angels attributed to Giulio Romano and a small *Madonna and Child and St John the Baptist* by Pinturicchio.

Near the Duomo

In Piazza Gabriotti by the Duomo is the trecento **Palazzo dei Priori** (or Comunale) designed by Angelo da Orvieto, a handsome but unfinished sandstone building. The **Torre Civica** (*open Tues–Sun 10–12.30 and 3–6.30; adm*) from the same century once held the city's medieval prisons and has magnificent views over the valley.

From a 14th-century **loggia**, Corso Cavour leads past the covered market, with an 18th-century print shop on top and a pretty 1890s Art Nouveau bank. Civic life was concentrated in Piazza Matteotti, overlooked by a very austere **Palazzo del Podestà** with double clocks on the façade, also by Angelo da Orvieto. In Piazza Costa, cloth is woven on traditional looms at the **Laboratorio e Collezione Tela Umbra** (*t 875 855 4337; open Tues–Sat 10–12 and 3.30–5.30, Sun and hols 10.30–1 and 3–5.30; adm*), founded in 1908 by Baron Leopoldo Franchetti. The adjacent museum tells the history of weaving.

The Collezioni Burri

t 075 855 4649; open Tues–Sat 9–12.30 and 2.30–6,
Sun 10.30–12.30 and 3–6; adm.

Alberto Burri (1915–95) was a doctor by profession and ended up a prisoner of war in Texas in 1943, where he turned to art to express the carnage he had witnessed, using whatever he could find. On his return to Italy, he continued to explore the evocative power of discarded materials and junk, most famously his sacking soaked in red paint that resembled giant bandages and his carefully composed pieces of twisted metal and charred wood. Burri was one of the great precursors of Abstract Expression and junk art in the USA, and of Italian Arte Povera; in later years, he went on to explore colour and other materials. The **Collezione Burri,** in the quattrocento Palazzo Albizzini at the top of Via Mazzini displays numerous works from 1943 to 1983. His large-scale works are exhibited in the tobacco-drying shed he used as a studio, the **Seccatoi Tabacchi** (*same hours*), south of town in Via Francesco Pierucci.

The North End of Town

The ruling Vitelli family simply could not have enough palaces; the Collezioni Burri is near their largest spread, the elegant **Palazzo Vitelli a Porta Sant'Egidio** built in 1540 by Giorgio Vasari. It has a beautiful façade facing a huge garden, and an interior lavishly frescoed by Cristoforo Gherardi (Il Doceno) and Prospero Fontana; it's now owned by a bank and used for concerts. Also along Via Albizzini is the 13th-century church of **San Francesco** with an 18th-century interior. Vasari designed the elaborate Cappella Vitelli and painted the altarpiece, although both are outdone by the fancy wrought-iron grille made by a local craftsman, Pietro di Ercolano. There's a majolica of *St Francis receiving the Stigmata* by the Della Robbia workshop, and a German-made wooden polychrome *Pietà* from the 1400s. The *Betrothal of the Virgin* (1504), Raphael's early masterpiece, was painted for this church, but Napoleon put it in the Brera, which won't give it back; Città di Castello grudgingly shows a copy. In the adjacent piazza is an 1860 monument celebrating the end of the Papal States.

Via San Bartolomeo heads north, passing a smaller Palazzo Vitelli on the way to the **Museo Civico** (*t 075 855 5687; open Mon–Tues 9–1 and 3–7, Wed–Sat 9–1*) and the Biblioteca Comunale. This contains fossils from the Pleistocene era, when the Tiber was a lake, and a small archaeological collection. In this part of town, around Via XI Settembre, there are three convents of closed orders of the Clarisse; at No.21, the nuns at **Santa Veronica** will show on request their pretty cloister and a small museum dedicated to their order and to St Veronica Giuliani (d. 1727), who lived here for 50 years in a state of almost continuous mystical experience and vision. Nearby is the non-conventual church of **Santa Maria delle Grazie,** which has a fresco of the *Transition of the Virgin* by Ottavino Nelli and a precious and highly venerated painting of the *Madonna della Grazie*, by Giovanni di Piemonte, a collaborator of Piero della Francesca; unfortunately, it's kept locked up and shown only twice a year, on 2 February and 26 August.

The Pinacoteca Comunale

From behind the Duomo, take Via di Modello/Via C. Battisti south to Via della Canoniera 22; t 075 852 0656; open April–Oct Tues–Sun 10–1 and 2.30–6.30; Nov–Mar Tues–Sun 10–12.30 and 3–5.30; adm.

This contains Città di Castello's only surviving Raphael, a half-ruined, processional standard of 1503, but there are plenty of other attractions, beginning with the building itself. The Palazzo Vitelli alla Cannoniera (one of the five Vitelli *palazzi* in town) was built in the 1520s by Antonio da Sangallo the Younger and Pier Francesco da Viterbo, decorated with *sgraffito* by Giorgio Vasari – a very nice façade, facing the inner gardens. The 16th-century frescoes inside are the work of Cola dell'Amatrice (on the stairs, celebrating the glory of the Vitelli family) and Doceno.

The star of the early paintings is a beautiful and recently restored 14th-century *Maestà* by an anonymous painter known as the Master of Città di Castello. Nearby hangs a fine *Madonna and Child* by Spinello Aretino. The next room has another *Madonna* by the Sienese Andrea di Bartolo, as well as some early choir stalls, while next there's a residual Gothic Venetian view of the same subject by Antonio Vivarini. Lorenzo Ghiberti, master of Florence's famous baptistry doors, puts in a rare guest appearance with an equally Gothic-style golden reliquary of St Andrew (1420). The other highlight in this room is a Florentine *Madonna and Two Angels* by Neri di Bicci. In the next room, is a *Coronation of the Virgin* from the workshop of Domenico Ghirlandaio; the *Head of Christ* is usually attributed to Giusto di Gand, a Flemish painter who worked in Urbino.

The next room has the Raphael standard, followed by altarpieces by a local boy, Francesco Tifernate and five marquetry sacristy cupboards. Many of these rooms contain frescoes by Doceno and reproductions of other works he produced during his stay in Città di Castello. The most powerful painting in the whole museum is a *San Sebastiano* by Luca Signorelli and his workshop – a fascinating work with fantasy Roman ruins and a truly surreal treatment of space. There's also a good comical kitsch piece, an anonymous *Quo Vadis?*, a strange Virgin by an unknown follower of Pontormo, and a room of works by Raffaellino del Colle.

The sculpture collection includes some early medieval woodcarving, or mixtures of painting and wooden sculpture, especially the altarpiece of the *Crucifixion with the Virgin Mary and the Magdalene*, the sun and moon – the wooden crucifix has now disappeared, but the work is strangely suggestive without it. Here, too, is a fine 14th-century Sienese relief on the Baptism of Christ and works by Della Robbia.

San Domenico

The first street to the left of the museum, Largo Mons Muzi, leads up to the enormous preaching church of **San Domenico**, finished in 1424. The façade was never finished but it has a handsome door on the left side; the gloomy interior has good 15th-century frescoes and choir stalls. Signorelli's *San Sebastiano* used to hang in the Renaissance chapels by the altar, along with Raphael's *Crucifixion*, which is now in the National Gallery in London and replaced here by a copy.

Around Città di Castello

Just 2km south of Città di Castello, in the Villa Cappelletti at **Garavelle**, the **Centro Tradizioni Popolari** (*t 075 855 2119; open winter Tues–Sun 9.30–12.30 and 2.30–5.30;*

summer Tues–Sun 8.30–12.30 and 3–7; adm) is a fascinating folk museum in an Umbrian farmhouse, furnished as it would have been a century ago, complete with blacksmith's forge, oil press, wine cellars and farm instruments.

Just to the east, Città di Castello has its own spa, the **Terme di Fontecchio**, where Pliny the Younger used to come to take the alkaline sulphurous waters. The current spa dates from the 19th century, and is open from March to December. There's some fine scenery along the SS257, especially 5km east of Città di Castello at the hill of **Belvedere**, site of the **Santuario della Madonna del Belvedere**, an octagonal domed Baroque church with a quirky façade and a venerated terracotta *Madonna and Child*.

West of Città di Castello, **Monte Santa Maria Tiberina** is a lovely medieval hill town in a lofty sublime setting. Once inhabited by the Etruscans, in 1355 the emperor Charles IV made this village an independent marquisate for the Del Monte family. A favour to the French earned them the right to call themselves the Bourbon Del Monte, and they ruled their little Ruritania until 1798 when Napoleon, who had no patience for anachronisms, especially with the name Bourbon on them, snatched it away. Today, fewer than 150 souls live here, but you can see what remains of the Del Monte family's medieval castle and some of their tombs in the parish church.

Citerna

If you head west from Città di Castello along the SS221 towards Arezzo, you will come across **Citerna**, a gem of a hill town that has aged like fine wine. Located on the border of Tuscany, peacefully set over the Tiber Valley on a densely wooded hill, Citerna was a Roman town, then rebuilt by the Lombards, fought over by its neighbours and restored after an earthquake in 1917. One unusual feature is the partially vaulted medieval passageway that circles much of the lower part of town. Further up, the church of **San Francesco** (*if locked, ask at Via Garibaldi 27, just down from the church, to be let in*), rebuilt in 1508, is the village's chief repository of art, with a late and rather worn fresco by Luca Signorelli and helpers, the *Madonna and Child, St Francis and St Michael*. The altars are decorated with Della Robbia ceramics that seeped over the Tuscan border, and there are two fine altarpieces by Raffaellino del Colle, the *Christ in Glory* and the *Madonna and St John the Evangelist*, as well as a *Deposition* by Pomarancio. Ask at the friendly bar on the piazza for someone with a key to the nearby **Casa Prosperi**, to see its extraordinary carved 16th-century fireplace. Up past the pretty Piazza Scipioni, the dark 18th-century church of **San Michele Arcangelo** (*key as for Casa Prosperi*) contains more colourful Della Robbia work, a *Crucifixion* by Pomarancio and a bell from a church destroyed in the earthquake, signed and dated 1267. In the last war, Citerna's castle on top of the town was blown up by the Germans, leaving the walls and brick tower, which offer a spectacular view as far as La Verna in Tuscany, where St Francis received the stigmata. A fountain by the walls commemorates the saint, who visited in 1224.

San Giustino

Further up the Tiber Valley, **San Giustino** has the beautiful **Castello Bufalini** (*open July–Sept Sat and Sun only 10.30–1 and 3.30–7.30; call t 075 852 2655 for info*), begun in

s a fortress by the *comune* of Città di Castello, which gave it in 1487 to the
ni family to complete (and pay for) the impressive walls and star-shaped
surrounded it. A century later, when war seemed unlikely, Giulio Bufalini
converted it into an elegant seigneurial villa, on plans by Vasari, complete with a
loggia and courtyard. He also planted one of the most beautiful Italian gardens in
Umbria inside the moat, with a maze and geometric hedges, fountains and
parterres. In 1989, the Bufalini donated the castle to the state; the gardens and the
ground floor of the castle, with rooms of antiques frescoed by the 16th-century
painter Cristofano Gherardi, are gradually being restored.

Gubbio

In a way, **Gubbio** (pop. 33,000) is what Umbria has always wanted to be: stony,
taciturn and mystical, a tough mountain town that fought its own battles until
destiny and the popes caught up with it – also a town of culture, one with its own
school of painters. For a city over 2,500 years old, it still seems like a frontier town, an
elemental place that sticks in the memory: the green mountainside, a rushing
stream, straight rows of rugged grey stone houses. On Gubbio's windy slopes, the
hard-edged brilliance of the Italian Middle Ages is clear and tangible.

Gubbio is also one of the few Italian hill towns that a stick-in-the-mud geologist
might recognize. Everyone has heard of the theory that the dinosaurs became
extinct after a large meteor struck the earth 65 million years ago and raised so much
dust that it blocked out the sun, making it too cool for the reptiles to survive. Some
of the strongest evidence for the theory was discovered just outside Gubbio, in the
Camignano Valley towards Scheggia, where there's a layer of sedimentary rock, dense
with the rare minerals of meteorites. It's thin, but it's chronologically correct and
thick enough to have done the dirty deed.

History

Gubbio was a city of the ancient Umbrii, perhaps even their political and religious
centre. In Roman times, it flourished as *Iguvium*, and, according to legend, was where
Rome exported its lunatics, which has left a lingering influence on the populace today.
Mad or not, the Eugubini, as the natives are known, certainly weren't stupid; when
unsolicited visits by the Goths, Huns and Avars left the place a mess, the survivors
moved their town to a more defensible site on the nearby hillside.

The chronicles paint a picture of medieval Gubbio as a tough, querulous *comune*. In
the 1150s, 12 Umbrian cities under Frederick Barbarossa combined to atttack it; the
city was saved by its bishop, later Sant'Ubaldo, who persuaded the emperor to grant
it its independence. The chroniclers also claimed for Gubbio a population of 50,000 –
probably double the real figure but still quite large for a medieval town. As in every
other city, there was continuous conflict between the *comune* and ambitious nobles.
One of them, Giovanni Gabrielli, became *signore* of the town in 1350, but only four
years later, Cardinal Albornoz and his papal army snatched it away from him. In 1387,

Getting There and Around

There are no trains, but around 10 APM **coaches** a day follow the beautiful SS298 to Perugia (40km/1hr) from the central Piazza Quaranta Martiri where schedules are posted (**t** 800 512141; Fontevegge Station **t** 075 501 0485, Fossaro di Vico Station **t** 075 919230). There are also **buses** to the closest train station, 20km southeast at Fossato di Vico on the FS Foligno–Ancona line to Rome and a line to Città di Castello–Arezzo–Florence.

There is a bus and train information office for all these at Via della Repubblica 13, **t** 075 922 0066. You can purchase bus tickets there.

Tourist Information

Gubbio: Piazza Oderisi 6, **t** 075 922 0693 or **t** 075 922 0790, **f** 075 927 3409, *info@iat. gubbio.pg.it, www.umbria2000.it.*
Post office: Via Cairoli 11, **t** 075 927 3925.

Market Day

Piazza Quaranta Martiri, *Tuesday*.

Shopping

Gubbio's artist craftsmen still turn out some of the most beautiful ceramics in Italy, hand-painted in colourful, original floral designs. Some is too big to fit in your suitcase – majolica lamps and telephone stands, for example – but there are plates in every size for a souvenir. A number of good places cluster Via dei Consoli.
Fabbrica Ranimi, Via dei Consoli. Arguably the most artistic work.
Fabbrica Mastro Giorgio, Via dei Consoli. A good alternative.
No.44, Via dei Consoli. A little further down the street, you will be able to find some less extravagant work at lower prices, including beautiful plaques and plates.

Gubbio also has a longstanding tradition in wrought iron work, perhaps even more difficult to carry home, but worth a look.

Where to Stay

Gubbio ✉ 06024

Gubbio gets pretty packed with tourists looking for the essential Umbria; reservations are essential in July and August.

Luxury–Very Expensive

****Relais Ducale, Via Galeotti, **t** 075 922 0157, **f** 075 922 0159, www.*mencarelligroup.com.* Recently opened in the heart of medieval Gubbio, occupying three historic buildings, linked by a lift. All sumptuously furnished with antiques and mod cons, while a shuttle provides transport to the garage on the edge of town.
****Park Hotel ai Cappuccini, Via Tifernate, **t** 075 9234, **f** 075 922 0323, *www.parkhotel aicappuccini.it*. A beautifully restored, award-winning Franciscan monastery; out of town with a cloister and chapel, pool, sauna and fitness centre.

Expensive

***Villa Montegranelli, 4km away at Loc Monteluiano, **t** 075 922 0185, **f** 075 927 3372, *www.villamontegranellihotel.it*. An 18th-century villa overlooking Gubbio, retaining many original features, such as the *piano nobile* and private chapel. The excellent restaurant serves dishes from Umbria and Puglia; for a real feast, order the *menu degustazione*.
***Bosone, Via XX Settembre 22, **t** 075 922 0688, **f** 075 922 0552, *www.men carelligroup.com*. Situated in a picturesque old palazzo off Piazza Grande. Rooms are comfortable, though not brilliant, and there's a garage.

it fell to Urbino's Dukes of Montefeltro, who ruled it well until their line became extinct in 1508. Gubbio remained part of the Duchy of Urbino until 1624, when it became part of the Papal States.

One famous visitor in 1206–7 was St Francis, who found the city plagued by wolves, one of which was ravaging the countryside and terrorizing the populace. Ignoring the townspeople's pleas and fears for his safety, Francis went out and had a word

Moderate

★★★Beniamino Ubaldi, Via Perugina 74, **t** 075 927 7773, **f** 075 927 6604, *www. rosatihotels.it*. Recently upscaled, in a seminarians' college just outside the walls; and yes, it has a bar (and restaurant, too).

★★★Gattapone, Via G. Ansidei 6, **t** 075 927 2489, **f** 075 927 2417, *www. mencarelligroup.com*. Another pleasant locale in the medieval centre, which has just been given a facelift.

★★★San Marco, Via Perugina 5, **t** 075 922 0234, **f** 075 927 3716, *www.hotelsanmarcogubbio. com*. Modern comforts in a former convent, with a pretty garden terrace. All rooms are en suite and there's parking nearby.

★★Dei Consoli, Via dei Consoli 59, **t** 075 927 3335, *www.urbaniweb.com*. Small and simple near Piazza Grande. It has a good restaurant in a medieval cellar, with tasty *spiedini* (meat on a spit).

Inexpensive

★★Oderisi, Via Mazzatinti 2, **t** 075 922 0662, **f** 075 922 0663, *www.rosatihotels.com*. Good, well-furnished rooms.

★Locanda del Duca, Via Piccardi 1, overlooking the river, **t** 075 927 7753. Simple rooms, some with bath. The restaurant (*closed Wed*), which serves roast duck and lamb, has outdoor tables in a pretty setting.

Ostello dell'Aquilone, Loc Ghigiano, **t** 075 927 1105 or 075 929 1144, **f** 075 922 0197, *aquilone@aquilone.it*. The youth hostel.

Eating Out

Gubbio has no good wines, but there are local herbal poisons like Amaro Iguvium and Liquore Ingeno to top off a meal.

Taverna del Lupo, Via Ansidei 21a, **t** 075 927 4368 (*expensive*). With a name recalling the legend of St Francis, in a medieval setting, this serves excellent, traditional fare such as boar sausage, game in the autumn and *truffle passatelli* (Gubbio is a land of white truffles, which are even more expensive than the black ones from southern Umbria), as well as delicious pasta dishes like lasagne with *prosciutto* and truffles and *fricassea*, a local speciality of mixed meats with cress. *Closed Mon, except in Aug and Sept.*

La Fornace di Mastro Giorgio, Via Mastro Giorgio, **t** 075 922 1836 (*expensive*). Another local classic in the workshop where the master ceramicist once created his famous ruby glaze. Serves some of Umbria's more esoteric specialities. *Closed Tues, Wed lunch and 10–31 Jan.*

Federico da Montefeltro, Via della Repubblica 35, **t** 075 927 3949 (*expensive–moderate*). Family-run, serving memorable mushroom and truffle dishes at outdoor tables in the summer. *Closed Thurs.*

Alla Balestra, Via della Repubblica 41, **t** 075 927 3810 (*moderate–cheap*). Features unusual dishes like *fondutina con tartufo*, homemade pasta, pizza and a good selection of meats. *Closed Tues.*

Funivia, on Monte Ingino, **t** 075 922 1259 (*cheap*). On a clear day, this offers fabulous views as well as delicious pasta with truffles or porcini mushrooms, and tasty *secondi* like grilled lamb. Good desserts and local wines. *Open Mar–Nov and Christmas holidays, closed Wed except in summer.*

San Francesco e Il Lupo, Via Cairoli 24, **t** 075 927 2344 (*cheap*). Local products, porcini mushrooms and truffles, or pizza. *Closed Tues, 10 days in Jan and 10–25 July.*

All'Antica Frantoio, Via Cavour 18, Largo Bargello, **t** 075 922 1780 (*cheap*). In a 13th-century oil mill, serving homemade soups and pasta, grilled meats and wood-oven pizza. *Closed Mon and 15–20 days Jan–Feb.*

with the wolf, brought it to town and made it promise to stop terrorizing Gubbio in exchange for regular meals – an agreement sealed with a shake of the paw. The wolf kept its part of the bargain and is immortalized in a bas relief over the door of a church on Via Mastro Giorgio. A few years ago, in another church, workmen discovered the skeleton of a giant wolf buried under a slab. Recently some of its descendants have been sighted, after a long absence, in the forests of northern Umbria.

Gubbio saw some terrible fighting in the Second World War. In 1943, after the Italians had surrendered, Umbria was occupied by the Germans, who were harried by partisans, based in the mountains above Gubbio. Although most of Umbria fell relatively quickly to the British and Commonwealth forces as they advanced north after the liberation of Rome on 4 June, the fighting was intense and progress slow in the north. Meanwhile, a number of vicious reprisals on innocent villagers took place around Gubbio, while the Germans took positions and pounded the allies; the battle for Gubbio took three weeks, only ending on 25 July.

All of Gubbio's churches are now open, except for San Domenico. The earthquake damage in 1997 was relatively minor compared to the one in 1982, which left some 1,500 people homeless.

Gubbio, From the Bottom Up

Most people approach Gubbio from the west, passing acres of open pastureland – once the centre of Roman *Iguvium*. In the middle stands a large, well-preserved 1st-century AD **Roman theatre** and **antiquarium** (*t 075 922 0992, f 075 922 3659; open April–Sept 8.30–7.30; Oct–Mar 8.30–sunset*), now used for summer performances of classical Greek and Roman drama and Shakespeare. From here, you get the best view of Gubbio: stone houses climb the slope in neat parallel rows, and the tall Palazzo dei Consoli on its massive platform dominates the centre.

Gubbio proper is entered via the big green **Piazza Quaranta Martiri**, named for the 40 citizens gunned down on this spot by the Nazis in reprisals for partisan activities. On the west end of the square, behind its unfinished façade, the mid 13th-century church of **San Francesco** (*t 075 927 3460, call in advance to visit*), with an octagonal campanile and a distinctive Gothic design with a triple apse, is the work of the Perugian architect Fra Bevignate. Inside are some good frescoes, especially the damaged series on the *Life of the Virgin* in the left apse, painted in 1408–13 and one of the greatest works by Gubbio's greatest painter, the International Gothic master Ottaviano Nelli. There is also a copy of Daniele da Volterra's *Deposition* on the third altar; to the right of the altar are 14th-century frescoes on the *Life of St Francis*. The oldest frescoes from the 1200s are high up in the main apse. In the recently restored cloister are bits of polychrome Roman mosaics found in Gubbio and more frescoes.

On the other side of the piazza is the **Loggia dei Tiratoio** (Weaver's Loggia), an arcade of 1603 under which newly woven textiles could be stretched to shrink evenly – one of the few such loggias to survive. The nearby 14th-century church, **Santa Maria dei Laici** (*usually locked*), has an *Annunciation*, the last painting of Baroque master Federico Barocci.

Piazza Grande and the Palazzo dei Consoli

From Piazza dei Quaranta Martiri, Via Piccardi ascends past picturesque medieval lanes on the banks of the Camignano, a rushing torrent in the spring and winter. Many of the houses and modest *palazzi* date back to the 13th century, here and there adorned with carved doors or windows, or 'Death's doors' as in Perugia. At the top is the magnificent **Piazza Grande** (or Piazza della Signoria), occupying a ledge of the hill, a balcony hovering over a steep drop and a stunning view of the town below.

The king of the piazza is the beautiful, enormous **Palazzo dei Consoli**, one of the most remarkable public buildings in Italy, begun in 1332 by Gubbio's master architect Gattapone, with a bit of help from Angelo da Orvieto (*consolo*, a word derived from the Roman *consul*, was a common title for an officer of a free medieval *comune*). Supported on the hill by a remarkable substructure of arches, the palazzo is graced with an elegant loggia, a slender campanile, square Guelph crenellations and asymmetrically arranged windows and arches. It faces the **Palazzo Pretorio** (now the *municipio*) designed by the same Gattapone to make the piazza a set piece.

The Palazzo dei Consoli, now the **Museo Civico** (*t 075 927 4298, f 075 923 7530, www.comune.gubbio.pg.it; open April–Sept daily 10–1 and 3–6; Oct–Mar daily 10–1 and 2–5; closed 13–15 May, 25 Dec and 1 Jan; adm*), boasts treasures from the 16th century BC to the 19th century AD. On the first floor, the enormous barrel-vaulted Sala dell'Arengo, where assemblies were held, is a cluttered, fascinating place that resembles an indoor flea market, with archaeological odds and ends, tombstones, sarcophagi and crossbows deposited every which way. There is a Roman inscription – Governor Gnaeus Satirus Rufus bragging how much he spent to embellish the town – and a collection of seals and coins from the days when Gubbio minted its own. One unique treasure, the bronze **Eugubine Tablets**, have far and away the most important inscriptions ever found in the Umbrian language and were discovered in the 15th century near the Roman theatre. Partly written in the Etruscan alphabet, and partly in the Latin, these codes of religious observances and rituals for Gubbio's priests are also a rare survival of a religious how-to textbook, with details on sacrifices (including human enemies) and how to read the future in a liver or in the flight of birds.

Medieval Gubbio made its living from ceramics, and in the 16th century, this tradition produced a real artist, **Mastro Giorgio Andreoli**. Born in 1498, he discovered a beautiful ruby and golden glaze for majolica plates (you'll notice the absence of red in most painted ceramics; it's very hard to do). Mastro Giorgio's secret died with him, and it was long one of Gubbio's deepest regrets that it had not a single example of his work to show. When it became known that Sotheby's had a plate by Mastro Giorgio to auction in 1991, the townspeople purchased it by public subscription and then did it again in 1996. The pieces are displayed in the loggia and show the *Fall of Phaeton* and *Circe*, and keep company with ceramic works made over the centuries, including red terracotta pharmaceutical jars. There are also fine views over Gubbio.

The **Pinacoteca** (*same hours as Museo Civico*, see *above*), up the stairs on the *piano nobile*, is just as quirky and charming, although there are few first-rate pictures: a 13th-century diptych in a Byzantine portable altar; some fine painted crucifixes; a detached 17th-century fresco on the legend of *St Francis and the Wolf*; a *Tree of Jesse* by a cinquecento Gubbio artist; the quattrocento *Madonna del Melograno* by Pier Francesco Florentini; a *Flight into Egypt* by Rutilio Manetti; and an anonymous work of the 1600s called the *Last Night of Babylon* – one of the best crazy paintings in Italy. The rooms of the Pinacoteca are an attraction in themselves; some haven't been remodelled since the 1500s.

The lower floor of the Palazzo dei Consoli houses the recently rearranged **Museo Archeologico** (*same hours as Museo Civico,* see p.484) with an Umbrian and Roman collection of bronzes and ceramics and other architectural odds and ends, and a Byzantine sarcophagus.

To the Duomo and Palazzo Ducale

From Piazza Grande, stepped **Via Galeotti**, one of the city's most resolutely medieval lanes, leads up to the winding Via Ducale and Gubbio's Duomo. On the way, note the old cellar under the cathedral housing a wine bibber's impossible dream: the **Botte dei Canonici**, a house-sized barrel from the 1500s that once held some 40,000 litres of wine, a masterpiece of the cooper's art (made without nails). The building on top, the 14th-century **Palazzo dei Canonici**, houses the **Museo Diocesano** (*t 075 922 0904, www.museogubbio.org; open winter 10–6; summer 10–7; adm*) with a damaged 14th-century fresco of the *Crucifixion* and a beautiful 16th-century Flemish cope, magnificently embroidered and presented to the cathedral by Pope Marcellus II, a native of Gubbio.

The 13th-century **Duomo**, which was refitted with a simple new front during the 1400s, is remarkable for the unusual pointed wagon stone vaulting of the nave, a Eugubine speciality and for its stained glass windows. Local talent is very well represented in the side chapels and in the presbytery there's a *Nativity* attributed to one of Pinturicchio's talented students, Eusebio di San Giorgio. The high altar is a Roman sarcophagus. Note the 16th-century choir stalls, painted to resemble intarsia by Benedetto Nucci and the 1556 carved throne (real) by Girolamo Maffei. From the Duomo, you can walk up and up and up to the Sanctuary of Sant'Ubaldo, following the route run in the race of the *Ceri* (*see* p.488), but it's much easier to take the *funivia*.

Opposite the cathedral on Via Federico da Montefeltro, the **Palazzo Ducale** (*t 075 927 5872; open Thurs–Tues 8.30–7; adm*) was designed in the 1470s for that great patron of artists and humanists, the *condottiere* Federico da Montefeltro, Duke of Urbino, by the Sienese architect Francesco di Giorgio Martini. The gentlemanly Federico was a paragon among Renaissance rulers (he received the Order of the Garter from Edward IV), and he took a paternalistic interest in the welfare of his subjects and frequently travelled to keep an eye on things.

He also liked to be lodged in style and built at least a dozen palaces in the northern Marche as homes away from home. His Gubbio address was one of the most stylish, a compact version of his famous palace in Urbino: the elegant and serene little courtyard in particular evokes its great model, with *pietra serena* details and the initials F.D. (Federico Duca). The palace was stripped of its furnishings before it was purchased by the state in 1957, but some fireplaces remain, along with the fine stairways, windows and original terracotta floor, one wooden ceiling, a few 15th-century intarsia doors and photos of the beautiful intarsia work of the little *studiolo* or ducal study, made by Giuliano da Maiano, and now on display in the Metropolitan Museum in New York. Some rooms have detached frescoes and paintings. Downstairs, you can examine the plumbing and old kitchen, the foundations of a Lombard palace from the 10th century. Upstairs, the loggia has a handsome frieze in *pietra serena* and lovely views down on the Palazzo dei Consoli.

Gubbio's West End

From Piazza Grande, Gubbio's main street, Via dei Consoli, leads past a number of ceramic shops to the very medieval and picturesque western quarter of town. Near Piazza Giordano Bruno, the **Bargello** (1302), the first public building in Gubbio, was a combined police station and governor's office; its round 16th-century **Fontana dei Matti** (Fountain of the Mad) used to be Gubbio's main water source and has the power to make you *loco* if you run around it three times. Here, too, is **San Domenico** (*closed for earthquake repairs*), an earlier Romanesque church taken over by the Dominicans in the 1300s. After an 18th-century remodelling, only bits of the trecento frescoes remain, along with an exceptional Renaissance intarsia reading stand. Vias Vantaggi and Gabrielli lead from here to the 13th-century **Palazzo del Capitano del Popolo**, a no-nonsense Romanesque structure, containing something every medieval town in Europe seems to have: a privately run museum of torture instruments. Nearby is one of the equally austere city gates, **Porta Metauro**, and a medieval tower fortress belonging to the Palazzo Gabrielli. **Santa Croce della Foce**, just outside the gate, is the site of the medieval Good Friday representation of the Passion.

Just inside the Porta Metauro is the entrance to the **Parco Ranghiasci-Brancaleoni**, which sweeps all the way up under the town walls to the Palazzo Ducale. Laid out as an English garden in 1841 by Francesco Ranghiasci (who married an Englishwoman), it was recently purchased and restored by the *comune* and offers the greatest possible contrast to the grey stone streets of the city. It has a pretty little covered bridge, neoclassical pavilions, big shady trees and a café.

The East End

At the east end of town, the 13th-century gatehouse of the **Porta Romana** is now a private museum (*t 075 922 1199; open daily 9.30–1 and 3.30–7.30; adm*) devoted to medieval gates, with a collection of old keys and a drawbridge mechanism, as well as a collection of Gubbio ceramics, which includes some from the workshop of Mastro Giorgio. Near the gate, two 13th-century churches contain works by Ottaviano Nelli. The now deconsecrated **Santa Maria Nuova** (*to visit, permission is needed from the Suprintendenza di Perugia, t 075 57411*) has his joyous, worldly *Madonna del Belvedere* and frescoes by his followers while, just outside the gate, **Sant'Agostino** has more frescoes by Nelli and his pupils: the *Life of St Augustine* in the triumphal arch and apse and, on the fifth altar on the right, *Sant'Ubaldo and Two Saints*. The *funivia* here ascends to Monte Ingino (*see p.487*).

Back within the Porta Romana, the **Arco di San Marziale**, marks the site of the ancient Umbrian gate. Via Dante leads down to a giant 18th-century tabernacle of Sant'Ubaldo at the crossroads with Corso Garibaldi. Near here, the **Palazzo Accoramboni** was the birthplace in 1557 of Vittoria Accoramboni. By age 16, she was not only married, but having an affair with Duke Paolo Giordano Orsini, who killed her husband to marry her (twice), before she was killed aged 28 by Orsini ruffians. Papal involvement and other sordid details made it juicy enough for the London stage – John Webster's play on Vittoria's life, *The White Devil*, appeared in 1608.

From Corso Garibaldi, Via Vincenzo Armanni descends to the church of **San Pietro**, with four Corinthian columns on the façade and a Renaissance interior. The first altar has a *Martyrdom of St Bartholomew* by the Sienese painter Rutilio Manetti, while the fourth has a Visitation by Giannicola di Paolo; the fifth was decorated by Raffaellino del Colle. In the left transept there's a 13th-century wooden statue of the Deposition.

Below San Pietro is the **Porta Vittoria**: if you follow Via della Piaggiola from here, you'll pass **Santa Maria della Piaggiola**, with an ornate Baroque interior, now used for concerts; there's a *Madonna and Child* by Ottaviano Nelli on the altar, although it's been repainted. Another Baroque church, **Santa Maria del Prato** (1662), is a copy of Borromini's San Carlino alla Quattro Fontane in Rome, just over the bridge to the right; it has recently been restored. If you continue along Via della Piaggiola, it's about a mile to the spot where Francis had his meeting with the wolf on Via Frate Lupo: the isolated **Chiesa della Vittorina** (*open Tues–Sun 9–12 and 4–7*) was built in the 13th century and the charming interior has another odd nave with pointed Gothic vaulting and some early frescoes, undisturbed by the remodelling in the 1500s. A bronze statue (1973) of the saint and wolf marks the famous encounter.

Monte Ingino

From the cathedral, you can make the stiff climb up Monte Ingino to the **Sanctuary of Sant'Ubaldo**, but it's much easier to take the *funivia* (*t 075 927 3881; open Oct 10–1.15 and 2.30–6; Nov–Feb Thurs–Tues 10–1.15 and 2.30–5; Mar Mon–Sat 10–1.15 and 2.30–5.30, Sun and hols 9.30–1.15 and 2.30–6; April–May Mon–Sat 10–1.15 and 2.30–6.30, Sun and hols 9.30–1.15 and 2.30–7; June Mon–Sat 9.30–1.15 and 2.30–7, Sun and hols 9–7.30; July–Aug daily 9–8; Sept Mon–Sat 9–8, Sun and hols 9–7.30*), which operates year-round from the Porta Romana. On display in the five-naved church, besides the ashes of the patron saint who saved Gubbio from the emperor, are the three *ceri* (*see* p.488). There's a café and restaurant where you can while away the hours or you can walk a bit further up for even more spectacular views from the **Rocca** (888m/2,913ft). At Christmas time, the entire slope of Monte Ingino is illuminated, using 12km of electric cable, to form 'the world's largest Christmas tree.'

Excursions from Gubbio

The area around Gubbio is not densely populated: expect long stretches of empty space punctuated by an occasional half-ruined castle, monastery or the very plainest of mountain villages. **Castel d'Alfiolo**, 6km south of Gubbio on the SS219, was converted from a family fortress to a Benedictine abbey in the 1100s; most of the buildings were redone in the 16th century, but the chapel and the main building conserve some good stone carving from the 1200s.

East of Gubbio, the SS298 passes through a lovely gorge with old water mills on the way to the **Parco Naturale del Monte Cucco** on the border of the Marches. This

The *Corsa dei Ceri*

Gubbio has retained some exceedingly medieval festivals that fill its solemn streets with colour and exuberance. On the last Sunday in May, crossbow-men from Sansepolcro come to compete in the *Palio della Balestra*, a fiercely fought contest dating back to 1461, with a procession, flag-throwing and music to warm things up. An even older custom is the Good Friday procession and a representation of the Passion, performed at the little church of Santa Croce della Foce just outside the city walls, with medieval chants and music played on wooden instruments called *battistrangoli*. Oldest of them all, however, is the *Corsa dei Ceri*, held every 15 May, the day before the feast of Sant'Ubaldo, the town's patron saint. Although first documented a couple of years after Ubaldo saved the city from Emperor Frederick and his Umbrian allies, over centuries the festival has taken on the uninhibited trappings of a pagan celebration that may have predated the good bishop's heroism. The *ceri* (candles) are three tall, wooden, octagonal towers some 13ft high, each topped by a wax saint representing one of the three guilds of Gubbio – Sant'Ubaldo (the builders), San Giorgio (the artisans) and Sant'Antonio Abate (the farmers).

The *ceri* are brought down from the sanctuary into Gubbio on 1 May. On May 15, following a mass, the three wax saints are brought out of the church of the Muratori and taken in a procession to the *ceri* in Piazza Grande, where they are affixed to the top of the 'candles'. A second procession then begins at Porta Castello and heads up to Piazza Grande, where the *ceri* are taken around town by their colourfully costumed teams. This is followed by a big fish banquet for participants and officials in the Palazzo dei Consoli. At 4.30 in the afternoon, there's another procession led by the bishop, in which the *ceri* are baptized with a jug of water. The race begins at 6, starting in Piazza Grande; 10 bearers hoist the supports of their respective *cero* on their shoulders and race pell-mell through the crowds up the streets (Via XX Settembre, Via Colomboni, Via Appennino to Porta del Monte, where they rest before continuing to the mountain-top church of Sant'Ubaldo). At intervals, the teams are replaced by fresh men – a neat trick done without slowing the remarkably quick pace. Ubaldo invariably wins (and what could be more Italian than a fixed race?). In the evening, the wax saints are returned to their home in the Muratori with the last procession of the day, by candlelight.

In 1943 during the German occupation, all-women teams carried the *ceri* (each weighs around 450lbs) and successfully made it all the way up to Sant'Ubaldo, for pride and to spite the Nazis – an experiment that hasn't been repeated since. Since the war, the *ceri* have become the symbol of Umbria, represented by the three red stripes on the region's coat of arms.

is a popular spot with the Eugubini on summer weekends, with pretty mountain meadows and beech forests around Pian di Ranco; it's also one of the best places in Umbria for hang-gliding, and in winter, people head up for the cross-country skiing. Descendants of Francis's Brother Wolf still roam on **Monte Cucco** (1,566m/5,137ft), one of Umbria's highest peaks, which in one of its flanks conceals one of the world's deepest (922m/3,025ft) subterranean systems, the 20km-long **Grotte di Monte**

Cucco, reached by a long iron stair (*closed to the public, but for guided tours of other caves, contact CENS, t 075 917 0400 or 075 917 0601, www.cens.it*). Remains of giant prehistoric cave bears have been found here and the innermost, darkest chambers are inhabited by a singular race of blind brown flies.

This mountainous region had a special pull on the holy men of the 10th and 11th centuries. San Romualdo, the nobleman turned monk and founder of the Order of the Camaldolese Benedictines, had a mystical vision of his vocation on Monte Sitria; the site is marked by the handsome Romanesque church of the **Abbazia di Santa Maria di Sitria**, located above **Scheggia**, the last Umbrian town on the Via Flaminia. Romualdo, although a great wanderer who founded abbeys as far as the Pyrenees, was also the moving spirit behind the **Monasterio della Fonte Avellana** (*visits Mon–Sat 9–11.30 and 3–5, Sun 3–4*), off the SS360, just over the border in the Marches in an isolated mountain setting. Founded in 979, this was an important centre of learning in the Middle Ages (Dante was one of many famous visitors) and almost nothing has changed here since the 12th century. Perhaps unique in Italy, it preserves the *scriptorium* where codices and manuscripts were copied.

Down the Via Flaminia

The Via Flaminia (SS3) was a Roman road of conquest; even in the Dark Ages, the Goths and Lombards kept it in repair, an important highway linking Ravenna, Spoleto and Rome. Somewhere along here, between Scheggia and Gualdo Tadino, the deciding battle in the bitter Greek–Gothic War took place in 552. The Goths, led by Totila, were coming up the road from the south, and were met here by the freshly arrived Byzantine forces under the eunuch general Narses, at the time nearly 80 years old. The Goths were outnumbered, and Totila did everything he could to stall battle until reinforcements arrived, even to the extent of ordering his most skilled horsemen to put on a display of dressage to entertain the Byzantines. But Narses was not to be fooled. His troops completely outflanked the Goths; Totila was mortally wounded, and although enough Goths fled to fight one last showdown with the Greeks near Cumae, their show was over. As for the octogenarian eunuch, he continued to besiege, battle and consolidate the position of his Emperor Justinian in Italy for a further nine years.

Gualdo Tadino

Tourist information t 075 915021; Pro Loco t 075 912172.

A stern old town, under the steep slopes of Monte Serra Santa, **Gualdo** has taken some big blows from earthquakes: the one in 1751 felled many public buildings and the 1997–98 one was pretty bad as well. Very slowly, progress is being made. Almost everyone is now back in proper homes, but many of Gualdo's churches are still off limits and some of the town's historic buildings are still under scaffolding.

In Gualdo's main square, **Piazza dei Martiri della Libertà** (recalling the civilians killed by the Germans in the Second World War), is a squat but well-proportioned

Duomo (*open to public*) with a good façade and rose window of 1256 and three doors, with an inscription mentioning the restoration after the 1751 earthquake; the 16th-century fountain on its side is attributed to Antonio da Sangallo. The 13th-century **Palazzo del Podestà**, remodelled in Baroque times, houses the new **Museum of Emigration** (*t 075 914 2445, www.emigrazione.it*); the earthquakes have caused many to emigrate from this region. Here, too, is the former church of **San Francesco** (*closed for restoration*), a copy of the basilica in Assisi, with a luminous interior and frescoes by Matteo da Gualdo, a local boy of the late quattrocento given to brilliant colouring (and, as critics liked to sniff a century ago, 'incorrect drawing'); others are by the school of Ottaviano Nelli. Another work by Matteo, a glowing triptych of the *Virgin and Child, with St Sebastian and St Roch* can be seen in the church of **Santa Maria dei Raccomandati** (*closed to public*) over on Piazza XX Settembre. Gualdo's castle, the **Rocca Flea** (*t/f 075 916078; open Oct–Mar Sat–Sun 10.30–1 and 3–6; April–June Thurs–Sun 10.30–1 and 3.30–6; July–Sept Tues–Sun 10.30–1 and 4–7.30*), was restored and improved by Emperor Frederick II, and is considerably larger than its name suggests. Restored before the quake as a **Museo Civico** (*same opening hours as Rocca Flea; adm*), it contains ceramics including Renaissance lustre-ware (like Gubbio, Gualdo has made it for centuries), archaeological finds and the town's painting collection, with a sumptuous polyptych by Niccolò Alunno, a *Coronation of the Virgin* by Sano di Pietro and more Matteo da Gualdo.

There's fine walking country in the mountains above Gualdo: take the road 8km east to **Valsorda**, a resort 3,333ft (1,015m) up and the base for the pilgrmage walk to the 12th-century sanctuary of **Santissima Trinità** (*open by request*) on Monte Serra Santa, now part of Monte Cucco park.

Gualdo has preserved four 13th-century gates, and in the last week of September, the townspeople from the four quarters, or 'gates', of Gualdo, don their medieval glad rags to play the *Giochi de le Porte* – archery and slingshot competitions and pell-mell donkey races around town.

Nocera Umbra

South of Gualdo Tadino, the hill town of **Nocera Umbra**, famous for its sparkling mineral water, was at the epicentre of the 1997–8 earthquakes, and it's a mess – virtually a ghost town. The *centro storico* is closed on one side, with access on the west side for families whose flats have been rebuilt there. Inside the barrier, every other building seems to be propped up with heavy scaffolding or steel girders. It makes you wonder how it could possibly be rebuilt, although restoration work has started and people who were living in the areas that received the most damage have had new accommodation built for them around Nocera. Many of the town's municipal institutions, banks and businesses are still housed in a huge container park down from the old town. While the modern parts are buzzing with life, the whole place has a very grim feel. For more information, contact **Comune di Nocera**, **t** 074 283 4011, **f** 074 281 2301.

The Valle Umbra: Spello to Spoleto

18

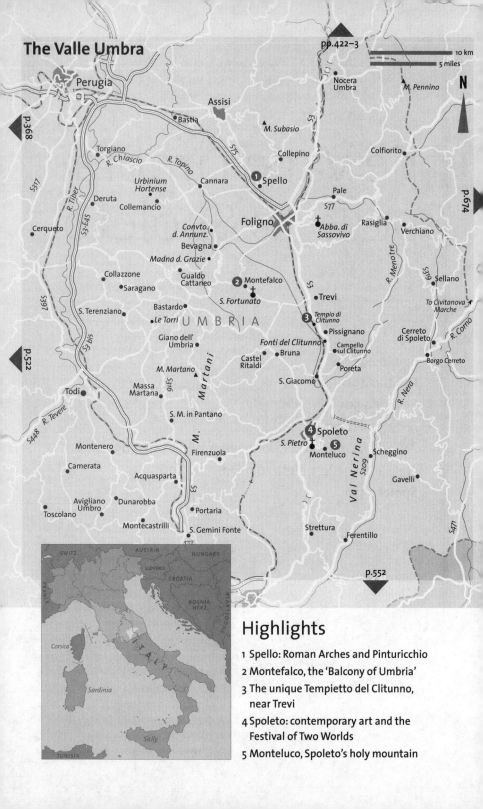

The Valle Umbra

pp.422–3

10 km
5 miles

N

p.368

p.674

p.522

p.552

Perugia

Assisi

Nocera Umbra

M. Pennino

Bastia

M. Subasio

Collepino

Colfiorito

Torgiano

R. Chiascio

R. Topino

1 Spello

R. Tiber

Urbinium Hortense

Cannara

Pale

S77

Rasiglia

Deruta

Collemancio

Foligno

† Abba. di Sassovivo

Verchiano

R. Menotre

Cerqueto

Convto. d. Annunz.

Bevagna

Sellano

Madna d. Grazie

To Civitanova Marche

Collazzone

Gualdo Cattaneo

2 Montefalco

Trevi

Saragano

† S. Fortunato

U M B R I A

Tempio di Clitunno

Cerreto di Spoleto

R. Corno

S. Terenziano

Bastardo

3

Borgo Cerreto

Le Torri

Pissignano

Giano dell' Umbria

Fonti del Clitunno

Campello sul Clitunno

M. Martano

Bruna

R. Nera

Castel Ritaldi

Poréta

Massa Martana

M. Martani

S. Giacomo

Todi

R. Tevere

S. M. in Pantano

4 Spoleto

Val Nerina

Montenero

Firenzuola

S. Pietro †

5 Monteluco

Scheggino

Camerata

Gavelli

Acquasparta

Avigliano Umbro

Dunarobba

Toscolano

Portaria

Strettura

Montecastrilli

S. Gemini Fonte

Ferentillo

SWITZ. AUSTRIA HUNGARY

FRANCE

SLOVENIA

CROATIA

Corsica

ITALY

BOSNIA HERZ.

YUGOSLAVIA

Sardinia

Sicily

TUNISIA

Highlights

1 Spello: Roman Arches and Pinturicchio

2 Montefalco, the 'Balcony of Umbria'

3 The unique Tempietto del Clitunno, near Trevi

4 Spoleto: contemporary art and the Festival of Two Worlds

5 Monteluco, Spoleto's holy mountain

Between Assisi and Spoleto spreads one of the largest patches of open country in the region. The sunny Valle Umbra, or Vale of Umbria as it is sometimes known, encompasses the valleys of the Teverone and the Topino (Little Mouse River) and has much in common with parts of southern Tuscany; the magnificent landscape seems almost consciously arranged by some geomantic artist to display each olive grove, vineyard, city and town to the best advantage. One Grand Tourist, the Abbé Barthélemy, wrote of the area, 'It is the most beautiful countryside in the world. I do not exaggerate.'

This area is littered with fascinating Roman and Lombard relics, thanks to that vital ancient thoroughfare, the Via Flaminia (SS3), the two branches of which joined in the remarkable but often overlooked town of Foligno before heading north to Gualdo Tadino. Besides some of Umbria's most beautiful hill towns, Spello, Montefalco and Trevi, the Valle Umbra is home to that unique relic of the Dark Ages called the Tempietto del Clitunno, and to glorious Spoleto, a genuine capital in those times, one of the most fascinating art towns in Italy, and now one of the trendiest, thanks to its famous festival of the Two Worlds. For tourist information for the whole of this area, see *www.valleumbra.com*.

Spello

Lovely medieval **Spello** (pop. 8,000) could be Assisi's little sister, dressed in the same pink and cream Umbrian stone, lounging on the same sort of gentle hillside under Mount Subasio, overlooking the Valle Umbra. It has a similar history, first as an Umbrian settlement, then as the Roman city with a fancy name, *Splendidissima Colonia Iulia Hispellum* or just *Hispellum* for short. The Lombards destroyed it, then made it part of the Duchy of Spoleto. In the Middle Ages, as a *comune*, Spello fought to keep free of Assisi, the same way Assisi resisted domination by the Perugians. This earned it a thumping from Frederick II, and when he was dead, Spello was swallowed up by Perugia. There's so much to see in nearby Assisi that relatively few tourists find their way up here, but like most little sisters, Spello has some charms of her own.

Porta Consolare

Spello has three excellently preserved Roman gates, including the main entrance to town, the **Porta Consolare**, with three arches and three worn statues from the time of the Roman republic, placed here in the 1600s after their discovery by the amphitheatre; in the Middle Ages, it was incorporated into the walls and given a tower.

Pinturicchio *et al*

From the gate, Via Consolare winds up into the centre, following the old Roman main street, passing an open chapel, the **Cappella Tega**, with faded Renaissance frescoes by L'Alunno. Where Via Consolare becomes Via Cavour stands Spello's chief monument, the late 13th-century church of **Santa Maria Maggiore** (*t 0742 301792; open winter daily 8.30–12.30 and 2.30–6; summer 8.30–12.30 and 3–7*), with its original

Getting Around

Spello is linked by **rail** (station 1km from town) and **bus** to Assisi, Perugia and Foligno.

Tourist Information

Spello: Piazza Matteotti 3, **t/f** 0742 301009, *prospello@libero.it*, *www.comune.spello.pg.it*. Open Mon–Sun 9.30–12.30 and 3.30–5.30, 4–6 in Aug.

Festivals

Festa dell'Olivo, *early December*. Spello's celebration of its olive oil production.
Corpus Domini, *late May–early June*. The town is decked out with intricately designed flower carpets, an *infiorata* – come in early morning to see the blooms at their best.

Where to Stay and Eat

Spello ✉ 06038
★★★★La Bastiglia, Via dei Molini 17, **t** 0742 651277, **f** 0742 301159, *fancelli@labastiglia. com* (*expensive*). Located in a charmingly restored mill, this stands out for its pleasant rooms, beautiful terrace, views and good restaurant. *Closed Wed*.
★★★★Palazzo Bocci, Via Cavour 17, **t** 0742 301021, **f** 0742 301464, *bocci@bcsnet.it* (*expensive*). Occupies an elegant, frescoed 17th-century building with beautiful rooms and a hanging garden; dining is *bello* and mellow in Spello under the vaulted ceiling at the hotel's restaurant **Il Molino**, **t** 0742 651305, just opposite, in Piazza Matteotti 6/7

– try homemade pasta or tender Umbrian meats cooked over the flames with a few glasses of Spello's own wines. *Closed Tues and 10–24 Jan*.
★★★Altavilla, Via Mancinelli 2, **t** 0742 301515, **f** 0742 651335, *www.hotelaltavilla.com* (*moderate*). A pleasant terrace and 24 well-furnished rooms run by the Prioetti family.
★★★Del Teatro, Via Giulia 24, **t** 0742 301140, **f** 0742 301612, *www.hoteldelteatro.it* (*moderate*). So-called for its proximity to the Teatro Comunale, this is a quiet, cheerfully furnished hotel with 11 well-equipped and comfortable rooms and wonderful views from the breakfast veranda.
★★Il Cacciatore, Via Giulia 42, **t** 0742 651141, **f** 0742 301603, *ilcacciatore@mclink.it* (*moderate*). Staying here costs you a bit more, but saves the walk to its very popular restaurant, with beautifully prepared homemade pasta and other dishes at decent prices. *Closed Mon and Nov*.
★★Il Portonaccio, Via Centrale Umbra 46, **t** 0742 651313, **f** 0742 301615, *www. ilportonaccio@libero.it* (*moderate*). Sound and inexpensive accommodation.
La Cantina, Via Cavour 2, **t** 0742 651775 (*moderate*). Seasonal variations and grilled barbecued meats. *Closed Wed*.

Cannara ✉ 06033
Casa delle Volpi, Vocabolo Ducale 50, **t/f** 0742 720361 (*inexpensive*). English owners offer self-catering lodgings outside town in a traditional farmhouse, with a spacious garden and excellent views over rolling hills to Assisi. Homemade breakfasts and dinners can be provided on request and cookery evenings are also available. Minimum stay 1 week.

Romanesque campanile and some 11th-century carving incorporated into its 17th-century façade. The interior was renovated at the same time, when it was given its fancy stuccoes and a hotchpotch of Baroque altars. The two holy water stoups are ancient Roman columns, and there are two late and mediocre frescoes by Perugino on the pilasters either side of the apse, an excellent pulpit with grotesques of 1545 sculpted by Simone di Campione, and fine inlaid choir stalls (1520), as well as a *baldacchino* by Tommaso di Rocco.

Best of all is the **Cappella Baglioni**, commissioned in 1500 by Troilo Baglioni, scion of Perugia's gangster family and brilliantly frescoed by Pinturicchio (make sure you have some €1 coins for the lighting). The three scenes, *Annunciation, Nativity* and *Dispute in the Temple*, are delightful, full of colour and incident, and include Pinturicchio's self-portrait hanging under the *Annunciation*. The floor is made of painted ceramics from Deruta (1516). More by Pinturicchio can be seen in the **Cappella del Sacramento**.

The adjacent Palazzo dei Canonici contains the **Pinacoteca Civica** (*t 0742 301497, Oct–Mar Tues–Sun 10.30–12.30 and 3–5, April–Sept 10.30–1 and 3–6.30; adm*), used as a repository for art from Spello's churches: there's woodcarving from the 13th and 14th centuries, including a fine *Madonna and Child* (1240) by an anonymous Umbrian sculptor; gold and silver work (a beautiful enamelled silver cross of 1398 by Perugian goldsmith Paolo Vanni); a portable diptych by Cola Petruccioli from the 1390s and Umbrian paintings by L'Alunno and his circle. Marcantonio Grecchi's *Madonna and Child with St Felice Vescovo and the Blessed Andrea Caccioli* includes a fine view of early 17th-century Spello.

For yet more Pinturicchio (he spent all of 1501 in Spello), the nearby 13th-century church of **Sant'Andrea** (*open Mon–Sat 8–12.30 and 3–7, Sun 3–7*) has a large *Madonna, Child and Saints* to the right of the crossing that he painted with another of Perugino's students, Eusebio di San Giorgio. There are also 13th–16th-century frescoes, and a high altar with a crucifix attributed to a follower of Giotto.

Souvenirs of Roman Hispellum

Walking the narrow, cobbled streets, hidden archways and stairways of Spello is a joy, although they're a bit steep. Press on past the rather anonymous Piazza della Repubblica, where the **Palazzo Comunale** (*visits can be arranged through the Assessorato alla Cultura, t 074 230 0039*) bears only traces of original work from the 1200s and contains a small archaeological collection in the atrium. Off the piazza, the Romanesque **San Lorenzo** (*c*. 1160) has an unusual façade full of bits from Roman and early medieval buildings and some curious paintings within by a 16th-century artist from Brussels, Frans van de Kasteele.

From here, ambitious climbers can continue up Via di Torre Belvedere to the top of Spello for the **Belvedere** and a lovely view over the Vale of Umbria. There are ruins of the 14th-century **Rocca**, built by the indefatigable Cardinal Albornoz. The small **Roman Arch** nearby was the entrance to *Hispellum*'s acropolis.

A circumnavigation of Spello's walls will show you the two other Roman gates: the **Porta Urbica** (near the Porto Consolare, by a well preserved stretch of 1st-century AD walls), and best of all, the **Porta Venere**, a beautiful, almost perfectly preserved monumental gate from the time of Augustus, flanked by a pair of tall cylindrical towers.

Outside the Walls of Spello

The Porta Venere is plainly visible from the road to Assisi and Perugia. Look the other way and you'll see the overgrown ruins of the **Roman amphitheatre**, perhaps more impressive when viewed from the Belvedere in the city than from ground level; it once seated 15,000. Just to the north of Spello is the charming, resolutely asymmetrical Romanesque church of **San Claudio** from the 12th century. Already in bad condition in 1997, it was then almost entirely destroyed by the earthquake and is still being restored. Just beyond, amid a lovely Italian garden, the **Villa Fidelia** at Via Flamina 72 (*t/f* 0742 651726) was built in the 1500s but has been fiddled with over the years; it now contains the **Collezione Straka-Coppa** (*reopens spring 2005; adm*), an ensemble of late Renaissance, Baroque and early 20th-century art, with a few big names sprinkled throughout (including a 16th-century *Madonna and Child* by Vincenzo Catena of Venice, Italy's first amateur painter), as well as silver and ceramics. Some 2.5km further along the same road is the **Chiesa Tonda**, or Santa Maria Rotonda, another geometric Renaissance temple (1517), with quirky Umbrian frescoes by Mezzastris, although it's now privately owned and off limits.

Beyond the 18th-century Porta Montanara 1km northeast of Spello, the cemetery church of **San Girolamo** (1474), has a portico and interior decorated by students and followers of Pinturicchio. Another road continues to the slopes of Monte Subasio and the walled medieval village of **Collepino**. Above town, the Romanesque church of **San Silvestro** was founded by St Romualdo in 1025; it has an interesting crypt and an altar carved out of a Roman sarcophagus. From here, an unpaved road continues over Subasio to the Eremo delle Carceri in Assisi (*see* pp.468–9).

West of Spello: Cannara and Urbinum Hortense

The fertile plain of Foligno, lying along the banks of the River Topino, was greatly appreciated in ancient times. **Cannara** was founded as a satellite of the large Roman town of Urbinum Hortense to the west, but has survived the centuries in better nick; it is known for its unique Vernaccia di Cannara, a sweet red dessert wine. There are two churches with good paintings of the Virgin, Child and Saints by Nicolò Alunno: one in **San Matteo** (1786) and the other in **San Giovanni**. The Municipio has fresco fragments and other finds from Urbinum Hortense.

West of Cannara, in a beautiful setting, the tiny walled village of **Collemancio** has a Romanesque church and Palazzo del Podestà in its core. From the public garden, a road leads up 0.5km to the ruins of Urbinum Hortense. Mentioned by Pliny the Younger, it has been partially excavated to unearth a temple, baths and a basilica, but the colourful mosaic found here is in the Museo Nazionale Romano in Rome.

Foligno

In **Foligno** (pop. 54,000), Umbria's third city, they point out the exact centre of a billiard table in the centre of a bar that stands in the centre of town, which is in the centre of Umbria, which is in the centre of Italy, which is in the centre of the Mediterranean, whose name means 'the middle of the world'. In September 1997, Foligno was in the middle again, this time of an earthquake. The whole world watched as its medieval Torre Comunale collapsed, while the Folignati wept and vowed to rebuild it just as it ('where it was, as it was' – the battle cry of major Italian restoration projects). A few of the townspeople are still living in containers, but nearly all are now back in their own homes or new houses. The tower will take longer, many *palazzi* are still under scaffolding, but most churches have now reopened.

Even before the disaster, not many people stopped for Foligno; in a sense, the town centre has also been a victim of its post-war prosperity and the ring of factories and modern suburbs that surrounds it is enough to discourage most travellers. But to pass on by is to miss one of the most distinctive Umbrian towns, neither as archaic nor as cute as Assisi, but memorable in its own way, a minor medieval capital

Getting There and Around

Foligno, 36km/30mins from Perugia and 158km/2½hrs from Rome, is one of the principal **rail** junctions for eastern Umbria.

Buses (the bus station is just up Viale Mezzetti) link it to Colfiorito, Montefalco, Bevagna, Trevi and Spoleto; FS bus services connect Foligno to Assisi, Perugia and Siena three times a day.

Hire a **bike** from **Baltistelli**, Via XX Settembre 88, **t** 0742 344059.

There is underground **parking** near Porta Romana, handy for the tourist office.

Tourist Information

Foligno: Corso Cavour 126, **t** 0742 354459/ 354165, **f** 0742 340545, www.umbria2000.it.

As in Assisi, the earthquake devastation has left many buildings unstable, with many places still under restoration.

Market Day

Via Nazario Sauro, *Tues and Sat.*

Festivals and Activities

Giostra della Quintana, *14–15 June, or nearest weekend*. A custom dating back to the 17th century, where knights from 10 rival districts of Foligno compete in jousting matches. The event is accompanied by plays performed in 300-year-old Umbrian dialect (of which you won't understand a word), and a more accessible historic cooking competition, as well as other games, a fair, parades, outdoor taverns and so on. *14–15 Sept* the 10 teams return to the field for a rematch.

Aeroclub, **t** 0742 670201. Foligno is one of Umbria's **gliding** and **hang-gliding** centres.

Centro Ippico CO.GI.VE, Fraz. Verchiano, **t** 0742 632846. Riding stables.

Where to Stay and Eat

Foligno ✉ 06034

★★★**Le Mura**, Via Bolletta 29, **t** 0742 357344, **f** 0742 353327, www.albergolemura.com (*moderate*). A comfortable, modern hotel on the northwest of town with a good restaurant, where you can watch the chef grilling meat or cooking *cialde* (wafer-thin layers of pizza-ish dough stuffed with cheese, vegetables or ham, prepared on the griddle). *Closed Tues.*

★★★**Villa Roncalli**, just south of the centre on Viale Roma 25, **t** 0742 391091, **f** 0742 391001 (*moderate*). A fashionable 17th-century villa hotel with a shady garden, pool, garage and comfortable rooms, and the city's finest restaurant (*expensive*) serving Umbrian dishes with a gourmet flair. *Closed Mon and 2 weeks in Aug and 2 weeks in Jan.*

★★**Albergo Valentini**, Via F. Ottaviani 19, **t** 0742 353990, **f** 0742 356243 (*inexpensive*). Situated near the station, this is family-run and more than adequate, with pleasant rooms and breakfast, but no restaurant.

Osteria del Teatro, Via Petrucci 8, **t** 0742 350745 (*moderate*). A delightful restaurant with vaulted ceiling, theatre posters and a garden, where you can enjoy *zucchini* fritters, deep-fried sage, pumpkin ravioli and excellent lamb and beef (the *tagliata* is particularly good). *Closed Mon.*

Da Remo, Via Filzi 10, **t** 0742 340522 (*cheap*). A Liberty-style villa near the station which has been a classic choice for the past four generations, serving tasty *strangozzi* (fat, homemade spaghetti) and roast kid simmered in Montefalco's Sagrantino wine. *Closed Mon.*

Il Bacco Felice, Via Garibaldi 73, **t** 0742 341019. A cosy *enoteca* where wine lovers can while away an evening over their favourite bottles, cheeses and other snacks.

Barbanera, Piazza della Repubblica. For a light snack, coffee or *aperitivo*, try this old *drogheria* with a wonderful old counter.

with a pinch of grandeur and an air of genteel dilapidation and hopelessness that the tremors have aggravated.

History

Foligno was the ancient Roman *Fulginum*, near the junction of the two branches of the Via Flaminia. This key location brought Christianity early to Foligno, thanks to St Felicianus, who was martyred in the 3rd century. In spite of its location on a plain, the city never disappeared in all the troubles that followed the crack-up of the Roman Empire: it survived attacks by the Saracens and Magyars to spring back up in the 12th century as a free *comune* with strongly Ghibelline tendencies. St Francis was a frequent visitor, and not long afterwards, it was the home of the Blessed Angela (1248–1309), a mystic whose direct communion with God and visions were recorded by her spiritual director in her autobiographical *Book of Divine Consolation*.

The Blessed Angela was 12 when the man suspected of being the Antichrist, the Emperor Frederick II, with his exotic Saracen army and dancing girls, held his parliament in Foligno, in defiance of the pope who had excommunicated him. This got the Folignati into trouble after his death, and the period of wars and civil disorders that followed resulted in the Trinci family's assuming power in 1305. Their rule, which saw Foligno dominating Assisi, Spello, Montefalco, Bevagna and Trevi, lasted until 1439, when in a moment of upheaval, Pope Eugenius IV sent in an army under Cardinal Giovanni Vitelleschi. Vitelleschi's family hated the Trinci and he had no qualms about executing the last lord and his followers and instituting direct papal rule. There was one bright spot before the town nodded off, when German printers brought their presses to Foligno in 1470, only six years after the first books were printed in Italy; the first printed edition of Dante's *Divina Commedia* – which was also the first printed book in the Italian language – came out in Foligno the following year.

Piazza della Repubblica

Piazza della Repubblica marks the centre of Foligno, with the Duomo facing the **Palazzo Comunale** (*closed for restoration*) – a rare architectural catastrophe. This was once a genuine 12th-century monument, until someone had the bright idea of pasting a neoclassical façade on it in the early 1900s, mercifully disguised by scaffolding at present. The tower survived with its original lantern with Ghibelline crenellations as one of Foligno's proudest landmarks, before it collapsed in the earthquake.

The Folignati can't leave well alone; in the 18th century, they commissioned Luigi Vanvitelli, court architect to the Kingdom of Naples, and the town's own Giuseppe Piermarini, designer of La Scala in Milan, to modernize their already grandiose **Duomo**. Fortunately, they didn't tamper with the two façades on either side of the L-shaped piazza: the **east front** (1133) is pink and white in Perugian style, with some 1900s Venetian mosaics and other modern improvements, but the original **south front** remains, featuring one of the finest portals in Umbria (1201). It's also one of the least orthodox, a strange testament to the syncretic religious and philosophical currents of that age. The reliefs include figures of the zodiac, a medieval bestiary and long panels with geometric patterns and grapevines. Frederick II appears left of the door, one of only two existing likenesses in Italy. Two porphyry lions hold up the doorway, and at the top of the arch, barely visible, is a Muslim star and crescent. There are more fantastical animals above the portal and a good rose window.

The portal was brand-new when young Francis of Assisi came here in 1205 and sold his father's stock of cloth and a packhorse to raise money for the restoration of San Damiano (*see* pp.494–5). He wouldn't, however, recognize the Duomo's interior, where the Cappella dell'Assunta is all that remains of the 12th-century original. The best art is in the sacristy, with a painting of the *Madonna and St John* by Alunno and busts of Bartolomeo and Diana Roscioli, recently attributed to Bernini. The cathedral also housed a remarkable life-sized silver statue of St Feliciano seated on a throne; much of it was taken to bits and stolen in 1982.

At the western end of the piazza, the much-altered **Palazzo Trinci** (*t 0742 357989 or 357697, f 0742 340496, www.comune.foligno.pg.it/cultura; open Tues–Sun 10–7; adm*) still has its elegant original Renaissance courtyard behind a neoclassical façade. Nearly all the interior dates from the period of Foligno's greatest *signore*, Ugolino III Trinci (ruled 1386–1415), who commissioned a precocious humanistic cycle of late Gothic frescoes, by Gentile da Fabriano and others, for the second floor. They are an early example of the reawakening of interest in the Classical past, especially notable for being far from the centre of action in Florence. The frescoes were undergoing restoration for years before the earthquake and emerged unscathed.

The palace **chapel** has frescoes on the *Life of Mary* (1424) by Ottaviano Nelli of Gubbio, who also painted the heroic Roman figures in the Sala dei Giganti. Frescoes in the loggia show the founding of Rome: most curious of all is a half-completed fresco and *sinopia* (preparatory sketch), *Rhea Silvia Being Buried Alive*; Rhea was the Vestal Virgin who gave birth to Romulus and Remus. The **Sala delle Arti Liberali e dei Pianeti** has allegorical figures of the liberal arts represented by women seated on thrones, and allegories of the planets. The corridor, which gave the Trinci access to the Duomo, has frescoes of ancient heroes and the *Seven Ages of Man*. Ugolino also collected ancient art: there's a rare high relief of the games in the Circus Maximus, busts of the emperors and a statue of Cupid and Psyche. The building also houses the **Pinacoteca Comunale** (*open 10–7, closed Mon; adm*), with an *Annunciation* attributed to Gozzoli, works by Pierantonio Mezzastris of Foligno and detached trecento frescoes.

Foligno's newest museum, the **Museo Multimediale dei Tornei delle Giustre e dei Giochi** (*t 0742 357697 and 0742 357989, f 0742 340496, open 10–7; closed Mon*), in Palazzo Trinci, has multimedia displays on Foligno's medieval pageant and similar jousts and tournaments elsewhere.

Down Via Gramsci

Palazzo Trinci is only the first of a long line of Folignati palaces that stretch out along Via Gramsci. Most of the noble residences were built in the 1500s and can now be seen newly restored after the earthquake and the preceding hundreds of years of neglect. The one nearest Palazzo Trinci, the 16th-century **Palazzo Deli**, is by far the most beautiful.

Foligno's other churches are well-endowed with art: **San Niccolò** in Via Scuola d'Arti e Mestieri has works by Foligno's own Niccolò di Liberatore, known as Alunno; in the Piazza San Domenico, **Santa Maria Infraportas** (*open daily 9–12 and 4–6, closed Sun pm*) is one of Foligno's oldest churches, with unusual 12th-century windows and portico, and frescoes by Mezzastris and others; the large, deconsecrated church of **San Domenico** (*open for musical events, t 0742 344563, Tues–Sat 10–12.30*) has good trecento frescoes, recently discovered but currently hidden by scaffolding. There are more Renaissance palaces along Via Mazzini and along Via Garibaldi, its northern extension, where the oratory known as the **Nunziatella** (*t 0742 357989/357687, f 0742 340496, cultura@comune.foligno.pg.it; open Tues–Sat 10–1 and 3–7*) has a fresco by Perugino.

Up the Menotre Valley

Directly east of Foligno, you can follow the valley of the little Menotre River into the mountains, a beautiful but seldom visited corner of Umbria that extends to the border with the Marches. This area was the worst hit by the earthquake. The collapsed buildings in the villages have been cleared, but it will take a few years for all the scaffolding, rubble and cranes to be removed. The villages are largely abandoned. Many families have moved to Foligno or even Rome and most likely will not come back. While the state gave immediate compensation to earthquake victims, it has been slower to invest in rebuilding village homes. In some cases, containers have been replaced by wooden chalets and there is some new building outside the old villages, but overall, the area is very demoralized. The villagers had little before, but what little they had, they lost. A number of modest roadside stalls sell the lentils, chick peas, red potatoes and onions indigenous to the region.

The SS77 from Foligno follows the valley but, just after crossing the Via Flaminia, a side road to the right (signposted Casale) heads in 5km to the **Abbazia di Sassovivo** (*closed for restoration*), an 11th-century Benedictine abbey with a remarkable cloister. The main road twists up into the mountains, passing some interesting caves and a pretty waterfall on the Menotre at **Pale**, 8km from Foligno, a village wedged between the rocks. Paper has been milled here since the 13th century and there's some good art in the church, although like most of the buildings, it's closed.

On the heights, just before the Marches border, the mountains level out to form the broad meadow or *valico* of **Colfiorito**, where the lofty green marshlands, 2,400ft (730m) above sea level, are a favourite spot for migrating birds; other parts of the *valico* are used for growing beans and lentils. Sadly, most of the hamlets around its rim have been abandoned since the earthquake. The rugged roadside 11th-century church, **Santa Maria di Pistia**, has porticoes on two sides to accommodate the country fairs held here in the Middle Ages. A side road turns off before Colfiorito (24km) heading south into pristine mountain scenery around **Rasiglia**, where the little **Santuario della Madonna delle Grazie** (*being rebuilt since the earthquake*) has walls covered with well-preserved, colourful quattrocento frescoes, many of them painted as *ex votos*. Further up is **Sellano**, in a beautiful setting, but all but abandoned now to cranes, scaffolding and concrete.

Bevagna

Located under the Martani Hills, on the original westerly route of the Via Flaminia, Roman *Mevania* has survived as **Bevagna** (pop. 2,400), a quiet, unspoiled, friendly town, where the main crops are flax and wine. Although low-key, it has some artistic gems. During its period as a free *comune* in the Middle Ages, before being taken over in 1371 by the Trinci family of Foligno, it built two of Umbria's best Romanesque churches. The earthquake left a number of people homeless; now nearly all are back in their homes. It also damaged the churches, which are now undergoing lengthy restoration. However, there are fewer external signs of damage than elsewhere.

Piazza Silvestri

Bevagna's pride and joy is its perfect **Piazza Silvestri**, a medieval and theatrical *pièce de résistance* which shows that the Bevanati tried hard to keep up with their bigger neighbours. It has a Corinthian column, a fountain and the impressive Gothic **Palazzo Comunale** of 1270, which was damaged by an earlier earthquake in 1832 and restored with a charming little theatre inside.

An archway connects it to the delightful church of **San Silvestro** (*closed for restoration*) built by an architect named Maestro Binello (who signed his work) and currently being restored with the help of funds raised by Prince Charles. The simple façade incorporates bits of Roman buildings, an 1195 inscription to Emperor Henry VII and a frieze over the door. The interior is essentially Romanesque, and like many

Tourist Information

Bevagna: Piazza Silvestri 1, **t/f** 0742 361667, *www.bevagna.it*. *Open daily 9.30–12.30 and 3–7*.

Festivals

Mercato delle Gaite, *mid-June*. A neo-medieval fair in which the four districts (*gaite*) vie to dress more authenticallly, while street stalls sell food and drink.

Where to Stay and Eat

Bevagna ✉ 06031

L'Orto degli Angeli, Via D. Alighieri 1, **t** 0742 360130, **f** 0742 361756, *www.ortoangeli.it* (*very expensive*). This property in the centre of town contains both a 2nd-century temple to Minerva (forming one wall of the restaurant), and the ruins of a Roman theatre, part of the delightful hanging garden. The Antonini Angeli Nieri Mongelli family home, it is full of family antiques and pictures. The restaurant (*expensive–moderate*) serves Umbrian classics with a creative twist. *Closed Tues*.

★★★Palazzo Brunamonti, Corso Matteotti 79, **t** 0742 361932, **f** 0742 361948, *www.brunamonti.com* (*moderate*). Another old palazzo, newly restored but more modestly furnished, with 16 comfortable bedrooms and frescoed public rooms.

Il Chiostro di Bevagna, Corso Matteotti 107, **t** 0742 361987, **f** 0742 369231, *www.ilchiostrodibevagna.com* (*moderate*). Simple but very charmingly furnished rooms, set in the frescoed cloister of the former Dominican Convent.

Da Nina, Piazza Garibaldi 6, **t** 0742 360024 (*moderate*). A simple but attractive lunch stop, serving truffles and good pasta dishes with porcini mushrooms and wild boar flavoured with tarragon. *Closed Tues*.

El Rancho, Via Flaminia 53, **t** 0742 360105 (*cheap*). A tempting array of local dishes and products at down-to-earth prices; eat outside in fair weather. *Closed Mon*.

12th-century buildings, it features a raised presbytery, leaving room for twin pulpits (*ambones*, now vanished) on either side of the steps and a small crypt underneath. The real surprise is the style of the capitals – they're in the Egyptian order, representing papyrus leaves the way Ionic and Corinthian capitals recall the leaves of the acanthus. Such columns are common in this area, but their presence has never been explained: maybe they were copied from the ruins of some Roman-era temple to Isis or Serapis. They are slightly curved, in *entasis* to look straight.

Across the piazza, the late 12th-century church of **San Michele Arcangelo** (*closed for restoration*) has a few Egyptian capitals, recycled from older buildings. Binello and Rodolfo built this about the same time as San Silvestro and to the same interior plan. St Michael and his dragon figure prominently on the façade, along with some re-used Roman friezes, a Cosmatesque arch, and a menagerie of cows, cats and such, similar to the portal in Foligno (by the same architects), while the crypt under the raised presbytery is supported by Roman columns. There are also two processional statues of Bevagna's patron saint Vincenzo, one of wood and the other of silver.

The third church on the piazza, **Santi Domenico e Giacomo** (*open 11–12.30 and 3.30–6.30*), has a Baroque interior with what must be the biggest alabaster window in Italy behind the altar. Of the church's original decoration, little remains but a radiant trecento *Virgin of the Annunciation* in the choir; there are also works by the Bevagna-born artist Il Fantino ('the Jockey', Ascensidonio Spacco, d. 1646). From here, Corso Matteotti follows the route of the old Via Flaminia, passing by an 18th-century pharmacy and a *municipio* of the same period, its ground floor home to the **Museo della Città** (*t 0742 360031, www.sistemamuseo.it; open April, May and Sept daily 10.30–1 and 2.30–6; June–July daily 10.30–1 and 3.30–7; Aug Mon–Sun 10.30–1 and 3–7.30; Oct–Mar Tues–Sun 10.30–1 and 2.30–5; adm; the 'circuito cittadino' ticket includes the museum, theatre and mosaics, see below*). This houses a fine collection of Roman artefacts and coins, busts and architectural fragments found in and around Bevagna, a collection of medieval manuscripts and a model of the Santuario della Madonna delle Grazie (*see p. 503*). There are also works by Dono Doni, Il Fantino and an *Adoration of the Magi* by Corrado Giacinto.

The Rest of Town

More remnants of Roman *Mevania* can be seen a few blocks further up the Corso, turning at Via Crescimbeni, where a **Roman Temple** was partially conserved when its columns were bricked in long ago. Nearby, at Via Porta Guelfa, there's a marine **mosaic** featuring a big lobster, sea horses and Tritons, once part of the 2nd-century baths (*t 0742 360031, or ask at the museum or tourist office*). A picturesque crescent of houses traces the curve of the amphitheatre, in Via dell'Anfiteatro, and there's a house at the end, in Via Dante Aligheri, with a fine Roman frieze.

At the highest point in Bevagna, the 13th-century church of **San Francesco** (*closed since the earthquake*) holds the stone on which Francis stood when he preached to the birds at Pian d'Arca, north of Bevagna. Steps from the church lead down to Piazza Garibaldi and Bevagna's best-preserved medieval gate, **Porta Cannara**.

Around Bevagna

More bits of Roman *Mevania* can be seen off the old Via Flaminia to Foligno (the SS316): the fossil-like imprint of another amphitheatre in a field and two ruined tombs. Just north of Bevagna, the **Convento dell'Annunziata** (*closed; badly damaged in the earthquake, restoration has started, call* **t** *0742 361234 for information*) has more works by Il Fantino and a pretty terracotta altarpiece of the *Annunciation*. A path from the convent leads down to a spring-fed lake. To the southwest of Bevagna stands yet another 16th-century shrine to the Virgin Mary, the **Santuario della Madonna delle Grazie** (*open 8–12 and 4–sunset*), designed by Valentino Martelli with a handsome octagonal dome and a pretty view over the area.

Montefalco

Only 7km from Bevagna but set much higher up in the hills, **Montefalco** (pop. 5,500) is another unspoilt gem. Known as the '*Ringhiera* (balcony) *d'Umbria*', the town offers splendid 360° views over to Assisi and Perugia and down the entire Valle Umbra as far as Spoleto. Another nickname, '*il lembo di cielo caduto in terra*' (heaven's hem fallen to earth), refers to its reputation as a factory for saints, extraordinary even by Umbrian standards; the celestial hosts count eight former Montefalconesi. Until 1240 it was known as Coccorone, and when Frederick II destroyed it and rebuilt

Tourist Information

Montefalco: At the museum, Via Ringhiera Umbra 6, **t/f** 0742 379598, *www. montefalco.it*. Open daily Nov–Feb Tues–Sun 10.30–1 and 2.30–5; Mar–May and Sept–Oct 10.30–1 and 2–6; June–July Mon–Sun 10.30–1 and 3–7; Aug 10.30–1 and 3–7.30.

Getting There

There are two **trains** a day to/from Foligno, and also SSIT **buses** (**t** 0743 212208, **f** 0743 47807, *www.spoletina.com*) to Montefalco from Bastardo, Bevagna and Perugia once a day, and from Foligno and Spoleto several times a day.

Where to Stay and Eat

Montefalco ✉ 06036
****Villa Pambuffetti, Via della Vittoria 20, **t** 0742 379417, **f** 0742 379245, *www. villapambuffetti.com* (*very expensive*).

A 19th-century villa owned by a local noble family, with 15 rooms, each decorated differently, some with family antiques. Set in a park with huge trees and an outdoor pool.
Ringhiera Umbra, Corso G. Mameli 20, **t/f 0742 379166, *ilverziere@tiscalinet.it* (*inexpensive*). Comfortable, near Piazza del Comune, with en suite baths in some of the rooms and a good restaurant (*moderate*).

Montefalco is perhaps best known for a couple of red wines, Sagrantino and Rosso di Montefalco. Sagrantino has a delicate aroma of blackberries; both are sold in many shops around town and used widely in its cuisine.
Coccorone, off the central square at Vicolo Fabbri, **t** 0742 379535 (*moderate*). Elegant and understated, with tempting *tagliatelle al tartufo* as a starter and braised woodcock, grilled pigeon and *pappardelle al sagrentino* as main dishes. *Closed Wed*.
Il Falisco, Via XX Settembre 14, **t** 0742 379185 (*cheap*). Local specialities such as beef fillet cooked in Sagrantino wine. *Closed Mon*.
Enoteca Cocconne, Piazza del Comune, **t** 0742 378902. Pleasant for a snack and a glass of wine on the piazza. *Closed Wed*.

it as a Ghibelline town, he named it after his imperial eagle. It later became part of the domain of the Trinci family, and then part of the Church's; today, it is practically synonymous with its fine Sagrantino wines and woven textiles.

San Francesco

Appropriately enough, the town of heaven's hem is capped by a monk's tonsure: the central, circular and partially arcaded **Piazza del Comune**, from where streets radiate down like spokes. One of these, Via Ringhiera Umbra, takes in the lovely Clitunno Valley, while descending to Montefalco's pride and joy: the frescoes in the deconsecrated 14th-century church of **San Francesco** (*t/f 0742 379598; open Nov–Feb Tues–Sun 10.30–1 and 2.30–5; Mar–May and Sept–Oct daily 10.30–1 and 2–6; June–July daily 10.30–1 and 3–7; Aug daily 10.30–1 and 3–7.30; adm*), now converted to a museum. The earthquake caused some structural damage to the apse, and although the frescoes themselves were unharmed, it was deemed a good moment for complete restoration; the work has now been completed.

Benozzo Gozzoli spent two years here (1450–52), painting the apse with the Life of St Francis. Montefalco's Franciscans did not let Gozzoli put in many of his usual fancies – though there are a few moppet children grinning out from the corners. Gozzoli does, however, indulge in his favourite cityscapes, including views of Montefalco (where Francis visited after preaching to the birds around Bevagna), and of Arezzo (where he cast out the devils). The panels along the bottom of the apse show portraits by Gozzoli of great Franciscans – a distinguished company of saints, popes and philosophers, including Duns Scotus. The cycle makes a fascinating contrast to the earlier and much better frescoes in Assisi, but Gozzoli's rather facile, charming and sentimental figures clearly struck a deep chord in the mid-15th century, because they became a model for a good deal of later Umbrian painting. Gozzoli also frescoed the first chapel, a triptych with the *Madonna and Saints and Crucifix*.

The other Renaissance fresco here is by Perugino, a restored run-of-the-mill Nativity with Lake Trasimeno. The aisles contain fine trecento painting, including a vivid and unique *Temptations of St Anthony*; there is a fond painting by Tiberio d'Assisi of a local favourite and exemplar of spiritual first aid, the *Madonna del Soccorso*, in which Our Lady is about to whack a devil with a big club, when he comes to snatch a child whose exasperated mother had exclaimed 'May the Devil take you!'

The **Pinacoteca** in San Francesco has an 18th-century statue of Foligno's Quintana Saracen, another *Madonna del Soccorso*, a *Madonna and Child* by the school of Melozzo da Forlì, and a beautiful painting, *SS. Vincent, Illuminata and Nicolas of Tolentino*, by Antonizzo Romano; another section has an ancient marble statue of Hercules found in the town, a medieval lion and a Renaissance river god.

The Rest of Town

Montefalco's people are a cheerful lot, contentedly looking down on to the rest of Umbria. Most live in tiny low houses jammed into narrow lanes; when it's nice, they sit out talking about the weather. After San Francesco, sights are few; two other churches contain frescoes by 14th–16th-century Umbrian painters – **Sant'Agostino** and **Sant'Illuminata** (*opening hours depend on the priest*). Montefalco retains medieval walls, including two gates: **Porta Sant'Agostino**, with a fresco of the Virgin and Saints, and **Porta Federico II**, decorated with the eagle.

Outside the Walls of Montefalco

Just outside the Porta Federico II, the large 17th-century church of **Santa Chiara da Montefalco** (*open 8–12 and 4–sunset*) was built around a much earlier chapel of Santa Croce. It has beautiful frescoes of 1333 on the life of Saint Clare of the Cross (*c.* 1268–1308). Clare was a follower of St Francis, a mystic visionary and special devotee of the Passion of Christ, famous for her charity, learning and prophecy; after she died, her heart was found to be branded with the sign of the cross.

The Franciscan convent of **San Fortunato** (*open 9.30–12 and 3.30–5*), just over 1km southeast of Montefalco's Porta Spoleto, enjoys a beautiful setting and still shelters a handful of friars; the thick ilex forest that surrounds it was planted as insulation against the winter winds. The church, dedicated to Fortunatus (d. 400), a priest famous for his charity to the poor, was founded over a Roman basilica in the 5th century. It was rebuilt in the 16th and later Baroqued inside, though it preserves interesting fresco fragments by Gozzoli: a lunette over the door, an *Adoration of the Child* and the *Enthroned St Fortunatus*. The cloister uses Roman columns and has a chapel frescoed by Tiberio d'Assisi on the *Life of St Francis*. The church in Turrita has an array of votive frescoes; just outside, there's a 19th-century **Santuario della Madonna della Stella** (*closed*), built in honour of a miracle-working 16th-century fresco.

Around Montefalco: Into the Monti Martani

At Montefalco begins a range of hills and lofty plateaux known as the Monti Martani, separating the Valle Umbra from the Tiber. This lies well off the main tourist trails. Places like **Gualdo Cattaneo**, west of Bevagna, knew their peak of importance under the Lombards (the name Gualdo comes from the German *wald* or wood). Its big cylindrical castle dates from 1494 – the work of Pope Alexander VI, built after his fiery son Cesare Borgia stormed through the area to show the Umbrians who was boss. When Gualdo's church was rebuilt in 1804, stonework from its 13th-century predecessor was preserved on its façade; the crypt is original as well. The apse has a fine *Last Supper* by Bevagna's early 17th-century master Fantino.

A pretty drive west of Montefalco leads to a market town bearing the unfortunate name of **Bastardo**, the gateway to other forgotten castles: **Le Torri** (a poor man's San Gimignano), Renaissance **Barattano** and a Lombard fort at **Saragano**.

Southeast of Bastardo, amid the olive groves on the slopes of the Monti Martani, the walled village of **Giano dell'Umbria** is one of several in the area founded by Norman knights who were granted the land after fighting as mercenaries for Pope Gregory VII in the 1080s – the whole area extending to Castel Ritaldi was known as Normandia in the Middle Ages. Originally it consisted of two fortified villages and it has two 13th-century churches on the same piazza, but only a single Palazzo

Pubblico; until the 1300s, Giano managed to remain independent in spite of being circled by all the local sharks. Of the churches, the Pieve has a Baroque interior and a recently restored painting by Andrea Polinori of the *Madonna and Child* (1620) who keeps company with a much venerated *Madonna and Child* painted 300 years earlier.

Just north of Giano, the red stone **Abbazia di San Felice** was founded by some of Umbria's early coenobitic monks. In the 8th century, the Benedictines moved in and rebuilt it, and since 1815, it has been reoccupied by a congregation dedicated to mission work. The Romanesque church, from the 12th century, has a handsome portal topped by a three-light window and an impressive apse with a gallery. Under the raised presbytery, the crypt has quaint old Roman and early medieval capitals and an ancient sarcophagus, holding the remains of the martyred bishop of Martana. San Felice's frescoed cloister is especially pretty.

Castel Ritaldi (14km south of Montefalco), has a castle from the 1200s. Just outside the village is the **Pieve di San Gregorio**, built in 1140, with a charming pink and white sculpted façade decorated with elaborate interwoven designs inhabited by little monsters; it has been restored by funds raised in New York. Nearby **Bruna** has a Renaissance church in the shape of a trefoil called **Santa Maria della Bruna** (1510).

Trevi and the Tempietto del Clitunno

No small town in Umbria makes a grander sight than **Trevi** (pop. 7,400), a nearly vertical village reminiscent of Positano on the Amalfi coast, hung on a steep and curving hillside draped with olive groves above the Via Flaminia. In case you were wondering, it has no connection with the famous fountain in Rome apart from the fact that both were at the intersection of three roads or *tre vie*. Trevi was part of the Duchy of Spoleto and seat of a bishop, and was destroyed by the Saracens and Magyars. Briefly an independent *comune*, its strategic position made it a prize fought over by Perugia and Foligno. Joining the Papal States in 1439 brought it prosperity, at least in the short run, as well as the fourth printing press in Italy in 1470. These days, there are no flies on Trevi: like its sister hill towns, it may look medieval, but it also dallies on the wild side of the international avant-garde.

Two Churches, Two Art Museums

Trevi's credentials as a free *comune* in the Middle Ages are in its small but proud **Palazzo Comunale** in Piazza Mazzini, built in the 14th century, with numerous later additions. From here, the stepped street Via Beato Placido Riccardi leads up past the Piazza della Rocca, lined with quattrocento palaces; further up stands the domed cathedral, **Sant'Emiliano**. Emiliano, an Armenian monk, served in the 4th century as bishop of Trevi, and he has been solemnly celebrated every 27 January since the Middle Ages with a procession of the Illuminata. His church (damaged by the quake, but now restored and open for Mass) has three Romanesque apses and a 15th-century portal, with the good bishop and a pair of lions carved in relief. The interior was last redone in the 19th century, but contains a beautiful altar of 1522,

Getting There and Around

There are buses to Trevi from Foligno several times a day (t 0743 212208, f 0743 47807, www.spoletina.com). There are also **trains**, but you have to get a bus up the hill. Trains go to Spello, Assisi and Perugia several times a day, and others to Spoleto, Terni, Narni and Rome.

Tourist Information

Trevi: Piazza Mazzini 5, t/f 0742 781150, www.protrevi.com. Open daily 9–1 and 3–7.

Where to Stay and Eat

Trevi ✉ 06039

*Il Terziere, Via Salerno 1, t/f 0742 78359, www.ilterziere.com (moderate). New, with lovely views and delicious dinners.

Il Pescatore, Via Chiesa Tonda 50, Loc Pigge, t 0742 381711, f 0742 381785, mau.mao @tiscali.it (inexpensive). A peaceful pensione, with nine pleasant rooms, near a babbling brook. Downstairs, the excellent **Taverna del Pescatore, t 0742 780920 (moderate), has an imaginative menu based on meat or fish, very good value and beautifully prepared. Closed Wed.

*La Cerquetta, Via Flaminia 144, Loc Parrano, t 0742 78366, f 0742 381455, cerquetta@ bcsnet.it (rooms inexpensive, meals cheap). Turns out reliable Umbrian food at very honest prices. Closed Sun.

In October, try Trevi's famous black celery (sedano nero); every Thursday morning in October there is a market devoted to it.

Campello sul Clitunno ✉ 06042

Campello sul Clitunno is a quiet alternative to Spoleto if you've come for the festival.

***Vecchio Molino, Via del Tempio 34, Loc Pissignano, t 0743 521122, f 0743 275097, www.vecchio-molino.it (expensive). Close to the Perugia–Spoleto road, but don't be put off by the location of this ex-water mill. Once inside, the sounds are of gurgling water; two streams run through the garden. Inside, old bits of mill are still in evidence and the bedrooms are decorated with antiques. Open April–Oct.

**Fontanelle, Via d'Elci 1, Loc Fontanelle, t 0743 521091, f 0743 275052, www.albergo fontanelle.it (inexpensive). A lovely hotel and restaurant surrounded by greenery. Rooms are comfortable and with bath; the restaurant serves Umbrian specialities like country prosciutto, strangozzi (homemade pasta) and platters of tender lamb, chicken and pigeon.

**Ravale, Via Virgilio, Loc Ravele, Fonti del Clitunno, t 0743 521320, f 0743 521023 (inexpensive). Simple rooms, and a restaurant-pizzeria (moderate).

Pettino da Palmario, Loc Pettino, above Campello, northeast towards Colle Pian Fienile, t 0743 276021. A family-run agriturismo with a deserved reputation for its truffles at affordable prices. Rooms available (moderate). Closed Tues.

carved by Rocco di Tommaso. Next door, the **Palazzo Lucarini** hosts the **Trevi Flash Art Museum** (t 0742 381021 open Tues–Sun 3–7; adm), a joint endeavour between Flash Art magazine and the comune, with works by contemporary Umbrian, Italian and foreign artists.

For the older stuff, make your way to **San Francesco**, a huge mid-14th century church with some original frescoes, on the site where Francis's preaching was drowned out by the braying of an 'indomitable ass'. 'Brother ass, do hush and let me preach to these people,' Francis said, and the animal 'put its head down on the ground and knelt, and remained silent until Francis had finished, much to the wonder of the people'. It holds Renaissance tombs, a Roman sarcophagus with the remains of St Ventura (d. 1310) and one of Lo Spagna's finest works, the Assumption with SS. Jerome, John the Baptist, Francis and Anthony of Padua, where the Virgin ascends to heaven over Foligno. This was originally in the chapel of the San Martino monastery (see p.508).

Access to the church is via its enormous convent, now home to the **Museo Civico** or Raccolta d'Arte di San Francesco (*t 0742 381628; open April, May and Sept Tues–Sun 10.30–1 and 2.30–6; June–July Tues–Sun 10.30–1 and 3.30–7; Aug daily 10.30–1 and 3–7.30; Oct–Mar Fri–Sun 10.30–1 and 2.30–5; adm*). There are good paintings by local artists, including an *Incoronazione di Maria* by Lo Spagna and scenes of the *Life of Christ* from polyptychs by Giovanni di Corraduccio, a charming 15th-century painter from Foligno. In 1999, a **Museo della Civiltà dell'Olivo** (*t 0742 381628; open Oct–Mar Fri–Sun 10.30–1 and 2.30–5; June–July Tues–Sun 10.30–1 and 3.30–7; Aug daily 10.30–1 and 3–7.30; April, May and Sept Tues–Sun 10.30–1 and 2.30–6; adm, includes visit to the Pinacoteca and San Francesco church*) was also opened in the convent. Trevi is famous for its olive oil: its conical hill is wrapped with majestic olive trees, including specimens believed to be well over 1,000 years old (especially the so-called Olivo da Sant'Emiliano, 3km south at Bovara). Olives reached Umbria by the 5th century BC, having been introduced by the Greeks in the Bay of Naples; like many Greek things, they were quickly adapted by the Etruscans and the rest is history.

Around Trevi

Although the town has many churches, the best two are just outside. From Piazza Garibaldi, outside the gate to the *centro storico*, Via Ciuffelli leads to the 14th-century Capuchin monastery and church of **San Martino** (*open 8–12 and 4–sunset*). Over the door is a lunette by Tiberio d'Assisi, whose *St Martin and the Beggar* is inside; the other prize painting is Pierantonio Mezzastris' *Madonna*.

South of Trevi, in an olive grove, is the votive church of the **Madonna delle Lacrime** (*closed*), built in 1487 to house a weeping statue of the Virgin – the first of many churches that went up during the great Marian renewal, inspired by the sermons of San Bernardino. The church, shaped like a Latin cross, has a fine sculpted portal by Giovanni di Gian Pietro of Venice; when the earthquake damage has been repaired, you'll be able to see the beautiful frescoes: the *Adoration of the Magi* by Perugino, an anonymous *Madonna and Child* of 1483 and a *Deposition* by Lo Spagna. Many of the locally prominent Valenti family have impressive tombs from the 1500s and 1600s.

Although the Roman villas and temples that once stood in sacred Clitunno (*see opposite*) are long gone, bits of them were reassembled in a mysterious little building called the **Tempietto del Clitunno** (*t 0743 275085; open summer 8.45–7.45, winter 8.45–5.45; adm*), on the SS3 just south of Trevi (keep your eyes peeled for the sign). Two centuries ago, this was believed to be a pagan temple converted to Christian use; Goethe dissented, believing it to be an original Christian work. For once this most misinformed of all geniuses got it right. The most recent studies put the Tempietto somewhere in the 6th century, or even as late as the 8th, making this obscure, lovely building in a way the last work of classical antiquity, Christian enough, but an architectural throwback to a world that was already lost.

The little track that runs below the temple was the original Roman Via Flaminia; travellers between Ravenna and Rome would look up and see the beautiful façade, with its two striking coloured marble columns and ornate pediment in an exotic, half-oriental late Roman style. The entrance, however, is round the side, leading into the portico and from there to the tiny sanctuary decorated with Byzantine frescoes of the 700s: Saints Peter and Paul flanking the altar, and above, two unforgettable, very spiritual angels inspired by the great mosaics of Ravenna, gazing inscrutably out from the depths of the Dark Ages. The dedication remains intact, on the architrave: 'Holy God of the Angels who made the Resurrection'.

The Fonti del Clitunno

Still on the SS3, 2km south of the Tempietto, you come to **Fonti del Clitunno** (*t 0743 521141; open Nov–Feb 10–1 and 2–4.30; Mar and Oct 9–6; 1–15 April and 16–30 Sept 9–7.30; 16–30 April 9–8; May–Aug 8.30–8; 1–15 Sept 8.30–7.30; adm*), a famous beauty spot for some 2,300 years. Through the poetry of Virgil and Propertius, all of Rome knew about Clitumnus, its eponymous river god, and the snow-white oxen raised here to serve as sacrifices. It was one of the great sights of the Grand Tour; in the 19th-century, it inspired Giosuè Carducci to write one of his best-known poems, baptizing Umbria green for evermore.

Salve, Umbria verde, e tu del puro fonte
nume Clitumno! Sento in cuor l'antica
patria e aleggiarmi su l'accesa fronte
gl'ital iddii.

Hail, green Umbria, and you, Clitunno, genius of the pure spring!
I feel in my heart the ancient fatherland, and the Italic gods
alighting on my fevered brow.

A score of underground springs rise up at the river's source, forming a landscape of astonishing crystal lagoons and islands, planted with weeping willows and poplars. Byron devoted a few stanzas of *Childe Harold's Pilgrimage* to the place (Canto 4), but today, the proximity of the busy Via Flaminia and the railway keep the springs from being quite the idyllic paradise evoked by the poets; still it comes pretty close if you come on a quiet weekday, late in the afternoon after the coach parties have moved on. Next to the park, part of the lagoon doubles as a delightful picnic ground and a well-stocked trout farm.

The village hanging on the steep slope above, **Campello sul Clitunno**, is built around the 16th-century **Chiesa della Bianca**, with frescoes by Lo Spagna inside. For a remarkable view over the Valle Umbra, take the steep little road that snakes up and up through the terraces of olives to the **Castello** (or Campello Alto), a tiny old place hunkered down in the walls.

South of Clitunno: San Giacomo

After Clitunno, the Via Flaminia passes under a grim square castle in **San Giacomo di Spoleto**, an outpost built in the 14th century by Cardinal Albornoz. Unlike the Cardinal's other Umbrian fortresses, this one was later converted into a residential neighbourhood, with tiny lanes lined with little houses. Opposite the castle walls stands the church of **San Giacomo**, founded in the 13th century and redone in the

16th, the date of its beautiful carved doorway and frescoes. The best of these are by Lo Spagna and show miracles accredited to St James the Greater that occurred along the road to Compostela: a young man, unjustly hanged, is discovered still to be alive when his parents returned to cut down his body. The parents hurry to tell the judge, who scoffs and says their son is as alive as the roast chickens on his table, whereupon the roast chickens fly away.

Spoleto

When composer Giancarlo Menotti was dreaming up the Festival of Two Worlds in the 1950s, he spent months travelling across central Italy looking for a pretty town where the best of modern culture could be displayed against a background that recalled the best of the past. **Spoleto** (pop. 36,000) was almost unknown then, a rather austere town of grey stone and cobbled streets, buried in one of the most obscure corners of darkest Umbria. But this one has a remarkable past; after its prominence in classical times, Spoleto became the seat of one of the most powerful states in Italy at the very beginning of the Middle Ages. It remained splendid enough through the golden years of the high Middle Ages and Renaissance to acquire its share of lovely monuments, and then it pricked its finger on a spindle and dozed like Sleeping Beauty. Shelley called it 'the most romantic city I ever saw'.

After its long sleep, Spoleto was ready for Menotti. More than ready, perhaps: even after the musicians pack their instruments and go, they leave behind a Spoleto full of special exhibitions and art workshops, its streets littered with jarring chunks of abstract sculpture. This experimental marriage of trendy art and the medieval hill town is not always a happy one, but it's done Spoleto no harm.

History

Ancient *Spoletium* was one of the Umbrii's most important cities. It was resettled as a Roman colony in 242 BC, only 24 years before an over-confident Hannibal came pounding at the gates, expecting an easy victory after his rout over the legions at Lake Trasimeno (*see* p.450). But *Spoletium* remained loyal to Rome and repulsed the Carthaginians and their allies; Hannibal, who had planned to go to Rome from there, was discouraged enough to make a fatal detour into the Marches instead.

Strategically located on the Via Flaminia midway between Rome and the late Imperial capital of Ravenna, Spoleto was one of the rare towns to prosper in the twilight of the empire. King Theodoric built it up for the Ostrogoths; Justinian's general, Belisarius, did the same for the Byzantines; the Goths under Totila made the city into a fortress, while the Lombards, arriving in 569, made it the base of their power, a duchy that at its height in the 700s controlled most of central Italy.

In 890, after Charlemagne, Duke Guido III made an armed play for the Imperial Crown, but had to be content with crowning himself King of Italy at Pavia. After Guido and his son Lamberto, the duchy fell into decline, and in the 11th century, the popes began to lean on Spoleto, claiming authority through that famous forgery, the

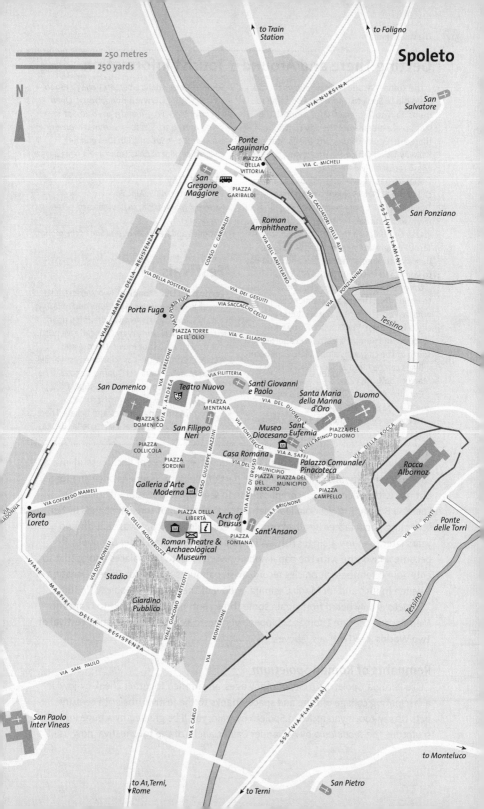

Spoleto

250 metres
250 yards

N

to Train Station
to Foligno

VIA NURSINA

San Salvatore

Ponte Sanguinario

PIAZZA DELLA VITTORIA

VIA C. MICHELI

VIA CACCIATORI DELLE ALPI

San Ponziano

SS3 (VIA FLAMINIA)

San Gregorio Maggiore

PIAZZA GARIBALDI

CORSO G. GARIBALDI

Roman Amphitheatre

VIA DELL'ANTITEATRO

VIA PONZIANINA

Tessino

VIALE MARTIRI DELLA RESISTENZA

VIA DELLA POSTERNA

VIA DEI GESUITI

VIA SACCACCIO CECILI

Porta Fuga

VIA DI PORTA FUGA

PIAZZA TORRE DELL'OLIO

VIA G. ELLADIO

VIA PIERLEONE

VIA FILITTERIA

VIA S. ANDREA

San Domenico

PIAZZA S. DOMENICO

Teatro Nuovo

PIAZZA MENTANA

Santi Giovanni e Paolo

VIA DEL DUOMO

Santa Maria della Manna d'Oro

Duomo

San Filippo Neri

PIAZZA COLLICOLA

PIAZZA SORDINI

VIA FONTECCA

Museo Diocesano

Sant' Eufemia

PIAZZA DEL DUOMO

VIA DELL'ARINGO

VIA DELLA ROCCA

Rocca Albornoz

Casa Romana

VIA A. SAFFI

Galleria d'Arte Moderna

CORSO GIUSEPPE MAZZINI

VIA DEL

VIA ARCO DI DRUSO

MUNICIPIO
PIAZZA DEL MUNICIPIO

Palazzo Comunale/ Pinacoteca

PIAZZA DEL MERCATO

PIAZZA CAMPELLO

VIA DELLE MONTEROZZE

PIAZZA DELLA LIBERTÀ

Arch of Drusus

Sant'Ansano

VIA E. BRIGNONE

VIA DEL PONTE

Ponte delle Torri

VIA MADONNA

Porta Loreto

Roman Theatre & Archaeological Museum

PIAZZA FONTANA

VIALE MARTIRI DELLA RESISTENZA

VIA DON BONELLI

Stadio

VIA MONTERONE

Giardino Pubblico

VIALE GIACOMO MATTEOTTI

Tessino

VIA SAN PAULO

VIA S. CARLO

SS3 (VIA FLAMINIA)

San Paolo inter Vineas

to A1, Terni, Rome

to Terni

San Pietro

to Monteluco

Getting There and Around

The Rome–Ancona railway follows the Via Flaminia to Spoleto. There are also some 10 **trains** daily to Perugia (63km/70mins); the station is a bit far from the city centre, but there are regular connecting buses. **State Railway Ticket Office**, Piazza Polvani, t 0743 48516 (*open daily 6am–8pm*).

Spoleto has its own intercity **bus** company, called the Società Spoletina di Imprese Trasporti (SSIT, t 0743 212208, f 0743 47807, *www.spoletina.com*) with connections from Piazza Garibaldi on the west of town to Assisi, Terni, Perugia and nearby villages. Regular buses go to Norcia and Foligno, and one a day to Rome and to Urbino in the Marches.

Long-term **parking** in the city centre is next to impossible; there's a convenient car park outside Porta Loreto on the west end of the city, a free one in Via Don Bonilli, by the stadium and Roman theatre, and another just south of the city walls along Viale Cappuccini.

Bikes can be hired at Scocchetti Cicli, Via Marconi 82, t 0743 44728.

Car hire: AVIS, Loc S. Chiodo 164, t 0743 46272, f 0743 220840.

Hertz, Via Cerquiglia 144, t/f 0743 46703, *hertzspoleto@tin.it*.

Tourist Information

Spoleto: Piazza della Libertà 7, t 0743 238920, f 0743 238941, *www.umbria2000.it. Open winter Mon–Fri 9–1 and 3.30–6.30, Sat 10–1 and 3.30–6.30, Sun 10–1; summer Mon–Fri 9–1 and 4–7, Sat and Sun 10–1 and 4–7.*
Post office: Piazza della Libertà 12, t 0743 43752.

Market Day

Via Cacciatori delle Alpi, *Fri.*
Farmers' market, Piazza del Mercato, *sporadically.*
Antiques and flea market, *2nd Sun of the month.*

Festivals

Festival dei Due Mondi (of Two Worlds): *held over 3 weeks between mid-June and mid-July.* Italy's leading arts festival, dreamed up in the mid 20th-century by Giancarlo Menotti. A veritable feast of music, theatre and dance. Contact the Associazione Festival dei Due Mondi, Piazza del Duomo, t 45028 220320 or freephone t 800 565600, f 0743 30436, *www.spoletofestival.it* for information, programmes and tickets. There is another box office at Piazza della Libertà.

'Donation of Constantine'. Not until 1198, though, was Innocent III successful in capturing the city, and in 1247, it became part of the papal domains once and for all. But not without occasional complications: in 1499 Spoleto was briefly ruled by Lucrezia Borgia, a 19-year-old just married to the second of three husbands by her scheming papal father. By all accounts, Lucrezia ruled well, but was sent off two years later to marry a bigger fish – Alfonso d'Este of Ferrara. Under the popes, it became a favourite with the papal nobility, who filled it with palaces and used it to entertain celebrities: chronicles record lavish banquets laid on for Queen Christina of Sweden in 1655 and for Maria Casimira, widow of the hero John Sobieski, in 1699.

Spoleto is only heard from again some three centuries later, thanks to Giancarlo Menotti and the late Thomas Schippers who bestowed on the town their **Festival of Two Worlds** (*see* 'Festivals', above).

Remnants of Roman *Spoletium*

Like Perugia, Spoleto is a city of many ages, all jammed together cheek-by-jowl in a fascinating collage of time and space. Thanks to the festival, the 20th century gets its say, too: if you arrive in Spoleto by train, you'll be greeted by a huge iron sculpture, the *Teodolapio* by Alexander Calder, a relic of the 1962 festival now used

Where to Stay

Spoleto ✉ 06049

During the festival, accommodation is tight in and around Spoleto. The tourist office in Spoleto has a list of private rooms and *agriturismo*, but it's vital to book ahead.

Con-Spoleto, Piazza della Libertà 7, t/f 0743 220773, *www.conspoleto.com*, can help with finding accommodation.

Very Expensive

****Dei Duchi, Viale Matteotti 4, t 0743 44541, f 0743 44543, www.hoteldeiduchi.com. An attractive contemporary hotel, popular among visiting artists and performers.

****San Luca, Via Interna delle Mura 21, t 0743 223 399, f 0743 223 800, *www.sanluca.com*. Another hotel in the historic centre, offering a sophisticated 19th-century ambience; some rooms are equipped with a hydromassage.

Expensive

****Albornoz Palace, Viale Matteotti 4, t 0743 221 221, f 0743 221 600, *www.albornoz palace.com*. Refined and stylish, with a pool, just outside the historic centre.

****Gattapone, Via del Ponte 6, t 0743 223447, f 0743 223448, *www.hotelgattapone.it*. The most spectacular: a stone house, clinging to the slope near the Rocca and the Ponte delle Torri, with good views. Eight spacious, finely furnished rooms.

Palazzo Dragoni, Via del Duomo 13, t 0743 222220, f 0743 222225, *www.palazzo dragoni.it*. A *residenza d'epoca* in a 16th-century building, retaining much of its original atmosphere; it's beautiful and central.

Moderate

***Charleston, Piazza Collicola 10, t 0743 220052, f 0743 221244, www.hotelcharleston.it. In a pretty 17th-century palazzo, with 18 comfortably furnished rooms in the *centro storico*.

***Clarici, Piazza della Vittoria 32, t 0743 223311, f 0743 222 010, *www.hotelclarici.com*. More modern, in the lower part of town, but still decorated with taste and style.

***Nuovo Clitunno, Piazza Sordini 6, t 0743 223340, f 0743 222663, *www.hotelclitunno. com*. A good option close to the centre of town.

to shade a taxi stand. Buses from the station leave you at central **Piazza della Libertà**, which is also the usual approach if you arrive by car. Just across from the tourist office, the open side of the piazza overlooks the **Roman theatre** (*open daily 8.30–7.30; adm*), built in the 1st century AD. In the 1950s it was restored as a venue for concerts and ballets during the music festivals; most of the theatre's impressive substructure of arches and tunnels has survived, as well as the pretty marble pavement in the *scena*.

In the Middle Ages, the stage building was replaced with the formidable church, charming cloister and Benedictine monastery of **Sant'Agata**. Now restored, the convent houses Spoleto's **Museo Archeologico** (*t 0743 223277; open daily 8.30–7.30; adm*) with inscriptions and architectural fragments, busts of Julius Caesar and Augustus and other distinguished Romans, and a stone found in a sacred grove dedicated to Jupiter, warning against profaning the place (or chopping wood). The convent refectory has a good cinquecento fresco of the *Last Supper*.

Continue east through Piazza Fontana and turn left, and you'll pass under the travertine **Arch of Drusus and Germanicus**, erected in AD 23 by Tiberius' son (Drusus would have made a good emperor – but he died, and the Roman world got Caligula instead). The arch marked the entrance to the Forum, and on the adjacent modern

Inexpensive

★★**Due Porte**, Piazza della Vittoria 5, t/f 0743 223666.

★★**Il Panciolle**, Via Duomo 4, t/f 0743 45677. Has a good restaurant (*moderate*) where meat is grilled over an open fire. *Closed Wed.*

Outside Spoleto

★★★**La Macchia**, Loc Licina 11, t/f 0743 49059 (*moderate*). Quiet and just north of the centre off Via Flaminia, this is good value. The style is modern, but the furniture in the 12 bedrooms is rustic and made locally. The restaurant specializes in the local *cucina spoletana*, and there's a nice garden.

★★**Ferretti**, Loc Monteluco 20, t 0743 49849, f 0743 222344 (*moderate*). A *pensione* with plenty of charm; some rooms have balconies looking out on to the pretty piazza.

Il Barbarossa, Via Licina 12, t 0743 43644, f 0743 222060, *www.countryhouse-ilbarbarossa.it.* (*inexpensive*). Good value for money; just outside the town walls and in the middle of an olive grove.

Pecoraro, Fraz Strettura 76 in Strettura, about 12km down the SS3 towards Terni, t 0743 229697, *www.ilpecoraro.it* (*inexpensive*). A very pretty and welcoming *agriturismo*,

where guests are treated like one of the family. There is also a small outdoor pool, a luxury in these parts. Very good home cooking (*moderate*) and strong, homemade grappas make this a memorable place to stay or eat. *Closed 15–30 Nov, 1–15 Feb*

There are several decent options if you head up to Monteluco:

★★★**Paradiso**, Loc Monteluco 19, t/f 0743 223 427, *www.albergoparadiso.net* (*inexpensive*). Offers a garden, great views, peace and quiet.

★★★**Michelangelo**, t 0743 47890, f 0743 40289, *www.michelangelohotel.net* (*inexpensive*). Large rooms and very friendly staff, near the top of the town. *Closed 7 Nov–7 Dec.*

Eating Out

Tartufo, Piazza Garibaldi 24, t 0743 40236 (*expensive–moderate*). The name is Italian for truffle and here the black diamonds of the Valnerina appear in various forms combined with pasta or eggs. Other dishes include pigeon breast, thick chickpea soup with river shrimps, *zucchini* flowers with aubergine, duck breast with potatoes and truffles. *Closed Sun eve, Mon and last 15 days of Jan and July.*

building, you can see the outline of the columns of a temple, as well as its actual foundations underneath. The church of **Sant'Ansano** (*t 0743 40305; open April–Oct daily 7.30–12 and 3.30–6.30; Nov–Mar 7.30–12 and 3–5.30*), built over a Paleochristian church and a Roman temple, incorporates more ancient fragments, although its original medieval appearance was sacrificed for fashion in the late 18th century. The 11th-century **crypt of San Isacco**, however, has stayed the same, decorated with rare frescoes in the Byzantine style: the *Beheading of John the Baptist, Christ in Glory*, the *Last Supper*, and the *Life of St Isaac the Hermit*, a 5th-century Syrian monk who took refuge near Spoleto. The crypt's columns are Roman and the capitals Lombard.

Via Arco di Druso empties into the Roman forum, now the **Piazza del Mercato**, where the glistening tomatoes and aubergines compete for your attention with the 18th-century **Fonte di Piazza**, a provincial version of Rome's Trevi Fountain, which incorporates Carlo Maderno's monument to Urban VII of 1626.

Pinacoteca Comunale and the Roman House

The **Pinacoteca** is due to reopen in a new location, in the Palazzo Rosani–Spada on Corso Mazzini, in spring 2003 and will share the building with a **Textile and Antique Costume Museum** (*ask at the tourist office for information*). Among the highlights at the Pinacoteca are works by Spoleto-born Lo Spagna, including his finest, the

Apollinare, Via S. Agata 14, **t** 0743 223256 (*moderate*). These romantic dining rooms are housed in a 13th-century Franciscan convent, which also has a few rooms, though the former occupants wouldn't recognize the elaborate concoctions that emerge from the kitchen, such as fillet of suckling pig with pecorino sauce. Booking recommended. *Closed Tues.*

Pentagramma, Via Martani 4, **t** 0743 223141 (*moderate*). A warm and welcoming place near Piazza della Libertà in a former stable, and a favourite festival rendezvous. It is owned by the daughter of Arturo Toscanini, and serves perfectly prepared local dishes: *spelt* soup, *strangozzi di Spoleto* (flat homemade pasta, with olive oil, garlic, tomato and basil), truffles and lamb. *Closed Mon and part of Jan and Aug.*

Sabatini, Corso Mazzini 54, **t** 0743 221831 (*moderate*). Another old favourite, offering good traditional Umbrian fare. *Closed Mon, 15–30 Jan and 1–15 Aug.*

Del Festival, Via Brignone 8, **t** 0743 220993 (*cheap*). A pretty dining room in the heart of Spoleto, with arched ceilings and a blazing fireplace in winter. As well as truffle dishes of every kind, the chef has a winning way

with desserts and gives regulars membership cards which guarantee them a 10% discount. *Closed Thurs and 1–15 Feb.*

Trattoria Pecchiarda, Vicolo San Giovanni 1, **t** 0743 221009 (*cheap*). Tucked off Via Porta Fuga, this place serves delicous dishes prepared with olive oil from the owner's grove, served with the owner's own white or red Colli Spoletini wine. *Open daily*

Sportellino, Via Cerquiglia 4, **t** 0743 45230 (*cheap*). Another central choice with a simple, homely atmosphere; try the generous mixed *antipasti*, gnocchi with truffles, grilled meats or *ossobuco* with peas. *Closed Thurs and 10 days in July or Aug.*

Outside Spoleto

Il Capanno, Loc Torrecola 6, **t** 0743 54119 (*moderate*). Some 10km south on the Via Flaminia. The menu is Umbrian, with some surprises such as *caramelline* stuffed with caciotta cheese, tomatoes and marjoram, also wild boar, venison and pork – all, of course, prepared with truffles. *Closed Mon.*

Palazzo del Papa, on the SS3 in Strettura, **t** 0743 54140 (*cheap*). A mere *trattoria*, despite its name, but some of the best home cooking around. *Closed Wed.*

Raphaelesque *Madonna, Child and Saints* (1512) painted for the Rocca Albornoz. Another of his commissions, an allegorical *Charity, Mercy and Justice*, was painted for Julius II even though they were hardly that pope's strong points; in 1824 the work was adjusted to fit a bust of another pope, Leo XII, a Spoleto native. There are portraits of the Teutonic dukes of long ago and coins from the days of the Lombard duchy, as well as a beautiful crucifix reliquary and painting of Christ in a lavish filigree frame by the Maestro di Sant'Alò, from the late 1200s. There's a bejewelled Byzantine-style icon from the 13th century and frescoes on the *Lives of SS. Peter and Paul*. Anyone who has read the conspiracy book *Holy Blood, Holy Grail* may want to take a close look at the *Magdalene* by Guercino.

The 1st-century BC **Casa Romana** (*t* 0743 224656, open daily mid-Oct–Mar 10–6; mid-Mar–mid-Oct 10–8; adm) on Via di Visiale is believed, perhaps fancifully, to have been the house of Emperor Vespasian's mother, Vespasia Polla. The atrium and well head, bedrooms, bath and beautiful mosaic floors survive.

Piazza Campello, the Rocca and the Ponte delle Torri

From Piazza del Municipio, Via Saffi climbs up to panoramic **Piazza Campello**. Here, you'll find another good fountain, the 17th-century **Mascherone**, with a huge, grotesque face spitting out the water from the Roman and medieval aqueduct. The monument on the square is from 1910, built to honour all the Spoletines who fought to free their city from the Papal States.

The symbol of the oppression looms just above: the **Rocca Albornoz** (*t 0743 43707 or 0743 238920; open 15–31 Mar Mon–Fri 10–1 and 3–6, Sat and Sun 10–6; April–mid-June and mid-Sept–Oct daily 10–1 and 3–7; mid-June–mid-Sept daily 10–8; Nov–Dec Mon–Fri 2.30–5, Sat–Sun 10–5; adm; guided tour only, lasting 45mins*), an impressive, six-towered citadel by Gattapone from Gubbio, commissioned in 1359 by that indefatigable papal enforcer Cardinal Albornoz, who made this his personal headquarters. Most of the stone used to build it is at least third-hand, first used in the Roman amphitheatre, then cannibalized by the Goth Totila for his fortress, then dragged up here. When Spoleto was firmly in the papal pocket, the Rocca became a popular country resort for the popes, frequented in particular by Julius II, accompanied on occasion by Michelangelo, who loved the peace of the surrounding hills. Until recently, the Rocca served as a prison (among its inmates was Mohammed Ali Agca, the would-be assassin of Pope John Paul II); when it is fully restored, there are plans to install a museum dedicated to the Duchy of Spoleto, a laboratory for the restoration of books and art, an exhibition and conference area and an open-air theatre. Ruins of a 7th-century church of **Sant'Elia** have been found on the hill, which will become a park; there are beautiful views of Spoleto and the valley below.

The pedestrian-only **Via del Ponte** from Piazza Campello leads down to one of the greatest engineering works of the 1300s, the spectacular 755ft **Ponte delle Torri**, a bridge and aqueduct of 10 towering arches built by Gattapone for Cardinal Albornoz, to guarantee the water supply to the Rocca. It dizzily spans the 260ft-deep ravine of the Tessino River far, far below, and was one of the unmissable sights for Grand Tourists, all of whom thought it was Roman; Turner painted a fine picture of it. The bridge does stand on a Roman foundation; you can walk across it to the towers that gave it its name, and to Monteluco's San Pietro (*see* p.520). From here, Via del Ponte circles around under the Rocca back to Piazza Campello.

Sant'Eufemia and the Museo Diocesano

Behind the Palazzo Comunale on Via Saffi, an archway leads into the small courtyard of the archbishop's palace, facing one of the finest Umbrian Romanesque churches, **Sant'Eufemia** (*t/f 0743 231022; open April–Sept Mon–Fri 10–1 and 4–7, Sat–Sun 10–6; Oct–Mar Mon and Wed–Fri 10–12.30 and 3–6, Sat–Sun 11–5; adm*), completed about 1140. It has a plain façade but its interior in luminescent white stone, is remarkable. Fragments of Roman buildings are built into the walls and columns in surprising ways, and it has an anachronistic *matroneum*, the Byzantine-style second-floor gallery where women were segregated during Mass – although this was a common practice in Rome and Ravenna, it's the only *matroneum* in Umbria. The altar, brought from Spoleto's first cathedral, is good Cosmatesque work, with symbols of the four Evangelists surrounding the Paschal lamb.

Part of Sant'Eufemia's convent, built over an important and still partly visible 1st-century Roman structure, became the Palazzo Arcivescovile, now home of the **Museo Diocesano** (*same opening hours as Sant'Eufemia, see above*). This has works garnered from the diocese, with an array of early painted crucifixes and trecento Madonnas, including a beautiful one by the First Master of Santa Chiara di Montefalco. Highlights among the later works are an *Adoration of the Child* by Domenico Beccafumi of Siena, the *Madonna delle Neve* by Neri di Bicci and a *Madonna and Child with SS. Montano and Bartolomeo* by Filippino Lippi. One room contains an excellent collection of medieval Umbrian sculpture, and there's a fascinating assortment of popular *ex votos* from the 16th to 19th centuries.

Via dell'Arringo

Via dell'Arringo, a grand, shallow stairway behind Sant'Eufemia, opens into the Piazza del Duomo. In early medieval times, the Spoletani gathered here to make communal decisions by acclamation after hearing speeches. It must have been this theatrical ensemble that sold Menotti on Spoleto, with its naturally tiered seating set against the cathedral façade and the Umbrian hills as a backdrop. Among the buildings, there's the **Teatro Caio Melisso** (*t 0743 222209, open for performances*), an exquisite little late 19th-century theatre, named after the Spoleto-born dramatist and librarian of the Emperor Augustus; the pink and white striped **Casa dell'Opera del Duomo** (1419); and an octagonal church, **Santa Maria della Manna d'Oro**, built after 1527 as a votive after the Sack of Rome, with four paintings by Sebastiano Conca. Note the Roman sarcophagus used as a fountain, the memorial to American conductor Thomas Schippers, who loved the view and festival so much that he asked to be buried here. Nearby is the 16th-century **Palazzo Racani**, designed by Giulio Romano – with faded *sgraffito* decoration in dire need of restoration.

The Duomo

*t 0743 44307; open Nov–Feb daily 8.30–12.30 and 3.30–6;
Mar–Oct daily 8.30–12.30 and 3.30–7.*

The magnificent Duomo was rebuilt after Emperor Frederick Barbarossa, the most powerful of papal enemies, razed its predecessor to the ground in 1155. Consecrated by the most powerful of medieval popes, Innocent III, in 1198, it has several unusual features. A graceful Renaissance portico (1491) incorporates two pulpits; four rose windows and four circular emblems of the Evangelists adorn its façade, surrounding a gold-ground Byzantine-style mosaic of *Christ Enthroned with Mary and John the Baptist* (1207), signed by Solsternus. The lower middle *rosone* is an exceptional example of the Cosmatesque work imported from Rome – stone or enamel chips in sinuous patterns. The campanile is built from Roman odds and ends.

The earthquake damaged the cathedral but the repair work is now complete. The Latin cross **interior** was unfortunately redone in the 1630s, a misguided gift to the city by the Barberini family of Rome: Maffeo Barberini had been Cardinal of Spoleto before he was elected Urban VIII in 1623, and his nephew, another Cardinal of Spoleto, funded the works and commemorated his uncle with the bronze bust by Bernini located just inside the central door. Several treasures survived the interior redesigners, including the fine Cosmati pavement in the central nave. Pinturicchio, not on one of his better days, painted the frescoes of the *Madonna and Saints* in the first chapel on the right with his usual amusing detail, such as St Jerome's lion frisking about the landscape. His pupil Jacopo Siculo painted the frescoes in the next chapel. In the right transept, a Baroque chapel by Giambattista Mola holds the 12th-century *Santissima Icone*, a highly venerated icon from Constantinople donated as a peace offering to Spoleto by Frederick Barbarossa. The chapel has two paintings by the Cavalier d'Arpino, who painted the dome of St Peter's.

In the apse are the exquisite, rich frescoes of the *Life of the Virgin* (1467–69), a masterpiece by Florentine Fra Filippo Lippi, now beautifully restored. Not only did Lippi paint larger-than-life figures, but he fitted them expertly into the space, through a canny use of perspective and architectural features, including columns and friezes from Spoleto itself. The splendid *Coronation of the Virgin*, in the upper part of the apse, is the best preserved of the cycle, crowded with the angel musicians and female figures that Lippi loved to paint, here in the guise of Sibyls and women from the Old Testament. Lippi portrayed himself (in a white habit with a black hat), his son Filippino (the young angel) and his assistants among the mourners in the central scene of the Virgin's death. The fun-loving monk (he ran off with a nun, but was permitted to leave his order and marry her) died in Spoleto while working on the project and the *Nativity* was finished by his chief helpers, Fra Diamanti and the Umbrian Pier Matteo d'Amelia. When Lippi's great patron Lorenzo de' Medici asked that the artist's body be returned to Florence, the Spoletini refused, claiming they had no notable dead while Florence had a great many. Lorenzo had to be content with commissioning a handsome Florentine tomb for him, now in the right transept.

In the left aisle, the original sacristy was converted into a chapel of reliquaries in the 1560s, with lavish intarsia cupboards made mostly by local craftsmen, although the two with architectural perspectives are by the great Fra Giovanni da Verona; the most important relic is a very rare letter in the hand of St Francis to Fra Leone. Hanging in the first altar on the left is a large and colourful *Crucifix*, dated 1187 and signed by Alberto Sotius, the first Umbrian artist whose name has come down to us.

Lower Spoleto

Some of the city's contemporary art has gone to the Palazzo Collicola on Via Collicola, now the **Galleria Civica d'Arte Moderna** (*t 0743 46434, f 0743 223349; open Wed–Mon 16 Oct–15 Mar 10.30–1 and 3–5.30, 16 Mar–15 Oct 10.30–1 and 3.30–7; adm*). Founded in 1953, the collection has works by Italy's top 20th-century masters (Pomodoro, Burri, Guttoso, Accardi) and showcases Spoleto's Leoncillo Leonardi (1915–68), who evolved a distinctive and colourful style executed in highly textured glazed terracotta. The gallery custodian keeps the key for the church of **Santi Giovanni e Paolo**, consecrated in 1178. It has excellent frescoes; on the left wall, note the scene, attributed to Alberto Sotio, of the *Martrydom of Thomas à Becket*, canonized only five years before (1170).

From here, Via Tobagi leads you to Spoleto's fanciest Baroque church, **San Filippo Neri**, with an ornate façade and lofty dome, designed by a local architect named Loreto Scelli who studied in Rome. It has a fine Baroque bust of St Philip Neri by the

Bolognese sculptor Alessandro Algardi and paintings by Sebastiano Conca and Gaetano Lapis da Cagli.

Via Filitteria leads into Via Sant'Andrea, site of the **Teatro Nuovo** (*Largo B. Gigli, t 0743 40265; closed for restoration*), headquarters of the Two Worlds festival and the older Festival of Experimental Opera. Down the steps from here, the colourful pink and white striped preaching church of **San Domenico** (*closed*) was built in the 13th century; the interior has been restored to its original medieval appearance and has a colourful crucifix hanging in the centre of the nave. The walls are decorated with interesting if fragmented 13th–15th-century frescoes: the first chapel has an especially good *Triumph of St Thomas Aquinas* from the early 1400s, representing the triumph of Aquinas' scholastic philosphy; in a little chapel in the right transept is a *Life of Mary Magdalene* and there's a *Madonna and Child* behind the high altar, both from the early 15th century. The crucifix over the altar is 14th-century. Near here is a fine fresco of the *Pietà*, and a painting of *St Peter Martyr*, the overly efficient Dominican inquistor who was axed in the head for his trouble.

From San Domenico, walk down Via Leone to the tall-towered 13th-century **Porta Fuga** (Put-to-flight Gate – as experienced by Hannibal in 217 BC) and along Via Saccocchio Cecili to take in a stretch of Spoleto's **walls**. The Umbrii built the 6th-century BC cyclopean base using huge blocks, later heightened by the Romans and all the other occupants of Spoleto up to the 15th century. The street ends in Piazza Cairoli; from here, Via dell'Anfiteatro leads past the ruined 2nd-century AD **Roman amphitheatre**, turned into a fortress by Totila and still part of a barracks.

Down on Piazza Garibaldi is the 12th-century **San Gregorio Maggiore** (*t 0743 44140; closed for restoration*); through the gate are the ruins of the Roman **Ponte Sanguinario** (Bloody Bridge), supposedly named after the Christians martyred in the amphitheatre, though more probably a corruption of the Latin name of a nearby gate, the *Sandapilarius*. It was built in the 1st century BC to carry the new Via Flaminia over the river and rediscovered in 1817.

Outside Spoleto

San Ponziano and San Salvatore

From the bridge and Piazza Vittoria, it's a short drive or an unpleasant 15-minute walk on the road under the *superstrada* to the cemetery, passing by way of 12th-century **San Ponziano** (*t 0743 40655; to visit, ring the bell of the custodian's house near the church*). Ponziano is Spoleto's patron, martyred here in 1169. The façade of his church, once faced with marble, is divided horizontally by a cornice and has a pretty Cosmatesque door and a round window surrounded by symbols of the Evangelists. The interior was redone by Giuseppe Valadier in 1788, but has preserved the original crypt. This has an upside-down Roman column, two turning posts (*metae*) from a Roman circus, three ancient sarcophagi and some fresco fragments. In the corridor, embedded like fossils in the wall, are huge Corinthian columns.

Even more Roman material went into building the charming **San Salvatore** (*t 0743 49606; open Nov–Feb 7–5; Mar–April and Sept–Oct 7–6; May–Aug 7–7*), just down from San Ponziano by the cemetery. Spoleto's oldest church, built in the 4th century, San Salvatore preserves its façade and apse despite subsequent rebuildings and loss of its marble facing; the three doors have fine marble architraves and three curious old windows. The fluted Corinthian columns in the interior originally supported a Roman temple; the fresco of the jewelled cross in the apse is 8th or 9th century.

Monteluco

Just east of town, beautiful, forested **Monteluco** is Spoleto's holy mountain. The name is derived from *lucus* (sacred wood), and in Roman times, it was forbidden to chop down the trees. In the 5th century, Isaac the Hermit from Antioch founded the first cenobitic community here; the Benedictines and the Franciscans followed.

You can get to Monteluco by car, by bus from Piazza della Libertà, or on foot over the Ponte delle Torri (*see* p.515–16). Near the bottom of the mountains stands the great Romanesque church of **San Pietro** (*t 0743 44882; open daily summer 9–6.30; winter 9–4.30; in the afternoon ring the custodian's bell near the church*), with a magnificent 12th-century façade, the last hurrah of the Lombard Dukes of Spoleto. The Lombards delighted in portraying real and imaginary animals: here is a fox playing dead to capture some too-curious chickens, battles with lions, oxen, peacocks, eagles, a wolf in monk's clothing, animals devouring one another and the occasional armoured knight; devils contest souls, and St Michael slays his dragon. On the top level are two bulls, statues of St Peter and St Andrew and reliefs of Christ washing St Peter's feet and Christ calling St Peter and St Andrew. An elaborate frieze of vines and plants links allegorical scenes; on the left, the pious could compare the post-mortem destinies of the righteous and the sinful. The interior was Baroqued in 1699.

A steep, hairpinning road leads up through ilex forests to the lonely 12th-century church of **San Giuliano** (*call the monastery of San Francesco to arrange a visit, t 0743 40711*), with a façade incorporating some 6th-century elements of its predecessor. In the 7th century, anchorites and hermits, refugees from the wars in the Holy Land, settled here and set up monasteries; St Francis, who tried to emulate them, came to meditate here and in 1218 founded the tiny monastery of **San Francesco** (*t 0743 40711 or 0743 47797; open daily 9–12 and 3–6*) near the summit of the mountain, a serene spot overlooking the countryside. Monteluco now has more summer villas and hotels than hermitages, but it's still a cool and tranquil place to spend an afternoon.

San Paolo Intervineas

1km or so southwest of Spoleto; take Via San Paolo off Via Martiri della Resistenza. Closed for restoration since the earthquake.

Founded in Paleochristian times and mentioned in the 6th century by St Gregory the Great, **San Paolo Intervineas** was rebuilt in the 10th century and again in 1234, when it was consecrated by Gregory IX as a church for a convent of Clarisse. It has a pretty façade with a rose window and frescoed lunette over the door; the interior contains a good series of frescoes from the period, including an account of the Creation, and an old altar.

The Tiber Valley: Todi, Orvieto, Amelia

19

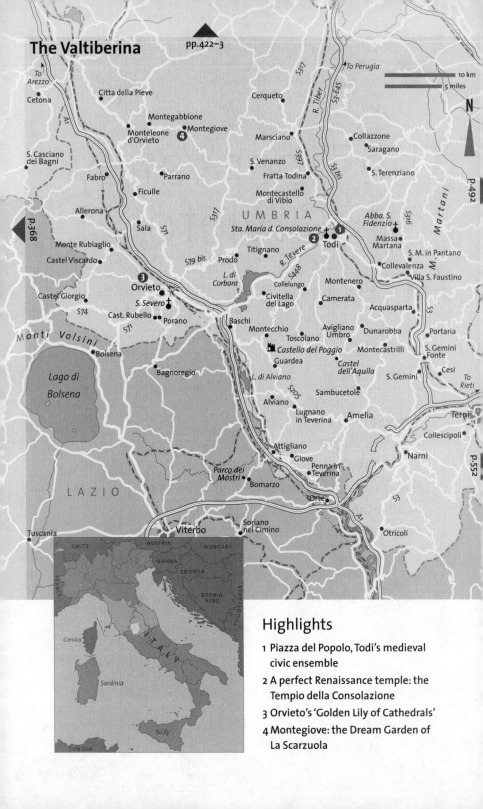

The Valtiberina

pp. 422–3

To Arezzo

To Perugia

10 km

5 miles

N

Cetona

Citta della Pieve

Cerqueto

Montegabbione

Monteleone d'Orvieto • Montegiove ④

Marsciano

Collazzone
Saragano

S. Casciano dei Bagni

Parrano

S. Venanzo
Fratta Todina

S. Terenziano

Fabro

Ficulle

Montecastello di Vibio

UMBRIA

Abba. S. Fidenzio

Allerona

Sta. Maria d. Consolazione

② ①
Todi

Massa Martana

S. M. in Pantano

Monte Rubiaglio

Sala

Titignano

Prodo

R. Tevere

Collevalenza

Villa S. Faustino

Castel Viscardo

L. di Corbara

Collelungo

Montenero

Camerata

Acquasparta

Orvieto ③

Civitella del Lago

Castel Giorgio

S. Severo

Cast. Rubello • Porano

Baschi

Montecchio
Toscolano

Avigliano Umbro

Dunarobba

Portaria

Monti Volsini

Bolsena

Bagnoregio

Castello del Poggio

Guardea

Montecastrilli

S. Gemini Fonte

Castel dell'Aquila

S. Gemini

Cesi

To Rieti

L. di Alviano

Sambucetole

Lago di Bolsena

Alviano

Lugnano in Teverina

Amelia

Terni

Collescipoli

Attigliano

Giove

Narni

LAZIO

Parco dei Mostri

Bomarzo

Penna in Teverina

Orte

Tuscania

Viterbo

Soriano nel Cimino

Otricoli

Highlights

1 Piazza del Popolo, Todi's medieval civic ensemble
2 A perfect Renaissance temple: the Tempio della Consolazione
3 Orvieto's 'Golden Lily of Cathedrals'
4 Montegiove: the Dream Garden of La Scarzuola

South of Perugia, Old Father Tiber flows below the proud medieval eagle's eyrie of Todi, then swells to form the Lago di Corbara and takes a sharp left under lofty hills to form the border with Lazio. This corner of Umbria closest to Rome has a character all its own, much of it concentrated in Orvieto, where mementos of Etruscans rub elbows with those of medieval popes and the papal nobility, under the shadow of one of Italy's great cathedrals. Amelia, wrapped in walls built by the ancient Umbrii, is the third most important hill town in the area, charming but often overlooked. In between the three big hill towns are vineyards and steep wooded ridges, a score of smaller villages and lovely churches, and a handful of unexpected oddities, from a fossil forest of sequoias at Dunarobba to a tiny jewel box theatre at Monte Castello di Vibio to the bizarre gardens of La Scarzuola at Montegiove.

Todi

Todi (pop. 17,200) may be small, but it has everything a self-respecting central Italian hill town needs. There's the hill in a gorgeous setting, a cathedral and medieval public buildings, one great Renaissance monument, a long and tortuous history, a saint (uncanonized, this time), and a proud comune escutcheon, a fierce eagle over the inevitable device 'SPQT'. In the past few years, it has consistently been voted the world's most liveable-in town by the University of Kentucky, an accolade that has brought American tycoons rushing to buy its villas and castles as holiday retreats, inviting comparisons with the Hamptons. But Todi was always a sophisticated little place, famous for its carpentry and woodworking. In April it hosts one of Italy's major antique fairs, the Rassegna Antiquaria d'Italia, and in August and September, the Mostra Nazionale dell'Artigianato, a national crafts fair. Since 1986, the festival has brought the town opera, ballet and stage companies from late July.

History

It was the eagle that showed the ancient Umbrii where to build the city they were to call the 'Border' or *Tuter*, above modern Todi, on what is now the Rocca. The border was an uncomfortable one with the Etruscans, who settled lower down around the Piazza del Popolo; one day, the Etruscans became kings of the whole hill when they surprised, slaughtered and enslaved their Umbrian neighbours. As *Colonia Julia Fida Tuder*, dedicated to the war god Mars for its role in the wars against Hannibal, the town prospered through Roman times, and its nearly impregnable site kept the barbarians out; there's no evidence that Todi was ever part of the Lombard duchy of Spoleto, and it's possible that it may have maintained its independence all along.

By the 1200s, Todi had accumulated a little empire, including Terni and Amelia, and its soldiers were kept in trim by constant dust-ups with their peers in Spoleto, Narni and Orvieto. In 1227, their *podestà* was the notorious Mosca dei Lamberti, who had been exiled from Florence after the killing of Buondelmonte dei Buondelmonti (*see* **Topics**, p.33); Dante would consign him to the Eighth Circle of Hell. But above all, Todi took special pride in its good deeds. In 1249, the *comune* founded the Ospedale della

Getting Around

Todi is linked by **bus** to Terni (33km/45mins; ATE, **t** 0744 492711, *www.actemi.it*), Perugia (41km/1hr; APM, **t** 800 512141, *www.apmon line.com*), Rome (130km/2½hrs), and by the FCU's little trains (**t** 075 575 4038, *www.fcu.it*) to Perugia and Terni.

Trains (FS, **t** 892 021, *wwwtrenitalia.com*) and **coaches** (to Perugia, Terni, Rome and Orvieto) come and go from down below, at Ponte Rio, **t** 075 894 2092, linked to the centre by city bus.

Unfortunately, there's only one **bus** a day between Todi and Orvieto (SULGA, **t** 800 099 661, *www.sulga.it*) , but it's a pleasant route that takes in the lovely scenery over the Tiber Valley. There are SSIT buses to Spoleto (**t** 074 321 2208 and 0743 212229 for timetables, *www.spoletina.com*).

Tourist Information

Todi: Piazza del Popolo 25, **t** 075 894 5416, **f** 075 894 2406, *info@iat.todi.pg.it. Open summer Mon–Sat 9.30–1 and 3.30–7, Sun and hols 10–1 and 3.30–7; winter closes at 6.* **Church opening hours**: *9–12.30 and 2.30–6.*

Where to Stay

Todi ✉ 06059

Very Expensive
Relais Todini, on the road to Collevalenza di Todi, **t** 075 887521, **f** 075 887182, *www.*

relaistodini.com. A 14th-century palazzo furnished with antiques, plus a heated pool, tennis, elegant restaurant and beautiful views. The 750-acre park has camels, kangaroos, zebras and penguins, horses or carriages to ride, and four lakes for boating.

Expensive
★★★★**Bramante**, Via Orvietana 48, **t** 075 894 8381, **f** 075 894 8074,*www.hotelbramante.it.* In a 13th-century convent just outside town. The setting is lovely, but the service and décor have become a bit run-down.
★★★★**Fonte Cesia**, Via L. Leoni 3, **t** 075 894 3737, **f** 075 894 4677, *www.fontecesia.it*. Stylish, accommodation in an 18th-century building near Piazza Jacopone in the historic centre.
Poggio d'Asproli, Loc Asproli 7 (15mins from Todi), **t/f** 075 885 3385, *poggiodasproli@tin.it*. Artist Bruno Pagliari has opened this 16th-century convent to guests, filled with antiques and his own colourful art. Pool, terrace and musical and theatrical evenings in the summer. Delightfully quirky, friendly and comfortable. Dinner on request.
San Lorenzo Tre, Via S. Lorenzo, **t/f** 075 894 4555. A *residenza d'época*, in a palazzo in town, with 19th-century furnishings.

Moderate
★★★**Villa Luisa**, Via A. Cortesi 147, **t** 075 894 8571, **f** 075 894 8472, *www.villaluisa.it*. A pleasant place near the centre, with parking and garden; all rooms have TV. The following are *agriturismo* around Todi. For a full list, ask at the tourist office.

Carità, where the poor were treated for free – even Florence wasn't to have the like until 1316 – and it produced one of the greatest Italian poets of the Middle Ages in Fra Jacopone (*see* p.527). By the end of the century, the government and the political effectiveness of the free *comune* were failing. The Atti family established themselves as *signori* during the early 1300s, but were pushed out by the Malatesta of Rimini and Francesco Sforza of Milan among others, until eventually, in the 1460s, the pope gobbled up the town definitively for the Papal States.

Piazza del Popolo

Todi's streets converge on its magnificent 13th–15th-century Piazza del Popolo, the centre of civic life since the Etruscans and Romans. In the 15th century, as Todi's existence as an independent city state came to an end, the square was preserved in aspic, leaving a medieval pageant in grey stone. The sternest building, the **Palazzo**

L'Arco, at Cordigliano, **t** 075 894 7534, *larco-rosaspina@libero.it*. Rooms with shared bath. *Open May–Sept*.

Poponi, Via delle Piagge 26, **t** 075 894 8233. Similar facilities. *Closed mid-Jan–mid-Feb*.

Castello di Porchiano, at Porchiano, **t** 075 885 3127, **f** 0635 3447 308. *Closed Feb*.

Monte Castello di Vibio ✉ 06057

***Il Castello, Piazza G. Marconi 5, **t** 075 878 0560, **f** 075 878 0676, *www.hotelilcastello.it* (*moderate*). The charming 15th-century Castello is the only place to stay and eat here. *Closed Jan, and Tues in Dec–Mar*.

Eating Out

Local specialities include pigeon, lamb and *porchetta*, and fat homemade spaghetti called *ombricelli* served *alla boscaiola* (tomatoes, piquant black olives and hot peppers). Seek out the dry white wine Grechetto di Todi, dating back to the Roman Republic.

Umbria, Via S. Bonaventura 13, **t** 075 894 2737 (*expensive*). Fine Umbrian cuisine with an enchanting Umbrian view. Meals begin with a delicious variety of *antipasti*, followed perhaps by *spaghetti alla tudertina*, and succulent grilled meat and fish, ranging from trout to boar. Book for a table with an unobstructed view. *Closed Tues*.

Antica Hosteria de la Valle, Via Ciuffelli 19, **t** 075 894 4848 (*moderate*). An atmospheric restaurant with a creative menu – be sure to book ahead. The *antipasto della casa* is recommended: cheese fondue flavoured with truffles, rustic pâté and a selection of *bruschette*. Seasonal vegetables, fruit and herbs feature strongly in dishes such as lamb cooked with orange. *Closed Mon*.

Italia, Via del Monte 27, **t** 075 894 2643 (*cheap*). An unpretentious and welcoming *trattoria*, with red tablecloths and a rustic feel, offering the usual fare plus a few specialities, most notably the *capriccio*, a pasta dish cooked in the oven, a bit like lasagne. *Closed Fri*.

Jacopone (Da Peppino), Piazza Jacopone 3, **t** 075 894 2366 (*cheap*). Similar Umbrian specialities, served by friendly staff. Try the *pasticcio alla jacopone*, a roll made of meat, vegetables and ricotta served sliced with either tomato or white truffle sauce. *Closed Mon and 15 days in July*.

Lucaroni, Via Cortesi 57, **t** 075 894 2694 (*cheap*). More sophisticated dishes, such as a delicious risotto with pigeon, black truffles and port and an excellent linguini with crab – a refreshing change after so many Umbrian meat dishes. *Closed Tues and 1–15 Nov or Aug*.

La Mulinella, Loc Pontenaia, 3km from the centre at Ponte Naia, **t** 075 894 4779 (*cheap*). Enjoy a fine view up towards Todi from the garden at this reliable old favourite, which will fill you up with tagliatelle with goose sauce, gnocchi with mushrooms and guinea fowl with chestnuts, at very fair prices. *Closed Wed and 1–15 Nov*.

dei Priori (1293–1337), has square battlements with a chunky tower, while the **Palazzo del Popolo** (1213), with swallow-tail crenellations, and its adjacent **Palazzo del Capitano** (1290) are all grace by comparison; these two, linked by a grand Gothic stairway, make up one of the most remarkable medieval town halls in Italy. These outer stairs emphasized how easy it was for the citizenry to have access to their local government, who invariably held their meetings on the first floor.

They now provide access to Todi's attic, the **Museo Pinacoteca di Todi** (*t/f 075 894 4148; open Oct–Feb Tues–Sun 10.30–1 and 2–4.30; Mar and Sept Tues–Sun 10.30–1 and 2–5; April daily 10.30–1 and 2.30–6; May–Aug Tues–Sun 10.30–1 and 2.30–6; adm; beware, the stairs can be slippery when wet*). On the fourth floor of the Palazzo del Popolo, this harbours fond civic memories: retired eagles, archaeological pieces, 16th-century scenes of charity by local painter Pietro Paolo Sensini, among portraits of saints and worthies connected to the city, a model of the Tempio della Consolazione from *c.* 1570, a fine *Coronation of the Virgin* by Lo Spagna, and paintings by a 16th-century so-so painter, Ferraù da Faenza, who spent a lot of time here. Todi is especially proud of a saddle it made for the ailing and pregnant Anita Garibaldi.

To the right of Palazzo del Capitano, a cypress was planted in 1849 in honour of Garibaldi's visit – a fleeting one, as the republic of Rome had just fallen to the French allies of the pope and they were pursuing the hero, his wife and a handful of loyal Garibaldini. Now named **Piazza Garibaldi**, this overlooks much of central Umbria.

On the far side of the Piazza del Popolo, the **Duomo** (*t 075 894 3041; open 28 Mar–Oct 8.30–12.30 and 2.30–6.30; Nov–27 Mar 8.30–4.30*) is enthroned atop another distinguished flight of steps. Begun in the 12th century and finished 200 years later, it has a handsome flat screen façade, fine rose window and delicately decorated portal, while the interior is embellished with good capitals, a Gothic arcade by a fourth aisle and a 14th-century altarpiece. Parishioners who turned round to gossip during Mass were confronted by a not-too-terrifying vision of the *Last Judgement* by Ferraù da Faenza, a reworking of Michelangelo's in the Sistine Chapel. The large crypt has been turned into a **lapidary museum** (*adm*), containing bells, a copy of Todi's patron deity *Mars*, now housed in the Vatican, and fragments of statue groups by the school of Giovanni Pisano.

To the left of the Duomo stands the 16th-century **Bishop's Palace** and the **Palazzo Rolli**, attributed to the younger Antonio da Sangallo; it was once the home of Paolo Rolli (d. 1765), who translated Milton into Italian.

Down to Porta Perugina

To the right of the Duomo, the road twists around, allowing a view of its beautiful apse. Some of Todi's **Etruscan-Roman walls** survive nearby, off Via Mure Antiche. Via Santa Prassede leads down to the pink and white church of **Santa Prassede**, from the 14th century, but with a Baroque interior. The early medieval town ended here; beyond, Via Borgo Nuovo descends steeply past the monastery of **San Francesco**, also from the 14th century, with an allegorical fresco on *Salvation* from the same period by the altar. Further down, a round tower marks the 13th-century **Porta Perugina**, through which there are views over the countryside. The only hitch is walking back up the hill.

San Fortunato and the Rocca

From Piazza del Popolo, Via Mazzini leads past the **Teatro Comunale** (1872) to Todi's other great monument, **San Fortunato** (*April–14 Oct 9–12.30 and 3–7, closed Mon am; 15 Oct–Mar Tues–Sun 9.30–12.30 and 3–5*). Located atop a broad stair in a prominent position, San Fortunato (1292) was one of many churches built during the late 13th-century Franciscan spending spree, when the Order received permission from the popes to administer as well as 'use' the substantial property it had received as donations from the pious. In Todi they built on a grand scale, but the façade remains unfinished. According to scurrilous legend, when the Orvietani heard that the Tuderini had commissioned Lorenzo Maitani to decorate it, they had the sculptor murdered to prevent Todi from having a church as good as their cathedral. The late Gothic central portal was completed only in the 1400s and has little figures hidden among the acanthus and decorative bands: there's St Francis receiving the stigmata and the damned in hell with a little salamander, who doesn't seem to mind because salamanders were believed to be fireproof. The statues on either side of the door are of the *Annunciation*; the beautiful angel has been attributed to Jacopo della Quercia. The airy, luminous and remarkably wide Gothic interior is one of the best in central Italy, divided into three naves of equal height. Large fragments of frescoes decorate many of the chapels, including a *Madonna and Child* (1432) by Masolino da Panicale, his only work in Umbria. The fine wooden choir is by Antonio Maffei of Gubbio (1590). But for the Tuderini the focal point is the **tomb** of the poet and mystic Jacopone da Todi in the crypt, the subject of much local if unofficial devotion. With his revolt against Boniface, Jacopone may have blown all hopes of ever being canonized, though Todi regards him as a saint, and in 1906, on the 600th anniversary of his death, erected the bronze statue in the niche at the bottom of San Fortunato's steps.

Next to San Fortunato stands the Palazzo Ludovico Atti, built for the town's *signori* and attributed to Galeazzo Alessi. From the garden to the right of the church, a lane leads up to the top of the town and the massive round tower of the Rocca, what remains of Todi's 14th-century citadel; the public gardens and belvedere offer an unforgettable view of the Tiber Valley and the Tempio della Consolazione. Here, too, is a Roman cistern converted into a chapel, known as the Carcere di San Cassiano for an account that it also at one point served as St Cassian's prison cell.

Piazza Mercato Vecchio and Santa Maria in Camuccia

The most impressive reminder of Roman *Tuder* is in the **Piazza Mercato Vecchio**: take the stepped Via San Fortunato down to Via Roma, walk through the handsome medieval **Porta Marzia** (made out of Roman pieces) and then turn left. A temple of *Tuder*'s patron Mars once stood near here, and in the old market square there is a series of imposing arches with a Doric frieze called the **Nicchioni** (niches) from an Augustan era basilica. Below the piazza is the little Romanesque church of **San Carlo** and the **Fontana Scarnabecco**, which was built in 1241 by a *podestà* from Bologna.

If you return to the Porta Marzia, continue down Via Roma and turn right, you'll come to **Santa Maria in Camuccia** (*open daily summer 8–1 and 3–8; winter 8–1 and 3–5*), a 13th-century church with Roman columns by the door; inside is the 12th-century wooden statue of the *Virgin and Child* known as the *Sedes Sapientiae* (Seat of Wisdom). From here, you can walk down to the Tempio della Consolazione (if you don't mind the slog back up the hill); you can also reach it by car on the ring road around Todi.

Tempio di Santa Maria della Consolazione

Open April–Oct Wed–Mon 9–1 and 2.30–6,
Nov–Mar Wed–Mon 10–12.30 and 2.30–6.

This is the most ambitious attempt in Umbria to create a perfect Renaissance temple, and it is a beautiful ornament for Todi, an ivory-coloured essay in geometric forms, isolated amid wooded slopes and farmlands. Dedicated to an apparition of the Virgin, the Tempio della Consolazione was begun by the unknown Cola da Caprarola in 1508 but shows the influence of the great Roman architect Bramante, who may indeed have helped with the design. Scholars attempting to unravel the building's origins found only more puzzles, as a picture of the temple was discovered among the architectural sketches of Leonardo da Vinci from 1489.

Begun in 1508, the church was not completed until 99 years later. By that time, every celebrity architect of the late Renaissance had stuck his oar in, including many who worked on St Peter's: Antonio da Sangallo the Younger, Baldassare Peruzzi, Vignola and Sanmicheli among others. In 1589 a Perugian architect, Valentino Martelli, designed the drum and dome. But unlike St Peter's in Rome, the Tempio's purity of form, geometrically harmonious restraint, patterns of semicircles and triangles and careful proportions of the fine dome and four apses (three polygonal and one semicircular) emerged as if the work of a single architect. Four Tudertini eagles guard the corners of the terrace and the classical interior, in the form of a Greek cross, is white, spacious and serene, with Baroque statues of the 12 Apostles and an elaborate altar with a 15th-century fresco of the *Madonna della Consolazione*.

Montesanto

t 075 894 8886; closed for restoration until 2006.

Another sacred site outside Todi's walls is the 13th–14th-century fortified **Convento di Montesanto**, on Viale Montesanto, 1km below the Porta Orvietana. A famous Etruscan bronze statue of Mars (probably made in Orvieto) was found here in what may have been an Etruscan temple. The great lime tree by the entrance is one of the oldest in Italy, planted in 1428 by San Bernardino di Siena. The church contains a massive 16th-century fresco of the *Nativity*, and another by Lo Spagna, and has lovely views over the Tempio della Consolazione.

Around Todi

North of Todi: Montecastello and The Smallest Theatre in the World

Todi's lovely surroundings are dotted with minor attractions. If you have to choose one, make it **Montecastello di Vibio,** 10km northwest, a walled medieval hill town high over the Tiber Valley, home to an American art school. When Montecastello became its own master under Napoleon, the village's nine leading families decided to commemorate the Revolution by pooling their money to build the delightful **Teatro della Concordia** (*t 075 878 0737, www.teatropiccolo.it; open Sat and Sun all year, Oct–May 10–12.30 and 3–6.30; June–Sept 10–12.30 and 4.30–7.30; daily at Christmas, New Year, Easter and July–Aug)* a miniature version of La Scala with its boxes, decorations and 99 seats. It closed in 1950, but was restored in 1993.

Beyond Montecastello

Just north of Montecastello, the little hill town of **Fratta Todina** was a bone of contention between Perugia and Todi before it became a favourite country retreat of the rich families of Todi; it has a handsome Franciscan convent called La Spineta. There's a 12th-century castle 7km further north in the industrial sprawl of **Marsciano**, built by its *signori* the Bulgarelli, who gave their fief to Perugia rather than let it fall into the grasping talons of Todi. North again, there's part of a fresco of *St Sebastian and the Plague Saints*, by a young Perugino (1478) in the parish church of **Cerqueto**.

There's a bridge over the Tiber at Marsciano to charming **Collazzone**, a near-intact walled medieval hill town that was once a Perugian outpost. Like Todi, it enjoys a lovely setting among olive groves and forests, so perhaps Jacopone, who spent his last years here in the monastery of San Lorenzo, wasn't too homesick. The monastery was restored by Todi's bishop Angelo Cesi and is now Collazzone's town hall. South, charming **San Terenziano** has a handsome Palazzo Cesi and a pink Romanesque church outside the centre; don't miss the crypt with its funny old capitals.

East of Todi: Massa Martana and Around

These days, pilgrims tend to ignore the Tempio della Consolazione and Montesanto, preferring the hideous **Santuario dell'Amore Misericordioso**, 6km east of Todi in **Collevalenza**. Founded in 1955 by Mother Speranza Alhama Valera (d. 1983), it was so popular that it had to be enlarged 10 years later.

East a further 10km is **Massa Martana**, behind a 10th-century gate and 13th-century walls; it was founded as *Vicus ad Martis*, a way-station along the western branch of the Via Flaminia. Unfortunately, Massa was the epicentre of the first earthquake – back in May 1997 – of the many that would shake Umbria for the next two years, and it will be a long time before its *centro storico* and its houses, town hall and theatre, are repaired. Still clad in scaffolding, it's a ghost town, with its one bar catering for the labourers. Like Orvieto, the town is built on a *rupe*, or spongey bluff made of tufa, which adds to the difficulty; it requires major infrastructure work and buttressing as well as the more obvious repairs to walls and roofs. Just outside the centre, the late Renaissance church, the octagonal **Santa Maria della Pace** (*now being restored*) is a minor jewel, with an interior reminiscent of the Tempio della Consolazione. West of Massa, in a beautiful setting, the pink and white 11th-century **Abbazia Santi Fidenzio e Terenzio** (*open church hours*) is built over the tomb to Umbria's first saints, who came from Syria to spread the Good Word and were martyred under Diocletian. The campanile stands on a twelve-sided pedestal of tufa blocks, cannibalized from a Roman structure; if it ever reopens, it has an unusual crypt and Lombard reliefs, and a marble pulpit from the 1200s.

South of Massa, **Santa Maria in Pantano** (*key at the house next door*) was built in the 7th or 8th century out of a Roman structure along the Via Flaminia. The oldest section is the apse; the adjacent campanile was converted from a medieval defensive tower. Inside are Roman bits and a Roman altar, columns erected in the 12th century and frescoes from the 14th century and earlier; it also has a beautiful wooden Christ on the cross, halfway down the nave. Further south, the little walled town of **Villa San Faustino** is synonymous in Umbria with its bottled mineral water. Just outside the walls, the **Abbazia di San Faustino** (*key kept next door*) was also built using Roman stone, this time in the 12th century. It's an old, mysterious place, set among other buildings cobbled together over the centuries. One was a Paleochristian funerary chapel built over **catacombs** (*recently restored; open Tues, Thurs, Sat and Sun 9–1*) dating back to the 4th century AD and decorated with Christian symbols of the fish and lamb.

Orvieto

Orvieto (pop. 20,700) owes much of its success to an ancient volcano. First this created the city's magnificent pedestal – a 325m (1,066ft), sheer-cliffed mesa, straight out of the American southwest – and then it enriched the hillsides below with a special mixture of volcanic minerals that form part of the secret alchemy of Orvieto's famous white wine. Although new buildings crowd the outskirts of Orvieto's unique crag, the medieval town on top, crowned by its stupendous cathedral, looks much the same as it has for the last 500 years.

History

Attracted by Orvieto's incomparable natural defences, the Etruscans settled it early and named it *Velzna* (or *Volsinium* as the Romans pronounced it). It was one of the 12 cities of the Etruscan confederation, and it fought frequently with the Romans until they laid it waste in 280 BC. Velzna/Volsinium must have been a wealthy place; historians record the Romans carrying home 2,000 statues after the sack. The Etruscans departed and founded a new Volsinium on the shores of Lake Bolsena, leaving behind their old city (*Urbs Vetus*, hence 'Orvieto'). Orvieto in the Middle Ages was an important stronghold of the Papal States – primarily for popes who could take refuge here when their polls went down with the fickle Romans.

The Duomo

t 0763 341167 (Cathedral direct line), f 0763 340336; open Nov–Feb 7.30–12.45 and 2.30–5.15; Mar and Oct 7.30–12.45 and 2.30–6.15; April–Sept 7.30–12.45 and 2.30–7.15. For Cappella di San Brizio, see p.535.

The 13th century may have been an age of faith, but it certainly wasn't an age of fools. The popes were having trouble putting over the doctrine of transubstantiation, an archaic, genuinely pagan survival that many in the Church found difficulty in accepting. But then the necessary miracle occurred, during a visit to Orvieto by Pope Urban IV in the 1260s. A Bohemian priest named Peter, while on his way to Rome, was asked to celebrate Mass in Bolsena, just to the south. Father Peter had long been sceptical about the doctrine of the Host becoming the body of Christ, but during this Mass, the Host itself answered his doubts by dripping blood on the altar linen.

Marvelling, Peter took the linen to show to the Pope, who declared it a miracle and instituted the feast of Corpus Christi. St Thomas Aquinas, also visiting Orvieto at the

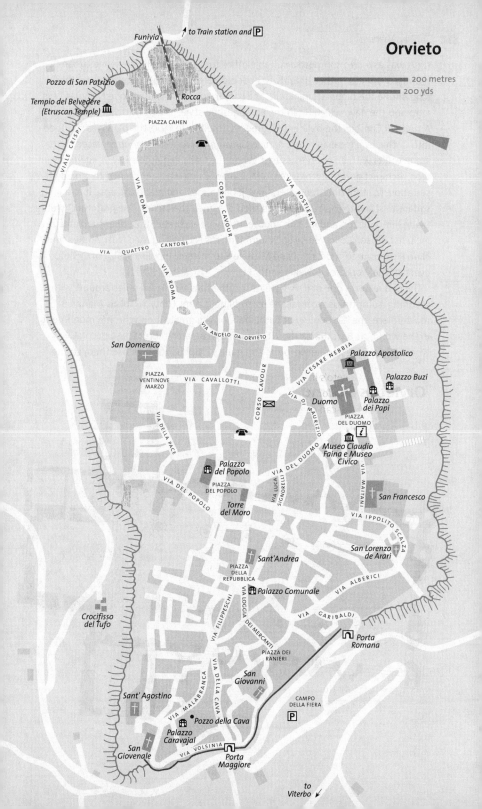

time, was asked to compose a suitable office for the new holy day, while Urban IV promised Orvieto (rather unfairly to poor old Bolsena) a magnificent new cathedral to enshrine the blood-stained relic. The cornerstone was laid by Pope Nicholas IV in 1290 and the nave was built in the Romanesque style, probably to a design by Arnolfo di Cambio, the builder of Florence cathedral. In 1300, the plan was changed into Gothic by a local architect named Giovanni di Uguccione, who replaced the stone vaults with an open truss roof. When the walls began to sway dangerously in 1305, architect and sculptor Lorenzo Maitani of Siena was summoned to remedy the situation. Maitani built four lateral flying buttresses and made the apse into a square to stabilize the building, and then designed the façade. The grateful Orvietani made him a citizen and let him choose his own assistants. Subsequent architects included his son, followed by such luminaries as Nicolò and Meo Nuti, Andrea and Nino Pisano, Andrea Orcagna and Michele Sammicheli. Ippolito Scalza of Orvieto oversaw the works for 50 years, until 1617.

The end result is one of Italy's greatest cathedrals, visible for miles around, with a stunning, sumptuous 170ft façade resembling a giant triptych. This is Maitani's masterpiece, the 'Golden Lily of Cathedrals' or 'the greatest polychrome monument in the world,' as Burckhart called it, designed as an architectural and decorative whole, the simple geometric forms and gables emphasized to make them strong

Orvieto's Duomo

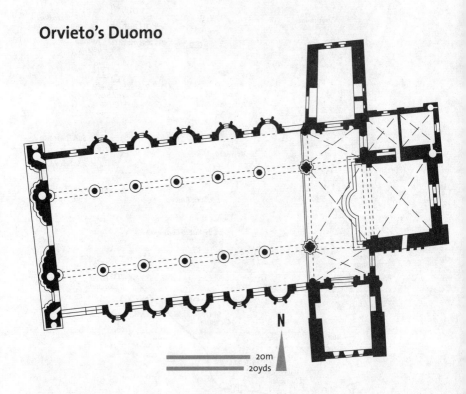

enough to take the lavish detail. Colour it certainly has, especially when the late afternoon sun inflames the dazzling Technicolor **mosaics** that fill every flat surface, although artistically there's not much to say about them – all were replaced after the façade was struck by lightning in 1795, except for the restored *Nativity of Mary* (1364) over the south door. The magnificent **rose window** (1360) is by the great Florentine artist Orcagna and is surrounded by 16th-century statues of the Apostles.

Close up, the richness and beauty of the sculptural detail is simply breathtaking. It is said that 152 sculptors worked on the cathedral in total, but it was Maitani himself who contributed the best work – the remarkable design and execution (along with his son Vitale, and Nicolò and Meo Nuti) of the **bas reliefs** (1320–30) on the lower pilasters that recount the story of the *Creation* to the *Last Judgement*. This Bible in stone captures the essence of the stories with vivid drama and detail – the *Last Judgement*, in particular. Maitani also cast the four bronze symbols of the Evangelists, the ox, eagle, man and winged lion, all ready to step right off the cornice of the façade, and the bronze angels in the lunette over the central portal, who pay homage to a *Madonna* by Andrea Pisano (*removed for restoration*). The bronze doors, portraying the *Works of Mercy* (1965) are by Emilio Greco. The 16th-century sibyls on the corners of the façade were sculpted by Fabiano Toti and Antonio Federighi.

In contrast with the soaring vertical lines of the façade, the cathedral's sides and little rounded chapels are banded with horizontal zebra stripes of yellow tufa and grey basalt. On the right (south side) is the oldest door, the Porta di Postierla, while on the left, the Porta del Corporale had three statues by Andrea Pisano in its lunette. Along with Pisano's *Madonna* from the Duomo, these are being restored by the **Opera del Duomo**, which has yet to decide whether to display them in its museum or replace them in their original positions.

One of the best times to come to Orvieto is in mid-May, when you can witness the Pentecost **Festa della Palombella**, a tradition founded by the Monaldeschi in 1404: a steel wire is suspended from the roof of the church of San Francesco (*see* p.541) to a wooden tabernacle on the porch of the cathedral, and on the stroke of noon, a white dove tied with red ribbons on an iron wreath-like contraption gets the ride of its life hurtling down to the tabernacle, greeted by a round of firecrackers to symbolize the flames of the Holy Spirit that lit up over the heads of the Apostles. The dove is later presented to the last couple to have been wed in the cathedral, who are charged to keep it as a pet until the end of its natural days. Another high day, **Corpus Christi** in early June, occasions a procession of the *Corporale* in its glittering reliquary through Orvieto, accompanied by the Orvietani in all their trecento finery.

The Interior

Filtered through stained glass and alabaster window, the muted light adds to the serene beauty of the striped Romanesque nave, divided into three by fine columns and capitals and rounded arches, topped in turn by a clerestory. The lack of clutter – much of the art has been stowed away in the Museo dell'Opera del Duomo – reveals the lovely proportions and the subtle asymmetries that give the interior its unique dynamism. Note how neither the five semicircular chapels on

Getting There and Around

Orvieto, or at least its lower version, Orvieto Scalo, lies on the main **railway** between Rome (121km/2hrs) and Florence (152km/2hrs); from Perugia it's 86km and just over an hour. Orvieto is also linked by ATC **coach**, t 0763 301224, with Amelia, Narni, Terni, Viterbo in Lazio, etc. The once daily trip to Todi (48km/2hrs) down the SS79 bis is magnificently scenic. All coaches stop by the funivia at the railway station.

There are **car parks** in Piazza Cahen and at the ex-Campo della Fiera under the cliff (from here take a lift up to the church of San Giovanni, or bus C to Piazza della Repubblica). If you book a table at a restaurant in the historic centre, you can park for free in Via Roma: the restaurant will give you a voucher to stick on the dashboard.

It may be easiest to park free by the station. From there, bus 1 makes the steep trip up a couple of times a day, or take the scenic *funivia* (built in 1888, when it ran on water power, restored in 1990 to run on electricity) that runs every 10–15 mins (*7.20am–8.30pm, Sun 8am– 8.30pm*) from the station to Piazza Cahen next to the Fortezza and Etruscan temple. From here, shuttle bus A will take you directly to the cathedral, or bus B will take you around the *centro storico* (save your tickets, and you get a discount at the Museo Faina).

Car Hire and Bike Hire

Avis, Viale I Maggio 46, Orvieto Scalo, t 0763 393007. *Open Mon–Fri 9–12.30 and 3–7, Sat 9–10, Sun open on request.*

Hertz, Via Sette Martiri 32f, Orvieto Scalo, t 0763 301303. *Open Mon–Fri 8.30–1 and 3–7, Sat 8.30–1, Sun open on request.*

For pedal and motorbikes try:

Gulliver, Strada del Piano 6a, Orvieto Scalo, t 0763 302969. *Open daily 24 hours.*

Ciclo e Trekking 'Natura e Avventura', t 0763 342484, f 0763 391625, *www.argoweb.it/ ciclotrekking*; also Via Montenibbio 35/37, Orvieto Scalo (near the staion), t/f 0763 301649. For bike tours in the surrounding countryside. *Open Mar–Oct.*

Tourist Information

Orvieto: Piazza del Duomo 24, t 0763 341772 and 0763 341911, f 0763 344433, *www.orvienet.it, www.umbria2000.it, www.comune.orvieto.tr.it. Open Mon–Fri 8.15–1.50 and 4–7, Sat and Sun 10–1 and 3–6.*

---

each wall nor the windows are centred between the arches of the aisles, nor the upper clerestory windows. The floor rises gently up to the altar, and each striped column is slightly shorter as you approach – producing a magical effect as you walk down the nave.

Of the details that remain, look for Gentile da Fabriano's delicate fresco of the *Madonna and Child* (1426) by the left door, near the baptismal font of 1407. Many of the side chapels have remains of votive frescoes. In the left transept, there's a *Pietà* (1579) by Ippolito Scalza, its figures carved from a single block of marble. Beyond is the **Cappella del Corporale**, built *c.* 1350 to house the famous relic and decorated by Sienese masters: the frescoes of the *Miracle of Bolsena* and *Crucifixion* by Ugolino di Prete Ilario (1360s) and, in a niche in the right wall, the exquisite *Madonna dei Raccomandati* (1339) by Lippo Memmi, the brother-in-law of Simone Martini. The altar, with Gothic tabernacle by Nicola da Siena and Orcagna, shelters the venerated blood-stained linen. To the left, encased, is the silver gilt **Reliquario del Corporale** (1338), echoing the façade of the cathedral and decorated with 12 enamelled scenes from the Life of Christ by goldsmith Ugolino di Vieri of Siena. In the nave, the cathedral's magnificent **organ**, built in 1584 is the second largest in Italy.

The **choir** frescoes, by Ugolino di Prete Ilario and other Sienese painters, have recently been restored. The intarsia **stalls** are by another Sienese, Giovanni

Their *Carta Orvieto Unica* costs €12.50 and admits you to the Capella San Brizio, Musei Archelogici C. Faina and Civico, Orvieto Underground, and the Torre del Moro; also a free round trip on the *funivia* plus minibus A or B or five hours' parking in the Campo della Fiera and lifts to the city centre. Available from the tourist office, relevant museums or at the booths in the car parks.
Post office: Largo M. Ravelli, **t** 0763 340914.

Where to Stay

Orvieto ✉ 05018

Very Expensive
****La Badia**, Loc. La Badia 8, 5km south on the Bagnoregio road, **t** 0763 301959, **f** 0763 305396, *www.labadiahotel.it*. Set in the hills, within an old abbey with lovely views up to the tufa-crowned citadel. It preserves much of its original ambience. In the grounds there's a pool and a tennis court.

Expensive
****Villa Ciconia**,Via dei Tigli 69, north along the SS71, **t** 0763 305582, **f** 0763 302077, *www.hotelvillaciconia.com*. A 16th-century villa, set in an oasis of green bordered by two rivers in the ugly sprawl of Orbetello Scalo, with a frescoed restaurant serving fine food.
****Maitani**, Via Maitani 5, **t** 0763 342012/3, **f** 0763 342011, *www.hotyelmaitani.com*. Just opposite the cathedral, offering comfortable rooms with bath, air conditioning, TV and parking.
****Palazzo Piccolomini**, Piazza dei Ranieri 36, **t** 0763 341743, **f** 0763 391046, *www.hotel piccolomini.it*. A gorgeous medieval palace in the historic centre, sumptuous and luxurious.
***Duomo**, Vicolo di Maurizio 7, **t** 0763 341887, **f** 0763 341105, *www.orvietohotelduomo.com*. Recently refurbished hotel near the cathedral.

Moderate
****Aquila Bianca**, Via Garibaldi 13, **t** 0763 341246, **f** 0763 342273, *www.gattei.it/ aquilabianca*. Old-fashioned but central, with a garage and wine cellar.
***Valentino**, Via Angelo da Orvieto 30/32, **t/f** 0763 342464, *www.valentinohotel.com*. In a 16th-century house near the old church of San Domenico, with mod cons and garage.
***Virgilio**, Piazza Duomo 5, **t** 0763 341882, **f** 0763 343797, *www.hotelvirgilio.com*.

Ammannati, and the **stained glass** is by Giovanni di Bonino from Assisi (1334). To the right is Ippolito Scalza's last work, an *Ecce Homo* (1608). In the little south transept, the **altar of the Magi** was sculpted by a young Sammicheli, before he went on to become Venice's great military architect.

The Cappella di San Brizio

*Open Nov–Feb Mon–Sat 8–12.45 and 2.30–5.15; Mar and Oct 8–12.45 and 2.30–6.15, April–Sept 8–12.45 and 2.30–7.15; also Oct–June Sun and hols 2.30–5.45; July–Sept Sun and hols 2.30–6.45; buy tickets at the tourist office; to reserve tickets, call **t** 0763 343592, **f** 0763 340336, opsmon@tin.it. Only 26 people admitted at a time.*

This contains one of the finest and most powerful fresco cycles of the Renaissance, but its genesis was hit and miss. In 1408, the Monaldeschi financed the construction of the Cappella Nuova, which became known as Cappella di San Brizio for the pretty 14th-century altarpiece of the *Madonna di San Brizio*. In 1447, they hired Fra Angelico to fresco it and he began with the ceiling vaults, completing two scenes near the altar – the serene *Christ in Judgement* and the *Prophets* – while his pupil Benozzo Gozzoli contributed the hierarchies of angels. Then the pope summoned Fra Angelico to Rome and he died before returning to finish the project.

Occupies a recently refurbished trecento building just across from the cathedral.

Inexpensive

None of these is anything special, but the price is right. There are plenty of *agriturismo* close by; the tourist office has a list.

Posta, Via Luca Signorelli 18, **t/f** 0763 341909. Off Corso Cavour in the historic centre, with a garage and a patch of garden.

Near the station in Orvieto Scalo:

Pergoletta, Via Sette Martiri 5, **t/f** 0763 301418. All rooms have TV; garage parking.

Picchio, Via G. Salvatori 17, **t/f** 0763 301144, *hotelpicchio@tin.it*. Even cheaper.

Eating Out

There are lots of good restaurants in Orvieto, although day-trippers from Rome and tourists have helped to keep some mediocre venues in business – choose with care. Besides Orvieto's famous wine, local specialities include *cinghiale in agrodolce* (sweet and sour boar) and *gallina ubriaca* (Umbrian 'drunken chicken').

I Sette Consoli, Piazza Sant'Angelo 1A, **t** 0763 343911 (*very expensive*). Using the best local ingredients with imagination, such as *pappardelle* with duck sauce or gnocchi with *zucchini* and mint; a fine selection of wines, too, and you can dine outside in the summer. The *menu degustazione* (*expensive*) with three wines is good. *Closed Sun eve winter only and Wed from Nov–Mar.*

Le Grotte del Funaro, Via Ripa Serancia 41, **t** 0763 343276 (*expensive*). An elegant restaurant in a set of tufa caves, with a terrace. Good, solid Umbrian cuisine, with especially good pasta and mixed grilled meats, and pizza at night. Open till 1am, with *enoteca* and piano. *Closed Mon except July–Aug; 1 week in Jan and 1 week in July.*

Osteria dell'Angelo, Piazza 29 Marzo 8a, **t** 0763 341805 (*expensive*). Sets off local ingredients with flair, with dishes such as goose liver and red turnip in puff pastry with raspberry vinegar, lamb with aubergine and good desserts. Good wine list. *Closed Sun eve, Mon and Tues lunch and 1–15 Aug.*

L'Asino d'Oro, Vicolo del Popolo 9, **t** 0763 344406 (*moderate*). The best place to eat – innovative cuisine with a menu that changes daily to give scope to the chef Lucio Sforza, who sometimes appears to explain the inspiration for his dishes. Tables under a

Years later, Perugino was commissioned to complete the work, but he left after a few days. Finally, in 1499, Luca Signorelli of Cortona, a student of Piero della Francesca and already sufficiently famous to have painted a fresco in the Sistine Chapel, was hired to complete the vaults. The patrons liked what they saw and commissioned him to fresco the walls. Signorelli made the end of the world his theme, and worked on the project until 1504. This chapel is, in many ways, the stylistic and psychological precursor of Michelangelo's *Last Judgement* in the Sistine Chapel; Signorelli's remarkable draughtsmanship and foreshortening, his dynamic male nudes inspired by Antonio Pollaiuolo and what he learned from Piero about simplifying nature and architecture into essential geometrical forms, give the frescoes tremendous power.

The six scenes in the Cappella di San Brizio are iconographically taken from the *Divine Comedy* and St Augustine's *City of God*. The first, the *Preaching of the Antichrist,* is a rare subject and evokes the confusion and turmoil in Florence after the Dominican preacher Savonarola was burned at the stake in 1498. If you look in the crowd attending the Antichrist (whose words are prompted by the Devil), you can see Dante's beaky profile and red hat as he stands with Petrarch and Christopher Columbus – symbolic of the beginning of the modern era – while in the background, around the Temple of Solomon, chaos and catastrophe are at work in the last throes of the Middle Ages. Far to the left of the Antichrist, the artist has portrayed himself and Fra Angelico dressed in black, watching the anarchy with a quiet detachment

pergola; simple stylish presentation and charming waiters. Open until 12am. *Closed Mon, 20 Oct–15 Dec and 15 Jan–15 Mar.*

Etrusca, Via Lorenzo Maitani 10, t 0763 344016 (*moderate*). Lovely traditional food in this cinquecento building near the cathedral; it comes top among the trattorias. *Open daily, no hols*

Maurizio, Via Duomo 78, t 0763 341114 (*cheap*). More inspired Umbrian pasta and other dishes at this long-time favourite. *Closed Tues and 15–31 Jan.*

La Volpe e L'Uva, Via Ripa Corsica 1, t 0763 341612 (*moderate–cheap*). A busy place, with some unusual *secondi* on the menu. *Closed Tues, Mon and Jan.*

Zeppelin, Via G. Garibaldi 28, t 0763 341447 (*moderate*). *www.ristorantezeppelin.it.* Not only can you eat lunch and dinner in this excellent restaurant, but you can also learn how to cook the dishes you are sampling on one of the resident cooking courses. The food is based on local traditions (*umbrichelli* with juniper-flavoured wild boar sauce and pecorino cheese, tagliolini with back truffles, pork fillet with peaches and wild fennel plus a choice of fish dishes) and there is an ample wine list.

Wine-tastings

For information on the local wine visit:

Consorzio per la Tutela dei Vini Doc Orvieto e Rosso Orvietano, Corso Cavour 36, t 0763 343790, f 0763 394980, *consvino@tiscali.net.*

Cantina Foresi, Piazza Duomo 2, t 0763 341611. The best place to taste and buy wines. *Open Nov–Mar daily 9.30–7.30, April–Oct 9 –9.*

Antinoni, Castello della Sala, Loc Sala, Ficulle, t 0763 86051, f 0763 86491. Famous for its Cervara. *Open daily 8–5, telephone first for reservations.*

Barberani, Loc. Cerreto (Lago di Corbara), Baschi, t 0763 341820, f 0763 340733. *Open Mon–Fri 8–1 and 2–5, weekends by appointment.*

Tenuta Le Velette, at Le Velette near Orvieto Scalo, t 0763 29090. *Open Mon–Sat by appointment.*

Cooperativa Vitivinicola per la Zona di Orvieto, Vini Cardeto, Sferravacallo, Orvieto, t 0763 300594, f 0763 300594, *cardecom@tin.it.* *Open Tues–Fri except hols and harvest; telephone first.*

Cantina Monrubo, Loc. Le Prese, Monterubraglio, t 0763 626064, f 0763 626074, *cantina.monrubio@tiscalinet.it. Open Mon–Fri 8–1 and 2–5 except hols and harvest.*

that seems almost chilling. Signorelli's mistress jilted him while he painted this, so he put her in the scene as the prostitute taking money. Overhead St Michael keeps the Antichrist from ascending to heaven.

Next to this is the *End of the World*, where a prophet foretells doomsday: the sea floods, the earth shakes, the stars fall from the firmament and the darkened sky is shot with streaks of fire. In the next scene, Signorelli gives us the *Resurrection of the Dead* in unforgettable, literal detail as the corpses and skeletons pull themselves out of the curiously glutinous earth and form new coats of flesh, although the fellow on the right merrily conversing with six skeletons adds a humorous touch. This is one of the most powerful nude studies of the quattrocento, only surpassed by the next scene, *The Damned Consigned to Hell*, a crowded writhing *Inferno* that seems to echo Sartre's 'Hell is other people'; even the cruel devils, one per person, are more or less human, except for their metallic colours, horns and shaggy hips (Signorelli made sure to put his mistress here, too, caught in the embrace of a flying devil). The *Blessed* in the next scene get to go to Paradise with the lovely angels (parts of this fresco, concealed by the 18th-century altar, can be seen by way of video) while the final scene shows the *Coronation of the Chosen*. Below the frescoes Signorelli painted medallions of Cicero, Homer (though since the restoration, he's been identified as Statius), Dante, Virgil, Ovid, Lucan and pre-Socratic philosopher Empedocles (to the right of the entrance). He also painted the scenes from the *Divine Comedy* and myth in the *tondi*, and the *Deposition*, where one mourner is Pietro Parenzo, who served Orvieto as *podestà* in the 13th century and was killed by heretics.

Piazza del Duomo

The cathedral shares the piazza with Ippolito Scalza's handsome **Palazzo Buzi** (1580) and the deteriorating neoclassical church of **San Giacomo Maggiore**, as well as other palazzi housing Orvieto's five museums. Opposite the cathedral, the 19th-century Palazzo Faina contains two of these, the **Musei Archeologici Claudio Faina e Civico** (*t 0763 341511, f 0763 341250, www.museofaina.it; open Oct–Mar 10–5; April–Sept 9.30–6; closed Mon from Nov–Feb; adm*). The ground floor, the Museo Civico, has terracotta decorations from the Belvedere temple – male figures, a warrior, a horse and the goddess Artemis that show a strong Greek influence. The Venus of Cannicella, an Archaic Greek statue made of Naxos marble from the 6th century BC, was found in Orvieto's oldest tombs; a giant warrior's head from the same period came from the Crocifisso del Tufo. A 4th-century BC sarcophagus is decorated with gruesome scenes from the Trojan War, of Achilles sacrificing Trojan prisoners to Patroclos, and Neoptolemos killing Polyxena, Priam's daughter, on Achilles' tomb.

The Museo Claudio Faina one of Italy's top private archaeological collections, was garnered in the last century by the Faina counts and donated to the city in 1954. It fills the two upper floors and is rich in finds from Orvieto's necropoli: there are 3,000 ancient coins, Etruscan gold, an excellent collection of vases and bronzes, a beautiful selection of the black and red figure Attic vases imported by wealthy Etruscans, *bucchero* ware, and an Etruscan sarcophagus with traces of its bright paint. The top floor has a good view of the cathedral. Concerts are held in the garden in summer. This museum is one of the few that has a specific children's 'programme'. Kids are given a special brochure (in English and Italian) with information and descriptions of the various exhibits plus a history of the museum and explanations on: What is archaeology? What does an archaeologist do? How did the exhibits get here? A quiz tests how much of the museum they have taken in.

The south side of the cathedral was the heartbeat of papal Orvieto. The austere, crenellated tufa **Palazzo Soliano** was begun by Boniface VIII in 1297, who didn't think the slightly older Palazzo Apostolico (*see* p.539) was up to snuff. It was finished in the 1500s and contains the **Museo dell'Opera del Duomo** (*t 0763 343592, f 0763 340336, due to reopen after restoration 2005*), with works that once filled the cathedral – statues by grand masters like Arnolfo di Cambio and Andrea Pisano, grand statues by little-known hands, especially the colossal *Apostles*, and two early Baroque figures of the Annunciation by Bernini's teacher, Francesco Mocchi. Paintings include a *Crucifixion* by Spinello Aretino, a *Madonna* by 13th-century master, Coppo di Marcovaldo, a *Self-portrait* and a *Magdalene* by Signorelli (very much like the one painted by his master Piero, in Arezzo), a reliquary of San Savino's head by Ugolino di Vieri and, most beautiful of all, two richly coloured *Madonnas* by Simone Martini. There are two beautiful sketches on parchment of the cathedral façade, one by Maitani, and an older one attributed to Arnolfo di Cambio. The ground floor houses the **Museo Emilio Greco** (*t 0763 344605, f 0763 344664; open daily*

April–Sept 10.30–1 and 2.30–6; Oct–Mar 10.30–1 and 2–5.30; adm; combined ticket available with the Pozzo di San Patrizio), with a large collection of works from 1947 up to the 1980s, donated by the sculptor.

Adjacent, the 13th-century **Palazzo Apostolico** (or Palazzo Papale), begun by Urban IV and finished in 1304, has been restored to hold the **Museo Archeologico** (*t/f 0763 341039; open daily 8.30–7, also 2 Aug–15 Sept Sat 8.30am–11pm; adm, combined ticket with Necropoli Etrusca available*), with an excellent collection of Etruscan bronzes, vases (including some fine Greek ones), mirrors, bronze armour and a fresco of an Etruscan butcher's stand. Best of all are two painted 4th-century BC tombs from Settecamini, reconstructed here. Both represent scenes of the banquet that all good Etruscans expected to find when they went into the underworld: those in the first tomb, of the Leinie, show scenes of the kitchen, as servants (all carefully named) prepare the meat. On the opposite wall the banquet takes place, presided over by the gods of the underworld, Pluto in a wolfskin cap and spear decorated with a serpent, and Persephone, holding a sceptre topped by a bird. The dead guest of honour arrives in a chariot with a demon.

Orvieto Underground

> *t 0763 344891, f 0763 391121, speleotecnica@libero.it. Scheduled visits daily at 11, 12.15, 4 and 5.15; call t 0763 334 0688 for tours in English or extra tours; adm. Tours depart from the tourist office at Piazza del Duomo 24.*

From within their obliging tufa, the residents of the *rupe* have excavated a shadow, alternative city, an underground labyrinth of galleries (or *grotte*) containing wine cellars, silos, wells, cisterns, ovens, aqueducts, little religious shrines, medieval rubbish pits, dovecotes and more.

Piazza del Popolo and Around

In contrast to its heavenly cathedral (Pope John XXIII said that on Judgement Day the angels would bear it up to Paradise), the rest of Orvieto is a solid medieval town, dotted with *palazzi* built for Roman and local bigwigs by many of the architects who worked on the cathedral. **Corso Cavour** has been Orvieto's main street since Etruscan times and where it meets Via del Duomo towers the 137ft **Torre del Moro** (*t 0763 344567; open Mar–April and Sept–Oct 10–7; May–Aug 10–8; Nov–Feb 10.30–1 and 2.30–5; adm*), built in the 12th century and affording a sublime view over the city. The big bell, decorated with 24 symbols of Orvieto's guilds, was cast in 1316; the cathedral builders timed their workday by it. Adjacent, the **Palazzo dei Sette** (1300) was built for the seven magistrates elected by the guilds to govern the *comune*.

One block to the north, in Piazza del Popolo is the **Palazzo del Popolo**, a tufa palace begun in 1250, with mullioned windows and an open loggia in the Lombard style. Turned into a prison and warehouse by the popes, the building has recently been restored and is now a conference centre. The restoration uncovered the sacred area of an Etruscan temple, a medieval aqueduct and a cistern. Also in the piazza,

Palazzo Simoncelli is the site of the new **Museo delle Ceramiche Medioevali Orvietane** (*check at tourist office for opening hours*). Orvieto was an important centre for the production of ceramics in the Middle Ages.

From here, Via della Pace leads back to a piazza with the church of **San Domenico**, built in 1233, just after St Dominic's canonization, making it the first Dominican church ever built. St Thomas Aquinas taught at the former monastery here and is recalled with several mementos in the **Cappella Petrucci**, built by Sammicheli below the church. None of these claims to fame, however, spared the church from a savage amputation of its naves in 1934 to make room for a barracks. The surviving transept held an elaborate, elegant *Tomb of Cardinal de Braye* (1285) by Arnolfo di Cambio, but even that has now been spirited away.

Four Churches and a Palazzo

From the Torre del Moro, Corso Cavour winds down through 16th-century *palazzi* and medieval buildings to **Piazza della Repubblica**, Orvieto's main square and site of the Etruscan and Roman forums. Here is the 12th-century church of **Sant'Andrea** with its unusual twelve-sided campanile, pierced by mullioned windows and topped by bellicose crenellations. The mosaic pavement of a 6th-century church was discovered underneath Sant'Andrea, and on an even lower level, there's an Etruscan street and buildings (*the sacristan has the key to the excavations*). Decorated with 14th-century frescoes, Sant'Andrea was the most important church in Orvieto before the construction of the cathedral and basks in the memory of the important events that took place within its walls: here Innocent III proclaimed the Fourth Crusade, and here in 1281, Charles of Anjou and his glittering retinue attended the coronation of Martin IV.

Piazza della Repubblica's 13th-century **Palazzo Comunale**, hidden behind a late Renaissance façade, is the starting point for exploring Orvieto's most picturesque medieval streets, such as Via Loggia dei Mercanti, lined with tufa houses; at its end, beyond Piazza dei Ranieri, the octagonal church, **San Giovanni**, was first built in 916 and rebuilt in 1687; it has a 14th-century detached fresco of the Madonna from the original church and a handsome cloister used for exhibitions. At this point, Orvieto's pedestal is almost sheer, and a narrow lane follows along the edge down and around to the oldest corner of the town and the delightful **San Giovenale**, begun in 1004, equipped with a fortified tower, frescoes from the 12th–15th centuries and charming old bits of ancient sculpture. The big adjacent Gothic church of **Sant'Agostino**, with its handsome door, has been restored as an exhibition space.

To Porta Maggiore

The picturesque Via Malabranca leads back to the centre by way of the 16th-century **Palazzo Caravajal**, designed by Ippolito Scalza, with its handsome portal and an inscription in Spanish, informing passers-by that the house was built for the comfort of the owner's friends. Here, too, is the 15th-century **Palazzo Filippeschi** (or Pietrangeli), the most beautiful in Orvieto. Florentine rather than Roman in style, it has such a lovely courtyard and portico that it has been attributed to Bernardo Rossellino. From here, Via della Cava descends to the old gate, **Porta Maggiore**; at the restaurant at Via della Cava 26, you can peer into the depths of the **Pozzo della Cava** (*t 0763 342373, f 0763 341029, www.pozzodellacava.it; open Tues–Sun 8am–8pm; adm*), a deep public well excavated by the Etruscans and used from 1428 to 1546.

San Lorenzo and San Francesco

The 13th-century Romanesque church of **San Lorenzo de Arari**, reached by Via Ippolito Scalza from Corso Cavour (or on Via Maitani from the Piazza Duomo) was named for its venerable altar (*ara*), supported by a cylindrical Etruscan altar, the whole protected by a lovely 12th-century stone *ciborium*. The Byzantine-style frescoes in the apse add an ancient feel, especially the elongated figures and staring eyes of *Christ Enthroned with Saints*, while other frescoes, from the 1330s and restored with more good will than skill, depict the *Life of St Lawrence*, who retains his sense of humour even while being toasted on the grill ('Turn me over, I'm done on this side,' he said). In the Middle Ages, when no body part was too kinky to stick in a reliquary, some churches claimed to have vials containing his melted fat.

Nearby in Piazza dei Febei, the 13th-century preaching church of **San Francesco** has been much changed over the centuries. Its size came in handy for important events – it was here that Boniface VIII canonized St Louis of France in 1297. Inside, it has a wooden *Crucifixion* attributed to Maitani or a close follower and some recently discovered 14th-century frescoes in the sacristy.

The Citadel, a Temple and St Patrick's Well

Orvieto's northeastern end and funicular terminus, **Piazza Cahen**, is dominated by the ruins of the **Rocca**, a citadel built in 1364 by Cardinal Albornoz. The people of Orvieto, always willing to host a pope or two (some 33 spent extended periods in the city), showed their appreciation of this direct attempt at papal domination by destroying it in 1390, so that only the walls, a gate and a tower survive, now encompassing a garden of umbrella pines. Views from the ramparts stretch from the shallow Paglia River to the Tiber Valley. Next to the citadel lies the massive podium of an Etruscan temple, the 5th-century BC **Tempio del Belvedere**, made of travertine: it had a double row of columns in front, a *pronaos*, and three *cellae*, a perfect example of the typical Etruscan-Italic temple described by Vitruvius. The podium was rediscovered by accident in 1828 and fragments of its terracotta decoration are in the Museo Civico.

Much of the temple's stone was cannibalized for the building of a nearby well, but it's hardly any old well: the ingenious **Pozzo di San Patrizio** (*Valle Sangallo, t 0763 343768, f 0763 344664; open April–Sept 10–6.45; Oct–Mar 10–5.45; adm, joint ticket with Museo Greco available*), designed in the 1530s by Antonio da Sangallo the Younger, is the most celebrated of all Orvieto's subterranean wonders. Its name comes from St Patrick's well in Ireland, where according to legend, Patrick found Paradise after passing through the depths of Hell.

The well was built on the orders of the calamitous Medici pope Clement VII. After surviving the sack of Rome – and sneaking out of the city disguised as a greengrocer – Clement became understandably paranoid about the security of the papal person.

He commissioned this unique work of engineering to supply Orvieto in the event of a siege; to reach the spring below, Sangallo had to dig the equivalent of seven storeys. To haul the water to the surface, he built two spiral stairs of 248 steps in a brick double helix – one for the water-carriers and their donkeys going down, another for going up, meeting at a narrow bridge at the base of the well. The stairs are lit by 72 windows on the central shaft. Bring a sweater; it is surprisingly cold and damp at the bottom (*open summer 10–7; winter 10–6; adm*). Despite the labour that went into its construction, the well was never needed. But it didn't harm the Church as much as another decision the hapless Clement made during his stay in Orvieto – his refusal to annul Henry VIII's marriage to Catherine of Aragon.

Around Orvieto

The base of Orvieto's bluff is pocked with Etruscan tombs that have been excavated off and on for centuries, and back in the finders-keepers age of archaeology, many of the most beautiful finds went to the Louvre and the British Museum. Unlike Perugia's impressive Ipogeo dei Volumni, few of these have any decoration; the tombs resemble streets of low houses, each sparsely furnished with a pair of benches where the urns of the departed were arranged. The most impressive is the 6th-century BC **Crocifisso del Tufo** (*t 0763 343611; open daily April–Sept 8.30–7, Oct–Mar 8.30–5; adm*), on the SS71 north of Orvieto; go by foot from the Porta Maggiore, where the austerity of its large tufa blocks are relieved by velvety moss and soft grassy roofs. Excavations began in the 1800s and continue slowly apace. So far over 100 rectangular chamber tombs have been found, one per nuclear family, sharing walls, each with a little entrance with the family and given names inscribed on the lintel. Originally they were closed with a stone door. Piles of clay and earth sealed the roofs, which would be topped with a *cippus* – the head of the warrior in the Museo Civico was one of these. By the unique wealth of inscriptions found here, it seems that Velzna was unusually multicultural for an Etruscan town – the oldest burials were of Greek origin, while other families have Latin, Umbrian and even Gothic names.

Still on the SS71, about 2.5km south from the Porta Romana, the 12th–13th-century Benedictine abbey of **Santi Severo e Martirio** (renovated in the 19th century and now partly a hotel, La Badia, *see* p.535), retains much of its original work – a Cosmatesque pavement and some trecento frescoes, as well as another dodecagonal campanile similar to the peculiar one at Sant'Andrea. Further south in Loc Porano, there's the painted Etruscan **Tomb of the Hescanas** near **Castel Rubello** (*open by request; the custodian lives nearby*), while just over the border in Lazio, medieval **Bagnoregio** is piled on a smaller version of Orvieto's tufa pedestal.

Hills, Lakes and Gardens around Orvieto

North of Orvieto

The rather empty territory high in the hills to the north of Orvieto on either side of the *autostrada* isn't one of Umbria's better-known regions – which may be part of its

Orvieto's Wine, in Legend and in a Glass

When Signorelli drew up his contract to fresco the Cappella di San Brizio, he made sure to add a certain clause: 'that he be given as much as he wanted of that wine of Orvieto'. And, fuelled on the stuff, Signorelli never painted better. First made by the Etruscans and Romans, and shipped down the Tiber at *Palianum*, near Baschi (where archaeologists have recently found large caches of amphorae), the wine legendarily saved the city from the barbarians, who partook so generously of the golden nectar that they found in the city's temples that all the locals had to do was gather up the drunks in the middle of the night and give them the old heave-ho.

Now refined over the centuries, Umbria's most famous wine is grown in 16 designated areas in the provinces of Terni and Viterbo, and consists of a careful mixture of grapes, with Tuscan Trebbiano and Verdello dominant. Light straw-coloured Orvieto DOC comes in four different varieties: dry (Orvieto secco), which now predominates because of the market, although you can still find the more authentic moderately dry (*abboccato*, often served with appetizers), medium-sweet (*amabile*) and sweet (*dolce*), made like a Sauternes from noble rot (*muffa nobile*). If made in the oldest growing zone, right near Orvieto, it's called Classico.

appeal. One possible destination, along the winding SS71 to Città della Pieve, is walled medieval **Ficulle**, founded by the Lombards and long home to potters who make earthenware wine pitchers (*panate*), oil containers (*ziri*) and bean pots (*pignatte*), which you can purchase. All the houses in Ficulle have little terracotta numberplates by the doors. The Collegiata in town was designed by Ippolito Scalza, while the little church of **Santa Maria Vecchia**, outside the walls, has 15th-century frescoes and preserves an ancient *cippus* from a mithraeum. Other residents of Ficulle are the Marchesi Antinori, who make the finest Orvietos and live six kilometres south at the imposing, beautifully preserved **Castello della Sala** (*open for visits if you call ahead Mon–Fri, t 0763 86051; closed Aug*), built by the Monaldeschi in the 1300s; it has a Gargantuesque cylindrical tower, linked to the square castle by a covered gallery. North, near Montegiove, up a signposted unpaved road through a forest, lie the gardens of **La Scarzuola** (*guided visits by appointment only, Convento della Scarzuola e Città Buzziana, t 0763 837463; minimum of 8 people per visit, lasts 2 hours; adm exp*). In 1956, the architect Tomaso Buzzi (1900–81) purchased a 13th-century Franciscan convent and its grounds to create a garden based on the beautiful woodcuts and descriptions in the celebrated *Hypnerotomachia Polifili* (Polyphilus' Dream of the Strife of Love), a nearly incomprehensible philosophical romance on love, beauty and architecture written by a Dominican friar named Francesco Colonna and published in Venice in 1499.

Buzzi's fantasy garden is very much in the offbeat Italian tradition: Renaissance gardens often had follies and water games, and not far from here, just over the border in Lazio, is the ultimate crazy garden, the 16th-century Monster Park at Bomarzo, while in southern Tuscany there's Niki de Sainte-Phalle's Giardino dei Tarocchi, full of large fantastical statues (*see p.312*). At La Scarzuola, Buzzi has created a series of ruins and stage sets meant to be viewed by following a special itinerary:

Where to Stay and Eat

Ficulle ✉ 05016

La Casella, an old hamlet in Ficulle near Parrano, **t/f** 0763 86684 or 0763 86588, *www.lacasella.com* (*very expensive – half board*). One of the nicest of the *agriturismo* places around, set in a 1,000-acre forest; lodgings are in 12 stone houses, and there are horses, a riding school, pool, tennis, mountain bikes, an antique billiards table and a good restaurant. A favourite summer activity is riding in the moonlight followed by a candlelit dinner in the forest.

Titignano ✉ 05010

Fattoria di Titignano, Loc Titignano, **t** 0763 308002, **f** 0763 308002, *www.titignano.com* (*moderate – half board*). A simple guesthouse on a working farm. Bedrooms and self-catering apartments are in the main house or in cottages in the grounds, and there's a pool. The restaurant (*cheap*) serves wonderful rustic food: lasagne with porcini mushrooms, *gallina ubriaca*, wild boar with olives; non-residents need to book in advance.

Baschi ✉ 05023

★★★Villa Bellago, Pian delle Monache 138, Lago di Corbara on SS448, **t** 0744 950521/2/3, **f** 0744 950524, *www.villabellago.it* (*expensive*). A handsome complex of three old farmhouses, set in its own grounds on the shore of Lake Corbara, with a pool and restaurant, where you can dine out on the terrace on their speciality: giant *bistecca alla fiorentina*.

Pomurlo Vecchio, Loc Pomurlo Vecchio (5km east of Baschi on the Montecchio road), **t** 0744 950190, **f** 0744 950500, *pomurlo vecchio@tiscalinet.it* (*inexpensive – half board*). An *agriturismo* on a 350-acre farm producing wine, oil, fruit, honey and jams. There are two apartments in the house – actually a tower – and 14 simply decorated double rooms in outbuildings (in better condition than the apartments), as well as a good pool and horse riding. Ideal for families. There is also a good restaurant using produce from the estate.

Baschi is best known for a restaurant that gourmets rank among Italy's top five: **Vissani**, on the SS448 Todi–Baschi towards Civitella del Lago, **t** 0744 950206, *info@ vissani.net* (*very expensive–expensive*). In this almost passionately religious inner sanctum of *cucina altissima*, you may dip your fork (but only if you've reserved a table in advance) into such marvels as oyster lasagne with basil, peppers with black truffles, parmesan and *foie gras* and chicken kiev stuffed with tongue and black truffles. Fabulous Italian and French cheeses and wines; fabulous bill, too! *Closed all day Wed, Thurs lunch and Sun eve.*

Montecchio ✉ 05020

Semiramide, Via Pian dell'Ara, **t** 0744 951008 (*inexpensive*). In lovely woods above Montecchio, in medieval Melezzole, this is a fine place to tuck into good basic Italian cooking: *bruschette*, homemade pasta with tomato-based sauces, or with asparagus or pigeon, all at fair prices. Family atmosphere. *Closed Tues, hols, 1 wk in Nov, 1 wk in Jan.*

there's even a transparent pyramid (predating the one at the Louvre) and a musical staircase. Although it's unfinished, Buzzi's nephew is continuing the project according to his uncle's plans. There is also a Franciscan church, with a fresco portrait of St Francis from the mid-13th century.

East and South of Orvieto: Lakes Corbara and Alviano

Between Orvieto and Todi, a dam stops up the Tiber to form the **Lago di Corbara**, Umbria's second largest lake and popular with fishermen. Both of the Orvieto–Todi routes are scenic drives: the slower SS79bis passes by **Prodo**, with its pink medieval castle, and by the turn-off for **Titignano**, a 16th-century fortified villa connected to a hamlet; the more southerly SS448 passes along the lake shore and **Civitella del Lago**, known for its restaurant Vissani (*see* p.541). The convent by the lake was founded by St Francis in 1218 on land donated by the Baschi family and rebuilt in 1703.

Nearby, at the confluence of the Paglia and the Tiber, stands their eponymous fief, **Baschi**, a hill town with a medieval centre enjoying spectacular views, in spite of its location directly over the Autostrada del Sole. Below lie the ruins of the ancient Roman port of *Palianum*, from where Orvieto's wine would be shipped down to Rome. Baschi's church of **San Nicolò**, designed by Ippolito Scalza (1584) has a lovely triptych by the Sienese painter Giovanni di Paolo and a Murano chandelier.

From Baschi, the SS205 climbs high over the valley of the Tiber, taking in splendid scenery on the way to **Montecchio** and the 15th-century **Castello del Poggio** (*t* 0744 903379; open 2nd Sat and 3rd Mon of month – mornings only). Set on a wooded hill, with beautiful views over Lakes Corbara and Alviano, the *castello* is reached by a hard-to-find road from the village of Guardea. This now peaceful area was a busy place in the Greek–Gothic wars; the castle was founded by the Byzantines and later occupied by the Normans, when they took over the Greek lands of southern Italy; it was restored by Antonio Sangallo the Younger and is now being restored again as a cultural centre and residence.

To the south, just off the SS205 is medieval **Alviano**, where St Francis hushed the swallows that drowned out his preaching. Alviano has a strong, square and perfectly preserved **castle** (1495–1506), with a fine Renaissance courtyard, built by the *condottiere* Bartolomeo d'Alviano. The courtyard is open during the day and houses the **Municipio Museum**. A scion of the Liviani family, Bartolomeo was employed by the Republic of Venice and gave such satisfaction that he was made the lord of the Venetian city of Pordenone. In 1651, his castle was purchased by the grasping Olimpia Pamphili, the sister-in-law of Pope Innocent X; in 1920 her family donated the castle to Alviano, which now uses it as a town hall. On the round tower, note the Medusa head designed to ward off enemies. The **chapel** in the castle courtyard is frescoed with scenes of St Francis and the swallows, while in the old storage cellars there's the **Museo della Civiltà Contadina,** dedicated to farm tools from the good old days. Alviano's charming parish **church** (1505) has kept most of its original features and has Umbria's only fresco (the *Madonna and Saints*) by the painter Pordenone. The commission came from Pentesilea Baglione, the widow of the *condottiere*; she is the elderly woman on the right. The church also contains one of Niccolò Alunno's finest paintings, the *Madonna in Gloria* (1480s).

The Tiber has been dammed near here to create another small artificial lake, the **Lago di Alviano**; its banks are nothing to look at now, but come back in a century or so. The surrounding marshes are protected as a **nature reserve**, complete with hides, where you can sit and watch the herons, bitterns and ducks (*open Sat 4–7, Sun and hols 10.30–12.30 and 4–7; adm; t 0744 903715 for guided tours at other times; entrance at Madonna del Porto, on Mutano–Scalo–Baschi road*).

Getting Around

Amelia is on the ATC **bus** routes from Terni, Orvieto and Orte. Less frequent buses from Amelia go on to Lugnano in Teverina, Attigliano and Alviano. **Cars** are forbidden in Amelia's centre on weekdays; park in one of the car parks outside the Porta Romana and catch the minibus into the centre.

Tourist Information

Amelia: Via Orvieto 1, t 0744 981453, *www. umbria2000.it. Open winter Mon and Sat 9–1, Tues–Fri 9–1 and 3.30–6.30; summer Mon and Sun 9–1, Tues–Sat 9–1 and 3.30–6.30.*
Pro Loco, Via della Repubblica 2, t 0744 982559.

Where to Stay and Eat

Amelia ✉ 05022
Not many tourists stay in Amelia, but you can do comfortably enough.
***Scoglio dell'Aquilone**, Via Orvieto 23, t 0744 982445, f 0744 983025 (*moderate*). A quiet place in the woods.

Il Carleni, Via Pellegrino Carleni 21, t 0744 983925, f 0744 978143 (*moderate*).
A delightful restaurant with panoramic views, serving traditional soups, game and mushroom dishes, as well as some more sophisticated choices (*foie gras*, crêpes with creamy *robiolla* cheese and spinach). *Open lunch 12–2.30; evenings for hotel guests only.* The owners have recently expanded their business to include a lovely hotel in the same palazzo; comfortable, rustic rooms (*moderate*), some of which have a little kitchenette.

Lugnano in Teverina ✉ 05020
****La Rocca**, Via Cavour 60, t 0744 900064 (*inexpensive*). A pleasant inn providing parking and good home-style cooking (*moderate*).
Youth hostel, Casale di Vallenera in Lugnano, t 0744 902674 (*cheap*). 25 beds available.
La Frateria dell'Abate Loniano, Loc San Francesco, t 0744 902180 (*moderate*).
An atmospheric restaurant in an ex-convent just outside Lugnano, serving good, hearty Umbrian fare in the restored 13th-century refectory. Some evenings the menus are dedicated to dishes with medieval origins. *Closed Wed*.

Amelia

Authorities as important as the Elder Pliny and Cato claimed that Ameria was among the oldest cities in Italy – perhaps founded in the 12th century BC, three centuries prior to Rome itself. It didn't take advantage of its head start, but was an important Roman *municipium* by 90 BC, and gave its name to the Via Armerina, linking Perugia and Todi to southern Etruria. When it became a comune in the Middle Ages, its sympathies lay with the Ghibellines, even after it was officially incorporated into the Papal States. In 1571 the whole town was excommunicated after refusing to pay a war tax that the popes had levied to raise money for an army to fight the Turks. In a beautiful setting on the ridge dividing the valleys of the Tiber and Nera, modern **Amelia** (pop. 11,200) is far enough off the busy *autostrada* to Rome to retain its tranquillity, at least in its *centro storico*, even if the surroundings are gritty and prosperous. Once there, reward yourself with one of the town's famous candied figs, made with cocoa and almonds.

The Walls, San Francesco and the Archeological Museum

The great age attributed by the Romans to Amelia is most tangible today in its **Mura Poligoni**, the 5th-century BC Cyclopean walls built by the Umbrii. Built without mortar, a section remains substantially intact, 12ft thick in places and standing some

25ft high near the Renaissance **Porta Romana**. These walls are about all that survived after the Goths devastated the town in 548, although parts of the Roman town can still be seen in bits of ancient masonry and columns in some of the houses; sections of Roman street paving have recently been revealed along Via della Repubblica.

Near the Porta Romana, the **Museo Archeologico** has recently opened in Palazzo Boccarini (*Piazza Augusta Vera 10, t 0744 978120; open Oct–Mar daily 10.30–1 and 3–5.30; April–June and Sept Tues–Sun 10.30–1 and 3.30–6; July–Aug daily 10.30–1 and 4–7; adm*). Its star exhibit is a restored bronze statue of Germanicus, father of Caligula, which was found near the town in 1963 and displayed for many years in the Museo Nazionale Archeologico in Perugia, which eventually agreed to its return. Also on display are relics of the Umbrii in Amelia and the **Pinacoteca**'s collection of paintings.

Just off Via della Repubblica, Piazza Vera opens up with the town war memorial and the church of **San Francesco** (or SS. Filippo e Giacomo), built in 1287 and remodelled inside in the 18th century. The one chapel that was left alone houses six fine Renaissance tombs of the Geraldini family, one of which (Matteo and Elisabetta) is by Agostino di Duccio, exquisite although somewhat worse for wear. The best-known member of the family, Alessandro Geraldini (1455–1525), lobbied in the court of Ferdinand and Isabella for Columbus' voyage, and was rewarded by being appointed Bishop of Santo Domingo, the first in the New World.

To Piazza Marconi and the Duomo

Continuing up Via della Repubblica, take the narrow stepped alley under the arch on the left to Amelia's most impressive palace, the **Palazzo Farrattini** (1520), designed by Antonio da Sangallo the Younger as a smaller version of the Palazzo Farnese in Rome; it incorporates two Roman mosaics inside. After this Via della Repubblica continues up steeply past more Renaissance *palazzi* to the **Arco della Piazza**, made up in the Middle Ages of Roman fragments and a frieze. Through here is Amelia's charming old main square, the rectangular **Piazza Marconi**, with its original paving, more proud Renaissance palaces, and the **Loggia dei Banditori**, from where public proclamations were read. **Palazzo Petrignani** has frescoed Mannerist and Baroque rooms, some by Zuccari (*to visit, call t 0744 976219*).

From here, Via Duomo ascends steeply towards the cathedral, passing by way of pretty Via Pellegrino Carleni as it rises into the medieval part of town. At the summit, the **Duomo** (*open daily 10–12 and 4–6.30*) was almost completely rebuilt in 1640 with a brick façade. The handsome dodecagonal **campanile** was built in 1050 as a Torre Civica, reusing Roman stones and a portion of another frieze. The cathedral features a worn Romanesque column, where Amelia's patron saint Firmina is said to have been bound and tortured to death under Diocletian in 303. It also contains reliefs by Agostino di Duccio's followers in the tomb of another Bishop Geraldini (1476), first chapel on the left. Another Duccio, this time the great Sienese Duccio di Buoninsegna, painted the cathedral's finest painting, an Assumption, but you have to come in May or between 15 and 20 August to see it on display. In the right transept, there's a *Last Supper* by Francesco Perini of Amelia (1538), and in the Oratorio del Sacramento there are two recently restored paintings by Niccolò Pomarancio. The octagonal chapel in the right aisle is said to be the work of Antonio da Sangallo. Here there are also two Turkish flags captured in the Battle of Lepanto in 1571 – most peculiar for a town that was excommunicated for refusing to contribute its share to the Christian cause. There are lovely views from the nearby belvedere.

Sant'Agostino to Piazza Matteotti and the Roman Cisterns

From the Duomo, Via Geraldini descends to the church of **Sant'Agostino** with a good, squarish Gothic façade rebuilt in 1477, a beautiful ogival doorway and a large rose window. The interior (*open am only*) was enthusiastically Baroqued and frescoed by Francesco Appiani in 1747–62. The first altar to the right has a *Vision of St John at Patmos* by Pomarancio. Of the older church, only the pavement remains, but recent work in the sacristy revealed some very curious sinopie from the 11th century. A *sinopia* is the rough sketch made for a fresco in red earth pigment: these show saints, floral patterns and stars in the vault that were never completed.

From here, Via Poserola descends to a little 13th-century gate, passing the large convent of **San Magno**; the church has a rare old organ of 1680, recently restored and now used for concerts. Heading the opposite way, Via Garibaldi passes medieval alleys and leads into Piazza Matteotti, home of Amelia's delightful **Palazzo Comunale.** Fragments of Roman *Ameria* decorate the courtyard and a *Madonna with Saints* presides in the Sala Consiliare (*open by request, ask in office hours: weekdays 10–12*), painted by Pier Matteo d'Amelia (d. 1508) who, through art history sleuthing, has been identified with the Master of the Gardner Annunciation. In 1996, a steep stair was built to allow access to the remarkable vaulted **Roman cisterns** beneath (*open Sat 3–6, Sun 10.30–12.30 and 3–6, or call Associazone I Poligonali, t 0744 978436, to arrange a visit*), capable of holding over 4,000 cubic metres. Built for emergencies in the 1st century BC, they comprise 10 chambers into which rainwater was channelled; another channel was used to release the waters periodically to keep them fresh.

Amelia has an especially delightful theatre, the **Teatro Sociale**, located under Piazza Matteotti. Built in 1783 on the model of La Fenice in Venice, its boxes and stalls are well preserved and still in use between the months of November and May; at other times, guided tours are available by appointment (*t 0744 976219/20*). Note how some of the boxes are equipped with cupboards for food; in the late 18th century, only a magnificently sung aria had the power to make an audience shut up or stop eating.

The surrounding hills are famous for their figs and wine: visit the Cantina dei Colli Amerini near Amelia at **Fornole** (*t 0744 989721, f 0744 989695; open Mon–Sat 9–1 and 3.30–6; closed Sun*). On the first Sunday in October, the wine is miraculously made to pour from Amelia's fountains.

Around Amelia

Lugnano in Teverina

Lugnano in Teverina (pop. 1,650), 11km northwest of Amelia, is a walled town on a ridge that was long a bone of contention between the *comuni* of Amelia, Orvieto and

Todi; in 1503 it was sacked by Cesare Borgia. Nowadays it attracts a few Romans and foreigners for summer holiday *villeggiatura*. The huge **Palazzo Pennone** was built in the 1500s by wealthy cardinals; now converted into the town hall, the palace has a little *antiquarium* on the first floor (*open Sat–Sun 10–12.30 and 3.30–6.30; adm; closes earlier in winter; outside these times, call* **t** *0744 902321*) containing fragments of frescoes and mosaics from a 1st-century BC Roman villa at Poggio Gramignano. Excavations began in 1988 in collaboration with the University of Tucson, Arizona. Among the finds was an infant cemetery which may be unique – dozens of babies died from malaria and were buried in a series of amphorae; their skeletons (still in the vessels) can be seen among the artefacts in the *antiquarium*.

Lugnano's main attraction is one of the finest, most exotic Romanesque churches around, the 12th-century **Collegiata di Santa Maria Assunta**. It has a striking roof and columned portico or *pronaos*, added in 1230 reusing older columns on a design derived from the ancient Roman basilica. The shallow arches above still bear a few traces of their once glorious Cosmati decoration and there is a fine large window in the form of a double wheel. On the wall to the left of the portico, a curious three-headed figure represents the Trinity.

The barrel-vaulted interior, not remodelled to everyone's taste, still retains its fine proportions. Like so many churches of the period, the presbytery at the end of the central nave is raised over the crypt. The pavement is beautifully worked and there are fine carved capitals along the nave; the third one to the left shows a scene of a Byzantine-style Mass and a man with a snake coming out of his mouth, symbolic of evil, almost like an editorial comment on the Great Schism. There are finely carved *ambones* (twin pulpits) and *transennas* from the original choir, with bas reliefs showing St Michael killing the dragon and two men exchanging the kiss of peace, and a rare *ciborium* restored in 1937. The apse has a fine tripytch of the Assumption by Nicolò Alunno, while the mannerist painter Livio Agresti from Forlì checks in with a rather surprising *Beheading of John the Baptist* of 1571, the chapel to the right.

South of Amelia: Penna in Teverina, Giove and a Dip into Lazio

Southeast of Amelia towards the Tiber and the big road and rail junction at Orte, **Penna in Teverina** is a charming old fortified town with houses built directly into the walls. It was disputed by Rome's eternal Punch and Judy factions, the Colonna and Orsini families, until the Colonna got tired of the show and simply sold it to the Orsini, who constructed a Palazzo Orsini in town with a fine 19th-century Italian garden attached (privately owned). Other relics of the same era are the Mammalocchi, allegorical herms in travertine standing at the entrance to villas on the road to Amelia.

North of Penna are a pair of crumbling medieval villages. **Giove** was smashed in 1503 by the troops of Cesare Borgia, who dismantled the walls and castles; what was left was rebuilt in the next century as an imposing and elegant **Palazzo Ducale** overlooking the Tiber; it was built by the Mattei, a great Roman family, and is still privately owned by their heirs. Members of great Roman families can be on the lazy and decadent side; one of the original features of this palace is the proto-parking garage ramp spiralling up to the first floor, big enough for horse-drawn carriages. The nearby hamlet of **Attigliano** is all but abandoned.

Most of the truly remarkable sights in these parts are over the border in **Lazio** – there is the **Monster Park** in the woebegone village of **Bomarzo**, a mad garden of colossal cinquecento sculptures that brings the neurosis of late Renaissance Italy right to the surface. Just to the south, the pretty Cimini hills shelter fine towns like **Soriano nel Cimino** and **San Martino al Cimino**, as well as beautiful, unspoiled **Lake Vico**, an ancient volcanic crater. **Caprarola**, nearby, sits in the shadow of one of the greatest, strangest and most arrogant of all Renaissance palaces, the Farnese, built with papal booty by Perugia's arch enemy Paul III.

North of Amelia

Much of the countryside north of Amelia towards Todi is *terra incognita*; today hamlets stand abandoned but, in Roman times, it was important enough for a road, the Via Falisca Armerina. Traces of this and a Roman bridge are by **Sambucetole**; the modern hamlet is under the abandoned old medieval town. Further north the road passes the tower of the medieval **Castel dell'Aquila**, and then forks: to the west, surrounded by forests, is the unusual circular walled village of **Toscolano**, once owned by Todi (note the eagle over the gate), and now used as the summer base for the Centro Europeo Toscolano, dedicated to the renewal of popular Italian music among other things. Just outside the centre, the chapel of the **Santissima Annunziata** contains recently restored frescoes attributed to Pier Matteo d'Amelia. A scenic road continues north to **Collelungo**, last outpost of the Monaldeschi on the frontier of Todi. The recently restored church has a Lombard-era altar and frescoes from the late 1200s.

The east fork of the road from Castel dell'Aquila leads to **Avigliano Umbro** with a castle-like water tower. North, little **Dunarobba** with its big 16th-century castle, once stood on the banks of the prehistoric Lago Tiberino that once filled the Tiber Valley to the brim. In the 1980s, diggers in a quarry nearby came upon 40 specimens of the 200,000-year-old ancestors of the sequoia that once stood on the lake shores. The mighty trunks of this **Foresta Fossile**, some standing 25ft high, were so well preserved that they were found still standing upright in thick clay. They are the most important palaeobotanical finds in the region and a research centre has been set up to study them (*visits by appointment with the Pro-Loco of Avigliano Umbro, t/f 0744 940348, www.forestafossile.it, or guided tours April–Oct Mon–Sat 9.30, 11.30, 3.30 and 5.30; adm*). The surrounding countryside is lovely, whether you head north to Todi or east towards **Montecastrilli**, a traditional fortified Umbrian hamlet that was an outpost of Todi for centuries.

The Valnerina: Narni to Norcia

20

The Valnerina

p.492

Highlights

1 Mountainous, medieval Narni and its Bridge of Augustus
2 Cascata delle Marmore: Europe's highest waterfall
3 S. Pietro in Valle: Byzantine-style frescoes
4 The mountain dream landscape of the Piano Grande
5 Norcia: boar salami and basilicas

The clear River Nera, one of the main tributaries of the Tiber, flows east off the slopes of the mighty Monti Sibillini across the southern edge of Umbria. Nera means 'black' in Italian, but the name actually derives from Naharkum, a tribe of the Umbrii, who were the valley's first known inhabitants. One of the very few facts we do know about them is that they did not get along at all with their cousins in Gubbio.

The Nera is the region's special river: 'There would be no Tiber if the Nera did not give it to drink,' is an old Umbrian saying; the Umbrians have long memories and know deep in their hearts that the ancient Romans learned all their simple and honest virtues from their ancestors, before they started conquering the world and running amok. Much of the Valnerina is still an Italian secret, although its black truffles and its saints (Benedict, Valentine and Rita) enjoy international reputations, and its superb, unspoiled and often dramatic natural beauty is now protected under the auspices of a natural park.

Narni, Terni and Around

Narni

Once an important stop on the Via Flaminia, **Narni** (pop. 21,000) is a fine old hill town in a dramatic position, guarding the steep gorge as you enter the Valnerina. Originally the Umbrian *Nequinum*, it renamed itself *Nahar* or *Narnia* after the river when it changed its allegiance to Rome in 299 BC. Pliny wrote of its unassailable defences, the Emperor Nerva was born here in AD 32, and the city can also claim a pope, John XIII (965–72), as well as a great *condottiere*, Gattamelata (1370–1443), who went on to fame and fortune in Venice. However, Narni tends to be overlooked; many people never bother to breach the modern industry and electrocarbon plant at Narni Scalo in the river valley to discover the fine town within – which, *pace* Foligno, is in reality, the closest to the geographic centre of Italy.

To Piazza Garibaldi

The sight in Narni that most engaged the Grand Tourist of the past two centuries, the romantically ruined **Ponte d'Augusto** (27 BC), is now just visible from the bridge at lower, industrial Narni Scalo or from the train window when you approach from the south. This lofty massive arch standing in the river is all that survives of a bridge that was famous even in Roman times for its size – it stretched 425ft and stood 90ft high – built to carry the newer Via Flaminia towards Terni and Spoleto. It fell into ruins in the Middle Ages, and until 1855, it had two arches and a much more picturesque setting. If it looks familiar, you may have seen Corot's famous painting in the Louvre.

Many of Narni's old city gates are intact, especially the eastern **Porta Ternana**, with its twin round towers built by Sixtus IV where the Via Flaminia entered Narni proper. This bustling ancient road served the city well throughout history, except in 1527, when the brutal mercenary troops of Charles V, having sacked Rome, were marching home and stopped to sack and pillage Narni as well. The Flaminia (here called the Via Roma) leads to Narni's main crossroads: the busy, colourful, irregularly shaped **Piazza Garibaldi**, overlooked by the side door of the cathedral and a neoclassical palace. The whole square was originally a Roman *piscina* and steps from the restored 15th-century fountain descend into a 12th-century cistern.

The Duomo and Around

From Piazza Garibaldi, main Via Garibaldi squeezes round the corner to the front of the Duomo and its elegant quattrocento portico, adorned by a classical frieze. Consecrated in 1145 by Pope Eugenius III, the cathedral's interior originally had three

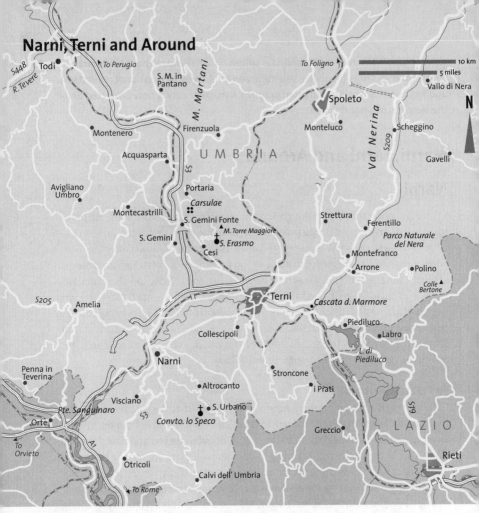

Narni, Terni and Around

[Map labels:]

S448 · Todi · To Perugia · S. M. in Pantano · M. Martani · To Foligno · Vallo di Nera · 10 km · 5 miles · R. Tevere · Spoleto · N

Montenero · Firenzuola · Monteluco · Scheggino · Val Nerina · S209

Acquasparta · UMBRIA · Gavelli

Avigliano Umbro · S3 · Portaria · Carsulae · Strettura · Ferentillo

Montecastrilli · S. Gemini Fonte · Parco Naturale del Nera

S. Gemini · M. Torre Maggiore · S. Erasmo · Cesi · Montefranco · Polino

S205 · Amelia · Arrone · Colle Bertone

Terni · Cascata d. Marmore

Collescipoli · Piediluco · Labro

Penna in Teverina · Narni · Stroncone · L. di Piediluco

Pte. Sanguinaro · Visciano · Altrocanto · i Prati · S3

Orte · S3 · S. Urbano · S79

To Orvieto · Convto. lo Speco · Greccio · LAZIO

A1 · Otricoli · Rieti

To Rome · Calvi dell' Umbria

naves, separated by a wide variety of capitals and columns reused from other buildings. A fourth nave was added in the 15th century, when most of its art was commissioned, although there are still remnants of original frescoes. There's a charming 15th-century fresco of the *Madonna and Child* by a local artist by the door. On the right, the third chapel has a Cosmati mosaic pavement and a Renaissance architectural perspective by a northern artist named Sebastiano Pellegrini.

The next chapel, the **Sacello dei Santi Giovenale e Cassio**, predates the cathedral by almost 800 years, founded around the tomb of Narni's first bishop, San Giovenale. Its marble screen was pieced together in the Renaissance from Paleochristian and Romanesque reliefs and Cosmati work, and on the upper wall, there's a 9th-century mosaic of the Redeemer. The niches contain 15th-century statues of Giovenale and a German-made *Pietà*. The inner chapel is made in part from the Roman wall and contains the 6th-century sarcophagus of the saint; there's a picture of him on the pilaster by the Sienese Vecchietta. The high altar was completed in 1714; there are a pair of marble pulpits and choir stalls from 1490 and, in the left nave, a large polychrome wooden statue of *Sant'Antonio Abate* by Vecchietta (1474). There are also two Renaissance funerary monuments to the left; Pietro Cesi's has been attributed to Bernardo da Settignano.

Opposite the Duomo, in little Piazza Cavour, is the **Pinacoteca** (*open daily 6pm–8pm and 9pm–11pm, Sat–Sun 11–3 also*), housed in the Palazzo del Vescovile. The picture gallery displays newly restored paintings owned by the cathedral and town, including an *Annunciation* by Benozzo Gozzoli. Tucked behind Piazza Cavour is the **Roman arch**, reworked into a medieval gate. To the right of the cathedral, off Via Garibaldi, the Via del Campanile leads to the sturdy Roman base of the cathedral's **bell tower**; the upper

Getting There and Around

Narni is easily reached by **train** from Rome (89km/1hr), Terni, Spoleto or Assisi on the main Rome–Ancona line; it is 15km from the main Florence–Rome rail and *autostrada* junction at Orte. Frequent buses link the station and the city on the hill.

ATC **buses, t** 0744 492711, *www.atcterni.it*, also departing from the station, connect Amelia, Terni, Otricoli and surrounding hamlets.

Tourist Information

Narni: Piazza dei Priori 3, **t/f** 0744 715362, *www.comune.narni.tr.it. Open daily 9.30–12.30 and 4.30–7*. Ask here about visits inside the narrow tunnel of the **Ponte Cardona**, part of a 1st-century Roman aqueduct 3km east of town.

Festivals

Festival of San Giovenale, Narni, *last week April and 1st week May*. This is medieval pageantry at its brightest. A torchlight procession takes place in full costume the night before the *Corsa dell'Anello* (*2nd weekend in May*) or 'Tournament of the Ring', in which knights from the town's three neighbourhoods, compete to pierce a ring suspended over the street with their lances – a popular medieval joust aimed to test skill, with undercurrents of a fertility rite once associated with the success of the year's crops.

Where to Stay and Eat

Narni ✉ 05035

Most of the hotels are down by the river and station at Narni Scalo.

Monte del Grano 1696, Loc San Vito, 15km south of Narni on the SS3bis, **t** 0744 749143 (*expensive*). An elegant, welcoming place serving creative dishes made with local ingredients including truffles. Don't miss desserts such as chocolate terrine with coffee-flavoured *zabaglione* or hazelnut ice cream with hot caramelized fruit. *Open Tues–Fri eves, Sat and Sun lunch and eves.*

Podere Costa Romana, SS. Flaminia, Strada per Itieli, **t** 0744 722495/335 5738210, **f** 0823 797118, *www.poderecostaromana.com* (*expensive*). This beautifully restored stone farmhouse, on a wooded hillside just outside Narni has been converted into comfortable apartments sleeping from 2–5. There is a big garden for general use and a pool overlooking the hills. You can opt for B&B (min 2 nights) or can be independent which is cheaper, but there is a minimum stay of a week.

★★★Dei Priori, Vicolo del Comune 4, **t** 0744 726843, **f** 0744 726844, *www.loggiadeipriori.it* (*moderate*). In a medieval palace, with very comfortable rooms – the best in the centre; its restaurant, La Loggia, **t** 0744 722744 (*moderate*), has long been popular, although of late it isn't quite what it was. *Closed Mon.*

Il Cavallino, Via Flaminia Romana 220, on the road to Terni, **t** 0744 761020 (*inexpensive*). A good, old-fashioned little inn with single rooms. *Closed Tues and part July.*

San Gemini ✉ 05029

★★★Locanda di Carsulae, Via Tibernia 2 Loc Fonte, on the SS3bis, at San Gemini Fonte, **t** 0744 630163, **f** 0744 333068, *www.gruppobacus.com* (*moderate*). Pleasant, either for food or sleep.

★★Duomo, Piazza Duomo 4, **t** 0744 630015 or 0744 630005, **f** 0744 630336, *www.gruppobacus.com* (*moderate*). Beds and a restaurant in the centre of town.

section was added in the 1400s and adorned with colourful ceramic plates. The 14th-century church of **San Francesco** near the top of the next street to the left, stands on the site of an oratory founded in 1213 by St Francis. It burnt down in a fire in 1998, but its fine façade remains and the interior is being restored.

Piazza dei Priori

Via Garibaldi, the main street since Roman times (note the pretty 19th-century restored Teatro Comunale), widens to form Piazza dei Priori, the centre of Narni's civic life in the Middle Ages. Here sits the **Palazzo del Podestà** (14th–15th centuries), now the seat of the *comune*, an old tower melded with three medieval tower houses and decorated with four bas reliefs depicting a joust, a lion and dragon, the beheading of Holofernes, and a hunt with falcons. The palace shows some cracks from Narni's very own earthquake in 2000, which left 250 people homeless. In the **Sala Consigliare** (*open Fri–Sun 10–1 and 3–7*) hangs Narni's finest painting, a magnificent *Coronation of the Virgin* (1486) by Florentine Domenico Ghirlandaio, in a beautiful frame with a *predella* showing *St Francis Receiving the Stigmata*, a *Pietà* and *St Jerome*.

The circular **fountain** dates from 1303. Opposite is the medieval **Casa Sacripanti**, with more reliefs, and the **loggia** and **clock tower** of the once massive 14th-century Palazzo dei Priori, built by Matteo Gattapone, all that survived the sack of Charles V's *Lands-knechten* in 1527; the pulpit was used for reading public proclamations.

At the end of the piazza and the beginning of Via Mazzini is the beautiful Romanesque façade of **Santa Maria in Pensole**, dated 1175 (*visit by appointment with the local caving club, the Associazione Culturale Subterranea, t 0744 722292, www.narni sotterranea.it; open Nov–Mar Sun 11–1 and 3–5; April–Oct Sat 3–6, Sun 10–1 and 3–6*), fronted with a handsome portico made with columns borrowed from older buildings and three beautiful doors with elaborate marble decoration. Other reused columns line the three naves, many of which have charming capitals. The church was built over the vaults (*in pensole*) of an 8th-century Benedictine church and a Roman cistern once believed to be a temple of Bacchus. Opposite here are two attractive palaces: the **Palazzo Bocciarelli**, dating from the 17th century, and the 16th-century **Palazzo Scotti**.

The iron fixtures in the walls, here and all around Narni, hold torches for the medieval pageant that takes place in May, in honour of San Giovenale (*see* 'Festivals', p.555), and still one of the most colourful festivals of the Umbrian calendar.

San Domenico

Further down tower- and palace-lined Via Mazzini, the deconsecrated 12th-century pink and white church and campanile of **San Domenico** (*open Nov–Mar Sun 11–1 and 3–5; April–Oct Sat 3–6, Sun 10–1 and 3–6*) is now the public library. The door is adorned with worn medallions of the 12 apostles and the walls inside have 13th- to 16th-century fresco fragments. On the east end is a wall memorial (1494) near a tabernacle by the workshop of Agostino di Duccio; on the left side are faint frescoes by the Zuccari family and the tusk of a prehistoric elephant found on the banks of the Nera in 1988.

The Dominicans' convent, demolished in the 1950s, was replaced by the **Giardino di San Bernardo**, with ruins of a lofty tower and an excellent view towards the

Roman-esque Abbey of San Cassiano over the narrow wooded gorge of the Nera. Near Narni the river takes on a shade of robin's-egg blue from the copper and lime deposits in the soil. The aforementioned Associazione Culturale Subterranea discovered an earlier church under the apse of San Domenico, dating from the 1100s with frescoes, another Roman cistern and a prison cell covered with 18th-century graffiti left by poor souls imprisoned by the Dominican-run Inquisition; the ensemble is known as the **Sotterranei della Chiesa di San Domenico** (*hours as S. Maria in Pensole,* see p.556).

Lower Narni, and the Rocca

At the end of Via Mazzini, in the Piazza Marzio, is the 15th-century well, the **Pozzo della Comunità**; from here you can follow the 15th-century walls along Via della Mura, or cut down the steps of Vicolo degli Orti to the most picturesque bit, around the tall tower of the **Porta della Fiera**. Via Gattamelata continues back to the centre, passing the so-called **House of Gattamelata** (No.113). The 'Honeyed Cat' (Erasmo da Narni) was born here in 1370 to a baker, and from these modest beginnings, he became such a successful, reliable and honest *condottiere* for Venice that he received the highest honour that the usually stingy Republic bestowed on anyone: a paid funeral and an equestrian statue by Donatello, the first since Roman times and one of Padua's gems.

Via Gattamelata continues to **Sant'Agostino** (*closed for restoration*), its severe façade decorated with a faded fresco in a niche, attributed to Antoniazzo Romano. The interior has good quattrocento frescoes, a *Crucifixion* by the school of Antoniazzo Romano and a *Madonna* by Pier Antonio d'Amelia; a fine Renaissance wooden crucifix and a lofty carved ceiling holding a 16th-century painting on the *Triumph of St Augustine* by Carlo Federico Benincasa of Narni.

From Piazza Garibaldi, Via del Monte winds up through a picturesque medieval neighbourhood, leading eventually to the four-square **Rocca Albornoz** (*open Fri–Sun 10–7*) that dominates all views of Narni from the plain of Terni. Built in the 1370s by the indefatigable Cardinal Albornoz, the Rocca's restoration programme has just recently been completed; the views, not surprisingly, are far and wide.

South of Narni

South of Narni, the ancient Via Flaminia (SS3) continues towards the Rome of the Caesars, now just a back road in an obscure corner of Umbria. At about the 83km mark, it passes through a small plain with rugged cliffs near the road, an ancient holy site known as **Grotte d'Orlando** (Roland's cave). Some badly worn Roman reliefs can be made out on the rocks and there are remains of an altar called 'Roland's Seat'. On a steep slope below the hamlet of **Visciano**, southwest of Narni off the Otricoli road, there's a lovely 11th-century church dedicated to Santa Pudenzia, surrounded by trees, with an exceptionally tall slender campanile. The portico has two Roman columns with fine capitals and some other Roman bits embedded in the walls. The polygonal apse is similar to those in Ravenna. Where the road branches off for Calvi, you'll see scanty remains of another Roman bridge, the **Ponte Sanguinario**.

The first Umbrian town a Roman would find along the Via Flaminia was **Otricoli** (16km from Narni), a town of the Umbrii destroyed by the Romans in the Social War in the 1st century BC. It was later rebuilt down on the then-navigable Tiber as the city and port of *Ocriculum*. When this became swampy in the Middle Ages, the inhabitants moved back up to their hill and what was once a thriving city became by the 18th century a wretchedly poor village. The rest of Otricoli is concentrated in a walled hill town with medieval streets, built of cannibalized Roman stone. The constantly rebuilt and reworked parish church of Santa Maria seems to have something from every century somewhere, from Roman columns within to a 19th-century campanile.

The ruins of **Ocriculum** (*always open*) are a mile below town, overlooking the Tiber. Excavations began under Pope Pius VI in 1776, enriching the Vatican Museum with an enormous head of Jupiter and other pieces, but little has happened since, and many ruins, including the big baths, a theatre, amphitheatre, funerary monuments and a section of the original Via Flaminia, are overgrown and crumbling from exposure.

Fine oak forests and scenery surround **Calvi dell'Umbria** (south of Narni, 11km east of Otricoli), the southernmost *comune* of Umbria, and prosperous until the plague crippled it in 1527. It was the home of Bernardo da Calvi, a follower of St Francis, who was martyred in the first Franciscan mission to Morocco; the church of San Francesco is built on land Bernardo donated to Francis. Calvi's pride, however, is the 16th-century *presepio* of unusually large terracotta figures in the church of Sant'Antonio.

To the southeast, 13km from Narni beyond Altrocanto and Sant'Urbano, the **Convento del Sacro Speco** (*guided tours 8–11.30 and 3–4.45, churchyard and cloisters open 8–11.30, 3–5 and 6–7.30; some parts closed for restoration*) was founded in 1213 by St Francis, who often stayed in a nearby cave; the legend goes that once when he fell ill here, an angel comforted him with sweet violin music. It was rebuilt in the 1300s and is one of Italy's most evocative Franciscan monuments. In recent years, it has been reoccupied by friars living according to the saint's First Rule.

San Gemini, Carsulae, Acquasparta and Cesi

North of Narni, the SS3bis to Todi passes two towns known for their waters since the Etruscans. The first, **San Gemini**, keeps its spa a few kilometres to the north; the old centre remains the essential Umbrian hill town, despite being thoroughly wrecked on two occasions, by the Saracens in 882, and by the Imperial mercenary army of the Constable of Bourbon in 1527, who was practising for the Sack of Rome. There's a convenient car park near the church of **San Francesco** (1291), with a carved portal and doors from the 14th century and frescoes from the 15th–17th centuries. In the medieval centre (take narrow Via Casventino) in Piazza Palazzo Vecchio, the restored 12th-century **Palazzo Pubblico** has an external stairway and encompasses an older defensive tower converted into a campanile in the 1700s; here, too, is the 13th-century **Oratorio San Carlo**, housing a striking, fresco-covered *ciborium*. Further along, the curiously shaped church of **San Giovanni Battista** started out in the 12th century as an octagon; it has a Romanesque door on its left side, with scant remnants of its Cosmati decoration and an inscription of 1199. Near San Gemini's 18th-century **gateway** stands its **cathedral**, with a tarted-up 19th-century interior.

Outside the gate, set in a pretty garden, the church of **San Nicolò** (*open winter Fri–Sun 9–1 and 2–5; summer 3–6*) was built as a dependency of the once mighty abbey of Farfa near Rieti, and is now privately owned; the frieze and lions on its portal are copies of the originals, which are now ensconced in the Metropolitan Museum in New York. The columns within have fine sculpted capitals, several of which came from Carsulae (*see* below), and among its 13th-century frescoes, most of which are detached, is the only known work of Rogerino da Todi.

The spa, **San Gemini Fonte**, is in a pretty park full of old oaks, where you can try the carbonated diuretic waters from May to October. Near here, under the steep green hills, are the remains of Imperial era **Carsulae** (*t 0744 334133, www.archeopg.act. beniculturali.it; open April–Sept 8.30–7.30; Oct–Mar 8.30–5.30; adm*), a Roman city that was abandoned and never rebuilt after an earthquake in the 800s. In its day, *Carsulae* was famous for its waters and wines. From the handsome gate built by Trajan (the locals' favourite spot for wedding photos), you can follow a stretch of the original Via Flaminia, dotted with funerary monuments, amongst which are two large and well-preserved tombs and a head of Claudius. There are the remains of a residential district, a theatre and an amphitheatre; in the pink marble forum are the bases of twin temples that may have been dedicated to the heavenly twins, the Dioscuri, and the basilica used as a council house or Curia. One temple was rebuilt in the 11th century to become a little chapel of **Santi Cosma e Damiano**.

North of San Gemini, the village of **Portaria** is known for its restaurants and for possessing one of the oldest post boxes in Italy (1674, under the clock tower).

Further north, **Acquasparta** (Latin *Ad Aquas Partas*) is another quiet spot to sort out your digestive problems, recommended by no less than St Francis; today, the waters Amerino and Furapane are bottled here. In the centre, is the **Palazzo Cesi**, from 1565. Owned by the University of Perugia, it has Renaissance frescoes and a beautiful courtyard filled with ancient inscriptions (*visits by appt, t 075 5851*). Here the Roman prince, Federico Cesi, established a country branch of the scholarly Accademia dei Lincei that he founded in Rome in 1609; his friend Galileo came out to visit for a month in 1624. Although the Accademia died with the prince, the idea caught on across Italy and most towns of any consequence managed to create a little academy of their own. Normally peaceful and very typical of the region, the town alarms its neighbours every summer by hosting, of all things, a German lieder-singing competition.

From Acquasparta, you can follow a mountain road, the SS418, across to Spoleto – just don't think you've somehow got lost in Tuscany when you see signs for Arezzo. There are pleasant picnic spots along the way, overlooking deep-set **Lake Arezzo**, and nearby, a Romanesque church with an unusual portico at **Firenzuola**.

On the last craggy slope of the Monti Martani, 6km east of San Gemini Fonte, **Cesi** thrived between the 12th and 16th centuries, although it lies under a much older town. The entrance, through the Porta Ternana, leads into the medieval centre and the church of **Santa Maria Assunta** (1515–25); there's a trecento wooden sculpture of the *Virgin and Child*, and underneath, a room that belonged to a former church on the site, frescoed with a *Crucifixion* of 1425 by Giovanni di Giovannello of Narni. Outside the second gate, the **Porta Tudertina**, a piazza has a handsome church of **Sant'Andrea**, built of Roman stones from Carsulae, as well as another impressive 16th-century Palazzo Cesi. A road twists up Monte Eolo to the site of the ancient town, with remains of the 6th-century BC walls and splendid views. **Sant'Erasmo**, a 12th-century church with a pretty window, stands near the remains of the medieval fortress. From here, an unpaved road continues to the top of **Monte Torre Maggiore** (1,121m/3,677ft).

Terni

Sprawling, mouldering, modern – you may not want to spend long in southern Umbria's capital, but at least muster some respect for **Terni**'s accomplishments. In 1867, as the city closest to the geographical centre of Italy, it was intended to be the nation's capital (this was before Rome was wrested from the occupying French), but even so, the idea flew like a penguin. If Italy's politicians couldn't appreciate Terni's location, far from the country's vulnerable coasts and frontiers, the military certainly did. Its location on the River Nera, and the vicinity of the Cascata delle Marmore, Europe's highest waterfall, sealed its destiny. In the 1870s, the beautiful thundering waters were diverted for cheap hydroelectric power, and Italy's first steel mill went up to build ships for its navy to pester Africa, pushing Umbria to lurch belatedly into the Industrial Revolution (even though Italy has no iron ore to speak of; the mill has never made a profit, but it's still there on the east end of town). The **Industrial Heritage Documentation Centre** offers guided tours on themes such as 'The City Factories' and 'The Culture and Conditions of a Worker's Life' (*t 0744 407187 and 0744 428753, antennapreessa@icsim.it; open Mon, Tues and Thurs 9–12 and 4–7, Wed, Fri 4–7, Sat 9–12*). The population doubled in less than a decade, then tripled, and today hovers around 110,000. Before the First World War, the city employed one-third of Umbria's workforce, and what had been an insignificant medieval town before Unification became Umbria's second city after Perugia, the Manchester of Italy. In the 1920s Terni scientists astounded the world with the first practical plastic. Terni also has the State Arms Factory (the rifle that killed John Kennedy was manufactured here); these three industries together proved enough of an attraction during the last war for Allied air forces to smash the place flat. They also keep Terni ardently Communist, the heart of Red Umbria, and a fun place to be on 1 May for a parade of humorous floats made by towns in the province.

For the past few years, Terni has hosted an Easter holiday instalment of the Umbrian Jazz Festival, with a special emphasis on gospel and spirituals. It has taken a new pride in its industrial past: the mills, now employing 3,000 and specializing in stainless and other speciality steels, have been tarted up. Major intersections and piazze are decorated with imposing rusty chunks of raw industrial art. And as Italian film-makers grow estranged from the high costs and confabulations of Rome and Cinecittà, they are falling into the seductive clasp of Terni: cheap, spacious and just over an hour's drive from the capital. Some of Italy's best special effects gizmos and wizardry are concentrated in the increasingly important Centro Multimediale di Terni, which lent its support to Roberto Benigni's *Pinnocchio* and *Life is Beautiful*, much of which was shot in the suburb of Papigno.

St Valentine's City

During the building of the steelworks, bulldozers uncovered an important Iron Age necropolis, and the mysterious Umbrii Naharkum were here around 7th century BC. Terni's name derives from their *Interamna Nahars* (from *inter amnes*, 'between two rivers', namely the confluence of the Nera and the torrential Serra). *Interamna* was conquered by the Romans in the 3rd century BC, and grew into a major station along the newer, easterly route of the Via Flaminia. It was traditionally considered the birthplace of the historian Tacitus, although scholars now quibble that Terni's was a more meagre Tacitus, Claudius Tacitus, one of the many Roman emperors for a day.

More certainly identified with the city is its first bishop, the martyred St Valentine, who was beheaded in 273. Several stories attempt to explain how he became the patron saint of lovers: one claims that he miraculously united a 4th-century Romeo and Juliet, a Christian and a pagan (who converted after matrimony); another that his feast day coincided with the traditional mating day of Umbrian birds. He was buried in a cemetery 2km south of the centre, where the first chapel was built; in the 17th century this was rebuilt rather modestly as the **Basilica di San Valentino**.

Valentine's mummified head was stolen in 1986, but was found three years later, unharmed, wrapped in newspaper under a park bench at the Cascata delle Marmore. Until then, the city seemed unaware of its patron's fame abroad. Now on 14 February it hosts the traditional Mass, market and fireworks, and also a full range of international chocs and schlock, as well as a jewellery exhibition and prize for the best piece dedicated to St Valentine. An 'Act of Love' prize is solemnly awarded by the city to a person or organization who has performed one (in 1996 it was dedicated to the memory of Itzhak Rabin), while modern lovers have an all-night Latino dance party. Terni also has a spring awakening festival, Cantamaggio, with processions and shows.

In the Heart of the City of Love

Much of the rest of Terni has relatively little to show in spite of a history of over 2,500 years. The post-war rebuilding, however, was left in the expert hands of architect Mario Ridolfi (d. 1984) who, after working on the reconstruction of Rome, moved here and laid out Terni's more pleasant residential districts, filling in the gaps left by the bombs. Of Roman Terni only part of the **amphitheatre** (32 AD) remains as a souvenir, in the south of the city near the pretty public gardens, where gladiators once tussled to the death before a crowd of 10,000, pensioners now play *bocce*.

The **Pinacoteca Comunale** (*in Palazzo Gazzoli, Via del Teatro Romano 16, t 0744 59421; open Tues–Sun 10–1 and 4–7; adm*) has a lot of paintings by Anonymous (a strange 16th-century *Circumcision*; a portrait of *St Charles Borromeo*, a light of the Counter Reformation, but here almost caricatured, with an enormous nose; and then, in the same Counter Reformation vein, a nightmarish scene of Franciscan martyrdoms in the Low Countries). The highlight is a *Marriage of St Catherine* from 1466 by Benozzo Gozzoli, inspired by Beato Angelico, and there is also a triptych of the *Madonna, Child and Saints* by Pier Matteo d'Amelia, a gonfalon from Siena and a *Crucifixion* painted by L'Alunno, a triptych by the late 14th-century Maestro della Dormitio di Terni, and small works by Chagall, Picasso, Carrà, Severini, Mirò, Kandinsky and Léger.

Getting Around

The SS209 from Terni to Visso is the main thoroughfare of the upper Valnerina; you can reach Norcia and Cascia by turning off at Sant'Anatolia di Narco or Triponzo, the latter offering the prettier routes. Both towns have frequent SSIT **buses** to Spoleto. From Terni, ATC buses, **t** 0744 492711, leave from the park near the station for Narni, the Cascata delle Marmore (bus 21), Piediluco (bus 24), Arrone, Ferentillo, Spoleto, Orvieto, Viterbo and Scheggino; another bus picks up passengers along the SS209 daily to Rome. Terni is the terminus of the FCU **train** line through Todi, Perugia and Città di Castello to Sansepolcro, **t** 0744 59741, and a stop on the FS's Rome–Ancona line, though from Rome you'll often have to change at Orte; from Assisi and the east usually requires a change at Foligno. For **bike** hire, contact Blob Service, Via G. di Pergarmo 66, **t** 0744 286686.

Tourist Information

Terni: Via Casian Bon 2/4, **t** 0744 423047, **f** 0744 427259, www.umbria2000.it. Open Mon–Sat 9–1 and 3–6.
Post office: Via del Plebiscito, **t** 0744 440 1839.

Market Day

Off Piazza Briccialdi, near the stadium, *Wed*.

Where to Stay

Terni ✉ 05100

Terni can be a good base for the Valnerina if you're dependent on public transport; it's also worth looking here for lodgings if Spoleto is filled up for the Two Worlds Festival.

★★★★**Garden**, Viale Bramante 6, **t** 0744 300041, **f** 0744 300414, www.gardenhotelterni.it (*expensive*). Terni's prettiest hotel, near the motorway exit, with plant-filled balconies, a pool and all the usual mod cons.

★★★★**Valentino**, Via Plinio il Giovane 5, **t** 0744 402550, **f** 0744 403335, www.hotelvalentino terni.it (*moderate*). Central with comfortable modern rooms, all air conditioned (important here in summer), and one of Terni's classiest restaurants, La Fontanella (*see* 'Eating Out,).

★★★**Hotel de Paris**, Viale Stazione 52, **t/f** 0744 58047, www.hoteldeparis.it (*moderate*). Right by the station; it has had a complete facelift.

★★★**Allegretti**, Strada dello Staino 7b, **t** 0744 426747, **f** 0744 401246 (*inexpensive*). A little way from the centre, immersed in green; rooms are adequate, with balconies.

★★★**Brenta II**, Via Montegrappa 51, **t/f** 0744 273957 (*inexpensive*). Nice modern rooms, all with bath, in one of Terni's shady, anonymous neighbourhoods, near the Nera and the Corso del Popolo.

There is another recommended alternative up at Lake Piediluco:

Best of all, there's a large collection of works by Terni's own **Orneore Metelli** (1872–1938), a shoemaker who spent his evenings painting, as Bernard Berenson said, the most naïve of naïve art. Metelli is Umbria's Grandma Moses and the two rooms of his paintings alone make a trip to this industrial city worthwhile: disarming, colourful scenes of Terni, its steel mill and its surroundings, of shoemakers, of Mussolini's motorcade, of Dante, even the Venus of Terni.

Nearby, the **Duomo**, founded in the 6th century, rebuilt in the 12th and completely redone in the 17th century, has a handsome portico and a pair of original portals, the front one topped with a 12th-century frieze. The interior has an elaborate high altar and a *Circumcision* by Livio Agresti. The 10th-century crypt, with Roman columns and altar, was restored in 1904. In the cathedral square is a fountain and Terni's most elegant palace, the **Palazzo Bianchini-Riccardi**, both from the 16th century.

From here, Via Aminale leads around to Terni's old main street, **Via Roma**, where a number of *palazzi* survived the bombing; a tower house marks the crossroads. Turn left here into Piazza Europa; at the south end is the massive **Palazzo Spada** (1546) by

***Vecchia Osteria**, just below Villalago, t 0744 369111, *www.vecchiaosteria.it* (*expensive*). Primarily a restaurant with six rooms (*moderate–inexpensive*). Serves traditional local fare and also more creative dishes. *In winter dinner only, summer lunch and dinner. Closed Mon.*

Eating Out

It's easy to eat cheaply in Terni; the pizza-by-the-slice and snack competition is fierce. And be sure to try Viparo, the local *aperitivo* with all the charm of flat rum and cola.

La Fontanella, Via Plinio il Giovane 3, t 0744 402550, f 0744 403335 (*expensive–moderate*). The restaurant of the Hotel Valentino (*see* opposite), featuring fresh, natural ingredients in tasty and imaginative dishes: watch them grill your chops through the glass before they are served.

Villa Graziani, 4km from the centre in Papigno, t 0744 67138 (*moderate*). An 18th-century place once graced by Byron; you can dine well on a mix of Umbrian specialities and Italian classics. *Closed Sun eve and Mon.*

Lu Somaru, Viale Cesare Battisti 106, t 0744 300486 (*moderate*). A popular choice on the western edge of the centre, offering Umbrian specialities, out in a garden in summer. *Closed Fri.*

La Piazzetta, Via del Leone 34, t 0744 58188 (*cheap*). This restaurant in the old part of town serves marinated fish *antipasti* or lamb *cacciatora* with potatoes and truffles. *Closed Sun.*

Stroncone ✉ 05039

Taverna di Portanova, t 0744 60496 (*moderate*). A family-run restaurant in a 14th-century building and serving an unusual speciality – a grain and vegetable *minestra*, from a medieval Franciscan recipe, alongside the usual Umbrian favourites, and a good wine list. *Eves only, closed Wed.*

Piediluco ✉ 05038

Tavoletta, Vocabolo Forca 4, t 0744 368196, (*moderate*). Piediluco's lakeside restaurant, off the SS79, serves food living up to its setting. Fish from both lake and sea figures strongly on the menu, but there is also plenty of meat. *Antipasti* and pasta dishes based around fish are especially good. Try fresh tagliatelle with *ragù* of lake fish and the trout with peppers, but leave room for a fabulous *torta di cioccolata. Closed Mon–Wed.*

Peppe Scappa, high over the lake on the Arrone road, t 0744 368416 (*moderate*). At the sign of a plate of spaghetti under a black nuclear cloud, this old pink *trattoria* serves up some of the tastiest and most reasonably priced Umbrian cuisine in the area. *Closed Mon.*

Antonio da Sangallo the Younger, perhaps his least inspired effort (some scholars have absolved him from all responsibility), now used as the town hall. To its right is the charming round church of **San Salvatore**, the oldest building in Terni, from the 5th century, which may have been a Roman temple to the Sun. In the 12th century, a nave and some frescoes were added.

From Piazza Europa, Via Cavour leads past the severe medieval **Palazzo Mezzancolli** back to Via Febbraio; off this is the Knights of St John's 12th-century church of **Sant'Alò**, with a pretty exterior, incorporating Roman and medieval fragments. Turn off on to Via Fratini, follow it north to Via Noblini and turn left for the 13th-century **San Francesco**. Its landmark campanile with colourful ceramic edgings (1345) is by Angelo da Orvieto, and inside in the Cappella Paradisi, are the Dominican friar Bartolomeo di Tommaso's fascinating and recently restored 15th-century frescoes based on Hell, Purgatory and Paradise as described in the *Divine Comedy*.

Piazza della Repubblica is the starting point for modern Terni's main thoroughfare, **Corso Tacito**, which passes through the piazza of the same name, decorated with a fountain by Mario Ridolfi (1932) with mosaics of astrological signs. The train station (now adorned with a ponderous piece of steel) is just north. Alternatively, from Piazza della Repubblica the Corso Vecchio, passes other signs of medieval Terni, around to **San Pietro in Trivio**, a church built in the 14th century and rebuilt in the 1700s, and rebuilt again after the war, yet somehow managing to retain some of its original frescoes. The nearby **Palazzo Carrara** is a 17th-century reconstruction of a medieval palace. It is no longer open to the public but its Iron Age collections are now housed in the new **Museo Archeologico** at Via Lungonera Savoia (*t 0744 22801; open Tues–Sun 10–1 and 4–7*), containing some of the Iron Age artefacts discovered under the steel mills. Another church along the Corso Vecchio, **San Lorenzo**, has Terni's oddest interior, with one short and one tall nave, and contains a good 16th-century painting on the *Martyrdom of San Biagio*. Opposite are a set of medieval tower houses known as the **Case dei Castelli**.

Santa Maria del Monumento (*open 8.30am–9.30am only*) is to the west near the cemetery, 1.5km along the extension of Via Cavour (Viale di Porta Sant'Angelo); partly built from a Roman funerary monument, it was enlarged in 1474. Inside, frescoes depict the legend of the golden apples and there is an early 16th-century *presepio*.

Around Terni

Overlooking Terni to the southwest is medieval hilltop **Collescipoli**. Long a defensive outpost of the city, it is now slowly being engulfed in urban sprawl. Among the churches, **Santa Maria Maggiore** has a handsome Renaissance door and one of the most beautiful Baroque interiors in Umbria, and an unusual painting on the *Death of St Joseph*. There are some popular votive frescoes and a *Coronation of the Virgin* (1507) painted by Evangelista Aquili in the church of **San Nicola da Bari**. The church of **Santo Stefano** has an odd bell tower, a *Crucifixion* and an inscription from 1093.

The pretty, old walled village of **Stroncone** lies at the crossroads 8km south of Terni, leading to a series of alpine meadows and chestnut forests called **I Prati**. Here there are grand views over Terni's plain from the highest point, **Cimitelle** (840m/2,756ft).

The Cascata delle Marmore and Lago di Piediluco

www.marmore.it. The falls are let down on the following schedule:
*Jan: Sat–Sun 12–1 and 3–4; **Feb**: Sat–Sun 11–1 and 3–5; **March**: Sat–Sun 11–1 and 4–9; Mon–Fri 12–1 and 4–5; **April**: Sat–Sun 10–1 and 4–9; Mon–Fri 12–1 and 4–5 **May**: Sat–Sun 10–1 and 3–10; Mon–Fri 12–1 and 4–5; **June–Aug**: Sat–Sun 10–1 and 3–10; Mon–Fri 11–1, 4–6 and 9–10pm; **Sept**: Sat–Sun 10–1 and 3–10; Mon–Fri 12–1, 4–5 and 8–9pm; **Oct**: Sat–Sun 11–1 and 3–7; Fri 3–5; **Nov–Dec**: Sat–Sun 12–1 and 3–4; Adm. Both top and bottom of the falls are easily reached by bus from Terni. For a closer encounter, contact **Centro Canoa e Rafting Le Marmore**, t 337 729154, f 06 8621 2249, www.raftingmarmore.com, which organizes guided canoeing and rafting down the Corno and Nera rivers.*

Terni, appropriately enough as the city of St Valentine, has its own Niagara Falls for honeymooners: the 413ft green and misty **Cascata delle Marmore**, 6km east of the city. Falling in three stages, this is one of Europe's tallest, most beautiful waterfalls – when it's running. Surprisingly, the Cascata is an artificial creation, albeit an ancient one. In 271 BC Curius Dentatus, best known as the conqueror of the Sabines, dug a channel to drain the marshlands of Rieti, diverting the River Velino into the Nera. Although the falls are usually swallowed up by hydroelectric turbines, the thundering waters are let down at regular times (*see* p.564), and illuminated after dark. The surrounding area is open for picnics at most times except in December and January.

There are two places from which to view the falls – from the Belvedere Inferiore down below on the SS209 (equipped with a large car park, tourist pavilion and a dozen *porchetta* vans, just beyond the tunnel) or from the Belvedere Superiore, in the village of Marmore. A path through the woods connects the two, although it's steep, prone to be muddy in the off season, and much nicer to walk down than up (the path at the bottom begins 100 yards downstream from the falls). There are some pleasant places to swim near the bottom, but you can't use them when the falls are on (the siren sounds 15 minutes before the falls are turned on to warn swimmers).

Up near Marmore, lovely **Lago di Piediluco** zigzags in and out of wooded hills, one of which is crowned by a 12th-century fortress. There are a couple of beaches, but the water is cold, a bit dirty and has dangerous undercurrents. There are other diversions; in recent years, the lake has become the capital of sport rowing in Italy and the site of international competitions. On its shores, the medieval village and modest resort of **Piediluco** is named after a sacred Roman grove of trees (*lucus*) and has a fine late 13th-century church, **San Francesco**, up a flight of steps. The bricked-up door has a striking frieze decorated with knots and lions; inside, the walls are decorated with 16th-century frescoes, among them a *Madonna and Two Saints* by Marcantonio di Antoniazzo. The stoup was a Roman capital and there's a Roman statue of a lady in a niche. Above the church is a ruined castle (1364) built by Cardinal Albornoz.

Perched high above the east shore of the lake is lovely **Labro**, former nest of noblemen on the run, and now colonized by Belgians after a Belgian architect bought and restored the entire village. Below the lake, the Arrone road passes **Villalago**, which has an outdoor theatre for summer events and lovely grounds for picnicking.

Up the Valley and Into the Mountains

The further you head up the Valnerina, the more wild and beautiful the scenery becomes, and the tastier the truffles. The Parco Naturale del Nera begins at the Cascata delle Marmore. This part of Umbria had just about finished repairs after tremors in 1979, when the 1997 earthquake caused fresh damage and closed a number of roads; most have since reopened, but the road from S. Anatolia di Nano to Monteleone di Spoleto is closed after Caso. Some villages are still undergoing repairs.

Arrone and Ferentillo

After the Cascata delle Marmore, the SS209 passes beneath the pretty townlets of **Torreorsina** and **Casteldilago** before arriving at the more substantial and picturesque

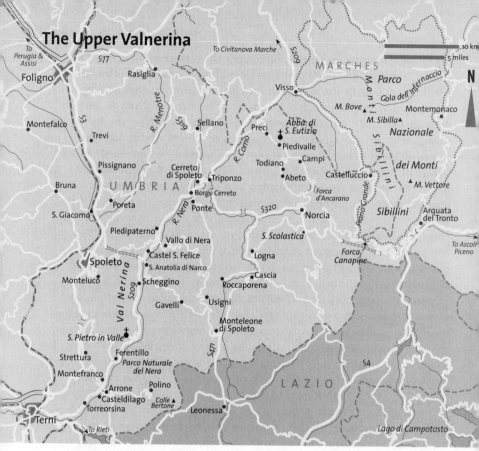

market village of **Arrone**, spilling over its isolated rock. In the centre, the church of **Santa Maria** has remarkably good frescoes, including a *Life of the Virgin*, by Vincenzo Tamagni and Giovanni di Spoleto, inspired by Lippo Lippi's work in Spoleto's Duomo. The *Madonna della Misericordia* (1544) by Jacopo Siculo is to the right of the main altar, and there's a *Supper at Emaus* by Caravaggio's school. In the apse left of the altar is a Renaissance terracotta of the *Madonna Suckling the Child, Between Two Saints*.

In the old days, Arrone and its neighbours indulged in some fierce warfare. The *signori* of Arrone, who built the landmark tower on top of the town (with a tree growing out of it), were bitter enemies of the lords of Polino. A pretty 10km drive along a winding road, passing at **Rosciano** under the great white arch of a Mussolini-built aqueduct, the Ponte Canale, brings you to **Polino**, Umbria's tiniest *comune*. It, too, has its feudal tower, as well as a monumental Baroque fountain and a road up to the **Colle Bertone** (1,223m/4,041ft), a modest winter sports resort and summer picnic area.

The biggest rivals of the lords of Arrone were the powerful abbots of **Ferentillo**, the next town up the Valnerina, guarded by twin 14th-century citadels on dramatic rocks that dominate the narrow valley like matching bookends; their sheer walls are as popular now with rock-climbers as Arrone's aqueduct is with rubber-banded leapers. In Precetto, the oldest quarter of Ferentillo, the crypt of **Santo Stefano** contains something you don't expect to find in Umbria: **mummies** (*t 0743 54395; open daily*

Nov–Feb 10–12.30 and 2.30–5; Mar and Oct 9.30–12.30 and 2.30–6.30; April–Sept 9–12.30 and 2.30–7.30; adm). Accidentally preserved by a microfungus in the soil, Ferentillo's most gruesomely fascinating corpses (complete with brown papery skin and organs, hair, whiskers, teeth and even eyeballs in some cases) are displayed in shiny glass cases. Among them are Chinese newlyweds who came here over 100 years ago on a pilgrimage to Rome and got cholera instead; two French prisoners who were hanged in the Napoleonic wars; a woman who died of bubonic plague, a lawyer stabbed 27 times and one of his murderers, a tidy shelf of skulls and an eagle, placed here as an experiment and perfectly mummified in less than a year. The nonchalant housewives who give the tours add to the surreal pleasure.

San Pietro in Valle

Ring in advance, t 0744 780316; church open 10.30–1 and 2.30–6.
The custodian's house is clearly marked on the road up to the abbey.

The former Benedictine abbey of Ferentillo, **San Pietro in Valle**, is 4km further up the valley on the beautiful slopes of Monte Solenne, and you won't find a more charming abbey to visit – or stay in, as it has recently been converted into a *residenza d'epoca*. Founded *c.* 710 by the Duke of Spoleto Faraoldo II, the abbey is on the site of a Syrian hermitage from the 6th century.

The abbey has an ornate 12th-century campanile embedded with 8th-century fragments, in a style more common to Rome than Umbria. The church is full of rare treasures. The nave is covered with recently restored **frescoes** from 1190, a rare and important early example of the Italian response to the Byzantine style – here already moving away from the stylized hierarchy to a more natural 'Latin style' where figures are individuals rather than types; the only comparable frescoes of the period are in the Roman church of San Giovanni a Porta Latina. The left wall has Old Testament scenes (note *Adam Naming the Animals* and *Noah*) and there are New Testament scenes on the right. The high **altar** (*c.* 740) is a rare example of Lombard work, sculpted on front and back, complete with a self-portrait of the sculptor, signed Ursus Magester. The apse contains good 13th-century frescoes, with a pretty *Madonna* by the school of Giotto. At the back there's a cylindrical altar, said to be Etruscan. Among the stone fragments on the wall is a real rarity – a bas relief of a monk with oriental features, believed to be one of the two Syrian monks who set up a hermitage here. The side door is usually open so you can peek into the charming two-storey **cloister**, built in the 12th century, where the hotel rooms are; the two 11th-century figures guarding the door of the church are Peter and Paul.

The views extend across the valley to the abandoned citadel of **Umbriano**, the legendary first city of Umbria. If you walk up there, be sure to make a lot of noise to scare off any unsuspecting vipers. It makes an unforgettable place for a picnic.

Up the Valnerina: Scheggino to Triponzo

Scheggino, the next town up the valley, occupies both banks of the Nera and is laced with tiny canals full of trout and a rare species of crayfish (*gamberettini*)

Tourist Information

Ferentillo: There are two organizations, both on Via della Vittoria: **Comune**, t 0744 780521, f 0744 780234 (*open daily 8.30–1*) and **Pro-Loco**, t 0744 780990 (*open daily 3.30–7*).

Activities

Valnerina Verticale Sport, Piazza Vittorio Emanuele 9, Ferentillo, t 0744 302451. Organizes rock-climbing at various levels around Ferentillo, Montefranco and Arrone.
Fiume Corno, t 0742 23146, *www.raftingumbria.it*. Rafting, kayaking, hiking and mountain bike tours in the Valnerina.

Where to Stay and Eat

Arrone ✉ 05031

★★Rossi, on the SS209, Loc Isola 7, t 0744 388372, f 0744 388305, *www.rossihotelristorante.it* (*inexpensive*). Sixteen modern en suite rooms, and one of the best local restaurants (*moderate*), with excellent *crostini*, spaghetti with truffles, grilled meats and a variety of trout dishes, served in a pretty garden in summer. Book ahead for the deservedly popular and completely overwhelming Thursday seafood feast. *Closed Fri.*
Locanda Paradiso, Via del Colle Buonacquisto 9, t 0744 368526 (*inexpensive*). Reliable pizza and basic fare. it also has a few simple rooms all with baths.

Ferentillo ✉ 05034

★★★Fontegaia, on the SS209, towards Ferentillo in Montefranco, t 0744 388621, f 0744 388598, *www.hotelfontegaia.it* (*moderate*). The most pretentious in the Valnerina; comfortable rooms, children's playground, beautiful gardens for dining *al fresco*, but it lacks charm. The restaurant is popular with locals for a special occasion, if a bit heavy-handed with the cream sauces: ostrich with marsala and ginger or *tagliatelle con graniciale* and *pecorino. Closed Tues–Thurs lunch, Mon.*
Abbazia San Pietro in Valle, Loc Macenano, t 0744 780129, f 0744 435522, *www.san*

pietroinvalle.com (*expensive*). A hotel and restaurant in the former abbey, with well-furnished rooms, some with frescoes, in the old monks' quarters – a very peaceful spot. *Open from 22 Mar–27 Oct.*
★★★Monterivoso, Via Case Sparse, 5 Loc Monterivoso on the mummy road (*see Santo Stefano, p.567*), t 0744 780772, f 0744 780725, *www.monterivoso.it* (*inexpensive*). An old mill, beautifully converted into a hotel in 1997, where antique-furnished rooms look out over the lawn – a pool is planned but the municipal one in Ferentillo, 3mins away, is especially nice; the restaurant is good, too.
Piermarini, Via della Vittoria 53, t 0744 780714 (*moderate*). Wonderful local dishes. Try *coratina di agnello* (lamb's innards) with asparagus, homemade pasta with truffles, lamb cutlets *scottadito* with olive foccacia, freshwater trout and river crayfish. There are mushrooms and chestnuts in the autumn. *Closed Sun eve and Mon.*
Pizzeria Collestate, in Collestate (from Montefranco, go up the mountain towards Spoleto (*inexpensive*); the pizzeria is signposted at the pass). Delicious pizza smothered in rocket and views over the lower Valnerina.
Vecchio Ponte, Via Circonvallazione 3, t 0744 380016 (*moderate*). More *tartufo*, *cinghiale* galore, by the river. Pizza at weekends. *Closed Wed.*
Ai Tre Archi, on the SS. Valnerina 29km, t 0744 780004 (*cheap*). Good, workman-like pasta dishes, such as *gnocchi al sugo di pecora* and pizza. *Closed Mon.*

Scheggino ✉ 06040

★★Del Ponte, Via Borgo 15, t 0743 61253, f 0743 61131 (*inexpensive*). A charming hotel on the River Nera, offering 12 rooms and delicious meals (*moderate*), based on crayfish and truffles. For a trip to Umbrian heaven, try the *fettuccine* with a sauce that combines both ingredients. *Closed Mon.*

Sant'Anatolia di Narco ✉ 06040

★★Tre Valli, Strada Valnerina, t 0743 613118, f 0743 61115 (*inexpensive*). Simple rooms.

imported from Turkey; it is also the fief of Italy's truffle tycoons, Paolo and Bruno Urbani, who thanks to the foresight of their grandfather Carlo control about 70 per cent of the Valnerina's black gold. Scheggino has 12th-century walls that famously repelled the notorious brigand Girolamo Brancaleoni in 1522. There are late frescoes by Lo Spagna in the apse of the church of **San Nicolò**, along with a *Madonna del Rosario* by Pierino Cesari and other late 16th-century works.

On the left bank of the Nera, 3km from Scheggino, **Sant'Anatolia di Narco** is another bailiwick of the black truffle. It's an ancient place: in the 19th century, a necropolis of Naharkum was discovered here, going back to the 8th century BC, making it one of the oldest of all Umbrii sites. Today fewer than 600 people live within its 14th-century walls. Its glory days as a medieval *comune* are recalled in an archway with a relief of a knight, all that survives of the 13th-century Palazzo del Comune. Nearby, the medieval church of **Sant'Anatolia** (*if locked, ask at the house next door for the key*) has been restored since the earthquake, revealing fragments of early frescoes. Just outside the west gate, the Porta di Castello, the pretty church of **Santa Maria delle Grazie** (*under restoration; the keyholders for Sant'Anatolia will show you to the priest's house for the key*) has a façade of 1572 and popular votive frescoes, as well as a beautiful fresco in the presbytery of the *Madonna and Child* by the 15th-century Master of Eggi.

Just up from Sant'Anatolia, medieval **Castel San Felice** is a pretty little hamlet on its hill, completely restored after 1979. You can visit the delightful 12th-century abbey church of **San Felice in Narco** (*t 0743 613427, f 0743 613420, get the key from Via Orichelle 34*), located on an unpaved road at the foot of the village. There is a great picnic spot just beond the church, by the little bridge over the Nera. The façade has an intricate rose window surrounded by Evangelist symbols, sculpted columns and capitals, Cosmatesque decoration and reliefs on the life of St Felice, who moved here with his father Mauro from Palestine in the 5th century. At the time the local inhabitants were having serious problems with a dragon; with the help of an angel, Felice dispatched it for them and performed other miracles. When he died, Mauro built an oratory over his grave. The interior is equally beautiful, containing a pair of *transennae* with Cosmatesque remains and some early 15th-century frescoes. The crypt contains the ancient sarcophagus of St Mauro and St Felice.

High over the left bank of the Nera, walled medieval **Vallo di Nera** has fortified walls, twisting steep cobbled streets, covered alleys, little piazzas and stone houses, all immaculately restored, and two churches with frescoes. One is the 13th-century **Santa Maria** (*key from the house through the gate to the left of the church, by the water fountain*), with a Gothic portal and frescoes by Cola di Pietro from Camerino and Francesco di Antonio, painted in 1383; other frescoes are votive and feature some delightful pigs. Even better are the beautifully coloured frescoes in pink and white **San Giovanni Battista** (*key kept next door or ask any local*) at the top of the village; these, on the *Life of the Virgin* (1536), are by Pinturicchio's assistant, Jacopo Siculo.

This upper part of the Valnerina has been decidedly less remote since the opening of a road and tunnel from Spoleto to Piedipaterno, replacing the old narrow winding road. The next village, **Borgo Cerreto**, lies at an important crossroads and has a late 13th-century Franciscan church, **San Lorenzo**, which was badly damaged in the earthquake and is still being restored. Above it, on a high hill, tiny **Ponte** overlooks the confluence of the Tissino and the Nera. In the 9th century, this village was big news, a major Lombard stronghold ruling both Cascia and Norcia. The views from Ponte are lovely and the **Pieve di Santa Maria Assunta** (1201) is also well worth a look; it has a beautifully carved rose window with symbols of the Evangelists and a *telamon* on its tall façade, and a fine apse decorated with hanging arches and funny little heads. The handsome interior (*the custodian lives in Via Nortosce*) was restored in 1940 and contains ancient fragments, a fine pavement and some damaged frescoes by the Umbrian school. From here, it is a steep but pretty walk up to the ruined castle.

Across the valley and just off the main road sits **Cerreto di Spoleto** high on its spur, offering splendid views towards Ponte. It was the birthplace of the humanist and Latin poet Giovanni Pontano (1426–1503), better known as Pontanus. While he was away attending university in Perugia, his family's home in Cerreto was burned down, so he went to live with relatives in Naples, advising the court and running the literary academy that was later to take his name, the Accademia Pontana. Cerreto has several fine *palazzi*, as well as a pretty main piazza with a 15th-century **Palazzo Comunale** and fountain; just beyond here is the tall 15th-century **Torre Civica**. Unfortunately, the churches were all damaged in 1997 and some are still clad in scaffolding, although most restoration is complete. **San Giacomo** (*now fully restored, ask nearby for key*) on the edge of the hill, has beautiful 15th-century frescoes.

Triponzo, the last Umbrian village in the Valnerina, was the epicentre of the 1979 earthquake, but is now inhabited again. The road continues on to Pontechiusita, and from there, you can pick up the road to Preci and Norcia (*see pp.573–6*).

Towards Monteleone di Spoleto and Cascia from Sant'Anatolia

A spectacular mountain road rises east of Sant'Anatolia di Narco to the hamlet of **Caso**, with a pair of interesting churches: **Santa Maria delle Grazie** (*ask in the village for the keys to both churches*) with frescoes by the school of Lo Spagna; and, outside the village, the Romanesque church of **Santa Cristina**, with frescoes from the 14th–16th centuries. Futher along, the road (*currently closed*) rises and rises to **Gavelli** (1,152m/3,780ft), a tiny village on the cliff with a 15th-century church of **San Michele Arcangelo** (*key kept next to door*), beautifully frescoed by Lo Spagna and his school. The remote hamlet of **Usigni**, signposted off the main road, has a remarkable 17th-century Roman-Baroque church, **San Salvatore** (*open Sun only*), attributed to Bernini. It was commissioned by Fausto Poli, who was born here and became a cardinal in the court of Urban VIII; he is best remembered for promoting the beatification of St Rita.

Further south, high above the Corno Valley, remote little **Monteleone di Spoleto** has a pretty setting that has been inhabited for centuries: a large 6th-century BC cemetery on the road from Usigni was discovered in 1902 and yielded a wooden chariot of Etruscan manufacture, decorated with magnificent bronze reliefs of the life of Achilles (now in the Metropolitan Museum in New York). Monteleone was ruled by Spoleto until 1559, but has suffered from earthquakes in 1703 and 1979. In the upper, semi-deserted part of town, a couple of fine quattrocento *palazzi* and a porticoed **Palazzo dei Priori** are testimony to its former importance. Here, too, is the massive

13th-century church and convent of **San Francesco** with a beautiful Gothic door. The recently restored interior has a fine high altar, an 18th-century painted ceiling decorated with symbols of the Madonna and fascinating remains of 15th-century frescoes, especially a magnificent *Christ in Majesty*. The arcaded cloister has more frescoes, as does the lower church, with a nice one of *St Anthony Abbot and the Animals*. For stupendous views over much of southern Umbria, take the remote SS471 south through the mountains to Leonessa in Lazio and follow the signs west to Labro, Lake Piediluco and the Cascata della Marmore near Terni.

Cascia

The narrow SS471 north from Monteleone takes you to the top of **Cascia** (pop. 4,000), a hill town that sees more pilgrims than truffles; more, in fact, than any Umbrian town except Assisi. Santa Rita, the 'Saint of Impossibilities', was born near here in 1381, but had to wait until 1900 to be canonized, and then hold on until the inauspicious period of 1937–47 for her sanctuary. Poor Rita! After a wretched marriage to a roughneck, who was killed by his enemies, she persuaded her two sons not to take vengeance; when they died soon afterwards of disease, she became a nun, only to develop such a foul-smelling sore on her forehead that none of the sisters would come near her. Then she received the Stigmata and spent the rest of her life in pain.

Cascia itself has known more than its share of bad luck. Originally the Roman *Cursula*, it was wiped out by an earthquake and refounded on a different site. This did not prevent other earthquakes from periodically destroying it, in 1599, 1703 and 1979. The Lombards and Saracens sacked it in the three digit years. Afterwards, Cascia was a freewheeling *comune* like the others, sometimes under Spoleto's sway, sometimes under the Emperor or the Trinci family in Foligno. When it came under the Church with the rest of Umbria in 1516 it rebelled, but was soon put in its place.

The Basilica of Santa Rita

The **Basilica di Santa Rita** (*open April 6.30am–7.30pm, May–Sept 6.30am–8pm*) has been described as the most vulgar in Christendom, a proto-Disney castle with a pseudo-Byzantine interior and ghastly frescoes. Rita's dried up body is displayed in a glass coffin, surrounded by votive offerings from the Terni and Rome football clubs, while every year tens of thousands of unhappily married women and other victims of bad luck come to pray for relief. An attempt to insert some art into the basilica, the high altar by Giacomo Manzù, doesn't really stand a chance. The **Monasterio di Santa Rita** (*t 0743 76221, www.santaritadacascia.com; open April–Sept 8–6 for guided tours*), to the left of the basilica, marks the spot where she spent her 40 years as a nun, the 15th-century cloister, her cell and miraculous rose bush.

The Rest of Town

Other spots around Cascia receive less devotion, but they offer more substance in the art department. The **Museo Comunale di Palazzo Santi**, in Via G. Palombi

Getting Around

The Società Spoletino, **t** 0743 212211, runs **buses** from Norcia, Spoleto, Terni, Foligno and Perugia to Cascia.

Tourist Information

Cascia: Piazza Garibaldi, **t** 0743 71147, *info@iat.cascia.pg.it. Open Mon–Sat 9–1 and 3.30–6.30, Sun 9–1.*

Market Day
Wed.

Where to Stay and Eat

Cascia ✉ 06043
★★★**Cursula**, Via Cavour 3, **t** 0743 76206, *www.hotelcursula.com* (*moderate*). Pleasant rooms and Umbrian fare in the restaurant.
★★**Centrale**, Piazza Garibaldi 36, **t** 0743 76736 (*inexpensive*). A handy location.
★★**Mini Hotel La Tavernetta**, Via Palombi, **t** 0743 71387, *www.minihotellatavernetta.com* (*inexpensive*). Family-run, with clean, comfy rooms and a restaurant (*moderate*) serving well-cooked dishes using wild mushrooms, salami, trout and lamb. *Closed Tues.*

(**t** 0743 751 010; open Oct–Mar Sat–Sun 10.30–1 and 3–5; April Sat–Sun 10.30–1 and 4–6; May–June Fri–Sun 10.30–1 and 4–6.30; July and Sept Tues–Sun 10.30–1 and 4–6.30; Aug daily 10.30–1 and 4–7; adm) housed in a 17th-century palace, has an archaeological collection and works of art from the town's churches, including some beautiful early medieval wooden sculpture. There's a lovely carved doorway and rose window on the Gothic church of **San Francesco** in Piazza Garibaldi; inside are frescoes from the 15th and 16th centuries, a fancy Baroque pulpit, Gothic choir stalls and the last painting by Niccolò Pomarancio, an *Ascension* (1596). There are more good frescoes and a pretty 14th-century statue of the *Virgin and Child* in the nearby **Collegiata di Santa Maria**, a large church founded in 856 but rebuilt several times since; one of the Romanesque lions that originally held up a porch is now a fountain, while the other peers out from a niche over the door.

Below Piazza Garibaldi, the austere church of **Sant'Antonio Abate** (*open same hours as Palazzo Santi*) is part of the museum. Despite frequent earthquake repairs over the centuries, it preserves in the apse a delightful 14th-century fresco cycle on the *Life of St Anthony Abbot*, attributed to the Maestro della Dormitio di Terni. The nun's choir contains another fine fresco cycle, on the *Passion of Christ* (1461) by Nicola da Siena. But most beautiful of all is the painted 15th-century wooden statue of the *Archangel Raphael with Tobias* by Antonio Rizzo's workshop.

Around Cascia

Above Cascia (follow the signs for Monteleone) are the ruins of its 15th-century citadel, destroyed by the papal army after the town's revolt. Below this, the pink and white 14th-century **Convento di Sant'Agostino** has more good 15th-century frescoes. The last site on the Rita trail is her birthplace, at **Roccaporena**, 6km west of Cascia in the Corna Valley. The setting, under a mighty rock renamed the Scoglio della Preghiera (the Cliff of Prayer) is exactly the kind of slightly other-worldly place you might expect a saint to be born. Rita's house was transformed into a church in 1630 by Cardinal Fausto Poli, the chief promoter of her beatification; a little chapel crowns the big rock like a cap.

Norcia and the Monti Sibillini

Here in its southeast corner, in the shadow of the Monti Sibillini, Umbria achieves its highest heights and widest open spaces. Norcia, in ancient times the northernmost of all Sabine towns, stands battered yet proud on its high plain, famous for its saint and its butchers. Because of the frequent earthquakes, an 18th-century law limited buildings to two storeys and the result looks like no other town in Umbria.

Norcia

Old **Norcia** (pop. 4,900) or, as the gate reads, VETUSTA NURSIA, depending on when you visit can seem bright and cheerful or morose and gloomy, barricaded like a Foreign Legion outpost in its 14th-century walls on the edge of the lofty Piano di Santa Scolastica, surrounded by mountains on all sides. Virgil called it *Frigida Nursia*, so one can imagine when he visited. But the last Roman emperor was still warm in his grave when this old, cold town offered the world St Benedict (480–543), the father of Western monasticism.

In the Middle Ages, Norcia was a *comune* to be reckoned with. Nor was it long before the Nursini lost their early reputation for sanctity; they were known at various times for witchcraft (there was a sorcerers' college here in the Middle Ages, when *nursino* or *norcino* became synonymous with 'wizard'), as well as pork butchers and surgery. Practitioners of both the latter were renowned for their expert knife work – after all, in the days when doing autopsies on cadavers was illegal, the famous surgeons of Preci (*see* p.577) practised on pigs. To this day, Norcia is synonymous with *prosciutto* (from both domestic pork and wild boar) and the best *norcinerie* in Umbria, as well as fine cheeses.

As a sideline to all this, the Nursini were also experts in the art of keeping male voices unnaturally pure and sweet. The parents of a boy with operatic potential would bring him to Norcia, where he would be drugged with opium and put in a very hot bath until he was quite insensible, when the dirty deed was done (the ducts leading to the testicles were severed, so that the organs would eventually shrivel and disappear). Too bad for the lad whose voice never made the grade, but those who did became the darlings of society and quite wealthy besides. Some were such charming primadonnas that Casanova wasn't the only one to keep falling in love with them. One of the last 'graduates' of Norcia, Domenico Mustafa (d. 1912), was director of the Sistine Chapel choir and stayed long enough to cut the only recording by a *castrato*.

Piazza San Benedetto

Norcia's history has been plagued by earthquakes: one in 1328 destroyed the medieval city and further quakes in 1703, 1730, 1859 and 1979 all took their toll on the city. However, it escaped any damage in the 1997 earthquake. The city's chief monuments are on the rounded **Piazza San Benedetto**, presided over by a stern statue of St Benedict from 1880. Directly behind him stands the 13th-century Gothic

Getting There and Around

Società Spoletino **buses** to Norcia run from Spoleto, Cascia, Perugia, Terni, Foligno, Rome and Ascoli Piceno in the Marches, call **t** 0743 212211 for schedules.

Tourist Information

Norcia: Piazza Garibaldi, **t** 0743 71147, *www.norcia.net*. There is also an information office for the **Monte Sibillini National Park**, the Casa del Parco, at Norcia, Via Solferino 22, t/f 0743 817090, *www.sibillini.net. Open daily 9.30–12.30.*

Preci: Via Santa Caterina, **t** 0743 93781, **f** 0743 937827, *comunedipreci@tin.it. Open Tues and Thurs 9–1 and 3–5; Mon, Wed and Fri 9–1.*

Market Day

Thurs.

Festivals

Truffle fair, *Feb.*

Feast of St Benedict, *20–21 March*. Crossbow tournament between six *quaite* or districts of town.

Sports and Activities

For outdoor activities, contact any of the organizations below.

Associazione Piangrande, Castelluccio, **t** 0743 817 279. For **mountain bike** excursions and **horse trekking**.

Cooperativa Monte Patino, Via Foscolo 2, Norcia, **t** 0743 817487. Organizes **hiking** trips, mountain biking and horse trekking.

Rafting Centre Monti Sibillini, c/o Ristorante dei Cacciatori, Biselli di Norcia, **t** 0742 23146.

Prodelta, Via delle Fate 3, Castelluccio, **t** 0743 821156. **Paragliding** and **hang-gliding** school.

Where to Stay and Eat

Norcia ✉ 06046

★★★Grotta Azzurra, Via Alfieri 12, **t** 0743 816513, **f** 0743 817342, *www.bianconi.com* (*moderate*). An inn since 1850, this is an attractive choice with a good restaurant serving traditional local fare but perhaps with a lighter touch, its mandatory truffled dishes competing with a tasty risotto with crayfish from the Nera, or *fettuccine* with trout, or delicious grilled mushrooms in season. *Closed Tues.*

Basilica di San Benedetto, with a charming portal, framed by statues of Benedict and Scholastica and painted angels, with a Madonna on top and a rose window. On the side of the church, a portico shelters 16th-century grain measures and ends at a sturdy campanile. The interior, remodelled in the 18th century, with unexceptional paintings and restored for the 2000 Jubilee, seems unduly modest for the shrine to the Patron Saint of Europe. In the crypt you can study the ruins of a late Roman house, which tradition says belonged to Europroprio Anicio and Abbondanza Reguardati, parents of twins Benedict and Scholastica, the first Western monk and nun.

The handsome **Palazzo Comunale**, also in the piazza, has a 13th-century campanile and portico of 1492, and a **Cappella dei Priori** containing a 15th-century silver reliquary of St Benedict. Next door and in the nearby streets are the boar and truffle gastronomic shops. These are Norcia's real attraction for Italians: brown, lumpy whole truffles, crusty salami tied up in string and tough weathered hams still sprouting tufts of black bristles ('*Two years old and never been in a refrigerator!*' boasts one sign).

The other side of the piazza is occupied by the square **Castellina** (*t 0743 817030; open Oct–April Tues–Sun 10–1 and 3–5; June, July and Sept daily 10–1 and 4–7; 21–31 Aug daily 10–1 and 4–7.30*), built over the ruins of an ancient temple. Designed in 1554 for

***Nuovo Hotel Posta**, Via C. Battisti 10, **t/f** 0743 817 434, *www.bianconi.com* (*hotel and restaurant moderate*).Closed for refurbishment, due to reopen summer 2005, ask at Grotta Azzurra (*see* opposite). A fine establishment, where the pleasant rooms all have bath and they serve the famous, hearty, robust fare of Castelluccio lentils, boar salami, *tortellini alla norcina* (with ricotta), lamb with truffles, topped off, if you dare, by a tumbler of Norcia's nasty grappa flavoured with black truffles.

Dal Francese, Via Riguardati 16, **t** 0743 816290 (*moderate*). The ideal place for a bumper meal in this corner of Umbria, where the truffle is king. Try the smoked turkey and homemade salami as *antipasto*, followed by a pasta medley of *tris al tartufo*, *gnocchi al tartufo* or *tortellini con crema di tordi* (thrushes) *e tartufi*. For a main course choose a trout dish, tender grilled lamb or *braciola in agrodolce con tartufi* (a chopin sweet-and-sour sauce with truffles). Good wine list, too. *Closed Fri except in summer.*

Restaurant Granaro del Monte, Via Alfieri 12, **t** 0743 816 513 (*moderate*). Specializes in grilled meats prepared before your very eyes over their large open fire. Precede this with *pappardelle* with truffles and ricotta or a velvety lentil soup.

Castelluccio di Norcia ✉ 06046

***Sibilla**, **t** 0743 821113 (*inexpensive*). You can spend a rural medieval interlude in one of the 11 rooms in this hotel, each with its own shower. There is also a restaurant (*moderate*). *Closed Tues.*

Taverna Castelluccio, Via dietro la Torre, **t** 0744 821100 (*moderate*). The best food in town, with Norcia-style *antipasti* and the village's famous lentils served in soup or with sausages. It also has a few reasonably priced rooms to rent. *Closed Wed, but open daily in summer.*

Il Guerin Meschino, Via Monte Veletta 22, **t/f** 0743 821125 (*moderate*). Fifteen bedrooms and five apartments available to rent on a working lentil farm.

For overnight stays in the mountains, there are plenty of *rifugi* – huts that offer modest accommodation and food for equally modest prices. For information, contact the park's headquarters:

Parco Nazionale dei Monti Sibillini, Largo G.B. Gaola Antinori 1, Visso (Mc), **t** 0737 972711, **f** 0737 972707, *parco@sibillini.net*, *www. sibillini.net*.

Pope Julius III by his favourite architect Vignola, its upper floor now houses the **Museo Civico Diocesano** (**t** *0743 817030; open Tues–Sun 10–12.30 and 3.30–6.30; adm*). This holds pretty and precious things, including a late 12th-century painted *Crucifixion* with the two Marys standing on either side of Christ, a not uncommon Romanesque conceit; there were originally two others, but they fell off. Another remarkable *Cross*, signed Petrus, was made half a century later. There's a life-sized *Deposition* group in wood from Ruccataniburo, dating from the late 1200s, high reliefs of the Madonna and Child, and paintings of the same by Antonio da Faenza (whose architectural training shows in his use of perspective) and others in the Salone, under its handsome panelled ceiling, along with a *Risen Christ* by Nicola da Siena. Another room has stone sculptures by Giovanni Dalmata (1469) from an altarpiece formerly in San Giovanni, and further on are two terracotta statues of the *Annunciation* by Luca Della Robbia. The loggia is dedicated to detached frescoes.

Next to the Castellina is Norcia's **Duomo**, built by Lombard masons in 1560 and remodelled in the 1700s; the massive campanile was rebuilt in 1859. The 17th-century chapel of the Madonna della Misericordia, shelters a venerated 16th-century fresco, *Madonna between SS. Scholastica and Benedict.*

The **Mostra Museo della Civiltà Contadina ed Artigiana del Passato**, at the Palazzo Cavallieri di Malta is a private collection (*in the winter, call the owner, Olderico Fratini, before visiting t 075 802145; open Sat 8–7 and Sun 9–7; adm*).

Elsewhere in Norcia

From the Castellina, Via Battisti leads to the 14th-century Gothic church of **San Francesco**, with a rose window and handsome portal; the interior has 16th-century frescoes and a fine painting by Jacopo Siculo, *Coronation of the Virgin*. Opposite is the building, now occupied by a restaurant, that once held the public pawn shop, the Monte di Pietà, founded in 1466. Norcia's straight main street, Corso Sertorio, runs just east of here; the town's recently rebuilt **Teatro Civico** (*t 0743 816022*) is in Piazza Vittorio Veneto, at the north end of the Corso by the handsome 19th-century **Porta Romana**. Just outside, a new partially underground building houses the **Cripto Portico Romano Museo Archeologico** (*same opening hours as Castellina*), displaying finds from the area.

From Corso Sertorio, Via Gioberti leads to the 15th-century church of **San Giovanni**, with its bell tower built into the walls. This is one of the most important churches in Norcia, with a good interior and art, but it has long been closed. From nearby Piazza Carlo Alberto with a fountain, turn down Via Umberto to see the most curious building in Norcia, the square limestone **Tempietto**, built on the street corner by local stonemason Vanni Tuzi in 1354. No one is quite sure what it was used for, but it has pretty reliefs. Via Umberto continues past here to Via Anicia, where a left turn will take you to the 13th-century Gothic church of **Sant'Agostino** (*open in summer*), with an ogival portal and a frescoed lunette from 1368 and good 15th- and 16th-century frescoes inside. The **Oratorio di Sant'Agostinuccio**, further up Via Anicia, belongs to a local confraternity and has a charming interior covered in fine woodwork of the early 1600s.

The cemetery church of **Santa Scolastica**, 3km south of Norcia, was built not long after the lifetime of the holy twins, according to tradition on the site of their mother's house. Significantly rebuilt in the 17th century, it has a late 14th-century fresco cycle illustrating the *Life of St Benedict*, discovered in a 1978 restoration. After the 1997 earthquake more of the same is urgently needed.

North of Norcia: the Valcastoriana

North of Norcia, the rugged Valcastoriana is one of the most remote of Umbrian valleys, making it a favourite residence for hermits in the early Middle Ages; in addition to its natural beauty, it has a fine collection of small churches, villages and an important abbey, all of which have suffered in recent earthquakes. The east of the valley is now part of Monti Sibillini National Park.

The road from Norcia (follow signs for Visso) rises through pines to the 3,307ft (1,008m) pass, the **Forca d'Ancarano**. Descending into the Valcastoriana it passes the delightful, beautifully restored and maintained church of **Santa Maria Bianca** (*signposted right; pick up the key at the nearby house*), rebuilt and added to over the centuries. Early Romanesque capitals support a 15th-century loggia and there's a funny old campanile. Inside, there's an ancient font and the high altar shelters the eponymous *Madonna* (1511), a marble in high relief attributed to the Florentine Francesco di Simone Ferrucci; votive frescoes adorn the walls.

The valley road continues towards Campi, although before reaching it, on the right, you'll see a sign for **Campi Castello**, a tiny hamlet with a pretty public wall fountain, all restored after 1979. Its handsome church, **Sant'Andrea** (*key at Via Entedia 15*), has a prominent portico that acts as a belvedere over the valley. Two rather sweet lions guard the Gothic door; a hotchpotch of votive paintings and colourful gilded wooden altars lines the attractive 16th-century interior. **Campi Basso**, back on the main road, is equally proud of its church of **San Salvatore**, near the main road by the cemetery. This has a lovely old asymmetrical façade with a pair of rose windows; inside are fine frescoes by Giovanni and Antonio Sparapane (1464) and an old immersion baptismal font.

To the north beyond Piedivalle, you'll see the sign for the **Abbazia di Sant'Eutizio** (*Museo dell'Abbazia t 0743 99659 or 0743 231635, f 0743 199659 or 0743 231036, www.museospoletonorcia.it; open Oct–Mar Mon–Fri 10–12.30 and 3–6, Sun and hols 11–5; April–Sept Mon–Fri 10–1 and 4–7, Sun and hols 10.30–1 and 3–6; closed Thurs; adm; if closed, the custodian is at the first door on the left inside the abbey, or ask at the bar*) up in its own little sub-valley. In the early Middle Ages, Sant'Eutizio owed much of its success to its remoteness: according to St Gregory the Great, it was founded by hermits Eutizio and Spes in the late 400s, who were visited by the young St Benedict. It became an abbey under Benedictine rule, and between the 800s and 1200s prospered under the Dukes of Spoleto who, along with emperors and popes, gave it large grants of land, so that by the first millennium it owned over a hundred villages and churches. It had a famous library (it had Umbria's oldest examples of vernacular Italian from the 11th century) and an infirmary renowned for the skill of its doctors, a skill later handed to Preci when the Benedictines were barred from practising surgery.

The abbey enjoys a beautiful setting, hugging the steep wooded mountain, with its campanile set high on a rock over the cloister. The Romanesque **church** with its rose window and handsome portal was rebuilt in 1190 by a Master Petrus, who gave it a majestic interior, with a single nave culminating in a lofty presbytery over the crypt. A fine funerary monument to St Eutizio stands behind the altar, attributed to Rocco da Vicenza (1514), and the intarsia choir stalls date from the 16th century. The abbey was restored after the 1997 earthquake as a hostel for pilgrims of the 2000 Jubilee; from the courtyard, you can visit the grottoes where the first hermits lived.

Preci, just up the road, was badly damaged in the earthquakes of 1979 and 1998, and much of it remains structurally unsound. A small fortified village rebuilt after an attack by Norcia in 1528, it has proud palaces built by its famous surgeons, who learned the art from the Benedictines and passed it down through generations into the 18th century. They had very sharp knives and tools and specialized in eye operations: when Queen Elizabeth I of England needed a cataract operation in 1588, Cesari Scacchi of Preci was summoned to do the job. A long list of popes and royalty similarly turned to Preci's surgeons. The museum displays surgical instruments from Preci's school, and a jumble of wooden sculpture, paintings (some from earthquake-damaged churches in the area), archaeological bits and pieces and ancient crafts.

From Preci, you can circle back to the Valnerina by way of Triponzo, or return to Norcia via the more remote but wonderfully scenic **Valle Oblita**, where only a handful of people live year-round, at **Abeto** and **Todiano**, both home to handsome *palazzi* and churches holding important Baroque canvases attesting to their former importance, when the inhabitants made their fortunes as itinerant pork butchers in Tuscany.

The Piano Grande and Castelluccio

Since 1993, all the territory east of Norcia has been encompassed in the majestic **Monti Sibillini National Park**, which Umbria shares with the Marches. A protected area of some 70,000 hectares, it is off the tourist track, remote and wildly beautiful.

You can see some of the most spectacular scenery along the narrow road from the church of Santa Scolastica south of Norcia (*see* p.576), which winds a magnificent 21km up to **Forca Canapine** (1,540m/5,055ft), high enough to support a modest ski station in the winter, with a refuge and hotel. If you're hurrying to Ascoli Piceno and the Adriatic, there's a fast new road and a tunnel, but it cuts out the glorious scenery.

On the same Forca Canapine road, 18km from Norcia, a road descends into one of the most poetic landscapes in all these pages, the best possible ending to a journey in Umbria. This is the sublime **Piano Grande**, a karstic basin, former glacial lake and now an extraordinary meadow measuring 16 square kilometres, surrounded by bare rolling hills and mountains that look as if they were covered with velvet in the late spring, when the entire meadow explodes into swathes of wildflowers that go on and on for miles, reaching their peak in June. It is a rarefied dream landscape (used by Franco Zeffirelli in his Franciscan film *Brother Sun, Sister Moon*), large enough to distort distances; the flocks that produce Norcia's famous cheese graze here and its fields produce the famous minute lentils of Castelluccio, which come in three colours and are among the tastiest and rarest in Italy.

A long straight road crosses the Piano Grande, then rises to the lentil village of **Castelluccio**, perched over the valley at 4,763ft (1,452m), the highest and altogether loneliest settlement in Umbria. Castelluccio had 700 inhabitants in 1951 and now has around 40; not so long ago, it was often entirely cut off by the winter snows, a problem now alleviated by ploughs. It is also the one old village in Umbria with no pretence to charm, but it does attract hikers, hang-gliders and cross-country skiers.

The Rooftop of Umbria: the Monti Sibillini

Castelluccio lies near an important crossroads under the dark, legendary **Monti Sibillini** (*see* **The Marches**, p.637), the most dramatic mountains in the Apennines. East of Castelluccio a secondary road skirts the slopes of **Monte Vettore** (2,476m/ 8,123ft), the tallest in the Sibillini, covered with snow for much of the year. Its summit (the usual approach is from the east, from the hamlet of Foce near Montemonaco in the Marches) is one of the very few places on the Italian peninsula where both the Adriatic and Tyrrhenian seas are visible, at least on a clear day.

The Marches

The Marches

To Ravenna

Rimini

Cattolica

S. Marino

Castedimezzo

Pesaro

Fano

Senigallia

Falconara
Marittima

Ancona

Adriatic

Sea

To Greece

20 km
10 miles

N

S. Leo

Montefeltro

Tavoleto

M. Carpegna

Sassocorvaro

Urbino

Mondavio

Piandimeleto

Urbania

Fossombrone

Ostra

Jesi

R. Esino

M. Conero

Sirolo
Numana

Sestino

VIA FLAMINIA

Alpe d. Lun

Mercatello
s. Metauro

Acqualagna

Pergola

Arcevia

Osimo

Loreto

Sansepolcro

Cagli

M. Petrano

Genga

Filottrano

Recanati

Citerna

Citta di Castello

Pietralunga

Sassoferrato

Cingoli

THE

MARCHES

Macerata

Civitanova March

Monte Sta.
Maria Tiberina

Scheggia

Fabriano

Cerreto d'Esi

S. Severino
Marche

Corridonia

S. Elpidio a Mare

Umbertide

Gubbio

Porto S. Giorgio

Tolentino

Massa
Fermana

Fermo

Montelabate

Pioraco
Camerino

S. Ginesio

Servigliano

Monterubbiano

Pedaso

Lago
Trasimeno

Perugia

Nocera Umbra

Sarnano

Montalto
di Marche

Grottamm

Assisi

Spello

Monti Sibillini

Amandola
Montefortino

Acquaviva
Picena

S. Benede
del Tron

Porto d'A

UMBRIA

Foligno

Verchiano

Visso

Ascoli
Piceno

M. Vettore

Pissignano

Triponzo

*Forca
Canapine*

Acquasanta
Terme

Civitella del
Tronto

Giuliana

To Pescara

SWITZ.

AUSTRIA

HUNGARY

FRANCE

SLOVENIA

CROATIA

BOSNIA-
HERZ.

YUGOSLAVIA

Corsica

ITALY

Sardinia

Sicily

TUNISIA

Highlights

1 Urbino and the perfect Renaissance palace

2 High castles of the Montefeltro

3 Romanesque churches and beaches under
  Monte Conero

4 The Monti Sibillini: rare wildflowers and
  scenery in the high Apennines

5 Refined, travertine Ascoli Piceno

Meglio un morto in casa che un marchigiano fuori della porta.
'Better a corpse in the house than a man from the Marches at the door.'

Old Italian saying

Now what could the inhabitants of this placid little region have done to earn such opprobrium from their countrymen? They aren't so bad, really; the saying comes from the old days when many of the Marchigiani served across the Papal States as the pope's tax collectors. Since then, their neighbours have more often ignored than insulted this obscure patch of territory along the Adriatic.

A *march*, or *mark*, in the Middle Ages meant a border province of the Holy Roman Empire, usually an unsettled frontier held by one of the Emperor's fighting barons. With no better name than that, one might expect this Italian region to be somewhat lacking in personality. In fact, this has always been the odd bit of central Italy. In ancient times, too, it was a border zone, shared by Umbrii, Gauls, Sabines and the Piceni, a stout-hearted little tribe that had for its totem the *picus*, or woodpecker, which was also the sacred bird of the war god Mars. Unencumbered by art and culture, they occupied much of the central Adriatic; their name lives on in their old capital, Ascoli Piceno. The Romans called it the *Annonaria*, for its annual production of cereals and cattle. Today, the Marchigiani still have a little identity problem, but it doesn't keep them awake at night. Their land, tucked between the Apennines and the sea, is one of the greenest, prettiest and most civilized corners of Italy, with two lovely Renaissance art towns in Urbino and Ascoli Piceno, lots of beaches, art and scores of fine old rosy brick towns in the valleys that lead up to the impressive snowy peaks of the Sibilline Mountains, one of the highest sections of the Apennines.

Today, the pope's old taxmen have a newly discovered talent for business. Their region in recent years has had one of the highest growth rates in Italy and has become a showcase of what Italians like to call their 'new model for capitalism': small firms, often family-run, with a close relationship to their employees and their community. They use their natural Italian talent to find something they can make better or more cheaply than anyone else – from shoes to electric guitars – and the results are often spectacular. This will not necessarily be evident to the visitor (just the occasional new power-line ruining a pretty panorama, as in Tuscany), but it has given the region a new feeling of pride: its citizens look on it as an updated version of the city states that made medieval Italy great.

For those with a fatal attraction towards central Italy, the Marches are the new frontier: new emerald landscapes and hill towns, new discoveries at the table, new surprises from the Renaissance, and fewer tourists to share them with. Prices are lower and the people are friendly to visitors, who are more of a novelty here than in their coachloads in Umbria's art cities.

The damages of the 1997 earthquake left many living in containers. Now most have moved into wooden chalets or new housing, which looks permanent. But restoration of churches, *palazzi* and museums has been much slower here than in the media spotlight of Umbria. Many sights are still closed (especially in Fabriano) and city streets are still lined with scaffolding in the worst-hit places.

Northern Marches: The Coast and Inland

The Coast North of Pesaro

If you get as far as Rimini, it's only a short drive down the coast to the northernmost resort in the Marches, **Gabicce Mare**, with one hundred hotels of its own. Gabicce calls itself, with a wee bit of exaggeration, the Capri of the Adriatic, for the promontory of Gabbice Monte that closes off its south end; take a good look, because such natural features on the coast will be rare from now on. The best views are from the corniche road hugging the coast, passing through **Casteldimezzo** and little medieval **Fiorenzuola di Focara**, both with beaches and popular seafood restaurants.

Inland, looming over the highway, the frontier of the Marches was defended by a pretty fortress, the **Rocca of Gradara** (*t 0541 964181; open Mon 8.30–2, Tues–Sun 8.30–7.15; adm, ticket office closes 45 mins before closing*), built in the 11th century, then rebuilt in the 1300s, when it was hotly contested between the Malatestas and Montefeltros of Urbino. Traditionally, this castle was the scene of the story of Francesca da Rimini and Paolo Malatesta, the tragic lovers consigned to hell by Dante in Canto 5 of the *Inferno*. Being within easy striking distance from Rimini has led the management to exploit the story to the hilt for tour groups, but it's fun if you're in the mood. It has a beautiful little chapel, with a ceramic altarpiece by Luca della Robbia.

The Northern Marches

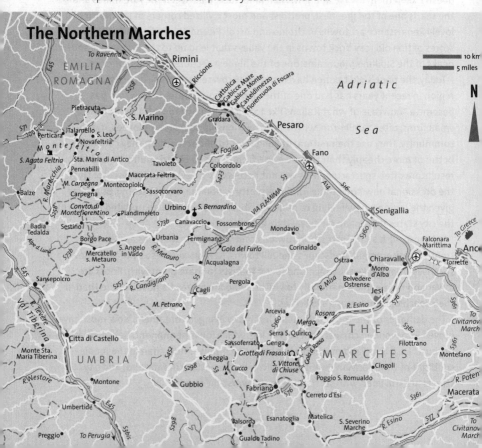

The Lilliputian Republic of San Marino

Even a small nation is large if it is placed on the rock of truth and
radiates the light of justice.
                John Paul II, in a 1997 pilgrimage to San Marino

If you drive up through the hills to the top of Monte Titano, you can visit the world's only sovereign and independent roadside attraction. Before Rimini became the Italian Miami Beach, the 50,000 citizens of **San Marino** made their living peddling postage stamps. Now, their streets crowded with day-trippers, they have been unable to resist the temptation to order some bright medieval costumes, polish up their picturesque mountain towns and open up souvenir stands selling wines, *mistra* – the local aniseed liqueur – ceramics, sweets and tat, and 'duty free' shops (sales taxes are much lower here than in Italy). Combine this with no sales limit and you have a mecca for shoppers; when you go back over the border, there will be customs taxes to fork out either.

The famous San Marinesi stamps, though nothing like the exquisitely engraved numbers of 40 years ago, are still prized by collectors and can be bought from the **Officio Filatelico e Numismatico di Stato**. In 1972 the country began to mint its own coins (including gold ones) again after a lapse of decades; nevertheless, the citizens of San Marino, who have one of the highest national average incomes in Europe, are making their living almost entirely from tourism.

The World's Smallest Republic

Also the oldest republic. According to legend, **San Marino** (61 sq km, pop. 27,000) was founded as a Christian settlement on the easily defensible slopes of Monte Titano by a stonecutter named Marinus, fleeing from the persecutions of Diocletian in the early 4th century. 'Overlooked', as the San Marinese put it, by the Empire and various states that followed it, the little community had the peace and quiet to evolve its medieval democratic institutions; its present constitution dates from 1243, when the first pair of 'consuls' was elected by a popular assembly. The consuls are now called Captains Regent, but little else has changed in 700 years. Twice, in 1503 and 1739, the republic was invaded by papal forces, and independence was preserved only by good luck and the intervention of St Agatha, now national co-patron. Napoleon, passing through in 1797, found San Marino amusing and, half-seriously, offered to enlarge its boundaries, a proposal that was politely declined. The republic felt secure enough to offer refuge to Garibaldi after the Roman revolt of 1849, and as an island of peace during the Second World War, it distinguished itself by taking in hundreds of thousands of refugees.

San Marino last made the news in the 1970s, when the Communists threatened to win the elections. The San Marino government decided that even emigrants were still citizens, with the right to vote and felt obliged to assist them. Thousands of San Marinese descendants in places like New Jersey were given free holidays at government expense to help tip the election. There has never been a similar threat since.

Most visitors enter San Marino from Rimini, at the hamlet called Dogana (Customs), although there are no border formalities now. The main road rises through a string of

Getting There and Around

San Marino is only 24km from Rimini and reached by regular **bus** from Rimini train station or in summer from the Piazza Tripolo or Marina Centro. There's a **funicular** up from Borgo Maggiore to San Marino town that may save parking stress: it runs 8am–6.30pm in winter, and 8am–9pm in July, 8am–1am August.

Tourist Information

San Marino town: Contrada Omagnano 20, t 0549 from Italy (t 00 378 549 from other countries) 882998, f 882575, www.visitsanmarino.com

Where to Stay and Eat

San Marino ✉ 47890, **t** 0549 from Italy; **t** 00 378549 from elsewhere.

San Marino can be refreshingly cool and fairly quiet in the summer, but book early.
★★★★Grand Hotel San Marino, Viale Onofri 31, t 0549 992400, f 0549 992951, www.grand hotel.sm (expensive). A modern hotel with luxurious rooms and lovely views, close to the Rocche.

★★★★Titano, Contrada del Collegio 31, t 0549 991006, f 0549 991375, www.hoteltitano. com (expensive–moderate). Situated in the historic centre, this has kept much of its 1890s décor, along with a pretty restaurant terrace. Closed Jan–Mar 10.

★★★Panoramic, Via Voltone 91, t 0549 992359, f 0549 990356 (moderate). Good views. Family-run with functional rooms. Closed Nov–mid-Dec.

★★★Quercia Antica, at the junction of Via Capannaccia and Via Cella Bella, t 0549 991 257, f 0549 990044, www.querciantica.com (moderate). Just outside the historic centre, with views and a good restaurant.

La Taverna Righi, Piazza Libertà 10, t 0549 991196 (expensive). The best food in the republic; refined versions of the traditional passatelli, seafood and vegetarian dishes, as well as some fancier innovative ones with foie gras. Closed Wed in winter, also 2 weeks in Jan.

La Fratta, Salita alla Rocca 14, t 0549 991594 (cheap). An old favourite with grand views from the terrace. Closed Wed exc June–Oct, Jan and Feb.

villages: San Marino, no tiny state like the Vatican City, is 12km long at its widest. On the slopes of Monte Titano (one of the mountains the mythological Titans piled up to reach heaven and overthrow the gods), **Borgo Maggiore** is the largest town in the republic, with most of the shops and the funicular up to the capital and citadel, also called **San Marino**. This is a steep medieval village and has wonderful views over Rimini and the coast. But even here nothing is as old as it looks; in main Piazza della Libertà, the **Palazzo Pubblico** (t 0549 885370, f 0549 882679, museodistato@omniway.sm; open daily Jan–Mar and Oct–Dec 8.50–5; April–Sept 8am–8pm; closed 25 Dec, 1 Jan and 2 Nov (pm); adm), full of guardsmen with brass buttons and epaulettes, is an 1894 reconstruction. If you're there in the summer, the changing of the guard takes place hourly (mid-May–Sept 8.30–6.30). The Grand Council meets in the Palazzo and the Captains Regent have their offices here, while other rooms are full of San Marino memorabilia. The **Museo-Pinacoteca San Francesco** (t 0549 885132; free) in the 14th-century convent at Contrada San Francesco 5, has the same opening times as do the medieval tower fortresses on the three peaks that give San Marino its famous silhouette – famous to philatelists anyhow and long the symbol of the republic. The first, the **Rocca Guaita** (t 0549 991369; joint adm optional), was restored in 1500 and used as a prison; the second, the **Rocca Cesta** (t 0549 991295), on the highest peak of Mt Titano, contains a collection of weapons from the 12th to 19th centuries; you cannot visit the interior of the third, the **Rocca Montale**.

A crop of flaky museums, mainly in San Marino town, has sprouted up in recent years to shake loose a few euros from the tourists – collections range from the most obvious stamps, coins and weapons to waxworks and the utterly bizarre Clessidra Atomica, a device which counts the number of atomic bombs being defused at any one time, complete with the sound of fluttering doves' wings with each defusion. And when you find you need a fix of Renaissance art or summer beach madness, or both, catch the bus over to Sigismondo Malatesta and Federico Fellini's Rimini.

Pesaro

Under the Byzantines, the five big ports of the central Adriatic were known as the Pentapolis – Rimini, Fano, Senigallia, Ancona and Pesaro. Pesaro is the nicest, with a handsome little historic centre.

A Stroll around Rossini's Hometown

Although it doesn't have many exceptional monuments, **Pesaro** (pop. 88,900) is lovely to walk through, both its older quarters and arcaded streets, and the new streets by the beach. These are full of trees and little villas from the 19th century – many in the Liberty style, including the small but outrageous **Villino Ruggieri**, with a cornice supported by terracotta lobsters designed by Giovanni Brega in 1907. Pesaro's castle, the **Rocca Costanza** (*t 0721 387474; closed for restoration*) in Piazzale Malteolti, was built in 1478 by Laurana, the designer of the palace at nearby Urbino.

The Sforzas of Milan ruled Pesaro for a time, and they sold it to the della Rovere, the family of Julius II, in 1512, right after their acquisition of Urbino. The big crenellated **Palazzo Ducale** (*t 0721 387474; open for guided tours by appt*) in central Piazza del Popolo had been completed by the Sforzas only a couple of years previously, although the prettiest thing in the square is the post office – with a terracotta portal of 1395, transferred here from a church. In the Sforza years, Pesaro rivalled Faenza as a producer of fine ceramics; you can see beautiful examples in the nearby **Pinacoteca** and **Museo delle Ceramiche**, Piazza Toschi Mosca 29 (*t 0721 387541, www. museicivicipesaro.it; open Sept–June Thurs–Sun 9.30–12.30 and 4–7, Tues and Wed 9.30–12.30; July–Aug Tues and Thurs 9.30–12.30 and 4–10.30, Wed and Fri–Sun 9.30–12.30 and 4–7; adm*); others come from Urbino, Castel Durante (Urbania), Deruta and Gubbio, including a few superb works by that city's celebrated Mastro Giorgio. Besides the majolica plates there are a few good pictures – and one very great one, a *Coronation of the Virgin* or Pala di Pesaro (1474) by Giovanni Bellini. Pesaro is proud to have given the world the composer Gioacchino Rossini in 1792 and you can visit his birthplace, the **Casa Rossini** (*t 0721 387357*) nearby at Via Rossini 34, with mementos of the maestro (*opening hours as for museums, see above*).

In nearby Via Mazza 97, the **Museo Oliveriano** (*t 0721 33344; open Sept–June Mon–Sat 9–12 on request; July–Aug Mon–Sat 4–7*) houses two Greek bronze ornaments from the 5th century BC, a Roman copy of a statue of a youth from the same period, an elegant 3rd-century Roman sarcophagus and votive offerings, a rare Etruscan-Latin

Getting There and Around

Pesaro's **train** station is on the southern edge of town on Viale Roma, about ½km from the centre. At least 10 **buses** a day go to Urbino, some via Fano and (usually) Fermignano. There are different companies, and conflicting schedules are posted, but all leave from or stop at Pesaro's train station.

Bus companies: AMI, **t** 0721 370734; SAPUM (part of AMI); Capponi, **t** 0721 67980; Bucci, **t** 0721 32401; Davani Arrigo Eredi, **t** 0721 23927; SOGET, **t** 0721 549620.

Tourist Information

Pesaro: Main office Piazzale Libertà 11, **t** 0721 69341, *iat.pesaro@regione.marche.it*.

Pesaro–Urbino province: Via Rossini 4, **t** 0721 359501.

Comune di Pesaro: Viale Trieste 164, **t** 0721 34073, *turismo@comune.pesaro.ps.it*. Freephone: **t** 800 222111 (Marche) and **t** 800 563800 (Pesaro).

Where to Stay

Pesaro ☒ **61100**

At first sight, Pesaro looks refined, even exclusive; it's a pleasant surprise to find that prices aren't over the top.

★★★★**Vittoria**, Via Vespucci 2, **t** 0721 34343, **f** 0721 65204, *www.viphotels.it (luxury)*. One of the 'Hundred Historic Hotels of Italy', a renovated century-old *belle époque* villa along the beach strip. Rooms, furnished with period beds, mirrors and wardrobes, have TV and air con; there's also a pool, sauna and billiards room.

★★★★**Savoy**, Viale Repubblica 22, **t** 0721 67440, **f** 0721 64429, *www.viphotels.it (very expensive)*. A modern hotel run by the same team as the Vittoria (*above*), in an attractive shady place, with all mod cons and a pool.

★★★**Villa Serena**, Via San Nicola 6, **t** 0721 55211, **f** 0721 55927, *www.villa-serena.it (expensive)*. South of Pesaro, occupying a 17th-century palace with fireplaces and antique furniture in the rooms, in a quiet, scenic park. *Closed two weeks in Jan.*

★★**Oasi San Nicola**, Via S. Nicola 8, **t** 0721 50849, **f** 0721 390428, *wwwoasisannicola.it. (expensive)*. In a quiet location south of town.

★★★**Des Bains**, Viale Trieste 221, **t** 0721 34957, **f** 0721 35062, *www.innitalia.com (moderate)*. More character than most modern hotels.

★★★**Due Pavoni**, Viale Fiume 79, **t/f** 0721 370 105, *www.hotelduepavoni.com (moderate)*. Near the *centro storico*, with sea views and a friendly welcome.

★★★**Principe**, Viale Trieste 180, **t** 0721 30222, **f** 0721 31636 *(moderate)*. On the waterfront,

inscription, and the *stele* of Novilara, with a peculiar relief of a sea battle from an Iron Age civilization similar to the Piceni. In adjacent Piazza Olivieri 5, you can see Rossini's piano and manuscripts at the **Conservatory** (**t** *0721 33671*) he founded, and during the Rossini festival in late summer take in one of his operas (your chance to hear *William Tell* in its entirety) at Pesaro's grand, five-tiered **Teatro Rossini** (*Piazza Lazzanini*, **t** *0721 387620*), inaugurated with *The Thieving Magpie* in 1816.

North of Pesaro

In the hills towards Gabicce Mare, 2km north of Pesaro, is the 18th-century **Villa Caprile** (*guided tours by request, call* **t** *0721 21440; open mid-June–mid-Sept 3–7; adm*), with pretty Italian gardens, fountains and a stuccoed gallery. For two years (1817–19) this was the residence of the Princess of Wales, mother of Queen Victoria, but today it hosts engineers of the Istituto Tecnico Agrario. Another 3km further on is **Villa Imperiale** (**t** *0721 69341; open mid-June–late Aug; Wed for guided tours; adm*), built for the Sforzas but enlarged by the della Rovere.

with modern, fairly comfortable rooms. Stands out more for its excellent, popular restaurant **Teresa** (*moderate, see* below).

There is a wide selection of one- and two-star places both along the beach and on the side streets. Viale Trento, running parallel to the beach one block from the sea, is scattered with inexpensive 'seasonal' hotels, popular with locals and backpackers in the summer.

***Abbazia, Viale Trento 147, t 0721 33694, *www.apahotel.it* (*inexpensive*). *Open Easter–Sept.*

**Holiday, Viale Trento 159, t 0721 34851, f 0721 370310 (*inexpensive*). *Open May–Sept.*

Eating Out

Local cuisine is, naturally, fishy, and includes delectables such as ravioli with sole fillets, *garagoli in porchetta* (shellfish tossed with olive oil, garlic, rosemary and wild fennel), stuffed cuttlefish, red mullet with *prosciutto*; a local meat recipe is *olivette alla pesarese* (slices of veal in prosciutto, rolled up and fried). All of the above go very nicely with the local white wine, Bianchello del Metauro.

Alceo, Strada Panoramica Ardizio 101, t 0721 51360 (*very expensive*). Come here for fresh fish dishes, homemade pasta and desserts, a friendly atmosphere and tables outside with sea views. *Closed Sun eve and Mon.*

Lo Scudiero, Via Baldassini 2, t 0721 64107 (*expensive*). Occupies the cellar of a 17th-century palace. Specialities include some imaginative dishes with seafood and pasta – they also do a good roast lamb. *Closed Sun and July.*

Antica Osteria La Guercia, Via Baviera 33, on the corner of the Piazza del Popolo, t 0721 33463 (*cheap*). The oldest in town, with all the classics, including homemade *strozzapreti* ('priest-chokers'). *Closed Sun.*

Il Cantuccio di Leo, Via Perfetti 18, t 0721 68088 (*cheap*). An *enoteca* in the centre with all kinds of dishes to go with its wines, such as boar terrines, cheeses (including French ones), pasta and meat courses; and it stays open until 2am. *Closed Tues and July.*

Teresa, Viale Trieste 180, t 0721 30222 (*moderate*). Enticing dishes at the Hotel Principe.

***Locanda da Ciacci, Via Roma 105, in Gallo, 12km from Urbino off the SS423, t 0722 355030, f 0722 355566, *www.locandaciacci. com* (*moderate–inexpensive*). A good stop between Pesaro and Urbino, housed in an attractive villa with pretty rooms upstairs and a farm producing most of the ingredients for the restaurant (*cheap*). The menu is seasonal, offering homemade pastas, *passatelli* and an ample range of meats, from grilled pork chops and sausages to stuffed pigeon and duck. *Closed Dec 24–25.*

Urbino

From Pesaro – and almost nowhere else – it is easy to reach the isolated mountain setting of **Urbino**. With its celebrated Ducal Palace and the memory of the honourable and refined Duke Federico who built it, Urbino is one of the monuments of the Italian Renaissance. Today its publicists go perhaps too far – 'the ideal city of the Renaissance' and 'most beautiful palace in the world', and so on and so on, a lack of modesty that wasn't at all Federico's style. Even so, Urbino does represent a certain facet of the Renaissance more clearly than any other Italian town: elegance, learning and intelligent patronage combined in a small place. Urbino's golden age may not have long outlasted the reign of Duke Federico and his son but, as an example of what a community can be, it exerts a fascination even today. Modern Urbino is above all a lively university town: its Università degli Studi is one of the largest private institutions in Italy – students outnumber the 'townies' by 22,000 to 15,000 – although they've been segregated on to a campus outside the centre.

Getting There and Around

There are frequent SOGET **buses** from Pesaro to Urbino (**t** 0721 371318). In Urbino, the bus depot is on Piazzale Mercatale, at the town's southern gate, with connections to most of the inland villages in Pesaro province. Arrivals and departures are listed on a board under the loggia in Piazza della Repubblica.
Bus companies: AMI, **t** 0722 376711; Bucci, **t** 0721 32401.

Tourist Information

Urbino: Piazza Rinascimento 1, **t** 0722 2613, **f** 0722 2441, *www.comune.urbino.ps.it*, *iat. urbino@regione.marche.it. Open Mon, Wed, Fri 9–1 and 3–6 Tues and Thurs, 3–6 ; 15 June–15 Sept also Sun 3–6.*

Where to Stay

Urbino ✉ 61029

Hotels here can be very crowded in summer, and even spring, so book ahead.
*****Albergo San Domenico**, Piazza Rinascimento 3, **t** 0722 2626, **f** 0722 2727, *www.viphotels.it* (*very expensive*). Luxurious, in an old convent in the main square.
*****Bonconte**, Via delle Mura 28, **t** 0722 2463, **f** 0722 4782, *www.viphotels.it* (*expensive*). On the city walls, with lovely views, 25 air conditioned rooms, a garage, private beach cabins and access to a sports club in Pesaro.
****Italia**, Corso Garibaldi 32, **t** 0722 2701, **f** 0722 322664, *www.albergo-italia-urbini.it* (*expensive*). Good and central, one block from the Ducal Palace.
****Raffaello**, Via S. Margherita 40, **t** 0722 4784, **f** 0722 328540, *www.albergoraffaello.com* (*expensive– moderate*). Nicely furnished rooms in an 18th-century house, on a quiet lane just above the Maestro's birthplace; no restaurant.
****Residence Dei Duchi**, Via G. Dini 2, **t** 0722 328226, **f** 0722 328009, *www.viphotels. it* (*moderate*). New, in a quiet scenic setting northwest of Urbino; rooms have air conditioning and satellite TV.

****Tortorina**, Via Tortorina 4, **t** 0722 308100, **f** 0722 327715, *www.hotel-tortorina.it* (*moderate–inexpensive*). Northeast of town, near the hospital, with a panoramic terrace and comfy rooms, furnished with antiques.
*San Giovanni, Via Barocci 13, **t** 0722 2827, **f** 0722 329055 (*inexpensive*). In an old palazzo with a good restaurant. *Closed part Dec–Jan.*
Locanda di Valle Nuova, La Cappella 14, Sagrata di Fermignano, **t/f** 0722 330303, *www.vallenuova.it* (*moderate*). Six simple, stylish rooms on a 185-acre organic farm in hills within sight of Urbino. The farm produces its own wine, wheat, fruit and veg plus beef, pork and poultry, much of which appears at mealtimes. There is a pool and horse riding on the property and lots of walking nearby. No smoking. *Closed second week Nov-early June.*
*Pensione Fosca, Via Raffaello 67, **t** 0722 329622, **f** 0722 329622. If you're looking to economize, this is the only option central Urbino has to offer, but there are several student and religious institutions in town that have space in summer; ask at the tourist office.

Eating Out

Taverna degli Artisti, Via Bramante 52, **t** 0722 2676 (*moderate*). Arrive early, or book ahead, for great food (including pizza) at great prices. Open until midnight. *Closed Tues.*
Vecchia Urbino, Via Vasari 3/5, **t** 0722 4447 (*moderate*). An elegant option in the historic centre, for a feast in the autumn-winter truffle-funghi season. *Closed Tues.*
Franco, Via del Poggio 1, **t** 0722 2492. Just off the top of the main square, serving good food at reasonable prices in the self-service area (*cheap*) and slightly fancier fare in the restaurant. *Closed Sun.*
Osteria L'Angolo Divino, Via Sant'Andrea 14 (off Via Cesare Battisti), **t** 0722 327559 (*moderate–cheap*). Here you can dine in a pretty room in an old palace, on old Urbino specialities – pasta with chick peas, bacon, lamb or breadcrumbs, and tasty *secondi* from the grill; also some vegetarian dishes. *Closed Sun eve and Mon lunch.*

History

Beginning in 1234, Urbino's fortunes were attached to those of the Montefeltros, mountain warlords from San Leo who gradually extended their influence in the northern Marches. Most were *condottieri* working throughout Italy, serving various masters. In 1443, Oddantonio da Montefeltro earned the title of Duke for his service before his assassination. His half-brother and successor, Federico (reigned 1444–82), was the most successful of the family *condottieri*, a crafty and respected warrior who earned the money for his famous palace serving Alfonso of Naples and the Pope.

In later years, Federico became one of the quattrocento's most celebrated patrons of art and literature, as well as a slow but close student of the classics and the new humanities. Federico learned Greek and Latin, and the library he assembled was one of the best in Europe. There was a bad side to Federico – his sack of Volterra while serving Lorenzo de' Medici was only one of his indiscretions on the job – but he ruled Urbino paternally and well, always liberal to those of his subjects in need, peering into every detail of his little state's economy and social life, and educating the sons of the poor. It is also said that he banished gambling and cursing, and made the people of Urbino exert themselves mightily to keep the place clean. His admirable wife, Battista Sforza, was a duchess beloved by her subjects, a lady capable of delivering an impromptu speech in impeccable Latin to welcome any surprise visitor; both were immortalized in Piero della Francesco's famous warts-and-all portraits now in the Uffizi. Their son, Guidobaldo I (1472–1508), was as enlightened a ruler as his father, married to the cultivated Elisabetta Gonzaga and maintaining a court idealized as the height of civilized existence in Baldassare Castiglione's *The Courtier* (1528). He was also clever enough to survive and prevail after Urbino's occupation by Cesare Borgia's papal army in 1497; in 1506 he found the Università degli Studi. When Guidobaldo died without an heir, the duchy fell to a nephew, Francesco Maria della Rovere, also related to Pope Julius II. When the della Rovere dukes died out in turn, they willed Urbino to the papacy in 1626, leading to its rapid decline.

Urbino experienced high drama in 1944. Towards the end of the war, many central Italian works of art had been brought to the town for safekeeping. During the retreat in August, a spiteful German commander planted enough explosives under the town walls to blow the whole place to smithereens. Only a few went off and the remainder were defused by the British after the liberation – a job that took over a week.

Up the Rampa Elicoidale

Under the grand city walls, **Piazzale Mercatale**, with its sandstone gate marks the front door to Urbino (with the bus station and a large car park). In the old days, this large open space hosted the Ducal stables and the market and, to make access easier for the good people of Urbino, Duke Federico had Francesco di Giorgio Martini link it directly to the centre of town with a semi-cylindrical bastion containing the **Rampa Elicoidale**, a great, winding, stepped ramp. Restructured in 1976, it still does the job, leaving you in Corso Garibaldi under the mid-19th-century **Teatro Sanzio**. Corso Garibaldi leads up to **Piazza della Repubblica**, the heart of Urbino; just up Via Vittorio Veneto you'll find the cathedral and the entrance to Urbino's five-star attraction...

Palazzo Ducale

t 0722 2760/322625 for group bookings; open Tues–Sun 8.30–7.15, Mon 8.30–2; visits every 15mins in winter; adm.

So many architects helped Federico build his dream house, it is difficult to divide the credit. Alberti may have been an original adviser, and the Dalmatian Luciano Laurana generally gets credit for most of the work and the elegant arcaded courtyard; Francesco di Giorgio Martini may have designed its two internal squares, while the finest part of it, the twin-turreted façade, is by Ambrogio Barocchi. That every Italian schoolboy should know this to be 'the most beautiful palace in the world' is an interesting reflection both on the Italians and on the quattrocento. Federico's palace is not finished, not symmetrical and not really even very grand; its aesthetic is utterly foreign to the tastes of the centuries that followed. For all that, it is a great building, and a test of one's faith in the genuine Renaissance – the 15th-century high noon of life and art, as opposed to the cinquecento of Spaniardism, surrender and neurotic excess. Many critics have regarded it, though unfinished, as the culmination of Renaissance architecture, not yet entirely enslaved to perspectivism or imitation of the ancients, but a creation of freedom and delight. The rosy brick palace made a comfortable residence for the Montefeltri and an exquisite decoration for Urbino.

The palace **façade**, overlooking the hills, consists of three tiers of balconies between two slender towers; the decorative trim is of Dalmatian limestone that hardens to look like marble. To enter it today, you'll need to go round the back through the **Cortile d'Onore**, a prototype for numerous other western Mediterranean courtyards. Much of the palace interior is occupied by the **Galleria Nazionale delle Marche**, a splendid collection whose finest works were originally the property of Duke Federico.

Piero della Francesca's amazing *Flagellation* is perhaps the best-known work in Urbino, an endlessly disturbing image that has troubled art scholars for centuries. Standing before a pavilion of fantasy classical architecture, three gentlemen in contemporary dress hold a serious discussion, indifferent to the scourging of Christ going on behind them – a bloodless scourging, for that matter. Piero, one of the luminaries of Federico's court, had already written a great Renaissance treatise on theoretical perspective; a complex system of foreshortening is the major feature of this work. The combination of a surreal, dream-like scene and a drily scientific visual presentation gives the painting its enigmatic quality – as noted by the critics, this is one of the instances where art blends into sorcery. The same room contains Piero's *Madonna di Senigallia*, another superb work; the Virgin looks as if she just stepped into a grey room, holding her baby; everyday things sit on the shelves and even the two angels look like a pair of homeowners – yet the domestic scene is rendered timeless, meditative and almost hypnotic through Piero's magic. Almost as strange a display of perspectivist wizardry as the *Flagellation* is the *Ideal City*, another of the museum's most famous works, often attributed to Laurana. The scene is a broad, paved square, lined with buildings in the new style, dominated by a large circular temple in the centre. Disturbingly, there are no people present – not one living thing in this display of vanishing point virtuosity – save a few pot plants on the balconies.

Not to be outdone by Piero, Paolo Uccello offers a similarly mysterious *Miracle of the Profaned Host* (*newly restored*) while Piero's student Luca Signorelli is represented by two dark and inspired paintings, the *Crucifixion* and *Pentecost*. Other works not to miss: a *Crucifixion* by Antonio Alberti de Ferrara, taking care to show off contemporary fashions, in armour as well as court dress; the *Annunciation* of Vicenzo Pagani (and a pagan-looking work it is, too); *La Muta*, a lovely portrait of a lady by Raphael, and his *St Catherine of Alexandra*, a recent acquisition; also fine works by Luca della Robbia, Giovanni Santi (Raphael's dad), Carlo Crivelli, Verrocchio and the Venetian Alvise Vivarini. The Spanish artist Pedro Berruguete contributes the famous *Portrait of Duke Federico*: the tough old warrior, with his broken nose, symbolically still wears his armour as he pores over a heavy book, with his little son Guidobaldo at his knee; note the badge of the Order of the Garter conferred on Federico by King Edward IV.

Some of the surviving interior decoration of the palace is wonderful – carved mantelpieces and window frames, intarsia doors, cornices and stuccoes, carved and painted ceilings, all bearing the monogram FE DUX and family emblems. Best of all is the intimate intarsia **Studiolo** of Duke Federico, which looks as if the scholarly *condottiere* might wander in at any moment. The inlaid wood designs are by Botticelli, Bramante and Francesco di Giorgio Martini, and they portray the 'Life of a Scholar' with mesmerizing *trompe-l'œil* effects.

The paintings above, representing philosophers and illustrious men, are by Berruguete and Giusto di Gand, although only half of the 28 are original – the rest are in the Louvre. Nearby, reached by a spiral staircase inside one of the façade's towers, are the **Cappella del Perdono**, with an ornate ceiling of hundreds of angel heads in stucco, and an equally fancy chamber called the **Tempietto delle Muse**. A *Last Supper* by Titian hangs in the duchess's bedroom, while the huge throne room, where Federico liked to entertain on a grand scale, has seven tapestries on the *Acts of the Apostles* from Raphael's cartoons.

The upper floor, the **Appartamento Roveresco**, has now opened again after earthquake restoration. Look for 16th- and 17th-century paintings and many portraits of the poor Italians dressed in black like their Spanish overlords. The best are by Urbino native Federico Barocci (1535–1612), a sensitive Mannerist considered the best Central Italian painter of his day; also seek out some *chiaroscuri* of the *Life of St Paul* by Claudio Ridolfi, colourful 18th-century ceramics and good woodcuts of Montefiore d'Asso from the early 1900s by Adolfo de Carolis.

The palace's 'underground' contains the working bits – the laundry, kitchens, ice rooms, storage, the 'Duchess's bath' and plumbing, with grafitti scrawled here and there on the walls. On the ground floor, Urbino's **Archaeology Museum** (*opening hours and adm as for Palazzo Ducale, see p.590*) has a vast 18th-century collection of Greek and Roman funeral inscriptions, and early Christian reliefs and symbols.

Other Sights Around Urbino

Adjacent to the Ducal Palace in Piazza Rinascimentale, the **cathedral** (*open daily 7.30–1 and 2–7*) was built at the same time as the Ducal Palace by Francesco di Giorgio Martini, but an earthquake in 1789 caused the collapse of its dome and it was completely rebuilt as a big dull neoclassical church; only the crypt, with a fine 16th-century *Pietà* by Giovanni Bandini (*open by request*), and a chapel in the left nave, frescoed with a *Last Supper* by Federico Barocci, survived from the original. The cathedral's collection of detached trecento frescoes, a bronze Paschal candelabra by Francesco di Giorgio Martini, a 13th-century bronze English lectern and artefacts are in the **Museo Albani** (*t* 0722 2850; *open daily summer* 9–12 *and* 2.30–6; *winter* 9–12 *and* 3–6; *adm*). The oldest thing in Piazza Rinascimentale is the Egyptian obelisk from 580 BC, in front of the former Montefeltro Palace, now **Palazzo dell'Università** and Gothic **San Domenico**, its handsome portal of 1451 crowned with a lunette by Luca della Robbia (the original is in the Palazzo Ducale); near the latter is a plaque marking the birthplace in 1471 of Virgilio Polidoro, a friend of Sir Thomas More and Erasmus and the bishop of Wells. Piero della Francesca may have modelled the portico of the *Flagellation* on that of **Palazzo Bonaventura-Odasi** in Via Valerio, near the cathedral; the plane tree outside is over 150 years old.

Though its streets are often steep, Urbino and its surrounding hills make an enchanting spot for walks. On Via Barocci (above Via Mazzini from Piazza della Repubblica), the little 14th-century **Oratorio di San Giovanni Battista** (*t* 347 671 1181 *(mobile); open Mon–Sat* 10–12.30 *and* 3–5.30, *Sun* 10–12.30; *closed mid-Jan to mid-Feb; adm*) has strikingly colourful frescoes of the *Crucifixion*, the *Madonna* and the *Life of John the Baptist* by the brothers Iacopo and Lorenzo Salimbeni (1416), artists from the little town of San Severino Marche heavily influenced by Giotto. On the same street, the **Oratorio di San Giuseppe** has a fine stucco *presepio* by a 16th-century Urbino artist, Federico Brandani (*t* 347 6711181; *open daily* 10–12.30 *and* 3.30–6).

Every Italian university has a **Botanical Garden** (*t* 0722 2428; *open Mon–Wed and Fri* 8–12.30 *and* 3–5.30, *Thurs and Sat* 7–12.30; *closed Sun and hols*), and Urbino's, with tropical plants founded in 1806, is down Via Bramante, below Piazza della Repubblica. Urbino's most famous native, Raphael (Raffaello Sanzio) was born in 1483 near the corner of Via Raffaele and Via Bramante; now a museum, the **Casa di Raffaello** (*t* 0722 320105; *open Mar–Oct Mon–Sat* 9–1 *and* 3–7, *Sun and hols* 10–1; *Nov–Feb Mon–Sat* 9–2, *Sun and hols* 10–1; *adm*) has little to see – a *Madonna* by the artist as a child and copies of his later works, and others by his pupil Giulio Romano and his father, Giovanni Santi. Santi not only taught Raphael the basics of painting but, as a humanist writer, instilled something in his son's famously sweet soul that later produced the very healthy, very human Madonnas and angels, whose beauty and dignity matched the best of the ancient Greeks – a major aesthetic concern of Renaissance patrons, especially popes. Santi died when Raphael was only 11 years old; afterwards he painted with Perugino and was executing independent commissions by the age of 17. There is a monument to Raphael from the 1890s up in **Piazzale Roma**, which offers lovely views over the hills, more along Viale Buozzi and yet more from the 14th-century **Fortezza Albornoz** – now a garden (*open daily* 9–6).

A pleasant half-hour walk from the west of town (2.5km) takes you to the church of **San Bernardino degli Zoccolanti** (*t* 0722 320539; *open daily* 8–6) by Francesco di Giorgio Martini (1491); inside are the simple yet starkly impressive black marble tombs of Dukes Federico and Guidobaldo I.

Northwest of Urbino: the Montefeltro

Urbino can be used as a base for excursions to the towns and villages in the rolling hills and mountains of the northern Marches – towns as serene and lovely as those in Tuscany, though much less known. Some of the most enchanting landscapes lie in the ancient fief of the Montefeltro. Off the beaten track to anywhere, far from railways and highways and awkward to reach by public transport, it is studded with remarkable rocky crags, each crowned by a castle from the days when the dukes of Urbino and the Malatesta of Rimini clobbered each other for control of the turf. It's an attractive region, just being discovered by outsiders (Umberto Eco has a house here); if you only make one stop, head for the Montefeltro's capital, San Leo (*see* p.596).

Sassocorvaro, Macerata Feltria and Piandimeleto

The winding roads from Urbino grow increasingly scenic as you approach **Sassocorvaro**, 'the Sentinel of the Montefeltro' (pop. 3,500). Built around a spur over the River Foglia, Sassocorvaro is topped by the striking 15th-century **Rocca Ubaldinesca** (*t 0722 76177; open Oct–Mar Sat–Sun 9.30–12.30 and 2.30–6; April–Sept daily 9.30–12.30 and 3–7; adm*), an elegant round citadel with bulging towers, one of Francesco di Giorgio Martini's finest designs, commissioned by Duke Federico for one of his top commanders, Ottaviano degli Ubaldini. A spiral stair from the courtyard leads to a little theatre, added in the 1800s, and a museum with exhibits on country life and crafts. There are also copies of some of Italy's greatest paintings, stored here for safety during the Second World War. Sassocorvaro's artificial lake, **Mercatale**, is named after the fairgrounds it drowned.

There are castles wherever you turn. Although the Montefeltro proper is north and west of Sassocorvaro, you may want to take a detour (18km) northeast to **Tavoleto**, a titbit snatched from Rimini by Duke Federico in 1462. Although the fortress that once defended Tavoleto collapsed in 1865, the fantastical **Castello dei Conti Petrangolini** (*closed*), with its 170ft tower and Ghibelline crenellations, bristles proudly intact.

To the northwest of Sassocorvaro, **Macerata Feltria** inherited the site of *Pitinum Pisaurense*, a Roman foundation of the 3rd century AD that was crushed in the wars of the 6th. The upper part of town around the Malatesta castle has kept its medieval allure, with its walls, gate and 11th-century **Palazzo del Podestà** and **Torre Civica** (*open June–Sept Tues–Sun 4.30–7.30; Oct–May Sat 3.30–6.30; at other times, call Signor Giuseppe Rossi t 0722 74546 or 73231; adm*), containing a hotchpotch of curiosities, including finds from Pitinum, Renaissance ceramics, a palaeontological collection and medieval tombs. Macerata Feltria's oldest church is on the fringe of town, the 11th-century **San Cassiano in Pitino**, decorated in the 17th century; Roman tombs lie in the garden.

If you're in no hurry, consider driving southwest to **Piandimeleto** (from the Latin *Planus Mileti*), another unspoiled town with a late 15th-century castle, the **Castello dei Conti Oliva**, retaining original fireplaces and fittings, and now defender of a pair of museums about farm work and the geology of the Marches (*t 0722 721528, www.comunepiandimeleto.pu.it; open Mon–Fri winter 2–6, summer 3–7, adm*). The church is worth a look for its 14th-century frescoes and Gothic tombs.

Getting There and Around

There are four or five Ferrovie Padane **buses** (t 0541 25474) daily from Rimini station to San Leo, via Pietracuta, Novafeltria and Pennabilli. Salvadori buses link Sassocorvaro to Pesaro.

There's a very pretty **drive** up from Sansepolcro on the SS258, over the Alpe della Luna. Baschetti buses (t 0575 749816) take this route from Arezzo and Sansepolcro to Rimini. If you're driving from Urbino, you have a choice of squiggly routes – following the signs to Sassocorvaro, Macerata Feltria and Montecopiolo is the most direct.

Tourist Information

Pennabilli: Piazza Garibaldi, Municipio 92841, t 0541 928659. Ask for the map of walking paths around the area.

San Leo: Palazzo Mediceo, Piazza Dante 14, t 0541 916306, *iat.sanleo@regione.marche.it. Open Mon–Fri 9–6.30, Sat and Sun 9–7.*

Carpegna: Piazza Conti 1, t 0722 77153.

Where to Stay and Eat

Carpegna ✉ 61021

Carpegna has the biggest concentration of accommodation in the Montefeltro.

***San Michele**, Via Amaducci 51, t 0722 77320, f 0722 77690, *www.hotelsmichele.com (moderate).* No TVs, but a pool. *Open June–Sept.*

***Ulisse**, Via Amaducci 16, t 0722 77119, f 0722 77482, *www.hotelulisse.it (inexpensive).* A modern hotel, next to the Palazzo dei Principi. *Closed 2 wks late Nov.*

*Onelia**, Via Amaducci 42/c, t/f 0722 77175 (*inexpensive*). More reasonable still. *Open June–Sept.*

Pennabilli ✉ 61016

Most hotels here require at least half board.

Parco, Via Marconi 14, t 0541 928446, f 0541 928498 (*inexpensive*). Family-run; surrounded by greenery. *Closed Nov–Jan.*

Piastrino, Via Parco Begni 9, t 0541 928569 (*expensive, cheaper without truffles*). The best food in town, in a country house with a garden, just outside the *centro storico*. Truffles are their forte. *Closed Tues.*

Sant'Agata Feltria ✉ 61019

Antenna, Monte Benedetto 32, t 0541 929626 (*expensive*). Renowned for almost 50 years as the best *trattoria* in the area, situated up in the *frazione* Monte Benedetto. The home-made pasta and tasty oven-baked ham are excellent; there's also a good-value set menu. If you call ahead in the autumn, you can feast on their *pièce de résistance* – chestnut-stuffed pheasant. *Closed Mon except July and Aug,and 3 wks in Jan.*

***Pian del Bosco**, Fraz Perticara Pian del Bosco, Narafeltria, signposted off the road from Narafeltria to Sant'Agata, t 0541 927600, f 0541 927700, *www.piandelbosco.com (moderate).* A charming farmhouse conversion with a pool, lively pizzeria and restaurant.

***Falcon Hotel**, Viale S. Girolamo 30, just outside Sant'Agata, t 0541 929090, f 0541 929830, *wwwfalconhotel.it (moderate).* Glossy new hotel, all mod cons and garden with a view.

San Leo ✉ 61018

Locanda San Leone, Strada Sant'Antimo 102, t 0541 912194, f 0541 912348, *www.locanda sanleone.it (expensive–moderate).* There are some rooms here, but if all you fancy is lunch on the way to Sant'Igne, the farm restaurant (*open to all*) serves lovely pasta with fresh eggs and other homegrown ingredients, including vegetarian dishes. *Restaurant closed Mon–Wed and Jan.*

****La Rocca**, Via G. Leopardi 16, t 0541 916241, f 0541 926914, *www.paginegialle.it/larocca sanleo (moderate).* This is run by the Rossi family, who offer simple rooms and good home cooking (*moderate*), which is gaining quite a following; truffles and mushrooms in season, and *secondi* such as *pasticciata alla Cagliostro* – beef marinated in wine, with carrots, celery, onions and cloves. *Closed Mon Sept–June; also closed Dec 12–early Feb.*

****Il Castello**, Piazza Dante Alighieri 11–12, t 0541 916214, f 0541 926926, *albergo-castello @libero.it (inexpensive).* Comfortable rooms; all the better for its excellent restaurant. *Closed mid-Nov–mid-Dec and all Feb.*

Il Bettelino, Via Montefeltro 4, t 0541 916265 (*cheap*). A bar-pizzeria-restaurant, worth knowing also for the inexpensive rooms available above it. *Closed Wed.*

Around Monte Carpegna and Pennabilli

North of Piandimeleto and west of Sassocorvaro rises the majestic profile of **Monte Carpegna** (1,415m/4,642ft). In 1996 this area, noted for its rare wild orchids, red lilies and falcons, became the **Parco Naturale del Sasso Simone e Simoncello**, named after two of its more prominent mesa-like crags, 'Big and Little Simon', just west of Carpegna.

From Piandimeleto, stop at the 13th-century **Convento di Montefiorentino** (*t 0722 71202; open daily 8–12 and 3.30–6; adm free*), near Frontino, where the church has a beautiful Renaissance **Cappella dei Conti Oliva**, attributed to Francesco di Simone Ferrucci, and contains the tombs of its patrons. **Carpegna**, 6km north, is the most popular resort on the mountain, built around the enormous, late Renaissance **Palazzo dei Principi Carpegna**; also see the little parish church **San Giovanni Battista**, built by travelling Lombard masters in 1182. From Carpegna a road wiggles up to a track just below the summit, for grandiose views across the Montefeltro and San Marino; in winter people come here to ski.

Pennabilli, just west, is an important market town under two crags, each capped by an 11th-century 'feather' or castle built by the Malatesta, named Penna and Billi. Billi, with a large convent clinging to its slope, now does service as a base for an iron cross, but Penna's castle is in pretty good nick, in the heart of the *centro storico*. Here you'll find a good Renaissance church, the **Santuario della Madonna delle Grazie** with pretty frescoes and a **Museo Diocesano** (*t 0541 928469; closed for renovation*) displaying art gathered from the Montefeltro's churches. Pennabilli runs a major antiques exhibition in July, but it likes new things, too; scattered across the town are houses decorated with contemporary art, mostly imitations of famous paintings. Amongst these are the *Path of Sundials*, by contemporary poet Tonino Guerra, and the *Petrified Gardens*, the latter up by the 12th-century tower, standing like an exclamation mark on the next hill, at **Bascio**. Another of Pennabilli's *frazioni*, **Pontemessa**, has the **Museo di Informatica e Storia del Calcolo** (*t 0541 928563, www.museoinformaticac.it; open 3rd Sun of each month 10–12.30 and 3.30–6.30, or by appointment; adm*), dedicated to the evolution of calculation, from ancient times to modern computers, with software to play with at the end.

A narrow mountain road runs north of Pennabilli to **Sant'Agata Feltria**, protected by the **Rocca Fregoso**, another fantastical castle built by Martini, balancing precariously on its rock. Inside (*t 0541 929111; open daily winter 10–1 and 3–7, summer 10–1 and 3–7.30; adm*) there are Renaissance frescoes, as well as some rather unexpected stained glass from various periods, and Liberty-style Art Nouveau ads and posters. The *municipio* houses a 17th-century wooden theatre, the **Teatro Angelo Mariani** (*t 0541 929714; open by request*), one of the oldest of its kind in Italy and still used today. Sant'Agata comes into its own in the autumn, when it holds a white truffle market on four consecutive Sundays, beginning with the second Sunday in October.

Just off the road from Sant'Agata to Novafeltria about 7km northeast, lofty **Perticara** (900m) is tucked under another rocky crag; it once made its living from mining sulphur. It keeps the now odour-free memory alive in its **Museo Storico Minerario** (*t 0541 927576; open summer Tues–Sun 10–1 and 4–7; winter Tues–Sat 9–1 an 3–7; adm*), containing the reconstruction of a gallery and an extensive mineral collection.

On the slopes of Mt Perticara 2km east, **Talamello** is another old hill town, where they make a much-loved cheese matured in pits called *formaggio di fossa Ambra di Talamello*, best eaten when it emerges from the pits in November and December. The church of **San Lorenzo**, at the highest point of town, has frescoes by Antonio da Ferrara (1473). **Novafeltria** is rather dull, but 4km south on the Pennabilli road, stop to visit **Santa Maria Antico**, a sandstone church from the 13th century, with a handsome marble lunette of the *Madonna del Soccorso* and another Madonna inside, complete with *Bambino*, by Luca della Robbia.

San Leo

The most extraordinary of all the Montefeltro's extraordinary castles hangs high over the one and only entrance into **San Leo**, a road that had to be cut into the living rock. According to legend, San Leo was founded in the 4th century by St Leo of Dalmatia, a companion of Marinus (who founded San Marino). Pepin, father of Charlemagne, donated it to the Church and it briefly served as 'capital of Italy' in the 960s, during the undistinguished reign of King Berengarius II, who after a siege of two years, surrendered both San Leo and Italy to the German emperor Otto, who returned San Leo to the Church. Dante slept here and gave San Leo a mention in *Purgatory*; St Francis also wandered through and preached so convincingly that one of his listeners, the Count di Chiusi, gave him his beloved La Verna as a retreat.

For all that, San Leo is tiny, a huddle of stone houses balanced on the gentle slope of the stupendous crag. Its rough-walled **Pieve** (*open daily 9–12.30 and 3–6; adm free*) is one of the oldest churches in the Marches; the *ciborium* over the altar has an inscription to Christ and the Madonna from the year 882, dedicated by Duke Orso, who ruled San Leo for Pope John VIII. Just above, the Romanesque **Duomo** (*closed for restoration*) was built by Lombard masters in 1173 to replace a 7th-century church, which in turn was built over a prehistoric shrine; its harmonious interior has very old capitals, including a few Roman ones; in the crypt, there's a bas relief and tomb of St Leo with a 6th-century inscription. The **Palazzo Mediceo** (*t 0541 916306 or 926967; open Mon–Sat 9–6, Sun 9–6.30; adm*) has temporary exhibits, and holds **Museo d'Arte Sacra** with artworks from the 14th–18th centuries, including a Botticelli-like *Madonna with SS. Leo and Marino* (1493) by Luca Frosino. The peaceful 13th-century church and convent of **Sant'Igne** (*t 0541 916277; visits by appointment only*), 2km from San Leo, was founded by St Francis on the spot where a miraculous light guided him to shelter when he was lost in the woods at night.

The Rocca di San Leo

Only one Pope, only one God, only one Fort – San Leo!
A Montefeltro saying

In Roman times, the tremendous pinnacle was known as *Mons Feretrius*, referring to Jove's lightning (another castle, atop nearby Majolo, was blasted into ruins by a thunderbolt in the 1600s). There was probably a temple on top, perhaps of the same

The Rise and Fall of Giuseppe Balsamo

Born into a poor family in Palermo in 1743, Giuseppe Balsamo began his career humbly enough by forging theatre tickets. The rest of his life reads as if it were concocted by a picaresque novelist on amphetamines. After outlandishly tricking a gullible goldsmith in Palermo with a ghost story, Giuseppe hooked up with a famous Armenian alchemist, Altolas, who took him to Greece, Egypt and Malta, where the Grand Master of the Knights let the two seek the philosopher's stone in his laboratory. Altolas accidently poisoned himself, but Giuseppe, thanks to a forged letter, next appears in Rome, financially supported by the Maltese ambassador in his business of manufacturing love potions. He found a 14-year-old Roman intriguer named Lorenza Feliciani to marry and, after several unsuccessful machinations, Giuseppe decided there was nothing to do but recreate himself with a new name: Count Alessandro Cagliostro, the greatest magician in Europe, born in Egypt and raised by alchemists, a man who personally assassinated Pompey and gave counsel to Jesus Christ.

After years of travelling around Europe, pimping for Lorenza, staying just ahead of the law or behind bars, and exciting debate as to whether he was a scoundrel, a sage, a prophet or the Antichrist, Cagliostro rocketed to fame and fortune in London in 1776 when he gave a couple the numbers that won them £2,000 in a lottery. All at once people were pounding on his door for his numbers, his elixir of Long Life and his love potions. When the numbers began to lose, Cagliostro retreated to the Continent, where he made a triumphal tour – he became a counsellor to Catherine the Great, healed the blind and crippled in Strasbourg, founded his own Masonic lodge and became the protégé of the Cardinal of Rohan in Paris, one of the most powerful men and biggest dupes in France. Rohan was tricked into financing a diamond necklace for Marie Antoinette by a group of swindlers, who took the money and ran; when the queen got the bill, she had Louis XVI toss Rohan and Cagliostro into the Bastille. Ironically, it was the one time that Cagliostro was innocent and he was soon acquitted of having anything to do with the affair.

Lorenza, however, had thought the gig was up and told the whole history of the Count's humble origins to a journalist in London. Cagliostro forgave her, and the two returned to Rome and lay low, until Cagliostro caused a sensation in Rome's Masonic Lodge in September 1789 when he hypnotized a girl who accurately predicted the start of the French Revolution. This caught the attention of the Inquisition and Lorenza, immune to her husband's love potions, confessed that the Count was guilty of Freemasonry. This was enough to get him condemned to death by the Holy Office, a sentence that Pope Pius VI commuted in 1791 to solitary confinement for life in the Rocca di San Leo. Cagliostro was first placed in a normal cell, but the prison guards were so terrified of his evil eye that he was moved to a tiny, dark, rat-infested pit where he slowly went mad. He died of apoplexy four years later. According to the accounts preserved in San Leo's archives, as an unrepentant heretic, his body was buried somewhere near the fortress, in unconsecrated ground. When Napoleon showed up a few years later, he freed the pope's prisoners and asked to pay his respects to Cagliostro's grave, but no one could find it.

Jove Feretro to whom the Roman Consul Marcellus dedicated the corpse of the leader of the Gauls in the 3rd century BC. *Mons Feretrius* gave its name to *Montefeltro*, the old name of San Leo, and in 1158, to the ducal family who relocated to Urbino. In the 15th century, the Urbino dukes commissioned Francesco di Giorgio Martini to replace the old fortifications on the summit with the most spectacular castle in Italy, hung on a breathtakingly sheer cliff. The castle overlooks the whole of the Montefeltro and the three landmark towers of San Marino: in the autumn, the region's landmark crags and castles rise over the rolling sea of fog like an enchanted archipelago.

Like the ducal palace at Urbino, Martini's **fortress** is a perfect representative building of the Renaissance: balanced, finely proportioned in its lines, a structure of intelligence and style. But it proved to be not quite as impregnable as it looks – in 1523, after a four-month siege, the troops of Lorenzo de' Medici the Younger (who was made Duke of Urbino by his uncle, Leo X) captured it on a dark and stormy night by using ropes and ladders to scale the west face of the rock, an exploit that Vasari frescoed on to the walls of Florence's Palazzo Vecchio. The Medici were succeeded by the delle Rovere dukes and, when they died out, by the Popes, under whom it became a notorious prison, the escape-proof Alcatraz of its day. Inside (*t 0541 926967/800 553800; open Mon–Sat 9–6, Sun 9–6.30; adm*), you can see Renaissance weapons, parts of the prison, the dungeon, charts of various nasty tortures, modern art, a series of illustrations of Dante's *Inferno*, and the cell where San Leo's most famous prisoner, Cagliostro, spent the last years of his life.

South of Urbino

The culture-loving dukes in Urbino had ants in their pants judging by how many *palazzi ducali* they required in their small realm. They took their artists and architects wherever they went, leaving behind some nice surprises tucked here and there.

The Upper Metauro Valley: Fermignano and Urbania

Fermignano, 5km south of Urbino, was the home town of Mrs Bramante and is also believed to have been the birthplace of her High Renaissance architect son Donato as well, in 1444 (although Urbania disputes that honour). Bramante met his much younger fellow Marchigiano Raphael in Rome, and is often credited with designing the architectural setting in Raphael's famous Vatican fresco, *The School of Athens* – a favour that Raphael returned by painting Bramante into the scene as the geometer Euclid. In the centre of town, don't look for any Bramantine monuments, but under a graceful medieval tower and bridge there is a little waterfall on the Metauro River.

In the upper Metauro Valley, just southwest of Urbino, **Urbania** was known as Castel Durante for most of its history; it was renamed in 1636 to flatter Pope Urban VIII and the name stuck. In the 15th century, Castel Durante was famous for its majolica, manufactured in over 30 workshops, and the town has changed little since. The Porta Cella Quarter, in particular, is evocative: a little octagonal temple, mostly destroyed in the last war, is said to have been an early work by Bramante. Urbania's **Palazzo Ducale**

Getting There and Around

Bucci **buses** (**t** 0721 32401, *www.mediaworks. it/bucci.htm*) from Pesaro serve Fossombrone and Cagli, via Fano, once daily, and there are buses from Urbino to Cagli, too.

Tourist Information

Urbania: Corso Vittorio Emanuele II 27, **t** 0722 313140.
Fossombrone: Via C. Battisti, **t** 0721 740377, or Piazza Dante, **t/f** 0721 716324, *uficioturismo@libero.it*.
Pergola: Corso Matteotti 47, **t** 0721 736469.
Fermignano: Via Bramante 3, **t** 0722 330523.
Cagli: Via Leopardi 3, **t** 0721 787457.

Where to Stay and Eat

Fermignano ✉ 61033

***Bucci, Via dell'Industria 13, **t/f** 0722 356050, *wwwpaginegialle.it/hotelbucci* (*moderate*). Modern, if fairly functional, in a quiet location. *Closed first 2 wks Sept.*

Urbania ✉ 61049

Big Ben, Corso Vittorio Emanuele 61, **t** 0722 319795 (*moderate*). Possibly *the* place to eat in Urbania; the locals have borrowed the name for their own tower. Porcini mushrooms, truffles and meat, pizzas and an *enoteca*, but no fish, in a 17th-century palace. *Closed for lunch, also Wed, 2 weeks in Jan and 2 weeks in July or Sept.*
Osteria del Cucco, Via Betto de' Medici 9, **t** 0722 317 412 (*moderate*). Family-run,

old-fashioned, serving delicious seasonal dishes with asparagus, fresh greens, truffles and mushrooms. *Closed Sun eve and Mon, 2 weeks in Jan and 2 weeks in July.*
Bramante, Via Roma 4, **t 0722 319562, **f** 0722 311140 (*inexpensive*). A pleasant hotel, always good value.

Fossombrone ✉ 61034

***Al Lago, Via Cattedrale 79, Loc San Lazzaro, **t** 0721 726 129, **f** 0722 726 12, *www.paginegialle. it/allago* (*expensive*). A pleasant, modern, family-run place, in a quiet spot by the bottom of the Gola del Furlo, with a large garden, tennis and pool. *Closed Christmas, restaurant closed Sat.*
Symposium Quattro Stagioni, Via Cartoceto 38, 30km from Pesaro: take the *superstrada* to Fano, then follow signs to Calcinelli and Cartoceto, **t** 0721 898320 (*very expensive*). One of the best restaurants in the region, with a lovely panoramic view. The chef takes traditional recipes and ingredients (white truffles, *passatelli, formaggio di fossa*), and does marvellous things with them. There are four *menu degustazione* choices, featuring fish, crustacea, game and truffles; also a wonderful cellar. *Open for lunch only Sat and Sun. Closed Mon and Tues, also Jan 1–Feb 8.*

Cagli ✉ 61043

Guazza, Piazza Federico da Montefeltro, **t** 0721 787 231 (*moderate*). You can't do better for a country lunch than here. Try the fragrant porcini mushrooms or local speciality, *fricò* – lamb, chicken and rabbit doused in wine and vinegar and fried with garlic; try it with the house wine. *Lunch only, closed Fri and July.*

began as a 13th-century castle and was transformed for Duke Federico by Francesco di Giorgio Martini and Gerolamo Genga into an elegant residence, with a long, arcaded gallery overlooking the Metauro Valley. In its heyday it hosted Ariosto, Tasso, Bembo and Cosimo I de' Medici's gallant father, Giovanni dalle Bande Nere; today, it hosts the **Museo Civico** and **Pinacoteca** (**t** 0722 313151; *open summer Tues–Sun 10–12.30 and 3–6.30; winter closes 30min earlier; adm*), with Castel Durante ceramics, a large collection of drawings and engravings and the remains of Duke Federico's famous library, including terrestrial and celestial globes by the famous geographer Mercatore (1541).

In Via Urbano VIII, the bishop's palace was another building that was beautifully 'Renaissanced' by Francesco di Giorgio Martini and Gerolamo Genga, and now contains the **Museo Diocesano** with more treasures: detached 14th-century frescoes, Romanesque capitals, a Paleochristian cross, paintings and more ceramics (*t 0722 319555; open summer Tues–Sun 9–12 and 4–7; winter on request; adm*). The best work, a *Crucifixion* by Pietro da Rimini of 1320, is still in the Baroque **cathedral**. Urbania, like Ferentillo in Umbria, also has naturally preserved **mummies**, next to the **Chiesa dei Morti** by San Francesco (*t 0722 319446; open daily 10–12 and 3–6; adm*). Just outside town on the Sant'Angelo in Vado road, the Montefeltro dukes would hunt in the **Parco Ducale** (*ask at the Pro Loco*), where you can see their villa containing some ceramics, begun by Francesco di Giorgio Martini and completed by Girolamo Genga.

Beyond Urbania, in all directions towards the Apennine peaks, villagers dream of the truffles they will find in the autumn, like their counterparts over the mountains in Umbria. The 'Sagra del Tartufo' in October is the big event of the year in **Sant'Angelo in Vado**, another exceptionally pretty village on the Metauro. Originally called *Tifernum Metaurensis* (to distinguish it from *Tifernum Tiberensis*, nearby Città di Castello in Umbria), it was the home of the Zuccari brothers, late Renaissance painters whose best works are in Rome. The small octagonal church of **San Filippo** has a wooden statue attributed to Lorenzo Ghiberti, who spent time wandering about the Marches in his early 20s, before the great Florentine baptistry door contest changed his life.

From here the SS73bis climbs over the mountains to Sansepolcro and Arezzo, passing the village of **Mercatello**; here one of the earliest Franciscan churches (13th-century San Francesco) has been converted into a museum with a collection of late medieval works (*t 0722 89593; open on request*). Further west, towards Sansepolcro, **Borgo Pace** and **Lamoli** are equally picturesque, out-of-the-way places.

Fossombrone

From Urbino, the SS73bis will take you southeast to the Metauro Valley and **Fossombrone** (pop. 9,500), a busy workaday town with laundry flapping in the alleys and not a wine bar or olive oil mill in sight. A Roman foundation that takes its name, *Forum Sempronii*, from the famous reformer Sempronius Gracchus, Fossombrone is strikingly built in tiers over the Metauro. It once had pretensions to grandeur: impressive if somewhat tattered palaces line the arcaded Corso Garibaldi, including a sometime ducal residence, the Corte Bassa. Near the top of the town, under the citadel, a huge stepped ramp ascends to the **Corte Alta** (you can also drive up), a pint-sized Palazzo Ducale begun by the Malatesta in the 13th century, and sold along with the rest of Fossombrone to Duke Federico of Urbino in 1466; and the Duke, as usual, got Francesco di Giorgio Martini and Girolamo Genga to remodel it according to the style he was rapidly becoming accustomed to. Now seat of the **Museo Civico** and **Pinacoteca Civica** (*t 0721 714645; open June–Sept Tues–Sun 10.30–12.30 and 4–7; Oct–May Sat 4–7, Sun 10.30–12.30 and 4–7; adm*), it has some good Renaissance pavements and ceilings, and houses a small archaeological museum with busts and fragments of Roman sculpture, ceramics and coins, as well as a collection of paintings and etchings by Dürer, Rembrandt and Tiepolo. There's a fine view over Fossombrone's tile roofs, punctured here and there with big cylindrical apses of churches. There's more art – 19th-century and modern Italian works (De Chirico, Umberto Boccioni,

Marino Marini, etc.) – in the **Museo Cesarini** (*t 0721 714650; opening hours as for other museums; adm, reduced ticket available for all three*), in the Renaissance Palazzo Pergamino on Via Pergamino 32, outside the centre towards Urbino.

The Gola del Furlo

Southwest 10km from Fossombrone, a little stream called the Candigliano has spent aeons pounding out a steep gorge, the **Gola del Furlo**, a wild, rocky landscape that provides a striking contrast to the gently sculpted farmlands beyond. A road has traversed the gorge since ancient times, including a small tunnel cut in the rock by the Consul Flaminius in 217 BC, when he laid out the Via Flaminia; traffic had increased so much by the 1st century AD that a larger tunnel, the 580ft (176m) **Galleria del Furlo**, was built by Emperor Vespasian and is still in use. Despite the traffic, the Furlo is home to wildlife, including a few specimens of Italy's rare *aquila reale* (royal eagle, *see* Monti Sibillini, p.637).

Mussolini built the tall dam and power plant at the end of the Gola del Furlo; later, passing through in one of his endless trips around Italy in his red Alfa Romeo, he became enamoured of the region and stopped in often for short holidays. To make him feel at home, the local fascists sculpted one of the Furlo's cliffs into the dictator's profile. It can still be seen, from a point near the village of **Acqualagna** – although it's a bit hard to make out, since resistance fighters blew his nose off with dynamite after the war. Acqualagna is famous for truffles, both black and white, a must-buy for gastronomes travelling in the region.

Cagli and Around

Cagli, 9km south of Aqualagna, is known for craftwork in wrought iron. It has its modest collection of monuments – late Gothic details in the cathedral and church of San Francesco, a late Renaissance portal by the Roman architect Vignola on **Sant'Angelo Minore**, a painting by Raphael's dad, Giovanni Santi in **San Domenico**, and yet another palace of Duke Federico (1463), now the town hall. They make a pleasant ensemble, all in the shadow of the **Torrione**, Cagli's landmark, an elliptical defence tower built for the insatiable Montefeltro dukes by the unflagging Francesco di Giorgio Martini. A road full of hairpin turns scales **Monte Petrano** (1,120m/3,634ft), which overlooks Cagli from the south, near the border with Umbria; a detour along the side road up to it will bring you out on to some green alpine meadows, full of wild flowers in the spring and sheep in the summer. The SS3, the Via Flaminia, continues south of Cagli into Umbria – towards Gubbio, with yet another ducal palace (*see* **Northern Umbria**, p.485) and the **Parco Naturale di Monte Cucco** and ancient hermitage of **Fonte Avellana** (*see* p.487).

Pergola (pop. 7,000), 20km east of Cagli, or south of Fossombrone, is the big town in the area, founded in the 13th century by the lords of Gubbio, who invited everyone in hilltop castles to move down into the little plain. Later part of the Duchy of Urbino, it won a gold medal for its bravery in the Risorgimento. Pergola also has a superb set of gilded bronze **Roman statues** (two female figures and two horsemen) from the 1st century AD, found just north in Cartoceto in 1946. These are displayed in the **Museo**

dei Bronzi Dorati e della Città di Pergola (*t 0721 734090, www.bronzidorati.com; open winter Tues–Sun 9.30–12.30 and 3.30–7.30, summer daily 9.30–1 and 4–8; adm*) on Largo San Giacomo. Pergola's **cathedral** was built in 1258, but overhauled in the 19th century; only a Gothic reliquary and a 14th-century *Crucifixion* escaped the renovation squads.

Back on the Coast: South from Pesaro

South of Pesaro, the string of Adriatic resorts continues. Fano and Senigallia are not merely seaside playgrounds, however, but also fine old towns, both members of the Byzantine/medieval Adriatic Pentapolis.

Fano

Older even than the Romans, **Fano** (pop. 54,000) took its name – *Fanum Fortunae* – from a famous temple of the goddess Fortuna. Under Roman rule, it became the most important of the Marches' coastal cities, being the terminus of the Via Flaminia from Rome. Curiously enough, Fano's *centro storico* still looks uncannily like the perfect provincial Roman town: just the right size, with its grid plan (there's even a copy of a Roman milestone at the meeting of the *cardo* and *decumanus*, modern Via Arco di Augusto and Corso Matteotti) and severe brick buildings – just imagine that the signs are in Latin, there are temples instead of churches and chariots instead of cars and you're back in the 2nd century.

Today, in the central Piazza XX Settembre, a statue of Fortune (now a copy) from the 1500s decorates the pretty **Fontana della Fortuna**. Behind it, the **Palazzo della Ragione** (1299) is an austere Romanesque Gothic hall, linked by an arch with the **Palazzo Malatestiano** (*t 0721 828362; open Wed, Fri and Sat 8.30–1.30, Tues, Thurs 8.30–1.30 and 3-6, Sun 10–1; adm*), a palace built in the 1420s, when Fano was ruled by Rimini's tyrant Pandolfino Malatesta III, father of bad boy Sigismundo. It has a lovely courtyard with crenellations, mullioned windows and a portico; the elegant loggia, attributed to Jacopo Sansovino, was added in 1544. Inside there's a small, good picture collection, including a fine polyptych (1420) by Venetian Michele Giambono, an *Enthroned Madonna* by Giovanni Santi, an unusually crowded *Annunciation* by a local 16th-century painter, Domenico Sacchetta, works by Renaissance tail-enders Guido Reni and Guercino (including the *Guardian Angel* that inspired Browning's sentimental classic of the same name after a visit in 1848), some small bronzes of the ancient Piceni and the original statue of Fortuna.

The church of **Santa Maria Nuova** (*open daily 10–12 and 4–6*), two blocks south on Via dei Pili, is decorated with stuccoes and altarpieces by Perugino (lovely *Annunciation* and *Madonna and Saints*) and Giovanni Santi, one with a small predella panel attributed to Raphael, who was there with his father; it's possible this is where he first met his future master. The Romans tell us Vitruvius built a famous basilica in Fano, and although time has obliterated all traces of it, the overgrown, roofless ruins of the 14th-century basilica of **San Francesco** offer an evocative replacement, especially where its massive Corinthian columns support the **Portico della Sopressa** – it does

Tourist Information

Fano: Viale Cesare Battisti 10, **t** 0721 803534,
f 0721 824292, *iat.fano@regione.marche.it.*
Open Mon–Sat 9–1 and 3–6, Sun 9–1.
Senigallia: Piazza Morandi 2, **t** 071 792 2725,
f 071 792 4930, *www.senigalliaturismo.it.*
*Open summer Mon–Sat 8.30–1.30 and
3–6.30, Sun 9–1; winter Wed, Fri and Sat 9–1,
Tues and Thurs 9–1 and 3–6.*
Corinaldo: Via del Velluto 20, **t** 071 679047.

Where To Stay and Eat

Fano and Senigallia don't offer anything
particularly outstanding – all are standard
beach hotels, and all are less than 30 years old.
Fano, however, wins points for the cheapest,
tastiest seafood in the Marches.

Fano ✉ 61032

****Augustus, Via Puccini 2, **t** 0721 809781,
f 0721 825517, *www.hotelaugustus.it*
(*moderate*). A central, family-run hotel,
which has recently had a facelift from head
to toe and offers all mod cons. The
restaurant serves fish as well as some more
creative dishes. *Restaurant closed Sun.*
***Angela, Viale Adriatico 13, **t** 0721 801239,
f 0721 803102, *www.hotelangela.it*
(*inexpensive*). Modern rooms overlooking
the beach. *Closed Christmas–New Year.*
***Astoria, Viale Cairoli 86, **t/f** 0721 803474,
www.promofano.net (*inexpensive*).
A pleasant hotel, situated on the best part of
the beach. *Open Easter–Oct.*
Mare, Viale C. Colombo 20, **t/f 0721 805 667
(*inexpensive*). If you're feeling nostalgic for
the homely *pensioni* of 20 years ago, try this
place just off the beach, where *mamma*
Anna cooks up some of the best and most
affordable seafood in Fano. *Restaurant*
(*moderate–cheap*) *closed Sun eve.*
Ristorantino Giulio, Viale Adriatico 100, **t** 0721
805680 (*moderate*). Another reliable little
favourite, serving fresh and tasty seafood in
the Marchigiano style: try the *fusilli con le
canocchie* (a local kind of shrimp). Book in
advanve. *Closed Tues and Nov.*
Pesce Azzurro, near the port at Viale Adriatico
48, **t** 0721 803165 (*cheap*). Unique in all Italy,

this was founded a decade ago by the
local fishermen's cooperative, designed to
promote the glories of 'blue fish' – not
just one specific type, but a variety of
sardines, anchovies, mackerel and other
small fish, all, despite their diminutive
size, very tasty! The degradation of the
Adriatic makes them harder to find with
each passing year, but at this self-service
restaurant, you can try them in three
courses, with the local Bianchello del
Metauro to wash them down. *Closed
Mon, and Oct–Mar.*

Senigallia ✉ 60019

****Duchi della Rovere, Via Corridoni 3,
t 071 792 7623, **f** 071 792 7784, *www.hotel
duchidellarovere.it* (*very expensive*). You can
spoil yourself at this stylish hotel, with all mod
cons, located by the park a couple of blocks
in from the beach. *Closed for Christmas.*
***La Vela, Piazzale N. Bixio 35, **t** 071 792 7444,
f 071 792 7445 (*expensive*). A nice place with
garden near the port; also the furthest hotel
from the railway line. *Open May–Sept only.*
***Cristallo, right by the *rotunda* at
Lungomare Alighieri 2, **t** 071 792 5767, **f** 071
792 5768, *www.h-cristallo.it* (*moderate*).
A typical resort hotel with lots of balconies
and a roof terrace for sun-drenched drinks.
Madonnina del Pescatore, Lungomare Italia 11,
7km south in Marzocca, **t** 071 698267, **f** 071
698484 (*very expensive*). Packed out for its
brilliant and creative seafood, and some of
the best desserts in all the Marches. Book
ahead. *Closed Mon, 2 middle weeks in Nov,
Easter week and 1 week in Sept.*
Uliasse, Via Banchina di Levante 6, **t** 071 65463
(*very expensive*). A classy restaurant serving
creative fish and seafood dishes including a
fabulous fish soup.
Osteria del Tempo Perso, Via Mastai 53,
t 071 60345 (*moderate*). Offers a change
from all the seafood, with a number of
vegetarian dishes that change with the
season, right in the *centro storico.*
Closed Tues in winter.
Osteria Del Teatro, Via Fratelli Bandiera 70,
t 071 60517 (*cheap*). Situated by Senigallia's
Teatro La Fenice, serving simple tasty dishes.
Eves only; closed Wed and June.

come as a surprise on the narrow Via S. Francesco. The portico holds the **Arche Malatestiane**: the Renaissance tomb of Pandolfo III Malatesta (1460) attributed to Alberti and, on the left, a more elaborate Gothic model in pink and white marble of his wife Paola Bianca (1421) by Filippo di Domenico.

Fano does preserve a genuine relic of its Roman days, a stately gate of the year AD 2, the **Arco di Augusto**, marking the end of the Via Flaminia. Next to the arch is the airy **Logge di San Michele** (1495), used for market stalls, and the church of **San Michele** with a relief carved on its façade showing how the arch looked before having its block knocked off with artillery in 1463. The besieging *condottiere*, eventually successful, who bombarded it was none other than Duke Federico of Urbino, working at that time for the pope; the defender was Sigismondo Malatesta of Rimini. Another corner of Fano's walls is occupied by a 15th-century **Rocca Malatestiana**, built by Pandolfo III, once used as a prison and now for special exhibitions.

Fano's **Lido**, modern and a little overbuilt, is one of the nicer resorts on the Adriatic, but the long, broad beach continues down the coast for miles, through the suburbs of Torrette and Marotta, and there's room for all, sprawling all the way to Senigallia.

Senigallia

Senigallia (pop. 41,000), next down the coast, was one of the first to change its orientation to a resort, boasting a long 'velvet beach', one of the nicest along this coastline, decorated with a pretty *rotunda* on piers and an enormous modern pyramid thingamabob on its north end. Before sun and fun, Senigallia was best known for its duty-free port, the site of an important annual trade fair that attracted some 500 ships from the 12th up to the 18th century.

The centre of town, divided by a canal, has an elegant fortress, the **Rocca Roveresca** (*t 071 63258; open daily 8.30–7.30; adm*), built by Laurana for Duke Federico's della Rovere son-in-law in 1480. It has sumptuous Renaissance interiors and was a nasty prison used by the popes. There's a fountain with four lions in the adjacent Piazza Ducale, with yet another down-at-heel 16th-century ducal palace, and from the same century, the **Palazzo Baviera**, now the town hall, with gloriously stuccoed ceilings. Prominent next to all this is a vast brick hemicycle of unfulfilled expectations called the **Foro Annonario** (the Roman name for the Marches), a market built in the 19th century after the great trade fair had already ended, as if wishing could somehow bring back the ships. Perhaps Senigallia still believed that producing a pope – Pius IX, or Pio Nono as the Italians call him – was equivalent to winning the sweepstakes and dreamed of all the goodies that would trickle down from Rome. Unfortunately, it was a lousy time to pontificate – although Pio Nono declared the doctrine of papal infallibility in 1869, Rome (as the last vestige of the old Papal States) fell to the Italians the next year, forcing Pius, and all subsequent popes until the Lateran accords, to become 'a prisoner' in the Vatican. The pope's family palace, the **Palazzo Mastai** (behind the *municipio*) has a small **Museo Pio Nono** (*t 071 60649; www. papapionono.it; open Mon–Sat 9–12 and 4–6; adm*). For a change of pace, at the **Collezione Ducati** (*t 071 660 9654; open Mon–Sat 10–12 and 5–7, Sun by request*) you can see examples of nearly every Ducati motorcycle ever produced.

You can seek out two bristling walled towns in the hinterland of Senigallia. The first, **Corinaldo** (21km) claims not only some of the best preserved fortifications in the Marches, but also the reliquary holding one arm of one of the region's newest saints, Maria Goretti (in her **Casa Natale**, well signposted out of the centre on Via Pregiegna). Maria was a pious illiterate 12-year-old girl knifed to death in 1902 when she refused the advances of a young swain. When she was canonized in 1950, she had nearly 50 miracles under her small belt, and her parents and murderer were among the crowd attending the Vatican ceremony. Another 9km bring you to **Mondavio**, the mountain of birds (*Mons avium*), with ancient walls crowned by a **Rocca**, built by Francesco di Giorgio Martini for Duke Federico in 1482; its studied elegance is only emphasized by what must be the queerest-shaped defence tower in all Italy. Within, the **Museo di Rievocazione Storica e Armeria** (*t 0721 97102; open daily 9–12 and 3–7; adm*) has a collection of arms and armour from the 15th to 18th centuries.

Back on the coast towards Ancona, at the mouth of the River Esino, **Falconara Marittima** is a dull industrial town with a beach, Ancona's airport and kiddie park, the Paese dei Bimbi. The original village, **Falconara Alta**, 2km inland, enjoys fine views and there's a heavily restored medieval castle up the river.

Inland from Falconara: Valle dell'Esino

The Esino is the one of the Marches' most important valleys, with a busy train line and road and clusters of industry. In ancient times the Esino marked the frontier between the Gauls to the north and the Piceni to the south. It was busy in the 12th century as well: near the bottom of the valley, 9km inland from Falconara, the Cistercians in 1126 built one of the very first Gothic churches in Italy, **Santa Maria di Castagnola** at **Chiaravalle** – Italian for *Clairvaux*, where St Bernard founded the Order only a few years previously. Funded by Countess Matilda of Tuscany, the church is as severe as Bernard himself, with only a rose window for decoration.

Jesi

The Valle dell'Esino is named for **Jesi** (pop. 40,000, pronounce it 'Yea si'), founded by the Umbrii and called *Aesis* by the Romans, set on a narrow ridge between well-preserved walls, with houses built on and over their tops, overlooking the industry that has made Jesi the 'little Milan of the Marches.' The *centro storico*, however, hasn't changed much since the 18th century, after centuries of evolution around a necklace of theatrical squares: in the uppermost, once the Roman forum/market square, Constance de Hauteville, at the age of 40 and after nine years of marriage to Emperor Henry VI of Hohenstaufen, was on her way home to Sicily on 26 December 1194 when she was unexpectedly assailed by labour pains. She at once ordered a huge tent to be erected in the square and invited in every matron in town and 19 churchmen to witness the birth and testify to the legitimacy of her son, the future Emperor Frederick II, the medieval *Splendor Mundis*. The discreetly Baroque square was renamed **Piazza Federico II** and the exact spot of the tent marked by an

Getting There and Around

There are several **trains** a day on the Ancona–Rome line, stopping at Jesi, Genga and Fabriano. Crognaletti **buses** (t 0731 204965) go between Ancona and Jesi (at least hourly Mon–Sat, several times on Sun), as well as between Jesi and much of the valley (Mon–Sat).

Tourist Information

Jesi: Piazza Repubblica 11, t 0731 59788, f 0731 58291, *www.comune.jesi.an/proloco. Open Mon–Sat 9–1 and 5–7.30.*
Arcévia: Corso Mazzini 105, t 0731 9127. *Open summer only.*
Sassoferrato: Piazza Matteotti 4, t 0732 956231.
Genga: at the **Grotte di Frasassi**, t 0732 97211.
Fabriano: Corso della Repubblica 70, t 0732 625067, f 0732 629791, *iat.fabriuano@regione.marche.it. Open Mon–Sat 9–1 and 3–6, Sun 9–1.*

Where to Stay and Eat

Jesi ⊠ 60035

Jesi is used to entertaining more business travellers than tourists.
****Federico II**, just outside town on the Via Ancona 10, t 0731 211079, f 0731 57221, *www.hotelfederico2.it* (*very expensive*). Modern, high-tech and luxurious, in a lovely garden.
***Italia**, Viale Trieste 28, t 0731 4844 or t 0731 59004, *www.italiarestaurant.it* (*moderate*). A few minutes' walk from the centre towards the station, this is a family-run place with air conditioned rooms and a good restaurant specializing in local recipes. *Restaurant closed Sun.*
***Mariani**, Via Orfanotrofio 10, t 0731 207286, f 0731 200011, *www.hotelmarianai.com* (*moderate*). A quiet and welcoming hotel in the centre, recently renovated.
OH frutti Emporio, Via Mura Orientali 3, t 0731 64409 (*expensive*). Dine on delectable seafood classics, simply but carefully prepared. *Closed Mon and 2 wks in Aug.*
Da Antonietta, Via Garibaldi 19, t 0731 207173 (*cheap*). The best kind of simple, delicious Italian home cooking. *Closed eves and Sun.*

La Rincrocca, Vicolo delle Pace 3 (near Piazza Federico II), t 0731 56174 (*cheap*). Tunisian and other North African dishes, Italian-style. *Closed lunch and Mon.*
Tana Liberatutti, Piazza Baccio Pontelli 1, t 0731 59237 (*cheap*). Set in a pretty medieval building with a garden. *Closed Sun and part of Aug.*

Serra San Quirico ⊠ 60048

La Pianella, Via Gramsci, t 0731 880054 (*moderate*). Above town in an old pine forest, serving tagliatelle in duck sauce and meats grilled over the fire. *Closed Mon and Jan.*
****K3**, Via Piedaspri 1, t/f 0731 86063 (*inexpensive*). Small, with a restaurant and pizzeria. *Restaurant closed Wed.*

Arcevia ⊠ 60100

*****Alle Terrazze**, Via Rocchi 24, t 0731 9391, f 0731 9948 (*moderate*). This has a lovely setting with great views, just outside the village, a new hydrotherapy pool and the chance for a stroll in the woods. It is also the town's best restaurant (*moderate–cheap*), a good place to savour the area's culinary treasure – truffles; when they're in season, it will be *spaghetti con tartufi*, everything else *con tartufi*, and you won't mind a bit. *Restaurant closed Mon.*

Fabriano ⊠ 60044

****Janus**, Piazzale Matteotti 45, t 0732 4191, f 0732 5714, *www.janusgroup.it* (*expensive*). An ugly, but well-equipped modern hotel near the historic centre, connected to Fabriano's finest restaurant, **La Pergola** (*moderate*). Try their *agnolotti* with meat, courgettes and truffles. *Closed Fri and sat lunch.*
*****Aristos**, Via Cavour 103, t 0732 22308, f 0732 21459, *hotel.aristos@libero.it* (*moderate*). Small and pleasant, in an old townhouse; free parking nearby. *Closed Aug.*
*****Old Ranch**, 3km outside the centre on Via Piaggia d'Olmo, t 0732 627610 (*inexpensive*). No cowboys here, but good food (*expensive*) and a handful of modern rooms in a 19th-century villa, run by the same family for decades. *Restaurant closed Tues and July.*
****Fulvio**, Poggio San Romualdo, 15km east of Fabriano, t 0732 74088 (*inexpensive*). One of Poggio's several small, plain hotels.

obelisk in 1845, flanked by eight lions from an older fountain. Arch-rival of the popes, Frederick later favoured Jesi and confirmed the town's ancient privileges. A few clues lead one to suspect that the citizens found their centuries of papal rule a grating experience: the former headquarters of the Inquisition in the piazza wears a plaque in honour of Giordano Bruno, 'Martyr to Free Thought', put up by the citizens in 1889. Opposite, a former seminary holds the small **Museo Diocesano** (*t 0731 56625, dioces imuseo@libero.it; open Oct–June Tues and Sat 10–12, Thurs 4.30–7.30; July–Sept Tues, Thurs and Fri 6pm–11pm; adm*), with works by Ercole Ramazzani, a student of Lorenzo Lotto.

In Piazza Colocci, the elegant **Palazzo della Signoria** with its clock tower was begun in 1486 by Francesco di Giorgio Martini and wears Jesi's proud *stemma* over the portal, a giant lion rampant, paws up, ready to box all comers; the papal keys added later have been carefully effaced. Overlooking the next square, irregular Piazza Indipendenza, is the 16th-century **Palazzo Ricci**, with its striking waffle-iron façade like the Gesù Nuovo in Naples. Near the entrance of the adjacent **Palazzo del Comune** there's the engraved text of a letter to Jesi from Stupor Mundis.

Besides the most extraordinary of all medieval emperors, Jesi also gave birth to Giambattista Pergolesi in 1710, who started composing at age 16 and died at age 26, but managed in that brief span to produce some perennial favourites of the Italian repertoire: the *Stabat Mater*, the *Frate 'nnammorato* and *La Serva Padrona*. Go through the arch to Piazza della Repubblica to see the fancy late 18th-century **Teatro Pergolesi** (*t 0731 538351/0731 538390, teatro.pergolesi@comune.jesi.an.it; open Mon–Sat 10–1, Tues and Thurs 4–6; or knock on the custodian's door in Vicolo del Teatro*). Up the stairs next door are the **Sale Pergolesiane** (*t 0731 538355; open Mon–Sat 10–1, Tues and Thurs 4–6*), with odds and ends from the composer's life.

Jesi's real treasure, the **Pinacoteca e Musei Civici** (*t 0731 538343; open Tues–Sat 10–1 and 4–7; Sun 10–1 and 5–8; adm*), is in a palace in Via XX Settembre. The Pianetti, the local noble family who built the palace in 1720, hired Placido Lazzarini to supply the decoration, and he gave them their money's worth in the delightful **Rococo gallery** overlooking the garden, 230ft of exuberant pink and lavender stuccoes, symbolizing the 'human adventure in time and space' – a catch-all for lobsters, drums, camels, snakes, and just about everything else. Apart from some Renaissance sculpture, ceramics, archaeological finds and a small modern art gallery, most of the collection is from the same period. The highlight is a set of paintings by Lorenzo Lotto, some of his finest work including the strange, beautifully lit *Annunciation* (1526) in two panels – Gabriel, his expression uncertain as he alights on earth, and Mary, in terror, even more uncertain – compare it to his more famous *Annunciation* in Recanati (*see* p. 625). Other works, all from the same period, include *Santa Lucia in Judgement*, with a good predella of scenes from the life of St Lucy; a *Sacra Conversazione*, with the Virgin and Saints, a soft, luxurious work in Lotto's finest style, and a *Visitation* with scattered petals on the floor. Lotto, a tempermental character wandering through the Marches (he was from Venice, until Titian's gang ran him out of town) had a hard time earning a living, perhaps because patrons never knew if they would get something great or mediocre from his brush; one wonders if the fallen petals and torn papers so often littering his paintings were the signature of a troubled soul.

Outside the walls the 13th-century Benedictine Gothic church of **San Marco** (*t 0731 4804; open Mon–Sat 8.30–11,30 and 4–5.30, Sun 9–11.30 and 4.30–5.30*) has exceptional early 14th-century frescoes by painters from Rimini, in the manner of Giotto.

Around Jesi

If you feel like dawdling in the surrounding hills, drive some 14km south from Jesi to **Filottrano**, another fine old brick town, and there's a surprise: the **Museo Beltrami** (*open Tues 3–6, Wed and Thurs 9–12 and 3–6, Fri 9–12; adm*), where antique carts and wagons share space with Mississippi Indian artefacts, collected by a local man named Giacomo Beltrami in the 1820s, while in exile for having served in the revolutionary government during the Napoleonic Wars.

North of Jesi, a very pretty drive skirts the hills, passing **Belvedere Ostrense** with its crumbling octagonal church, the **Madonna del Sole**, and **Ostra** (18km) a typically pink brick village in its little walls. Nearby **Morro d'Alba** has a well-preserved medieval centre, more picturesque walls and a **Museo Utensilia** (*t 0731 63000, open mid-June–mid-Sept Tues–Thurs and Sun 5–8, Sat 5–8 and 9–11; mid-Sept–mid-June Sun 10.30–12.30 and 3–6; adm*) devoted to old farm tools.

The Upper Valle dell'Esino to the Grotte di Frasassi

From Jesi, the SS76 winds up through the rolling vineyards that produce the excellent DOC region Verdicchio dei Castelli di Jesi – crisp and clear with green highlights, quaffed young and cold, a great thirst-quencher and just the ticket with seafood, especially the local *brodetto di pesce*. It's powerful stuff: in 410, the Visigoth king Alaric took along several barrels 'to improve his manly vigour' when he passed through: he then sacked Rome. The main castles of the Castelli di Jesi, **Rosora** and **Mergo**, are here on the SS76, before the looming mountains are sliced by another dramatic limestone gorge, **Gola della Rossa**, with the fabulous Grotte di Frasassi waiting on the west end.

However, if you're not hurrying, you can best take in this beautiful area on a circular route, turning north up the side road just before the entrance to the gorge, to **Serra San Quirico**, a 14th-century village that stands sentinel over the gorge, shaped like a ship riding the sheer rocks. Part of its defences include lanes covered by houses, the *copertelle*. From here, the road winds to the medieval village of **Arcevia**, the impregnable 'Pearl of the Mountains' perched on a crag, with a fortified gate, Palazzo Comunale and tower, and nine other towers, too. The church of **San Medardo** (*closed for renovation*) is surprisingly rich, with a wooden choir of 1490, a majolica altar by Giovanni della Robbia (1512), and a polyptych and *Baptism of Jesus* by Luca Signorelli. Arcevia's public gardens, dedicated to Leopardi, once belonged to a 16th-century villa.

From Arcevia, it's 12km west to **Sassoferrato** (pop. 8,000), a venerable town along the Marena best known for the artist who took its name, Giovanni Battista Salvi, born here in 1609. His deliberately archaic paintings are more reminiscent of Perugino than his own century; the church of **Santa Chiara** has two *Madonnas* by his hand, although his best work resides in Rome.

Mosaics, marbles and other bits excavated from the first town on this site, Umbrii-Roman *Sentinum*, are in the **Museo Archeologico Sentinate** (*t 0732 956230/1; closed until mid-2005*), in the 14th-century Palazzo dei Priori in Piazza Matteotti. *Sentinum* witnessed two battles that changed the course of history: the defeat by the Romans of the Gauls and Samnites in 295 BC, securing their possession of Central Italy, and one that resulted in the death of Totila in 553, marking the end of the Greek Gothic wars that ravaged the country.

A panoramic road descends from Sassoferrato to the castle and village of **Genga**, birthplace of Pope Leo XII (1823–29), fondly remembered in the **Museo d'Arte Sacra** (*t 0732 97211, closed for restoration*) in Largo Leone XII, along with a quattrocento tryptych, and a *Madonna* from Canova's workshop. Further down, near Genga railway station and the west end of the Gola della Rossa, are a series of magnificent caves, the **Grotte di Frasassi** (*t 0732 97211 (info), t 0732 90080 (bookings), www.frasassi. com; to reach them, take the Genga-Sassoferato motorway exit or hop on a train to Genga San Vittore Terme; open Nov–Feb Mon–Fri 11-3, Sat 11–4.30, Sun and hols 9.30–6; Mar–July and Sept daily 9.30–6; Aug daily 8–6.30; July 20–Aug 25 also open nightly 8pm–10.30pm; closed Dec 4, Dec 25, Jan 1 and Jan 10–30; tours last 70mins; adm exp , also inc adm to Museo d'Arte Sacra di Genga and Museo Speleopaleontologico*). The caves are the largest karstic complex discovered in Italy, extending over 18km, with a spectacular display of glistening pastel stalactites reflected in calcareous pools; the tour takes in the first mile. The massive Grotta Grande del Vento, the 'Cave of the Winds', rises 787ft from the ground – but was only discovered in 1971. It's worth bearing in mind that the temperature inside is about 14°C, so bring a sweater.

Near Genga station and a spa with a sulphurous spring, San Vittore Terme is an impressive temple from the 10th century, showing an unusual combination of Romanesque and Byzantine influences, square in shape, decorated with Lombard blind arcades, a triple apse and corner towers, an octagonal cupola and a huge, squat campanile. The church's former abbey contains a **Museo Speleopaleontologico** (*opening hours/adm as for Grotte di Frasassi, see above, closed until early 2005*), dedicated to the natural history of the caves, and there's a rather less spectacular cave, a half-mile walk uphill, called the **Grotta del Santuario** (*open daily dawn–dusk*), named for its octagonal domed church by Valadier (1828) with a *Madonna* sculpted by Canova.

Fabriano, City of Paper

Handsome, medieval **Fabriano**, the capital of the upper Esine (pop. 28,700), was another victim of the 1997 earthquake; although little actually crumpled, many buildings were left unsound. A lot of scaffolding remains and many of the museums and churches are closed. Away from the media spotlight on Umbrian towns like Assisi, funds have been less readily available and restoration is slow.

Fabriano was one of the first cities in Europe to manufacture paper, back at the end of the 12th century – an art that passed from Central Asia to Egypt in the 9th century, and was then introduced into Spain by the Moors, who were making it in Andalucía by the 1150s. Two centuries later, Fabriano is recorded as exporting a million sheets a year, especially to Florence and Venice, both leaders in the medieval book trade: today Fabriano's biggest mill, Miliani, rolls out an amazing 600 miles of paper a day. The watermark (*filigrana*), and various other papermaking techniques were invented here and, typical of the tenacity of craftwork in many Italian towns, Fabriano still makes its living from the stuff, using modern methods as well as the old-fashioned artisan techniques. The most important use for speciality paper is, of course, banknotes; besides supplying the Italian treasury, Fabriano paper changes hands each day from Kashmir to the Congo. On the edge of the historic centre, by the public gardens, the convent of San Domenico has been restored by the Miliani mill as the **Museo della Carta e della Filigrana** (*t 0732 709297, www.museodellacarta.com; open Tues–Sat 10–6, Sun 10–12 and 2–5; adm*) to tell you how it's done. The museum has the key for the church of **San Domenico** (*closed for restoration, open for Santa Lucia on 13 Dec*), with frescoes from the 1300s, notably those in the Chapel of Sant'Orsola.

The town centre is a beautiful stage set: the arcaded **Piazza del Comune**, with a crenellated **Palazzo del Podestà** (1250), a Palazzo Comunale and **Fontana Sturinalto** (1281–1351), strangely reminiscent of those in Perugia. Opposite stands a 19th-century theatre and the 17th-century Loggia di San Francesco (currently shored up with breeze blocks and covered in scaffolding) housing the **Grande Museo** (*t 0732 5726; closed for restoration, opens early 2005*). This promises seven rooms of horror, including an electronic King Kong, dinosaurs and other life-size 'creatures of horror', as well as masks, mysteries, birds, tools, crime, prehistory and memories of old Fabriano.

Fabriano was home to a school of painting that produced one of Italy's most influential International Gothic artists, Gentile da Fabriano (*c.* 1370–1427), master of the famous *Adoration of the Magi* in the Uffizi, though his major works (frescoes in the Lateran in Rome and the Doge's palace in Venice) have been lost. If he left anything in Fabriano, it's been lost as well, but there are paintings by other 14th-century members of the school (Allegretto Nuzi, Antonio da Fabriano and Francesuccio di Cecco) along with some detached frescoes and 16th-century Flemish tapestries in the **Pinacoteca Civica Bruno Molajoli** (*t 0732 709255, pinacoteca.civica@comune.fabriano.an.it*). This is closed for restoration, but many of its works are on display in the **Deposito Altrezzato Opera d'Arte** in Via Fontanelle (*t 0732 709230/709319, deposito.altrezzano@comune.fabriano.an.it; open Tues–Sun 10–12.30 and 3–7*), which also houses works moved from churches after the earthquake. The Pinacoteca occupies the former **Ospedale di Santa Maria** (1456) with a fine portico facing Piazza della Cattedrale and the glisteningly restored 14th-century **Cattedrale Basilica di San Venanzio**. Rebuilt in 1607, it retains some original chapels and its tall polygonal apse; there are frescoes on the *Life of St Lawrence* by Fabriano's Allegretto Nuzi and others in a chapel on the left by Orazio Gentileschi, who worked in the Marches in 1615.

Piazza della Cattedrale is one of the prettiest squares in tidy Fabriano. Note the proud 'SPQF' on the fountain and decorative blacksmith's plaque; you'll spot several of these in memory of the ironworking that was Fabriano's stock in trade before it moved on to paper; these days, Fabriano has branched out again, this time into making household appliances.

Around Fabriano

On weekends, the Fabrianese head to the hills to **Poggio San Romualdo** (936m/ 3,070ft), 15km east up a hairpinning road, with woodlands, meadows and a handful of places to sleep and eat. The itinerant St Romualdo founded the nearby **Abbazia di San Salvatore in Val di Castro** in 909 – the crypt remains, though the church was rebuilt in the 1100s.

The Marches' second Verdicchio-growing region, DOC Verdicchio di Matelica, begins just south of Fabriano. Places to aim for include handsome **Cerreto d'Esi**, southeast of Fabriano, encircled by garden walls with the remains of a Byzantine gate and a leaning silo-shaped tower, supposedly built in the time of Justinian. **Matelica**, 7km south (quite badly hit by the earthquake and still being stabilized), is surrounded by industry but its centre is typically Marchigiano, with all the essentials of urban life: a pretty main square, the Piazza Mattei, a civic palace, the **Palazzo Pretorio**, with Roman ruins inside and a clock tower from 1270 (with later touches), a loggia and a 17th-century fountain. The Palazzo Ottoni holds the *municipio*, the **Museo Archeologico** (*www.matelica.sinp.net, open Tues–Fri 11–1; Sat–Sun 11–1 and 5–7; adm*), whose prize exhibit is 2,000-year-old Greek marble globe, thought to be a solar clock, and a **Pinacoteca** (*same hours*). Behind the Palazzo Ottoni, there are pretty Roman mosaics from the 1st century AD (*ask for the key at the tourist office under the loggia, t 0737 85671*).

In the spanking new **Enoteca Comunale e Centro Analisi Sensoriale** (*open Tues–Sun 9–1; Tues, Wed, Fri and Sat 4–7*), under the loggia on Piazza Mattei, you can taste local wines or get a chemical analysis of your *cinghiale* sausages. Matelica also has a fine picture gallery, the **Museo Piersanti**, at Via Umberto I 11 (*t 0737 84445; open Easter–July and Sept–Oct Tues–Sun 10–12 and 5–7; Aug daily 10–12 and 5–7; Nov–Easter Sat–Sun 10–12 and 4–6; adm*), with an exceptional *Crucifixion* by Antonio da Fabriano (1452), and works by Federico Barocci, Guercino and the followers of Raphael; there are other good paintings in the church of **San Francesco**, including a quattrocento triptych by Francesco di Gentile de Fabriano – presumably a relative of the great Gentile.

Esanatoglia, to the west, is very quiet, except for May and June when it roars with the **Coppa Mille Dollari Apiro**, its world champion cross-country motorcycle races.

Ancona

'Filthy hole: like rotten Cabbage. Thrice swindled.'
James Joyce

Just before the city, the mountains once more reach the sea, providing a splendid setting for the mid-Adriatic's biggest port, a crescent-shaped harbour under the steep promontory of Monte Guasco. Here colonists from Syracuse founded the city in the 5th century BC. It was the furthest north the ancient Greeks went in the Adriatic and the colony was never a great success until Roman emperors built it up, especially Trajan, who hired his favourite architect, Apollodoro of Damascus, to lay out the port and town. After the fall of the Roman Empire, Ancona became the leading city of the Byzantine Pentapolis, and along with the other Adriatic ports, was given to the

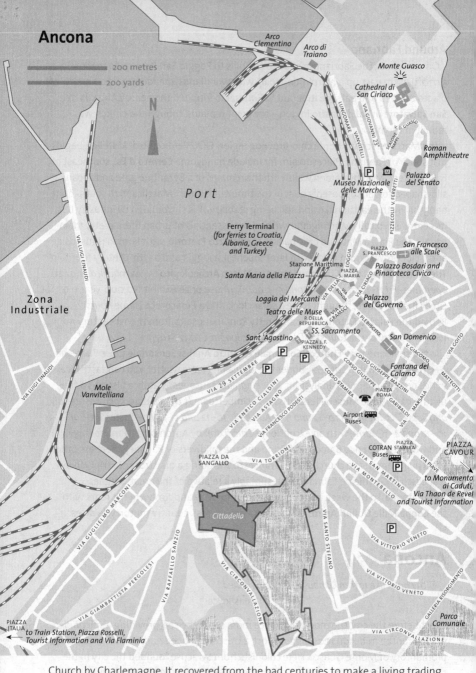

Ancona

200 metres
200 yards

N

Arco Clementino

Arco di Traiano

Monte Guasco

Cathedral di San Ciriaco

Port

Roman Amphitheatre

Palazzo del Senato

Museo Nazionale delle Marche

LUNGOMARE VANVITELLI

VIA GIOVANNI 23°

K. D. GUASCO

SALONE DEI PAPPI

PIZZECOLI V. FERRETTI

Ferry Terminal (for ferries to Croatia, Albania, Greece and Turkey)

Stazione Marittima

Santa Maria della Piazza

Loggia dei Mercanti

Teatro delle Muse

Sant'Agostino

PIAZZA S. FRANCESCO

San Francesco alle Scale

Palazzo Bosdari and Pinacoteca Civica

VIA DELLA LOGGIA

PIAZZA S. MARIA

VIA CIRIACO

VIA DELLA BONDA

VIA ERAMSCI

Palazzo del Governo

P. PLEBISCITO

SS. Sacramento

P. DELLA REPUBBLICA

PIAZZA J. F. KENNEDY

San Domenico

V. GIACOMO

Fontana del Calamo

CORSO GIUSEPPE MAZZINI

VIA GOITO

VIA MATTEOTTI

Zona Industriale

VIA LUIGI EINAUDI

VIA LUIGI EINAUDI

Mole Vanvitelliana

VIA 29 SETTEMBRE

VIA ENRICO CIALDINI

VIA ASTAGNO

VIA FRANCESCO PODESTI

CORSO STAMIRA

CORSO GIUSEPPE GARIBALDI

VIA MARSALA

PIAZZA ROMA

Airport Buses

COTRAN Buses

PIAZZA STAMIRA

PIAZZA CAVOUR

VIA PIAVE

PIAZZA DA SANGALLO

VIA TORRIONI

VIA SAN MARTINO

VIA MONTEBELLO

to Monumento ai Caduti, Via Thaon de Revel and Tourist Information

Cittadella

VIA SANTO STEFANO

VIA VITTORIO VENETO

VIA GUGLIELMO MARCONI

VIA GIAMBATTISTA PERGOLESI

VIA RAFFAELLO SANZIO

VIA CIRCONVALLAZIONE

VIA VITTORIO VENETO

VIA CIRCONVALLAZIONE

GALLERIA RISORGIMENTO

Parco Comunale

PIAZZA ITALIA

to Train Station, Piazza Rosselli, Tourist Information and Via Flaminia

Church by Charlemagne. It recovered from the bad centuries to make a living trading with Dalmatia and the east, although its never-ending battles, with Venice on the seas and on land against the emperors, as well as the lords of Jesi, Rimini and Macerata, never allowed it the leisure to blossom as a maritime republic in the style of Venice, Pisa or Genoa, even though it was independent in all but name. Only in 1532 did the Medici pope Clement VII reassert the authority of the Church, moving in a papal army and constructing a citadel to house them.

Our own century has been murderous to Ancona. The Austrians bombarded it in 1915, an earthquake damaged it in 1930, and the British and Americans bombed it again, thoroughly, in 1944. Then came a major flood, a serious earthquake in 1972, and after that, a landslide that caused the abandonment of parts of the old town. For all its troubles, **Ancona** (pop. 101,000) has come up smiling. The port is prospering, and even though most of the population now lives in newer faceless districts to the south and west, the city is devoting its attention to the restoration of the historic centre.

Around the Port

Most of Ancona's monuments have survived the recent misfortunes, although many are a little the worse for wear. At its western end, the long curve of the port is anchored by the **Mole Vanvitelliana**, a pentagonal building designed in 1733 by Neapolitan architect Luigi Vanvitelli, the court architect of the Bourbons at Naples. Although it looks like a fortress, the Mole really served as Ancona's *lazaretto* or quarantine station; it now hosts temporary exhibitions. At the other end of the port, the tall, graceful **Arco di Traiano** was built in AD 115, in honour of Ancona's imperial benefactor; the sculptural reliefs have disappeared, but it is one of the better preserved in Italy. Nearby, Pope Clement XII had Vanvitelli erect an **Arco Clementino** to himself (1733) as Ancona's papal benefactor (he declared the city a duty-free port).

At the centre of the port, the elegant 15th-century Venetian Gothic **Loggia dei Mercanti**, the merchants' exchange, is the best souvenir of Ancona's heyday as a free maritime city. Just in from here, Ancona's 19th-century **Teatro delle Muse** (*t 071 52525/071 207841*), now restored after bomb damage in 1943, and the church of **Santissimo Sacramento**, dominate the Piazza Repubblica. Corso Garibaldi leads back to where Ancona's business centre has gravitated, around the broad Piazza Cavour. In Piazza Kennedy around the corner, 15th-century **Sant'Agostino** has an elaborate Venetian Gothic portal. At twilight, you can walk from here along Via Cialdini to Piazza da Sangallo, just under Clement VII's citadel, to see 'the most beautiful sunset in the world', according to Goethe, who was so overwhelmed by the sun, art and sex that nearly everything he wrote about it in his *Italian Travels* was either mush or wrong.

To see the oldest quarters of Ancona, you'll have to climb a little as well, starting up Via Gramsci. Off on a little square to the left, the 13th-century church of **Santa Maria della Piazza** (*open daily 7.30–7*) has a great late Romanesque façade with figures of musicians and soldiers and odd animals carved by a 'Master Phillippus'. A window has been installed in the pavement to allow you to see underneath, to the extensive ruins of the church's predecessors, from the 5th and 6th centuries.

Up and to the right of this, under the Renaissance decorative arch of the handsome **Palazzo del Governo** (designed by Francesco di Giorgio Martini in 1484) extends the elongated **Piazza del Plebiscito**, graced with a statue of Clement XII (1738), who was determined to leave his mark on Ancona, if not on history. At the top of the piazza, ramps and steps lead up to **San Domenico** (*open daily 8–12 and 3–7.30*), built in the 13th century, rebuilt in 1788, and frequently battered and repaired. Step in to see

Getting There and Around

By Air

Ancona's Raffaello Sanzio **airport** is 10km north at Falconara, **t** 071 28271 or **t** 071 282 7491, *www.ancona-airport.com*, with daily flights from Rome, Milan, London and Munich, and several flights a week from Bucharest and Moscow.

In Ancona, the terminal for **airport buses** is on Piazza Cavour. CONERO buses run hourly from the airport to Ancona and Falconara (tickets from the *tabacchi* in the airport).

There are regular **trains** from the airport to Ancona, Jesi, Fabriano and Foligna.

Airport **taxis t** 071 918221.

By Rail

Ancona lies at the intersection of the Adriatic coast and Ancona–Rome routes, with no long waits in either direction. The **station** is west of the port on Piazza Rosselli (bus no.1 or 3 to or from Piazza Repubblica near the port). A few trains go on to Ancona Marittima station on the port itself.

Rail info: t 892021 (enquiries) or **t** 071 42250 (bookings) 199 166177, *www.trenitalia.com*.

By Bus

RENI buses (**t** 071 804 6430, **f** 071 286 8409) to the Conero Riviera via Camerano depart from Piazza Cavour. For towns in the province (Jesi, Recanati, Osimo, Castelfidardo, Loreto, Senigallia, and in summer, Portonovo), CONERO buses (**t** 071 280 2092, *www.conerobus.it*) leave from Piazza Cavour; many also stop at the railway station.

By Sea

There are plenty of **ferries** for Greece, Albania, Croatia and Turkey. If you're heading to Greece, taking the ferry from here is moderately better than making the long train trip down to Brindisi, Bari or Otranto. Fares are only slightly higher; both are overnight trips. All the ferry companies have offices in the Stazione Marittima; these often open only at sailing times.

Agencia Marittima, Via XXIX Settembre 10, **t** 071 5021 1621, **f** 071 202296 (bookings),

ticket.adn@frittellimaritime.it. Can help to find a service or company.

To Croatia (Split and Dubrovnik):

SNAV, t 071 207 6116, **f** 071 54859, *www.snav.it*. Hydrofoil, summer only.

Jadrolinja, Booking office Piazza Repubblica 20, **t** 071 204305, **f** 071 200211; Stazione Marittima, **t** 071 207 1465, **f** 071 207 9272, *www.jadrolinja.hr*.

SEM, Via della Loggia 6, **t** 071 55218, **f** 071 20618.

For hydrofoils out to the islands on the Dalmatian coast:

Miatrade, Via della Loggia 1, **t** 071 204516, **f** 071 56256.

For Croatia, Albania and Montenegro:

Adriatica, (also Greece) Via XXIX Settembre 10, **t** 071 5021 1621, **f** 071 202296, *www.adriatica.it*.

To Greece (Corfu and Patras):

Minoan Lines, Via Astagno 1, **t** 071 201708, **f** 071 201933, Stazione Marittima **t** 071 56789, **f** 071 200207, *www.minoan.it*. The nicest boats, but slightly higher fares.

Anek Lines, Via XXIX Settembre 2, **t** 071 207 2346, **f** 071 207 7904, *www.anekitalia.com*; Stazione Marittima **t** 071 207 2275, **f** 071 207 6387.

Superfast, Via XXIX Settembre 2/0, **t** 071 202033/4, **f** 071 200885; Stazione Marittima **t** 071 207 0218, *www.superfast.com*.

Marlines (also to Turkey), c/o SATIMA, Via di Vittorio 8, **t** 071 286 6713, **f** 071 286 6734. Also **Adriatica** (*see* above).

To Turkey:

Topas, Piazza S. Maria 2, **t** 071 202806, **f** 071 52956. Also **Marlines** (*see* above).

Car Rental

Avis, t 071 44241.
Hertz, t 071 41314.
Maggiore Budget, t 071 42624.

Tourist Information

Ancona: Via Thaon de Revel 4, **t** 071 358991, **f** 071 358 0592, *www.comune.ancona.it*. Open *Mon–Sat 9–1 and 3–6, Sun 9–1*.
Branch offices: at the railway station, on Piazza Rosselli (no telephone);
in the port, **t** 071 201183, summer only.

Where to Stay

Ancona ✉ 60100

Well, Goethe spent a night or two here, but unless you're just coming or going, you may prefer to head on down to the Conero Riviera to find yourself a quieter base (*see* p.617).

Very expensive

★★★★**Grand Hotel Palace**, Lungomare Vanvitelli 24, **t** 071 201813, **f** 071 207 4832, *www.alberghiancona.it*. The finest hotel, by the port near Arco di Traiano. Comfy and small, in a 17th-century palace, with a roof garden with magnificent views over the port, but no restaurant.

★★★★**Grand Hotel Passetto**, Via Thaon de Revel 1, **t** 071 31307, **f** 071 32856, *www.hotel passetto.it*. Similar; central but modern, with a pool in summer.

Moderate

★★★**Fortuna**, Piazza Rosselli 15, **t** 071 42663, **f** 071 42662, *www.hotelfortuna.it* The nicest near the station; convenient and comfortable if you're coming and going.

★★★**Della Rosa**, Piazza Rosselli 3, **t** 071 42651, **f** 071 41388, *www.hoteldellarosa.it*. Near the station; nice rooms, not all en suite.

★★**Viale**, Viale della Vittoria 23, **t/f** 071 201861. More tranquillity and lower prices, nearly 1km out of the centre.

Inexpensive

★★**Dorico**, Via Flaminia 8, **t/f** 071 42761. By the station; simple rooms, with or without bath.

★★**Gino**, Via Flaminia 4, **t** 071 42179 (hotel), **t** 071 43310 (restaurant), *hotel.gino@ tiscalinet.it*. Its restaurant (*moderate*) has excellent fresh seafood. *Closed Sun.*

Eating Out

The dish to try here is *stoccafisso all'anconetana*, dried cod exquisitely prepared in a casserole with tomatoes, potatoes and marjoram. Nearly every port in Italy developed a taste for dried cod in the Middle Ages, when barrel-loads from England and the Baltic passed through in exchange for wine; here it's preferred even to the day's catch from the Adriatic. Another local speciality is *brodetto*, a soup made with many kinds of fish.

Very Expensive–Expensive

La Moretta, Piazza Plebiscito 52, **t** 071 202317. This handsome 19th-century building has long been a favourite with the townspeople for its excellent *stoccafisso all'anconetana* and *spaghetti agli scampi*. *Closed Sun.*

Passetto, Piazzale IV Novembre, **t** 071 33214. An excellent seafood place with a seaside terrace, offering a less pricy set menu featuring meat dishes, including wine. *Closed Sun eve, Mon and 2nd–3rd weeks Aug.*

Moderate

Carloni, Via Flaminia 247, out of Ancona to the north at Torrette, **t** 071 888239. Another hot spot for seafood; reasonable prices, it sits right between the sea and the rail tracks, so your mussels rattle when trains pass. *Closed Mon.*

Corte, Via della Loggia 5, **t** 071 200806. Set in an elegant 18th-century palace near the port, with a very pretty summer garden, and excellent gourmet dishes, including fish. *Closed Sun and Jan.*

Cheap

Like any self-respecting port, Ancona has dozens of *trattorie* where you can put away some less grandiose marine delights at inconceivably low prices.

La Cantinetta, Via Gramsci, **t** 071 201107. Just around the corner, this offers a foretaste of Greece if you're hopping on a ferry, complete with Greek seamen fingering worry beads. It is one of the most popular places in town, though certainly not for its décor; it's famed for its *stoccafisso*, its nightly fish fry, traditional *vincisgrassi* and, oddly enough, lemon sorbet. *Closed Mon.*

Da Irma, Piazza S. Primiano, **t** 071 53110. A classic family-run *trattoria* with simple traditional cooking, right by the port. *Closed Tues.*

Osteria del Pozzo, Via Bonda 2, **t** 071 207 3996. Elegant and right in the middle of the port; try the mixed fry or seafood pasta of the day. *Closed Sun and Aug.*

Titian's *Crucifixion* (1558) on the high altar, and Guercino's *Annunciation*, just to the left. Below it, on Corso Mazzini, Ancona is proud of the pretty **Fontana del Calamo** with its 13 spouts designed by Pellegrino Tibaldi in 1560.

To the left of Santa Maria della Piazza, at Via Pizzecolli 17, the late Renaissance **Palazzo Bosdari** houses the small collection of Ancona's **Pinacoteca Comunale** (*t 071 222 5041; open Tues–Sat 9–7, Mon 9–1, Sun 3–7; adm*). Here is a masterpiece of the eccentric but endearing Carlo Crivelli: a *Madonna col Bambino*, complete with Crivelli's trademark apples and cucumbers hanging overhead. Other Madonnas include one in a *Sacra Conversazione* by Lorenzo Lotto (one of his good ones) and one of Titian's, floating smugly on a cloud, and a 16th-century view of Ancona by Andrea Lilli. Another two blocks up takes you to **San Francesco delle Scale**, another theatrically set church on a stair, with another charming Gothic portal and, inside, a large lush altarpiece of the *Assumption* by Lotto.

On Monte Guasco

Further up, Via Pizzecolli changes its name to Via del Guasco, in an area where bits of decorative brickwork from Roman Ancona's theatre peek out between and under the ruined buildings. This was the area hardest hit by the earthquake and landslide, and only in 1988 did the **Museo Archeologico Nazionale delle Marche** reopen (*t 071 202602; open Tues–Sun 8.30–7.30; adm*), in a 16th-century palace at Via Feretti 6. Its rich archaeological collection includes some exceptional Greek vases and metalwork, Etruscan bronzes, gold and amber from Gaulish and Piceni tombs, as well as an extensive collection of Roman finds (*the Roman and medieval sections are currently being rearranged*). Also damaged in 1972 was the 13th-century **Palazzo del Senato** around the corner, Ancona's capital when it was a self-governing *comune*.

Ancona's pink and white **Cattedrale di San Ciriaco** (*t 071 52688; open daily autumn– winter 8–12 and 3–6, spring–summer 8–12 and 3–7*) crowns Monte Guasco, the ancient Greek acropolis, once the site of a famous temple of Venus. To reach it, either climb the long garden stairway, the **Scalone Nappi,** or catch the no.11 bus from Piazza Cavour or Piazza Repubblica to the top, or drive up from the port. Unusually for a church this far north, the 11th-century cathedral shows a strong influence from the Puglian Romanesque. The fancy Gothic porch is by Margaritone d'Arezzo and the sculpted portals and detached campanile were both added about 1200. Inside, the marble columns came originally from the Temple of Venus, some crowned with Byzantine capitals; there's an unusual polygonal cupola and a 12th-century, elaborately carved altar screen in the right transept. The cathedral is dedicated to St Cyriacus, the converted Jew who revealed the whereabouts of the True Cross to St Helen (*see* **Florence**, Santa Croce, p.163) and, in a clever piece of 4th-century propaganda, was said to have been martyred by the virtuous but non-Christian Emperor Julian the Apostate; the saint's perfectly pickled body is contained in the Rococo casket. There is a small **Museo Diocesano** (*t 071 200391 /071 52688; open winter Sun 4–6, April–Sept Sun 5–7, at other times by appointment*) with a fine 4th-century Christian sarcophagus, reliquaries and architectural fragments from the cathedral (9th–12th century).

Around Ancona: The Conero Riviera

The arm of the Apennines that stretches down to shelter Ancona's port creates a short but beautiful stretch of Adriatic coast. South of Ancona, the cliffs of **Monte Conero** (572m/1,876ft) plunge steeply into the sea, forcing the railway and coastal highway to bend inland, and isolating beautiful beaches and coves only a few kilometres from Ancona; it's now a Parco Naturale and is very crowded in summer.

Tourist Information

Sirolo: *iat.sirolo@regione.marche.it.*
Piazza Dante, **t** 071 933 1749.
Via Peschiera, **t** 071 933 0611.
Numana: Piazza del Santuario, **t** 071 933 0612, *iat.numana@regione.marche.it.* *Open April–Sept only.*

Where to Stay and Eat

Portonovo ✉ 60020

★★★★**Fortino Napoleonico**, Via Poggio 166, **t** 071 801450, **f** 071 801454, *www.hotelfortino.it* (*very expensive*).This award-winning hotel incorporates a fortress built in the Napoleonic Wars; it's quiet and modern, with its own beach, tennis courts and pool. The restaurant is one of the Marches' finest, with two beautiful dining rooms and immaculate service; don't miss the painting of the staff and guests decked out in Napoleonic garb. Eight superb courses include stuffed olives and scampi, sole stuffed with spinach, cream and smoked salmon, shrimps with fennel and orange, gnocchi with caviar, and more.
★★★★**Emilia**, Collina di Portonno, **t** 071 801145, **f** 071 801330, *www.hotelemilia.com* (*expensive*). Luxurious, in a lovely setting. Artists are invited to stay free in exchange for a painting and the place has many pictures, including one by Graham Sutherland. *Closed Christmas–mid-Feb.*
★★★**Internazionale**, Via Portonovo 149, **t** 071 801 001, **f** 071 801 082, *www. hotel-internazionale* (*moderate*). A sturdy stone building in the trees, with ravishing views above the bay, its own beach and a good restaurant.
Il Laghetto, near Portonovo's lake, **t** 071 801183 (*moderate*). A great place to feast on fish and *frutti di mare*, prepared in some unusual

ways. *Closed Mon and mid-Jan–end Feb, also Sun lunch Sept–Jan.*

Sirolo ✉ 60020

★★★**Locanda Rocco**, Via Turnione 1, **t/f** 071 933 0558, *www.locandarocco.it* (*very expensive*). A charming, stylish 14th-century inn. The restaurant (*expensive*) with terrace serves modern Italian cuisine. *March, April, May, Oct only. Closed Tues Mar–May and Nov–Feb*
★★★**Monte Conero**, built around the Badia di San Pietro, **t** 071 933 0592, **f** 071 933 0365, *www.hotelmonteconero.it* (*expensive*). A great place to get-away-from-it-all, in a sublime setting near the top of the headland, with a pool, restaurant (*moderate–cheap*) and tennis. *Closed mid-Nov–mid-Mar.*

Numana ✉ 60026

Numana has some pretty dismal spots, but there are one or two worth knowing.
★★★**Gigli Eden**, Via Morelli 11, **t** 071 933 0652, **f** 071 933 0930, *www.giglihotels.it* (*moderate*). A little pricy, but it's worth the bill, having nice rooms with a view, two pools, tennis and huge grounds with plenty of trees. There's a secluded private beach, but it's a climb back up. *Closed Nov–Easter.*
★★★**Majestic**, Via Roma 4, **t** 071 933 0614, **f** 071 933 0167 (*moderate*). In the centre, within walking distance of the beach, with simple, comfortable rooms; full board is optional in summer. *Closed Oct–March.*
★★**Teresa a Mare**, Via del Golfo 26, **t/f** 071 933 0623, *www.rivieradelconero.it* (*expensive*). *Closed Oct–Easter.*

For something a little more rustic:
Il Granaio di Valcastagno, Via Valcastagno 10, **t** 071 739 1580, **f** 071 739 2776, *www.val castagno.com* (*expensive*). In the farm buildings of an 18th century noble's house, with sailing and riding. *Minimum stay one week in summer.*

Portonovo

From the city, the Conero road between sea and mountain passes after some 7km the cliff of Trave, so-called for a rock formation that resembles a beam (*trave*), dropping sheerly down to the sea. A little further on, a side road to the left leads down to **Portonovo**, tucked under the cliffs and the most beautiful place for a swim in these parts, with a pebble beach. Besides the beach, three campsites and a little lake, there's a lovely church of the 1030s, once part of a Benedictine abbey, and built in the same style as Ancona cathedral. The recently restored **Santa Maria di Portonovo** (*t 071 56307; open summer Tues–Sun 4–7; winter Sun 10–12*) is one of the better Romanesque churches in the north; Dante mentions it – 'the House of Our Lady on the Adriatic coast' in the 21st canto of *Paradiso*. Portonovo has a small fortress, the Fortino Napoleonico (now a hotel: *see* 'Where to Stay and Eat', p.617), and a watchtower built by Pope Clement XII in 1716 – even at that late date, there was worry about pirates. Much earlier, some of the local pirates hung out at the nearby **Grotta degli Schiavi** – *schiavi* in this case meaning Slavs, not slaves, refugees from across the Adriatic. The grotto faces a sheltered cove popular with divers.

South of Portonovo, the road curves inland around **Monte Conero** proper. A road from Sirolo leads to the mountain's summit and the remains of an 11th-century Camaldolese abbey, **San Pietro**, with interesting capitals, now partially a hotel (*see* 'Where to Stay and Eat', p.617). On its inland slopes, Conero is green and luxuriant; in this direction the view takes in a wide stretch of the Apennines, as far south as the highest peak in the range, the Gran Sasso d'Italia in Abruzzo. Somebody, apparently, was enjoying it 100,000 years ago; near the summit archaeologists dug up the oldest traces of human settlement yet discovered in the Marches.

Sirolo and Numana

On the southern slope of Conero are two attractive but often very crowded resorts. **Sirolo** is a medieval village on the cliffs high above the sea, its highest point marked by a 15th-century church and a former Franciscan convent; near its entrance are two holm oaks planted by St Francis himself in 1215. Sirolo has a beach nearby and the lovely beach of **Due Sorelle**, behind the sea rocks under the stretch of jagged white cliffs called **Sassi Bianchi**. Merging with Sirolo, **Numana** has Numana Alta, with a beach tucked under the cliff, while Numana Bassa has a long sandy one and boats out to the swimming holes off the Due Sorelle islets. The Greeks arrived in Numana in the 8th century BC to set up a trading counter with the Piceni, and it grew into an important town, a bishopric from the 5th to the 15th centuries. At its centre, Piazza del Santuario, the **Santuario del Crocifisso** (*t 071 933 1026; open daily 9.30–12 and 4–7*) is a pilgrimage site for its miraculous icon, a crucifix painted by St Luke and St Nicodemus (a less pious opinion calls it a Byzantine-inspired work from 13th-century Poland). Numana also has an **Antiquarium** (*t 071 933 1162; open daily 8.30–7.30; adm*) at Via La Fenice 4, where artefacts show the evolution of the Piceni culture. Just inland are pretty rolling hills, dotted with oaks and pale pink villas, all along the narrow roads set up by the local wine consortium of DOC Rosso Conero. The wine is robust and full of character, based on Montepulciano grapes; Marchetti is a reputed label.

Sweet Music: Castelfidardo and Osimo

South of Ancona, the slightly dishevelled town of **Castelfidardo** is the accordion capital; they say the instrument was invented here in the 1870s. The **Museo Internazionale della Fisarmonica**, Via Mordini (*t 071 7808 288; open winter Mon–Sat 10–12 and 4.30–6.30, Sun 10–12; summer Mon–Sat 10–12 and 4–7, Sun 10–12; adm*) will fill in any gaps in your knowledge. The accordion industry's peak year was 1953, when 200,000 were exported from Italy alone. In October the town hosts the International Accordion Soloists' Competition. In 1860, the town witnessed a comic-opera skirmish: the Battle of Castelfidardo, where King Vittorio Emanuele II vanquished the rag-tag legions of the pope, allowed the Piemontese to look heroic in completing Italy's year of unification – after the hard work had been done by Garibaldi and his Thousand. A monument to the Piemontese General Cialdini, on a cypress-lined avenue, commemorates the event.

Venerable **Osimo**, 3km up the road, began life as a capital of the Piceni in the 9th century BC and was occupied by the Greeks of Ancona, and then by the Romans, who called it *Auximum*. Its neighbours call people from Osimo '*senza teste*' because of the 12 headless Roman statues in the entrance and *atrium* of the 17th-century **Palazzo Comunale,** overlooking the piazza that once held Osimo's forum.

At the highest point in town, the 13th-century Romanesque-Gothic cathedral of **San Leopardo** (*t 071 715396, open daily 8–1 and 4–8*), dedicated to Osimo's first bishop has some quirky medieval details: a rose window circled with little monsters, a fine *tympanum* carved with the Virgin and Apostles, who seem to be humming, with a figure resembling Jack in the beanstalk on top, and a second door framed by two snakes, slithering up to share an egg. The style of the reliefs over the portals, with the eyes 'holed in', seems to have been copied from the 4th-century Luni marble sarcophagus in the crypt, showing the story of Noah, Jonah and a hunt; there's also a 4th-century sarcophagus of St Leopardo, and a late medieval tomb of St Vitaliano and a wide variety of second-hand capitals holding up the vault. Next to the cathedral, the 12th-century **baptistery** (*now the Museo Diocesano, t 071 715396 or t 071 723 1808; open June Sat 4–7, Sun 10–12 and 4–7, other days by appt; July–mid-Sept daily 10–12 and*

Tourist Information

Castelfidardo: Piazza della Repubblica 6, **t** 071 782 2987, *proloco@tiscalinet.it.*
Osimo: Via Bordimare 9, **t** 071 714440.

Where to Stay and Eat

Castelfidardo ✉ 60022

★★★★**Parco**, Via Donizetti 2, **t** 071 782 1605, **f** 071 782 0309, *www.hotelparco.net* (*moderate*). Near the town's pretty park; mod cons but no restaurant.

Osimo ✉ 60027

★★★**Cristoforo Colombo**, on the SS16, 6km east, **t** 071 710 8990, **f** 071 710 8994, *www. cristoforo-colombo.com* (*expensive*). Comfortable and home to the best local restaurant (*see below*).
★★★**La Fonte**, Via Fonte Magna 33, **t** 071 714767, **f** 071 713 3547 (*moderate*). A quiet, functional place, with lovely views, by the Roman walls.
Cantinetta del Conero, next to Cristoforo Colombo Hotel, SS16, **t** 071 710 8651 (*moderate*). Worth knowing for the good, fresh fish. *Closed Sat and 2 wks in Aug.*

4–8; Aug also Fri and Sat 9pm–11pm; adm) has a remarkably ornate frescoed ceiling of 1629 and a splendid bronze baptismal font by the Jacometti brothers of Recanati.

Down from Piazza del Comune, in early 17th-century **Palazzo Gallo** (now the Cassa di Risparmio bank), ask to see the Salone delle Feste, frescoed by Pomarancio with the *Judgement of Solomon*. Behind it, a huge brick 13th-century Franciscan church acquired baroque decoration inside when it became the **Santuario di San Giuseppe da Copertino**, dedicated to the flying friar from Puglia (d. 1663) who, as a nearly daily occurrence, would soar from the church door over the heads of his parishioners to the altar. One of Italy's most popular 17th-century saints, Giuseppe spent his last years in the convent here, which now has a little museum of his life. One chapel has an elaborate *Enthroned Virgin and Saints* by Antonio Solario. Below this, in Via Fonte Magna, are the remains of a Roman wall and **fountain** or *nymphaeum*. Piazza Dante is the site of the 17th-century **Palazzo Campana**, containing Osimo's **Museo Civico** (*t 071 714621; open 15 June–15 Sept Tues–Sat 5pm–8pm, Sun 10–12.30 and 5–7; winter Tues–Sat 5.30–7, Sun 10–12.30 and 5.30–7; free guided tours*) with a handful of paintings, including the beautiful, retro (for 1464) golden polyptych by the Viviani brothers of Venice (formerly in the Mayor's office).

The Southern Marches

'Infinite Places': Loreto, Recanati and Around

The local tourist offices have concocted this slogan from one of Leopardi's most famous poems, the *Colle dell'Infinito*, referring to the never-ending panorama of hills from his native Recanati melting in the distance. You can do all four towns in a day, perhaps beginning or ending at a pretty Adriatic resort, Porto Recanati.

Porto Recanati

In 1229, Emperor Frederick II rewarded Recanati's fidelity with a port and long sandy beach, and threw in the **Castello Svevo**; nearly destroyed in an attack by Turkish pirates in 1518, it was rebuilt and still serves as a focal point for **Porto Recanati**. In 1927, the castle courtyard was made into the Arena Beniamino Gigli, after the great tenor whose summer villa still stands at Montarice, along the Loreto road; in the summer, it hosts films, plays and opera. One castle tower now holds the **Pinacoteca Moroni** (*t 071 759 1283, open Mon–Fri 4–7*) with mainly 19th- and early 20th-century paintings (especially by the *Macchiaoli*), and minor works by Zurbaran, Ribera, Rosso Fiorentino, Millet, Maratta and Salvator Rosa.

Just south of Porto Recanati, along the SS16, archaeologists are excavating the Roman colony of **Potentia** (*t 071 759971 or t 071 979 9084, free guided tours Mon pm and Fri pm*), dating from 184 BC and lasting into the 5th century as a bishopric. There are remains of a temple, portico, houses with frescoed walls and mosaic pavements, a bridge and a noble's tomb. Near here, the **Abbey of Santa Maria in**

Potentia dates from the 12th century, although only its Romanesque apse survives intact; a rest stop for pilgrims to Loreto for hundreds of years, Napoleon gave it to his sister Pauline and her husband, Prince Camillo Borghese as a villa, and so it has remained (*visits as for Potentia*).

Loreto

The inventor of the accordion, the story goes, got his inspiration when an Austrian pilgrim on his way to **Loreto** left behind a button-box as a gift. This town (pop. 10,780) has been one of the most popular pilgrimage sites in Europe since the 1300s.

Like Urbino, Loreto is a small but concentrated dose of Renaissance fine art. Its story is a mystery of the faith. During the 1200s, the Church found itself threatened on all

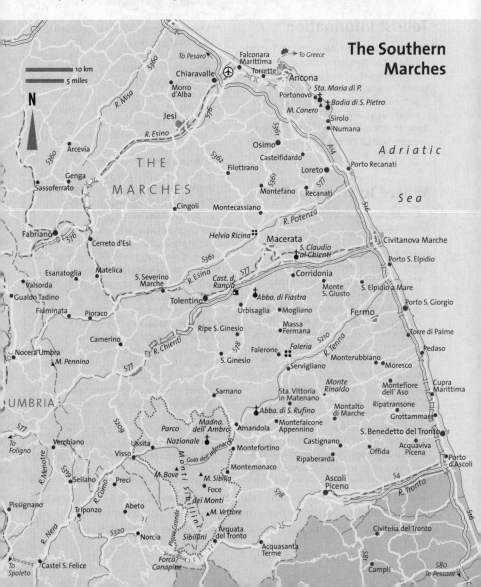

Getting There and Around

Buses link Loreto station with the town. CONERO buses (t 071 202766) from Ancona run frequently to Loreto and Recanati via Osimo and Castelfidardo; CONTRAM buses (t 0737 63401/0737 632402) link Porto Recanati to Loreto, Recanati and Macerata, along the coast, and there's one bus a day linking Loreto to Camerino and Tolentino and Sarnano.

Port Recanati train station, t 071 979 9162.
Loreto train station, t 071 978668.

Tourist Information

Porto Recanati: Corso Matteotti 111, t/f 071 979 9084, *iat.portorecanti@regione.marche.it*. Open Mon–Sat 9–1 and 4–7, Sun 9–1.

Loreto: Via Solari 3, t 071 970276, f 071 970020, *iat.loreto@regione.marche.it*. Open Mon–Sat 9–1 and 4–7, Sun 9–1.

Recanati: Piazza G. Leopardi 31, t/f 071 981471, *recanti.iat@tin.it*. Open Mon–Sat 9–1, Thurs and Sat also 4–7.

Where To Stay and Eat

Another stretch of beach with plenty of accommodation.

Porto Recanati ✉ 62017

★★★★**Enzo**, Corso Matteotti 21–23, t 071 759 0734, f 071 979 9029, *www.hotelenzo.it* (*expensive*). Top for creature comforts and near the port, with minibars, air conditioning, a good restaurant and a garage.

★★★**Bianchi Vincenzo**, Via Garibaldi 15, t 071 979 9040, f 071 7599 8231, *www.hotelbianchi. com* (*moderate*). Good for families, with its suites (some with kitchenettes) which sleep up to five. *Closed mid–Dec–mid-Jan.*

★★★**Giannino**, Via C. Colombo 25 (Lungomare nord) t 071 979 9141 f 071 979 9289, *www.conerohotelgiannino.com* (*moderate*). North of the centre, but situated on the sea with pretty views, this has modern seaside rooms in a nice and quiet location.

Il Diavolo del Brodetto, Lungomare 136, t 071 979 9251 (*expensive*). The best place to eat fresh fish on this stretch of coast. Simple *antipasti di mare, spaghetti alle cozze* and *frittura di pesce fresco* – right on the sea front. Get there early or book. *Closed Mon.*

Fatatis, Via Vespucci 2, t 071 979 9366 (*moderate, meat cheaper than fish*). Excellent Marchigiano cuisine on a pretty, panoramic terrace. *Closed Mon 1–10 Jan.*

Loreto ✉ 60025

Some of the most pleasant choices are outside the centre.

★★★★**Villa Tetlameya**, Via Villa Costantina 187, Loreto Archi, t 071 978863, f 071 976639, *www.loretoitaly.com* (*expensive*). An elegant 19th-century villa that has the most comfortable rooms in the area, as well as one of the best restaurants (*see below*).

★★★**Blu Hotel**, Via Villa Constantina 89, t 071 978501, f 071 978439, *www.hotelbluloreto.it* (*moderate*). Nearby, with simple but pleasant rooms.

★★★**Vecchia Fattoria**, Via Manzoni 19, t 071 978976, f 071 978962, *lavecchiafattoriasrl@ virgilio.it* (*inexpensive; restaurant moderate*). The local favourite for weddings and banquets. *Closed Mon.*

In the centre hotels are invariably clean, quiet and respectable, with a crucifix above every bed. Many are run by religious orders.

★★★**Casa del Clero Madonna di Loreto**, Via Asdrubali 104, t 071 970298, f 071 750 0532, *www.lopretoalberghi.it* (*inexpensive*). With 32 rooms, all with bath.

★★**Centrale**, Via Solari 7, t 071 970173, f 071 750 0219 (*inexpensive*). A more secular atmosphere, slightly cheaper. *Closed Jan.*

Andreina, Via Buffolareccia 14, t 071 970124 (*moderate*). This place has been here for donkey's years, serving grilled meats and Marchigiano specialities. *Closed Tues and end of June 2 wks.*

Zì Nene, Via Villa Costantina 187, at the Villa Tetlameya (*moderate*). Classic sea-food and historical Marchigiano recipes. *Closed Mon.*

sides by heretical movements and freethinkers. The popes responded in various subtle ways to assimilate and control them; creating the Franciscan movement was one, and the encouragement of the cult of the Virgin Mary another. Conveniently enough, a legend of a miracle in the Marches gained wide currency. Mary's house in Nazareth – site of the Annunciation and where the Holy Family lived after their return from Egypt – was transported by a band of angels to a hill in Istria on 10 May 1291, then decided to fly off again on 9 December 1294, this time landing in these laurel woods (*loreti*) south of Ancona. Supposedly the house had bestirred itself in protest over Muslim reoccupation of the Holy Land; the popes were thumping the tub for a new Crusade and Loreto was just coincidentally located on the route to the Crusader ports on the Adriatic. Among the thousands of devout pilgrims to make their way here were Galileo, Montaigne and Descartes.

Since the 1960s, archaeologists and scholars had a closer look. When they compared the Santa Casa with other buildings in the grotto of Nazareth (now in the Basilica of the Annunciation) they found that the stones of the Holy House are similar to those in the Grotto, that they date from the same period, and that the Hebrew-Christian graffiti cut in the stones of the Holy House is very similar to that in Nazareth. The Holy House, they also found, has no foundation, but sits in the middle of an old road. But it appears angels had little to do with its removal: a recently discovered document dated September 1294 refers to the dowry given by the Nikeforos Angelo, king of Epirus, to his daughter when she wed Philip of Taranto, son of the Angevin King of Naples, Charles II, which included 'the holy stones carried away from the House of Our Lady.' When the Crusaders lost Palestine in 1291, apparently Nikeforos had the house in Nazareth dismantled and took the stones with him to keep them from falling into Muslim hands, and they ended up here.

The Santuario della Santa Casa

t 071 970104, www.santuarioloreto.it; Basilica open daily Oct–Mar 6.45am–7pm April–Sept 6.15am–8pm; Santa Casa closed 12.30–2.30.

Beginning in 1468, the simple church that originally housed the **Santa Casa** was reconstructed and embellished in a huge building programme that took over a century to complete. Corso Boccalini, lined with the inevitable souvenir stands, leads from the town centre up to the sanctuary, which suddenly materializes in all its glory when you turn a corner and enter the enclosed **Piazza della Madonna**, with the church, a great fountain by Carlo Maderno, one of the architects of St Peter's, the **Palazzo Apostolico**, and its elegant **loggia** by Bramante, enclosing the square. This being a papal production, a big bronze statue of Sixtus V, in front of the church doors, dominates the piazza – many of the most important figures in the Roman art world had a hand in the work. In the summer, this space is often filled up with white trainloads of sick people, in the hopes that Loreto's Madonna may succeed where modern medicine has fallen short.

The sanctuary's understated façade is typical early Roman Baroque, though a little ahead of its time (1587); no one is perfectly sure to whom they should ascribe it, since so many architects had a hand in the work. Giuliano da Sangallo built the cupola, almost a copy of Brunelleschi's great dome in Florence, Bramante did the side chapels, and Sansovino and Sangallo the Younger also contributed. One of the best features is the series of reliefs on the bronze doors by the Lombardis and other artists; another is the circle of radiating brick **apses** on the east end, turreted like a Renaissance castle; be sure to walk around for a look. Apparently the original architects really did intend the back of the church, overlooking the town walls, to function as part of the fortifications, a bookend to Antonio da Sangallo the Younger's round bastion by Piazza Garibaldi at the far end of town. The only unfortunate element in the ensemble is the ungainly neoclassical **campanile**, topped with a bronze-plated garlic bulb. Luigi Vanvitelli designed it in the 1750s. Don't blame the architect for the proportions; the tower had to be squat and strong to hold the 15-tonne bell.

Chapels line the walls inside, embellished by the faithful from nations around the world, including the United States and Mexico. The sedate Spanish chapel is one of the better ones, the Knights of Malta's chapel has one of the goriest Crucifixes in all Italy, and the English chapel holds a memory of the lyric poet Richard Crashaw, who served as canon here until his death in the 1640s. A good deal of Loreto's art was swiped by Napoleon, and consequently, most of the paintings in the interior are from the last two centuries; the two **sacristies** on the right aisle have fine frescoes by Luca Signorelli and Melozzo da Forli (with 3-D angels, and a beautiful *Christ entering Jerusalem*). Under the dome, you'll see the object of the pilgrims' attention. The **Santa Casa**, a simple brick room with traces of medieval frescoes, contains the venerated black Madonna of Loreto, sculpted out of cedar in 1921, after the original was destroyed in a fire. The house was sheathed in marble by Bramante to become one of the largest and most expensive sculptural ensembles ever attempted. In size and plan it is rather like Michelangelo's original project for the famous tomb of Pope Julius II; its decoration includes beautiful reliefs by Sansovino, Sangallo, della Porta and others, showing scenes from the *Life of Mary*. The reliefs on the back show the airborne house removal that made Loreto's Virgin the patroness of the airline industry; Charles Lindbergh took her image with him (along with a kitten and a ham sandwich) on his historic transatlantic flight.

The **Sala del Tesoro** (1610) off the left nave has a ceiling frescoed with the *Life of Mary* by Pomarancio, who won the (rigged) competition over Caravaggio, only to get his face knifed by a gangster hired by Caravaggio. Napoleon and his troops looted the treasures but many were eventually returned, only to fall victim to a spectacular robbery in 1974. The upper floor of the Apostolic palace houses what the crooks missed in the **Museo Pinacoteca** (*t 071 974 7198; open Nov–Mar Tues–Sun 10–1 and 3–6; April–Oct 9–1 and 4–7; contribution requested*), especially the dramatic late paintings by Lorenzo Lotto, who spent his last years in Loreto, took orders and died in 1556. There are some Flemish tapestries from cartoons by Raphael and a superb collection of ceramics, many from the 16th-century workshop of Orazio Fontana. Just by the basilica there's a Polish war cemetery, with over 1,000 graves of men who died on the Adriatic front.

The rest of Loreto is devoted to the pilgrim trade and pastry shops (**Pirri** is good) selling almond sweets such as *amaretti di Loreto* and *dolci del Conero*. From the 1600s until the 1940s, a Loreto pilgrim's favourite souvenir was either an envelope containing

Holy Dust (i.e. daily sweepings from the Holy House) or a tattoo of the Virgin, but now there's just the usual plaster models, pictures and plastic catapults.

Recanati

South of Loreto, rising above a massive ring of sprawl, Recanati (pop. 19,300) is a sombre town within brick walls. It was born in the late 12th century, when three Ghibelline lords of surrounding hilltops decided to unite to form a single town, an endeavour blessed by Emperor Frederick II. In later years, Recanati was the birthplace of Italy's greatest modern poet, Giacomo Leopardi (1798–1837), and the town has made a discreet industry out of this melancholy soul, His family, still residing in the **Casa Leopardi**, in Piazzale Sabato del Villaggio, permits visits to the library (*t 071 757 3380, www.giacomoleopardi.it; open daily winter 9.30–12.30 and 2.30–5.30; summer 9–7; adm*), where young Giacomo spent much of his dismal childhood, with original manuscripts and archives. Fans can study the poet's death mask and first editions in the neighbouring **Centro Nazionale di Studi Leopardiani** (*t 071 757 0604, www.leopardi.it; open Mon–Fri 10–1 and 4.30–8; Sat 10–1*). Below, the gardens of the **Colle dell'Infinito** take in the view of Leopardi's famous poem. The Capuchin church by the palace contains a rather unusual 18th-century Madonna, *Our Lady of the Salad*.

Recanati's main square, Piazza Leopardi, is presided over by a statue of the poet. The swallowtail crenellations of the **Torre del Borgo** commemorate the town's Ghibelline origins, as does the golden seal that Frederick II conceded to Recanati housed in the **Pinacoteca** (*t 071 757 0410; open summer Tues–Sun 9–12 and 3–7; winter Tues–Fri 9–12 and 3–7, Sat–Sun 9–1 and 3–8; adm*); highlights are a polyptych and three other works by Lorenzo Lotto, including one of the most original, colourful, if silliest *Annunciations* (1528) ever painted – even Mary's cat can't bounce out of the scene fast enough. Another section has the operatic wardrobe and other relics of the tenor Beniamino Gigli (1890–1957). **Gigli's tomb**, a fair-sized pyramid with full *Aida* trappings, lords it over the town cemetery in Viale Dalmazia. Get there through the **Porta Marina**, erected in honour of a visit by Pius VI in 1782, although Napoleon had the papal friezes knocked off prior to his own triumphal entry into Recanati.

North of Piazza Leopardi, Recanati's cathedral was completely made over in the 1700s, though there are a few interesting paintings, reliquaries and archaeological fragments in the **Museo Diocesano** (*t 071 981122, closed for restoration*), in the 14th-century bishop's palace and later papal prison. The 12th-century **Santa Maria in Castelnuovo** retains its campanile façade and a lunette over the door.

Montefano, 11km west, is a hill town guarded by the **Castello di Montefiore**, built by Recanati in the 15th century, with a tower dominating the landscape for miles around. Montefano was the birthplace of Pope Marcello II, whose pontificate may have been one of the briefest – it lasted all of 22 days in 1555 – but it was long enough to get him a lovely requiem mass from Palestrina and a marble bust on Montefano's **Palazzo Comunale**, which also houses a charming 19th-century **Teatro della Rondinella** (*t 0733 850001; open for performances*), a provincial version of Venice's La Fenice.

Getting There and Around

Macerata's **train** station is down in the suburbs and is linked to Piazza della Libertà by city buses. CONTRAM **buses** (**t** 0737 63401, **f** 0737 632402, *www.contram.sinp.net)* to the province leave from the Giardini Diaz, west from the centre, off Viale Puccinotti. **Pagliani, t** 0733 231368. Buses to Rome. **APM, t** 0733 29351, **f** 0733 293 5213, *www. apmgroup.it.* Local buses.

Tourist Information

Macerata: Piazza della Libertà 12, **t** 0733 234807, **f** 0733 266631, *iat.macerata@ regione.marche.it. Open Mon–Sat 9–1 and 3–6, Sun 9–1.*
Cingoli: Via L. Ferri 17, **t** 0733 602444, *iat.cingoli@ regione.marche.it. Open June and 16–30 Sept daily 9–1, Thurs and Sat also 4–7; July–15 Sept daily 9–1 and 4–8.*

Where To Stay and Eat

Macerata ✉ **62100**
****Claudiani, Via Ulissi 8, **t** 0733 261400, **f** 0733 261380, *www.hotelclaudiani.it*
(*expensive*). A new, modern hotel inside the walls of an old palace in the historic centre, with all four-star comforts.
***Da Rosa, Via Armaroli 94, **t/f** 0733 232670 (*moderate*). A pleasant enough place to lay your head, in the centre very near Piazza della Libertà; there's a restaurant of the same name at No.17.
Arena, Vicolo Sferisterio 16, **t 0733 230931, **f** 0733 236059 (*moderate*). Small but good, right next to the Sferisterio.

Macerata is the place to try *vincisgrassi*, a kind of lasagne with a rich sauce of chicken livers, gizzards and brains, mushrooms, ground meat and wine, topped with béchamel sauce. Before you fetch your Latin dictionary, know that the name comes from the Austrian General Windischgrätz (from the Napoleonic Wars) who must have liked it a lot, although others say it was invented by a famous Macerata chef in the 18th century to fatten up skinny princes (*Principrassi*).
Da Rosa, Via Armaroli 17, **t** 0733 260124 (*moderate*). A good *trattoria* and pizzeria with a menu that changes daily, linked to the hotel of the same name. *Closed Sun and over Christmas.*
Da Secondo, Via Pescheria Vecchia 26, **t** 0733 260912 (*moderate*). Macerata's finest

The Pocket Province of Macerata

You won't find a more out-of-the-way corner in central Italy. This hilly enclave lacks great attractions (when the provinces of Italy were being divided up in 1860, Macerata was involved in a bitter quarrel with the commissioner in charge of fixing the borders, so he took away half of its traditional territory – Loreto, Fabriano and other famous places – in revenge). Still, the towns that remain to Macerata put up a good front, with stout medieval walls or a Romanesque tower to lure you in. Many of its villages and towns also have fine works of art in their little museums.

Macerata

High on its hill, **Macerata** is a pleasant medieval-looking town (pop. 43,000). The town's major landmark is a huge colonnaded hemicycle and outdoor theatre called the **Arena Sferisterio** (**t** *0733 234333; open 10.30–1 and 5–8*), built in the 1820s by local subscription for a game, *pallone a bracciale,* that required a long wall on one side – a game played in Macerata since the 15th century. *Pallone* reached its peak of popularity not long after the construction of the Sferisterio, losing out to new sport – football – 'which still excites portions of the Italian population' as a local booklet on Macerata

restaurant is in the centre of town; besides *vincisgrassi*, you can order the famous *fritto misto* of lamb and vegetables – do book ahead as it's always crowded; there are lovely views, too, and a terrace. *Closed Mon and part of Aug.*

Osteria dei Fiori, Via Lauro Rossi 61, t 0733 260142 (*cheap*). Another good, popular choice found in between the Sferisterio and Piazza della Libertà, with its own version of *vincisgrassi*, or stuffed boned pigeon, *fritto misto* along with other hearty favourites. *Closed Sun and mid-Aug–mid-Sept.*

Montecassiano ✉ 62010

****Villa Quiete, Valle Cascia, 3km south of Montecassiano, t/f 0733 599559, *www.gestionihotels.it* (*expensive*). An 18th-century country house, set in beautiful grounds amidst industrial sprawl, where the rooms are furnished with antiques and decorated with masterful simplicity. It's quite special: if they could pick it up and move it to Tuscany, they could charge three times the room rate. There's a very good restaurant, too.

****Roganti, Valle Cascia, on the S77, t 0733 598639, f 0733 598964, *www.recinahotel.it* (*expensive*). If the Quiete is full, this is nearby

and in the same price range, with comfortable rooms and a garden.

Cingoli ✉ 62011

***Miramonti, Via dei Cerquatti 31, t 0733 604027, f 0733 602239, *www.hotelmiramonti cingoli.it* (*moderate*). Modern, small and fairly cosy; there's a tennis court and some lovely views over the sea and Apennines.

***Diana, Via Cavour 21, t 0733 602313, f 0733 603479 (*moderate*). A family-run place housed in an 18th-century palace in the historic centre of Cingoli; the rooms are fairly simple. *Closed Feb and Oct.*

***Antica Taverna alla Selva, Via Cicerone 1, San Vittore, t 0733 617119, f 0733 617128, *www.tavernaallaselva.it* (*inexpensive*). For something more remote, drive 12km north to the hamlet of San Vittore on the banks of the River Musone, where you'll find this country inn with a good restaurant. *Closed Wed and Jan.*

La Terrazza, Via Fra Bevignate 65, t 0733 603957 (*moderate*). Marchigiano staples.

There are some pleasant places to eat on the road to Cingoli's lake.

Le Cascatelle, Fraz. Villa Pozzo, t 0733 616129 (*cheap*). By a bubbling river; good mixed grill and salads. *Open summer only.*

drily puts it. But the builders of the Sferisterio endowed it with excellent acoustics, making for one of the grandest opera settings south of Verona; the Macerata Opera Festival (*t 0733 230735, f 0733 261570, www.macerataopera.org; box office at Piazza Mazzini 10; open daily summer 9.30–1 and 4–8; winter 10–1 and 5–8*), founded in 1921 and running from mid-July to mid-August, is one of the most popular summer music events in Italy.

Nearly as many people could fit into **Piazza della Libertà**, decorated with Macerata's proudest monuments: a Tuscan **Loggia dei Mercanti** (1505), built by Papal Legate Alessandro Farnese, future Pope Paul III; the 17th-century **Palazzo del Comune** with an *atrium* decorated with statues and inscriptions from *Helvia Ricina* (*see* p.628); and an elegant 18th-century **Teatro Rossi**, created by the great Bibbiena family of theatre designers.

Corso della Repubblica leads down to Piazza Vittorio Veneto, where Macerata's museums are in an old Jesuit College: the **Museo Civico e Pinacoteca** (*t 0733 256361; open Mon 4–7, Tues–Sat 9–1 and 4–7.30, Sun 9–1; adm*) has another *Madonna* by Crivelli (no cucumbers, but lovely), works by Sassoferrato, Parmigiano, and a curious *Idealized Portraits of Michelangelo as Moses and Raphael as a Prophet* by Taddeo Zuccari, and modern works, especially by the Futurists Cagli and Maceratese painter Ivo Pannaggi.

Adjacent is the **Museo delle Carrozze** (*same hours as Museo Civico*, see p.627), with carriages from the 16th to 20th centuries; a Risorgimento collection is being added.

The privately run **Museo Tipologico del Presepio** (*open by request, t 0733 234035*), with 4,000 Christmas crib figures from the 17th century to the present, is at Via Maffeo Pantaleoni 4, near the Sferisterio. There's an excellent collection of modern Italian artists, including Manzu, de Chirico, Carrá, Messina, de Pises, Morandi, Balla, and more by Ivo Pannaggi in the **Palazzo Ricci Gallery**, Via D. Ricci 1 (*t 0733 232802; open Tues and Thurs 4–6, Sat 10–12; adm free*). The noble Ricci family who owned this palace produced the intriguing Matteo Ricci, born here in 1522, the eldest of 11 sons. He became a Jesuit against his father's will and ended up in China, where he spent his last 20 years under the name of Li Matou, dressed like a Buddhist monk, reputed to be 'a second Confucius' for his writings and understanding of Chinese culture; the Ming emperor Wan Li made him a court scholar, and on his death in 1610, declared a day of national mourning. Ricci wrote in Chinese as well as Italian: among his works are *The Ten Paradoxes* (still read in China), *A Chinese Map of the World*, *Eight Songs for the Harpsichord*, *Treatise on the Constellations* and the semi-autobiographical *The Entry of the Society of Jesus and Christianity into China*.

Santa Maria degli Vergini (1582), 2km outside the Porta Picena, is a domed Renaissance church in the form of a Greek cross, with a rich stucco interior, a fine *Nativity* by Tintoretto (1587) and a stuffed crocodile.

Around Macerata and West to Cingoli

You could spend an afternoon on a treasure hunt around Macerata; each village has a little something to see. North 4km on the SS361 towards Osimo, at **Helvia Ricina**, a Roman town decimated by the Visigoths in 408, it's the romantically overgrown ruin of an ancient theatre. Press on a little further to **Montecassiano**, where the church Santa Maria Assunta has an elaborate Della Robbia altar of 1527.

Southeast of Macerata, just off the SS485, there's a 7th-century church **San Claudio al Chienti**, built over the ruins of a Roman villa, with a pair of round *campanili*; it was reworked in the 12th century and restored in the 20th, after being used as a farm.

Corridonia, 4km south, on the ancient site of *Paulsulam*, was renamed in 1931 after Filippo Corridoni, a union leader who died in 1915 in the First World War: there's a monument to him, made of melted Austrian cannons, and a display on his life in the town hall. The **Pinacoteca** (*t 0733 431832; open by request*), in an 18th-century parish house, has a *Madonna* by Carlo Crivelli, in a wreath of angels, works by the Vivarini brothers and a painting attributed to Sassetta. Monte San Giusto's church of **Santa Maria Telusiano**, 10km east of town, has a *Crucifixion* by Lorenzo Lotto (1531).

Southwest on the SS77 and SS78, the **Abbadia S. Maria di Chiaravalle di Fiastra** (*t 0733 202942; open Sept–June Sat–Sun 10–12.30 and 3–5.30; July–Aug daily 10–12.30 and 3–6.30; adm*) was founded by Cistercians in 1142; now a bit over-restored and reinhabited by Cistercians since 1985, it retains some 15th-century frescoes. The World Wide Fund for Nature runs part of it as a **museum** (*opening times by request*) including exhibitions of country life and crafts, local flora and fauna, with a working *cantina* and exhibition of archaeological finds from Urbs Salvia. Medieval **Urbisaglia** inherited the name and enjoys a panoramic setting with its 14th-century castle; below is the largest archaeological site in the Marches, the ruins of **Urbs Salvia**, including a well-preserved amphitheatre from AD 75, a sacred area encircled by a *cryptoporticus* frescoed with hunting scenes, a huge theatre, an aqueduct, cistern, gates and walls (*to visit, contact the archeological museum, t 0733 50107, f 0733 50367*). Medieval **Mogliano**, a centre for weaving wicker furniture, is 9km southeast; its church, **Santa Maria,** was frescoed in 1548 by Lorenzo Lotto.

In the rather empty land to the west, **Rambona** has a church founded in the 8th century by Lombard queen Ageltrude over the Roman temple of *Ara Bona*; remodelled in the 11th century and frescoed in the 16th, it has Ageltrude's original dedication and some Roman architectural fragments. Further northwest, in increasingly beautiful country, quiet, noble **Cingoli** (22km from Macerata) is a small summer resort. By tradition Cingoli receives the last ray of sun this side of the Apennines; it also has the largest artificial lake in central Italy (its size is its only attraction).

The cathedral has some good painting and a bust of Pius VIII, a native son (1761–1830); the famous views that earned Cingoli's reputation as the '**Balcony of the Marches**' are from behind the apse of San Francesco, while outside the gate, Roman-esque **Sant'Esuperanzio** (*closed for restoration*) has an attractive portal of 1299, a polyptych by Giovanni Antonio da Pesaro, and a *Christ at the Column* by Sebastiano del Piombo. More art is displayed in the **Pinacoteca** (*t 0733 602877; closed for earthquake restoration – due to re-open early 2005*), at Via Mazzini 10. Most of the paintings can be viewed in the church of **San Domenico** (*t 0733 602877; open by request only*). Despite the difficulty of seeing Cingoli's art, it is a charming town, whose main piazza is reminiscent of a French village, lined with lime trees and the brightly coloured chairs of a café terrace.

The tiny **Museo Archeologico** (*t 0733 603399; open Mon–Wed 8.30–1.30, Thurs–Sun 3–7; adm*) in the Palazzo del Comune (with a façade attributed to the great Venetian Tullio Lombardo) has items from prehistoric times up to Roman *Cingulum*, and for something different, there's the **Museo Internazionale del Sidecar**, Corso da Valcarecce 13, holding over a hundred types of them, collected by a dedicated nut named Costantino Frontalini (*call him on t 0733 602651 to see them, www.sidecar.it*).

The Chienti Valley

Up the valley from Macerata is a stately array of hill towns, where you'll find the region's finest trecento frescoes (in Tolentino), a small version of Urbino, with a Renaissance dukedom and university (Camerino), and a museum of plaster mushrooms (Pioraco), along with lovely mountain scenery towards the Umbrian border.

Tolentino

One of the larger Marchigiano hill towns (pop. 18,350), **Tolentino** is prosperous and modern on the outside, with a walled medieval centre. The city is known for two Nicholases. One, Niccolò da Tolentino, was a *condottiere* who earned an equestrian

Tourist Information

Tolentino: Piazza Libertà 18, t/f 0733 972937, *proloco.tolentino@utente.sinp.net.*

San Severino Marche: Piazza del Popolo, t/f 0733 638414.

Sarnano: Largo E. Ricciardi, t 0733 657144, f 0733 657343, *iat.sarnano@regione. marche.it. Open Mon–Sat 9–1 and 3–6, Sun 9–1; June–Sept also Sun 4–7.*

Camerino: Piazza Cavour 19, t 0737 632534.

Where To Stay and Eat

Tolentino ✉ 62029

★★★★**Hotel 77**, outside the centre on Viale B. Buozzi 90, t 0733 967400, f 0733 960147, *www.hotel77.com* (*expensive*). Very cosy and up-to-date, with a garden, garage and every comfort.

★★**Milano**, Via Roma 13, t 0733 973014, f 0733 973077 (*inexpensive*). An older, more modest choice, in the centre.

Iuby Park, Contrada Cisterna 55, t 0733 969347 (*cheap*). In Tolentino's urban sprawl, in an 18th-century villa named after Napoleon's general Joachim Murat. Good classics washed down with Verdicchio. Also has five small but comfortable bedrooms, some with frescoed ceilings.

San Severino Marche ✉ 62027

Il Giardino degli Ulivi, Via Crucianelli 54, Sant'Angelo, near Castelraimondo off the SS361 en route to Camerino, t 0737 642121, f 0737 642600 (*moderate*). A charming *agriturismo*, either for a stay or for lunch, with seven rooms in a well-restored farm surrounded by lovely hilly countryside. The restaurant prepares delicious traditional fare. *Closed Nov–Dec, restaurant closed Tues.*

★★★**Due Torri**, Via S. Francesco 21, t 0733 645419, f 0733 645139, *www.duetorri.it* (*inexpensive*). A pretty hotel in an old stone house at the top of town, family-run since 1932. The restaurant (*cheap*) serves excellent *vincisgrassi* and good grills. *Closed Mon.*

Camerino ✉ 62032

★★★**I Duchi**, Via V. Favorino 72, t/f 0737 630440 (*moderate*). The best option here: a modern, family-run place in the *centro storico*.

★★**Roma**, Piazza Garibaldi 6, t 0737 632592, f 0737 630125 (*inexpensive*). Simple, central, some rooms without bath.

Osteria dell'Arte, Via Arco della Luna 4, t 0737 633 558 (*moderate–cheap*). Renovated, but one of the oldest restaurants in town, with an unusual array of pasta (with wild fennel or in a pigeon-based *ragù*) and good rabbit and trout. *Closed Fri and 2 weeks in Jan.*

fresco in Florence's cathedral by Andrea del Castagno; the second was a miracle-working Augustan preacher, San Nicola da Tolentino (1245–1305), one of his special concerns is souls in Purgatory. His **Santuario di San Nicola** (*t 0733 976311; open 9–12 and 3–7*) is one of the most popular pilgrimage destinations in central Italy. Even if you don't have a favour to ask, stop to see the impressive portal (1430s), designed by the Florentine Nanni di Bartolo, in a restrained Baroque façade with a big smiling sun. Inside, the Baroqued nave has an ornate gilded casement ceiling by Filippo di Firenze (1603–28); there's an *Annunciation* by Guercino in the first chapel to the right, while to the right of the high altar is the **Cappella dei Santi Braccia** (the Chapel of the Holy Arms) – these parts of the saint were taken off for juju when he died, and kept here in reliquaries until his body, hidden for six centuries, was rediscovered during excavations in 1932; note the 19th-century 3-D view of heaven in the dome, the iron coffer that once held Nicola's arms, and a votive painting of him putting out a fire in the Doge's Palace in Venice.

In the late 13th century, a noble lady paid for the construction of an oratory, now called the **Cappellone**, where an artist known only as the 'Maestro di Tolentino' (Berenson attributed them to Giuliano da Rimini), working between 1310 and 1325, covered the walls from top to bottom in Giotto-style frescoes: richly coloured, intense, inspired work that bears comparison with the best trecento painting in Tuscany, with the four Evangelists, each coaching a Doctor of the Church up amongst the stars in the ceiling, and on the walls, a band dedicated to the life of Mary, Jesus and San Nicola – painted over a century before he was canonized in 1446. In the centre is the stone sarcophagus of the saint, over his reconstructed remains down in the modern crypt. Around the cloister, wreathed in wisteria, are a series of **museums** (*open daily 9–12 and 3–7*) displaying ceramics (Italian and foreign) and art from Tolentino's churches – including 14th-century nativity figures, a *Madonna* by Simone de Magistris, a fascinating collection of painted *ex votos*, each detailed in a catalogue by the entrance – and a giant *presepio*, a spooky diorama of the life of St Nicholas.

Tolentino's central Piazza della Libertà is just a block up, decorated with a fine assortment of palaces and a fascinating **clock tower** that will tell you the phases of the moon, the canonical hour and the day. Upstairs in the 16th-century **Palazzo Sangallo** (by Antonio da Sangallo the Younger) is the world's first **Museum of Caricatures** (*www.biennaleumorismo.org; open summer Tues–Sun 10–1 and 3.30–7; winter Tues–Sun 10–1 and 3–6*), with satirical cartoons from ancient times to the present. Tolentino also hosts a biennial International Festival of Humour in Art (*Octobers in odd-numbered years, contact the museum for details*). In February 1797 Napoleon stayed in the **Palazzo Bezzi-Parisani**, Via della Pace 20 (off the next piazza to the north), where he signed the peace Treaty of Tolentino, returning the Papal States to the Pope; the room has been kept as it was that fateful day and now houses a small **Museo Napoleonico** (*closed since the earthquake; for info, call t 0733 969797*).

Down Corso Garibaldi from Piazza della Libertà, Tolentino's **cathedral** was begun in the 8th century, has a campanile from 1100, but was palatially restored in the 1820s, with alabaster windows and chandeliers. The wooden statue of the dead Christ (1200) is carried in Tolentino's Good Friday processions. Just left of the altar, the sarcophagus of the town's patron, San Catervo (*c.* 350) is a masterpiece of Palaeochristian art, showing the Good Shepherd, the saints and the Adoration of the Magi, the latter dressed in Phrygian caps. Near the door to the right of the altar, the saint's original mausoleum, built by his wife, was found in 1990 (under the glass in the floor), along with a 9th-century Byzantine fresco of the Prudent Virgins. Just outside the centre, Tolentino bottles its own mineral water at **Santa Lucia**, a spa and sauna open year-round. The town also owns the brick **Castello della Rancia**, 5km from the centre on the SS77 (*t 0733 973349; open mid-Oct–mid-Mar Sat, Sun and hols 10–1 and 3–6; mid-Mar–mid-Oct Tues–Sun 10–1 and 3.30–7; adm*), a 12th-century farm once belonging to the abbey of Fiastra, transformed into a castle in 1357 with a huge tower and swallowtail crenellations; it houses archaeological finds (Greek and Etruscan ceramics and bronzes), as well as holding exhibitions and special events.

Up into the Hills South of Tolentino: San Ginesio and Sarnano

Perched high on its green hill, walled **San Ginesio**, 18km south, has views stretching from the Conero and through the Sibillini to the Gran Sasso, the tallest of the Apennines over in the Abruzzo. Its **Collegiata**, in the main piazza, has a peculiar

Gothic façade decorated with terracotta lace and fine quattrocento works inside by Simone de Magistris, Lorenzo Salimbeni and Pietro Alemanno. Behind it, there's a picture gallery (*t 0733 656022; open summer daily 10–1 and 3.30–7; winter by request*) installed in the 15th-century church of **San Sebastiano**, with a lively scene of a battle between San Ginesio and Fermo from 1440, back when town rivalries could be dangerous to one's health. San Ginesio's walls still stand and outside the main gate is a large medieval stone pilgrims' hospice.

Further south, **Sarnano** has spruced itself up as a small radioactive spa – the waters have been known since Roman times – offering all the important mud, water and aerosol tortures. It has an attractive medieval centre to give its spa guests something to explore, plus yet another tiny **Pinacoteca** (*t 0733 659923; open Mon, Wed and Thurs 10–1 and 4–6.30, Tues and Fri 10–1; adm*) in the Palazzo Comunale on Via Leopardi; look for the *Last Supper*, an exceptional work by Simone de Magistris, (*c.* 1600) and a *Madonna* (with cucumber) by Carlo Crivelli's brother Vittore. On top of the medieval town, Piazza Alta has a number of fine buildings and Santa Maria Assunta, with 15th-century frescoes by Niccolò Alunno and Pietro Alemanno. There are scenic drives in every direction from Sarnano, either west towards the mountains or south to Amandola, an enchanting route (*see* p.637).

San Severino Marche

Northwest of Tolentino, a road leads to **San Severino Marche** (pop. 13,000), a town that hasn't risen from its slumbers since Totila the Goth sacked its predecessor *Septempeda* in 545; the oldest parts of town, in the medieval Castello on Montenero, are almost abandoned, but make a brave sight when the two towers are lit up at night. In the early 1400s, the town was a minor artistic centre, hometown of International Gothic masters Iacopo and Lorenzo Salimbeni. On Via Salimbeni, you can inspect some of their frescoes at the **Pinacoteca Tacchi-Venturi** (*t 0733 638095; open summer Tues–Sun 9–1 and 4.30–6.30; winter Tues–Sat 9–1; adm*) which has Pinturicchio *Madonnas* and works by Alunno, Girolamo di Giovanni of Camerino, and Carlo Crivelli's brother Vittore; also a polyptych by the great pre-Renaissance Venetian painter Paolo Veneziano (his only work south of the Veneto) and many others, alongside archaeological finds from Roman Septempeda and Piceni tombs from the 6th–4th centuries BC. The Salimbeni brothers and the Baroque painter Pomarancio also left frescoes in the crypt of 11th-century church **San Lorenzo in Doliolo** on Via di Piagge, and others in the church of the **Misericordia**, in the elliptical **Piazza del Popolo**, encircled with porticoes. The **Duomo** (10th century, but often remodelled) is a steep hike to the Castello, a quiet place. The baptistry has frescoes by the Salimbeni.

West of San Severino, **Pioraco**, like Fabriano, was a paper-making town and the cloister of the 15th-century church of **San Francesco in Largo Leopardi** now has a little **Museo della Carta e della Filigrana** (*t 0737 42715; open summer Mon–Sat 10–1 and 3–7; winter Sat–Sun 10.30–12.30 and 4.30–6; adm*), including a paper-making workshop using 14th-century techniques. The Palazzo Comunale has a **Museo dei Fossili** and the **Museo dei Funghi**, with models of every mushroom 'personally created by Offerl

Spitoni' (*t 0733 42142; both open summer Tues–Sun 10–1 and 3–7; winter Sat–Sun 10.30–12.30 and 4–6*). Further west, **Fiuminata** is lush and green with waterfalls; the next town west is Nocera Umbra (*see* p.490).

Camerino

Camerino (pop. 7,300) passed the time during the Middle Ages in endless fighting with arch-enemy Fabriano just to the north (and, like Fabriano, was hit by the quake; there is still some scaffolding, but overall the town is pretty solid). Set on a ridge, it was ruled by the Da Varano dukes from the 14th to 16th centuries, who managed to give it something in 1355 that the larger and more prosperous Fabriano never had: a **university**, still in business today. In main Piazza Cavour, the Da Varano's elegant Renaissance **Palazzo Ducale** has an Urbino-style courtyard and several frescoed halls (now used as a law faculty), and just below, by way of a 16th-century stairway, the lovely **Botanical Garden** (*t 0737 403084; open Mon–Fri 9–1 and 3–5*), planted with fine old trees, as well as the usual plants and herbs. The palace shares the square with the **Duomo**, rebuilt in 1832 after an earthquake in 1799 knocked over its predecessor; the crypt, however, preserves a beautiful 14th-century tomb of **Sant'Ansovino** (a Carolingian bishop of Camerino) in red and pink marble. Like Fabriano, Camerino also produced a home-grown crop of artists, including a quattrocento painter named Girolamo di Giovanni, whose works may be seen next to the Duomo in the **Museo Diocesano** (*t 0737 630 400; closed for earthquake restoration*) along with a king-size Gian Battista Tiepolo, the *Madonna and St Philip Neri* (1740), paintings by Giovanni Boccati (another native) and a trecento fresco of the *Madonna di Altino*. Down the Corso from here, the Palazzo Comunale incorporates the town's **theatre** (1856); a Roman *cryptoporticus* was recently discovered under the stage.

Girolamo di Giovanni's masterpiece, the *Annunciation and Deposition* (both on the same panel, in 1462) is in the **Pinacoteca** (*t 0737 402310; open Oct–Mar Tues–Sun 10–1 and 3–6; April–Sept Tues–Sun 10–1 and 3.30–7; adm*), in the former church complex of San Domenico north of Piazza Cavour. This church saw a brutal murder, ordered by Cesare Borgia in 1502, when good duke Giulio Cesara da Varano and three of his sons were strangled at Mass; two of the youngest managed to escape and one returned to become duke again. Further north, the church of **San Venanzio** has a fine 14th-century Gothic portal (the rest was rebuilt following the earthquake).

The mountainous Alte Valli del Fiastrone to the south are peppered with castles, towers and fortresses, but most striking is the ruined white castle just east of Camerino, the **Rocca di Varano**, from the 1200s. The isolated church of **San Giusto**, from the same period, is 3km away.

Around Fermo

After Monte Conero, the Adriatic won't show you another stretch of beautiful coastline until the Gargano peninsula in Puglia. That does not seem to impede the

Getting There and Around

Three START **buses** (call freephone **t** 800 443040, *www.startspa.it*) run daily from Fermo down the coast to Porta d'Ascoli, then head inland to Ascoli Piceno and Rome. STEAT buses (**t** 800 630715, *www.steat.it*) provide a service from Fermo to Macerata.

Tourist Information

Porto San Giorgio: Via Oberdan 6, **t** 0734 67461, *iat.portosangiorgio@regione.marche.it*. Open Mon–Sat 9–1, Tues and Thurs also 3–6.
Fermo: Piazza del Popolo 6, **t** 0734 228738, **f** 0734 228325, *iat.fermo@regione.marche.it*. Open Mon–Thurs 9–1 and 3–6, Fri–Sat 9–1.
Parco Nazionale dei Monti Sibillini, *www.sibillini.net*.
Amandola: Via Indipendenza 73, **t/f** 0736 848598.
Montemonaco: Via Roma, **t** 0736 856462.

Where to Stay and Eat

Porto San Giorgio ✉ 63017

****David Palace**, Lungomare Gramsci Sud 503, **t** 0734 676848, **f** 0734 676468, *www.hotel david palace.it* (*expensive*). A new seaside hotel at the upper end of this range, with a beach and a gourmet restaurant set around the pool.
***Rosa Meublé**, Lungomare Gramsci 177, **t/f** 0734 678485 (*moderate*). Simple and quieter than most; no restaurant. *Open all year.*
Damiani e Rossi, Via della Misericordia 1, **t** 0734 674401 (*moderate*). The best place to eat, but no fish; some vegetarian dishes. *Menu degustazione* only. *Closed Mon and Tues in winter; open daily Aug for dinner only.* For fish, take your pick of the places along the seafront.

Fermo ✉ 63023

Good restaurants are rare in central Fermo, although there are several pizzerias.
***Astoria**, Viale Veneto 8, **t** 0734 228601,

f 0734 228602, *www.hotelastoriafermo.it* (*moderate*). Modern; the comfiest in the centre, with a good restaurant.
****Casina delle Rose**, on Piazzale Girfalco 16, **t/f** 0734 228932 (*moderate*). Near the cathedral; grand views and a good restaurant.

Servigliano ✉ 63029

***San Marco**, Via Garibaldi 14, **t** 0734 750761, **f** 0734 750740 (*inexpensive*). A reliable little stopover. *Closed 2 weeks in Jan.*

Montefalcone Appennino ✉ 63029

Da Quintilia Mercuri, Via Corradini 9, **t** 0734 79158 (*moderate–cheap*). Dine really well at this tiny place; try the *fritto* of lamb, olives, artichokes, cream and honey. *Closed Wed.*

Amandola ✉ 63021

***Hotel Paradiso**, Piazza Umberto I 7, **t** 0736 847468, **f** 0736 847726, *www.sibillinihotels.it* (*moderate*). A stylish family-run hotel in the centre, set in a park with a tennis court, plus the town's best restaurant. *Closed Tues.*
Youth hostel, Via Indipendenza 73, **t** 0736 848598 (*inexpensive*). An exceptionally nice hostel, with en-suite rooms in an old palace. *Closed Nov–Mar.*

Montemonaco ✉ 63048

Plenty of unpretentious but comfortable hotels, though prices tend to be over the odds.
***Guerrin Meschino**, Via Rocca, Loc Rocca, **t/f** 0736 856356, *www.guerrinmeschino.com* (*inexpensive*).
****La Colombella**, Via Stradone 86, **t** 0736 856155 (*inexpensive*). Reasonable rooms, with or without bath.
****Hotel Monte Azzurri**, Via Roma 18, **t** 0736 856127, *www.hotelmonteazzurri.com* (*inexpensive*). *Closed 2 wks in Jan.*
La Cittadella dei Sibillini, at Loc La Cittadella, **t** 0736 856361, **f** 0736 844262, *www. lacittadelladeisibillini.it* (*moderate*). Eighteen rooms and a pool. A lovely, hospitable place with a menu of hearty dishes and a good choice of wines. *Closed Feb–Mar.*

tourist sprawl of humble but growing resorts along the sands, all pleasant enough but unspectacular, and all sliced by railways and busy highways: the largest, **Civitanova Marche**, is a big industrial port, mainly of note for its gridlocked traffic.

Porto Sant'Elpidio and Porto San Giorgio

If you escape the traffic jams of Civitanova, **Porto Sant'Elpidio** preserves a bit of its old centre, but you are best off heading inland 9km for **Sant'Elpidio a Mare**, which conserves some pretty things within its walls and seven gates, including the stout 91ft **Torre Gerosolimitana** built by the crusading Knights of St John in Piazza Matteotti, with 14th-century carvings on one side. Adjacent, the 17th-century **Collegiata** has paintings by Pomarancio and Palma Il Giovane, and, behind the altar, a beautiful 3rd-century BC Roman sarcophagus in Greek marble, with a scene of a lion hunt. Also in Piazza Matteotti, the church of **Maria Santissima della Misericordia** (late 1500s) has a colourful ceiling frescoed by Pomarancio and paintings by Andrea Boscoli, including the latter's beautiful *Marriage of the Virgin* (1603) in the presbytery, as well as *two* 18th-century organs. Here, too, is the **Palazzo Comunale**, with a façade by Pellegrino Tibaldi, a tryptych by Garofalo and a *Madonna* by Domenichino. Close by, in the Concento dei Filippini on Corso Baccio, the **Pinacoteca Civica Crivelli** (*t 0734 859279, www.sisstemamusea.it; open summer Tues–Sun 5.30–7.30; winter Sat–Sun 4–7; adm*) is home to art by Crivelli. The **Museo della Calzatura** in Palazzo Montalto (*t 0734 810840, open July–Sept Wed–Sun 4.30–7.30; adm*) traces the local shoemaking industry from medieval clogs and papal slippers to the shoes of football heroes – a must-see for all devotees of Prada shoes, made down the road.

Back down the coast, the next resort south is **Porto San Giorgio**, Fermo's port. It has a rare Saracen tower with embattlements (above Villa Pelagallo, built by Napoleon's brother Jerome) and the romantically overgrown **Rocca Tiepolo**, built by Lorenzo Tiepolo, who went on to be elected Doge of Venice. The Festa del Mare on the second Sunday in July is the biggest fish fry in the Marches, with a frying pan 16ft across.

Fermo

The old town of **Fermo** (pop. 35,000), 6km above Porto San Giorgio, is set against a dramatic mountain backdrop. The Piceni town of *Firmum*, later a close ally of Rome, gained importance and lost it several times; during the 10th century, it was the capital of a duchy that included all the southern Marches. Fermo's handsome, brick-arcaded **Piazza del Popolo** has been its drawing room, and between 1398 and 1826, it was also seat of its university. The Baroque **Palazzo degli Studi** at the square's end, still holds the university's superb library – now the town library – with a beautiful world globe made in 1722 (*can be visited during library hours*).

Opposite, another corner of the piazza is closed by the 15th-century **Palazzo Comunale**, with a mildly eerie bronze statue of Pope Sixtus V, by a 16th-century sculptor, Accursio Baldi, inviting you in to the **Pinacoteca** (*t 0734 284327; open daily mid-June–Sept 10–1 and 3.30–7.30, Thurs until 11.30pm; Oct–mid-June 9.30–1 and 3.30–7; adm, joint ticket available for Pinacoteca, Roman cisterns and Science museums*). Works include a moving *Nativity* by a young Rubens; local records recall a Fermo priest commissioning it in 1608 for the grand sum of 1,700 *scudi*. Other works include the delightful fairytale *Story of St Lucy* by Jacobello del Fiore (1410), a polyptych by Andrea da Bologna and a 15th-century Flemish tapestry of the Annunciation.

Under the Via degli Aceti there is a singular relic of Roman times: the **Piscina Epuratoria** (*same hours as Pinacoteca; adm*), an enormous underground reservoir built in AD 41–61 to both hold and clarify rain and spring water.

Behind the Palazzo Comunale, Via Perpenti leads down to the Gothic church of **San Francesco**, with 15th-century frescoes and a tomb by Andrea Sansovino; further down in Viale Trento, the 18th-century Villa Vitali houses the **Museo di Scienze Naturali** and the **Museo Polare** (*t 0734 226166; both open Mon–Fri 9–12.30 and 3.30–6.30, Sat–Sun 3.30–7.30; adm*), with a collection of stuffed birds, and examples of polar flora and fauna, tools and sculptures from Greenland, and photos all gathered by Silvio Zavatti during his five Arctic expeditions (1959–69). Don't miss the villa's romantic gardens.

On top of Fermo, there's **Piazza del Girfalco**. Parasol pines grow where the castle once stood, but the **Duomo**'s still there, begun in 1227, but massively expanded and remodelled in the 1780s. Fortunately the restorers left the attractive, asymmetrical front rose window and portals alone – note the lobster carved on the left. Inside is a fine 1366 tomb, a Palaeochristian sarcophagus in the crypt and, in the sacristy, a superb 12th-century Islamic embroidered silk chasuble that belonged to St Thomas à Becket – but they can't really explain how they got it. Near the south end of the Piazza del Popolo, old Roman storehouses contain the **Museo Archeologico** (*t 0734 217140; open mid-June–Sept 10–1 and 3.30–7.30, Thurs until 11.30pm; Oct–mid-June Tues–Sun 9.30–1 and 3.30–7; adm*) with Roman artefacts. A pre-Roman collection (before the Piceni, Fermo was the site of a Vilanova culture settlement from the 9th century BC) is on display at the **Palazzo dei Priori**, also in Piazza del Popolo.

South of Fermo

The hills around Fermo are engraved by the valleys of three small rivers – the Tenna, the Ete Vivo and the Aso to the south. A pretty road heads south for **Monterubbiano** and **Moresco** (16km), a pair of picturesque hill towns above the Aso Valley; the latter is supposedly named after the Saracen mercenaries who accompanied the 11th-century Norman chieftain Robert Guiscard in his campaigns to boot the Byzantines out of Italy. Its churches have frescoes by a late 16th-century painter, Vincenzo Pagani.

Southwest of Fermo (23km), north off the SS210, a 1st-century BC Roman theatre is used for occasional summer performances at **Faleria** (Roman *Falerio Picenus*); other surviving bits include an aqueduct, tombs, cistern and villas, although they could be better signposted. High above, **Falerone**, the medieval town which replaced it, has a quattrocento merchants' loggia, a clock tower with a tiny museum and a painting by Vittore Crivelli in the church of **San Fortunato**.

Massa Fermana, 8km north of Falerone, must have been a very strategic spot at one point to someone, judging by its massive 14th-century gate, the **Porta di Sant'Antonio**, complete with loggia and tower. The parish church of **San Lorenzo** houses Carlo Crivelli's oldest work to be found in the Marches, a polyptych of 1468 (no cucumbers and only two apples), and a much later work by his brother Vittore. The *municipio* has a **Pinacoteca** (*t 0734 760126; open Mon–Fri 8–2, Sat–Sun 5.30–7.30; adm*) with paintings by Vincenzo Pagani, and a 15th-century wooden choir.

Further west, **Servigliano** is a rare old town that's *not* on a hill; note how the cemetery just west resembles a miniature version of the town. The scenery becomes increasingly dramatic up the SS210; even more so if you have time to drive south for **Santa Vittoria in Matenano**, then follow the road west to **Montefalcone Appennino** before rejoining the SS210 at **San Martino al Faggio**. Here, the **Abbazia di San Rufino** (13th-century) is built over a 9th–10th-century crypt with early frescoes, holding the remains of St Rufino, a farmboy who could plough thousands of acres in one night. Farmers approach his tomb down on their knees when they have hernias; Rufino is apparently a wiz at curing them.

On the edge of the Monti Sibillini National Park, the biggest town in these parts is **Amandola** (pop. 4,100), formed in the Middle Ages when residents of the surrounding castles decided to band together. It has a Romanesque bridge, just off the SS210, and in town, the church of **San Francesco**, with a 13th-century Byzantine-style fresco of *Christ the King*. The convent has an intriguing **Museo della Civiltà** (*t 0736 840704; closed for restoration*), an accumulation of everything the locals used until a few decades ago, down to the kitchen sink. The first week of September sees a very sprightly International Theatre Festival in the streets.

The Monti Sibillini

Above Amandola rises the dark, legendary range of the **Monti Sibillini**, the most striking mountains in the Apennines, wearing snow-capped peaks from late October to late May. The region has been designated as a National Park to protect the numerous species of flora and fauna thriving there; it is still the haunt of wolves and now of bears, who have migrated up from the Abruzzo. There is the odd wildcat and marten, and about 50 pairs of royal eagles (the entire Italian population of this bird is estimated at a mere 300). In late May and early June they are covered with wild flowers and orchids, including some rare ones.

Further up above Amandola, there are two small summer resorts to use as bases, both well served by buses, **Montefortino** and **Montemonaco** (988m/3241ft). Montefortino has a small **Pinacoteca** (*t 0736 859101; open July–mid-Sept Tues–Sun 10.30–12.30 and 5–7; 15–30 Sept Sat–Sun 10.30–12.30 and 5–7; Oct Sat 3–7, Sun 10.30–12.30 and 3–7; adm*) with a polyptych by Pietro Alemanno and a spooky painting of Circe the sorceress from the 1700s; from here, a road goes up the pretty valley of the Ambro to the **Santuario della Madonna dell'Ambro**, frescoed in 1610 with pictures of the 12 sibyls by Martino Bonfini.

Medieval Montemonaco, a pretty walled town further up, is even closer to the mountains. You can walk in a couple of hours to the 'Cave of the Sibyl' (the lair of Tannhäuser's Venus) or, much more striking, follow the thundering Tenna River up the stark, wild, narrow **Gola dell'Infernaccio**, 'Shabby Little Hell Gorge', a 3-hour walk from the road (*summer only*).

A drive east of Montemonaco to Foce (9½km) gets you within trekking distance of the highest peak, **Monte Vettore** (2,475m/8,121ft), snow-covered until June, and its uncanny **Lago di Pilato** (1,949m/6,393ft), receptacle of much of the mountains' weirdness. It lies on the border of Umbria and the Marches (*see* **The Valnerina**, p.551–578) and is a four-hour hike from the road, really feasible only in July, August and early September. Bring a map or tag along with some Italians who know the way. The lake is associated with Pontius Pilate, who either threw himself into its waters to drown in remorse, or according to another story, was condemned to death by Tiberius

The Sibyl of the Mountains

One of the most popular medieval Italian romances was *Guerino il Meschino* ('Guerino the Wretch'), written in 1391 by Andrea da Barberino. Guerino, a bold and clever young orphan in search of his parents, meets the Devil in a mountain pass above Norcia. The Devil, playing the role of a pimp, advises Guerino to go up into the mountains and seek out Sibilla, a lovely fairy whose cave is a bower of bliss. The price of her charms, of course, is his soul.

Guerino, however, doesn't hesitate, and finds that Sibilla is everything the Devil promises. He also finds out her true identity: she is the Cumean Sibyl from Campania, the most famous of the dozen prophetic wise women who were honoured by the Church for their predictions of Christ's birth and Passion, thus earning a place on Michelangelo's Sistine Chapel ceiling, on Siena Cathedral's inlaid floor, and elsewhere before the Counter Reformation put on the brakes. In the *Aeneid*, the Cumean Sibyl was visited by Aeneas as he went to found Rome and she offered him a brief tour of Hell; she was later visited by the last king of Rome, Tarquin, coming to purchase the nine Sibylline books of prophesy. When he tried to barter down the price, the Sibyl threw three of the precious books into the fire; when he still tried to bargain, she threw in three more until, in a panic, he paid the original price for the last three. In *Guerino il Meschino*, we learn something else about her: that she had expected God to have chosen her to be the virgin mother of His son and was miffed when He chose Mary, then a nobody. When the new Christianity she had predicted took hold, the Sibyl left her cave in Campania and took refuge in a cave in the mountains that were named in her honour.

Guerino discovers in the nick of time that Sibilla and her ladies turn into monsters on Saturdays, and after spending a year in their pleasant company, he goes to Rome to seek the Pope's absolution. The Humanist Aeneas Silvius (the future Pope Pius II) identified Sibilla as the goddess Venus, and the popular tale inspired several variants, all casting their spell of magical eroticism and forbidden knowledge over the Monti Sibillini. The most famous story these days, thanks to Wagner, is *Tannhäuser*. Soon great numbers of amorous pilgrims and necromancers were making their way to Norcia, the lake and the cave (near Montemonaco), such that by the 1490s, Rome threatened to excommunicate anyone who went to visit the Sibyl. So many people continued to defy the pope with their profane pilgrimages that the long corridors descending into the Sibyl's magical realm were filled in during the 17th century, and dynamited in the 19th to keep all the wickedness within from ever escaping. But in Montemonaco they still know where it is, if you're interested.

and asked for his body to be placed in a cart and driven by oxen to go where they would, whereupon they dumped his body in this lake. Others say a lake as red as blood formed here at the moment of the Crucifixion (the lake does really turn red on occasion, thanks to a species of algae). Peaks and crags in these parts are named after Christ and the Devil, and right by the lake, there's a rock called 'the Policeman' to keep mischief to a minimum. Originally, however, this was the Lake of the Sibyl. Amulets and weird carvings were found on its shores, perhaps left by members of Norcia's college of sorcerors (*see* p.573), who would trudge up here to baptize their grimoires and so double their powers. No one is quite sure how the Mountains of the Sibyls got their name; ancient writers record no such oracular priestesses in these parts (the closest were at *Cumae*, near Naples, and at Tivoli). Italy, however, is full of stories about them and these mountains supposedly gave birth to the legend of Wagner's *Tannhäuser*.

The Riviera delle Palme

The coast, down to San Benedetto del Tronto, dubbed the Riviera delle Palme for its thousands of palms, is especially popular with German and Austrian package tours. The palms lend a tropical air while inland more fine hill towns peer over the sea.

By the Sea

The Riviera delle Palme starts at modest **Cupra Marittima**, where the main attraction besides the beach is the **Museo Malacologico Piceno**, Via Adriatica Nord 240 (*t 0735 777550, www.malacologio.org; open daily June–Aug 4–10.30; April–May and Sept Tues, Thurs, Sat–Sun 3.30–7; Oct–Mar Thurs, Sat–Sun 3–6.30; adm*) with an enormous collection of seashells, as well as displays of buttons, cameos and other shell handicrafts. If you need an art fix, there's **Montefiore dell'Aso**, on its hill 11km inland, where the **Collegiata di Santa Lucia** has three paintings by Carlo Crivelli and the carved 13th-century **Portale della Pinnova** in the apse. Montefiore was also the home town of Adolfo de Carolis (1847–1928), a friend of Gabriele D'Annunzio, who shared some of D'Annunzio's romantic, decadent, nationalist excesses and whose woodcuts, engravings and paintings fill a room at Via Garibaldi 38 (*t 0735 938103; open summer Tues–Sun 4–8, winter Tues–Sun 3–7*).

Next down the coast is **Grottammare**, bigger, with a small medieval core. It was the birthplace of Felice Peretti, Pope Sixtus V (d. 1590) – he who excommunicated Elizabeth I and helped finance the Invincible Armada; there's a portrait of him in the church of **Santa Lucia**. A road leads to **Ripatransone** (12km), 'the Belvedere del Piceno', an old, walled town which claims the narrowest alley in all Italy, just off Piazza XX Settembre (only 15 inches wide – don't get stuck!), as well as a pair of museums: the **Museo Civico C. Cellini**, in the 17th-century **Palazzo Comunale** (*t 0735 99329; open Tues–Sun 9.30–12.30 and 4–8; adm; joint adm to Museo and Pinacoteca also available – see below*) with prehistoric, Etruscan, Greek and Roman finds, and a **Pinacoteca**, at Corso Vittorio Emanuele 130 (*t 0735 99329; open on request*), featuring Vittore Crivelli, Vincenzo Pagani and others, as well as a big batch of plaster casts. There are some

Tourist Information

Grottammare: Piazza Pericle Fazzini 6, t/f 0735 631087, *iat.grottammare@regione.marche.it, open Mon–Sat 8.30–1, Tues, Thurs and Fri also 3–6.*

San Benedetto del Tronto: Viale delle Tamerici 5, t 0735 592237, f 0735 582893, *iat.sanbenedetto@regione.marche.it. Open Mon–Sat 9–1 and 4–7, Sun 9–1.*

Where to Stay and Eat

Grottammare ✉ 63013

****Parco dei Principi**, Lungomare De Gasperi 70, t 0735 735066, f 0735 735080, *www.hotel parcodeiprincipi.it* (*moderate*). A big modern seaside resort hotel, with a pool and tennis. *Closed over Christmas.*

***Villa Helvetia**, Via F. Salvi 1, t 0735 631293, f 0735 735491, *www.grottamare.it/villaheletia* (*moderate*). It's not on the sea, but has an old-fashioned charm, despite recent renovations.

***Roma**, Lungomare De Gasperi 30, t 0735 631145, f 0735 633249, *www.hotelroma grottamare.com* (*inexpensive*). A good, family-run choice, set back a bit from the beach with a garden. *Open April–Sept.*

★Villa Parco, Lungomare della Repubblica 48, t 0735 631015, f 0735 730147 (*inexpensive*). Overlooking the beach, with a fine view.

Up in Alta Grottamare:

Osteria dell'Arancio, Piazza Peretti, t 0735 631059 (*moderate*). Tables outdoors and excellent local cooking; you'll need to book ahead. *Eves only, closed Wed in winter.*

Locanda Borgo Antico, Via Santa Lucia 1, t 0735 634357 (*moderate*). In the same area, with a delicious *menu degustazione* with wine. *Closed Tues and Nov.*

San Benedetto del Tronto ✉ 63039

San Benedetto has a huge choice of ugly modern hotels, including many in the inexpensive range:

****Bahia**, Lungomare Europa 98, t 0735 81711, f 0735 81654, *www.hotelbahia.it* (*moderate*). This one is right on the sea. *Open May–Oct.*

***Miami Beach**, Viale Europa 40, t/f 0735 82115 (*moderate*). *Closed Oct–April.*

Lelii, Via Roma 81, t 0735 587320 (*cheap*). Go to the old part of town and get a table here for one of the best *brodetto di pesce* (the local mixed fish stew); they also do a wide choice of other seafood dishes at kind prices. *Closed Sun in winter.*

Ristorantino da Vittorio, Via Liberazione 31, t 0735 81114, *www.davittorio.net* (*expensive*). Offers delicious seafood in a more refined garden setting near the centre. *Closed Mon.*

picturesque 15th-century houses in Via Garibaldi and other bits that reward a walk around town; recently a Roman amphitheatre was discovered outside the walls.

The smarter and bigger **San Benedetto del Tronto** (pop. 42,000) is 5km south of Grottammare. San Benedetto started off as a Benedictine monastery, grew into a large fishing port and is now a modern resort, where you can find white sandy beaches, discos, restaurants and hotels galore, graced by thousands of palm trees. You get a vague idea of what pre-resort San Benedetto was like in the little streets between the train tracks and main highway. **The Museo Ittico** (*t 0735 588850, www.museo itticocapriotti.it; open summer Tues–Sat 6–midnight; winter Mon–Sat 9–12 and 4–6; adm*) by the fish market in the port has 3,500 stuffed fish, as well as an aquarium of live ones, and fossils of extinct ones, and near the *municipio* in Via De Gasperi a collection of 200 Phoenician, Carthaginian, Greek and Roman amphorae in the **Museo delle Anfore** (*t 0735 592177; open winter Mon–Sat 9–12 and 4–6; summer Tues–Sun 6–midnight; adm*). To the south San Benedetto merges seamlessly into Porto d'Ascoli, marking the end of the Roman Via Salaria and beginning of the Abruzzo.

Inland from San Benedetto, the medieval town of **Acquaviva Picena** (7km) is defended by a **Rocca** (*t 0735 764407; open June and Sept Tues–Sun 10.30–12.30 and 4–7; July–Aug Thurs–Tues 10.30–12.30, 5–8 and 9–11.30pm, Wed 10.30–12.30 and 4pm–12.30am; Oct–May Sat, Sun and hols 10.30–12.30 and 3–5; adm*) with four big towers, now home to a collection of armour; its church of San Rocco has a pretty terracotta frieze. Further west, hilltop **Offida** (pop. 5,300) is an ancient place whose name goes back to the Etruscan Ophyte. It overlooks two valleys, is famous for bobbin lace and puts on a good carnival.

Offida's handsome 14th-century **Palazzo Comunale**, on Corso Serpente Aureo (Golden Snake), has a proud Ghibelline tower, a double gallery, a little theatre and the local **Pinacoteca** (*t 0736 888609; open July–mid-Sept 10–12.30 and 4–8; mid-Sept–June Sat–Sun 10–12.30 and 3–6; adm*), with handsome works by Crivelli and his follower Pietro Alemanno (*St Lucy crowned by Angels*, with her eyes in a dish) and Simone de Magistris (*The Three Realms*, 1589). Outside the centre, the Romanesque–Gothic church of **Santa Maria della Rocca** has beautiful, recently restored trecento frescoes by the Bolognese school. The Roman sarcophagus under the altar has a relief of the Roman God Silvanus; walk around the back for a striking view of the apse.

To the west and north of Offida, you can find truly obscure places, like **Castignano**, its hill dramatically eroding away. A 5th-century BC Piceni *stele* found on the site (now in Ascoli's Archaeology Museum) confirms its age. The 14th-century parish church **Santi Pietro e Paolo** has frescoes in the crypt by Vittore Crivelli, and a painted terracotta *Addolorata* from Scandinavia on the altar, from the 15th century, showing the Virgin's heart stabbed with knives of sorrow. In 1993 a fresco of the *Last Judgement* was discovered behind a Baroque altar; someone wrote the dates of solar eclipses in the corner in 1485 and 1537. Another church, **Sant'Egidio**, houses the *Ostensorio Reliquario*, one of the masterpieces of Ascoli Piceno's 15th-century goldsmiths.

Montalto di Marche is worth a stop for the little **Museo Diocesano** (*t 0736 828688; open on request; adm*) in Piazza Sisto V. Its treasure is one of the most beautiful reliquaries ever made – an exquisite shrine of gold, enamel, gems and cameos made in Paris in 1390, and donated to the town by Pope Sixtus V; the 16th-century Palazzo Comunale contains a small **Pinacoteca** (*t 0736 828015; open Sat–Sun 5.30–7.30; adm*) with a painting of Sixtus V and old photos of the area. Further to the northwest, in **Monte Rinaldo**, an impressive 2nd-century BC **Hellenistic-Roman temple** has been discovered, its columns re-erected under a modern transparent roof.

Ascoli Piceno

Urbino, at the northern end of the Marches, and **Ascoli** (pop. 54,000) at the southern, compete for your attention as almost polar opposites. Urbino gets most of the praise and partisans of Ascoli may find that somewhat unfair. While Urbino was paternalistically led by its enlightened, aesthetic Dukes, Ascoli, with its long heritage as a free *comune*, has always had to fend for itself. The difference shows; Ascoli is a beautiful city, but beautiful in a gritty, workaday manner like Florence. It has taken some hard knocks in its 2,500 years, which have no doubt added to its character.

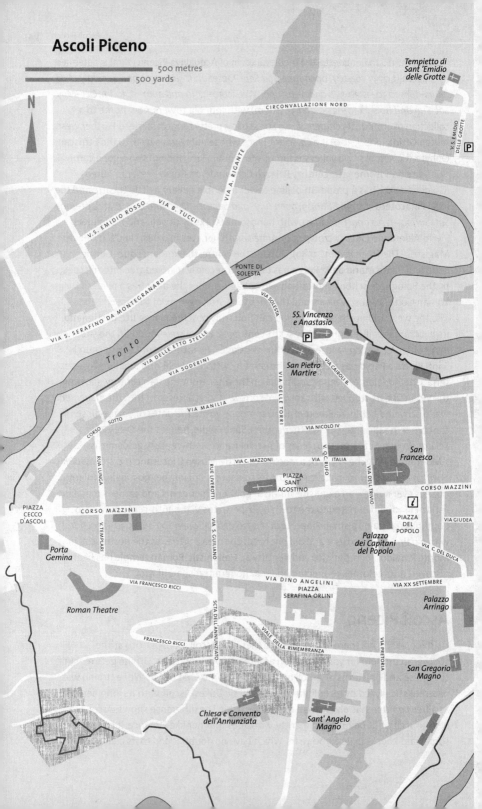

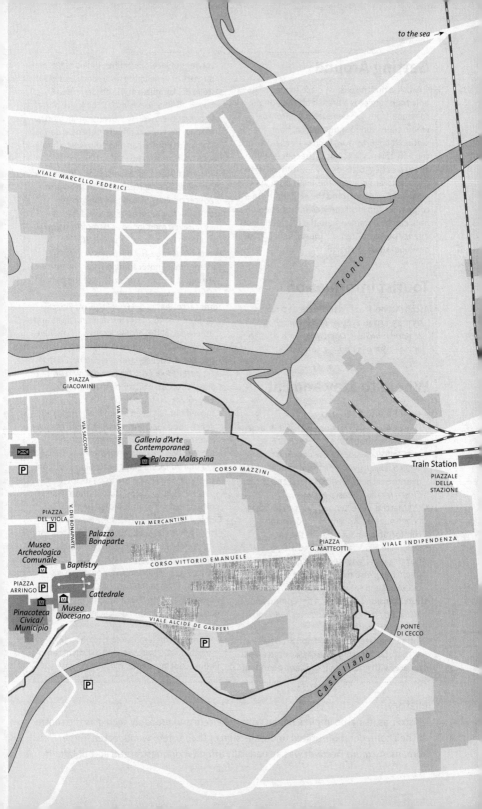

Getting Around

Ascoli is not the easiest place to reach. The only **train** service is a branch off the Adriatic coastline, from San Benedetto del Tronto, where trains run roughly once an hour. The station (**t** 0736 341004) is on Viale Marconi in the new town. START **buses** (freephone **t** 800 443040 or **t** 0736 263053, *www.startspa.it*) for the coast, Fermo and Rome, leave from Viale Alcide de Gasperi behind the cathedral; other companies run local services. Information on both can be obtained from the Brunozzi Travel Agency on Corso Trento e Trieste, near Piazza del Popolo, **t** 0736 262128.

Tourist Information

Ascoli Piceno: Piazza del Popolo 1, **t** 0736 253045, **f** 0736 252391, *iat.ascolipiceno@regione.marche.it*. Open Mon–Fri 8.30–1.30 and 3–7, Sat 9–1 and 3–7, Sun 9–1.

Where to Stay and Eat

Ascoli Piceno ✉ 63100

One of Ascoli's attractions is that it is largely undiscovered, but that also less choice.

★★★★Gioli, Via Alcide De Gasperi 14, **t/f** 0736 255550 (*expensive*). A pleasant, modern hotel near the cathedral, with parking and garden. *Closed for Christmas.*

★★★★Marche, Viale Kennedy 34, **t** 0736 45475, **f** 0736 342812 (*moderate*). Modern and comfortable; about 1.5km to the east.

★★★Pennile, Via Spalvieri, **t** 0736 41645, **f** 0736 342755, *www.hotelpednnile.com* (*moderate*). Also modern, in the same area, but quiet and set in pines.

★Hotel Pension Le Dune, Via del Commercio 210/a, **t** 0736 342575 (*moderate*). Ten simple rooms with bathrooms.

Cantina dell'Arte, Rua della Lupa 8, **t** 0736 255620, **f** 0736 255191 (*inexpensive*). In an old palace, with adequate rooms and abundant servings of local specialities, grilled meats and pitchers of wine in the restaurant. *Closed Sun.*

Ostello dei Longobardi, Via dei Soderini 26 **t** 0736 261862 (*inexpensive*). The youth hostel, in one of the medieval towers on the north of town. Very cheap, offes bunk beds in dorms. The tourist office can also help you to find a B&B or *agriturismo* nearby.

To most Italians, Ascoli means one thing: *olive all'ascolana*. The Marches is the third biggest producer of olives in Italy and the groves around Ascoli produce the best and fattest – they are even mentioned as part of Trimalcio's banquet in Petronius's *Satyricon*. Stuffed, breaded and fried, the olives are wonderful.

Gastronomia Enoteca Migliori, on Piazza Arringo 2, **t** 0736 250042. One of the best places to sample the above.

Tornasacco, Piazza del Popolo 36, off Piazza Arringo, **t** 0736 254151 (*moderate*). Olives and other specialities *all'ascolana* await you here, alongside *tagliatelle* with lamb sauce, very good local cheeses and *charcuterie*. *Closed Fri, part of July, Christmas and New Year.*

Gallo d'Oro, Corso Vittorio Emanuele 54, **t** 0736 253520 (*moderate*). This has just moved but has been doing business for 30 years; good food and a tourist menu of *olive all'ascolana, funghi porcini* and *tartufi*. *Closed Sun, Christmas–New Year.*

C'era una Volta, Via Piagge 336, 6km south on the Colle San Marco road, **t** 0736 261780 (*cheap*). Hearty soups, stuffed gnocchi and olives fried with lamb. *Closed Tues.*

Cefelò, **t** 0736 254525 (*cheap*). Also worth trying, with *olive all'ascolana* and succulent meats from the grill, *baccalà* in winter. *Closed Tues and Sept.*

La Liva, Piazza della Viola 13, **t** 0736 259358 (*cheap*). A small *trattoria* offering a good menu, including the famous olives, fried artichokes and other delicacies. *Closed Tues pm and Weds.*

Dell'Arengo, Via Tamasacco 5, **t** 0736 254711. Another little *trattoria* with excellent, simple home cooking. *Closed Mon.*

History

Ascoli, as its name implies, began with the Piceni and probably served as the centre of their confederation, united under the sign of their totem woodpecker. To the Romans, *Asculum Picenum* was an early ally after its conquest in 286 BC, but later it

proved a major headache. Asculum fought Rome in the Samnite Wars and actually
initiated the pan-Italian revolt of the Social Wars.

The Romans took the city in 89 BC and razed it to the ground for good measure,
refounding it soon afterwards with a colony of veterans. The street plan has hardly
changed since; it is one of the most perfect examples in Italy of a rectilinear Roman
castrum. In the Dark Ages, Ascoli's naturally defensible position between steep
ravines helped avert trouble. Its citizens, too, showed admirable determination,
defeating Odoacer's Goths on one occasion, and the Byzantines and Saracens on others.
Despite periods under the rule of Lombards, Franks, Normans and various feudal lords,
Ascoli emerged by the 1100s as a strong, free *comune*. Reminders of this glorious
period are everywhere: in the 13th-century Palazzo del Popolo, the clutch of tall, noble
towers like those of San Gimignano, and in Ascoli's famous festival, the **Quintana**, a
jousting contest whose rules were laid down in the statutes of 1378. With the advent of
papal rule in the 15th century, Ascoli lost its freedom immediately and its prosperity
gradually, only recovering some of its wealth and importance in the last 100 years.

Piazza del Popolo

Like Rome, Ascoli is built of travertine. The central **Piazza del Popolo** is one of the
most beautiful squares in Italy. It's a real town square, too, full of children riding bikes
and playing football. This is no grand architectural ensemble, neither monumental
nor symmetrical. But the travertine paving shines like marble; the low brick arcades
that surround it give the square architectural unity and a setting for two fine
buildings bearing statues of Popes, who keep an eye on the bustling action in the
square. The first, the 13th-century **Palazzo dei Capitani del Popolo**, was begun in the
1200s and redone in the late 16th century, after its papal governor set it on fire to
discomfit his enemies. It has a façade by Ascoli's best-known architect and artist, Cola
dell'Amatrice, and a statue of Paul III over its huge portal; in 1982 excavations revealed
buildings dating back to the Roman republic. Next door, try a homemade *amaretto* at
the Art Nouveau **Caffè Meletti**, one of few to resist the siren song of stainless steel
and bright lights. At the narrow end of the piazza, the church of **San Francesco**
(*c. 1260; open daily 9.30–12.30 and 4–7.30*) turns its back on the square; the apse and
transepts are the best part of the building, an austere ascent of Gothic bays and
towers under a low dome added in the late 15th century. Over the south door is a
statue of Pope Julius II. The façade, around the corner, isn't much to look at; a flat
square of travertine with a plain rose window. It does have a sculpted portal, guarded
by a pair of sarcastic-looking lions. Within are some grand and simple Gothic vaults.
The southern end of the façade adjoins the **Loggia dei Mercanti**, built by the Wool
Corporation – a medieval-style manufacturers' cooperative – in the early 1500s.

Northern Quarters and Around the Edges of Town

On the northern side, one of two Franciscan cloisters has become the town's busy,
colourful **market** (*mornings*). The street in front of San Francesco is the centre of
activity in Ascoli, the **Via del Trivio**; follow it north to Ascoli's oldest and prettiest
neighbourhoods, on the cliffs above the lovely Tronto Valley, which skirts the northern

reaches of the town and makes an ideal picnic spot. Parts of the town walls, still visible in places, show the diamond-shaped brickwork (*opus reticulatum*) characteristic of Roman construction. It's here on the northern stretches that you'll find most of the city's surviving towers. Ascoli has as many of these medieval family fortresses as San Gimignano in Tuscany, though they are not as well known; the tallest is the **Torre degli Ercolani** on Via Soderini. Piazza Ventidio Basso, the medieval commercial centre, has two good churches: 11th-century **Santi Vincenzo e Anastasio** (*t 0736 252205; open on request*), with a façade divided into 64 squares that once framed frescoes, still has some Romanesque carvings around the portal. The second church, gloomy Gothic 13th-century **San Pietro Martire**, has a portal from 1523 by Cola d'Amatrice; both have a few 14th-century frescoes inside. From here, picturesque Via di Solestà, lined with tower houses, leads to the northern tip of Ascoli; a doughty single-arched Roman bridge, the 1st-century **Ponte di Solestà**, carries traffic across to the northern suburbs without a creak. If you cross it, and walk along the river bank to the east, you will see signs for the church of **Sant'Emidio delle Grotte**, on the street of the same name, an elegant 1623 Baroque façade that closes the front of a cave; it's here that St Emidio, Ascoli's patron, was martyred; the site became the city's earliest place of Christian worship.

At the western entrance to town, on Corso Mazzini, a little Roman gate of the first century AD survives, the **Porta Gemina**, spanning the Via Salaria (the square just outside is named after Cecco d'Ascoli, an acquaintance of Dante, a poet, doctor, astrologer and reputed magician, who got in trouble with the Inquisition and died under its hands in 1327). On the fringes of the city, other Roman remains are everywhere; just south of the Porta Gemina, on Via Angelini, there are traces of the **Roman Theatre**, near the remains of a fortress built by the popes in 1564. From here, Via Ricci leads up to the Parco della Rimembranza, with two medieval churches of the **Annunziata** (with a large fresco by Cola dell'Amatrice in the Refectory and more Roman remains in the 'Grotte') and **Sant'Angelo Magno**, the latter with frescoes of eight sibyls in the nave, painted in 1712 in honour of the nearby mountains and 10th–11th-century frescoes of the *Old Testament*, the oldest in the city. Finally, there's **San Gregorio Magno**, built over a Roman temple of Vesta, with two columns and walls in *opus reticulatum*, just behind Ascoli's town hall in Piazza Arringo.

Piazza Arringo

Ascoli's oldest square, monumental Piazza Arringo, has lost much of its old lustre in its service as a municipal car park. One end is held down by the **cathedral**, dedicated to Sant'Emidio (*t 0736 259774; open 7–12 and 3.30–6.30*), a 12th-century building similar to San Francesco, but with a façade from the 1530s, also by Cola dell'Amatrice. The interior was tarted up in the 19th century, but in the chapel on the south side, you can see the beautiful and recently restored polyptych by Carlo Crivelli, one of his masterpieces; in the crypt, there's a curious Gothic tomb of a knight; another, left of the altar, shows the deceased leaning forwards on his books, as if lazily attending Mass.

The **Museo Diocesano** (*t 0736 252883; open July–Aug daily 10–1 and 3.30–7, Sept–June, Mon–Fri 9.30–1 and Sat 9.30–1 and 3.30–7; adm*), in the adjacent bishop's palace, has two rare statues in travertine of Adam and Eve (1300), from a pulpit; works by Cola dell'Amatrice (whose style changed tremendously after he went to Rome to see the Raphaels); a Carlo Crivelli (three apples); a beautiful 15th-century arm reliquary, of St Emidio made in Ascoli and, stealing the show, a room of frescoes on the *Life of Moses* by a mid-1500s painter from Vicenza, Marcello Fogolino. The 10th-century octagonal **baptistry**, to the side of the cathedral, stands resolutely in the middle of one of Ascoli's busiest streets. Facing the cathedral, behind the dragons and seahorses in the twin Renaissance fountains, is the 13th-century **Palazzo Arringo**, hidden behind an imposing 17th-century Baroque façade. It holds the **Pinacoteca Civica** (*t 0736 298213; open summer daily 9–1 and 3.30–7.30; winter daily 9–1 and 3–7; adm*), with paintings by Cola dell'Amatrice and other local artists, Simone de Magistris, Pietro Alemanno, Titian, Guido Reni Van Dyck, Crivelli of course, drawings by Pietro Cortona and Guercino, collections of ceramics and musical instruments, and a 13th-century English-made cope that Pope Nicolas IV (a native of Ascoli) gave to the cathedral in 1288.

Across the square, in Palazzo Panichi, the **Museo Archeologico** (*t 0736 253562; open Tues–Sun 8.30–7.30; adm*) has some bronzes of the ancient Piceni and some of the stones they hurled at the Romans, engraved with curses; there are also Roman mosaics and a plan of the city in Roman times, as well as Lombard jewellery and relics from a medieval necropolis. A walk through the streets north of Piazza Arringo will take you past some of the palaces of medieval Ascoli, with many curious carvings and morally uplifting inscriptions on the old houses; one, the **Palazzo Bonaparte** on Via Bonaparte, was built by a prominent family of the 1500s that local legend claims as the ancestors of the Bonapartes; Napoleon himself said he didn't know if it was true.

The 16th-century **Palazzo Malaspina** at Corso Mazzini 224 is one of the fancier buildings and houses a **Civica Galleria d'Arte Contemporanea** (*t 0736 248662; open Tues–Sun 9–1 and 4–7; adm*); its paintings, sculptures and graphic works form a good introduction to Italian modern art, from futurist Gino Severini to Lucio Fontana, a central figure of Arte Povera. Down this long street, at Corso Mazzini 39, you can also visit the recently rearranged **Museo di Storia Naturale** (*t 0736 277540; open Mon–Sat 9–1, also Tues and Thurs 3–5; adm*), with exhibits on the natural history of the Marches.

West Towards Umbria

This is the surest year-round route over the Sibillini on the Roman Via Salaria. The mountains outdo any manmade sights, and if you need a break, there's **Aquasanta Terme**, where the Roman legions used to rest. It has a medieval bridge that looks like new and a natural spring, where 15 million litres of hot sulphuric water burst out of the ground in a cave – André Gide recommended it highly.

Further up, **Arquata del Tronto** is a lovely village under a 13th-century Rocca. In one of its *frazioni*, **Capodacqua**, is a little octagonal church, **Madonna del Sole**, attributed to Cola dell'Amatrice, who may also have painted the frescoes within.

Beyond Arquata, the spectacular mountain route twists over the **Forca Canapine** pass (1,500m/4,920ft), a balcony over the southern Apennines; in late May, it's covered with purple crocuses, and continues through a mountain meadow, the **Piano Grande** (*see* p.578). The newer route is faster, plunging through a massive tunnel.

Glossary

acroterion: decorative protrusion on the rooftop of an Etruscan, Greek or Roman temple. At the corners of the roof they are called *antefixes*.

ambones: twin pulpits (singular: *ambo*), often elaborately decorated.

ambulatory: aisle around the apse of a church.

atrium: entrance court of a Roman house or early church.

badia: abbey or abbey church (also *abbazia*).

baldacchino: baldachin, a columned stone canopy above the altar of a church.

basilica: a rectangular building, usually divided into three aisles by rows of columns. In Rome this was the common form for law courts and other public buildings, and Roman Christians adapted it for their early churches.

borgo: from the Saxon *burh* of Santo Spirito in Rome: a suburb or village.

bucchero ware: black, delicately thin Etruscan ceramics, usually incised or painted.

Calvary chapels: a series of outdoor chapels, usually on a hillside, that commemorate the stages of the Passion of Christ.

campanile: a bell tower.

campanilismo: local patriotism; the Italians' own word for their historic tendency to be more faithful to their home towns than to the abstract idea of 'Italy'.

campo santo: a cemetery.

cardo: the transverse street of a Roman *castrum*-shaped city.

carroccio: a wagon carrying the banners of a medieval city and an altar; it served as the rallying point in battles.

cartoon: the preliminary sketch for a fresco or tapestry.

caryatid: supporting pillar or column carved into a standing female form; male versions are called *telamones*.

castrum: a Roman military camp, always neatly rectangular, with straight streets and gates at the cardinal points. Later the Romans founded or refounded cities in this form, hundreds of which survive today (Lucca, Aosta, Florence, Pavia, Como, Brescia, Ascoli Piceno, Ancona are clear examples).

cavea: the semicircle of seats in a classical theatre.

cenacolo: fresco of the *Last Supper*, often on the wall of a monastery refectory.

chiaroscuro: the arrangement or treatment of light and dark areas in a painting.

ciborium: a tabernacle; the word is often used for large, free-standing tabernacles, or in the sense of a *baldacchino* (q.v.).

comune: commune or commonwealth, referring to the governments of the free cities of the Middle Ages. Today it denotes any local government, from the Comune di Roma down to the smallest village.

condottiere: the leader of a band of mercenaries in late medieval and Renaissance times.

confraternity: a religious lay brotherhood, often serving as a neighbourhood mutual-aid and burial society, or following some specific charitable work (Michelangelo, for example, belonged to one that cared for condemned prisoners in Rome).

contrapposto: the dramatic, but rather unnatural twist in a statue, especially in a Mannerist or Baroque work, derived from Hellenistic and Roman art.

convento: a convent *or* monastery

Cosmati work: or *Cosmatesque*: referring to a distinctive style of inlaid marble or enamel chips used in architectural decoration (pavements, pulpits, paschal candlesticks, etc.) in medieval Italy. The Cosmati family of Rome were its greatest practitioners.

crete: found in the pasturelands of southern Tuscany, chalky cliffs caused by erosion. Similar phenomena are the *biancane*, small chalk outcrops, and *balze*, deep eroded ravines around Volterra.

cupola: a dome.

decumanus: street of a Roman *castrum*-shaped city parallel to the longer axis, the central, main avenue called the Decumanus Major.

Dodecapolis: the federation of the 12 largest and strongest Etruscan city states (*see* **History and Art**, p.10).

duomo: cathedral.

ex voto: an offering (a terracotta figurine, painting, medallion, silver bauble or whatever) made in thanksgiving to a god or Christian saint; the practice has always been present in Italy.

forum: the central square of a Roman town, with its most important temples and public buildings. The word means 'outside', as the original Roman Forum was outside the first city walls.

fresco: wall painting, the most important Italian medium of art since Etruscan times. It isn't easy; first the artist draws the *sinopia* (q.v.) on the wall. This is covered with plaster, but only a little at a time, as the paint must be on the plaster before it dries. Leonardo da Vinci's endless attempts to find clever short-cuts ensured that little of his work would survive.

Ghibellines: one of the two great medieval parties (*see Guelphs*), the supporters of the Holy Roman Emperors.

gonfalon: the banner of a medieval free city; the *gonfaloniere*, or flag-bearer, was often the most important public official.

graffito: originally, incised decoration on buildings, walls, etc.; only lately has it come to mean casually-scribbled messages in public places.

Greek cross: in the floor plans of churches, a cross with equal arms. The more familiar plan, with one arm extended to form a nave, is called a *Latin Cross*.

grisaille: painting or fresco in monochrome.

grotesques: carved or painted faces used in Etruscan and later Roman decoration; Raphael and other artists rediscovered them in the 'grotto' of Nero's Golden House in Rome.

Guelphs (*see Ghibellines*): the other great political faction of medieval Italy, supporters of the Pope.

intarsia: decorative inlaid wood or marble.

loggia: an open-sided gallery or arcade.

lozenge: the diamond shape – this, along with stripes, is one of the trademarks of Pisan architecture.

lunette: semicircular space on a wall, above a door or under vaulting, either filled by a window or a mural painting.

matroneum: the elevated women's gallery around the nave of an early church, a custom adopted from the Byzantines in the 6th and 7th centuries.

narthex: the enclosed porch of a church.

naumachia: mock naval battles, like those staged in the Colosseum.

opus reticulatum: Roman masonry consisting of diamond-shaped blocks.

palazzo: not just a palace, but any large, important building (though the word comes from the Imperial *palatium* on Rome's Palatine Hill).

Palio: a banner, and the horse race in which city neighbourhoods contend for it in their annual festivals. The most famous is at Siena.

Pantocrator: Christ 'ruler of all', a common subject for apse paintings and mosaics in areas influenced by Byzantine art.

pietra dura: rich inlay decoration that uses semi-precious stones, perfected in post-Renaissance Florence.

pieve: a parish church.

pluteo: screen, usually of marble, between two columns, often highly decorated.

podestà: in medieval cities, an official sent by the Holy Roman Emperors to take charge; their power, or lack of it, depended on the strength of the *comune*.

predella: smaller paintings on panels below the main subject of a painted altarpiece.

presepio: a Christmas crib.

putti: flocks of plaster cherubs with rosy cheeks and bottoms that infested much of Italy in the Baroque era.

quattrocento: the 1400s – the Italian way of referring to centuries (*duecento, trecento, quattrocento, cinquecento*, etc.).

sbandieratore: flag-thrower in medieval costume at an Italian festival; sometimes called an *alfiere*.

sinopia: the layout of a fresco (q.v.), etched by the artist on the wall before the plaster is applied. Often these are works of art in their own right.

stele: a vertical funeral stone.

stigmata: a miraculous simulation of the bleeding wounds of Christ, appearing in holy men like St Francis in the 12th century, and Padre Pio of Puglia in our own time.

telamone: (*see caryatid*).

thermae: Roman baths.

tondo: round relief, painting or terracotta.

transenna: a marble screen separating the altar area from the rest of an early Christian church.

travertine: hard, light-coloured stone, sometimes flecked or pitted with black, sometimes perfect. The most widely used material in ancient and modern Rome.

triptych: a painting, especially an altarpiece, in three sections.

trompe l'œil: art that uses perspective effects to deceive the eye – for example, to create the illusion of depth on a flat surface, or to make columns and arches painted on a wall seem real.

tympanum: the semicircular space, often bearing a painting or relief, above the portal of a church.

voussoir: one of the stones of an arch.

Know your Medici

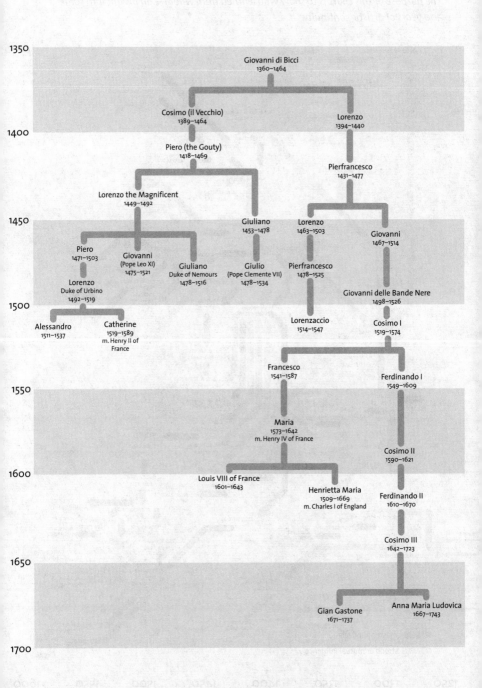

Masters and Students: the Progress of the Renaissance

The purpose of this chart is to show who learned from whom – an insight into some 300 years of artistic continuity.

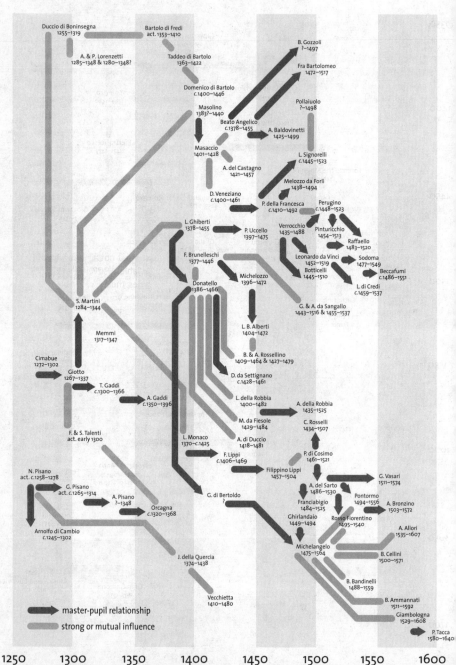

Duccio di Boninsegna
1255–1319

Bartolo di Fredi
act. 1353–1410

A. & P. Lorenzetti
1285–1348 & 1280–1348?

Taddeo di Bartolo
1363–1422

Domenico di Bartolo
c.1400–1446

Masolino
1383?–1440

Beato Angelico
c.1378–1455

B. Gozzoli
?–1497

Fra Bartolomeo
1472–1517

Pollaiuolo
?–1498

A. Baldovinetti
1425–1499

Masaccio
1401–1428

A. del Castagno
1421–1457

L. Signorelli
c.1445–1523

D. Veneziano
c.1400–1461

Melozzo da Forlì
1438–1494

P. della Francesca
c.1410–1492

Perugino
c.1448–1523

L. Ghiberti
1378–1455

P. Uccello
1397–1475

Verrocchio
1435–1488

Pinturicchio
1454–1513

Raffaello
1483–1520

F. Brunelleschi
1377–1446

Leonardo da Vinci
1452–1519

Botticelli
1445–1510

Sodoma
1477–1549

Beccafumi
c.1486–1551

Michelozzo
1396–1472

L. di Credi
c.1459–1537

Donatello
1386–1466

G. & A. da Sangallo
1443–1516 & 1455–1537

S. Martini
1284–1344

Memmi
1317–1347

L. B. Alberti
1404–1472

B. & A. Rossellino
1409–1464 & 1427–1479

Cimabue
1272–1302

Giotto
1267–1337

T. Gaddi
c.1300–1366

A. Gaddi
c.1350–1396

D. da Settignano
c.1428–1461

L. della Robbia
1400–1482

A. della Robbia
1435–1525

F. & S. Talenti
act. early 1300

L. Monaco
1370–c.1425

M. da Fiesole
1429–1484

C. Rosselli
1434–1507

A. di Duccio
1418–1481

F. Lippi
c.1406–1469

P. di Cosimo
1461–1521

N. Pisano
act. c.1258–1278

G. Pisano
act. c.1265–1314

A. Pisano
?–1348

Orcagna
c.1320–1368

Filippino Lippi
1457–1504

G. Vasari
1511–1574

A. del Sarto
1486–1530

Pontormo
1494–1556

A. Bronzino
1503–1572

Arnolfo di Cambio
c.1245–1302

G. di Bertoldo
?

Franciabigio
1484–1525

Ghirlandaio
1449–1494

Rosso Fiorentino
1495–1540

A. Allori
1535–1607

Michelangelo
1475–1564

B. Cellini
1500–1571

J. della Quercia
1374–1438

B. Bandinelli
1488–1559

B. Ammannati
1511–1592

Vecchietta
1410–1480

Giambologna
1529–1608

P. Tacca
1580–1640

master-pupil relationship

strong or mutual influence

1250   1300   1350   1400   1450   1500   1550   1600

Language

The fathers of modern Italian were Dante, Manzoni and television. Each did their part in creating a national language from an infinity of regional and local dialects; the Florentine Dante, the first 'immortal' to write in the vernacular, did much to put the Tuscan dialect in the foreground of Italian literature. Manzoni's revolutionary novel, *I Promessi Sposi* (*The Betrothed*), heightened national consciousness by using an everyday language all could understand in the 19th century. Television in the last few decades is performing an even more spectacular linguistic unification; although the majority of Italians still speak a dialect at home, school and work, their TV idols insist on proper Italian.

Perhaps because they are so busy learning their own beautiful but grammatically complex language, Italians are not especially apt at learning others. English lessons, however, have been the rage for years, and at most hotels and restaurants there will be someone who speaks some English. In small towns and out-of-the-way places, finding an Anglophone may prove more difficult. The words and phrases below should help you out in most situations, but the ideal way to come to Italy is with some Italian under your belt; your visit will be richer and you're much more likely to make some Italian friends.

Pronunciation

Italian words are pronounced phonetically. Every vowel and consonant (except 'h') is sounded. Consonants are the same as in English, except the 'c' which, when followed by an 'e' or 'i', is pronounced like the English 'ch' (*cinque* thus becomes 'cheenquay'). Italian 'g' is also soft before 'i' or 'e' as in *gira*, pronounced 'jee-ra'. 'H' is never sounded; 'z' is pronounced like 'ts'. The consonants 'sc' before

the vowels 'i' or 'e' become like the English 'sh' as in 'sci', pronounced 'shee'; 'ch' is pronouced like a 'k' as in Chianti, 'kee-an-tee'; 'gn' as 'ny' in English (*bagno*, pronounced 'ban-yo'; while 'gli' is pronounced like the middle of the word 'million' (Castiglione, pronounced 'Ca-steely-oh-nay').

Vowel pronunciation is: 'a' as in English 'father'; 'e' when unstressed is pronounced like 'a' in 'fate' as in *mele*, when stressed can be the same or like the 'e' in 'pet' (*bello*); 'i' is like the 'i' in 'machine'; 'o' like 'e', has two sounds, 'o' as in 'hope' when unstressed (*tacchino*), and usually 'o' as in 'rock' when stressed (*morte*); 'u' is pronounced like the 'u' in 'June'.

The accent usually (but not always) falls on the penultimate syllable. Also note that, in the big northern cities, the informal way of addressing someone as you, *tu*, is widely used; the more formal *lei* or *voi* is commonly used in provincial districts.

Useful Words and Phrases

yes/no/maybe *sì/no/forse*
I don't know *Non lo so*
I don't understand (Italian) *Non capisco (l'italiano)*
Does someone here speak English? *C'è qualcuno qui che parla inglese?*
Speak slowly *Parla lentamente*
Could you assist me? *Potrebbe aiutarmi?*
Help! *Aiuto!*
Please/Thank you (very much) *Per favore/ (Molte) grazie*
You're welcome *Prego*
It doesn't matter *Non importa*
All right *Va bene*
Excuse me *Mi scusi*
Be careful! *Attenzione!*
Nothing *Niente*
It is urgent! *È urgente!*
How are you? *Come sta?*

Well, and you? *Bene, e Lei?*
What is your name? *Come si chiama?*
Hello *Salve or ciao (both informal)*
Good morning *Buongiorno (formal hello)*
Good afternoon, evening *Buonasera (also formal hello)*
Good night *Buonanotte*
Goodbye *Arrivederla (formal), arrivederci/ciao (informal)*
What do you call this in Italian? *Come si chiama questo in italiano?*
What?/Who?/Where? *Che?/Chi?/Dove?*
Where is/are... *Dov'è/Dove sono...*
When?/Why? *Quando?/Perché?*
How? *Come?*
How much? *Quanto?*
I am lost *Mi sono smarrito*
I am hungry/thirsty/sleepy/tired *Ho fame/sete/sonno/stanco*
I am sorry *Mi dispiace*
I am ill *Mi sento male*
Leave me alone *Lasciami in pace*
good/bad *buono bravo/male cattivo*
hot/cold *caldo/freddo*
slow/fast *lento/rapido*
up/down *su/giù*
big/small *grande/piccolo*
here/there *qui/lì*

Transport

airport *aeroporto*
bus stop *fermata*
bus/coach *autobus/pullman*
railway station *stazione ferroviaria*
train *treno*
platform *binario*
port *porto*
port station *stazione marittima*
ship *nave*
car *macchina*
taxi *tassì*
ticket *biglietto*
customs *dogana*
seat (reserved) *posto (prenotato)*

Travel Directions

One (two) ticket(s) to Naples, please *Un biglietto (due biglietti) per Napoli, per favore*
one way *semplice/andata*

return *andata e ritorno*
first/second class *Prima/seconda classe*
I want to go to... *Desidero andare a...*
How can I get to...? *Come posso andare a...?*
How do I get to the town centre? *Come posso raggiungere il centro città?*
Do you stop at...? *Ferma a...?*
Where is...? *Dov'è...?*
How far is it to...? *Quanto siamo lontani da...?*
What is the name of this station? *Come si chiama questa stazione?*
When does the next ... leave? *Quando parte il prossimo...?*
From where does it leave? *Da dove parte?*
How long does the trip take...? *Quanto tempo dura il viaggio?*
How much is the fare? *Quant'è il biglietto?*
Have a good trip *Buon viaggio!*

Driving

near/far *vicino/lontano*
left/right *sinistra/destra*
straight ahead *sempre diritto*
forwards/backwards *avanti/indietro*
north/south *nord/sud*
east *est/oriente*
west *ovest/occidente*
round the corner *dietro l'angolo*
crossroads *bivio*
street/road *strada/via*
square *piazza*
car hire *noleggio macchina*
motorbike/scooter *motocicletta/Vespa*
bicycle *bicicletta*
petrol/diesel *benzina/gasolio*
garage *garage*
This doesn't work *Questo non funziona*
mechanic *meccanico*
map/town plan *carta/pianta*
Where is the road to...? *Dov'è la strada per...?*
breakdown *guasto/panne*
driving licence *patente di guida*
driver *guidatore*
speed *velocità*
danger *pericolo*
parking *parcheggio*
no parking *sosta vietata*
narrow *stretto*
bridge *ponte*
toll *pedaggio*
slow down *rallentare*

Numbers

one *uno/una*
two/three/four *due/tre/quattro*
five/six/seven *cinque/sei/sette*
eight/nine/ten *otto/nove/dieci*
eleven/twelve *undici/dodici*
thirteen/fourteen *tredici/quattordici*
fifteen/sixteen *quindici/sedici*
seventeen/eighteen *diciassette/diciotto*
nineteen *dicianove*
twenty *venti*
twenty-one *ventuno*
thirty *trenta*
forty *quaranta*
fifty *cinquanta*
sixty *sessanta*
seventy *settanta*
eighty *ottanta*
ninety *novanta*
hundred *cento*
one hundred and one *centouno*
two hundred *duecento*
one thousand *mille*
two thousand *duemila*
million *milione*

Days

Monday *lunedì*
Tuesday *martedì*
Wednesday *mercoledì*
Thursday *giovedì*
Friday *venerdì*
Saturday *sabato*
Sunday *domenica*

Time

What time is it? *Che ora è?*
day/week *giorno/settimana*
month *mese*
morning/afternoon *mattina/pomeriggio*
evening *sera*
yesterday *ieri*
today *oggi*
tomorrow *domani*
soon *fra poco*
later *dopo/più tardi*
It is too early *È troppo presto*
It is too late *È troppo tardi*

Shopping, Services, Sightseeing

I would like... *Vorrei...*
How much is it? *Quanto costa questo?*
open/closed *aperto/chiuso*
cheap/expensive *a buon prezzo/caro*
bank *banca*
beach *spiaggia*
bed *letto*
church *chiesa*
entrance/exit *entrata/uscita*
hospital *ospedale*
money *soldi*
newspaper (foreign) *giornale (straniero)*
pharmacy *farmacia*
police station *commissariato*
policeman *poliziotto*
post office *ufficio postale*
sea *mare*
shop *negozio*
tobacco shop *tabaccaio*
WC *toilette/bagno*
men *Signori/Uomini*
women *Signore/Donne*

Useful Hotel Vocabulary

I'd like a single/twin/double room please
    *Vorrei una camera singola/doppia/
    matrimoniale, per favore*
with/without bath *con/senza bagno*
for two nights *per due notti*
We are leaving tomorrow morning *Partiamo
    domani mattina*
May I see the room/another room, please?
    Posso vedere la camera/un'altra camera?
Is there a room with a balcony? *C'è una
    camera con balcone?*
There isn't (aren't) any hot water/soap/light/
    toilet paper/towels *Manca (Mancano)
    acqua calda/sapone/luce/carta igienica/
    asciugamani*
May I pay by credit card? *Posso pagare con
    carta di credito?*
Fine, I'll take it *Bene, la prendo*
Is breakfast included? *E' compresa la prima
    colazione?*
What time do you serve breakfast? *A che ora
    è la colazione?*

For a list of vocabulary relating to Italian
food and drink, *see* **Food and Drink**, p.46.

Further Reading

Carmichael, Montgomery, *In Tuscany* (Burns & Oates, 1910).

Goethe, J.W., *Italian Journey* (Penguin Classics, 1982). An excellent example of a genius turned to mush by Italy; good insights, but big, big mistakes.

Hutton, Edward, *Florence, Assisi and Umbria Revisited*, in *Unknown Tuscany*, and *Siena and Southern Tuscany* (Hollis & Carter, 1995). Modern travel classics.

McCarthy, Mary, *The Stones of Florence* and *Venice Observed* (Penguin, 1986). Brilliant evocation of Italy's two great art cities, with an understanding that makes many other works on the subject seem sluggish and pedantic; don't visit Florence without it.

Morton, H.V., *A Traveller in Italy* (Methuen & Co., 1964). Among the most readable and delightful accounts of Italy in print. Morton is a sincere scholar and a true gentleman.

Raison, Laura (ed), *Tuscany: An Anthology* (Cadogan, 1983). An excellent selection of the best by Tuscans and Tuscany-watchers.

Spender, Matthew, *Within Tuscany* (Viking, 1992). Poet Stephen Spender's son, on everything from porcupines to Pontormo's bowel movements.

Williams, Egerton R., *Hill Towns of Italy* (Smith, Elder, 1904). An Englishman goes exploring in Tuscany and Umbria.

Art and Literature

Boccaccio, Giovanni, *The Decameron* (Penguin, 1972). The ever-young classic by one of the fathers of Italian literature. Its irreverent worldliness still provides a salutary antidote to whatever dubious ideas persist in your mental baggage.

Burckhardt, Jacob, *The Civilization of the Renaissance in Italy* (Harper & Row, 1975). The classic on the subject (first published in 1860); the mark against which scholars still level their poison pens of revisionism.

Castiglione, Baldassare, *The Book of Courtier* (Wordsworth Editions Ltd., 2000).

Cellini, B., *Autobiography of Benvenuto Cellini* (Penguin, translated by George Bull, 1999). Fun reading about the vicious competition of the Florentine art world by a swashbuckling braggart and world-class liar.

Clark, Kenneth, *Leonardo da Vinci* (Penguin, 1993).

Dante, Alighieri, *The Divine Comedy* (plenty of good translations). Few poems have ever had such a mythical significance for a nation. Anyone serious about understanding Tuscany or Italy and their world view will need more than a passing acquaintance with Dante.

Gardner, Edmund G., *The Story of Florence, The Story of Siena*; also **Gordon, Lina Duff**, *The Story of Assisi* and *The Story of Perugia* and **Ross, Janet**, *The Story of Pisa* (J.M. Dent, 1900s). All part of the excellent and highly readable Medieval Towns series.

Ghibert/Linscott, *Complete Poems and Selected Letters of Michelangelo* (Princeton Press, 1984).

Gordon, Lina Duff, *The Story of Assisi* (see Gardner, Edmund G. above)

Hale, J.R. (ed), *A Concise Encyclopedia of the Italian Renaissance* (Thames and Hudson, 1981). An excellent reference guide, with many concise, well-written essays. Also *Florence and the Medici: The Pattern of Control* (1977), which describes just how the Medici did it.

Hibbert, Christopher, *Rise and Fall of the House of Medici* (Penguin, 1965). One of the classics – compulsive reading.

Hook, Judith, *Siena* (Hamish Hamilton, 1979). A bit weak on art, but good on everything else.

Leonardo da Vinci, *Notebooks* (Oxford, 1983).

Levey, Michael, *Early Renaissance* (1967) and *High Renaissance* (both Penguin). Old-fashioned accounts of the period, with a breathless reverence for the 1500s – but still full of intriguing interpretations.

Masson, Georgina, *Frederick II of Hohenstaufen* (Secker & W., 1973).

Murray, Linda, *The High Renaissance* and *The Late Renaissance and Mannerism* (Thames and Hudson, 1977). Excellent introduction to the period; also Peter and Linda Murray, *The Art of the Renaissance* (1963).

Origo, Iris, *The Merchant of Prato* (Penguin, 1963). Everyday life in 14th-century Tuscany with the father of modern accounting, Francesco di Marco Datini. Also *Images and Shadows*; *War in the Val d'Orcia*, about a Tuscan childhood and life during the war.

Petrarch, Francesco, *Canzoniere and Other Works* (Oxford, 1985). The most famous poems by the 'First Modern Man'.

Procacci, Giuliano, *History of the Italian People* (Penguin, 1973). An in-depth view from the year 1000 up to the present – also an introduction to the wit and subtlety of the best Italian scholarship.

Richards, Charles, *The New Italians* (Penguin, 1995). An observant and amusing study of life in Italy during and since the political upheaval and financial scandals of the early 1990s.

Ross, Janet, *The Story of Pisa* (see Gardner, Edmund G., p.656)

Symonds, John Addington, *A Short History of the Renaissance in Italy* (Smith, Elder, 1893). A condensed version of the authority of a hundred years ago, still fascinating today.

Vasari, Giorgio, *Lives of the Painters, Sculptors and Architects* (Everyman, 1996). Readable, anecdotal accounts of the Renaissance greats by the father of modern art history.

Index

Main page references are in **bold**. Page references to maps are in *italics*.

Answers to 'A Florentine Puzzle' (*see* **Topics**, p.32)

1 Façade of **San Miniato**

2 **Baptistry**, interior apse

3 Windows at the rear of **San Iacopo sopr'Arno**, visible from Santa Trinita

4 Windows, **Orsanmichele**

5 Façade, **Santa Croce** (inspired by Orcagna's tabernacle in Orsanmichele)

6 Baptistry doors (Pisano's and Ghiberti's first set); portico of the Bigallo, interior apse, **Santa Croce**

7 **Loggia dei Lanzi**

8 Rucellai Chapel, **San Pancrazio**